The Gallup Poll

Public Opinion 2014

Other Gallup Publications Available from SR Books:

The Gallup Poll Cumulative Index: Public Opinion, 1935–1997
ISBN 0-8420-2587-1 (1999)

The Gallup Poll: Public Opinion Annual Series

2010 (ISBN 978-1-4422-0991-6)
2009 (ISBN 978-1-4422-0519-2)
2008 (ISBN 978-1-4422-0105-7)
2007 (ISBN 0-7425-6239-5)
2006 (ISBN 0-7425-5876-2)
2005 (ISBN 0-7425-5258-6)
2004 (ISBN 0-7425-5138-5)
2003 (ISBN 0-8420-5003-5)
2002 (ISBN 0-8420-5002-7)
2001 (ISBN 0-8420-5001-9)
2000 (ISBN 0-8420-5000-0)
1999 (ISBN 0-8420-2699-1)
1998 (ISBN 0-8420-2698-3)
1997 (ISBN 0-8420-2697-9)
1996 (ISBN 0-8420-2696-0)
1995 (ISBN 0-8420-2695-2)
1994 (ISBN 0-8420-2560-X)
1993 (ISBN 0-8420-2483-2)

1992 (ISBN 0-8420-2463-8)
1991 (ISBN 0-8420-2397-6)
1990 (ISBN 0-8420-2368-2)
1989 (ISBN 0-8420-2344-5)
1988 (ISBN 0-8420-2330-5)
1987 (ISBN 0-8420-2292-9)
1986 (ISBN 0-8420-2275-0)
1985 (ISBN 0-8420-2249-X)
1984 (ISBN 0-8420-2234-1)
1983 (ISBN 0-8420-2220-1)
1982 (ISBN 0-8420-2214-7)
1981 (ISBN 0-8420-2200-7)
1980 (ISBN 0-8420-2181-7)
1979 (ISBN 0-8420-2170-1)
1978 (ISBN 0-8420-2159-0)
1972–77 (ISBN 0-8420-2129-9, 2 vols.)
1935–71 (ISBN 0-394-47270-5, 3 vols.)

International Polls

The International Gallup Polls: Public Opinion, 1979
ISBN 0-8420-2180-9 (1981)

The International Gallup Polls: Public Opinion, 1978
ISBN 0-8420-2162-0-9 (1980)

The Gallup International Opinion Polls: France, 1939, 1944–1975
2 volumes ISBN 0-394-40998-1 (1976)

The Gallup International Opinion Polls: Great Britain, 1937–1975
2 volumes ISBN 0-394-40992-2 (1976)

The Gallup Poll

Public Opinion 2014

EDITED BY
FRANK NEWPORT

ROWMAN & LITTLEFIELD
Lanham • Boulder • New York • Toronto • Plymouth, UK

ACKNOWLEDGMENTS

The Gallup Poll represents the efforts of a number of talented and dedicated individuals. I wish to express my gratitude to James Clifton, Chairman and CEO of Gallup, whose continuing vision and commitment to the value of social and economic analysis of the poll data undergirds all that is in this volume. I also acknowledge the central role of the poll staff, including Jeffrey Jones, Gallup Poll Managing Editor; Lydia Saad, Gallup Poll Senior Editor; Alyssa Brown, Art Swift, and Tracey Sugar, who compiled the chronology; and all of the authors whose names appear on the by-lines within this volume. Kimberly Clarke edited text, selected the graphs and managed the assembly of materials and the publication process. Professor Fred Israel, City University of New York, George Gallup Jr. (1930–2011), and Alec Gallup (1928–2009) deserve special credit for their contributions to the first 37 volumes in this series.

Published in the United States of America by Rowman & Littlefield Publishers, Inc.
A wholly owned subsidiary of The Rowman & Littlefield Publishing Group, Inc.
4501 Forbes Boulevard, Suite 200, Lanham, Maryland 20706, www.rowman.com

Unit A, Whitacre Mews, 26-34 Stannary Street, London SE11 4AB

ISSN 0195-962X

Cloth ISBN-13: 978-1-4422-5404-6 eISBN: 978-1-4422-5405-3

Printed in the United States of America

∞™ The paper used in this publication meets the minimum requirements of American National Standard for Information Sciences—Permanence of Paper for Printed Library Materials, ANSI/NISO Z39.48-1992.

CONTENTS

Introduction.. vii

The Sample ix

Descriptions of Gallup Economic Measures Used in This Volume xiii

About the Gallup-Healthways Well-Being Index.. xv

State of the States Polls... xv

2014 Chronology xvii

Polls...1

Index..485

INTRODUCTION

The Gallup Poll: Public Opinion 2014 contains the findings of the more than 500 Gallup Poll reports released to the American public during the year 2014. The latest volume reveals the attitudes and opinions of individuals and key groups within the American population concerning national and international issues and events of the year, and reports on Americans' views of the economy, their personal financial situation and well-being, and the political arena.

The 2014 volume is the most recent addition to the 41-volume Gallup collection, *Public Opinion, 1935–2014*, the largest compilation of public opinion findings ever published. The Gallup collection documents the attitudes and opinions of Americans on national and international issues and events from Franklin D. Roosevelt's second term to the present.

Shown in detail are results of tens of thousands of questions that the Gallup Poll—the world's oldest and most respected public opinion poll—has asked of the public over the last eight decades. Results of the survey questions appear in the Gallup Poll reports reproduced in the 41 volumes. These reports, the first of which was released on October 20, 1935, have been provided on a continuous basis since that time, most recently as daily updates on Gallup's website, gallup.com.

The 41-volume collection documents public opinion from 1935 to the present in the following six separate and distinct areas:

1. *Measuring the Strength of Support for the President, Political Candidates, and Political Parties.* For over seventy years, Gallup has measured, on a continuous basis, the strength of support for the president, for the congressional opposition, and for various political candidates and parties in national elections.

2. *Monitoring the Economy.* An important Gallup Poll objective has been monitoring the U.S. economy in all of its permutations from the perspective of the American consumer. Gallup now measures unemployment and job creation and assesses American's views on economic conditions, the job market, and personal financial concerns on a daily basis—providing a continuous record of this vital component of the U.S. economy.

3. *Gauging and Charting the Public's Mood.* From its earliest days the Gallup Poll has sought to determine, on an ongoing basis, Americans' satisfaction or dissatisfaction with the direction in which the nation appeared to be headed and with the way they thought that their personal lives were progressing. This process also has involved regular assessments of the people's mood regarding the state of the nation's economy as well as the status of their personal finances, their jobs, and other aspects of their lives.

4. *Recording the Public's Response to Major News Events.* Gallup has recorded the public's attitudes and opinions in response to major news events of the last seven decades. Examples include Adolf Hitler's invasion of the Soviet Union, the bombing of Pearl Harbor, the dropping of the atomic bomb on Hiroshima, the assassination of President John F. Kennedy, the moon landing, the taking of U.S. hostages in Iran, the O.J. Simpson trial verdict, the impeachment of President Bill Clinton, the 9/11/01 terrorist attacks, the Iraq war, Hurricane Katrina and its aftermath, and the election of the nation's first black president in 2008.

5. *Measuring Americans' Views on Key Policy Issues.* A primary ongoing Gallup polling activity has been to document the collective will of the American people in terms of major policy issues and initiatives under consideration by elected representatives. Gallup routinely measures Americans' priorities, including monthly assessments of the most important problem facing the nation, interest in and awareness of issues and pending legislation, and overall sentiments on pressing national issues.

6. *Tracking America's Well-Being and Health.* Since 2008, Gallup has tracked America's subjective well-being and personal health assessments on a daily basis as part of the Gallup-Healthways Well-Being Index.

Two of the most frequently asked questions concerning the Gallup Poll are: Who pays for or provides financial support to the Poll? And who determines which topics are covered by the Poll or, more specifically, who decides which questions are asked on Gallup surveys? Since its founding in 1935 the Gallup Poll has been underwritten by Gallup itself, in the public interest, and by the nation's media. The Gallup Poll also receives financial support from subscriptions to Gallup Analytics, this annual volume, and partners with innovative businesses who are vitally interested in understanding human attitudes and behavior.

Suggestions for poll questions come from a wide variety of sources, including print and broadcast media, from institutions as well as from individuals, and from broad editorial consideration of the key and pressing issues facing the nation. In addition, the public themselves are regularly questioned about the problems and issues facing the nation as they perceive them. Their answers establish priorities and provide an up-to-the-minute list of topic areas to explore through the Poll.

The Gallup Poll, as it is known today, began life on October 20, 1935, as a nationally syndicated newspaper feature titled "America Speaks—The National Weekly Column of Public Opinion." For brevity's sake, the media quickly came to refer to the column as the Gallup Poll, after its founder and editor-in-chief, Dr. George H. Gallup. Although Dr. Gallup had experimented during the 1934 congressional and 1932 presidential election campaigns to develop more accurate techniques for measuring public opinion, including scientific sampling, the first Gallup survey results to appear in print were those reported in the initial October 20, 1935, column.

Although the new scientific opinion polls enjoyed almost immediate popular success, their initial efforts were met with skepticism from many quarters. Critics questioned, for example, how it was possible to determine the opinions of the entire American populace based on only 1,000 interviews or less, or how one knows whether people were telling the truth. The credibility of the polls as well as their commercial viability was enhanced significantly, however, when Gallup correctly predicted that Roosevelt would win the 1936 presidential election in a landslide, directly contradicting the forecast of the Literary Digest Poll, the poll of record at that time. The Digest Poll, which was not based on scientific sampling procedures, claimed that FDR's Republican challenger, Alfred M. Landon, would easily win the election.

Over the subsequent eight decades scientifically based opinion polls have gained a level of acceptance to where they are used today to investigate virtually every aspect of human experience in most nations of the world.

In 2008 Gallup began an unprecedented program of daily tracking surveys, interviewing 1000 national adults virtually each day of the year, as part of the Gallup-Healthways Well-Being Index project. Daily interviewing allows Gallup to track important health, well-being, political and economic indicators on a continuous basis, and also creates large databases used for detailed analysis of small demographic, political and regional subgroups. The benefits of this major initiative in survey research procedures will be apparent to the reader as he or she reviews the content of this volume.

Frank Newport

THE SAMPLE

Most Gallup Poll findings are based on telephone surveys. The majority of the findings reported in Gallup Poll surveys are based on samples consisting of a minimum of 1,000 interviews.

Design of the Sample for Telephone Surveys

The findings from the telephone surveys are based on Gallup's standard national residential and cell telephone samples, consisting of directory-assisted random-digit telephone samples utilizing a proportionate, stratified sampling design. The random-digit aspect of the residential telephone sample is used to avoid "listing" bias. Numerous studies have shown that households with unlisted telephone numbers are different from listed households. "Unlistedness" is due to household mobility or to customer requests to prevent publication of the telephone number. To avoid this source of bias, a random-digit procedure designed to provide representation of both listed and unlisted (including not-yet-listed) numbers is used.

Beginning in 2008, Gallup began including cell phone telephone numbers in its national samples to account for the growing proportion of Americans who are "cell phone only." Cell phone samples are also based on random-digit-dial procedures using lists of all cell phone exchanges in the United States.

Telephone numbers for the continental United States are stratified into four regions of the country. The sample of telephone numbers produced by the described method is representative of all telephone households within the continental United States.

Only working banks of telephone numbers are selected. Eliminating nonworking banks from the sample increases the likelihood that any sampled telephone number will be associated with a residence.

Within each household contacted on a residential landline, an interview is sought with the adult eighteen years of age or older living in the household who has had the most recent birthday (this is a method commonly employed to make a random selection within households without having to ask the respondent to provide a complete roster of adults living in the household). In the event that the sample becomes disproportionately female (due to higher cooperation rates typically observed for female respondents), the household selection criteria are adjusted to select only the male in the household who has had the most recent birthday (except in households where the adults are exclusively female). Calls made on cell phones do not use the same respondent selection procedure since cell phones are typically associated with a single individual rather than shared among several members of a household.

A minimum of three calls (and up to six calls) is attempted to each selected telephone number to complete an interview. Time of day and the day of the week for callbacks are varied to maximize the chances of reaching a respondent. All interviews are conducted on weekends or weekday evenings in order to contact potential respondents among the working population.

The final sample is weighted so that the distribution of the sample matches current estimates derived from the U.S. Census Bureau's Current Population Survey (CPS) for the adult population living in households with a landline or cellular telephone in the continental United States.

Weighting Procedures

After the survey data have been collected and processed, each respondent is assigned a weight so that the demographic characteristics of the total weighted sample of respondents match the latest estimates of the demographic characteristics of the adult population available from the U.S. Census Bureau. Gallup weights data to census estimates for gender, race, age, Hispanic ethnicity, educational attainment, region, population density, and phone status.

The procedures described above are designed to produce samples approximating the adult civilian population (eighteen and older) living in private households. Survey percentages may be applied to census estimates of the size of these populations to project percentages into numbers of people. The manner in which the sample is drawn also produces a sample that approximates the distribution of private households in the United States. Therefore, survey results also can be projected to numbers of households.

Sampling Tolerances

In interpreting survey results, it should be borne in mind that all sample surveys are subject to sampling error— that is, the extent to which the results may differ from what would be obtained if the whole population surveyed had been interviewed. The size of such sampling errors depends largely on the number of interviews. The design of the survey methodology, including weighting the sample to population estimates, should also be taken into account when figuring sample error.

The following tables may be used in estimating the maximum sampling error of any percentage. The computed allowances have taken into account the effect of the sample design and weighting upon sampling error for a typical Gallup poll. They may be interpreted as indicating the maximum range (plus or minus the figure shown) within which the results of repeated samplings in the same time period could be expected to vary, 95 percent of the time, assuming the same sampling procedure, the same interviewers, and the same questionnaire.

Table A shows how much allowance should be made for the sampling error of a percentage near 50% (which produces the largest uncertainty or sampling error; sampling error decreases as the percentages move further away from 50% in either direction).

Let us say a reported percentage is 49% for a group that includes 1,000 respondents. We go to the column for a sample size of 1,000. The number here is 4, which means that the 49 percent obtained in the sample is subject to a maximum sampling error of plus or minus 4 points. Another way of saying it is that very probably (95 chances out of 100) the average of repeated samplings would be somewhere between 45 and 53, with the most likely figure being the 49 obtained.

In comparing survey results in two samples, such as for men and women, the question arises as to how large must a difference between them be before one can be reasonably sure that it reflects a real difference. In Table B, the number of points that must be allowed for in such comparisons is indicated.

Here is an example of how the table would be used: Let us say that 50 percent of men respond a certain way and 40 percent of women also respond that way, for a difference of 10 percentage points between them. Can we say with any assurance that the 10-point difference reflects a real difference between men and women on the question? The sample contains approximately 500 men and 500 women.

TABLE A
Recommended Allowance for Sampling Error of a Percentage

In Percentage Points (at 95 in 100 confidence level)*
Sample Size

	1,000	750	500	250	100
Percentages near 50	4 (3.6)	4	5	7	11

*The chances are 95 in 100 that the sampling error is not larger than the figures shown.

TABLE B
Recommended Allowance for Sampling Error of the Difference

In Percentage Points (at 95 in 100 confidence level)*
Percentages near 50

	750	500	250
Size of sample			
750	6		
500	6	7	
250	8	8	10

*The chances are 95 in 100 that the sampling is not larger than the figures shown.

Since the percentages are near 50, we consult Table B, and since the two samples are about 500 persons each, we look for the number in the column headed "500" that is also in the row designated "500." We find the number 7 here. This means that the allowance for error should be 7 points, and that in concluding that the percentage among men is somewhere between 3 and 17 points higher than the percentage among women, we should be wrong only about 5 percent of the time. In other words, we can conclude with considerable confidence that a difference exists in the direction observed and that it amounts to at least 3 percentage points.

DESCRIPTIONS OF GALLUP ECONOMIC MEASURES USED IN THIS VOLUME

Gallup's **Employment/Underemployment Index** provides continuous monitoring of U.S. employment and underemployment and serves as a key adjunct to the U.S. government's monthly tracking. This index—based on the combination of responses to a set of questions about employment status—is designed to measure U.S. employment accurately, in accordance with International Conference of Labour Statisticians standards. Based on an individual's responses to the question series (some of which are asked of only a subset of respondents), Gallup classifies respondents into one of six employment categories: employed full time for an employer; employed full time for self; employed part time, but do not want to work full time; employed part time, but want to work full time; unemployed; and out of the workforce. Using these categorizations, Gallup further divides the workforce into those who are employed and those who are underemployed. Employed respondents are those in the workforce who are either employed full time or working part time but do not want to work full time. Underemployed respondents are those in the workforce who are either unemployed or employed part time but want to work full time. Gallup interviews 1,000 Americans daily—or about 30,000 per month. Because of its daily tracking of other political, business, and well-being measures, Gallup provides insights not available from any other source on the health, well-being, optimism, financial situations, and politics of those who are working or seeking work.

Gallup's **Economic Confidence Index** is based on the combined responses to two questions asking Americans, first, to rate economic conditions in this country today and, second, whether they think economic conditions in the country as a whole are getting better or getting worse. The resulting index correlates at a .96 level with the Reuters/University of Michigan Index of Consumer Sentiment and at a .84 level with the Conference Board's Consumer Confidence Index. Gallup's Economic Confidence Index is updated daily, based on interviews conducted the previous night, as well as weekly, providing a far more up-to-date assessment than the monthly reports from the two traditional indices, which are often weeks old when issued. Further, Gallup's monthly sample of about 15,000 consumers far exceeds the Reuters/Michigan sample of 500 and the Conference Board's sample of about 3,500 mail-in surveys.

Gallup's **Job Creation Index** is based on employed Americans' estimates of their companies' hiring and firing practices. Gallup asks its sample of employed Americans each day whether their companies are hiring new people and expanding the size of their workforces, not changing the size of their workforces, or letting people go and reducing the size of their workforces. The resulting index—computed on a daily and a weekly basis by subtracting the percentage of employers letting people go from the percentage hiring—is a real-time indicator of the nation's employment picture across all industry and business sectors. Gallup analysis indicates that the Job Creation Index is an excellent predictor of weekly jobless claims that the U.S. Labor department reports each Thursday. The index has about a 90% chance of predicting the direction of seasonally adjusted initial weekly jobless claims and a better-than-90% chance of predicting the direction of seasonally adjusted initial claims on a four-week average basis. It also has a better-than-80% probability of projecting the direction of the unemployment rate as reported by the Labor Department on the first Friday of every month. In some ways, Gallup's Job Creation Index is more meaningful than the government's weekly new jobless claims measure, given that not everyone who is laid off files for unemployment. The index may also pick up hiring trends days or weeks before they are manifested in the official unemployment rate or other lagging indicators. Finally, the index measures job creation (hiring) and job loss (letting go) on a continuous basis. This provides additional real-time insight not available from broadly aggregated indicators and unemployment data.

Gallup's **Consumer Spending** measure is calculated from responses to a basic question asking Americans each day to estimate the amount of money they spent "yesterday," excluding the purchase of a home or an automobile, or normal household bills. The result is a real-time indicator of discretionary retail spending, fluctuations in which are sensitive to shifts in the economic environment. Gallup's average monthly estimate of spending is correlated at the .65 level with the U.S. government's report of total U.S. retail sales (not seasonally adjusted) and exhibits similarly positive and substantial correlations to other government measures of retail sales. These positive correlations indicate that changes in Gallup's spending estimates are related to changes in both direction and magnitude of actual consumer spending as reported by the government. Further, Gallup's Consumer Spending measure provides estimates on a continuing basis, giving an early read on what the government eventually reports roughly two weeks after the close of each month. Gallup's continuous surveying allows for analysis of spending patterns on a daily and a weekly basis, which is particularly important to understanding seasonal variations in spending. The spending measure allows business and investment decisions to be based on essentially real-time information.

ABOUT THE GALLUP-HEALTHWAYS WELL-BEING INDEX®

The **Gallup-Healthways Well-Being Index** includes more than 2.2 million surveys and captures how people feel about and experience their daily lives. Levels of well-being correlate with healthcare (utilization and cost) and productivity measures (absenteeism, presenteeism, and job performance), all critical to organizational and economic competitiveness.

Well-Being Index data provide a comprehensive view of well-being across five elements:

Purpose: Liking what you do each day and being motivated to achieve your goals

Social: Having supportive relationships and love in your life

Financial: Managing your economic life to reduce stress and increase security

Community: Liking where you live, feeling safe and having pride in your community

Physical: Having good health and enough energy to get things done daily

STATE OF THE STATES POLLS

A number of stories included in this volume are based on Gallup's "State of the States" series, analyses that examine state-by-state differences on the political, economic, and well-being measures that Gallup tracks each day.

State of the States stories are based on aggregated data for six-month or full-year time periods, providing large enough samples for meaningful analyses of responses in each of the 50 states and the District of Columbia.

2014 CHRONOLOGY

January 2014

January 6   Janet Yellen confirmed as Federal Reserve chairman

January 8   NJ Governor Chris Christie pulled into bridge scandal

January 11   Former Israeli prime minister Ariel Sharon dies

February 2014

February 2   Seattle Seahawks win first Super Bowl in franchise history

February 7   The 2014 Sochi Winter Olympics begin

February 20   Ukraine protests take violent turn

February 24   Budget cuts shrink army to pre–World War II size

March 2014

March 1   Russia dispatches troops to Crimea

March 8   Malaysia Airlines flight disappears

March 16   Crimea votes to secede from Ukraine

March 22   Washington State mudslide kills dozens

March 31   UN report predicts dire effects of climate change

April 2014

April 1   Japan lifts decades-old arms ban

April 2   Supreme Court rules on campaign contributions

April 11   Sebelius resigns as secretary of health and human services

April 14   Mass kidnapping in Nigeria sparks international outrage

April 16   South Korean ferry sinks, leaving hundreds missing

April 27-29   Tornadoes strike the southeast, killing dozens

May 2014

May 5   Boko Haram takes responsibility for kidnapping

May 19   Two more states legalize same-sex marriage

May 25   Billionaire businessman wins presidential election in Ukraine

June 2014

June 11   Members of ISIS take control of Mosul

June 30   Supreme Court rules against contraceptives mandate

July 2014

July 2   Unemployment rate lowest since September 2008

July 9   Chinese hackers gain access to U.S. employee data

July 16	U.S., EU place new sanctions on Russia
July 17	Passenger jet crashes in eastern Ukraine
July 22	Two rulings jeopardize key Affordable Care Act component
July 31	Ebola outbreak hits West African countries

August 2014

August 5	U.S. general killed in Afghanistan
August 6	Offensive by Ukrainian military continues
August 7	U.S. launches limited airstrikes on ISIS
August 9	Police shooting of unarmed teenager sparks outrage in Ferguson, Missouri
August 11	Actor and Oscar winner Robin Williams commits suicide
August 16	State of emergency declared in Ferguson

September 2014

September 18	Scotland votes to remain with UK
September 19	White House security breach causes Secret Service fallout
September 25	U.S. Attorney General Eric Holder announces resignation
September 30	First U.S. Ebola case confirmed

October 2014

October 1	Secret Service director resigns after security breach
October 8	First U.S. Ebola patient dies
October 29	14 million vehicles involved in Takata air bag recall

November 2014

November 11	China and U.S. reach landmark agreement on climate change
November 4	Republicans take control of Senate, retain control of House in midterm elections
November 4	Two more states legalize marijuana
November 20	Obama takes executive action on immigration
November 24	Chuck Hagel resigns as defense secretary
November 24	Missouri grand jury makes decision not to indict police officer Darren Wilson in Michael Brown shooting
November 12	Spacecraft lands on comet and makes history

December 2014

December 1	Holder announces plan to address racial profiling
December 20	Two New York City police officers killed

January 02, 2014

U.S. UNINSURED STILL RATE EXCHANGE EXPERIENCE NEGATIVELY

Twenty-six percent of uninsured Americans have visited an exchange website

by Jeffrey M. Jones

PRINCETON, NJ—Uninsured Americans who have visited a health insurance exchange website mostly say their experience was negative rather than positive, by 59% to 39%. That reading, from Gallup Daily tracking throughout December, is only a slight improvement from Gallup's combined October and November polling, when 63% reported a negative experience and 33% a positive one.

Uninsured Americans' Ratings of Health Insurance Exchange Websites

All in all, was your experience using the health exchange website(s) -- [ROTATED: very positive, positive, negative, (or) very negative]?

	Very positive	Positive	Negative	Very negative	Total positive	Total negative
	%	%	%	%	%	%
Dec 2013	7	32	30	29	39	59
Oct/Nov 2013	4	29	34	29	33	63

Gallup Daily tracking

GALLUP

The latest figures are based on Dec. 1–29 Gallup Daily tracking interviews with more than 1,500 uninsured Americans, including roughly 450 who have visited a health insurance exchange website. Since the exchanges opened on Oct. 1, the federally run websites have been plagued by technical problems, while the state-run exchanges have reportedly performed better. Among uninsured Americans who have visited an exchange, 24% say they went to a federal exchange, 20% to a state exchange, 17% to both, and 37% are unsure.

The Obama administration set a goal of having the major technical problems with the federal exchanges fixed by Nov. 30. Thus, all of the recent interviews followed that date. However, some of the respondents interviewed in December may have visited exchanges prior to Nov. 30. Still, the update suggests the website fixes have not dramatically improved the customer experience for uninsured Americans seeking health insurance to comply with requirements of the Affordable Care Act, also known as "Obamacare."

One in Four Uninsured Have Visited Exchanges

Currently, 26% of uninsured Americans say they have visited a health insurance exchange website, up from 20% in October and November polling.

The health insurance exchanges were set up as part of the healthcare law to allow Americans to compare insurance plan specifics and to see if they qualify for a government subsidy to help offset insurance premiums. With the exchanges as the primary new way to get insurance, assuming most Americans intend to comply with the law, one might have expected many more than 26% of uninsured Americans to have visited exchange websites.

Since the December result covers interviews across the entire month, it could slightly underestimate the actual percentage of uninsured Americans who have visited an exchange site if proportionately more visited near the end of the month to meet the deadline for having insurance coverage effective Jan. 1, 2014.

Also, prior Gallup tracking has shown that less than half of uninsured Americans who plan to get insurance say they will do so through an exchange, perhaps opting instead to take an employer-sponsored plan or get covered on a family member's plan. In addition, roughly 30% of uninsured Americans say they are more likely to forego insurance and pay the government fine than to sign up for insurance.

Implications

The Obama administration recently announced that roughly 2 million Americans have signed up for insurance through a federal or state health insurance exchange. Most of those enrollments happened in December, particularly in the latter part of the month given the deadline to have coverage effective Jan. 1. The rise in exchange visits in December could, to some degree, reflect improvements in the health insurance exchange websites, as people who wanted to sign up for insurance were more easily able to do so. Also, the increased exchange website traffic may be due to procrastination on the part of those seeking insurance. Uninsured Americans still have time in 2014 to sign up for insurance and avoid paying a fine, so exchange visits may continue to increase.

However, the fact that most uninsured Americans who have visited the exchanges report a negative experience is problematic, particularly given the Obama administration's efforts to improve the federal sites. If uninsured Americans continue to have bad experiences with the exchanges, it could hinder the Obama administration's goal to insure as many Americans as possible.

Survey Methods

Results for this Gallup poll are based on telephone interviews conducted Dec. 1–29, 2013, on the Gallup Daily tracking survey, with a random sample of 1,563 adults, aged 18 and older, living in all 50 U.S. states and the District of Columbia, who do not currently have health insurance.

For results based on the total sample of uninsured adults, the margin of sampling error is ±3 percentage points at the 95% confidence level.

January 03, 2014

OBAMA'S JOB APPROVAL DECLINED STEADILY THROUGHOUT 2013

Budget battles, NSA revelations, and healthcare law rollout all contributed

by Lydia Saad

PRINCETON, NJ—President Barack Obama wrapped up 2013 with an average 41% approval rating in December, unchanged from November. However, his monthly job approval declined steadily through most of 2013, including a three-percentage-point drop in March.

Gallup's three-day rolling averages of Obama's job approval rating are especially helpful in identifying the events that likely contributed to his overall decline in popularity.

January and February Looked Bright

Obama started the year with approval ratings generally where they left off in 2012—in the middle to upper 50s. These included consecutive days in early January at 56%—his highest three-day rating of 2013.

President Barack Obama's Job Approval Rating in 2013

% Approve, based on monthly averages in Gallup Daily tracking

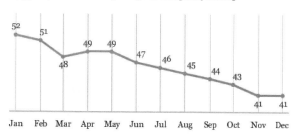

GALLUP

Obama's approval rating fell to the high 40s for two days in mid-January, soon after he outlined new gun control policies formulated in response to the Newtown school shootings. Although the specific proposals were popular, Americans had a mixed reaction to his overall plan, with barely half wanting their members of Congress to support it.

His approval rating rebounded around the time he was sworn in for a second term, reaching 53% in the first three days after the Jan. 20 inauguration, and it remained at 50% or more through February.

President Barack Obama's Job Approval Ratings -- January-February 2013

% Approve, based on three-day rolling averages in Gallup Daily tracking

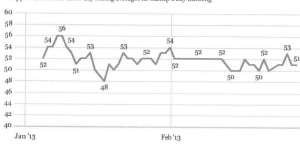

GALLUP

Sequester, NSA Revelations Cost Obama

With March came the federal government's budget sequestration and an immediate downtick in Obama's approval rating to 46%, in the first three days of the sequester. His approval rating stayed below 50% for most of March, and ultimately averaged 48% for the month, down three points from February's 51%.

Obama's rating improved slightly to 49% and 50% in early April; it then jumped to between 51% and 53% in the days after the April 15 Boston Marathon bombing and subsequent Boston memorial for the victims, at which Obama spoke. Obama received an average 49% approval rating for all of April, up one point from March.

Obama's approval rating ranged from 48% to 51% for most of May. The May 3 Bureau of Labor Statistics jobs report, which showed a downtick in the nation's unemployment rate from 7.6% to 7.5%, may have helped him maintain a steady 49% average for the month.

President Barack Obama's Job Approval Ratings -- March-April 2013

% Approve, based on three-day rolling averages in Gallup Daily tracking

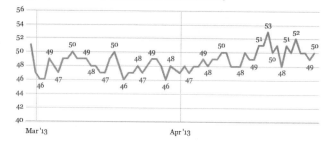

GALLUP

June brought more challenges for Obama, with *The Guardian*, a British newspaper, issuing a series of reports starting on June 5 about the existence of secret NSA spy programs, including surveillance of American citizens. On June 9, *The Guardian* revealed the identity of its source, former NSA contractor Edward Snowden, and during the second week of June, Obama's approval rating dipped from 49% to 45%—his lowest rating of the year to that point. His approval briefly surged to 50% on the first two days of his weeklong Africa trip in late June, but quickly reverted to 45% by month's end. His average approval rating for the month was 47%, down two points from May.

President Barack Obama's Job Approval Ratings -- May-June 2013

% Approve, based on three-day rolling averages in Gallup Daily tracking

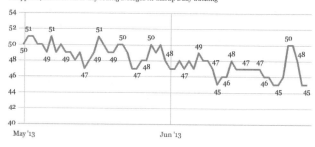

GALLUP

The Guardian continued to expose U.S. government spy programs through the summer, with the revelations sparking outcries against the Obama administration from certain members of Congress and world leaders. Meanwhile, Obama's approval rating sank a point per month, hitting 44% in September.

It is possible that other issues contributed to his declining approval. Obama's comments on the not-guilty verdict for George Zimmerman in the Trayvon Martin murder trial in mid-July received heavy media coverage. The budget conflict in Congress leading up to the October shutdown dominated political news in September. And Obama addressed the nation that month about the need to intervene in Syria to help prevent the use of chemical weapons on civilians. The government's U.S. unemployment rate improved slightly over the summer—yet evidently, given the decline in Obama's approval rating, this good news was more than offset by other issues.

The Shutdown/Health Exchange One-Two Punch

After weeks of failed efforts at a compromise budget bill in Congress, the federal government was forced into a partial shutdown on Oct. 1, and, similar to what happened in March with sequestration,

Obama's approval rating immediately fell four points—from 45% in the last three days of September to 41% in the first three days of October.

President Barack Obama's Job Approval Ratings -- July-September 2013
% Approve, based on three-day rolling averages in Gallup Daily tracking

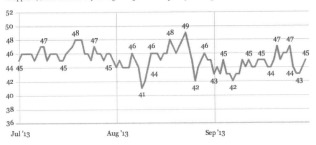

This period also spanned the Oct. 1 opening of federal health insurance exchange websites, which gave Americans access to a new health insurance marketplace under the new healthcare law. However, the website had major technical problems, and many Americans lost their health insurance because it didn't comply with the law. This prompted some to charge that Obama intentionally misled the public about their freedom to retain their own healthcare plans. Likely as a result, Obama's average approval rating fell further in late October and into November. Underscoring this, Obama brushed up against his own record-low approval rating of 38% (from 2011) with three 39% ratings in November and, as a result, it fell two points overall in November after a one-point drop in October.

December brought better news for the White House by comparison—including significant, if not perfect, repairs to the federal health exchange website upon its relaunch after Thanksgiving, a positive jobs report on Dec. 6, and the stock market's string of record-high closings. Obama spoke at Nelson Mandela's memorial service in South Africa on Dec. 10, but otherwise made little news in December. For that, he received a reprieve from declining job approval, as his average rating held steady at 41% for the month. This was aided by a late-month increase in his approval to 44%.

President Barack Obama's Job Approval Ratings -- October-December 2013
% Approve, based on three-day rolling averages in Gallup Daily tracking

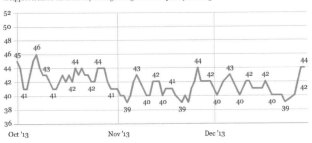

Historical Precedents for Recovery

It is common for presidents to have an extended period of decline in approval at the start of a presidency. It's the reality check after the honeymoon, and Obama also experienced this. It is also common to see extended downturns in approval following a major job approval rally such as George H.W. Bush experienced after the 1991 Gulf War, and George W. Bush experienced after 9/11.

It has been less common to see sustained periods of significant decline during the normal course of a presidency, such as what Obama experienced this year, his fifth in office. The few examples of these from recent presidencies are:

- Reagan suffered a particularly protracted decline at the beginning of his presidency, with a normal period of decline from his initial approval rating lengthened by the 1981–1982 recession. Then, given an improving economy, he amply recovered in time to win re-election in 1984.
- Later in Reagan's presidency, between 1986 and 1987, he suffered three quarters of decline over the Iran-Contra affair, falling from the 60s to below 50%, but this was followed by only a partial recovery for most of 1988. Only at the tail end of his presidency did his approval rebound to the 63% seen in the fall of 1986.
- George H.W. Bush's rating fell for three quarters in 1992—mainly owing to the economy—after it had already spent the three previous quarters coming down from its 1991 Gulf War high. This spelled the end of his presidency.
- George W. Bush's rating dropped for six quarters from 2005—his fifth year in office—through the first half of 2006 as the Iraq war became increasingly unpopular, and for three more quarters between 2006 and 2007. It never recovered.

Thus, recent polling history doesn't offer any firm conclusions about what a year of decline portends for a president; there is precedent for recovery, but also for stagnation.

Separately, Gallup trends show that two-term presidents typically receive less support in their second term than their first, what some have dubbed a "second-term curse." Even in the short term, it's unlikely Obama will get much of a boost out of his upcoming State of the Union address, given how little his past addresses have been associated with increases in approval.

Prior Gallup analysis shows that Obama's overall job approval rating is highly linked to his approval rating on the economy. This means that under normal circumstances, if his overall job rating is to increase, not only does the economy have to improve but Americans also have to acknowledge it and give Obama credit for it. In 2013, despite BLS reports of reduced unemployment, a soaring stock market, and other positive economic signs, Americans maintained both a net-negative view of the economy and a negative view of Obama's handling of it. Clearly, they are looking for stronger economic growth before relinquishing their negative posture on the economy—something Obama will need to focus on.

At the same time, Obama's 2013 decline did not chiefly stem from economic problems, but political ones: budget conflicts with Congress, revelations that his administration sanctions a national security program involving extensive covert monitoring of Americans' phone and computer data, and negative public reaction to the rollout of the Affordable Care Act. As long as these issues linger, particularly without major progress felt on the economy, Obama's job rating could continue to languish in 2014 and beyond.

January 06, 2014
U.S. CONSUMER SPENDING IN DECEMBER HIGHEST SINCE 2008
Americans spent $96 per day on average in December

by Frank Newport

PRINCETON, NJ—Americans reported spending $96 per day in December—the highest monthly average since September 2008, when the reality of the depth of the recession and economic crisis began to be felt across the nation. This is also the highest average for any December across the six years that Gallup has been tracking daily spending.

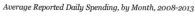

Average Reported Daily Spending, by Month, 2008-2013

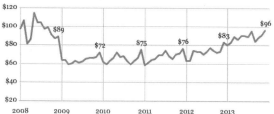

Figures shown are for December of each year

GALLUP'

The results are based on Dec. 1–29 Gallup Daily tracking. Each night since January 2008, Gallup has asked Americans to say how much they spent the prior day, aside from normal household bills and major durables such as homes or cars. These data provide an indicator of Americans' discretionary spending. Self-reports of spending, which dropped modestly in the fourth quarter of 2008, dropped dramatically in the first quarter of 2009. But after remaining low for several years, spending began to rise at the end of 2012 and has continued to trend generally upward during 2013, ending the year with an average that was $16 per day higher than Gallup found at the beginning of 2013.

Spending in December is typically the highest of any month because of Christmas holiday spending. The one exception to this came in 2008, with depressed December spending reflecting the effects of the recession. The $96 spending average in December 2013 was up from $91 in November and is the highest of 2013, just above the $95 August average.

Implications

The trend in consumer spending over the past six years presents a clear pattern. Spending was at its highest point in the first three quarters of 2008—the year in which Gallup started tracking daily spending—including the monthly high to date of $114 measured in May. Then came the economic collapse. Spending dropped to its nadir of $58 by January 2011. Since then, it has gradually increased, and spending last year clearly was the most robust since 2008.

Consumer spending is one of the main engines of economic growth, and its trajectory in the months ahead will be an important indicator of the economy's health. If the current trends continue, average daily spending could break through the $100 mark on a routine basis, and thus denote a return to levels that characterized spending in pre-recession times.

Still, continued spending growth is not a certainty. Other attitudinal data show that Americans are still more likely to say they prefer to save rather than spend, and many continue to claim that spending less is the "new normal" in their lives. Additionally, Gallup's measure of job creation slipped slightly at the end of the year, suggesting some caution in concluding that the economy is on a straight linear upward trajectory.

Survey Methods

Results for this Gallup poll are based on telephone interviews conducted Dec. 1–29, 2013, on the Gallup Daily tracking survey, with a random sample of 13,193 adults, aged 18 and older, living in all 50 U.S. states and the District of Columbia.

For results based on the total sample of national adults, the margin of sampling error is ±1 percentage point at the 95% confidence level.

The margin of error for the spending mean is ±$4.

January 06, 2014
AMERICANS' TECH TASTES CHANGE WITH TIMES
Internet-connected devices growing in popularity

by Andrew Dugan

WASHINGTON, D.C.—The International Consumer Electronics Show (CES) this week allows technology developers to showcase the latest gadgets that may become must-haves for many Americans. As attendees get a glimpse of the industry's future, Gallup finds that the devices Americans own have changed over the past decade, with ownership of laptops (64%) and iPods/MP3 players (45%) up most dramatically from 2005. Meanwhile, far smaller proportions of Americans now own VCRs and basic cellphones, which were a staple to many in the past.

Possession of Electronic Devices in the U.S.

For each of the following, please say whether it is something you, personally, have, or do not have. How about --

Sorted by Yes, have (2013)

	Yes, have (2005)	Yes, have (2013)	Change from 2005
	%	%	pct. pts.
A DVD player or Blu-ray player	83	80	-3
Wireless Internet access, or Wi-Fi, in your home	--	73	n/a
Cable TV	68	68	0
A laptop computer	30	64	+34
A smartphone, that is, a cellular phone that has built-in applications and Internet access, such as an iPhone or Android	--	62	n/a
A VCR	88	58	-30
A desktop computer	65	57	-8
A basic cellular phone that is not a smartphone	78	45	-33
An iPod or MP3 music player	19	45	+26
A video game system, such as Xbox or PlayStation	36	41	+5
An Internet streaming service like Hulu, Netflix, or Roku	--	39	n/a
A tablet computer such as an iPad or Kindle Fire	--	38	n/a
Satellite TV	30	34	+4
An E-reader, such as a Kindle or Nook	--	26	n/a

n/a = Not applicable
Dec. 5-8, 2013

GALLUP'

These results come from a Dec. 5–8 Gallup telephone survey of 1,031 national adults, with roughly half of the respondents reached on cellphones and half on landlines.

Technology and consumer electronics is a dynamic field; devices that are commonplace can quickly become obsolete as new products emerge. That Gallup did not ask about a number of electronic products and services in 2005 that were included in the current update is testimony to these changes.

Compared with 2005, fewer Americans today have desktop computers, VCRs, and basic cellphones, while there have been substantial increases in ownership of MP3 players and laptops, with slight increases in ownership of video game systems and satellite TV. Meanwhile, most Americans say they have Internet access at home through Wi-Fi (73%) or have smartphones with Web access (62%).

Still, even in the face of such rapid innovation, some items have showed remarkable staying power since 2005. Ownership of cable TV (68%) has not changed, even as speculation abounds that Internet streaming services such as Hulu, Netflix, or Roku could displace cable. Essentially the same share of Americans own DVD or Blu-ray players as in 2005, 80%, and this is the most commonly owned electronic device.

Generational Differences in Technology Ownership

The youngest American adults—those aged 18 to 29—favor a different portfolio of technology devices than their older compatriots do. Smartphone ownership among the young is nearly universal (88%), and it is the most common device among this group. Eighty-three percent of 18- to 29-year-olds have wireless Internet access at home, and another 79% have a laptop.

Technological Device Ownership Among Young Americans
18 to 29 years of age

	% Yes, have
Smartphone	88
Wireless Internet access in home	83
Laptop computer	79
DVD player or Blu-ray player	77
Video game system	64
IPod or MP3 player	63
Cable TV	62
Internet streaming service	62
VCR	41
Desktop computer	41
Tablet computer	34
Satellite TV	32
E-reader	25
Basic cellular phone that is not a smartphone	24

Dec. 5-8, 2013

GALLUP

Less common among younger Americans are items that are familiar to individuals of a different generation—about four in 10 younger Americans have a VCR (41%), and an identical percentage have a desktop computer. Meanwhile, a basic cellphone, which 86% of 18- to 29-year-olds owned in 2005, is now the least commonly owned technology device among this age group (24%).

This is not to say that older generations have been left behind as technology changes. Recent research suggests that the largest growth in Facebook over the past year came from the oldest cohort of Americans, aged 65 and older. But older Americans are most likely to have older forms of technology, including cable TV (74%) and the now essentially obsolete VCR (74%), although 70% own DVD players. A majority of Americans aged 65 and older own a basic cellphone (61%), while one-quarter own a smartphone.

About half of older Americans have wireless Internet access in their homes. Portable Internet-based or Internet-providing devices are less popular with American seniors: one-quarter have tablet computers, while 16% have an iPod or MP3 player and 15% have an Internet streaming service. Video game systems are the least popular electronic product among older Americans, at 10%.

Technological Device Ownership Among the Oldest Americans
65+ years of age

	% Yes, have
Cable TV	74
VCR	74
DVD player or Blu-ray player	70
Basic cellular phone that is not a smartphone	61
Desktop computer	58
Wireless Internet access in home	51
Laptop computer	41
Satellite TV	41
Smartphone	25
Tablet computer	25
E-reader	20
IPod or MP3 player	16
Internet streaming service	15
Video game system	10

Dec. 5-8, 2013

GALLUP

All in all, the five devices that skew the youngest are smartphones, video game systems, Internet streaming services, iPod or MP3 players, and laptop computers. And the five devices that skew the oldest are satellite TV, cable TV, desktop computers, VCRs, and basic cellphones.

Technology Use and Age Skew

	18 to 29	65+	Gap in ownership, 18 to 29 minus 65+
	% Yes, have	% Yes, have	pct. pts.
SKEW YOUNGEST			
Smartphone	88	25	+63
Video game system	64	10	+54
Internet streaming service	62	15	+47
IPod/MP3 player	63	16	+47
Laptop computer	79	41	+38
SKEW OLDEST			
Satellite TV	32	41	-9
Cable TV	62	74	-12
Desktop computer	41	58	-17
VCR	41	74	-33
Basic cellphone	24	61	-37

Dec. 5-8, 2013

GALLUP

Bottom Line

The week's CES show could unveil another electronic device that will soon be ubiquitous in American life. Of course, in the process, these new devices will begin displacing other popular technology. The constantly evolving nature of the technology scene is why so many people find it exciting, and as this Gallup poll shows, technology ownership has changed dramatically since 2005. Portable Internet-connected devices such as laptops and smartphones are generally more favored, while older forms of technology such as desktop computers, VCRs, and basic cellphones are falling out of fashion.

Survey Methods

Results for this Gallup poll are based on telephone interviews conducted Dec. 5–8, 2013, on the Gallup Daily tracking survey, with a random sample of 1,031 adults, aged 18 and older, living in all 50 U.S. states and the District of Columbia.

For results based on the total sample of national adults, the margin of sampling error is ±4 percentage points at the 95% confidence level.

January 08, 2014
RECORD-HIGH 42% OF AMERICANS IDENTIFY AS INDEPENDENTS
Republican identification lowest in at least 25 years

by Jeffrey M. Jones

PRINCETON, NJ—Forty-two percent of Americans, on average, identified as political independents in 2013, the highest Gallup has measured since it began conducting interviews by telephone 25 years ago. Meanwhile, Republican identification fell to 25%, the lowest over that time span. At 31%, Democratic identification is unchanged from the last four years but down from 36% in 2008.

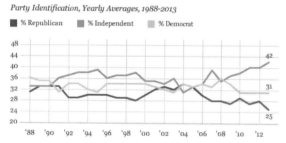

Party Identification, Yearly Averages, 1988-2013

■ % Republican   ■ % Independent   ■ % Democrat

Based on multiple day polls conducted by telephone

GALLUP

The results are based on more than 18,000 interviews with Americans from 13 separate Gallup multiple-day polls conducted in 2013.

In each of the last three years, at least 40% of Americans have identified as independents. These are also the only years in Gallup's records that the percentage of independents has reached that level.

Americans' increasing shift to independent status has come more at the expense of the Republican Party than the Democratic Party. Republican identification peaked at 34% in 2004, the year George W. Bush won a second term in office. Since then, it has fallen nine percentage points, with most of that decline coming during Bush's troubled second term. When he left office, Republican identification was down to 28%. It has declined or stagnated since then, improving only slightly to 29% in 2010, the year Republicans "shellacked" Democrats in the midterm elections.

Not since 1983, when Gallup was still conducting interviews face to face, has a lower percentage of Americans, 24%, identified as Republicans than is the case now. That year, President Ronald

Reagan remained unpopular as the economy struggled to emerge from recession. By the following year, amid an improving economy and re-election for the increasingly popular incumbent president, Republican identification jumped to 30%, a level generally maintained until 2007.

Democratic identification has also declined in recent years, falling five points from its recent high of 36% in 2008, the year President Barack Obama was elected. The current 31% of Americans identifying as Democrats matches the lowest annual average in the last 25 years.

Fourth Quarter Surge in Independence

The percentage of Americans identifying as independents grew over the course of 2013, surging to 46% in the fourth quarter. That coincided with the partial government shutdown in October and the problematic rollout of major provisions of the healthcare law, commonly known as "Obamacare."

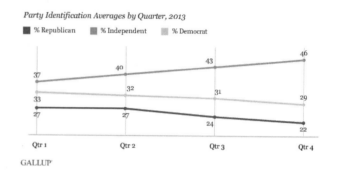

Party Identification Averages by Quarter, 2013

■ % Republican   ■ % Independent   ■ % Democrat

GALLUP

The 46% independent identification in the fourth quarter is a full three percentage points higher than Gallup has measured in any quarter during its telephone polling era.

Democrats Maintain Edge in Party Identification

Democrats maintain their six-point edge in party identification when independents' "partisan leanings" are taken into account. In addition to the 31% of Americans who identify as Democrats, another 16% initially say they are independents but when probed say they lean to the Democratic Party. An equivalent percentage, 16%, say they are independent but lean to the Republican Party, on top of the 25% of Americans identifying as Republicans. All told, then, 47% of Americans identify as Democrats or lean to the Democratic Party, and 41% identify as Republicans or lean to the Republican Party.

Democrats have held at least a nominal advantage on this measure of party affiliation in all but three years since Gallup began asking the "partisan lean" follow-up in 1991. During this time, Democrats' advantage has been as high as 12 points, in 2008. However, that lead virtually disappeared by 2010, although Democrats have re-established an edge in the last two years.

Implications

Americans are increasingly declaring independence from the political parties. It is not uncommon for the percentage of independents to rise in a non-election year, as 2013 was. Still, the general trend in recent years, including the 2012 election year, has been toward greater percentages of Americans identifying with neither the Republican Party nor the Democratic Party, although most still admit to leaning toward one of the parties.

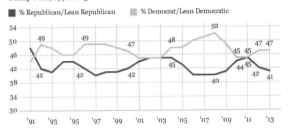

Party Identification (Including Independent Leanings), Annual Averages, Gallup Polls, 1991-2013

■ % Republican/Lean Republican   ▒ % Democrat/Lean Democratic

Note: Gallup began regularly measuring independents' party leanings in 1991.

GALLUP°

The rise in political independence is likely an outgrowth of Americans' record or near-record negative views of the two major U.S. parties, of Congress, and their low level of trust in government more generally.

The increased independence adds a greater level of unpredictability to this year's congressional midterm elections. Because U.S. voters are less anchored to the parties than ever before, it's not clear what kind of appeals may be most effective to winning votes. But with Americans increasingly eschewing party labels for themselves, candidates who are less closely aligned to their party or its prevailing doctrine may benefit.

Survey Methods

Results are based on aggregated telephone interviews from 13 separate Gallup polls conducted in 2013, with a random sample of 18,871 adults, aged 18 and older, living in all 50 U.S. states and the District of Columbia.

For results based on the total sample of national adults, the margin of sampling error is ±1 percentage point at the 95% confidence level.

January 09, 2014
U.S. PAYROLL TO POPULATION RATE FALLS TO 42.9% IN DECEMBER
Unemployment rate declines to 7.4%

by Ben Ryan and Frank Newport

WASHINGTON, D.C.—The U.S. Payroll to Population employment rate (P2P), as measured by Gallup, fell to 42.9% in December, from 43.7% in November. The current rate is the lowest Gallup has measured since March 2011.

Gallup's P2P metric estimates the percentage of the U.S. adult population aged 18 and older that is employed full time by an employer for at least 30 hours per week. P2P is not seasonally adjusted. However, because of seasonal fluctuations, year-over-year comparisons are often helpful in evaluating whether monthly changes are attributable to seasonal hiring patterns or true growth (or deterioration) in the percentage of people working full time for an employer. The P2P rate for December 2013 is down from 44.4%

in December 2012 and 43.8% in December 2011, but is higher than the 42.4% of December 2010.

U.S. Payroll to Population Employment Rates
Monthly trend, January 2010-December 2013

■ % of adult population employed full time for an employer

Gallup Daily tracking

GALLUP°

The most recent results are based on Gallup Daily tracking interviews with approximately 26,000 Americans, conducted Dec. 1–29 by landline and cellphone. Gallup does not count adults who are self-employed, working part time, unemployed, or out of the workforce as payroll-employed in the P2P metric.

Seasonally Unadjusted Unemployment 7.4% in December

Unlike Gallup's P2P rate, which is a percentage of the total U.S. population, traditional employment metrics, such as the unemployment rates Gallup and the U.S. Bureau of Labor Statistics (BLS) report, are a percentage of the workforce. Gallup defines the "workforce" as adults who are working or actively looking for work and available for employment. The U.S. workforce participation rate in December was 65.8%, down from November's 66.9% and from 66.8% in December 2012.

Without seasonal adjustment, Gallup's December unemployment rate was 7.4%. Gallup's seasonally adjusted U.S. unemployment rate for December, using an estimate of the government's likely adjustment factor, is 7.6%, down from 8.6% in November. Gallup calculates this rate by applying the adjustment factor the government used for the same month in the previous year, which in December 2012 was an increase of 0.2 percentage points. The exact adjustment the government uses for December 2013 will not be known until Friday's BLS release. The government's unemployment estimates are relatively stable from month to month; Gallup's measure of unemployment tends to exhibit more monthly fluctuation.

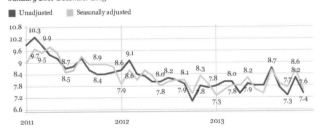

Gallup Adjusted and Unadjusted U.S. Unemployment Rate Trend, January 2011-December 2013

■ Unadjusted   ▒ Seasonally adjusted

Gallup Daily tracking; Gallup seasonally adjusts its unemployment data using the initial BLS seasonal adjustment for the same month in the prior year

GALLUP°

Underemployment, as measured without seasonal adjustment, was 17.2% in December, little changed from 17.3% in November, and from 17.1% in December 2012. Gallup's U.S. underemployment rate combines the percentage of adults in the workforce who are unemployed (7.4% in December) with the percentage of those who are employed part time but looking for full-time work (9.8%).

Gallup's U.S. Underemployment Rate, Monthly Averages

Not seasonally adjusted

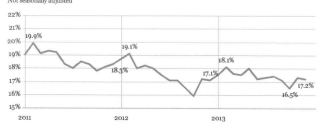

Gallup Daily tracking
January 2011-December 2013

GALLUP®

Bottom Line

The overall percentage of the U.S. adult population that was employed full time for an employer dropped in December to 42.9%, a low point since 2011. Further, the 34.2% of all Americans who were not in the workforce is up from what Gallup has measured over the past four years.

At the same time, Gallup's seasonally adjusted U.S. unemployment rate—the closest comparison it has to the official BLS numbers—decreased in December. However, it is important to note that Gallup's adjusted number is based on past BLS seasonal adjustments, and those adjustments may not be the same this month. Additionally, while both Gallup and BLS data are based on robust surveys, the two have important methodological differences. Although Gallup's employment numbers highly correlate with BLS rates, Gallup's numbers tend to have more month-to-month variability, and the unemployment rate that BLS reports each month does not always track precisely with Gallup's estimate.

Gallup's U.S. Unemployment Measures, December 2013

	Most recent month (December 2013)	Previous month (November 2013)	Month a year ago (December 2012)
Employed full time for employer (P2P)*	42.9%	43.7%	44.4%
Employed full time self*	5.1%	5.3%	4.5%
Workforce participation rate*	65.8%	66.9%	66.8%
Unemployment rate (unadjusted)**	7.4%	8.2%	7.7%
Unemployment rate (adjusted)**	7.6%	8.6%	7.9%
Employed part time wanting full time**	9.8%	9.1%	9.4%
Underemployment rate**	17.2%	17.3%	17.1%

*Metrics represent percentages of the U.S. population
**Metrics represent percentages of the U.S. workforce

Note: Workforce participation rate is defined as the percentage of all Americans aged 18 or older who have a job or are actively seeking work. Gallup seasonally adjusts its unemployment data using the initial BLS seasonal adjustment for the same month in the prior year.

GALLUP®

Survey Methods

Results for this Gallup poll are based on telephone interviews conducted Dec. 1–29, 2013, on the Gallup Daily tracking survey, with a random sample of 26,381 adults, aged 18 and older, living in all 50 U.S. states and the District of Columbia.

For results based on the total sample of national adults, one can say with 95% confidence that the margin of sampling error is ±1 percentage point.

January 09, 2014

U.S. ECONOMIC INDICATORS IMPROVE IN 2013
Gallup's economic confidence, job creation, and consumer spending measures rise

by Brendan Moore

WASHINGTON, D.C.—Three key Gallup consumer-based measures of the U.S. economy showed overall growth in 2013, despite monthly fluctuations. Gallup's U.S. Economic Confidence Index averaged −16 for 2013, up five points from 2012; its Job Creation Index averaged +20, up two points from 2012; and average daily self-reported spending increased to $88, up $16 from 2012.

Annual U.S. Economic Trends, 2008-2013

Economic confidence, job creation, and consumer spending

	2008	2009	2010	2011	2012	2013	Change, '13 vs. '12
Economic Confidence Index	-48	-35	-28	-37	-21	-16	+5
Job Creation Index	18	-1	7	14	18	20	+2
Average consumer spending	$96	$64	$65	$68	$72	$88	+$16

Gallup Daily tracking

GALLUP®

Despite Monthly Swings, U.S. Economic Confidence Rose in 2013

Americans' confidence in the economy improved in 2013, including high points of −7 in May and −8 in June—the best two months since Gallup began tracking this measure daily in 2008. But there were also some large downturns occurring around pivotal political events. For example, amid the federal government shutdown and partisan bickering over the federal debt limit, the Economic Confidence Index plunged as low as −35 in October. Despite these setbacks, the index for 2013 is the highest Gallup has measured since Daily tracking began in 2008, even though it was still in negative territory.

Gallup Economic Confidence Index -- Monthly Averages

January 2008 through December 2013

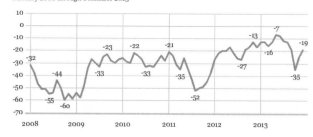

Gallup Daily tracking

GALLUP®

The index represents Americans' net optimism about the economy, combining their views about current economic conditions and their perceptions of the economy's direction. The index has a theoretical maximum of +100 if all Americans think the economy is "excellent" or "good" and improving, and a theoretical minimum of −100 if all believe the economy is "only fair" or "poor" and getting worse.

By income level, the largest increase in confidence last year was among those with annual household incomes of $90,000 or more. The index among this group improved by seven points to −5 in 2013. By comparison, confidence among Americans with annual household incomes below $90,000 rose three points to −18.

Democrats were more positive than negative about the economy last year, with an index of +13. Meanwhile, Republicans' index remained entrenched in negative territory, averaging −44. Democrats have been significantly more optimistic than Republicans about economic conditions since early 2009—shortly after President Barack Obama took office. Although Republicans' confidence is significantly lower than Democrats', Republicans' index improved seven points in 2013, while the Democrats' average score was unchanged from 2012.

U.S. Job Creation Improved Slightly Last Year

Gallup's Job Creation Index averaged +20 for 2013, up slightly from +18 in 2012, and the highest annual average in Gallup's six-year history of tracking this measure.

Job Creation Index Among All U.S. Workers – Monthly Averages, January 2008-December 2013

Based on the percentage of U.S. workers who say their employer is hiring workers and expanding the size of its workforce minus the percentage who say their employer is letting workers go and reducing the size of its workforce

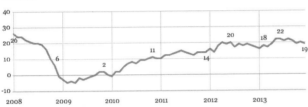

Gallup Daily tracking

GALLUP

The index is a measure of net hiring in the U.S., based on responses from a nationally representative sample of full- and part-time workers. In 2013, an average of 36% of all workers said their employer was hiring employees and expanding the size of its workforce, while 16% said their employer was letting workers go and reducing the overall size of its workforce, resulting in the +20 net hiring score.

The Midwest region registered the highest score of +22, while the East had the lowest, at +17. The West, however, had the greatest improvement in 2013, rising five points to +20.

U.S Consumer Spending—Highest Since 2008

Americans' self-reported daily spending increased significantly to a monthly average of $88 in 2013, up $16 from 2012. Last year's average is the highest Gallup has measured since 2008, when spending averaged $96.

Gallup's consumer spending measure is based on Daily tracking of a question that asks Americans how much they spent the prior day, aside from normal household bills and major durables such as homes or cars.

Average Reported Daily Spending, by Month, 2008-2013

Figures shown are for December of each year

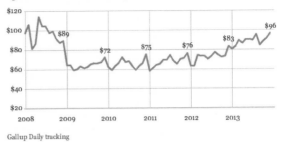

Gallup Daily tracking

GALLUP

Spending last year increased across income groups. Americans with household incomes of $90,000 or more increased their average daily spending by $26, to $153 in 2013. Americans with lower household incomes increased their spending by $16, to an average of $76 per day. The increases in average daily spending levels among upper-, middle-, and lower-income groups are the largest annual increases since Gallup began tracking Americans' spending habits daily in 2008.

Implications

The U.S. economy in 2013 showed signs of improvement in several areas, according to Gallup Daily tracking of key economic metrics. Americans are more confident in current economic conditions and the future direction of the economy than they were in the previous five years; net hiring improved, as reported through Gallup's Job Creation Index; and consumer spending—a strong indicator of future GDP growth—shot up significantly.

Key traditional, non-Gallup economic indicators also improved last year. U.S. economic output as reported by the Bureau of Economic Analysis increased as the year went on, with third quarter real GDP growing by an annual rate of 4.1%, after 2.5% growth in the second quarter and 1.1% in the first quarter. In addition, the U.S. stock market had a year of record highs, with roughly a 30% gain in the S&P 500, and housing prices appreciated as continuing low interest rates boosted demand.

While the 2013 economic data are a positive sign that the U.S. economy is recovering from the 2008–2009 economic recession, it is still unclear whether the economy is fundamentally strong, especially considering the support it received from the Federal Reserve during the past two years. The Fed took an aggressive stance on stimulating the economy from mid-2012 through 2013 by keeping interest rates historically low via its bond purchasing program—but a few weeks ago, the Fed announced that beginning in January, it would start to taper its monthly buying.

This has the potential to drive up interest rates, increasing borrowing costs for home buyers and potential and existing business owners—which in turn could negatively affect housing markets, consumer spending, and job creation. The Fed has indicated it will seek to keep short-term interest rates low until unemployment drops a bit more or until inflation becomes a concern; however, it is unlikely that the U.S. will continue to experience the record-low interest rates seen in 2013.

In addition to worries about future interest rate hikes and the associated risks, the labor market is also a pressing concern. While the unemployment rate as reported by the Bureau of Labor Statistics has declined since 2010, the U.S. still has a ways to go before getting back to pre-recession levels of around 4.5% to 5%. Gallup found that unemployment was lower in 2013 compared with recent years but its Payroll to Population rate—the percentage of adults employed full time by an employer—showed no improvement in 2013. This may be attributable to more Americans dropping out of the workforce or more becoming self-employed.

Survey Methods

Results for this Gallup poll are based on telephone interviews conducted Jan. 2–Dec. 29, 2013, on the Gallup Daily tracking survey, with a random sample of adults, aged 18 and older, living in all 50 U.S. states and the District of Columbia.

Economic confidence results are based on interviews with 178,071 U.S. adults.

Spending results are based on interviews with 178,520 U.S. adults.

Job Creation results are based on interviews with 208,759 employed adults.

For results based on the total sample of national adults, the margin of sampling error is ±1 percentage point at the 95% confidence level.

January 10, 2014
LIBERAL SELF-IDENTIFICATION EDGES UP TO NEW HIGH IN 2013
Fifteen-percentage-point conservative advantage ties as smallest to date

by Jeffrey M. Jones

PRINCETON, NJ—Americans continue to be more likely to identify as conservatives (38%) than as liberals (23%). But the conservative advantage is down to 15 percentage points as liberal identification edged up to its highest level since Gallup began regularly measuring ideology in the current format in 1992.

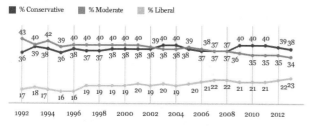

Ideological Self-Identification, Annual Averages

How would you describe your political views -- [ROTATED: very conservative, conservative, moderate, liberal or very liberal]?

■ % Conservative ▓ % Moderate ▒ % Liberal

Based on annual averages of Gallup multiday telephone polls

GALLUP

The figures are based on combined data from 13 separate Gallup polls, including interviews with more than 18,000 Americans, conducted in 2013.

When Gallup began asking about ideological identification in all its polls in 1992, an average 17% of Americans said they were liberal. That dipped to 16% in 1995 and 1996, but has gradually increased, exceeding 20% each year since 2005.

The rise in liberal identification has been accompanied by a decline in moderate identification. At 34% in 2013, it is the lowest Gallup has measured, and down nine points since 1992. Moderates had been the largest ideological group throughout the 1990s, and competed with conservatives for the top spot during the 2000s. Since 2009, conservatives have consistently been the largest U.S. ideological group.

The percentage of conservatives has always far exceeded the percentage of liberals, by as much as 22 points in 1996. With more Americans identifying as liberals in recent years, and conservative identification holding steady, the conservative advantage of 15 points ties the 2007 and 2008 gaps as the smallest.

Democrats Increasingly Likely to Identify as Liberal

The shift toward greater liberal self-identification has been led by Democrats. Currently, 43% of Democrats say they are liberal, a nearly 50% increase from 29% in 2000. Over the same period, the percentage of Democrats identifying as moderate is down to 36% from 44%, and conservative identification is down to 19% from 25%.

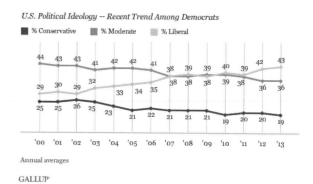

U.S. Political Ideology -- Recent Trend Among Democrats

■ % Conservative ▓ % Moderate ▒ % Liberal

Annual averages

GALLUP

From 2000 through 2006, Democrats were much more likely to describe their ideology as moderate than as liberal. In 2007, the year the Democratic Party regained control of both houses of Congress for the first time since 1994, the two lines converged, with Democrats equally likely to call themselves moderates or liberals. Now, in each of the last two years, Democrats have been more likely to describe their views as liberal than as moderate.

These changes are a telling indicator of the shift in the Democratic Party from a party that was more ideologically diverse to one that is increasingly dominated by those from the left end of the ideological spectrum.

In fact, the rise in liberal identification among all Americans is due exclusively to the changes among Democrats. Independents are no more likely now than in the past to describe their political views as liberal. The main change in independents' views is that they increasingly call themselves conservative. That could be related to recent developments in party identification, with fewer Americans now identifying as Republicans and more as independents. Thus, the change in independents' ideological preferences may be attributable to former Republicans, who are more likely to be politically conservative, now residing in the independent category.

Republicans have become more likely to describe their political views as conservative over the past 13 years, from 62% in 2000 to 70% in 2013. The percentage of Republicans saying their political views are moderate has dropped by an equivalent amount, from

31% to 23%. To some degree that may be a function of declining Republican Party identification in the U.S., now at a 25-year low of 25%. The smaller group of present Republican identifiers is likely more ideologically homogeneous than the larger group of Republican identifiers from a decade ago.

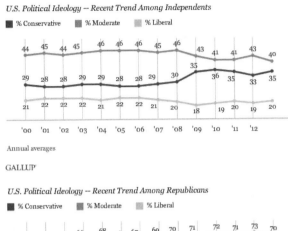

U.S. Political Ideology -- Recent Trend Among Independents

■ % Conservative   % Moderate   % Liberal

Annual averages

GALLUP'

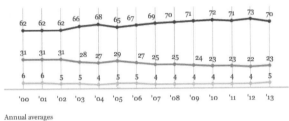

U.S. Political Ideology -- Recent Trend Among Republicans

■ % Conservative   % Moderate   % Liberal

Annual averages

GALLUP'

The increasing percentages of Republicans and independents who identify as political conservatives has helped keep the overall percentage of conservatives stable in recent years, offsetting the decline in conservative identification among Democrats. The drop in U.S. moderates is because of declines among all three major political party groups.

Implications

Americans' perceptions of their political views—if not the views themselves—are undergoing unmistakable change, contributing to greater political polarization in the country. Now, the plurality of Democrats consider themselves to be politically liberal, whereas a decade ago, Democrats were most likely to say they were moderate. That could be because Democrats are now more comfortable calling themselves "liberal"—a term that was less popular in the recent past—even if their current and past views on issues are similar. But it could also reflect an evolution in their views to favor more traditionally liberal issue positions.

Meanwhile, Republicans, who have always been overwhelmingly conservative, have become increasingly so. One manifestation of that may have been a series of primary election challenges for long-serving GOP members of Congress by candidates aligned with the Tea Party movement.

These data confirm the tendency for Americans who identify with the two major parties to be more ideologically homogeneous than was the case in the past, a tendency that appears to be matched by the increasing polarization between Democratic and Republican members of Congress.

The changes in ideological identification among party groups has resulted in a rise in the percentage of Americans overall who call themselves liberal and a decrease in the percentage of moderates. Even though the percentage of conservatives has generally held steady, the rise in liberal identification leaves conservatives with their smallest advantage over liberals in the last two decades. If the trends in Democratic self-identification continue, that gap will likely continue to shrink over time, and could lead to further polarization in U.S. politics.

Survey Methods

Results are based on aggregated telephone interviews from 13 separate Gallup polls conducted in 2013, with a random sample of 18,871 adults, aged 18 and older, living in all 50 U.S. states and the District of Columbia.

For results based on the total sample of national adults, the margin of sampling error is ±1 percentage point at the 95% confidence level.

January 13, 2014
MINORITY, YOUNG STUDENTS MORE ENTREPRENEURIALLY INCLINED
Tomorrow's entrepreneurs have few opportunities to learn necessary skills

by Robin Myers and Preety Sidhu

WASHINGTON, D.C.—About half of all racial and ethnic minority students (50%) say they plan to start their own business, compared with 37% of white students, according to recent findings from the Gallup-Hope Index.

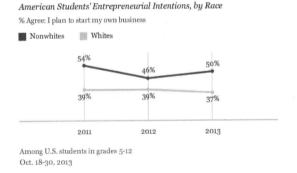

American Students' Entrepreneurial Intentions, by Race

% Agree: I plan to start my own business

■ Nonwhites   Whites

Among U.S. students in grades 5-12
Oct. 18-30, 2013

GALLUP'

The results are based on a telephone survey conducted Oct. 18–30, 2013, with a nationally representative sample of 1,009 U.S. students in grades 5–12.

Older Students Less Likely Than Younger Ones to Have Entrepreneurial Intentions

Students' desire to start their own business is lower among high schoolers than middle schoolers, and, more generally, decreases with each grade level. Roughly half of students in grades 5–8 (51%) say they plan to start their own business, compared with a third (33%) of those in grades 9–12.

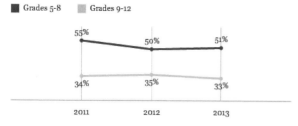

American Students' Entrepreneurial Intentions, by Grade

% Agree: I plan to start my own business

■ Grades 5-8   ■ Grades 9-12

55%   50%   51%
34%   35%   33%

2011   2012   2013

Among U.S. students in grades 5-12
Oct. 18-30, 2013

GALLUP'

Overall, four in 10 U.S. students express plans to start a business. Slightly fewer (38%) say they will invent "something that changes the world." Students' interest in starting their own business is similar to the level found in 2012, but down from 2011. Their belief that they will invent something world-changing declined in 2013 after holding steady in 2012.

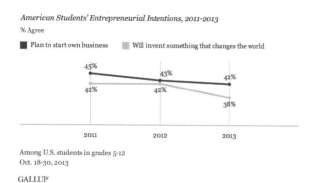

American Students' Entrepreneurial Intentions, 2011-2013

% Agree

■ Plan to start own business   ■ Will invent something that changes the world

45%   43%   42%
42%   42%   38%

2011   2012   2013

Among U.S. students in grades 5-12
Oct. 18-30, 2013

GALLUP'

Students Express Lack of Opportunities to Match Entrepreneurial Aspirations

Relatively few students report participating in workplace activities that could give them valuable workplace skills and experience. Seventeen percent of all middle school and high school students say they work at least one hour weekly. With little exposure to the workforce, few youth have any experience at all in the workforce or that would help them build a business later in their lives.

The majority of students do appear to have opportunities at school to gain at least some preparation for the business world. In 2013, more than half (55%) of students said their school teaches them about money and banking, and slightly fewer, 47%, said their school offers classes on how to start or run a business. Additionally, students widely agree that the more education they attain, the more money they will make.

Implications

American youth have an incredible amount of economic energy. They have the hope and desire to jump-start the U.S. economy. There are essentially 1.5 million students with the potential to build all-important small to medium-sized businesses. But according to the Gallup-Hope Index, less than half are learning about how to start and run their own business at their school. It is crucial to identify

these students early and cultivate their entrepreneurial energy, if Americans expect to maintain the global advantage in entrepreneurship the U.S. has enjoyed. Creating opportunities for young minority entrepreneurs may provide a much-needed foundation for helping such businesses flourish.

U.S. Students' Experiential and Entrepreneurial Educational Opportunities in 2013

	% Agree/Yes
The more education, the more money I will make	88%
My school teaches me about money and banking	55%
My school offers classes in how to start and run a business	47%
Worked at least one hour at a paying job last week	17%
Currently interning with a local business	5%
Currently running your own business	3%

Among U.S. students in grades 5-12
Oct. 18-30, 2013

GALLUP'

Small business is frequently the entry point for entrepreneurs, and the impact could be magnified if the nation could prepare its young innovators to capitalize on their ideas. Though larger businesses had the highest net gain in job creation in the last quarter of 2012, the smallest businesses (those with one to 49 employees) created nearly twice the number of jobs. The smallest businesses tend to close at a higher rate than larger establishments, but their potential is seen in the sheer number of employees they hired at the end of 2012. The power of these small businesses to affect the economy is enormous if they can maintain profitability and their employee levels. Simply put, if U.S. communities are to be thriving places to live and learn well into the future, America needs a strategy that includes investment in its youngest and most hopeful members—its youth.

To bolster these numbers, identifying these students and increasing their educational opportunities may increase entrepreneurship. Educators, community and business leaders, and policymakers all have a role in formulating plans to encourage students' entrepreneurial aspirations. Through advisory boards and individual programs, leaders can develop local efforts that help students connect with mentors in their community, with learning opportunities such as workshops or internships, and with jobs that help them unite their entrepreneurial intentions with the experiences they need to bring their innovative ideas to life.

At no other time in the recent past has it been more important for America to invest in tomorrow's entrepreneurs.

Methodology

The Gallup-HOPE Index findings are based on results from a nationally representative telephone survey of 1,009 students in grades 5–12. Telephone interviews were conducted from Oct. 18–30, 2013. Participants were selected based on eligibility criteria determined from previous contact on the Gallup Daily tracking survey and based on their consent to be recontacted. Gallup contacted respondents who indicated they had children under the age of 18 and screened for the appropriate grade level and garnered consent from the parent or guardian to allow their children to participate. The weighted subset of households with parents of school-aged children in grades 5 through 12 who granted permission to be recontacted served as the sampling frame for this study.

January 13, 2014
ONE IN FOUR AMERICANS SATISFIED
WITH DIRECTION OF U.S.
Republicans' satisfaction has increased since last month

by Joy Wilke

PRINCETON, NJ—Twenty-three percent of Americans say they are satisfied with the way things are going in the U.S. at this time, unchanged from December and within one percentage point of the 24% average for 2013. This month's reading is seven points higher than last year's low of 16% in October, which came during the government shutdown, but is lower than the April 2013 high of 30%.

In general, are you satisfied or dissatisfied with the way things are going in the United States at this time?

% Satisfied

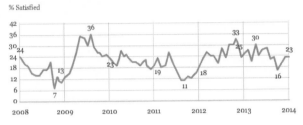

GALLUP

These results, from a Jan. 5–8 Gallup poll, represent a leveling off from the two-month rebound that occurred after the major drop in satisfaction in October. Last year's monthly satisfaction readings varied widely. The current reading is slightly below the 25% measured last January.

Republican Satisfaction Increases This Month

Democrats remain significantly more likely than independents or Republicans to be satisfied, as has been the case each month since President Barack Obama took office in 2009. This pattern is not unusual; Americans who identify with the party of the sitting president typically are more satisfied than those who don't identify with his party.

Twelve percent of Republicans say they are satisfied with the way things are going in the U.S. in January, up from 5% last month. This is toward the high end of recent Republican satisfaction, which has ranged between 3% and 14% since Obama was inaugurated. On average, 9% of Republicans were satisfied with the way things were going in the country in 2013, putting this month's reading slightly above last year's norm.

Democrats' satisfaction with the country's direction stands at 40% in January, unchanged from December and in line with Democrats' average 39% satisfaction throughout 2013.

Satisfaction among independents has been relatively flat for three months, standing at 19% in January, compared with 20% in the final two months of 2013.

Implications

Americans' attitudes about the nation's direction in the first month of the new year are in line with their average satisfaction last year. However, the recovery in satisfaction from the significant drop in October stalled this month, and the majority of Americans remain dissatisfied with the way things are going in the U.S. at this time.

Satisfaction With the Way Things Are Going in the U.S., by Party

% Satisfied

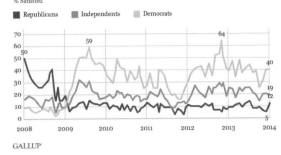

GALLUP

While Republicans are more positive than they were about where the country is headed, they remain more dissatisfied overall than either independents or Democrats. The improvement this month likely does not signal a coming resurgence in Republicans' satisfaction, as it falls within the range that Gallup has seen over the past few years.

Survey Methods

Results for this Gallup poll are based on telephone interviews conducted Jan. 5–8, 2014, on the Gallup Mood of the Nation Survey, with a random sample of 1,018 adults, aged 18 and older, living in all 50 U.S. states and the District of Columbia.

For results based on the total sample of national adults, the margin of sampling error is ±4 percentage points at the 95% confidence level.

January 15, 2014
GOVERNMENT ITSELF STILL CITED
AS TOP U.S. PROBLEM
Narrowly leads the economy, unemployment, healthcare

by Lydia Saad

PRINCETON, NJ—Americans start the new year with a variety of national concerns on their minds. Although none is dominant, the government, at 21%, leads the list of what Americans consider the most important problem facing the country. The economy closely follows at 18%, and then unemployment/jobs and healthcare, each at 16%. No other issue is mentioned by as much as 10% of the public; however, the federal budget deficit or debt comes close, at 8%.

Most Important Problem Facing the U.S.

What do you think is the most important problem facing this country today?

	Jan 5-8, 2014
	%
Dissatisfaction with government/Congress/politicians; poor leadership/corruption/abuse of power	21
Economy in general	18
Unemployment/Jobs	16
Poor healthcare/hospitals; high cost of healthcare	16
Federal budget deficit/Federal debt	8
Ethics/Moral/Religious/Family decline; dishonesty	5
Lack of money	4
Gap between rich and poor	4
Education/Poor education/Access to education	4
Poverty/Hunger/Homelessness	4
Foreign aid/Focus overseas	3
Immigration/Illegal aliens	3
Lack of respect for each other	2
Welfare	2

Shown are problems mentioned by at least 2%.

GALLUP

Americans' current telling of the top problems facing the country comes from a Jan. 5–8 Gallup poll. The rank order is similar to what Gallup found in December, although the percentage mentioning unemployment has risen four percentage points to 16%.

Mentions of the government as the top problem remain higher than they were prior to the partial government shutdown in October. During the shutdown, the percentage naming the government as the top problem doubled to 33% from 16% in September.

Compared with a year ago, mentions of government are up slightly. Mentions of healthcare, on the other hand, have quadrupled—from 4% in January 2013 to 16% today, likely related to highly visible problems with the rollout of the 2010 healthcare law. At the same time, references to the federal deficit or debt have declined from 20% to 8%, while mentions of the economy in general have dipped from 21% to 18%, and mentions of unemployment/jobs are the same, at 16%.

Recent Trend in Top Five "Most Important" U.S. Problems

What do you think is the most important problem facing this country today? (open-ended and coded)

■ % Government/Politicians ■ % Economy in general ■ % Healthcare
■ % Unemployment/Jobs □ % Federal budget deficit/Federal debt

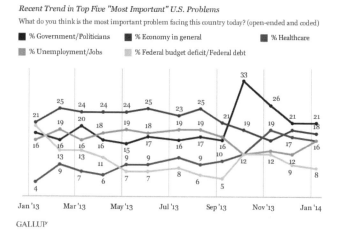

GALLUP

The noteworthy increase in healthcare mentions over the past year stems from increases among all party groups, but particularly Republicans, among whom concern rose from 4% to 24%. Concern about healthcare as the top problem was up half as much among independents (+10 points) and Democrats (+9 points).

Year-to-Year Change in Mentions of Healthcare as Top U.S. Problem

	January 2013	January 2014	Change
	%	%	Pct. pts.
U.S. adults	4	16	+12
Men	3	13	+10
Women	4	19	+15
18 to 34 years	2	13	+11
35 to 54 years	3	15	+12
55 and older	6	19	+13
Republicans	4	24	+20
Independents	3	13	+10
Democrats	5	14	+9

GALLUP

Concern about the federal budget deficit peaked last January after the deficit figured prominently in the "fiscal cliff" budget negotiations, but has since declined. This has occurred across the political spectrum, but more sharply with Americans aged 55 and older than among younger adults.

Year-to-Year Change in Mentions of Federal Budget Deficit/Federal Debt as Top U.S. Problem

	January 2013	January 2014	Change
	%	%	Pct. pts.
U.S. adults	20	8	-12
Men	23	9	-14
Women	18	8	-10
18 to 34 years	17	9	-8
35 to 54 years	20	11	-9
55 and older	24	6	-18
Republicans	27	16	-11
Independents	23	8	-15
Democrats	13	3	-10

GALLUP

Healthcare and Federal Budget Deficit Are Outsized Problems Among GOP

Government is the No. 1 concern among all three party groups, although Republicans and independents are more likely than Democrats to cite it. Mentions of healthcare as a problem are much higher for Republicans than for independents and Democrats.

The federal budget deficit also troubles Republicans more than the other groups, while unemployment sparks more concern with independents and Democrats than with Republicans. The economy in general ranks high among all three party groups, with roughly equal percentages naming it.

Four other issues are mentioned by at least 5% of any party group, and of these, the "gap between rich and poor" shows the most disparity. This issue that President Barack Obama has focused on is cited by 6% of Democrats and 5% of independents, but only 1% of Republicans.

Top Issues Mentioned as Most Important Problem in U.S., by Party ID
Jan. 5-8, 2014

	Republicans' top issues	Independents' top issues	Democrats' top issues
1	26% Government	23% Government	18% Government
2	24% Healthcare	19% Economy	17% Economy
3	20% Economy	18% Unemployment	17% Unemployment
4	16% Federal deficit	13% Healthcare	14% Healthcare
5	11% Unemployment	8% Federal deficit	6% Education
6	7% Ethics/Morals	5% Rich-poor gap	6% Rich-poor gap
7	4% Lack of money	5% Lack of money	5% Ethics/Morals
8	4% Education	4% Education	3% Lack of money
9	1% Rich-poor gap	4% Ethics/Morals	3% Federal deficit

Based on issues mentioned by 5% or more of at least one group

GALLUP

Bottom Line

The issues that concern Americans at the start of 2014, and as Obama prepares to deliver the second State of the Union address of his second term, are similar to those Gallup measured in December, and not wildly different from those last January. While the top five issues today also figured prominently in January 2013, their relative positioning has shifted in ways that could affect how Obama frames his message. Concern about unemployment, while up slightly from December, is the same as it was a year ago, and both the economy and problems with government remain top issues. At the same time, concern about healthcare is up, likely resulting from issues with the rollout of the Affordable Care Act, while concern about the federal deficit has dwindled.

Survey Methods

Results for this Gallup poll are based on telephone interviews conducted Jan. 5–8, 2014, with a random sample of 1,018 adults, aged 18 and older, living in all 50 U.S. states and the District of Columbia.

For results based on the total sample of national adults, the margin of sampling error is ±4 percentage points at the 95% confidence level.

January 15, 2014
MORE AMERICANS WORSE OFF FINANCIALLY THAN A YEAR AGO
Yet most expect to be better off within a year

by Andrew Dugan

WASHINGTON, D.C.—More Americans, 42%, say they are financially worse off now than they were a year ago, reversing the lower levels found over the past two years. Just more than a third of Americans say their financial situation has improved from a year ago.

Change in Personal Financial Situation Over the Past Year -- 2005-2014 Trend

Next, we are interested in how people's financial situation may have changed. Would you say that you are financially better off now than you were a year ago, or are you financially worse off now?

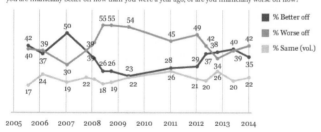

(vol.) = Volunteered response

GALLUP'

These results come from Gallup's annual "Mood of the Nation" poll, conducted Jan. 5–8. Gallup has found that Americans' economic confidence, self-reported consumer spending, and perceptions of job creation improved in 2013. Despite Americans' more positive views of the overall U.S. economy in 2013, nearly two-thirds believe their personal financial situation deteriorated or was stable over the past year.

Though down from mid-2013, the percentage of Americans saying they are financially better off than a year ago is nearly in line with the historical average (38%), spanning 1976–2014. On the other hand, the share of Americans saying they are financially worse off compared with a year ago is, by historical standards, high— eight percentage points above the average. The record high of 55% occurred in May and September 2008, the year (and, in the latter case, the month) of the global financial meltdown.

Americans' Assessments of Personal Financial Situation

Next, we are interested in how people's financial situation may have changed. Would you say that you are financially better off now than you were a year ago, or are you financially worse off now?

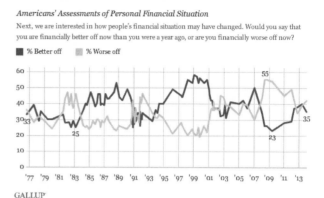

GALLUP'

Most Americans Have High Economic Hopes for Year Ahead

While many Americans say the past year was a financial dud, a majority (55%) predict that at this time next year they will be financially better off. Optimism about the future may still be the predominant feeling, but the overall positivity of the nation's personal financial predictions appears to be easing, compared with the average during the past decade.

Outlook for Personal Financial Situation Over the Next Year -- 2005-2014 Trend

Looking ahead, do you expect that at this time next year you will be financially better off than now, or worse off than now?

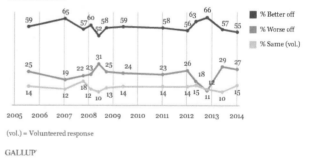

(vol.) = Volunteered response

GALLUP'

Bottom Line

Despite a sustained, if sluggish, economic recovery that has lasted nearly five years, most Americans report being no better off financially than they were a year ago. Indeed, the share of Americans saying last year put them in a worse financial position is on the higher end of the 1976–2014 trend. Although this would seem to suggest that many Americans begin this year in a state of financial unease, a majority instead believe the next year will be financially uplifting. As previous years show, Americans are typically more positive about their future compared with their assessments of the past, a testament to the enduring sense of optimism many Americans share about their financial future.

Results for this Gallup poll are based on telephone interviews conducted Jan. 5–8, 2014, on the Gallup Daily tracking survey, with a random sample of 1,018 adults, aged 18 and older, living in all 50 U.S. states and the District of Columbia.

For results based on the total sample of national adults, one can say with 95% confidence that the margin of sampling error is ±4 percentage points.

January 16, 2014
AMERICANS' SATISFACTION WITH ECONOMY SOURS MOST SINCE 2001
Public more satisfied on most other issues today than 13 years ago

by Joy Wilke and Frank Newport

PRINCETON, NJ—Americans are now more satisfied with many issues than they were 13 years ago, but they are significantly less satisfied with the economy and the role the U.S. plays in world affairs. The 40-percentage-point drop in Americans' satisfaction with the economy, along with a 21-point drop in the world affairs issue, contrasts with gains in satisfaction on issues such as the position of gays and lesbians in society, taxes, the nation's military strength, and race relations.

Americans' Satisfaction With Where the Nation Stands on Issues

Next, we'd like to know how you feel about the state of the nation in each of the following areas. For each one, please say whether you are -- very satisfied, somewhat satisfied, somewhat dissatisfied, or very dissatisfied. If you don't have enough information about a particular subject to rate it, just say so.

% Very/Somewhat satisfied

	Jan 10-14, 2001	Jan 5-8, 2014	Difference
	%	%	pct. pts.
The acceptance of gays and lesbians in the nation ^	35	53	18
The amount Americans pay in federal taxes	26	38	12
The nation's military strength and preparedness	61	72	11
The state of race relations	44	55	11
The availability of affordable healthcare	29	38	9
The nation's energy policies	32	40	8
The quality of medical care in the nation	48	56	8
The nation's policies to reduce or control crime	45	51	6
The level of immigration into the country today	32	38	6
The Social Security and Medicare systems	38	42	4
The nation's laws or policies on guns	38	40	2
The quality of public education in the nation	40	39	-1
The quality of the environment in the nation	56	55	-1
The nation's efforts to deal with poverty and homelessness	30	27	-3
The nation's policies regarding the abortion issue	43	38	-5
The role the U.S. plays in world affairs	61	40	-21
The state of the nation's economy	68	28	-40

^ 2001 wording: The acceptance of homosexuality in the nation

GALLUP'

These data are from Gallup's annual Mood of the Nation survey, conducted Jan. 5–8. Gallup has measured satisfaction with these measures periodically since January 2001. The comparison to those baseline data 13 years ago provides an important measure of how the American public's views have and have not changed from that time, just as the dot-com boom was coming to a close and before the 9/11 terrorist attacks fundamentally altered many aspects of American life.

One of the most interesting findings from this 13-year comparison is that satisfaction has actually improved or stayed statistically the same on most issues measured over that period. As noted, Americans are statistically less satisfied today than in 2001 with only the economy and the role the U.S. plays in world affairs. Twenty-eight percent of Americans say they are satisfied with the state of the economy, compared with 68% in January 2001. And 40% of Americans currently say they are satisfied with where the nation stands on the role of the U.S., down from 61% in 2001. Clearly the aftermath of 9/11, including the ensuing wars in Afghanistan and Iraq and the more recent pullback from those engagements, may have affected these views—particularly in comparison with early 2001, when the U.S. was unencumbered by any major involvement in foreign wars.

The largest increase in satisfaction since 2001 has come in terms of the acceptance of gays and lesbians, now at 53% satisfaction, vs. 35% 13 years ago. This shift mirrors the significantly increased acceptance of legalized same-sex marriage over the same time period.

In addition to the increase in Americans' satisfaction with taxes, the strength of the military, and race relations, the comparison to 2001 also shows an increase in satisfaction with two healthcare measures: the availability of affordable healthcare and the quality of medical care in the nation. The role of the highly visible Affordable Care Act in shifting these attitudes is not precisely clear.

Democrats' and Republicans' Satisfaction Differs on Most Issues

Democrats express higher levels of satisfaction than Republicans on all but two of the 18 issues Gallup asked about this year, likely because a Democrat occupies the White House. Republicans are significantly more satisfied than Democrats on the quality of the environment and gun policy. These disparities reflect basic partisan differences on fundamental aspects of these issues. Republicans are less likely than Democrats to believe that global warming is a problem, for example, or to believe that stricter gun control laws are necessary.

Reflecting the highly contentious Affordable Care Act that has occupied so much partisan debate over the last several years, the survey shows that healthcare tops the list of issues on which Democrats and Republicans do not see eye to eye. Fifty-six percent of Democrats vs. 31% of Republicans say they are at least somewhat satisfied with the availability of affordable healthcare in the U.S. However, six in 10 from each party express satisfaction with the quality of medical care that is available.

Democrats and Republicans also express large differences in satisfaction when asked about the level of immigration into the U.S., with a majority of Democrats (53%) saying they are satisfied, compared with 29% of Republicans.

Democrats are more satisfied than Republicans on issues related to the military and national security. Democrats are more likely to be satisfied with the role of the U.S. in world affairs (56% vs. 36%), the nation's military strength and preparedness (85% vs. 65%), and the nation's security from terrorism (75% vs. 66%).

In addition to the quality of medical care, partisans express similar levels of satisfaction with the status of poverty and homelessness, the quality of public education, crime, and race relations in the nation.

Satisfaction on National Issues, by Party ID
% Very/Somewhat satisfied

	Republicans	Democrats	Republicans minus Democrats
	%	%	Pct. pts.
The quality of the environment in the nation	69	46	23
The nation's laws or policies on guns	51	33	18
The nation's efforts to deal with poverty and homelessness	32	28	4
The quality of medical care in the nation	62	63	-1
The quality of public education in the nation	42	43	-1
The nation's policies to reduce or control crime	55	59	-4
The state of race relations	54	58	-4
The nation's energy policies	41	49	-8
The amount Americans pay in federal taxes	36	44	-8
The nation's security from terrorism	66	75	-9
The acceptance of gays and lesbians in the nation	49	59	-10
The Social Security and Medicare systems	41	51	-10
Government surveillance of U.S. citizens	33	44	-11
The nation's policies regarding the abortion issue	28	47	-19
The role the U.S. plays in world affairs	36	56	-20
The nation's military strength and preparedness	65	85	-20
The state of the nation's economy	21	43	-22
The level of immigration into the country	29	53	-24
The availability of affordable healthcare	31	56	-25

Jan. 5-8, 2014

GALLUP

Implications

The U.S. has seen numerous changes since early 2001, but Americans' satisfaction with many aspects of the state of the nation over that time is quite similar. The biggest change in satisfaction has been with the state of the economy—now much lower than it was then, at the end of the dot-com boom and before the major recession of 2008–2009. The impact of the 9/11 terrorist attacks and their aftermath are most likely associated with Americans' decreased satisfaction with the position of the U.S. in the world.

At the same time, perhaps in parallel with recent shifts in attitudes toward legalized same-sex marriage across the nation, Americans as a whole are now much more satisfied with the position of gays and lesbians than they were 13 years ago. Increased satisfaction with military strength reflects the positive position of the military in the nation's eyes, while increased satisfaction with taxes may reflect the lingering impact of the Bush tax cuts.

Americans are also more satisfied with healthcare and medical treatment now than in 2001. Although much of the 2010 Affordable Care Act's impact has yet to be felt, it's possible that this contentious piece of legislation has affected these attitudes.

Survey Methods

Results for this Gallup poll are based on telephone interviews conducted Jan. 5–8, 2014, with a random sample of 1,018 adults, aged 18 and older, living in all 50 U.S. states and the District of Columbia.

For results based on the total sample of national adults, the margin of sampling error is ±4 percentage points at the 95% confidence level.

January 16, 2014
AMERICANS RATE ECONOMY AS TOP PRIORITY FOR GOVERNMENT
Other high-priority issues include education, healthcare policy

by Frank Newport and Joy Wilke

PRINCETON, NJ—Americans have a distinct sense of priorities for issues facing the nation in the next year, with more saying it is extremely or very important for the president and Congress to address the economy than any other issue.

Priorities for the U.S. President and Congress
Next, how important is it to you that the president and Congress deal with each of the following issues in the next year -- is it -- extremely important, very important, moderately important, or not that important? How about -- [RANDOM ORDER]?

% Extremely/Very important

	%
The economy	89
Education	81
Healthcare policy	77
Social Security and Medicare	73
Terrorism	72
Poverty and homelessness	69
The military and national defense	68
Crime	68
Taxes	62
The distribution of income and wealth	57
Energy policy	56
The environment	55
Gun policy	54
World affairs	52
Immigration	50
Government surveillance of U.S. citizens	42
Abortion	39
Race relations	39
Policies toward gays and lesbians	27

Jan. 5-8, 2014

GALLUP

In addition to the economy, education, healthcare policy, Social Security, and terrorism are issues at least 70% of Americans deem important. These priority rankings are from Gallup's annual Mood of the Nation survey, conducted Jan. 5–8.

Americans' importance rankings extend from 89% for the economy to 27% for policies toward gays and lesbians. In fact, the three lowest-rated issues are social policies—the other two being race relations and abortion. Americans also give government surveillance of U.S. citizens a low priority rating, despite the continuing and controversial revelations about the data-snooping actions of the National Security Agency.

Americans assign a higher priority to "poverty and homelessness" than to "the distribution of income and wealth." This suggests that this current hot-button issue for President Barack Obama and other elected officials resonates more with the public when it focuses on those at the bottom end of the spectrum rather than on wealth distribution across the whole population.

Priorities Often Differ From Overall Dissatisfaction With the Status of an Issue

Gallup has previously reported the wide range of satisfaction levels Americans have with the status of these issues in the U.S. today.

The juxtaposition of these two ways of rating the list of issues—satisfaction with the status of the issue and the issue's priority for the president and Congress—provides a unique perspective on how Americans view policy priorities.

The accompanying graph maps each issue on Americans' relative level of dissatisfaction with it (the vertical axis) and their relative priority for it (the horizontal axis).

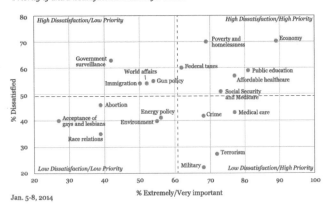

Priority of and Dissatisfaction With Major Issues

Jan. 5-8, 2014

GALLUP

Americans express above-average dissatisfaction with six issues to which they also give above-average priority ratings for the government, making these the issues that Americans presumably would want their government to focus on most immediately. The economy stands out among this group—it's one of two issues about which Americans express the least satisfaction, and is the single issue with the highest priority rating. Other issues in this "high focus" quadrant are poverty and homelessness, taxes, education, affordable healthcare, and Social Security and Medicare.

Americans assign high priority to four issues with which they are generally satisfied—reflected in their below-average *dissatisfaction* scores. In other words, the public believes these issues are under control at the moment, in essence saying, "Keep up the good work." These include the quality of medical care, terrorism, the strength of the military, and crime.

Americans are dissatisfied with four other issues to which they give below-average priority for the president and Congress. Importantly, these include government surveillance of its citizens—an issue about which Americans express dissatisfaction, but also one to which they give a lower priority. Others in this group include gun policy, world affairs, and immigration.

Finally, there is a group of issues about which Americans express relatively low dissatisfaction but at the same time low government priority. Clearly these are issues that Americans believe deserve the least government focus at this time. This group includes race relations, the environment, gay and lesbian acceptance, energy policy, and abortion.

Bottom Line

The economy tops the list when Americans are asked how important it is that the government in the next year address a series of issues facing the nation—and it is one of two issues about which Americans express the greatest dissatisfaction. The economy thus remains the single issue out of 19 tested that Americans would be most likely to entreat their government to deal with. Five other issues are also in this high-focus category, given that the public is dissatisfied with them and assigns them a high priority: poverty and homelessness, taxes, education, the availability of affordable healthcare, and Social Security and Medicare.

The public appears to be relatively satisfied with the quality of medical care, the military, efforts to fight terrorism, and crime, but the importance assigned to each of these suggests that they should continue to be a government "maintenance" focus.

All other issues tested have below-average priority, albeit with differing levels of satisfaction. Of these, perhaps the most notable is government surveillance of its citizens. Americans are dissatisfied when asked about surveillance, but at the same time do not see that it should be one of the most important priorities for their government. The two hot-button issues of immigration and gun policy also fit into this high dissatisfaction/low priority category.

Survey Methods

Results for this Gallup poll are based on telephone interviews conducted Jan. 5–8, 2014, with a random sample of 1,018 adults, aged 18 and older, living in all 50 U.S. states and the District of Columbia.

For results based on the total sample of national adults, the margin of sampling error is ±4 percentage points at the 95% confidence level.

January 17, 2014
DESPITE HIGH STOCK PRICES, HALF IN U.S. WARY OF INVESTING
Americans divided on whether investing in the stock market is a good or bad idea

by Art Swift

WASHINGTON, D.C.—Half of Americans say investing $1,000 in the stock market right now would be a bad idea, even though the Dow Jones Industrial Average and Standard & Poor's 500 index have recently hit record highs. Forty-six percent of Americans say investing $1,000 in the stock market would be a good idea.

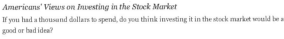

Americans' Views on Investing in the Stock Market

If you had a thousand dollars to spend, do you think investing it in the stock market would be a good or bad idea?

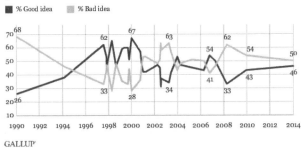

GALLUP

Despite a Dow closing record high of 16,576 this past New Year's Eve, and an average that has stayed well above 16,000 throughout January, Americans appear skittish about pouring money into what appears to be a bull market, according to a Gallup poll conducted Jan. 5–8. In January 2000, when the Dow was at a then-record high of 11,500, Americans were much more likely to say investing in the stock market was a good idea than they are today. A record-high 67% of Americans that month said investing was a good idea.

After the onset of the 2008–2009 Great Recession, the percentage of Americans who believed investing in the markets was a bad idea swelled to 62%. While that percentage has dropped, Americans' confidence in buying stocks has clearly not returned to levels seen during the heady days of the early 2000s.

Stock Ownership Among Americans Still Near Record Low

Fifty-four percent of Americans now say they own stock, little changed from the 52% who said so last April—which was the lowest in Gallup's 16-year trend of asking this question in its current format. Stock ownership is far lower than it was during the dot-com boom of 2000, when 67% said they owned stock—a record high. While staying above 60% for much of the 2000s, the ownership percentage fell into the 50% range as the Great Recession took hold and has not yet rebounded. Despite economic booms and busts, however, a majority of Americans have maintained an investment in the markets in the past 15 years.

Americans' Ownership of Stocks

Do you, personally, or jointly with a spouse, have any money invested in the stock market right now -- either in an individual stock, a stock mutual fund, or in a self-directed 401(k) or IRA?

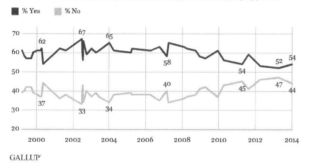

GALLUP

Although fewer Americans now own stocks, those who do, not surprisingly, are much more likely than non-owners to believe investing in the market is a good idea, 59% to 30%.

Bottom Line

During the dot-com boom of the late 1990s and early 2000s, confidence in investing in the stock market was higher than it is today and more people said they were invested in the market. With a federal budget surplus, low unemployment, and consistently high GDP growth, the record stock market of 2000 appeared to mirror the strong American economy.

The Dow is 5,000 points higher today than it was in 2000, but confidence in the markets is much lower, as is participation. The unemployment rate as reported by the Bureau of Labor Statistics is hovering around 7% in 2014, GDP growth is roughly 2% to 3%, and the government is mired in a large amount of debt. Given these factors, Americans may not believe that the current economy is as strong as the market suggests. Alternatively, they may believe the current market is inflated beyond reasonable measures. As 2014 unfolds, it will be interesting to observe whether the stock market continues its record pace and Americans regain confidence in investing or if a correction occurs, resulting in a decline in stock values.

Survey Methods

Results for this Gallup poll are based on telephone interviews conducted Jan. 5–8, 2014, with a random sample of 1,018 adults, aged 18 and older, living in all 50 U.S. states and the District of Columbia.

For results based on the total sample of national adults, the margin of sampling error is ±4 percentage points at the 95% confidence level.

January 20, 2014

IN U.S., 67% DISSATISFIED WITH INCOME, WEALTH DISTRIBUTION

Democrats and independents are more dissatisfied than Republicans

by Rebecca Riffkin

WASHINGTON, D.C.—Two out of three Americans are dissatisfied with the way income and wealth are currently distributed in the U.S. This includes three-fourths of Democrats and 54% of Republicans.

Satisfaction With Income and Wealth Distribution in the U.S.

Next, I'm going to read some aspects of life in America today. For each one please say whether you are -- very satisfied, somewhat satisfied, somewhat dissatisfied, or very dissatisfied. How about the way income and wealth are distributed in the U.S.?

	% Very satisfied	% Somewhat satisfied	% Somewhat dissatisfied	% Very dissatisfied
National adults	7	25	28	39
Republicans	11	34	26	28
Independents	5	23	27	43
Democrats	6	18	32	43

Jan. 5-8, 2014

GALLUP

President Barack Obama spoke about income disparities in a Dec. 4, 2013, speech, saying he wanted to prioritize lowering income disparity and increasing opportunities, particularly for the poor, during the rest of his second term. He most likely will return to that topic in his State of the Union speech at the end of the month. Gallup's Jan. 5–8 Mood of the Nation survey included a question asking Americans how satisfied they are with income and wealth distribution in the U.S. Few, 7%, report that they are "very satisfied" with the distribution, while 39% of Americans say they are "very dissatisfied."

Attitudes about the distribution of income and wealth are highly related to partisanship. Republicans, at 45% very or somewhat satisfied, express the highest satisfaction with the current wealth disparity in the U.S. Democrats are much less satisfied, at 24%, with independents closer in satisfaction to Democrats, at 28%. Furthermore, almost half (43%) of Democrats and independents express strong dissatisfaction with the current state of wealth and income distribution.

Dissatisfaction With the Opportunity to Get Ahead Remains High

The same poll updated a long-time Gallup trend, finding that 54% of Americans are satisfied, and 45% dissatisfied, with the opportunity for an American "to get ahead by working hard." This measure has remained roughly constant over the past three years, but Americans are much less optimistic about economic opportunity now than before the recession and financial crisis of 2008 unfolded. Prior to that, at least two in three Americans were satisfied, including a high of 77% in 2002.

Satisfaction With Americans' Opportunities to Get Ahead by Working Hard, 2001-2014 Trend

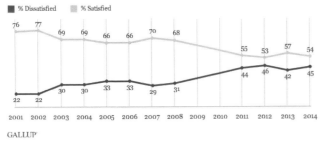

■ % Dissatisfied   ▨ % Satisfied

GALLUP

In contrast to the question about income distribution in the same poll, satisfaction with the opportunity to get ahead does not show a significant partisan split, with 61% of Republicans and 60% of Democrats saying they are satisfied. Among independents, 45% are satisfied and 53% are dissatisfied. Independents are the only group in which a majority are dissatisfied with opportunities to get ahead by working hard.

Satisfaction With the Opportunity to Get Ahead by Working Hard, by Party ID

Next, I'm going to read some aspects of life in America today. For each one, please say whether you are -- very satisfied, somewhat satisfied, somewhat dissatisfied, or very dissatisfied. How about the opportunity for a person to get ahead by working hard?

	% Very satisfied	% Somewhat satisfied	% Somewhat dissatisfied	% Very dissatisfied
Republicans	19	42	22	17
Independents	18	27	29	24
Democrats	25	35	23	15

Jan. 5-8, 2014

GALLUP

Bottom Line

Obama will almost certainly touch on inequality in his State of the Union address on Jan. 28. This will certainly resonate in a general sense with the majority of Americans who are dissatisfied with income and wealth distribution in the U.S. today. Members of the president's party agree most strongly with the president that this is an issue, but majorities of Republicans and independents are at least somewhat dissatisfied as well.

Although Americans are more likely to be satisfied with the opportunity for people to get ahead through hard work, their satisfaction is well below where it was before the economic downturn. Accordingly, improvement in the U.S. economy could bring Americans' views back to pre-recession levels.

Survey Methods

Results for this Gallup poll are based on telephone interviews conducted Jan. 5–8, 2014, on the Gallup Daily tracking survey, with a random sample of 1,018 adults, aged 18 and older, living in all 50 U.S. states and the District of Columbia.

For results based on the total sample of national adults, the margin of sampling error is ±4 percentage points at the 95% confidence level.

January 20, 2014
MANY BABY BOOMERS RELUCTANT TO RETIRE
Engaged, financially struggling boomers more likely to work longer

by Jim Harter and Sangeeta Agrawal

This article is part of an ongoing series analyzing how baby boomers—those born from 1946 to 1964 in the U.S.—behave differently from other generations as consumers and in the workplace. The series also explores how the aging of the baby boomer generation will affect politics and well-being.

WASHINGTON, D.C.—True to their "live to work" reputation, some baby boomers are digging in their heels at the workplace as they approach the traditional retirement age of 65. While the average age at which U.S. retirees *say* they retired has risen steadily from 57 to 61 in the past two decades, boomers—the youngest of whom will turn 50 this year—will likely extend it even further. Nearly half (49%) of boomers still working say they don't expect to retire until they are 66 or older, including one in 10 who predict they will never retire.

Baby Boomers' Expected Age of Retirement

At what age do you expect to retire?

	Baby boomers
64 or younger	27%
65	24%
66 or older	39%
Never	10%

Dec. 6-29, 2013
Gallup Daily tracking

GALLUP

Concerns about money likely play a significant role in explaining why so many baby boomers see themselves working longer. Even before the 2008–2009 recession, financial advisers were warning that some baby boomers were carrying too much debt, saving too little, and relying too heavily on Social Security to retire comfortably. And then came the economic collapse—a perfect storm of layoffs, pension and stock losses, and plummeting home values—which was particularly ill-timed for boomers who might otherwise have been in financial shape to retire on schedule with the start of their Social Security benefits.

Gallup finds that baby boomers who strongly agree that they currently "have enough money to do everything [they] want to do" expect to retire at age 66. Boomers who strongly disagree with this statement predict they will retire significantly later, at age 73.

Baby Boomers Who Feel They "Have Enough Money to Do Everything They Want to Do" Plan to Retire Earlier

On a five-point scale, where "5" means strongly agree and "1" means strongly disagree, please rate your level of agreement with the following items.

You have enough money to do everything you want to do.

	Baby boomers' expected retirement age
Strongly disagree (1)	73 years old
2	70 years old
3	70 years old
4	67 years old
Strongly agree (5)	66 years old

Dec. 6-29, 2013
Gallup-Healthways Well-Being Index

GALLUP

Engaged Boomers Slightly More Likely to Delay Retirement

Aside from financial considerations, boomers' notoriously hard-charging work ethic and drive to get ahead may make it difficult for them to envision downshifting into the slower pace of retired life. But being wired for work doesn't necessarily guarantee that all baby boomers are engaged employees who are involved in, enthusiastic about, and committed to their jobs. About one in three (31%) employed boomers are engaged at work, compared with 38% of traditionalists (those born before 1946), 30% of Generation X workers, and 28% of millennials. However, baby boomers who expect to retire after age 65 are slightly more engaged (34%) in their jobs than boomers overall.

Engagement by Generation, 2013

	Millennials (1980-1996)	Generation X (1965-1979)	Baby boomers (1946-1964)	Tradition-alists (1900-1945)	Baby boomers planning to work past age 65
Engaged	28%	30%	31%	38%	34%
Not engaged	55%	50%	49%	47%	44%
Actively disengaged	17%	20%	20%	15%	22%

Gallup Daily tracking

GALLUP

Baby Boomers Still a Substantial Part of the Workforce

As the largest generation born in U.S. history, baby boomers' sheer numbers coupled with their reluctance to retire will likely ensure that their influence endures in the workplace in the coming years. Although the first wave of boomers became eligible for early retirement under Social Security about six years ago, the generation still constitutes about one-third (31%) of the workforce, similar to percentages for millennials (33%) and Generation X (32%).

Percentage of Each Generation in the Workforce, 2013

	Millennials (1980-1996)	Generation X (1965-1979)	Baby boomers (1946-1964)	Traditionalists (1900-1945)
% in the workforce	33%	32%	31%	4%

Gallup Daily tracking

GALLUP

Bottom Line

Whether by choice or necessity, baby boomers will remain a sizable proportion of the workforce in the years ahead, with many expecting to work past the average U.S. retirement age of 61 and even the traditional retirement age of 65. As they continue to age and work, it is important that their organizations build workplaces with outstanding managers who leverage the experiences of older workers by positioning them to do what they do best—listening to their insights and opinions, and continuing to develop their talents into strengths.

By investing in baby boomers' engagement, employers will reap the benefits that an engaged workforce brings to their bottom line. No matter what their age, engaged workers tend to have higher well-being, better health, and higher productivity than their not-engaged and actively disengaged counterparts. A targeted effort to engage baby boomers could have important ramifications for healthcare costs and productivity for individual workplaces and the overall U.S. economy.

Survey Methods

Results from working adults reported in this article are based on telephone interviews conducted Jan. 3–Dec. 29, 2013, on the Gallup Daily tracking survey, with a random sample of 85,572 working adults, aged 18 and older, living in all 50 U.S. states and the District of Columbia. For results based on the total sample of working adults, the margin of sampling error is ±1 percentage point at the 95% confidence level.

Baby boomers' views about the age they expect to retire are based on telephone interviews conducted Dec. 6–Dec. 29, 2013, on the Gallup Daily tracking survey, with a random sample of 1,929 adults born between 1946 and 1964, and living in all 50 U.S. states and the District of Columbia.

Baby boomers' view about having enough money to do what they want are based on telephone interviews conducted Dec. 6–29, 2013, as part of the Gallup-Healthways Well-Being Index survey, with a random sample of 1,929 adults born between 1946 and 1964, and living in all 50 U.S. states and the District of Columbia.

For results based on the total sample of baby boomers born 1946–1964, the margin of sampling error is ±4 percentage points at the 95% confidence level.

January 21, 2014
OBAMA AVERAGES 45.8% JOB APPROVAL IN YEAR FIVE
Most recent quarterly average is 41.2%

by Jeffrey M. Jones

PRINCETON, NJ—President Barack Obama averaged 45.8% job approval during his fifth year in office. That is down more than two percentage points from his fourth-year average, and slightly better than his career-low 44.4% in his third year.

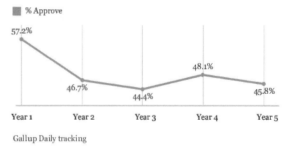

Barack Obama's Yearly Job Approval Averages

■ % Approve

Gallup Daily tracking

GALLUP

The results are based on more than 175,000 Gallup Daily tracking interviews conducted throughout Obama's fifth year in office, from Jan. 20, 2013 (also the start of his second term), through Jan. 19, 2014.

On the heels of his re-election victory, Obama's fifth year started off strongly, with consistent majority approval. However,

Americans' approval of Obama declined over the course of 2013. His latest Gallup Daily tracking job approval rating, based on Jan. 17–19 interviewing, is 40%, just two points above his personal low approval rating.

From a historical perspective, Obama's fifth-year approval average is in the lower range. It is similar to George W. Bush's 45.7%, but lower than those for Dwight Eisenhower, Ronald Reagan, and Bill Clinton. Obama's fifth-year average exceeds Richard Nixon's 41.1% in the year ending Jan. 19, 1974. Nixon's fifth-year approval rating reflected declining support as the Watergate scandal unfolded, but his fifth year ended well before he resigned from office.

Elected Presidents' Fifth-Year Job Approval Averages

President	Dates of fifth year in office	Average job approval rating	Number of polls
Eisenhower	Jan 20, 1957–Jan 19, 1958	62.8%	15
Nixon	Jan 20, 1973–Jan 19, 1974	41.1%	21
Reagan	Jan 20, 1985–Jan 19, 1986	60.4%	15
Clinton	Jan 20, 1997–Jan 19, 1998	57.9%	19
G.W.Bush	Jan 20, 2005–Jan 19, 2006	45.7%	42
Obama	Jan 20, 2013–Jan 19, 2014	45.8%	351

Data shown are for presidents elected to their first and second terms. Harry Truman averaged 51.1% in his fifth year in office (January 1949–January 1950) and Lyndon Johnson averaged 43.9% in his fifth year in office (January 1967–January 1968).

GALLUP

Obama's Most Recent Quarter Nearly Matches His Worst

In the just-completed 20th quarter of Obama's presidency, from Oct. 20, 2013–Jan. 19, 2014, Obama averaged 41.2% job approval. That is slightly above his worst quarter, the 11th of his presidency, in which an average 41.0% of Americans approved of him.

Barack Obama's Quarterly Job Approval Averages

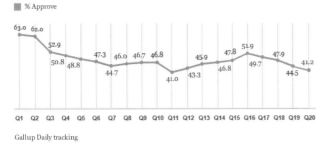

■ % Approve

Gallup Daily tracking

GALLUP

Obama's approval ratings dropped in every quarter of his fifth year in office, with the declines exceeding three points in each of the last two quarters. Prior to the recent four-quarter skid, Obama's average approval rating had improved for five quarters in a row.

Obama's 20th-quarter average exactly matches that for George W. Bush in the same quarter. While Obama was struggling with the rollout of major provisions of the healthcare law, Bush was struggling with the response to Hurricane Katrina, opposition to his nomination of Harriet Miers to the Supreme Court, and the Iraq war. Nixon, however, had the lowest 20th-quarter average in Gallup's records, 28.0%, as the Watergate scandal intensified. Eisenhower, Clinton, and Reagan received approval averages at or near 60% at a similar point in their presidencies.

Elected Presidents' 20th-Quarter Job Approval Averages

President	Dates of 20th quarter in office	Average job approval rating	Number of polls
Eisenhower	Oct 20, 1957–Jan 19, 1958	59.0%	2
Nixon	Oct 20, 1973–Jan 19, 1974	28.0	5
Reagan	Oct 20, 1985–Jan 19, 1986	63.5	4
Clinton	Oct 20, 1997–Jan 19, 1998	59.0	6
G.W.Bush	Oct 20, 2005–Jan 19, 2006	41.2	12
Obama	Oct 20, 2013–Jan 19, 2014	41.2	83

Data shown are for presidents elected to their first and second terms. Harry Truman averaged 37.0% in his 20th quarter in office (January–April 1950) and Lyndon Johnson averaged 38.5% in his 20th quarter in office (July–October 1968).

GALLUP

Implications

Obama's fifth year in office, which included the troubled rollout of his signature healthcare law and a government shutdown, was a difficult one. His approval ratings nosedived after re-election in a similar way to those of George W. Bush and, to a more extreme degree, Nixon, after they were re-elected. Neither of those two presidents recovered from that point on. Bush's quarterly ratings never averaged as high as 40% after his 20th quarter in office, and Nixon's held below 30% until he resigned from office. Both trends were attributable to unusual circumstances, however, with Nixon's second term plagued by scandal and Bush's by a protracted and unpopular war soon to be followed by an economic crisis.

There is no guarantee that Obama will suffer a similar fate. In the short term, however, all recent elected presidents except Clinton saw at least some decline in their 21st quarter in office, and only Clinton had a sixth-year approval average higher than his fifth-year average. From a historical perspective, then, the prospects for Obama's approval rating to improve are not great, although improvement would not be unprecedented.

Survey Methods

Results for this Gallup poll are based on telephone interviews conducted Oct. 20, 2013–Jan. 19, 2014, on the Gallup Daily tracking survey, with a random sample of 42,335 adults, aged 18 and older, living in all 50 U.S. states and the District of Columbia.

For results based on the total sample of national adults, the margin of sampling error is ±1 percentage point at the 95% confidence level.

January 21, 2014
BABY BOOMERS PUT MORE MONEY THAN TRUST IN BANKS
Nearly one in four boomer customers are dissatisfied with industry

by Daniela Yu and Julie Ray

This article is part of an ongoing series analyzing how baby boomers—those born from 1946 to 1964 in the U.S.—behave differently from other generations as consumers and in the workplace. The series also explores how the aging of the baby boomer generation will affect politics and well-being.

WASHINGTON, D.C.—Baby boomers make up the largest share of banking customers in the U.S., according to a December Gallup poll. Nearly nine in 10 baby boomers (89%) currently have at least one checking, savings, or money market account at a bank or another financial institution. But Gallup's 2013 retail banking study shows that just 12% of baby boomers with active bank accounts trust banks a "great deal," with the majority placing only "some" or "very little" trust in these institutions.

Banking Baby Boomers' Trust in Banks

How much confidence do you, yourself, have in banks?
Among those with active bank accounts

	A great deal	Quite a lot	Some	Very little
Generation Y/Millennials (1980-1996)	25%	34%	33%	8%
Generation X (1965-1979)	18%	29%	42%	11%
Baby boomers (1946-1964)	12%	34%	42%	11%
Traditionalists (1900-1945)	15%	43%	34%	9%

Based on November 2013 retail banking study of 11,809 adults with bank accounts

GALLUP'

On top of this, baby-boomer bank customers are among the least satisfied of any generation with the banking industry overall; nearly one in four in this generation are dissatisfied, with 9% not satisfied at all and another 14% dissatisfied. Both of these findings are similar to what Gallup found in its 2011 and 2012 retail banking studies, suggesting banks have failed to win baby boomers' trust or satisfy them in the past several years.

Banking Baby Boomers' Satisfaction With Banking Industry

How satisfied are you with the banking industry overall?
Among those with active bank accounts

	Not at all satisfied	2	3	4	Extremely satisfied
Generation Y/Millennials (1980-1996)	5%	10%	27%	35%	24%
Generation X (1965-1979)	6%	12%	32%	32%	18%
Baby boomers (1946-1964)	9%	14%	31%	34%	12%
Traditionalists (1900-1945)	7%	12%	28%	41%	12%

Based on November 2013 retail banking study of 11,809 adults with bank accounts

GALLUP'

This lukewarm trust and satisfaction is not a healthy sign for the industry. Boomers are also as likely as or more likely than younger generations to be wealthy and to be business owners—two target customers for banks and their products. Twenty-nine percent of baby-boomer banking customers have more than $100,000 in investable household assets, compared with 19% of Generation X and 12% of Generation Y. Traditionalists may be the wealthiest cohort, but the 39% with this much in investable assets represents a much smaller segment of the population. Sixteen percent of boomers and 15% of Generation X report they currently own a business, while only 6% of Generation Y and 9% of traditionalists are business owners.

Majority of Baby Boomers Bank Online

One surprising area where banks may be able to engage their baby-boomer customers is in their online service options. While some banks may assume their older customers are less likely to use digital relationships for their banking needs, Gallup's 2013 retail banking study shows that 75% of banking baby boomers used online services in the past six months. Nearly as many of these boomers

(71%) use online banking services at least weekly, as frequently as Generation X (70%) and Generation Y (72%) do. This suggests that baby boomers value the speed and convenience of online banking as much as younger generations do.

Bottom Line

While millennials are a hot topic in all kinds of banking strategy meetings, Gallup's research shows that baby boomers, because of their sheer numbers, are still the largest and arguably the most influential generation because of its strongest purchasing power with regard to various banking businesses, such as retail, wealth management, and even business banking.

Given boomers' significant purchasing power, banks' failure to earn this large demographic's trust and satisfaction may be costing them money. Fully engaged customers are banks' most valuable customers because they are emotionally attached and rationally loyal, while actively disengaged customers are emotionally detached and antagonized, and seek out opportunities to talk to others about their negative experiences. The 2013 retail banking study shows that 12% of banking baby boomers are actively disengaged with their primary bank. If banks can convert their actively disengaged customers to fully engaged customers, Gallup research shows it could open up a market of at least $82 billion in deposits and $443 billion in investable assets in the U.S.

Banks need to design and sell financial products and services for baby boomers that are based on their life cycle needs and economic situations—for example, they might want to offer retirement planning products and advice, organize platforms for baby boomers to learn new tech apps, or help with choosing a health insurance product or wealth transfer planning.

At the same time, similar to customers in all other generations, baby boomers deeply appreciate individualized, customized service. Because baby boomers are such a large, diverse group, their banking needs can vary significantly. Each customer has his or her unique needs, and banks need to be fully aware of differences among individuals.

Survey Methods

Results for this Gallup poll are based on telephone interviews conducted Dec. 13–14, 2013, on the Gallup Daily tracking survey, with a random sample of 1,014 adults, aged 18 and older, living in all 50 U.S. states and the District of Columbia.

For results based on the total sample of national adults, the margin of sampling error is ±3 percentage points at the 95% confidence level.

January 22, 2014
IN U.S., 65% DISSATISFIED WITH HOW GOV'T SYSTEM WORKS
Republicans and independents most likely to be dissatisfied

by Justin McCarthy

WASHINGTON, D.C.—Sixty-five percent of Americans are dissatisfied with the nation's system of government and how well it works, the highest percentage in Gallup's trend since 2001. Dissatisfaction is up five points since last year, and has edged above the previous high from 2012 (64%).

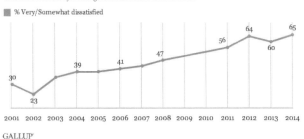
These findings are from Gallup's annual Mood of the Nation poll, conducted Jan. 5–8, 2014. The trend line on this measure shows remarkable change over time, rising from fewer than one in four Americans expressing dissatisfaction in 2002, after the 9/11 terrorist attacks, to the current situation in which almost two-thirds are dissatisfied.

Republicans and Independents Less Satisfied, Democrats Remain Consistent

Republicans and independents are largely responsible for the overall decrease in satisfaction with government effectiveness in recent years. Satisfaction among Republicans and independents began to wane during President George W. Bush's final year in office. This may have reflected mounting public dissatisfaction with the Iraq war, coupled with the Democratic takeover of Congress after the 2006 midterm elections. Both groups' satisfaction plummeted still more between 2008 and 2011, and has since dipped further. Republicans' satisfaction went from a peak of 79% in 2005 to a low of 28% in each of the past two years. Meanwhile, Democrats' satisfaction has been remarkably steady, generally hovering near 50%, and is essentially the same as it was in 2004 under a Republican president.

Democrats' satisfaction might have been much higher today, with a Democrat in the White House, if not for the twin problems of the economy and partisan gridlock that have tarnished the government's image among both parties. Satisfaction among Republicans, which has directly correlated with the party of the president in office, continues at its depressed level, with this year's reading tying the record low from 2013. Satisfaction among independents, meanwhile, has gone down 10 percentage points during that same time.

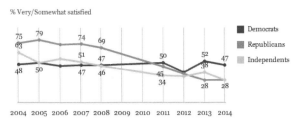
Dissatisfaction Carries Over to Americans' Views on Government Size and Power

One reason Americans are dissatisfied with how the government system is working is that they believe it is too big and powerful. Two-thirds of Americans (66%) are unhappy with the size and power of the federal government. These views potentially hamper President Barack Obama's ability to propose large-scale government solutions in his State of the Union speech next week. However, this problem is not a new one for the president. Roughly two-thirds of Americans have expressed this view consistently since at least 2011, after the measure jumped a full 10 points between 2008 and 2011.

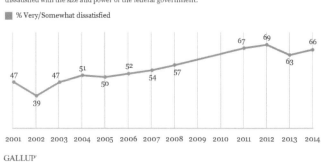
Bottom Line

Obama and the elected representatives in Congress have faced a tough audience in the American public in recent years, with the majority dissatisfied with the performance of government and concerned about its size and power. This year will be no different as the president prepares to speak to the nation next week. And even a slight majority of those in his own party are generally dissatisfied with how government is working. This dissatisfaction is also reflected in Gallup's separate question measuring Americans' perceptions of the most important problem facing the country; dysfunctional government is the top category mentioned this month.

Outside of the president's party, unhappiness with federal government size and effectiveness has only grown during his time in office. Republican satisfaction with the government's effectiveness dropped dramatically after Obama's 2008 election, while that of independents fell a bit more gradually.

Survey Methods

Results for this Gallup poll are based on telephone interviews conducted Jan. 5–8, 2014, with a random sample of 1,018 adults, aged 18 and older, living in all 50 U.S. states and the District of Columbia.

For results based on the total sample of registered voters, the margin of sampling error is ±4 percentage points at the 95% confidence level.

January 22, 2014

BABY BOOMERS NOT MAXIMIZING THEIR STRENGTHS

Strengths differ slightly by generation

by Brandon Rigoni, Jim Asplund, and Susan Sorenson

This article is part of an ongoing series analyzing how baby boomers—those born from 1946 to 1964 in the U.S.—behave differently from other generations as consumers and in the workplace. The series also explores how the aging of the baby boomer generation will affect politics and well-being.

WASHINGTON, D.C.—Despite U.S. baby boomers' considerable years of experience in the workforce, they are no more likely than younger generations to say that they are able to use their strengths to do what they do best throughout the day. Overall, working baby boomers say they use their strengths to do what they do best an average of 6.9 hours a day, on par with 6.8 hours for Generation Xers and 6.7 hours for millennials.

Daily Strengths Usage in Hours Among U.S. Working Adults, by Generation

About how many hours out of the day yesterday were you able to use your strengths to do what you do best?

	Less than 4 hours	4-6 hours	7-9 hours	10+ hours	Average hours per day
Millennials	30%	29%	20%	22%	6.7
Generation X	26%	31%	22%	21%	6.8
Baby boomers	24%	30%	24%	22%	6.9
Traditionalists	25%	34%	22%	20%	6.8
U.S. WORKING ADULTS	26%	30%	22%	21%	6.8

Aug. 20-Dec. 30, 2013

GALLUP

These results from Gallup-Healthways Well-Being Index surveys from Aug. 20 to Dec. 30, 2013, show that baby boomers are not alone. More than half of U.S. working adults overall do not use their strengths throughout the day, with 56% saying they use them for six hours or fewer each day.

Gallup defines strengths as activities for which one can consistently provide near-perfect performance. Individuals who report using their strengths have higher productivity, self-confidence, well-being, hope, and altruism. Gallup has spent more than a half-century studying human strengths, as chronicled in *StrengthsFinder 2.0*—the book with the longest stay on Amazon's Top 100.

Baby Boomers in Workplace to Stay

Gallup finds that about one in two boomers intend to delay their retirement, meaning they likely will remain an influential part of the workforce in the years ahead. Employers can make the most of these surplus years by ensuring that boomers have more targeted opportunities to use their innate talents and accumulated expertise to achieve their full potential at work.

Additional Gallup research shows that organizations that help their employees identify their innate talents and position them in roles to use their strengths achieve higher performance outcomes, including greater productivity and profitability and lower turnover.

Baby Boomers Have a Talent for Developing Others

Gallup's Clifton StrengthsFinder assessment tests respondents for 34 specific strengths and identifies each individual's top five strengths. More than 9.7 million adults have taken the StrengthsFinder assessment worldwide, and the most common strengths in the StrengthsFinder database differ slightly by generation within this database.

While certain strengths overlap among these generational profiles, the Developer strength stands out as uniquely powerful among the baby boomers who have taken the assessment. People high in the Developer strength are adept at recognizing and cultivating potential in others. They excel at monitoring signs of improved performance and find personal satisfaction in helping others succeed.

Top Five Strengths, by Generation

	Millennials	Generation X	Baby Boomers	Traditionalists
1.	Adaptability	Input	Responsibility	Responsibility
2.	Input	Achiever	Achiever	Harmony
3.	Responsibility	Responsibility	Adaptability	Empathy
4.	Achiever	Learner	Developer	Consistency
5.	Context	Relator	Empathy	Achiever

GALLUP

Although the Gallup StrengthsFinder database is not a random sample of all Americans, the prevalence of the Developer strength among baby boomers who are in the database suggests that a focus on the attributes of Developers could be used fruitfully by companies and managers who deal with boomers in the years ahead.

Bottom Line

Baby boomers have weathered sweeping economic, societal, and technological changes that have shaped the modern workplace, honing their talents, skills, and expertise along the way. They also have staying power, with many of them intending to remain in the workforce beyond traditional retirement age. Factor in the talent for developing others that seems to be prevalent in baby boomers who have taken the StrengthsFinder assessment, and it seems clear that these workers have the potential to bring even more value to their workplaces if they had more opportunities to use their strengths.

Developers make natural mentors, trainers, managers, and leaders, and with their wealth of work and life experiences, baby boomers would seem ideally suited to assume these roles at this point in their careers. This does not necessarily mean that every boomer has strong Developer talent and should automatically be promoted to management. Rather, companies should make an effort to identify and learn more about boomers' individual strengths and position them in mentoring roles where they can easily share their expertise. Once they have the opportunity to fully develop their strengths, it would come naturally to baby boomers strong in Developer to act as catalysts in helping younger workers reach their potential.

Survey Methods

For how many hours working Americans use their strengths to do what they do best each day are based on telephone interviews conducted as part of the Gallup-Healthways Well-Being Index survey Aug. 20–Dec. 30, 2013, with a random sample of 76,141 working adults, aged 18 and older, living in all 50 U.S. states and the District of Columbia.

For results based on the total sample of national adults, the margin of sampling error is ±0.4 percentage points at the 95% confidence level.

January 23, 2014

IN U.S., UNINSURED RATE SHOWS INITIAL DECLINE IN 2014

Uninsured rate drops most among the unemployed and nonwhites

by Jenna Levy

WASHINGTON, D.C.—The U.S. uninsured rate is 16.1% so far in January, modestly down from 17.3% in December after the Affordable Care Act's requirement for Americans to have health insurance took effect on Jan. 1. The percentage of uninsured adults aged 18 and older for Jan. 2–19 is slightly lower than what Gallup has measured in any month since December 2012.

Monthly Averages of Uninsured Americans, January 2008-January 2014

Do you have health insurance coverage?

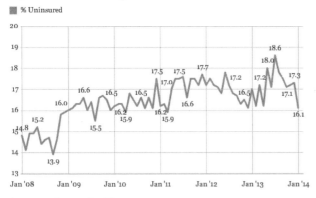

January 2014 data was collected Jan. 2-19
Gallup-Healthways Well-Being Index

GALLUP

These data are based on over 9,000 interviews with American adults collected Jan. 2–19, 2014, as part of the Gallup-Healthways Well-Being Index. This is a preliminary snapshot of the uninsured rate in January 2014, after several provisions of the Affordable Care Act, commonly known as "Obamacare," took effect. The long-term impact of the Affordable Care Act on the uninsured will take months to determine.

Uninsured Rate Drops Most Among Unemployed, Nonwhites

The uninsured rate so far in January has declined more among those who are unemployed than it has among those who are employed. The unemployed remain the subgroup with the highest uninsured rate at 34.1%, but the initial decline among this group suggests the healthcare law may be working as intended for unemployed adults. Additionally, the uninsured rate has fallen more among nonwhites than whites. The uninsured rate among nonwhites so far in January is 26.5%, compared with 29.1% in December 2013.

These preliminary results indicate that, so far, uninsured rates have not declined disproportionately among younger Americans, who continue to be more likely to be uninsured than older Americans.

Implications

Preliminary results from the first 19 days of January show the U.S. uninsured rate has modestly declined since the health insurance mandate went into effect at the beginning of the year. The uninsured rate has fluctuated at other points over the past several years, so it is unclear if this small decline is a reflection of the provisions of the Affordable Care Act that took effect on Jan. 1, or if this is part of a trend based on other reasons.

Percentage of Uninsured Americans, by Subgroup

	December 2013	Jan. 2-19, 2014	Difference
	%	%	(pct. pts.)
National adults	17.3	16.1	-1.2
Employed	18.8	17.8	-1.0
Unemployed	40.8	34.1	-6.7
Not in workforce	11.8	10.6	-1.2
White	12.3	11.3	-1.0
Nonwhite	29.1	26.5	-2.6
18-34 years	24.7	24.5	-0.2
35-64 years	19.0	17.0	-2.0
65 years and older	2.1	1.5	-0.6
Male	18.9	18.3	-0.6
Female	15.9	14.0	-1.9
Less than $36,000	31.0	29.6	-1.4
$36,000-$89,999	11.4	9.6	-1.8
$90,000+	7.2	5.6	-1.6

Gallup-Healthways Well-Being Index

GALLUP

Still, with only 2.1 million Americans newly enrolled in plans through the exchanges as of Dec. 28, 2013, the Obama administration and other proponents of the new healthcare law have a long way to go in hopes of reaching the goal of increasing the number of Americans who have health coverage.

Gallup will continue to track the U.S. uninsured rate in the weeks and months ahead.

Survey Methods

Results are based on telephone interviews conducted as part of the Gallup-Healthways Well-Being Index survey Jan. 2–19, 2014, with a random sample of 9,145 adults, aged 18 and older, living in all 50 U.S. states and the District of Columbia.

For results based on the total sample of national adults, the margin of sampling error is ±1 percentage points at the 95% confidence level.

January 23, 2014

OBAMA'S FIFTH YEAR JOB APPROVAL RATINGS AMONG MOST POLARIZED

Job approval 82% among Democrats, 11% among Republicans

by Jeffrey M. Jones

PRINCETON, NJ—The partisan gap in President Barack Obama's job approval rating was 71 percentage points during his fifth year in office, with 82% of Democrats and 11% of Republicans approving, on average. That is down from a 76-point gap during his re-election year, but continues to reflect the high degree of political polarization in presidential job ratings during his time in office.

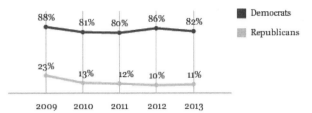

Barack Obama's Approval Ratings, by Political Party

Democrats
Republicans

88% 81% 80% 86% 82%

23% 13% 12% 10% 11%

2009 2010 2011 2012 2013

Note: Gallup's presidential years begin on Jan. 20 of each year and end on Jan. 19 of the following year.

GALLUP'

The results are based on more than 175,000 Gallup Daily tracking interviews conducted throughout Obama's fifth year in office, from Jan. 20, 2013, through Jan. 19, 2014.

Obama's fifth year in office ranks as the fourth-most polarized presidential year in Gallup's records, which date back to the Eisenhower presidency. In fact, all five of Obama's years in office rank among the 10 most polarized, with his fourth year edging out George W. Bush's fourth year in office for the top overall spot. Four of Bush's years in office rank among the 10 most politically polarized in terms of presidential job approval.

Largest Party Gaps in Presidential Approval Ratings, 1953-2013

President	Year in office	Dates of year	Average approval, Republicans	Average approval, Democrats	Average party gap
Obama	4	1/2012-1/2013	10%	86%	76 pts
G.W. Bush	4	1/2004-1/2005	91%	15%	76 pts
G.W. Bush	5	1/2005-1/2006	86%	14%	72 pts
Obama	5	1/2013-1/2014	11%	82%	71 pts
G.W. Bush	6	1/2006-1/2007	79%	9%	70 pts
Obama	2	1/2010-1/2011	12%	81%	69 pts
Obama	3	1/2011-1/2012	12%	80%	68 pts
G.W. Bush	7	1/2007-1/2008	73%	7%	66 pts
Obama	1	1/2009-1/2010	23%	88%	65 pts
Clinton	4	1/1996-1/1997	23%	85%	62 pts
G.W. Bush	8	1/2008-1/2009	67%	6%	61 pts
Reagan	4	1/1984-1/1985	89%	29%	60 pts

Note: Gallup's presidential years begin on Jan. 20 of each year and end on Jan. 19 of the following year.

GALLUP'

This recent era of extreme party polarization in views of the president began in Bush's fourth year in office, and has continued uninterrupted. Each year since 2004, the average party gap in presidential job approval has been 60 percentage points or greater. The only other two years with that degree of polarization were Ronald Reagan's and Bill Clinton's re-election years.

Obama's Fifth Year Slightly Less Polarized Than Bush's Fifth Year

Obama's first, second, third, and fourth years in office were the most polarized for any president's first, second, third, or fourth years. However, the 71-point party gap in ratings of Obama's job approval during his fifth year in office is slightly less than the 72-point gap found in Bush's fifth year. After Obama, the next largest fifth-year gap was 53 points for Clinton.

Apart from Nixon, whose fifth year was marred by the Watergate scandal, most presidents got similarly high ratings from their party's supporters in their fifth year, ranging from 82% for Obama

to 88% for Reagan. The differences in polarization are attributable to the ratings presidents received from supporters of the opposition party. Bush and Obama had approval ratings of 14% and 11% from Democrats and Republicans during their fifth year in office, respectively. Reagan, Clinton, and Eisenhower received approval ratings of at least 30% from the opposition party during the fifth year of their administrations.

Party Gaps in Presidential Approval Ratings, Fifth Year in Office, Elected Presidents

President	Dates of fifth year in office	Average approval, Republicans	Average approval, Democrats	Average party gap
G.W. Bush	1/2005-1/2006	86%	14%	72 pts
Obama	1/2013-1/2014	11%	82%	71 pts
Clinton	1/1997-1/1998	31%	84%	53 pts
Reagan	1/1985-1/1986	88%	36%	52 pts
Nixon	1/1973-1/1974	67%	24%	43 pts
Eisenhower	1/1957-1/1958	86%	47%	39 pts

Note: Gallup's presidential years begin on Jan. 20 of each year and end on Jan. 19 of the following year.

GALLUP'

Implications

Obama is on course to have the most politically polarized approval ratings of any president, with an average 69-point gap during his presidency, a full eight points higher than was the case with Bush. There have always been party differences in presidential ratings, but these have become more extreme in recent decades, averaging 34 points before Reagan's presidency and 58 points after. This is due more to presidents receiving comparatively lower approval ratings from the opposition party than it is from extremely high support from their own party, though both are factors.

Obama's highly polarized ratings, then, may have as much to do with the era in which he is governing as they do with his actions as president. Both Obama and Bush made overtures toward bringing politically divided Americans together, but the evidence suggests neither succeeded. That said, it is not clear that presidents will be very successful in gaining significant support from the opposition party, regardless of what they do in the current political environment.

January 23, 2014
BABY BOOMERS TO PUSH U.S. POLITICS IN THE YEARS AHEAD
Baby boomers' politics vary significantly by age

by Frank Newport, Jeffrey M. Jones, and Lydia Saad

This article is part of an ongoing series analyzing how baby boomers—those born from 1946 to 1964 in the U.S.—behave differently from other generations as consumers and in the workplace. The series also explores how the aging of the baby boomer generation will affect politics and well-being.

PRINCETON, NJ—Baby boomers constitute 32% of the U.S. adult population and, by Gallup's estimate, 36% of the electorate in 2012, eclipsing all other generational groups. Baby boomers have dominated U.S. politics on the basis of their sheer numbers since the late 1970s, when most of the group had reached voting age. Taken as a whole, baby boomers' political leanings are slightly less Democratic than the adult population's, perched between the strong Democratic orientation of the youthful millennials and the more Republican orientation of the older Greatest and Silent generations.

Party ID, With Leaners, by Generation: 2013

	All Americans	Millennial (1980-1996)	Gen X (1965-1979)	Baby boom (1946-1964)	Silent	Greatest
Democrat/ Lean Democratic	48%	53%	46%	46%	43%	46%
Republican/ Lean Republican	42%	35%	42%	44%	50%	47%
Net Democratic	6 pts.	18 pts.	4 pts.	2 pts.	-7 pts.	-1 pt.

GALLUP

If the party preferences of each generational group were to hold steady in the coming years as the Democratic-leaning baby boomers gradually replace the more Republican Silent and Greatest generations, the country as a whole would likely become more Democratic. That assumes today's children will lean at least slightly Democratic when they reach young adulthood, and thus that Americans who today are younger than 18 grow up to be as Democratic as the young voters they replace.

One difficulty with that projection, however, is that baby boomers' party identification was not steady in the past, so it may change again in the future. Gallup polling at 10-year intervals since 1993 shows baby boomers leaned Democratic in 1993, were divided with a slight Republican tilt in 2003, and remained divided but with a slight Democratic tilt in 2013. These findings are based on party ID that includes independents' leanings, available in Gallup data since 1992.

These 10-year shifts partly mirrored changes in the population as a whole. As ever-changing political dynamics in the country have created broad swings in the strength of each major party, baby boomers' political affiliation has also changed. Thus, boomers' politics could in theory change again in the years ahead, making predictions difficult.

Party ID by Generation -- 1993, 2003, 2013

	1993		2003		2013	
	Rep/ Lean	Dem/ Lean	Rep/ Lean	Dem/ Lean	Rep/ Lean	Dem/ Lean
	%	%	%	%	%	%
All Americans	40	49	46	45	42	48
Millennial	--	--	43	47	35	53
Gen X	42	49	46	44	42	46
Baby boom	41	48	46	45	44	46
Silent	41	50	46	46	50	43
Greatest	39	51	43	50	47	46

GALLUP

Baby Boomers Not Monolithic

The above analysis is based on baby boomers as a group—taking the average political views of Americans born between 1946 and 1964 as one broad population segment. Boomers, however, are not monolithic; their political preferences are actually quite different *within* the 19-year boomer age span.

Gallup's large database of Daily tracking interviews allows for an examination of baby boomers' party preferences in yearly increments. The accompanying chart shows the net Democratic

identification for boomers at each age in 2013, defined as the percentage of those of each age who identify with or lean toward the Democratic Party minus those who identify with or lean toward the Republican Party.

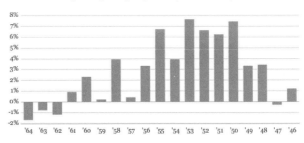

Democratic Advantage in 2013 Among Baby Boomers, Based on Year of Birth

GALLUP

Although the preponderance of baby boomers lean Democratic, the net political advantage varies from a seven- to eight-percentage-point Democratic one for some ages to a one- to two-point Republican tilt for others. Further, both the youngest boomers (born from 1962 to 1964) and the oldest boomers (born in 1946 and 1947) tend to be significantly less Democratic than the middle-year boomers. In particular, boomers born between 1950 and 1953 appear to have the highest Democratic orientation, along with those born in 1955.

These data can be compared with data for baby boomers six years ago, in 2008—the first year of Gallup tracking that allows for this detailed type of age-by-age examination of the population. The overall political environment was more Democratic in 2008, with the average Democratic advantage among boomers at +11.6 points in contrast to the +2.8 points in 2013. Still, it appears that the relative structure of boomers' political orientation by age was similar then to what it was in 2013. Those born in the earliest boomer years and those in the latest boomer years were the least Democratic, while those born from the late 1940s through the mid-1950s were the most Democratic. In short, the relative differences across boomer age groups held roughly constant even as the views of all boomers shifted in a less Democratic direction.

Democratic Advantage in 2008 Among Baby Boomers, Based on Year of Birth

GALLUP

Boomers' Politics Reflect Age-Specific Historical Imprints

There are many reasons why a particular age cohort of Americans displays a specific political orientation. A key factor could be the political and social environment that prevailed as the segment was reaching adulthood. Thus, for example, the Depression and World War II years affected today's greatest generation, while the Internet has affected today's millennials.

The most Democratic segment of boomers in 2013—generally, those born between 1950 and 1955—entered adulthood in 1968–1973. This was at the height of the Vietnam War and as race riots were going on in the U.S. It was also at the height of the hippie era, epitomized by the Woodstock festival, and a period of rapid liberalization of Americans' social views.

The youngest boomers, particularly those born in 1960 and later, would have come of age in a different political environment, one marked by the stagflation and tax revolt of the late 1970s, questions about U.S. strength in world affairs, and specific events such as the Iranian hostage crisis and Ronald Reagan's election in 1980. This group is not only less Democratic than baby boomers as a whole but also significantly less Democratic than the U.S. population.

Thus, the politics of baby boomers are not straightforward. While in the aggregate, boomers are slightly less Democratic than the U.S. population, within the boomer group there appear to be diverse subgroups, associated with the distinct political environments each experienced as they were coming of age politically.

These intra-boomer differences only further complicate the problem of trying to predict what baby boomers' politics will be in their golden years. The next wave of baby boomers to turn 65 will be those born between 1950 and 1955. This group came of age at a highly transformative period in U.S. history, and according to the resilience of their Democratic leanings since 2008, may have the most fixed political views of any boomers. Thus, barring any major political realignment in the country as a whole, they could carry these leanings into their senior years. This would cause seniors more broadly to tilt more Democratic in the short term.

By 2021 and thereafter, however, the more conservative bloc of younger boomers will be entering the ranks of seniors, and—depending on the broader political dynamics affecting them—could shift the balance again.

Of course, boomers will also be subject to the multifaceted ramifications of becoming a "senior citizen" as they age and thus, they may bend to forces that shift their political orientations in new ways as they enter this final stage of life.

Bottom Line

Predicting the politics of the highly important baby boom generation over the next decade as the group moves into its senior years is highly speculative. But one thing is certain. Baby boomers, holding the distinction of the largest generation in the U.S. population, will continue to exert disproportionate influence over the U.S. political process for at least the next 25 years.

January 24, 2014
RECORD LOW SAY OWN REPRESENTATIVE DESERVES RE-ELECTION
Less than a fifth of registered voters say most in Congress deserve re-election

by Andrew Dugan and Brad Hoffman

WASHINGTON, D.C.—The enduring unpopularity of Congress appears to have seeped into the nation's 435 congressional districts, as a record-low percentage of registered voters, 46%, now say the U.S. representative in their own congressional district deserves

re-election. Equally historic, the share of voters saying most members of Congress deserve re-election has fallen to 17%, a new nadir.

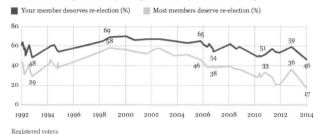

Americans' Views on Whether Their Member, Most Members of Congress Deserve Re-Election
Please tell me whether you think each of the following political officeholders deserves to be re-elected, or not.
How about the U.S. representative in your congressional district/most members of Congress?

■ Your member deserves re-election (%)   ▪ Most members deserve re-election (%)

Registered voters

GALLUP'

These findings are from Gallup's annual Mood of the Nation poll, conducted Jan. 5–8, 2014. The percentage of voters saying most members of Congress deserve re-election has been below its historical average of 39% since early 2008. The figure has plummeted since mid-2011, with a brief improvement—to 36%—in November 2012, attributable to a surge in Democratic support at the time of the national election.

The legendary Speaker of the House Tip O'Neill famously coined the phrase "all politics is local," a dictum that guided his Democratic majorities against Republican electoral waves in the 1980s. More generally, the saying describes the local versus national phenomenon that also occurs when the public is asked about such things as healthcare, education, and crime. But now that adage rings less true as voters see their own U.S. representative in the same way that they see most other members of Congress—as not deserving re-election.

Can 2014 Be a "Wave" Election?

The 17% of voters who now say most of Congress deserves re-election is well below the roughly 40% threshold that has historically been associated with major electoral turnover. With this in mind, Congress could be in for a major shake-up. Judging by net seats lost in an election as a percentage of the overall number of seats, 2010, 1994, and 2006 register as the top three recent elections. All of these years had election-year averages of 41% or fewer voters saying most of Congress deserved re-election, with the Republican-wave election of 2010 registering the lowest, 30%—still 13 percentage points higher than the current reading.

The political direction of any potential electoral wave is difficult to determine, however, as self-identified registered voters of both parties largely agree that most members of Congress do not deserve re-election. Eighteen percent of Republicans, the majority party in the House, say most members deserve re-election, identical to the percentage of Democrats saying so.

Thus, voters' wrath appears not to be directed toward one party in particular, as much as toward any incumbent member of Congress.

Implications

Consistent with abysmally low congressional approval ratings and widespread dissatisfaction with the nation's system of government, the proportion of registered voters saying Congress deserves re-election has hit an all-time low of 17%. While Congress as an institution is no stranger to voter disenchantment, American voters are usually more charitable in their assessments of their own representatives in the national legislature. But even this has fallen to a new trough.

Do Most Members of Congress Deserve Re-Election?

Election-year averages, registered voters

	Yes (%)	Net seats turned over in an election (% of overall membership)	Overall membership change (% of overall membership)
2014	17	?	?
2012	36	2	17
2010	30	15	21
2008	37	6	12
2006	39	7	12
2004	51	1	9
2002	57	2	12
2000	55	0	9
1998	57	1	9
1994	41	12	15
1992	35	2	20

Sources: Gallup polls, House of Representatives, & Congressional Research Service

GALLUP'

Typically, results like these have presaged significant turnover in Congress, such as in 1994, 2006, and 2010. So Congress could be headed for a major shake-up in its membership this fall.

However, unlike those three years, when one party controlled both houses of Congress, the beneficiary of the anti-incumbent sentiment is not clear in the current situation, in which one party controls the House and the other, the Senate. Partisans on both sides of the aisle are displeased with Congress. But with so few voters saying they are willing to re-elect their own representative, it suggests that many officeholders will be vulnerable, if not in the general election, then perhaps in the host of competitive primaries soon to take place.

Survey Methods

Results for this Gallup poll are based on telephone interviews conducted Jan. 5–8, 2014, with a random sample of 1,018 adults, aged 18 and older, living in all 50 U.S. states and the District of Columbia.

For results based on the total sample of national adults, the margin of sampling error is ±4 percentage points at the 95% confidence level.

January 27, 2014
HAWAIIANS, D.C. RESIDENTS MOST APPROVING OF OBAMA IN 2013
Wyoming and West Virginia residents least approving

by Jeffrey M. Jones

PRINCETON, NJ—Residents of 11 states and the District of Columbia gave President Barack Obama job approval ratings above 50% in 2013. Hawaii had the highest approval rating among the 50 states at 61%, while more than eight in 10 District of Columbia residents also approved. In three states—Wyoming, West Virginia, and Utah—fewer than three in 10 residents approved.

Top States, Obama Job Approval

	% Approve
District of Columbia	80.8
Hawaii	61.3
Maryland	57.0
Rhode Island	56.7
New York	56.7
Vermont	56.6
Massachusetts	56.5
New Jersey	56.4
California	55.8
Connecticut	55.1
Delaware	54.4
Illinois	53.7

Gallup Daily tracking, January-December 2013

GALLUP'

Bottom States, Obama Job Approval

	% Approve
Wyoming	22.5
West Virginia	25.1
Utah	27.3
South Dakota	31.7
Idaho	32.1
Oklahoma	32.1
Montana	33.1
Alaska	33.5
Arkansas	34.9
Kentucky	35.1
Kansas	35.1
North Dakota	35.5

Gallup Daily tracking, January-December 2013

GALLUP'

The results are based on more than 178,000 Gallup Daily tracking interviews conducted nationwide throughout 2013. Each state's sample had a minimum of 500 respondents, and Gallup interviewed at least 1,000 residents in 40 different states. The state samples were weighted to ensure they were demographically representative of the state's adult population.

Obama's average approval rating declined about two percentage points nationally in 2013 versus 2012, and his approval rating in most states showed at least some decline. In three states—Washington, Minnesota, and Michigan—his job approval dropped below the majority level. His approval rating did not improve by a statistically significant amount in any state.

Throughout Obama's presidency, the most approving and least approving states have mostly stayed the same. In addition to the District of Columbia, seven states have been among the 10 most approving each year since 2009—Hawaii, Maryland, New York, Massachusetts, Connecticut, Vermont, and California. New Jersey, Rhode Island, and Delaware have ranked among the 10 most approving states in all but one year of Obama's presidency. Hawaii has ranked first among states each year, and Maryland has been second in all but one year.

Eight states have ranked among the 10 least approving every year Obama has been in office—Wyoming, Idaho, West Virginia, Alaska, Utah, Oklahoma, Montana, and Arkansas. Wyoming residents gave Obama his lowest average state approval rating in three of the five years he has been president, and Utah residents did so twice.

Approval ratings of Obama vary regionally, with the highest ratings generally coming from Northeastern and Mid-Atlantic states, and his lowest approval ratings tending to come from states in the Mountain West and parts of the South.

Implications

Obama's relative popularity in each state takes on added significance this year because of November's midterm elections. In particular, Republicans hope to regain party control of the Senate for the first time since 2006.

Republican candidates in states in which Obama is unpopular will attempt to link their Democratic challenger to the president to help their election prospects. In contrast, Democratic candidates in states in which Obama is popular may benefit politically from the association, which may include a visit from Obama to the state to campaign on the candidate's behalf.

Obama's job approval ratings could change significantly between now and the elections, so while the 2013 averages provide a good indication of his strongest and weakest states, they may not be indicative of his ratings in November, when the elections take place. For example, Obama's current job approval ratings in most states are likely a few points lower now than their 2013 averages, given that he has averaged 41% job approval so far in January, compared with the 46% average for his fifth year in office.

Survey Methods

Results for this Gallup poll are based on telephone interviews conducted Jan. 2–Dec. 29, 2013, on the Gallup Daily tracking survey, with a random sample of 178,527 adults, aged 18 and older, living in all 50 U.S. states and the District of Columbia.

For results based on the total sample of national adults, the margin of sampling error is ±1 percentage point at the 95% confidence level.

Margins of error for individual states are no greater than ±6 percentage points, and are ±3 percentage points in most states. The margin of error for the District of Columbia is ±6 percentage points.

January 28, 2014
STARK RACIAL DIFFERENCES IN VIEWS ON U.S. STATUS
Nonwhites more positive about state of U.S.; whites less positive

by Justin McCarthy

WASHINGTON, D.C.—Overall, Americans are as likely to be positive (39%) about the current state of the country as they are to be negative (40%). However, the gap between whites' and nonwhites' views of where the country stands is wider than at any point in recent history, with nonwhites now almost twice as likely as whites to view the nation's situation positively.

Americans' Positive Views on the Nation's Current Standing, by Race

We'd like you to imagine a ladder with steps numbered from zero at the bottom to 10 at the top. Suppose the top of the ladder represents the best possible situation for our country and the bottom represents the worst possible situation. Please tell me the number of the step on which you think the United States stands at the present time.

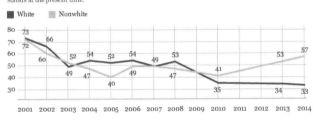

NOTE: Positive ratings were counted as ratings from six to 10.

GALLUP'

These findings are from Gallup's annual Mood of the Nation poll, conducted Jan. 5–8, 2014, which asked Americans to rate the present standing of the U.S. using a zero-to-10 ladder scale, with 10 being the best possible situation for the country and zero being the worst. Scores from six to 10 are considered positive, and scores from zero to four are considered negative; five is neutral.

The question does not refer to the presidency, yet the elected official occupying the White House has dramatically affected the way particular demographic groups have viewed the country in recent years. From the tail end of President Bill Clinton's presidency in January 2001 through the start of the last full year of George W. Bush's presidency in January 2008, whites' and nonwhites' ratings of the nation's standing were generally similar, although whites tended to be slightly more positive than nonwhites. The greatest gap between the two groups' views was 12 points in 2005, just after Bush's re-election.

This changed after the 2008 presidential election, when differences between the two racial groups started to get larger. Between 2008 and 2010, the views of whites and nonwhites soured, likely reflecting the major economic challenges that erupted in late 2008. However, whites' views declined much more than nonwhites', resulting in a six-point gap in 2010 with nonwhites more positive than whites.

More than half of whites (53%) were positive about the country's current trajectory in January 2008—10 months before the presidential election. After President Barack Obama's first year in office, that percentage fell to 35%. Four years later, that figure is roughly the same.

Conversely, nonwhites have been increasingly positive about the United States' standing. While their assessments of current conditions dipped with the rest of the country's in 2010, nonwhites' views have increased 16 percentage points since then.

Republicans Slightly More Positive Than Last Year

Republicans are more positive about the nation's present situation now (29%) than they were last year (21%). They continue, however, to be the least positive group, with their positivity hovering below that shown by independents (33%) and Democrats (54%).

Americans' Positive Views on the Nation's Current Standing, by Party ID
% Positive

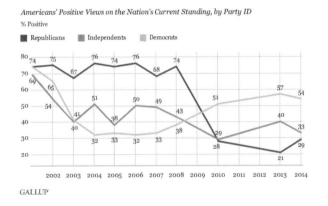

GALLUP'

Republicans' positive views about the nation's trajectory are dramatically worse than they were during the Bush presidency, when their ratings consistently dwarfed the optimism of independents and Democrats. Today, Republicans' numbers are even lower than the subdued positive reactions Democrats gave during the Bush era and have been consistently low throughout Obama's term.

For Many Americans, the Future Is Bright, but the Past Was Even Brighter

As they have since 2002, Americans view the nation's future—and its past—more favorably than its present. While nearly four in 10 view the current situation positively, exactly half (50%) view the future positively and 53% reflect positively on the past. Historically, this has not always been the case. From 1985 to 2002, Americans viewed the future more positively than the past.

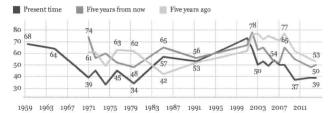

Americans' Positive Views on the Nation's Past, Present and Future Standing

We'd like you to imagine a ladder with steps numbered from zero at the bottom to 10 at the top. Suppose the top of the ladder represents the best possible situation for our country and the bottom represents the worst possible situation. Please tell me the number of the step on which you think the United States stands?

■ Present time ■ Five years from now ■ Five years ago

NOTE: Positive ratings were counted as ratings from six to 10.

GALLUP

Demographics by race and political identification followed similar trends in their views of the future as they did for the present time, but with higher levels of optimism. Americans of all demographics have historically viewed the future more positively than the present.

Bottom Line

As the president prepares to make his fifth State of the Union speech Tuesday, he will have to address these many, diverging sentiments about the state of the nation within the electorate as a single audience.

Since Obama's election, whites' and nonwhites' views about the nation's trajectory have moved in opposite directions. For non-whites, his election could have signaled an inclusion they had not felt before, whereas for whites, who largely identify as Republicans, Obama's big-government views and policies such as the Affordable Care Act could have played a major role in their pessimism about where the nation is and where it will go.

Though only a slight increase, the small uptick in Republicans' positive thoughts could serve as a small gift to Obama as he attempts to rise above the second-lowest yearly job approval rating he has received since entering office and could signal that the opposing party's low optimism has already bottomed out. Republicans remain the least positive about America's current prospects, but the extreme lows could be abating, as the end of Obama's second term is closer at hand.

Survey Methods

Results for this Gallup poll are based on telephone interviews conducted Jan. 5–8, 2014, with a random sample of 1,018 adults, aged 18 and older, living in all 50 U.S. states and the District of Columbia.

For results based on the total sample of national adults, the margin of sampling error is ±4 percentage points at the 95% confidence level.

January 28, 2014
AMERICANS' MOODS STILL IMPROVE ON HOLIDAYS AND WEEKENDS
Average daily happiness increased in 2013; stress levels held steady

by Lindsey Sharpe

WASHINGTON, D.C.—The happiest day of 2013 fell on Thanksgiving Day, Nov. 28, with 70% of Americans reporting that they felt a lot of happiness and enjoyment without a lot of stress and worry. Thanksgiving has been one of the top three happiest days every year since 2008. Following closely last year were Memorial Day and Christmas Day.

The results for each year comprise more than 175,000 surveys, conducted daily as part of the Gallup-Healthways Well-Being Index. As part of the survey, interviewers read respondents a series of emotions and ask them to say whether they experienced each one "during a lot of the day yesterday." Gallup's U.S. Mood Index tracks the percentage of U.S. adults who, reflecting on the day before they were surveyed, say they experienced a lot of happiness and enjoyment without a lot of stress and worry, and vice versa.

As is common, the majority of the year's happiest days fell on holidays and weekends. During these times, Americans are more likely to spend additional hours socializing with friends and family, which can increase enjoyment and decrease stress levels.

Gallup-Healthways Daily Mood: Happiest Days of 2013

Asked of American adults

	% With a lot of happiness/enjoyment without a lot of stress/worry	Day of the week	Key events
Nov 28	70	Thursday	Thanksgiving Day
May 27	65	Monday	Memorial Day
Jun 8	64	Saturday	–
Sep 28	64	Saturday	–
Dec 25	64	Wednesday	Christmas Day
Jan 19	62	Saturday	Saturday prior to Martin Luther King Day
Mar 31	62	Sunday	Easter Sunday
May 12	62	Sunday	Mother's Day
Jun 9	62	Sunday	–
Jun 16	62	Sunday	Father's Day

Gallup-Healthways Well-Being Index

GALLUP

High-Stress Days Often Coincide With Negative News

Following a typical pattern, high-stress days in 2013 often accompanied high-profile negative news events, though other factors may be more influential in driving daily stress levels.

In 2013, the most stressful day of the year was Monday, June 3. While stress likely stemmed from beginning the workweek, this day also coincided with the beginning of the WikiLeaks trial involving Chelsea Manning (known at the time of the trial as Bradley Manning), who released classified military documents to the anti-secrecy website WikiLeaks in the largest security breach in U.S. history.

Feb. 21 and 28 followed closely in terms of high stress levels, as the U.S. federal government headed toward automatic budget sequestration and associated spending cuts, which negatively affected Americans' economic confidence.

Later in the year, Americans reported feeling a lot of stress and worry in September amid reports of potential U.S. involvement in the Syrian civil war.

Gallup-Healthways Daily Mood: Most Stressed Days of 2013
Asked of American adults

	% With a lot of stress/worry without a lot of happiness/enjoyment	Day of the week	Key events
Jun 3	20	Monday	WikiLeaks/Manning trial begins
Feb 21	19	Thursday	--
Feb 28	18	Thursday	U.S. government approaches budget sequestration
Apr 8	17	Monday	--
May 22	17	Wednesday	--
Sep 10	17	Tuesday	Obama delivers remarks making the case for U.S. action in Syria
Sep 16	17	Monday	UN confirms use of chemical warfare in Syria; gunman kills 12 at Washington Navy Yard
Dec 9	17	Monday	--

Gallup-Healthways Well-Being Index

GALLUP'

Americans' Daily Happiness Ticked Up Slightly, While Stress Stayed Level

On average, 48.4% of Americans reported feeling a lot of happiness and enjoyment without a lot of stress and worry in 2013, a slight uptick from 48.0% in 2012. Americans' happiness is down from 2011 and the same as in 2010.

Those experiencing the opposite—a lot of stress and worry without a lot of happiness and enjoyment—remained stable at 11.0%, where it has hovered throughout the past six years. Americans' self-reported stress levels peak during the workweek, decline slightly on Fridays, and fall even more on weekends.

Gallup-Healthways Daily Mood: Yearly Averages, 2008-2013
Asked of American adults

■ % With a lot of happiness/enjoyment without a lot of stress/worry

░ % With a lot of stress/worry without a lot of happiness/enjoyment

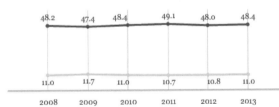

48.2	47.4	48.4	49.1	48.0	48.4
11.0	11.7	11.0	10.7	10.8	11.0
2008	2009	2010	2011	2012	2013

Gallup-Healthways Well-Being Index

GALLUP'

Implications

Despite 2013 being a year filled with economic and political uncertainty in the U.S. and around the world, stress levels remained steady and happiness increased slightly.

While mood is not indicative of a person's well-being, following the daily mood of the nation can provide insight into two of the elements that make up a person's well-being—social relationships and physical health. When adults spend more time socially, happiness and enjoyment levels increase. Stress, on the other hand, can adversely affect physical health.

The happiest days of 2013 fell on holidays and weekends, when people tend to spend more hours interacting socially with friends and family, while the most stressful days fell within the workweek. Gallup research shows that engaged employees report lower stress levels and better moods during the workweek than "not engaged" or "actively disengaged" employees. Business leaders can bolster well-being by engaging employees and creating a work environment that is conducive to employees being able to form and develop social relationships. Gallup research also shows that boosting social well-being in the workplace will benefit the employer, as well as the employee, by increasing productivity and improving overall well-being.

Survey Methods

Results are based on telephone interviews conducted as part of the Gallup-Healthways Well-Being Index survey Jan. 3–Dec. 29, 2013, with a random sample of 175,000 adults, aged 18 and older, living in all 50 U.S. states and the District of Columbia.

For results based on the total sample of national adults, the margin of sampling error is ±1 percentage point at the 95% confidence level.

January 28, 2014

DEMOCRATS AND REPUBLICANS DIFFER ON TOP PRIORITIES FOR GOV'T

Democrats prioritize education; Republicans focus on terrorism as a top issue

by Joy Wilke and Frank Newport

PRINCETON, NJ—American politics over the last decade has become notoriously polarized, with congressional Republicans and Democrats disagreeing on the best way to address healthcare, immigration, taxes, and a host of other issues. But supporters of both parties do agree that the economy should be a top priority, with 91% of Democrats and 88% of Republicans saying it is extremely or very important that the president and Congress deal with that issue this year. There is less agreement on the other issues the federal government should focus on.

These results are from Gallup's annual Mood of the Nation survey, conducted Jan. 5–8.

In addition to the economy, the four top issues that Democrats rate as high priorities are education, poverty and homelessness, healthcare policy, and Social Security and Medicare. At least three in four Democrats rate each of these issues as extremely or very important for the federal government to deal with.

By contrast, at least three in four Republicans feel that terrorism, the military and national defense, and healthcare should be high-priority issues for the president and lawmakers this year. Education, at 70% extremely or very important, rounds out Republicans' top five priorities.

Overall, Democrats and Republicans share seven of each other's top 10 priorities—the economy, education, healthcare, terrorism, crime, Social Security and Medicare, and poverty. Democrats, but not Republicans, rank the distribution of wealth, the environment, and gun policy as top priorities. Republicans rank the military, taxes, immigration, and world affairs in their top 10.

Top 10 Priority Issues, by Party Identification

Next, how important is it to you that the president and Congress deal with each of the following issues in the next year?

% Extremely/Very important

	Democrats/Democratic leaders	Republicans/Republican leaders
	%	%
1.	The economy (91)	The economy (88)
2.	Education (91)	Terrorism (77)
3.	Poverty and homelessness (82)	The military and national defense (76)
4.	Healthcare policy (79)	Healthcare policy (75)
5.	Social Security and Medicare (77)	Education (70)
6.	Distribution of income/wealth (72)	Taxes (69)
7.	Crime (71)	Social Security and Medicare (67)
8.	The environment (71)	Crime (65)
9.	Terrorism (68)	Immigration (54)
10.	Gun policy (64)	World affairs (53)
		Poverty and homelessness (53)

Jan. 5-8, 2014

GALLUP

Partisans Most Divided on Prioritizing the Environment, Distribution of Wealth

Democrats overall assign a significantly higher priority than do Republicans to nine of the 19 issues measured. This almost certainly reflects differences in underlying partisan views of how involved the government should be in fixing societal problems, with Democrats significantly more likely than Republicans to say government should be used to fix problems.

Democrats are particularly more likely to assign a high priority to government efforts to address the environment, with a 39-percentage-point gap separating the parties.

Democrats and Republicans also differ substantially in their rankings of the distribution of income and wealth (with Democrats 34 points higher) and poverty and homelessness (29 points). Democrats are also more likely than Republicans to prioritize education, gun policy, race relations, policies toward gays and lesbians, energy policy, and Social Security and Medicare.

Republicans are more likely than Democrats to say the president and Congress should prioritize the military and national defense (15 points), and taxes (13 points). Republicans also assign a higher priority to terrorism, government surveillance, and immigration.

Altogether, three issues can be considered **bipartisan priorities**, receiving extremely/very important ratings from at least 70% of Democrats and Republicans. These include the economy, education, and healthcare policy.

Four issues are **Democratic priorities**, which at least 70% of Democrats rate highly but are rated significantly lower (and lower than 70%) by Republicans: the distribution of income and wealth, poverty and homelessness, Social Security and Medicare, and the environment.

Two issues are **Republican priorities**, rated above 70% by Republicans, but not as high by Democrats: the military and national defense, and terrorism.

Differences in Issue Priorities Between Democrats and Republicans

% Saying issues should be extremely/very important for the president and Congress to deal with in the next year

		Democrats/ Democratic leaders	Republicans/ Republican leaders	Difference
		%	%	pct. pts.
1.	The environment	71	32	39
2.	The distribution of income and wealth	72	38	34
3.	Poverty and homelessness	82	53	29
4.	Education	91	70	21
5.	Gun policy	64	43	21
6.	Race relations	48	29	19
7.	Policies toward gays and lesbians	37	18	19
8.	Energy policy	63	49	14
9.	Social Security and Medicare	77	67	10
10.	Crime	71	65	6
11.	Healthcare policy	79	75	4
12.	The economy	91	88	3
13.	World affairs	53	53	0
14.	Abortion	38	42	-4
15.	Immigration	47	54	-7
16.	Government surveillance of U.S. citizens	37	45	-8
17.	Terrorism	68	77	-9
18.	Taxes	56	69	-13
19.	The military and national defense	61	76	-15

Jan. 5-8, 2014

GALLUP

Bottom Line

As President Barack Obama prepares to deliver his State of the Union address Tuesday evening, he will be facing a national audience that, regardless of partisanship, agrees on one thing: the economy should be the government's highest priority. Democrats and Republicans alike also put education and healthcare policy among their top five priorities. Beyond that, however, the two groups disagree, with Democrats prioritizing poverty and homelessness, income inequality, Social Security and Medicare, and the environment, while Republicans prioritize the military and defense and terrorism.

Survey Methods

Results for this Gallup poll are based on telephone interviews conducted Jan. 5–8, 2014, with a random sample of 1,018 adults, aged 18 and older, living in all 50 U.S. states and the District of Columbia.

For results based on the total sample of national adults, the margin of sampling error is ±4 percentage points at the 95% confidence level.

For results based on the total sample of Democrats, the margin of sampling error is ±5 percentage points at the 95% confidence level.

For results based on the total sample of Republicans, the margin of sampling error is ±5 percentage points at the 95% confidence level.

January 29, 2014

NOT AS MANY U.S. STATES LEAN DEMOCRATIC IN 2013

Parties now about equal in state party leanings, 17 to 14

by Lydia Saad

PRINCETON, NJ—Blue states outnumbered red states in the U.S. last year, 17 to 14, according to Gallup Daily tracking of party preferences. That three-state advantage for the Democrats is down from a seven-state lead for the Democrats in 2012, and well short of their 30-state lead in 2008—Gallup's first year of state measurement. Still, it's larger than the near-tie in the party balance of states found in 2011.

Political Composition of the 50 U.S. States

Based on annual state averages of party affiliation from Gallup Daily tracking
District of Columbia not included

	'08	'09	'10	'11	'12	'13	Change, 2012-2013
Solid Democratic	29	23	13	11	13	12	-1
Lean Democratic	6	10	9	7	6	5	-1
Competitive	10	12	18	15	19	19	0
Lean Republican	1	1	5	7	3	2	-1
Solid Republican	4	4	5	10	9	12	+3
Total Democratic	35	33	22	18	19	17	-2
Total Republican	5	5	10	17	12	14	+2
Net Democratic	+30	+28	+12	+1	+7	+3	

Notes:
-- Solid states are defined as those in which one party has at least a 10-percentage-point advantage over the other in party affiliation (identification + leaning).
-- Leaning states are those in which one party has more than a 5-point but less than a 10-point advantage in party affiliation.
-- Competitive states are those in which the parties are within 5 points of each other in party affiliation.

GALLUP'

The biggest change in the party profile of the states in 2013 was the Republicans' gain of three solidly Republican states—meaning those where Republicans outnumbered Democrats by at least 10 percentage points. Those additions were South Carolina, South Dakota, and Oklahoma. However, this was partly offset by a net loss of one Republican-leaning state. At the same time, Democrats had net losses of one solid and one Democratic-leaning state, while the number of competitive states was unchanged.

Overall, the most Democratic-leaning states in 2013 were New York, Hawaii, Rhode Island, Massachusetts, and Maryland, all showing 20-point or better Democratic advantages in party identification. Gallup considers another seven states to be "solidly Democratic," by virtue of their 10-point or better Democratic advantage.

The most Republican-leaning states were Wyoming, Utah, North Dakota, Idaho, Kansas, and Alaska, all with 20-point or more Democratic deficits. Another six states qualify as solidly Republican, with Democratic deficits ranging from −10 to −17.

The results are from Gallup Daily tracking from January through December 2013, and are based on interviews with more than 178,000 U.S. adults, with each state's data weighted to match U.S. Census demographic parameters for that state's adult population. The state sample sizes range from 447 for the District of Columbia to 17,355 for California. All but the District of Columbia have at least 500 respondents, and 40 states have at least 1,000.

Solidly Democratic States in 2013

	Democratic advantage^
	Pct. pts.
District of Columbia	58
New York	25
Hawaii	24
Rhode Island	23
Massachusetts	21
Maryland	20
Vermont	19
California	18
Illinois	17
Delaware	17
New Jersey	16
Connecticut	16
New Mexico	11

Gallup Daily tracking, January-December 2013

^ % Democrat/Lean Democratic minus % Republican/Lean Republican

Solidly Republican States in 2013

	Democratic advantage^
	Pct. pts.
Wyoming	-40
Utah	-32
North Dakota	-25
Idaho	-24
Kansas	-21
Alaska	-20
South Dakota	-17
Nebraska	-16
Montana	-13
Oklahoma	-13
Alabama	-11
South Carolina	-10

Gallup Daily tracking, January-December 2013

^ % Democrat/Lean Democratic minus % Republican/Lean Republican

GALLUP'

Gallup determines the party orientation of each state by subtracting the total percentage of adults identifying as or leaning Republican from those identifying as Democrats or leaning Democratic, thus creating a "Democratic advantage" figure. Positive values indicate a state is more Democratic than Republican, while negative values indicate it is more Republican than Democratic. Taking the partisan leanings of independents into account gives a better picture of the parties' relative strength in each state, as independents who lean toward a particular party typically vote for that party's candidates. Additionally, the percentage of total independents (before leaners are allocated to the parties) varies widely by state, from 30% in Kentucky to 55% in New Hampshire, which may mask latent partisanship.

Red States Hang Together; Blue States Rim the Coasts

Republican states are clustered in the center of the country stretching west to the Rockies, with another bundle located in the Southeast. Democratic states are more dispersed, although largely grouped along the East and West Coasts, as well as around the Great Lakes.

Party ID by State, 2013

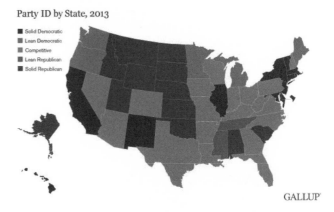

GALLUP'

As seen in 2012, only a handful of states share a border with a state oriented to the opposing party, underscoring the extreme regional separation of the parties. The Democratic states of Oregon and Washington share a border with Republican Idaho, and the Republican Dakotas border Democratic-leaning Minnesota.

Democratic New Mexico barely touches Republican Utah on its northwest corner and the panhandle of Oklahoma on its northeast corner.

Despite the Republicans' gain in the states last year, the overall political orientation of the country stayed about the same in 2013, with the Democrats enjoying a six-point advantage—47% vs. 41%—over Republicans. That compares with a five-point advantage—47% vs. 42%—in 2012. Part of the reason for this seeming discrepancy is that some of the Democratic Party's largest gains last year were in highly populous states, and ones where the Democrats already held a strong lead. They gained three points each in California, New Jersey, and New York, and one point in Illinois. Thus, while helping to increase Democratic ID nationally, these gains did not add to the number of Democratic states.

Implications

Leading up to the 2014 midterm elections, when 36 Senate seats and 36 governorships will be on the line, Gallup's 2013 polling saw the Republican Party making slight gains in the party orientation of the states, with three more states now in the GOP's column than in 2012. That modest shift still leaves Democratic states outnumbering Republican states. But it reflects a gradual shrinking of the Democrats' dominance since 2008, the year Barack Obama first won the presidency.

The resulting four-state lead for Democrats in 2013 is far less than their 12-state lead in 2010—a year with a wave election that swept out 63 House Democrats and established the current Republican majority. In that same vein, Democrats appear disadvantaged in protecting this year's Senate majority, as they will be attempting to protect seats in three solidly Republican states (South Dakota, Montana, and Alaska), as well as in a host of truly competitive states. Thus, the political climate appears relatively auspicious for Republicans. But given potential differences in partisanship between the state adult population and the voting electorate, state partisanship doesn't always match state voting patterns, and doesn't account for the influence of incumbency or specific issues in a given race.

Further, to the extent state partisanship is instructive in forecasting how statewide elections play out, it remains to be seen how the 2013 patterns might change in 2014. The elections will be held more than 10 months into the year, and more than a year after most of the 2013 data were collected. Of particular note, a major change in Obama's job approval rating by this fall could affect party ID nationally, could trickle down to state partisanship figures, and potentially affect at least some statewide races.

Survey Methods

Results for this Gallup poll are based on telephone interviews conducted Jan. 2–Dec. 29, 2013, on the Gallup Daily tracking survey, with a random sample of 178,527 adults, aged 18 and older, living in all 50 U.S. states and the District of Columbia.

For results based on the total sample of national adults, the margin of sampling error is ±1 percentage point at the 95% confidence level.

Margins of error for individual states are no greater than ±6 percentage points, and are ±3 percentage points in most states. The margin of error for the District of Columbia is ±6 percentage points.

January 29, 2014
FED CHAIRMAN BERNANKE LEAVES WITH MIXED VERDICT
About as many Americans approve of Bernanke as disapprove

by Andrew Dugan

WASHINGTON, D.C.—Presiding over the darkest days the U.S. economy has experienced since the Great Depression, Federal Reserve Chairman Ben Bernanke leaves office this week as one of the most influential economic policymakers in the country's recent history. But the American public is divided on how Bernanke has handled his job, with 40% approving and 35% disapproving. One in four have no opinion. By contrast, Bernanke's predecessor, the better-known Alan Greenspan, left office with a strong majority approving of his performance.

Judging the Nation's Top Central Banker

Do you approve or disapprove of the way Ben Bernanke/Alan Greenspan has handled his job as Federal Reserve Chairman?

	Approve	Disapprove	No opinion
	%	%	%
Ben Bernanke^	40	35	25
Alan Greenspan^^	65	21	14

^ Jan. 25-26, 2014
^^ Jan. 20-22, 2006

GALLUP

These data come from a Jan. 25–26 Gallup poll, just ahead of Bernanke's final day on Friday. Bernanke has implemented a vast array of controversial and in some instances novel policy choices. These included acting as the "lender of last resort" to the beleaguered banking system, maintaining low interest rates for an extended period of time, and, most notably, engaging in the money-supply-expanding, bond-purchasing policy known as "quantitative easing" that has quadrupled the size of the Fed's balance sheet.

Republicans Most Likely to Disapprove of Bernanke

Appointed by a Republican president and then re-appointed by a Democratic one, Bernanke might seem like the rare public official with bipartisan appeal. However, Democrats are far more likely to say they approve of the outgoing Fed chairman (59%) than are Republicans (28%). Independents are divided, with 35% approving and 38% disapproving.

Approval of Ben Bernanke and Alan Greenspan, by Party ID

	Republicans	Independents	Democrats
	%	%	%
BERNANKE ^			
Approve	28	35	59
Disapprove	53	38	19
No opinion	19	28	23
GREENSPAN ^^			
Approve	75	62	60
Disapprove	13	24	26
No opinion	13	14	14

^ Jan. 25-26, 2014
^^ Jan. 20-22, 2006

GALLUP

In a separate question that Gallup has asked throughout Bernanke's tenure, confidence in Bernanke's ability "to do or to recommend the right thing for the economy" tracked closely with the party of the president he served. Under George W. Bush, Republicans were more likely to express confidence in Bernanke; under Barack Obama, Democrats were more supportive.

Greenspan, who also was initially appointed by a Republican president but served presidents of both parties, had a higher approval rating with Republicans (75%) than Democrats (60%) when he left office during Bush's presidency.

Higher-Income Americans Most Likely to Approve of Bernanke

A majority of Americans living in households with annual incomes of $90,000 or more, 54%, approve of Bernanke's performance as Fed chairman, while 35% disapprove. Lower- and middle-income Americans show a closer divide between approval and disapproval, with generally higher rates of no opinion.

Approval of Ben Bernanke, by Annual Household Income

	Less than $24,000	$24,000 to <$60,000	$60,000 to <$90,000	$90,000+
	%	%	%	%
Approve	34	36	43	54
Disapprove	36	34	42	35
No opinion	30	31	16	11

Jan. 25-26, 2014

GALLUP

Bernanke and other officials at the Federal Reserve have long insisted that the controversial quantitative easing program was designed to help the overall economy, but many critics charge that it has only benefited the wealthy by boosting the prices of assets disproportionately owned by upper-income Americans, such as equities. These data suggest that the wealthy were more aware and more appreciative of Bernanke's performance.

Implications

Bernanke's consequential legacy may take decades to fully assess, but he has already won many plaudits from an array of economists, policymakers, and financial analysts. *Bloomberg Businessweek* said of Bernanke's tenure that "the U.S. can consider itself fortunate he was there," while a columnist in *U.S. News and World Report* wrote, "the Fed chairman literally saved the country from another Great Depression." Former Obama economic adviser Austan Goolsbee recently praised Bernanke's performance, while even the more skeptical *Wall Street Journal* allowed that Bernanke's response to the financial crisis deserved "the benefit of the doubt."

The American public is divided on Bernanke's job performance. Many of the commentaries applauding Bernanke's actions focus on what might have happened had the Fed chairman not intervened, but most Americans are more likely to judge Bernanke, like other public officials, on the results of his policy decisions, rather than what might have been. While even a man as powerful as Bernanke cannot control all of the interrelated forces that drive the economy, Americans' views on his job as top central banker have been shaped by the speed and breadth of the recovery. And for many, the economic recovery remains underwhelming.

Survey Methods

Results for this Gallup poll are based on telephone interviews conducted Jan. 25–26, 2014, on the Gallup Daily tracking survey, with a random sample of 1,020 adults, aged 18 and older, living in all 50 U.S. states and the District of Columbia.

For results based on the total sample of national adults, the margin of sampling error is ±4 percentage points at the 95% confidence level.

January 30, 2014
MORE UNINSURED PLANNING TO GET INSURANCE FROM EXCHANGES
Fifty-six percent plan to use an exchange, first time above majority

by Jeffrey M. Jones

PRINCETON, NJ—Fifty-six percent of uninsured Americans who plan to get health insurance say they will do so through a government health insurance exchange. That figure has steadily increased since Gallup began tracking uninsured Americans' intentions in October.

One possible factor in the growing popularity of exchange-based plans versus other sources is improvements made to the federal exchange website to correct a wide array of technical issues that plagued the site. Another factor may be that previously uninsured Americans who now have health insurance for 2014 had other options, such as insurance through an employer or signing up on a spouse's or parent's plan. Those options may not be as available to those who remain uninsured.

Expected Source of Health Plan -- Uninsured Americans Who Say They Are Likely to Get Insurance

Do you plan to get health insurance specifically through a state or federal health insurance exchange, or not?

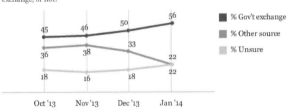

■ % Gov't exchange
■ % Other source
□ % Unsure

Gallup Daily tracking

GALLUP

The latest results are based on Jan. 2–28 Gallup Daily tracking interviews with more than 1,500 Americans who currently do not have health insurance.

Currently, 53% of all uninsured Americans say they plan to get insurance, while 38% say they are more likely to pay the fine the government will assess most Americans who lack health insurance.

The percentage planning to get insurance is down from 60% of the then-uninsured pool in December. This decline may be attributable as much to the shrinking uninsured population as to changes in uninsured Americans' intentions for obtaining insurance. In other words, fewer Americans are now uninsured, and those who remain uninsured as time goes on are least motivated to get insurance.

Likewise, fewer of those who were uninsured in January (72%) were aware of the federal requirement to have health insurance than was true for those who were uninsured in December (80%).

Gallup previously reported a drop in the uninsured rate, from 17.3% in December to 16.1% in early January, a figure that remains unchanged through Jan. 28 interviewing. If the uninsured rate continues to drop in the coming months, the percentage of uninsured Americans aware of the requirement and the percentage planning to get insurance may also continue to decline.

Uninsured Exchange Visits, Familiarity Still Lacking

A fairly small minority of the uninsured, 23%, say they have visited, or have attempted to visit, a federal or state health insurance exchange website. That number is little changed from 26% in December, and 20% in October and November, when many Americans had difficulty accessing the sites because of technical issues.

Perhaps surprisingly, exchange website visits are no more common, 21%, among uninsured Americans who plan to get insurance. Thus, apparently many of those who plan to get insurance have yet to take specific steps toward doing so.

Because relatively few uninsured Americans have visited insurance exchange websites, it follows that 67% claim to be unfamiliar with these exchanges. Thirty-one percent of uninsured Americans say they are "very" or "somewhat familiar" with the exchanges.

Implications

A small but notable drop in the percentage of Americans who are uninsured in January, the first month new health plans went into effect, is a positive sign the Affordable Care Act is making progress toward its goal of getting more Americans covered. Another positive sign may be the increasing percentage of the remaining pool of the uninsured who are planning to get insurance through the exchanges that were created by the law.

Still, both trends represent only modest improvements, and it may get harder to convince the remaining uninsured population to sign up for health insurance in the coming months. Gallup will continue to track the U.S. uninsured rate, and uninsured Americans' intentions for obtaining insurance, in the months ahead. Both measures will continue to gauge the early outcomes of one of the more significant recent pieces of domestic legislation.

Survey Methods

Results for this Gallup poll are based on telephone interviews conducted Jan. 2–28, 2014, on the Gallup Daily tracking survey, with a random sample of 1,593 adults, aged 18 and older, living in all 50 U.S. states and the District of Columbia, who do not have health insurance.

For results based on the total sample of uninsured adults, the margin of sampling error is ±3 percentage points at the 95% confidence level.

January 30, 2014
AMERICANS' DISSATISFACTION WITH GUN LAWS HIGHEST SINCE 2001
Increase in proportion who are dissatisfied and want less strict laws

by Rebecca Riffkin

WASHINGTON, D.C.—Americans' dissatisfaction with U.S. gun laws and policies has increased to 55%, nearly matching the high of 57% in 2001. Forty percent are satisfied, down from the historical average of 47% since Gallup began asking this question in this way in 2001.

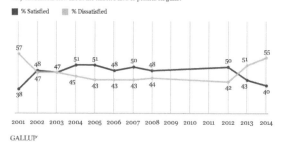

Americans' Satisfaction With Gun Laws and Policies

Overall, Americans' satisfaction with gun laws ranks near the middle of a list of 19 issues measured in Gallup's 2014 update of its annual Mood of the Nation survey. The highest levels of satisfaction were with the nation's military strength and ability to deal with terrorism; the lowest were with poverty and homelessness and the state of the nation's economy.

Americans may be dissatisfied with gun laws because they believe they should be stricter, or because they believe the laws are too strict as they are. Therefore, Gallup asks those who are dissatisfied with gun laws to choose among explanations for their dissatisfaction. Those who are dissatisfied have historically leaned heavily in the direction of wanting stricter rather than less strict laws.

But this year, the gap between those wanting stricter gun laws and those wanting less strict laws narrowed as a result of a sharp increase in the percentage of Americans who want *less* strict laws, now at 16% up from 5% a year ago. Support for making gun laws stricter fell to 31% from 38% last January. The January 2013 poll was conducted shortly after the December 2012 Sandy Hook school shooting tragedy, which sparked some state governments to consider new gun laws and a robust national discussion about the issue.

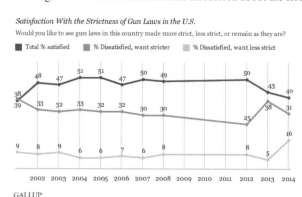

Satisfaction With the Strictness of Gun Laws in the U.S.

More Americans "Very Dissatisfied" With Current U.S. Gun Laws Than Ever Before

In addition to overall dissatisfaction with gun laws rising, more Americans this year are "very dissatisfied" (35%) versus "somewhat dissatisfied" (20%). The 15-percentage-point gap between these views is the largest in Gallup's trend.

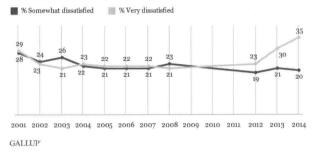

Americans' Dissatisfaction With Gun Laws

Next, we'd like to know how you feel about the state of the nation in each of the following areas. For each one, please say whether you are -- very satisfied, somewhat satisfied, somewhat dissatisfied, or very dissatisfied. How about the nation's laws or policies on guns?

■ % Somewhat dissatisfied   ▨ % Very dissatisfied

GALLUP

Implications

In the wake of multiple shootings around the U.S. over the last few years, President Barack Obama pledged in his 2014 State of the Union address that he would continue trying to prevent shootings in shopping malls, movie theaters, and schools. Several states introduced legislation in 2013 to restrict gun ownership, although similar legislation failed at a national level.

Americans have become more dissatisfied with gun laws over the past year, but this is attributable to a greater percentage who say gun laws are too strict, rather than not being strict enough. Americans' changing views could set the course for future gun law debates and legislation.

Survey Methods

Results for this Gallup poll are based on telephone interviews conducted Jan. 5–8, 2014, with a random sample of 1,018 adults, aged 18 and older, living in all 50 U.S. states and the District of Columbia.

For results based on the total sample of national adults, the margin of sampling error is ±4 percentage points at the 95% confidence level.

January 31, 2014
WYOMING RESIDENTS MOST CONSERVATIVE, D.C. MOST LIBERAL
"Conservative advantage" down from last year

by Art Swift

WASHINGTON, D.C.—Wyoming was the most conservative U.S. state in 2013, replacing Alabama, which fell to 10th place. The District of Columbia was once again the most liberal area in the United States, with Vermont and Massachusetts having the highest percentage of liberals among the 50 states.

Top 10 Conservative States

State	% Conservative
Wyoming	51.4
Mississippi	47.9
Idaho	47.5
Utah	46.9
Montana	45.2
Arkansas	45.2
South Carolina	45.1
Oklahoma	45.0
Tennessee	44.9
Alabama	44.7

Gallup Daily tracking, January-December 2013

GALLUP

Top 10 Liberal States

State	% Liberal
District of Columbia	38.1
Vermont	32.4
Massachusetts	30.2
Delaware	29.3
New York	28.2
Hawaii (tie)	27.9
Oregon (tie)	27.9
Maine	27.3
California	27.1
New Jersey	26.5

Gallup Daily tracking, January-December 2013

GALLUP

Overall, Americans were much more likely to self-identify as conservatives than as liberals last year, though that gap shrank from previous years.

The most conservative states are located primarily in the South and West, while the most liberal states are found on the East and West Coasts of the United States, with the exception of Hawaii. The top 10 liberal states all voted for President Barack Obama in 2008 and 2012, while the top 10 conservative states all voted for the Republican nominees—John McCain and Mitt Romney, respectively—in those years.

For the most part, the top conservative states align with the most Republican states in the union, and the top liberal states, with the most Democratic areas. Yet Kansas and Nebraska, two of the most solid Republican states, do not fall among the top 10 conservative states. Similarly, the Democratic states of Maryland, Illinois, Connecticut, and New Mexico are not among the top 10 liberal states, but Gallup found that they were among the solid Democratic states in 2013.

Conservative Advantage Still Predominant, Yet Down From 2012

The national "conservative advantage," defined as the percentage of residents self-identifying as conservative minus the percentage self-identifying as liberal in each state, was at 14.6 percentage points in 2013. Given that national advantage, only three states (Hawaii, Massachusetts, and Vermont) have a negative score, along with the District of Columbia, meaning they have more liberals than conservatives.

In 2012, the conservative advantage overall was 15.9 points, suggesting that the gap between conservative and liberal self-identification is narrowing.

Bottom Line

There may have been more "blue" states than "red" states in 2013, but a clear majority of Americans are ideologically at the center or right of center. How do Democrats continue to win elections if so few Americans identify themselves as liberal? The answer may lie with moderates, which, as a voting bloc, are solidly Democratic. If moderates begin voting with Republicans in the near or long-term future, there may indeed be a Republican revival on the national level.

Yet while less than a quarter of Americans consider themselves ideologically liberal, the term has been steadily increasing in popularity over a generation. This may be attributable to Americans becoming more comfortable with the term again. Once a popular staple of the civil rights and protest era of the 1960s and 1970s, the term "liberal" was later derided on the national stage—for example, when George H.W. Bush scornfully used the term against Michael Dukakis in the 1988 presidential election. With the passage of time, perhaps this moniker is experiencing a rebirth of sorts.

Survey Methods

Results for this Gallup poll are based on telephone interviews conducted Jan. 2–Dec. 29, 2013, on the Gallup Daily tracking survey, with a random sample of 178,527 adults, aged 18 and older, living in all 50 U.S. states and the District of Columbia.

For results based on the total sample of national adults, the margin of sampling error is ±1 percentage point at the 95% confidence level.

Margins of error for individual states are no greater than ±6 percentage points, and are ±3 percentage points in most states. The margin of error for the District of Columbia is ±6 percentage points.

January 31, 2014

STATE OF THE UNION: THE PUBLIC WEIGHS IN ON 10 KEY ISSUES

Where Americans stand on immigration, energy, minimum wage, and other issues

by Frank Newport, Jeffrey M. Jones, and Lydia Saad

PRINCETON, NJ—President Barack Obama recommended a number of actions in his 2014 State of the Union address Tuesday. Some steps he will take using executive orders; others were requests for congressional legislative action.

Gallup data reveal how Americans' views line up with 10 of these issues.

1. Immigration

"If we are serious about economic growth, it is time to heed the call of business leaders, labor leaders, faith leaders, and law enforcement—and fix our broken immigration system."

Immigration is a relatively low-priority issue for Americans, with 50% saying it is extremely or very important for the president and Congress to address the issue this year. Three percent name immigration as the most important problem facing the nation.

Thirty-eight percent of Americans are satisfied with the level of immigration into the U.S., and 54% are dissatisfied. Most of those who are dissatisfied want to see immigration levels decreased. Although more Americans are dissatisfied than satisfied, satisfaction is the highest it has been since Gallup first asked this question in 2001.

Americans widely favor a variety of proposals to address illegal immigration, including tightening security at U.S. borders, requiring business owners to check new employees' immigration status, extending the number of short-term work visas for skilled workers, and giving illegal immigrants in the U.S. a path to citizenship.

2. Minimum Wage

"Today, the federal minimum wage is worth about 20% less than it was when Ronald Reagan first stood here. Tom Harkin and George Miller have a bill to fix that by lifting the minimum wage to $10.10.

This will help families. It will give businesses customers with more money to spend. It doesn't involve any new bureaucratic program. So join the rest of the country. Say yes. Give America a raise."

Americans overwhelmingly support increasing the minimum wage. Gallup found in November that 76% of Americans favor a specific proposal to raise the minimum wage to $9 an hour. The president on Tuesday proposed a more generous raise to $10.10 an hour. Gallup has historically found that public support for increasing the minimum wage generally exceeds 75%. Democrats are more likely than Republicans to support hikes in the minimum wage.

Relatively few Americans mention the minimum wage as the best way to fix the U.S. economy, instead focusing on job creation and tax cuts.

3. Energy and the Environment

"My administration will keep working with the [natural gas] industry to sustain production and job growth while strengthening protection of our air, our water, and our communities. . . . Let's continue that progress with a smarter tax policy that stops giving $4 billion a year to fossil fuel industries that don't need it, so that we can invest more in fuels of the future that do. . . . That's why I directed my administration to work with states, utilities, and others to set new standards on the amount of carbon pollution our power plants are allowed to dump into the air."

Obama's call for greater environmental protection via government action is likely to receive a mixed reaction from the American public. A long-term Gallup trend shows that fewer Americans now (47%) than in the past say the government is doing too little to protect the environment. Another 16% say the government is doing too much, while approximately one-third say the government is doing about the right amount. There are, as might be expected, major partisan differences, with Democrats much more likely than Republicans to say the government is doing too little.

More generally, neither Democrats nor Republicans classify the environment as a top priority for the president and Congress. The environment is tied for the seventh-highest-rated priority—out of a list of issues—among Democrats, while it is near the bottom of the list among Republicans. In fact, the partisan gap in prioritization of the environment, 39 points, is higher than for any other issue tested or measured in this way.

Obama clearly recognizes that there is a tradeoff between "sustaining production and job growth" and "protection of our air, our water, and our communities." Gallup measures of the public's preferences on the two sides of this tradeoff over the past 13 years show that at this point, neither perspective prevails—about equal numbers of Americans choose protection of the environment and development of U.S. energy sources.

The president proposed more investment in nontraditional fuels. The public would appear to agree with this emphasis. Given a tradeoff between developing alternative energy such as wind and solar power and the production of more oil, gas, and coal supplies, Americans lean heavily toward the former, by 59% to 31%.

4. Invest in Infrastructure

"Moreover, we can take the money we save with this transition to tax reform to create jobs rebuilding our roads, upgrading our ports,

unclogging our commutes—because in today's global economy, first-class jobs gravitate to first-class infrastructure."

The general concept of spending government money to create jobs rebuilding and working on the nation's infrastructure resonates with Americans.

A Gallup survey conducted last March showed that 77% of Americans would vote for a federal government program that would put people to work on urgent infrastructure programs. A slightly different version of that question included the phrase "spend government money" to put people to work on infrastructure, and that version produced 72% support.

5. Affordable Care Act

"But let's not have another forty-something votes to repeal a law that's already helping millions of Americans like Amanda. The first forty were plenty. We got it. We all owe it to the American people to say what we're for, not just what we're against. . . . That's why, tonight, I ask every American who knows someone without health insurance to help them get covered by March 31st."

Americans cite the Affordable Care Act, commonly known as Obamacare, as the single greatest achievement, as well as the single biggest failure, so far in the president's administration. The controversial nature of this signature legislation may help explain why the president gave it only a brief mention in his speech, defending the need for the law, and challenging Republicans to cease their efforts to repeal the measure. He also called for the uninsured to sign up for health insurance.

It is clear that the public as a whole is more negative than positive about the legislation. Gallup's last measure, in January, showed 54% disapprove of the law, while 38% approve, the most negative assessment in Gallup's trend. Additionally, the plurality of Americans say Obamacare has had a more negative than positive effect on them personally, and that it will have a more negative effect on them and on the country in the future.

These negative attitudes, however, do not necessarily mean that the public wants the law repealed, as Obama appeared to recognize in his speech. Thirty-two percent of Americans in December wanted the law repealed entirely, while the rest were divided between wanting the law expanded, cut back, or kept as is. The majority of Americans, in short, would apparently agree with Obama's position that efforts to repeal the law should be curtailed, and four in 10 would apparently be favorably predisposed to suggestions for ways to amend and improve the law.

In terms of Obama's plea that the uninsured should sign up for healthcare, Gallup found that the percentage of uninsured adults fell slightly in January. But the uninsured rate still has a long distance to go before it shrinks into the desired single-digit range.

6. Foreign Trade/Bringing Jobs Home

"Both Democrats and Republicans have argued that our tax code is riddled with wasteful, complicated loopholes that punish businesses investing here, and reward companies that keep profits abroad. Let's flip that equation. Let's work together to close those loopholes, end those incentives to ship jobs overseas, and lower tax rates for businesses that create jobs here at home. . . . We need to work together on tools like bipartisan trade promotion authority to protect our workers, protect our environment, and open new markets to new

goods stamped 'Made in the USA.' China and Europe aren't standing on the sidelines. Neither should we."

Many Americans support bringing jobs home to the U.S. Gallup has asked Americans twice over the past five years to say in their own words what would be the best way to create more jobs in the U.S. The most frequently mentioned response in both instances was keeping manufacturing jobs in the U.S. and not sending them overseas.

The president specifically referenced in his speech the idea of changing the tax code to encourage businesses to bring jobs home. A separate referendum-type question last March asked Americans if they would vote for or against a law that would lower tax rates for businesses and manufacturers that "create jobs in the United States." An overwhelming 79% said they would vote for such a law. This proposition receives strong support across the political spectrum, and thus suggests that this component of Obama's recommendations would be well received.

The idea of taking steps to increase "Made in U.S.A." goods also resonates with the public. An April poll showed that 45% of Americans were already making a special effort to buy products made in the U.S.

7. Reform Surveillance Programs

"So even as we aggressively pursue terrorist networks—through more targeted efforts and by building the capacity of our foreign partners—America must move off a permanent war footing. That's why I've imposed prudent limits on the use of drones—for we will not be safer if people abroad believe we strike within their countries without regard for the consequence. That's why, working with this Congress, I will reform our surveillance programs—because the vital work of our intelligence community depends on public confidence, here and abroad, that the privacy of ordinary people is not being violated."

After hailing the success of anti-terrorism efforts, Obama made a glancing reference to reforming the federal government's surveillance programs, intimating that this is needed to restore Americans' belief that "the privacy of ordinary people is not being violated."

Americans don't seem to be clamoring for action on the issue. In fact, less than half of Americans, 42%, rated government surveillance of citizens as an extremely or very high priority for the president and Congress this year. However, government spying programs are a latent public concern, and therefore a potential liability for Obama. Sixty-three percent of Americans say they are very or somewhat dissatisfied with the government's surveillance of U.S citizens. And 53% last June said they disapproved of the government's building a database of U.S. telephone and Internet records. That was shortly after Edward Snowden, a former National Security Agency contractor, publicly revealed this spy program.

Further, political independents—whose votes will be crucial in tight House and Senate contests this fall—are particularly critical of government surveillance. Half of independents, compared with 36% of Republicans and 21% of Democrats, say they are "very dissatisfied" with this aspect of the nation right now. Thus, by indicating that he respects personal privacy and wants to rein in any possible government overreach, Obama may be trying to limit Republican candidates' ability to paint Democrats as the "surveillance party."

8. Gun Violence

"Citizenship means standing up for the lives that gun violence steals from us each day. I have seen the courage of parents, students, pastors, and police officers all over this country who say 'we are not afraid,' and I intend to keep trying, with or without Congress, to help stop more tragedies from visiting innocent Americans in our movie theaters, shopping malls, or schools like Sandy Hook."

Without mentioning specific proposals, Obama pledged to work "with or without Congress" to help prevent future tragedies involving gun violence. Gallup trends suggest that the window for capitalizing on Americans' post–Sandy Hook concern about the issue may be over. Public support for passing stricter gun laws spiked in the first month after the December 2012 tragedy, but by October 2013, it had nearly reverted to pre-Newtown levels. Additionally, while satisfaction with existing gun laws is down, that mostly reflects those who are dissatisfied because they believe gun laws are too strict, rather than not strict enough.

Still, Obama may have public opinion on his side when it comes to advancing specific measures to strengthen regulations regarding the sale and purchase of guns and ammunition. Gallup polling over the past year has found broad public support for many such proposals, such as 65% support for a law expanding background checks for gun purchases, 60% support for reinstating and strengthening an expired ban on assault rifles, and 54% in favor of limiting the sale of high-capacity magazines.

9. New Retirement Savings Vehicle MyRA

"Let's do more to help Americans save for retirement. Today, most workers don't have a pension. A Social Security check often isn't enough on its own. And while the stock market has doubled over the last five years, that doesn't help folks who don't have 401(k)s. That's why, tomorrow, I will direct the Treasury to create a new way for working Americans to start their own retirement savings: MyRA. It's a new savings bond that encourages folks to build a nest egg. MyRA guarantees a decent return with no risk of losing what you put in."

MyRA is a new proposed way for Americans to save for retirement to supplement Social Security. Fewer Americans expect to live comfortably in retirement than did so before the recession. And six in 10 nonretirees do not expect to receive a Social Security benefit when they retire.

The major retirement funding sources for today's retirees, Social Security and pensions, are not the same sources nonretirees expect to rely on when they stop working.

Nonretirees expect retirement savings plans such as 401(k)s to be their major retirement funding source. However, not all nonretirees have access to 401(k) plans or funding sources other than Social Security; this is particularly true of low-income workers. Without alternative funding sources, future retirees may be forced to continue working beyond retirement age—increasing numbers already expect to—or make do on what Social Security provides.

The importance to Americans of having a way to grow tax-deferred savings for retirement was evident in a 2012 Wells Fargo-Gallup Investor and Retirement Optimism Index survey, in which 83% of investors rated 401(k) and other tax-advantaged accounts as highly important to saving for retirement. The same poll found majorities of investors calling it extremely or very important for the federal government to take a number of steps that could encourage more Americans to use 401(k) accounts; thus, it seems likely investors would welcome the establishment of a new tax-deferred option.

10. Limits on Drones

"I've imposed prudent limits on the use of drones—for we will not be safer if people abroad believe we strike within their countries without regard for the consequence."

Americans generally oppose the use of drones to attack suspected terrorists who are either U.S. citizens or living on U.S. soil. But a majority of Americans do support using drones against suspected terrorists (not identified as U.S. citizens) living in other countries. Americans are particularly opposed to using drones in the United States, even against suspected terrorists who are not U.S. citizens.

Gallup will continue to monitor public opinion on the key issues raised in the president's speech in the weeks and months to come.

February 03, 2014
MISSISSIPPI MOST RELIGIOUS STATE, VERMONT LEAST RELIGIOUS
Average religiousness of states continues to range widely

by Frank Newport

PRINCETON, NJ—Religiousness across the U.S. in 2013 remained similar to previous years. With 61% of its residents classified as very religious, Mississippi held on to its position as the most religious state, while Vermont, with 22% very religious residents, remained the least religious. The most religious states were in the South, except for Utah, while the least religious states were clustered in New England and the West.

Most Religious States, Based on % Very Religious

State	Very religious
Mississippi	61%
Utah	60%
Alabama	57%
Louisiana	56%
South Carolina	54%
Tennessee	54%
Georgia	52%
Arkansas	51%
North Carolina	50%
Oklahoma	49%
Kentucky	49%

Gallup Daily tracking, January-December 2013

GALLUP

Least Religious States, Based on % Very Religious

State	Very religious
Vermont	22%
New Hampshire	24%
Maine	27%
Massachusetts	28%
Oregon	31%
Nevada	32%
Washington	32%
Connecticut	32%
Hawaii	32%
District of Columbia	32%

Gallup Daily tracking, January-December 2013

GALLUP

These state-by-state results are based on more than 174,000 interviews conducted as part of Gallup Daily tracking in 2013, including more than 500 interviews conducted in each state and 442 in the District of Columbia.

Gallup classifies Americans as very religious if they say religion is an important part of their daily lives and that they attend religious services every week or almost every week. More than four in 10 Americans nationwide (41%) fit this classification in 2013. Twenty-nine percent of Americans were nonreligious, saying religion is not an important part of their daily lives and that they seldom or never attend religious services. The remaining 29% were moderately religious, saying religion is important in their lives but that they do not attend services regularly, or that religion is not important but that they still attend services.

Gallup began tracking religion using this measure in 2008, and the nationwide proportions of Americans in each of the three religious categories have remained generally stable since then. The percentage "very religious" is slightly higher in 2013 than it was in 2012, 2011, and 2008, while the percentage of nonreligious Americans is slightly lower in 2013 than in any previous year.

Although there have been minor changes in the rank-order of the most religious and the least religious states between 2008 and 2013, the broad pattern has remained similar year after year. Ten of the 11 most religious states in 2013 are in the South. The exception is Utah, a majority of whose residents identify as Mormons—the most religious of any major religious group in the country.

The 10 least religious states in 2013 are from two areas—New England and the West—plus the District of Columbia. The New England states of Vermont and New Hampshire continue to be the least religious states in the union.

Religiosity by Year: 2008-2013

	Very Religious	Somewhat Religious	Nonreligious
	%	%	%
2013	41.4	29.2	29.4
2012	40.1	28.9	31.1
2011	40.5	28.4	31.1
2010	41.5	28.2	30.3
2009	41.6	28.3	30.1
2008	40.9	28.7	30.4

GALLUP

Implications

The U.S. remains a religious nation—with about seven in 10 Americans classified as very or moderately religious—and the nation's residents as a whole are about as religious now as they were in 2008. The religiousness of the nation's residents, however, does vary substantially by state and region. The most religious areas continue to be the South, the state of Utah, and the Midwestern Plains states, while the least religious areas are mostly in New England, the Pacific Northwest, and other Western states.

These regional variations are quite stable and look generally the same now as they did six years ago. They reflect basic state cultures that are highly persistent, even as states experience demographic changes through births, deaths, and migration.

The differences in religiousness across states can have several causes. For example, the Southern states have a higher percentage of Protestants than the national average, and Protestants have above-average religiousness. The New England states have a higher percentage of those with no religious identity at all, and these residents are of course much lower than average on the religiousness scale. Still, previous research shows that even among those in the different regions who have the same religious identity, state-level cultural differences still affect average religiousness. Protestants in Mississippi are more religious than Protestants in Vermont, and those with no religious identity in Mississippi are more religious than those with no religious identity in Vermont.

Additionally, although states vary significantly in their racial and ethnic composition, differences in religiosity between states persist even among residents of the same races. Whites in Mississippi are more religious than whites in Vermont, and blacks in New England are less religious than blacks in the South.

Utah is the exceptional state. Mormons are the most religious of any category or denomination Gallup routinely measures, and Utah's majority Mormon population clearly explains why Utah stands out so remarkably from its much less religious neighboring states.

Survey Methods

Results for this Gallup poll are based on telephone interviews conducted Jan. 2–Dec. 29, 2013, on the Gallup Daily tracking survey, with a random sample of 174,699 adults, aged 18 and older, living in all 50 U.S. states and the District of Columbia.

For results based on the total sample of national adults, the margin of sampling error is ±1 percentage point at the 95% confidence level.

Margins of error for individual states are no greater than ±6 percentage points, and are ±3 percentage points in most states. The margin of error for the District of Columbia is ±6 percentage points.

February 04, 2014
U.S. ECONOMIC CONFIDENCE CONTINUED TO IMPROVE IN JANUARY
Index improves for third consecutive month

by Justin McCarthy

WASHINGTON, D.C.—Gallup's Economic Confidence Index improved slightly for the month of January, climbing to −16 from −19 in December. Although a disheartening jobs report and steep stock market losses negatively affected Americans' confidence in the short term, Americans' economic confidence improved for the third month in a row after dipping to −35 during the federal government shutdown in October.

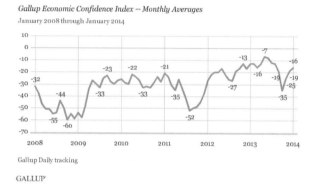

Gallup Economic Confidence Index -- Monthly Averages
January 2008 through January 2014

Gallup Daily tracking

GALLUP

Last month's rise in confidence may surprise some, given the dismal December statistics from the Bureau of Labor Statistics and the worst January performance from the Dow in five years, but Americans have continued to become more confident in the nation's economic circumstances since October's federal government shutdown.

The January results are based on Gallup Daily tracking interviews conducted by landline and cellphone with more than 15,000 U.S. adults.

The Gallup Economic Confidence Index is the average of two components: Americans' views on the current economic situation and their economic outlook. The current economic conditions component of the index averaged −18 in January, based on 18% rating the economy as excellent or good versus 36% rating it poor. The economic outlook component was −13 in January, with 41% of Americans saying the economy is getting better and 54% saying it is getting worse.

Upper-Income Americans at Highest Level of Confidence Since July 2013

Confidence among Americans with an annual household income of at least $90,000 reached −1 for the month of January, a peak it hasn't seen since July of last year. Though still a negative figure, it reflects a six-point increase from December's −7 reading. Those living in

lower- and middle-income households remain less confident in the economy, but also experienced an increase in economic confidence, to −18 from −22 in December.

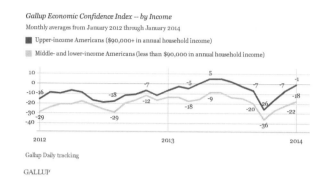

Gallup Economic Confidence Index -- by Income
Monthly averages from January 2012 through January 2014
■ Upper-income Americans ($90,000+ in annual household income)
▨ Middle- and lower-income Americans (less than $90,000 in annual household income)

Gallup Daily tracking

GALLUP

Implications

There was no shortage of bad economic news for the first month of 2014, and although Gallup did observe short-term movement in confidence in response to these events, the broader January readings might indicate that Americans' confidence in the economy is not strictly tied to jobs reports and the stock market. Those negative reports may have been counteracted to some degree by positive reports on consumer spending and GDP growth.

Still, economic confidence in February may be a bit fragile, with the stock market continuing to slide after steady gains throughout 2013, and uncertainty about whether this week's January jobs report will be more positive than December's was.

Survey Methods

Results for this Gallup poll are based on telephone interviews conducted Jan. 1–31, 2014, on the Gallup Daily tracking survey, with a random sample of 15,240 adults, aged 18 and older, living in all 50 U.S. states and the District of Columbia.

For results based on the total sample of national adults, the margin of sampling error is ±1 percentage point at the 95% confidence level.

February 04, 2014
MAJORITY OF AMERICANS STILL DISAPPROVE OF HEALTHCARE LAW
Attitudes toward law and its long-run potential still tilt negative

by Andrew Dugan

WASHINGTON, D.C.—President Barack Obama defended his signature legislative achievement, the Affordable Care Act, before Congress and the nation last week in his State of the Union address, but public opinion toward the law is little changed since November. Americans are still more likely to disapprove (51%) than approve (41%) of the law.

The latest results, from a Gallup poll conducted Jan. 31–Feb. 1, show that even though many provisions of the law are now in effect, Americans' views of the Affordable Care Act, commonly known as "Obamacare," still tilt negative.

Do you generally approve or disapprove of the 2010 Affordable Care Act, signed into law by President Obama that restructured the U.S. healthcare system?

■ % Approve   % Disapprove

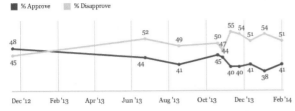

November 2012 wording: Do you generally approve or disapprove of the 2010 Affordable Care Act, also known as "Obama-care," that restructured the U.S. healthcare system?

GALLUP

Underpinning this lack of overall support is the fact that most Americans believe the law so far has had no effect (64%) or a harmful effect (19%) on their family. These opinions are broadly consistent with Gallup polling dating back to February 2012, when fewer provisions of the law were in place.

Effect of Healthcare Law on You and Your Family So Far

As you may know, a few of the provisions of the healthcare law have already gone into effect. So far, has the new law -- [ROTATED: helped you and your family, not had an effect, (or has it) hurt you and your family]?

■ Helped (%)   ■ Had no effect (%)   ■ Hurt (%)

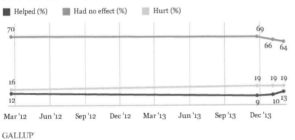

GALLUP

Americans Remain Pessimistic About Health Law's Long-Term Effects

While it likely will take some time to measure the full impact of the law, most Americans predict that the law will not personally benefit them or help improve the national healthcare situation. Less than a quarter of U.S. adults (24%) say that in the long run, the healthcare law will make their family's healthcare situation better, while nearly four in 10 (37%) say it will make their healthcare situation worse. About a third (34%) say it will have no effect.

Notably, views that the law would make Americans' own healthcare situation worse had been declining through October, as the botched rollout of the healthcare website occurred, but ticked up in November. However, this percentage has now receded to levels observed before the troubled rollout of the website.

Effect of Healthcare Law on You and Your Family in the Long Run

In the long run, how do you think the healthcare law will affect your family's healthcare situation? Will it -- [ROTATED: make things better, not make much difference, (or will it) make things worse]?

■ % Make worse
■ % No difference
■ % Make better

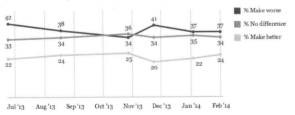

GALLUP

Americans are slightly more optimistic that, in the long run, the law will make the healthcare situation in the U.S. better. Thirty-five percent hold this view, though a heftier 45% believe it will make the national healthcare situation worse. One in seven (14%) say the comprehensive law will not make much difference.

Effect of Healthcare Law on U.S. Healthcare in the Long Run

In the long run, how do you think the healthcare law will affect the healthcare situation in the U.S.? Will it -- [ROTATED: make things better, not make much difference, (or will it) make things worse]?

■ % Make worse
■ % No difference
■ % Make better

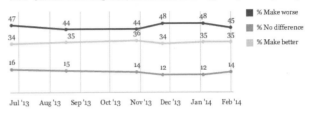

GALLUP

Implications

Even if the Affordable Care Act fulfills its purpose of improving the overall health of the nation by expanding individuals' access to insurance, public opinion of the law itself remains sickly. Americans' disapproval of the law has declined slightly since its peak late last year during the flawed rollout of the federal health exchange website, but a majority still disapprove of the law, and few believe it will make their current or future healthcare situation better.

Survey Methods

Results for this Gallup poll are based on telephone interviews conducted Jan. 31–Feb. 1, 2014, on the Gallup Daily tracking survey, with a random sample of 1,017 adults, aged 18 and older, living in all 50 U.S. states and the District of Columbia.

For results based on the total sample of national adults, the margin of sampling error is ±4 percentage points at the 95% confidence level.

February 05, 2014
MISSISSIPPI AND ALABAMA MOST PROTESTANT STATES IN U.S.
Rhode Island is most Catholic, Utah most Mormon, and New York most Jewish

by Frank Newport

PRINCETON, NJ—Fifty-one percent of Americans identified as Protestant or other non-Catholic Christian in 2013, making this by far the largest major religious grouping in the country. All 10 of the most Protestant states are located in the South. Nine of these states are at least 70% Protestant, including the two most highly Protestant states, Mississippi and Alabama, each with a 77% Protestant population.

These state-level findings come from a nationally representative sample of more than 178,000 U.S. adults interviewed as part of Gallup Daily tracking from January through December 2013.

Each state's results are based on more than 500 interviews, with 447 taking place in the District of Columbia.

Most Protestant States

State	Protestant
Mississippi	77%
Alabama	77%
Arkansas	76%
Tennessee	76%
South Carolina	75%
Oklahoma	73%
West Virginia	71%
Georgia	71%
North Carolina	70%
Kentucky	68%

Gallup Daily tracking, January-December 2013

GALLUP

Least Protestant States

State	Protestant
Utah	11%
Rhode Island	20%
New Jersey	29%
Massachusetts	29%
New York	31%
Connecticut	34%
California	37%
Idaho	38%
Nevada	38%
New Hampshire	39%
Vermont	39%
Hawaii	39%

Gallup Daily tracking, January-December 2013

GALLUP

Gallup measures Americans' religious identity by asking, "What is your religious preference—are you Protestant, Roman Catholic, Mormon, Jewish, Muslim, another religion, or no religion?" If Americans name another religion, they are asked, "Would that be a Christian religion or is it not a Christian religion?"

The Protestant percentage is based on those who say they are Protestant or who identify with "another religion" and, upon probing, indicate that it is a Christian faith other than Catholic or Mormon. Americans' recognition of the "Protestant" label has declined in recent years, but the term provides a useful way of describing Americans who are non-Catholic, non-Mormon Christians. The 2013 percentage of the population identifying as Protestant (51%) is down slightly from 54% in 2008.

The least Protestant state is heavily Mormon Utah, which is only 11% Protestant. Other states with low representations of Protestants are in New England and the Middle Atlantic, along with the Western states of California, Idaho, Nevada, and Hawaii.

Rhode Island Has Highest Percentage of Catholics

More than half of Rhode Island's population (54%) is Catholic, making it the most Catholic state in the union, and the only state in which the Catholic population is at least twice the national average (24%). The next four most Catholic states are also on the East Coast, including New Jersey, Massachusetts, Connecticut, and New York. The least Catholic states are generally the highly Protestant Southern states, along with Utah.

Most Catholic States

State	Catholic
Rhode Island	54%
New Jersey	44%
Massachusetts	41%
Connecticut	40%
New York	37%
New Mexico	33%
California	32%
Wisconsin	32%
Illinois	30%
Pennsylvania	29%
New Hampshire	29%
North Dakota	29%
Nebraska	29%

Gallup Daily tracking, January-December 2013

GALLUP

Least Catholic States

State	Catholic
Mississippi	8%
Alabama	8%
Tennessee	8%
Arkansas	8%
West Virginia	9%
South Carolina	9%
Oklahoma	9%
Utah	9%
Georgia	11%
North Carolina	11%

Gallup Daily tracking, January-December 2013

GALLUP

The 24% of Americans identifying themselves as Catholic in 2013 conforms to the generally stable percentage of the population identifying themselves this way since 2008.

In addition to the high representation of Catholics on the East Coast (including the top five states plus New Hampshire), above-average proportions of Catholics are found in nearby Pennsylvania, four Midwestern states—Wisconsin, Illinois, North Dakota, and Nebraska—and two states with high Hispanic populations, New Mexico and California.

On the other hand, nine of the 10 least Catholic states are in the South, with the bottom four—Mississippi, Alabama, Tennessee, and Arkansas—all having just 8% Catholic populations. Of these 10 states, only Utah is not in the South, reflecting its predominantly Mormon population.

Mormons and Jews

Mormons represent about 2% of the U.S. adult population, but are concentrated in a small number of states. Utah, at 60% Mormon, is followed by Idaho (24%) and Wyoming (9%). All other states have 5% or fewer Mormons, and 11 states have so few Mormons that their percentage in Gallup's 2013 interviewing rounds to zero.

Most Mormon States

State	Mormon
Utah	60%
Idaho	24%
Wyoming	9%
Nevada	5%
Montana	5%
Arizona	4%
Hawaii	4%
Alaska	4%
Washington	3%
Colorado	3%
Oregon	3%

Gallup Daily tracking, January-December 2013

GALLUP

About 2% of the U.S. population identifies itself as Jewish, but unlike Mormons, Jews are much more evenly distributed across the states. The highest Jewish concentration of any state—in New York—is just 7%. Other states with slightly higher-than-average Jewish populations include New Jersey (5%) and Massachusetts (4%), in addition to the District of Columbia (4%).

Most Jewish States

State	Jewish
New York	7%
New Jersey	5%
Massachusetts	4%
District of Columbia	4%
Maryland	3%
Connecticut	3%
Florida	3%
Nevada	3%

Gallup Daily tracking, January-December 2013

GALLUP

The distribution across the states of the two large religious classifications of Americans has remained generally stable over the past five years, with the highest proportions of Protestants in the South, while Catholics are more highly concentrated in the Middle Atlantic and New England regions, along with several states with higher Hispanic populations and a few states in the Midwest. Two other religious groups that are much smaller constitute about 2% of the population each, with Mormons concentrated in Utah and Idaho, and Jewish Americans most likely to be found in several Middle Atlantic and New England states, plus the District of Columbia. A large group of Americans, about 18% in 2013, have no formal religious identity.

Survey Methods

Results for this Gallup poll are based on telephone interviews conducted Jan. 2–Dec. 29, 2013, on the Gallup Daily tracking survey, with a random sample of 178,521 adults, aged 18 and older, living in all 50 U.S. states and the District of Columbia.

For results based on the total sample of national adults, the margin of sampling error is ±1 percentage point at the 95% confidence level.

Margins of error for individual states are no greater than ±6 percentage points, and are ±3 percentage points in most states. The margin of error for the District of Columbia is ±6 percentage points.

February 06, 2014
AMERICANS' FAMILIARITY WITH HEALTHCARE LAW UNCHANGED
Nearly a third of the country not too or not at all familiar with the law

by Andrew Dugan

WASHINGTON, D.C.—Americans' familiarity with the Affordable Care Act has remained static since last August, even after new provisions of the law have taken effect and the Obama administration has tried to promote understanding of it. A majority of Americans (68%) are very or somewhat familiar with the law, while a third of the country is not too or not at all familiar with it. Gallup found nearly identical familiarity numbers last August.

Americans' Familiarity With the Affordable Care Act

Still thinking about the 2010 Affordable Care Act, how familiar are you with the healthcare law — very familiar, somewhat familiar, not too familiar, or not familiar at all?

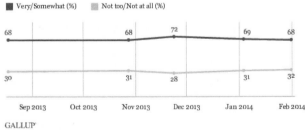

These results come from a Jan. 31–Feb. 1 Gallup poll. While a majority of Americans may disapprove of the still-unfolding healthcare law, commonly known as "Obamacare," nearly one in three are not too or not at all familiar with the measure.

Republicans More Familiar Than Democrats With the Law

Despite their general opposition to the law, Republicans are significantly more likely to say they are familiar with it than are independents or Democrats. The percentage of Republicans who have some degree of familiarity with the legislation (78%) is markedly above the 64% of Democrats who say they have a similar level of knowledge.

Americans' Familiarity With the Healthcare Law, by Self-Identified Party Affiliation

	Republican (%)	Independent (%)	Democrat (%)
Very familiar	25	15	19
Somewhat familiar	53	50	45
Not too familiar	18	21	19
Not familiar at all	3	13	16

Jan. 31-Feb. 1, 2014

GALLUP

This party dynamic partially helps explain why familiarity with the ACA appears to breed contempt. Nearly six in 10 Americans (58%) who say they are very or somewhat familiar with the law disapprove of it. By contrast, those not too or not at all familiar with the law are more divided in their opinions of the law—44% of this group approve and 35% disapprove, with 23% unsure.

Bottom Line

Whether it's the well-publicized website glitches, the focus on Obama's erroneous declaration that "if you like your plan, you can keep it," the requirement that most Americans have health insurance, or the law's brief appearance in last week's State of the Union address, the ACA has been the center of attention for some time.

But this has not translated into more Americans saying they are familiar with the ACA. This watershed legislation that will change the face of the U.S. healthcare system, for better or worse, remains somewhat of a mystery for a significant portion of the nation.

Survey Methods

Results for this Gallup poll are based on telephone interviews conducted Jan. 31–Feb. 1, 2014, on the Gallup Daily tracking survey, with a random sample of 1,017 adults, aged 18 and older, living in all 50 U.S. states and the District of Columbia.

For results based on the total sample of national adults, the margin of sampling error is ±4 percentage points at the 95% confidence level.

February 07, 2014
TEXAN HISPANICS TILT DEMOCRATIC, BUT STATE LIKELY TO STAY RED
Hispanics statewide are less likely to be Democratic than other U.S. Hispanics

by Andrew Dugan

WASHINGTON, D.C.—Texas Hispanics are decidedly Democratic in their political party preferences, 46% to 27%, but that 19-percentage-point Democratic advantage is much smaller in Texas than the average 30-point gap Democrats enjoy among the Hispanic population in the other 49 states. And white Texas residents are decidedly more Republican (61%) than the average among whites residing in other states (48%), complicating whether Texas will turn into a "blue" Democratic state in future elections.

Political Preferences by Race
Among those living in Texas and elsewhere

	Living in Texas	Living in all other states
	%	%
Hispanics		
Republican/Lean Republican	27	21
Independent, no lean	20	21
Democrat/Lean Democrat	46	51
Non-Hispanic Whites		
Republican/Lean Republican	61	48
Independent, no lean	12	12
Democrat/Lean Democrat	26	38

Aggregated 2013 data

GALLUP

With an increasingly large minority population, including the second-largest Hispanic population of any state, Texas has the potential to see a once-in-a-generation political re-alignment, which could transform the nation's largest reliably Republican state.

These latest results come from 2013 Gallup Daily tracking poll data, which consists of 16,028 Hispanics nationwide, including 2,536 Hispanics residing in Texas. The Lone Star state is experiencing significant changes in its population—it is one of the top destinations for state-to-state migration—and these data provide a crucial, updated look into Texan Hispanics' political preferences over the past year.

Texas holds a gubernatorial race this year, and some Democratic operatives are hoping Texas' evolving demographic makeup will allow them to more effectively compete for the governor's mansion. In 2010, Gov. Rick Perry was re-elected handily, defeating his Democratic opponent by 13 percentage points.

In Texas, GOP Making Small But Meaningful Gains With Hispanics

Relative to 2008—the year of President Barack Obama's landslide presidential victory—Texan Hispanics have gradually become more Republican, even as the percentage of Hispanics identifying with or leaning toward the Republican Party has remained relatively stable nationwide. The six-percentage-point gap between the percentage of Texan Hispanics and Hispanics living in all other states who identify or lean GOP is the highest it has been in over six years.

Hispanic Party Identification -- Republican Party
Identify or lean Republican

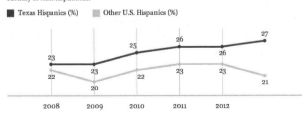

Aggregated 2013 data

GALLUP

Meanwhile, Hispanics living in Texas have followed the broad national trend in terms of primarily identifying as Democrats. The 46% of Texan Hispanics who now lean or identify Democratic is seven points below the 2008 crest; by contrast, U.S. Hispanics living in the other 49 states report support of the Democratic Party that has declined by a slightly smaller four points between 2008 and 2013.

Hispanic Party Identification -- Democratic Party
Identify or lean Democratic

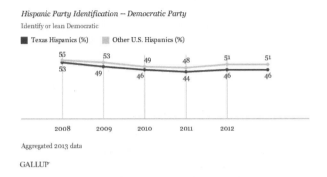

Aggregated 2013 data

GALLUP

Voter Participation and Texan Hispanics

Voter registration among Hispanics lags behind other major racial and ethnic groups in Texas, as it does across the rest of the nation. The average Hispanic adult in Texas is more likely to say they are *not* registered to vote than are registered, with 43% saying they are registered. No other major race or ethnic group in Texas is so poorly represented in the state's voter registration—82% of whites and 77% of blacks say they are registered. Additionally, 50% of non-Texan Hispanics are registered to vote, marking another indication of the challenges faced by those who hope to take political advantage of Texas' large Hispanic population.

Self-Reported Voter Registration in Texas by Race/Ethnicity

	%
Non-Hispanic whites	64
Blacks	13
Hispanics	19
Other	5

Aggregated 2013 data (rounding causes total to add to 101)

GALLUP

This translates into an eligible electorate that remains predominantly white. Among self-reported registered voters in Texas, 64% are non-Hispanic white, 13% are black, and less than a fifth (19%) are Hispanic, further evidence of Hispanics being poorly represented on the state's voter files.

White Texans Continue to Flock to the Republican Party

While Texas has a sizeable proportion of Hispanics living in its borders, nearly half of the population (46%) is non-Hispanic white. This group has grown more heavily Republican over the past five years, a fact that no doubt contributed to President Obama's large 2012 defeat in Texas, larger even than his 2008 drubbing. Currently, 61% of white Texans identify or lean Republican, up four points from 2008. White Texans are also far more likely to identify or lean Republican than are whites living in other states, 48% of which tilt Republican. During this same time period, the overall U.S. white population increased from 44% self-identifying or leaning Republican in 2008 to 48% in 2013.

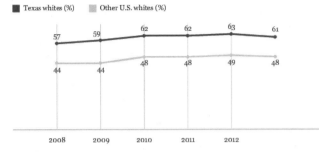

Non-Hispanic Whites Party Identification -- Republican Party

Identify or lean Republican

■ Texas whites (%) ▨ Other U.S. whites (%)

Texas whites: 57, 59, 62, 62, 63, 61

Other U.S. whites: 44, 44, 48, 48, 49, 48

2008 2009 2010 2011 2012

Aggregated 2013 data

GALLUP'

Implications

Long-suffering Texas Democrats appear to have some hope that their political fortunes in the Lone Star state could soon reverse. The growing Hispanic population, along with the solidly Democratic African-American population, present the best path for the party to move Texas out of its consistent "red state" category and into a more competitive position. Texan Hispanics are more likely to identify as Democrat than Republican, and this could prove advantageous to Democrats.

At the same time, the path toward victory for Democrats may not be as smooth or linear as this logic might suggest. Hispanics in Texas are more likely to identify as Republican than are Hispanics elsewhere, and the Republican Party in Texas has seen more growth in Hispanic support over the past five years than the Democratic Party. While this has not changed the overall equation—Democrats still lead big among Texan Hispanics—it does suggest the GOP may be more competitive with this bloc than many assume.

Nor is it clear that Hispanics alone can alter the political trajectory of Texas. While nearly 38% of the Texas population is Hispanic—over double the national rate—political participation among this group is not high. So while Texas is a majority minority state in terms of population, differences in political participation by racial and ethnic group—despite those groups' political leanings—continue to make Texas a solidly Republican state.

It follows that the biggest challenge for Democrats hoping to turn Texas blue may be in registering and turning out minority voters in that state. But the Democratic Party's relatively poor standing with white Texans will continue to impede its ability to compete on a statewide basis for the foreseeable future.

Survey Methods

Results for this Gallup poll are based on telephone interviews conducted Jan. 1–Dec. 31, 2013, on the Gallup Daily tracking survey, with a random sample of 178,527 adults, aged 18 and older, living in all 50 U.S. states and the District of Columbia.

For results based on the total sample of national adults, one can say with 95% confidence that the margin of sampling error is ±1 percentage points.

February 07, 2014
HIGHEST UNINSURED STATES LESS LIKELY TO EMBRACE HEALTH LAW
Medicaid expansion, state exchanges uncommon among highest uninsured states

by Dan Witters

WASHINGTON, D.C.—Texas, Arkansas, Mississippi, Florida, and Louisiana are the states with the highest percentage of uninsured adult residents, but Arkansas is the only one of the five that has chosen to expand Medicaid and to set up its own state exchange in the health insurance marketplace. Of the 12 states with the highest uninsured rates, eight have thus far decided not to expand Medicaid or establish state-based exchanges.

Highest 2013 Uninsured Rates and Medicaid Expansion With State Exchange

State	% of residents without health insurance	Medicaid expansion and state exchange in 2014?
Texas	27.0	No
Arkansas	22.5	Yes
Mississippi	22.4	No
Florida	22.1	No
Louisiana	21.7	No
California	21.6	Yes
Georgia	21.4	No
Oklahoma	21.4	No
Montana	20.7	No
Arizona	20.4	Yes
Kentucky	20.4	Yes
North Carolina	20.4	No

Gallup-Healthways Well-Being Index, January-December 2013

GALLUP'

Nationally, 17.3% of U.S. adults reported being without health insurance in 2013, a percentage that has slowly increased from 14.8% in 2008. These data, collected as part of the Gallup-Healthways Well-Being Index, are based on respondents' self-reports of health insurance status based on the question, "Do you have health insurance coverage?"

Some states have chosen to implement state-federal "partnership" exchanges. For purposes of this analysis, these partnerships are counted along with the state exchanges. Only two states, North Dakota and New Jersey, have decided to expand Medicaid without also administering a state-based exchange, while several others continue to debate its expansion.

In contrast to the states with the highest rates of uninsured residents, the 11 states with the lowest percentage of uninsured are considerably more likely to have already approved Medicaid expansion and state exchanges. All five states with an uninsured rate below 10%—Massachusetts, Hawaii, Vermont, Minnesota, and Iowa—have elected to do so. Pennsylvania, Wisconsin, and Kansas are the three of the 11 that have not.

Lowest 2013 Uninsured Rates and Medicaid Expansion With State Exchange

State	% of residents without health insurance	Medicaid expansion and state exchange in 2014?
Massachusetts	4.9	Yes
Hawaii	7.1	Yes
Vermont	8.9	Yes
Minnesota	9.5	Yes
Iowa	9.7	Yes
Delaware	10.5	Yes
Pennsylvania	11.0	No
Wisconsin	11.7	No
Connecticut	12.3	Yes
Michigan	12.5	Yes
Kansas	12.5	No

Gallup-Healthways Well-Being Index, January-December 2013

GALLUP'

Overall, 16.2% of adults report that they lack health insurance in states that have thus far chosen Medicaid expansion and state exchanges, compared with 18.7% among adults in states that are implementing one or neither.

Overall Uninsured Rates Among States With and Without Medicaid Expansion Plus State Exchanges

	States with Medicaid expansion and state exchange	States with only one or neither
% Uninsured (weighted by population)	16.2%	18.7%

Gallup-Healthways Well-Being Index, January-December 2013

GALLUP

Regional Differences Continue to Shape the U.S. Insurance Situation

States with the lowest percentages of uninsured residents continue to cluster in the East and upper Midwest, while states with the highest uninsured rates are in the South and the West. For the sixth straight year, Texas has the highest rate of uninsured residents, while Massachusetts has the lowest.

Implications

As states grapple with how to implement the Affordable Care Act, a pattern has emerged that reveals that states with the highest rates of uninsured residents are among the least likely to expand Medicaid and to establish state-based exchanges. Utah's apparent recent decision to expand Medicaid means that for the first time, a majority of states (plus the District of Columbia) plan to do so. Thus far, however, most states headed by Republican governors have decided against voluntary state action, preferring to pursue other means of lowering uninsured rates among their residents.

While a majority of Americans continue to disapprove of the law, preliminary data suggest that its intended effects are beginning to occur, with a small decline in the percentage who are uninsured reported in mid-January. And, for the first time since October, when Gallup began regularly tracking uninsured Americans' plans for getting insurance, a majority of the uninsured now plan to get their insurance from exchanges.

Survey Methods

Results are based on telephone interviews conducted as part of the Gallup-Healthways Well-Being Index survey Jan. 2–Dec. 29, 2013, with a random sample of 178,068 adults, aged 18 and older, living in all 50 U.S. states and the District of Columbia.

The margin of sampling error for most states is ±1 to ±2 percentage points, but is as high as ±4 points for states with smaller population sizes such as Wyoming, North Dakota, South Dakota, Delaware, and Hawaii.

February 10, 2014
ECONOMIC CONFIDENCE STILL HIGHEST IN D.C. IN 2013
Confidence improved in most states; West Virginia still least confident

by Justin McCarthy

WASHINGTON, D.C.—Although scores on Gallup's Economic Confidence Index improved in most U.S. states in 2013, the index remained negative in all 50. Only the District of Columbia had a positive index. Indexes were least negative in Massachusetts, Minnesota, and California. They were most negative in West Virginia, followed by Alaska.

Top 10 States, Gallup Economic Confidence Index, 2013	Index score
District of Columbia	19
Massachusetts	-1
Minnesota	-2
California	-5
Texas	-8
Nebraska	-9
Maryland	-9
Iowa	-9
Connecticut	-10
North Dakota	-10
Washington	-10
Wisconsin	-10

Gallup Daily tracking, January-December 2013

GALLUP

Bottom 10 States, Gallup Economic Confidence Index, 2013	Index score
West Virginia	-44
Alaska	-32
Wyoming	-29
Kentucky	-28
Arkansas	-27
Idaho	-27
Oklahoma	-26
Montana	-25
Tennessee	-25
Alabama	-24
Louisiana	-24

Gallup Daily tracking, January-December 2013

GALLUP

These results are based on Gallup Daily tracking interviews with 178,071 national adults conducted from January through December 2013, and represent averages for the year. Gallup conducted interviews with at least 500 residents in every state and interviewed 1,000 or more in 41 states. In the District of Columbia, 462 interviews were conducted.

The Gallup Economic Confidence Index is a composite of Americans' ratings of current U.S. economic conditions and their perceptions of the economy's direction. The index has a theoretical maximum of +100 (if all respondents rate the economy "excellent" or "good" and say it is getting better) and a theoretical minimum of −100 (if all rate the economy "poor" and say it is getting worse).

Most of the top 10 states in economic confidence in 2013 were the same as in 2012, but the rankings changed. Massachusetts (index score of −1) climbed five spots to top the list in 2013. California, Connecticut, Nebraska, and Wisconsin were new to the top 10, replacing Hawaii, South Dakota, and Virginia (because of ties, there were 12 states on the list in 2013, vs. 11 in 2012). Hawaii (−12 index score) and South Dakota (−21) were among the few states to experience decreases in their index scores last year. Hawaii's index, though still above the national average of −16, dropped three points, and South Dakota's index dropped 10 points.

The District of Columbia (+19) is the clear outlier in economic confidence, having the only positive reading for 2013 and well above the readings for even the most optimistic states. Its confidence has taken a hit, however, since 2012, when its index was +29. Likely factors in the 10-point drop include October's federal government shutdown as well as the sequestration spending cuts that occurred earlier in the year.

Other states with indexes significantly above the national average were Minnesota (−2), California (−5), and Texas (−8), as well as Nebraska, Maryland, and Iowa (all at −9). Connecticut, North Dakota, Washington, and Wisconsin, at −10, also made the top 10.

Bottom 10 States Largely the Same as in 2012

Of the bottom 10 states, all but Alaska and Louisiana were repeats from 2012, while some of the rest changed spots. The majority of the bottom 10 states are now in the South and West after being more geographically diverse in 2012. The indexes in Missouri and Vermont each improved by 11 points, enough to propel them out of the bottom 10. Mississippi, which improved six points, also broke out of the bottom 10.

West Virginia remains the least economically confident state (−44), having owned the title for the past four years. Alaska plunged to become the second-least economically confident state (−32), despite not being in the bottom 10 in 2012. Its index change of −6 between 2012 and 2013 falls within the margin of error. However, its index fell while most other states' indexes gained.

Eight of the states in the bottom 10 in 2013 were also in the bottom 10 in approval of President Barack Obama's job performance, underscoring the sometimes-political nature of economic confidence. Gallup has long observed that economic confidence is a complex consumer attitude that reflects real-world economic factors, but is also sensitive to the U.S. political environment, with members of the current president's party typically expressing more confidence than members of the opposing party.

Improvements in 2013 Were More Tempered Than the Increases in 2012

Individual state increases in economic confidence in 2013 were not as sweeping as those seen in 2012, when 48 of the 50 states saw gains in confidence, and the national average improved by 16 points. In 2013, the improvements were smaller, though noteworthy in a number of states.

The index in Connecticut improved most, climbing 14 points and securing a spot in the top 10—a distinction the state didn't share in 2012. The index in California, which also scored a new slot in the top 10, increased 13 points last year, as did Nevada's index. Massachusetts, which was near the middle of the top 10 in 2012, saw its index jump 12 points in 2013, earning it the title of most economically confident state of the year (−1).

Implications

Though U.S. economic confidence improved overall, it continues to vary widely across states. Forty-three points separate the most confident and least confident states, underscoring how different the nation's economic situation looks, depending on where Americans live.

Political sentiments play a role in confidence, as eight of the bottom 10 economic confidence states are also among the 10 lowest-ranking presidential approval states for Obama. Conversely, five of the highest-ranking economic confidence states are in the top 10 for presidential approval.

While confidence is negative for states across the nation, these polarized political divisions could play out in a variety of elections in 2014, as most states hold gubernatorial elections and all states have congressional elections. Candidates running on Republican tickets can attempt to paint this economic dissatisfaction as the fault of the Democratic president. Democratic candidates, on the other hand, will have to be sensitive to the low levels of economic confidence across the country—particularly for Democrats running in the bottom 10 states.

Survey Methods

Results for this Gallup poll are based on telephone interviews conducted Jan. 2–Dec. 29, 2013, on the Gallup Daily tracking survey, with a random sample of 178,071 adults, aged 18 and older, living in all 50 U.S. states and the District of Columbia.

For results based on the total sample of national adults, the margin of sampling error is ±1 percentage point at the 95% confidence level.

Margins of error for individual states are no greater than ±6 percentage points, and are ±3 percentage points in most states. The margin of error for the District of Columbia is ±6 percentage points.

February 10, 2014
CONGRESSIONAL JOB APPROVAL AT 12% IN FEBRUARY
Republicans significantly more positive than independents or Democrats

by Frank Newport

PRINCETON, NJ—Americans' approval of the way Congress is handling its job is at 12% in February, roughly unchanged since December, and only three points higher than the all-time low of 9% recorded last November.

Congressional Job Approval
Recent trend

■ % Approve

GALLUP

These results are from a Gallup poll conducted Feb. 6–9.

Americans' approval of Congress has been relatively stable for the last three months, at a level that is slightly below the 14% average congressional job approval rating for 2013, which in turn was the lowest annual average in Gallup's history. Congress' job approval has averaged below 20% for each of the past four years, well below the historical average of 33%.

The record-low reading last November came on the heels of Congress' inability to pass a budget plan, which in turn resulted in the government shutdown. Approval ratings are up slightly from that nadir, but appear to have settled down at continued low levels.

Republicans Rate Congress More Highly Than Democrats, Independents Do

Congressional job approval could have particular relevance in this midterm election year. In February 2010, the last midterm year, approval of Congress was 18%. At that point, Democrats controlled the House and the Senate, which was reflected in a 30% approval rating among Democrats, contrasted with a much lower 13% among independents and 11% among Republicans. In November of that year, the Republicans gained a large number of seats in the House and took control of it in January 2011.

Since then, control of Congress has been divided, although Republicans (23%) this month give Congress a significantly higher rating than independents (9%) or Democrats (7%) do. Republicans also gave Congress a higher rating in January, contrasting with much of 2013, when partisan differences showed a more varied pattern.

Party ratings of Congress fluctuate from month to month, partly because of the smaller sample sizes of each partisan group in each month's survey, but the current margin between Republicans and Democrats is the largest since the GOP controlled both houses in 2006. It remains to be seen whether this uptick in Republican approval will be sustained throughout this election year or is more of a short-term phenomenon.

Congressional Job Approval by Party

	Approve	Disapprove	No Opinion
	%	%	%
Republicans	23	71	7
Independents	9	84	7
Democrats	7	89	3

Feb. 6-9, 2014

GALLUP

Implications

Americans continue to have low opinions of the job their elected representatives in Congress are doing, one of a number of measures reflecting the general displeasure the nation's citizens have for their government right now. All members of the House and about a third of the Senate are up for re-election this November, but with control of these two bodies in the hands of different parties, it remains difficult to predict how Americans' negative feelings will affect their decisions in the voting booth.

Survey Methods

Results for this Gallup poll are based on telephone interviews conducted Feb. 6–9, 2014, with a random sample of 1,023 adults, aged 18 and older, living in all 50 U.S. states and the District of Columbia.

For results based on the total sample of national adults, the margin of sampling error is ±4 percentage points at the 95% confidence level.

February 11, 2014
DECADE AFTER "FREEDOM FRIES," U.S. OPINION OF FRANCE STRONG
Sentiment near record high as French president makes state visit

by Art Swift

WASHINGTON, D.C.—As French President Francois Hollande visits the U.S. this week, including being honored at the first state dinner of President Barack Obama's second term, 78% of Americans view France favorably. This represents a full restoration of France's U.S. image more than 10 years after it tumbled to 34% favorable in 2003, when France refused to back the U.S.-led invasion of Iraq.

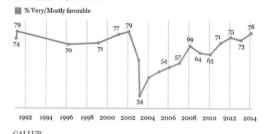

Americans' Views of France
What is your overall opinion of France? Is it very favorable, mostly favorable, mostly unfavorable, or very unfavorable?
■ % Very/Mostly favorable

GALLUP

Overall favorability toward France in the U.S. is near the record of 79% measured in 1991 and 2002. The 1991 reading may have reflected Americans' appreciation for France's active participation in the 1991 Gulf War, and the 2002 poll came shortly after the 9/11 terrorist attacks, when Americans may also have welcomed French moral support.

However, France's opposition to the United States' call for U.N. support for the Iraq war in 2003 upended the country's image in the U.S. Not only did 64% of Americans view France unfavorably in a March 2003 Gallup poll, but 39% viewed their longtime ally *very* unfavorably. Outrage toward France spurred numerous restaurants to rename French fries "freedom fries." Those restaurants included three House of Representatives cafeterias, which also renamed French toast "freedom toast."

As the 2000s wore on, Americans' opinions of France improved, with favorable views doubling to 69% by 2008. In 2011, favorability ratings reached the 70% range, where they have since remained. The positive sentiment comes at a time when Hollande is embroiled in scandal at home over a bitter split with his partner.

Four in 10 French Approve of U.S. Leadership

Although Gallup's World Poll does not ask the French for their views of the U.S. as a country, it does ask them to evaluate U.S. leadership, which has a bearing on their support for U.S.-French cooperation. French opinion of U.S. leadership has not always been rosy. After reaching single digits toward the end of the Bush presidency in the late 2000s, French approval of U.S. leadership quadrupled at the start of Obama's presidency, peaking at 55% approval in 2010. French support has dropped more recently, standing at 40% in April–June 2013, just below Obama's approval rating among Americans at the same time. A sizable portion of the French people, however—34%—have no opinion about U.S. leadership.

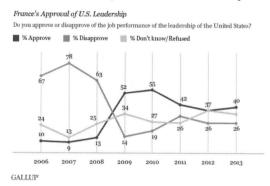

France's Approval of U.S. Leadership
Do you approve or disapprove of the job performance of the leadership of the United States?
■ % Approve ■ % Disapprove ■ % Don't know/Refused

GALLUP

Part of these more negative thoughts may be linked to ongoing tensions that have existed throughout Obama's presidency, which include Obama's not yet closing the detention facility at Guantanamo Bay, not pulling U.S. troops out of Afghanistan, and the drone strike policies of the U.S. military. Obama and Hollande announced in the *Washington Post* this week a "renewed alliance" between France and the U.S., citing a commitment to work together on pressing issues of mutual interest, including nuclear talks with Iran.

Bottom Line

The American-French alliance dates back to the American Revolutionary War and was solidified during the French Revolution of 1789. This partnership endured two world wars but was tested during the Iraq war of the last decade. Americans' support for France, which dipped sharply in 2003–2004, has returned to highs last seen in the 1990s and early 2000s.

Gallup trends show that more than half of French residents disapprove of U.S. leadership or do not offer an opinion. This suggests that the mutual warm feelings Obama and Hollande discuss in their *Washington Post* piece may take a while to resonate with the French public. It remains to be seen whether Hollande's state visit will bolster feelings toward U.S. leadership in his homeland, or whether Obama's lackluster approval ratings will receive a boost, domestically, as well.

Survey Methods

Results for this Gallup poll are based on telephone interviews conducted Feb. 6–9, 2014, with a random sample of 1,018 adults, aged 18 and older, living in all 50 U.S. states and the District of Columbia.

For results based on the total sample of national adults, the margin of sampling error is ±4 percentage points at the 95% confidence level.

February 12, 2014
U.S. UNINSURED RATE DROPS SO FAR IN FIRST QUARTER OF 2014
Rate among 26- to 34-year-olds continues to fall

by Jenna Levy

WASHINGTON, D.C.—The percentage of uninsured Americans fell to 16.0% so far in the first quarter of 2014 from 17.1% in the fourth quarter of 2013.

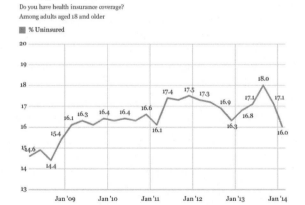

Percentage Uninsured in the U.S.
Do you have health insurance coverage?
Among adults aged 18 and older
■ % Uninsured

Quarter 1, 2008-Feb. 10, 2014
Gallup-Healthways Well-Being Index

GALLUP

These data are based on more than 19,000 interviews with Americans from Jan. 2–Feb. 10, 2014, as part of the Gallup-Healthways Well-Being Index. While more than a month remains in the first quarter, these preliminary data show the uninsured rate appears to be on track to drop to the lowest quarterly level measured since 2008.

The uninsured rate also dropped to the low–16% range in late 2012 before rising again in 2013, suggesting that there may be inherent variability in the rate or random fluctuation due to sampling error. Still, if the uninsured rate continues to fall over the next several months, it may suggest that the Affordable Care Act's requirement for most Americans to have health insurance, which took effect on Jan. 1, is responsible for the decline.

Percentage of Uninsured 26- to 34-Year-Olds Continues to Fall

The percentage of uninsured 26- to 34-year-olds, which has been dropping since the third quarter of 2013, is now 25.7%. Americans in this age group have had the highest uninsured rate since 2011. The uninsured rate among 26- to 34-year-olds has been declining faster than it has among any other age group.

The uninsured rate among 18- to 25-year-olds declined slightly so far in 2014 to 23.3%. The uninsured rate for this age group has generally been steady since December 2010, after the Affordable Care Act provision allowing young adults under age 26 to remain on their parents' health insurance plans took effect. Prior to that provision's implementation, 18- to 25-year-olds were the most likely to lack health insurance among all age groups.

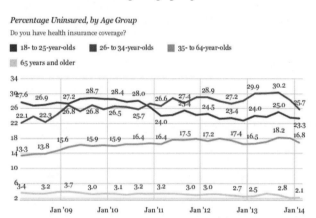

Percentage Uninsured, by Age Group
Do you have health insurance coverage?
■ 18- to 25-year-olds ■ 26- to 34-year-olds ■ 35- to 64-year-olds
■ 65 years and older

Quarter 1, 2008-Feb. 10, 2014
Gallup-Healthways Well-Being Index

GALLUP

More Americans Have Medicaid, Fewer Are Covered Through Employers

The percentage of Americans who report they are insured through Medicaid has increased to 7.4% from 6.6% in the fourth quarter of 2013. This uptick may be because some states have chosen to participate in the Medicaid expansion under a provision of the Affordable Care Act.

Meanwhile, fewer Americans now say they get their primary insurance through a current or former employer—43.5% down from 45.5% in the fourth quarter of 2013. More Americans now say they have a plan fully paid for by themselves or a family member—18.0% versus 17.2% at the end of last year.

Type of Primary Health Insurance Coverage in the U.S.

Is your primary health insurance coverage through a current or former employer, a union, Medicare, Medicaid, military or veteran's coverage, or a plan fully paid for by you or a family member?
Among those who have health insurance

	Quarter 4 2013 %	Jan. 2–31, 2014 %
Current or former employer	45.5	43.5
Medicare	20.1	20.5
Plan fully paid for by you or a family member	17.2	18.0
Medicaid	6.6	7.4
Military or veteran's	4.4	4.3
A union	2.6	2.5
(Something else)	1.9	2.0

Gallup-Healthways Well-Being Index

GALLUP'

Implications

The percentage of uninsured Americans has marginally decreased since the requirement to have health insurance went into effect at the beginning of 2014. It remains unclear if this decline is an effect of the Affordable Care Act, or if the percentage who lack health insurance coverage is decreasing for other reasons.

Even though the uninsured rate is falling more rapidly among 26- to 34-year-olds than it is among other age groups, these young adults still remain the most uninsured age group. Perhaps this is because 26- to 34-year-olds do not have the option to remain on their parents' insurance plans that those under age 26 have.

The Obama administration and other proponents of the healthcare law have continued their appeal to younger Americans to sign up for health insurance through the exchanges established for the Affordable Care Act. Young Americans are critical to the success of the healthcare law; the White House previously said 40% of new health insurance enrollees would need to be younger adults. Young adults' premiums would help subsidize the cost of healthcare for older enrollees who tend to have more health problems.

Some provisions of the healthcare law have yet to take effect, such as the requirement that employers provide health insurance coverage to their workers by 2015 or 2016. These provisions will likely affect the percentage of Americans who are uninsured, as well as the type of insurance that Americans have.

Gallup will continue to track the U.S. uninsured rate in the weeks and months ahead.

Survey Methods

Results are based on telephone interviews conducted as part of the Gallup-Healthways Well-Being Index survey Jan. 2–Feb. 10, 2014, with a random sample of 19,293 adults, aged 18 and older, living in all 50 U.S. states and the District of Columbia.

For results based on the total sample of national adults, the margin of sampling error is ±1 percentage points at the 95% confidence level.

February 12, 2014
NORTH DAKOTA LEADS IN JOB CREATION FOR FIFTH STRAIGHT YEAR
Rhode Island replaced Maine in 2013 as state with lowest Job Creation Index

by Lydia Saad

PRINCETON, NJ—For the fifth consecutive year, North Dakota topped all other states in employee perceptions of job creation at their workplaces in 2013, as measured by the Gallup Job Creation Index. North Dakota's +40 index score easily surpasses the District of Columbia's and South Dakota's second-place +30 scores. Rhode Island workers saw the least job creation, with a +12 score.

Top States, Gallup Job Creation Index

	Job Creation Index
North Dakota	40
District of Columbia	30
South Dakota	30
Delaware	29
Nebraska	29
Minnesota	28
Texas	27
Michigan	25
Iowa	25
Arizona	23
Wisconsin	23
Hawaii	23

Gallup Daily tracking, January-December 2013

GALLUP'

Bottom States, Gallup Job Creation Index

	Job Creation Index
Rhode Island	12
New Mexico	13
Vermont	13
West Virginia	14
New York	15
Connecticut	15
Maine	16
North Carolina	16
New Hampshire	16
Kentucky	16
Alabama	16
Arkansas	16

Gallup Daily tracking, January-December 2013

GALLUP'

Gallup's Job Creation Index is a measure of net hiring, determined by asking full- and part-time U.S. workers, aged 18 and older, whether their employer is hiring new people and expanding the size of its workforce, not changing the size of its workforce, or letting people go and reducing the size of its workforce. The index score is the difference between reported "hiring" and "letting go."

North Dakota has ranked No. 1 among U.S. states for job creation in each of the last five years, and it has appeared in Gallup's top 10 in all six years since the inception of the Gallup Job Creation Index in 2008.

Two states have enjoyed a five-year run in the top tier: Nebraska and Texas. South Dakota, Iowa, and the District of Columbia have been in the top group each of the past four years, since 2010. Minnesota first appeared in the group in 2012, while five other states—Delaware, Michigan, Arizona, Wisconsin, and Hawaii—are making their first appearance.

Two states—Rhode Island and Connecticut—have the unwanted distinction of appearing in the bottom tier for job creation every year since 2008. New York has been in the low-ranking group each of the past four years, New Mexico each of the past three years, and West Virginia for the past two years. Vermont, New Hampshire, Maine, and North Carolina have made occasional appearances, while 2013 was the first year for Kentucky, Alabama, and Arkansas.

Nationally, net hiring increased slightly in 2013, with the Job Creation Index averaging +20 during the year, up from +18 in 2012. The index was relatively stable in most states, but rose by significantly more than the average in a handful—most notably Delaware (up 15 points to +29), Florida (up seven points to +22), and California (up seven points to +21).

Job Creation Index Linked With Standard of Living Perceptions

Three of the five states with the longest track records at the top of the state job creation ranking—North Dakota, South Dakota, and Nebraska—are strongly Republican in party affiliation. All three states with a long track record (at least four years) at the bottom—Rhode Island, Connecticut, and New York—are heavily Democratic. However, apart from this, there is little correspondence between net hiring and partisan affiliation in the states.

At the same time, there is a strong connection between employee reports of net hiring and Americans' perceptions of their standard of living. States with higher Job Creation Index scores tend to have higher standard-of-living scores, and vice versa. There is a lesser, but still strong, relationship between the Job Creation Index and Americans' confidence in the national economy, as measured by Gallup's Economic Confidence Index.

Bottom Line

Nationally, reported job creation was fairly flat in 2013, with Gallup's overall Job Creation Index inching up two points to +20. Within the states, the index varied in a 28-point range from +12 in Rhode Island to +40 in North Dakota. Many of the states in the highest and lowest tiers carried over from 2012; but there was also some shuffling. Most notably, net hiring in Delaware as reported by workers residing in that state rose sharply, enough to convert Delaware from one of the lowest-ranking states to one of the highest. Whether that represents a statistical anomaly or a sign of real improvement in the jobs picture in that state will become clear in 2014.

Along the same lines, from 2008 through 2011, West Virginia had been one of the highest-ranking states. It then dropped to one of the lowest in 2012, and remained there in 2013—thus confirming the 2012 finding. How much of this is due to reported declines in coal production in that state is unclear, but it bears watching in 2014.

The good news about the Gallup Job Creation Index nationally is that it has recovered from the net-negative reading Gallup recorded in 2009, and since then nearly all states have shown substantial improvement.

Thus far in 2014, the index remains near +20. However, as was seen in 2013, even if that score persists, important state-level shifts could be happening.

Survey Methods

These results are based on telephone interviews conducted as part of Gallup Daily tracking Jan. 2–Dec. 29, 2013, with a random sample of 208,758 adults, aged 18 and older, employed full or part time, living in all 50 U.S. states and the District of Columbia.

For results based on the total sample of employed adults, the margin of sampling error is ±1 percentage point at the 95% confidence level.

Margins of error for individual states are no greater than ±6 percentage points, and are ±3 percentage points in most states. The margin of error for the District of Columbia is ±6 percentage points.

February 13, 2014
AMERICANS' VIEWS OF RUSSIA, PUTIN ARE WORST IN YEARS
Clear majority view the Russian president and his nation unfavorably

by Art Swift

WASHINGTON, D.C.—As host nation Russia dominates the world stage at the Winter Olympics in Sochi, Americans clearly do not think highly of the country or its president, Vladimir Putin. Putin and Russia score the highest unfavorable ratings—63% and 60%,

respectively—that Gallup has recorded for them in the past two decades.

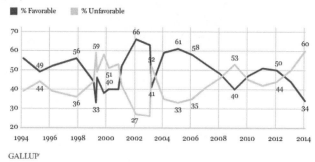

Americans' Opinions of Russia

What is your overall opinion of Russia? Is it very favorable, mostly favorable, mostly unfavorable, or very unfavorable?

■ % Favorable   ■ % Unfavorable

GALLUP

These sentiments, based on a survey conducted Feb. 6–9, continue the downward trajectory in Americans' opinions since Putin returned to Russia's presidency in 2012. These results align with Gallup's findings last fall when Americans, for the first time in 14 years of Gallup polling on the topic, said they consider Russia an enemy, not an ally. In the past year, Russia has faced scrutiny for granting former National Security Agency contractor Edward Snowden asylum, involving itself in the Syrian civil war, and restricting gay and lesbian civil rights. The threat of terrorism at the Olympics and the allegedly substandard conditions at the Winter Games have also been big media stories in the past several months.

While their unfavorable ratings of Russia are at an all-time high, Americans' perceptions of the world power have not always been positive in the years since the former Soviet Union collapsed in 1991. In 1999, Russia's bombing of the former Soviet republic of Chechnya, along with its opposition to the NATO war in Kosovo, likely soured American opinion toward Russia. Another spike in anti-Russian opinion occurred in March 2003 (52% unfavorable) when Russia refused to back the U.S. in the Iraq war, claiming that only the United Nations could settle the dispute.

Gallup first asked Americans about Russia in 1994, more than two years after the Soviet Union's collapse. Since then, Americans have expressed the most positive views in 2002, with 66% rating the country favorably.

Clear Majority Also Does Not View Putin Favorably

Not surprisingly, Americans' views of Russia and Putin are parallel, perhaps because Putin and Russia have become synonymous. More than six in 10 Americans currently have an unfavorable opinion of Putin, the highest negative rating in the four times Gallup has asked about him since he became president for the first time in 1999. Putin's op-ed criticizing the U.S. in the *New York Times* last September may have contributed to this low opinion. In the op-ed, he claimed that President Barack Obama's statement about American exceptionalism was "extremely dangerous." Obama had said that the ability of the U.S. to intervene in geopolitical conflict when needed is "what makes us exceptional." Just after the publishing of the op-ed, Gallup found that 54% of Americans viewed Putin unfavorably.

Americans at the time endorsed Putin's plan to rid Syria of chemical weapons, but apparently that validation did not improve feelings overall. Tension between Russia and Ukraine, along with ongoing concerns about the threat of terrorism at the Olympics and Russia's anti-gay legislation, may be adding to Putin's unfavorability.

Americans' Views of Putin

Do you have a favorable or unfavorable opinion of Vladimir Putin?

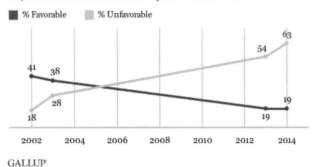

GALLUP

Bottom Line

Over the past year, Russia has pursued a much more aggressive stance on the world stage than at any other time in the new millennium. In his first term in office, Putin was viewed more favorably than unfavorably by the American public, but Americans now see him in a clearly unfavorable light.

Russia itself, which the U.S. long viewed with suspicion during the Cold War days, has traveled a more complicated path since. While American sentiments have been mostly favorable over the past 20 years, it is obvious that Americans will react strongly at moments when Russia clashes with the U.S. The Chechnya conflict, the Iraq war, and now a multitude of factors—Snowden, Syria, Putin's taking issue with American "exceptionalism," Ukraine, and Russia's anti-gay policies—distinctly affect Americans' views of Russia and its leader.

Survey Methods

Results for this Gallup poll are based on telephone interviews conducted Feb. 6–9, 2014, on the Gallup Poll Social Series, with a random sample of 1,018 adults, aged 18 and older, living in all 50 U.S. states and the District of Columbia.

For results based on the total sample of national adults, the margin of sampling error is ±4 percentage points at the 95% confidence level.

February 13, 2014
ALASKANS MOST POSITIVE ABOUT STANDARD OF LIVING
Gallup's U.S. Standard of Living Index improved in nearly all states

by Justin McCarthy

WASHINGTON, D.C.—Among residents of the 50 states, Alaskans were the most satisfied with and optimistic about their standard of living in 2013, according to Gallup's Standard of Living Index. Alaska's average index score of 53 was similar to the scores in

North Dakota and Hawaii, but far outpaced West Virginia's bottom-ranking score of 22. The national index improved to 38 in 2013, up from 34 in 2012, with marginal improvements in nearly all states.

Top 10 States, Gallup Standard of Living Index, 2013	Index score
Alaska	53
North Dakota	52
Hawaii	51
District of Columbia	51
Nebraska	49
South Dakota	48
Texas	48
Minnesota	47
Iowa	46
California	45
Massachusetts	45

Gallup Daily tracking, January–December 2013

GALLUP

Bottom 10 States, Gallup Standard of Living Index, 2013	Index score
West Virginia	22
Maine	31
Rhode Island	32
Alabama	33
Missouri	33
North Carolina	33
Kentucky	33
Pennsylvania	33
Michigan	34
New York	34
Ohio	34
Connecticut	34
Mississippi	34

Gallup Daily tracking, January–December 2013

GALLUP

These results are based on Gallup Daily tracking interviews with 178,068 U.S. adults conducted from January through December 2013—approximately 500 per day—and are thus averages for the year. For these questions, Gallup conducted interviews with at least 500 residents in every state and interviewed 1,000 or more in 41 states. In the District of Columbia, 462 interviews were conducted.

The Standard of Living Index is a composite of Americans' satisfaction with their standard of living on the basis of two questions: one asking whether they are satisfied with their current standard of living, and the other asking whether their standard of living is getting better or worse. The index has a theoretical maximum of 100 (if all respondents say they are satisfied with their standard of living and say it is getting better) and a theoretical minimum of −100 (if all respondents are dissatisfied with their standard of living and say it is getting worse).

Following Alaska in the top 10 were North Dakota (52), Hawaii (51), and the District of Columbia (51). These states were joined by Nebraska (49), South Dakota (48), Texas (48), and Minnesota (47), all of which ranked in the top 10 in 2012.

West Virginia had the lowest Standard of Living Index reading (22), a distinction it also held in 2012. Also in the bottom 10 were Maine (31) and Rhode Island (32), both repeats from 2012.

Standard of Living and Its Relationship to Economic Confidence and Job Creation

Generally speaking, states that ranked highest in economic confidence and job creation also reported their standard of living to be higher. Of the top 10 states with the highest economic confidence and job creation, eight from each list were in the top 10 for standard of living.

North Dakota, which surpassed all other states in perceptions of job creation in 2013, found itself at No. 2 for standard of living. The District of Columbia, Nebraska, South Dakota, Texas, and Minnesota also scored high in state rankings for both the Job Creation and Standard of Living Indexes.

Vermont Residents See Biggest Improvement

The most improved state was Vermont, which climbed 19 points from last year to an index reading of 39. Vermont had been on the lower end of the bottom 10 in 2012, but its standard of living improved so greatly in 2013 that it is no longer on the bottom 10 list. This may be attributed to Vermont's jump of 11 points in the Economic Confidence Index from 2012 to 2013.

Marked improvements in perceived standard of living were also seen in Iowa (46) and Massachusetts (45), both of which improved 11 points from 2012. California (45) improved by nine points. None of these three were in the top 10 in 2012, but improved so greatly that they comprised the latter end of the top 10 in 2013. Iowa, Massachusetts, and California all experienced gains in either the Economic Confidence or Job Creation Index last year.

In the District of Columbia, the Standard of Living Index dropped 11 points in 2013, which was the only decrease from 2012. Still, it ranks among the states with the highest Standard of Living Index scores.

The Last Frontier: An Unlikely Leader in Standard of Living

Despite standard of living's correlations with the Job Creation and Economic Confidence Indexes, one state—Alaska—has been a true outlier for standard of living.

Considering its dismally low score in economic confidence, Alaska may seem an improbable state to lead the pack on the Standard of Living Index. Though high rankings in standard of living usually indicate higher scores for job creation and/or economic confidence, Alaska is an extreme exception, ranking among the lowest in the nation for economic confidence. It was also one point away from being included in the bottom 10 for job creation.

Alaska's high standard of living reading could reflect its unique distinction of being the only state with neither a state income tax nor a state sales tax. In fact, three of the seven states with no income tax—Alaska, South Dakota, and Texas—have been in the top 10 for the past three years. Two others, Washington and Wyoming, were just a few points short of being in the 2013 top 10. Alaska only fell to second place in standard of living in 2012, when it was superseded by the District of Columbia. With the exception of 2012, Alaska has led this list each year since 2009.

Additionally, Alaska has a unique landscape ripe for many of nature's most exciting outdoor activities, and this may provide a physical environment conducive to a high standard of living for Alaskans. Removed from the continental United States, residents in Alaska may define "high standard of living" differently, partly factoring in the life-enriching opportunities that nature freely provides.

Implications

Perceptions of job creation and economic confidence clearly have an impact on standard of living in the United States. For Alaskans, however, these perceptions might be irrelevant toward their views on their standard of living, as their lives are virtually untaxed by their state government and they are removed from the fast pace of the continental U.S.

Though the lowest-ranking states remained largely the same from 2012, nearly all states witnessed increases, reflecting the national four-point increase to a reading of 38. It may be said that states that improve perceptions of economic confidence and/or job creation could realize concurrent gains in standard of living ratings over time.

Survey Methods

Results for this Gallup poll are based on telephone interviews conducted Jan. 2–Dec. 29, 2013, on the Gallup Daily tracking survey, with a random sample of 178,068 adults, aged 18 and older, living in all 50 U.S. states and the District of Columbia.

For results based on the total sample of national adults, one can say with 95% confidence that the margin of sampling error is ±1 percentage point.

Margins of error for individual states are no greater than ±6 percentage points, and are ±3 percentage points in most states. The margin of error for the District of Columbia is ±6 percentage points.

February 13, 2014
U.S. SMALL-BUSINESS OWNERS' OPTIMISM UP SHARPLY
Optimism jumps to as high as it has been since 2008

by Frank Newport

PRINCETON, NJ—U.S. small-business owners are substantially more optimistic than they have been in several years. The Wells Fargo/Gallup Small Business Index in January increased to +45, up from +24 in October and the most positive score since the third quarter of 2008. However, optimism is still below the high levels recorded pre-recession.

Wells Fargo/Gallup Small Business Index

The Small Business Index consists of owners' ratings of their business' current situation and their expectations for the next 12 months, measured in terms of their overall financial situation, revenue, cash flow, capital spending, number of jobs, and ease of obtaining credit.

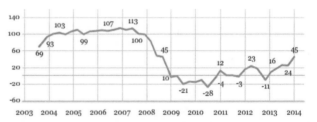

Index conducted since August 2003 and quarterly from December 2003-January 2014

GALLUP

These results are from the most recent update of the Wells Fargo/Gallup Small Business Index, based on telephone interviews with 603 small-business owners conducted Jan. 6–10, 2014.

Small-business owners are modestly more optimistic in terms of their future expectations across most of the six key components that comprise the index, including more positive expectations about hiring in the coming year.

More specifically:

- Expectations for hiring in the next 12 months rose from 16% in the fourth quarter of 2013 to 22% in the current poll.
- Expectations for having good cash flow also increased in January, with 57% rating cash flow expectations for the next 12 months as "good," compared with 52% in the fourth quarter of 2013.
- Expectations for increases in revenue in the next 12 months rose to 48% in the current survey from 44% last quarter.

- More small-business owners rated their cash flow in the past 12 months as "good" than did so in the fourth quarter of 2013 (52% vs. 46%, respectively).
- Fewer small-business owners reported having difficulty obtaining credit in the most recent poll (23%) than did so in the fourth quarter of last year (27%).

Implications

After reaching low points in 2009 and 2010, and again late in 2012, the Wells Fargo/Gallup Small Business Index has generally been on the rise throughout the last five quarters, and is now as high as it has been since mid-2008. Despite this significant improvement, however, this indicator remains substantially below where it was in pre-recession years—as is true with other Gallup economic measures.

A key to improved U.S. job creation in the months to come will be whether small-business owners' greater optimism translates into actual steps to expand their businesses—including investing more in their businesses and hiring more workers.

Survey Methods

Results for the total data set are based on telephone interviews conducted Jan. 6–10, 2014, with a random sample of 603 small-business owners, living in all 50 U.S. states and the District of Columbia.

For results based on the total sample of small-business owners, the margin of sampling error is ±4 percentage points at the 95% confidence level.

Sampling is done on a random-digit-dial basis using Dun & Bradstreet sampling of small businesses having $20 million or less in sales or revenues. The data are weighted to be representative of U.S. small businesses within this size range nationwide.

In addition to sampling error, question wording and practical difficulties in conducting surveys can introduce error or bias into the findings of public opinion polls.

February 13, 2014
IN U.S., 14% OF THOSE AGED 24 TO 34 ARE LIVING WITH PARENTS
Marital status, educational attainment, and job status biggest predictors

by Jeffrey M. Jones

PRINCETON, NJ—Fourteen percent of adults between the ages of 24 and 34—those in the post-college years when most young adults are trying to establish independence—report living at home with their parents. By contrast, roughly half of 18- to 23-year-olds, many of whom are still finishing their education, are currently living at home.

Just in terms of your current circumstances, are you currently living at home with your parents, or not?
Based on U.S. adults under age 35

	% Yes
All U.S. adults under age 35	29
18 to 23 years old	51
24 to 34 years old	14

Gallup Daily tracking, Aug. 7-Dec. 29, 2013

GALLUP

The results are based on Gallup Daily tracking interviews conducted from Aug. 7 through Dec. 29, 2013, in which adults younger than 35 were asked about their current living arrangements. This article focuses on the 14% who are beyond college age and living at home.

An important milestone in adulthood is establishing independence from one's parents, including finding a job, a place to live and, for most, a spouse or partner, and starting one's own family. However, there are potential roadblocks on the path to independence that may force young adults to live with their parents longer, including a weak job market, the high cost of living, significant college debt, and helping care for an elderly or disabled parent.

A statistical model that takes into account a variety of demographic characteristics indicates that three situational factors are most likely to distinguish the group of 24- to 34-year-olds living at home from their peers:

They are much less likely to be married.

They are less likely to be working full time and more likely to be unemployed or underemployed.

They are less likely to have graduated from college.

Being married is, by a large margin, the most important predictor of whether individuals between the ages of 24 and 34 live with their parents or have their own place. The vast majority of young adults living at home, 75%, are single and have never married, twice the rate among those of the same ages who are living on their own. A plurality, 46%, of those no longer living with their parents are married.

Marital Status, by Living Arrangement
Based on U.S. adults aged 24 to 34

	Living at home with parents	Not living at home with parents	Difference
	%	%	pct. pts.
Single/Never married	75	35	40
Married	12	46	-34
Domestic partnership	6	11	-5
Divorced/Separated	7	7	0

Gallup Daily tracking, Aug. 7-Dec. 29, 2013

GALLUP

Divorce or marital separation does not appear to be a major factor in whether young adults move back home, because 7% of both those living and those not living with their parents are divorced or separated. And although the vast majority of those who are living with their parents are currently not married, nearly one in five have added a spouse (12%) or partner (6%) to their parents' household.

Being married may better explain why young adults move out of their parents' home than why single adults live at home. For those living at home, their situation may have more to do with their job or income status than their marital status. Being single, however, may make living with parents a more feasible option for young adults than it would be if they were married.

Employment status ranks as the second-most-important predictor of young adults' living situation once they are beyond college age. Specifically, 67% of those living on their own are employed full time, compared with 50% of those living with their parents.

The unemployment rate, as calculated by Gallup, among those in the workforce is twice as high for post-college-aged adults living with their parents as it is for their counterparts who are not living with their parents, 14.6% vs. 7.1%.

Employment Status, by Living Arrangement

Based on U.S. adults aged 24 to 34

	Living at home with parents	Not living at home with parents	Difference
	%	%	pct. pts.
Employed full-time	50	67	-17
Employed part-time	18	11	7
Unemployed	12	6	6
Out of workforce	20	16	4
Unemployment rate (as a percentage of workforce)	14.6	7.1	7.5
Underemployment rate (as a percentage of workforce)	32.8	15.4	17.4

Gallup Daily tracking, Aug. 7-Dec. 29, 2013
Note: The underemployment rate is the percentage of the workforce who are unemployed or employed part time but wanting full-time work.

GALLUP'

The underemployment rate, which combines the percentage unemployed with the percentage working part time but wanting full-time work, is 32.8% among those living at home and 15.4% among those living on their own. In other words, among young adults who live with their parents and are working or actively looking for work, nearly one in three are in a substandard employment situation.

Education is also an important predictor of whether young adults are living at home: those with higher educational attainment are more likely to have their own place to live, and those with less formal education are more likely to be living at home. Still, a substantial number of those living at home, 28%, are college graduates.

Educational Attainment, by Living Arrangement

Based on U.S. adults aged 24 to 34

	Living at home with parents	Not living at home with parents	Difference
	%	%	pct. pts.
High school or less	41	34	7
Some college	31	28	3
College graduate	28	38	-10

Gallup Daily tracking, Aug. 7-Dec. 29, 2013

GALLUP'

Perhaps because of employment differences, those living on their own tend to report that they live in higher-income households. To some degree, that reflects the greater likelihood that those living on their own are married, and likely to have a second source of income from their spouse. Analysis of the effect of income on where young adults live is also complicated by the fact that Gallup measures income at the household rather than individual level, and income reports from those living under their parents' roof may include parental income as well as respondent income.

Twenty-four- to 34-year-olds living at home do not differ substantially from those of the same age living on their own in terms of gender, race, region, or prior military service.

Implications

A 2012 report from Ohio State University sociologists showed that it is increasingly common for young adults to live at home with their parents. The high costs of housing and a relatively weak job market are key factors that may force, or encourage, young adults to stay at home.

Perhaps it is comforting that by the time U.S. adults pass college age, the vast majority have left their parents' homes and found a place of their own to live. The biggest impetus for leaving home seems to be marriage, easily the strongest predictor of one's living arrangement among those between the ages of 24 and 34. This indicates that if the marriage rate increases in the future, the percentage living with their parents may decline. Earlier Gallup research suggests that most unmarried Americans do have a goal of getting married someday.

Also, those who have secured full-time employment or have earned college degrees are more likely to have gotten a place of their own to live. An improving job market and economy should lead to a decrease in the percentage of young adults living with their parents.

A key question is to what extent those living at home are better off or worse off than their contemporaries who are out on their own, and what implications that has for society in general and the economy in particular. Gallup will explore differences in well-being between young adults living with parents and those living on their own in an upcoming story.

Survey Methods

Results for this Gallup poll are based on telephone interviews conducted Aug. 7–Dec. 29, 2013, on the Gallup Daily tracking survey, with a random sample of 3,445 adults, aged 18–34, living in all 50 U.S. states and the District of Columbia, who report they are currently living at home with their parents.

For results based on the total sample of adults living at home with their parents, the margin of sampling error is ±2 percentage points at the 95% confidence level.

For results based on the total sample of 1,076 adults aged 24–34 who are living at home with their parents, the margin of sampling error is ±4 percentage points at the 95% confidence level.

February 14, 2014
WASHINGTON, D.C., LEADS NATION IN PAYROLL TO POPULATION
West Virginia has lowest P2P

by Ben Ryan

WASHINGTON, D.C.—Washington, D.C., had the highest Payroll to Population (P2P) rate in the country in 2013, at 55.7%. A cluster of states in the Northern Great Plains and Rocky Mountain regions—North Dakota, Nebraska, Minnesota, Wyoming, Iowa, Colorado, and South Dakota—all made the top 10. West Virginia (36.1%) had the lowest P2P rate of all the states.

Bottom 10 States, Payroll to Population

States with the lowest P2P rates

	P2P rate %
West Virginia	36.1
Mississippi	37.1
New Mexico	37.4
Hawaii	37.7
Florida	38.3
Michigan	38.9
Montana	39.2
South Carolina	39.6
North Carolina	40.1
Oregon	40.2
Idaho	40.2

Gallup Daily tracking, January-December 2013

GALLUP'

Gallup's P2P metric tracks the percentage of the adult population aged 18 and older that is employed full time for an employer for at least 30 hours per week. The differences in P2P rates across states may reflect several factors, including the overall employment situation and the population's demographic composition. States with large older and retired populations, for example, would have a lower percentage of adults working full time. West Virginia and Florida—both in the bottom 10—have some of the largest proportions of older residents, with more than half of each state's adult residents older than 50 (52.9% and 51.5%, respectively), and both states rank in the bottom 10 states on the P2P index. Regardless of the underlying reason, however, the P2P index provides a good reflection of a state's economic vitality.

Midwestern States Had Lowest Underemployment Rates

As with Payroll to Population rates, states in the Midwest—including North and South Dakota, Minnesota, Nebraska, and Iowa—were among those with the best underemployment rates in 2013.

Gallup's U.S. underemployment rate combines the percentage of adults in the *workforce* that is unemployed with the percentage of those working part time but looking for full-time work. While P2P reflects the relative size of the *population* that is working full time for an employer, the underemployment rate reflects the relative size of the *workforce* that is not working at capacity, but would like to be.

Lowest Underemployment States

	Underemployment rate
	%
North Dakota	10.1
South Dakota	11.0
Minnesota	11.8
Nebraska	12.2
Iowa	12.6
Alaska	12.7
New Hampshire	12.8
Montana	13.5
Wyoming	13.5
Colorado	14.1

Gallup Daily tracking, January–December 2013

GALLUP'

Highest Underemployment States

	Underemployment rate
	%
California	22.0
Nevada	21.7
New Mexico	20.6
Arizona	20.6
Michigan	20.4
New York	20.4
Mississippi	20.2
Georgia	19.9
Florida	19.8
Hawaii	19.6
North Carolina	19.6

Gallup Daily tracking, January–December 2013

GALLUP'

California and Nevada have the highest percentages of their workforces not working at desired capacity. Their rates are about twice those of states at the other end of the spectrum, such as North Dakota (10.1%). Other states hard hit by the recession and declining housing market, including Florida and Arizona, rank among the states with the highest underemployment rates.

Bottom Line

North Dakota, South Dakota, Nebraska, Iowa, and Minnesota ranked in the top 10 states on P2P rates in 2013, and in the bottom 10 for underemployment, as well as in the top 10 on Gallup's Job Creation Index, highlighting the strong job markets in the Midwest.

In contrast, Mississippi, Florida, New Mexico, Hawaii, Michigan, and North Carolina ranked in the bottom 10 states on P2P rates, and are among the states with the highest underemployment rates. There is more overlap between the top 10 P2P states and low underemployment states than there is among the bottom 10 P2P states and

high underemployment states on the two measures. That is mainly because many of the states with low P2P rates also have low workforce participation rates. They still have much room for both job growth and labor force mobilization.

Gallup's "State of the States" series reveals state-by-state differences on political, economic, and well-being measures Gallup tracks each day. New stories based on full-year 2013 data will be released throughout February.

Survey Methods

Results are based on telephone interviews conducted as part of Gallup Daily tracking from Jan. 2–Dec. 29, 2013, with a random sample of 356,586 adults, aged 18 and older, selected using random-digit-dial sampling.

For results based on the total sample of national adults, one can say with 95% confidence that the maximum margin of sampling error is less than ±1 percentage point.

Margins of error for individual states are no greater than ±6 percentage points, and are ±3 percentage points or less in most states.

February 14, 2014
YOUNG ADULTS LIVING AT HOME LESS LIKELY TO BE "THRIVING"
Living at home also affects overall well-being

by Frank Newport

PRINCETON, NJ—Young adults between the ages of 24 and 34 who live at home with their parents are significantly less likely to be "thriving" than those in the same age group who don't live with their parents.

Thriving, Struggling, Suffering, by Living Arrangement, Among U.S. Adults Aged 24 to 34

Controlling for gender, race and ethnicity, region, socioeconomic status, employment, and marital status

	Living at home with parents	Not living at home with parents
	%	%
Thriving	51	57
Struggling	48	42
Suffering	1	1

Gallup-Healthways Well-Being Index, Aug. 7-Dec. 29, 2013

GALLUP'

These results are based on Gallup Daily tracking interviews conducted from Aug. 7–Dec. 29, 2013, in which adults younger than 35 were asked about their current living arrangements. Fourteen percent of those between the ages of 24 and 34 report that they live at home with their parents.

Gallup classifies Americans as "thriving," "struggling," or "suffering," according to how they rate their current and future lives on a ladder scale with steps numbered from 0 to 10, based on the Cantril Self-Anchoring Striving Scale. People are considered thriving if they rate their current lives a 7 or higher and their lives in five years an 8 or higher.

Previous Gallup research shows that young adults who live at home are significantly less likely to be married, to be employed full time, and to have a college education than those who are the same age but don't live at home. Because all three of these characteristics are related to how people evaluate their lives, it is not surprising to find that those living at home are less likely to be thriving.

However, even after accounting for marital status, employment, education, and a number of other demographic variables, those living at home between the ages of 24 and 34 still are less likely to be thriving. This suggests that while living with one's parents may have some benefits for young people who have not yet found their full footing in society, the net effect of living at home lowers young adults' perceptions of where they stand in life.

In other words, even among young adults who have equal status in terms of being single, not being employed full time, and not having a college education, those who do not live at home are more likely to be thriving than those living at home. Something about living at home appears to drive down young adults' overall life evaluations.

Same Living-at-Home Deficit Found on Gallup-Healthways Well-Being Index

A broader measure of well-being, the Gallup-Healthways Well-Being Index, which is based on physical and emotional health and other factors, as well as life evaluations, reflects the same pattern. The index summarizes more than 50 different well-being items and is calculated on a scale of 0 to 100, where a score of 100 represents ideal well-being. Young adults living at home have a Well-Being Index score of 63.73, while the score for those not living at home is 65.36.

Well-Being, by Living Arrangement, Among U.S. Adults Aged 24 to 34

Controlling for gender, race and ethnicity, region, socio-economic status, employment, marital status

	Living at home with parents	Not living at home with parents
	%	%
Gallup-Healthways Well-Being Index	63.73	65.36
Life Evaluation	49.24	54.63
Emotional Health	78.78	79.14
Physical Health	79.76	80.60
Work Environment	45.91	44.51
Healthy Behaviors	57.23	59.82
Basic Access	71.47	73.47

Gallup-Healthways Well-Being Index, Aug. 7–Dec. 29, 2013

GALLUP

Those aged 24 to 34 who live at home generally do at least marginally worse than those who do not live at home on five of the six domains of well-being—life evaluation, physical health, emotional health, healthy behaviors, and basic access to things that promote healthy living. Those living at home but who are in the workforce score marginally better on the work environment index than those not living at home.

Interestingly, among Americans aged 18 to 23, those living at home do slightly better than those who are not living at home in terms of physical health and access to basic necessities, perhaps reflecting their parents' influence. On the other hand, these advantages for those living at home disappear among those aged 24 to 34.

Bottom Line

This research on the well-being of young adults living at home with their parents is the first of its kind at Gallup, although research conducted at Ohio State and elsewhere suggests that living at home is increasingly common among those younger than 35 today.

The data show that those between the ages of 24 and 34 who live at home tend to be unattached—in the sense that they are not married and less likely to have a full-time job—and also to be less well-educated. This research underscores the idea that living at home may have some emotional costs for young adults—particularly in terms of their perceptions that they are not enjoying the best possible life, beyond those associated with being unemployed or unmarried.

Times may change. If marriage rates rebound, the job market for young adults improves, and more young Americans go to college, then living at home may be less common in the years ahead. If that happens, young Americans' overall well-being may improve.

Survey Methods

Results for this Gallup poll are based on telephone interviews conducted as part of the Gallup-Healthways Well-Being Index survey from Aug. 7–Dec. 29, 2013, with a random sample of 3,445 adults, aged 18 to 34, living in all 50 U.S. states and the District of Columbia, who report they are currently living at home with their parents.

For results based on the total sample of adults living at home with their parents, the margin of sampling error is ±2 percentage points at the 95% confidence level.

For results based on the total sample of 1,076 adults aged 24 to 34 who are living at home with their parents, the margin of sampling error is ±4 percentage points at the 95% confidence level.

February 17, 2014
IN U.S., BORDER SECURITY, IMMIGRANT STATUS EQUALLY IMPORTANT
Americans gave border security higher priority in past

by Jeffrey M. Jones

PRINCETON, NJ—Americans now assign about equal importance to the two major aspects of immigration reform being debated in Washington. Forty-four percent say it is extremely important for the U.S. to develop a plan to deal with the large number of immigrants already living in the United States, and 43% say it's extremely important to halt the flow of illegal immigrants into the country by securing the borders. This is a shift from the past, when Americans were consistently more likely to rate border security as extremely important.

Percentage Rating Government Actions on Illegal Immigration as "Extremely Important"

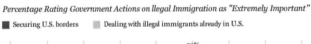
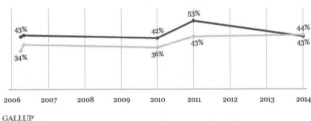

GALLUP

These results are based on a Feb. 6–9 Gallup poll. President Barack Obama has made immigration reform a priority this year, although the prospects of such legislation passing in an election year are dim. Since George W. Bush's second term as president, Washington leaders have tried unsuccessfully to pass comprehensive immigration legislation that deals with both border security and illegal immigrants already living in the U.S.

Compared with 2011, Americans of all partisan orientations have come to view border security as less important. Meanwhile, their views on the importance of devising a plan to deal with illegal immigrants already in the United States have been largely stable.

Party Ratings of Importance of Illegal Immigration Actions, 2011 vs. 2014

Figures are percentage rating each action as "extremely important"

	2011	2014	Change
	%	%	pct. pts.
Securing U.S. borders to halt flow of illegal immigrants			
Republicans	68	56	-12
Independents	50	44	-6
Democrats	42	31	-11
Dealing with illegal immigrants already in the U.S.			
Republicans	51	50	-1
Independents	44	43	-1
Democrats	37	41	+4

GALLUP

"Forced Choice" Tilts Toward Resolving Illegal Immigrants' Status

The equal importance Americans place on the two main immigration challenges does not give government leaders much guidance as to which they should attempt to resolve first if they opt for a piecemeal approach to immigration reform. However, Gallup has historically asked Americans to choose which of the two is more important. Prior to 2012, Americans tended to favor border security, in line with the higher percentages rating it as extremely important. Since then, Americans have tilted in the direction of addressing the status of illegal immigrants already in the U.S. Still, the gap is small, suggesting this is not an overwhelming preference, and that a strategy that attempts to deal with both issues may be preferable.

Forced Choice -- Main Focus of Immigration Legislation

If you had to choose, what should be the main focus of the U.S. government in dealing with the issue of illegal immigration -- [ROTATED: developing a plan for halting the flow of illegal immigrants into the U.S., (or) developing a plan to deal with immigrants who are currently in the U.S illegally]?

■ Securing U.S. borders   ▦ Dealing with illegal immigrants in U.S.

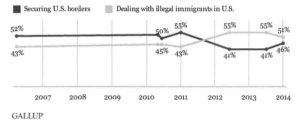

GALLUP

Republicans place a greater priority on securing U.S. borders, by 55% to 42%. Meanwhile, Democrats think the government should focus on resolving the status of illegal immigrants living in the U.S., 59% to 40%.

But Republicans are less likely to prioritize border security than in the past. In 2011, they favored border security by 67% to 32%—helping explain the recent shift in Americans' views about what the government should focus on.

Implications

In a broad sense, Americans do not assign as high a level of urgency to immigration reform as to other issues the government could work on, such as the economy, education, and healthcare policy. Still, they do think it is important for the government to take steps to deal with the two major challenges presented by the current immigration situation—keeping illegal immigrants out and resolving the legal status of the millions of illegal immigrants already living in the U.S.

In the past, Americans gave a higher priority to securing U.S. borders, but they now rate dealing with illegal immigrants already in the country as equally important, if not more so, when forced to choose. The relative importance of the two would matter less if Congress and the president were able to agree on comprehensive legislation that dealt with both issues. And that may still be a possibility in the future, but it seems unlikely to happen this year. Whether the chances improve next year may depend on which party gains seats in this fall's congressional elections.

Survey Methods

Results for this Gallup poll are based on telephone interviews conducted Feb. 6–9, 2014, with a random sample of 1,023 adults, aged 18 and older, living in all 50 U.S. states and the District of Columbia.

For results based on the total sample of national adults, the margin of sampling error is ±4 percentage points at the 95% confidence level.

February 18, 2014
AMERICANS' MIDEAST COUNTRY RATINGS SHOW LITTLE CHANGE
Israel alone is viewed highly favorably; Iran viewed least favorably

by Lydia Saad

PRINCETON, NJ—Americans' views of eight important Mideast countries were fairly stable over the past year, after a decade that saw shifts in several of their ratings. Roughly seven in 10 Americans continue to view Israel favorably—making it by far the most positively reviewed Mideast country of those Gallup tested. Just under half view Egypt and a third view Saudi Arabia favorably, while less than 20% have a favorable view of the remaining five, including Libya, the Palestinian Territories, Iraq, Syria, and Iran.

Recent Trend in Very Favorable/Mostly Favorable Views of Mideast Countries

Next, I'd like your overall opinion of some foreign countries. What is your overall opinion of [country]? Is it very favorable, mostly favorable, mostly unfavorable, or very unfavorable?

	Feb 1-3, 2010	Feb 2-5, 2011	Feb 2-5, 2012	Feb 7-10, 2013	Feb 6-9, 2014
	%	%	%	%	%
Israel	67	68	71	66	72
Egypt	58	40	47	40	45
Saudi Arabia	35	37	42	36	35
Libya	--	--	25	20	19
Palestinian Authority	20	19	19	15	19
Iraq	23	25	24	19	16
Syria	--	--	17	14	13
Iran	10	11	10	9	12

GALLUP

Positive views of Israel, Egypt, and the Palestinian Territories are up slightly from 2013; however, the shifts are not statistically significant and, in any case, current attitudes are similar to those found in 2012.

These results are based on Gallup's 2014 World Affairs poll, conducted Feb. 6–9. Gallup's annual World Affairs poll measures Americans' views on a variety of foreign policy issues, as well as the favorable and unfavorable images of a number of countries. The poll was initiated in 2001 and is updated each February.

At 13%, Syria's minimal U.S. favorable rating is similar to what it was a year ago, but down slightly from 2012, continuing a gradual slide in that country's image since 2005.

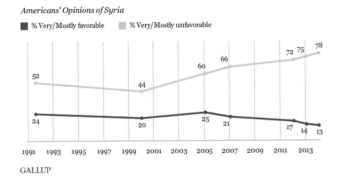

Americans' Opinions of Syria

As the U.S. and other world powers are engaged in high-level talks with Iran over its nuclear program, Gallup finds little change in the overall percentage viewing Iran favorably, remaining near 85%. However, there has been some decline in the percentage viewing Iran very unfavorably, now at 42%, down from 52% in 2012.

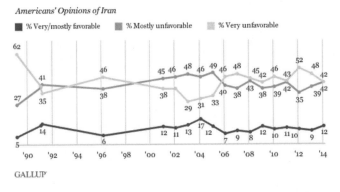

Americans' Opinions of Iran

Egypt's U.S. image had been quite positive from 1991 through 2009, but grew mixed around the time of the 2011 popular uprising in that country that drove President Hosni Mubarak from power. Egypt continued to experience tumult, including violent clashes between supporters and opponents of the democratically elected President Mohamed Morsi in December 2012, which may have been the reason for the spike in Americans' negative reviews of Egypt in 2013. Although Morsi was removed from power in July, the relative calm in Egypt in recent months may help explain the decline since last year in the percentage of Americans viewing it unfavorably.

Views of Libya and Iraq are mostly negative, but less so than in 2001. Americans' negativity toward Libya eased after its former leader, Moammar Gadhafi, took responsibility for the 1988 Pan Am bombing over Lockerbie, Scotland, and agreed to eliminate its weapons of mass destruction in 2003. Attitudes soured again after

Libyan rebels killed the U.S. ambassador and other officials in a raid on the U.S. consulate in Benghazi, Libya, in September 2012. But views have since stabilized at a level still better than before Gadhafi's capitulation.

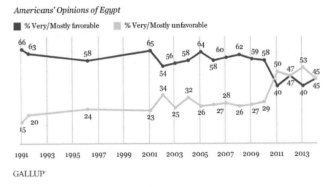

Americans' Opinions of Egypt

Americans' favorability toward Iraq has been gradually sinking since it hit a recent high in 2009, immediately after Iraqi governorate elections, and just two months after President George W. Bush signed a status-of-forces agreement that laid out a timeline for the withdrawal of U.S. forces. However, as with Libya, views continue to be more positive after the landmark event in the U.S.-Iraq relationship, which was the start of the U.S. invasion of Iraq.

Older Americans More Partial to Israel

The poll reveals modest generational differences in how the Mideast countries are viewed. Gallup finds young adults, those aged 18 to 34, holding somewhat more positive views of several of the Arab countries than do adults 55 and older. This applies to Libya, Egypt, Iran, Syria, Iraq, and the Palestinian Territories. At the same time, older Americans have more favorable views of Israel, while there is no difference by age in views of Saudi Arabia.

The two countries, Libya and Egypt, that experienced successful Arab Spring revolutions—inspired in part by frustrated young adults—are most likely to receive positive evaluations from the youngest Americans. In particular, Egypt, which has seen massive youth-led protests even after the Arab Spring and as recently as July of last year that helped force President Mohamed Morsi from power, is most favorably viewed by 18- to 34-year-old adults.

Americans' Views of Mideast Countries, by Age

% Very/Mostly favorable

	18 to 34	35 to 54	55+	Gap, 55+ vs. 18 to 34
	%	%	%	
Israel	64	72	81	+17
Saudi Arabia	35	35	37	+2
Palestinian Authority	24	18	16	-8
Iraq	20	20	9	-11
Syria	21	13	8	-13
Iran	20	11	6	-14
Egypt	57	40	42	-15
Libya	28	16	12	-16

Feb. 6-9, 2013

GALLUP'

Bottom Line

Events in the Middle East often trigger modest to significant changes in how Americans view the various countries. By the same token, a year absent major political or military incidents on the scale of the Arab Spring, the Iraq war, or the Benghazi incident produces stability in U.S. attitudes, as seen this past year. Gallup's 2014 World Affairs survey finds no significant changes in the mostly positive image Israel enjoys among Americans, or in the more negative images of several of the major Arab countries.

As is typical, Gallup finds some generational differences in the country ratings. The greatest of these is toward Israel—with adults 55 and older more positive by 17 percentage points than young Americans. The gap by age is nearly as wide for Libya, however, with young adults the more positive of the two groups.

Survey Methods

Results for this Gallup poll are based on telephone interviews conducted Feb. 6–9, 2014, with a random sample of 1,023 adults, aged 18 and older, living in all 50 U.S. states and the District of Columbia.

For results based on the total sample of national adults, the margin of sampling error is ±4 percentage points at the 95% confidence level.

February 19, 2014
MORE AMERICANS NOW VIEW AFGHANISTAN WAR AS A MISTAKE
Republicans most likely to say the war was not a mistake

by Frank Newport

PRINCETON, NJ—For the first time since the U.S. initially became involved in Afghanistan in 2001, Americans are as likely to say U.S. military involvement there was a mistake as to say it was not.

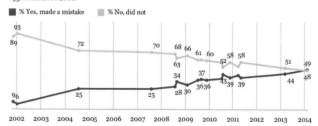

Looking back, do you think the United States made a mistake sending troops to fight in Afghanistan in 2001?

■ % Yes, made a mistake   % No, did not

2001–2011 question wording: Thinking now about U.S. military action in Afghanistan that began in October 2001, do you think the United States made a mistake in sending military forces to Afghanistan, or not?

GALLUP

Gallup first asked Americans about U.S. intervention in Afghanistan in November 2001, just after the U.S. sent armed forces into that country in an effort to retaliate against those who had harbored the al Qaeda terrorists responsible for the 9/11 attacks. At that point, fewer than one in 10 Americans said U.S. involvement there was a mistake—the most positive assessment of any war since Gallup first asked the "mistake" question during the Korean War in 1950. Clearly, in the turbulent atmosphere and general "rally effect"

environment that followed 9/11, Americans were overwhelmingly supportive of the decision to send the U.S. military to Afghanistan.

Americans' perceptions that U.S. involvement in Afghanistan was a mistake rose as the war continued, although there were some ups and downs over the years. The "mistake" percentage reached 25% in 2004, and surpassed 30% for the first time in 2008, and 40% in 2010. Now, in Gallup's Feb. 6–9, 2014, World Affairs survey, conducted some 12 years and four months after action in Afghanistan began, Americans' views essentially split down the middle, with 49% saying involvement there was a mistake and 48% saying it was not.

Still, the more than 12-year span during which less than half of Americans thought the U.S. made a mistake in entering Afghanistan has been remarkably long, relative to past U.S. interventions.

- Although only one in five Americans in the late summer of 1950 initially thought U.S. involvement in Korea was a mistake, less than six months later—after the Chinese Communists had poured over the Yalu River into North Korea, turning the war into a bloody stalemate—attitudes shifted dramatically: 49% said U.S. involvement was a mistake, while 38% said it was not.
- Gallup first asked Americans about the Vietnam War in late August/early September 1965, with 24% saying military involvement there was a mistake. A little more than two years later, in October 1967, as U.S. troop presence and casualties in that war escalated rapidly, 47% viewed involvement there as a mistake, compared with 44% who did not.
- And it took just a year and three months from the March 2003 start of the Iraq war for a plurality of Americans to first say involvement there was a mistake, although opinions about that war fluctuated until late 2005, after which they were more consistently negative.

Four Wars: Timeline Until Plurality Said War Was a Mistake

	Mistake to be involved militarily	Not a mistake
	%	%
AFGHANISTAN		
Nov 8–11, 2001*	9	89
Feb 6–9, 2014**	49	48
IRAQ		
Mar 24–25, 2003*	23	75
Jun 21–23, 2004**	54	44
VIETNAM		
Aug 27–Sep 1, 1965*	24	60
Oct 6–11, 1967**	47	44
KOREA		
Aug 20–25, 1950*	20	65
Jan 1–5, 1951**	49	38

* First survey asking if military involvement was a mistake
** First survey in which a plurality said military involvement was a mistake

GALLUP

Republicans Remain Less Likely to See Afghanistan as a Mistake

Republicans and independents who lean Republican are significantly less likely than Democrats and Democratic leaners to say the war in Afghanistan was a mistake. U.S. involvement in Afghanistan began under a Republican president, George W. Bush, but it has continued under Barack Obama, a Democratic president. Therefore, Republicans' higher levels of support may be related to a Republican president's initiation of the war, or an ideological inclination to support military involvement.

Looking back, do you think the United States made a mistake sending troops to fight in Afghanistan in 2001?

By party ID

	Yes, a mistake %	No, not a mistake %
Republicans/Republican leaners	36	62
Democrats/Democratic leaners	59	40

Feb. 6-9, 2014

GALLUP

Implications

Afghanistan has become America's longest war, stretching over 12 years since U.S. military forces were first sent in 2001, with well over 35,000 troops still there. Americans were initially more supportive of involvement in Afghanistan than they were for any recent major military intervention. They also maintained a generally supportive posture toward U.S. involvement in Afghanistan for a longer period of time than was the case for other wars. But Americans' waning patience with the conflict has finally reached the point at which Americans are as likely to say the war was a mistake as to say it was not.

The Obama administration plans to draw down the number of troops in Afghanistan significantly by the end of this year. Once that happens, and the war essentially ends, Americans' assessments of whether intervention was a mistake will largely depend on the political course Afghanistan takes, including whether terrorist cells are able to regroup there.

Gallup research conducted in Afghanistan shows that Afghans rate their lives as poorly on several dimensions as residents of any country in the world. These findings may suggest that U.S. involvement in that country was not a success from the Afghan people's perspective, although it is not clear what Afghans' attitudes were before the war began.

Survey Methods

Results for this Gallup poll are based on telephone interviews conducted Feb. 6–9, 2014, with a random sample of 1,023 adults, aged 18 and older, living in all 50 U.S. states and the District of Columbia.

For results based on the total sample of national adults, the margin of sampling error is ±4 percentage points at the 95% confidence level.

February 19, 2014
NORTH KOREA LEAST FAVORABLE AMONG NATIONS
Iran no longer least favorable in Americans' eyes

by Joy Wilke

PRINCETON, NJ—Americans rate North Korea the least favorably of 22 countries rated in Gallup's 2014 World Affairs poll, with 11%

having a favorable opinion of the country. North Korea took over the bottom spot from Iran, whose rating rose from 9% to 12% this year. North Korea's favorability has not exceeded 15% since 2002, consistently making it one of the lowest rated. But this is the first time since 2004 that it has been alone in last place.

Americans' Favorability Rating of North Korea Since 2000

Next, I'd like your overall opinion of some foreign countries. What is your overall opinion of North Korea? Is it very favorable, mostly favorable, mostly unfavorable, or very unfavorable?

% Very/mostly favorable

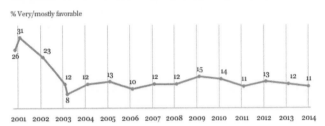

GALLUP

North Korea's position at the bottom of the list is mainly attributable to a slight improvement in Americans' opinions of Iran. Iran had been the worst-rated country since 2004. North Korea now immediately trails Afghanistan (14%), Syria (13%), and Iran (12%).

The current data come from the 2014 update of Gallup's annual World Affairs survey, conducted Feb. 6–9. The poll was conducted shortly before the United Nations announced the results of a year-long study concluding that North Korea has committed crimes against humanity, which could lead to the arrest of the North Korean leader Kim Jong-un, as well as drive Americans' perceptions of the country even lower. Americans' opinions of the country fell sharply in 2002, when President George W. Bush labeled the country a member of the "axis of evil" in his State of the Union Address, and have not recovered.

In contrast, Americans have much more positive attitudes toward South Korea, with 64% viewing the country favorably. Americans' views of South Korea have steadily grown more positive since its initial sub-50% favorable rating in 2001.

Americans' Favorability Rating of South Korea Since 2000

Next, I'd like your overall opinion of some foreign countries. What is your overall opinion of North Korea? Is it very favorable, mostly favorable, mostly unfavorable, or very unfavorable?

%Very/mostly favorable

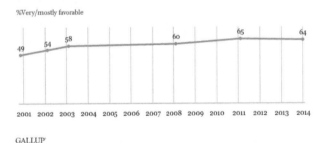

GALLUP

Majority View Conflict Between North and South as a Critical U.S. Threat

The conflict between North and South Korea escalated last year after North Korea's nuclear tests prompted U.N. condemnation and the country's withdrawal from all non-aggression pacts with South

Korea. More recently, the two sides have been talking, and while tensions flared over the South's refusal to cancel joint military exercises with the U.S., negotiators agreed Friday to go forward with a cross-border reunion of 200 people.

A majority of Americans, 53%, see the conflict between North and South Korea as a "critical threat" to the "vital interests of the U.S. in the next 10 years." Another 36% see the conflict as an important, but not critical threat, while 8% see it as not an important threat.

Republicans and Democrats are more likely than independents to consider the conflict as a critical threat. Conservatives are slightly more likely than moderates and liberals to view the conflict as critical.

Americans' Perceptions of the Threat of the Conflict Between North and South Korea

Next, I am going to read you a list of possible threats to the vital interests of the United States in the next 10 years. For each one, please tell me if you see this as a critical threat, an important but not critical threat, or not an important threat at all. How about the conflict between North and South Korea?

	Critical threat	Important but not critical threat	Not an important threat at all
	%	%	%
All adults	53	36	8
Republicans	57	34	7
Independents	47	38	10
Democrats	59	34	7
Conservatives	58	30	7
Moderates	51	40	8
Liberals	51	40	7

Feb. 6-9, 2014

GALLUP

Bottom Line

Recent coverage of North Korea in the American press has ranged from news of last year's nuclear threats and political posturing to the unusual friendship between former NBA star Dennis Rodman and Kim Jong-un, events that did nothing to improve the country's image in the American public's eyes. Americans have had an overwhelmingly unfavorable view of North Korea for many years. Even before Bush included North Korea in the "axis of evil" in 2002, roughly six in 10 Americans viewed the country unfavorably. However, by 2003, North Korea's U.S. image had soured further, and has never recovered. Today, with tensions high between North and South Korea, Americans see the conflict as a threat to vital U.S. interests.

The report of the U.N. panel, which concluded that human rights abuses have occurred in North Korea, has brought the country into the international spotlight once again, and could push its image in the U.S. even lower. Though with about one in 10 Americans giving the country a favorable rating, there is not much farther for it to fall.

Survey Methods

Results for this Gallup poll are based on telephone interviews conducted Feb. 6–9, 2014, with a random sample of 1,023 adults, aged 18 and older, living in all 50 U.S. states and the District of Columbia.

For results based on the total sample of national adults, the margin of sampling error is ±4 percentage points at the 95% confidence level.

February 20, 2014
NORTH DAKOTA NO. 1 IN WELL-BEING, WEST VIRGINIA STILL LAST
Well-being has steadily increased in 11 states since 2010

by Dan Witters

WASHINGTON, D.C.—North Dakota residents had the highest well-being in the nation in 2013, according to the Gallup-Healthways Well-Being Index. South Dakota trailed its northern neighbor in second place, with its highest score in six years of measurement. Hawaii held the top spot for the previous four years, but fell slightly last year. West Virginia and Kentucky had the two lowest well-being scores, for the fifth year in a row.

Well-Being: Top 10 States in 2013

State	Well-Being Index score
North Dakota	70.4
South Dakota	70.0
Nebraska	69.7
Minnesota	69.7
Montana	69.3
Vermont	69.1
Colorado	68.9
Hawaii	68.4
Washington	68.3
Iowa	68.2

January-December 2013
Gallup-Healthways Well-Being Index

GALLUP

Well-Being: Bottom 10 States in 2013

State	Well-Being Index score
West Virginia	61.4
Kentucky	63.0
Mississippi	63.7
Alabama	64.1
Ohio	64.2
Arkansas	64.3
Tennessee	64.3
Missouri	64.5
Oklahoma	64.7
Louisiana	64.9

January-December 2013
Gallup-Healthways Well-Being Index

GALLUP

North Dakota rejoined the top 10 well-being states in 2013 after being among that group from 2009 to 2011. South Dakota was among the top 10 in well-being for the first time since 2010, while Washington last appeared in 2008.

These state-level data are based on more than 178,000 interviews with American adults across all 50 states, conducted from January–December 2013. Gallup and Healthways started tracking state-level well-being in 2008. The Gallup-Healthways Well-Being Index score for the nation and for each state is an average of six sub-indexes, which individually examine life evaluation, emotional health, work environment, physical health, healthy behaviors, and access to basic necessities.

The Well-Being Index is calculated on a scale of 0 to 100, where a score of 100 represents ideal well-being. Well-Being Index scores among states varied within a nine-point range in 2013. The Well-Being Index score for the nation in 2013 dipped to 66.2 from 66.7 in 2012, and matches the previous low, measured in 2011.

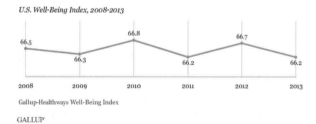

U.S. Well-Being Index, 2008-2013

66.5 — 66.3 — 66.8 — 66.2 — 66.7 — 66.2

2008   2009   2010   2011   2012   2013

Gallup-Healthways Well-Being Index

GALLUP

Based on U.S. Census Bureau regions, Midwestern and Western states earned nine of the 10 highest well-being scores in 2013, while Southern states had eight of the 10 lowest well-being scores. The regional pattern of well-being is similar to previous years.

West Virginia at the Bottom on Five Out of Six Key Areas of Well-Being

In addition to North Dakota's having the highest overall Well-Being Index score, it was the top state on two of the six well-being sub-indexes: Work Environment and Physical Health. At the opposite end of the spectrum was West Virginia, which ranked last on all sub-indexes except Work Environment.

Nebraska topped all other states on the Life Evaluation Index, with a score that was 17 points higher than West Virginia's. Alaska boasted the highest Emotional Health Index score, while Vermont led all states in Healthy Behaviors for the second straight year. Massachusetts had the best score on the Basic Access Index for the fourth straight year, which is partially a result of having the highest percentage of residents with health insurance in the nation.

States With the Highest and Lowest Scores on the Well-Being Sub-Indexes

Well-Being sub-index	Highest sub-index	Lowest sub-index
Life Evaluation	Nebraska (56.3)	West Virginia (39.3)
Emotional Health	Alaska (82.9)	West Virginia (73.8)
Work Environment	North Dakota (60.7)	Mississippi (41.0)
Physical Health	North Dakota (79.6)	West Virginia (68.7)
Healthy Behaviors	Vermont (71.7)	West Virginia (58.4)
Basic Access	Massachusetts (86.9)	West Virginia (77.8)

Gallup-Healthways Well-Being Index, 2013

GALLUP

Eleven States' Well-Being Index Scores Have Improved Steadily Since 2010

Well-being has been fairly stable nationally since 2008. However, since 2010, the first full year after the Great Recession officially ended, 11 states' well-being scores have shown year-over-year improvement, with the largest gains seen in Nevada, Montana, Vermont, Nebraska, Iowa, and Maine. Four of these states—Montana, Vermont, Nebraska, and Iowa—also were among the top 10 well-being states in 2012 and 2013, making their continued improvement notable given their already high Well-Being Index scores.

States Showing Improvement Each Year Since 2010, and Whether They Finished in the Top 10 in Well-Being in 2012 and 2013

State	Total improvement from 2010 to 2013	Top 10 in 2012 and 2013?
Nevada	+2.4 points	No
Montana	+2.0	Yes
Vermont	+2.0	Yes
Nebraska	+1.9	Yes
Iowa	+1.3	Yes
Maine	+1.3	No
Arizona	+1.0	No
Wisconsin	+1.0	No
Mississippi	+0.7	No
Texas	+0.6	No
California	+0.6	No

Gallup-Healthways Well-Being Index

GALLUP

Implications

Overall well-being in the U.S. and within states has been fairly steady since 2008, although the national Well-Being Index score fell in 2013. The nation's well-being declined despite improvement in economic confidence in most states. Still, steady growth in 11 states' well-being scores since 2010 illustrates that sustained improvements in well-being are possible regardless of national trends. Four states in particular—Montana, Vermont, Nebraska, and Iowa—demonstrate that steady progress is possible, even among the top 10 well-being states.

Gallup's research has shown that people take a variety of factors into account when evaluating their well-being. Job creation, for example, is related to well-being; Gallup's job creation rankings for 2013 are correlated with the well-being rankings. The 2013 Payroll to Population (P2P) state rankings are also correlated with top and bottom well-being states. North Dakota, which has benefited economically from the surge in its oil industry, was the top state in both job creation and P2P in 2013. And other behavioral factors, such as smoking rates, generally line up with well-being at the state level as well.

Regardless of metrics such as employment and job creation, all states rely on strong leadership to spearhead their well-being efforts. Iowa's Healthiest State Initiative, for example, is a privately led, government-supported program designed to improve Iowa's well-being, and has received Gov. Terry Branstad's support since its inception. This sort of steady advocacy for higher well-being can serve as a positive example for other leaders to follow as states try to improve their residents' well-being in 2014.

Survey Methods

Results are based on telephone interviews conducted as part of the Gallup-Healthways Well-Being Index survey Jan. 2–Dec. 29, 2013, with a random sample of 178,072 adults, aged 18 and older, living in all 50 U.S. states and the District of Columbia.

For results based on the total sample of national adults, the margin of sampling error is ±1 percentage point at the 95% confidence level.

The margin of sampling error for most states is ±1 to ±2 percentage points, but is as high as ±4 points for states with smaller populations, such as Wyoming, North Dakota, South Dakota, Delaware, and Hawaii.

February 20, 2014
AMERICANS VIEW CHINA MOSTLY UNFAVORABLY
A majority again rate China as world's leading economic power

by Andrew Dugan

WASHINGTON, D.C.—Despite the announcement of historic reforms late last year that would shift China's economy to a more consumer-driven model, Americans still see China in the same, mostly unfavorable, way they did in early 2013. Forty-three percent of U.S. adults say they have a very or mostly favorable opinion of China, while 53% see it very or mostly unfavorably.

These results come from the Feb. 6–9 Gallup World Affairs poll.

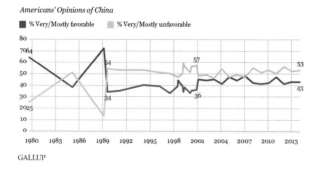

Americans' Opinions of China

■ % Very/Mostly favorable   ■ % Very/Mostly unfavorable

GALLUP

Most analysts expect China to be the United States' foremost strategic and economic rival in the decades to come. That is a dramatic shift from 1979, the first year Gallup asked this question, when China's GDP was not even one-tenth of U.S. GDP. That year, 64% of Americans saw China favorably. Impressions fluctuated strongly between positive and negative until the televised crackdown on Tiananmen Square protests in June 1989. Americans' favorable ratings of China plummeted to 34% late that year—the lowest to date at that time. Notably, since China joined the World Trade Organization in 2001 and trade with the U.S. expanded dramatically, China's favorable rating has fluctuated in a narrow range between 41% and 48%.

Majority Rate China as Leading Economic Power

The U.S. still boasts a GDP almost twice that of China, but the majority of Americans (52%) believe China is the world's leading economic power. Less than one-third (31%) believe the U.S. is the leading economic power, while another 16% choose Japan, India, Russia, or the European Union.

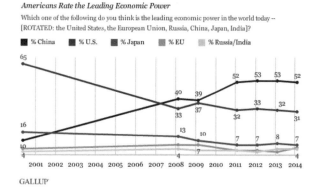

Americans Rate the Leading Economic Power

Which one of the following do you think is the leading economic power in the world today -- [ROTATED: the United States, the European Union, Russia, China, Japan, India]?

■ % China   ■ % U.S.   ■ % Japan   ■ % EU   ■ % Russia/India

GALLUP

Attitudes on this question have not changed since 2011, but longer term, belief that China is the world's leading economic power has skyrocketed since 2000. Then, just one in 10 Americans named China as the superior economic power; now, a reliable majority do. This is likely attributable to China's impressive economic performance over the last 13 years—its economy often growing by double digits over this time span—and the United States' often underwhelming, crisis-ridden economy.

China's Economic and Military Power Concerns Americans

Though Gallup last year found that most Americans regard China as more friend than foe, many Americans regard China's military strength and economic power as a threat to the vital interests of the

U.S. Americans are more likely to perceive China's economy (52%) than its military (46%) as a "critical" threat to U.S. vital interests over the next 10 years, suggesting that, for now, U.S. residents see China's growing influence through more of an economic lens.

China's Power as a Threat to U.S. Vital Interests

Next, I am going to read you a list of possible threats to the vital interests of the United States in the next 10 years. For each one, please tell me if you see this as a critical threat, an important but not critical threat, or not an important threat at all.

	Critical %	Important but not critical %	Not important %	No opinion %
The economic power of China	52	36	10	2
The military power of China	46	41	11	2

Feb. 6-9, 2014

GALLUP

Still, a plurality (46%) do see China's military—which has the world's largest standing army, though its defense budget is less than one-fifth that of the U.S.—as a critical threat, down slightly from 51% last year, but elevated from the 39% who held this view the first time Gallup asked this question, in 2004. Another 41% of Americans currently say China's military is "an important but not critical" threat to U.S. vital interests.

Bottom Line

John F. Kennedy in a 1959 speech noted that "When written in Chinese, the word 'crisis' is composed of two characters—one represents danger and one represents opportunity." Americans clearly see the potential for danger in China, in its looming economic and military power.

At the same time, China may also represent an opportunity. Unfavorable opinions of China have softened from lows observed during Tiananmen Square and other tense moments in Sino-American relations. Most Americans, as has largely been the case since 2008, see China as the world's leading economic power, a tectonic image shift for a country once regarded as poor. And despite their generally unfavorable views of China, more Americans see China as a friend or an ally, rather than an enemy. How American public opinion shifts with regard to this rising Asian power will continue to measure which possibility—opportunity or danger—Americans believe is more the reality.

Survey Methods

Results for this Gallup poll are based on telephone interviews conducted Feb. 6–9, 2014, with a random sample of 1,023 adults, aged 18 and older, living in all 50 U.S. states and the District of Columbia.

For results based on the total sample of national adults, the margin of sampling error is ±4 percentage points at the 95% confidence level.

February 20, 2014
FAR FEWER AMERICANS NOW SAY
IRAN IS NO. 1 U.S. ENEMY
Nuclear agreements may be fueling change

by Jeffrey M. Jones

PRINCETON, NJ—Half as many Americans view Iran as the United States' greatest enemy today as did two years ago. As a result, China now edges out Iran and North Korea atop the list.

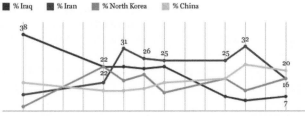

What one country anywhere in the world do you consider to be the United States' greatest enemy today? [OPEN-ENDED]

■ % Iraq ■ % Iran ▨ % North Korea ▨ % China

GALLUP

Americans' Perceptions of Greatest U.S. Enemy, by Age and Party ID

	China	North Korea	Iran
	%	%	%
AGE			
18 to 34 years	21	20	9
35 to 54 years	19	16	18
55+ years	21	13	20
PARTY ID			
Republicans	19	16	20
Independents	23	11	16
Democrats	17	24	12

Feb. 6-9, 2014

GALLUP

After the top three countries, 9% of Americans mention Russia, 7% name Iraq, 5% Afghanistan, and 3% Syria.

Gallup first asked this open-ended question in 2001, and opinions have shifted over that time. In the 2001 survey—10 years after the Persian Gulf War but before the 2003 Iraq war began—Americans named Iraq as the greatest U.S. enemy by a large margin.

By 2005, with the U.S. nearly two years into the Iraq war, Iraq and North Korea tied as the greatest enemy, with 22% mentioning each country. The next year, Iran surged to the top of the list, with 31% of all mentions, and it remained the most often cited enemy until this year.

The drop in mentions of Iran as the greatest enemy in this year's poll has been accompanied by increases in the percentages mentioning North Korea (from 10% in 2012 to 16%), Russia (from 2% to 9%), and Syria (from less than 1% to 3%). The percentage mentioning China, however, has stayed virtually the same. Thus, China now tops the list mainly because Americans' views on the nation's enemies are more divided among several countries rather than focused on one dominant country, as in recent years.

Iran reached an agreement last November with several of the world's largest nations, including the United States, to limit its nuclear activity. Those nations in return agreed to ease some of the sanctions on Iran. That agreement may be the main reason the American public is taking a less antagonistic view of Iran.

This week, Iran and the same countries agreed to a framework for continued negotiations toward a comprehensive agreement on Iran's nuclear capabilities.

Importantly, although Americans are less likely to regard Iran as the greatest U.S. enemy, their basic favorable and unfavorable opinions of Iran have improved only slightly this year, and remain overwhelmingly negative.

Key Subgroups' Perceptions of the Nation's Greatest Enemy Are Similar

Americans in all major subgroups are less likely now than in 2012 to name Iran as the United States' greatest enemy. Groups that were among the most likely to view Iran as the top enemy, such as men, older Americans, and college graduates, tend to show the greatest declines.

There are not major differences by subgroup in current perceptions of the greatest U.S. enemy. Older Americans and Republicans are a bit more likely than younger Americans and Democrats to name Iran as the top enemy. In turn, younger Americans and Democrats more commonly view North Korea as the No.1 enemy.

Implications

Americans' perceptions of the United States' greatest enemy have varied over time, usually in response to developments on the world stage. As such, the sharp drop in their likelihood of naming Iran as the United States' top enemy is probably tied to Iran's continued willingness to agree to international limitations on its nuclear capabilities.

However, Iran's reluctance to agree to limitations in the past has made U.S. and world leaders cautious about whether Iran will uphold its end of any agreement. Indeed, the Senate is preparing a measure to impose new sanctions on Iran if it does not curtail its nuclear program.

With fewer Americans currently regarding Iran as the greatest enemy, China now tops the list, ranking just slightly ahead of Iran and North Korea. Americans in general view China much more positively than Iran, though on balance, still negatively. They may regard China's emerging economic power to be as threatening, if not more so, than the potential military threats from Iran and North Korea.

Survey Methods

Results for this Gallup poll are based on telephone interviews conducted Feb. 6–9, 2014, with a random sample of 1,023 adults, aged 18 and older, living in all 50 U.S. states and the District of Columbia.

For results based on the total sample of national adults, the margin of sampling error is ±4 percentage points at the 95% confidence level.

February 21, 2014
HILLARY CLINTON MAINTAINS
POSITIVE IMAGE IN U.S.
American public's opinion of Vice President Joe Biden is mixed

by Art Swift

WASHINGTON, D.C.—A clear majority of Americans, 59%, still view Hillary Clinton favorably a year after she left her post as secretary of state. Clinton's current rating is noticeably lower than the 64% she averaged while serving in President Barack Obama's cabinet.

Favorability Ratings of Hillary Clinton

■ % Favorable ░ % Unfavorable

GALLUP

The last time she had a higher unfavorable than favorable rating in the U.S. was in February 2008, when she was running for the Democratic presidential nomination against Obama. The latest findings come from a Gallup poll conducted Feb. 6–9.

Clinton, an enduring figure on the U.S. political stage, has seen her favorability ratings rise and fall since she was introduced to the American public during Bill Clinton's 1992 presidential campaign. The first time Gallup asked Americans about her, in March 1992, 39% viewed her favorably, 26% unfavorably, and 35% either did not know who she was or had no opinion of the then-first lady of Arkansas. Since then, Hillary Clinton's favorability peaked at 67% in late 1998, just after her husband was impeached by the House of Representatives during the Monica Lewinsky scandal, and her rating remained high through most of 1999.

During her time as a U.S. senator, 2001–2009, her favorability rating leveled off, fluctuating within the 40% and 50% range. Clinton enjoyed a long period of high favorable ratings during her time as secretary of state, staying above 60% during her entire time in Obama's cabinet. Clinton dipped below 60% last June, several months after she left public life, but her ratings remain high.

Americans Still Divided in Their Opinions of Vice President Biden

Joe Biden's image, on the other hand, is not as positive as Hillary Clinton's. Currently, 46% of Americans have a favorable image of the vice president, while 42% view him unfavorably. Biden's favorability exceeded 50% from October 2008 to January 2009, during the end of his successful campaign with Obama and just prior to his inauguration into office. Biden's favorability has been in the 40% range for the entirety of his time as vice president, with unfavorability ratings in the same range.

Favorability Ratings of Joe Biden

■ % Favorable ░ % Unfavorable

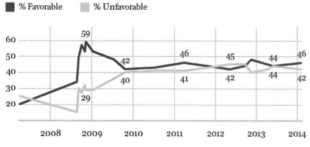

GALLUP

While Gallup has been asking about Clinton since 1992, it has been polling about Biden only since 2007, as he was preparing for the Democratic primary race the next year. The longtime senator from Delaware has been a fixture in public life, however, since 1972, when he was elected to the U.S. Senate just shy of his 30th birthday.

Implications

While the 2016 presidential election is more than 2 ½ years away, it is possible that the battle for the Democratic nomination will begin in earnest after the midterm elections this November. Clinton and Biden, two Democratic Party luminaries who have run for president before, are leading contenders, although both have yet to declare their candidacy.

It is also possible that the race will start later because of their high name recognition with the American public. This survey did not measure a head-to-head match-up or Americans' views on their potential candidacies, but these results show that Americans have long had a more positive image of Clinton than of Biden. Biden's favorables have consistently trailed those of his boss, Obama, while roughly 10% to 15% of Americans still have not heard of or have no opinion of the vice president. Conversely, Clinton was consistently a popular member of Obama's cabinet, with higher favorable ratings than the president for all of the time she served in his administration.

Survey Methods

Results for this Gallup poll are based on telephone interviews conducted Feb. 6–9, 2014, with a random sample of 1,023 adults, aged 18 and older, living in all 50 U.S. states and the District of Columbia.

For results based on the total sample of national adults, the margin of sampling error is ±4 percentage points at the 95% confidence level.

February 21, 2014
AMERICANS REMAIN POSITIVE ABOUT FOREIGN TRADE
Views on trade currently differ by education but not by party

by Lydia Saad

PRINCETON, NJ—After years of being generally skeptical about foreign trade, or at best divided over it, Americans now firmly view trade as a benefit to the U.S. economy. Similar to last year, 54% of Americans say trade represents an opportunity for economic growth through increased U.S. exports, while 38% consider it a threat to the economy from foreign imports.

What Americans Think Foreign Trade Means for the Country

What do you think foreign trade means for America? Do you see foreign trade more as -- an opportunity for economic growth through increased U.S. exports or a threat to the economy from foreign imports?

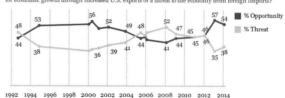

GALLUP

The latest findings are based on Gallup's 2014 World Affairs survey, conducted Feb. 6–9 with 1,023 U.S. adults.

North American leaders gathered this week to mark the 20th anniversary of the North American Free Trade Agreement (NAFTA) and discuss further commercial integration and expansion into the Asia-Pacific region. The Obama administration has been working to reach two major new free trade deals with Europe and 11 Pacific-facing countries, although Vice President Joe Biden recently indicated these efforts may be on hold because Senate Democrats do not support it.

Americans' perceptions of foreign trade may partly stem from their confidence in the U.S. economy. Public skepticism about foreign trade peaked in 2008, when 52% saw it mainly as a threat whereas 41% saw it as an opportunity. At the same time, the Gallup Economic Confidence Index was highly negative, at −32. Americans were evenly divided on trade for the next few years, through 2012, as economic confidence remained quite negative. Then, in 2013, along with an uptick in confidence, Americans turned sharply positive about trade. And that pattern holds today.

Recent Trends in Positive Views of Trade vs. Gallup Economic Confidence Index

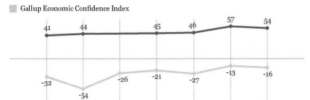

Views on foreign trade are based on Gallup World Affairs survey, conducted each February. Gallup Economic Confidence Index scores are monthly averages for January of each year.

GALLUP

Another factor may be the country's narrowing trade deficit. In 2008, when a comparatively low percentage of Americans saw foreign trade as an opportunity (41%), the U.S. was running a seasonally adjusted trade deficit of $816 billion. In 2013, the deficit was a much lower $688 billion.

Partisan Gaps on Trade Have Varied by President

Current public attitudes about trade mirror those Gallup recorded in the first decade after NAFTA went into effect in 1994, after a robust debate in Congress and a narrow House vote in favor of the measure. President Bill Clinton strongly endorsed and encouraged ratification of the agreement, but there were also strong proponents and detractors on both sides of the political aisle. In particular, Clinton had to rely on more Republican than Democratic votes to get the measure through Congress.

Shortly before President George H. W. Bush signed the NAFTA agreement in 1992, Republicans were significantly more likely than Democrats to see foreign trade as an opportunity: 49% vs. 36%. However, by 1994, with Clinton backing the measure and reaching a side agreement meant to add some protections for American workers, Democrats' support grew to nearly match Republicans': 58% of Republicans and 54% of Democrats called foreign trade an opportunity.

The partisan gap on foreign trade remained narrow at the start of George W. Bush's presidency, but it widened as his term progressed,

possibly indicating that Democrats have greater fear of foreign trade policies under Republican leadership. By 2008, as the country faced mounting economic problems, support for foreign trade waned among Republicans, falling to nearly match Democrats' lower support. Since then, and throughout Barack Obama's presidency, Democrats and Republicans have expressed nearly identical support for foreign trade as an opportunity, with agreement surging among both parties, as well as among independents, in 2013, and remaining high this year.

View Foreign Trade Mainly as an Opportunity for the U.S. -- by Party ID

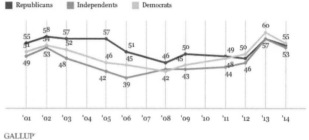

Trade More of a Socioeconomic Than a Partisan Issue

Gallup trends since 2001 find Americans' perceptions of foreign trade far more divided along educational lines than by political party. College graduates and those with postgraduate education are significantly more likely to see foreign trade as an opportunity for the U.S. than are those with no college or even some college education.

View Foreign Trade Mainly as an Opportunity for the U.S. -- by Education

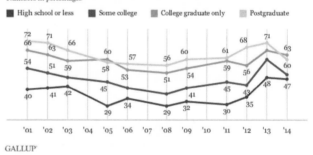

Bottom Line

As the Obama administration strives to reach watershed free trade agreements with the European Union and a collection of Pacific Ocean–facing nations forming a new bloc known as the Trans-Pacific Partnership, Americans view foreign trade positively today, mainly seeing it as an opportunity for economic growth through exports rather than as a threat to the economy through imports. This positive outlook is similar to what Gallup found in 2013, but represents a sharp reversal of the more mixed, or even negative, view Americans had of trade during the prior eight years.

The change likely stems from the increase in Americans' confidence in the economy since the depths of the 2008–2009 recession. It may also reflect Democrats' greater confidence in foreign trade when a Democrat is in the White House. Meanwhile, Americans with lower education—a group most likely to feel their livelihood is at risk when U.S. manufacturing dries up—remain far more skeptical of the merits of foreign trade than their more educated counterparts.

Results for this Gallup poll are based on telephone interviews conducted Feb. 6–9, 2014, with a random sample of 1,023 adults, aged 18 and older, living in all 50 U.S. states and the District of Columbia.

For results based on the total sample of national adults, the margin of sampling error is ±4 percentage points at the 95% confidence level.

February 24, 2014

FEWER AMERICANS THINK OBAMA RESPECTED ON WORLD STAGE

Slim majority still think world views U.S. favorably

by Jeffrey M. Jones

PRINCETON, NJ—For the first time, more Americans think President Barack Obama is not respected by other world leaders than believe he is. Americans' opinions have shifted dramatically in the past year, after being relatively stable from 2010 to 2013.

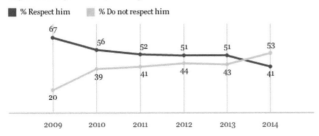

Americans' Perceptions of President Obama's World Standing

Do you think leaders of other countries around the world have respect for Barack Obama, or do you think they don't have much respect for him?

■ % Respect him   ▨ % Do not respect him

GALLUP

The results are based on Gallup's annual World Affairs poll, conducted Feb. 6–9. Although opinions about a president's perceived world standing often track with his job approval rating, a majority of Americans still thought world leaders respected Obama in 2010 and 2011, when his job approval was similar to what it is now. Thus, the recent decline may be more tied to specific international matters from the past year, such as the revelation the U.S. was listening in on foreign leaders' phone calls, the situation in Syria, increased tensions with Russia, and an uneasy relationship between Obama and Israeli Prime Minister Benjamin Netanyahu.

Though the current data represent a personal low for Obama, they are not the lowest Gallup has measured since the question was first asked in 1994. That was reached in 2007, when 21% of Americans thought world leaders respected President George W. Bush. President Bill Clinton's ratings in 1994 and 2000 were similar to Obama's current ratings.

Democrats and independents are mainly responsible for the slide in Obama's ratings. Independents now, by a wide margin, believe world leaders do not respect Obama. Republicans were already largely convinced world leaders don't respect the president.

Changes in Perceptions of President Obama's World Standing, by Political Party

Do you think leaders of other countries around the world have respect for Barack Obama, or do you think they don't have much respect for him?

	% Respect him	% Do not respect him
DEMOCRATS		
2013	80	14
2014	69	28
Change (pct. pts.)	-11	+14
INDEPENDENTS		
2013	49	45
2014	34	57
Change (pct. pts.)	-15	+12
REPUBLICANS		
2013	21	74
2014	19	77
Change (pct. pts.)	-2	+3

GALLUP

Slim Majority Still Thinks U.S. Viewed Favorably

At the same time that Americans think other world leaders view Obama more negatively, Americans still think the international community views the U.S. as a country favorably (51%) rather than unfavorably (47%).

Americans have been more optimistic about the United States' worldwide image since 2010 than they were from 2005 to 2009, years when more thought the world viewed the U.S. unfavorably than favorably. Americans were much more likely to think the rest of the world viewed the U.S. favorably in the early 2000s. Opinions began to change in the lead-up to the 2003 Iraq war.

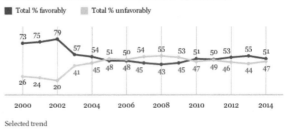

Americans' Perceptions of How U.S. Rates in the Eyes of the World

In general, how do you think the United States rates in the eyes of the world -- very favorably, somewhat favorably, somewhat unfavorably, or very unfavorably?

■ Total % favorably   ▨ Total % unfavorably

Selected trend

GALLUP

Americans Still Dissatisfied With U.S. Position in the World

Sixty-one percent of Americans are dissatisfied, and 37% are satisfied, with the position of the United States in the world today. That level of dissatisfaction has generally persisted since 2007. The last time a majority of Americans were satisfied was in 2003, just after the U.S. toppled Saddam Hussein's regime in Iraq. By 2004, once it was clear the U.S. would be in a long-term engagement in Iraq, a majority became dissatisfied.

Implications

Americans' perceptions of how other nations view the U.S. have not changed in the past year, but their opinions of how world leaders view the president have. Now, Americans believe other world leaders generally do not respect Obama. This could be related to a series of tense moments in the past year between Obama and prominent foreign leaders, many of whom are close U.S. allies.

Satisfaction With United States' Position in the World

On the whole, would you say that you are satisfied or dissatisfied with the position of the United States in the world today?

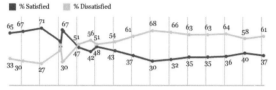

■ % Satisfied   ░ % Dissatisfied

Trend since 2000

GALLUP'

Americans themselves are not overly positive about the way the president is handling foreign affairs specifically, with 40% approving of his job in that area, one percentage point above his low last November.

Obama has had some success in foreign policy lately, most notably the progress the U.S. and other nations are having in getting Iran to agree to limits on its nuclear capabilities. But Obama faces several challenges, including winding down U.S. involvement in Afghanistan, the ongoing civil war in Syria, and North Korea's continued actions. To the extent Obama manages these challenges successfully, Americans' views of his competence on international matters, and of world leaders' opinions of him, could improve.

Survey Methods

Results for this Gallup poll are based on telephone interviews conducted Feb. 6–9, 2014, with a random sample of 1,023 adults, aged 18 and older, living in all 50 U.S. states and the District of Columbia.

For results based on the total sample of national adults, the margin of sampling error is ±4 percentage points at the 95% confidence level.

February 25, 2014
BUSINESS LEADERS SAY KNOWLEDGE TRUMPS COLLEGE PEDIGREE
American public puts more emphasis on college major and institution

by Valerie J. Calderon and Preety Sidhu

WASHINGTON, D.C.—When hiring, U.S. business leaders say the amount of knowledge the candidate has in a field, as well as applied skills, are more important factors than where a candidate attended school or what their college major was.

For Business Leaders: Please tell me if each of the following factors are very important, somewhat important, not very important, or not at all important to managers making hiring decisions for organizations. How about...?

	% Very important	% Somewhat important	% Not very important	% Not at all important
Amount of knowledge the candidate has in the field	84	14	2	0
Candidate's applied skills in the field	79	16	2	2
Candidate's college or university major	28	42	22	8
Where the candidate received his or her college degree	9	37	40	14

Source: 2013 Gallup-Lumina Foundation Business Leaders Poll on Higher Education

GALLUP'

Business leaders were asked to rank the level of importance four distinct factors have on hiring. Eighty-four percent of business leaders said the amount of knowledge a candidate has in a particular field was "very important," followed by 79% who said applied skills were very important. These two reasons far outweighed the importance of a candidate's college major (28%) or where the candidate received his or her college degree (9%).

These findings are from a Nov. 25–Dec. 16, 2013, telephone survey with 623 U.S. business leaders conducted by Gallup on behalf of Lumina Foundation. The sample for the business leader study is nationally representative of businesses in the United States, with minimum quotas by sales revenue. The study gauges business leaders' perceptions of higher education in this country. The business leader poll was conducted concurrently with the third annual Gallup-Lumina Poll report on Higher Education.

American Public Perceives Importance of University and Major Differently

Reflecting on the same four factors, the American adult population broadly agrees with the opinions of business leaders in terms of the importance of knowledge and applied skills in the field. About eight in 10 U.S. adults say that knowledge and applied skills in the field are very important to managers making hiring decisions for organizations. The average American, however, rates the candidate's college major and where the candidate received his or her degree as higher in importance than business leaders do. Nearly half of U.S. adults (47%) say the candidate's college or university major is a very important factor to hiring managers, and 30% say where the candidate received his or her college degree is very important.

For the American Public: Please tell me if each of the following factors are very important, somewhat important, not very important, or not at all important to managers making hiring decisions for organizations. How about...?

	% Very important	% Somewhat important	% Not very important	% Not at all important
Candidate's college or university major	47	43	8	2
Where the candidate received his or her college degree	30	50	16	4
Amount of knowledge the candidate has in the field	80	17	2	1
Candidate's applied skills in the field	76	22	1	0

Source: 2013 Gallup-Lumina Foundation Poll on Higher Education

GALLUP'

Implications

Business leaders say that the managers responsible for making hiring decisions are far less concerned with where job candidates earn their degrees, or even the type of degree itself, than they are with what knowledge and skills a candidate brings to the table. This corresponds with recent insights into how large, high-tech corporations like Google conduct their hiring. At Google, hiring managers say certain types of skills and talents are what matter most, more than a particular type of college degree or even having a college degree at all.

As opportunities to access postsecondary degrees, certificates, and credentials continue to evolve and become more accessible through innovative learning models, Americans will be able to expand and use their knowledge in the workplace more quickly and efficiently in the future. Further, there may be more emphasis on what potential employees know and their style of working, rather than on the candidate's degree per se. Thus, while college is still important to business leaders, Americans—who tend to rate the importance of where and what type of degree was attained higher than do business leaders—need to recognize that college alone is not enough. Getting a job and achieving long-term success in one's career may increasingly depend on demonstrating real value to employers through experience and targeted learning—and increasingly less on degrees, even if they are from prestigious universities. Higher education institutions have a tremendous opportunity to partner with businesses to bring relevant, responsive, and timely learning opportunities to workplaces in this country and worldwide.

Survey Methods

This article includes results from two surveys conducted by Gallup on behalf of Lumina Foundation.

The first study reported includes findings from the Gallup-Lumina Foundation Poll on Higher Education, a quantitative survey conducted to understand the perceptions of the general American population about several important issues pertaining to higher education, including degree attainment, quality and value, costs, and innovative learning models. To achieve these objectives, Gallup conducted 1,012 interviews from a random sample of individuals 18 years and older residing in landline telephone–only households, cellphone-only households, and dual-user households.

Gallup conducted surveys in English only from Nov. 25–Dec. 15, 2013. Up to three calls were made to each household to reach an eligible respondent.

The data set was statistically adjusted (weighted) using the following variables: race/ethnicity, gender, education, and age as defined by the most recent data from the Current Population Survey conducted by the U.S. Census Bureau. The final overall results are representative of the U.S. adult population 18 years and older.

The questionnaire was developed in consultation with representatives from Lumina Foundation and Gallup. All interviewing was supervised and conducted by Gallup's interviewing staff. For results based on the total sample size of 1,012 adults, one can say with 95% confidence that the margin of error attributable to sampling and other random effects is ±4 percentage points. For subgroups within this population (e.g., education level, gender, and income), the margin of error would be greater.

The second study reported includes findings from the Gallup-Lumina Business Leaders Poll on Higher Education, a quantitative survey conducted to understand the perceptions of business leaders about the quality and effectiveness of American higher education institutions in preparing graduates for the workforce. Gallup conducted 623 interviews with business leaders in executive and senior roles at their company. The sample was from Dun and Bradstreet. A simple stratified random sample design was used for sampling businesses. Businesses were grouped into five strata based on sales revenue ($50,000–$499,999/$500,000–$4.9Million/$5M–$14.9M/$15M–$49.9M/$50M–$100M+). Businesses with larger sales revenue were oversampled to ensure enough completes for analysis. Weights were calculated to take into account sampling rate and also the non-response rate by sales revenue and census region.

February 25, 2014
SOLID MAJORITY OF AMERICANS SAY UN DOING A POOR JOB
Two-thirds of Republicans give U.N. a poor mark

by Andrew Dugan and Nathan Wendt

WASHINGTON, D.C.—More Americans believe the U.N. is doing a poor rather than good job in trying to solve the problems it has had to face, by 57% to 35%. This rating is slightly worse than a year ago, when 50% said the U.N. was doing a poor job, and thus continues a decade-long trend of low public confidence in the U.N.

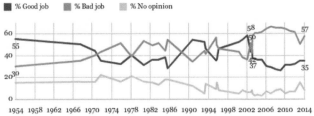

Americans Rate the Job Performance of the United Nations

Do you think the United Nations is doing a good job or a poor job in trying to solve the problems it has had to face?

GALLUP

These results come from the Feb. 6–9 Gallup World Affairs Poll. The U.N. has been struggling to help bring the bloody, three-year Syrian civil war to a close, with the most recent U.N.-sponsored peace talks in Geneva widely seen as a failure, to the point that the U.N. envoy for Syria, Lakhdar Brahimi, publicly apologized to the Syrian people that the peace conference did not yield any progress.

With such intractable conflicts as Syria dogging the U.N., it may not be surprising that many Americans would consider the international body—originally proposed by U.S. President Franklin Roosevelt and established with strong U.S. support—ineffective. However, Americans' negative evaluation of the U.N.'s functioning is nothing new. After the U.S. failed to win U.N. support for the invasion of Iraq in March 2003, the percentage of Americans who said the U.N. was doing a good job fell 13 points to 37%, and hit a nadir of 26% in 2009. It has failed to climb above 40% since then.

Prior to the Iraq war, Americans' reviews of the international body waxed and waned. Opinions were generally positive in the 1950s and 1960s—not long after the institution was created—before falling off in the 1970s, a decade marked by continued war in Vietnam, a war between Israel and several Arab nations, and OPEC's oil embargo of the U.S. American attitudes became more positive in the early 1990s, when the U.N. Security Council maintained a unified front against Iraq's invasion of Kuwait.

The recent decline after the invasion of Iraq in Americans' rating of the U.N. tracks closely with the public's falling satisfaction with the U.S. position in the world. Americans' satisfaction with the nation's position and their positive ratings of the U.N.'s job performance have each not exceeded 50% since 2003, which may suggest that Americans are broadly uncomfortable with both the United States' and the U.N.'s abilities to positively shape world affairs.

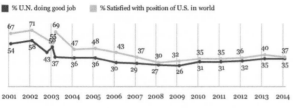
Republicans Far More Likely Than Democrats to Give U.N. Poor Ratings

Similar to the pattern in previous years, Republicans are far more likely than Democrats or independents to say the United Nations is doing a poor job. Republicans and independents are much more likely to say the U.N. is doing a poor job than a good job, while Democrats are more evenly divided.

Performance of United Nations and Self-Identified Party Affiliation

Do you think the United Nations is doing a good job or a poor job in trying to solve the problems it has had to face?

	Republican %	Independents %	Democrat %
Good job	26	34	42
Bad job	67	58	49

Feb. 6-9, 2014

GALLUP

Americans Divided on Role U.N. Should Play

The U.N.'s charter declares that one of its main goals is "to maintain international peace and security," but adults in the U.S. are divided over just how the U.N. should go about this. A plurality (37%) say the U.N. should play a major role, in which the U.N. establishes policies, but individual countries still act separately when they disagree. Another 32% believe the U.N. should play a minor role, with the U.N. serving mostly as a forum for communication between nations, but with no policymaking role. A quarter say the U.N. should play a leading role in which all countries are required to follow the U.N.'s policies.

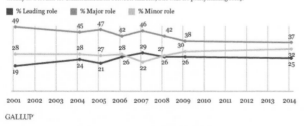

The Role of U.N. in World Affairs Today

Now thinking more specifically, which of the following roles would you like to see the United Nations play in world affairs today -- should it play -- [ROTATED: a leading role where all countries are required to follow U.N. policies, a major role, where the U.N. establishes policies, but where individual countries still act separately when they disagree with the U.N., (or should it play) a minor role, with the U.N. serving mostly as a forum for communication between nations, but with no policymaking role]?

GALLUP

While attitudes about the U.N.'s role have remained fairly stable over the past half decade, fewer Americans now say the U.N.

should play a major role in international affairs than said this in 2001, 37% vs. 49%, respectively.

Implications

President John F. Kennedy, in his inaugural address, famously called the U.N. "our last best hope" to preserve world peace, but today most Americans seem less than hopeful. Nearly six in 10 say the U.N. is doing a poor job, in line with attitudes observed over the past decade. While some of this may reflect Americans' frustration with the general state of the world, including their own country's standing in it, the public's negative assessment of the U.N.'s performance is hardly new.

Americans are divided on what role the U.N. should have in international affairs—a leading, major, or minor one. Such confusion on how much power the U.N. should have may be one reason for its perceived ineffectiveness. The U.N.'s charter is broad, and the media may be less likely to report partial successes such as progress toward achieving some of the Millennium Development Goals than it is to report the U.N.'s role in fostering international peace and security. Whatever the reasons, residents of the United States, a nation that contributes 22% of the U.N.'s budget, feel the international body is doing a poor job.

Survey Methods

Results for this Gallup poll are based on telephone interviews conducted Feb. 6–9, 2014, with a random sample of 1,023 adults, aged 18 and older, living in all 50 U.S. states and the District of Columbia.

For results based on the total sample of national adults, the margin of sampling error is ±4 percentage points at the 95% confidence level.

February 26, 2014
BOEHNER'S FAVORABILITY RETURNS TO PRE-SHUTDOWN LEVELS
Thirty-two percent view speaker favorably, 50% unfavorably

by Justin McCarthy

WASHINGTON, D.C.—After suffering record-low favorability for his tenure as House speaker in October, John Boehner's image among Americans has rebounded to pre-shutdown levels. Still, Boehner, who on Tuesday attended his first private meeting with President Barack Obama since late 2012, continues to be viewed more unfavorably (50%) than favorably (32%).

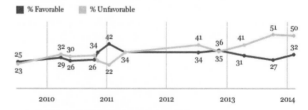

Favorability Ratings, John Boehner

Next, we'd like to get your overall opinion of some people in the news. As I read each name, please say if you have a favorable or unfavorable opinion of these people -- or if you have never heard of them. How about Speaker of the House, John Boehner^?

Note: Never heard of/No opinion responses not shown
^ 2009-2011 wording: House Republican leader, John Boehner

GALLUP

The latest results are from a Feb. 6–9 Gallup poll. Gallup first asked Americans about Boehner's image in 2009, when a quarter (25%) viewed him favorably and 23% viewed him unfavorably, with the rest, 52%, having never heard of him or having no opinion. Over the years, Americans have generally viewed Boehner more unfavorably than favorably, except in January 2011—when he took the speaker's gavel after Republicans won control of the House of Representatives—and again in November 2012, when Americans were more favorable than unfavorable by one percentage point.

For Boehner, 2014 could be a turning of the page as he recovers from the October federal government shutdown, which resulted in his party's receiving the lowest party favorability ratings ever recorded by Gallup, and a drop in his own image to 27% favorable and 51% unfavorable. His favorability has now edged back up to where it was in April of last year (31%), and he recently allowed a vote on the debt ceiling increase with no attached legislation—a move Boehner had never previously made as speaker. Boehner had set the tone for 2013 by telling his party in January of that year that he was done negotiating with the president one-on-one, and hadn't met with him since December 2012.

New Year, New Favorability Ratings, New Relationship

As Obama and Boehner met in the Oval Office Tuesday, the president clearly had the upper hand in terms of image. Like Boehner's favorability ratings, the president's ratings took a dip in late 2013 and have begun to recover this year. But unlike Boehner's, Obama's ratings have tended to be much more positive than negative over the years since he first ran for the presidency, though well below those from his initial year as president and his personal high after he won the 2008 election. In the February survey, Obama's favorable vs. unfavorable ratings were 52% to 46%.

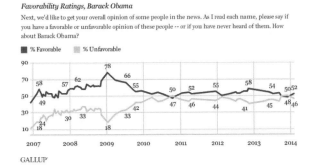

Favorability Ratings, Barack Obama

Next, we'd like to get your overall opinion of some people in the news. As I read each name, please say if you have a favorable or unfavorable opinion of these people -- or if you have never heard of them. How about Barack Obama?

GALLUP

The president and the speaker have consistently sparred on a variety of fiscal issues since Boehner became speaker, and the two hadn't met privately since their unsuccessful attempt at a bargain as the "fiscal cliff" loomed in 2012. Last year's political drama didn't improve their relationship by any means, and culminated in October's government shutdown, leaving Obama with his second-lowest favorability rating since taking office in 2009. With both of their favorability ratings on the rise since the shutdown, 2014 could serve as a restart for Boehner and Obama.

Bottom Line

Boehner and Obama's relationship has likely never been more ready for negotiating, as both reconnect after a hard year of gridlock. But while the stalemate over raising the debt ceiling has let up, other disagreements such as immigration might not be overcome.

Ultimately, 2013 wasn't just a bad year for the speaker and the president; it was also a bad year for Americans, who watched their government partially halt for 16 days, sending their confidence in the economy downward and convincing them that government itself was the nation's biggest problem.

At this point, Americans see Obama in a much more favorable light than they see Boehner, giving the president considerable power in the court of public opinion as the two leaders joust on a series of issues and policy proposals facing the country. This has been typical of president-speaker relationships, with presidents commanding much higher favorability from the nation that elected them to the job. Boehner is no exception to this, and lower favorability usually comes with his role in the political process.

Survey Methods

Results for this Gallup poll are based on telephone interviews conducted Feb. 6–9, 2014, on the Gallup Daily tracking survey, with a random sample of 1,023 adults, aged 18 and older, living in all 50 U.S. states and the District of Columbia.

For results based on the total sample of national adults, the margin of sampling error is ±4 percentage points at the 95% confidence level.

February 26, 2014
MANY BUSINESS LEADERS DOUBT U.S. COLLEGES PREPARE STUDENTS
Few leaders believe U.S. colleges and universities are the best

by Preety Sidhu and Valerie J. Calderon

WASHINGTON, D.C.—Business leaders have doubts that higher education institutions in the U.S. are graduating students who meet their particular businesses' needs. More than one-third of business leaders agree with the statement "higher education institutions in this country are graduating students with the skills and competences that my business needs." About a third disagree with this statement—including 17% who strongly disagree—while another third is neutral.

On a five-point scale, where 5 means strongly agree and 1 means strongly disagree, please indicate your level of agreement with each of the following statements.

Higher education institutions in this country are graduating students with the skills and competencies that MY business needs.

1 Strongly disagree	2	3	4	5 Strongly agree
17%	17%	34%	22%	11%

Source: 2013 Gallup/Lumina Foundation Business Leaders Poll on Higher Education

GALLUP

These findings are from a Nov. 25–Dec. 16, 2013, telephone survey with 623 U.S. business leaders that Gallup conducted on behalf of Lumina Foundation. The sample for the business leader study is nationally representative of businesses in the U.S., with minimum quotas by sales revenue. The study gauges business leaders' perceptions of higher education in this country. The business leader poll was conducted concurrently with the third-annual Gallup/Lumina Poll report on higher education.

Few Business Leaders Believe U.S. Colleges and Universities Are the Best

When asked to react to two statements about the quality of higher education in the country, 37% of business leaders agree the U.S. has the highest quality college and university system in the world, including 19% who strongly agree. Nearly as many—32%—disagree.

The perceived deficiencies of the American higher education system, however, do not mean that employers are turning elsewhere when hiring. Slightly more than one in 10 business leaders agree that their business must hire foreign-born workers as a result of a shortage of American workers with necessary skills, including 4% who strongly agree. But 57% strongly disagree with this statement.

On a five-point scale, where 5 means strongly agree and 1 means strongly disagree, please indicate your level of agreement with each of the following statements.

	%1 Strongly disagree	2	3	4	5 Strongly agree
This country has the highest quality higher education system in the world.	14%	18%	32%	18%	19%
Our business must hire foreign-born workers due to a shortage of American workers with the skills we need.	57%	16%	14%	7%	4%

Source: 2013 Gallup/Lumina Foundation Business Leaders Poll on Higher Education

GALLUP'

Although most business leaders disagree that they need to hire foreign-born workers, a majority, 61%, would favor a policy of issuing green cards to foreign-born international students who graduate from U.S. higher education institutions. And 36% would oppose it.

Would you favor or oppose a policy that says a green card will be issued to foreign-born international students who graduate from a U.S. higher education institution?

	%
Favor	61%
Oppose	36%

Source: 2013 Gallup/Lumina Foundation Business Leaders Poll on Higher Education

GALLUP'

Implications

There is a disconnect between what business leaders need and what higher education institutions think they are producing. A separate Gallup study for Inside Higher Ed finds that 96% of chief academic officers at higher education institutions say their institution is very or somewhat effective at preparing students for the world of work. Quite the reverse, business leaders say that college graduates do not have the skills that their particular businesses need such as applicable knowledge and applied skills in the field. Even though leaders are not yet turning to foreign-born workers when hiring, they favor increasing green card policies for foreign-born international graduate students in the U.S.

There is clearly room to increase collaboration, with a strong majority of business leaders favoring an increased level of collaboration between higher education institutions and businesses. An increased level of collaboration will benefit both business leaders and higher education institutions in preparing students with the right knowledge and applied skills so that they are ready for the real world and have the best opportunity to find a good job.

Survey Methods

This article includes results from the U.S. Business Leaders poll conducted by Gallup on behalf of Lumina Foundation.

The study reported includes findings from the Gallup/Lumina Business Leaders Poll on Higher Education, a quantitative survey conducted to understand the perceptions of business leaders about the quality and effectiveness of American higher education institutions in preparing graduates for the workforce. Gallup conducted 623 interviews with business leaders in executive and senior roles at their company. The sample was from Dun & Bradstreet. A simple stratified random sample design was used for sampling businesses. Businesses were grouped into five strata based on sales revenue ($50,000–$499,999/$500,000–$4.9 million/$5 million–$14.9 million/$15 million–$49.9 million/$50 million–$100 million+). Businesses with larger sales revenue were oversampled to ensure enough completes for analysis. Weights were calculated to take into account sampling rate and the non-response rate by sales revenue and census region.

Gallup conducted surveys in English only from Nov. 25–Dec. 16, 2013. Up to five calls were made to each business to reach an eligible respondent.

The questionnaire was developed in consultation with representatives from Lumina Foundation and Gallup. All interviewing was supervised and conducted by Gallup's full-time interviewing staff. For results based on the total sample size of 623 business leaders, one can say with 95% confidence that the margin of error attributable to sampling and other random effects is ±6 percentage points.

In addition to sampling error, question wording and practical difficulties in conducting surveys can introduce error or bias into the findings of opinion polls. Reported frequencies may not add up to 100% in some cases due to rounding or the exclusion of "don't know" and "refused" results.

Smaller and larger business groups were created for the Lumina Foundation leader project based on annual revenue. For this study, businesses with less than $5 million in annual revenue are classified as small businesses, and businesses with more than $5 million in annual revenue are classified as large businesses.

February 27, 2014
U.S. OBESITY RATE TICKS UP TO 27.1% IN 2013
Percentage "morbidly obese" rose slightly to a new high of 3.8%

by Rebecca Riffkin

WASHINGTON, D.C.—In the U.S., 27.1% of adults were obese in 2013, the highest rate measured since Gallup and Healthways began tracking in 2008. The obesity rate increased by nearly a full percentage point over the average rate of 26.2% found in 2012. As more Americans moved into the obese category in 2013, slightly fewer Americans were classified as overweight or as normal weight.

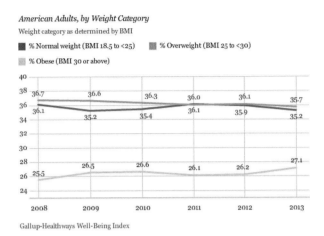

American Adults, by Weight Category
Weight category as determined by BMI

■ % Normal weight (BMI 18.5 to <25)   ■ % Overweight (BMI 25 to <30)
■ % Obese (BMI 30 or above)

Gallup-Healthways Well-Being Index

GALLUP

The Gallup-Healthways Well-Being Index, which uses respondents' self-reports of their height and weight to calculate body mass index (BMI) scores, differs slightly from government reports of obesity, which are based on actual heights and weights found in clinical measurements. A recent government report based on the National Health and Nutrition Examination Survey found that 34.9% of adults, aged 20 years or older, in the study were obese. This rate had not significantly changed between 2003 and 2012.

Gallup and Healthways began tracking U.S. adults' weight daily in 2008. Individual BMI values of 30 or above are classified as "obese," 25 to 29.9 are "overweight," 18.5 to 24.9 are "normal weight," and 18.4 or less are "underweight." For the past six years, nearly two-thirds of Americans have had BMIs higher than is recommended, while roughly 35% of Americans have been in the "normal weight" category.

The World Health Organization further classifies BMIs of 30.00 or higher into one of three classes of obesity:

- Obese class I = 30.00 to 34.99
- Obese class II = 35.00 to 39.99
- Obese class III = 40.00 or higher

Those with BMIs of 40 or higher—obese class III—are often considered "morbidly obese." According to Americans' self-reports of height and weight, the percentage of morbidly obese has been slowly rising since 2011, and is now the highest Gallup has recorded, at 3.8%.

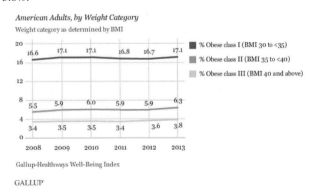

American Adults, by Weight Category
Weight category as determined by BMI

■ % Obese class I (BMI 30 to <35)
■ % Obese class II (BMI 35 to <40)
■ % Obese class III (BMI 40 and above)

Gallup-Healthways Well-Being Index

GALLUP

The percentage of Americans in obese class II has also been on the rise, reaching a record high of 6.3% in 2013. The percentage

in obese class I has varied, but the 17.1% who fall into this group matches the highest rate recorded since tracking began. Thus, the overall increase in obesity in 2013 reflects an upward shift among all three obesity groups.

The majority of Americans who are obese fall into obese class I, which means they have less weight to lose to move into the overweight or, ideally, the normal weight category. But the increase in the percentage in the U.S. who fall into obesity classes II and III is troubling, given the fiscal and physical costs of obesity.

All Demographic Groups See Stable or Increasing Obesity Rates

The obesity rates across all major demographic and socioeconomic groups in the U.S. increased at least marginally in 2013 compared with 2012, with the exception of 18- to 29-year-olds. These increases ranged from 0.6 percentage points among Americans living in the East to 1.8 points for 45- to 64-year-olds.

Percentage Obese in U.S. Among Various Demographic Groups
Sorted by largest change to smallest
Among adults aged 18 and older

	2012	2013	Difference
	%	%	(pct. pts.)
Aged 45-64	30.7	32.5	1.8
Annual income $36,000-$89,999	26.0	27.7	1.7
Midwest	27.4	28.6	1.2
Women	25.0	26.2	1.2
Annual income less than $36,000	30.4	31.5	1.1
South	28.1	29.2	1.1
Aged 65+	25.2	26.3	1.1
Blacks	34.9	35.8	0.9
NATIONAL ADULTS	26.2	27.1	0.9
Whites	25.1	26.0	0.9
West	23.2	24.1	0.9
Aged 30-44	28.1	28.9	0.8
Men	27.3	28.1	0.8
Annual income $90,000+	21.2	22.0	0.8
Hispanics	27.1	27.8	0.7
East	25.0	25.6	0.6
Aged 18-29	17.2	17.2	0

Gallup-Healthways Well-Being Index

GALLUP

Some of the groups with the highest obesity rates saw the largest increases from 2012 to 2013. The obesity rate increased by more than one point among Americans who make less than $36,000 a year, 45- to 64-year-olds, and those living in the South. The obesity rate among black Americans, already the highest rate recorded among major demographic groups, rose 0.9 points to 35.8% in 2013.

Implications

Obesity is linked to increased health risks and lower productivity rates among workers of all industries. A high obesity rate can hold a country back, both in national well-being and in economic productivity.

Obesity increases the risk of many serious and costly medical conditions and leads to increased healthcare costs and workplace absenteeism, which negatively affect the U.S. economy. If more Americans become obese, these costs will continue to climb.

Americans' eating habits worsened in 2013, which may have contributed to the uptick in the obesity rate along with the fact that

Gallup found Americans were exercising less in the first half of 2013. Furthermore, while many Americans say they want to lose weight, few are actively trying to do so.

President Barack Obama and first lady Michelle Obama have emphasized the importance of healthy eating and exercise, especially for children, throughout their time in the White House. Further, national restaurant chains are providing more healthy options in their children's meals, like fruit and vegetable options as sides. Though the rate of childhood obesity—which the Gallup-Healthways Well-Being Index does not track—has dropped over the last decade, it is yet to be seen whether it will lead to lower adult obesity rates in the years to come.

That the obesity rate increased across almost all demographic groups in 2013 suggests this is not an issue in one region, age group, or income bracket; it is a national problem.

Survey Methods

Results are based on telephone interviews conducted as part of the Gallup-Healthways Well-Being Index survey Jan. 2–Dec. 29, 2013, with a random sample of 178,072 adults, aged 18 and older, living in all 50 U.S. states and the District of Columbia.

For results based on the total sample of national adults, the margin of sampling error is ±0.3 percentage points at the 95% confidence level. For the various subgroups, the sampling error will range from ±0.5 to ±1.5 percentage points.

February 27, 2014
AMERICANS REMAIN DIVIDED ON MILITARY SPENDING
Views are not as extreme in either direction as in other years

by Frank Newport

PRINCETON, NJ—As the Obama administration announces plans for further decreases in military spending, Gallup surveys show no broad consensus among Americans that the U.S. is spending too much or too little on the military. Americans' views of the money spent on national defense and the military have held fairly steady in recent years, with 37% now saying the nation spends too much and 28% saying it spends too little. The rest say spending is about right.

There is much discussion as to the amount of money the government in Washington should spend for national defense and military purposes. How do you feel about this? Do you think we are spending too little, about the right amount, or too much?

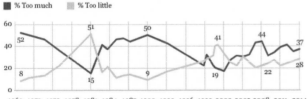

"About the right amount" not represented on graph

GALLUP

The most recent data are from Gallup's Feb. 6–9 World Affairs poll. Americans' attitudes on military spending have fluctuated since 1969, with occasional spikes in the "too much" and the "too little" viewpoints. Americans' current views are fairly moderate, with the percentages saying "too much" and "too little" falling about midway in the historical ranges.

These attitudes have taken on a renewed importance as Secretary of Defense Chuck Hagel announced a far-reaching Pentagon defense plan Monday that would, among other things, cut the Army's size to its lowest level since before World War II.

Historically, Americans were most likely to believe the nation was spending "too much" on the military in 1969 (52%) and in the early 1970s, just after the peak of U.S. involvement in the Vietnam War. This belief also reached as high as 50% in 1990 after the major military buildup under Presidents Ronald Reagan and George H.W. Bush. Public concern that military spending was too high rose to 44% in the final year of the George W. Bush administration as the nation's military spending increased for the wars in Afghanistan and Iraq.

Americans were most likely to say the government was spending "too little" on the military in January 1981, just as Reagan was taking office after having won the election partly because of his emphasis on the need to build up America's military. Similarly, the "too little" percentage peaked in 2000 and early 2001 as George W. Bush campaigned for and won the presidency after a period of lower military spending during the Clinton administration.

Democrats Most Likely to Perceive Too Much Military Spending

As has historically been the case, there are political differences in views on defense spending. Democrats and independents are most likely to believe the nation is spending too much, while Republicans are most likely to say it is spending too little. Even so, current attitudes are not extreme on either side of the political equation, with slightly more than half of Democrats saying there is too much spending, and 49% of Republicans saying there is too little.

Views of Amount of Defense Spending, by Political Party

	% Too much	% About right	% Too little
Democrats	51	32	15
Independents	37	33	26
Republicans	20	29	49

Feb. 6-9, 2014

GALLUP

Americans Still Say U.S. Is No. 1 Military Power

U.S. military involvement around the world escalated sharply after September 2001, owing to the fight against terrorism, the major buildup involved in fighting wars in Afghanistan and Iraq, and increased use of special operations forces, which, by one count, are active in more than 100 countries. Throughout this period, a majority of Americans have continued to say the U.S. is the No. 1 military power in the world, although the extent of that belief has varied significantly.

Gallup has asked this question only periodically since 1993, with the high points coming that year and again in January 2010. A slim majority felt the U.S. was No. 1 militarily in 1999, near the end of the Clinton administration. The percentage has ranged between 50% and 54% in the past three years.

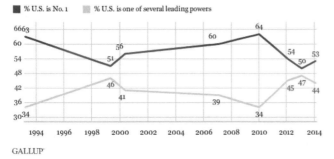

Do you think the United States is No. 1 in the world militarily, or that it is only one of several leading military powers?

■ % U.S. is No. 1   ▨ % U.S. is one of several leading powers

GALLUP

Democrats and Republicans have nearly identical views that the U.S. is No. 1 militarily; independents are a bit more skeptical. These views are similar to those measured last year.

Do you think the United States is No. 1 in the world militarily, or that it is only one of several leading military powers?

By party identification

	Republicans	Independents	Democrats
	%	%	%
U.S. is No. 1	57	49	58
U.S. is only one of several leading powers	41	48	41

Feb. 6-9, 2014

GALLUP

Bottom Line

U.S. spending on defense as a percentage of GDP has varied substantially in the 70 years since the huge military outlays of World War II. Spending increased from post–World War II levels during the Korean War, stayed relatively high during the Cold War and Vietnam War years that followed, began to fall during the 1970s, rose slightly during the Reagan administration, fell during the Clinton years, rose significantly during the last decade, and has now begun to fall again.

The American public's views on military spending have also varied, generally in reaction to these shifts. Americans were most likely to view spending as too high during Vietnam and the 1980s and early '90s, and most likely to view it as too little after the drop in spending in the 1970s and 1990s. Since 2002, Americans' views that the U.S. is spending too much increased concomitant with actual spending increases that followed 9/11 and U.S. involvement in two wars. Now, as the U.S. begins once again to decrease military spending, the public's attitudes are divided. Given these cuts, it would not be unusual if at some point the public once again began to say military spending had dropped too low, potentially making military preparedness a 2016 presidential campaign issue.

Survey Methods

Results for this Gallup poll are based on telephone interviews conducted Feb. 6–9, 2014, with a random sample of 1,023 adults, aged 18 and older, living in all 50 U.S. states and the District of Columbia.

For results based on the total sample of national adults, the margin of sampling error is ±4 percentage points at the 95% confidence level.

February 27, 2014
AMERICANS STILL DOUBT MIDEAST PEACE IS IN THE CARDS
Sympathy for Israel remains high; plurality support two-state answer

by Lydia Saad

PRINCETON, NJ—Despite intensive efforts by the Obama administration to help the Israelis and Palestinians agree on a framework for peace negotiations by late April, and Secretary of State John Kerry's frequent trips to the region, Americans are as doubtful as ever that Israel and its Arab neighbors will ever settle their differences and live in peace. Exactly one-third now believe this will happen, down from 38% in 2012, while 64% believe peace will never be reached. Current optimism is on the low end of what Gallup has found in the last two decades.

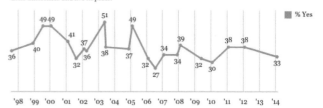

Outlook for Arab-Israeli Peace
Do you think there will or will not come a time when Israel and the Arab nations will be able to settle their differences and live in peace?

■ % Yes

GALLUP

The poll was conducted Feb. 6–9, prior to a recent report that Palestinian leader Mahmoud Abbas walked out of talks in Paris last week over the United States' proposal for the division of Jerusalem and other issues. Kerry has since indicated that the deadline for reaching an agreement on the framework for peace may have to be extended, possibly indefinitely, although President Barack Obama is meeting with Israeli Prime Minister Benjamin Netanyahu at the White House Monday to try to keep the momentum going.

The United States has long supported a "two-state solution" to the Israeli-Palestinian conflict, based on mutually agreed-upon terms establishing Palestine as an independent state. In 2011, Obama spoke in favor of using the region's pre–1967 borders—before Israel gained control of the West Bank and Gaza Strip in the Six-Day War—as the starting point.

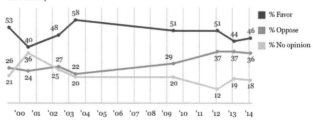

Support for Independent Palestinian State
Do you favor or oppose the establishment of an independent Palestinian state on the West Bank and the Gaza strip?

■ % Favor
■ % Oppose
▨ % No opinion

GALLUP

By 46% to 36%, more Americans agree than disagree with the goal of having an independent Palestinian state on the West Bank and Gaza Strip, with 18% expressing no opinion. However, support has waned since 2003, when 58% backed it. Since then, support has held steady among Democrats (55% in 2003 vs. 56% today), while it has fallen from 60% to 41% among Republicans, and from 59% to 43% among independents.

Although Americans tend to favor a Palestinian state encompassing the West Bank and Gaza Strip, most say their sympathies lie with the Israelis. In fact, Americans have favored Israel over the Palestinians consistently since 1988, and since 2000 an outright majority have typically favored Israel. At no time has sympathy for the Palestinians exceeded 20%.

Currently, 62% sympathize more with the Israelis and 18% more with the Palestinians, while 21% are neutral or unsure.

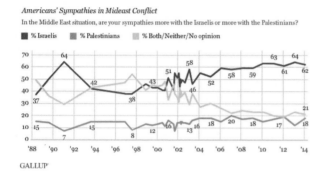

Americans' Sympathies in Mideast Conflict
In the Middle East situation, are your sympathies more with the Israelis or more with the Palestinians?

■ % Israelis   ■ % Palestinians   ■ % Both/Neither/No opinion

GALLUP'

The partisan gap in views toward Israel has been quite pronounced since 2002, early in George W. Bush's presidency. Republicans' sympathy for Israel expanded that year, perhaps reflecting the strengthening of U.S.-Israeli relations after 9/11. It expanded further in early 2003, when Israel backed Bush's initiative to invade Iraq at a time when France and other nations were resisting, then shrank during a brief period of public optimism about peace that spring when agreement on a "road map" for resolving the conflict seemed near.

Republicans' sympathy for Israel has since swelled, reaching 80% or higher in recent years, while Democrats' sympathy has risen less sharply. Independents' views have been closer to Democrats' views since 2002.

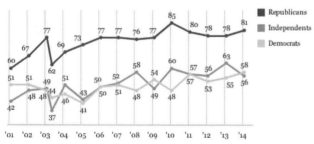

Trend in Sympathy for Israel -- by Party ID
Percentage sympathizing more with the Israelis than the Palestinians in Mideast conflict

■ Republicans
■ Independents
■ Democrats

Selected trend: Results from annual February World Affairs survey, plus May 2003 survey

GALLUP'

Support for Israel Differs Along Generational Lines

While majorities of all age groups say their sympathies lie more with the Israelis, and few side with the Palestinians, barely half of young adults, those aged 18 to 34, currently favor Israel on this question, compared with 58% of 35- to 54-year-olds and 74% of those 55 and older.

Additionally, Gallup trends document that older Americans have grown increasingly likely to side with Israel in the conflict, while support from younger adults and those in between has been flat or risen more modestly.

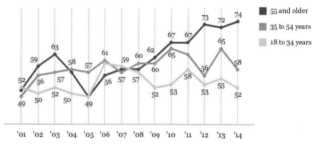

Trend in Sympathy for Israel -- by Age
Percentage sympathizing more with the Israelis than the Palestinians in Mideast conflict

■ 55 and older
■ 35 to 54 years
■ 18 to 34 years

Selected trend: Results from annual February World Affairs survey

GALLUP'

Bottom Line

Americans have seemingly become hardened pessimists about the Israeli-Palestinian conflict, with the majority consistently skeptical that peace in the region will ever be attained. Although their pessimism has diminished at times, there is no hint of that today even as the Obama administration is deeply involved in brokering peace talks after a three-year hiatus.

Israel continues to enjoy greater support in the U.S. than do the Palestinians. Relatedly, Gallup finds Israel enjoying a high favorable rating among Americans, while the Palestinian authority and several Arab countries are viewed more negatively. Still, far more Americans support the creation of a Palestinian state, or at least have no opinion about it, than reject it, indicating that U.S. leaders pursuing a two-state solution are on the right track.

Survey Methods

Results for this Gallup poll are based on telephone interviews conducted Feb. 6–9, 2014, with a random sample of 1,023 adults, aged 18 and older, living in all 50 U.S. states and the District of Columbia.

For results based on the total sample of national adults, the margin of sampling error is ±4 percentage points at the 95% confidence level.

February 28, 2014
TERRORISM, IRANIAN NUKES CONSIDERED GREATEST THREATS TO U.S.
Islamic fundamentalism rising as perceived threat

by Art Swift

WASHINGTON, D.C.—More than a decade after the 9/11 terror attacks, Americans rank international terrorism as the greatest threat to the U.S. in the next 10 years, along with Iran's development of nuclear weapons. Majorities also perceive Islamic fundamentalism, the conflict between North and South Korea, and China's economic power as critical threats. Fewer Americans see Russia's military power as a critical threat to the U.S. in the coming decade.

Threats to the Vital Interests of the United States in Next 10 Years

I am going to read you a list of possible threats to the vital interests of the United States in the next 10 years. For each one, please tell me if you see this as a critical threat, an important but not critical threat, or not an important threat at all.

	% Critical threat	% Important, not critical
International terrorism	77	19
Development of nuclear weapons by Iran	76	18
Islamic fundamentalism	57	27
Conflict between North Korea and South Korea	53	36
Economic power of China	52	36
Military power of China	46	41
Conflict between Israel and the Palestinians	46	42
Military power of Russia	32	49
Conflict between India and Pakistan	28	48

Feb. 6-9, 2014

GALLUP

Americans are less likely this year than last to perceive the development of Iranian nuclear weapons as the greatest threat to the U.S. in the next decade, with the percentage falling from 83% last year to 76%, tying terrorism. This might be partly attributable to the ongoing nuclear talks between the U.S., Iran, and several other nations over the last several months.

Russia's military power is viewed as less of a threat, though the belief that it is a critical threat has been rising over the past decade. Americans are nearly twice as likely to view Russia's military power as a critical threat now (32%) as they were 10 years ago, when 18% of Americans said Russian military power was a critical threat, 50% said it was important but not critical, and 29% said it was not important.

International Terrorism Enduring as Threat in Last Decade

A clear majority of Americans have consistently viewed international terrorism as a critical threat since Gallup began asking this question 10 years ago, although slightly fewer perceive this today. This comes nearly a year after the terror attack in Boston and as questions remain about the 2012 attack on a U.S. consulate in Benghazi, Libya.

Americans' Views on the Threat of International Terrorism

	% Critical threat	% Important, not critical
Feb 6-9, 2014	77	19
Feb 7-10, 2013	81	17
Feb 1-3, 2010	81	16
Feb 9-12, 2004	82	16

GALLUP

Islamic Fundamentalism Prominent, Steadily Rising as Threat

Over the past decade, the perceived threat of Islamic fundamentalism to American interests has risen. Now, 57% of Americans believe

Islamic fundamentalism is a critical threat to vital U.S. interests in the next 10 years, up four percentage points from last year and six points from 2004.

Americans' Views on the Threat of Islamic Fundamentalism

	% Critical threat	% Important, not critical
Feb 6-9, 2014	57	27
Feb 7-10, 2013	53	28
Feb 9-12, 2004	51	31

GALLUP

Fewer See Israeli-Palestinian Conflict as a Critical Threat

In light of ongoing Israeli-Palestinian negotiations for a peace framework, and amid Secretary of State John Kerry's frequent trips to the region, less than half of Americans (46%) believe the Israeli-Palestinian conflict will be a critical threat to U.S. interests in the next decade. This belief has been steady in recent polls, but is down from 58% in 2004. About as many Americans believe this is a critical threat as say it is an important but not critical one.

Americans' Views on the Threat of the Conflict Between Israel and the Palestinians

	% Critical threat	% Important, not critical
Feb 6-9, 2014	46	42
Feb 7-10, 2013	44	44
Feb 1-3 2010	47	41
Feb 9-12 2004	58	32

GALLUP

Bottom Line

Predicting the future is always difficult. Unforeseen crises often occur, while feared, expected events often never materialize. In geopolitical terms, Americans have remained relatively consistent in what they believe could constitute a critical threat to the U.S. in the next 10 years—nuclear weapons or terrorism from abroad.

International terrorism, which has manifested itself worldwide from time to time in the new millennium, has always ranked near the top of the list of perceived threats, even though no major international terrorist attacks have occurred in the U.S. since 9/11. There has been a seven-point drop this year in Americans' belief that the development of nuclear weapons by Iran will pose a threat to vital U.S. interests, and it remains to be seen whether that percentage will continue to drop if the nuclear peace talks between the U.S., Iran, Britain, France, Russia, China, and Germany are successful.

Survey Methods

Results for this Gallup poll are based on telephone interviews conducted Feb. 6–9, 2014, with a random sample of 1,023 adults, aged 18 and older, living in all 50 U.S. states and the District of Columbia.

For results based on the total sample of national adults, the margin of sampling error is ±4 percentage points at the 95% confidence level.

March 03, 2014
MICHELLE OBAMA MAINTAINS POSITIVE IMAGE
Average favorable rating tops Hillary Clinton's as first lady

by Alyssa Brown

WASHINGTON, D.C.—First lady Michelle Obama's positive public image may be an asset as she advocates for major changes to nutrition labels and tries to help Democrats retain control of the Senate in the coming midterm elections. Sixty-six percent of Americans have a favorable opinion of the first lady, unchanged from a year and a half ago and on par with her ratings since her husband's inauguration in January 2009.

Americans' Opinions of Michelle Obama

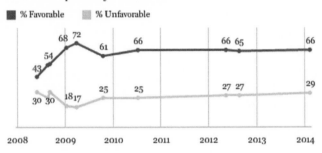

Note: Never heard of/No opinion responses are not shown.

GALLUP'

As first lady, her favorables have remained close to that pre-inaugural level, even as the president's favorable rating has declined. As such, she remains more popular than her husband, who managed a 52% favorable rating in Gallup's most recent survey. The first lady has focused on her "Let's Move" campaign to fight childhood obesity and on supporting military families—issues that may engender public support and help her rise above the partisan politics that have worn on the president's rating.

Favorable Ratings of Michelle Obama and Barack Obama

	Michelle Obama	Barack Obama
	%	%
National adults	66	52
Democrats	92	88
Independents	61	47
Republicans	43	18
Men	59	48
Women	73	57

Feb. 6-9, 2014

GALLUP'

First ladies are typically viewed more positively than presidents, likely because their roles are often more ceremonial and invite less criticism compared with the president's active political and policy-making role. Laura Bush and Barbara Bush were each viewed more favorably than their husbands while they were in the White House. The recent exception is Hillary Clinton, whose favorable ratings

were generally lower than Bill Clinton's until the Monica Lewinsky scandal.

Michelle Obama has a more positive image than her husband does across all partisan and gender groups, but does particularly well on a relative basis among Republicans. This suggests she could be an important campaign resource for the Democratic Party this year as it fights to keep control of the U.S. Senate in the coming midterm elections.

Michelle Obama's Image Better Than Hillary Clinton's as First Lady

Michelle Obama's 66% average favorability rating exceeds Hillary Clinton's 56% average rating during Clinton's time as first lady, but trails those of Laura Bush and Barbara Bush (73% and 77%, respectively). Clinton's role in trying to pass a controversial national healthcare reform law may have contributed to her comparatively lower ratings, while the rally effect after 9/11 may have given Laura Bush's ratings a boost. Gallup began measuring favorability in its current format in 1992, so only the last four first ladies' ratings can be compared in this way.

Average Favorable and Unfavorable Ratings of First Ladies

	Favorable	Unfavorable	No opinion	Number of polls
	%	%	%	
Michelle Obama	66	25	7	6
Laura Bush	73	15	12	9
Hillary Clinton	56	37	7	51
Barbara Bush	77	10	13	2

GALLUP'

As the Obama administration seeks to encourage young Americans to sign up for health insurance and apply for financial aid, and the Democratic Party tries to maintain control of the Senate, the first lady's lately unshakeable positive public image could be an asset to each in the coming months.

Survey Methods

Results for this Gallup poll are based on telephone interviews conducted Feb. 6–9, 2014, with a random sample of 1,023 adults, aged 18 and older, living in all 50 U.S. states and the District of Columbia.

For results based on the total sample of national adults, the margin of sampling error is ±4 percentage points at the 95% confidence level.

March 04, 2014
MISSISSIPPIANS MOST OBESE, MONTANANS LEAST OBESE
Chronic diseases are more prevalent in the most obese states

by Jenna Levy

WASHINGTON, D.C.—Mississippi had the highest obesity rate in the U.S. in 2013, at 35.4%, while Montana has the lowest rate, at 19.6%. The obesity rate has generally increased across the U.S. each year since 2008.

Ten States With Highest Obesity Rates		Ten States With Lowest Obesity Rates	
	% Obese		% Obese
Mississippi	35.4	Montana	19.6
West Virginia	34.4	Colorado	20.4
Delaware	34.3	Nevada	21.1
Louisiana	32.7	Minnesota	22.0
Arkansas	32.3	Massachusetts	22.2
South Carolina	31.4	Connecticut	23.2
Tennessee	31.3	New Mexico	23.5
Ohio	30.9	California	23.6
Kentucky	30.6	Hawaii	23.7
Oklahoma	30.5	New York	24.0

January-December 2013
Gallup-Healthways Well-Being Index

GALLUP

January-December 2013
Gallup-Healthways Well-Being Index

GALLUP

From 2010 through 2012, West Virginia maintained the highest obesity rate nationwide while Colorado had the lowest. Five states—Mississippi, West Virginia, Louisiana, Arkansas, and Kentucky—have been listed among the 10 states with the highest obesity rates in the nation since 2008. Colorado, Massachusetts, Connecticut, and California have routinely been states with lower levels of obesity—all four have made the list of the 10 states with the lowest obesity rates in the nation each year since 2008.

The national obesity rate, as computed by respondents' self-reported height and weight in the Gallup-Healthways Well-Being Index, has increased to 27.1% from 26.2% in 2012, and is up 1.6 percentage points from 25.5% in 2008, Gallup's initial year of tracking. Americans who have a BMI of 30 or higher are classified as obese.

More than two in 10 adults were obese in nearly every state in 2013, with the exception of Montana. Three in 10 adults were obese in 11 states—Mississippi, West Virginia, Delaware, Louisiana, Arkansas, South Carolina, Tennessee, Ohio, Kentucky, Oklahoma, and Alaska—compared with only five states in 2012. Obesity rates continue to be highest in Southern and Midwestern states and lowest in Western and Northeastern states, a trend that has been ongoing since Gallup and Healthways began tracking the obesity rate in 2008.

Chronic Diseases Are More Prevalent in the Most Obese States

Those living in the 10 states with the highest levels of obesity are more likely to report having had a diagnosis of chronic disease at some point in their lives, including high blood pressure, high cholesterol, depression, diabetes, cancer, and heart attacks, than are those living in the 10 states with the lowest obesity rates. Gallup-Healthways data show an average 35.8% of Americans living in the 10 states with the highest obesity rates report a high blood pressure diagnosis, while 26.4% of Americans living in the 10 least obese states say the same—a difference of 9.4 points.

Average Lifetime Disease Rates for States With the Highest and Lowest Obesity Levels

	Ten most obese states avg. %	Ten least obese states avg. %
High blood pressure	35.8	26.4
High cholesterol	28.2	23.2
Depression	20.7	16.6
Diabetes	14.3	9.6
Cancer	7.8	7.6
Heart attack	5.0	3.5

January-December 2013
Gallup-Healthways Well-Being Index

GALLUP

Residents in Least Obese States Eat Healthier and Exercise More

Americans living in the 10 states with the lowest rates of obesity also report higher instances of healthy eating and exercise than do those who live in the 10 states with the highest obesity levels. For example, an average 66.7% of those living in the 10 least obese states say they ate healthy all day yesterday compared with 60.8% of those living in the 10 most obese states.

Average Exercise and Healthy Eating Rates for States With the Highest and Lowest Obesity Levels

	Ten most obese states avg. %	Ten least obese states avg. %
Ate healthy all day yesterday	60.8	66.7
Ate 5+ servings of fruits/vegetables at least 4 of last 7 days	55.8	59.6
Exercised for 30 minutes or more at least 3 of last 7 days	49.6	56.1

January-December 2013
Gallup-Healthways Well-Being Index

GALLUP

Bottom Line

As the rate of obesity among U.S. adults continues to increase across all 50 states, health issues and costs associated with the chronic diseases that can accompany obesity will continue to rise. Gallup-Healthways Well-Being Index data show Americans are not eating as healthily or exercising as often as in past years, which might play a role in the increase of national and state obesity rates.

"While there are a variety of factors that are often correlated with rising obesity rates, such as an unhealthy food environment, poor eating habits, increasing portion sizes, and inactivity, experts agree that the health consequences of obesity are real," Dr. James E. Pope, Senior Vice President and Chief Science Officer at Healthways said. "Research has shown that the average healthcare costs for an obese individual are over $1,300 more annually than someone who is not obese. Although slowing and even reversing this trend may seem daunting, even modest weight loss of 5% to 10% of initial body weight can lower the health risks associated with obesity," added Pope.

The American Medical Association in June 2013 recognized obesity as a disease, which may affect the way medical professionals discuss and treat obesity. Additionally, the CDC released new data reporting obesity rates among children aged two to five years have dropped 43% in the past decade. Although the Gallup-Healthways Well-Being Index does not track childhood obesity rates, the CDC data is an encouraging sign that progress is being made in this area. Efforts to curb childhood obesity in America may positively affect adult obesity rates across all states in the years ahead. Specifically, these efforts may lead to fewer Americans entering adulthood overweight, while also encouraging overweight adults to make healthier lifestyle choices.

Survey Methods

Results are based on telephone interviews conducted as part of the Gallup-Healthways Well-Being Index survey Jan. 2–Dec. 29, 2013, with a random sample of 178,072 adults, aged 18 and older, living in all 50 U.S. states and the District of Columbia.

The margin of sampling error for most states is ±1 to ±2 percentage points, but is as high as ±4 points for states with smaller populations, such as Wyoming, North Dakota, South Dakota, Delaware, and Hawaii.

March 04, 2014

HAVING CHILDREN MAJOR DRIVER OF SPENDING PATTERNS IN U.S.

Average daily spending falls once children turn 18

by Joy Wilke

WASHINGTON, D.C.—Americans who have at least one child under the age of 18 report spending $29 more daily, on average, than those without younger children. Parents with younger children across all age and income groups report higher spending levels.

Average Daily Spending by Parental Status

Next, we'd like you to think about your spending yesterday, not counting the purchase of a home, motor vehicle, or your normal household bills. How much money did you spend or charge yesterday on all other types of purchases you may have made, such as at a store, restaurant, gas station, online, or elsewhere?

	Average daily spending
Do not have children under age 18	$79
Have children under age 18	$108
DIFFERENCE	$29

Gallup Daily tracking, January-December 2013

GALLUP'

These results are based on 2013 Gallup Daily tracking, which asks Americans about the amount of money they spent on purchases "yesterday," excluding normal household bills and major purchases. Americans without children under 18 reported average daily spending of $79, while Americans with children reported a $108 daily average.

A multivariate analysis confirms that this difference in spending is significant when controlling for income, age, education, and marital status. That is, even among adults in the same income group, for example, there is an incremental bump in spending as a result of having children under 18. This could be the result of having more people in the house to provide basic necessities for, including food and clothing. In addition, there is a whole separate class of expenses that are common for parents, including children's extracurricular activities, books, toys, and games. Overall, the presence of children is clearly related to a higher outflow of money on a daily basis.

Americans' Daily Spending Declines Once All Their Children Turn 18

Once children move beyond the age of 18, their parents' spending appears to drop back down, approaching the levels found among those without children. This holds true across most income and age groups. In all demographic groups but one, spending is lowest among those without children, rises among those who have children under the age of 18, and then falls among those whose children are aged 18 or older.

Average Daily Spending of Americans With and Without Children, by Income and Age

	Do not have children	Have children under 18	Have children 18 or older
MONTHLY INCOME			
Less than $3,000	$53	$80	$55
Between $3,000 and $7,499	$73	$103	$88
$7,500 or more	$121	$171	$151
AGE			
18 to 29	$61	$100	--
30 to 49	$86	$110	$82
50 to 64	$81	$106	$92
65+	$69	$137	$77

Gallup Daily tracking, January-December 2013

GALLUP'

Having More Children Under 18 Linked to Higher Daily Spending

The total number of children under the age of 18 also affects the amount Americans spend. Aside from those with no children younger than 18, parents with one child in this age category spend the least ($96 per day), while those with five or more spend the most on average ($145). Overall, there is a clear, upward trend: the more children under 18 there are in a household, the more money parents spend on a daily basis.

Americans' Average Daily Spending, by Number of Children Younger Than 18

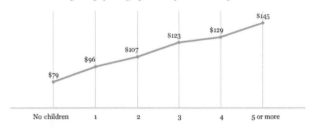

Gallup Daily tracking, January-December 2013

GALLUP'

Bottom Line

Gallup research shows that marital status affects daily spending. These data show that having children younger than 18 has an effect on daily spending that goes above and beyond other demographic factors such as income, age, and marital status.

The drop in U.S. fertility rates in recent years, documented by the Centers for Disease Control and Prevention, therefore may have had a negative effect on consumer spending. The good news for the economy is that Gallup research also shows that there may be a pent-up fertility demand in the American population. If the fertility rate does increase in the years ahead, consumer spending may increase correspondingly.

Survey Methods

Results for this Gallup poll are based on telephone interviews conducted Jan. 2–Dec. 29, 2013, on the Gallup Daily tracking survey, with a random sample of 172,556 adults, aged 18 and older, living in all 50 U.S. states and the District of Columbia.

For results based on the total sample of national adults, the margin of sampling error is ±1 percentage point at the 95% confidence level.

For results based on the total sample of Americans with children under 18, the margin of sampling error is ±1 percentage point at the 95% confidence level.

March 05, 2014

SECRETARY OF STATE KERRY'S FAVORABILITY RISING IN THE U.S.

A majority of Americans have favorable opinion of him one year into his term

by Art Swift

WASHINGTON, D.C.—As Secretary of State John Kerry traveled to Kiev, Ukraine, this week to show solidarity with the interim

Ukrainian government, a recent Gallup poll finds that a majority of Americans have a generally favorable view of the secretary. Fifty-five percent in the U.S. view Kerry favorably, up seven percentage points since last September.

Favorability of U.S. Secretary of State John Kerry

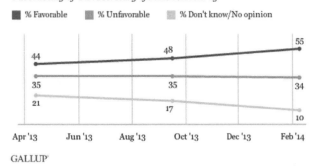

GALLUP'

These results come from Gallup's annual World Affairs poll, conducted in February. The survey preceded the current crisis in Ukraine but followed the deal the U.S. and other countries reached with Iran to temporarily freeze parts of its nuclear program in exchange for the relaxation of some Western sanctions.

Gallup last asked Americans about Kerry in September 2013, when he was in the midst of U.S. debate over military action in Syria. At that time, Kerry said Syria's use of chemical weapons on its own people was "undeniable" and announced that the U.S. was pondering intervention in the conflict. At that time, 48% of Americans viewed Kerry favorably, while 35% viewed him unfavorably. In April 2013, two months into his tenure as secretary of state, 44% of Americans regarded Kerry favorably. So in less than a year, as more and more Americans have felt they knew enough about Kerry to rate him, his favorable ratings have risen 11 percentage points, while his unfavorable ratings have stayed essentially constant.

Gallup has asked about Kerry's favorability periodically since 1999, covering his time as senator from Massachusetts and Democratic presidential nominee in 2004. His current 55% favorable rating ranks on the high end of those ratings, with his personal best of 61% coming after his victories in the 2004 Iowa caucuses and New Hampshire primary that made him the clear front-runner for the 2004 Democratic nomination. At the time of the general election that year, 52% viewed him favorably and 43% unfavorably.

After First Year, Kerry Favorability Lower Than That of Most Recent Secretaries of State

While Kerry is enjoying the popular approval of a majority of Americans one year into his tenure, his favorable rating is lower than ratings of four of the last five secretaries of state at comparable points in office. Kerry's immediate predecessor, Hillary Clinton, had a 61% favorable rating after approximately one year in office. More than 60% of Americans also favored Condoleezza Rice and Madeleine Albright a year into their terms. Colin Powell enjoyed a high 85% favorability rating roughly one year into his service as secretary of state. That measure, taken in April 2002, at least partly reflected Americans' rallying for the government after 9/11, resulting in high approval ratings for the Bush administration and Congress.

Kerry's favorability ratings after his first year in office eclipsed only those of President Bill Clinton's first secretary of state, Warren Christopher. The late secretary, who served in Clinton's cabinet from

1993 to 1997, had a favorable rating of 41% after roughly his first year in office, with 21% of Americans viewing him unfavorably and 39% either not having heard of or having no opinion of Christopher.

Americans' Views of U.S. Secretaries of State

After approximately one year in office

	% Favorable	% Unfavorable	% Don't know/ No opinion
John Kerry (Feb 6-9, 2014)	55	34	10
Hillary Clinton (Jul 8-11, 2010)	61	35	4
Condoleezza Rice (Aug 18-20, 2006)	61	26	13
Colin Powell (Apr 29-May 1, 2002)	85	9	6
Madeleine Albright (Feb 20-22, 1998)	62	15	23
Warren Christopher (Jan 6-8, 1994)	41	21	39

GALLUP'

Bottom Line

Much of the world is focused on Kerry this week as the U.S. and Russia engage in brinkmanship over Russia's military involvement in Ukraine. In his year in office, Kerry has been involved in not only the Ukrainian crisis but also the chemical weapons situation in Syria, developing a framework for peace talks between Israel and the Palestinians, and nuclear peace talks with Iran. Although the question wording identified Kerry as secretary of state, Americans may also remember him as a longtime senator from Massachusetts or as the failed presidential candidate from 2004. Still, as this series of world conflicts persists, Kerry's favorable ratings as secretary of state are rising.

The secretary will be faced with a variety of challenges this spring. Kerry was supposed to be focused this month on achieving progress on Mideast peace, possibly reaching a historic agreement on the framework for peace talks, and now he is mired in a Cold War–like geopolitical conflict he likely never envisioned when he became secretary.

Survey Methods

Results for this Gallup poll are based on telephone interviews conducted Feb. 6–9, 2014, on the Gallup Daily tracking survey, with a random sample of 1,023 adults, aged 18 and older, living in all 50 U.S. states and the District of Columbia.

For results based on the total sample of national adults, the margin of sampling error is ±4 percentage points at the 95% confidence level.

March 06, 2014
NUMBER OF AMERICANS SAYING ACA HAS HURT THEM INCHES UP
Stark contrast along party lines on whether the law has helped or hurt

by Justin McCarthy

WASHINGTON, D.C.—Although several parts of the Affordable Care Act have yet to be implemented, 23% of Americans say the healthcare law has hurt them or their families, while 10% say it has helped them so far. Still, the majority of Americans (63%) feel the law has had no impact on them or their families.

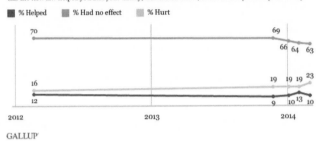

The Affordable Care Act's Perceived Effect on Families

As you may know, a few of the provisions of the healthcare law have already gone into effect. So far, has the new law helped you and your family, not had an effect, or has it hurt you and your family?

■ % Helped   ■ % Had no effect   ▨ % Hurt

GALLUP'

This update is from Gallup polling conducted between Feb. 28 and March 2, just prior to the Obama administration's announcement this week that insurance companies will be able to delay until next year the requirement that they cancel or replace policies that don't conform to the provisions of the law often referred to as "Obamacare."

The 23% who feel the law has hurt them is the highest percentage for the question since Gallup began asking Americans about it in 2012, and is up from 19% in previous polling.

Party Affiliation Plays a Big Role in Americans' Responses

When Americans answer the question about the law's impact on them and their families, their political orientation substantially affects their responses. Republicans are more than five times as likely (39%) as Democrats (7%) to say the ACA has had a negative impact. One in four independents (25%) say the law has hurt them or their families.

The Affordable Care Act's Perceived Effect on Families, by Party ID

As you may know, a few of the provisions of the healthcare law have already gone into effect. So far, has the new law helped you and your family, not had an effect, or has it hurt you and your family?

	Democrats	Independents	Republicans
	%	%	%
Helped	17	10	3
No effect	71	60	57
Hurt	7	25	39

Feb. 28-March 2, 2014

GALLUP'

A Divided But Largely Negative Outlook for the Law's Long-Term Impact

Despite the extraordinary emphasis on fixing problems with the healthcare exchanges that marred the initial rollout of the law, and a national campaign to enroll more Americans through the exchanges, most Americans remain unconvinced that the law will be beneficial to their families in the long run. By 40% to 21%, Americans say the law is more likely to make their families' healthcare situations worse rather than better, with the rest saying it will make little difference.

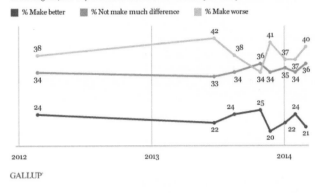

Americans' Views of the ACA's Ability to Improve Families' Healthcare Situations

In the long run, how do you think the healthcare law will affect your family's healthcare situation?

■ % Make better   ■ % Not make much difference   ▨ % Make worse

GALLUP'

Americans Continue to Disapprove Rather Than Approve of Law

Americans continue to be more negative than positive when asked about their overall attitudes toward the law. Approval has hovered around the 40% mark in recent months, down from as high as 48% just after the November 2012 election, reflecting the problems with the healthcare exchanges, and the widespread and highly publicized policy cancellations Americans received as the law began to take effect. Disapproval of the ACA has hovered at or slightly above the 50% mark since last summer, with some survey-to-survey fluctuations.

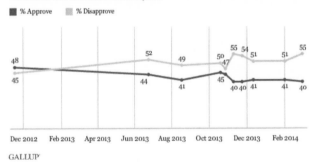

Americans' Views of the Affordable Care Act

Do you generally approve or disapprove of the 2010 Affordable Care Act, signed into law by President Obama that restructured the U.S. healthcare system?

■ % Approve   ▨ % Disapprove

GALLUP'

Bottom Line

For a White House that has made healthcare reform one of its core missions, the relatively low approval ratings for the Affordable Care Act are surely disappointing, though they are certainly nothing new. What may be more disappointing is the growing percentage of Americans who feel the law has already hurt them and their families, though, at 23%, this remains relatively small in absolute terms. Additionally, it is not clear whether some of these, particularly Republicans, have actually been harmed by the law or are more generally expressing their disapproval of it.

Open enrollment for healthcare ends later this month, and the ACA's legacy will likely be judged in the long term rather than by Americans' initial reactions to its implementation. So, low approval ratings and a compromised rollout could be a thing of the past if Americans covered under the ACA ultimately like their healthcare once the law goes into full effect.

Results for this Gallup poll are based on telephone interviews conducted Feb. 28–March 2, 2014, on the Gallup Daily tracking survey, with a random sample of 1,533 adults, aged 18 and older, living in all 50 U.S. states and the District of Columbia.

For results based on the total sample of national adults, the margin of sampling error is ±3 percentage points at the 95% confidence level.

March 07, 2014
VERMONT NO. 1 IN FREQUENT EXERCISE, PRODUCE CONSUMPTION
Americans exercised less in 2013 but maintained produce consumption level

by Lindsey Sharpe

WASHINGTON, D.C.—Adults living in Vermont (65.3%) are the most likely in the U.S. to report exercising three or more days a week for at least 30 minutes. Hawaii is in second place (62.2%), while Montana and Alaska follow closely behind (60.1% each). Residents of Delaware, West Virginia, and Alabama are the least likely to report that they exercise frequently.

Exercise: Top 10 States in 2013

In the last seven days, on how many days did you: Exercise for 30 or more minutes?

State	% 3 or more days
Vermont	65.3
Hawaii	62.2
Montana	60.1
Alaska	60.1
Colorado	59.8
Oregon	58.0
Idaho	57.7
New Mexico	57.4
Nebraska	56.3
North Dakota	56.0

January-December 2013
Gallup-Healthways Well-Being Index

GALLUP'

Exercise: Bottom 10 States in 2013

In the last seven days, on how many days did you: Exercise for 30 or more minutes?

State	% 3 or more days
Delaware	46.5
West Virginia	47.1
Alabama	47.5
New Jersey	47.7
Rhode Island	48.2
Tennessee	49.2
New York	49.3
Ohio	49.3
Indiana	49.4
South Carolina	49.7

January-December 2013
Gallup-Healthways Well-Being Index

GALLUP'

Six states, Vermont, Hawaii, Montana, Alaska, Colorado, and New Mexico, have ranked among the top 10 states for frequent exercise every year since Gallup and Healthways began tracking Americans' exercise habits in 2008. Vermont has taken the top spot three times, in 2013, 2009, and 2008, while Alaska was ranked first in both 2012 and 2010. On the other hand, four states—Indiana, Ohio, New Jersey, and Alabama—have ranked in the bottom 10 every year since 2008.

The results are from the Gallup-Healthways Well-Being Index from January through December 2013, and are based on interviews with more than 178,000 U.S. adults, with each state's data weighted to match U.S. Census demographic parameters for that state's adult population. The state sample sizes range from 547 for North Dakota to 17,053 for California. All have at least 500 respondents and 40 states have at least 1,000.

The national average for regular exercise decreased slightly to 51.6% in 2013 from 52.7% in 2012, but remains in line with the averages reported in previous years. According to NOAA's National Climatic Data Center, 2013 brought the coldest and wettest weather on record since 2009. This contrasts with 2012, which was the warmest year on record and considerably drier than 2013 was. These changes in weather may be related to Americans' exercising less frequently in 2013 than in 2012. Frequent exercise declined at least marginally in 31 states in 2013 compared with 2012, while it increased in 19 states.

The incidence of frequent exercise in a state is a function of many factors, including the age of the population, the availability of outdoor activities, and state-specific cultural factors that help determine the most popular recreational or leisure time activities. Additionally, many Americans are physically active as part of their work, and state-by-state differences in the type of work that residents do could affect the averages.

Vermont Residents Remain Most Likely to Eat Produce, Oklahomans the Least

For the second year in a row, Vermont residents are the most likely to report consuming produce frequently, with 67.8% of residents reporting that they eat at least five servings of vegetables four or more days per week. Montana (63.0%) and Washington (61.8%) residents follow closely behind. Oklahoma, Louisiana, and Missouri residents are the least likely to report consuming produce frequently.

Healthy Eating: Top 10 States in 2013

In the last seven days, on how many days did you: Eat five or more servings of vegetables four or more days per week?

State	% 4 or more days
Vermont	67.8
Montana	63.0
Washington	61.8
Oregon	61.4
New Mexico	61.1
Colorado	60.6
Wyoming	60.3
Maine	59.9
Arizona	59.9
Alaska	59.8

January-December 2013
Gallup-Healthways Well-Being Index

GALLUP'

Healthy Eating: Bottom 10 States in 2013

In the last seven days, on how many days did you: Eat five or more servings of vegetables four or more days per week?

State	% 4 or more days
Oklahoma	52.3
Louisiana	53.3
Missouri	53.8
Delaware	54.3
West Virginia	54.5
Arkansas	54.6
Iowa	55.4
Kansas	55.5
Texas	55.5
Ohio	55.6

January-December 2013
Gallup-Healthways Well-Being Index

GALLUP'

Vermont, Oregon, and Maine have ranked in the top 10 for frequent produce consumption every year since Gallup and Healthways started tracking Americans' produce consumption in 2008. While no state has ranked within the bottom 10 every year since 2008, seven states—Texas, Iowa, Arkansas, Louisiana, Oklahoma, Nebraska, and North Dakota—have been in the bottom 10 for five out of six years.

The nationwide average for regular produce consumption was 57.7% in 2013. The estimate has been highly stable since Gallup began tracking it in 2008, ranging narrowly between 56.0% and 57.8%.

Implications

With obesity rates rising in almost every state in 2013, it is important that state and local leaders address the decrease in exercise in 2013 and the unchanged level of regular produce consumption.

"There are tangible policies that cities and states can adopt to create an environment where the healthy choice is the easy choice—environments where fruits and vegetables are abundant and easy to access and people can easily exercise and move naturally in their communities," said Dan Buettner, National Geographic Fellow and Founder, Blue Zones, LLC. "When leadership makes it a priority to bring in policies that promote an environment of healthy choices, then it's not surprising that better outcomes ensue."

There are six states that rank in the top 10 for both frequent exercise and regular produce consumption, and five of them—Montana, Colorado, New Mexico, Vermont, and Oregon—also ranked in the bottom one-third in state obesity rates. While obesity is a complex condition, state and local policies and programs that encourage frequent exercise and healthy eating can reduce state and national obesity rates.

Survey Methods

Results are based on telephone interviews conducted as part of the Gallup-Healthways Well-Being Index survey Jan. 2–Dec. 29, 2013, with a random sample of 178,072 adults, aged 18 and older, living in all 50 U.S. states and the District of Columbia.

The margin of sampling error for most states is ±1 to ±2 percentage points, but is as high as ±4 points for states with smaller populations, such as Wyoming, North Dakota, South Dakota, Delaware, and Hawaii.

March 07, 2014
EVEN WEALTHY AMERICANS NOT IMMUNE TO MONEY WORRIES
Four in 10 with highest incomes don't feel good about the money they have to spend

by Andrew Dugan

WASHINGTON, D.C.—While Americans' average daily self-reported spending increased in 2013, many Americans nonetheless expressed anxiety about how much money they had to spend. Less than half (45%) said they felt "pretty good" about it. Lower-income Americans were least likely to feel good about their amount of disposable income, but even wealthier Americans—who were more likely to feel good—were not immune to money worries.

Are you feeling pretty good these days about the amount of money you have to spend, or not?

By self-reported annual household income

	% Yes	% No
U.S. ADULTS	45	54
Annual income <$48,000	35	64
$48,000 to <$90,000	50	50
$90,000 to <$240,000	59	40
$240,000 or more	59	40

Gallup Daily tracking, 2013

GALLUP'

These findings are based on Gallup Daily tracking throughout 2013 with more than 178,000 U.S. adults, aged 18 and older. The spending question is one of eight that Gallup asks daily to measure Americans' attitudes toward finances and spending.

More Than One in Four Wealthy Americans Unable to Make Major Purchase

In 2013, three in 10 Americans who reported annual household incomes less than $48,000 said they would be able to make a major purchase, such as a car, appliance, or furniture, if needed, compared with at least 61% of those in higher-income groups. But among those in the $240,000+ category, barely seven in 10 said they would be able to handle such a purchase, underscoring that some of even the highest-income Americans may be leading financially precarious lives.

On the other hand, there is a wide divide between Americans in the lowest income bracket and the others on whether they have enough money to buy the things they need: a majority (54%) of Americans in households with annual incomes less than $48,000 agree with this, compared with at least 80% of those with higher incomes.

Financial Security in the U.S.
Do you have enough money to buy the things you need, or not?

Would you be able right now to make a major purchase, such as a car, appliance, or furniture, or pay for a significant home repair if you needed to?

	Enough money to buy things you need	Able to make a major purchase
	% Yes	% Yes
U.S. ADULTS	68	47
Annual income <$48,000	54	30
$48,000 to <$90,000	80	61
$90,000 to <$240,000	87	75
$240,000 or more	85	72

Gallup Daily tracking, 2013

GALLUP'

Majority Not Feeling Better About Financial Situation

At 1.9% for 2013, U.S. economic growth remained well below the 3% level that economists say will provide the "escape velocity" that will power the recovery. In this low-growth environment, the majority of Americans (55%) interviewed in 2013 said they were not feeling better about their financial situation. The poorest Americans were particularly pessimistic, with 37% saying they felt better about their financial situation. However, even for those earning between $48,000 and $89,999, less than half were upbeat about their finances. Remarkably, only small majorities of Americans in the two highest income groups say they are feeling better about their financial situation, showing that many wealthier Americans still experience some financial angst.

Are you feeling better about your financial situation these days, or not?
By self-reported annual household income

	% Yes	% No
U.S. ADULTS	43	55
Annual income <$48,000	37	61
$48,000 to <$90,000	48	51
$90,000 to <$240,000	53	44
$240,000 or more	55	43

Gallup Daily tracking, 2013

GALLUP'

Bottom Line

No amount of income appears to spare Americans from common financial worries. Four in 10 of the highest-income Americans say they are not feeling better about their financial situations, and more than a quarter of them say they would not be able to handle a major purchase or home repair.

Income is important in overall financial well-being, of course, and the poorest Americans are the most sensitive to financial issues such as the ability to buy necessities and feeling good about spending capabilities. All in all, the economic recovery struggled on in 2013, but many Americans, regardless of income, weren't feeling better.

Survey Methods

Results for this Gallup poll are based on telephone interviews conducted Jan. 2–Dec. 29, 2013, on the Gallup Daily tracking survey, with a random sample of 178,527 adults, aged 18 and older, living in all 50 U.S. states and the District of Columbia.

For results based on the total sample of national adults, the margin of sampling error is ±1 percentage point at the 95% confidence level.

March 11, 2014
MOST AMERICANS PAYING CLOSE ATTENTION TO CRISIS IN UKRAINE
Two-thirds at least somewhat worried about specter of U.S. military involvement

by Joy Wilke

WASHINGTON, D.C.—More than two-thirds of Americans, 68%, say they are paying "very" or "somewhat" close attention to Russia's involvement in the situation in Ukraine. This is somewhat higher than the 61% of Americans who have paid close attention to key news events Gallup has asked about over the past two decades, but about in line with the level of attention paid to other recent international events, such as the political crisis in Egypt in 2011.

Americans' Attention to Key International and Domestic Events

How closely are you following the news about ...

(Sorted by date)

	% Following "very" or "somewhat" closely
Russia's involvement in the situation in Ukraine (March 2014)	68
The fiscal cliff, the combination of major tax increase and spending cuts (November 2012)	71
The proposed building of the Keystone XL pipeline, which could carry oil from Canada to Texas (March 2012)	49
U.S. military finding and killing Osama bin Laden (May 2011)	83
The situation in Libya (March 2011)	71
The political crisis and demonstrations in Egypt (February 2011)	69
Classified documents on war in Afghanistan leaked on the Internet (July 2010)	53
The oil spill in the Gulf of Mexico off the coast of Louisiana (May 2010)	87
The tsunami that struck parts of Asia (January 2005)	89
Terrorist attacks on New York City and Washington, D.C. (September 2001)	97

GALLUP

These data, collected March 6–9, as Russian forces continued to control several Ukrainian military sites, suggest that these events have generated above-average attention from most Americans, compared with other news events Gallup has asked about since 1991. Attention to the crisis in Ukraine is on par with the attention paid to such events as the crises in Egypt in February 2011 (69% paying close attention) and Libya in March 2011 (71%) but below attention to the killing of Osama bin Laden (83%) or the BP oil spill in the Gulf of Mexico (87%). By comparison, the events in Gallup's database that garnered the highest levels of attention were the 9/11 terrorist attacks, Hurricane Katrina, and the beginning of the war with Iraq in 2003, all of which at least 95% of Americans were following closely.

Older Americans Following Situation in Ukraine More Closely Than Younger Americans

Older Americans report paying more attention than younger Americans to Russia's involvement in the situation in Ukraine. Eighty-two percent of those 65 or older report they are paying "very" or "somewhat" close attention, compared with 49% of those aged 18 to 29.

The size of the generational gap in attention paid to the situation in Ukraine is approximately the same as it has been for other recent international events, suggesting that this gap likely reflects younger Americans' relative indifference toward international events, rather than older generations' memory of Russian aggression during the Cold War.

Americans' Attention to the Situation in Ukraine, by Age

How closely are you following the news about Russia's involvement in the situation in Ukraine?

	% Very/ Somewhat closely	% Not too closely/ Not at all
18 to 29	49	51
30 to 49	63	37
50 to 64	79	21
65+	82	18

March 6-9, 2014

GALLUP

Majority of Americans Worry That Ukraine Situation Could Lead to U.S. Military Involvement

Two-thirds of Americans report they are "very" or "somewhat" worried that the current political crisis in Ukraine could develop into a larger regional conflict, leading to U.S. military action. Those who report they are following the news about the crisis closely are more likely to say they are worried than those who are not following the news closely. Younger adults are slightly less likely to be worried than those who are older.

Americans' Worry About U.S. Military Involvement in Ukraine

How worried are you that the current situation in Ukraine will develop into a larger regional conflict that could lead to the U.S. military getting involved?

	% Very/ Somewhat worried
National adults	66
Following the news about Ukraine very/somewhat closely	73
Not closely following the news about Ukraine	51
18 to 29	60
30 to 49	66
50 to 65	70
65+	68

March 6-9, 2014

GALLUP

Implications

As interim Ukrainian Prime Minister Arseniy Yatsenyuk plans to travel to the U.S. to meet with President Barack Obama this week, and as Crimea prepares for a referendum on whether to join Russia, Americans are paying more attention to news of the crisis in that country than they have, on average, for major news stories in recent decades. Additionally, the majority of Americans are at least somewhat concerned over the prospect that the U.S. military may become involved in the region as a result of the situation.

As Gallup has previously reported, Americans' favorability ratings of Russia and its president, Vladimir Putin, have recently dropped to record lows. If Russia's aggression toward Ukraine continues, Americans' image of the country and its president may fall even further.

Survey Methods

Results for this Gallup poll are based on telephone interviews conducted March 6–9, 2014, with a random sample of 1,048 adults, aged 18 and older, living in all 50 U.S. states and the District of Columbia.

For results based on the total sample of national adults, the margin of sampling error is ±4 percentage points at the 95% confidence level.

March 12, 2014
CLIMATE CHANGE NOT A TOP WORRY IN U.S.
U.S. concerns with the quality of the environment dropped in 2014

by Rebecca Riffkin

WASHINGTON, D.C.—Twenty-eight U.S. senators held an all-night "talkathon" Monday to call attention to climate change, an issue that only 24% of Americans say they worry about a great deal. This puts climate change, along with the quality of the environment, near the bottom of a list of 15 issues Americans rated in Gallup's March 6–9 survey. The economy, federal spending, and healthcare dominate Americans' worries.

Americans' Level of Worry About National Problems -- 2014 Rank Order

Next, I'm going to read a list of problems facing the country. For each one, please tell me if you personally worry about this problem a great deal, a fair amount, only a little, or not at all? First, how much do you personally worry about ... [RANDOM ORDER]?

	Great deal	Fair amount	A little/ not at all
	%	%	%
The economy	59	29	11
Federal spending and the budget deficit	58	22	20
The availability and affordability of healthcare	57	20	23
Unemployment	49	28	23
The size and power of the federal government	48	20	31
The Social Security system	46	29	24
Hunger and homelessness	43	33	23
Crime and violence	39	31	29
The possibility of future terrorist attacks in the U.S.	39	24	37
The availability and affordability of energy	37	30	33
Drug use	34	29	37
Illegal immigration	33	24	42
The quality of the environment	31	35	34
Climate change	24	25	51
Race relations	17	26	56

Question asked of a half sample
March 6-9, 2014

GALLUP

This was the first year Gallup included "climate change" in the list of worries tested in the annual March Environment survey. Americans are less worried only about race relations than they are about climate change. The majority of Americans say they worry about these two issues "only a little" or "not at all"; more than half of Americans worry about the other 13 issues at least "a fair amount."

Thirty-one percent of Americans indicate that they worry "a great deal" about the quality of the environment this year, marking the lowest level of worry about the environment more broadly since Gallup began measuring this in 2001. Americans were most concerned about the environment in 2007, when 43% worried a great deal.

Americans' Worry About the Environment Over Time

Next, I'm going to read a list of problems facing the country. For each one, please tell me if you personally worry about this problem a great deal, a fair amount, only a little, or not at all? How much do you personally worry about the quality of the environment?

■ % Worry a great deal

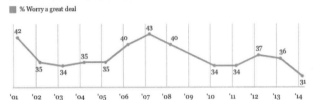

NOTE: March 2014 data asked of a half sample

GALLUP

Worries Differ Greatly Between Political Parties

Americans from the two major political parties express different levels of worry about a number of the issues tested, including climate change and the environment. Among Democrats and Democratic leaners, 45% say they worry a great deal about the quality of the environment. This percentage drops to 16% among Republicans and Republican leaners.

Gallup finds a 26-percentage-point difference in worry about climate change, with Democrats again more likely than Republicans to worry a great deal. Democrats, conversely, are much less worried than Republicans about the size and power of the federal government, and about federal spending and the budget deficit.

*Americans' Concern About U.S. Issues -- by Party Leaning^*

% Worry a great deal

	Republicans/ Republican leaners	Democrats/ Democratic leaners	Difference, Republicans minus Democrats
	%	%	Pct. pts.
The size and power of the federal government	67	29	+38
Federal spending and the budget deficit	74	44	+30
Illegal immigration	43	26	+17
The economy	67	54	+13
The possibility of future terrorist attacks in the U.S.	43	35	+8
The Social Security system	49	43	+6
The availability and affordability of healthcare	57	57	0
Unemployment	50	52	-2
Crime and violence	38	42	-4
Drug use	31	37	-6
The availability and affordability of energy	32	40	-8
Race relations	12	23	-11
Hunger and homelessness	33	53	-20
Climate change	10	36	-26
The quality of the environment	16	45	-29

^ Ranked by "Difference"
March 6-9, 2014

GALLUP

Republicans over the last few years have been more worried than Democrats about the economy and governance issues, while Democrats have been comparatively more worried with social issues such as race relations and homelessness. Although more Democrats than Republicans worry about the environment, climate change, and race relations, these are not major worries for most Democrats. The affordability and availability of healthcare and unemployment are two economic issues that Republicans and Democrats worry about equally.

Implications

Climate change and the quality of the environment rank near the bottom of a list of concerns for Americans, who are instead far more worried about more basic economic issues such as the economy, federal spending, and the affordability of healthcare. Concerns about the environment typically rank low among all Americans, but the current level of worry is even lower than in the past.

It is unclear whether or to what extent the senators' actions Monday will raise Americans' concern about climate change or the environment. But unless Americans' concern increases, the likelihood of the public's support for significant legislative action on environmental matters is small.

Survey Methods

Results for this Gallup poll are based on telephone interviews conducted March 6–9, 2014, on the Gallup Daily tracking survey, with a random sample of 513 adults, aged 18 and older, living in all 50 U.S. states and the District of Columbia.

For results based on the total sample of national adults, the margin of sampling error is ±6 percentage points at the 95% confidence level.

March 12, 2014
AMERICANS SLIGHTLY MORE UPBEAT ABOUT COUNTRY'S DIRECTION
One-quarter of Americans satisfied with how things are going in the country

by Justin McCarthy

WASHINGTON, D.C.—One in four Americans (25%) are satisfied with the way things are going in the country at this time—a low figure in an absolute sense but the highest since last July. Still, nearly three times as many Americans remain dissatisfied with how things are going in the U.S.

In general, are you satisfied or dissatisfied with the way things are going in the United States at this time?

% Satisfied

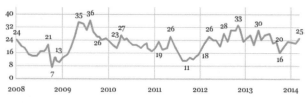

Trend since 2008

GALLUP'

These results are from a March 6–9 Gallup poll, which show that Americans' satisfaction with the country's direction is gradually recovering from a recent low of 16% in October, during the federal government shutdown.

Satisfaction with the nation's direction has generally hovered in the 20s since early 2012. The highest satisfaction reading in recent years (33%) came in November 2012, just days before Barack Obama's re-election.

Gallup has asked this question since 1979. Satisfaction reached an all-time high of 71% in February 1999 amid the dot-com boom. The lowest reading (7%) was measured in October 2008 as the nation grappled with the early effects of the 2008 global financial crisis. Less than 40% of Americans have been satisfied with the way things are going in the U.S. since 2005, and satisfaction was last above the majority level in January 2004.

Satisfaction Varies by Political Identification

Americans' satisfaction levels with the way the country is going have historically varied according to the political party they identify with and the party of the president in office. This month, with a Democratic president in office, Democrats report the highest satisfaction levels (40%). Independents are half as likely to be satisfied with the country's direction (21%), and Republicans are the least satisfied (12%).

Satisfaction With the Way Things Are Going in the U.S., by Party ID

% Satisfied

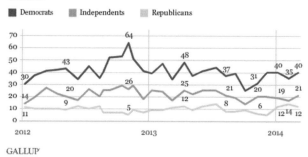

GALLUP'

Bottom Line

Satisfaction with how things are going in the U.S., like other measures such as economic confidence, has recovered from its decline during the federal government shutdown. Still, with just 25% of the nation's residents satisfied with the way things are going, the nation as a whole remains deeply negative. These attitudes, coupled with continuing low congressional approval, may significantly influence the outcome of the midterm elections this November, although it is not clear exactly how voters will take out their frustrations, given that Congress is under divided party control.

Satisfaction was slightly lower (23%) in March 2010, the last congressional midterm year, when Republicans took control of the House, and only slightly higher in March 2006 (29%), the year Democrats took control. Satisfaction was significantly higher in March 2002 (61%), before the midterms in which Republicans gained control of the Senate and retained control of the House, reflecting in part the continuing rally effect that followed the 9/11 terrorist attacks the previous September.

Much of the explanation for low satisfaction is low economic confidence, which has been quite negative in recent years. Economic confidence could be even more influential in determining the future course of satisfaction because another shutdown seems unlikely in the near future.

Survey Methods

Results for this Gallup poll are based on telephone interviews conducted March 6–9, 2014, on the Gallup Daily tracking survey, with a random sample of 1,048 adults, aged 18 and older, living in all 50 U.S. states and the District of Columbia.

For results based on the total sample of national adults, the margin of sampling error is ±4 percentage points at the 95% confidence level.

March 13, 2014
AMERICANS CITE JOBS, ECONOMY, GOV'T AS TOP U.S. PROBLEMS
Three responses are dominant in American minds as the most important problems

by Rebecca Riffkin

WASHINGTON, D.C.—Three issues—unemployment, the economy in general, and dissatisfaction with government—dominate when Americans name the most important problem facing the nation. Nineteen percent mention unemployment or jobs, 18% say dissatisfaction with government, and 17% the economy in general. Unemployment edged out the other two issues in February, but dropped slightly in March.

Recent Trend in Top Five "Most Important" U.S. Problems
What do you think is the most important problem facing this country today? (open-ended and coded)

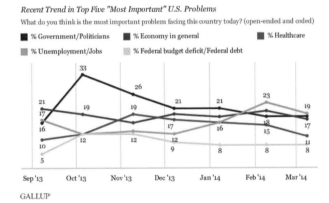

GALLUP'

In the midst of the federal government shutdown in October 2013, dissatisfaction with government and politicians jumped up to the top of the "most important problem" list. But mentions of dysfunctional government settled back down by February and are now on par with mentions of the economy and unemployment.

In the latest poll, conducted March 6–9, the percentage who cite healthcare dropped to where it was in October, while concerns about the federal budget remained stable for the third month in a row. The percentages mentioning other issues such as education, ethics, and poverty remain at levels similar to February's.

Americans mentioned a few other issues related to recent news developments more frequently than in the previous month, although still only a small percentage mentioned them. One percent of

Americans named the situation with Russia as the most important problem, and 2% listed war. Russia was not mentioned in February, while 1% mentioned war last month. These small increases may be linked to recent international developments such as the conflict in Ukraine. Gallup research shows that Americans are paying a relatively high level of attention to the situation in Ukraine, but clearly they do not perceive the situation as grave enough to consider it a top problem.

Most Important Problem Facing the U.S.
What do you think is the most important problem facing this country today?

	Feb 6-9, 2014	Mar 6-9, 2014
	%	%
Unemployment/Jobs	23	19
Dissatisfaction with government/Congress/politicians; poor leadership/corruption/abuse of power	18	18
Economy in general	20	17
Poor healthcare/hospitals; high cost of healthcare	15	11
Federal budget deficit/Federal debt	8	8
Education/Poor education/Access to education	4	5
Ethics/Moral/Religious/Family decline; Dishonesty	5	4
Foreign aid/Focus overseas	2	4
Poverty/Hunger/Homelessness	3	4
Immigration/Illegal aliens	6	4
Lack of money	3	3
Gap between rich and poor	2	3

Shown are the top 12 responses in March

GALLUP'

In a separate question that Gallup recently reported, Americans said they worried most about the economy, federal spending, and healthcare, and then unemployment, when asked to rate their level of worry about 15 issues. Together, these findings confirm the primacy of the economy and unemployment, as well as government, as the issues that most concern Americans today.

Implications

Unemployment, the economy, and the government dominate as Americans' top concerns about the major issues facing the country. Separately, Gallup recently reported that Americans say they worry most about the economy, federal spending, and healthcare when asked to rate their level of worry about 15 issues. Together, these findings confirm that regardless of how the question is asked, the economy and government are the issues that most concern Americans today.

International issues in the news, such as the large-scale protests in Venezuela and the crisis in Ukraine, are currently not major concerns for most Americans. President Barack Obama has pledged to lessen wage gaps and make other measures to combat income inequality, but the public remains more concerned with finding good jobs and lowering the unemployment rate.

Survey Methods

Results for this Gallup poll are based on telephone interviews conducted March 6–9, 2014, with a random sample of 1,048 adults, aged 18 and older, living in all 50 U.S. states and the District of Columbia.

For results based on the total sample of national adults, the margin of sampling error is ±4 percentage points at the 95% confidence level.

March 13, 2014
IN U.S., SMOKING RATE LOWEST IN UTAH, HIGHEST IN KENTUCKY
Smoking rate in Alaska has dropped the most since 2008

by Justin McCarthy

WASHINGTON, D.C.—Utah remains the state with the lowest percentage of smokers (12.2%), a distinction it has held since Gallup and Healthways began tracking smoking habits in 2008. Kentucky (30.2%) and West Virginia (29.9%) have the highest smoking rates in the nation, as has been the case since 2008.

States With the Lowest Smoking Rates
Do you smoke?

	% Yes
Utah	12.2
California	15.0
Minnesota	15.8
Massachusetts	16.3
New Jersey	16.9
Maryland	17.0
Washington	17.0
Rhode Island	17.1
Colorado	17.4
Arizona	17.5

January-December 2013
Gallup-Healthways Well-Being Index

GALLUP

States With the Highest Smoking Rates
Do you smoke?

	% Yes
Kentucky	30.2
West Virginia	29.9
Mississippi	27.0
Oklahoma	25.2
Ohio	25.0
Missouri	24.7
Indiana	24.7
Louisiana	24.1
Tennessee	23.6
Michigan	23.2

January-December 2013
Gallup-Healthways Well-Being Index

GALLUP

These results are based on interviews conducted Jan. 2–Dec. 29, 2013 with more than 178,000 Americans in all 50 states and the District of Columbia as part of the Gallup-Healthways Well-Being Index.

Utah's low smoking rate is due in large part to the religious composition of its residents. Six in 10 Utah residents identify themselves as Mormon, and in 2013 just 5% of Mormons living in Utah smoked, while smoking among the next three most represented groups in Utah—those with no religious identity, Protestants, and Catholics—were at or above national smoking averages for each group.

While smoking rates declined in nearly all states from 2008—the first year Gallup and Healthways collected enough data on smoking habits to allow state-level estimates—to 2013, the states with the top 10 highest and lowest smoking rates are largely the same as they were six years ago. Nationally, the smoking rate fell to 19.7% in 2013 from 21.1% in 2008.

States with the lowest smoking rates are generally located in the Northeast and the West, while states with the highest smoking rates are predominantly located in the South and Midwest.

When comparing the 2008 and 2013 smoking rates for each state, Alaska, North Dakota, Rhode Island, Illinois, and Nevada saw the most improvement. The smoking rate in each of these states is at least four percentage points lower in 2013 than it was in 2008, well above the 1.4-point drop nationally.

Most Improved Smoking Rates, 2008 vs. 2013
% Who smoke

	2008 %	2013 %	Change (pct. pts.)
Alaska	25.2	18.7	-6.5
Rhode Island	22.7	17.1	-5.6
North Dakota	24.1	18.5	-5.6
Illinois	22.5	18.1	-4.4
Nevada	24.7	20.3	-4.4

Gallup-Healthways Well-Being Index

GALLUP

States With Smoking Bans Tend to Have Lower Smoking Rates

Thirty-three states have outright bans on smoking in private worksites and restaurants, and 27 states have bans on smoking in bars, according to the Centers for Disease Control and Prevention. Some states, like California, have provisions for ventilated rooms. Others, like Missouri, have provisions for designated smoking areas. These figures do not include smoking bans that localities have put in place.

Nine of the 10 states with the lowest smoking rates have outright bans on smoking in all three of these settings, with California allowing for ventilated rooms.

Statewide Bans in States With the Lowest Percentage of Smokers, 2013
Outright bans (B) = Banned
Ventilated (V) = Designated smoking areas allowed for the specified site if separately ventilated

	Workplace	Restaurants	Bars	No statewide bans
Utah	B	B	B	
California	V	V	V	
Minnesota	B	B	B	
Massachusetts	B	B	B	
New Jersey	B	B	B	
Maryland	B	B	B	
Washington	B	B	B	
Rhode Island	B	B	B	
Colorado	B	B	B	
Arizona	B	B	B	

Centers for Disease Control and Prevention
State Tobacco Activities Tracking and Evaluation (STATE) System

GALLUP

Bans are significantly less common in the 10 states with the highest smoking rates. Kentucky, West Virginia, and Mississippi—the states with the three highest smoking rates—do not have statewide bans in any of the three settings.

Statewide Bans in States With the Highest Percentage of Smokers, 2013
Outright bans (B) = Banned
Ventilated (V) = Designated smoking areas allowed for the specified site if separately ventilated
Designated (D) = Designated smoking areas required or allowed for the specified site

	Workplace	Restaurants	Bars	No statewide bans
Kentucky				X
West Virginia				X
Mississippi				X
Oklahoma	D	V		
Ohio	B	B	B	
Missouri	D	D	D	
Indiana	B	B		
Louisiana	B	B		
Tennessee	B	D		
Michigan	B	B	B	

Centers for Disease Control and Prevention
State Tobacco Activities Tracking and Evaluation (STATE) System

GALLUP

Bottom Line

Since Gallup began asking Americans whether they smoke or not in 1944, the percentage of smokers has declined by more than half. Still, about one in five Americans in 2013 said they smoke.

There is still wide variation in smoking rates across states; roughly one in three residents in Kentucky and West Virginia are smokers, compared with 12% of residents in Utah. Statewide bans on smoking, or lack thereof, are a strong indicator of where a state ranks relative to the national average.

Notably, in 2013, Gallup found that most smokers want to quit, and the majority have tried to stop, often numerous times. Americans may benefit from state-level, policy-based interventions that would discourage smoking through various laws, bans, and taxes, and may assist residents in quitting through state-run helplines and websites. States that have more comprehensive statewide bans have lower overall smoking rates, although the precise way that these policies affect smoking rates is unclear.

"The past 20 years saw an intense public health push to address tobacco use in the U.S., ranging from legislation around smoke-free zones to the development of pharmaceutical products to leveraging the Internet to drive cessation. However the dramatic loss of state funding for tobacco control across the country could endanger these gains," said Nathan Cobb M.D., Assistant Professor of Medicine at Georgetown University of Medicine and Chief Medical Officer of MeYou Health.

"To pick up the slack will require innovative thinking around social marketing to continue the denormalization of smoking and more cost effective mechanisms to drive cessation and abstinence for those people wishing to quit," Cobb said.

The frontier for future smoking-related debate is widening, however, as e-cigarettes are a new tobacco product that have provoked unchartered legislative battles in states. Corporations, too, are entering the fray with CVS recently deciding that it will eventually end tobacco sales.

Survey Methods

Results are based on telephone interviews conducted as part of the Gallup-Healthways Well-Being Index survey Jan. 2–Dec. 29, 2013, with a random sample of 178,067 adults, aged 18 and older, living in all 50 U.S. states and the District of Columbia.

For results based on the total sample of national adults, the margin of sampling error is ±1 percentage point at the 95% confidence level.

The margin of sampling error for most states is ±1 to ±2 percentage points, but is as high as ±4 points for states with smaller populations, such as Wyoming, North Dakota, South Dakota, Delaware, and Hawaii.

March 13, 2014
IN U.S., MOST DO NOT SEE GLOBAL WARMING AS SERIOUS THREAT
Nearly two in three believe global warming will happen during their lifetimes

by Jeffrey M. Jones

PRINCETON, NJ—The majority of Americans continue to believe that the effects of global warming are happening or will begin to happen during their lifetimes. At the same time, many fewer, currently 36%, believe global warming will pose a serious threat to their way of life during their lifetimes.

The results are based on Gallup's annual Environment poll, conducted March 6–9. Only about half of those who expect global warming to occur during their lifetimes, 51%, believe it will pose a serious threat to their way of life. This explains the gap between

Americans' perceptions that global warming is occurring and that it will be a threat.

Expectations for Global Warming During Lifetime
Which of the following statements reflects your view of when the effects of global warming will begin to happen -- [ROTATED: they have already begun to happen, they will start happening within a few years, they will start happening within your lifetime, they will not happen within your lifetime, but they will affect future generations, (or) they will never happen]?

Do you think that global warming will pose a serious threat to you or your way of life in your lifetime?

■ % Is happening/Will happen during lifetime   ▨ % Will pose serious threat to way of life

GALLUP

Although the gap between the perceived occurrence and perceived threat of global warming remains wide, it is narrower than in the past. The percentage of Americans who believe global warming's effects will happen during their lifetimes is the same now as it was in 1997, when Gallup first asked the question, and is among the lower readings over that 17-year span. During that same period, the percentage who believe global warming will threaten their way of life has increased from 25% to 36%.

Gallup's 2008 survey marked the peak in the belief that global warming will happen during one's lifetime (75%) and that it will seriously threaten one's way of life (40%).

Currently, 54% of Americans say the effects of global warming have already begun to happen, with 3% saying they will begin in a few years and 8% saying they will happen during their lifetimes. Another 16% expect that global warming's effects will not start in their own lifetimes but will affect future generations. This leaves 18% saying the effects will never happen, double the 9% who said this in 1997.

Expectations That Global Warming's Effects Will Occur
Which of the following statements reflects your view of when the effects of global warming will begin to happen -- [ROTATED: they have already begun to happen, they will start happening within a few years, they will start happening within your lifetime, they will not happen within your lifetime, but they will affect future generations, (or) they will never happen]?

	%
Already begun	54
Will begin within a few years	3
Will begin within lifetime	8
Will not begin within lifetime, but will affect future generations	16
Will never happen	18
No opinion	2

March 6-9, 2014

GALLUP

Older Americans Less Likely to See Global Warming as Threat

Americans younger than 65 are much more likely than senior citizens to believe global warming will seriously threaten their way of life. Whereas 18% of seniors say global warming will be a threat to the way they live, roughly four in 10 of those in younger age groups do.

Expectations That Global Warming Will Seriously Threaten One's Way of Life, by Age Group

	18 to 29 years	30 to 49 years	50 to 64 years	65+ years
	%	%	%	%
Yes, will	43	42	37	18
No, will not	57	57	63	82

March 6-9, 2014

GALLUP

That difference could be due to practical considerations; senior citizens can rightly expect that they have fewer years left on earth than younger Americans, and therefore to believe that long-term issues such as global warming will not affect them personally. Senior citizens are also the age group least likely to believe that global warming will happen during their lifetimes. However, these differences are not entirely a function of seniors' recognition of their advanced age, as those 65 and older are also most skeptical that the effects of global warming have already begun.

Expectations That Global Warming's Effects Will Occur, by Age Group

	18 to 29 years	30 to 49 years	50 to 64 years	65+ years
	%	%	%	%
Already begun	58	62	52	38
Will begin within a few years	6	1	2	3
Will begin within lifetime	14	5	7	6
Will affect future generations	11	13	14	27
Will never happen	10	16	22	24
NET: During lifetime	78	68	61	47

March 6-9, 2014

GALLUP

Notably, although young Americans are the most likely age group to believe that the effects of global warming will occur during their lifetimes, they are no more likely than 30- to 49-year-olds, and just slightly more likely than 50- to 64-year-olds, to believe global warming will seriously threaten their way of life.

Seniors' greater skepticism about global warming may be influenced by their Republican-leaning politics; party identification is a major factor in Americans' views of global warming. Democrats are nearly twice as likely as Republicans to believe the effects of global warming will occur in their lifetimes, and nearly three times as likely to believe it will seriously threaten their way of life.

Expectations That Global Warming's Effects Will Occur and Threaten One's Way of Life, by Political Party

	Democrats	Independents	Republicans
	%	%	%
WHEN EFFECTS WILL OCCUR			
Already begun	73	51	36
Will begin within a few years	4	2	2
Will begin within lifetime	6	10	4
Will affect future generations	13	14	22
Will never happen	3	19	34
NET: During lifetime	83	63	42
SERIOUS THREAT TO WAY OF LIFE			
Yes	56	32	19
No	44	67	81

March 6-9, 2014

GALLUP

Implications

Most Americans believe global warming's effects will occur during their lifetimes, though this sentiment is no higher than it was 17 years ago, and is down from a peak of 75% in 2008. At the same time, although Americans largely do not view global warming as a likely threat to their way of life, they are more likely to believe this now than in the 1990s.

Americans' belief that global warming is not a serious threat to their way of life may help explain why they see it and the environment more generally as a lower priority for government than issues that affect them more immediately, like the economy and healthcare. However, Americans' average concern about global warming may shift in the future, even if there is no obvious change in environmental conditions, as today's more skeptical older Americans are replaced by younger Americans who are more likely to view global warming as occurring and as a potentially serious threat to their way of life.

Survey Methods

Results for this Gallup poll are based on telephone interviews conducted March 6–9, 2014, with a random sample of 1,048 adults, aged 18 and older, living in all 50 U.S. states and the District of Columbia.

For results based on the total sample of national adults, the margin of sampling error is ±4 percentage points at the 95% confidence level.

March 14, 2014
U.S. INVESTORS' OPTIMISM TICKS UP
Investor confidence surged among retirees; unchanged among non-retirees

by Lydia Saad

PRINCETON, NJ—U.S. investors' economic views warmed a bit in the past quarter, even as frigid temperatures across much of the country kept job growth and retail sales in check. The Wells Fargo/Gallup Investor and Retirement Optimism Index rose to +37 in February from +25 in November. Still, the index remains slightly below its May 2013 level of +43, measured amid last year's bull market, as well as its 2011 and 2012 high points.

Wells Fargo/Gallup Investor and Retirement Optimism Index

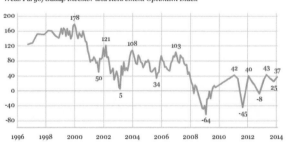

GALLUP

The Wells Fargo/Gallup Investor and Retirement Optimism Index is a measure of broad economic and financial optimism among U.S. investors with $10,000 or more in any combination of stocks, bonds, mutual funds, self-directed IRAs, and 401(k)s. The index has been conducted quarterly since 2011 and, prior to that, was conducted quarterly from October 1996 through December 1998, and monthly from February 1999 to October 2009. The current results are based on interviews conducted Feb. 6–16 with 1,011 investors, including 358 retirees and 650 non-retirees.

Gains Seen More on Personal Than on Economic Dimension

Both components of the index improved in the latest quarter, with a 10-point jump to +45 from +35 in the personal component, and a five-point increase to −5 from −10 in the economic component. Improvement in the personal dimension mainly stems from heightened investor confidence in being able to maintain or increase their income over the next year. Most of the improvement in the economic dimension comes from increased investor optimism about economic growth, with little change in their optimism about unemployment, inflation, or the stock market.

Wells Fargo/Gallup Investor and Retirement Optimism Index -- Recent Trend in Personal vs. Economic Dimensions

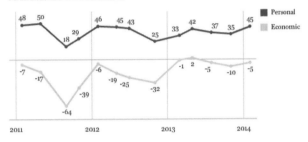

GALLUP'

Optimism Rises Mainly on Strength of Retirees' Improved Outlook

Optimism surged in the past quarter among retirees, rising to +41 in February from +6 in November. It was fairly steady among non-retirees, sitting at +35, similar to the previous reading of +32. This pattern of greater movement among retirees could be partly because optimism fell significantly more among retirees than among non-retirees between May and November of last year, possibly in reaction to low interest rates, as well as the federal budget showdown in September, and the resulting federal government shutdown in October. Now, with the stock market largely maintaining last year's gains, retirees may be feeling more confident about their finances as well as about the economy more broadly.

Wells Fargo/Gallup Investor and Retirement Optimism Index
Recent trend, by retirement status

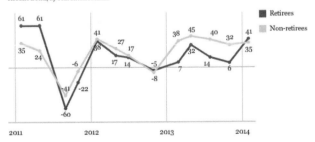

GALLUP'

Just in the past quarter, retirees' optimism increased the most in terms of their outlook for maintaining or increasing their income in the next 12 months. Their net optimism score (percentage optimistic minus percentage pessimistic) on this rose 20 points to +38. Their net optimism about economic growth and the stock market improved nearly as much, while their outlook for inflation rose 10 points. Notably, retired investors' expectations for unemployment have not improved.

Wells Fargo/Gallup Investor and Retirement Optimism Index -- Retired Investors
Recent change in net optimism for each index component^

	2013 -- Q4 (November 2014)	2014 -- Q1 (February 2014)	Change
PERSONAL DIMENSION			
Ability to maintain or increase your income in next 12 months	18	38	+20
Ability to achieve investment goals in next five years	24	31	+7
Ability to achieve investment targets in next 12 months	29	33	+4
ECONOMIC DIMENSION			
Economic growth	-12	4	+16
Performance of the stock market	26	41	+15
Inflation	-12	-2	+10
Unemployment rate	-17	-16	+1

^ Net optimism = percentage very/somewhat optimistic minus percentage very/somewhat pessimistic

GALLUP'

Bottom Line

Just as economic confidence among Americans as a whole has improved somewhat since last fall, U.S. investors' optimism has advanced modestly, rising 12 points to +37 in February. Investor optimism is not quite as high as it was last May, when the stock market was still surging, or as high as at several other points since 2011, but it has partially rebounded from its post-government-shutdown dip last fall. The reason for the rebound is not entirely clear, but given that it occurred almost entirely among retirees who, as a group, were consistently less confident than non-retirees in 2013, it could represent a delayed recovery for this group from last year's political shocks, aided by continued strength on Wall Street.

Survey Methods

Results for the Wells Fargo/Gallup Investor and Retirement Optimism Index are based on questions asked Feb. 6–16, 2014, on the Gallup Daily tracking survey, of a random sample of 1,011 U.S. adults having investable assets of $10,000 or more.

For results based on the entire sample of investors, one can say with 95% confidence that the maximum margin of sampling error is ±3 percentage points at the 95% confidence level.

March 14, 2014
AMERICANS DON'T ATTRIBUTE COLDER WEATHER TO CLIMATE CHANGE
Many more say colder temperatures due to normal yearly variation

by Jeffrey M. Jones

PRINCETON, NJ—Two in three Americans say their local area is experiencing colder-than-usual temperatures this winter, and one in four say their area is experiencing drought. When asked why they think these extreme weather events are happening, many more say they are attributable to normal yearly variation in temperature or rainfall than to human-caused climate change or global warming.

Americans' Experience of Extremes in Local Weather and the Perceived Cause

	%
WINTER TEMPERATURES IN LOCAL AREA	
Colder than usual	66
(Due to normal variation in temperatures)	(46)
(Due to human-caused climate change)	(19)
(Unsure)	(1)
About the same	19
Warmer than usual	13
EXPERIENCING DROUGHT	
Yes	25
(Due to normal variation in rainfall)	(15)
(Due to global warming)	(9)
(Unsure)	(1)
No	75

March 6-9, 2014

GALLUP

Gallup's March 6–9 Environment poll asked Americans to report on weather conditions in their local areas. Extreme cold and snow have blanketed the Northeast and Midwest all winter, with frigid temperatures and snowfall extending into the Deep South at times. Also, California and the Southwestern part of the country have experienced drought conditions.

Democrats are much more inclined than Republicans to attribute the extreme weather to global warming or climate change. Forty-seven percent of Democrats and Democratic-leaning independents who perceive colder temperatures in their areas attribute this to climate change, compared with 11% of Republicans and Republican-leaning independents who perceive colder temperatures.

Meanwhile, 51% of Democrats and Democratic leaners experiencing drought attribute it to global warming, compared with 14% of Republicans.

Those political patterns on global warming are consistent with the Republican-Democratic divide on global warming attitudes more generally.

Extreme Weather Patterns Apparent by Region

Americans certainly appear to be aware of the more extreme temperature ranges the country has been experiencing in recent years, with many reporting colder-than-usual temperatures this year, compared with an even higher percentage who reported warmer-than-usual temperatures two years ago.

Specifically, 66% of Americans say their local area is experiencing colder winter temperatures than normal this winter, a sharp contrast to 2013 (19%) and 2012 (4%). In 2012, 79% said winter temperatures were warmer than usual.

Winter Temperatures Compared With Prior Winters

Next, I'd like you to think about the weather in your local area this winter season compared to past winters. Have temperatures in your local area been -- [ROTATED: colder than usual this winter, about the same, (or) warmer than usual this winter]?

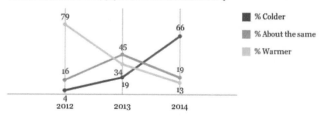

GALLUP

Perceptions that the temperatures have been colder than usual vary by region. There is widespread consensus among Eastern and Midwestern residents that temperatures have been colder this winter, with 87% in each region holding that view. A majority of Southern residents, 68%, say the same about local temperatures in their part of the country. In contrast, 41% of Western residents say temperatures have been *warmer* where they live, consistent with the record warmth that California has seen this winter.

Winter Temperatures Compared With Prior Winters, by Region

Next, I'd like you to think about the weather in your local area this winter season compared to past winters. Have temperatures in your local area been -- [ROTATED: colder than usual this winter, about the same, (or) warmer than usual this winter]?

	East	Midwest	South	West
	%	%	%	%
Colder	87	87	68	26
About the same	9	10	21	31
Warmer	1	3	9	41

March 6-9, 2014

GALLUP

Overall, drought is affecting far fewer Americans, with 25% saying their area is suffering from a shortage of rainfall. That small national percentage is likely because drought conditions are largely confined to one part of the country—65% of Western residents say they are experiencing drought, compared with between 4% and 20% in the other regions of the country.

Local Area Experiencing Drought, by Region

Is your local area experiencing a drought, that is, a serious shortage of rainfall this year, or not?

	East	Midwest	South	West
	%	%	%	%
Yes, is	4	11	20	65
No, is not	96	87	80	35

March 6-9, 2014

GALLUP

Implications

Recent years have brought extreme weather to the United States and raised the possibility that it is evidence of global warming's effects. But Americans tend not to attribute this winter's colder weather in most of the country, or the drought in the Southwestern part of the country, to global warming or climate change. Rather, they are more likely to view these as simply normal variations in weather patterns, though Republicans are much more likely than Democrats to believe this. The belief that temperature extremes are part of normal variation is not new; almost eight in 10 Americans in 2012 thought that the temperatures that winter had been warmer than usual, but most of those also said this reflected normal variations rather than the effect of global warming.

Americans' views of what is causing this winter's weather may be influenced by their relative lack of concern about global warming or climate change, with only about four in 10 predicting it will seriously threaten their way of life. If Americans were more likely to see global warming as an immediate threat, they might be more willing to see it as a cause of current weather patterns.

Survey Methods

Results for this Gallup poll are based on telephone interviews conducted March 6–9, 2014, with a random sample of 1,048 adults, aged 18 and older, living in all 50 U.S. states and the District of Columbia.

For results based on the total sample of national adults, the margin of sampling error is ±4 percentage points at the 95% confidence level.

March 17, 2014
IN U.S., 66% SATISFIED HEALTH SYSTEM WORKS FOR THEM
One-third of those without insurance are satisfied

by Frank Newport

PRINCETON, NJ—Two-thirds of Americans are satisfied with the way the healthcare system is working for them today. Health insurance status is a major determinant of this satisfaction, but even one-third of those who don't have health insurance still say they are satisfied.

Are you satisfied or dissatisfied with how the healthcare system is working for you?

	Satisfied	Dissatisfied	No opinion
	%	%	%
National adults	66	32	3
Have health insurance	72	26	2
Do not have health insurance	33	59	8

March 10-15, 2014

GALLUP

This question was asked during March 10–15 interviewing as a basic summary indicator of how well the healthcare system is working for individual Americans.

Healthcare insurance status is the most important dividing factor in Americans' perceptions of how the healthcare system is working for them, although by no means is having insurance a perfect

determinant of their satisfaction. Seventy-two percent of those with health insurance say they are satisfied with the system, leaving about one-quarter who are not. And one-third of those who do not have health insurance still say they are satisfied.

As with any summary question, it is impossible to measure exactly what Americans take into account when they answer. However, research conducted in last November's Gallup Poll Social Series survey on healthcare showed broadly similar results when Americans were asked three questions involving access to healthcare, and the cost and quality of their own healthcare. Overall, 79% rated the quality of healthcare they received as excellent or good, 69% rated their personal healthcare coverage as excellent or good, and 59% were satisfied with the total cost they paid for healthcare.

Thus, Americans may be averaging these three aspects of the healthcare system in answering whether they are satisfied with the way the healthcare system is working for them. Additionally, when this question was asked of a different sample but with the added phrase "including your access to healthcare, and the cost and quality of healthcare you receive," responses were almost identical, reinforcing the conclusion that the basic question represents a valid overall summary measure.

Young and Old Most Likely to Be Satisfied

Although younger Americans are less likely to have health insurance than those who are aged 30 to 64, they are more likely than this middle-aged group to be satisfied with the way the healthcare system is working for them. Seniors aged 65 and older, all of whom are eligible for Medicare, are the most satisfied.

Are you satisfied or dissatisfied with how the healthcare system is working for you?
By age

	Satisfied	Dissatisfied	No opinion
	%	%	%
18 to 29	73	26	1
30 to 49	60	38	2
50 to 64	56	39	4
65+	80	17	4

March 10-15, 2014

GALLUP

The higher satisfaction level among younger Americans may at least partly reflect that young people tend to be the healthiest—and therefore may be more inclined to indicate that the system is working fine as far as they are concerned. Additionally, young people may have lower premiums if they don't have families, and they might not have to pay for coverage if they are carried on their parents' policies.

Democrats Significantly More Likely to Be Satisfied

This general satisfaction question does not mention the Affordable Care Act by name, nor does it mention insurance or politics. Regardless, there is a political aspect to the responses. More than three in four Democrats are satisfied with how the healthcare system is working for them, compared with roughly six in 10 independents and Republicans. It is probable that some respondents think about the ACA when *any* question about healthcare is asked. Previous research shows Democrats are much more likely to approve of the law than anyone else, and some of this attitudinal foundation probably becomes a part of responses to the satisfaction question.

Are you satisfied or dissatisfied with how the healthcare system is working for you?

By party ID

	Satisfied	Dissatisfied	No opinion
	%	%	%
Republicans	61	38	1
Independents	59	36	5
Democrats	78	20	2

March 10-15, 2014

GALLUP

Implications

Most Americans do not believe the healthcare system in this country is in crisis. This may in part reflect the current finding that about two-thirds of Americans are satisfied with the way the healthcare system is working for them, including majorities in most subgroups except those who do not have health insurance.

At the same time, a clear majority of Americans now say they disapprove of the Affordable Care Act. Their disapproval could be because many don't see the need to change the system, and worry that the new legislation will affect a process they currently are satisfied with. President Barack Obama famously argued that under the ACA, those who liked their existing health insurance could keep it. However, in recent months, he has had to backtrack from that statement as news reports suggest that under the new law, some insured Americans may face changes in their policies, including coverage and cost. Their new policies, though they may provide a higher level of benefits, may end up costing them more than their old ones did.

Of course, much of the rationale for the new law involved helping Americans with no health insurance who would clearly benefit from change. With one in three Americans, including the majority of those without insurance, dissatisfied with the way the system is working for them, there is obvious need for this type of help. And, it may be that some of those who approve of the law have a satisfactory health insurance situation, but are motivated by charitable impulses rather than their own self-interest.

Still, Americans' satisfaction with the way the healthcare system is working for them appears to be one of the headwinds facing broad acceptance of the ACA. When a system is seen as working well, it is usually more difficult to propose major changes to it—particularly when those affected may be worried about unanticipated or negative consequences from those changes.

Survey Methods

Results for this Gallup poll are based on telephone interviews conducted March 10–15, 2014, on the Gallup Daily tracking survey, with a random sample of 1,542 adults, aged 18 and older, living in all 50 U.S. states and the District of Columbia.

For results based on the total sample of national adults, the margin of sampling error is ±3 percentage points at the 95% confidence level.

AMERICANS MOST LIKELY TO SAY GLOBAL WARMING IS EXAGGERATED
Sixty percent say most scientists believe global warming is occurring

by Andrew Dugan

This article is the fourth in a series that will analyze Gallup's latest March update on Americans' views on climate change and examine how these views have changed over time. The series will explore public opinion on the severity and importance of climate change, its causes and effects, the extent of Americans' understanding of the issue, and much more.

WASHINGTON, D.C.—Even as most Americans report experiencing abnormal weather conditions lately, more than four in 10 say the seriousness of global warming is generally exaggerated in the news. These sentiments are lower than the record 48% who believed this four years ago, but higher than any year before Barack Obama became president.

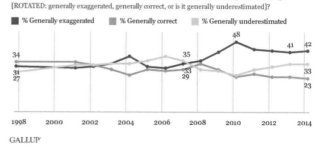

Americans Rate the Seriousness of Global Warming

Thinking about what is said in the news, in your view is the seriousness of global warming -- [ROTATED: generally exaggerated, generally correct, or is it generally underestimated]?

■ % Generally exaggerated ■ % Generally correct ■ % Generally underestimated

GALLUP

Though the largest share of Americans specifically describe reports on the seriousness of global warming as exaggerated, a slim majority collectively see these reports as generally correct (23%) or generally underestimated (33%). On this basis, most Americans seem to accept that global warming is at least as serious a problem as news reports say it is. Viewed still another way, fully three-quarters of the country believe that reports about global warming are mistaken—for better or worse.

These results come from Gallup's annual Environment poll, conducted March 6–9. Since 2011, attitudes about the perceived seriousness of global warming have been steady, but public opinion has changed notably since Gallup first asked the question in 1997. Fewer Americans now say the seriousness of global warming is generally correct; at the same time, the percentage finding the threat generally exaggerated has increased, and since 2009 has consistently been at or above 40%, a mark it never reached in the years before.

Views on Seriousness of Global Warming Vary by Party

Opinions about global warming vary by party identification, with Democrats typically more worried than Republicans about global warming and its potentially harmful effects on the environment. Democrats are most likely to say the seriousness of global warming is generally underestimated in the news, with about half (49%) saying so. Another 32% of Democrats believe reports about global warming are generally correct. Less than one-fifth (18%) find that the seriousness of global warming is generally exaggerated.

Seriousness of Global Warming by Self-Identified Political Affiliation

Thinking about what is said in the news, in your view is the seriousness of global warming -- [ROTATED: generally exaggerated, generally correct, or is it generally underestimated]?

	Republicans	Independents	Democrats
	%	%	%
Generally exaggerated	68	45	18
Generally correct	15	21	32
Generally underestimated	15	32	49

March 6-9, 2014

GALLUP

When GOP Sen. Jeff Sessions recently said the threat of global warming has been subjected to "a lot of exaggeration," he spoke for a commanding majority of self-identified Republicans. Nearly seven in 10 (68%) agree that the threat is generally exaggerated, while 15% say it is generally correct and 15% say it is generally underestimated. Views among independents break closer to national numbers.

Six in 10 Say Most Scientists Believe Global Warming Is Happening

While political disagreements on the veracity and severity of global warming continue, a broad swath of Americans (60%) agree that most scientists believe global warming is occurring, with only 8% saying most scientists believe that global warming is *not* occurring. Still others, 29%, are unsure if a scientific consensus exists at all.

While these findings differ little from last year, the percentage of Americans saying most scientists believe global warming is real did dip in the early years of the Obama administration. Those figures have since rebounded, but not to 2007–2008 levels.

Americans' Views on Whether Scientists Believe Global Warming Is Happening

Just your impression, which one of the following statements do you think is most accurate -- most scientists believe that global warming is occurring, most scientists believe that global warming is NOT occurring, or most scientists are unsure about whether global warming is occurring or not?

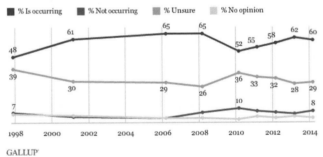

GALLUP

Partisanship is a major factor in these attitudes as well. Forty-two percent of Republicans say most scientists believe global warming is occurring, compared with 82% of Democrats. Another 43% of Republicans believe most scientists aren't sure about global warming, a position only 14% of Democrats accept.

Implications

The American public has a complicated view of global warming—most believe it is happening, but most do not think it will seriously affect their way of life and many do not attribute severe or unusual

weather events to this phenomenon. While a majority view the reported seriousness as generally correct or underestimated, a sizable and, since 2009, heightened percentage see the threat as generally exaggerated.

The seriousness of global warming is viewed through the all-too-familiar prism of political party affiliation, suggesting this issue will continue to divide Americans rather than serve as a cause that will allow "Congress to come together and develop a bipartisan road map to confront this problem," as Democratic Sen. Mark Udall recently said. It is unlikely the two parties can agree on any road map when they can't even agree on whether or where they need to go.

Survey Methods

Results for this Gallup poll are based on telephone interviews conducted March 6–9, 2014, on the Gallup Daily tracking survey, with a random sample of 1,048 adults, aged 18 and older, living in all 50 U.S. states and the District of Columbia.

For results based on the total sample of national adults, the margin of sampling error is ±4 percentage points at the 95% confidence level.

March 18, 2014

A STEADY 57% IN U.S. BLAME HUMANS FOR GLOBAL WARMING

Even as more Americans say they're informed, blame on humans hasn't grown

by Lydia Saad

PRINCETON, NJ—More Americans believe increases in the Earth's temperature over the last century are due to pollution from human activities (57%) than to naturally occurring changes in the environment (40%). The balance of views on this issue is essentially unchanged from 2013, but reflects broader agreement with the idea that mankind is responsible for global warming than was the case from 2010 through 2012, when barely half believed it. Agreement that human activities are responsible has yet to return, however, to the 61% level seen as recently as 2007.

Perceived Cause of Global Warming

And from what you have heard or read, do you believe increases in the Earth's temperature over the last century are due more to -- [the effects of pollution from human activities (or) natural changes in the environment that are not due to human activities]?

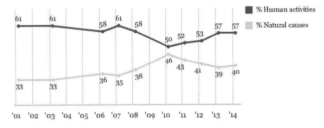

GALLUP

This trend comes from Gallup's annual Environment poll, a nationally representative telephone survey conducted each March since 2001. The 2014 update was conducted March 6–9.

Americans' prevailing view that human activity is responsible for global warming doesn't necessarily translate into concern over the issue. The percentage of Americans worried about global warming (as well as "climate change") still ranks low relative to other issues, and barely a third expect global warming to pose a serious threat in their own lifetime.

A Record 33% Say They Understand Global Warming "Very Well"

In the same survey, Gallup asks Americans to describe their general understanding of global warming, with 33% this year—a record high—saying they understand global warming "very well," up from 27% in 2013 and triple the level seen in the initial 1992 measure.

The proportion understanding the issue "fairly well" has also increased over the long term, from 42% in 1992 to 51% today, while the percentage who don't understand has dropped by more than half, from 44% to 16%.

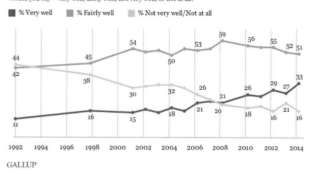

How Well Do You Understand Global Warming?
Next, thinking about the issue of global warming, how well do you feel you understand this issue? Would you say -- very well, fairly well, not very well, or not at all?

GALLUP

The Most Knowledgeable Are the Least Likely to Blame Humans

Leading climate science researchers in the U.S. and globally—including those at the International Panel on Climate Change, a U.N. body that is at the forefront of climate research—are convinced that elevated levels of carbon dioxide and other byproducts of fossil fuel use are the reason the Earth's temperature has warmed. Nevertheless, Americans who say they are highly knowledgeable about global warming are no more likely than those who profess little knowledge of the issue to believe humans are to blame.

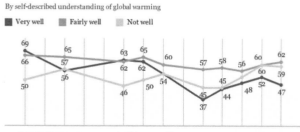

Trend in % Believing Global Warming Is Caused by the Effects of Pollution From Human Activities
By self-described understanding of global warming

GALLUP

In fact, in recent years, those with the highest level of knowledge—those saying they understand the global warming issue very well—are the least likely to believe global warming is the result of

pollution from human activities. This is somewhat of a change from 2001 to 2007, when the most informed Americans were generally among the most likely of all knowledge groups to consider pollution the cause.

The pattern changed sharply between 2007 and 2010, when the most informed group became the most skeptical. That period spanned the release of some hacked emails in 2009 that global-warming skeptics say proved climate researchers were suppressing scientific information—a controversy that ultimately became known as "Climategate."

During about the same period, between 2008 and 2010, Republicans became much more likely to claim a solid understanding of global warming, while high understanding among Democrats remained relatively low. Since then, Democrats' knowledge has surged, while Republicans' has been fairly steady. Self-reported knowledge about the global warming issue is, however, up among all three political groups compared with a decade ago.

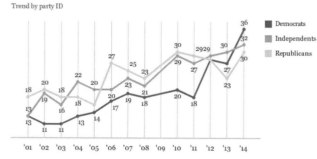

Understand Global Warming Issue "Very Well"
Trend by party ID

GALLUP

College Education Not a Strong Predictor of Blaming Human Activities

Apart from political party, Gallup finds little relation between Americans' levels of formal education and their agreement with the idea that human activities cause global warming—a central tenet of climate change science. College graduates are just slightly more likely than adults without a college degree to believe human activities are to blame.

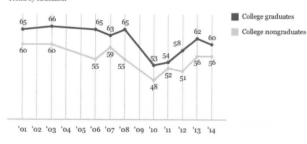

Percentage Believing Global Warming Is Caused by Human Activities
Trend by education

GALLUP

Perceived Cause of Global Warming Depends on Politics

Far more than knowledge, politics dictate the degree to which Americans believe humans are responsible for global warming, with

Democrats much more likely to hold this position than are Republicans. And as Gallup trends document, the partisan gap on this has widened in recent years.

Believe Rise in Earth's Temperature in Last Century Due Mainly to Human Activities
Trend by party ID

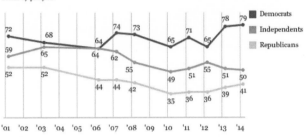

GALLUP

Bottom Line

Three times as many Americans say they understand global warming "very well" as said this two decades ago, rising to a record high 33% this year. And a combined 84% now profess to understand it very or fairly well, up from 53% in 2001. Despite this increased knowledge, slightly fewer Americans today than in 2001 agree with global warming proponents that the Earth's warming is "anthropogenic"—in other words, the result of humans' influence on nature. The 57% who believe humans are the cause is up from the low point recorded in 2010 (50%), but still not back to earlier levels.

Importantly, public skepticism about the human role in global warming is not based on lack of education. College-educated Americans are barely more likely than those without a college degree to ascribe global warming to humans. Nor do Americans who consider themselves knowledgeable on the subject show more support for the pollution theory. Rather, as is the case with so many other measures of public attitudes on global warming, politics are the guiding force, with most Democrats accepting the prevailing scientific view that pollution is the cause and most Republicans believing it is a natural climatic cycle, not man-made.

Survey Methods

Results for this Gallup poll are based on telephone interviews conducted March 6–9, 2014, with a random sample of 1,048 adults, aged 18 and older, living in all 50 U.S. states and the District of Columbia.

For results based on the total sample of national adults, the margin of sampling error is ±4 percentage points at the 95% confidence level.

March 19, 2014
AMERICANS' OUTLOOK FOR U.S. ENVIRONMENTAL QUALITY STEADY
Republicans more likely than Democrats to say environment is excellent or good

by Rebecca Riffkin

WASHINGTON, D.C.—Half of Americans think the quality of the environment in the U.S. is getting worse, a view that has remained

stable for the past five years. Americans were more pessimistic about the environmental outlook before Barack Obama became president in 2009.

Right now, do you think the quality of the environment in the country as a whole is getting better or getting worse?

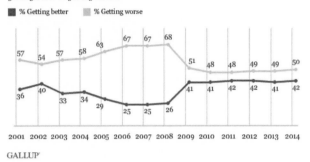

GALLUP

The latest update is from Gallup's March 6–9 Environment poll. Although Americans' perceptions about the outlook for the environment became more positive five years ago, the public remains somewhat more negative than positive about where environmental quality is headed.

Democrats and Republicans are equally likely to say the environment is getting better—with 42% in each party saying so—while independents are only one percentage point less positive. Prior to 2009, Democrats were much less positive about the outlook for the environment than Republicans were. After that, perceptions among the two party groups converged, and over the last three years, their views have been almost identical.

Outlook for the Quality of the Environment in the U.S. -- by Party ID
% Getting better

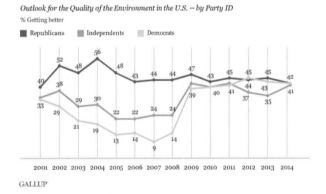

GALLUP

Thus, a Democrat's taking over the presidency significantly increased rank-and-file Democrats' positive attitudes about the environment, but so far, it has not had a correspondingly negative effect on Republicans' attitudes, compared with where they were during George W. Bush's second term.

Views of the Current Quality of the Environment Fall Slightly

Americans' ratings of current environmental quality dipped slightly this year. Forty-four percent rate its quality as "good" or "excellent," down from 48% last year—which was an all-time high since Gallup began tracking this question in 2001. Views of environmental quality mainly have been stable over time, and did not show a big change when Obama took office in 2009. However, these views have been slightly more positive since 2010 than they were from 2005 to 2009.

How would you rate the overall quality of the environment in this country today --
as excellent, good, only fair, or poor?

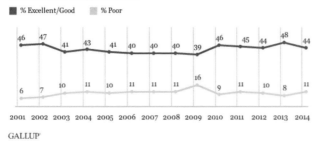

■ % Excellent/Good ■ % Poor

46 47 41 43 41 40 40 40 39 46 45 44 48 44

6 7 10 11 10 11 11 11 16 9 11 10 8 11

2001 2002 2003 2004 2005 2006 2007 2008 2009 2010 2011 2012 2013 2014

GALLUP'

Democrats have historically perceived the quality of the environment as worse than Republicans and independents have. But the percentage of Democrats who rated the environment as "excellent" or "good" increased between 2009 and 2010, and has stayed at or above that level since then.

Ratings of the Quality of the Environment in the U.S. -- by Party ID

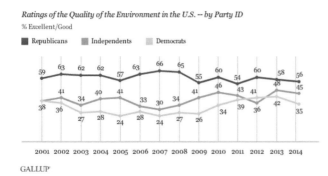

% Excellent/Good

■ Republicans ■ Independents ■ Democrats

59 63 62 62 57 63 66 65 55 60 54 60 58 56

41 34 40 41 33 30 34 41 46 43 41 48 45

38 36 27 28 24 28 24 27 26 34 39 36 42 35

2001 2002 2003 2004 2005 2006 2007 2008 2009 2010 2011 2012 2013 2014

GALLUP'

Although Republicans have historically seen the environment in the most positive light, they are less positive now than when Bush was president. In contrast, Democrats and independents rate environmental conditions more positively now than they did during most years under Bush.

Implications

Overall, Americans remain more negative than positive about the environment. They are less likely to see environmental quality in the U.S. as "excellent" or "good" (44%) than to see it as "only fair" or "poor" (55%). Additionally, half feel the environment is getting worse. More broadly, Americans are not very concerned with the environment, at least compared with other issues.

Americans' views of environmental quality in the U.S. generally appear to be linked to their party identification. Even though Republicans and Democrats now have similar opinions regarding the outlook for environmental quality, Democrats' optimism on this measure has increased dramatically since Obama became president. Independents are also now more optimistic. Republicans' outlook, however, is down at least somewhat from the heights it achieved during Bush's first term.

Democrats' views of the current quality of the environment in the U.S. have improved during Obama's presidency, while Republicans' are down from the mid-60% excellent/good range they reached when Bush was president. Thus, the future course of Americans' attitudes on the environment may depend on which party's candidate wins the presidency in 2016.

Survey Methods

Results for this Gallup poll are based on telephone interviews conducted March 6–9, 2014, with a random sample of 1,048 adults, aged 18 and older, living in all 50 U.S. states and the District of Columbia.

For results based on the total sample of national adults, the margin of sampling error is ±4 percentage points at the 95% confidence level.

March 19, 2014
IN U.S., 28% SAY NOW IS A GOOD TIME TO FIND A QUALITY JOB
Highest since 2008, though well below pre-recession peak

by Frank Newport

PRINCETON, NJ—Americans' perceptions that now is a good time to find a quality job continue to inch up, but remain far less positive than they were before the 2008–2009 recession. Gallup's March reading finds that 28% of Americans say now is a good time to find a quality job, up from 27% in February, and now the highest reading on this measure since January 2008.

Percentage in U.S. Saying Now Is a Good Time to Find a Quality Job

Thinking about the job situation in America today, would you say that it is now a good time or a bad time to find a quality job?

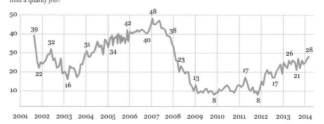

39 32 22 16 31 34 42 48 40 38 23 13 8 17 8 17 21 26 28

2001 2002 2003 2004 2005 2006 2007 2008 2009 2010 2011 2012 2013 2014

GALLUP

Americans' outlook for quality jobs—as well as several other core state-of-the-nation indicators—are tracked monthly as part of the Gallup Poll Social Series. The latest update is based on Gallup's March 6–9 survey.

One can take a positive or negative historical view of the current 28% who say it's a good time to find a job. The good news: the current reading reflects a continuing, but slow rise from the all-time lows of 8% recorded in November 2009 and November 2011, and is now the highest reading since January 2008.

The not-so-good news is that the 28% figure is low on an absolute basis, and low compared with where it was in the mid-2000s. On the first point, when two-thirds of the population says it is a bad time to find a quality job, this clearly does not describe an optimal economic environment. The most positive levels Gallup has recorded on this measure since 2001 were in January 2007—when 48% said it was a good time, and 47% a bad time to find a good job—a year or more before the full effects of the banking crisis and recession began to be evident.

Those who are in the workforce—currently employed, or unemployed and looking for work—are a bit more positive about the job market than the broader U.S. population, with 31% saying it is a good time to find a quality job.

Americans' political persuasion affects their views of the job market, as it has to varying degrees over the past 13 years. Republicans were substantially more positive than Democrats during most of George W. Bush's presidency, and Democrats are now the most positive with Barack Obama in the White House, although the gap between parties is not nearly the same as it was under Bush. In this latest poll, 25% of both Republicans and independents say it's a good time to find a quality job, contrasted with 35% of Democrats.

Is Now a Good Time or a Bad Time to Find a Quality Job?

By party ID

	Yes	No
	%	%
Republicans	25	73
Independents	25	70
Democrats	35	62

March 6-9, 2014

GALLUP

Younger Americans have in recent years been most positive about the job market, while older Americans have been the least positive. In the most recent survey, more than four in 10 18- to 29-year-olds say it's a good time to find a quality job, contrasted with no more than one in five of those 50 and older.

Is Now a Good Time or a Bad Time to Find a Quality Job?

By age

	Yes	No
	%	%
18 to 29	43	57
30 to 49	31	64
50 to 64	20	76
65+	18	78

March 6-9, 2014

GALLUP

Although job prospects may be better among those with higher education, those who have postgraduate education are actually less positive about the job market than those having less education, with only 20% of the former group saying it's a good time to find a quality job.

Implications

Americans now rate unemployment, along with dysfunctional government and the economy in general, as the most important problems facing the country. The data reported here, showing that fewer than three in 10 Americans say it is a good time to find a quality job, reinforce the public's decidedly negative views of the jobs situation today.

It has been more than five years since the full effect of the banking crisis and recession hit the nation's economy. While perceptions of the job market have certainly improved from their nadir in 2009

and 2011, when only 8% thought it was a good time to find a quality job, they are nowhere near where they were prior to the recession and—based on research conducted by others—are far behind the levels seen during the last economic "good times" in this country, during the dot-com boom of the late 1990s. This measure of the average American's view of the job market will provide an excellent barometer of economic progress going forward.

Survey Methods

Results for this Gallup poll are based on telephone interviews conducted March 6–9, 2014, with a random sample of 1,048 adults, aged 18 and older, living in all 50 U.S. states and the District of Columbia.

For results based on the total sample of national adults, the margin of sampling error is ±4 percentage points at the 95% confidence level.

March 20, 2014
HOUSTON LEADS U.S. METRO AREAS ON JOB CREATION INDEX
San Diego ranked lowest among 50 largest metro areas

by Andrew Dugan

WASHINGTON, D.C.—Among the nation's 50 largest U.S. metropolitan areas, Houston ranks as the best environment for job creation and San Diego ranks as the worst, based on reports of hiring activity versus layoffs from workers who live in those areas.

Top Large MSAs, Gallup Job Creation Index

	Job Creation Index Score
Houston-Sugar Land-Baytown, TX	32
Columbus, OH	29
Salt Lake City, UT	28
Orlando-Kissimnmee, FL	28
Phoenix-Mesa-Scottsdale, AZ	28

Gallup Daily tracking, January 2012-December 2013

GALLUP

Bottom Large MSAs, Gallup Job Creation Index

	Job Creation Index Score
San Diego-Carlsbad-San Marcos, CA	12
New York-North New Jersey-Long Island, NY-NJ-PA	13
Providence-New Bedford-Fall River, RI-MA	13
Sacramento--Arden-Arcade--Roseville, CA	14
Riverside-San Bernardino-Ontario, CA	14
Los Angeles-Long Beach-Santa Ana, CA	14

Gallup Daily tracking, January 2012-December 2013

GALLUP

Gallup's Job Creation Index score is based on the percentage of workers who say their employer is hiring and expanding its workforce versus the percentage saying their employer is letting people go and reducing its workforce. Houston's top score of +32 on the index is based on 44% of Houston-area workers saying their employer was hiring and expanding versus 12% saying their employer was letting people go and reducing in 2012–2013.

San Diego, at the bottom of the list, had 32% of its workforce saying companies are hiring and 20% saying companies are letting people go.

These results are based on Gallup Daily tracking conducted throughout 2012–2013 in the 50 most populous metropolitan statistical areas (MSAs). Gallup interviewed at least 1,000 working adults in each of these MSAs, with as many as 14,252 in the New York City metro area. Each MSA sample is weighted to match the demographic characteristics of that area. Gallup previously conducted an analysis examining the 2012 data alone. Because of changes in interviewing in 2013, the 2012 and 2013 data are reported together to have large enough samples to report updated figures for each MSA.

Houston climbed to the top of the Job Creation Index list after being just outside the top five in 2011, displacing Oklahoma City. While Houston's progress on this front is notable, Charlotte, N.C., had nominally the highest overall change in its index score, from 13 in 2011 to 26 in 2012–2013. Other cities that saw similar improvements include Austin, Texas, Salt Lake City, and Minneapolis.

Top Five Net Positive Growth in Job Creation Index Score Rankings

	2011 Job Creation Index score	2012-2013 Job Creation Index score	Net change*
Charlotte-Gastonia-Concord, NC-SC	13	26	+13
Houston-Sugar Land-Baytown, TX	20	32	+12
Austin-Round Rock, TX	15	27	+12
Salt Lake City, UT	18	28	+10
Minneapolis-St. Paul-Bloomington, MN-WI	15	25	+10

*2012-2013 Job Creation Index score minus 2011 Job Creation Index score

GALLUP'

An increase in reported hiring fueled Houston's ascent to the top of the Job Creation Index rankings in 2012–2013, with 44% of Houston-area workers saying companies in the area are hiring, up from 39% in 2011. Houston's hiring percentage ties with Orlando, Fla., as the nation's highest; Los Angeles is at the bottom of the list, at 31%. The reason Houston tops Orlando in the overall ranking is that fewer workers in Houston reported layoffs, at 12%, and a higher 15% of Orlando-based workers said the company or employer they work for is letting people go.

Top and Bottom Metropolitan Areas for Hiring and Letting Workers Go

HIGHEST	% Hiring	HIGHEST	% Letting go
Houston-Sugar Land-Baytown, TX	44	Virginia Beach-Norfolk-Newport News, VA-NC	21
Orlando-Kissimmee, FL	44	San Diego-Carlsbad-San Marcos, CA	21
Columbus, OH	43	Providence-New Bedford-Fall River, RI-MA	20
San Antonio, TX	43	Jacksonville, FL	20
Salt Lake City, UT	41	Las Vegas-Paradise, NV	19
LOWEST		**LOWEST**	
Los Angeles-Long Beach-Santa Ana, CA	31	Houston-Sugar Land-Baytown, TX	12
New York-North New Jersey-Long Island, NY-NJ-PA	32	Salt Lake City, UT	13
San Diego-Carlsbad-San Marcos, CA	32	Phoenix-Mesa-Scottsdale, AZ	13
Sacramento--Arden-Arcade--Roseville, CA	32	Nashville-Davidson-Murfreesboro-Franklin, TN	13
Buffalo-Niagara Falls, NY	33	Minneapolis-St. Paul-Bloomington, MN-WI	13

Gallup Daily tracking, January 2012-December 2013

GALLUP'

Bottom Line

In general, metro areas in Texas proved able in terms of creating jobs, with large cities such as San Antonio and Austin making the top 10 list of MSAs with the highest Job Creation Index scores. California, on the other hand, saw several of its cities ranked toward the bottom, with San Diego last on the list.

But there is room for cheer for residents living in all of these 50 metro areas because the Job Creation Index was still in positive territory in 2012–2013, meaning all of these important population centers were, generally speaking, hiring. Given the considerable size of these 50 metro areas, this uniform net hiring is also a good thing for the U.S. economy overall.

Survey Methods

Results are based on telephone interviews conducted as a part of Gallup Daily tracking Jan. 1, 2012–Dec. 3, 2013, with a random sample of 150,521 adults, aged 18 and older, employed full or part time, living in the 50 largest metropolitan statistical areas (MSAs) by population.

Margins of error for individual MSAs are no greater than ±4 percentage points and are ±3 percentage points in most MSAs.

March 20, 2014
AMERICANS AGAIN PICK ENVIRONMENT OVER ECONOMIC GROWTH
Partisan gap over priority largest recorded

by Art Swift

WASHINGTON, D.C.—Americans are more likely to say protection of the environment should be given priority, even at the risk of curbing economic growth. Since 2009, during the economic downturn, Americans generally prioritized economic growth over the environment, except for immediately after the BP oil spill in the Gulf of Mexico in May 2010.

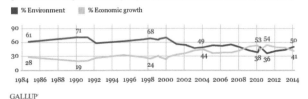

Prioritizing Environmental Protection vs. Economic Growth, 1984-2014

With which one of these statements about the environment and the economy do you most agree -- [ROTATED: protection of the environment should be given priority, even at the risk of curbing economic growth (or) economic growth should be given priority, even if the environment suffers to some extent]?

■ % Environment ▨ % Economic growth

GALLUP'

In a March 6–9 Gallup Poll Social Series survey on the environment, Americans said the environment is a priority over economic growth by a 50%-to-41% margin. In the 30 years that Gallup has asked this question, Americans have almost always chosen the environment over economic growth as a priority.

The percentage of Americans who prioritized the environment swelled to 71% in 1990 and 1991, with the lowest percentage for economic growth occurring in 1990, at 19%. That year is notable for the mass revival of Earth Day, begun in 1970 by Wisconsin Sen. Gaylord Nelson as a way to boost environmental awareness. The 20th anniversary of Earth Day attracted hundreds of conservational groups that pressured businesses for tighter environmental regulations.

Democrats and Republicans Far Apart on Environment and Economic Growth Priorities

Democrats and Republicans are sharply divided as to whether the environment should be given priority, even at the risk of curbing economic growth. Two-thirds of Democrats say the environment should be prioritized higher, while about one-third of Republicans say the same thing. This is the largest partisan gulf since 1997, mainly as result of the sharp rise among Democrats prioritizing the environment higher than economic growth. Both parties give higher priority to the environment than they did prior to the 2008–2009 economic recession.

Republicans' Views of Prioritizing the Environment vs. Economic Growth

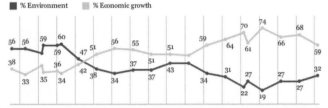

A majority of both Republicans and Democrats prioritized the environment prior to George W. Bush becoming president in 2001. The drop in Republican support for the environment over economic growth coincided with President Bush placing less of a priority on the environment. During this era, the Bush Administration did not take part in the Kyoto Protocol, citing that the cost was prohibitive to the U.S. economy. Since 2001, Republicans have chosen economic growth over the environment, with the largest gap between the two parties occurring in 2011, when economic growth was favored over the environment by a margin of 74%-to-19%. However, there has been a slight increase in the percentage of Republicans prioritizing the environment and a slight decrease in the percentage prioritizing economic growth in the last year.

Democrats' Views of Prioritizing the Environment vs. Economic Growth

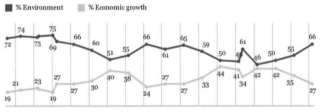

The percentage of Democrats choosing the environment over economic growth surged 11 percentage points in the past year and 20 points since 2011. This increase suggests that Democrats may believe the economy is improving and it is now acceptable to favor protecting the environment, even if it curbs economic growth. As the leader of the Democratic Party, President Barack Obama has made climate change one of his top priorities for his second term. The 66% of Democrats who prioritize the environment over economic growth is the highest since 2000.

Younger Americans Choose Environment, Older Americans Choose Economic Growth

Among age groups, Americans aged 18 to 29 are most likely to say the environment should be given priority over economic growth, by a 60%-to-30% margin. Americans aged 65 and older, on the other

hand, say economic growth should be prioritized, by a margin of 50%-to-39%. Both 30- to 49-year-olds and 50- to 64-year-olds prioritize the environment over economic growth, but the gap between the two topics narrows as the age group becomes older.

Environment vs. Economic Growth as Priority, by Age

With which one of these statements about the environment and the economy do you most agree -- [ROTATED: protection of the environment should be given priority, even at the risk of curbing economic growth (or) economic growth should be given priority, even if the environment suffers to some extent]?

	% Environment	% Economic growth
18-29	60	30
30-49	52	41
50-64	49	41
65+	39	50

Gallup poll, March 6-9, 2014

Bottom Line

When Americans prioritize the environment over economic growth, it could be a sign that they perceive a healthier U.S. economy. Gallup's Economic Confidence Index has rebounded since the Great Recession, suggesting Americans believe that the U.S. economy is improving. Perhaps the gap between Republicans and Democrats on the issue of prioritizing the environment or economic growth since 2001 can be explained by the increasing polarization between the two parties over the issue of climate change and global warming.

Survey Methods

Results for this Gallup poll are based on telephone interviews conducted March 6–9, 2014, on the Gallup Daily tracking survey, with a random sample of 1,048 adults, aged 18 and older, living in all 50 U.S. states and the District of Columbia.

For results based on the total sample of national adults, the margin of sampling error is ±4 percentage points at the 95% confidence level.

March 21, 2014
CLINTON'S TOP SELLING POINT IN 2016: FIRST FEMALE PRESIDENT
Top negatives are not being qualified; continuing Obama's agenda

by Frank Newport

PRINCETON, NJ—Americans say the best or most positive thing about a possible Hillary Clinton presidency—if she were to run and be elected in 2016—would be her serving as the first female president in the nation's history. Other positives mentioned by at least 5% of Americans are her experience, that she would bring about change from the previous two administrations, that she would adhere to a Democratic agenda, and that she would be the best choice.

Suppose Hillary Clinton is elected president in 2016. In your view, what would be the best or most positive thing about a Hillary Clinton presidency?

	March 15-16, 2014
PERSONAL CHARACTERISTICS	%
Would be first woman president	18
Experience/Foreign policy experience	9
Best choice	5
Capable/Competent/Qualified	3
Intelligent/Smart/Educated	2
Bill Clinton would be back in White House/Help, advise her	2
Like her/Want her to win	1
Open, honest government	1
Would be good for common people	1
ISSUES	%
Healthcare issue/reform	3
Jobs/Employment issue	2
Agree with her politics/Approve of her actions	2
Economy	2
Will help immigrants/Bring diversity	2
Would balance the budget	1
Would end the wars	1
POLITICAL	%
Change from Obama/Bush administrations	8
Democratic agenda/platform	6
OTHER/DON'T KNOW	%
Other	9
Nothing	27
No opinion	22

GALLUP

These results are from a Gallup survey conducted March 15–16, which asked a nationally representative sample of Americans to say what would be the best and the worst things about a possible Clinton presidency, if she were to be elected in 2016.

A little less than half of Americans did not give a substantive answer in response to the positive question, and about the same percentage didn't give a substantive answer to the negative question. This is in large part because the majority of Republicans have no specific thoughts about the best thing about a Clinton presidency, and a majority of Democrats do not have specific responses to the question about the worst aspects of a Clinton presidency.

Americans' substantive responses can be grouped into three broad categories: personal characteristics, specific issues, and political considerations.

Clearly Clinton's "unique selling proposition" is that she would be the first woman president. Nearly one in five Americans mention this historic possibility as a positive, including 22% of women, 27% of 18- to 29-year-olds, and 30% of Democrats. A Gallup analysis of a similar question, asked of a representative Gallup Panel sample in 2007, also found that Americans were more likely to mention her being the first woman president than any other positive factor.

Americans mention a number of other positives dealing with her personal characteristics—including her experience, and the perception that she is capable, qualified, and intelligent. Notably, 2% mention that a positive outcome of a Hillary Clinton presidency would be that Bill Clinton would be back in the White House—the same outcome that 3% of Americans see as a negative if she were to be elected.

Americans also indicate as a positive feature of a potential Clinton presidency the change it would provide from the Obama and Bush administrations, and, separately, that it would continue a Democratic agenda and platform.

Relatively few Americans mention specific issues as the best thing about a Clinton presidency. Among those mentioned are healthcare—her signature issue when she became first lady after her husband was elected president in 1992—jobs, the economy, and immigration.

Diverse View of Negatives Associated With a Hillary Clinton Presidency

Americans' views of the possible negatives that would be associated with a Hillary Clinton presidency are more diverse than the positive responses. No one single issue dominates to the degree that her being the first woman president does on the plus side.

And, what would be the worst or most negative thing about a Hillary Clinton presidency?

	March 15-16, 2014
PERSONAL CHARACTERISTICS	%
Not qualified/Would not succeed	6
Don't want a woman president	4
Getting elected in first place/That she won	4
Dishonest/Does not tell truth	3
Bill Clinton would be back in White House	3
Just don't like her	3
Handling of Benghazi incident	2
Clinton scandals, baggage	2
Too liberal/A socialist	2
Her past history (non-specific)	2
Country not ready for woman president	1
Other countries would view us negatively	1
Too old	1
Would be unfairly/harshly criticized by opponents, the media	1
ISSUES	%
Healthcare views/Wants socialized medicine/Gov't system	3
Ability to deal with foreign policy	3
Government spending/Deficit	2
Dislike her views on immigration	1
Her views on the wars	1
Favors welfare, handouts	1
Would continue bad economy	1
Would raise taxes	1
Would not help with employment/jobs	1
Wants gun control	1
Pro-abortion	1
POLITICAL	%
Continuation of Obama's path/agenda/No change	6
She's a Democrat	4
Her views/agenda (non-specific)	3
Gridlock with Republicans/Nothing would get done	2
OTHER/DON'T KNOW	%
Other	5
Everything	2
Nothing	22
No opinion	25

GALLUP

Americans volunteer a varied list of personal characteristics when asked to think about the negatives if Clinton were to be president. These include a simple perception that she is not qualified, negative reactions to the fact that she would be a woman president, views that she is dishonest, and the fact that her husband, Bill, would be back in the White House.

Two percent of Americans, including 4% of Republicans, specifically mention Clinton's handling of the Benghazi, Libya, incident that occurred while she was secretary of state—an incident in which the American ambassador and three other Americans were killed. Another 2% mention past scandals and baggage without being specific.

A number of Americans say the most negative thing about a Clinton presidency would be that she is a Democrat and would continue Obama's Democratic policies and agenda.

As was the case on the positive side of the ledger, specific mentions of her positions on issues are widely diversified with no one issue dominating. Some Americans mention her views on healthcare and foreign policy, while others talk about her views on government spending and the deficit.

Democrats Focus on the Positives, Republicans on the Negatives

Fifty-nine percent of Democrats do not name anything or answer "nothing" in response to the question about negatives associated with a Clinton presidency, while 72% of Republicans do the same when asked to name the most positive thing about a Clinton presidency. Independents are generally close to the sample average in terms of their giving an opinion on both questions—54% did not have a response or said nothing for the positive outcomes and 48% for the negative outcomes.

Still, all three partisan groups who do offer a response mention the fact that she would be the first woman president—albeit in significantly different percentages. Democrats are the most effusive in their responses, and talk in significant numbers about her experience and that she would further the Democratic agenda. Republicans have fewer positives to offer, but do mention that a Clinton presidency would represent a change from Obama, in addition to her being the first woman president. Independents, in addition to mentioning her being the first woman president, talk about her experience and the change from Obama.

Mentions of Best Things About Hillary Clinton Presidency, by Party

Republicans		Independents		Democrats	
%		%		%	
Change in administration	11	First female president	17	First female president	30
First female president	7	Her experience	8	Her experience	16
Her experience	4	Change in administration	5	Democratic agenda	13
Healthcare issue	3	Best choice	4	Best choice	10
Economy	2	Will help immigrants	4	Change in administration	10
Capable/ Competent	2				

GALLUP

The most frequently mentioned negative views of a Clinton presidency offered by Republicans include that she would be continuing Democratic control of the White House, that she is a Democrat in general, that she got elected in the first place, that she is not qualified, and that she is dishonest. Independents are more likely

than Democrats and Republicans to mention her specific views on healthcare, and that Bill Clinton would be back in the White House as negatives. Democrats who do offer a view on the negatives associated with a Clinton presidency talk most about not wanting a woman president, her qualifications, that the polarized and contentious nature of fights with Congress would continue, that Bill would be back in the White House, and her scandals and baggage.

Mentions of Worst Things About Hillary Clinton Presidency, by Party

Republicans		Independents		Democrats	
%		%		%	
Continuation of this path	11	Continuation of this path	7	Don't want a female president	6
Getting elected in the first place	9	Not qualified	6	Not qualified	5
Not qualified	8	Views on healthcare	4	Bill Clinton back in White House	4
She's a Democrat	8	Her views/ political agenda	4	Standoff between Republicans and Democrats	4
Dishonest/ Does not tell the truth	7	Bill Clinton back in White House	4	Clinton scandals, baggage	3
		Dishonest/ Does not tell the truth	4		

GALLUP

Implications

From the American public's perspective, Hillary Clinton's greatest selling point going into the 2016 presidential election, should she decide to run, would be the historic fact that, if elected, she would be the first female president in the nation's history. Other positive perceptions that she and her campaign team could, in theory, use to her advantage are the views that focus on her experience and intelligence. At the same time, Clinton's team would have to grapple with the fact that many Americans have acquired a negative view of some of her personal characteristics over the years, disagree with her positions on issues, and are simply opposed to having another Democrat in the White House.

Survey Methods

Results for this Gallup poll are based on telephone interviews conducted March 15–16, 2014, with a random sample of 1,024 adults, aged 18 and older, living in all 50 U.S. states and the District of Columbia.

For results based on the total sample of national adults, the margin of sampling error is ±4 percentage points at the 95% confidence level.

March 21, 2014
MISSISSIPPIANS' STRUGGLES TO AFFORD FOOD CONTINUED IN 2013
Residents in Alaska, New Hampshire, and Minnesota struggled least

by Rebecca Riffkin

WASHINGTON, D.C.—For the sixth consecutive year, Mississippians were the most likely in the U.S. to report struggling to afford food. In 2013, 25.1% report there was at least one time in the last 12 months when they did not have enough money to buy the food they or their families needed. Residents in West Virginia, Louisiana, and Alabama were also among the most likely to struggle to afford food. Residents of Alaska, New Hampshire, and Minnesota were among the least likely to have this problem.

States Where Residents Are Most Likely to Struggle to Afford Food	% Not enough money for food	States Where Residents Are Least Likely to Struggle to Afford Food	% Not enough money for food
Mississippi	25.1	Alaska	11.0
West Virginia	23.0	New Hampshire	11.3
Louisiana	23.0	Minnesota	11.6
Alabama	22.9	Iowa	12.3
Arkansas	22.5	North Dakota	12.9
North Carolina	22.2	Nebraska	14.5
Kentucky	21.8	South Dakota	14.6
Georgia	21.5	Wisconsin	15.1
Oklahoma	21.2	Massachusetts	15.2
Arizona	21.1	Illinois	15.2

January-December 2013
Gallup-Healthways Well-Being Index

January-December 2013
Gallup-Healthways Well-Being Index

GALLUP'

GALLUP'

These findings are from surveys conducted with more than 178,000 U.S. adults in 2013 as part of the Gallup-Healthways Well-Being Index. Gallup asks 500 Americans each day if there have been times in the past 12 months when they did not have enough money to buy food that they or their families needed.

In 16 states, at least one in five residents said they struggled to afford the food that they or their families needed at least once in the past 12 months. In seven states, less than 15% of residents reported the same struggles in 2013.

Alabama has been among the 10 states most likely to report struggling to afford food in each of the six years Gallup and Healthways have tracked this measure. Louisiana, Arkansas, and Georgia are also frequent visitors on this list, with each state appearing five times since tracking began. Other repeat states among the 10 most likely to report struggling to afford food are West Virginia, North Carolina, South Carolina, Kentucky, and Oklahoma—each making the list four of the last six years. This is the first time Arizona has been among the 10 states reporting the highest percentage of residents who struggled to afford food.

Those states with the lowest percentage of residents who reported struggling to afford food show more movement from year to year than those states with the highest rates. Only Minnesota and North Dakota have been listed among the states with the lowest food hardship rates for all six years of tracking. South Dakota, Massachusetts, Wisconsin, and Iowa have been in this group for five of six years. Alaska, the state with the lowest percentage in 2013, has appeared among this group once before, in 2009, when 15.4% of its residents reported struggling to afford food.

As a nation, Americans were slightly more likely to struggle to afford food in 2013 compared with prior years. In 2013, 18.9% struggled to afford food nationally, compared with 18.2% in 2012 and 17.8% in 2008, the lowest rate Gallup has recorded since tracking began in 2008.

Americans' growing struggles to afford food may be linked to a rise in food prices across the country, particularly meat prices, while national incomes have largely flat-lined since the recession. Trouble affording food may also be linked to the national rise in unhealthy eating habits in 2013 and the uptick in the obesity rate.

Residents in Southern States Report Struggling More to Afford Food

There are wide disparities across regions in the percentage of residents who at times lacked the money to purchase the food they or their families needed. Southern states tend to have higher percentages of residents who report struggling, whereas Midwestern states report lower percentages.

Implications

More Americans in 2013 reported struggling to afford food than in 2012. While seven states reported less than 15% of residents struggling, 16 states—more than twice as many—reported that at least one in five residents struggled in 2013.

To address this issue, states try to help their struggling residents afford food by offering food assistance programs. However, Congress passed an update to the Farm Bill in early 2014 that cuts approximately $8 billion from national food assistance programs over the next decade. This could make it harder for states to help their residents who struggle to afford food. Some states are trying to fight these cuts to continue to provide food assistance for their residents, but rising food prices nationally could make food affordability an even bigger issue in the coming year, regardless of the cuts.

While food assistance programs help residents avoid going hungry, providing quality jobs and increasing average income could do more to help citizens have the money they need to afford food.

Gallup's "State of the States" series reveals state-by-state differences on political, economic, and well-being measures Gallup tracks each day. New stories based on full-year 2013 data will be released in the coming months.

Survey Methods

Results are based on telephone interviews conducted as part of the Gallup-Healthways Well-Being Index survey Jan. 2–Dec. 29, 2013, with a random sample of 178,067 adults, aged 18 and older, living in all 50 U.S. states and the District of Columbia.

For results based on the total sample of national adults, the margin of sampling error is ±1 percentage points at the 95% confidence level.

The margin of sampling error for most states is ±1 to ±2 percentage points, but is as high as ±4 points for states with smaller populations, such as Wyoming, North Dakota, South Dakota, Delaware, and Hawaii.

March 24, 2014
U.S. WHITES MORE SOLIDLY REPUBLICAN IN RECENT YEARS
Party preferences more polarized by race and ethnicity under Obama

by Jeffrey M. Jones

PRINCETON, NJ—Whites and nonwhites have long shown differing political party preferences, with nonwhites widely favoring the Democratic Party and whites typically favoring the Republican Party by at least a small margin. In recent years, however, the margins in favor of the Republican Party among whites have been some of the largest.

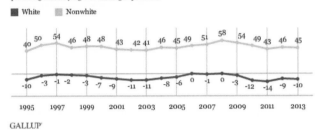

Democratic Advantage in Party Affiliation, Whites vs. Nonwhites, 1995-2013

Democratic advantage is the percentage identifying as or leaning Democratic minus the percentage identifying as or leaning Republican

■ White ▪ Nonwhite

White: 40 50 54 46 48 48 43 42 41 46 45 49 51 58 54 49 43 46 45

Black: -10 -3 -1 -2 -3 -7 -9 -11 -11 -8 -6 0 -1 0 -3 -12 -14 -9 -10

1995 1997 1999 2001 2003 2005 2007 2009 2011 2013

GALLUP

The results are based on yearly aggregates of Gallup poll data since 1995, the first full year that Gallup regularly measured Hispanic ethnicity. For this analysis, Gallup defines whites as non-Hispanic whites, and nonwhites as blacks, Hispanics, Asians, and all other races combined.

The net Democratic advantage represents the percentage of each racial/ethnic group identifying as Democratic minus the percentage identifying as Republican. Positive scores indicate that a group is more Democratic than Republican; negative scores indicate the reverse.

The trend lines in white and nonwhite party preferences often move in the same direction, but with a sizable gap maintained between them. For example, both racial groups drifted in a more Republican direction from 2001 to 2003, after the 9/11 terrorist attacks. Whites and nonwhites became increasingly Democratic in the last years of the Bush presidency, with whites as likely to favor the Democratic Party as the Republican Party from 2006 to 2008. Since 2009, whites and nonwhites have trended more Republican.

In recent years, party preferences have been more polarized than was the case in the 1990s and most of the 2000s. For example, in 2010, nonwhites' net party identification and leanings showed a 49-point Democratic advantage, and whites were 12 percentage points more Republican than Democratic. The resulting 61-point racial and ethnic gap in party preferences is the largest Gallup has measured in the last 20 years. Since 2008, the racial gaps in party preferences have been 55 points or higher each year; prior to 2008, the gaps reached as high as 55 points only in 1997 and 2000.

Party Preferences More Polarized Under Obama Than Under Bush or Clinton

The increasing racial polarization in party preferences is evident when comparing the data by presidential administration. Nonwhites' average party preferences have been quite stable across the last three administrations, consistently showing a roughly 47-point Democratic advantage under Clinton, Bush, and Obama. On average, 69% of nonwhites have identified as Democrats or said they were independents who leaned Democratic, and 21% have identified as Republicans or leaned Republican.

Meanwhile, whites have become increasingly Republican, moving from an average 4.1-point Republican advantage under Clinton to an average 9.5-point advantage under Obama.

Democratic Party Advantage, Whites vs. Nonwhites, 1995-2013

	Clinton years, 1995-2000	Bush years, 2001-2008	Obama years, 2009-2013
NON-HISPANIC WHITES			
% Democratic/Lean Democratic	42.7	43.2	40.8
% Republican/Lean Republican	46.8	48.6	50.3
Democratic advantage	-4.1	-5.4	-9.5
NONWHITES			
% Democratic/Lean Democratic	68.7	68.9	68.4
% Republican/Lean Republican	21.2	22.0	21.2
Democratic advantage	+47.5	+46.9	+47.2

Note: 1995 is the first full year in which Gallup regularly measured Hispanic ethnicity.

GALLUP

This polarization could ease by the time Obama's term finishes, in three years. However, given the already large racial gap in party preferences in his first five years, unless there is a dramatic shift among whites toward the Democratic Party or among nonwhites toward the GOP in the next three years, party preferences will end up more racially polarized in Obama's presidency than in his two predecessors' administrations.

Implications

Over the last two decades, whites have tended to favor the Republican Party and nonwhites have overwhelmingly favored the Democratic Party. During the last few years, those racial and ethnic divisions have grown, mostly because whites have drifted more toward the GOP. Thus, party preferences by race during the Obama years, though similar in nature to the past, have seen some movement that has resulted in slightly greater racial polarization than before.

It is unclear precisely what role Obama's race has played in these changes. However, the shifts do not appear to be an immediate reaction to his becoming president. Whites became slightly more Republican during 2009, the first year of Obama's presidency. However, the biggest movement came during the next year, when Obama signed the healthcare overhaul into law but saw his approval rating sink and his party lose its large majority in the House in that year's midterm elections. Further, whites were about as likely to favor the Republican Party at points during George W. Bush's presidency as they are now.

Whites are somewhat less likely to align with the Republican Party now than they were in 2010 and 2011, but they still show a roughly 10-point advantage in that direction. Although whites remain the majority racial group in the U.S., the Democrats' decisive advantage among racial and ethnic minorities allows them to more than offset the Republicans' advantage among whites, and thus enjoy the advantage, nationally.

With the U.S. becoming increasingly racially and ethnically diverse, the balance of political power may shift toward the Democrats unless Republicans increase their advantage among a shrinking white majority, or cut into Democrats' advantage among nonwhite voters.

Survey Methods

Results are based on yearly aggregated data from multiple day Gallup telephone polls conducted between 1995 and 2013. Each yearly aggregate is based on a minimum of 18,000 interviews with adults age 18 and older.

For results based on the total sample of national adults in any given year, the margin of sampling error is ±1 percentage point at the 95% confidence level.

For results based on the total sample of non-Hispanic whites in any given year, the margin of sampling error is ±1 percentage point at the 95% confidence level.

For results based on the total sample of nonwhites in any given year, the margin of sampling error is a maximum of ±2 percentage points at the 95% confidence level.

March 24, 2014
SAN JOSE AND D.C. TIE FOR HIGHEST IN ECONOMIC CONFIDENCE
Jacksonville still area with lowest confidence; slightly up from 2012

by Justin McCarthy

WASHINGTON, D.C.—Among the 50 largest U.S. metropolitan areas, Washington, D.C., remained the most confident in the U.S. economy in 2012–2013, but it now shares the top spot with San Jose, Calif. Both averaged a +4 score on Gallup's Economic Confidence Index over the past two years; they were among the three areas with net positive economic confidence on this measure. Jacksonville, Fla., had the lowest economic confidence (-25).

Top Five Metro Areas, Gallup Economic Confidence Index
Among the 50 largest MSAs

	Index score
Washington-Arlington-Alexandria, DC-VA-MD-WV	4
San Jose-Sunnyvale-Santa Clara, CA	4
San Francisco-Oakland-Fremont, CA	3
Minneapolis-St. Paul-Bloomington, MN-WI	-2
Seattle-Tacoma-Bellevue, WA	-4

January 2012-December 2013
Gallup Daily tracking

GALLUP'

Bottom Five Metro Areas, Gallup Economic Confidence Index
Among the 50 largest MSAs

	Index score
Jacksonville, FL	-25
Pittsburgh, PA	-24
Oklahoma City, OK	-23
Cincinnati-Middletown, OH-KY-IN	-23
St. Louis, MO-IL	-21
Providence-New Bedford-Fall River, RI-MA	-21

January 2012-December 2013
Gallup Daily tracking

GALLUP'

These results are based on Gallup Daily tracking conducted throughout 2012–2013 in the 50 most populous U.S. metropolitan statistical areas (MSAs). Gallup interviewed at least 12,000 adults in each of these MSAs, with the highest number of interviews, 15,443, conducted in the New York City metro area. Each MSA sample is weighted to match the demographic characteristics of that area.

Gallup's Economic Confidence Index is a composite of Americans' ratings of current U.S. economic confidence conditions and their perceptions of the economy's direction. The index has a theoretical maximum of +100 (if all respondents rate the economy as "excellent" or "good" and say it is getting better), and a theoretical minimum of −100 (if all rate the economy as "poor" and say it is getting worse). Nationwide, the Gallup Economic Confidence Index averaged −16 in 2013.

Washington, D.C., had a −5 score for the economic conditions component, but its +13 score for economic optimism boosted its overall index reading to positive territory, putting it ahead of the other metro areas. San Jose, too, had a negative score for the economic conditions component (−8), but was buoyed by its positive readings for optimism (+16), which brought its index to the top of the list.

Jacksonville had a dismal economic outlook score (−21), but an even more dismal score for current conditions (−28), which sank the MSA to the very bottom of the list. Pittsburgh, coming in second-lowest in overall confidence, had a −26 economic outlook score and a −23 score for current economic conditions.

Bottom Line

Though economic confidence is still negative in most MSAs, most areas saw slight increases when factoring in the 2013 data. And fortunately for areas near the bottom such as Jacksonville and Pittsburgh, MSA confidence levels have shown some resilience. Buffalo, N.Y., for example, whose dismal confidence readings put it at the bottom in 2011, has climbed to the relatively average reading of −18 for 2012–2013.

Survey Methods

Results are based on telephone interviews conducted as a part of Gallup Daily tracking Jan. 1, 2012–Dec. 3, 2013, with a random sample of 164,754 adults, aged 18 and older, living in the 50 largest metropolitan statistical areas (MSAs) by population.

Margins of error for individual MSAs are no greater than ±4 percentage points and are ±3 percentage points in most MSAs.

March 24, 2014
AMERICANS VIEW OBAMA BETTER ON ENVIRONMENT THAN ENERGY
Opinions on his handling of these two issues tick down in 2014

by Andrew Dugan

WASHINGTON, D.C.—About half of Americans say President Barack Obama is doing a good job of protecting the nation's environment, while fewer—about four in 10—say the president is doing a good job on improving the nation's energy policy or making America prosperous. Americans have rated the president more highly on the environment than on energy or prosperity across the six times Gallup has asked this question.

*Do you think Barack Obama is doing a good job or a poor job in handling each of the following issues as president?^*
% "Good job"

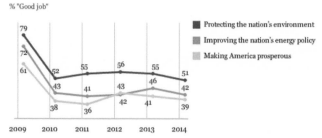

■ Protecting the nation's environment
■ Improving the nation's energy policy
■ Making America prosperous

Question asked in March of each year
^2009 question asked: "Do you think Barack Obama will do a good job or a poor job" in each area.

GALLUP'

These results come from Gallup's annual March Environment survey, conducted March 6–9 this year. Obama's 51% positive rating for protecting the nation's environment is down slightly from the 55% and 56% ratings seen in each of the prior three years. Still, the current rating exceeds the roughly four in 10 who say Obama is doing a good job of making America prosperous or improving the nation's energy policy. Obama's relative strength on the environment may present limited opportunities for him to widen his overall support base, however, as Americans rank environmental concerns among the lowest when compared with other problems facing the nation.

Gallup first measured these dimensions about Obama's job performance in March 2009, when Obama was still in his honeymoon period after having been inaugurated just a couple of months earlier, and when his overall job approval rating was 62%. In that survey, respondents were asked to predict whether Obama *would* do a good or a poor job in each area as president and gave largely optimistic forecasts. By 2010, just a little over a year into his term, he had lost a great deal of support based on Americans' views of his actual performance.

Nonetheless, Obama is better positioned on these three issues at this point in his presidency than was his predecessor, George W. Bush. In March 2006, during Bush's sixth year in office, a third of the country said he was doing a good job of protecting the environment, while a quarter rated him this way on improving the nation's energy policy and 39% on making America prosperous. These differences partly reflected Bush's lower job approval rating of 37% in March 2006, vs. Obama's 44% in the March 6–9 Environment survey.

Bush began his presidency with lower expectations on these three measures, and over the course of his tenure, his performance on these matters was largely evaluated poorly. An average of 38% of Americans from 2002 to 2008 gave Bush praise on protecting the environment, compared with 32% on improving the nation's energy policy and 43% on making America prosperous. Currently, Obama's averages since 2010 are higher on two of these issues—54% for environmental protection and 43% for improving the nation's energy policy. On making America prosperous, an average of 39% say Obama has done a good job, four points lower than Bush's average during his presidency.

2001-2008 Ratings of George W. Bush -- % "Good Job"

Do you think George W. Bush is doing a good job or a poor job in handling each of the following issues as president?^

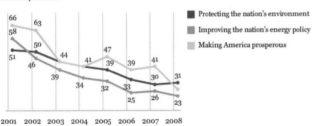

Question asked in March of each year
^2001 question asked: "Do you think George W. Bush will do a good job or a poor job" in each area.

GALLUP'

All Partisan Groups Give Obama Highest Approval on Environment

Across the three major U.S. political groups, Obama receives the highest support on protecting the environment, including 73% of Democrats, 47% of independents, and 32% of Republicans who

say he is doing a good job. While support falls somewhat among all three groups on improving the nation's energy policy, it falls much further among independents and self-identified Republicans than among Democrats on making America prosperous. One in three independents (32%) and 12% of Republicans say Obama has done a good job of making America prosperous, vs. 70% of Democrats.

Has President Obama Done a Good Job or a Bad Job of Handling the Following Issues
% Good job, by self-identified party affiliation

	Democrats	Independents	Republicans
	%	%	%
Protecting the nation's environment	73	47	32
Improving the nation's energy policy	66	37	19
Making America prosperous	70	32	12

March 6-9, 2014

GALLUP'

Bottom Line

Roughly half of the nation still believes Obama is doing a good job of protecting the nation's environment, notably higher than the percentage saying he is doing a good job of improving the nation's energy policy or making America prosperous. In fact, Obama's stewardship on the environment eclipses his overall approval rating, suggesting this issue is a relative strength for the president. However, given the low level of importance most Americans assign the environment compared with other pressing issues of the day, this advantage may have limited political utility.

Survey Methods

Results for this Gallup poll are based on telephone interviews conducted March 6–9, 2014, on the Gallup Daily tracking survey, with a random sample of 1,048 adults, aged 18 and older, living in all 50 U.S. states and the District of Columbia.

For results based on the total sample of national adults, the margin of sampling error is ±4 percentage points at the 95% confidence level.

March 25, 2014
PROVO-OREM, UTAH, LEADS U.S. COMMUNITIES IN WELL-BEING
San Jose-Sunnyvale-Santa Clara, Calif., tops large communities

by Dan Witters

WASHINGTON, D.C.—Provo-Orem, Utah, has the highest Well-Being Index score (71.4) in the U.S. across 189 communities Gallup and Healthways surveyed in 2012–2013. Also in the top 10 are Boulder, Colo.; Fort Collins-Loveland, Colo.; Honolulu, Hawaii; and San Jose-Sunnyvale-Santa Clara, Calif.

At 59.5, Huntington-Ashland, W.Va.-Ky.-Ohio, is the only community with a Well-Being Index score below 60. Huntington-Ashland also trailed all other metros in 2008, 2010, and 2011; its score of 58.1 in 2010 remains the lowest on record across five reporting periods spanning six years of data collection.

"Metropolitan Statistical Areas" as defined by the U.S. Office of Management and Budget

Community	Well-Being Index composite score
Provo-Orem, UT	71.4
Boulder, CO	71.3
Fort Collins-Loveland, CO	71.1
Honolulu, HI	70.7
San Jose-Sunnyvale-Santa Clara, CA	70.6
Ann Arbor, MI	70.4
Naples-Marco Island, FL	70.4
San Luis Obispo-Paso Robles, CA	70.4
San Francisco-Oakland-Fremont, CA	70.2
Lincoln, NE	70.1

2012-2013 data collection
Gallup-Healthways Well-Being Index

GALLUP'

Charleston, W.Va., has the second-lowest score of 60.0. Redding, Calif.; Spartanburg, S.C.; Beaumont-Port Arthur, Texas; and Hickory-Lenoir-Morganton, N.C.; round out the bottom six—with the last three communities tied with a score of 62.2. None of these metro areas are strangers to the bottom 10 list, with each community having appeared at least once on the list in a prior reporting period.

Bottom 11 Communities, Overall Well-Being

"Metropolitan Statistical Areas" as defined by the U.S. Office of Management and Budget

Community	Well-Being Index composite score
Huntington-Ashland, WV-KY-OH	59.5
Charleston, WV	60.0
Redding, CA	62.0
Spartanburg, SC	62.2
Hickory-Lenoir-Morganton, NC	62.2
Beaumont-Port Arthur, TX	62.2
Columbus, GA-AL	62.3
Shreveport-Bossier City, LA	62.9
Mobile, AL	62.9
Evansville, IN-KY	62.9
Chattanooga, TN-GA	62.9

2012-2013 data collection
Gallup-Healthways Well-Being Index

GALLUP'

The regional breakdown in well-being scores is largely consistent with Gallup and Healthways state-level results, which find well-being generally higher in the Midwest and West, and lower in the South. West Virginia, which is home to at least a portion of the two lowest-rated metro areas (Huntington-Ashland and Charleston), ranked last in the nation for well-being among states for the fifth consecutive year in 2013. The state of California ranked 17th in overall well-being in 2013, but it nevertheless boasts three metros in the top 10 for 2012–2013.

The Metropolitan Statistical Areas (MSAs) described in this article are defined by the U.S. Office of Management and Budget. In many cases, more than one city is included in the same MSA, and the same MSA can cross state borders (such as Huntington-Ashland). All reported MSAs encompass at least 300 completed surveys in 2012–2013, and Gallup has weighted each of these samples to ensure it is demographically representative of that MSA.

The Gallup-Healthways Well-Being Index score is an average of six sub-indexes, which individually examine life evaluation, emotional health, work environment, physical health, healthy behaviors,

and access to basic necessities. The overall score and each of the six sub-index scores are calculated on a scale from 0 to 100, where a score of 100 represents the ideal. Gallup and Healthways have been tracking these measures daily since January 2008.

Ann Arbor Still No. 1 in Life Evaluation; Honolulu Best Off Emotionally

Although Provo-Orem has the highest overall well-being score, it does not lead in any of the six domains of well-being that we measured in 2012 and 2013. Residents of Ann Arbor, Mich., rated their current and future lives the best, for the second year in a row, and those of Huntington-Ashland rated theirs the worst.

Holland-Grand Haven, Mich., is the metro area with the highest Physical Health Index in the nation, displacing Fort Collins-Loveland, Colo., the community that held the spot in 2011. San Luis Obispo-Paso Robles, Calif., has the highest Work Environment Index score. Holland-Grand Haven, Mich., led the nation in access to basic necessities as it did in 2008–2010 (Gallup and Healthways did not conduct enough surveys in Holland-Grand Haven to report on it in 2011).

Best and Worst Scoring Communities, Gallup-Healthways Well-Being Sub-Indexes

Among 189 U.S. Metropolitan Statistical Areas surveyed

Well-Being Sub-Index	Best	Score	Worst	Score
Life Evaluation	Ann Arbor, MI	61.7	Huntington-Ashland, WV-KY-OH	34.6
Emotional Health	Honolulu, HI	83.4	Huntington-Ashland, WV-KY-OH	73.1
Work Environment	San Luis Obispo-Paso Robles, CA	59.1	Fayetteville, NC	38.5
Physical Health	Holland-Grand Haven, MI	80.9	Huntington-Ashland, WV-KY-OH	66.2
Healthy Behaviors	Salinas, CA	71.5	Charleston, WV	58.2
Basic Access	Holland-Grand Haven, MI	89.7	McAllen-Edinburg-Mission, TX	71.8

2012-2013 data collection
Gallup-Healthways Well-Being Index

Compare well-being across large, medium, and small metro areas.

Residents of Huntington-Ashland rated their lives about half as well as those in Ann Arbor, and also described their physical health at levels far below what is found among residents of Holland-Grand Haven. Including its nation-leading score of 89.7 in the Basic Access Index, Holland-Grand Haven is the only community to boast a top ranking in more than one sub-index, although lower ratings in Life Evaluation and Work Environment kept it out of the top 10 overall.

Huntington-Ashland had the worst Emotional Health Index score, the third sub-index on which it ranks last nationally. Honolulu has been the top-rated U.S. metro area in the Emotional Health Index each measurement period since 2010 and has never ranked lower than second on this domain.

Healthy behaviors were least prevalent in Charleston and most prevalent in Salinas, Calif. Salinas reclaimed the top spot it occupied in 2010 after dropping to second place in 2011.

McAllen-Edinburg-Mission, Texas, residents reported the worst access to basic necessities for the fourth measurement period in a row, due in part to just 47% of residents who reported having health insurance, by far the lowest percentage in the nation. The metro area in the U.S. with the lowest score on the Basic Access Index has come from the state of Texas across all five reporting periods.

San Jose and San Francisco Top All Large Communities in Well-Being

San Jose-Sunnyvale-Santa Clara residents reported the highest well-being among the nation's 52 largest (1 million or more residents) communities, followed by San Francisco-Oakland-Fremont, Calif., and Washington, D.C.-Arlington-Alexandria, Va.-Md.-W.Va. These three metros are commonly among the top of the list of large cities each year. San Jose-Sunnyvale-Santa Clara's overall rank of fifth across well-being areas of all sizes is the highest ever for a large metro area. Minneapolis-St. Paul-Bloomington, Minn.-Wis., also typically ranks in the top five, while Denver-Aurora, Colo., makes its first appearance on the list this year.

Louisville-Jefferson County, Ky.-Ind., which was ranked 50th among large metros in 2011, took over the bottom spot, displacing Las Vegas-Paradise, Nev., for the large metro area with the lowest well-being, due mostly to its residents' low physical, emotional, and healthy behaviors scores. Jacksonville, Fla., repeated its ranking of 51st from 2011.

Las Vegas-Paradise residents again reported the worst access to clean and safe water in the U.S. among large communities—a recurring pattern for this metro area and a principle reason why it is ranked last nationally in basic access for the fifth-straight reporting period among large communities. In general, the six-point gap in well-being between the highest and lowest-rated large communities is half as large as the 11-point gap found between the highest and lowest scores amid all 189 reportable communities that Gallup and Healthways surveyed.

Top Five and Bottom Five Large Communities, Overall Well-Being

Out of 52 Metropolitan Statistical Areas with at least 1 million residents

Top five communities	Well-Being Index composite score	Bottom five communities	Well-Being Index composite score
San Jose-Sunnyvale-Santa Clara, CA	70.6	Louisville-Jefferson County, KY-IN	64.1
San Francisco-Oakland-Fremont, CA	70.2	Jacksonville, FL	64.3
Washington-Arlington-Alexandria, DC-VA-MD-WV	70.1	Detroit-Warren-Livonia, MI	64.4
Minneapolis-St. Paul-Bloomington, MN-WI	69.7	Providence-New Bedford-Fall River, RI-MA	64.5
Denver-Aurora, CO	69.5	Tampa-St. Petersburg-Clearwater, FL	64.6

2012-2013 data collection
Gallup-Healthways Well-Being Index

GALLUP

Implications

With about 80% of Americans living in urban or suburban areas, the role of cities in spearheading the well-being of the U.S. is significant. City leadership—be it government, business, faith-based, community-based, or education—plays a critical role in the success or failure of a city to embrace and sustain a culture of well-being.

"There are tangible policies that communities can adopt to actively cultivate and improve residents' well-being," said Dan Buettner, National Geographic Fellow and founder of Blue Zones LLC. "Policies that nudge people into healthy activities—where it is easy to walk to the store, bike to a friend's house, get access to fresh produce, and be surrounded by healthy-minded, supportive friends—are ones that make the healthy choice, the easy choice. Sustained transformation depends on building an environment and establishing social policies that support and reinforce these programs."

Communities such as Boulder (highest average rank across all reporting periods since 2008), Provo-Orem (most religious city, which helps its overall well-being), and San Jose-Sunnyvale-Santa Clara (the highest-ever rating for a large metro) can serve as best-practice examples for leaders of other cities. Key elements of community well-being, such as learning new and interesting things, providing safe places to exercise, routine trips to the dentist, and smoking cessation, are all key vanguards of high well-being locations. Leaders can leverage these learnings and advocate their execution in their own communities.

Survey Methods

Results are based on telephone interviews conducted as part of the Gallup-Healthways Well-Being Index survey Jan. 2–Dec. 29, 2012, and Jan. 2–Dec. 30, 2013, with a random sample of 531,630 adults, aged 18 and older, living in metropolitan areas in the 50 U.S. states and the District of Columbia, selected using random-digit-dial sampling. Two years of data were aggregated together to enable the same number of reportable cities as in prior years, when the overall annual data collection exceeded 350,000 interviews per year compared to 178,072 interviews conducted in 2013. At least 300 cases are required per metro area for reporting.

The metro areas referenced in this article are based on the Metropolitan Statistical Areas (MSAs) as defined by the U.S. Office of Management and Budget. In many cases, more than one city is included in the same MSA. The San Jose, Calif., metropolitan statistical area, for example, also includes the smaller nearby cities of Sunnyvale and Santa Clara in addition to San Jose itself. Each respondent is attributed to his or her MSA based on the self-report of his or her ZIP code, and all metro areas had at least 300 completed surveys in the 2012–2013 data collection period.

Maximum expected error ranges for the Well-Being Index and the sub-index scores vary according to MSA size, ranging from less than 1 point for the largest cities represented to ±1.5 points for the smallest cities.

Interviews are conducted with respondents on landline telephones and cellular phones, with interviews conducted in Spanish for respondents who are primarily Spanish-speaking. Each sample of national adults includes a minimum quota of 50% cellphone respondents and 50% landline respondents, with additional minimum quotas by time zone within region. Landline telephone and cellphone numbers are selected using random-digit-dial methods. Landline respondents are chosen at random within each household on the basis of which member had the most recent birthday.

Samples are weighted to match MSA demographics of gender, age, race, Hispanic ethnicity and education. Demographic weighting targets are based on the most recent Nielsen demographic estimates for the aged 18 and older population in each MSA. All reported margins of sampling error include the computed design effects for weighting.

In addition to sampling error, question wording and practical difficulties in conducting surveys can introduce error or bias into the findings of public opinion polls.

For more details on Gallup's polling methodology, visit www.gallup.com.

March 26, 2014
U.S. SENIORS HAVE REALIGNED WITH THE REPUBLICAN PARTY
Seniors move from a reliably Democratic
to a reliably Republican group

by Jeffrey M. Jones

PRINCETON, NJ—U.S seniors—those aged 65 and older—have moved from a reliably Democratic group to a reliably Republican one over the past two decades. From 1992 through 2006, seniors had been solidly Democratic and significantly more Democratic than younger Americans. Over the last seven years, seniors have become less Democratic, and have shown an outright preference for the Republican Party since 2010.

Democratic Advantage in Party Affiliation, by Age, 1992-2013

Figures represent the % Democrats/Democratic-leaning independents minus the % Republicans/Republican-leaning independents

■ 18 to 64   ■ 65+

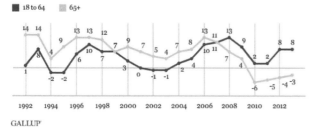

GALLUP

In 1992, 53% of senior citizens, on average, identified as Democrats or said they were independents but leaned Democratic, while 39% identified as Republicans or leaned Republican, resulting in a 14-percentage-point Democratic advantage in seniors' party affiliation. Last year, 48% of seniors identified as or leaned Republican, and 45% Democratic, a three-point Republican advantage.

By comparison, younger Americans, those aged 18 to 64, shifted from +1 point Democratic in 1992 to +8 Democratic in 2013, and tended to show greater Democratic advantages from 2006 to 2013 than prior to that. The changes in younger Americans' party affiliation generally follow those among the broader U.S. adult population between 1992 and 2013.

Senior citizens' changing political preferences are also apparent in their recent presidential vote preferences, according to Gallup's final pre-election polls. Senior voters favored the Democratic candidate in each election from 1992 through 2004, including a 17-point margin for Bill Clinton in 1992, the highest among age groups. In each of the last two elections, by contrast, seniors were the only age group to support the Republican candidate over Barack Obama.

Today's Seniors Were Once Democrats

Gallup's analysis reveals that the changes in seniors' party preferences are attributable in part to attitudinal change among today's seniors as they have aged. This is evident in survey results from 1993 and 2003 that show the party preferences of today's seniors when they were 10 or 20 years younger.

In 1993, Americans then aged 45 to 79 represented the age group that today is 65 to 99. At that time, 20 years ago, those

45 to 79 were highly Democratic, with a 12-point advantage in favor of the Democrats. That gap was larger than the average seven-point Democratic advantage among younger age groups that year.

Ten years later, all age cohorts had become more Republican and were fairly balanced politically. Today's seniors, who were aged 55 to 89 in 2003, were the only age cohort to tilt Democratic at that time. The 2013 results show that today's seniors have continued to move in a Republican direction, while the younger age cohorts have gone back in a Democratic direction.

Partisan Preferences of Age Cohorts Over Time

	% Democratic/ Lean Democratic	% Republican/ Lean Republican	Democratic advantage
CURRENTLY 65+ YEARS OLD			
2013 Gallup data, those aged 65 to 99	45	48	–3
2003 Gallup data, those aged 55 to 89	47	45	2
1993 Gallup data, those aged 45 to 79	51	39	12
CURRENTLY 50 TO 64 YEARS OLD			
2013 Gallup data, those aged 50 to 64	46	44	2
2003 Gallup data, those aged 40 to 54	45	46	–1
1993 Gallup data, those aged 30 to 44	48	41	7
CURRENTLY 30 TO 49 YEARS OLD			
2013 Gallup data, those aged 30 to 49	47	41	6
2003 Gallup data, those aged 20 to 39	44	46	–2
1993 Gallup data, those aged 18 to 29	49	42	7
CURRENTLY 18 TO 29 YEARS OLD			
2013 Gallup data, those aged 18 to 29	53	35	18

Note: 1993 data are based on 2013 age minus 20 years, and 2003 data are based on 2013 age minus 10 years. Minimum age of Gallup respondents is 18.

GALLUP

Race a Factor in Seniors' Shifting Allegiances

U.S. party preferences are strongly polarized along racial lines, and one reason seniors are more Republican now is that they are racially distinct from other age groups. Eighty-five percent of those 65 and older are non-Hispanic whites, according to Gallup estimates, compared with 77% of 50- to 64-year-olds, 66% of 30- to 49-year-olds, and 54% of 18- to 29-year-olds.

Whites 18 to 29 are slightly Democratic, but whites in all older age groups lean Republican by 10- to 13-point margins. At the same time, nonwhites in all age groups are overwhelmingly Democratic. Nonwhite seniors, in fact, are the most strongly Democratic of any age group.

Party Affiliation by Age and Race, 2013

	18 to 29 years old	30 to 49 years old	50 to 64 years old	65+ years
	%	%	%	%
NON-HISPANIC WHITES				
Democratic/Lean Democratic	45	38	40	40
Republican/Lean Republican	43	51	50	53
Gap	2	–13	–10	–13
NONWHITES				
Democratic/Lean Democratic	62	66	71	76
Republican/Lean Republican	25	20	20	18
Gap	37	46	51	58

Based on aggregated Gallup data, January-December 2013

GALLUP

The mainly white racial composition of seniors has not changed much in recent years, whereas younger age groups have become increasingly diverse. In 1995, the first year Gallup routinely measured both race and Hispanic ethnicity, 89% of seniors were non-Hispanic white, four points higher than today. But other age groups are now substantially more diverse than in 1995, showing declines of between nine and 17 points in the percentage of the group that is non-Hispanic white.

An earlier Gallup analysis showed that whites have become more firmly aligned with the Republican Party in recent years. Because seniors are predominantly white, the "Republicanization" of whites is more evident among this group.

However, white seniors have not always been as Republican as younger whites. From 1995 until 2008, whites aged 65 and older averaged a three-point greater preference for the Democratic Party than the Republican Party. In contrast, all other age groups of whites showed predominantly Republican preferences during those years.

Implications

It is not uncommon for subgroups to show variation in their party preferences over periods of time, usually in response to the political events of the day, such as the Republican surge after the 9/11 terrorist attacks or the Democratic surge in the latter years of the Bush administration.

But when change becomes more sustained and lasting, it is a sign of a political realignment. Although those are rare events, there have been some examples in recent decades, such as regional realignments in party preferences among Southerners and New Englanders. Now it appears U.S. seniors may be undergoing a realignment of their own.

Race appears to be a significant factor in seniors' Republican realignment, because whites have become more solidly Republican in recent years, seniors are overwhelmingly white, and white seniors today are Republican-aligned, while white seniors in the past were Democratic-aligned.

The timing of the shift raises the possibility that it is motivated by recent events that have more closely linked race and political party than was the case in the past, including the mid-2000s debate over immigration, and the election and presidency of Barack Obama. Because seniors did not show an outright preference for the Republican Party until 2010, Obama's second year in office, it may not have been just Obama's race, per se, but also his policies and performance in office that have turned seniors "red."

Once Obama leaves office, his influence on party preferences among racial and age groups may become clearer, if he is succeeded by a white president from either party. Should the current trends in party preference by age persist, it suggests a political realignment among seniors has taken place. If the current trends by age shift in the other direction, it suggests the shift was temporary, likely tied to the Obama era.

Survey Methods

Results are based on yearly aggregated data from multiple day Gallup telephone polls conducted between 1995 and 2013. Each yearly aggregate is based on a minimum of 18,000 interviews with adults age 18 and older.

For results based on the total sample of national adults in any given year, the margin of sampling error is ±1 percentage point at the 95% confidence level.

For results based on the total sample of Americans age 65 and older in any given year, the margin of sampling error is ±1 percentage point at the 95% confidence level.

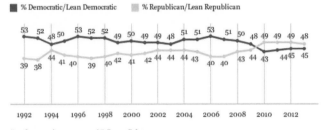

Party Affiliation, Americans Aged 65 and Older, 1992-2013

Based on yearly aggregates of Gallup poll data

GALLUP

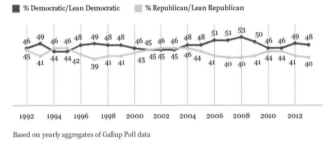

Party Affiliation, Americans Aged 18-64, 1992-2013

Based on yearly aggregates of Gallup Poll data

GALLUP

March 26, 2014
AMERICANS SEE POPE IN FAVORABLE LIGHT
Francis essentially matches John Paul II's soaring popularity at end of his tenure

by Frank Newport

PRINCETON, NJ—President Barack Obama meets Thursday for the first time with Pope Francis, whose image among Americans has become more favorable over the first year of his papacy. More than three in four Americans currently view the pope favorably.

Favorable Ratings of Pope Francis

	Favorable	Unfavorable	Never heard of/ No opinion
	%	%	%
Feb 6-9, 2014	76	9	16
Apr 11-14, 2013	58	10	31

GALLUP

Obama and Pope Francis, meeting at the Vatican, are expected to focus on the concerns both men have about inequality and the rising gap between rich and poor in the world today. Obama might well hope to benefit from his association with the popular pope. In the same February poll in which Pope Francis received his 76% favorable, 9% unfavorable rating from Americans, Obama's image was much more divided, at 52% favorable and 46% unfavorable.

A Gallup survey conducted the month after Pope Francis' election on March 13, 2013, showed that Americans' initial impressions of him were positive, although more than three in 10 had never heard of him or didn't have an opinion. As he has become better known over the past year, including being named *TIME's* Person of the Year in December, Pope Francis' favorable rating has increased. His low unfavorable percentage has remained essentially constant.

Pope Francis was elected after Pope Benedict XVI resigned in February 2013. Benedict ended his papacy in a significantly less popular position among Americans than when he was elected in 2005. At his most popular, in 2008, Benedict had a 63% favorable, 15% unfavorable rating in the U.S. But by 2010, dogged by his handling of the priest abuse scandals both before and after he became pope, nearly as many Americans saw Benedict unfavorably as favorably.

Favorable Ratings of Pope Francis, Pope Benedict XVI, Pope John Paul II

	Favorable	Unfavorable	Never heard of/ No opinion
	%	%	%
POPE FRANCIS			
Feb 6-9, 2014	76	9	16
Apr 11-14, 2013	58	10	31
POPE BENEDICT XVI			
Mar 26-28, 2010	40	35	25
Apr 18-20, 2008	63	15	22
Jun 1-3, 2007	52	16	32
Dec 16-18, 2005	50	11	39
Apr 29-May 1, 2005	55	12	33
POPE JOHN PAUL II			
Feb 25-27, 2005	78	11	11
Oct 6-8, 2003	73	17	10
Apr 29-May 1, 2002	61	26	13
Dec 28-29, 1998	86	8	6
Aug 8-10, 1993	64	15	21

GALLUP

In contrast with Benedict, his predecessor, Pope John Paul II, had a highly favorable image among Americans from the time Gallup started measuring his rating in 1993. John Paul averaged a 72% favorable rating; his highest rating was 86% in December 1998 and his lowest was 61% in late April/early May 2002.

Catholics Highly Positive, but So Are Other Americans

Pope Francis enjoys the highly positive ratings that would be expected among American Catholics, but Protestants—the largest religious group in the U.S.—also see him in a favorable light. More than seven in 10 of those who do not claim an official religious identity also view Pope Francis favorably.

American Catholics' views of Francis are similar to their views of Pope John Paul II in the February 2005 survey conducted just before his death. At the time, 93% rated John Paul II favorably, and 4% unfavorably. By contrast, Catholics gave Pope Benedict a significantly lower 61% favorable rating in 2010.

Favorable Ratings of Pope Francis

	Favorable	Unfavorable	Never heard of/ No opinion
	%	%	%
NATIONAL ADULTS	76	9	16
Catholics	89	3	8
Protestants	78	7	14
No religious identity	73	9	18

Feb. 6-9, 2014

GALLUP

Bottom Line

About one year after he was elected pope, Americans are essentially as positive about Francis as they were about Pope John Paul II shortly before he died. By contrast, Pope Benedict's image had deteriorated to a much less positive position in the years before he resigned in 2013.

Survey Methods

Results for this Gallup poll are based on telephone interviews conducted Feb. 6–9, 2014, with a random sample of 1,023 adults, aged 18 and older, living in all 50 U.S. states and the District of Columbia.

For results based on the total sample of national adults, the margin of sampling error is ±4 percentage points at the 95% confidence level.

March 27, 2014
IN U.S., RECORD 68% VIEW RUSSIA AS UNFRIENDLY OR AN ENEMY
Putin's favorability dips below 10%; Ukraine perceived as friend

by Art Swift

WASHINGTON, D.C.—After a tumultuous winter in which Russia has been at odds with the West over Crimea, more than two-thirds of Americans say Russia is either unfriendly (44%) or an enemy (24%) to the U.S. This is a departure from sentiments in recent years and a record high since 1999.

Americans' Perceptions of Russia as Friend or Foe

Please say whether you consider Russia an ally of the United States, friendly, but not an ally, unfriendly, or an enemy.

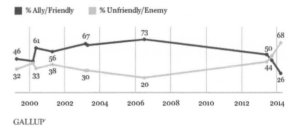

The March 22–23 survey was conducted after Crimea voted to secede from Ukraine, and Russian President Vladimir Putin announced that Crimea had joined the Russian Federation. From 1999 to the middle of last year, Americans viewed Russia more positively than negatively. As recently as June 2013, 52% of Americans said Russia was an ally or friendly.

Americans' negative views are a fairly recent development after an increasingly tense period in U.S.-Russian relations, starting when Putin granted temporary asylum to Edward Snowden, the former National Security Agency contractor who went public with his insider knowledge of the agency's surveillance secrets. Putin also intervened in the Syrian chemical weapons conflict last fall, ultimately brokering a peaceful solution, and chastised President Barack Obama in an op-ed in the *New York Times*.

This winter, the Sochi Olympics drew immense attention to Russia, including its anti-gay policies, its difficulties in preparing for the Winter Games, and fears about possible terrorist attacks at the global competition. But the situation in the Crimean region of Ukraine has garnered the most recent headlines because Putin called into question the sovereignty of the territory.

Ukraine Seen as an Ally or Friendly to the U.S.

At the same time, 64% of Americans believe Ukraine is an ally (17%) or friendly (47%) nation to the U.S. This is the first time Gallup has asked this particular question about Ukraine, and Americans' support is softer than what Gallup sees for other nations that are often considered allies. For example, 86% of Americans in the same poll say France is an ally or a friendly nation, and 92% perceive Great Britain this way.

Americans' Views of Ukraine

Please say whether you consider Ukraine an ally of the United States, friendly, but not an ally, unfriendly, or an enemy.

	Ally	Friendly, but not an ally	Unfriendly	An enemy	No opinion
Mar 22-23, 2014	17%	47%	16%	6%	14%

GALLUP

Putin's Favorable Ratings Drop to All-Time Low

The Russian president's favorable rating dropped to 9% in the most recent poll, down 10 percentage points since February. His unfavorable rating rose six points to 69%. Though he has never been popular in the U.S., Americans viewed Putin more favorably than unfavorably in 2002 and 2003, during his first term in office.

Americans' Opinions of Russian President Vladimir Putin

Do you have a favorable or unfavorable opinion of Vladimir Putin?

■ % Favorable   % Unfavorable

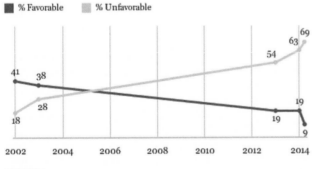

GALLUP

Bottom Line

This week, Obama said that while he doesn't foresee the U.S. and Russia entering a new "Cold War," it is a priority to protect Ukraine. The tensions engendered by Russia's interest in Crimea have directly affected Americans' views of Russia and Putin, which are now at historical lows. While it is unclear what the next step will be in the Crimean conflict—and in the region at large—Americans' dramatically souring views are reminiscent of the Cold War, despite Obama's dismissals.

The further development this week that the U.S. and other G7 nations have effectively kicked Russia out of the conclave is a sign that strained U.S.-Russia relations will likely continue in the near term.

Survey Methods

Results for this Gallup poll are based on telephone interviews conducted March 22–23, 2014, on the Gallup Daily tracking survey, with a random sample of 1,012 adults, aged 18 and older, living in all 50 U.S. states and the District of Columbia.

For results based on the total sample of national adults, the margin of sampling error is ±4 percentage points at the 95% confidence level.

March 27, 2014
HALF OF AMERICANS SAY U.S. HEADED BACK TO COLD WAR
Those who lived through Cold War more likely to say it is returning

by Rebecca Riffkin

WASHINGTON, D.C.—Fifty percent of Americans believe the U.S. and Russia are currently heading back toward a Cold War. During his trip to Europe, President Barack Obama acknowledged increasing tension with Russia but said he has no interest in entering into another Cold War.

Americans' Views About the Return of a Cold War

Do you think the United States and Russia are heading back toward a Cold War, or not?

	% Yes, are	% No, are not
2014 Mar 22-23	50	43
1991 Feb 22	25	64

Note: The 1991 question used "Soviet Union" instead of "Russia" in the question wording.

GALLUP

Spurred by increased international apprehensions of Russia's annexation of Crimea, Gallup asked Americans on March 22–23 if they felt the U.S. was returning to a Cold War. Gallup asked the same question in February 1991 polling and found a quarter of Americans saying they thought the U.S. and the Soviet Union were heading back toward a Cold War, while 64% did not think this.

The 1991 polling took place as tensions were easing in the decades-long Cold War, prior to the breakup of the Soviet Union at the end of that year. In January and February 1991, the U.S. Congress voiced anger over Soviet crackdowns on independence fighters in the Baltic region.

Older Americans More Likely to Say a Cold War Is Returning

Older Americans are much more likely than younger Americans to say the U.S. and Russia are heading back toward a Cold War. Sixty-four percent of Americans aged 65 and older say a Cold War is returning, almost 30 percentage points higher than the percentage of 18- to 29-year-olds who hold this same view.

Americans' Views About the Return of a Cold War, by Age

Do you think the United States and Russia are heading back toward a Cold War, or not?

	% Yes, are	% No, are not
18-29	36	58
30-49	48	48
50-64	54	37
65+	64	26

March 22-23, 2014

GALLUP

This difference in opinions between ages could be linked to Americans' experiences with the Cold War. The oldest Americans in the 18- to 29-year-old age group would have been five years old when one of the death knells of the Cold War occurred—the falling of the Berlin Wall in 1989. Overall, many in this younger age group were not alive at all during the Cold War. Americans who are older than 65, however, were at least 40 as the Cold War ended, and they grew up when tensions between the U.S. and Soviet Union dominated American foreign policy.

Americans of different ages are also paying different levels of attention to the situation in Ukraine. Nearly 80% of Americans aged 65 and older are very or somewhat closely following the news about the situation between Russia and Ukraine, while 42% of Americans aged 18 to 29 report paying the same amount of attention.

Nearly 60% of Americans who are very or somewhat closely following the situation between Russia and Ukraine say the U.S. is heading back toward a Cold War, while 36% of those whose who are not closely following the conflict say the same.

More Republicans Think the U.S. Is Heading Back Toward a Cold War

Fewer than half of Democrats and independents feel the U.S. is heading back toward a Cold War, compared with more than two-thirds of Republicans who say the same.

Americans' Views About the Return of a Cold War, by Party ID

Do you think the United States and Russia are heading back toward a Cold War, or not?

	% Yes, are	% No, are not
Democrat	44	51
Independent	47	45
Republican	67	27

March 22-23, 2014

GALLUP

These party differences could be linked to the finding that U.S. seniors are more likely to be Republican. They also may be associated with Republicans' historic views of the importance of the U.S. military and support for defense spending.

Implications

The Cold War, from roughly 1945 to 1991, was a watershed moment in American history. This period redefined America's defense system and led to decisions to enter into military conflicts in Korea and Vietnam. While the U.S. and the Soviet Union never directly engaged in battle, this competition led to an unprecedented arms race between the two nations. The icy tensions between the U.S. and the former Soviet Union affected countries worldwide for decades.

Russia's recent annexation of part of Ukraine as well as its support for Iran and Syria have put it at odds with the U.S. During his visit to Europe, President Obama said he does not feel the U.S. is returning to the Cold War, but currently, at least half of Americans do not appear to agree with him. Even if U.S.-Russia tensions do not escalate to the point they did during the Cold War era, for the immediate future, Russia may be the most challenging foreign policy issue facing the U.S.

Survey Methods

Results for this Gallup poll are based on telephone interviews conducted March 22–23, 2014, with a random sample of 1,012 adults, aged 18 and older, living in all 50 U.S. states and the District of Columbia.

For results based on the total sample of national adults, the margin of sampling error is ±4 percentage points at the 95% confidence level.

March 28, 2014
ALABAMANS STRUGGLE MOST TO AFFORD HEALTHCARE AND MEDICINE
Iowans and Minnesotans are least likely to struggle with healthcare costs

by Justin McCarthy

WASHINGTON, D.C.—One in four Alabamans (24.5%) said in 2013 that there were times in the past 12 months when they did not have enough money to pay for the healthcare and/or medicine they and their families needed—the highest percentage in the nation. Residents of West Virginia and Mississippi followed closely behind. At the other end, Iowa and Minnesota tied for the lowest percentage of residents who were unable to afford needed healthcare or medicine, at 12.2%.

These results are based on interviews conducted Jan. 2–Dec. 29, 2013, with more than 178,067 Americans in all 50 states and the District of Columbia as part of the Gallup-Healthways Well-Being Index.

Gallup asks Americans each day if there have been times over the past 12 months in which they did not have enough money to pay for healthcare and/or medicine they or their families needed. In 2013, 18.6% of Americans said they had trouble affording healthcare or medicine. The national average has held steady in recent years after a slight drop from the 19.7% average found in 2008.

States Where Residents Struggle the Most to Afford Healthcare or Medicine

State	% Without enough money for healthcare and/or medicine
Alabama	24.5
West Virginia	23.8
Mississippi	23.2
Kentucky	22.5
North Carolina	22.3
Arkansas	22.3
Oklahoma	21.7
South Carolina	21.3
Florida	21.1
Texas	21.0
Arizona	21.0

January-December 2013
Gallup-Healthways Well-Being Index

GALLUP

States Where Residents Struggle the Least to Afford Healthcare or Medicine

State	% Without enough money for healthcare and/or medicine
Iowa	12.2
Minnesota	12.2
Hawaii	12.6
North Dakota	12.9
Massachusetts	13.0
South Dakota	14.3
Wisconsin	14.3
Connecticut	14.6
Maryland	14.7
Alaska	14.9

January-December 2013
Gallup-Healthways Well-Being Index

GALLUP

In 2008, 24 states reported 20% or more of their residents said they could not afford needed healthcare. By 2013, this dropped to 16 states.

States with the highest percentages of residents who could not afford needed healthcare and/or medicine are predominantly in the South, where overall well-being scores lagged compared with the rest of the country. States where residents were least likely to struggle to afford these basic necessities are more geographically diverse.

Though it still falls among the bottom state rankings, Mississippi has seen the greatest improvement since 2008 in the percentage of residents who have trouble paying for healthcare or medicine. The percentage who struggled in Mississippi has steadily declined from 30.1% in 2008 to 23.2% in 2013.

Affording Healthcare Linked to Uninsured Rates

States with higher percentages of residents who struggled to afford healthcare or medicine also tend to have higher uninsured rates, lower ratings of the standard of living, or both. All 10 states with the highest percentage of residents who struggled to afford healthcare or medicine had uninsured rates that exceeded the national average of 17.3% in 2013, and most were among the list of states with the highest uninsured rates in 2013.

States Where Residents Struggle Most to Afford Healthcare or Medicine, by Uninsured Rates

State	% Uninsured	Among top 10 highest uninsured rates in U.S.?
National average	17.3	
Alabama	17.7	No
West Virginia	17.6	No
Mississippi	22.4	Yes
Kentucky	20.4	Yes
North Carolina	20.4	Yes
Arkansas	22.5	Yes
Oklahoma	21.4	Yes
South Carolina	18.7	No
Florida	22.1	Yes
Texas	27.0	Yes
Arizona	20.4	Yes

January-December 2013
Gallup-Healthways Well-Being Index

GALLUP

Lacking healthcare coverage, however, is not a perfect predictor of Americans' ability to afford needed healthcare in a given state. Though the uninsured rates in Alabama and West Virginia are above average, they were not among the top 10 states lacking insurance coverage. Still, they topped the list of states with high percentages of residents who struggled to afford healthcare or medicine in 2013. For these two states, their low standard of living ratings suggest that residents' financial struggles may play a role in their ability to pay for healthcare. Alabama and West Virginia also rank among the poorest states in the nation based on per capita income.

Bottom Line

The majority of Americans in all 50 states say there were no times in the past 12 months when they could not pay for healthcare or medicine. However, substantial numbers of Americans did struggle to pay these costs, including at least one in five residents in 16 states.

States with higher uninsured rates are clearly more at risk of having higher percentages of residents who cannot meet their healthcare needs. States are making decisions on how to navigate the Affordable Care Act's ongoing implementation. If states successfully reduce the number of residents without insurance, it may in turn help reduce the percentage who say they cannot afford what they need in terms of healthcare.

But insurance isn't the entire problem for many Americans—it's their personal financial situation that hinders them from purchasing the medicine or care they need. This is a challenge for all states, as Americans' views of their personal finances fell and their future expectations for their finances remained stagnant in 2013. While insuring more Americans may be one part of helping residents to afford the healthcare and medicine they need, addressing the need for jobs and increasing median income may also be necessary.

Survey Methods

Results are based on telephone interviews conducted as part of the Gallup-Healthways Well-Being Index survey Jan. 2–Dec. 29, 2013, with a random sample of 178,067 adults, aged 18 and older, living in all 50 U.S. states and the District of Columbia.

The margin of sampling error for most states is ±1 to ±2 percentage points, but is as high as ±4 points for states with smaller population sizes such as Wyoming, North Dakota, South Dakota, Delaware, and Hawaii.

March 28, 2014
YOUNG AMERICANS' AFFINITY FOR DEMOCRATIC PARTY HAS GROWN
Majority have consistently aligned with Democratic Party since 2006

by Jeffrey M. Jones

PRINCETON, NJ—Young adults—those between the ages of 18 and 29—have typically aligned themselves with the Democratic Party, but they have become substantially more likely to do so since 2006.

From 1993 to 2003, 47% of 18- to 29-year-olds, on average, identified as Democrats or said they were independents but leaned to the

Democratic Party, while 42% were Republicans or Republican leaners. That time span included two years in which young adults tilted Republican, 1994 and 1995, when Republicans won control of Congress. Since 2006, the average gap in favor of the Democratic Party among young adults has been 18 percentage points, 54% to 36%.

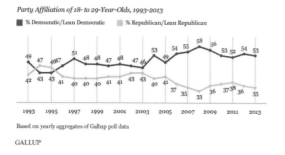

Party Affiliation of 18- to 29-Year-Olds, 1993-2013

■ % Democratic/Lean Democratic ■ % Republican/Lean Republican

Based on yearly aggregates of Gallup poll data

GALLUP

This Democratic movement among the young has come at a time when senior citizens have become more Republican. The broader U.S. population has shown more variability in its party preferences in recent years, shifting Democratic from 2005 to 2008, moving back toward the Republican Party from 2009 to 2011, and showing modest Democratic preferences in the last two years.

Younger Americans Now More Racially Diverse

A major reason young adults are increasingly likely to prefer the Democratic Party is that today's young adults are more racially and ethnically diverse than young adults of the past. U.S. political preferences are sharply divided by race, with nonwhite Americans of all ages overwhelmingly identifying as Democrats or leaning Democratic.

Gallup estimates that 54% of 18- to 29-year-olds are non-Hispanic white and 45% nonwhite, compared with 71% non-Hispanic white and 29% nonwhite in 1995, the first full year Gallup measured Hispanic ethnicity.

In 2013, 62% of nonwhite Americans between the ages of 18 and 29 were Democrats or Democratic leaners, while 25% were Republicans or Republican leaners. That 37-point Democratic advantage, though sizable, is slightly lower than the average 42-point advantage from 1995 through 2013.

But young adults are not more Democratic solely because they are more racially diverse. In recent years, young white adults, who previously aligned more with the Republican Party, have shifted Democratic. From 1995 to 2005, young whites consistently identified as or leaned Republican rather than Democratic, by an average of eight points. Since 2006, whites aged 18 to 29 have shown at least a slight Democratic preference in all but one year, with an average advantage of three points.

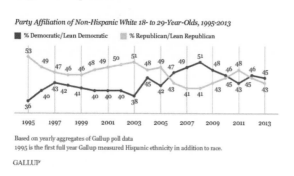

Party Affiliation of Non-Hispanic White 18- to 29-Year-Olds, 1995-2013

■ % Democratic/Lean Democratic ■ % Republican/Lean Republican

Based on yearly aggregates of Gallup poll data
1995 is the first full year Gallup measured Hispanic ethnicity in addition to race.

GALLUP

Young whites first shifted to a pro-Democratic position in 2006, perhaps because of frustration with George W. Bush and his policies. Barack Obama's presidential campaign also may have attracted younger whites, given the candidate's relative youth, particularly since Republicans nominated the much older John McCain as their presidential candidate. Young whites are not as high on the Democratic Party now as they were in 2008, but they remain more likely to prefer it to the Republican Party.

Implications

Recent decades have brought significant shifts in Americans' political allegiances, in the short term and the long term. While young adults have generally been more likely to align themselves with the Democratic Party than the Republican Party, they are now much more solidly Democratic than prior generations of young adults.

To a large extent, this reflects the increasing racial and ethnic diversity of the U.S. population, particularly among the youngest generations of Americans. And that growing diversity creates challenges for the Republican Party, given nonwhites' consistent and strong support for the Democratic Party. To some degree, Republicans have been able to offset the growing diversity and win elections by increasing their support among Americans aged 30 and older, particularly white senior citizens. But the GOP may find itself in an increasingly weak position against the Democrats unless it can broaden its appeal to younger and nonwhite Americans.

Survey Methods

Results are based on yearly aggregated data from multiple day Gallup telephone polls conducted between 1993 and 2013. Each yearly aggregate is based on a minimum of 18,000 interviews with adults age 18 and older.

For results based on the total sample of national adults in any given year, the margin of sampling error is ±1 percentage point at the 95% confidence level.

For results based on the total sample of Americans age 18 to 29, the margin of sampling error is ±3 percentage points at the 95% confidence level for 2007 and ±2 percentage points at the 95% confidence level for all other years.

March 28, 2014
POLITICS AFFECT UNINSURED AMERICANS'
INSURANCE INTENTIONS
Democrats twice as likely as Republicans
to say they will get insurance

by Frank Newport

PRINCETON, NJ—Three-quarters of uninsured Democrats say they still plan on getting insurance rather than pay a fine, double the percentage of uninsured Republicans. This strongly partisan divide in Americans' intentions to comply with the Affordable Care Act's individual mandate is in line with what Gallup has found in previous months, underscoring the ongoing political nature of the public's relationship with the ACA.

The sharp political divide in these views highlights a key challenge facing the Obama administration and other ACA proponents:

that Americans view the legislation not on its merits or benefits to the individual, but rather through strictly political lenses.

Insurance Intentions Among Political Groups: Get Insurance or Pay Fine?

	Republicans	Independents	Democrats
	%	%	%
MARCH 2014^			
Get insurance	38	52	75
Pay fine	58	39	18
FEBRUARY 2014			
Get insurance	35	54	70
Pay fine	58	39	22
JANUARY 2014			
Get insurance	39	50	70
Pay fine	52	41	23

^ Reflects data collected March 1-26

GALLUP

The degree to which uninsured Americans' actual purchases of health insurance will match their self-reported intentions is not clear. Gallup will report additional research in April that will shed light on the demographic makeup and health status of those who are newly insured since January, focusing particularly on whether Democrats have been more likely than Republicans to sign up.

Uninsured Americans' Intentions for Getting Health Insurance

Starting this year, Americans without health insurance either have to get health insurance or pay a fine. Given what you know, as of right now, would you say you are -- [ROTATED: more likely to get health insurance (or) more likely to pay the fine]?

■ % More likely to get insurance ■ % More likely to pay fine

	Oct '13	Nov '13	Dec '13	Jan '14	Feb '14	Mar '14
insurance	61	63	60	54	55	56
fine	30	29	31	38	37	36

Note: March numbers reflect data collected March 1-26, 2014

GALLUP

Republicans' lower representation in the ranks of those who say they are uninsured somewhat mitigates the effect of uninsured Republicans' being less likely to plan to sign up. Sixteen percent of the pool of the uninsured in the March 1–26 sample identify as Republican, compared with 25% of the overall 18 and older population. Democrats represent 27% of the uninsured, slightly below their representation in the population. Independents, at 51%, are the biggest component of the uninsured, compared with 41% of the entire adult sample.

The preponderance of Democrats and independents in the uninsured sample helps explain why more than half of the total pool of uninsured continue to say they will get insurance rather than pay a fine, similar to January and February readings.

These data were collected March 1–26, in the last official month for enrollment in a health insurance plan, although the deadline has been extended for those who say they began the process of enrollment before the end of the month. With more than half of the uninsured still intending to get insurance even as the deadline approaches, there could be a last-minute rush to sign up. It is also possible that these self-reported intentions are more general reactions to the idea of the law itself rather than accurate predictors of behavior, and include the possibility that some intend to get insurance at an indefinite future time.

Implications

The Affordable Care Act, as is evidenced by the popular sobriquet "Obamacare" tying it directly to a sitting president, remains highly political. Not only are Americans' attitudes about the law itself highly partisan, but so are uninsured Americans' self-reported intentions to sign up for the health insurance that the law requires.

If politics are prompting some uninsured Republicans to refuse to get insurance even in the face of having to pay a fine, this would likely be distressing for the law's proponents, who presumably would want Americans to consider the law on its merits rather than its political origins. The survey results suggest that one approach that might work for ACA advocates would be to shift the discussion away from politics, perhaps using high-profile apolitical public spokespeople and focusing on the law's merits rather than on the politics of those who oppose it.

Survey Methods

Results for this Gallup poll are based on telephone interviews conducted March 1–26, 2014, with a random sample of 1,322 adults who do not have health insurance, aged 18 and older, living in all 50 U.S. states and the District of Columbia.

For results based on the total sample of uninsured adults, the margin of sampling error is ±3 percentage points at the 95% confidence level.

April 01, 2014
POLITICS ARE BIGGEST FACTOR IN
VIEWS OF HEALTHCARE LAW
Party ID is most influential predictor of support

by Andrew Dugan and Frank Newport

WASHINGTON, D.C.—With Monday's deadline for enrolling in an insurance plan past, no other factor—including race, income, personal ideology, gender, or education—is as relevant to Americans' opinions on the Affordable Care Act as their party affiliation. This remains the foremost predictor of whether an individual will disapprove of the ACA.

The Odds of Disapproving of the Healthcare Law

Republicans are as much as **17 times** more likely to disapprove than Democrats

Independents are as much as **5 times** more likely to disapprove than Democrats

Whites are as much as **4 times** more likely to disapprove than nonwhites

Conservatives are as much as **6 times** more likely to disapprove than liberals

Moderates are as much as **2 times** more likely to disapprove than liberals

Based on a multivariate analysis of aggregated Gallup data, August 2013-March 2014   GALLUP'

These results stem from an aggregated set of surveys in which Gallup measured approval of the ACA. The data span August 2013 to March 2014 and include interviews with 13,797 U.S. adults. Overall support for the ACA remained low throughout this period, even as the various components of the law rolled out.

Of the majority of Americans who disapprove, nearly seven in 10 are self-identified Republicans or individuals who lean toward the GOP. Democrats and Democratic leaners make up less than a fifth of those who disapprove of the law. The remaining 14%, based on their survey responses, cannot be classified as Republicans or Democrats.

Party Affiliation of Those Who Approve and Disapprove of Healthcare Law

	% of those who approve	% of those who disapprove
Republican/Lean Republican	10	67
Independent/Don't know/Refused	9	14
Democratic/Lean Democratic	78	17

Aggregated Gallup data, August 2013-March 2014

GALLUP'

While party identification highly predicts support, other factors also play a role, including race and ideology, though not to the same degree. Characteristics such as income and employment status, which one might think are important when it comes to support for legislation aiming to help the uninsured get insurance, are not significant predictors.

The larger data set did not contain information about individuals' reported health insurance status or descriptions of their health, but a subset of the data consisting of 3,572 interviews conducted

in 2014 did. When health insurance status or ratings of one's own health were included, neither proved significant. Again, self-identified party affiliation was by far the most influential factor.

Party ID Trumps All When Assessing Future Impact of Law

Likewise, party affiliation is the biggest determinant of one's views toward the ACA when Americans are asked if the healthcare law will make their family's healthcare situation worse. Republicans are about 16 times more likely than Democrats to say the healthcare law will negatively affect their family's healthcare in the long run, with independents nearly five times more likely than Democrats to do this.

When projecting the long-term effect of the healthcare law on the nation, Republicans are about 22 times more likely than Democrats to say the law will make things worse. Independents are four times as likely as Democrats to say the law will make things worse.

Implications

The healthcare law is highly political. From its initial party-line passage, to its continued lightning-rod status for Republican politicians and candidates, to its informal label of "Obamacare" forever linking the law to the Democratic president, the ACA has remained a centerpiece of the nation's political debate, even as it becomes more firmly established in law. But the extraordinary importance of party identification in predicting a person's support for the legislation raises the question of whether the ACA can ever escape its polarizing branding and be accepted by policymakers—present and future—as settled law, rather than an ongoing political battle.

The healthcare law will undoubtedly be debated over the course of this year's midterm elections that could leave the Republican Party in control of both houses of Congress. But unless the GOP is able to obtain a difficult two-thirds majority in the House and the Senate, efforts to repeal or drastically alter the law will likely be unsuccessful at least through the 2016 presidential election, ensuring it remains a political football for the next few years.

Survey Methods

Results for this Gallup poll are based on telephone interviews conducted Aug. 17, 2013–March 2, 2014, on the Gallup Daily tracking survey, with a random sample of 13,797 adults, aged 18 and older, living in all 50 U.S. states and the District of Columbia.

For results based on the total sample of national adults, the margin of sampling error is ±1 percentage point at the 95% confidence level.

April 02, 2014
AMERICANS STILL FAVOR ENERGY
CONSERVATION OVER PRODUCTION
Americans look to conservation and
renewable energy for solutions

by Brendan Moore and Stafford Nichols

WASHINGTON, D.C.—Americans still prefer energy conservation over production. After dwindling in recent years, Americans' long-standing preference for emphasizing conservation over production in U.S. energy policy has rebounded, now matching levels seen in prior years. Currently 57% of Americans say the U.S. should emphasize conservation in its approach to solve the nation's energy problems, up from 51% in 2013 and 48% in 2011. About one-third in the U.S. now favor greater emphasis on energy production as the solution.

Americans' Preferences for U.S. Energy Policy

Which of the following approaches to solving the nation's energy problems do you think the U.S. should follow right now -- [ROTATED: emphasize production of more oil, gas, and coal supplies (or) emphasize more conservation by consumers of existing energy supplies]?

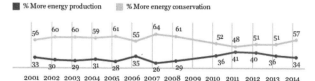

Notes: Trend from 2001-2014 Gallup Environmental polls (Gallup did not ask question in 2009)

GALLUP

This latest update is from Gallup's March 6–9, 2014, Social Series Environment poll. Since Gallup began asking the question in 2001, Americans have consistently named energy conservation over production. The highest percentage favoring conservation (64%) was recorded in 2007, while the lowest was in 2011, at 48%.

Alternative Energy Favored Over Traditional

A separate question in the survey, asked of a different subset of respondents, finds 64% of Americans prefer an emphasis on the development of alternative energy production, such as wind and solar power, to an emphasis on production of traditional fossil fuels. That is up from 59% in 2013. On this point, nearly one-third of Americans would rather the country pursue increased production of oil, gas, and coal supplies to these alternative energy options— roughly the same level of support seen in recent years.

Young Americans are highly likely to emphasize the development of alternative energy, and the older age groups each successively favor it less. In fact, slightly less than half of Americans aged 55 and older favor alternative energy, roughly equal to the support in that age group for traditional fossil fuels (44%).

Americans' Preference for Energy Development, by Age

Which of the following approaches to solving the nation's energy problems do you think the U.S. should follow right now -- [ROTATED: emphasize production of more oil, gas, and coal supplies (or) emphasize the development of alternative energy such as wind and solar power]?

	Alternative energy	Oil, gas, coal
All Americans	64%	32%
18-34 years	80%	20%
35-54 years	65%	29%
55+ years	49%	44%

March 6-9, 2014

GALLUP

Americans Favor Green Policies

Americans' collective interest in alternative energy sources is reinforced by the responses to a question asking Americans if they favor or oppose nine specific proposals dealing with energy and the environment. Two-thirds of Americans favor increased government spending to develop solar and wind power, and spending more to develop alternative fuels for cars has the same level of support.

Additionally, more than 60% of Americans favor a variety of proposals that would regulate or limit fossil fuel emissions, including setting higher pollution standards for business and industry. These results are consistent with Gallup's earlier findings that Americans prioritize the environment over economic growth.

At the same time, the majority of Americans favor the idea of opening up land owned by the federal government for oil exploration. This break from a more conservationist view is consistent with Americans' support for other proposals to increase oil and gas production, including support of offshore drilling.

Expanding the use of nuclear energy is the only proposed policy that the majority of Americans oppose, albeit by a slim margin. Attitudes toward this question have remained more or less unchanged since 2001, when 51% of Americans opposed it, except for a brief increase in favorability in 2006.

Environmental and Energy Proposals

I am going to read some specific proposals. For each one, please say whether you generally favor or oppose it. How about...[RANDOM ORDER]?

	% Favor	% Oppose
Spending more government money on developing solar and wind power	67	32
Spending government money to develop alternate sources of fuel for automobiles	66	33
Setting higher emissions and pollution standards for business and industry	65	35
More strongly enforcing federal environmental regulations	64	34
Imposing mandatory controls on carbon dioxide emissions/other greenhouse gases	63	35
Setting higher auto emissions standards for automobiles	62	35
Opening up land owned by the federal government for oil exploration	58	41
Setting stricter standards on the use of techniques to extract natural gas from the earth, including "fracking"	58	37
Expanding the use of nuclear energy	47	51

March 6-9, 2014

GALLUP

Implications

Americans continue to see alternative energy and energy conservation as better approaches to addressing the nation's energy problems than producing greater supplies of traditional energy like oil, coal, and gas.

In recent months, President Barack Obama has announced several new initiatives that tighten environmental regulations, such as increasing the fuel economy standards for heavy-duty vehicles and a strategy to cut methane emissions. The Obama administration's 2015 budget proposes significant funding for environmental research, including a new $1 billion climate resilience fund meant to help communities across the country adapt to the impact of climate change.

However, these proposed changes will come under considerable scrutiny from congressional Republicans. Gallup has consistently found that Democrats are typically more in favor of environmental regulations, while Republicans often oppose them. While Obama has promised to use unilateral executive orders to initiate new policies, the 2015 federal budget cannot pass without bipartisan support.

Results are based on telephone interviews conducted March 6–9, 2014, with a random sample of 1,048 adults, aged 18+, living in all 50 U.S. states and the District of Columbia. For results based on this sample of national adults, the margin of sampling error is ±4 percentage points at the 95% confidence level.

For results based on the sample of 535 national adults in Form A and 513 national adults in Form B, the margins of sampling error are ±6 percentage points.

April 04, 2014
BOULDER, COLO., RESIDENTS STILL LEAST LIKELY TO BE OBESE
Nearly two in five are obese in Huntington-Ashland, the highest rate in the nation

by Rebecca Riffkin

WASHINGTON, D.C.—Boulder, Colo., continues to have the lowest obesity rate in the nation, at 12.4%. Boulder has had the lowest obesity rate nearly every year since Gallup and Healthways began measuring in 2008, with the exception of 2009. Residents of Huntington-Ashland, W.Va.-Ky.-Ohio, were the most likely to be obese in 2012–2013, at 39.5%.

Least Obese U.S. Communities

Among the 189 U.S. Metropolitan Statistical Areas surveyed

Community	% Obese
Boulder, CO	12.4
Naples-Marco Island, FL	16.5
Fort Collins-Loveland, CO	18.2
Charlottesville, VA	18.7
Bellingham, WA	18.7
San Diego-Carlsbad-San Marcos, CA	19.3
Denver-Aurora, CO	19.3
San Jose-Sunnyvale-Santa Clara, CA	19.5
Bridgeport-Stamford-Norwalk, CT	19.6
Barnstable Town, MA	19.6

January 2012-December 2013
Gallup-Healthways Well-Being Index

GALLUP'

Most Obese U.S. Communities

Among the 189 U.S. Metropolitan Statistical Areas surveyed

Community	% Obese
Huntington-Ashland, WV-KY-OH	39.5
McAllen-Edinburg-Mission, TX	38.3
Hagerstown-Martinsburg, MD-WV	36.7
Yakima, WA	35.7
Little Rock-N Little Rock-Conway, AR	35.1
Charleston, WV	34.6
Toledo, OH	34.2
Clarksville, TN-KY	33.8
Jackson, MS	33.8
Green Bay, WI	33.0
Rockford, IL	33.0

January 2012-December 2013
Gallup-Healthways Well-Being Index

GALLUP'

Adult obesity rates are above 15% in all but one of the 189 metro areas that Gallup and Healthways surveyed in 2012 and 2013. The U.S. Department of Health and Human Services' Healthy People 2010 program had a goal of reducing obesity to 15% in each state. No state and only one U.S. metro area has achieved this goal.

Huntington-Ashland has been among the 10 most obese communities every year since 2008. The obesity rate for the most obese metro area in 2008—Binghamton, N.Y., at 34.6%—is lower than the obesity rates found in five most obese cities from 2012 to 2013.

These data reflect the state level results for 2013, which found that Mississippi and West Virginia were the most obese states and Montana and Colorado were the least. Three areas in Colorado—Boulder, Fort Collins-Loveland, and Denver-Aurora—were among the communities with the 10 lowest obesity rates.

Nationwide, the U.S. obesity rate increased to 27.1% in 2013, the highest Gallup and Healthways have recorded since tracking began in 2008. Obesity rates have increased in many communities since 2011, including a 3.5-percentage-point uptick in Huntington-Ashland.

Gallup and Healthways track U.S. obesity levels as part of the Gallup-Healthways Well-Being Index, using Americans' self-reported height and weight to calculate Body Mass Index (BMI) scores. BMI scores of 30 or higher are considered obese.

Gallup interviewed at least 300 adults aged 18 and older in each of 189 MSAs. Each MSA sample is weighted to match the demographic characteristics of that area. Gallup categorizes U.S. metro areas according to the U.S. Office of Management and Budget's definitions for Metropolitan Statistical Areas (MSAs).

Memphis Is Most Obese Large Community

Among large communities with populations above 1 million, Memphis, Tenn.-Miss.-Ark., had the highest obesity rate, at 31.9%, while Denver-Aurora and San Diego-Carlsbad-San Marcos, Calif., tied for the lowest at 19.3%.

The average obesity rate for all large communities was 25.7%, almost two points below the national average. None of the large communities designated as having the highest obesity rates ranked among the communities of all sizes with the 10 highest obesity rates. These findings suggest that residents in smaller communities are more likely to be obese than those living in larger communities.

Least Obese Major U.S. Communities

Community	% Obese
Denver-Aurora, CO	19.3
San Diego-Carlsbad-San Marcos, CA	19.3
San Jose-Sunnyvale-Santa Clara, CA	19.5
San Francisco-Oakland-Fremont, CA	19.7
Boston-Cambridge-Quincy, MA-NH	20.5
Miami-Fort Lauderdale-Pompano Beach, FL	21.8
Washington-Arlington-Alexandria, DC-VA-MD-WV	22.2
Minneapolis-St. Paul-Bloomington, MN-WI	22.7
Los Angeles-Long Beach-Santa Ana, CA	22.7
Seattle-Tacoma-Bellevue, WA	22.8

January 2012-December 2013
Gallup-Healthways Wellbeing Index

GALLUP'

Most Obese Major U.S. Communities

Community	% Obese
Memphis, TN-MS-AR	31.9
San Antonio, TX	31.1
Richmond, VA	28.8
New Orleans-Metairie-Kenner, LA	28.7
Columbus, OH	28.7
Rochester, NY	28.6
Louisville-Jefferson County, KY-IN	28.4
Oklahoma City, OK	28.4
Detroit-Warren-Livonia, MI	28.1
Cleveland-Elyria-Mentor, OH	28.0

January 2012-December 2013
Gallup-Healthways Wellbeing Index

GALLUP'

Implications

Not only is Colorado the state with the second-lowest obesity rate in the nation, but three of its metro areas—Boulder, Fort Collins-Loveland, and Denver-Aurora—are listed among the 10 communities with the lowest obesity rates. This may be because Colorado is known for its outdoor spaces and activities, which attracts active residents and encourages residents to live healthy lifestyles. Colorado has ranked among the top 10 states for frequent exercise every year since Gallup began tracking.

In two U.S. communities, Huntington-Ashland and McAllen-Edinburg-Mission, Texas, nearly two in five residents are obese. Nationally, obesity rates may be rising because of healthy eating habits worsening in 2013. Obesity is linked to lower worker productivity, which could negatively affect local and national economies.

"Rising obesity rates have significant health consequences for both individuals and communities of all sizes. Numerous social, environmental, economic, and individual factors may all contribute to physical inactivity and consumption of less healthy foods, two lifestyle behaviors linked to obesity," says Janna Lacatell, Healthways Lifestyle Solutions Director. "In order to combat the trend and encourage individuals to make healthier choices, community-based policy and environmental approaches can, and should, be used."

Programs focused on making healthy eating habits and active lifestyles the easy choice for residents could do a lot to help lower obesity rates in communities across the country. With the national obesity rate at an all-time high, a focus on lowering obesity rates at the local level could be an effective way to reduce the obesity rate and its negative effects on the economy and individuals.

Survey Methods

Results are based on telephone interviews conducted as part of the Gallup-Healthways Well-Being Index survey Jan. 2–Dec. 29, 2012, and Jan. 2–Dec. 30, 2013, with a random sample of 531,630 adults, aged 18 and older, living in metropolitan areas in the 50 U.S. states and the District of Columbia, selected using random-digit-dial sampling. Two years of data were aggregated together to enable the same number of reportable cities as in prior years, when the overall annual data collection exceeded 350,000 interviews per year compared to 178,072 interviews conducted in 2013. At least 300 cases are required per metro area for reporting.

The metro areas referenced in this article are based on the Metropolitan Statistical Areas (MSAs) as defined by the U.S. Office of Management and Budget. In many cases, more than one city is included in the same MSA. The San Jose, Calif., metropolitan statistical area, for example, also includes the smaller nearby cities of Sunnyvale and Santa Clara in addition to San Jose itself. Each respondent is attributed to his or her MSA based on the self-report of his or her ZIP code, and all metro areas had at least 300 completed surveys in the 2012–2013 data collection period.

Maximum expected error ranges for the Well-Being Index and the sub-index scores vary according to MSA size, ranging from less than 1 point for the largest cities represented to ±1.5 points for the smallest cities.

April 04, 2014
AMERICANS SHOW LOW LEVELS OF CONCERN ON GLOBAL WARMING
Worry about other environmental problems increasing

by Frank Newport

This article is the sixth in a series that will analyze Gallup's latest March update on Americans' views on climate change and examine how these views have changed over time. The series will explore public opinion on the severity and importance of climate change, its causes and effects, the extent of Americans' understanding of the issue, and much more.

PRINCETON, NJ—The United Nations Intergovernmental Panel on Climate Change issued a new report this week warning of the existing and potentially severe adverse future impact of climate change, yet most Americans continue to express low levels of concern about

the phenomenon. A little more than a third say they worry "a great deal" about climate change or about global warming, putting these concerns at the bottom of a list of eight environmental issues.

Percentage of Americans Worrying "a Great Deal" About Environmental Problems

I'm going to read you a list of environmental problems. As I read each one, please tell me if you personally worry about this problem a great deal, a fair amount, only a little, or not at all. First, how much do you personally worry about -- ?

	Mar 7-10, 2013	Mar 6-9, 2014	Change, 2013-2014 (pct. pts.)
Pollution of drinking water	53%	60%	+7
Contamination of soil and water by toxic waste	46%	53%	+7
Pollution of rivers, lakes, and reservoirs	46%	53%	+7
Air pollution	40%	46%	+6
Extinction of plant and animal species	35%	41%	+6
The loss of tropical rain forests	37%	41%	+4
Climate change	33%	35%	+2
Global warming	33%	34%	+1

GALLUP

Americans' concerns about global warming and climate change have held steady over the past year, while concerns about other environmental threats tested by Gallup have increased. The percentage expressing a great deal of worry about pollution of drinking water, as well as contamination of soil and water by toxic waste, increased by seven percentage points. Worry about climate change and global warming, on the other hand, went up by no more than two points versus last year.

Americans' generally low level of concern about global warming compared with other environmental issues is not new; warming has generally ranked last among Americans' environmental worries each time Gallup has measured them with this question over the years. Concern about pollution of drinking water has generally been at the top of the list.

Gallup has tracked worry about global warming using this question format since 1989. The percentage of Americans expressing a great deal of worry has varied over that period, partly reflecting major global warming news events along the way. The highest levels of worry occurred in April 2000 (40%) and March 2007 (41%). On the other hand, worry reached its lowest points in October 1997 (24%), March 2004 (26%), and March 2011 (25%). The current 34% worry is essentially the same as it was in 1989.

Percentage of Americans Worrying "a Great Deal" About Global Warming

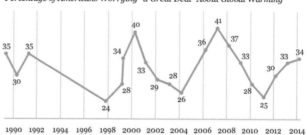

Wording prior to 2009: the "greenhouse effect" or global warming

GALLUP

Politics Remain Major Predictor of Worry About Global Warming

Politics remain a powerful predictor of Americans' worries about global warming, with more than half of Democrats saying they worry about it a great deal, compared with 29% of independents and

16% of Republicans. This political differentiation of global warming attitudes is not isolated; other research shows that in today's political environment, Republicans are much more likely to say that concerns about global warming are exaggerated and that warming's effects will not affect them personally in their lifetimes, and are less likely to say scientists believe global warming is occurring.

Young Americans aged 18 to 29 are more worried about global warming than older adults, particularly those 50 and older. If these young people hold on to these attitudes as they age, and if future generations of Americans hold the same levels of higher concern, then the nation's overall levels of worry about warming will rise.

Worry about global warming is not related to education in any systematic way; those with postgraduate education are no more worried than those with a high school education or less. This conforms with prior research showing that education bears little relation to Americans' believing that human activities are the cause of global warming.

How Much Do You Personally Worry About Global Warming?

	A great deal	Fair amount	Only a little/ Not at all
	%	%	%
National adults	34	22	43
18 to 29	38	32	30
30 to 49	41	19	40
50 to 64	32	18	50
65+	24	23	52
Postgraduate	36	19	45
College graduate	27	28	45
Some college	31	26	42
High school or less	38	19	43
Republicans	16	22	63
Independents	29	19	51
Democrats	56	27	18

March 6-9, 2014

GALLUP'

Implications

A major challenge facing scientists and organizations that view global warming as a major threat to humanity is that average citizens express so little concern about the issue. Many climate change activists have attempted to raise awareness in recent years, as evidenced by the recent U.N. report. Former Vice President Al Gore has been active in raising the alarm about the potentially disastrous impact of global warming, including in a documentary and a book. But the data at the national level show that none of this has changed Americans' worry about the issue in any lasting way—perhaps reflecting the strong counter-position taken by many conservative thought leaders, and the "Climategate" controversies.

A lack of formal education in general is clearly not a factor in Americans' failure to be more concerned about global warming; Americans who have not attended college are no less concerned than those with a college degree or postgraduate education.

Politics are important in understanding American attitudes about global warming. The issue has become highly politicized in recent years, and that polarization shows up across a number of indicators. At the core, Democrats appear to have widely accepted the warnings about global warming, and well over half today say they worry about it a great deal. On the other hand, less than 20% of Republicans worry a great deal, while almost two-thirds say they worry only a little or not at all. So long as global warming remains a politically charged issue, it will likely lag behind other environmental issues as a public concern.

Finally, pollution of drinking water is Americans' greatest environmental worry, and this shows that environmental concerns are—understandably—quite personal, and that worries are highest when issues have a direct effect on daily lives. Some have argued that the extreme cold spells this past winter and the drought in the West are a result of climate change, but Gallup research shows that the majority of Americans think these are normal weather variations.

The United Nations report mentions calamitous outcomes from continuing global warming that would affect the world's food supply, economies, and ways of life. If any of these possibilities materializes, they may have a distinct impact on Americans' concerns.

Survey Methods

Results for this Gallup poll are based on telephone interviews conducted March 6–9, 2014, with a random sample of 1,048 adults, aged 18 and older, living in all 50 U.S. states and the District of Columbia.

For results based on the total sample of national adults, the margin of sampling error is ±4 percentage points at the 95% confidence level.

April 04, 2014
ILLINOIS RESIDENTS LEAST TRUSTING OF THEIR STATE GOVERNMENT
North Dakota, Wyoming, and Utah rank at the top

by Jeffrey M. Jones

PRINCETON, NJ—Illinois residents trust their state government to handle their state's problems far less than residents in any other state. Twenty-eight percent of Illinois residents trust their state government "a great deal" or "a fair amount." In contrast, at least 75% of North Dakota, Wyoming, and Utah residents trust their state governments.

States With Highest Trust in State Gov't

	% Great deal/ Fair amount of trust
North Dakota	77
Wyoming	76
Utah	75
South Dakota	74
Nebraska	73
Texas	72
Alaska	71

Gallup 50-state poll, June-December 2013

GALLUP'

States With Lowest Trust in State Gov't

	% Great deal/ Fair amount of trust
Illinois	28
Rhode Island	40
Maine	40
Pennsylvania	46
Louisiana	48
California	49
Maryland	49

Gallup 50-state poll, June-December 2013

GALLUP'

The results are based on a special 50-state Gallup poll conducted June–December 2013, including interviews with at least 600 residents in every state. This poll allows Gallup for the first time to report trust in state government at the state level. Gallup has previously measured Americans' trust in their state governments on a national basis. The most recent national estimate, from September 2013, finds 62% of all Americans having a great deal or fair amount of trust in their state government.

The accompanying map identifies states as having above-average, average, or below-average trust, compared with the 50-state average of 58%.

Trust is generally higher in states in the upper Midwest and Plains states, and in the northern Mountain region states.

Trust in State Government, by State

- Above average trust
- Average trust
- Below average trust
- No data

Gallup 50-state poll, June-December 2013

GALLUP

In general, trust is lower in more populous states than in less populous states. The 10 most populous states and 10 least populous states differ by 11 percentage points in state government trust, with the middle population states in between. Larger states have larger economies and more citizens needing services, and often more diverse populations, so they may be more challenging to govern than smaller states.

Trust in State Government by Population Size, 2013

	Average % trust
Ten most populous states	52.1
Second 10 most populous states	58.4
Third 10 most populous states	57.0
Fourth 10 most populous states	60.8
Ten least populous states	63.1

Trust data from Gallup 50-state poll, June-December 2013
Population size based on 2013 census estimates.

GALLUP

The population size-trust relationship may help explain the finding that trust in state government tends to be higher in Republican-leaning states than Democratic-leaning ones, since larger states tend to be Democratic and smaller states Republican. Using Gallup's 2013 data on state party affiliation, average trust in state government is 67% in solidly Republican or Republican-leaning states, 58% in competitive states, and 53% in solidly Democratic or Democratic-leaning states.

All of the 10 most populous states are either Democratic or competitive, according to Gallup's party affiliation estimates. The most populous solid or leaning Republican state is Tennessee, which ranks 17th in population size. North Dakota, Wyoming, South Dakota, and Alaska rank among the top states in trust and the bottom states in population, and are all Republican-oriented states. Additionally, there are many other cultural, economic, and demographic factors that correlate with population size and politics that could help explain the trust-partisanship relationship.

Although Illinois' exceptionally low trust level does bring down the averages for both Democratic states and most populous states, those groups of states would still rank lower than other states if Illinois were excluded.

Corruption a Factor in Illinois Residents' Lack of Trust

Illinois' position at the bottom of the list in residents' trust in state government is not surprising, given that its last two governors, Rod Blagojevich and George Ryan, were sentenced to jail for crimes committed while in office. Two prior Illinois governors from the 1960s and 1970s also went to jail.

Additionally, the Illinois economy remains shaky and the state government continues to struggle to balance the budget, even after a significant income tax increase a few years ago. That tax hike is set to expire, but the governor is pushing to make it permanent. Last year, the state also passed controversial pension reforms for state workers that are being challenged in court.

In addition to Illinois, in six other states—Rhode Island, Maine, Pennsylvania, Louisiana, California, and Maryland—less than a majority of residents express trust in their state governments. Many of these less-trusting states have had poor economies in recent years. Louisiana, like Illinois, has a history of corruption among its elected leaders.

Healthy economies are generally associated with higher levels of trust in state government. Five of the six states with the lowest unemployment rates in the nation have trust scores of 73% or greater. Vermont is the exception. Despite its low unemployment rate, just 57% of Vermonters trust their state government.

Implications

Trust in government is a key commodity for a democratic government to function well. Voters must believe that those they elect to public office will act in the best interests of the citizens, and elected leaders who do not engender their constituents' trust will likely not serve for long. Trust in state government varies widely at the state level, with population, economic, political, and historical factors all seemingly related to how much citizens trust the leaders responsible for governing their state.

Survey Methods

Results for this Gallup poll are based on telephone interviews conducted June 27–Dec. 4, 2013, with a random sample of approximately 600 adults per state, aged 18 and older, living in all 50 U.S. states.

For results based on the total sample of adults per state, the margin of sampling error is ±5 percentage points at the 95% confidence level.

April 07, 2014
IN U.S., UNINSURED RATE LOWEST SINCE 2008
Uninsured rate declines most among blacks
and lower-income Americans

by Jenna Levy

WASHINGTON, D.C.—In the U.S., the uninsured rate dipped to 15.6% in the first quarter of 2014, a 1.5-percentage-point decline from the fourth quarter of 2013. The uninsured rate is now at the lowest level recorded since late 2008.

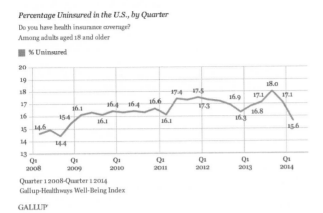

Percentage Uninsured in the U.S., by Quarter

Do you have health insurance coverage?
Among adults aged 18 and older

■ % Uninsured

Quarter 1 2008-Quarter 1 2014
Gallup-Healthways Well-Being Index

GALLUP

The uninsured rate has been falling since the fourth quarter of 2013, after hitting an all-time high of 18.0% in the third quarter—a sign that the Affordable Care Act, commonly referred to as "Obamacare," appears to be accomplishing its goal of increasing the percentage of Americans with health insurance coverage. Even within this year's first quarter, the uninsured rate fell consistently, from 16.2% in January to 15.6% in February to 15.0% in March. And within March, the rate dropped more than a point, from 15.5% in the first half of the month to 14.5% in the second half—indicating that enrollment through the healthcare exchanges increased as the March 31 deadline approached.

The results from the first quarter are based on more than 43,500 interviews with U.S. adults from Jan. 2 to March 31, 2014, as part of the Gallup-Healthways Well-Being Index.

Fewer Americans Across Age Groups Uninsured in 2014

The Obama administration has made young adults' enrollment in a health insurance plan a top priority, as healthcare experts say 40% of new enrollees must be young and healthy for the Affordable Care Act to be successful. However, Gallup's quarterly trends indicate the uninsured rate dropped by about the same amount among adults aged 26 to 64 as it did among those aged 18 to 25—two points. The uninsured rate among 18- to 25-year-olds fell to 21.7% in the first quarter; the rate fell to 26.4% among those aged 26 to 34, and to 16.1% among those aged 35 to 64.

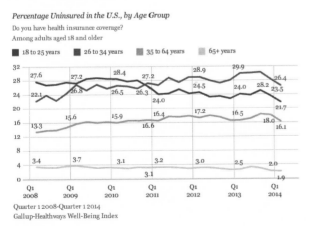

Percentage Uninsured in the U.S., by Age Group

Do you have health insurance coverage?
Among adults aged 18 and older

■ 18 to 25 years   ■ 26 to 34 years   ■ 35 to 64 years   ■ 65+ years

Quarter 1 2008-Quarter 1 2014
Gallup-Healthways Well-Being Index

GALLUP

While the Department of Health and Human Services' April Enrollment Report has not yet been released, Gallup's findings correspond with the government's last report, showing only 25% of new enrollees as of Feb. 28 were in the 18-to-34 age range.

Uninsured Rate Falls Most Among Lower-Income Americans and Blacks

The uninsured rate for every major demographic group declined in the first quarter of 2014. The uninsured rate for lower-income Americans dropped 3.2 points to 27.5%—the largest decline within any key subgroup—while the uninsured rate for blacks fell 3.3 points to 17.6%. Hispanics remain the subgroup most likely to lack health insurance, with an uninsured rate of 37.0%, though their rate dropped 1.7 points in the first quarter.

Percentage Uninsured in the U.S., by Subgroup

Do you have health insurance coverage?
Among adults aged 18 and older

	Quarter 4 2013 %	Quarter 1 2014 %	Net change (pct. pts.)
National adults	17.1	15.6	-1.5
18 to 25 years	23.5	21.7	-1.8
26 to 34 years	28.2	26.4	-1.8
35 to 64 years	18.0	16.1	-1.9
65+ years	2.0	1.9	-0.1
White	11.9	10.7	-1.2
Black	20.9	17.6	-3.3
Hispanic	38.7	37.0	-1.7
Less than $36,000 annual household income	30.7	27.5	-3.2
$36,000 to $89,999 annual household income	11.7	10.7	-1.0
$90,000+ annual household income	5.8	4.7	-1.1

Gallup-Healthways Well-Being Index

GALLUP

Implications

The uninsured rate fell 1.5 percentage points to 15.6% over the last quarter, as the open enrollment period to purchase healthcare coverage through the state and federal marketplaces closed on March 31. This quarterly figure represents the average percentage of adults without health insurance since provisions requiring Americans to have insurance established by the Affordable Care Act went into effect on Jan. 1 of this year. The current figure as of today is likely lower given that uninsured rates declined throughout the quarter, including in late March.

President Barack Obama announced on April 1 that 7.1 million Americans have signed up for health insurance plans through federal and state-run marketplaces. This figure includes a late surge in consumers signing up for coverage at the end of March, as HHS reported that as of Feb. 28, only 4.2 million Americans had signed up for plans. In fact, the healthcare exchanges experienced such an influx of insurance-seeking consumers over the last week of the enrollment period that the federal exchange site HealthCare.gov had to undergo maintenance to handle the traffic.

The Obama administration also announced that Americans unable to sign up by March 31 could request an extension through April 15, which could further drive down the uninsured rate in the second quarter of 2014. Additionally, other provisions of the healthcare law have not yet gone into effect, such as the requirement for employers to provide health insurance to their employees by 2015. These provisions also may affect the uninsured rate over time.

Moreover, Medicaid has likely added millions to its enrollment due to its expansion, although—as with the exchanges themselves—it remains unclear how many were previously insured and moved to Medicaid as a less expensive option. Regardless, the decline in the percentage of uninsured over the course of the first quarter almost certainly includes the effects of expanded Medicaid eligibility policies. It is also likely, in turn, that not all new enrollees will ultimately pay their insurance premiums, which would result in a subsequent change in status from insured to uninsured at some point later in 2014.

Gallup will continue to track the U.S. uninsured rate in the months ahead.

EDITOR'S NOTE: The estimates of the uninsured rates in the first half and the second half of March in the text have been changed from an earlier publication.

Survey Methods

Results are based on telephone interviews conducted as part of the Gallup-Healthways Well-Being Index survey Jan. 2–March 31, 2014, with a random sample of 43,562 adults, aged 18 and older, living in all 50 U.S. states and the District of Columbia.

For results based on the total sample of national adults, the margin of sampling error is ±1 percentage point at the 95% confidence level.

April 07, 2014
AMERICANS SAY COLLEGE DEGREE LEADS TO A BETTER LIFE
Say higher education must evolve to meet students' needs

by Valerie J. Calderon and Susan Sorenson

WASHINGTON, D.C.—Americans believe in the importance of postsecondary education, with more than nine in 10 (94%) saying a postsecondary degree or credential is at least somewhat important and 70% saying it is very important, similar to last year's findings. However, most also say higher-education institutions must evolve to better serve the needs of today's students.

Importance of Postsecondary Degree

How important is having a certificate or degree beyond high school?

	% U.S. adults	% With high school diploma or less	% With some college	% With college degree or certificate
Very important	70	66	60	77
Somewhat important	24	26	33	20
Not very important	4	5	3	3
Not at all important	1	1	3	<0.5

Source: 2013 Gallup-Lumina Foundation Poll on Higher Education

GALLUP

These results are from a Nov. 25–Dec. 15, 2013, study by Gallup and the Lumina Foundation with a random sample of U.S.

adults. While Americans in every age group are equally likely to see the importance of higher education, more than three-quarters (77%) of those who have completed postsecondary education themselves say it is very important to attain a certificate or degree, compared with 60% who have some college experience and 66% who have a high school diploma or less education.

Postsecondary Certificate or Degree Essential for Good Job and Good Life

Americans value higher education at least partly because of the perception that it opens the door to wider career opportunities and an improved standard of living. Nearly three in four Americans (73%) agree or strongly agree that having a certificate, certification, or degree beyond high school is essential for getting a good job. Furthermore, most U.S. adults (74%) see having a postsecondary degree or credential as a pathway to a better quality of life.

Postsecondary Degree Essential for a Good Job and a Better Life

On a five-point scale, where 5 means strongly agree and 1 means strongly disagree, please indicate your level of agreement with each of the following statements about higher education and the workforce.

	% 1 Strongly disagree	% 2	% 3	% 4	% 5 Strongly agree
Certificate, certification, or degree beyond high school is essential for getting a good job	5	6	16	29	44
Postsecondary degree or credential leads to a better quality of life	3	6	17	34	40

Source: 2013 Gallup-Lumina Foundation Poll on Higher Education

GALLUP

American Public Says Higher Education Institutions Need to Change

While the majority of Americans believe postsecondary degree attainment is vital to living a good life in this country, most—89%—say higher education institutions need to change to better serve the needs of today's students. At this point, about half (49%) of U.S. adults see evidence that such change is actually happening.

Higher Education and Signs of Change

	% Yes	% No
Do higher education institutions need to change to better serve the needs of today's students?	89	10
Do you see evidence that higher education institutions are changing to better meet the needs of today's students?	49	48

Source: 2013 Gallup-Lumina Foundation Poll on Higher Education

GALLUP

Americans aged 18 to 34—those closest to traditional college age—are the most likely to say they see signs of change (58%), compared with 50% of those aged 35 to 49 and 42% of those 50 or older.

Signs of Change in Higher Education, by Age

Do you see evidence that higher education institutions are changing to better meet the needs of today's students?

	Total, U.S. adults	Aged 18 to 34	Aged 35 to 49	Aged 50 to 64	Aged 65+
Yes	49%	58%	50%	42%	42%

Source: 2013 Gallup-Lumina Foundation Poll on Higher Education

GALLUP

Implications

Today's postsecondary graduates often leave school deeply in debt and with relatively limited prospects for high-paying work. Still, most U.S. adults believe that a postsecondary degree or certificate is the key to a better job and a better quality of life, with the caveat that reforms are needed to make the current system more conducive to students' needs.

To hold their value in Americans' eyes, colleges and universities may consider focusing on preparing students for good careers that will improve their lives without overburdening them with debt. This may mean redesigning higher education to make it more affordable and accessible. Stronger collaboration between businesses and academic institutions may help students gain the real-world skills they need to get hired.

Reforms like these may be already under way at some institutions, as about half of Americans report seeing some evidence of change. However, with nearly nine out of 10 U.S. adults saying the higher-education system needs to evolve, more work could be done to align these institutions to the demands of the 21st-century workforce.

Survey Methods

Results from the study are based on telephone interviews conducted as part of the Gallup-Lumina Foundation Poll on Higher Education Nov. 25–Dec. 15, 2013, with a random sample of 1,012 adults, aged 18 and older living in all 50 U.S. states and the District of Columbia.

For results based on the total sample size of 1,012 adults, one can say with 95% confidence that the margin of error attributable to sampling and other random effects is ±4 percentage points. For subgroups within this population (e.g., education level, gender, and income), the margin of error would be greater.

April 08, 2014

AMERICANS' TRUST IN ONLINE HIGHER ED RISING

Traditional universities and community
colleges have edge on quality

by *Valerie J. Calderon and Susan Sorenson*

WASHINGTON, D.C.—Americans' trust in the quality of online colleges and universities is steadily rising. More U.S. adults, 37%, now agree or strongly agree that these institutions offer high-quality education than did so in 2011 (30%) when Gallup first asked this question. Roughly one in four (27%) disagree or strongly disagree.

Quality of Education Offered by Online Colleges and Universities

On a five-point scale, where 5 means strongly agree and 1 means strongly disagree, please indicate your level of agreement with the following statement: Online colleges and universities offer high-quality education.

	% Agree/ Strongly agree	% Neutral	% Disagree/ Strongly disagree
2013	37	34	27
2012	33	39	25
2011	30	35	31

Source: Gallup-Lumina Foundation Poll on Higher Education

GALLUP

These findings are from a Nov. 25–Dec. 15, 2013, study by Gallup and Lumina Foundation with a random sample of more than 1,000 U.S. adults. The research shows that while online higher education institutions have made progress on this measure, they still operate at a deficit compared with other traditional educational institutions. Far more Americans agree or strongly agree that community colleges (58%) and traditional colleges and universities (77%) offer high-quality education compared with online institutions.

Quality of Education Offered by Traditional Colleges and Universities and Community Colleges

On a five-point scale, where 5 means strongly agree and 1 means strongly disagree, please indicate your level of agreement with the following statements:

	% Agree/ Strongly agree	% Neutral	% Disagree/ Strongly disagree
2013			
Traditional colleges and universities offer high-quality education.	77	19	5
Community colleges offer high-quality education.	58	30	13
2012			
Traditional colleges and universities offer high-quality education.	76	20	4
Community colleges offer high-quality education.	54	36	10
2011			
Traditional colleges and universities offer high-quality education.	71	23	6
Community colleges offer high-quality education.	58	31	11

Source: Gallup-Lumina Foundation Poll on Higher Education

GALLUP

Business Leaders Have Varying Perspectives on Hiring Online Graduates

Americans seem to have relatively more confidence in the graduates of online colleges and universities than in the quality of the institutions themselves. More than half of Americans (59%) say that, all else being equal, employers are at least somewhat likely to hire a candidate who has a degree from an online higher education provider over a candidate with the same degree from a traditional institution, though just 15% say they are very likely to select such a candidate.

Likelihood to Hire Candidate With Online Degree vs. Degree From Traditional Institution

All else being equal, how likely are [are employers/is YOUR business] to hire a candidate who has a degree from an online higher education provider OVER a candidate with the same degree from a traditional higher education institution -- very likely, somewhat likely, not very likely, or not at all likely?

	U.S. adult population: employers*	U.S. business leaders: employers**	U.S. business leaders: YOUR business**
Very likely	15%	13%	14%
Somewhat likely	44%	41%	33%
Not very likely	32%	34%	33%
Not at all likely	8%	10%	17%

*2013 Gallup-Lumina Foundation Poll on Higher Education
**2013 Gallup-Lumina Foundation Business Leaders Poll on Higher Education

GALLUP

In a separate 2013 Gallup-Lumina Foundation Business Leaders Poll on Higher Education, U.S. business leaders were asked the same question regarding the likelihood that employers would hire a candidate with a degree from an online higher education provider over a candidate with the same degree from a traditional institution. A similar proportion of business leaders polled (54%) say employers are at least somewhat likely to do so. However, a smaller percentage (47%) say they are at least somewhat likely to hire such a candidate for their own business.

Implications

Online colleges and universities continue to evolve, as do Americans' and business leaders' opinions about them. While perceptions about the quality of education at these institutions appear to be improving, attitudes toward community colleges and traditional universities remain far more positive at this point. And although more than half of business leaders and Americans in general say companies might be somewhat more likely to hire an online graduate over an equally qualified traditional college graduate, only about one in eight business leaders and one in seven U.S. adults overall say it is very likely. This represents room for improvement in the online education business.

Although online colleges and universities are still in their nascent stage, these findings seem to indicate an increasing acceptance of Internet-based education as a viable alternative to other more traditional institutions. As online colleges continue to grow and adapt to the needs of students and the marketplace, they have the potential to lower costs and increase accessibility to higher education, while imparting knowledge and skills that may be more relevant to today's high-tech employers. Online colleges, however, must continue closing the gap in regard to perceived quality if they aim to someday rival traditional colleges and universities.

Survey Methods

This article includes results from two surveys conducted by Gallup on behalf of Lumina Foundation.

Results from the first study reported are based on telephone interviews conducted as part of the Gallup-Lumina Foundation Poll on Higher Education Nov. 25–Dec. 15, 2013, with a random sample of 1,012 adults, aged 18 and older, living in all 50 U.S. states and the District of Columbia.

For results based on the total sample of 1,012 adults, one can say with 95% confidence that the margin of error attributable to sampling and other random effects is ±4 percentage points. For subgroups within this population (e.g., education level, gender, and income), the margin of error would be greater.

Results from the second study reported are based on telephone interviews conducted as part of the Gallup-Lumina Foundation Business Leaders Poll on Higher Education Nov. 25–Dec. 16, 2013, with a sample of 623 business leaders in executive and senior roles. The sample was obtained from Dun and Bradstreet and was stratified based on sales revenue. Businesses with larger sales revenue were oversampled to ensure enough completes for analysis. Interviews were conducted in English only.

For results based on the total sample of 623 business leaders, one can say with 95% confidence that the margin of error attributable to sampling and other random effects is ±6 percentage points.

Samples were weighted to correct for unequal selection probability and nonresponse by sales revenue and census region.

April 09, 2014
NEW YORK TRI-STATE REGION GRIPES MOST ABOUT STATE TAXES
Wyoming and Alaska residents are the least negative about what they pay

by Lydia Saad

PRINCETON, NJ—Residents of New York, New Jersey, and Connecticut are the most likely of any state's residents to say the amount they pay in state taxes is "too high." Roughly three in four adults in each of these say their state taxes are too high, four times higher than the 19% saying this in Wyoming, whose residents are least likely to say their state taxes are too high.

State Residents Most Negative About Their State's Taxes	% State taxes too high
New York	77
New Jersey	77
Connecticut	76
Illinois	71
Rhode Island	70
Maryland	67
Massachusetts	65
Nebraska	63
Vermont	63
California	62

Gallup 50-state poll, June-December 2013

GALLUP

State Residents Least Negative About Their State's Taxes	% State taxes too high
Wyoming	19
Alaska	21
South Dakota	27
Nevada	28
Florida	33
Delaware	34
North Dakota	35
Montana	36
Idaho	39
Colorado	39
Texas	39

Gallup 50-state poll, June-December 2013

GALLUP

While the states whose residents are most likely to say state taxes are too high include a fairly even mix of populous and less populous states, most of the states where residents are least likely to begrudge their taxes are small. The main exceptions to this are Florida and Texas, both highly populous U.S. states that boast no state income tax.

These findings are from a 50-state Gallup poll, conducted June–December 2013, that included at least 600 representative interviews with residents aged 18 and older in each state. They are based on respondents' answers to the question: "Do you consider the amount of state taxes you have to pay as too high, or not too high?"

On average, 50% of residents across all states say their taxes are too high. Nineteen states are within five percentage points of that figure. Seventeen states are above the average range, with six of these—New Jersey, New York, Connecticut, Illinois, Rhode Island, and Maryland—being well above the norm. Two-thirds or more in these states say their taxes are too high.

At the other end of the spectrum, 14 states are significantly less negative about their taxes than the 50-state average, with Nevada, South Dakota, Alaska, and Wyoming—where fewer than one-third in each state say their taxes are too high—the least negative.

From a broad regional perspective, Americans' dissatisfaction with their own state's taxes tends to be highest in the Northeast, as residents in all states in this region except New Hampshire tilt negative. But several other states in which large majorities say taxes are too high are scattered around the country. The states whose residents are least likely to say taxes are too high are primarily found in the Northern Plains, Rockies, and South, but Alaska, Delaware, and New Hampshire also belong in this group.

View That State Taxes Are Too High, by State

■ Most likely to say "too high"
■ Above average
▨ Average
▨ Below average
▨ Least likely to say "too high"

Gallup 50-state poll, June–December 2013
Note: No data available for the District of Columbia

GALLUP

While there is some regionalism to Americans' satisfaction with their state taxes, a greater factor relating to residents' views of their state tax burden appears to be the taxes themselves. Those living in states with higher combined state and local tax burdens (including income taxes, sales taxes, property taxes, and inheritance taxes) are much more likely to say their state taxes are too high than are those living in states with relatively low tax burdens.

In particular, according to the most recent Tax Foundation estimates, residents in five states—New York, New Jersey, Connecticut, California, and Wisconsin—pay 11% or more of their income, on average, in state and local taxes. And Gallup's state data find 69% of the residents in these, on average, saying their state taxes are too high, well above the 50% average for all states. By contrast, in Wyoming, Alaska, South Dakota, Texas, Tennessee, and Louisiana—the six states averaging less than 8% in state and local taxes—the average level of concern that taxes are too high is just 34%.

View of State Taxes, by Total State and Local Tax Rate

	Average % saying state taxes are too high
Taxes are 11% or higher	69%
Taxes are 10% to 10.9%	59%
Taxes are 9% to 9.9%	50%
Taxes are 8% to 8.9%	43%
Taxes are less than 8%	34%

Trust data from Gallup 50-state poll, June–December 2013
Tax rates are total state/local tax burden in 2011, as reported by the Tax Foundation

GALLUP

Bottom Line

As tax filing day approaches, the dread taxpayers feel may vary by state. Although taxpayers everywhere face the same federal income tax woes, those in states where the vast majority believe their state's taxes are too high may be more distressed at this time of year than those elsewhere.

Although few likely relish paying their taxes, it is notable that in 26 states, fewer than half of residents say their state taxes are too high. So while the saying goes that only death and taxes are certain, evidently complaining about taxes isn't.

Survey Methods

Results for this Gallup poll are based on telephone interviews conducted June–December 2013, with a random sample of approximately 600 adults per state, aged 18 and older, living in all 50 U.S. states.

For results based on the total sample of adults per state, the margin of sampling error is ±5 percentage points at the 95% confidence level.

April 09, 2014
NORTH DAKOTA RESIDENTS MOST POSITIVE ABOUT THEIR SCHOOLS
Nevada and New Mexico earn lowest ratings

by Susan Sorenson and Stephanie Kafka

WASHINGTON, D.C.—Nearly nine in 10 North Dakotans rate the quality of their state's public K–12 education as excellent or good—the highest ratings nationwide. Public school systems in Iowa, Minnesota, Nebraska, and South Dakota trail behind North Dakota closely, with at least 80% of residents rating their states' schools this highly.

States Where Residents Most Frequently Rate Quality of Education as Excellent or Good

Overall, how would you rate the quality of public education provided in grades K through 12 in this state -- as excellent, good, only fair, or poor?

	% Excellent/good
North Dakota	87
Iowa	83
Minnesota	81
Nebraska	80
South Dakota	80
Wyoming	79
Massachusetts	78
Kansas	78
Wisconsin	78
Montana	78

June–December 2013

GALLUP

States Where Residents Least Frequently Rate Quality of Education as Excellent or Good

Overall, how would you rate the quality of public education provided in grades K through 12 in this state -- as excellent, good, only fair, or poor?

	% Excellent/good
New Mexico	41
Nevada	42
Louisiana	45
Hawaii	46
Illinois	49
California	50
Mississippi	52
Oregon	54
Arizona	55
West Virginia	57

June–December 2013

GALLUP

The results are based on a special 50-state Gallup poll conducted June–December 2013, including interviews with at least 600 residents in every state. This poll allows Gallup for the first time to report Americans' perceptions of schools at the state level.

North Dakota has topped several of Gallup's recent state-by-state measures, including well-being, trust in state government, and job creation, to name a few. The state's strong performance on these and other measures is largely fueled by its newfound oil wealth and resulting economic boom, which also helped to fund record school spending in 2013. Residents' positive perceptions about school quality may reflect this investment in education as well as a general sense of optimism about the state's overall direction.

More than 1,000 miles to the south and west, half as many residents in Nevada (42%) and New Mexico (41%) rate their public schools as excellent or good, the lowest scores in the U.S. However, residents in Illinois, Hawaii, and Louisiana took a similarly dim view of their own schools, with less than 50% ranking them as excellent or good.

Respondents likely consider several factors when rating school quality in their states, including student outcomes. U.S. Department of Education data for 2010–2011 show that while eight of the top states in Gallup's measure had graduation rates of 80% or higher, four of the lowest-ranking schools in Gallup's measure—New Mexico, Nevada, Louisiana, and Oregon—fell into the bottom 20% of states with the lowest graduation rates in the U.S.

States With Top School Quality Ratings Also Highest in Preparing Pupils for Work

Residents in states that gave the highest rankings to the quality of their public schools were also the most likely to say these schools are preparing students for success in the workplace. Though in a slightly different order than they appeared in the quality rankings, each of the same top states received a 70% or higher rating on the student preparation question. The consistency in ratings of quality and student workforce preparedness suggests that residents may equate a quality education with one that prepares young people well for the workforce.

States Where Residents Most Frequently Say Public School System Prepares Students for Success in Workplace

Do you believe your state public school system prepares students for success in the workplace?

	% Yes
South Dakota	83
North Dakota	82
Iowa	81
Nebraska	79
Minnesota	76
Wisconsin	75
Wyoming	75
Montana	73
Kansas	71
Massachusetts	71

June-December 2013

GALLUP

States Where Residents Least Frequently Say Public School System Prepares Students for Success in Workplace

Do you believe your state public school system prepares students for success in the workplace?

	% Yes
Nevada	48
New Mexico	51
California	52
Oregon	54
Illinois	55
Hawaii	56
Arizona	57
Louisiana	58
Idaho	59
New York	60

June-December 2013

GALLUP

In five of the states dominating the top quality and student preparedness rankings, including both Dakotas, Iowa, Nebraska, and Wyoming, unemployment rates in 2013 were under 5%—some of the lowest seen in the U.S. Residents in these states might be more likely to see students as prepared for success in the workplace because people in general have a relatively easier time finding employment in these job markets. By contrast, five of the bottom-ranking states had unemployment rates of 7% or higher.

Bottom Line

The different ratings of school quality across the U.S. may reflect, in part, the varying economic realities of each state. Because this is the first time Gallup has measured these data, it is not known how ratings of education by state were affected by the economic downturn and improving economy since then. But with most of K–12 education dollars coming from local and state budgets, spending on public schools is largely tethered to a state's economic highs and lows. Therefore it is likely that states in good economic shape can afford to spend more to keep class sizes small, attract talented teachers with better pay, and maintain and improve their facilities, while schools in struggling state economies contend with overcrowded classrooms and deteriorating infrastructure, conditions that could lead to lower perceptions of quality.

Still, funding is just one of many interconnecting elements that combine to make a school system successful. Residents of the group

of states appearing at the top of both of Gallup's rankings seem to feel that their schools have found a winning formula of providing a quality education that prepares students for a successful career. As leaders struggle to come up with ways to make the nation's education system more competitive on a global stage, a closer look at the schools that top Gallup's quality and preparedness rankings may yield insights and best practices that other states can adopt to boost their own performance.

Survey Methods

Results for this Gallup poll are based on telephone interviews conducted June–December 2013, with a random sample of approximately 600 adults, aged 18 and older, living in all 50 U.S. states.

For results based on the total sample of adults per state, the margin of sampling error is ±5 percentage points at the 95% confidence level.

April 11, 2014
CITY SATISFACTION HIGHEST IN FORT COLLINS-LOVELAND, COLO.
High satisfaction linked to more optimism that area is improving

by Rebecca Riffkin

WASHINGTON, D.C.—Fort Collins-Loveland, Colo. (94.9%) and San Luis Obispo-Paso Robles, Calif. (94.1%) residents were the most likely to be satisfied with the city or area where they live in 2012–2013. Residents of Rockford, Ill. (72.8%) and Stockton, Calif. (73.3%) had the lowest satisfaction rates. On an absolute basis, satisfaction is high in every community, with only seven out of 189 communities Gallup surveyed in 2012–2013 having satisfaction scores below 75%.

Most Satisfied U.S. Communities

Among the 189 U.S. Metropolitan Statistical Areas surveyed

Community	% Satisfied with city
Fort Collins-Loveland, CO	94.9
San Luis Obispo-Paso Robles, CA	94.1
Holland-Grand Haven, MI	93.4
Billings, MT	93.1
Boulder, CO	92.8
Barnstable Town, MA	92.3
Provo-Orem, UT	92.3
Des Moines-West Des Moines, IA	92.2
Madison, WI	91.9
Honolulu, HI	91.7

January 2012-December 2013
Gallup-Healthways Well-Being Index

GALLUP

Least Satisfied U.S. Communities

Among the 189 U.S. Metropolitan Statistical Areas surveyed

Community	% Satisfied with city
Rockford, IL	72.8
Stockton, CA	73.3
Bakersfield, CA	74.0
Flint, MI	74.2
Jackson, MS	74.4
Binghamton, NY	74.6
Scranton-Wilkes-Barre, PA	74.9
Columbus, GA-AL	76.6
Trenton-Ewing, NJ	76.9
Fayetteville, NC	77.1

January 2012-December 2013
Gallup-Healthways Well-Being Index

GALLUP

Gallup and Healthways asked Americans how satisfied they were with the city or area in which they lived as part of the Gallup-Healthways Well-Being Index. Gallup interviewed at least 300 adults aged 18 and older in 189 metropolitan areas throughout 2012–2013. Each sample was weighted to match the demographic characteristics of that area.

Nationally, 85.0% of Americans in 2012–2013 said they are satisfied with the city or area in which they live, which is consistent with the averages recorded since Gallup and Healthways began tracking this measure in 2008.

The satisfaction levels in the lowest-rated U.S. communities have improved since 2008, when the lowest rated community, Memphis, Tenn.-Miss.-Ark., had 68.8% of its residents satisfied with the area where they lived. In 2012–2013, the Memphis area did not fall among the lowest-rated communities, with 79.7% of residents satisfied.

Fort Collins-Loveland has been among the communities with the highest satisfaction levels three times since Gallup and Healthways began tracking in 2008, with its satisfaction rate coming in above 90% in each reporting period. Satisfaction among residents is a common characteristic of cities with high well-being, and the two measures are generally aligned most years.

Optimism Higher in Communities Where Residents Are Already Satisfied

Nationally, 59.7% believe the city or area where they live is getting better, which is higher than Gallup and Healthways have found in past years. In 2009, 53.9% of Americans said their city or area was getting better—the lowest national average Gallup has recorded for this question.

Residents of Binghamton, N.Y., are the least optimistic that their city is getting better, as has been the case since 2008, with the exception of 2009 when it was second from last. The 36.5% of Binghamton residents who said the area is getting better in 2012–2013 is an improvement from the low of 27.8% recorded in 2011.

Fort Collins-Loveland, the most satisfied city in 2012–2013, just barely missed ranking in the top 10 for city optimism in 2012–2013, with 72.7% of residents saying the area is getting better. Fort Collins-Loveland did rank among the top 10 for city optimism in 2010 and 2011.

10 Communities About Which Residents Are Most Optimistic

Among the 189 U.S. Metropolitan Statistical Areas surveyed

Community	% City where you live getting better
Sioux Falls, SD	77.7
Des Moines-West Des Moines, IA	76.6
Lafayette, LA	76.1
Provo-Orem, UT	75.5
Holland-Grand Haven, MI	74.8
McAllen-Edinburg-Mission, TX	74.2
Greenville-Mauldin-Easley, SC	74.1
Fayetteville, Springdale-Rogers, AR-MO	74.1
Kennewick-Pasco-Richland, WA	73.2
Raleigh-Cary, NC	72.8

January 2012-December 2013
Gallup-Healthways Well-Being Index

GALLUP

10 Communities About Which Residents Are Least Optimistic

Among the 189 U.S. Metropolitan Statistical Areas surveyed

Community	% City where you live getting better
Binghamton, NY	36.5
Scranton-Wilkes-Barre, PA	38.0
Rockford, IL	39.7
Huntington-Ashland, WV-KY-OH	40.3
Flint, MI	40.6
Reading, PA	41.4
Stockton, CA	41.5
Utica-Rome, NY	43.0
Trenton-Ewing, NJ	44.3
Redding, CA	45.4

January 2012-December 2013
Gallup-Healthways Well-Being Index

GALLUP

In communities with higher satisfaction rates, residents are more likely to be optimistic that the area is improving than are residents of communities with lower satisfaction rates.

Among the 10 communities with the lowest levels of satisfaction, six are also on the list of communities with the 10 lowest levels of optimism. Three of the communities with the highest levels of satisfaction among residents are among the 10 communities where residents are most likely to say the community is getting better. In Rockford, the community with the lowest satisfaction rate, 39.7% of residents said the community is improving—the third-lowest score in the nation.

Implications

In every U.S. community, the majority of residents are satisfied with the city or area where they live. These high satisfaction rates are understandable because residents who are dissatisfied with where they were living would likely relocate to another area, if they had the means to.

Satisfaction rates vary from almost 95% of residents being satisfied in Fort Collins-Loveland to less than 73% in Rockford. These satisfaction levels may vary because of job opportunities or residents' overall well-being. Fort Collins-Loveland and San Luis Obispo-Paso Robles were among the communities with the highest Well-Being Index scores in 2012–2013. However, neither Rockford nor Stockton were among the communities with the lowest Well-Being Index scores.

Cities that have a higher percentage of dissatisfied residents are also less likely to be seen as improving by those who live there. This means that residents who are unhappy with their communities also don't think their communities are getting better, and residents who are happy with the city or area where they live do feel their community is improving.

Fort Collins-Loveland residents' satisfaction with their community may be linked to the community's success in other aspects of life. In 2012–2013, Fort Collins-Loveland ranked high in terms of communities where residents have easy access to fruit and vegetables. It was also one of the towns that inspired Main Street, U.S.A. at Disneyland.

Rockford, on the other hand, has seen better times. While the city used to be a major manufacturing hub, many companies have since closed local plants. And Woodward Inc., a maker of aircraft fuel system components, though founded in Rockford, has moved its headquarters to Fort Collins. Rockford has recently been plagued by high unemployment and high property taxes, and the community ranked third on the 2013 Forbes List of America's Most Miserable Cities because of a three-decade decline in their manufacturing based economy.

Survey Methods

Results are based on telephone interviews conducted as part of the Gallup-Healthways Well-Being Index survey Jan. 2–Dec. 29, 2012, and Jan. 2–Dec. 30, 2013, with a random sample of 531,630 adults, aged 18 and older, living in metropolitan areas in the 50 U.S. states and the District of Columbia, selected using random-digit-dial sampling. Two years of data were aggregated together to enable the same number of reportable cities as in prior years, when the overall annual data collection exceeded 350,000 interviews per year compared to 178,072 interviews conducted in 2013. At least 300 cases are required per metro area for reporting.

The metro areas referenced in this article are based on the Metropolitan Statistical Areas (MSAs) as defined by the U.S. Office of Management and Budget. In many cases, more than one city is included in the same MSA. The San Jose, Calif., metropolitan statistical area, for example, also includes the smaller nearby cities of Sunnyvale and Santa Clara in addition to San Jose itself. Each respondent is attributed to his or her MSA based on the self-report of his or her ZIP code, and all metro areas had at least 300 completed surveys in the 2012–2013 data collection period.

Maximum expected error ranges for the Well-Being Index and the sub-index scores vary according to MSA size, ranging from less than 1 point for the largest cities represented to ±1.5 points for the smallest cities.

April 11, 2014
AMERICANS REMAIN NEGATIVE
TOWARD HEALTHCARE LAW
Forty-three percent approve, 54% disapprove

by Jeffrey M. Jones

PRINCETON, NJ—With the open enrollment period for obtaining health insurance through a federal government exchange now over, Americans' views on the broader healthcare law remain more negative than positive. Currently, 43% approve and 54% disapprove of the law, commonly known as "Obamacare." The approval figure is a bit higher than Gallup's estimates since last November, but disapproval is essentially unchanged.

Do you generally approve or disapprove of the 2010 Affordable Care Act, signed into law by President Obama that restructured the U.S. healthcare system?

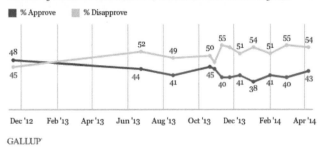

The March 31 deadline for obtaining health insurance through an exchange was a major milestone in the law's implementation. The White House reports more than 7 million Americans enrolled in health insurance plans. Gallup's tracking polling also shows a decline in the percentage of Americans without health insurance during the first quarter of this year.

Even so, Americans' generally negative views of the law have changed little over the past year as more and more of its provisions have gone into effect. For example, 45% of Americans expect the law to make the U.S. healthcare situation worse in the long run, compared with 37% who believe the law will make the situation better, with only minor variations on each percentage since June.

Americans' overall approval of the law and expectations for its long-term effects on the healthcare system continue to be strongly related to their party affiliation. A vast majority of Democrats, 79%, approve of the law, and 69% think it will make the healthcare situation better. In contrast, 87% of Republicans disapprove of the law, and 77% think it will make the healthcare situation worse.

In the long run, how do you think the healthcare law will affect the healthcare situation in the U.S.? Will it -- [ROTATED: make things better, not make much difference, (or will it) make things worse]?

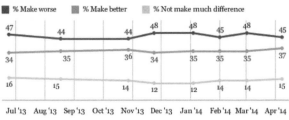

Independents are more negative than positive toward the law. They disapprove of the law by 65% to 32%, and 53% believe the law will make the healthcare situation worse compared with 26% who say better.

Majority of Americans Unaffected by Law

Most Americans, 64%, say their own healthcare situation has so far not been affected by the provisions of the ACA law already in effect. This percentage has declined only slightly from 70% in February 2012 even as more of the law has since been implemented.

More Americans continue to say the law has hurt (18%) rather than helped (15%) them, although that is a closer division than in past Gallup surveys.

As you may know, a few of the provisions of the healthcare law have already gone into effect. So far, has the new law -- [ROTATED: helped you and your family, not had an effect, (or has it) hurt you and your family]?

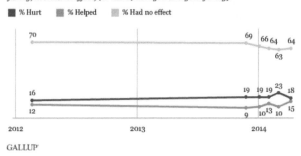

Americans are more likely to think the law will affect their own healthcare situation in the long run, with 32% expecting it to make their situation worse and 24% saying better. Americans have always predicted the law would do more to harm than help their healthcare situation, but the current eight-percentage-point gap is the lowest yet.

In the long run, how do you think the healthcare law will affect your family's healthcare situation? Will it -- [ROTATED: make things better, not make much difference, (or will it) make things worse]?

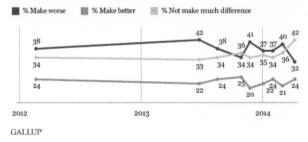

The plurality, 42%, now expect the healthcare law will not make much difference to their healthcare situation either way. That is up from prior surveys and suggests that as more of the law has taken effect, Americans are more likely to see that it is not affecting them—and has not made their situation worse.

These changes are a result of a shift in Republicans' views. Republicans are now more likely than in the prior survey to predict the law's long-term impact on their family will be negligible and less likely to believe it will be harmful. Perhaps with more of the law's provisions now in effect, and little evidence it has actually hurt their healthcare situation, Republicans' views may be more informed by their experience rather than their negative opinions about the law more generally.

Effect of Healthcare Law on the Individual and His or Her Family in the Long Run, by Political Party

	% Make worse	% Make better	% Not make much difference
REPUBLICANS			
Apr 7-8, 2014	51	3	43
Feb 28-Mar 1, 2014	72	3	23
DEMOCRATS			
Apr 7-8, 2014	9	47	43
Feb 28-Mar 1, 2014	16	39	43
INDEPENDENTS			
Apr 7-8, 2014	39	17	40
Feb 28-Mar 1, 2014	38	20	39

GALLUP

Implications

Americans continue to evaluate the Affordable Care Act negatively, and their basic opinions of the law have been fairly stable over the past year. That may suggest Americans have already made up their mind about the law, for the most part reflecting their underlying political orientation, and the law's implementation is not going to influence how they feel about the law.

Yet there is some evidence that Americans' perceptions of how the law might affect their own situation both in the short-term and long-term are changing and becoming less negative. Those shifts would make sense if the law works as intended to bring more people into the health insurance system and to make it more affordable for those struggling to pay for it, while not materially affecting the healthcare of those who have it and can afford it.

Still, many of the provisions of the law have yet to go into effect, and the Obama administration has delayed the dates that many are scheduled to take effect, most notably the requirement that employers with at least 50 workers must offer full-time employees health insurance. That, too, has the potential to influence Americans' views about whether the law is beneficial, neutral, or harmful to their own situation.

Survey Methods

Results for this Gallup poll are based on telephone interviews conducted April 7–8, 2014, on the Gallup Daily tracking survey, with a random sample of 1,009 adults, aged 18 and older, living in all 50 U.S. states and the District of Columbia.

For results based on the total sample of national adults, the margin of sampling error is ±4 percentage points at the 95% confidence level.

April 11, 2014
PARENTS LEAN IN FAVOR OF COMMON CORE, BUT MANY UNAWARE
Most support uniform standards, computerized tests, and teacher evaluation

by Mitchell Ogisi and Lydia Saad

PRINCETON, NJ—Nearly a year into the widespread implementation of the Common Core State Standards—an initiative that specifies what U.S. public school students should know in English and math at each grade level—35% of public school parents have a positive impression of the new education framework and 28% have a negative impression. Thirty-seven percent haven't heard of it or don't know enough to say.

U.S. Public School Parents' Overall Impressions of Common Core Standards

For those who have heard a great deal/fair amount/a little about Common Core:
And from what you know about them, do you have a positive or negative impression of the Common Core standards? Is that very [positive/negative], or somewhat [positive/negative]?

	Public school parents	Parents familiar with Common Core
	%	%
Very positive	9	13
Somewhat positive	26	39
Somewhat negative	15	23
Very negative	13	19
No opinion	4	6
Not heard of	33	--
Total positive	35	52
Total negative	28	42
No opinion/Not heard of	37	6

Results based on parents of students in public school, grades K-12

April 3-9, 2014

GALLUP

Among those who say they have heard at least a little about the Common Core standards, views tilt positive, by 52% to 42%. However, relatively few parents feel strongly about Common Core. Even among parents familiar with the standards, just 13% view them very positively, while slightly more—19%—view them very negatively.

These results are from Gallup Daily tracking April 3–9, and are based on interviews conducted with 639 parents, aged 18 and older, who have children in public school from kindergarten through high school.

Forty-five states plus the District of Columbia initially signed on to the Common Core standards, which were developed by a consortium of governors and state education commissioners, and partially funded by The Bill and Melinda Gates Foundation. President Barack Obama has endorsed the standards, and states that adopt them are eligible for federal Race to the Top education grants. Thirty-three of the states, plus the District of Columbia, implemented the standards in or before the 2013–2014 school year, while 11 states are slated to start next fall. Indiana just became the first state to withdraw from the program, citing budgetary as well as substantive concerns.

Two-Thirds of Parents Have Heard About Common Core

Some critics of Common Core have argued that the standards were crafted without sufficient involvement from parents, teachers, and local school boards, thus taking the public by surprise. In fact, fewer than four in 10 parents (38%) appear to be knowledgeable about the standards, saying they have heard either a great deal or a fair amount about them. Nearly as many—31%—have heard nothing, while another 30% have heard only a little.

Parents in states that have already implemented Common Core are only slightly more familiar with it than those in other states, and their overall views toward the standards are about the same.

U.S. Public School Parents' Awareness of Common Core

How much, if anything, have you heard about the new national standards for teaching reading, writing, and math in grades K through 12, known as the Common Core State Standards -- a great deal, a fair amount, only a little, or nothing at all?

	Public school parents	Parents in states that have implemented Common Core standards^
	%	%
A great deal	16	16
A fair amount	22	26
Only a little	30	27
Nothing	31	29
No opinion	2	1

All results based on parents of students in public school, grades K-12

^Includes parents in 33 states plus the District of Columbia that implemented Common Core standards in the 2013-2014 school year, or earlier.

April 3-9, 2014

GALLUP

Parents Hopeful About the Standards, the Testing, and Teacher Assessment

Even if public school parents are largely unfamiliar with the standards, they give positive ratings to the key Common Core components.

Three in four parents (73%) say having one set of educational standards across the county for reading, writing, and math will be positive for education. Nearly two-thirds (65%) believe using standardized computer-based testing to measure all students' performance and progress will have a positive effect. And 67% believe linking teacher evaluations to their students' Common Core test scores will be positive.

Additionally, at least twice as many parents say each component will be very positive for education as say it will be very negative.

Parents' Views on Specific Aspects of Common Core

Now I'd like to mention several aspects of the Common Core. For each, please tell me if you think it will have a very positive, somewhat positive, somewhat negative, or very negative impact on education in the United States?

	Very positive	Somewhat positive	Somewhat negative	Very negative
	%	%	%	%
Having one set of educational standards across the country for reading, writing, and math	37	36	15	10
Using standardized computer-based tests to measure all students' performance and progress	26	39	20	13
Linking teacher evaluations to their students' Common Core test scores	30	37	16	14

Based on parents of students in public school, grades K-12

April 3-9, 2014

GALLUP

Opposition Runs Deeper Among Republican Parents

There has been ample opposition to Common Core on the political right and left. Some Republican governors and prominent conservatives have decried what they see as a loss of local control over curriculum. At the same time, some teacher groups, including the New York City teachers' union, have concerns about loss of teacher control over curriculum, as well as Common Core–aligned standards and tests that they consider educationally and developmentally inappropriate.

When it comes to parents, however, the criticism mainly comes from the right. Among public school parents, 26% of those who are Republican or lean Republican have a positive impression of Common Core; 42% view it negatively. By contrast, 45% of Democratic and Democratic-leaning parents view Common Core positively, while 23% view it negatively.

Overall Impression of Common Core Standards Among Public K-12 Parents -- by Party ID

	Republican/ Lean Republican	Democratic/ Lean Democratic
	%	%
Very positive	4	13
Somewhat positive	22	32
Somewhat negative	20	15
Very negative	22	8
Not heard of/No opinion	31	33
Total positive	26	45
Total negative	42	23

April 3-9, 2014

GALLUP

At the same time, the majority of Republican and Democratic parents, alike, believe each of the three main aspects of Common Core will be positive for education rather than negative. But Republicans are somewhat less positive than Democrats on each item.

Reviews of Common Core Among Public K-12 Parents -- by Party ID

Views of whether each aspect will have a positive or negative impact on education in the U.S.

	Republican/ Lean Republican	Democratic/ Lean Democratic
Uniform national standards	%	%
Positive impact	64	85
Negative impact	34	15
Standardized computer-based student assessment tests		
Positive impact	58	70
Negative impact	41	29
Linking teacher evaluations to student test scores		
Positive impact	60	71
Negative impact	37	27

April 3-9, 2014

GALLUP

Bottom Line

State leaders pushed for the development of the Common Core State Standards to ensure that all K–12 students are challenged to meet the same high educational standards needed for success in college and entry-level jobs. On one level, the program has been successful, achieving buy-in from 44 states. But there is still a long way to go, including full implementation of the standards, launching the testing component, and using the test scores to evaluate teachers and principals. Already, critics of the program are proving their muscle by slowing down or reversing implementation in some states; and if this were to reach critical mass, it could derail the whole enterprise. But whether the critics speak for parents, generally, seems in doubt.

Parents play a critical role in their children's education, and their views about whether the Common Core standards and the associated curriculum and testing make sense are important. At this initial stage, parents' overall reaction is positive, though importantly, a substantial minority say they have never heard of the standards. After more parents observe the effects of Common Core firsthand, their views could change.

Regardless, because the standards will likely change the way many students are educated, it will be essential for school districts to clearly inform parents about the standards and any associated changes in expectations for students, so that parents can do their part in helping them adapt and succeed.

Survey Methods

Results for this Gallup poll are based on telephone interviews conducted April 3–9, 2014, on the Gallup Daily tracking survey, with a random sample of 639 public school K–12 parents, aged 18 and older, living in the 50 U.S. states and the District of Columbia. The margin of sampling error for results based on the total sample is ±5 percentage points at the 95% confidence level.

For results based on the 466 K–12 public school parents who familiar with the Common Core standards, the margin of sampling error is ±6 percentage points at the 95% confidence level.

For results based on the total sample of 382 parents living in the 33 states that have already implemented the Common Core standards, the margin of sampling error is ±7 percentage points at the 95% confidence level.

April 14, 2014
MORE THAN HALF OF AMERICANS SAY FEDERAL TAXES TOO HIGH
Fifty-four percent say they are fair, the lowest since 2001

by Rebecca Riffkin

WASHINGTON, D.C.—As many Americans scramble to prepare their taxes ahead of the April 15 deadline, a majority, 52%, say the amount they have to pay in federal income tax is "too high," while 42% say it is "about right." The percentage who say their taxes are too high has hovered around 50% since 2003, although the current 52% is up from 46% two years ago.

Americans' Views on Their Federal Income Taxes

Do you consider the amount of federal income tax you have to pay as too high, about right, or too low?

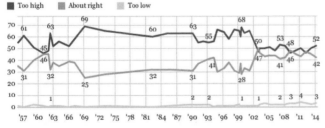

January 2003 poll asked of a half sample

GALLUP

Americans' current views of the amount they pay in taxes represent a significant change from prior to 2003, when they were much more likely to say their taxes were too high. The lower percentage since 2003 who say their taxes are too high most likely reflects the effect of the 2001 and 2003 income tax cuts passed during George W. Bush's administration. Prior to Bush's presidency, as many as 69% of Americans felt their taxes were too high, while as little as a quarter felt they were about right.

Few Americans have ever described their taxes as being "too low," with at most 4% saying this in the nearly 60 years Gallup has asked the question.

Americans' views on their federal taxes are similar to their views of their state taxes. A recent Gallup 50-state survey found that 50% of residents across all states, on average, believe their state taxes are too high.

A Slight Majority of Americans Say Their Taxes Are Fair

While a slim majority of Americans say their federal tax burden is too high, roughly the same percentage also say their taxes are fair. However, the view that taxes are fair is becoming less common, and, at 54% this year, is down to its lowest point since 2001—after peaking at 64% in 2003.

Americans' Perceptions of Their Income Taxes, 1997-2014

Do you regard the income tax which you will have to pay this year as fair?

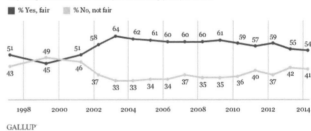

GALLUP

The majority of Americans have not always felt their taxes were fair. In 1999, slightly more Americans said their taxes were not fair (49%) than fair (45%). But this was the only year in which Americans were more likely to say their taxes were unfair.

Gallup also asked this question in the 1940s, mostly during World War II. During the war, Americans were overwhelmingly likely to say their taxes were fair, most likely out of a sense of patriotism as the nation was spending a large percentage of citizens' tax money to fight the war.

Americans' perceptions of their taxes being fair peaked in February 1944 at 90%. In 1946, after the war had concluded, the percentage regarding their taxes as fair dropped to 60%.

Democrats More Likely Than Republicans to See Taxes as Fair

Democrats are the only partisan group in which a majority, 55%, say their taxes are "about right." A majority of Republicans and independents say their taxes are "too high." Furthermore, Democrats (69%) are significantly more likely than Republicans (46%) and independents (51%) to say their taxes are fair.

These patterns are largely consistent with what Gallup found last year. However, the pattern has changed from prior to Barack Obama's presidency, when Americans across partisan groups felt similarly about whether their taxes were too high. In 2006, for example, 47% of Republicans and 47% of Democrats reported their taxes were too high, while 50% of independents said the same.

Democrats More Likely Than Other Party Groups to Say Their Taxes Are Fair

Do you consider the amount of federal income tax you have to pay as too high, about right, or too low?
Do you regard the income tax which you will have to pay this year as fair?

	Republicans	Independents	Democrats
	%	%	%
Too high	57	58	37
About right	38	36	55
Too low	1	3	5
Yes, fair	46	51	69
No, not fair	49	44	28

April 3-6, 2014

GALLUP

Views of tax fairness did reflect partisan differences in 2006. While the majority of Democrats, 56%, reported their taxes were fair, this was less than the percentage of Republicans who said this at the time. The percentage of Democrats who say their taxes are fair in 2014 is higher than the percentage who did in 2006. Republicans, at 65% fair, were much more likely to view their taxes as fair in 2006 than they are today. In 2006, 60% of independents felt their taxes were fair.

Upper-Income Americans Least Likely to Say Taxes Are Fair

Six in 10 upper-income Americans—those earning $75,000 or more annually—believe their taxes are too high, and the majority consider what they pay unfair. By contrast, barely half of middle- and lower-income Americans think their taxes are too high, and the majority consider them fair.

Americans' Views of Federal Income Taxes Paid, by Annual Income

Do you consider the amount of federal income tax you have to pay as too high, about right, or too low?
Do you regard the income tax which you will have to pay this year as fair?

	Less than $30,000 per year	$30,000 to $74,999 per year	$75,000+ per year
	%	%	%
Too high	49	46	61
About right	41	47	37
Too low	3	4	1
Yes, fair	58	60	47
No, not fair	33	37	51

April 3-6, 2014

GALLUP

Implications

As Americans across the country file their taxes, they either celebrate receiving a refund or dread how much they owe. This year, 52% of Americans feel they pay too much, the highest since before the height of the Great Recession in October 2008. However, it remains lower than what Gallup found from the 1960s through the 1990s.

The slight increase this year in Americans' views that their taxes are too high may reflect an actual increase in taxes, either direct or indirect, that has occurred recently. Specifically, the expiration of the Bush tax cuts increased taxes and eliminated some previous deductions. Upper-income Americans, particularly, may feel their taxes are too high now because their taxes actually may have increased. The uptick also may reflect overall discontent with the federal government, Congress, and high-profile laws such as the Affordable Care Act.

As political leaders discuss ways to simplify the tax code, the federal government also may want to revisit the amount of money Americans pay in taxes.

Survey Methods

Results for this Gallup poll are based on telephone interviews conducted April 3–6, 2014, on the Gallup Daily tracking survey, with a random sample of 1,026 adults, aged 18 and older, living in all 50 U.S. states and the District of Columbia.

For results based on the total sample of national adults, the margin of sampling error is ±4 percentage points at the 95% confidence level.

April 14, 2014
AS TAXES RISE, HALF IN U.S. SAY MIDDLE-INCOME PAY TOO MUCH
A near-record high of 23% say lower-income Americans pay too little

by Andrew Dugan

WASHINGTON, D.C.—Nearly half of Americans, 49%, believe middle-income people—a group many Americans consider themselves part of—pay too much in taxes, up from 42% a year ago and the highest Gallup has found since 1999. At the same time, the 42% who say middle-income Americans pay their "fair share" in taxes is down 11 percentage points from last year. This is also the first time since 2007 that a higher percentage of the public says middle-income Americans are paying too much rather than their fair share.

Americans' Views on Tax Burden of the Middle-Income

As I read off some different groups, please tell me if you think they are paying their FAIR share in federal taxes, paying too MUCH or paying too LITTLE? First, how about middle-income people?

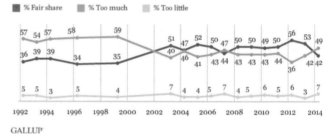

GALLUP

These results are from Gallup's annual Economy and Personal Finance poll, conducted April 3–6.

While the April 15 tax deadline may not be the most popular day on the nation's calendar, over the past decade, stable pluralities and sometimes majorities have said that middle-income Americans pay their fair share in taxes, rather than too much or too little. But the perception has grown since 2012 that middle-income Americans pay too much in taxes; this comes as income taxes increase for the first time in 20 years, though mainly for the top earners. President Barack Obama and Congress allowed the Bush tax cuts on the marginal rates for the highest income earners to expire last year, which increased the tax rate for 2013 income from 35.0% to 39.6%. Other taxes, such as capital gains taxes, have also increased, and the bill is now coming due for many taxpayers.

Though the bulk of the higher tax rates affect those in the top income bracket—$400,000 for individuals and $450,000 for married couples—there has not been a noticeable climb in the proportion of Americans who believe upper-income people pay too much. That figure stands at 13% today, essentially unchanged from 11% last year. A robust majority, 61%, believe that upper-income people pay too little, while about a quarter believe they pay their fair share.

Americans' Views on Tax Burden of the Upper-Income

As I read off some different groups, please tell me if you think they are paying their FAIR share in federal taxes, paying too MUCH or paying too LITTLE? First, how about upper-income people?

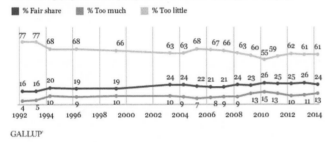

GALLUP

At the other end of the income spectrum, a plurality of Americans, 41%, say lower-income people pay too much in taxes. A third of Americans say the lower-income pay their fair share, while 23% say they pay too little, one point off the record high from 2012.

More broadly, Gallup's two-decade trend shows a clear increase in the percentage of Americans who believe the lower-income pay too little in taxes. The figure varied from 8% to 12% throughout the 1990s and the first half of the 2000s. It then jumped to between 13% and 17% in the late 2000s, and has consistently been near or above 20% since 2010.

Americans' Views on Tax Burden of the Lower-Income

As I read off some different groups, please tell me if you think they are paying their FAIR share in federal taxes, paying too MUCH or paying too LITTLE? First, how about lower-income people?

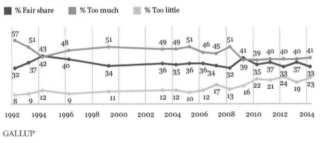

GALLUP

Republicans More Likely Than Democrats to Say Lower-Income Pay Too Little

Tax rates—how high they are and who should pay them—are a central debate in American politics. Not surprisingly, self-identified Republicans and Democrats disagree on how Uncle Sam treats the upper- and lower-income groups. A plurality of Republicans (40%) believe lower-income individuals pay too little in federal income taxes, far higher than the 22% of independents and 11% of Democrats who think so.

Republicans are also much less likely than Democrats or independents to believe upper-income people are paying too little (45%), though still a plurality think this. By contrast, 61% of independents and 76% of Democrats believe upper-income Americans pay too little.

Tax Burdens of Different Income Groups, by Self-Identified Party Affiliation

As I read off some different groups, please tell me if you think they are paying their FAIR share in federal taxes, paying too MUCH or paying too LITTLE? First, how about -- ?

	Republicans %	Independents %	Democrats %
LOWER-INCOME PEOPLE			
Fair share	33	31	35
Too much	25	44	52
Too little	40	22	11
MIDDLE-INCOME PEOPLE			
Fair share	43	40	45
Too much	49	51	45
Too little	6	7	8
UPPER-INCOME PEOPLE			
Fair share	31	23	17
Too much	21	14	5
Too little	45	61	76

April 3-6, 2014

GALLUP

One area of accord is with respect to middle-income people. Republicans (49%), independents (51%), and Democrats (45%) are about equally as likely to say middle-income earners pay too much in taxes—a reminder of why politicians design tax-cut proposals to help the middle class more than any other group.

Two-Thirds of Americans Believe Corporations Pay Too Little in Taxes

As is typical, most Americans say corporations pay too little in taxes (66%). Fewer than one in 10 say corporations pay too much (8%). Despite this broad consensus, prominent Republicans and Democrats, including Obama and Republican Dave Camp, chairman of the tax-writing House Ways and Means Committee, have offered separate proposals to reduce the corporate tax rate.

Americans' Views on Tax Burden of Corporations

As I read off some different groups, please tell me if you think they are paying their FAIR share in federal taxes, paying too MUCH or paying too LITTLE? First, how about corporations?

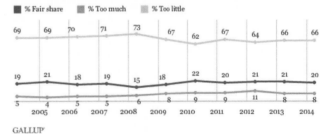

GALLUP

Implications

More Americans now think the middle class is paying too much in taxes than at any time since the 2001 tax cuts. The reasons for the shift are not obvious. Although some Americans' federal income tax rates have increased in the past year, those increases were largely confined to the highest earners. The payroll tax increase, taking effect in January 2013 paychecks, may have influenced Americans' perceptions of their income taxes, though those effects would have been first felt last year. News reports about higher tax rates for some taxpayers may have influenced Americans' perceptions of middle-income taxes, or perhaps the ongoing debate between Obama and Republicans about efforts to reduce income equality are having an effect. Also, many Americans consider themselves middle class, even if they fall on the higher end of the income distribution, and this could help explain the spike.

An interesting trend is the growing proportion of Americans who believe lower-income individuals pay too little. This comes after a presidential election in which some attention was paid to the so-called "47%" who pay no income tax because of their low income levels. While this issue caused some trouble for Republican presidential nominee Mitt Romney, who spoke dismissively of this segment of the population in a secretly recorded video, it appears that an expanding number of Americans do believe the lowest-income earners should pay more in taxes.

Survey Methods

Results for this Gallup poll are based on telephone interviews conducted April 3–6, 2014, on the Gallup Daily tracking survey, with a random sample of 1,026 adults, aged 18 and older, living in all 50 U.S. states and the District of Columbia.

For results based on the total sample of national adults, the margin of sampling error is ±4 percentage points at the 95% confidence level.

April 15, 2014
MCALLEN, TEXAS, RESIDENTS LEAST LIKELY TO FEEL SAFE
McAllen-Edinburg-Mission residents also most likely to struggle to afford housing

by Justin McCarthy

WASHINGTON, D.C.—Less than half of those living in the McAllen-Edinburg-Mission, Texas, community (48.5%) said they feel safe walking alone at night in the area where they live in 2012–2013, the lowest percentage among the 189 metro areas that Gallup and Healthways surveyed. Residents were most likely to feel safe walking unaccompanied after dark in Holland-Grand Haven, Mich. (85.7%), followed by Fort Collins-Loveland, Colo. (84.9%) and Provo-Orem, Utah (84.7%).

Least Safe Metro Areas

Do you feel safe walking alone at night in the city or area where you live?

	% Yes
McAllen-Edinburg-Mission, TX	48.5
Yakima, WA	51.3
Stockton, CA	52.2
Modesto, CA	54.2
Columbus, GA-AL	54.2
Mobile, AL	54.5
Fayetteville, NC	56.0
Memphis, TN-MS-AR	56.3
Huntington-Ashland, WV-KY-OH	56.7
Fresno, CA	57.2

January 2012-December 2013
Gallup-Healthways Well-Being Index

GALLUP

Safest Metro Areas

Do you feel safe walking alone at night in the city or area where you live?

	% Yes
Holland-Grand Haven, MI	85.7
Fort Collins-Loveland, CO	84.9
Provo-Orem, UT	84.7
Honolulu, HI	83.7
Sioux Falls, SD	83.1
Des Moines-West Des Moines, IA	82.4
Barnstable Town, MA	82.2
Portland-South Portland-Biddeford, ME	82.2
San Luis Obispo-Paso Robles, CA	80.4
Boulder, CO	80.4

January 2012-December 2013
Gallup-Healthways Well-Being Index

GALLUP

McAllen-Edinburg-Mission was the only community where less than half of residents said they felt safe walking alone at night.

Nationally, an average 70.5% of Americans in 2012–2013 felt safe walking alone in the communities they live in. This measure gives a sense of Americans' personal security in the area they live, which is most likely linked to local crime rates. This measure also may also be related to the age, gender, and demographic and economic composition of the metro areas, as well as security factors such as law enforcement presence and street lighting.

These results are from the Gallup-Healthways Well-Being Index interviews with at least 300 adults aged 18 and older in each of 189 metro areas over a two-year span, from January 2012 through December 2013. Each metro area sample is weighted to match the demographic characteristics of that area. Gallup categorizes U.S. metro area according to the U.S. Office of Management and Budget's definitions for Metropolitan Statistical Areas (MSAs).

Link Between Feeling Safe Walking Alone and Being Able to Afford Housing

Community rankings for perceived safety are related to community rankings for a number of other well-being measures affected by socioeconomic factors, but one of the most striking and illustrative is the relationship with the ability to afford housing.

Three communities—McAllen-Edinburg-Mission; Modesto, Calif.; and Columbus, Ga.-Ala.—are among the bottom 10 for both measures, with McAllen-Edinburg-Mission at the very bottom of both lists. Three of the top 10 safest communities also appear on the list of 10 communities that are least likely to struggle to afford housing—Holland-Grand Haven; Sioux Falls, S.D.; Portland-South Portland-Biddeford, Maine.

Bottom 10 Communities: Enough Money to Provide Adequate Shelter or Housing

Have there been times in the past 12 months when you did not have enough money to provide adequate shelter or housing for you or your family?

	% No
McAllen-Edinburg-Mission, TX	75.5
El Paso, TX	82.1
Miami-Fort Lauderdale-Pompano Beach, FL	82.4
Spartanburg, SC	83.4
Visalia-Porterville, CA	84.5
Jackson, MS	84.6
Columbus, GA-AL	85.2
Los Angeles-Long Beach-Santa Ana, CA	85.6
New York-North New Jersey-Long Island, NY-NJ-PA	85.7
Modesto, CA	85.8

January 2012-December 2013
Gallup-Healthways Well-Being Index

GALLUP

Top 10 Communities: Enough Money to Provide Adequate Shelter or Housing

Have there been times in the past 12 months when you did not have enough money to provide adequate shelter or housing for you or your family?

	% No
Ann Arbor, MI	96.0
Madison, WI	95.2
Olympia, WA	95.1
Youngstown-Warren-Boardman, OH-PA	94.9
Holland-Grand Haven, MI	94.8
Portland-South Portland-Biddeford, ME	94.6
Lancaster, PA	94.2
Sioux Falls, SD	94.1
Cedar Rapids, IA	94.0
Davenport-Moline-Rock Island, IA-IL	93.8

January 2012-December 2013
Gallup-Healthways Well-Being Index

GALLUP

Nationally, 89.5% of Americans, on average, said they had no trouble paying housing costs over the past year. Among the 10 communities where residents felt least safe walking alone, all but one community fell below the national average for residents being able to afford housing in the past year.

Though each measure's ranking is often indicative of how it will rate on the other, one major exception is Huntington-Ashland, W.Va.-Ky.-Ohio. Residents there were among the least likely nationally to feel safe walking alone, but are above the national average in saying they had no trouble paying for housing costs over the past year.

Ten Least Safe Communities: Percentage of Residents With Enough Money to Afford Shelter

	Enough money for adequate shelter or housing	Below national average
	%	
National average	89.5	
McAllen-Edinburg-Mission, TX	75.5	Yes
Yakima, WA	87.5	Yes
Stockton, CA	87.5	Yes
Modesto, CA	85.8	Yes
Columbus, GA-AL	85.2	Yes
Mobile, AL	86.2	Yes
Fayetteville, NC	87.3	Yes
Memphis, TN-MS-AR	86.3	Yes
Huntington-Ashland, WV-KY-OH	90.4	No
Fresno, CA	85.9	Yes

January 2012-December 2013
Gallup-Healthways Well-Being Index

GALLUP'

When looking at the 50 communities where residents felt safest walking alone at night, all but one were above that national average in reporting they did not struggle to afford shelter. Of the 50 communities where residents were least likely to feel safe walking alone at night, 32 of them fell below the national average in terms of struggling to pay for shelter. This underscores the general relationship between economic measures and crime, given the general finding that crime rates are higher in low-income areas across the country.

Bottom Line

While the two measures ask entirely different questions, it's no coincidence that the communities where residents were least likely to feel safe at night are also among the list of communities where residents were more likely to struggle with housing costs, among other problems. The factors that contribute to both of these problems are often rooted in socioeconomic status and are likely traced back to poverty and the discontent that comes with it.

A key question arising from these data is whether residents' inability to afford decent housing contributes to their reports of feeling less safe walking alone at night, or if being priced out of the housing market is merely a reflection of the same underlying poverty issues that foster poor safety and security at the community level. The latter possibility is more likely when considered in the context of other related factors, such as health insurance coverage. McAllen-Edinburg-Mission and other communities where residents were less likely to report feeling safe at night are also toward the top of the list for uninsured rates.

Maintaining public safety is one of the most important functions of government and integral to a free society. Both safety and affordable housing are likely related to broader poverty issues, and thus deserve policymakers' attention.

Survey Methods

Results are based on telephone interviews conducted as part of the Gallup-Healthways Well-Being Index survey Jan. 2–Dec. 29, 2012, and Jan. 2–Dec. 30, 2013, with a random sample of 531,630 adults, aged 18 and older, living in metropolitan areas in the 50 U.S. states and the District of Columbia, selected using random-digit-dial sampling. Two years of data were aggregated together to enable the same number of reportable cities as in prior years, when the overall annual data collection exceeded 350,000 interviews per year compared to 178,072 interviews conducted in 2013. At least 300 cases are required per metro area for reporting.

The metro areas referenced in this article are based on the Metropolitan Statistical Areas (MSAs) as defined by the U.S. Office of Management and Budget. In many cases, more than one city is included in the same MSA. The San Jose, Calif., metropolitan statistical area, for example, also includes the smaller nearby cities of Sunnyvale and Santa Clara in addition to San Jose itself. Each respondent is attributed to his or her MSA based on the self-report of his or her ZIP code, and all metro areas had at least 300 completed surveys in the 2012–2013 data collection period.

Maximum expected error ranges for the Well-Being Index and the sub-index scores vary according to MSA size, ranging from less than 1 point for the largest cities represented to ±1.5 points for the smallest cities.

April 16, 2014
UNINSURED RATE DROPS MORE IN STATES EMBRACING HEALTH LAW
Medicaid expansion, state exchanges linked to faster reduction in uninsured rate

by Dan Witters

WASHINGTON, D.C.—The uninsured rate among adults aged 18 and older in the states that have chosen to expand Medicaid *and* set up their own exchanges in the health insurance marketplace has declined significantly more this year than in the remaining states that have not done so. The uninsured rate, on average, declined 2.5 percentage points in the 21 states (plus the District of Columbia) that have implemented both of these measures, compared with a 0.8-point drop across the 29 states that have taken only one or neither of these actions.

Changes in States' Uninsured Rates Between 2013 and Quarter 1, 2014

	% Uninsured, 2013	% Uninsured, Q1 2014	Change (pct. pts.)
States that have expanded Medicaid AND implemented exchanges or partnerships	16.1	13.6	-2.5
States that have NOT expanded Medicaid and/or implemented exchanges or partnerships	18.7	17.9	-0.8

Gallup-Healthways Well-Being Index

GALLUP'

As Gallup previously reported, the states that have chosen to expand Medicaid and set up their own healthcare exchanges had a lower average uninsured rate to begin with: 16.1% compared with 18.7% for the remaining states—a difference of 2.6 points. The already notable gap between the two groups of states widened in the first quarter to 4.3 points.

Nationally, 17.3% of U.S. adults reported being without health insurance in 2013, a rate that had slowly increased from 14.8% in 2008. The uninsured rate peaked at 18.0% in the third quarter of

2013—the three months immediately preceding the opening of the healthcare exchanges—and has since declined to 15.6%.

These data, collected as part of the Gallup-Healthways Well-Being Index, are based on Americans' self-reported insurance status in response to the question, "Do you have health insurance coverage?"

Some states have chosen to implement state-federal "partnership" exchanges, for which states run certain functions and make key decisions based on local market and demographic conditions. For the purposes of this analysis, these partnerships are included with the state exchanges. Only four states—North Dakota, New Jersey, Ohio, and Arizona—have decided to expand Medicaid without also administering a state-based exchange, while several others continue to debate expanding eligibility.

Implications

While a majority of Americans continue to disapprove of the Affordable Care Act, also known as "Obamacare," the uninsured rate appears to be declining, as the law intended. In turn, the states (including the District of Columbia) that have implemented two of the law's core mechanisms—Medicaid expansion and state health insurance exchanges—are realizing a rate of decline that is substantively greater than what is found among the remaining states that have not done so. Consequently, the gap that previously existed between the two groups has now expanded.

Many states continue to debate implementing these measures. Nebraska's state government recently voted down Medicaid expansion, while New Hampshire voted to expand, effective July 1. Perhaps no state is being watched more closely than Utah, a conservative state with a Republican governor, Gary Herbert, that is considering Medicaid expansion but under revised, more flexible terms than what the Affordable Care Act provides. These plans, which include a three-year block grant to cover about 110,000 low-income residents with private insurance, plus cost sharing and work requirements, have fueled ongoing conversations with federal officials at the Centers for Medicare & Medicaid Services. The resolution of these negotiations and Utah's final decision may ultimately pave the way for more conservative-leaning states to follow, which could prove to be the best source of continued decline in the national uninsured rate in the months ahead.

Survey Methods

Results for 2013 are based on telephone interviews conducted as part of the Gallup-Healthways Well-Being Index survey Jan. 2–Dec. 29, 2013, with a random sample of 178,068 adults, aged 18 and older, living in all 50 U.S. states and the District of Columbia. Results for 2014 are based on telephone interviews conducted with 43,562 respondents between Jan. 2 and March 31, 2014.

The margin of sampling error for the two reported groups in 2013 is ±0.3 percentage points. The margin of error for both reported groups in 2014 is ±0.6 percentage points.

April 16, 2014
HIGHER FINES COMPEL UNINSURED AMERICANS TO SIGN UP
Healthy less willing to sign up for insurance than unhealthy

by Charlie Richter and Stafford Nichols

WASHINGTON, D.C.—Uninsured Americans' likelihood of signing up for insurance differs depending on the amount of the fine they would have to pay for not carrying insurance. At a hypothetical $95 fine level, uninsured Americans are as likely to say they would not get insurance (46%) as to say they would (47%). At a $500 fine level, the percentage saying they would get insurance jumps to 60%, but this percentage levels off at a $1,000 fine level at 62%.

Uninsured More Likely to Sign Up for Health Insurance at Higher Fines

If you know the annual fine for not having insurance was --- [RANDOM: fine level] would you be ...?

	More likely to get health insurance	More likely to pay the fine
$95	47%	46%
$500	60%	32%
$1,000	62%	28%

Jan. 2-April 3, 2014

GALLUP

The results are based on interviews with 4,829 Americans without health insurance as part of Gallup Daily tracking from Jan. 2–April 3, 2014. Uninsured Americans were randomly assigned to three groups, each testing respondents' likelihood to sign up for insurance under different fine conditions of $95, $500, and $1,000.

Under the Affordable Care Act, also commonly known as "Obamacare," U.S. adults and their dependents must have health insurance or pay a fine. In 2014, the fine is $95 or 1% of household income, whichever is greater. The fine increases to $325, or 2% of taxable income, in 2015 and $695, or 2.5% of income, in 2016. These Gallup Daily tracking results provide a broad indication of how consumers would react to the three thresholds of fines.

Likelihood to Sign Up for Insurance, Based on Self-Reported Health Status

If you know the annual fine for not having insurance was -- [RANDOM: fine level] would you be ...?

	Excellent/Very good	Good	Fair/Poor
$95			
More likely to get health insurance	42%	50%	47%
More likely to pay the fine	54%	44%	41%
$500			
More likely to get health insurance	53%	63%	66%
More likely to pay the fine	40%	31%	26%
$1,000			
More likely to get health insurance	59%	66%	64%
More likely to pay the fine	33%	28%	23%

Jan. 2-April 3, 2014

GALLUP

Healthy Less Likely Than Sick to Sign Up, Regardless of Fine Amount

Health insurance companies and stakeholders believe the most important factor in the future pricing and overall affordability of health insurance plans could be uninsured healthy individuals signing up for insurance at similar rates to less healthy uninsured individuals. With this concept in mind, Gallup asked respondents to self-report their health as "excellent," "very good," "good," "fair," or "poor." This measurement has proven to correlate with self-reporting of chronic and expensive health conditions like obesity, high blood pressure, and depression.

Across the various fine levels, adults with excellent or very good self-reported health are less likely to say they would sign up for health insurance than adults with poorer health. However, increasing the fine does increase the likelihood that healthier adults will enroll in a plan. At the $1,000 level, a solid majority of Americans in all health groups measured report being more likely to sign up for insurance than paying the fine.

Fine Levels Affect Democrats and Republicans Equally

The data show that respondents' political affiliation plays a role in their stated likelihood of signing up for health insurance. At each fine level, those who identify as Republican are about half as likely to report a willingness to sign up for health insurance as those who identify as Democrat.

Republicans Less Likely to Sign Up for Health Insurance

If you knew the annual fine for not having insurance was -- [RANDOM: fine level] would you be ...?

	Democrat	Independent	Republican
$95			
More likely to get health insurance	65%	42%	29%
More likely to pay the fine	29%	51%	66%
$500			
More likely to get health insurance	79%	58%	36%
More likely to pay the fine	16%	33%	55%
$1,000			
More likely to get health insurance	78%	61%	43%
More likely to pay the fine	15%	30%	47%

Jan. 2-April 3, 2014

GALLUP'

These political affiliation findings are consistent with earlier Gallup reports on how party identification affects Americans' attitudes toward the Affordable Care Act and uninsured Americans' intentions to get insurance.

Implications

The increase in the Affordable Care Act fine next year to a minimum $325, or 2% of one's yearly household income, could compel a significant amount of still-uninsured Americans who did not sign up during the open enrollment period to do so in 2015. This increase could begin to taper off between the 2015 and 2016 tax years if the average fine moves between $500 and $1,000. At this point, there is a distinct possibility that the growth in the insurance coverage rate will either slow down or stall based on expected future fine levels. However, other factors such as public support for the Affordable Care Act and targeted marketing campaigns may help to close the insurance coverage gap even as the fines lose some of their ability to influence decision making.

Survey Methods

Results for this Gallup poll are based on telephone interviews conducted between Jan. 2–April 3, 2014, on the Gallup Daily tracking survey, with a random sample of 4,929 adults, aged 18 and older,

living in all 50 U.S. states and the District of Columbia, who do not currently have health insurance.

Each experimental fine level ($95, $500, or $1,000) was asked of a randomly selected third of the overall sample, approximately 1,600 uninsured Americans per condition. For results based on these samples of uninsured Americans, the margin of sampling error is ±3 percentage points at the 95% confidence level.

April 16, 2014
NEWLY INSURED IN 2014 REPRESENT ABOUT 4% OF U.S. ADULTS
Half of newly insured obtained health insurance through exchanges

by Frank Newport

PRINCETON, NJ—Four percent of Americans are newly insured this year, reporting that they have health insurance now but did not last year. A little more than half of that group, or 2.1% of the U.S. population, got their new insurance through health exchanges. The rest got it using some other mechanism.

Insurance status as of April 2014

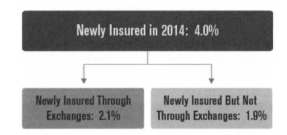

Based on interviews March 4-April 14, 2014   GALLUP'

These findings are based on interviewing with more than 20,000 U.S. adults, aged 18 and older, conducted as part of Gallup Daily tracking from March 4–April 14. Gallup asked those who have health insurance if their policy is new for 2014, and if so, whether they had insurance last year and if they got their new insurance through a federal or state health exchange.

Overall, 11.8% of U.S. adults say they got a new health insurance policy in 2014. One-third of this group, or 4% nationally, say they did not have insurance in 2013. Another 7.5% got a new policy this year that replaced a previous policy. The rest either did not respond or were uncertain about their previous insurance status.

The key figure is the 4% who are newly insured in 2014, which most likely represents Americans' response to the individual mandate requirement of the Affordable Care Act (ACA). This estimate of the newly insured broadly aligns with the reduction Gallup has seen in the national uninsured rate from 2013 to the first days of April 2014. However, the calculation of the newly insured does not take into account those who may have been insured in 2013 but not in 2014.

The ACA envisioned that the new healthcare exchanges would be the main place where uninsured Americans would get their insurance this year, but it appears that a sizable segment of the newly insured Americans used another mechanism. These sources presumably include employee policies, Medicaid, and other private policies not arranged through exchanges.

Newly Insured Younger Than General Population

The newly insured are, on average, much younger than the overall population, with most younger than age 65. Within the 18 to 64 age range, the newly insured are slightly more overrepresented in the 18 to 29 age category than in the 30 to 49 and 50 to 64 age categories. These data suggest that the ACA's efforts to add previously uninsured young people to the ranks of the insured have been modestly successful.

The newly insured who signed up outside of the exchanges are substantially younger than those who signed up through the exchanges.

Profiles of Newly Insured, by Age

	All newly insured in 2014	Newly insured in 2014 through exchanges	Newly insured in 2014 not through exchanges	National adult population*
18-29	30	24	37	21
30-49	38	39	37	34
50-64	30	35	23	26
65+	3	2	3	19

*Gallup Daily tracking, March 4-April 14, 2014

GALLUP'

Newly Insured Have Lower Incomes

The newly insured have lower-than-average annual household incomes, as might be expected. This skew toward the lowest income categories is particularly prevalent among those who signed up through the exchanges, who are significantly more likely than the overall population to be in the less than $24,000 household income category. This low-income skew among those who used the exchanges is partly related to their being less likely to be employed full time and more likely to be out of the workforce than those who obtained insurance outside of the exchanges.

Profiles of Newly Insured, by Income

	All newly insured in 2014	Newly insured in 2014 through exchanges	Newly insured in 2014 not through exchanges	National adult population*
Less than $24,000	38	42	33	23
$24,000-$59,999	37	36	39	31
$60,000-$89,999	9	6	13	14
$90,000+	5	4	8	16

*Gallup Daily tracking, March 4-April 14, 2014

GALLUP'

Self-Reported Health of Newly Insured Mirrors National Average

The self-reported health status of the newly insured as a group is not significantly different from the health status of the overall population. Given that those aged 65 and older describe their health in somewhat less positive terms than younger people, and given that the newly insured are mostly younger than 65, this is particularly important. The intent of the individual mandate, broadly speaking, was to bring healthy people—with their lower probability of needing to use their insurance—into the healthcare system. A strong skew among the newly insured toward healthier Americans has apparently not yet materialized.

Profiles of Newly Insured, by Self-Reported Health Status

	All newly insured in 2014	Newly insured in 2014 through exchanges	Newly insured in 2014 not through exchanges	National adult population*
Excellent	16	12	21	21
Very good	26	25	28	29
Good	34	36	31	29
Fair	15	14	16	13
Poor	6	8	3	5

*Gallup Daily tracking, March 4-April 14, 2014

GALLUP'

Newly Insured Skew Democratic in Political Orientation

All of the newly insured are more likely to identify with or lean toward the Democratic Party than the overall national adult population. Those who signed up through exchanges are the most likely to tilt Democratic and not Republican.

This political skew in those who have signed up for health insurance reflects two phenomenon. First, being young and having a low income are both associated with a Democratic political orientation. Second, the relationship between Americans' political orientation and their views toward the ACA is well-documented. It is likely that previously uninsured Democrats are more inclined to be sympathetic to the aims of the legislation and to sign up for insurance than are uninsured Republicans.

Profiles of Newly Insured, by Partisanship

	All newly insured in 2014	Newly insured in 2014 through exchanges	Newly insured in 2014 not through exchanges	National adult population*
Republican/ lean	24	19	30	39
Democratic/ lean	54	58	49	43

*Gallup Daily tracking, March 4-April 14, 2014

GALLUP'

Survey Methods

Results for this Gallup poll are based on telephone interviews conducted March 4–April 14, 2014, on the Gallup Daily tracking survey, with a random sample of 20,804 adults, aged 18 and older, living in all 50 U.S. states and the District of Columbia.

For results based on the total sample of national adults, the margin of sampling error is ±1 percentage points at the 95% confidence level. For results based on the total sample of 649 adults who are newly insured, the margin of sampling error is ±5 percentage points at the 95% confidence level. For results based on the samples of 356 and 292 adults who are newly insured through exchanges and newly insured not through exchanges, respectively, the margins of sampling errors are ±7 percentage points at the 95% confidence level.

April 17, 2014
AMERICANS SOLD ON REAL ESTATE AS BEST LONG-TERM INVESTMENT
Lower-income Americans prefer gold to stocks, savings accounts, bonds

by Rebecca Riffkin

WASHINGTON, D.C.—Americans today are more likely to think real estate is the best option for long-term investments than in the past, ranking it ahead of gold and stocks.

Which of the following do you think is the best long-term investment -- [ROTATED: bonds, real estate, savings accounts or CDs, stocks or mutual funds, (or) gold]?

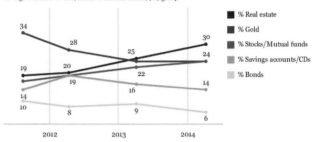

■ % Real estate
■ % Gold
■ % Stocks/Mutual funds
■ % Savings accounts/CDs
▨ % Bonds

April 2012 question asked to a half sample

GALLUP'

Perceived Best Investment, by Income

Which of the following do you think is the best long-term investment -- [bonds, real estate, savings accounts or CDs, stocks or mutual funds, (or) gold]?

	Real estate	Gold	Stocks/ Mutual funds	Savings accounts/CDs	Bonds
	%	%	%	%	%
$75,000 and over	38	18	30	7	7
$30,000 to $74,999	26	26	25	16	6
Less than $30,000	28	31	13	17	7

April 3-6, 2014

GALLUP'

These results are from Gallup's April 3–6 Economy and Personal Finances poll that asked Americans to choose the best option for long-term investments: real estate, stocks and mutual funds, gold, savings accounts and CDs, or bonds. Prior to 2011, Gallup asked the same question, but did not include gold as an option.

Gold was the most popular long-term investment among Americans in 2011—a time when gold was at its highest market price and real estate and stock values were lower than they are today. Gold prices dropped significantly after that and it lost favor with Americans. The 24% of Americans who currently name gold as the best long-term investment ties with the 24% who choose stocks.

Bonds have been Americans' least favored investment option for as long as Gallup has been asking the question. Savings accounts and CDs, on the other hand, have been more popular in the past. In September 2008, before gold was an option and at a time when the real estate and stock markets were tanking, savings accounts were the most popular long-term investment among Americans.

This year, the housing market has been improving across the U.S., and home prices have recently been rising after a steep drop in 2007 during the subprime mortgage crisis. This current improvement in prices may be why more Americans now consider real estate the best option for long-term investments. In 2002, during the real estate boom that preceded the mortgage crisis and before gold was offered as an option in the question, half of Americans said real estate was the best investment choice.

Stock values have also been improving in recent years, aided particularly by the bull market in 2013. The 24% of Americans who regard stocks as the best long-term investment is also higher now, up from 19% in 2012. Still, Americans are modestly more likely to say real estate is the better investment today, perhaps because of the recent volatility in the stock market.

Lower-Income Americans the Only Subgroup to Favor Gold

Lower-income Americans, those living in households with less than $30,000 in annual income, are the most likely of all income groups to say gold is the best long-term investment choice, at 31%. Upper-income Americans are the least likely to name gold, at 18%.

Upper-income Americans are much more likely to say real estate and stocks are the best investment, possibly because of their experience with these types of investments. Upper-income Americans are most likely to say they own their home, at 87%, followed by middle (66%) and lower-income Americans (36%). Gallup found that homeowners (33%) are slightly more likely than renters (24%) to say real estate is the best choice for long-term investments.

Stock investors are also more likely to favor stocks as the best long-term investment; 34% of them say that stocks are the best option compared with 13% of Americans who don't own stocks. Upper-income Americans are again the most likely to own stocks (82%), followed by middle- (57%) and lower-income Americans (16%).

Young Americans Place More Faith in Savings Accounts and CDs

Americans between 18 and 29 years old are almost evenly split, with about one-quarter each saying real estate, stocks, gold, and savings accounts are the best choices for long-term investments. However, the 23% who said savings accounts is much higher than the percentage who gave this same answer in older age groups.

Perceived Best Investment, by Subgroup

Which of the following do you think is the best long-term investment -- [bonds, real estate, savings accounts or CDs, stocks or mutual funds, (or) gold]?

	Real estate	Gold	Stocks/ Mutual funds	Savings accounts/CDs	Bonds
	%	%	%	%	%
18 to 29 years	25	21	24	23	7
30 to 49 years	34	21	23	14	6
50 to 64 years	30	28	23	10	6
65+ years	31	23	28	7	8
Republicans	30	26	26	12	5
Independents	33	25	19	14	6
Democrats	27	19	30	14	6

April 3-6, 2014

GALLUP'

These differences again could reflect actual home ownership and familiarity with the real estate purchasing process. Less than 30% of Americans between 18 and 29 own their home, compared with 68% of 30- to 49-year-olds, 73% of 50- to 64-year-olds, and 83% of those aged 65 and older. Younger Americans could favor savings accounts because they've largely become financially independent adults during a time of volatile housing and stock markets. This age group's relative preference to savings accounts is in line with findings from 2013.

Implications

With housing prices improving across the country, Americans are regaining faith that real estate is the best choice for long-term investments. But home ownership is also associated with views of real estate as an attractive investment opportunity. This leaves groups with lower home ownership rates, like lower-income and younger Americans, still looking elsewhere for investment options.

Likewise, stock values have been improving and Americans are more likely now than in recent years to say stocks are the best investment, though more still choose real estate. That could be partly attributable to more Americans owning a home than owning stocks, but could also be related to recent volatility in stocks this year, especially during the time the survey was conducted.

Different investment options historically offer different levels of risk and different rewards. Savings accounts and bonds are historically safe, but do not offer as high of returns, and Americans typically don't regard those as the best investments. While stocks can be more volatile, they also can offer huge returns. What Americans view as the best choice for investing reflects myriad factors and is influenced by how the investment is currently performing and respondents' biases toward where they are invested.

Survey Methods

Results for this Gallup poll are based on telephone interviews conducted April 3–6, 2014, with a random sample of 1,026 adults, aged 18 and older, living in all 50 U.S. states and the District of Columbia.

For results based on the total sample of national adults, the margin of sampling error is ±4 percentage points at the 95% confidence level.

April 17, 2014
ON ECONOMY, AMERICANS LESS CONFIDENT IN FEDERAL LEADERS
Record low for Obama, Democratic and Republican leaders in Congress

by Justin McCarthy

WASHINGTON, D.C.—Less than half of Americans (42%) have confidence in President Barack Obama on doing or recommending the right thing for the economy—the lowest figure Gallup has on record for him. New lows in confidence were also found for Democratic leaders (35%), while Republican leaders in Congress received the lowest mark on record for either party (24%). Americans have more confidence in business leaders and state governors than federal political leaders.

Americans' Confidence in Economic Leaders

Please tell me how much confidence you have in each to do or to recommend the right thing for the economy -- a great deal, a fair amount, only a little, or almost none. How about ... ?

	Great deal/ Fair amount	Only a little/ Almost none
	%	%
Business leaders	52	43
State governors	51	45
President Barack Obama	42	57
Federal Reserve Chair Janet Yellen	37	43
Democratic leaders in Congress	35	61
Treasury Secretary Jack Lew	30	48
Republican leaders in Congress	24	71

April 3-6, 2014

GALLUP

Gallup's current Economic Confidence Index score (–17) is virtually the same as where it was one year ago (–16), but Americans have less confidence in their elected officials to deal with the economy than they did a year ago. The depressed confidence in political leaders may be a lingering effect of October's federal government shutdown.

This is the first time President Obama's rating has fallen below the 50% mark on the question of Americans' confidence in his ability to recommend the right thing for the economy. Apart from his first honeymoon year in office when he garnered 71% confidence on this question, the president has had the confidence of between 50% and 57% of the American people when it comes to his economic dealings.

These findings are from Gallup's annual Economy and Personal Finance survey conducted April 3–6, 2014. Gallup has asked this question each year since 2001 for the president, congressional leaders, and the U.S. Federal Reserve chair.

Confidence in President Obama on the Economy

% Great deal/Fair amount of confidence

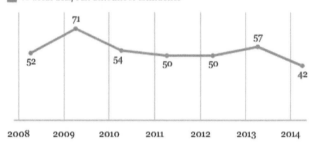

*2008 wording: Senator Obama

GALLUP

President Obama's current rating on the question took a 15-percentage-point dive from last year, and it is now the same as his current job approval score. Compared with his predecessor, Americans have the same degree of confidence now as they did in then-President George W. Bush during his sixth year in office (44%).

Federal Reserve Board Chair Janet Yellen (37%) and Treasury Secretary Jack Lew (30%), both Obama appointees, stimulate less confidence among the American public currently than the president does. Both, however, are relatively new to their jobs, and Americans' lack of familiarity with them may keep their scores lower.

Confidence in Congressional Leaders on the Economy, by Party

% Great deal/Fair amount of confidence

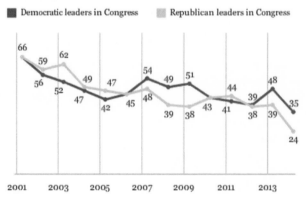

GALLUP

Confidence on Economic Issues Even More Dismal for Leaders in Congress

Americans have even lower confidence in congressional leaders of both parties than the president, as is typically the case. However, their confidence in congressional leaders on economic matters is the lowest Gallup has measured to date.

Democratic congressional leaders experienced a new low, at 35%, falling 13 points from last year. For Republicans, who took the brunt of the political fallout from the shutdown, only a quarter (24%) of Americans have confidence in their party's leaders in Congress, down from 39% in 2013.

Business Leaders, Governors Retain Higher Confidence on Economy

Leaders in business rank highest in Americans' confidence on economic recommendations (52%), slightly down from the 54% they received in both 2010 and 2011.

Americans' view state governors more confidently on economic issues (51%) than their federally elected counterparts in Washington, though less so than the finding of 58% in 2011 when Gallup last asked Americans to rate governors.

State governors may be rated higher because Americans generally express more trust in state government than in federal government. Americans may also see state governors, as well as business leaders, in less overtly political terms than federal political leaders.

Bottom Line

It has been six months since the federal government shutdown, and its aftermath still creates tremors throughout the collective American psyche.

Though confidence in the economy itself has recovered from the shutdown, confidence in the elected officials who strongly influence the economy seems to not have recovered. This is evident in the lack of change from last year's Economic Confidence Index reading versus the dramatic drop in confidence in elected leaders' economic recommendations.

While many election reporters expect 2014 to be a good midyear election year for the Republican Party, Gallup's data don't give that indication, as congressional Republicans received the lowest confidence score for either party on record for issues pertaining to the economy. But Democrats—including the president himself—saw their ratings drop as well. This reflects a national loss of confidence for elected officials across the board as all remember Congress' willingness to play political chicken with the U.S. economy.

Survey Methods

Results for this Gallup poll are based on telephone interviews conducted April 3–6, 2014, on the Gallup Daily tracking survey, with a random sample of 1,026 adults, aged 18 and older, living in all 50 U.S. states and the District of Columbia.

For results based on the total sample of national adults, the margin of sampling error is ±5 percentage points at the 95% confidence level.

April 21, 2014
AMERICANS CONTINUE TO ENJOY SAVING MORE THAN SPENDING
Gap largest among lower-income Americans and Southerners

by Brendan Moore

WASHINGTON, D.C.—The majority of Americans continue to enjoy saving money more than spending it, by 62% to 34%. The 2014 saving-spending gap is the one of the widest since Gallup began tracking Americans' preferences in 2001.

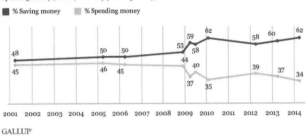

Americans' Enjoyment of Saving and Spending

Thinking about money for a moment, are you the type of person who -- [ROTATED: more enjoys spending money (or who) more enjoys saving money]?

These results are from Gallup's April 3–6 Economy and Personal Finance poll.

It may be surprising that the gap between self-reported enjoyment of saving and enjoyment is as wide as it is in 2014, considering the recent signs of positive momentum in the U.S. economy. Prior to the Great Recession, the saving-spending enjoyment gap was much smaller than it is now. After the onset of the economic downturn, the divergence widened considerably over the next couple of years, including 2010, when the gap stretched as wide as 27 percentage points. But then there was a short-lived narrowing of the gap to 19 points in 2012 before it increased again in 2013 and 2014.

While this question does not measure actual spending or saving, it provides important insight into the psychology of the American consumer's approach to money. At this point, the trend suggests that Americans have shifted their mindset significantly more toward the view that saving is the more enjoyable behavior, not spending.

Region and Income Linked With Saving vs. Spending

Americans' views vary little across the standard demographic segments of the U.S. population such as age, race, education, and political party.

But there are noticeable differences in saving versus spending preferences by region. The South has the largest tilt toward "saving" over "spending"—by 73% to 23%. The West has the smallest disparity, with only 51% favoring saving to 45% spending.

There are also significant differences by household income level, with those in the lowest income category (earning less than $20,000 a year) more than three times as likely to favor saving (73%) over spending (21%). The gap narrows to 63% to 36% among the highest income bracket (earning $75,000 or more per year).

Views on Spending vs. Saving, by Financial Outlook Groups

There is a sizable gap in self-reported enjoyment of spending and saving between stock market investors and non-investors, with self-identified investors more likely than non-investors to report enjoying spending, 38% versus 29%, respectively.

Thinking about money for a moment, are you the type of person who --
[ROTATED: more enjoys spending money (or who) more enjoys saving money]?

	Spending money	Saving money
	%	%
18 to 29	33	64
30 to 49	37	61
50 to 64	34	63
65+	34	62
White	35	61
Nonwhite	32	64
East	39	59
Midwest	37	60
South	23	73
West	45	51
Less than $20,000	21	73
$20,000 to $29,000	37	62
$30,000 to $49,000	39	59
$50,000 to $74,999	41	58
$75,000+	36	63
High school or less	30	68
Some college	41	55
College graduate only	33	65
Postgraduate	34	61
Republicans	34	64
Independents	31	66
Democrats	41	55

April 3-6, 2014

GALLUP

But for the most part, Americans' preferences for spending or saving do not tend to be linked to their views of the U.S. economy or to the severity of their financial worries. Americans who are more optimistic about the U.S. economy show little difference in enjoyment of spending or saving compared with Americans who are more negative.

Differences in Saving vs. Spending, by Economic and Financial Outlook Group

Thinking about money for a moment, are you the type of person who -- [ROTATED: more enjoys spending money (or who) more enjoys saving money]?

	Spending money	Saving money
	%	%
Those who rate the U.S. economy as excellent/good	35	61
Those who rate the U.S. economy as fair/poor	34	63
Those who say the U.S. economy is getting better	38	58
Those who say the U.S. economy is getting worse	32	66
Financial worry index: 0 (low)	32	64
Financial worry index: 1 to 2	37	60
Financial worry index: 3 to 5	36	59
Financial worry index: 6 to 7 (high)	30	69
Stock investor: Yes	38	59
Stock investor: No	29	67

April 3-6, 2014

GALLUP

There is also remarkably little difference in these self-reports based on worry about financial problems. Those who are most worried about finances are only slightly more likely to say they enjoy saving than those who are least worried.

Implications

The majority of Americans continue to report enjoying saving more than spending. However, this trend is not necessarily indicative of actual behavior. While the number of Americans to report greater enjoyment of saving has been increasing in recent years, so has personal consumption. Although Americans, since 2009, have been significantly more likely to enjoy saving, or perhaps more likely to feel guilty about spending, their views have not been evident in their real-world behavior.

This disconnection between desired state and actual behavior could have significant implications.

On a macro level, economists would typically view increases in personal consumption as a positive sign of an improving economy. But if the increases in spending are occurring out of necessity, not desire, and Americans take on more debt or deplete their savings, the picture may not be quite as rosy. Data from the U.S. Department of Commerce show that the 2013 average personal savings rate was 4.5%, the lowest since 2007 and low historically. The U.S. average personal savings rate in the 1970s was 11.8%, 9.3% in the 1980s, and 6.7% in the 1990s.

Stagnant wage growth and the overall sluggish recovery from the Great Recession perhaps have contributed to decreasing personal savings. While Gallup data indicate a stronger preference to save than to spend, in reality Americans seem to be having difficulty putting together a safety net. This has more than likely contributed to the lingering pessimism about the U.S. economy.

Survey Methods

Results for this Gallup poll are based on telephone interviews conducted April 3–6, 2014, with a random sample of 1,026 adults, aged 18 and older, living in all 50 U.S. states and the District of Columbia.

For results based on the total sample of national adults, the margin of sampling error is ±5 percentage points at the 95% confidence level.

April 21, 2014

YOUNG ADULTS CITE COLLEGE COSTS AS THEIR TOP MONEY PROBLEM
General mentions of college expenses at decade high, energy costs dip

by Lydia Saad

PRINCETON, NJ—Paying tuition or college loans far exceeds other money matters as the top financial challenge young adults in the U.S. say they face today. More than one in five adults aged 18 to 29 mention college costs as the biggest financial problem their families are dealing with, well exceeding the percentage of older Americans who identify this as their top issue.

These findings are based on Gallup's annual Economy and Personal Finance poll, conducted April 3–6, in which respondents were asked to name, in their own words, the top financial problem facing their families.

Top Financial Problems Facing Family, by Age
April 3-6, 2014

	18 to 29 years	30 to 49 years	50 to 64 years	65 and older
1.	College expenses/ loans 21%	College expenses/ loans 14%	Healthcare 15%	Healthcare 15%
2.	Lack of money/low wages 15%	Lack of money/low wages 14%	Bills/Credit cards/Debt 14%	Lack of money/low wages 13%
3.	Housing 14%	Healthcare 13%	Lack of money/low wages 12%	Cost of living/ Inflation 12%
4.	Bills/Credit cards/Debt 10%	Bills/Credit cards/Debt 10%	Cost of living/ Inflation 12%	Bills/Credit cards/Debt 7%
5.	Lack of work or job 8%	Cost of living/ Inflation 10%	Retirement savings 11%	Retirement savings 7%
6.	Gas/Transportation costs 6%	Lack of work or job 8%	Lack of work or job 10%	Housing 6%
7.	Cost of living/ Inflation 5%	Housing 6%	Housing 9%	Lack of work or job 3%
8.	Healthcare 4%	Taxes 5%	College expenses/ loans 7%	Taxes 3%
9.	Retirement savings 2%	Retirement savings 4%	Gas/Transportation costs 3%	College expenses/ loans 1%
10.	Taxes 1%	Gas/Transportation costs 3%	Taxes 2%	Gas/Transportation costs 1%

GALLUP

While college expenses outpace all other financial concerns among the youngest adults, it ties with overall lack of money or low wages as the top concern of those aged 30 to 49. And it ranks near the bottom of the top 10 financial problems that older Americans name, mentioned by 7% of 50- to 64 year-olds and 1% of seniors—those aged 65 and older.

Housing costs also emerge as a relatively bigger concern for younger adults (14%) than those aged 30 and older (9% or less). At the same time, at 5%, cost of living/inflation is a particularly low concern for young adults, perhaps because this age group has not been paying bills long enough to experience as much change in prices as have older adults.

What is the most important financial problem facing your family today?
Recent trend

	Apr 3-6, 2014	Apr 4-7, 2013	Apr 9-12, 2012
	%	%	%
Lack of money/Low wages	13	14	18
Healthcare costs	12	10	12
College expenses	11	9	7
Paying bills/credit cards/Debt	10	11	9
High cost of living/Inflation	10	11	11
Cost of owning/renting a home	8	9	12
Unemployment/Loss of job	8	7	9
Retirement savings	6	6	4
Taxes	3	5	5
Gas/Transportation costs	3	1	1
State of the economy	3	1	1
Lack of savings	2	2	3
Interest rates	2	1	*
Social Security	1	1	1
Utility/Energy costs	1	5	11
Controlling spending	1	1	1
Stock market/Investments	1	1	1
Other	5	2	4
None	12	13	11
No opinion	3	5	4

*Adds to more than 100% as a result of multiple mentions

GALLUP

Despite the availability of Medicare for seniors, healthcare is the chief concern of adults aged 65 and older as well as those aged 50 to 64, mentioned by 15% of both groups. However, other issues come close, including paying bills—for 50- to 64-year-olds—and lack of money—for seniors.

Concern about retirement savings spikes to 11% among pre-seniors—those aged 50 to 64—and it remains an issue for 7% of seniors. But it is barely referenced by those aged 18 to 29 or 30 to 49, a possible sign that these younger age groups are not as focused on retirement savings as they should be.

Many Issues Stretching Family Finances

Among Americans nationally, several issues, including lack of money, healthcare costs, college expenses, debt, and the high cost of living, cluster at the top of the list of responses—each mentioned by at least 10% of adults. Between 5% and 10% mention housing costs, unemployment, and saving for retirement.

Americans' top-of-mind mentions of utility/energy costs are now at an all-time low—1% versus as high as 29% in 2008. At the same time, the 11% mentioning college expenses—mainly tuition and college loans—is at an all-time high.

Notably, despite evidence that the rate of those with no health insurance has dropped to a five-year low, the percentage of Americans mentioning healthcare costs as their top financial worry is up slightly from 2013 and largely similar to its level found over the past five years.

Most Important Financial Problem -- Trend in Selected Mentions

■ % Healthcare costs ■ % College expenses ■ % Utility/Energy costs

GALLUP

Meeting Basic Needs Leads Low-Income Americans' Concerns

Americans in households making less than $30,000 a year are most likely to cite lack of money, difficulty paying their rent or mortgage, and difficulty paying bills or debt as their family's primary financial problems. Middle-income Americans' perspectives are slightly different, as they are focused more on the cost of living/inflation and healthcare expenses.

Upper-income Americans also struggle with healthcare costs, but they otherwise focus on two concerns that are unique to their income-level: college expenses and retirement savings.

Bottom Line

Simply not having enough income or money and the challenge of paying bills are high-ranking concerns for every generation. However, beyond these common challenges, Americans' financial woes tend to be age-specific. Young adults are especially focused on financing higher education, seniors on paying for healthcare and affording the ever-rising cost of living, and middle-aged adults on healthcare, lack of income, and simply keeping up with bills.

Top Financial Problems Facing Family, by Household Income
April 3-6, 2014

	Less than $30,000	$30,000-$74,999	$75,000 and more
1.	Lack of money/wages 23%	Cost of living 15%	College expenses/loans 16%
2.	Housing 17%	Healthcare 14%	Healthcare 13%
3.	Bills/Credit cards/Debt 14%	Lack of money/wages 11%	Retirement savings 12%
4.	Healthcare 10%	Bills/Credit cards/Debt 11%	Lack of money/wages 8%
5.	Lack of work/job 9%	College expenses/loans 8%	Bills/Credit cards/Debt 8%
6.	College expenses/loans 8%	Lack of work/job 8%	Cost of living 8%
7.	Cost of living 4%	Housing 8%	Lack of work/job 6%
8.	Gas/Transportation costs 4%	Retirement savings 4%	Housing 4%
9.	Retirement savings 1%	Gas/Transportation costs 4%	Taxes 4%
10.	Taxes 1%	Taxes 3%	Gas/Transportation costs 3%

GALLUP

Looking at the population differently, upper-income Americans clearly have less concern than low- and middle-income Americans do about important financial matters, such as paying their mortgage or keeping up with bills and the cost of living. Still, a sizable segment of all income groups worries about healthcare costs, and for many affluent Americans, college expenses and retirement represent serious financial problems.

Knowing these differences could help lawmakers and financial advisers better serve consumers' financial needs. And if consumers become familiar with what others of a similar age or income-level are concerned about, it might help them better understand and cope with their own financial challenges.

Survey Methods

Results for this Gallup poll are based on telephone interviews conducted April 3–6, 2014, with a random sample of 1,026 adults, aged 18 and older, living in all 50 U.S. states and the District of Columbia.

For results based on the total sample of national adults, the margin of sampling error is ±4 percentage points at the 95% confidence level.

April 21, 2014
OBAMA JOB APPROVAL UP SLIGHTLY IN MOST RECENT QUARTER
Averages 42.4%, up from 41.2%

by Jeffrey M. Jones

PRINCETON, NJ—President Barack Obama's job approval rating averaged 42.4% during his 21st quarter in office, a slight improvement from 41.2% in the prior quarter, but still one of his lowest quarterly averages as president.

These results are based on Gallup Daily tracking interviews conducted Jan. 20 through April 19. The slight improvement in Obama's average approval rating comes after four consecutive

quarters of decline following a 51.9% rating in his 16th quarter, which included his re-election in November 2012.

Barack Obama's Quarterly Job Approval Averages

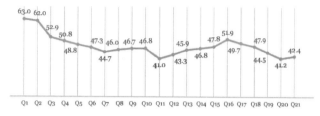

Gallup Daily tracking

GALLUP

Even with the improvement, Obama has had only two quarterly averages that were lower than the one just concluded—41.0% in his 11th quarter (July 20–Oct. 19, 2011) and 41.2% in the 20th quarter.

Obama's 21st quarter average ranks fourth of the six for the post–World War II presidents elected to two presidential terms. It is significantly lower than those of Bill Clinton, Ronald Reagan, and Dwight Eisenhower, but higher than those of George W. Bush and Richard Nixon. Nixon's 26% average came as he was embroiled in the Watergate scandal, and Bush's as the Iraq war was becoming increasingly unpopular.

Quarterly Job Approval Averages for Presidents During Their 21st Quarter in Office, Presidents Elected to Two Terms

President	Dates of 21st quarter	21st quarter job approval average	Number of polls
Eisenhower	Jan 20-Apr 19, 1958	53.0%	5
Nixon	Jan 20-Apr 19, 1974	26.1%	7
Reagan	Jan 20-Apr 19, 1986	62.5%	2
Clinton	Jan 20-Apr 19, 1998	63.3%	9
G.W. Bush	Jan 20-Apr 19, 2006	38.5%	8
Obama	Jan 20-Apr 19, 2014	42.4%	87

Harry Truman and Lyndon Johnson were not elected to their first term in office but were elected to a second term and served a 21st quarter in office. Truman averaged 41.3% approval from April 20- July 19, 1950, and Johnson averaged 45.3% approval from Oct. 20, 1968-Jan. 19, 1969.

GALLUP

Compared with the entire set of 273 presidential quarters for which Gallup has collected data since 1945, Obama's 21st quarter average ranks in the 21st percentile. That is, 20% of all presidential quarterly averages have been lower, and 79% have been higher.

Obama's job approval rating has averaged 48% throughout his presidency to date, which is better than Harry Truman's, Gerald Ford's, and Jimmy Carter's averages during their entire presidencies but lower than the averages for other post–World War II presidents. Obama has 11 quarters remaining in his presidency.

Implications

Despite the uptick in Obama's approval ratings during the last quarter, Obama's average approval rating remains low by historical standards, and could be troublesome for the Democratic Party heading into this fall's midterm elections. While most presidents' parties lose seats in the president's second midterm, the losses have been greater for less popular presidents than more popular presidents. Obama's party may be spared big losses in the House given the large number of seats that flipped from Democratic to Republican during his first midterm election in 2010, but many Senate Democrats remain vulnerable to defeat after having been elected in 2008, a strong Democratic year.

Obama's job approval rating has been higher in the last weeks of the quarter than in the earlier weeks, including his current rating of 44% for the week ending April 20. If Obama's job approval average stays at that slightly higher level during his next quarter, or increases, he would be the only twice-elected president other than Reagan to show even marginal improvement in his 22nd quarter average approval rating from his 21st.

Survey Methods

Results for this Gallup poll are based on telephone interviews conducted Jan. 20–April 19, 2014, on the Gallup Daily tracking survey, with a random sample of 44,167 adults, aged 18 and older, living in all 50 U.S. states and the District of Columbia.

For results based on the total sample of national adults, the margin of sampling error is ±1 percentage point at the 95% confidence level.

April 22, 2014

ONE IN FOUR IN U.S. ARE SOLIDLY SKEPTICAL OF GLOBAL WARMING

Nearly 40% are "Concerned Believers" in global warming, others are mixed

by Lydia Saad

PRINCETON, NJ—Over the past decade, Americans have clustered into three broad groups on global warming. The largest, currently describing 39% of U.S. adults, are what can be termed "Concerned Believers"—those who attribute global warming to human actions and are worried about it. This is followed by the "Mixed Middle," at 36%. And one in four Americans—the "Cool Skeptics"—are not worried about global warming much or at all.

Gallup Global Warming Opinion Groups

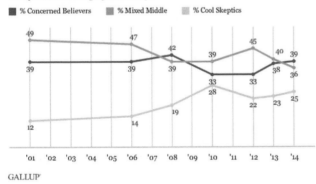

GALLUP

The rate of Concerned Believers has varied some over the past decade and half, but is currently identical to the earliest estimate, from 2001. Over the same period of time, the ranks of Cool Skeptics have swelled, while the Mixed Middle—once the largest group—has declined modestly.

These groupings stem from a special "cluster" analysis of four questions that measure Americans' belief and concerns about human-induced global warming, all of which have been asked together on Gallup's annual Environment survey seven times since 2001. The latest results are from the March 6–9, 2014, Environment poll. However, the groupings derive from analysis of seven years of combined data.

Gallup has recently reported on a number of the individual trends included in the cluster analysis as part of its Climate Change series. This analysis provides a unique way of summarizing Americans' overall stance on global warming.

Perceived Cause of Global Warming Is Major Discriminator

Concerned Believers and Cool Skeptics are of entirely different mindsets when it comes to how much they worry about global warming. Concerned Believers say they worry "a great deal" or a "fair amount" about the issue, while Cool Skeptics worry only "a little" or "not at all." Additionally, Concerned Believers think media reports about the issue are either correct or underestimated, while Cool Skeptics think they are exaggerated. And, most starkly, 100% of Concerned Believers say the rise in the Earth's temperature over the last century is due to the effects of pollution, while 100% of Cool Skeptics say it is due to natural changes in the environment. Finally, two-thirds of Concerned Believers believe global warming will pose a serious threat to their own way of life in the future, while 100% of Cool Skeptics disagree.

Americans in the Mixed Middle are individuals who hold a combination of views. For instance, some believe humans are the cause of the Earth's warming, but aren't worried about it. Others say global warming is a natural phenomenon, but that it will pose a serious risk in their lifetime. In one way or another, those in the Mixed Middle fail to line up with the orthodoxy on either side of the climate science issue.

Gallup Global Warming Opinion Groups -- Detail of 2014 Attitudes
March 6-9, 2014

	Concerned Believers	Mixed Middle	Cool Skeptics
	%	%	%
How much personally worry about global warming?			
...A great deal	67	24	
...A fair amount	33	26	
...Only a little		31	31
...Not at all		19	69
...No opinion		1	
Seriousness of global warming in the news:			
...Underestimated	58	30	
...Correct	42	19	
...Exaggerated		46	100
...No opinion		5	
Cause of the rise in Earth's temperatures:			
...Effects of pollution from human activities	100	51	
...Natural changes in environment		41	100
...No opinion		8	
Will global warming pose a serious threat to your way of life in your lifetime?			
...Yes	65	30	
...No	35	68	100
...No opinion		2	

GALLUP

Global Warming Clusters Differ by Gender, Age, and Politics

Concerned Believers are more likely to be women than men, 60% vs. 40%. Cool Skeptics skew even more strongly male—34% female vs. 66% male—while the Mixed Middle is just slightly more female than the overall U.S. adult population.

Global warming groups are also highly differentiated by age and politics. The majority of Concerned Believers are younger than 50, and identify as or lean toward the Democratic Party, whereas the majority of Cool Skeptics are 50 years or older and are more likely to identify as or lean Republican. Similarly, the plurality of believers are self-described liberals, while two-thirds of skeptics call themselves conservative.

Notably, education is not a strong discriminator for the polarized groups, as a little over one-third of each group has no college experience, roughly 30% has some, and about one-third has a college degree or some advanced education. On the other hand, lack of college education *is* a distinguishing characteristic of the Mixed Middle, with nearly half this group reporting no more than a high school diploma, and less than one-quarter finishing college.

Gallup Global Warming Opinion Groups -- Demographic Profile

March 6-9, 2014

	Concerned Believers	Mixed Middle	Cool Skeptics
	%	%	%
Men	40	45	66
Women	60	55	34
18 to 29	23	27	10
30 to 49	39	29	34
50 to 64	25	21	33
65 and older	14	23	23
High school or less	37	48	35
Some college	29	28	30
College graduate	14	12	17
Postgraduate	19	10	18
Republicans/Lean Republican	18	42	80
Democrats/Lean Democratic	76	44	11
Conservative	18	33	65
Moderate	38	42	24
Liberal	42	23	9

GALLUP'

Bottom Line

Gallup's "cluster analysis" of Americans' views on four key global warming questions finds the public naturally breaking into three groups. The two at the extremes are near polar opposites of each other, disagreeing about the cause of global warming and how it's presented in the news, as well as having sharply different personal reactions to the issue.

The ranks of skeptics expanded between 2008 and 2010 due to the decline in concern about global warming as documented in Gallup's original trends. In particular, the percentage of Americans believing that global warming is caused by pollution from human activities dropped sharply in 2010. The same pattern has been seen with personal worry about global warming and the perception that the seriousness of the issue is exaggerated in the news. All of these findings are likely linked to the high profile "Climategate" controversy that emerged in late 2009, raising questions about the objectivity of some leading climate science researchers, as well as the legitimacy of some of their findings.

The broader, and perhaps more important, point is that even while skepticism rose—causing a corresponding increase in the percentage of Americans who can be categorized as "Cool Skeptics"—the percentage of "Concerned Believers" has recovered to pre-Climategate levels, while the Mixed Middle has dwindled. As with many issues in the past decade, Americans' views have grown more polarized.

Survey Methods

Results for this Gallup poll are based on telephone interviews conducted March 6–9, 2014, on with a random sample of 1,048 adults, aged 18 and older, living in all 50 U.S. states and the District of Columbia.

For results based on the total sample of national adults, the margin of sampling error is ±4 percentage points at the 95% confidence level.

April 22, 2014
RETIREMENT REMAINS AMERICANS' TOP FINANCIAL WORRY
Middle-aged Americans most concerned about retirement

by Andrew Dugan

WASHINGTON, D.C.—A firm majority of Americans, 59%, are worried about not having enough money for retirement, surpassing eight other financial matters. A majority of Americans have reported being "very" or "moderately" worried about retirement savings every year since 2001, illustrating that saving for retirement disquiets Americans in both good and bad economic times.

Americans' Top Financial Concerns

Next, please tell me how concerned you are right now about each of the following financial matters, based on your current financial situation -- are you very worried, moderately worried, not too worried, or not worried at all?

	Very worried/ Moderately worried	Not too worried/ Not at all worried
	%	%
Not having enough money for retirement	59	35
Not being able to pay medical costs in the event of a serious illness or accident	53	45
Not being able to maintain the standard of living you enjoy	48	52
Not having enough money to pay off your debt	40	48
Not being able to pay medical costs for normal healthcare	39	57
Not having enough to pay your normal monthly bills	36	62
Not having enough money to pay for your children's college	35	31
Not being able to pay your rent, mortgage, or other housing costs	31	64
Not being able to make the minimum payments on your credit cards	16	65

Ranked by percentage very worried/moderately worried
April 3-6, 2014

GALLUP'

These results are from Gallup's annual Economy and Personal Finance poll, conducted April 3–6 this year.

The next top concern, not being able to pay medical costs in the event of a serious illness or accident, worries 53% of Americans. This is down from a record high of 62% in 2012.

Third on the list of Americans' top financial worries is not being able to maintain the standard of living they enjoy, with nearly half of the country's adults citing this concern. Together, retirement savings, unexpected medical costs, and maintaining one's standard of living typically top the list of the eight financial items that Gallup has tracked annually since 2001. Concerns about all three are down modestly from two years ago, but are still higher than they were before the Great Recession.

Americans' Top Financial Concerns, 2001 to 2014
% Very/Moderately worried

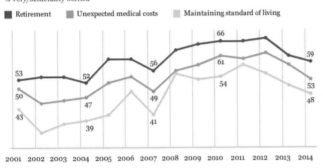

GALLUP

Notably, four in 10 American adults say they are very or moderately worried about not having enough money to pay off their debt. This is the first time Gallup has included this financial issue. With as much as $1 trillion in outstanding student loan debt circulating in the U.S. today—not to mention other prevalent types of debt such as credit cards—debt concerns are clearly weighing on a significant proportion of the country.

Of the nine concerns tested, the bottom two concerns—not being able to pay one's rent or mortgage, and not being able to make minimum payments on credit card bills—are those most likely to indicate immediate insolvency. This finding suggests that most common financial problems are related more to savings and future expenditures than day-to-day living.

Middle-Aged Americans Most Worried About Retirement

Personal financial concerns vary significantly across age groups. The top problem for the broadly defined group of middle-aged Americans—those aged 30 to 64—is not having enough money for retirement, in line with previous findings. For this group, about seven in 10 worry about not having enough money for retirement.

Young Americans aged 18 to 29 worry most about paying medical costs in the event of a serious illness or accident (52%), perhaps a result of the comparatively high uninsured rate for younger Americans or the lack of savings typically characterizing that age group. An equal share of 18- to 29-year-olds (52%) say they are worried about being able to maintain their standard of living. And nearly half of 18- to 29-year-olds worry about being able to pay off debt, perhaps a consequence of the massive amount of student loan debt that many young adults carry. Possibly befitting their youth and their longer distance in years from retirement, this group is least

concerned about having enough money when they retire compared with other age groups—despite dire predictions about the future of Medicare and Social Security.

Americans' Top Financial Concerns, by Age
% Very/Moderately worried

	18 to 29	30 to 49	50 to 64	65+
	%	%	%	%
Not having enough money for retirement	50	70	68	37
Not having enough money to pay for your children's college	46	55	23	8
Not being able to pay medical costs in the event of a serious illness or accident	52	54	58	43
Not having enough money to pay off your debt	47	45	42	20
Not being able to maintain the standard of living you enjoy	52	44	52	41
Not being able to pay medical costs for normal healthcare	35	37	46	33
Not having enough to pay your normal monthly bills	40	33	38	29
Not being able to pay your rent, mortgage, or other housing costs	40	30	31	20
Not being able to make the minimum payments on your credit cards	14	17	18	15

Ranked by percentage very/moderately worried among 30- to 49-year-olds
April 3-6, 2014

GALLUP

Older Americans, those aged 65 or older, also worry most about being able to pay medical costs in the event of a serious illness or accident, though few in this age group lack health insurance. However, given the formidable cost of protracted, continual medical care that often characterizes older Americans' later years, many senior citizens may feel their health insurance alone cannot handle such a financial burden. Generally speaking, though, senior citizens are much less concerned about most of these financial problems than are their younger counterparts. The majority of older Americans appear to have retirement financing under control; 37% worry about having enough money in their retirement, by far the lowest percentage of any age group. Senior citizens are least concerned about not having enough money to pay for their children's college education (8%)—presumably because older Americans already faced that challenge.

For Americans across all age groups, the ability to make minimum payments on credit card bills does not generate much concern.

Bottom Line

Retirement may be a time that many working adults look forward to, but it is paradoxically a source of stress in the here and now. A strong majority of Americans, particularly those aged 30 to 64, worry about having enough money for retirement, and this concern has regularly topped the list of Americans' top financial problems. The only other personal financial concern that a majority of Americans are very or moderately worried about is the ability to pay medical costs in the event of a serious accident or illness.

For a country that now has a life expectancy at birth of 78.7 years, retirement savings for post-work years is considered a matter of national importance. These concerns led President Barack Obama to propose a retirement savings account for working adults—MyRA—during this year's State of the Union address. It remains to be seen whether this new type of savings plan, which will be available in late 2014, will ultimately alleviate some Americans' concerns about retirement.

Additional insights on retirement are available through the Wells Fargo/Gallup Investor and Retirement Optimism Index. The Index provides quarterly updates on U.S. investors' economic optimism, as well as their views on a variety of savings and retirement issues.

Survey Methods

Results for this Gallup poll are based on telephone interviews conducted April 3–6, 2014, with a random sample of 1,026 adults, aged 18 and older, living in all 50 U.S. states and the District of Columbia.

For results based on the total sample of national adults, the margin of sampling error is ±4 percentage points at the 95% confidence level.

April 24, 2014

OPTIMISM FOR RISING U.S. HOME VALUES IS HIGHEST SINCE 2007

Majority, 56%, expect average home prices to rise in local area

by Jeffrey M. Jones

PRINCETON, NJ—Americans' growing optimism about the housing market continues, with 56% of Americans now expecting average home prices in their local area to increase. That is up from 33% just two years ago, and from a low of 21% in January 2011, but still below the readings of 60% or higher prior to the housing market downturn.

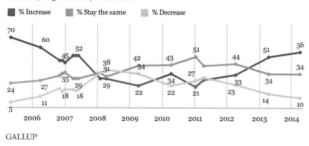

Over the next year, do you think that the average price of houses in your area will increase, stay the same, or decrease?

GALLUP

The results are based on Gallup's annual Economy and Personal Finance poll, which has tracked Americans' perceptions of the housing market annually since 2005.

From 2008 to 2011, Americans were typically more likely to expect local home values to decrease rather than increase. By April 2012, public optimism about home values outweighed pessimism by 33% to 23%. Now, more than five times as many Americans believe local home values will increase (56%) rather than decrease (10%).

Those living in the West—including the state of California where real estate values are among the fastest rising in the nation—are most likely to think home values will increase, at 72%. By comparison, 44% of Eastern residents expect home prices to increase. A slight majority of Southern (54%) and Midwestern residents (53%) agree.

Americans' views of local home values may also be influenced by their own experiences. The poll estimates 64% of Americans are homeowners. Of this group, 74% say their home is now worth more than when they bought it, up from 63% last year and 53% in 2014. Even with the increase, though, these perceptions have still not

fully recovered to what Gallup measured in 2006 and 2007, when upwards of 90% of homeowners said their home value exceeded the purchase price.

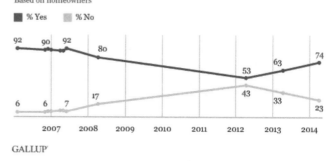

Is your home worth more than when you bought it, or not?

GALLUP

Three in Four Americans Endorse Buying a Home at Present Time

Seventy-four percent of Americans say it is a good time to buy a house, while 24% call it a bad time. That ranks among the most positive readings Gallup has found on this question.

Americans' optimism on this measure dropped sharply to 52% saying it was a good time to buy a house in 2006, just as home values were reaching their peak during the housing bubble. During the next two years, as home values plummeted, Americans continued to be less positive about buying a home. That changed in 2009, as depressed home values meant houses were a better buy than at the peak. Since then, the percentage of Americans who say it is now a good time to buy a house has been near 70%, but showing marginal increases in each of the past three years.

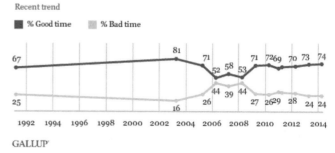

For people in general, do you think that now is a GOOD time or a BAD time to buy a house?

Recent trend

GALLUP

At 81%, homeowners are more likely than renters (60%) to say it is a good time to buy a house.

Implications

Americans continue to be more positive about the housing market than they were in the aftermath of the housing market downturn. This comes at a time when home values remain below where they were during the peak of the market in early 2006, though values are rising again. As a result, there has been a sharp increase over the last two years in the percentage of homeowners who say their house is worth more than when they bought it, which means it is likely that fewer homeowners are "underwater" on their mortgages than in recent years.

Americans' views of the housing market were clearly shaken during the downturn, but have mostly recovered today, with nearly three in four now saying it is a good time to buy a house. That could reflect the realization that the worst of the housing crisis is over, but that values have not yet risen to a level where homes are over-priced.

These more positive views of the housing market may help foster a situation in which home buying activity increases and home values continue to rise over the next year.

Survey Methods

Results for this Gallup poll are based on telephone interviews conducted April 3–6, 2014, with a random sample of 1,026 adults, aged 18 and older, living in all 50 U.S. states and the District of Columbia.

For results based on the total sample of national adults, the margin of sampling error is ±4 percentage points at the 95% confidence level.

For results based on the total sample of 737 homeowners, the margin of sampling error is ±5 percentage points at the 95% confidence level.

April 24, 2014

MONTANANS, ALASKANS SAY STATES AMONG TOP PLACES TO LIVE

Ill., R.I. residents most likely to say states are among worst places to live

by Justin McCarthy

WASHINGTON, D.C.—When asked to rate their state as a place to live, three in four Montanans (77%) and Alaskans (77%) say their state is the best or one of the best places to live. Residents of Rhode Island (18%) and Illinois (19%) are the least likely to praise their states.

Top: Residents' Views of Their State as Best Place to Live

How would you describe the state where you live?

	Best or one of the best possible states to live
Montana	77%
Alaska	77%
Utah	70%
Wyoming	69%
Texas	68%
Hawaii	68%
New Hampshire	67%
North Dakota	66%
Colorado	65%
Vermont	61%
Oregon	61%
Minnesota	61%

June-December 2013

GALLUP'

Bottom: Residents' Views of Their State as Best Place to Live

How would you describe the state where you live?

	Best or one of the best possible states to live
Rhode Island	18%
Illinois	19%
Mississippi	26%
Louisiana	27%
Michigan	28%
New Mexico	28%
New Jersey	28%
Maryland	29%
Missouri	29%
Connecticut	31%

June-December 2013

GALLUP'

Residents of Western and Midwestern states are generally more positive about their states as places to live. With the exception of the New England states of New Hampshire and Vermont, all of the top 10 rated states are west of the Mississippi River. In addition to Montana and Alaska, Utah (70%), Wyoming (69%), and Colorado (65%) are among the 10 states that residents are most likely to say their state is among the best places to reside. Most of these states have relatively low populations, including Wyoming, Vermont, North Dakota, and Alaska—the four states with the smallest populations in the nation. Texas, the second most populated state, is the major exception to this population relationship. Although it is difficult to discern what the causal relationship is between terrain and climate and positive attitudes, many of the top 10 states are mountainous with cold winters. In fact, the two states most highly rated by their residents—Montana and Alaska—not only are among the nation's coldest states but also border Canada.

With the exception of New Mexico, all of the bottom 10 states are either east of the Mississippi River or border it (Louisiana and Missouri). New Jersey (28%), Maryland (29%), and Connecticut (31%) join Rhode Island among the bottom 10.

The results are based on a special 50-state Gallup poll conducted June–December 2013, including interviews with at least 600 residents in every state. For the first time, Gallup measured whether residents view their states as "the best possible state to live in," "one of the best possible states to live in," "as good a state as any to live in," or "the worst possible state to live in."

Few Americans say their states are the single best or worst places to live. Rather, the large majority of respondents say their states were either "one of the best" or "as good a state as any" place to live.

One in Four Illinois Residents Say Their State Is the Worst Place to Live

Illinois has the unfortunate distinction of being the state with the highest percentage of residents who say it is the *worst* possible place to live. One in four Illinois residents (25%) say the state is the worst place to live, followed by 17% each in Rhode Island and Connecticut.

Throughout its history, Illinois has been rocked by high-profile scandals, investigations, and resignations from Chicago to Springfield and elsewhere throughout the state. Such scandals may explain why Illinois residents have the least trust in their state government across all 50 states. Additionally, they are among the most resentful about the amount they pay in state taxes. These factors may contribute to an overall low morale for the state's residents.

Texans Most Likely to View the Lone Star State as the Very Best

Although Texas trails Montana and Alaska in terms of its residents rating it as the best or one of the best places to live, it edges out Alaska (27%) and Hawaii (25%) in the percentage of residents who rate it as the single best place to live.

Texans' pride for their state as the single best place to live is not surprising when viewed in the context of other measures. According to Gallup Daily tracking for 2013, Texans rank high on standard of living and trust in their state government, and they are less negative than others are about the state taxes they pay. The same is true for Alaska and, to a lesser extent, Hawaii, which had relatively average scores for trust in state government and state taxes, but ranked high for standard of living. The three also have distinct histories, geographies, natural resources, and environmental features that may contribute to residents' personal enjoyment and pride in their locale.

Bottom Line

Residents with the most pride in their state as a place to live generally boast a greater standard of living, higher trust in state government, and less resentment toward the amount they pay in state taxes. However, the factors that residents use to determine whether their state is a great place to live are not always obvious. West Virginia, for example, falls far behind all other states on a variety of metrics, including economic confidence, well-being, standard of living, and stress levels. Still, over a third of West Virginians feel their state is among the best places to live, giving it a ranking near the middle of the pack.

Survey Methods

Results for this Gallup poll are based on telephone interviews conducted June–December 2013, with a random sample of approximately 600 adults per state, aged 18 and older, living in all 50 U.S. states.

For results based on the total sample of adults per state, the margin of sampling error is ±5 percentage points at the 95% confidence level.

April 28, 2014
ONE-THIRD OF AMERICANS HAVEN'T VISITED DENTIST IN PAST YEAR
Men, blacks, those with lower incomes, and Southerners less likely to see dentist

by Dan Witters

WASHINGTON, D.C.—About one in three U.S. adults say they did not visit the dentist at some point in the past 12 months. The 64.7% in 2013 who said they did visit the dentist at least once in the previous year is essentially unchanged from the rate found in 2008. Women are more likely than men to report visiting the dentist annually.

Percentage of U.S. Adults Who Have Visited the Dentist Over the Previous 12 Months

	2008	2013	Change
	%	%	Pct. pts.
All U.S. adults	65.7	64.7	-1
Men	63.5	62.0	-1.5
Women	67.8	67.2	-0.6

Gallup-Healthways Well-Being Index

GALLUP

These findings are based on interviews with 178,072 American adults conducted during 2013 and with 354,645 adults conducted during 2008 as part of the Gallup-Healthways Well-Being Index. Respondents were asked whether they had visited the dentist in the previous 12 months. Results for all years between 2008 and 2013 are similar.

The American Dental Association recommends that adults develop a plan for dental visits with their dentist, but say even those at low risk of oral disease benefit from at least annual cleanings. Thus, one in three American adults do not meet this minimum level of dental care.

Blacks, Hispanics, and Young Adults Least Likely to Visit Dentist

Among racial and ethnic groups, 55% of both blacks and Hispanics report visiting the dentist in the past year. Whites and Asians, in contrast, each are at about 70%, demonstrating that there is a notable racial and ethnic divide. Dental visit rates across most groups are similar to levels found in 2008, although there has been a small decline among blacks since that time.

In contrast, there are much smaller differences across age groups in reported dental behaviors. Young adults aged 18 to 29 are the least likely to have visited the dentist, but only marginally less so than those who are middle aged or older. An improved rate among seniors since 2008 is offset by a similarly sized decline among those 30 to 44.

Percentage of U.S. Adults Who Have Visited the Dentist Over the Previous 12 Months, by Age and Race/Ethnicity

	2008	2013	Change
	%	%	Pct. pts.
AGE			
18 to 29	62.9	62.4	-0.5
30 to 44	67.7	64.2	-3.5
45 to 64	69.0	66.7	-2.3
65+	59.1	63.4	+4.3
RACE/ETHNICITY			
Asians	70.3	69.6	-0.7
Whites	68.7	68.4	-0.3
Hispanics	53.7	55.2	+1.5
Blacks	58.0	55.0	-3.0

Gallup-Healthways Well-Being Index

GALLUP

Dental Habits Improve With Income

The most pronounced differences in dental habits are those across income groups. Those who earn $120,000 or more annually in household income are about twice as likely as those who earn less than $12,000 to say they visited the dentist in the past 12 months, 82.3% vs. 42.7%, respectively. Dental visit rates have held steady since 2008 for top earners, while they have declined for all other groups, particularly for low- and middle-income households with incomes between $24,000 and $60,000 per year.

Percentage of U.S. Adults Who Have Visited the Dentist Over the Previous 12 Months, by Annual Household Income

	2008	2013	Change
	%	%	Pct. pts.
Less than $12,000	43.4	42.7	-0.7
$12,000 to <$24,000	47.2	45.4	-1.8
$24,000 to <$36,000	58.2	55.5	-2.7
$36,000 to <$48,000	67.3	63.1	-4.2
$48,000 to <$60,000	72.6	69.6	-3.0
$60,000 to <$90,000	78.2	75.8	-2.4
$90,000 to <$120,000	82.6	80.7	-1.9
$120,000+	82.1	82.3	+0.2

Gallup-Healthways Well-Being Index

GALLUP

Annual Dental Visits Least Common in the South

Dental visit rates are essentially unchanged in all regions compared with 2008. As was the case in 2008, 2013 rates are lowest in the South (60.0%) and highest in the East (68.9%).

Percentage of U.S. Adults Who Have Visited the Dentist Over the Previous 12 Months, by Region

	2008	2013	Change
	%	%	Pct. pts.
East	70.0	68.9	-1.1
Midwest	66.8	66.9	+0.1
West	67.2	65.5	-1.7
South	61.0	60.0	-1.0

Gallup-Healthways Well-Being Index

GALLUP'

Married Adults Much More Likely Than Nonmarried to Visit Dentist

Marital status also influences dental decisions, with those who are married much more likely to report visiting the dentist annually than those who are not married. Those who are separated are the least likely to report visiting the dentist, and rates have dropped the most among this group—nearly six percentage points—since 2008.

Percentage of U.S. Adults Who Have Visited the Dentist Over the Previous 12 Months, by Marital Status

	2008	2013	Change
	%	%	Pct. pts.
Married	71.2	70.9	-0.3
Single	62.3	60.7	-1.6
Divorced	59.3	55.9	-3.4
Domestic partner	55.5	54.6	-0.9
Widowed	53.6	53.6	0
Separated	52.4	46.6	-5.8

Gallup-Healthways Well-Being Index

GALLUP'

Implications

Poor oral care can lead to many potential negative health outcomes. Recent medical research has indicated that when combined with other risk factors, poor oral health may be linked to both heart disease and stroke, possibly due to dislodged oral bacteria entering into the bloodstream. Maternal periodontal disease, too, has been linked to preterm births, and may increase risks for other diseases such as atherosclerosis, rheumatoid arthritis, and diabetes, among others.

The percentage of adults visiting a dentist in the past year varies widely across the major U.S. racial/ethnic boundaries, and may reflect several factors, including household income. Having health insurance coverage—which is related to income—also appears to be a meaningful factor in dental visits, although the Affordable Care Act may help minimize the disparities in professional dental care among income groups. According to the American Dental Association's Health Policy Resources Center, as many as 17 million adults

could gain some form of dental coverage via the ACA over the next several years.

Regardless of income or insurance status, however, poor oral health is preventable. Health literacy, access, and motivation can all increase the likelihood of routine dental visits and help reduce the negative health outcomes associated with not visiting the dentist.

Survey Methods

Results are based on telephone interviews conducted as part of the Gallup-Healthways Well-Being Index survey Jan. 2–Dec. 29, 2013, with a random sample of 178,072 adults, and Jan. 2–Dec. 30, 2008, with a random sample of 354,645 adults, aged 18 and older, living in all 50 U.S. states and the District of Columbia.

For results based on the total sample of national adults, the margin of sampling error is ±1 percentage point at the 95% confidence level.

The margin of sampling error for most demographic groups is less than ±1 percentage point, but is as high as ±2 points for groups with smaller populations, such Asians or those who are separated from their spouse.

April 28, 2014

AVERAGE U.S. RETIREMENT AGE RISES TO 62
Younger Americans are more likely to expect to retire before age 55

by Rebecca Riffkin

WASHINGTON, D.C.—The average age at which U.S. retirees report retiring is 62, the highest Gallup has found since first asking Americans this question in 1991. This age has increased in recent years, while the average age at which non-retired Americans expect to retire, 66, has largely stayed the same. However, this age too has slowly increased from 63 in 2002.

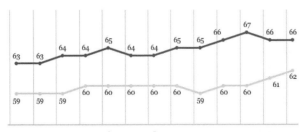

Americans' Actual vs. Expected Age of Retirement

■ Average expected retirement age among non-retirees

▧ Average actual retirement age among retirees

GALLUP'

These trends in Americans' actual vs. expected age of retirement are from Gallup's annual Economy and Personal Finance survey, conducted April 3–6, 2014. As part of that survey, Gallup asks retired Americans to report the age at which they retired, and non-retired Americans the age at which they expect to retire.

Americans' average self-reported age of retirement has slowly moved upward. Gallup conducted several polls in the early 1990s and found that the average retirement age was 57 in both 1991 and 1993. From 2002 through 2012, the average hovered around 60. Over the past two years, the average age at which Americans report retiring has increased to 62.

Retirement age may be increasing because many baby boomers are reluctant to retire. Older Americans may also be delaying retirement because of lost savings during the Great Recession or because of insufficient savings even before the economic downturn.

Meanwhile, the average age at which non-retired Americans expect to retire has also increased over time, from 60 in 1995 to 66 this year. Furthermore, in 1995, more non-retired Americans expected to retire younger—15% expected to retire before age 55, compared with 4% in 2014.

The age at which Americans expect to retire has been consistently higher than the average age at which they actually retire since Gallup began tracking both. This likely reflects changes in Social Security eligibility as well as the more challenging economic circumstances working Americans currently face. Today's workers are also less likely to have an employer-sponsored pension, and they may still be recovering financially from the Great Recession.

Young Americans Most Likely to Expect to Retire Before Age 55

About 30% of non-retired Americans in all age groups expect to retire before the age of 65. But 11% of 18- to 29-year-olds expect to retire before age 55, a much higher percentage than other groups. This could be because younger Americans, given the many years they have until retirement, may not understand the financial realities and challenges of funding retirement that middle-aged Americans are more familiar with.

Americans' Average Expected Age of Retirement

At what age do you expect to retire?

	Under 55	55 to 59	60 to 64	65	Over 65
18- to 29-year-olds	11%	4%	15%	26%	36%
30- to 49-year-olds	3%	7%	19%	33%	29%
50- to 64-year-olds	1%	5%	23%	18%	40%

Asked of non-retirees
April 3-6, 2014

GALLUP

The majority of all age groups expect to retire at age 65 or older. This includes 62% of 18- to 29-year-olds, 62% of 30- to 49-year-olds, and 58% of 50- to 64-year-olds. At the same time, an optimistic 15% of the youngest age group expect to retire before age 60. Adults closer to that age are naturally less likely to think they will be ready for retirement by that point.

The pressure to be financially prepared for retirement is evident in the recent Gallup finding that saving for retirement is Americans' top financial worry.

According to a 2011 Wells Fargo/Gallup Investor and Retirement Optimism Index survey, the value of investments is the key factor determining when pre-retired investors say they will retire, followed by their health, the cost of healthcare, and inflation. However, according to a more recent Wells Fargo/Gallup survey, U.S. investors are highly cautious about retirement savings, saying they would prefer secure investments with low growth potential over investments with high growth potential and a risk of lost principal.

Implications

Although Gallup has always found a consistent gap in the age at which retired Americans report retiring and the age at which non-retirees expect to retire, both averages have crept up over the past decade. This likely reflects the changing landscape of retirement, including longer life spans, changes in Social Security benefits and employer-sponsored retirement plans, and lifestyle choices such as a desire to keep working after reaching the traditional retirement age.

Given these trends, Americans' average retirement age being lower than their expected retirement age may reflect today's retirees hailing from a different generation. In the future, the average retirement age and expected retirement age may converge as current workers retire later in life.

Survey Methods

Results for this Gallup poll are based on telephone interviews conducted April 3–6, 2014, with a random sample of 1,026 adults, aged 18 and older, living in all 50 U.S. states and the District of Columbia.

For results based on the total sample of national adults, the margin of sampling error is ±4 percentage points at the 95% confidence level.

For results based on the sample of 334 retirees, the margin of sampling error is ±7 percentage points.

For results based on the sample of 692 non-retirees, the margin of sampling error is ±5 percentage points.

April 28, 2014

IN U.S., MOBILE TECH AIDS INTERPERSONAL COMMUNICATION MOST
Nearly nine in 10 say their communication has increased "a lot" or "a little"

by Jeffrey M. Jones

PRINCETON, NJ—Mobile technology, including the use of smartphones and tablet computers, has affected many aspects of Americans' lives, but most notably their communication with friends and family. Sixty-two percent of Americans say mobile technology has increased their interpersonal communication "a lot," with another 27% saying it has increased it "a little." Two-thirds of U.S. workers say they are now working at least a little more outside of working hours as a result of mobile technology. Slightly less than half of Americans say mobile technology has increased their political activity.

Increase in Activities as a Result of Mobile Technology

	Increased a lot	Increased a little	Not increased at all
	%	%	%
Communication with friends and family	62	27	12
Amount of work you do outside out of regular working hours ^	32	36	32
Involvement in election campaigns and other political activities	17	28	55

^Based on adults employed full or part time
March 21-23, 2014

GALLUP

The results are from a March 21–23 Gallup poll designed to assess how much mobile technology has affected Americans' behavior in the personal, political, and work areas.

The poll finds that seven in 10 Americans use either a smartphone or a tablet, devices that didn't exist 20 years ago, making the high level of reported use of a mobile device one of the most dramatic shifts in generations in the way Americans communicate and access information. These mobile devices have many implications for Americans' daily personal and work lives, allowing them to stay in touch with others outside of the home and office, and changing the way they approach their jobs.

Because mobile technology usage is higher among younger Americans, it is not surprising that younger adults are more likely than older Americans to report that mobile technology is having a greater effect across their personal, work, and political lives. But it is not just the under-30 crowd whose lives are being most affected. Those between the ages of 30 and 49 are just as likely as 18- to 29-year-olds to report that their interpersonal communication, work outside of working hours, and political involvement have increased a lot with the rise of mobile technology.

Those older than 50, particularly those 65 or older, are less likely to have been affected to a large degree by mobile technology.

Increase in Activities as a Result of Mobile Technology, by Age

Percentage whose activity has increased "a lot"

	18 to 29 years	30 to 49 years	50 to 64 years	65+ years
	%	%	%	%
Communication with friends and family	76	71	55	37
Amount of work you do outside out of regular working hours ^	37	37	25	15
Involvement in election campaigns and other political activities	21	19	14	12

^ Based on adults employed full or part time
March 21-23, 2014

GALLUP

Implications

Mobile technology has certainly increased Americans' opportunities to stay in touch and perform tasks that at one time could be accomplished only by sitting at a computer or using a landline phone. More than anything, it has increased nearly all Americans' communication with friends and family at least a little bit. Although it has had a less profound effect on the frequency with which Americans participate in the political process and work outside of regular working hours, it still has substantially affected their behavior in these areas.

Given the greater likelihood of younger Americans than older Americans to say mobile technology has increased their activity in the interpersonal, work, and political spheres, it is likely mobile technology will foster even greater activity in these areas in the future.

The increased ability to communicate with friends and family that mobile technology affords is presumably a positive, although some may complain of "communication overload" with the constant text messages, social media posts, and emailing that cause one's mobile device to beep, vibrate, or make noise throughout the day.

Whether the ability to do more work away from an employee's place of business is a positive or a negative is an intriguing question that will be answered in greater depth in a forthcoming analysis on gallup.com. Americans are less likely to report that their political

activity has increased as a result of mobile technology compared with the other areas tested, but, as Gallup will explore in a future report, the ability to reach potential voters and campaign contributors on a 24-hour basis has the potential to change how candidates and elected officials go about their business.

Survey Methods

Results for this Gallup poll are based on telephone interviews conducted March 21–23, 2014, on the Gallup Daily tracking survey, with a random sample of 1,505 adults, aged 18 and older, living in all 50 U.S. states and the District of Columbia.

For results based on the total sample of national adults, the margin of sampling error is ±3 percentage points at the 95% confidence level.

For results based on the total sample of 855 adults employed full or part time, the margin of sampling error is ±4 percentage points at the 95% confidence level.

April 29, 2014
MOBILE TECHNOLOGY IN POLITICS MORE POTENTIAL THAN REALITY
Little substantive difference in political contact among Americans

by Frank Newport

PRINCETON, NJ—Although most Americans now own mobile communication devices or otherwise have access to the Internet, no more than 23% have used them for a variety of political interactions. These results suggest that the potential use of mobile communication for connecting voters and potential voters to politics has yet to be fully realized.

Political Connection via Mobile Devices

I'm going to read a list of ways in which Americans sometimes connect electronically with campaigns, elected officials, and other political groups. For each, please tell me if within the last 30 days you have ...

	% Yes (National adults)
Received electronic communications from political interest groups through email, social media, or text message	23
Shared, "liked," or retweeted posts or links that express political opinions similar to your own	23
Received requests on your smartphone or other electronic device from interest groups asking you to contact your elected representative or take some action on a bill being considered in Congress or the state legislature	22
Received electronic communications from elected officials or candidates for office through email, social media, or text message	21
Received electronic communications from political parties through email, social media, or text message	20
Posted your opinions about politics and political issues, elected officials, elections, or candidates for office on Twitter, Facebook, or other Internet sites	16
Received instant electronic notification on your smartphone or other electronic device about political rallies or political protests in your area	9
Made a monetary donation to political candidates or political interest groups using your smartphone or tablet -- that is, using PayPal or having the dollar amount charged to your Amazon, Google, phone company, or other account	4

April 1-2, 2014

GALLUP

These results are from an April 1–2 Gallup poll assessing how mobile technology has affected Americans' political and election involvement.

The poll finds that about seven in 10 Americans use either a smartphone or a tablet, and that overall 83% are connected to the Internet through a phone, tablet, or personal computer. The use of these new mobile communication devices, and more generally the use of the Internet, have dramatically affected most aspects of Americans' lives—and politics, in theory, should be no exception. Political candidates, political parties, and those advising and running election campaigns have most certainly become aware that mobile devices represent a new frontier of political contact above and beyond the traditional use of media advertisements, phone calls, and direct mail.

Still, at this point, the majority of Americans have yet to be affected by the use of mobile technology for political purposes. Between 20% and 23% of those interviewed report receiving electronic communication from political interest groups, using social media to share political opinions posted by someone else, receiving electronic requests to contact elected representatives on behalf of a cause, or receiving direct electronic communications from elected officials or from political parties. Slightly fewer, 16%, say they post their own political opinions directly on social media. Less than 10% say they have received instant communication about an incipient or ongoing political rally or political protest or made a monetary donation using a smartphone or tablet.

Political Differences

The presidential campaign of Barack Obama in 2012 was widely reported to have successfully taken advantage of new technology both in terms of "big data" collection of voter information, and in terms of repeated contact with voters using both traditional and new electronic modes of communication. That technological advantage continues to be evident to some degree today, more than two years later. Democrats nationwide are modestly more likely than Republicans to report receiving political messages from either political parties or political advocacy groups in the last 30 days. Also, Democrats are four times as likely as Republicans to say they have donated to a campaign using a smartphone or tablet—although at 8% and 2%, respectively, these rates are still quite small. Republicans are slightly more likely to report sharing or "liking" posts or links that represent their opinions.

As would be expected, independents are less likely than either partisan group to report receiving political communication through their electronic devices.

None of the partisan differences seen here are especially large—suggesting that Republicans could potentially close the "mobile communication" gap by 2016, although whether they can do so for the 2014 midterm cycle is unclear.

Younger Americans More Likely to Be Politically Connected via Social Media

Young Americans are more likely than those who are older to engage in the two political activities involving social media—sharing or retweeting posts or links, and posting opinions on social media and other Internet sites. Otherwise, there is little difference by age in participation in the other political activities.

Political Connection via Mobile Devices, by Partisanship

% Yes

	Republicans %	Independents %	Democrats %
Received electronic communications from political interest groups through email, social media, or text message	23	19	31
Shared, "liked," or retweeted posts or links that express political opinions similar to your own	28	21	23
Received requests on your smartphone or other electronic device from interest groups asking you to contact your elected representative or take some action on a bill being considered in Congress or the state legislature	25	18	25
Received electronic communications from elected officials or candidates for office through email, social media, or text message	21	18	24
Received electronic communications from political parties through email, social media, or text message	19	16	28
Posted your opinions about politics and political issues, elected officials, elections, or candidates for office on Twitter, Facebook, or other Internet sites	20	14	17
Received instant electronic notification on your smartphone or other electronic device about political rallies or political protests in your area	8	7	15
Made a monetary donation to political candidates or political interest groups using your smartphone or tablet -- that is, using PayPal or having the dollar amount charged to your Amazon, Google, phone company, or other account	2	3	8

April 1-2, 2014

GALLUP

Republicans Slightly More Likely to Use Mobile Devices

Republicans are slightly more likely than Democrats to report using a smartphone or tablet on a daily basis. Still, despite this disparity in overall use, Democrats are as likely as Republicans to be heavy users of mobile devices (4+ hours per day). Apparently, the advantage Democrats may have in this regard among younger Americans, who are among the heaviest users of mobile technology, is somewhat offset by the greater use among those with higher incomes, who tend to be Republican. Overall, the data underscore the conclusion that there are not major partisan-based differences in the ability to reach voters and potential voters using mobile devices.

Hours Spent Using Smartphones and Tablets

How many hours a day, if any, do you typically spend using smartphones and tablet computers?

	Republicans %	Independents %	Democrats %
Do not use	28	30	33
Less than one hour	11	6	9
One to three hours	35	37	33
Four or more hours	26	27	26

April 1-2, 2014

GALLUP

Bottom Line

This is a midterm election year, and political activity has picked up in a number of states with early primaries and high-profile Senate and gubernatorial elections. This activity is certainly not at the level of where it will be in the fall, or in particular of where it will be in 2016, a presidential election year. Therefore, the current measures of political activity using mobile devices as of early April—with a little more than four in 10 having had one of eight possible types of political contact—most likely represent a floor or minimum level. Given the high penetration of these devices in the American population in general, the potential is there for a significantly increased use later this year and in future elections. Democrats have a slight advantage in terms of ongoing contact with potential voters at this point, but both parties will no doubt be actively working to increase their advantage in the months and years ahead.

Survey Methods

Results for this Gallup poll are based on telephone interviews conducted April 1–2, 2014, on the Gallup Daily tracking survey, with a random sample of 1,017 adults, aged 18 and older, living in all 50 U.S. states and the District of Columbia.

For results based on the total sample of national adults, the margin of sampling error is ±4 percentage points at the 95% confidence level.

For results based on the total sample of 661 smartphone or tablet users, the margin of sampling error is ±5 percentage points at the 95% confidence level.

April 30, 2014

HALF IN ILLINOIS AND CONNECTICUT WANT TO MOVE ELSEWHERE
Montana, Hawaii, Maine boast lowest rate of residents wanting to leave

by Lydia Saad

PRINCETON, NJ—Every state has at least some residents who are looking for greener pastures, but nowhere is the desire to move more prevalent than in Illinois and Connecticut. In both of these states, about half of residents say that if given the chance to move to a different state, they would like to do so. Maryland is a close third, at 47%. By contrast, in Montana, Hawaii, and Maine, just 23% say they would like to relocate. Nearly as few—24%—feel this way in Oregon, New Hampshire, and Texas.

States Where the Most Residents Would Leave if They Could	% Yes, would move
Illinois	50
Connecticut	49
Maryland	47
Nevada	43
Rhode Island	42
New Jersey	41
New York	41
Massachusetts	41
Louisiana	40
Mississippi	39

Gallup 50-state poll, June-December 2013

GALLUP

States Where the Fewest Residents Would Leave if They Could	% Yes, would move
Montana	23
Hawaii	23
Maine	23
Oregon	24
New Hampshire	24
Texas	24
Colorado	25
Minnesota	25
South Dakota	26
Wyoming	27

Gallup 50-state poll, June-December 2013

GALLUP

These findings are from a 50-state Gallup poll, conducted June–December 2013, which includes at least 600 representative interviews with residents aged 18 and older in each state. Gallup measured residents' interest in moving out of state by asking,

"Regardless of whether you *will* move, if you had the opportunity, would you *like* to move to another state, or would you rather remain in your current state?"

Thirty-three percent of residents want to move to another state, according to the average of the 50 state responses. Seventeen states come close to that 50-state average. Another 16 are above the average range, including three showing an especially high desire to move. In fact, in these three—Illinois, Connecticut, and Maryland—roughly as many residents want to leave as want to stay.

At the other end of the spectrum, 17 states are home to a below-average percentage of residents wanting to leave. This includes the previously mentioned six states—Montana, Hawaii, Maine, Oregon, New Hampshire, and Texas—where fewer than one in four want to move, the lowest level recorded.

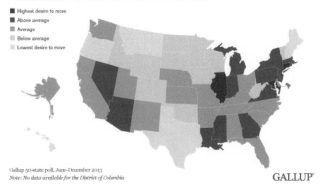

State Residents' Desire to Move to a Different State

■ Highest desire to move
■ Above average
■ Average
■ Below average
■ Lowest desire to move

Gallup 50-state poll, June-December 2013
Note: No data available for the District of Columbia

GALLUP

Nevada Residents Show Greatest Intention to Move in Next 12 Months

In the same poll, Gallup asked state residents how likely it is they *will* move in the next 12 months. On average across all 50 states, 6% of state residents say it is extremely or very likely they will move in the next year, 8% say it is somewhat likely, 14% not too likely, and 73% not likely at all.

The combined percentages reporting they are extremely, very, or somewhat likely to move out of state ranges from 8% in Maine, Iowa, and Vermont to 20% in Nevada. Although these figures are still high relative to the actual percentage of Americans who move out of state each year, they provide a basis for evaluating each state's risk of losing population that is somewhat stronger than the sheer desire of its residents to move.

States With Largest Proportion of Residents Planning to Move Within 12 Months	% Extremely/Very/ Somewhat likely to move
Nevada	20
Illinois	19
Arizona	19
Maryland	17
Louisiana	17
Idaho	17
South Carolina	17
Mississippi	16
New York	16
Connecticut	16
North Carolina	16

Gallup 50-state poll, June-December 2013

GALLUP

States With Smallest Proportion of Residents Planning to Move Within 12 Months	% Extremely/Very/ Somewhat likely to move
Maine	8
Iowa	8
Vermont	8
Minnesota	9
West Virginia	9
Texas	9
Pennsylvania	9
Indiana	9
Kentucky	10
North Dakota	10

Gallup 50-state poll, June-December 2013

GALLUP

Of course, all states enjoy an influx of new residents as well as outflows, so these intention-to-move data are only part of the population-change picture, but an important one.

Those saying it is at least somewhat likely they will move were asked to say why, in their own words. The biggest factor residents give for planning to move is for work or business reasons—the 50-state average is 31%. This is followed by family or other social reasons (19%), weather or location (11%), and then seeking a better quality of life or change (9%).

In most states, it is not possible to view these answers because there are too few respondents, but in each of the 11 states with the highest percentages wanting to leave, roughly 100 answered the question. The breakdown of the open-ended responses for these 11 states is shown in the accompanying graph.

States With Biggest Proportion of Residents Who Plan to Move Within 12 Months:
Top Reasons Given for Planning to Move

	Work-/ Business-related	Family/ Friends	Weather/ Location	Quality of life/ Change	School-related	Cost of living	Taxes
	%	%	%	%	%	%	%
Nevada	30	22	11	10	8	5	--
Illinois	26	6	17	15	6	9	8
Arizona	32	20	11	4	9	4	--
Maryland	17	17	13	7	6	7	8
Louisiana	39	19	5	10	5	9	1
Idaho	23	21	15	7	15	1	--
S. Carolina	49	15	3	15	8	2	--
Mississippi	50	17	3	13	4	1	--
New York	15	16	8	5	6	21	14
Conn.	21	13	7	12	10	12	6
N. Carolina	37	11	7	15	4	6	2
50-state average	31	19	11	9	8	5	3

Based on open-ended answers to question: What is the main reason you are planning or likely to move?
Gallup 50-state poll, June-December 2013

GALLUP

While not all of the percentage differences among the states are statistically significant because of small sample sizes, a few important ones stand out. Residents of Mississippi and South Carolina who indicate they are likely to move are significantly more likely to cite work- or business-related reasons than are their counterparts in other states. The cost of living is a greater relative factor for residents in Connecticut and New York, while taxes are a uniquely important factor in New York, Illinois, and Maryland.

Bottom Line

State leaders have important reasons for wanting to see their state populations grow rather than shrink. A growing population usually means more commerce, more economic vitality, and a bigger tax base to pay for state services. A shrinking population not only hurts government coffers but also can weaken a state politically by virtue of the potential loss of U.S. House members through redistricting every 10 years.

Gallup's 50-state poll finds some states far better positioned than others to retain residents, and thus possibly attract new ones. This is evident in the wide variation in the percentages of state residents who say they would leave their state if they could, as well as in the percentages who say they plan to move in the next year.

Nevada, Illinois, Maryland, Louisiana, Mississippi, New York, and Connecticut all appear particularly vulnerable to losing population in the coming few years: high percentages of their residents say

they would leave if they could, and larger-than-average percentages say they are at least somewhat likely to do so in the coming year. At the other end of the spectrum, Texas, Minnesota, and Maine have little to fear. Residents of these states are among the least likely to want to leave and few are planning to leave in the next 12 months.

If these states sound familiar to readers of Gallup's previous 50-state poll articles, it's because several of them also appear at the top or bottom of the states for resident satisfaction with state taxes, state government, and overall perceptions of how their state compares to others as a place to live. Texas is in the top 10 on all three, while Illinois, Rhode Island, and Maryland rank in the bottom 10 on all three.

In upcoming articles, Gallup will analyze interstate migration patterns in greater detail, looking at where residents who are likely to move say they would move to.

Survey Methods

Results for this Gallup poll are based on telephone interviews conducted June–December 2013, with a random sample of approximately 600 adults in each state, aged 18 and older, living in all 50 U.S. states and the District of Columbia.

For results based on the total sample of adults per state, the margin of sampling error is ±5 percentage points at the 95% confidence level.

April 30, 2014
MOST U.S. WORKERS SEE UPSIDE TO STAYING CONNECTED TO WORK
More than one-third frequently check work email after business hours

by Jim Harter, Sangeeta Agrawal, and Susan Sorenson

WASHINGTON, D.C.—Full-time U.S. employees are upbeat about using their computers and mobile devices to stay connected to the workplace outside of their normal working hours. Nearly eight in 10 (79%) workers view this as a somewhat or strongly positive development.

U.S. Employees' Views on Working Remotely After Business Hours

As far as you are concerned, is the ability for you to use your computer, tablet, or smartphone to work remotely outside of normal business hours and stay in touch with work remotely a positive development or a negative development?

	Strongly positive	Somewhat positive	Somewhat negative	Strongly negative
U.S. full-time employees	42%	37%	13%	8%

Gallup Daily tracking, March 24-April 8, 2014

GALLUP

These findings are from Gallup Daily tracking interviews, conducted March 24–April 8, 2014, with 3,865 U.S. workers employed full-time by an employer.

While a strong majority of working Americans view the ability to work off-hours remotely in a positive light, far fewer say they regularly connect with work online after hours. Slightly more than one-third (36%) say they frequently do so, compared with 64% who say they occasionally, rarely, or never do. The relatively low percentage who check in frequently outside of working hours nearly matches the 33% of full-time workers who say their employer expects them to check email and stay in touch remotely after the business day ends.

Among those who frequently check email away from work, 86% say it is a somewhat or strongly positive development to be able to do so. However, this is only slightly higher than the 75% of less frequent email checkers who view the technology change positively. Even among employees for whom staying connected is compulsory, 81% view this development in a somewhat or strongly positive light.

Men, Younger Employees Check Work Email More Frequently

Frequent checking of messages outside of work hours is more common among men (40%) than women (31%). It is also slightly more prevalent among millennials (38%) and those in Generation X (37%), compared with baby boomers (33%). Employees with a college degree or higher are more than twice as likely to regularly check work email versus those with less than a college degree (48% vs. 23%), and the highest earners are about twice as likely as the lowest (53% vs. 25%) to say they do the same. The education and income differences could reflect the greater likelihood of Americans in high education and income groups to be employed in white-collar or professional occupations where email communication is likely a more crucial aspect of the job.

U.S. Full-Time Employees' Remote Working Habits

How often do you normally check your work email outside of normal working hours -- frequently, occasionally, rarely, or never?

	Frequently	Occasionally, rarely or never
Male	40%	60%
Female	31%	70%
Millennials (1980-1996)	38%	62%
Generation X (1965-1979)	37%	63%
Baby boomers (1946-1964)	33%	67%
Less than a college degree	23%	77%
Some college	41%	59%
College degree or higher	48%	52%
$24,000->$36,000	25%	75%
$36,000->$48,000	30%	70%
$48,000->$60,000	31%	69%
$60,000->$90,000	38%	62%
$90,000->$120,000	43%	57%
$120,000 or more	53%	47%

Gallup Daily tracking, March 24-April 8, 2014

GALLUP'

Nearly All Working Americans Use Computers and/or Other Mobile Devices

The ubiquity of Web-enabled technology in U.S. workers' homes and lives could be a factor in their willingness to connect with employers outside of working hours. Gallup estimates 80% of full-time U.S. workers have a smartphone with Internet access, 87% have a laptop or desktop computer, and 49% have a tablet computer. In all, 96% of full-time American employees say they use at least one of these types of devices.

Computer, Smartphone, and Tablet Usage Among U.S. Employees

Do you personally use any of the following?

	U.S. workers
Laptop or desktop computer	87%
Smartphone	80%
Tablet	49%
Total who use at least one of these devices	96%

Gallup Daily tracking, March 24-April 8, 2014

GALLUP'

When asked how much time in a typical seven-day week they spend working remotely using a computer or other electronic device, such as a smartphone or tablet, employees who report checking their email frequently say they spend nearly 10 hours working remotely. Those who occasionally, rarely, or never check job-related email outside of work report spending nearly four hours a week working remotely.

Bottom Line

Despite technology's tendency to blur the lines between employees' work hours and off-hours, most full-time workers in the U.S. take a positive view about using their devices to stay in touch with work after normal business hours. Nearly all workers say they have access to the Internet on at least one device, whether a smartphone, laptop, desktop, or tablet, so it may be that they enjoy the convenience of easily checking in from home instead of putting in late hours at the office. They may also appreciate the freedom this technology offers them to meet family needs, attend school events, or make appointments during the day, knowing they can monitor email while out of the office or log on later to catch up with work if needed.

While about one-third of employees currently say they frequently check email after work, that a clear majority of workers feel positive about the ability to do so is encouraging for employers looking for more ways to integrate mobile devices into the way their companies work. Given that those who frequently check messages away from work also log twice as many hours remotely as those who occasionally, rarely, or never check email out of the office, enabling more employees to do so may play a role in increasing productivity.

Survey Methods

Results for this Gallup poll are based on telephone interviews conducted March 24–April 8, 2014, on the Gallup Daily tracking survey, with a random sample of 3,865 full-time working adults, aged 18 and older, living in all 50 U.S. states and the District of Columbia.

For results based on the total sample of national full-time working adults, the margin of sampling error is ±4 percentage points at the 95% confidence level.

May 01, 2014
STATES IN NORTHEAST LEAD NATION IN DENTIST VISITS
Residents of Southern states still least likely to visit dentist annually

by Lindsey Sharpe

WASHINGTON, D.C.—For the third year in a row, Connecticut residents were the most likely to say they visited a dentist in the last 12 months. It is one of only three states, the others being Massachusetts and Rhode Island, where nearly three in four residents visited a dentist. Just over half of the residents in Mississippi say the same, coming in last for dental care among the 50 states.

Top 10 States for Dentist Visits, Last 12 Months

State	%
Connecticut	74.9
Massachusetts	74.5
Rhode Island	73.8
Alaska	72.6
Wisconsin	72.4
Minnesota	71.9
North Dakota	71.4
Utah	71.4
Delaware	70.9
South Dakota	70.7

January-December 2013
Gallup-Healthways Well-Being Index

GALLUP'

Bottom 10 States for Dentist Visits, Last 12 Months

State	%
Mississippi	53.0
Oklahoma	55.2
Louisiana	55.3
Arkansas	56.1
Texas	56.3
West Virginia	56.6
Tennessee	56.9
Kentucky	58.6
Missouri	59.0
Arizona	59.3

January-December 2013
Gallup-Healthways Well-Being Index

GALLUP'

Five states, Connecticut, Massachusetts, Rhode Island, Wisconsin, and Minnesota, have ranked in the top 10 states for dental visits every year since Gallup and Healthways began daily tracking in 2008. Connecticut has taken the top spot four times—from 2011 through 2013, and in 2009. On the other hand, eight states—Mississippi, Oklahoma, Louisiana, Arkansas, Texas, West Virginia, Tennessee, and Kentucky—have ranked in the bottom 10 every year since 2008.

Nationally, 64.7% of Americans in 2013 said they visited the dentist at least once in the past 12 months. This is essentially unchanged from 65.4% in 2012, and remains in line with the averages reported in previous years since 2008.

These findings are based on interviews with more than 178,000 American adults conducted during 2013 as a part of the Gallup-Healthways Well-Being Index. Respondents were asked whether they visited the dentist in the last 12 months.

Annual Dentist Visits Most Common in Northeast, Least Common in South

The state-level results illustrate that dental visits vary by geographic region. Residents of Eastern states are the most likely to report visiting the dentist in the past year and hold the top three positions in the state rankings. Residents in the Midwest are the second-most likely to report visiting the dentist in the past year, and four Midwestern states are included within the top 10 for 2013. Residents of Southern states are the least likely to go to the dentist and make up eight of the bottom 10 states for dental visits.

Dentist Visits Related to Having Money for Healthcare and Insurance Rates

Residents of the 10 states with the highest dental visit rates are somewhat more likely to say they have enough money to pay for healthcare than residents in the 10 states with the lowest dental visit rates, 84.8% vs. 77.6%. Further, the bottom 10 states for dental visits have a significantly higher average uninsured rate at 20.5% than the top 10 states for dental visits (12.6%). Previous Gallup research shows that the likelihood of visiting the dentist annually increases with income, which bolsters the connection between obtaining professional dental care and affordability.

State Dentist Visits, Enough Money to Pay for Healthcare, and Health Insurance, by Quintiles

	Average % who visited dentist in last 12 months	Average % with enough money to pay for healthcare	Average % who are uninsured
Top quintile	72.5	84.8	12.6
Bottom quintile	56.6	77.6	20.5

Gallup-Healthways Well-Being Index
January-December 2013

GALLUP'

Implications

The American Dental Association recommends visiting the dentist regularly to maintain oral health, noting that the frequency should be determined by a dentist based on an individual's personal risk profile. Even those with a low risk profile should have at least one dental visit per year, while those at higher risk benefit from more frequent visits. In 11 states, less than 60% of residents reported that they visited the dentist at least once in the last year, revealing a wide disparity between actual dental visits and best practice oral care.

A relationship between dental visits and income exists, and those states with fewer reported visits also have, on average, a relatively lower percentage of residents with enough money to pay for healthcare and a higher percentage of uninsured residents.

It is possible that the full implementation of the Affordable Care Act and the declining percentage of uninsured Americans will boost annual dental visit rates. Some adult coverage options that were available for purchase through the federal and state exchanges included dental coverage, in addition to stand-alone dental insurance options. However, there is no fine associated with not having dental coverage under the ACA.

Even if previously uninsured Americans do not obtain dental insurance along with health coverage, physicians may advise them to consider their oral care as a critical aspect of their overall health.

Survey Methods

Results are based on telephone interviews conducted as part of the Gallup-Healthways Well-Being Index survey Jan. 2–Dec. 29, 2013, with a random sample of 178,072 adults, aged 18 and older, living in all 50 U.S. states and the District of Columbia.

The margin of sampling error for most states is ±1 to ±2 percentage points, but is as high as ±4 points for states with smaller populations, such as Wyoming, North Dakota, South Dakota, Delaware, and Hawaii.

May 01, 2014
FOR MANY, MOBILE TECHNOLOGY INCREASING RETAIL SHOPPING
Young adults more likely to say mobile tech increasing retail shopping

by Jeffrey M. Jones

This article is part of a weeklong series analyzing how mobile technology is affecting politics, business, and well-being.

PRINCETON, NJ—Although online and smartphone shopping are a clear threat to traditional brick-and-mortar retail stores, more than half of Americans say the amount of shopping they do in person at retail stores has not been affected by mobile technology. While a not insignificant 19% admit they now shop less at retail stores as a result of the rise of mobile technology, 22% say they are now doing more shopping in person at retail stores.

Effect of Mobile Technology on In-Person Retail Shopping

Has mobile technology increased, decreased, or not affected the amount of shopping you do in person at retail stores?

	Increased	Decreased	Not changed
Mar 21-23, 2014	22%	19%	59%

GALLUP

The results are based on a March 21–23 Gallup poll that measured the extent to which mobile technology, including smartphones and tablet computers, is transforming Americans' lives. Gallup has examined the effect of mobile technology on U.S. political life, employee engagement, and interpersonal communication.

Technological advances have created challenges for retailers, in part because Internet sellers can often offer the same product at cheaper prices because of lower overhead costs. Less expensive online pricing has led to concerns of retail store "showrooming," when consumers visit retail stores to examine a product, but then they purchase it online.

However, retailers have also taken advantage of electronic communications by allowing customers to pick up items they bought online in the store. And retailers have made the most of electronic communications and social networking websites to target customers arguably more effectively than they have been able to do with traditional mail, print, radio, and television advertising.

At this point, with roughly seven in 10 Americans using some form of mobile technology, the effects of mobile technology on in-store retail shopping seem to balance each other out, at least based on consumers' self-reports.

Notably, 18- to 29-year-olds are nearly twice as likely to say that mobile technology has led to an increase (29%) rather than a decrease (15%) in their shopping at retail stores. For all other age groups, it is a wash.

Effect of Mobile Technology on In-Person Retail Shopping, by Age

	Increased	Decreased	Not affected
18-29 years	29%	15%	56%
30-49 years	24%	23%	52%
50-64 years	17%	20%	62%
65+ years	16%	16%	67%

March 21-23, 2014

GALLUP

The exact reason for younger adults doing more in-person shopping is not clear, but one factor may be that Gallup has found 18- to 29-year-olds are much less likely than older adults to have credit cards, which would limit their ability to shop online.

Upper-income Americans are the only income group that reports a net decrease in their in-person retail shopping as a result of mobile technology, as slightly more say they are shopping less (28%) rather than more (23%) at stores. This income group is also the least likely to say their shopping habits have not changed.

Effect of Mobile Technology on In-Person Retail Shopping, by Annual Household Income

	Increased	Decreased	Not affected
Less than $36,000	20%	15%	65%
$36,000-less than $90,000	20%	20%	60%
$90,000 or more	23%	28%	49%

March 21-23, 2014

GALLUP

That upper-income Americans are more likely to report their retail shopping habits have been affected by mobile technology is consistent with the finding that upper-income Americans are more likely to possess technology devices such as smartphones and tablets.

Implications

Although a significant subset of Americans say they are now doing less in-person shopping at retail stores as the result of the rise of mobile technology, just as many say they are now doing more in-person shopping. What is unclear is whether consumers are spending more online than at retail stores overall and how much of their spending they used to do in stores is being transferred to online.

Presumably, those who are shopping more in person may be looking up products online and then buying them in person. Or, they may have been prompted to go to a local store by a sale or special offer sent by email, text message, or social networking site to their smartphone or tablet.

While Internet shopping offers the convenience of not having to travel to a store to buy items a consumer may need or want, in-person shopping is still the preferred channel for many consumers who want to interact with the product itself before purchasing. Retail stores also provide immediate gratification for consumers who can return home and use or enjoy the items they purchased rather than waiting several days for the items to be delivered to them after purchase.

Survey Methods

Results for this Gallup poll are based on telephone interviews conducted March 21–23, 2014, on the Gallup Daily tracking survey, with a random sample of 1,505 adults, aged 18 and older, living in all 50 U.S. states and the District of Columbia.

For results based on the total sample of national adults, the margin of sampling error is ±3 percentage points at the 95% confidence level.

May 02, 2014
USING MOBILE TECHNOLOGY FOR WORK LINKED TO HIGHER STRESS
Heavier users carry more stress, but also rate lives better

by Dan Witters and Diana Liu

WASHINGTON, D.C.—U.S. workers who email for work and who spend more hours working remotely outside of normal working hours are more likely to experience a substantial amount of stress on any given day than workers who do not exhibit these behaviors. Nearly half of workers who "frequently" email for work outside of normal working hours report experiencing stress "a lot of the day yesterday," compared with the 36% experiencing stress who never email for work.

Daily Stress by Email Usage and Remote Working Habits
"Did you experience stress a lot of the day yesterday?"

Mobile technology behavior	Lowest frequency	Second lowest frequency	Second highest frequency	Highest frequency
Checks email outside of working hours:	Never	Rarely	Occasionally	Frequently
	36%	40%	41%	48%
Hours spent per week working remotely:	None	1-2 hours	3-6 hours	7+ hours
	37%	41%	43%	47%

Gallup-Healthways Well-Being Index
Controlling for age, gender, race/ethnicity, income, education, region, marital status, and children in household

GALLUP

Time spent working remotely outside of working hours aligns similarly, with 47% of those who report working remotely at least seven hours per week having a lot of stress the previous day compared with 37% experiencing stress who reported no remote work time.

These data were collected from March 24 through April 10, 2014, as part of the Gallup-Healthways Well-Being Index for a special Gallup study exploring the effects of mobile technology on politics, business, and well-being in the United States. Gallup interviewed 4,475 working U.S. adults, and the findings hold true after controlling for age, gender, income, education, race/ethnicity, region, marital status, and children in household.

Workers Who Use Mobile Technology Rate Their Lives Better

In seeming contrast to the relationship between the use of mobile technology for work and its relationship to elevated daily stress, workers who email or work remotely outside of normal working hours also rate their lives better than their counterparts who do not. As with stress, frequency of emailing outside of work and hours spent working remotely are closely linked to the percentage of respondents who are "thriving."

Life Evaluation "% Thriving" by Email Usage and Remote Working Habits

Mobile technology behavior	Lowest frequency	Second lowest frequency	Second highest frequency	Highest frequency
Checks email outside of working hours:	Never	Rarely	Occasionally	Frequently
	54%	56%	61%	63%
Hours spent per week working remotely:	None	1-2 hours	3-6 hours	7+ hours
	52%	61%	61%	63%

Gallup-Healthways Well-Being Index
Controlling for age, gender, race/ethnicity, income, education, region, marital status, and children in household

GALLUP

Gallup classifies Americans as "thriving" according to how they rate their current and future lives on a ladder scale with steps numbered from 0 to 10 based on the Cantril Self-Anchoring Striving Scale. Those who rate their present life a 7 or higher and their life in five years an 8 or higher are classified as thriving.

Employers' Expectations Drive Mobile Technology Use

Regardless of well-being related outcomes such as daily stress and life evaluations, employers' expectations play a clear role in employees' mobile technology use. Sixty-two percent of workers who have employers that expect work-related mobile use say they use email frequently outside of working hours, compared with 23% of those whose employers have no such expectations. Just 5% of workers say they never email outside of work even in the existence of such employer expectations, compared with 30% who never email in the absence of those employer expectations. A similar pattern exists for remote work.

Mobile Technology Use Among Workers by Employer Expectations

	Employer expects mobile use	Employer does not expect mobile use
Frequently	62%	23%
Occasionally	23%	23%
Rarely	9%	20%
Never	5%	30%

Gallup-Healthways Well-Being Index
Controlling for age, gender, race/ethnicity, income, education, region, marital status, and children in household

GALLUP

Implications

The unusual dichotomy in key well-being outcomes—daily stress and life satisfaction—and work-related mobile technology use provides evidence that such behaviors can both positively and negatively influence employees' well-being. Even after controlling for all key demographics, workers who leverage mobile technology more often outside of work are much more likely to be stressed on any given day, while simultaneously being more likely to rate their lives better.

It is possible that by emailing or working remotely outside of normal hours, workers associate such behaviors with greater professional success and accomplishment, thus elevating how they think about and evaluate their lives more generally. At the same time, the elevated levels of stress associated with these behaviors may fall into what some refer to as "productive stress." For some workers this type of stress may be a desirable emotional state that is associated with greater urgency and more productive work days. Job type may also be a factor in these results; more personally rewarding occupations for many people also may be the type that demand more mobile technology use and that typically come with elevated stress levels.

Survey Methods

Results for this study are based on telephone interviews conducted March 24–April 10, 2014, as a part of the Gallup Daily tracking survey and the Gallup-Healthways Well-Being index with a random sample of 4,475 working adults, aged 18 and older, living in all 50 U.S. states and the District of Columbia.

For results based on the total sample of national adults, the margin of sampling error is ±1.8 percentage points at the 95% confidence level. For results based on the employer expectations sub-groups, the margin of sampling error is ±2.5 to 3.0 percentage points.

Workers were asked, "How often do you normally check your work email outside of normal working hours—frequently, occasionally, rarely, or never?" and "Now, I'd like you to think about any time you may spend doing your job remotely using a computer or other electronic device, such as a smartphone or tablet. In a typical seven-day week, about how many total hours, if any, do you spend working remotely?"

May 02, 2014
FEWER WILL RELY ON 401(K) IN RETIREMENT THAN PRE-RECESSION
Retired Americans rely on Social Security as a major source of income

by Rebecca Riffkin

WASHINGTON, D.C.—Prior to the Great Recession, most Americans planned to rely on a 401(k), IRA, Keogh, or other retirement savings account when they retire. Today, 48% of Americans say they would rely on a 401(k) account in retirement—a percentage that (48%) has not rebounded to pre-recession levels.

Reliance on Retirement Savings Accounts as a Major Source of Retirement Income

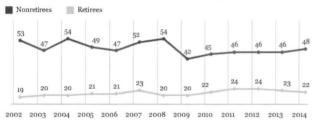

% Relying on a 401(k), IRA, Keogh, or other retirement savings account as a major source of income today (retirees) and in retirement (nonretirees)

GALLUP

In April 2008, 54% of Americans who had yet to retire expected to rely on a 401(k) as a major source of income. This dropped to 42% in 2009, in the depths of the recession, but has been rebounding ever since.

During the recession, many working Americans saw the value of their 401(k) accounts drop, which may have made them skeptical that they would be able to rely on these accounts as a source of retirement income. Stocks and 401(k) accounts have recovered much of their value since then, and simultaneously, the percentage of nonretired Americans who plan to use these retirement accounts as a source of income has increased.

The percentage of nonretired Americans who plan to rely on a 401(k) is far higher than the percentage of retired Americans who do rely on a 401(k) or other retirement savings account, currently 22%. The recession did not affect retired Americans' reliance on

401(k)s and other retirement savings accounts as much as it affected nonretirees' projected reliance on these accounts.

The Role of Social Security in Retirement Income

Historically, Social Security has been more of a prominent factor in the incomes of retired Americans than in the retirement plans of nonretired Americans. Over the 12 years Gallup has been tracking this measure, between 50% and 61% of retirees have considered Social Security a major source of income. By contrast, between 25% and 34% of nonretirees have expected it to be a major income source when they reach retirement.

Reliance on Social Security as a Major Source of Retirement Income

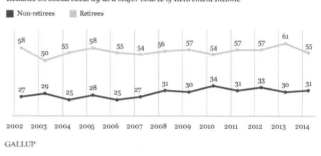

GALLUP

Since the recession began, more nonretirees have expected Social Security to be a major source of retirement income than did so before 2008. From 2002 to 2007, between 25% and 29% of nonretirees expected it to be a major source of income, compared with 30% to 34% from 2008 to 2014. This may reflect the higher volatility in the stock and housing markets, as fewer Americans felt comfortable trusting their retirement income to these sources and instead considered Social Security the safer option.

However, an additional 51% of nonretired Americans do expect to rely on Social Security as a *minor* source of income. So while nonretired Americans mostly don't expect to rely on it as a major source of income, most expect it to fund their retirement to some degree—not a surprising finding, given that Social Security is currently guaranteed for most working Americans.

Implications

For many Americans, saving for retirement is a scary prospect. It is the top financial worry for 59% of Americans. Already-retired Americans largely use sources that are outside of their control, like Social Security and employer-sponsored pension plans, as a source of income. But Americans who are still working toward retirement generally expect 401(k) accounts, IRAs, CDs, and other savings accounts to be major sources of retirement funds. Americans generally have more control over these types of savings plans, in terms of how much money they contribute and where that money is saved or invested. Still, this could be problematic because of studies showing how few workers today have adequately built up their savings to the point at which they can actually rely on them in retirement.

A recent Wells Fargo/Gallup Investor and Retirement Optimism survey found that investors are generally risk-averse when it comes to retirement savings, favoring security over larger growth potential. This could influence the amount today's working Americans have saved when they approach their desired retirement age.

Time will tell if this switch to self-controlled retirement savings plans is successful for working Americans. One-third of nonretirees still plan to rely on Social Security as a major income source, and half plan to rely on Social Security as a minor source. But there may be looming problems for the Social Security system, because the 65-and-older population is essentially going to double in the years ahead as the huge group of baby boomers move into their later years. Many baby boomers are reluctant to retire, whether because they enjoy working or because they can't afford to. It is worth monitoring how their plans change when these baby boomers eventually decide to stop working and retire.

Survey Methods

Results for this Gallup poll are based on telephone interviews conducted April 3–6, 2014, with a random sample of 1,026 adults, aged 18 and older, living in all 50 U.S. states and the District of Columbia.

For results based on the total sample of national adults, the margin of sampling error is ±4 percentage points at the 95% confidence level.

For results based on the sample of 334 retirees, the margin of sampling error is ±7 percentage points at the 95% confidence level.

For results based on the sample of 692 nonretirees, the margin of sampling error is ±5 percentage points at the 95% confidence level.

May 05, 2014
U.S. UNINSURED RATE DROPS TO 13.4%
Uninsured rate down nearly four percentage points since late 2013

by Jenna Levy

WASHINGTON, D.C.—The uninsured rate for U.S. adults in April was 13.4%, down from 15.0% in March. This is the lowest monthly uninsured rate recorded since Gallup and Healthways began tracking it in January 2008, besting the previous low of 13.9% in September of that year.

Percentage Uninsured in the U.S., by Quarter
Do you have health insurance coverage?
Among adults aged 18 and older

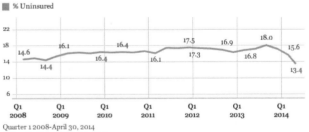

Quarter 1 2008–April 30, 2014
Gallup-Healthways Well-Being Index

GALLUP

The uninsured rate peaked at 18.0% in the third quarter of 2013, but has consistently declined since then. This downward trend in the uninsured rate coincided with the health insurance marketplace exchanges opening in October 2013, and accelerated as the March 31 deadline to purchase health insurance coverage approached—and passed—for most uninsured Americans. The Obama administration decided in late March to extend the deadline to April 15 for those who had already begun the enrollment process.

The uninsured rates for the first quarter of 2014 and the month of March are averages for the entire quarter and month, and do not necessarily reflect the uninsured rate for the day of the March 31 deadline. The April estimate better captures the impact of late sign-ups since all interviewing occurred after that critical date.

These data are based on more than 14,700 interviews with Americans from April 1–30, 2014, as part of the Gallup-Healthways Well-Being Index.

Uninsured Rate Falls Most Among Blacks, Hispanics, Lower-Income Americans

The uninsured rate was lower in April than in the fourth quarter of 2013 across nearly every key demographic group. The rate dropped more among blacks than any other demographic group, falling 7.1 percentage points to 13.8%. Hispanics were expected to disproportionately benefit from the Affordable Care Act—commonly referred to as "Obamacare"—because they are the subgroup with the highest uninsured rate. Although the percentage of uninsured Hispanics, at 33.2%, is down 5.5 points since the end of 2013, this rate is still the highest by far across key demographic groups.

Similarly, the uninsured rate among lower-income Americans—those with an annual household income of less than $36,000—has also dropped by 5.5 points, to 25.2%, since the fourth quarter of 2013.

Young Americans were an important target in public outreach efforts for enrollment because they can potentially subsidize the cost of insurance for those who are older and presumably less healthy. The uninsured rate among 18- to 25-year-olds fell 4.5 points, to 19.0%, from the fourth quarter of 2013. However, the uninsured rate declined even more among 35- to 64-year-olds, falling 4.8 points to 13.2%. The uninsured rate among 26- to 34-year-olds continued to decline, but at a rate more similar to the national average. These data do not show a disproportionately high rate of decline among younger Americans.

Percentage Uninsured in the U.S., by Subgroup
Do you have health insurance coverage?
Among adults aged 18 and older

	Quarter 4 2013 %	Quarter 1 2014 %	April 1–30, 2014 %	Net change from Q4 2013 to Apr 30, 2014 (pct. pts.)
National adults	17.1	15.6	13.4	-3.7
18 to 25 years	23.5	21.7	19.0	-4.5
26 to 34 years	28.2	26.4	24.5	-3.7
35 to 64 years	18.0	16.1	13.2	-4.8
65+ years	2.0	1.9	2.2	+0.2
White	11.9	10.7	9.0	-2.9
Black	20.9	17.6	13.8	-7.1
Hispanic	38.7	37.0	33.2	-5.5
Less than $36,000 annual household income	30.7	27.5	25.2	-5.5
$36,000 to $89,999 annual household income	11.7	10.7	9.0	-2.7
$90,000+ annual household income	5.8	4.7	3.2	-2.6

Gallup-Healthways Well-Being Index

GALLUP

Implications

The uninsured rate was 2.2 points lower in April than in the first quarter of 2014, reflecting the surge in late health insurance sign-ups to meet the official March 31 deadline. This figure represents the average percentage of adults without health insurance since provisions established under the Affordable Care Act requiring Americans to have insurance went into effect on Jan. 1 of this year.

Several factors may determine whether the uninsured rate declines, ticks up, or levels off in the coming months. Factors that may push the uninsured rate down include more states choosing to expand Medicaid and more Americans electing to buy insurance as penalty amounts increase. Gallup research shows that the uninsured rate, on average, has dropped more in states that have elected to expand Medicaid and run their own healthcare exchanges than in states that have not. Gallup also has found that higher fines would prompt more Americans to sign up for health insurance.

On the other hand, it is likely that some newly insured Americans will not pay their premiums and will rejoin the ranks of the uninsured. It is also possible that the uninsured rate could hold steady until early 2015, when those currently without insurance sign up for policies going into effect at the beginning of next year.

Additionally, other provisions of the healthcare law have not yet gone into effect, such as the requirement for employers to provide health insurance to their employees by 2015. These provisions also may affect the uninsured rate over time.

Survey Methods

Results are based on telephone interviews conducted as part of the Gallup-Healthways Well-Being Index survey, April 1–30, 2014, with a random sample of 14,704 adults, aged 18 and older, living in all 50 U.S. states and the District of Columbia.

For results based on the total sample of national adults, the margin of sampling error is ±1 percentage point at the 95% confidence level.

May 05, 2014
FEWER IN U.S. SAY THEY ARE SPENDING LESS
Majority of those spending less say pattern will be new normal

by Brendan Moore

WASHINGTON, D.C.—Thirty-seven percent of Americans say they have been spending less money in recent months than they used to, continuing the improvement in the trend since 2010. At the same time, 30% of Americans say they are spending more money, up from 17% in 2010, and 32% say they are spending the same amount.

Americans' Spending Habits

In general, would you say you have been spending -- [ROTATED: more money, the same amount, (or) less money] -- in recent months than you used to?

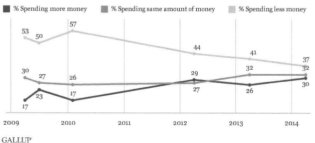

GALLUP

These data are from Gallup's annual Economy and Personal Finance survey, conducted April 3–6.

Americans' reports of changes in their spending habits are not in line with their preferences. In the same poll, Americans by a wide margin say they enjoy saving over spending. Although they say they prefer to save rather than spend—which would suggest lower spending—the percentage of Americans who report spending less has declined precipitously in recent years, suggesting the "new normal" pullback in spending during the recession and immediate postrecession period is ending.

These findings are consistent with trends in Gallup's monthly spending data, which also show much higher levels of reported spending now than in 2009–2011. Gallup does not ask about recent saving behavior, though it is possible that Americans are saving more *and* spending more if incomes are rising.

Majority of Those Spending Less Say It Will Become the New Normal

Most Americans who are spending less see it becoming their new, normal behavior. The 37% of Americans who report spending less includes 27% who see this change as their new, normal pattern, while only 10% see this as a temporary change.

Percentage of Americans Who Are Spending Less and Whether This Is a New Normal or Temporary

	Apr 20-21, 2009	Jul 10-12, 2009	Feb 1-3, 2010	Apr 9-12, 2012	Apr 4-14, 2013	Apr 3-6, 2014
SPENDING LESS MONEY	53	50	57	44	41	37
-- Will become new, normal pattern	32	32	38	33	31	27
-- Temporary changes in spending patterns	21	18	19	11	10	10

GALLUP

The percentage of Americans who say they are spending less and that it is their new normal is down from 38% in 2010. Since 2009, Americans who are spending less have been much more likely to say this is their new normal rather than a temporary change. As might be expected, the downtick in the overall percentage who are spending less has come mostly from those who say their spending less was temporary. This percentage has declined sharply from more than 20% in 2009 to only 10% now. In short, it appears that the temporary negative effect of the recession and economic downturn on spending is winding down, leaving only the hard core of those who claim to have settled into a new, normal pattern of spending less.

Conversely, of the 30% of Americans who report spending more in recent months, the majority see the change as only temporary (19%) rather than their new normal (11%). This is potentially worrying from an economic standpoint because the overall trend suggests that these spending increases are not going to be sustained but are only short-term spikes out of necessity.

Percentage of Americans Who Are Spending More and Whether This Is a New Normal or Temporary

	Apr 20-21, 2009	Jul 10-12, 2009	Feb 1-3, 2010	Apr 9-12, 2012	Apr 4-14, 2013	Apr 3-6, 2014
SPENDING MORE MONEY	17	23	17	29	26	30
-- Will become new, normal pattern	6	8	7	12	10	11
-- Temporary changes in spending patterns	11	15	10	17	16	19

GALLUP

Economic momentum is rooted in increasing levels of consumer spending, which accounts for roughly 70% of U.S. gross domestic product. While there was improvement in consumer spending this past year, there's still some apprehension and lack of confidence in the U.S. economy's direction, though clearly economic confidence is much greater than in 2009–2011.

Increased spending is a key to continued economic growth. And while Gallup's consumer spending estimates suggest the "new normal" period of spending may be ending—if not over—at the same time, in the last few months consumer spending, though robust, has been flat.

Survey Methods

Results for this Gallup poll are based on telephone interviews conducted April 3–6, 2014, on the Gallup Daily tracking survey, with a random sample of 1,026 adults, aged 18 and older, living in all 50 U.S. states and the District of Columbia.

For results based on the total sample of national adults, the margin of sampling error is ±5 percentage points at the 95% confidence level.

May 06, 2014
LIFE IN COLLEGE MATTERS FOR LIFE AFTER COLLEGE
New Gallup-Purdue study looks at links among college, work, and well-being

by Julie Ray and Stephanie Kafka

WASHINGTON, D.C.—When it comes to being engaged at work and experiencing high well-being after graduation, a new Gallup-Purdue University study of college graduates shows that the type of institution they attended matters less than what they experienced there. Yet, just 3% of all the graduates studied had the types of experiences in college that Gallup finds strongly relate to great jobs and great lives afterward.

The Undergraduate Experience: Support and Experiential and Deep Learning

	% Strongly agree
Support	
I had at least one professor at [College] who made me excited about learning.	63%
My professors at [College] cared about me as a person.	27%
I had a mentor who encouraged me to pursue my goals and dreams.	22%
Strongly agree with all three support statements	14%
Experiential	
I worked on a project that took a semester or more to complete.	32%
I had an internship or job that allowed me to apply what I was learning in the classroom.	29%
I was extremely active in extracurricular activities and organizations while attending [College].	20%
Strongly agree with all three experiential statements	6%
Strongly agree with all six statements	3%

Based on Web surveys of nearly 30,000 college graduates with Internet access from Feb. 4–March 7, 2014.
Gallup-Purdue Index

GALLUP

These results are based on the inaugural Gallup-Purdue Index, a joint-research effort with Purdue University and Lumina Foundation to study the relationship between the college experience and college graduates' lives. The Gallup-Purdue Index is a comprehensive, nationally representative study of U.S. college graduates with Internet access. According to a 2013 Census Bureau report, 90% of college graduates in the U.S. have access to the Internet. Gallup conducted the Web study Feb. 4–March 7, 2014, with nearly 30,000 U.S. adults who had completed at least a bachelor's degree.

Support in College, Experiences Tied to Workplace Engagement, Well-Being

The study found that the type of schools these college graduates attended—public or private, small or large, very selective or less selective—hardly matters at all to their workplace engagement and current well-being. Just as many graduates of public colleges as graduates of not-for-profit private colleges are engaged at work—meaning they are deeply involved in, enthusiastic about, and committed to their work. And just as many graduates of public as not-for-profit private institutions are thriving—which Gallup defines as strong, consistent, and progressing—in all areas of their well-being.

Instead, the study found that support and experiences in college had more of a relationship to long-term outcomes for these college graduates. For example, if graduates recalled having a professor who cared about them as a person, made them excited about learning, and encouraged them to pursue their dreams, their odds of being engaged at work more than doubled, as did their odds of thriving in all aspects of their well-being. And if graduates had an internship or job in college where they were able to apply what they were learning in the classroom, were actively involved in extracurricular activities and organizations, and worked on projects that took a semester or more to complete, their odds of being engaged at work doubled as well.

The odds of being engaged at work are:

2.6x Higher if ... [College] prepared me well for life outside of college.	**2.4x** Higher if ... [College] passionate about the long-term success of its students.
2.2x Higher if ... I had a mentor who encouraged me to pursue my goals and dreams.	**2.0x** Higher if ... I had at least one professor at [College] who made me excited about learning.
1.9x Higher if ... My professors at [College] cared about me as a person.	**2.3x** Higher if ... graduates experience all three
2.0x Higher if ... I had an internship or job that allowed me to apply what I was learning in the classroom.	**1.8x** Higher if ... I was extremely active in extracurricular activities and organizations while attending [College].
1.8x Higher if ... I worked on a project that took a semester or more to complete.	**2.4x** Higher if ... graduates experience all three

The odds of thriving in all areas of well-being are:

4.6x Higher if ... Engaged at work	**2.0x** Higher if ... Emotionally attached to school
2.5x Higher if ... [College] prepared me well for life outside of college.	**1.9x** Higher if ... [College] passionate about the long-term success of its students.
1.7x Higher if ... I had a mentor who encouraged me to pursue my goals and dreams.	**1.7x** Higher if ... My professors at [College] cared about me as a person.
1.5x Higher if ... I had at least one professor at [College] who made me excited about learning.	**1.9x** Higher if ... graduates experience all three
1.5x Higher if ... I had an internship or job that allowed me to apply what I was learning in the classroom.	**1.4x** Higher if ... I was extremely active in extracurricular activities and organizations while attending [College].
1.1x Higher if ... I worked on a project that took a semester or more to complete.	**1.3x** Higher if ... graduates experience all three

Yet few college graduates that Gallup studied achieve the winning combination. Only 14% of graduates strongly agree they were supported by professors who cared, who made them excited about learning, and who encouraged their dreams. Further, just 6% of graduates strongly agree they had an internship or job that allowed them to apply what they were learning, worked on a long-term project, and were actively involved in extra-curricular activities. Those who strongly agree to having had all six of these experiences during their time in college are the rarest of all (3%).

Bottom Line

When a student is trying to decide between an elite Ivy League school, a large public university, or a small private college, what should he or she consider to help make the decision? When an employer is evaluating two recent graduates from different backgrounds and institutions, which educational background should distinguish one applicant over the other, and why? When colleges and universities are setting internal strategies, designing new programs and curricula, deciding what performance measures faculty should be compensated for, and working to attract future students, what are they to do?

The data in this study suggest that, as far as future worker engagement and well-being are concerned, the answers could lie as much in thinking about aspects that last longer than the selectivity of an institution or any of the traditional measures of college. Instead, the answers may lie in *what* students are doing in college and *how* they are experiencing it. Those elements—more than many others measured—have a profound relationship to a graduate's life and career. Yet too few are experiencing them.

Survey Methods

Results for the Gallup-Purdue Index are based on Web surveys conducted Feb. 4–March 7, 2014, with a random sample of 29,560 respondents with a bachelor's degree or higher, aged 18 and older, with Internet access, living in all 50 U.S. states and the District of Columbia.

The Gallup-Purdue Index sample was compiled from two sources: the Gallup Panel and the Gallup Daily Tracking survey.

The Gallup Panel is a proprietary, probability-based longitudinal panel of U.S. adults that are selected using random-digit-dial (RDD) and address-based sampling methods. The Gallup Panel is not an opt-in panel. The Gallup Panel includes 60,000 individuals. Panel members can be surveyed by phone, mail, or Web. Gallup Panel members with a college degree, with access to the Internet, were invited to take the Gallup-Purdue Index survey online.

The Gallup Daily tracking survey sample includes national adults with a minimum quota of 50% cellphone respondents and 50% landline respondents, with additional minimum quotas by time zone within region. Landline and cellular telephone numbers are selected using RDD methods. Landline respondents are chosen at random within each household on the basis of which member had the most recent birthday. Gallup Daily tracking respondents with a college degree, who agreed to future recontact, were invited to take the Gallup-Purdue Index survey online.

Gallup-Purdue Index interviews are conducted via the Web, in English only. Samples are weighted to correct for unequal selection probability and nonresponse. The data are weighted to match national demographics of gender, age, race, Hispanic ethnicity, education, and region. Demographic weighting targets are based on the most recent Current Population Survey figures for the aged 18 and older U.S. bachelor's degree or higher population.

All reported margins of sampling error include the computed design effects for weighting.

For results based on the total sample of bachelor's degree or higher respondents, the margin of sampling error is ±0.9 percentage points at the 95% confidence level.

For results based on employee engagement of bachelor's degree or higher respondents, the margin of sampling error is ±1.0 percentage points at the 95% confidence level.

In addition to sampling error, question wording and practical difficulties in conducting surveys can introduce error or bias into the findings of public opinion polls.

May 07, 2014
U.S. JOB CREATION CONTINUES TO RISE IN APRIL
Nongovernment job creation reaches record high

by Rebecca Riffkin

WASHINGTON, D.C.—Gallup's U.S. Job Creation Index continued to climb to +25 in April from +23 in March. The index in April is one point shy of the all-time high found in January 2008, the first month Gallup began tracking hiring daily. The index is based on employee reports of hiring and layoffs at their workplaces.

Job Creation Index Among All U.S. Workers -- January 2008-April 2014

Based on the percentage of U.S. workers who say their employer is hiring workers and expanding the size of its workforce minus the percentage who say their employer is letting workers go and reducing the size of its workforce

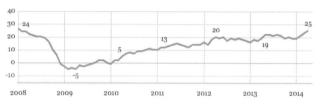

Based on monthly averages

Gallup Daily tracking
Values shown are for April 2014 and April of each year from 2008 to 2014

GALLUP

The U.S. Job Creation Index had a strong start in early 2008, but it began to fall later that year as the economy plunged into a recession. The index fell to a record low of −5 in both February and April 2009. Since then, the index has slowly recovered and registered averages in the low twenties starting in early 2012. It hovered in the high teens and low twenties through 2012 and 2013 before steadily rising in 2014.

The results for April are based on interviews with more than 16,000 full- and part-time workers. The index score of +25 reflects 39% of employees nationwide saying their employers are hiring workers and expanding the size of its workforce and 14% of employees saying their employers are letting workers go and reducing the size of their workforce. The percentage of employees who report their employers are letting workers go is the lowest Gallup has recorded, tied with 14% measured in January 2008. A remaining 41% of U.S. workers in April say their company is not changing the size of its workforce.

U.S. Workers' Reports of Hiring and Letting Go -- January 2008-March 2014

Monthly averages

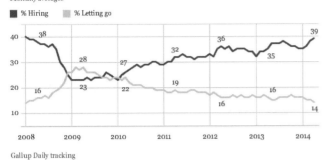

Gallup Daily tracking

GALLUP

Nongovernment Job Creation Reaches New High

Nongovernment job creation increased to +28 in April from +26 in March and is the highest Gallup has recorded since it began asking about government vs. nongovernment work in August 2008. Government job creation—based on reports from those who identify their place of employment as local, state, or federal government—was +12, similar to the +13 recorded the last two months. Since 2010, nongovernment workers have reported a more positive hiring situation than government workers have.

Gallup's U.S. Job Creation Index, by Type of Employer

Monthly averages

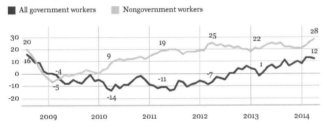

Values shown are for August 2008 and April of each year from 2009 to 2014
Gallup Daily tracking

GALLUP

Within the government employment sector, the job creation situation remains most positive at the state level (+20) followed by the local level (+13). The federal government trails behind both, with an index of −1.This score indicates that the federal government is basically at a standstill in terms of net hiring.

The overall U.S. Job Creation Index is primarily driven by nongovernment workers' perceptions of the hiring situation in their workplaces because more workers are employed in the nongovernment sector than in the government employment sector. Nongovernment net hiring tends to rise early in the year—as has been the case in 2014—but then generally levels off or drops slightly later in the year.

Implications

The recent rise in employee reports of hiring is a positive sign that the economic slowdown may be ending. More companies may be doing better than in recent years and thus are looking to increase the size of their workforces. Gallup's measure of the U.S. Payroll to Population employment rate was also up slightly in April, which

supports the rise in job creation, but the first quarter average in 2014 is down somewhat from the first quarter average in 2013. The current U.S. Job Creation Index signals that roughly the same percentage of employers are hiring new workers and increasing their staff now as they were in early 2008 before the recession took hold and before the stock market crash later that year.

Survey Methods

Results for this Gallup poll are based on telephone interviews conducted April 1–30, 2014, on the Gallup Daily tracking survey, with a random sample of 16,641 employed adults, aged 18 and older, living in all 50 U.S. states and the District of Columbia.

For results based on the total sample of workers, the margin of sampling error is ±1 percentage point at the 95% confidence level.

May 08, 2014
UTAHANS MOST LIKELY TO DONATE MONEY AND TIME
Residents of Southern and Southwestern states among least likely

by Justin McCarthy

WASHINGTON, D.C.—Utah leads U.S. states in reported charitable giving, with nearly half of its residents saying they had donated money *and* volunteered their time to an organization in the previous month. Residents in several Southern and Southwestern states—as well as New York—were among the least likely to say they did both.

Highest Percentages of Charitable Giving, by State

Have you done any of the following in the past month? How about -- Donated money to a charity? Volunteered your time to an organization?

	Donated money	Volunteered time	Yes to both
Utah	71%	56%	48%
Minnesota	66%	53%	41%
Hawaii	67%	46%	39%
South Dakota	66%	46%	39%
New Hampshire	70%	49%	38%
Kansas	62%	45%	38%
Illinois	70%	41%	37%
Montana	62%	47%	36%
Idaho	60%	45%	36%

Gallup 50-state poll, June-December 2013

GALLUP

These data come from a 50-state Gallup poll conducted June–December 2013, with at least 600 residents in each state. Gallup asked Americans whether they personally had donated money to charity or volunteered time to an organization in the previous month.

Overall, residents in all states were more likely to donate their money than their time, which is consistent with what Gallup has previously observed at the national and global levels. Utah and Minnesota are the only states where majorities of residents say they have done each in the past month.

High giving (48% to 36%)
Medium giving (35% to 30%)
Low giving (29% to 24%)

Gallup 50-state poll, June-December 2013
Note: No data available for the District of Columbia

GALLUP'

The percentage of those donating money *and* volunteering time was below 30% in 10 states—Nevada, Kentucky, New York, Mississippi, Arizona, Arkansas, North Carolina, West Virginia, Rhode Island, and Louisiana. New York and Rhode Island residents ranked fairly high on donating their money, but fell behind in volunteering their time.

Lowest Percentages of Charitable Giving, by State

Have you done any of the following in the past month? How about -- Donated money to a charity? Volunteered your time to an organization?

	Donated money	Volunteered time	Yes to both
Nevada	57%	32%	24%
Kentucky	56%	30%	24%
New York	65%	36%	26%
Mississippi	58%	34%	26%
Arizona	60%	35%	26%
Arkansas	56%	38%	28%
North Carolina	55%	36%	28%
West Virginia	60%	37%	28%
Rhode Island	68%	34%	29%
Louisiana	57%	39%	29%

Gallup 50-state poll, June-December 2013

GALLUP'

Link Between a State's Charitable Giving and Its Well-Being

Gallup has found that people with higher well-being are more likely to give back to their communities—whether it be their time, money, or help to strangers—and this relationship is true as well for states with lower well-being scores.

States with the lowest charitable giving percentages also had generally lower Gallup-Healthways well-being scores than states with higher giving averages. Of the most charitable states, all were above the national average for well-being; whereas only two of the least charitable states—Arizona and Nevada—were above the national average.

Bottom Line

While certain states outshine others in giving back to their communities, Americans as a whole do show impressive figures for their acts of kindness compared with the rest of the world. Although it is possible that giving to others helps foster higher well-being in the individuals taking part in those kinds of activities, it is also possible

that citizens with higher well-being are more likely to become active in their communities. Thus, by supporting their residents' well-being, state and local leaders could help communities reap a dividend in greater civic involvement.

Survey Methods

Results for this Gallup poll are based on telephone interviews conducted June–December 2013, with a random sample of approximately 600 adults per state, aged 18 and older, living in all 50 U.S. states.

For results based on the total sample of adults per state, the margin of sampling error is ±5 percentage points at the 95% confidence level.

May 08, 2014
FOUR YEARS IN, GOP SUPPORT FOR TEA PARTY DOWN TO 41%
Support for the movement nationwide drops to 22%

by Frank Newport

PRINCETON, NJ—About four in 10 Republicans and Republican-leaning independents classify themselves as supporters of the Tea Party, while 11% are opponents and 48% are neither. This continues to be a significant drop from the Tea Party's high-water mark in November 2010, when 61% of Republicans were supporters of the Tea Party.

Americans' Tea Party Affiliation -- by Party ID

Today vs. November 2010

	National adults	Republicans/ Leaners	Democrats/ Leaners
	%	%	%
Apr 24-30, 2014			
Supporter	22	41	7
Opponent	30	11	49
Neither/No opinion	48	48	43
Nov 4-7, 2010			
Supporter	32	61	9
Opponent	30	5	55
Neither/No opinion	38	34	36

GALLUP'

In the past three and a half years, levels of support and opposition for the Tea Party among Democrats and Democratic-leaning independents have changed relatively little.

These data are from a April 24–30 Gallup survey and underscore both the existing division of opinion in relationship to the Tea Party among Republicans and the shift in support since the last midterm election.

The role of the Tea Party in the selection of Republican nominees for Senate and House seats this year continues to be a high-profile issue. The Tea Party was perceived as suffering a setback on Tuesday, when Thom Tillis, the candidate widely perceived as representing the GOP establishment in the North Carolina Republican Senate primary, soundly defeated Greg Brannon, who was positioned as the Tea Party's choice. Tillis will now face incumbent North Carolina Democratic Sen. Kay Hagan in the fall general election.

The drop in support for the Tea Party among Republicans is mainly responsible for the drop in support among all Americans since November 2010, from 32% to today's 22%. Support has fluctuated in the intervening time period, but has been remarkably steady at 22% in the last three Gallup polls conducted since September of 2013. The percentage of Americans who classify themselves as Tea Party opponents, however, has risen to 30%, tied with two measurements in 2010 as the highest in the history of tracking this question.

Americans' Tea Party Affiliation

Do you consider yourself to be -- [ROTATED: a supporter of the Tea Party movement, an opponent of the Tea Party movement], or neither?

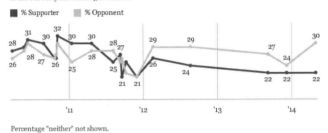

Percentage "neither" not shown.

GALLUP'

Republican Tea Party Supporters Are Core, Conservative Republicans

The broad group of Republicans who are supporters of the Tea Party are remarkably similar to other Republicans across most demographic categories—including race and ethnicity, income, age, education, or region of country. Republican Tea Party supporters are somewhat more likely to be weekly church attenders and slightly more likely to be men.

What then are the key factors that separate Republicans who support the Tea Party and those who do not? The answer to that question revolves mainly around ideology. Over half of Republicans who self-identify as conservatives are supporters of the Tea Party. Support for the Tea Party drops to 23% among moderate and liberal Republicans.

Americans' Tea Party Affiliation -- By Party ID and Ideology

	Supporter	Opponent	Neither/ No opinion
	%	%	%
National adults	22	30	48
Conservative Republicans	54	6	41
Moderate/ Liberal Republicans	23	19	58
Pure independents	14	13	73
Conservative Democrats	13	25	63
Moderate Democrats	7	46	47
Liberal Democrats	4	67	30

April 24-30, 2014

GALLUP'

Ideology also plays a role in determining Democrats' attitudes toward the Tea Party. Conservative Democrats are relatively indifferent to the Tea Party, while moderate, and in particular liberal, Democrats are much more likely to classify themselves as opponents.

Tea Party Republicans Are Most Focused on the Midterm Elections

Republicans in general are usually more tuned in to midterm elections than those who are not Republicans—but it is clear that within the broad group of those who identity with or lean toward the Republican party, Tea Party supporters are significantly more focused than other Republicans. Republican Tea Party supporters have given the election more thought, and also are significantly more likely to say they are more enthusiastic about voting, than either other Republicans or non-Republicans.

Thought Given to Election and Enthusiasm About Voting, by Tea Party Support Groups

	Republican Tea Party supporters	All other Republicans	All non-Republicans
	%	%	%
Given quite a lot of thought to midterm elections	43	26	19
More enthusiastic about voting this year	52	35	29
Less enthusiastic about voting this year	39	60	58

April 24-30, 2014

GALLUP'

Bottom Line

The number of Tea Party supporters among Republicans has dropped by a third since November 2010, and opposition to the Tea Party in the general population has returned to its all-time high—suggesting that the Tea Party will have less potential to affect elections this year than was the case in the last midterm election in 2010.

Tea Party support, more than anything else, appears to substantially correlate with the more straightforward characteristics of being a core, conservative Republican. Thus, these trends may suggest that the GOP is on a more moderate track in general. Clearly Mitt Romney's presidential nomination in 2012 was evidence of waning Tea Party support, and currently the Tea Party cannot even claim majority support of the GOP base, further hindering its influence to remake the party in its own image. The results of several high-profile primary contests later this month will be important indicators of the reality of the Tea Party's influence. Still, whatever else happens, Tea Party supporters will continue to be a presence in American politics because of their apparent motivation and interest in election outcomes, factors that, more than likely, will translate into support for candidates, and higher Election Day turnout.

Survey Methods

Results for this Gallup poll are based on telephone interviews conducted April 24–30, 2014, with a random sample of 1,513 adults, aged 18 and older, living in all 50 U.S. states and the District of Columbia.

For results based on the total sample of national adults, the margin of sampling error is ±3 percentage points at the 95% confidence level.

May 08, 2014
THREE IN 10 VOTERS SAY THEY WILL VOTE TO OPPOSE OBAMA
As in 2010, almost two-thirds of Republicans say they will vote to oppose Obama

by Andrew Dugan

WASHINGTON, D.C.—Three in 10 registered voters say when they vote for a candidate in the fall midterm elections, it will be to send a message that they oppose U.S. President Barack Obama, equal to the amount who said this before the Republican wave election of 2010. Nearly a quarter, 24%, say they are voting to support Obama, also similar to 2010. The largest number of voters, however, say their vote will not be a reflection on the president.

Voting to Send the President a Message of Support or Opposition, Among Registered Voters

Will your vote for a candidate be made in order to send a message that you SUPPORT Barack Obama, be made in order to send a message that you OPPOSE Barack Obama, or will you NOT be sending a message about Barack Obama with your vote?

	% Message to support	% Message to oppose	% Not a message
BARACK OBAMA			
Apr 24-30, 2014	24	30	43
Oct 28-31, 2010	22	30	44
GEORGE W. BUSH			
Nov 2-5, 2006	18	31	46
Oct 31-Nov 3, 2002	28	15	53
BILL CLINTON*			
Oct 29-Nov 1, 1998	24	19	54
Oct 23-25, 1998	24	20	53
Sep 23-25, 1998	24	18	55
Sep 11-12, 1998	20	17	60

*1998 wording: What effect, if any, will the Monica Lewinsky matter have on your vote for Congress in November? Will your vote for a candidate be made in order to send a message that you SUPPORT Bill Clinton, be made in order to send a message that you OPPOSE Bill Clinton, or will you NOT be sending a message about Bill Clinton with your vote?

GALLUP'

These results come from an April 24–30 Gallup poll. With various election primaries concluding, such as in North Carolina this past Tuesday, the 2014 midterm campaigns are intensifying. Many political analysts agree that the battle for control of the Senate will be the main element of suspense in the forthcoming election, and President Obama's middling poll numbers will present a challenge to Democratic candidates. Obama himself joked about this at the White House Correspondents' Association Dinner, saying his daughter Sasha "needed a speaker at career day and she invited Bill Clinton."

Obama does appear to be playing more of a role in voters' decisions at the ballot box than was the case for George W. Bush or Bill Clinton during their respective presidencies. A majority (54%) of voters say they will vote to send a message of support (24%) or opposition (30%) to the president, whereas less than a majority said that about either Bush or Clinton.

More voters say they are casting their ballot to *oppose* Obama than *support* Obama—a difference that is similar to Obama's first

midterm election in 2010 and President Bush's 2006 midterm election. In both cases, the incumbent president had an approval rating below 50% at the time of the contest, much like Obama's approval rating today.

In October 2010, those voting to oppose President Obama, then in his first term and enjoying Democratic majorities in both chambers of Congress, was eight percentage points higher than those who said they were voting to support the president. Obama's late October approval rating was 45%. The election ended in a Republican rout that hampered the president's ability to enact his agenda, after two years of ambitious, albeit controversial, legislation.

Likewise, in November 2006, more voters said they were voting to oppose (31%) the second-term President Bush than support him (18%). This gap was reflected in the final election results, with Democrats taking back both chambers of Congress for the first time since 1994.

By contrast, years where more voters say they are voting to support the president than oppose him have been marked by congressional gains for the president's party. Just prior to 2002 midterms, 28% of voters said they were voting to support the then-popular Bush as opposed to 15% who were voting to oppose him. That year, Republicans won the midterm elections, reclaiming the Senate and strengthening their House majority.

In 1998, the sixth year of Clinton's presidency, more voters said they were voting to support him than not. In addition, Clinton enjoyed a strong approval rating. Democrats picked up a few House seats that year, bucking the historical trend that typically dooms the party of a second-term president.

More Than Six in 10 Republicans Voting to Oppose President Obama

President Obama prominently figures in to the message self-identified Republican voters are trying to send. More than six in 10 Republicans (64%) say their vote will be a message of opposition to the president. This is on par with the situation in November 2010, illustrating that Republican resistance to the president is as strong today as it was before that pivotal election.

Voting to Send the President a Message in 2014, by Self-Reported Party Affiliation

Among registered voters

	Republicans	Independents	Democrats
Message that you support Obama	2%	11%	54%
Message that you oppose Obama	64%	31%	6%
Not sending a message	30%	55%	38%

April 24-30, 2014

GALLUP'

A majority of self-identified Democrats (54%) say they will be voting to support the president, which is about where it was in 2010. This also indicates one of Obama's problems: Only slightly more than half of Democrats are motivated to vote in support of him, while almost two-thirds of Republicans are willing to vote against him. More independents say they will vote to oppose the president (31%) than to support him (11%).

Implications

President Obama recently said he has run his "last campaign," but that does not mean he will not have a considerable presence—for good or ill—in at least one more election.

Of course, it is early in the 2014 election cycle. Senate Democrats are hopeful that legislation their members introduced, such as increasing the minimum wage and taking action on climate change issues, will ignite popular support for Democratic candidates. Republicans, meanwhile, see reason that their support could widen—and Obama's popularity diminish—especially with regard to the healthcare law. And, of course, both sides will closely watch the economy's progress. If economic growth increases, Obama and Democrats could benefit; if not, their electoral prospects could worsen.

Survey Methods

Results for this Gallup poll are based on telephone interviews conducted April 24–30, 2014, on the Gallup Daily tracking survey, with a random sample of 1,336 registered voters, aged 18 and older, living in all 50 U.S. states and the District of Columbia.

For results based on the total sample of registered voters, the margin of sampling error is ±3 percentage points at the 95% confidence level.

May 09, 2014
MORE AMERICANS THINK THEY WILL RETIRE COMFORTABLY
For the first time since 2007, half expect to have enough money

by Rebecca Riffkin

WASHINGTON, D.C.—Half of Americans who are not yet retired think they will have enough money to live comfortably after they retire. This is the first time since 2007 that more Americans think they will be able to live comfortably than fear they will not be able to—although they are only slightly more likely to believe this.

Half of Nonretired Americans Think They Will Have a Comfortable Retirement
When you retire, do you think you will have enough money to live comfortably, or not?
Asked of nonretired adults

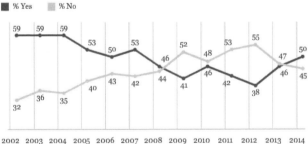

GALLUP'

Prior to 2008, a majority of nonretired Americans consistently thought they would be able to live comfortably in retirement. But this dropped to 46% early during the U.S. recession in 2008, and stayed below 50% until this year. In 2012, fewer than four in 10 nonretirees thought they would have enough money to live comfortably in retirement.

Notably, whereas 50% of nonretirees expect to live comfortably in retirement, this is lower than the 77% of current retirees

who say they have enough money to live comfortably. The percentage of retirees who report they are currently living comfortably also slightly exceeds the percentage of nonretirees who say they are currently living comfortably (69%), representing a consistent pattern over time.

Americans Closest to Retirement Age Are Most Mixed

Americans who are approaching retirement age, those aged 50 to 64, are more divided about whether they will have the money to live comfortably after retirement than those who are 18 to 49 years of age.

Confidence in Retiring Comfortably, by Age
When you retire, do you think you will have enough money to live comfortably, or not?

Age	% Yes	% No
18 to 29	52	44
30 to 49	51	44
50 to 64	45	48

Asked of nonretirees

GALLUP'

Americans who are closest to the conventional retirement age are generally worried about retirement. They are the age group most likely to think they will retire after age 65. Furthermore, 68% of 50- to 64-year-olds are very or moderately worried about having enough money for retirement, although this is similar to the percentage of 30- to 49-year-olds who say the same.

Implications

For the first time since before the recession, nonretirees are slightly more likely to think they will have enough money to live comfortably after retirement than think they will not have enough. Retirement worries are greatest among Americans aged 50 and older who are approaching retirement age and least among younger Americans.

This uptick in confidence in having enough money to retire comfortably may be related to the recent rises in the stock market. And while 401(k) accounts, which most nonretired Americans plan to rely on for income when they retire, dropped in value during the financial crisis, many are regaining their value, which could be easing Americans' fears about having a comfortable retirement.

Survey Methods

Results for this Gallup poll are based on telephone interviews conducted April 3–6, 2014, with a random sample of 1,026 adults, aged 18 and older, living in all 50 U.S. states and the District of Columbia.

For results based on the total sample of national adults, the margin of sampling error is ±4 percentage points at the 95% confidence level.

For results based on the sample of 334 retirees, the margin of sampling error is ±7 percentage points at the 95% confidence level.

For results based on the sample of 692 nonretirees, the margin of sampling error is ±5 percentage points at the 95% confidence level.

May 09, 2014

MORE IN U.S. HAVE SELF-FUNDED HEALTH COVERAGE, MEDICAID

Healthcare law's core coverage types are both more prevalent now

by Jenna Levy and Dan Witters

WASHINGTON, D.C.—More Americans aged 18 to 64 report getting health insurance coverage through a plan paid for by themselves or a family member or through Medicaid in April than in the latter half of 2013. Overall, the percentage of Americans under age 65 without health insurance has dropped nearly five percentage points to 16.3% from the 21.2% measured from Aug. 1–Sept. 30, 2013.

Percentage of 18- to 64-Year-Olds With Self-Funded Plans or Medicaid, by Quarter

Is your insurance coverage through a current or former employer, a union, Medicare, Medicaid, military or veteran's coverage, or a plan fully paid for by you or a family member?

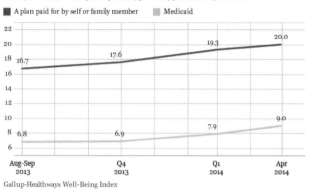

■ A plan paid for by self or family member   ▨ Medicaid

Gallup-Healthways Well-Being Index

GALLUP

These data were collected as a part of the Gallup-Healthways Well-Being Index, and are based on a nationally representative sample of at least 14,000 interviews with U.S. adults each month. Respondents were asked, "Is your primary health insurance coverage through a current or former employer, a union, Medicare, Medicaid, military or veteran's coverage, or a plan fully paid for by you or a family member?" Respondents who said they had a secondary form of health insurance were also asked, "Thinking about this secondary health insurance coverage, is it through a current or former employer, a union, Medicare, Medicaid, military or veteran's coverage, or a plan fully paid for by you or a family member?" Gallup used results for both primary and secondary types of insurance to form a combined estimate on insurance type.

Gallup and Healthways began asking about insurance types using the current question wording in August 2013. Gallup found 16.7% of 18- to 64-year-olds were covered by self-purchased health insurance Aug. 1–Sept. 30, 2013, and that figure has been ticking upward since the state and federal healthcare marketplace exchanges established under the Affordable Care Act opened in October 2013.

As the enrollment period for purchasing health insurance under the Affordable Care Act wound down in April, 20.0% of Americans aged 18 to 64 reported having a health insurance plan fully paid for by themselves or a family member. This is up slightly from 19.3% in the first quarter of 2014. Americans aged 18 to 64 who report having health insurance through Medicaid rose to 9.0% in April from 6.9% in the fourth quarter of 2013. At the same time, the percentage of those under age 65 who are uninsured is sharply lower in April

compared with the first quarter of 2014, and this figure has declined by more than five points since late 2013.

The percentage of Americans aged 18 to 64 who report having health insurance either through Medicare, military or veteran's coverage, or a union has been fairly stable over the last nine months. However, the percentage of Americans covered by a plan provided through a current or former employer decreased slightly in the first quarter of 2014. This decline could be due to several factors—employers may be dropping coverage for their employees, workers could be opting out of their employers' plans, or some Americans may be leaving the full-time workforce altogether. Regardless, this figure for the month of April was a bit higher than the first quarter of this year.

Type of Health Insurance Coverage in the U.S.

Is your insurance coverage through a current or former employer, a union, Medicare, Medicaid, military or veteran's coverage, or a plan fully paid for by you or a family member? Among 18- to 64-year-olds

	August-September 2013 %	Quarter 4 2013 %	Quarter 1 2014 %	April 2014 %
Current or former employer	44.4	44.2	42.5	43.1
A plan paid for by self or family member	16.7	17.6	19.3	20.0
Medicaid	6.8	6.9	7.9	9.0
Medicare	6.4	6.1	6.3	7.3
Military or veteran's	4.3	4.6	4.8	4.6
A union	2.8	2.5	2.6	2.5
(Something else)	3.8	3.5	3.7	4.0
No insurance	21.2	20.8	19.0	16.3

Gallup-Healthways Well-Being Index

GALLUP

Overall, the percentage of uninsured Americans among all age groups dropped to 13.4% in April, the lowest monthly measurement since Gallup and Healthways began ongoing tracking in January 2008. The uninsured rate is lower among all adults than it is among those ages 18 to 64 because seniors are eligible for Medicare. Thus, few seniors report not having health insurance.

Implications

The percentage of Americans aged 18 to 64 who are covered by health insurance that they themselves or a family member purchased has been on the rise since the Affordable Care Act's individual mandate and health insurance exchanges went into full effect this year. This increase is likely a direct result of the state and federal health insurance exchanges opening, which gave Americans the opportunity to compare various types of health insurance coverage and purchase individual and family plans. The exchanges were most likely to help those not offered or not eligible for health insurance through their employer, a union, or military and veteran's coverage, and those ineligible for Medicare and Medicaid. Given the way the law is structured, the gains seen in health insurance coverage are most likely to occur in the self-funded and Medicaid categories.

The increase in those reporting having Medicaid for health insurance likely reflects the Medicaid expansion enacted under the Affordable Care Act. A total of 21 states plus the District of Columbia have enacted locally managed state exchanges or state-federal partnerships, coupled with Medicaid expansions. These states have seen lower uninsured rates than those that have not enacted these measures.

Results are based on telephone interviews conducted as part of the Gallup-Healthways Well-Being Index survey August 2013 through April 2014 with a random sample of 118,000 adults aged 18 and older, living in all 50 U.S. states and the District of Columbia. Quarter 3 2013 results were only from the months of August and September, and were comprised of 24,927 respondents. Quarter 4 2013 results were comprised of 34,333 respondents. Quarter 1 2014 results were comprised of approximately 34,753 respondents. April 2014 results were comprised of approximately 11,695 respondents.

For results based on the total sample of 18- to 64-year-olds for each reported time period, the margin of sampling error is no more than ±1 percentage point at the 95% confidence level.

May 12, 2014
VOTER ENTHUSIASM DOWN SHARPLY FROM 2010
Republicans, Democrats less enthusiastic about voting

by Jeffrey M. Jones

PRINCETON, NJ—A majority of U.S. registered voters, 53%, say they are less enthusiastic about voting than in previous elections, while 35% are more enthusiastic. This 18-percentage-point enthusiasm deficit is larger than what Gallup has measured in prior midterm election years, particularly in 2010 when there was record midterm enthusiasm.

Compared to previous elections, are you more enthusiastic about voting than usual, or less enthusiastic?

Based on registered voters

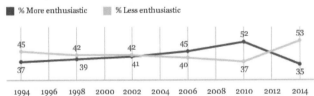

■ % More enthusiastic ▨ % Less enthusiastic

Note: Data for 1994 through 2010 based on annual averages. Data for 2014 based on April 24-30, 2014, Gallup poll.

GALLUP

Among registered voters, 42% of Republicans and Republican-leaning independents currently say they are more enthusiastic than usual about voting, while 50% are less enthusiastic, resulting in an eight-point enthusiasm deficit. But Democrats are even less enthusiastic, with a 23-point deficit (32% more enthusiastic vs. 55% less enthusiastic).

Typically, the party whose supporters have an advantage in enthusiasm has done better in midterm elections. Republicans had decided advantages in enthusiasm in 1994, 2002, and especially 2010—years in which they won control of the House of Representatives or expanded on their existing majority. Democrats had the advantage in 2006, the year they won control of the House. Neither party had a decided advantage in 1998, a year Democrats posted minimal gains in House seats.

More or Less Enthusiastic About Voting – Past Midterm Election Years, by Political Party
Based on registered voters

	% More enthusiastic	% Less enthusiastic	Net enthusiasm
2010			
Republicans/Republican leaners	62	28	+34
Democrats/Democratic leaners	44	44	0
2006			
Republicans/Republican leaners	41	40	+1
Democrats/Democratic leaners	52	38	+14
2002			
Republicans/Republican leaners	46	38	+8
Democrats/Democratic leaners	39	44	-5
1998			
Republicans/Republican leaners	41	39	+2
Democrats/Democratic leaners	38	43	-5
1994			
Republicans/Republican leaners	44	41	+3
Democrats/Democratic leaners	33	48	-15

Note: Data represent annual averages.

GALLUP

Although there is an apparent link between voter enthusiasm and midterm election outcomes, the mechanism through which that occurs is unclear. To some degree, greater enthusiasm may mean greater motivation to vote among the more enthusiastic party. However, Gallup has not been able to demonstrate that is the case, partly because changes in party affiliation from one midterm year to the next correlate with changes in enthusiasm by party.

Irrespective of whether a voter plans to turn out, enthusiasm may also be an expression of voters' optimism or pessimism about whether their party will have a strong or weak showing in the election.

Americans Not Highly Engaged in Election

A separate measure, one that historically has been predictive of turnout, asks Americans how much thought they have given to the election. Currently, 26% of Americans say they have given "quite a lot" or "some" thought to this year's midterm elections, much lower than Gallup's initial measurement in 2010 (37%) but on par with early readings in 2006 (28%) and 1998 (29%).

Not surprisingly, Americans usually give more thought to the election as it draws nearer—but in midterm election years, that typically has represented only about half of the public right before the election. The lower level of engagement at this point compared with similar points in prior years may indicate that overall voter turnout will be lower than in the last two midterm election years.

Currently, 37% of Republicans say they have given at least some thought to the election, compared with 24% of Democrats. Republicans' scores on this measure almost always exceed those for Democrats, so the size of the advantage is what matters for predicted turnout. The current 13-point Republican advantage in election thought is slightly smaller than the 2010 average of 15, but larger than the 2006 and 2002 averages of two and four points, respectively. That suggests Republicans may enjoy an above-average advantage in turnout this year, although perhaps not as significant as in 2010.

Implications

The thought and enthusiasm measures together suggest a mixed picture for Republicans. On one hand, it seems clear that 2014 will not be a repeat of 2010, when record Republican enthusiasm presaged major gains for the party in Congress. This year, Republicans' reported enthusiasm pales in comparison not only to 2010 but also to every other midterm election year.

However, Republicans still maintain advantages in thought given to the election and in voter enthusiasm compared with Democrats, and these advantages normally point to a better year for Republicans than Democrats. There is some uncertainty about how that will play out this year given that both Republicans and Democrats say they are less enthusiastic than usual about voting—something that has occasionally occurred in past midterm election years but never over the course of an entire midterm campaign.

Survey Methods

Results for this Gallup poll are based on telephone interviews conducted April 24–30, 2014, with a random sample of 1,513 adults, aged 18 and older, living in all 50 U.S. states and the District of Columbia.

For results based on the total sample of national adults, the margin of sampling error is ±3 percentage points at the 95% confidence level.

For results based on the total sample of 1,336 registered voters, the margin of sampling error is ±3 percentage points at the 95% confidence level.

May 13, 2014
U.S. SMALL-BUSINESS OWNERS' OPTIMISM CONTINUES TO EDGE UP
Wells Fargo/Gallup Small Business Index now at highest level since 2008

by Frank Newport

PRINCETON, NJ—U.S. small-business owners' optimism about their businesses continues to grow, with the Wells Fargo/Gallup Small Business Index rising slightly to +47 in the second quarter of 2014, up from +45 in the first quarter. The index is now at its highest level since 2008, although it is still significantly lower than in the pre-recession years from 2003 through 2007.

Wells Fargo/Gallup Small Business Index
The Small Business Index consists of owners' ratings of their business' current situation and their expectations for the next 12 months, measured in terms of their overall financial situation, revenue, cash flow, capital spending, number of jobs, and ease of obtaining credit.

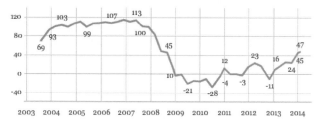

Index conducted since August 2003 and quarterly from December 2003-April 2014

GALLUP

These results are from the most recent update of the Wells Fargo/Gallup Small Business Index, based on telephone interviews with 600 small-business owners conducted March 31–April 4, 2014.

The rise in the index in late March and early April is the result of an increase in the future expectations score, based on owners' responses to a series of questions about anticipated conditions over the next 12 months. This score is now at +33, higher than at any point since the start of 2008. The present situation score, based on owners' assessments of their current situation, had jumped significantly in the first quarter, but has since decreased slightly to +14. Small-business owners' future expectations and assessments of their present situation nevertheless remain well below pre-recession levels.

Wells Fargo/Gallup Small Business Index
Scores for present situation and future expectations

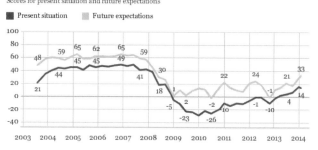

Index conducted since August 2003 and quarterly from December 2003-April 2014

GALLUP

One factor that has contributed to the uptick in small-business owners' optimism is their more positive attitudes about their ability to obtain credit. At this juncture, 32% of owners say it will be easy to obtain credit over the next year—up from 29% in the previous quarter—while another 37% say it will be about average. At the same time, 26% say it will be difficult to obtain credit; this is the lowest percentage recorded since the third quarter of 2008.

Wells Fargo/Gallup Small Business Index
Ease of obtaining credit over next 12 months

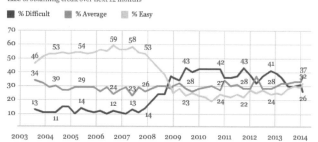

Index conducted since August 2003 and quarterly from December 2003-April 2014

GALLUP

From a longer-range perspective, there have been extreme shifts in small-business owners' views of credit since 2003. Up until 2008, about half or more of small-business owners felt that obtaining credit was easy. That changed dramatically as the recession unfolded, with the percentage saying that credit would be easy to obtain dropping to a low of 19% in the third quarter of 2010. The current view of credit availability thus represents a near-term improvement, but is far removed from the much more positive pre-recession era outlook.

Implications

U.S. small-business owners continue to recover from the major body blows suffered during the Great Recession. Owners' assessments of both their present situation and expectations for the future have recovered from lows registered in previous years, and the Wells Fargo/Gallup Small Business Index is now as high as it has been since 2008. However, attitudes have yet to recover to where they were pre-recession, and even if the current rate of improvement continues, it will be a long time until owners regain the optimism levels of 10 years ago.

Some of the more prominent political debates at the state and federal levels involve proposed policy changes relating to healthcare, immigration, and the minimum wage—all of which could have profound effects on small-business owners. The outcome of these debates could dictate whether small-business owners become more positive or negative in the coming years. Still, the fundamental need for any small business is actual customers willing to spend dollars, and the changes in dollars spent in the months ahead remain the most important factor likely to affect owners' views.

About the Wells Fargo/Gallup Small Business Index

Since August 2003, the Wells Fargo/Gallup Small Business Index has surveyed small-business owners on current and future perceptions of their business' financial situation. The index consists of two dimensions: 1) owners' ratings of the current situation of their businesses, and 2) owners' ratings of how they expect their businesses to perform over the next 12 months.

The overall Small Business Index is computed using a formula that scores and sums the answers to 12 questions—six about the present situation and six about the future. An index score of 0 indicates that small-business owners, as a group, are neutral—neither optimistic nor pessimistic—about their companies' situation. The overall index can range from −400 (the most negative score possible) to +400 (the most positive score possible), but in practice spans a much more limited range. The highest index reading was +114 in the fourth quarter of 2006, and the lowest reading was −28 in the third quarter of 2010.

Survey Methods

Results for the total data set are based on telephone interviews conducted March 31–April 4, 2014, with a random sample of 600 small-business owners, living in all 50 U.S. states and the District of Columbia.

For results based on the total sample of small-business owners, the margin of sampling error is ±4 percentage points at the 95% confidence level.

Sampling is done on a random-digit-dial basis using Dun & Bradstreet sampling of small businesses having $20 million or less in sales or revenues. The data are weighted to be representative of U.S. small businesses within this size range nationwide.

In addition to sampling error, question wording and practical difficulties in conducting surveys can introduce error or bias into the findings of public opinion polls.

May 14, 2014
AHEAD OF MIDTERMS, ANTI-INCUMBENT SENTIMENT STRONG IN U.S.
Twenty-two percent of voters say most members of Congress deserve re-election

by Jeffrey M. Jones

PRINCETON, NJ—The environment for congressional incumbents seeking re-election may be more challenging in 2014. With six months to go before the midterms, 22% of U.S. registered voters say most members of Congress deserve re-election, and 72% say they do not. The "deserve re-election" figure is on pace to be the lowest Gallup has measured in an election year.

Please tell me whether you think each of the following political officeholders deserves to be re-elected, or not. How about -- most members of Congress?

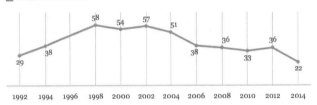

1992-2012 figures are final reading before election. 2014 figures are based on an April 24-30 poll. The question was not asked in 1996.

GALLUP

These results are based on an April 24–30 Gallup poll of 1,336 registered voters. The percentage of voters saying most incumbents deserve re-election is up slightly from the 17% Gallup measured in January. But even with the slight increase, the current 22% is lower than Gallup has measured in any other election year. The only other sub-30% readings before this year were 29% in October 1992 and 28% in both March 2010 and June 2010.

Democratic registered voters (28%) are slightly more likely than Republican registered voters (22%) to say most members of Congress deserve re-election. Independent voters, at 16%, are least likely to believe this.

U.S. voters as a whole are more positive about their own member of Congress than about most members of Congress, as they have been since Gallup first asked these items in 1992. Currently, 50% of voters say their own member deserves re-election. This, too, is slightly more positive than in January (46%), but is similar to levels observed at the time of the elections in 1992, 1994, 2006, and 2010. Most of these years saw relatively high turnover in Congress.

Please tell me whether you think each of the following political officeholders deserves to be re-elected, or not. How about -- the U.S. representative in your congressional district?

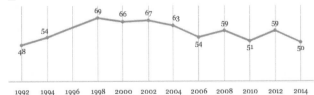

1992-2012 figures are final reading before election. 2014 figures are based on an April 24-30 poll. The question was not asked in 1996.

GALLUP

Republican (53%), Democratic (52%), and independent (47%) registered voters are about equally likely to say their own member deserves re-election.

The weak re-election figures also correspond with Congress' feeble job approval rating, at 15% in the new May 8–11 Gallup poll. That is also on the low end of what Gallup has measured in past election years.

Congressional Shake-Up on the Horizon?

A logical consequence of such dim views of Congress and its incumbents is that voters may take out their frustrations at the ballot box. Incumbent members of Congress are generally quite successful in getting re-elected, with roughly nine in 10 of those who seek re-election winning. However, the re-election rate tends to be lower in years when voters are less apt to think their own member or most members of Congress deserve re-election.

For example, in 1992 and 2010, when roughly 30% of registered voters thought most members of Congress deserved re-election and half thought their own member did, the incumbent re-election rate in the House of Representatives was lower than 90%. In turn, in the 1998–2002 elections, when U.S. voters were much more positive toward Congress, the re-election rates were 96% or higher.

Relationship of "Deserves Re-Election" Measures to Incumbent Re-Election Rates, 1992-2012 Elections for House of Representatives

Year	% Most members deserve re-election	% Own member deserves re-election	% of House members who sought and won re-election
2012	36	59	90
2010	33	51	85
2008	36	59	94
2006	38	54	94
2004	51	63	93
2002	57	67	96
2000	54	66	98
1998	58	69	98
1994	38	54	90
1992	29	48	88

1992-2012 figures on deserves re-election are final readings before election. The question was not asked in 1996.

GALLUP

One way to summarize the relationship between the "deserves re-election" measures and congressional turnover is to compute correlations, which provide a measure of association between two variables. Correlations near 1.0 indicate a strong positive relationship between the variables and scores near zero indicate no relationship whatsoever. The correlation between Gallup's "most members deserve re-election" item at the time of the election and actual incumbent re-election rates is .83 in all elections since 1992, and .87 in the five midterm elections in that time period. The correlation between the "own member" item and incumbent re-election rates is .86 in all elections and .87 in midterm elections.

Thus, the relatively low percentages of American voters saying members of Congress deserve re-election suggest that incumbents may be less successful than usual in winning re-election this year, being vulnerable to defeat by a challenger from their own party in their primary election or from the opposition party in the general election.

Implications

Even though the vast majority of congressional incumbents who are seeking re-election this year will win, the likelihood of an incumbent

winning appears as if it is on track to be lower than usual. The percentage of registered voters who think most members of Congress and their own member deserve re-election are at or near lows compared with prior election years, which indicates a more challenging environment for incumbents.

It is possible that voters' attitudes toward Congress will change between now and November, and thus more will believe congressional representatives deserve re-election. Historically, though, these measures do not change much during an election year, and when they have—such as in 1992 and 2006—they have generally become more negative rather than more positive.

Divided party control of Congress is a complicating factor for voters looking to take out their frustrations on Congress by voting against incumbents, with a Republican majority in the House of Representatives and a Democratic majority in the Senate. The same situation presented itself in the 2012 elections, when the incumbent re-election rate was 90% in a year in which voters were only a bit more positive than now toward incumbents.

Survey Methods

Results for this Gallup poll are based on telephone interviews conducted April 24–30, 2014, with a random sample of 1,336 registered voters, aged 18 and older, living in all 50 U.S. states and the District of Columbia.

For results based on the total sample of registered voters, the margin of sampling error is ±3 percentage points at the 95% confidence level.

May, 14, 2014
NEARLY ALL HAWAIIANS SAY THEIR LOCALE IS GOOD FOR MINORITIES
Texas and Alaska also rank high, while West Virginians are least positive

by Lydia Saad

PRINCETON, NJ—Ninety-five percent of Hawaii's residents consider the city or area in which they live to be a good place for racial and ethnic minorities, earning the Aloha State the top spot in Gallup's 50-state ranking on this measure. Texans and Alaskans are nearly as positive, with more than 90% saying their locales are good places for minorities to live.

States With Above-Average Social Climate for Minorities

Is the city or area where you live a good place or not a good place to live for racial or ethnic minorities?

	% Good place
Hawaii	95
Texas	92
Alaska	91
New Mexico	88
Washington	88
New Jersey	88
Delaware	87
Nevada	87

Gallup 50-state poll, June-December 2013

GALLUP

These results come from a 50-state Gallup poll conducted June–December 2013, with at least 600 residents in each state.

Nearly nine in 10 residents in an additional five states—New Mexico, Washington, New Jersey, Delaware, and Nevada—see their social climates as positive for minorities, all above Gallup's 50-state average of 83%.

West Virginians Are Least Positive About Climate for Minorities

No state performs terribly on this measure; in fact, solid majorities in all states think where they live is good for minorities. However, residents in 13 states register below-average scores of between 74% and 79%. West Virginia, at 74%, is the only state in which fewer than three-quarters of its residents are positive. Other states approaching this threshold are Missouri (76%), Vermont (77%), and Arkansas (77%).

States With Below-Average Social Climate for Minorities

Is the city or area where you live a good place or not a good place to live for racial or ethnic minorities?

	% Good place
West Virginia	74
Missouri	76
Vermont	77
Arkansas	77
New Hampshire	78
Mississippi	78
Kentucky	78
Michigan	78
Wyoming	78
Pennsylvania	78
Oklahoma	78
Louisiana	78
Idaho	79

Gallup 50-state poll, June-December 2013

GALLUP'

Parts of South Least Confident About Climate for Minorities

Five of the 13 states where residents are less likely than average to believe their communities are good places for racial and ethnic minorities are in the nation's South. These include Louisiana, Arkansas, Oklahoma, Mississippi, and Kentucky. But all other regions of the U.S. are also represented in the bottom-ranking states.

Beyond geography, there is a racial aspect to the states where residents perceive their communities as most and least hospitable to minorities.

All of the eight top-ranking states have relatively large minority populations of one race/ethnicity or another. Two—Texas and New Mexico—have large Hispanic populations. Two others—Hawaii and Washington—have large Asian or Native Hawaiian populations. And New Jersey and Nevada have fairly high proportions of Hispanics and Asians relative to the country as a whole. Just one state, Delaware, has a relatively high black population.

On the other hand, of the 13 states scoring below average for perceived minority well-being, none has a large Hispanic or Asian population, while four—Mississippi, Louisiana, Arkansas, and Michigan—have relatively high proportions of black residents, and Oklahoma has a fairly high proportion of Native Americans.

State Residents' Rating of Their Area as Good Place for Racial/Ethnic Minorities

■ Above-average rating
■ Average rating
■ Below-average rating

Gallup 50-state poll, June-December 2013
Note: No data available for the District of Columbia

GALLUP'

Still, racial composition alone does not determine residents' views of how hospitable their area is for minorities, because a number of the more racially diverse states such as Florida, Alabama, Arizona, Colorado, and New York fall near the average in Gallup's ranking as a good place for minorities.

Additionally, all states with large Hispanic or Asian/Native Hawaiian populations rank average or above average. By contrast, several states with large black populations rank below average, with most others average, and only one above average.

Bottom Line

Solid majorities of adult residents in every state in the union consider their area a good place for racial and ethnic minorities, ranging from 74% in West Virginia to 95% in Hawaii.

However, there is a clear race-related pattern, whereby states with large Hispanic or Asian populations all rank average or above average as good for racial/ethnic minorities, whereas states with large black populations tend to rank average or below average—with Delaware the only exception. While a key to understanding these differences may involve analyzing the results within each state according to residents' racial/ethnic backgrounds, that is not possible with the 50-state survey because of sample size.

Survey Methods

Results for this Gallup poll are based on telephone interviews conducted June–December 2013, with a random sample of approximately 600 adults per state, aged 18 and older, living in all 50 U.S. states.

For results based on the total sample of adults per state, the margin of sampling error is ±5 percentage points at the 95% confidence level.

May 15, 2014
MANY AMERICANS VIEW CONGRESSIONAL LEADERS NEGATIVELY
Republican leaders net higher favorability among Tea Party supporters

by Joy Wilke

WASHINGTON, D.C.—Americans' views of each of the four leaders of the House of Representatives and Senate continue to be more negative than positive. The two House leaders remain better known nationally than the two Senate leaders.

Favorability of Congressional Leaders

Next, we'd like to get your overall opinion of some people in the news. As I read each name, please say if you have a favorable or unfavorable opinion of these people -- or if you have never heard of them. How about...?

	% Favorable	% Unfavorable	% Never heard of/ No opinion	Net favorable (pct. pts.)
Speaker of the House, John Boehner	31	45	23	-14
Senate Democratic Leader, Harry Reid	27	41	32	-14
House Democratic Leader, Nancy Pelosi	33	49	18	-16
Senate Republican Leader, Mitch McConnell	23	40	37	-17

April 24-30, 2014

GALLUP

These are the results of an April 24–30 Gallup survey, which also shows that many Americans report they have never heard of or have no opinion of the congressional leaders.

House Leaders' Favorability Remains Low

John Boehner, who has served as the Republican leader of the House since 2006 and became speaker in 2011, enjoyed generally positive and neutral net favorability ratings between 2009 and 2011. His highest net favorable rating was in January 2011 when he became speaker, but fell later that same year. His rating has recovered somewhat from its lowest point during the government shutdown in late 2013, when Americans' unfavorable opinions of him outweighed favorable attitudes by 24 points.

Americans' views of Democratic leader Nancy Pelosi, who served as speaker from 2007 to 2011, remained mostly positive through 2008. She also enjoyed a surge in positivity in early 2007 when she became speaker. Since 2009, however, her unfavorable ratings have consistently overshadowed her favorable ratings by at least 12 points.

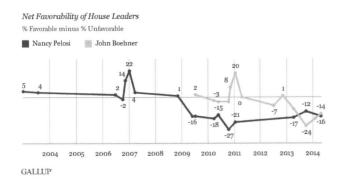

Net Favorability of House Leaders
% Favorable minus % Unfavorable

■ Nancy Pelosi ■ John Boehner

GALLUP

Favorability of Senate Leaders Remains Low

Democratic leader Harry Reid's net favorable now stands at −14, off its peak of +8 in 2006. Reid has not received a positive net favorable since 2007. Republican Mitch McConnell's net favorable is slightly worse at −17. Gallup has yet to measure a net positive score for McConnell since first asking about him in March 2010.

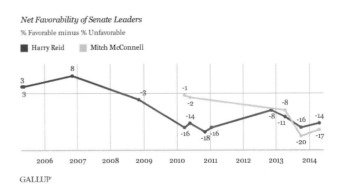

Net Favorability of Senate Leaders
% Favorable minus % Unfavorable

■ Harry Reid ■ Mitch McConnell

GALLUP

Tea Party Republicans Express Higher Support for GOP Leadership

The Tea Party continues to be an important component of the Republican Party, although its support has been dwindling. With its anti-establishment rhetoric and positioning, members of Congress aligned with the Tea Party have, at times, been at odds with the GOP leadership. Despite this, Republican leaders Boehner and McConnell get more positive ratings among self-identified Republicans who support the Tea Party than they garner among Republicans who do not.

Boehner currently has a net favorability rating of +32 among Republican supporters of the Tea Party, compared with a score of +9 among Republicans who do not support the Tea Party. Since 2010, Republican Tea Party supporters have consistently expressed more positive attitudes toward Boehner than non–Tea Party Republicans have. The gap between them is now 23 percentage points separating the groups' attitudes, down from a widest difference of 45 points in 2011.

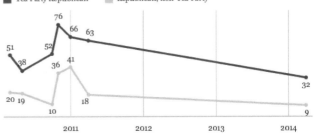

Favorability of John Boehner by Tea Party Status
% Favorable minus % Unfavorable

■ Tea Party Republican ■ Republican, non-Tea Party

Includes Republicans and independents who lean Republican

GALLUP

A similar pattern holds for Republicans' support of McConnell. Since 2010, Republicans who are Tea Party supporters have reported higher net favorability of McConnell, compared with non–Tea Party supporters.

As previous Gallup research shows, the Tea Party draws much of its support from Americans who are similar ideologically to traditional Republicans, whereas non–Tea Party Republicans are more likely to identify as liberal or moderate. This could explain the higher levels of support for Republican leadership among Tea Party supporters, despite the historical tensions between the Tea Party and the Republican establishment.

Favorability of Mitch McConnell by Tea Party Status

% Favorable minus % Unfavorable

■ Republican, Tea Party supporter ▨ Republican, non-Tea Party supporter

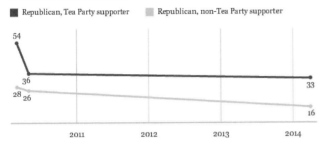

Includes Republicans and independents who lean Republican

GALLUP'

Implications

The current media narrative suggests Tea Party voters could be trouble for establishment candidates. These findings, however, suggest that Boehner's defeat of two Tea Party challengers in the Ohio Republican primary may have been at least partly attributable to his favorable image among Tea Party voters nationwide. Further, there is evidence that the gap in opinions between Tea Party Republicans and Republican non–Tea Party supporters may be shrinking.

McConnell receives higher net favorable ratings among Tea Party Republicans than among Republicans who do not support the Tea Party. This could be a positive sign for McConnell, who faces a Tea Party challenger in the Kentucky Republican primary on May 20. However, the Republican leader of the Senate remains relatively obscure to most Americans.

Survey Methods

Results for this Gallup poll are based on telephone interviews conducted April 24–30, 2014, on the Gallup Daily tracking survey, with a random sample of 1,513 adults, aged 18 and older, living in all 50 U.S. states and the District of Columbia.

For results based on the total sample of national adults, the margin of sampling error is ±3 percentage points at the 95% confidence level.

May 15, 2014
VIEW OF DEATH PENALTY AS MORALLY OK UNCHANGED IN U.S.
Lethal injection still widely viewed as most humane method

by Jeffrey M. Jones

PRINCETON, NJ—The recent news about the botched execution of an Oklahoma death row inmate has not affected the way Americans view the death penalty. Sixty-one percent say the death penalty is morally acceptable, similar to the 62% who said so in 2013, although both figures are down from a high of 71% in 2006.

The results are based on Gallup's annual Values and Beliefs poll, conducted May 8–11. On April 29, an Oklahoma death row inmate given a lethal injection appeared to suffer for an extended period of time until finally dying of a heart attack. That incident led to the postponement of a second execution scheduled in Oklahoma that day and raised questions about the methods used to execute prisoners.

Americans' Views of Death Penalty as Morally Acceptable

Next, I'm going to read you a list of issues. Regardless of whether or not you think it should be legal, for each one, please tell me whether you personally believe that in general it is morally acceptable or morally wrong. How about -- [RANDOM ORDER]?

■ % Acceptable ▨ % Wrong

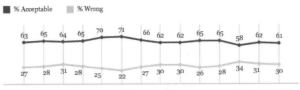

GALLUP'

The case did not fundamentally alter Americans' perceptions of the death penalty, however, with a solid majority viewing it as morally acceptable. This percentage is similar to the 60% who say they favor the death penalty as punishment for murder in Gallup's October update.

But the longer-term trends reveal that Americans have become less supportive of the death penalty. Gallup first asked the moral acceptability question in 2001, with an average 66% saying it was acceptable between 2001 and the peak in 2006. Over the last three years, the percentage saying it is morally acceptable has averaged 60%.

Similarly, Americans' support for the death penalty as a punishment for murder is also trending downward. Support reached a high of 80% in 1994, but it has generally slipped since then.

Americans Still Say Lethal Injection Most Humane Form of Execution

Lethal injection has been the most common method state officials have used to execute death row inmates for many years. The American public generally approves of that approach, as the poll finds Americans overwhelmingly saying lethal injection is the most humane way to administer the death penalty. The 65% holding this view compares with between 4% and 9% who endorse another method—the electric chair, gas chamber, firing squad, or hanging—as the most humane way to execute someone sentenced to death.

Gallup has asked this question twice before, and although 23 years have elapsed since the question was last asked, the results today have changed little. In 1991, 67% said lethal injection was the most humane method for administering the death penalty, and in 1985, 56% said this.

Americans' Views of Most Humane Way to Administer Death Penalty

Apart from your opinion about the death penalty, what form of punishment do you consider to be the most humane -- the electric chair, the gas chamber, lethal injection, firing squad or hanging?

	2014	1991	1985
	%	%	%
Lethal injection	65	67	56
Firing squad	9	3	3
Hanging	5	3	2
Electric chair	4	9	16
Gas chamber	4	6	8
None (vol.)	10	6	7
No opinion	3	5	9

GALLUP'

A majority of those who view the death penalty as morally acceptable and those who view it as morally wrong say lethal injection is the most humane way to execute prisoners. However, this belief is more common among those who say the death penalty is acceptable. Notably, roughly one in four of those who say the death penalty is morally wrong volunteer that "no method" is the most humane way to execute someone.

Americans' View of Most Humane Way to Administer the Death Penalty, by View of the Death Penalty

	View death penalty as morally acceptable	View death penalty as morally wrong
	%	%
Lethal injection	71	57
Firing squad	11	5
Hanging	6	3
Electric chair	4	3
Gas chamber	4	4
None of these (volunteered)	2	24

May 8-11, 2014

GALLUP

Implications

The drawn-out death of the Oklahoma prisoner reignited the debate over whether the death penalty violates the Constitution's prohibition of "cruel and unusual" punishment. The U.S. Supreme Court invalidated state death penalty statutes in the 1972 case *Furman v. Georgia*, deciding that death sentences were often arbitrary and consequently were a form of cruel and unusual punishment. Later, in the 1976 *Gregg v. Georgia* judgment, the Supreme Court ruled that states' rewritten statutes did pass constitutional muster, leading to a resumption of the death penalty in the U.S.

Americans have long supported the death penalty, with majorities saying they favor it as a penalty for murder and believe it is morally acceptable. While both of these Gallup trends show diminished support for the death penalty in recent years, the trends were in place well before the Oklahoma case.

Survey Methods

Results for this Gallup poll are based on telephone interviews conducted May 8–11, 2014, with a random sample of 1,028 adults, aged 18 and older, living in all 50 U.S. states and the District of Columbia.

For results based on the total sample of national adults, the margin of sampling error is ±4 percentage points at the 95% confidence level.

May 16, 2014
DEMOCRATIC PARTY STILL SEEN MORE FAVORABLY THAN GOP
Both parties face "upside down" net favorable ratings

by Andrew Dugan

WASHINGTON, D.C.—Americans view the Democratic Party more favorably than the Republican Party, even though both parties

have a net unfavorable rating. Democratic Party favorable ratings have held steady since last June, while Republican favorables have increased slightly from their all-time low last year. Still, if the Republicans' current favorability ratings hold, they will be the lowest ever for either party in an election year.

Republican and Democratic Party Favorables, 1992-2014

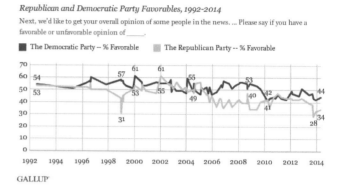

These ratings are based on a Gallup poll conducted April 24–30, 2014, in which the Democratic Party had a favorable rating of 44%, compared with 34% favorable for the Republican Party. Views of both parties have not changed markedly from the last update in December 2013, and the Republican Party's favorability has improved only modestly from the all-time low of 28% observed during the October government shutdown.

Overall, the GOP has a net favorability rating of −25 (34% favorable and 59% unfavorable), and this score has been negative since April 2011, averaging −15 percentage points. More broadly, the GOP has suffered from mostly negative or low positive scores since October 2005, about a year into President George W. Bush's second term, when his approval rating began to sink. The GOP boasted mostly positive net favorable scores prior to that, except for late 1998 and early 1999 during the Clinton impeachment vote and subsequent Senate trial.

Republican and Democratic Party Net Favorable Ratings, 1992-2014

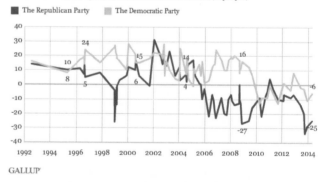

The Democrats' net favorable rating stands at −6 (44% favorable and 50% unfavorable), marking the fifth consecutive poll, dating to June 2013, in which Americans have viewed this party more unfavorably than favorably. The Democrats' net favorable rating throughout Barack Obama's presidency has alternated between episodes of positivity, such as in 2009 and in late 2012, and negativity, such as throughout 2010 and 2011. Prior to Obama's presidency, the Democratic Party had nearly always been viewed more positively than negatively—averaging a 15-point net favorable rating between

1992 and 2008, despite holding Congress or the presidency for no more than half of that time. In political polling parlance, both major political parties are currently "upside down" with the American public, meaning they have net negative approval ratings.

It has been almost a decade since Americans simultaneously viewed *both* parties more favorably than not, in July 2005.

Party With Higher Favorables Not Always Election Winner

The Democrats currently lead their Republican rivals in overall favorable ratings, but even if they are able to maintain this position throughout the 2014 midterm election cycle, it hardly augurs success for the party. There have been several instances in the eight elections from 1996 to 2012 (the 1998 midterm contest is excluded) in which the more popular party has failed to dominate the November elections.

Party Favorable Averages in Election Years

Averages of favorable ratings for all polls conducted in an election year prior to the election

Election year	Republican Party favorable average (%)	Democratic Party favorable average (%)	Election results
2014	34	44	?
2012	42	47	President Barack Obama re-elected, Democrats pick up seats in House and Senate
2010	41	43	Republicans take control of House and pick up 6 Senate seats
2008	41	54	Obama elected president, Democrats gain seats in House and Senate
2006	40	52	Democrats take control of Congress for first time since 1994
2004	51	52	President Bush re-elected, Congress remains in Republican control
2002	56	56	Republicans take control of Senate, strengthen majority in the House
2000	52	57	Bush wins election in a contest decided by Supreme Court, Democrats pick up Senate seats making party break 50-50
1996	52	57	Clinton wins re-election, Congress remains in Republican control

GALLUP'

Election results appear to more clearly favor one party in years when a majority of the country sees that party but not the other in a favorable light. This happened in 2006 and 2008, when the Democrats enjoyed majority average favorable ratings, while about four in 10 Americans had a favorable opinion of the Republican Party. Both elections were Democratic sweeps, with the 2008 elections giving Democrats control over both Congress and the White House for the first time since 1994.

The Republican rout in the 2010 midterms was not foreshadowed in the party's 41% average favorable rating that year, which was essentially no better than perceptions of the party in the election years of 2006 and 2008. However, views of the Democratic Party in 2010 had tumbled from the 2008 average by 11 points, indicating growing disenchantment with the ruling party. Even though the Democrats' 2010 average favorable rating was an insignificant two points higher than the Republicans', Republicans won the House handily and gained Senate seats.

Implications

The Democratic Party maintains a slender lead in favorability over the Republican Party, but both parties are "upside down" in net favorability. The fact that the public does not see either party positively suggests both parties will likely face some difficulties in convincing voters to give them their support this November. But for now, the Republican Party may have the most reason for concern: if its favorability rating hovers in the range in which it currently resides, this will be the lowest favorability rating either party has ever held in an election year. Given the GOP's big hopes this fall—including claiming a Senate majority—this low rating could cast cold water on these lofty objectives.

Survey Methods

Results for this Gallup poll are based on telephone interviews conducted April 24–30, 2014, on the Gallup Daily tracking survey, with a random sample of 1,513 adults, aged 18 and older, living in all 50 U.S. states and the District of Columbia.

For results based on the total sample of national adults, the margin of sampling error is ±3 percentage points at the 95% confidence level.

May 16, 2014
SATISFACTION WITH DIRECTION OF U.S. REMAINS AT 25%
Republicans still less satisfied than Democrats and independents

by Justin McCarthy

WASHINGTON, D.C.—Americans are as satisfied with the way things are going in the U.S. as they have been for the past five months. One in four (25%) say they are satisfied with the current direction of the country, while 74% express dissatisfaction.

In general, are you satisfied or dissatisfied with the way things are going in the United States at this time?

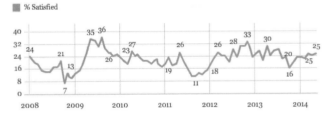

Trend since 2008

GALLUP'

Americans' satisfaction with the country's direction has remained flat over the past year, with the major exception of a drop to a low of 16% in October 2013 during the U.S. federal government shutdown. Otherwise, satisfaction has not strayed from the 20% range since April of last year when it reached 30%. This month's 25% is essentially the same as the 24% from April and the 25% reading in March. The latest findings are from a May 8–11 Gallup poll.

The high point for Americans' satisfaction with the country's direction during the Obama administration came in August 2009, when more than a third (36%) of Americans were satisfied with the direction of the country. The president entered office when 13% of Americans were content with the track the country was on. The lowest this figure reached under his leadership was 11% in August and September 2011, during a time of great economic angst.

Gallup has asked this question since 1979. Satisfaction reached an all-time high of 71% in February 1999 amid the dot-com boom. The lowest reading (7%) was measured in October 2008 as the nation grappled with the early effects of the 2008 global financial crisis.

Republicans Still Least Satisfied

Democrats (35%) and independents (24%) continue to be more satisfied with the state of the nation than Republicans (15%). Although low, the current level of satisfaction among Republicans is, by one percentage point, at its highest level since January 2009 when President Barack Obama was inaugurated.

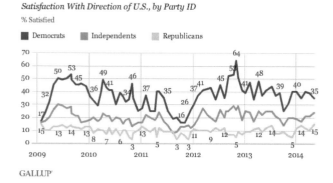

Satisfaction With Direction of U.S., by Party ID
% Satisfied

GALLUP'

Democrats' and Republicans' satisfaction with the country is strongly tied to whether the president in office is in their party. Since Obama's inauguration, Republican satisfaction has been consistently dismal, reaching its lowest of 3% on three separate occasions. Relatively speaking, however, Republicans have had a better outlook for the country's direction in 2014, with levels not dipping below 10% so far this year. In previous years, however, levels went long stretches below the 10% mark—from June to December in 2011, from August 2012 to February 2013, and from August to December 2013. Republican satisfaction has averaged 13% so far this year, after averaging below 10% each year from 2010 to 2013.

Democrats' satisfaction levels, meanwhile, have fallen slightly from last month's 39%. Still, their current satisfaction reading falls in the six-point margin they have maintained since December 2013. Independents' satisfaction levels have also stayed within a six-point margin on the question since December last year.

Bottom Line

Because 2014 has so far been largely devoid of any major political battles or sideshows, the waves of public opinion have been mostly calm and steady. Perhaps during a midterm election year partisan tensions could spark movement in the public's view of what kind of track the country is on. Also, to the extent the signs of economic recovery continue and strengthen, Americans may become more satisfied with national conditions more generally.

Though they are likely to continue being the least optimistic about the nation's direction, Republicans' pessimism may have bottomed out in the aftermath of last year's government shutdown, which jeopardized their party's image politically. One possible key for the outcome of the midterm elections is whether independents' level of satisfaction increases, decreases, or holds steady between now and November. An increase would likely be helpful to the Democratic Party, while a decrease could aid the Republicans' cause.

Survey Methods

Results for this Gallup poll are based on telephone interviews conducted May 8–11, 2014, with a random sample of 1,028 adults, aged 18 and older, living in all 50 U.S. states and the District of Columbia.

For results based on the total sample of national adults, the margin of sampling error is ±4 percentage points at the 95% confidence level.

May 19, 2014
JOBS, GOVERNMENT, AND ECONOMY REMAIN TOP U.S. PROBLEMS
Twenty percent mention unemployment or jobs, up from 14% in April

by Rebecca Riffkin

WASHINGTON, D.C.—Twenty percent of Americans name unemployment or jobs as the most important problem facing the country in May, up from 14% who mentioned these issues in April. Dysfunctional government (19%) and the economy in general (17%) also rank among the top problems.

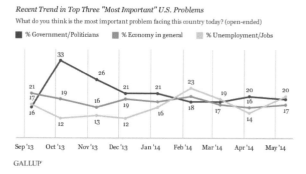

Recent Trend in Top Three "Most Important" U.S. Problems
What do you think is the most important problem facing this country today? (open-ended)

■ % Government/Politicians ■ % Economy in general ■ % Unemployment/Jobs

GALLUP'

These three issues—jobs, economy, and government—have been at the top of the "most important problem" list since the beginning of the year. Mentions of government and politicians rose sharply to 33% in October amid the partial government shutdown, but have dipped back down.

Mentions of the environment as the most important problem have ticked up to 3% in May from an average of 1% over the past six months. The increase may be related to recent news coverage highlighting the negative effects of global warming and climate change on the environment.

Most Important Problem Facing the U.S.
What do you think is the most important problem facing this country today?

	Apr 3-6, 2014	May 8-11, 2014
	%	%
Unemployment/Jobs	14	20
Dissatisfaction with government/Congress/politicians; Poor leadership/Corruption/Abuse of power	20	19
Economy in general	16	17
Poor healthcare/hospitals; High cost of healthcare	15	11
Federal budget deficit/Federal debt	9	8
Ethics/Moral/Religious/Family decline; Dishonesty	5	6
Education/Poor education/Access to education	6	5
Poverty/Hunger/Homelessness	5	4
Foreign aid/Focus overseas	4	4
Gap between rich and poor	3	3
Immigration/Illegal aliens	4	3
Environment/Pollution	1	3
Race relations/Racism	1	3

Responses listed by at least 3% of Americans are shown.

GALLUP'

Democrats Say Unemployment Is Top Problem, Republicans Say the Economy

Democrats are most likely to name jobs or unemployment as the country's most important problem, whereas Republicans' top response is the economy more generally. Democrats, Republicans, and independents are about equally likely to cite dissatisfaction with government. The federal budget deficit is a much larger concern among Republicans (16%) than among independents (7%) and Democrats (3%).

Top 13 "Most Important" Problems, by Party Identification
May 8–11, 2014

	Republicans %	Independents %	Democrats %
Unemployment/Jobs	17	20	25
Dissatisfaction with government/Congress/ politicians; Poor leadership/Corruption/Abuse of power	17	22	21
Economy in general	21	17	13
Poor healthcare/hospitals; High cost of healthcare	15	13	6
Federal budget deficit/Federal debt	16	7	3
Ethics/Moral/Religious/Family decline; Dishonesty	10	5	1
Education/Poor education/Access to education	1	6	6
Poverty/Hunger/Homelessness	3	4	5
Foreign aid/Focus overseas	3	4	4
Gap between rich and poor	*	3	6
Immigration/Illegal aliens	5	4	2
Environment/Pollution	*	2	7
Race relations/Racism	*	2	6

* Less than 0.5%

GALLUP

Democrats are much more likely to mention the environment as the top problem than are independents and Republicans. Democrats are more likely than Republicans to list several social issues, such race relations, the gap between rich and poor, and education. At least 6% of Democrats cite these issues compared with 1% or fewer Republicans. On the other hand, Republicans are more likely than Democrats to list moral and ethical decline and the economy in general as the most important problem.

Bottom Line

Americans are about equally likely to name unemployment and dissatisfaction with government as the most important problems facing the U.S., with the economy in general following closely behind. These issues have ranked at the top of the most important problem list since the beginning of 2014.

Despite recent congressional budget compromises, nearly one in five Americans still cite government itself as the nation's top problem. And even though U.S. workers report an increase in net hiring, unemployment and jobs remain at the top of the list.

Survey Methods

Results for this Gallup poll are based on telephone interviews conducted May 8–11, 2014, with a random sample of 1,028 adults, aged 18 and older, living in all 50 U.S. states and the District of Columbia.

For results based on the total sample of national adults, the margin of sampling error is ±4 percentage points at the 95% confidence level.

May 19, 2014
REPUBLICANS HAVE EDGE ON TOP ELECTION ISSUE: THE ECONOMY
Democrats have advantage on Affordable Care Act and economic inequality

by Frank Newport

PRINCETON, NJ—American voters rate the economy as the most important issue to their vote for Congress this year, and give the Republicans in Congress a slight edge over the Democrats as best able to handle it. Voters give four other issues lower, but still above-average, importance—the federal deficit, taxes, the Affordable Care Act, and income and wealth inequality. Voters see Republicans as better able to handle the first two, while Democrats have the edge on the latter two.

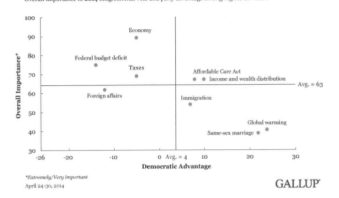

Issues in 2014 Elections
Overall importance to 2014 congressional vote and party advantage among registered voters

Extremely/Very important
April 24–30, 2014

GALLUP

These results are from an April 24–30 Gallup survey. Registered voters were asked to rate the importance of nine issues to their vote for Congress, and then asked to indicate which party would do a better job on each issue. The accompanying graph displays the ranking of these nine issues on both of these dimensions simultaneously. The higher the issue is on the vertical axis, the more important voters say it is to their vote, while the further to the right it is, the greater the perceived Democratic advantage.

- Republicans clearly have an advantage on three economic issues, all of which voters place above-average importance on—the "economy," the federal budget deficit, and taxes. The economy is the single most important issue tested, with 89% of voters rating it as extremely or very important. Forty-eight percent of voters say the Republicans can do the best job on the economy, while 43% say this about the Democrats.
- The other two issues to which voters attach slightly above-average importance are the Affordable Care Act and income and wealth inequality. Democrats have an eight- and 10-percentage-point advantage on these, respectively.
- Voters give the remaining four issues below-average importance. Republicans have the perceived advantage on handling foreign affairs, while voters give Democrats the advantage on immigration, same-sex marriage, and global warming. The Democratic advantage is particularly strong on same-sex marriage and global warming, although these two issues receive the lowest importance ratings of any of the issues tested.

Inequality, Same-Sex Marriage, Global Warming More Important to Democrats

Republicans and Democrats rate the importance of four of the issues similarly, including agreeing on the economy's importance. Democrats are significantly more likely than Republicans to rate global warming, same-sex marriage, and income and wealth inequality as important. Although same-sex marriage and global warming may have lower potential payoff in terms of the overall voting population, given their below-average importance ratings, they may still be campaign issues that Democrats can use to motivate their voting base.

Republicans give two issues a higher level of importance than do the Democrats—the federal budget deficit and taxes.

Importance of Issues to Congressional Vote This Year -- by Party

% Extremely/Very important, based on registered voters

	Republicans/ Leaners	Democrats/ Leaners
	%	%
The economy	91	87
The federal budget deficit	86	65
The way income and wealth are distributed in the U.S.	59	76
The Affordable Care Act, also known as "Obamacare"	67	70
Taxes	74	64
Foreign affairs	65	61
Immigration	55	56
Same-sex marriage	33	47
Global warming	16	63

April 24-30, 2014

GALLUP

Implications

American voters have a clearly differentiated sense of which issues will or will not be important to their vote for Congress this year. They give economy-related issues, including the distribution of income and wealth, along with the Affordable Care Act, above-average importance. Hot-button issues such as immigration and global warming, and issues that have been much in the news recently, such as foreign affairs and immigration, have below-average importance.

There is universal agreement across party lines on the importance of the economy this year, and Republicans have a slight perceptual advantage as the party best able to handle the issue, perhaps partly stemming from the blame the voters may place on the party that currently controls the White House. On the other hand, opinions diverge on the importance of issues such as global warming and same-sex marriage, with Democrats much more focused on these issues than Republicans are. While these issues may not have broad salience, they may work well as issues Democrats can use to motivate their voter base—vitally important in midterm elections in which turnout can be as important as changing people's minds about who can best handle an issue.

Survey Methods

Results for this Gallup poll are based on telephone interviews conducted April 24–30, 2014, with a random sample of 1,336 registered voters, aged 18 and older, living in all 50 U.S. states and the District of Columbia.

For results based on the total sample of registered voters, the margin of sampling error is ±3 percentage points at the 95% confidence level.

May 20, 2014

MOST U.S. SMALL-BUSINESS OWNERS WOULD DO IT ALL OVER AGAIN

Owners say greatest reward is independence, greatest challenge is generating revenue

by Frank Newport

PRINCETON, NJ—More than eight in 10 U.S. small-business owners say they would still become a small-business owner if they had it to do over again. This sentiment has changed little over the past 11 years, which suggests that the difficulties many small businesses experienced during the Great Recession did not cause owners to regret their decision to start a business.

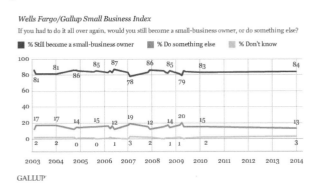

Wells Fargo/Gallup Small Business Index

If you had to do it all over again, would you still become a small-business owner, or do something else?

These results are from the most recent update of the Wells Fargo/Gallup Small Business Index, based on telephone interviews with 600 small-business owners conducted March 31–April 4, 2014.

From August 2003 through the first quarter of 2010, the Wells Fargo/Gallup Small Business Index regularly asked small-business owners about their decision to start a business, but did not ask this question in the intervening years until this most recent update.

One of the key reasons many small-business owners would do it all over again is that they clearly value the independence they get from their choice of career, which no doubt is a part of their satisfaction with their career choice. When asked to name the most rewarding thing about starting and running their own business, over four in 10 talk about being their own boss and being the decision-maker. Other responses mentioned by more than 10% of respondents include having a sense of job satisfaction, having family time and schedule flexibility, and interacting with customers.

Wells Fargo/Gallup Small Business Index

What would you say has been the most rewarding thing about starting and running your own business? (Open-ended)

	Total %
Being my own boss/Independence/Being the decision-maker	42
Job satisfaction/Sense of accomplishment/Pride	17
Work my own schedule/Flexible/Having more family time	12
Interacting with customers	11
Financial rewards/Money	7
Creating jobs/Employment	2
Community involvement/Giving back to community	1
Working with family	0
Other	3
None/Nothing	4
Don't know	1

March 31-April 1, 2014

GALLUP

At the same time, small-business owners recognize that it's a tough job. When asked about their biggest challenges, the majority of responses focus on the nuts and bolts of keeping a business running, such as generating revenue and a customer base, securing cash flow, obtaining credit and funds, and marketing and getting the word out about their business. Other responses that smaller percentages of owners mention include frustration with government regulations, employee issues, and dealing with uncertainty.

Wells Fargo/Gallup Small Business Index

Thinking now about when you started your small business, what would you say was the biggest challenge you faced when you opened your small business? (Open-ended)

	Total %
Securing accounts/Generating revenue/Customer base	23
Cash flow	15
Credit financing/Availability of funds	10
Bureaucracy/Licensing requirements/Government regulations	8
Advertising/Marketing/Getting the word out/Reputation	8
Unknown factors/Learning curve/Uncertainty	7
Employee issues/Hiring/HR issues	6
Paperwork/Organization/Managing/Getting started	3
Expenses/Maintenance/Repairs/Spending	2
Finding quality vendors/Inventory/Product line	2
Personal sacrifice/Long hours	2
Competing with other businesses	2
Taxes/Fees	1
Labor costs/Health insurance/Benefits	1
The economy/The market	1
Technology/Website	1
Other	1
None/Nothing	5
Don't know	2

March 31-April 1, 2014

GALLUP'

Implications

Small-business owners obviously like their choice of career, with 84% indicating that if they had it to do over again, they would still opt to start their own business. These attitudes have not fluctuated much over the past decade or so, and apparently the recession—which caused owners' optimism to fall dramatically—still did not affect their satisfaction with their decision to start a business. Owners' sense of freedom and independence derived from their entrepreneurship apparently overcomes the challenges of finding and keeping customers and maintaining enough cash flow to keep the business afloat.

Survey Methods

Results for the total data set are based on telephone interviews conducted March 31–April 4, 2014, with a random sample of 600 small-business owners, living in all 50 U.S. states and the District of Columbia.

For results based on the total sample of small-business owners, the margin of sampling error is ±4 percentage points at the 95% confidence level.

Gallup utilizes a Dun & Bradstreet sample of small businesses nationwide having $20 million or less in sales or revenue. The data are weighted to be representative of U.S. small businesses within this size range nationwide as well as by census region.

May 21, 2014
SAME-SEX MARRIAGE SUPPORT REACHES NEW HIGH AT 55%
Nearly eight in 10 young adults favor gay marriage

by Justin McCarthy

WASHINGTON, D.C.—Americans' support for the law recognizing same-sex marriages as legally valid has increased yet again, now at 55%. Marriage equality advocates have had a string of legal successes over the past year, most recently this week in Pennsylvania and Oregon where federal judges struck down bans on gay marriage.

Do you think marriages between same-sex couples should or should not be recognized by the law as valid, with the same rights as traditional marriages?

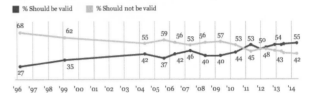

Note: Trend shown for polls in which same-sex marriage question followed questions on gay/lesbian rights and relations
1996-2005 wording: "Do you think marriages between homosexuals ... "

GALLUP'

Two successive Gallup polls in 2012 saw support climb from 53% to 54%, indicating a steady but slight growth in acceptance of gay marriages over the past year after a more rapid increase between 2009 and 2011. In the latest May 8–11 poll, there is further evidence that support for gay marriage has solidified above the majority level. This comes on the heels of gay marriage proponents' 14th legal victory in a row.

When Gallup first asked Americans this question about same-sex marriage in 1996, 68% were opposed to recognizing marriage between two men or two women, with slightly more than a quarter supporting it (27%). Since then, support has steadily grown, reaching 42% by 2004 when Massachusetts became the first state to legalize it—a milestone that reached its 10th anniversary this month.

In 2011, support for gay marriage vaulted over the 50% mark for the first time, and since 2012, support has remained above that level. In the last year, however, support has leveled off a bit. Currently, 17 states and the District of Columbia have legalized same-sex marriage, while several states wait in legal limbo as they appeal judge rulings overturning state bans.

Among the most dramatic divisions in opinion on the issue are between age groups. As has been the case in the past, support for marriage equality is higher among younger Americans; the older an American is, the less likely he or she is to support marriage for same-sex couples. Currently, adults between the ages of 18 and 29 are nearly twice as likely to support marriage equality as adults aged of 65 and older.

Support for Legal Same-Sex Marriage by Age, 1996, 2013, and 2014

	% Should be legal, 1996	% Should be legal, 2013	% Should be legal, 2014	Change, 1996-2014 (pct. pts.)
18 to 29 years	41	70	78	+37
30 to 49 years	30	53	54	+24
50 to 64 years	15	46	48	+33
65+ years	14	41	42	+28

GALLUP'

Opinions also differ dramatically along party lines. Democrats (74%) are far more likely to support gay marriage as Republicans are (30%), while independents (58%) are more in line with the national average. Though Republicans still lag behind in their support of same-sex marriage, they have nearly doubled their support for it since Gallup began polling on the question in 1996.

Support for Legal Same-Sex Marriage by Political Subgroup, 1996, 2013, and 2014

	% Should be legal, 1996	% Should be legal, 2013	% Should be legal, 2014	Change, 1996-2013 (pct. pts.)
All Americans	27	53	55	+28
Democrat	33	69	74	+41
Independent	32	58	58	+26
Republican	16	26	30	+14
Liberal	47	80	82	+35
Moderate	32	60	63	+31
Conservative	14	28	31	+17

GALLUP

An important region on the radar of gay marriage advocates is the South, where a condensed cluster of bans on same-sex marriage exists. All southern states have constitutional bans on same-sex marriage, from Louisiana in 2004 through North Carolina in 2012, though bans have been challenged in Arkansas and Kentucky. The South (48%) is the only region where same-sex marriage support falls below the 50% mark. Support is highest in the East, where two-thirds (67%) of residents support gay marriage.

Support for Same-Sex Marriage, by Region

	% Should be valid
East	67
West	58
Midwest	53
South	48

May 8-11, 2014

GALLUP

Bottom Line

For proponents of marriage equality, years of playing offense have finally paid off as this movement has reached a tipping point in recent years—both legally and in the court of public opinion. The latest gains are in Pennsylvania and Oregon, with court challenges in Utah, Oklahoma, and Virginia likely to be determined soon. Having spent years trying to influence state lawmakers to take action, gay marriage supporters' game strategy has officially pivoted to challenging state bans in court. One key question in the legal battle is the constitutionality of voter-approved state bans.

Younger Americans are more supportive of same-sex marriage, and this will likely continue to drive overall support at the gradual pace it has increased over recent years. While the map of gay marriage is regionally diverse, it is not so in the South, where traditional marriage advocates still hold a majority of support. Public opinion in southern states will be a barometer to observe, as the bulk of future legal battles will play out there in the months and years to come.

Survey Methods

Results for this Gallup poll are based on telephone interviews conducted May 8–11, 2014, with a random sample of 1,028 adults, aged 18 and older, living in all 50 U.S. states and the District of Columbia.

For results based on the total sample of national adults, the margin of sampling error is ±4 percentage points at the 95% confidence level.

May 22, 2014
IN U.S., ADULT OBESITY RATE NOW AT 27.7%
Blacks are still most likely to be obese among demographic groups

by Justin McCarthy

WASHINGTON, D.C.—In the U.S., the adult obesity rate is 27.7% thus far in 2014. This compares with the 27.1% average in 2013—the highest annual rate Gallup and Healthways have measured since beginning to track obesity in 2008.

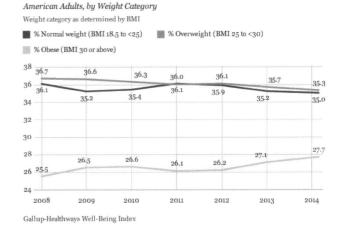

American Adults, by Weight Category
Weight category as determined by BMI

Gallup-Healthways Well-Being Index

GALLUP

The Gallup-Healthways Well-Being Index, which uses respondents' self-reports of their height and weight to calculate body mass index (BMI) scores, differs slightly from government reports of obesity, which are based on actual heights and weights found in clinical measurements. Individual BMI values of 30 or above are classified as "obese," 25 to 29.9 are "overweight," 18.5 to 24.9 are "normal weight," and 18.4 or less are "underweight." For the past six years, nearly two-thirds of Americans have had BMIs higher than are recommended, while roughly 35% of Americans have been in the "normal weight" category.

Thirty-five percent of Americans are classified having a normal weight so far in 2014, while 35.3% of adults are considered "overweight." Meanwhile, underweight Americans make up a very small 2.1% of the adult population.

The obesity rate was 25.5% in 2008 when Gallup and Healthways first began tracking it. The percentage of obese adults has fluctuated since then, but it is now 2.2 percentage points higher than it was in 2008.

Blacks Adults Still Have Highest Obesity Rate

Across major demographic categories, obesity rates are higher or stable thus far in 2014 compared with 2013. As has previously been the case, blacks (35.5%) are the most likely to be obese among all demographic groups. Meanwhile, young adults aged 18 to 29 years (17.0%) and high-income Americans (23.1%), those who earn $90,000 or more annually, remain the groups least likely to be obese.

The obesity rate among older Americans aged 65 and older ticked up 1.6 points so far in 2014 to 27.9%, the largest increase among subgroups.

Percentage Obese in U.S. Among Various Demographic Groups

Sorted by largest change to smallest

Among adults aged 18 and older

	2013	2014	Difference
	%	%	(pct. pts.)
Aged 65+	26.3	27.9	1.6
East	25.6	26.8	1.2
Annual income $90,000+	22.0	23.1	1.1
West	24.1	25.1	1.0
Midwest	28.6	29.6	1.0
Women	26.2	26.9	0.7
NATIONAL ADULTS	27.1	27.7	0.6
Whites	26.0	26.6	0.6
Aged 45-64	32.5	33.0	0.5
Aged 30-44	28.9	29.3	0.4
Annual income less than $36,000	31.5	31.9	0.4
Men	28.1	28.4	0.3
Hispanics	27.8	28.1	0.3
Annual income $36,000-$89,999	27.7	27.7	0.0
Aged 18-29	17.2	17.0	-0.2
Blacks	35.8	35.5	-0.3
South	29.2	28.7	-0.5

Gallup-Healthways Well-Being Index

2014 data from Jan. 1-May 19

GALLUP'

Bottom Line

Reducing obesity rates could unlock a bevy of economic and societal benefits including lower costs to employers. But despite the issue's ample media attention—including first lady Michelle Obama's "Let's Move" campaign—obesity rates have not declined.

"While it is difficult to identify long-term trends from short-term data, these data suggest, at best, no retreat in the obesity epidemic and, at worst, a deterioration," said Janna Lacatell, Healthways Lifestyle Solutions Director. "Given that obesity leads to higher rates of serious health conditions like diabetes and hypertension, and has been shown to cause disease onset at younger ages, this is a significant public health concern. Further, populations that have a disproportionately high obesity rate, such as African Americans and southerners, also have disproportionately higher diabetes rates."

Focusing on preventing and reducing obesity at the local level could be key to addressing this national health issue. Communities may want to emulate localities like Boulder, Colorado, where residents tend to be very active and obesity rates are significantly lower than is found in other communities across the country.

Survey Methods

Results are based on telephone interviews conducted as part of the Gallup-Healthways Well-Being Index survey Jan. 1–May 19, 2014, with a random sample of 64,546 adults, aged 18 and older, living in all 50 U.S. states and the District of Columbia.

For results based on the total sample of national adults, the margin of sampling error is ±1 percentage point at the 95% confidence level.

May 22, 2014

MOST U.S. VOTERS OK WITH SPLIT-PARTY CONTROL OF CONGRESS

Just as many favor divided control as one-party control

by Jeffrey M. Jones

PRINCETON, NJ—Roughly as many U.S. registered voters say it is better for the country to have divided-party control of Congress as say it is better to have one party in control of both the House and Senate. The remainder say it makes no difference or have no opinion.

Registered Voters' Preference for One-Party or Divided-Party Control of Congress

As you may know, the U.S. Congress consists of two houses -- the House of Representatives and the Senate. Regardless of which party you prefer, do you think it is better for the country -- [ROTATED: to have one political party control both the House of Representatives and the Senate, does it make no difference either way, (or do you think it is better) to have one political party control the House of Representatives and the other control the Senate]?

One party control both House and Senate	Makes no difference	One party control House, other control Senate	No opinion
32%	24%	36%	8%

April 24-30, 2014

GALLUP'

The major story line in the 2014 midterm elections seems to be whether the Republicans can win enough seats in the Senate to have full-party control of Congress. Political experts generally do not believe Democrats will win enough seats in the House to take control of that chamber.

Republicans have held majority control in the House since 2011, but with Democrats controlling the Senate, Congress has had difficulty passing legislation on some of the major issues facing the country. The split control has contributed to a dearth of legislation this session. The current 113th Congress is on pace to be one of the least productive in history, based on the number of bills passed into law.

Also, Congress' approval ratings have been historically low in recent years, as is trust in the legislative branch of the federal government. Americans who are critical of Congress commonly mention "gridlock," "partisanship," or lack of action as reasons why they disapprove. Also, "dissatisfaction with government" has ranked among the top issues in recent years when Gallup has asked Americans to name the most important problem facing the country.

Nevertheless, Americans do not appear to see one-party control of Congress as a solution to those ills or a desirable situation in general.

Americans' views on the matter do not appear to be based on strategic responses by partisan voters. It is possible Republicans will say they prefer one-party control of Congress because it appears there is a reasonable chance that Republicans could win control of both houses after this year's elections. And, in turn, Democrats might say they prefer divided control as that appears it may be the best-case scenario for their party this election year. However, both Democrats and Republicans are about evenly split on the desirability of one-party versus divided-party control of Congress. True to their more anti-partisan outlook, independents show a clearer preference for divided control of Congress.

Preference for One-Party or Divided-Party Control of Congress, by Party Identification, Registered Voters

As you may know, the U.S. Congress consists of two houses -- the House of Representatives and the Senate. Regardless of which party you prefer, do you think it is better for the country -- [ROTATED: to have one political party control both the House of Representatives and the Senate, does it make no difference either way, (or do you think it is better) to have one political party control the House of Representatives and the other control the Senate]?

	One party control both House and Senate	Makes no difference	One party control House, other control Senate	No opinion
Democrat	37%	23%	32%	8%
Independent	27%	27%	40%	6%
Republican	35%	20%	36%	9%

April 24-30, 2014

GALLUP

Younger and older voters have different views on whether it is better to have one party controlling both houses of Congress. Those aged 18 to 29, who are more likely to be politically independent, believe it is better to have divided control, while older voters are much more likely to endorse the idea of one party controlling both houses.

Preference for One-Party or Divided-Party Control of Congress, by Age, Registered Voters

As you may know, the U.S. Congress consists of two houses -- the House of Representatives and the Senate. Regardless of which party you prefer, do you think it is better for the country -- [ROTATED: to have one political party control both the House of Representatives and the Senate, does it make no difference either way, (or do you think it is better) to have one political party control the House of Representatives and the other control the Senate]?

	One party control both House and Senate	Makes no difference	One party control House, other control Senate	No opinion
18-29 years	27%	26%	43%	4%
30-49 years	28%	25%	39%	7%
50-64 years	34%	26%	35%	5%
65+ years	41%	20%	27%	12%

April 24-30, 2014

GALLUP

Implications

If Republicans can maintain their majority in the House and win a majority of Senate seats after the 2014 midterm elections, it could mean that Congress would have an easier time passing legislation than it has in the last few years. However, that would not necessarily solve the issue of government gridlock in the short term, given that President Barack Obama would have to sign any legislation a Republican House and Senate pass.

Passing new legislation and getting it signed into law is easiest when one party is in control of the White House and both houses of Congress, as was the case in 1992–1993, 2003–2006,

and 2009–2010. But each of those recent reigns of one-party control were short-lived as Americans, likely uncomfortable with U.S. policy going too far to the left or too far to the right, gave control of one or both houses of Congress to the other party in the next midterm election.

Thus, it appears Americans' reluctance to back one-party control of Congress, despite their obvious frustration with the work Congress is doing, may stem from their desire for moderation in U.S. policy over a Congress that can more easily pass legislation and get things done.

Survey Methods

Results for this Gallup poll are based on telephone interviews conducted April 24–30, 2014, with a random sample of 1,336 registered voters, aged 18 and older, living in all 50 U.S. states and the District of Columbia.

For results based on the total sample of registered voters, the margin of sampling error is ±3 percentage points at the 95% confidence level.

May 22, 2014
U.S. STILL SPLIT ON ABORTION: 47% PRO-CHOICE, 46% PRO-LIFE
No decline in voters who prioritize abortion issue, now at 19%

by Lydia Saad

PRINCETON, NJ—Americans remain divided on the abortion issue, with 47% of U.S. adults describing their views as "pro-choice" and 46% as "pro-life," continuing a pattern seen since 2010.

U.S. Adults' Position on Abortion

With respect to the abortion issue, would you consider yourself to be pro-choice or pro-life?

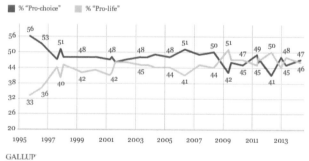

GALLUP

These results are based on Gallup's annual Values and Beliefs survey, conducted May 8–11. Gallup's trend on this question stretches back to 1995, when Americans tilted significantly more toward the pro-choice label. The balance generally remained more in the pro-choice direction until 2009 when for the first time more Americans identified as pro-life than pro-choice. Since then, these attitudes have fluctuated some, but remain roughly split.

Abortion Views Are Most Unified in the East

Americans' identification with the two abortion politics labels differs somewhat by gender and age, with women and 18- to 34-year-olds tilting pro-choice, and men and Americans aged 55 and older tilting pro-life. Middle-aged adults are evenly split on the issue.

Regionally, Easterners are the most unified, with 59% calling themselves pro-choice, whereas in all other regions, no more than 50% identify with either label. However, Southerners lean toward the pro-life position (49% to 41%), while those in the Midwest and West are about evenly split.

By far the biggest differences in these views are political, with over two-thirds of Republicans calling themselves pro-life and about as many Democrats identifying as pro-choice. Independents fall squarely in the middle.

Americans' Position on Abortion

By gender, age, region, and party ID

	"Pro-choice"	"Pro-life"
	%	%
U.S. adults	47	46
Men	44	51
Women	50	41
18-34 years	50	40
35-54 years	48	46
55+ years	44	50
East	59	35
Midwest	46	50
South	41	49
West	48	47
Republican	27	69
Independent	46	45
Democrat	67	28

May 8-11, 2014

GALLUP

The Moderate Middle Position Down to 50%

A second long-term Gallup trend, this one measuring Americans' views on the extent to which abortion should be legal, finds 50% saying abortion should be "legal only under certain circumstances," or in other words, favoring limited abortion rights. This stance has prevailed since 1975. However, a combined 49% of Americans takes a more hardline position, including 28% saying abortion should be legal in all circumstances and 21% believing it should be illegal in all circumstances.

Support for the strong anti-abortion rights position has hovered around 20% since 2011, just below the record-high 23% seen in 2009. Support for strong pro-abortion rights is a notch below the highest levels seen from 1990 to 1995, when it consistently exceeded 30%, but support is up from four to five years ago, when it had dipped into the low 20s.

The abortion issue seemingly has been sidelined over the past several election cycles as a series of weighty issues—including the Iraq war, the economy, and healthcare reform—have dominated political debate. It is thus remarkable that the percentage of voters

saying a candidate's position on abortion is paramount to their vote has not only remained constant but also increased slightly.

Degree to Which Abortion Should Be Legal

Do you think abortions should be legal under any circumstances, legal only under certain circumstances, or illegal in all circumstances?

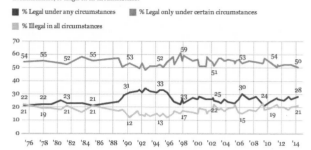

Values are shown for dates closest to election in midterm election years.
Note: The trend includes two polls conducted by Gallup/Newsweek: January 1985 and July 1992.

GALLUP

Nineteen percent of U.S. registered voters currently say candidates for major offices must share their views on abortion to get their vote. This number slightly eclipses the 16% to 17% seen since 2004 and is significantly higher than the 13% to 14% that Gallup recorded between 1992 and 2000. Only once, in May 2001, was the figure higher, at 21%.

Impact of Abortion Issue on Vote for Major Offices

Thinking about how the abortion issue might affect your vote for major offices, would you [only vote for a candidate who shares your views on abortion, (or) consider a candidate's position on abortion as just one of many important factors, (or) not see abortion as a major issue]?

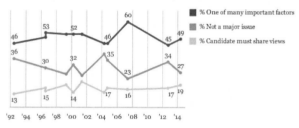

Based on registered voters

GALLUP

Gallup finds more pro-life voters than pro-choice voters saying they will only back candidates who share their views, 24% vs. 16%. Thus, the pro-life side has more intensity on the issue. However, because there are more pro-choice than pro-life registered voters (50% to 44%), this equates to 11% of all registered voters saying they will only vote for pro-life candidates and 8% saying they will only vote for pro-choice candidates—not a great advantage or disadvantage for either side.

Impact of Abortion Issue on Vote, by Position on Abortion

Based on registered voters

	Registered voters	"Pro-choice"	"Pro-life"
	%	%	%
Only vote for a candidate who shares your abortion views	19	16	24
Consider candidate's position on abortion as one of many important factors	49	50	50
Don't see abortion as a major issue	27	32	21
No opinion	4	2	5

May 8-11, 2014

GALLUP

U.S. public opinion on abortion has displayed great stability in recent years, with Americans dividing about evenly into the "pro-choice" and "pro-life" camps. Separately, Gallup finds roughly half of Americans retain a nuanced view about the legality of abortion, saying it should be legal only in certain cases. However, the percentages on the extremes—those favoring total legality or illegality—have crept up, presumably to the delight of their respective comrades in the Republican and Democratic parties.

In January, Jeremy W. Peters in a *New York Times* article described abortion as an "unexpectedly animating issue in the 2014 midterm elections," and referred back to the reported success that abortion rights groups had in 2012, both with modeling and targeting "women's health" voters. Indeed, Gallup finds that a quarter of Republican voters (24%) and 19% of Democratic voters claim they will only vote for a candidate who shares their views on abortion, making these voters prime targets for party turnout efforts. While their impact could result in a draw on the abortion issue, it is a battle neither party can afford to ignore.

Survey Methods

Results for this Gallup poll are based on telephone interviews conducted May 8–11, 2014, with a random sample of 1,028 adults, aged 18 and older, living in all 50 U.S. states and the District of Columbia.

For results based on the total sample of national adults, the margin of sampling error is ±4 percentage points at the 95% confidence level.

For results based on the total sample of 888 registered voters, the margin of sampling error is ±4 percentage points at the 95% confidence level.

May 23, 2014
AMERICANS SAY ARMY MOST IMPORTANT BRANCH TO U.S. DEFENSE
Marine Corps considered most prestigious branch by wide margin

by Dave Goldich and Art Swift

WASHINGTON, D.C.—Americans believe that the U.S. Army is the most important service branch to national defense, followed closely by the Air Force. Fewer than one in five choose the Marine Corps or the Navy. The Army has edged out other military branches in Gallup surveys conducted throughout the last decade.

Most Important Branches of the U.S. Military

Which of the five branches of the armed forces in this country would you say is the most important to our national defense today?

	Army	Air Force	Marines	Navy	Coast Guard
May 8-11, 2014	26%	23%	19%	17%	3%
Jun 9-12, 2011	25%	17%	24%	11%	3%
May 21-23, 2004	25%	23%	23%	9%	4%
Apr 22-24, 2002	18%	36%	16%	17%	1%
May 18-20, 2001	18%	42%	14%	15%	---

GALLUP

Army Still Most Important, Likely Because of Conflicts in Iraq and Afghanistan

Gallup started asking Americans about the importance of U.S. military branches in the 1940s, using a variety of questions over the years. Americans until the mid-2000s always viewed the Air Force as the most important branch of the military. And while it still ranks high today, it no longer dominates. This shift in opinion most likely stemmed from the heavy ground combat in Iraq and Afghanistan in the 2000s and early 2010s. The Army, the largest branch of the military, has likely improved its standing in the U.S. public's eyes as a result of the role it played in these conflicts. Because the United States is far removed geographically from Europe, Asia, and the Middle East, historically air power and sea power have enjoyed prominence among Americans in terms of national defense.

Marines Continue to Lead in Prestige; Coast Guard Trails Other Branches

Importance does not necessarily equal prestige, however. While the Army has held a thin lead in perceived importance to the United States' national defense over the last decade, the Marine Corps has consistently been considered the nation's most prestigious military branch, widening its lead over the Air Force and Army during the same period. Currently, nearly half of Americans (47%) say the Marines are the most prestigious, with the Air Force a distant second, at 17%.

Most Prestigious Branches of the U.S. Military

Which of the five branches of the armed forces in this country would you say is the most prestigious and has the most status in our society today?

	Marines	Air Force	Army	Navy	Coast Guard
May 8-11, 2014	47%	17%	15%	12%	2%
Jun 9-12, 2011	46%	15%	22%	8%	2%
May 21-23, 2004	44%	20%	15%	8%	5%
Apr 22-24, 2002	39%	28%	13%	13%	1%
May 18-20, 2001	36%	32%	11%	14%	---

GALLUP

Prior to 9/11 and the Iraq and Afghanistan wars, a May 2001 Gallup poll found that Americans narrowly considered the Marine Corps the most prestigious military branch over the Air Force. Since 2002, the American public's admiration for the Marines has clearly increased. This might be attributable to the Marines' conspicuous presence in movies, television, and other forms of media. Further, the Marine Corps, being a smaller force, may be considered to be more "elite" with higher standards.

Despite successful Navy SEALs raids that killed al Qaeda leader Osama bin Laden in 2011 and helped rescue the captain of the merchant marine vessel *Maersk Alabama* from pirates in an incident that was the basis of the movie *Captain Phillips*, the Navy's image has not benefited—12% in the U.S. say the Navy is the most prestigious branch. Perhaps related to its more modest presence on the defense landscape, only 2% of Americans say the Coast Guard is the most prestigious.

Bottom Line

The U.S. has long held a fascination with its military, which prior to the first decades of the 20th century consisted entirely of ground and naval forces. Air power clearly came into its own during World War II, the wars in Korea and Vietnam, and particularly in the Gulf War in 1991. For all of that time, Americans consistently viewed the Air Force as the most important branch of the military.

Since the very first years of the new millennium, the Army has received top billing as the most important branch, likely a result of the pressing combat operations in the Middle East and Central

Asia. This may also be related to the Army's sheer size, with the large number of bases it has nationwide, the prominence of the branch in ongoing news reports about the wars, and the likelihood of Americans knowing soldiers heading to or returning from deployments.

As ground combat forces have seen a decreased role in the last few years, unmanned aerial vehicles (UAVs) or drones have become increasingly visible and important for national defense efforts. Although other branches use UAVs, the Air Force may benefit more from this development because of its primary use of air power, and this may contribute toward an increased appreciation of the Air Force. Similarly, the announcement of an updated U.S. strategy "rebalancing" toward Asia in 2011 has coincided with Americans' higher regard for the importance of the U.S. Navy for national defense.

Americans don't necessarily view the branches as the same in importance and prestige. They clearly see the Marine Corps as the most prestigious. The Marines have benefited from being viewed as an expeditionary force central to U.S. wars over the last century, along with an omnipresent advertising campaign touting "the few, the proud." The trend of prestige has been rising since the beginning of the 21st century, and may continue in the next few years.

Survey Methods

Results for this Gallup poll are based on telephone interviews conducted May 5–8, 2014, on the Gallup Daily tracking survey, with a random sample of 1,028 adults, aged 18 and older, living in all 50 U.S. states and the District of Columbia.

For results based on the total sample of national adults, the margin of sampling error is ±4 percentage points at the 95% confidence level.

May 27, 2014
AMERICANS SAY BIG BUSINESS HELPS OVERSEAS, LESS SO AT HOME
Majority says large U.S. companies do poor job helping grow U.S. economy

by Frank Newport

PRINCETON, NJ—Americans see large U.S. companies as having a more positive effect overseas than they do domestically. While 66% of Americans believe that large U.S. companies do a good job creating good jobs for citizens in other countries where they do business, far fewer, 43%, say the companies do a good job of creating jobs for Americans.

These data are based on a Gallup survey with 1,005 U.S. adults conducted April 30–May 1.

Americans in general have a less-than-stellar image of "big business," with just 22% in previous polls saying they have "a great deal" or "quite a lot" of confidence in big business. This is one of the lowest confidence ratings of any of the institutions Gallup has tested. Americans' poor ratings of the effectiveness of large U.S. companies in creating U.S. jobs could be one of the underlying reasons for this overall negative image.

Americans do seem to recognize that large U.S. companies contribute in some areas. Americans are most positive about large

companies' ability to create important new products and technologies. But the other two areas in which the majority of Americans give large companies "good" ratings both have to do with their contributions overseas: creating jobs for citizens of other countries and creating better lives for people in communities outside the U.S. where U.S. companies do business. These are the only three issues of the eight tested on which more than half of Americans rate the job that large U.S. companies are doing as "good."

Turning now to businesses, how would you rate the job large U.S. companies are doing at each of the following -- very good, good, poor, or very poor?

	% Good	% Poor
Creating important new products and technologies	79	19
Creating good jobs for citizens in other countries where U.S. companies do business	66	26
Creating better lives for people in communities outside the U.S. where U.S. companies do business	56	34
Promoting U.S. values and ideals around the world	49	46
Protecting the environment	48	50
Helping grow the U.S. economy	44	54
Creating good jobs for Americans	43	54
Balancing the best interests of the U.S. and Americans with the best interests of the company	43	54

April 30-May 1, 2014

GALLUP

Americans are roughly split on how well large U.S. companies promote U.S. values and ideals worldwide and the job they do protecting the environment.

The American public rates large U.S. companies less positively on the remaining three areas tested, which all relate to these companies' domestic contributions. These include helping grow the U.S. economy, creating good jobs for Americans, and balancing the best interests of the U.S. and Americans with the best interests of the company.

Clearly the public is skeptical of the benefits provided by America's large companies for their home country or the people therein—even while conceding that these organizations create new products and technologies and help the countries overseas where they operate.

Small Is Better Than Big

Previous research shows that 65% of Americans have a great deal or quite a lot of confidence in small business, contrasted with the 22% who have confidence in big business. Asked in the current survey whether big businesses or small businesses make the greater contribution to developing new products and technologies in the U.S., Americans again prefer small over big by 60% to 35%, respectively. Even though Americans rate large U.S. companies positively overall for their creation of new products, they get much less credit on this dimension when compared with small businesses.

As far as you know, which do you think makes greater contributions to developing new products and technologies in the U.S., big businesses or small businesses?

Big businesses	Small businesses	Both equally	No opinion
35%	60%	2%	2%

April 30-May 1, 2014

GALLUP

Implications

Large U.S. companies clearly have an image problem. A majority of Americans perceive that large U.S. companies do a poor job in terms of creating jobs domestically, helping grow the American economy, and putting the interests of the country ahead of their own.

Thus, one significant challenge large U.S. companies face in their efforts to improve their image at home is convincing Americans that they are the backbone of the U.S. economy as much as they are economies overseas.

Demonstrating their economic contribution domestically compared with small businesses is another challenge. Americans have a positive image of small businesses and give them more credit than big businesses for creating new products and technologies in the U.S. To counter this perception, large businesses clearly need to document the degree to which they are behind many of the innovations and products that grow the U.S. economy. They also need to remind the public that growth among large companies usually leads to development in the small businesses that supply them and that small businesses gain when large companies increase workforces.

Survey Methods

Results for this Gallup poll are based on telephone interviews conducted April 30–May 1, 2014, with a random sample of 1,005 adults, aged 18 and older, living in all 50 U.S. states and the District of Columbia.

For results based on the total sample of national adults, the margin of sampling error is ±4 percentage points at the 95% confidence level.

May 28, 2014
CONSERVATIVE LEAD ON SOCIAL AND ECONOMIC IDEOLOGY SHRINKING
On social issues, 34% identify as conservative and 30% as liberal

by Jeffrey M. Jones

PRINCETON, NJ—More Americans continue to identify themselves as conservatives than as liberals on economic and social matters. However, the conservative advantage on each dimension is shrinking from higher points in recent years, down to 21 points on economic policy and four points on social policy.

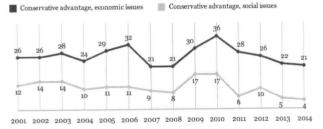

Ideological Identification on Social vs. Economic Issues, 2001-2014

Figures are the percentage identifying as conservative minus the percentage identifying as liberal

■ Conservative advantage, economic issues ■ Conservative advantage, social issues

GALLUP'

The results are based on Gallup's annual Values and Beliefs poll, conducted May 8–11. Currently, 34% of Americans say they

are conservative, 35% say moderate, and 30% say liberal on social issues. On economic issues, 42% say they are conservative, 34% say moderate, and 21% say liberal. The four-point conservative lead on social ideology and 21-point lead on economic ideology rank as the smallest Gallup has measured in the 14 years it has asked Americans to describe their views on those issue dimensions separately, although the 21-point conservative lead on economic policy was also found in 2007 and 2008.

The trends toward lower conservative advantages were evident as far back as 2004 on social ideology and 2007 on economic ideology, though both were interrupted in 2009 and 2010 when President Barack Obama and a Democratic Congress passed left-leaning legislation, most notably the Affordable Care Act. In those years, the percentage of Americans describing themselves as conservative on the two dimensions moved back up, most likely in reaction to their perceptions of the more liberal administration. Since then, however, the trends have continued moving in a less conservative direction.

In the same poll, using Gallup's standard ideology question, 37% of Americans describe their political views overall as conservative, 25% as liberal, and 35% as moderate. That 12-point conservative-liberal gap falls in between the 21-point gap on economic issues and the four-point gap on social issues. But this general measure of ideology has also shown that the conservative-over-liberal advantage has been narrowing in recent years.

Americans' increasingly liberal views on social issues are apparent in trends showing that the public is exhibiting greater support for gay marriage, legalizing marijuana, and having a baby outside of marriage, and diminished support for the death penalty.

Democrats Increasingly Say Their Social and Economic Views Are Liberal

A solid majority of Republicans and Republican-leaning independents identify their social and economic attitudes as conservative. Democrats and Democratic-leaners show less consensus, with pluralities saying their social views are liberal and their economic views moderate.

Self-Identified Ideology, Social and Economic Issues, by Political Party Affiliation

	% Conservative	% Moderate	% Liberal	Conservative advantage (% conservative minus % liberal)
REPUBLICANS/ REPUBLICAN LEANERS				
Economic issues	70	19	9	61
Social issues	60	28	11	49
DEMOCRATS/ DEMOCRATIC LEANERS				
Economic issues	20	43	35	-15
Social issues	11	40	47	-36

May 8-11, 2014

GALLUP'

In recent years, Republicans' views on social issues have been steady, while Democrats have been increasingly likely to identify their social views as liberal, particularly in the past four years. This means that Democrats are largely driving the shrinking conservative advantage on social issues among all Americans.

Ideological Identification on Social Issues, by Political Party, 2001-2014

Figures are the percentage identifying as conservative minus the percentage identifying as liberal

■ Conservative advantage, Republicans   ▓ Conservative advantage, Democrats

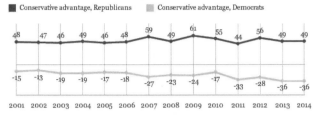

2001 2002 2003 2004 2005 2006 2007 2008 2009 2010 2011 2012 2013 2014

Note: Party groups include those who identify as independents but say they lean to the party.

GALLUP

On economic issues, Democrats were more likely to identify as conservatives than as liberals from 2001 to 2006. Since 2007, the reverse has been true in all but one year. Republicans, too, have shown movement on economic ideology, showing higher average conservative advantages from 2009 to 2014 than before.

Ideological Identification on Economic Issues, by Political Party, 2001-2014

Figures are the percentage identifying as conservative minus the percentage identifying as liberal

■ Conservative advantage, Republicans   ▓ Conservative advantage, Democrats

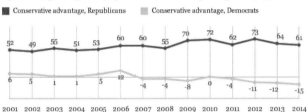

2001 2002 2003 2004 2005 2006 2007 2008 2009 2010 2011 2012 2013 2014

Note: Party groups include those who identify as independents but say they lean to the party.

GALLUP

To some degree, the Republican and Democratic trends in economic ideology offset each other, but because there are more Democrats and Democratic leaners than Republicans and Republican leaners, the national numbers are being pulled in a slightly more liberal direction.

Implications

Conservatism is still the dominant ideology in the U.S. when Americans are asked to describe their political views overall and when asked about their views on economic and social issues separately. However, the conservative advantages are shrinking, in large part because of Democrats' increasing likelihood of describing their views as liberal rather than conservative or moderate.

With the conservative advantage on social issues down to four points, it is possible in the next few years there will be more Americans describing themselves as socially liberal than as socially conservative. This movement is consistent with trends Gallup has seen on specific issues, perhaps most notably Americans' views toward gay rights and legalizing marijuana.

Conservatives maintain a healthy advantage on economic issues, so if more Americans ever do come to view themselves as economic liberals than as economic conservatives, it would not be anytime soon. The ideological trends are clearly heading in a more liberal direction, but as was the case in 2009 and 2010, they could be disrupted or even potentially reversed, depending on the course of the nation's policies.

Survey Methods

Results for this Gallup poll are based on telephone interviews conducted May 8–11, 2014, with a random sample of 1,028 adults, aged 18 and older, living in all 50 U.S. states and the District of Columbia.

For results based on the total sample of national adults, the margin of sampling error is ±4 percentage points at the 95% confidence level.

May 28, 2014
AMERICANS' VIEWS ON ORIGINS OF HOMOSEXUALITY REMAIN SPLIT
Most say being gay or lesbian starts at birth

by Justin McCarthy

WASHINGTON, D.C.—In a year when the movement for same-sex marriages continues to make strides across the U.S., Americans remain divided on how people come to be gay or lesbian. More than a third of Americans (37%) believe people become gay as a result of factors such as their upbringing and environment, while 42% say people are born gay. This latter belief is down slightly from 2013, when nearly half (47%) believed people were gay at birth.

Origins of Homosexuality: Innate or Environmental?

In your view, is being gay or lesbian -- [ROTATED: something a person is born with, (or) due to factors such as upbringing and environment]?

■ % Born with   ▓ % Due to upbringing and environment

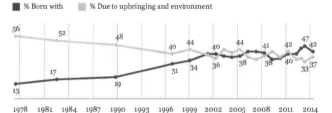

1978 1981 1984 1987 1990 1993 1996 1999 2002 2005 2008 2011 2014

1977-2008 wording: In your view, is homosexuality -- [ROTATED: something a person is born with, (or is homosexuality) due to factors such as upbringing and environment]?

GALLUP

These results are from Gallup's annual Values and Beliefs poll, conducted May 8–11. Americans' views on this question have evolved over time. When Gallup first asked about the origins of same-sex orientation in 1977, over half of Americans (56%) attributed it to an individual's upbringing and environment, while 13% believed it to be something a gay person is born with.

This gap in opinions narrowed over the time, and by 2001, Americans were more likely to believe in homosexuality as occurring at birth (40%) for the first time, though only by one percentage point. Since then, Americans have been roughly equally divided over this question, although with some year-to-year fluctuations in the precise percentages. Although this pattern appeared to be changing last year, when the belief that people are born gay rose to an all-time high of 47% after a slight increase in 2012, this year's slight downtick in the "born with" belief halted the trend.

The scientific community does not agree on one unified viewpoint regarding the issue of a person's sexual orientation. According to the American Psychological Association, "there is no consensus among scientists about the exact reasons that an individual develops a heterosexual, bisexual, gay, or lesbian orientation."

An Increase in the Upbringing and Environment Belief Across Demographics

Though the plurality of Americans believe that being gay is present a birth, there continues to be large differences in perspectives across demographic, religious, and political dimensions. Those with college educations, whites, females, liberals, Democrats, high-income earners, and those who seldom or never attend church are the most likely to believe that being gay or lesbian is something people are born with. Most of these differences among the various demographic groups were evident in previous years, with nonwhites' belief in the upbringing and environment theory substantially higher this year than last year.

Bottom Line

The contention on this question of a person's sexual orientation possibly reflects a lack of input from the scientific community, which historically has not shied away from offering its opinion on lesbian, gay, bisexual, or transgender (LGBT) issues and questions. The American Psychiatric Association removed homosexuality from its manual of mental disorders in 1973, giving credence to the nascent gay rights movement at the time.

U.S. public opinion about gays has changed drastically in recent decades on the issues of marriage equality and LGBT acceptance as a whole, possibly related to the fact that three in four Americans say they have a friend, relative, or coworker who has told them that he or she is gay. Though being gay as the result of genetics or other factors before birth has become a considerably more mainstream belief and is now mentioned by a plurality of Americans, it is still one held by slightly less than half of the U.S. population. This disagreement seems likely to continue as long as the scientific community remains agnostic about the question.

Survey Methods

Results for this Gallup poll are based on telephone interviews conducted May 8–11, 2014, with a random sample of 1,028 adults, aged 18 and older, living in all 50 U.S. states and the District of Columbia.

For results based on the total sample of national adults, the margin of sampling error is ±4 percentage points at the 95% confidence level.

May 29, 2014
DESPITE ENROLLMENT SUCCESS, HEALTHCARE LAW STILL UNPOPULAR
Affordable Care Act is most popular among blacks, least among whites

by Andrew Dugan

WASHINGTON, D.C.—Although the Obama administration is boasting higher-than-expected enrollment for the Affordable Care Act, Americans' attitudes toward the healthcare law have changed only marginally since the open enrollment period ended for 2014. A steady 43% of Americans approve of the 2010 Affordable Care

Act, also known as "Obamacare," while a majority continue to disapprove of it, roughly where sentiment was before the enrollment window officially closed on March 31.

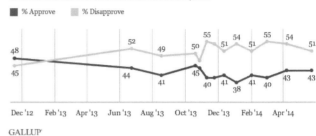
Approval of the U.S. Healthcare Law

Do you generally approve or disapprove of the 2010 Affordable Care Act, signed into law by President Obama, that restructured the U.S. healthcare system?

GALLUP

These data are based on interviews with 2,538 Americans in a May 21–25 Gallup poll.

At the moment, there appears to be a rare lull in media scrutiny and political acrimony toward the healthcare law. The opportunity to buy individual health insurance policies through federal or state-run exchanges officially came to a close on March 31, 2014. The number enrolled now exceeds 8 million, and the high tally gave the impression of a good finish to what had been a very bad start, plagued by a botched website launch in early October and then reports of canceled insurance policies due to new, Affordable Care Act–inspired regulatory standards.

Nonetheless, public opinion about the healthcare law has been relatively steady throughout this front-and-center saga, mostly immune to both the good and bad developments. Approval of the law fell to 38% in early January 2014, when the federal exchange website's glitches continued to plague the rollout of the marketplaces. Approval ratings improved slightly once the website was fixed and the public relations fiasco receded.

Net approval of the Affordable Care Act now stands at −8 points, reflective of the fact that more Americans disapprove than approve. This is the least negative tilt measured since the −3 recorded in late October 2013.

Fewer than four in 10 adults (37%) say the law will ultimately make the healthcare situation better in the U.S., consistent with past measures. A plurality of Americans (44%) say it will make things worse, and another 16% say it won't make much of a difference.

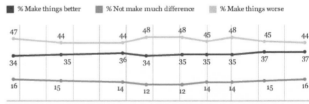
Long-Term Impact of Healthcare Law on the U.S.

In the long run, how do you think the healthcare law will affect the healthcare situation in the U.S.? Will it -- [ROTATED: make things better, not make much difference, (or will it) make things worse]?

GALLUP

Blacks Most Approving of Law, Whites Least

Approval of the healthcare law is intimately tied to a person's politics, with 79% of Democrats approving versus 8% of Republicans.

Race and ethnicity also play some role in approval of the Affordable Care Act. Non-Hispanic white Americans are, by far, the least supportive of the law, with 35% approving. By contrast, 76% of black Americans approve of the law, while less than a fifth disapprove. Meanwhile, 57% of Hispanics—a group intently targeted by the law—approve, and one-third disapprove.

The Obama administration made a concerted effort to try to enroll Hispanics, the least likely of the three major racial/ethnic groups to report having health insurance, with President Barack Obama appearing on two Spanish-language television networks earlier this year to discuss the issue.

Approval of the U.S. Healthcare Law, by Race

Do you generally approve or disapprove of the 2010 Affordable Care Act, signed into law by President Obama, that restructured the U.S. healthcare system?

	% Approve	% Disapprove
Blacks	76	18
Hispanics	57	33
Whites	35	61

May 21-25, 2014

GALLUP

Black Americans are also most likely to see the law as making the healthcare situation in the U.S. better, with 64% saying so. Lesser shares of Hispanics (41%) and whites (31%) believe the law will improve the U.S. healthcare situation.

Long-Term Impact of Healthcare Law on the U.S., by Race

In the long run, how do you think the healthcare law will affect the healthcare situation in the U.S.? Will it -- [ROTATED: make things better, not make much difference, (or will it) make things worse]?

	% Make things better	% Not make much difference	% Make things worse
Blacks	64	18	13
Hispanics	41	22	28
Whites	31	14	53

May 21-25, 2014

GALLUP

Implications

The past eight months have been eventful for the Affordable Care Act. The unresponsive federal health exchange website that blemished the start of the open enrollment period became a huge liability for the Obama administration and its signature domestic achievement, and matters only worsened once Americans began receiving notification letters of canceled policies. But the issues with the website were eventually resolved, and the number of people enrolled exceeded initial expectations, giving the law's supporters something of a happy ending.

Throughout this ordeal, public opinion has remained mostly static and oriented against the healthcare law, suggesting that most Americans have made up their minds on this issue and see no reason to revisit their opinion. This is likely a consequence of the polarizing effect of the law—Republicans are solidly opposed, while the bulk of Democrats support it. It's uncertain what role this still unpopular law will play in the midterm elections; Americans say the

economy and unemployment overshadow healthcare in terms of the most important problem facing the U.S. But many Republican candidates competing against Democratic incumbent senators in states such as North Carolina, Arkansas, and Louisiana are highlighting their opposition to the law. Some Democrats may try to embrace and defend it, while others may try to change the topic of discussion.

Survey Methods

Results for this Gallup poll are based on telephone interviews conducted May 21–25, 2014, on the Gallup Daily tracking survey, with a random sample of 2,538 adults, aged 18 and older, living in all 50 U.S. states and the District of Columbia.

For results based on the total sample of national adults, the margin of sampling error is ±3 percentage points at the 95% confidence level.

May 29, 2014
FEW AMERICANS SAY HEALTHCARE LAW HAS HELPED THEM
Those with new insurance policies in 2014 more likely to have positive views

by Frank Newport

PRINCETON, NJ—About one month after the new healthcare exchanges closed with over 8 million new enrollees, there has been little substantial change in Americans' perception that the healthcare law has helped them. Most Americans say the law has had no impact on their healthcare situation, while those who do perceive an effect are more likely to say it has hurt them rather than helped them.

Healthcare Law's Perceived Impact on Americans and Their Families

As you may know, a number of the provisions of the healthcare law have already gone into effect. So far, has the new law -- [ROTATED: helped you and your family, not had an effect, (or has it) hurt you and your family]?

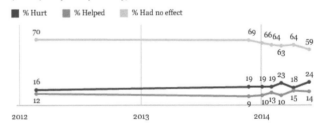

Wording from 2012 to April 2014: As you may know, a few of the provisions of the healthcare law have already gone into effect. So far, has the new law -- [ROTATED: helped you and your family, not had an effect, (or has it) hurt you and your family]?

GALLUP

These data are based on interviews with over 2,500 Americans in a May 21–25 Gallup poll.

The majority of Americans have reported that the Affordable Care Act has had little effect on their personal situations since Gallup first asked this question in early 2012. In more recent months, after the exchange-based enrollment opened up, Americans have gradually become more likely to indicate that the law has had an effect—both positive and negative. The current 24% who say the law has hurt them is by one percentage point the highest measured, while the 14% who say the law has helped them is also within one point of being the highest measured on that dimension. In all instances, across seven different surveys, Americans have been at least marginally more likely to say the law has hurt them and their families than to say it has helped them.

Americans' views on how the healthcare law has affected them personally are predictably partisan, as are almost all attitudes about Obamacare. The biggest partisan effect is evident among Republicans, with 41% claiming that the law has hurt them and their family. Democrats have opposite views, although more subdued, with 23% saying that the law has helped them, while over two-thirds say it has had no effect.

Effect of Healthcare Law on Americans and Their Families, by Political Party

	Helped	Not had an effect	Hurt
	%	%	%
Republican	2	54	41
Independent/Other/Don't know	13	57	26
Democrat	23	68	6

May 21-25, 2014

GALLUP

The goal of the law was to provide an insurance policy to the uninsured, particularly young, low-income, and minority Americans. There is, however, little difference in the perceived benefit of the law among those aged 18 to 64. But, those younger than 30 are more likely than those who are older to say the law has both helped and hurt them.

Americans living in households with very low incomes (less than $24,000 a year) are slightly more likely than those with higher incomes to say that the law has helped them, and slightly less likely to say that it has hurt them. Still, as many of this low-income group say the law has hurt them as say it has helped them.

Effect of Healthcare Law on Americans and Their Families, by Income Level

	Helped	Not had an effect	Hurt
	%	%	%
Less than $24,000 per year	20	56	20
$24,000 to less than $60,000 per year	11	59	29
$60,000 to less than $90,000 per year	12	64	23
$90,000 or more per year	11	63	25

May 21-25, 2014

GALLUP

Americans who say they obtained a new insurance policy in 2014 are significantly more likely than those who are insured but with the same policy as last year to say the new law has helped them, at 27% to 11%, respectively. Some of those who bought new policies this year did so because of mechanisms in the law, which others did so as a result of other factors, such as changing jobs. The number of Americans interviewed in this survey who have a new policy this year but were uninsured last year are more likely than average to say they have benefited from the law, although their representation in the sample is quite small, making precise estimates of their attitudes difficult.

Americans who are currently uninsured by definition did not take advantage of the exchanges to get insurance, and, at this point, they are substantially more likely to say the new law has hurt them rather than helped them.

Effect of Healthcare Law on Americans and Their Families, by Insurance Status

	Helped	Not had an effect	Hurt
	%	%	%
Insured/New policy for 2014	27	44	27
Insured/Policy had before beginning of year	11	65	22
Uninsured	13	48	31

May 21-25, 2014

GALLUP

More Negative Than Positive Views About Long-Term Effect of Healthcare Law

Americans continue to be more pessimistic than optimistic when asked to ponder the effect of the healthcare law on their family's healthcare situation "in the long run." About four in 10 say it will make no difference in the long run, while slightly fewer say that it will make their situation worse. Americans are least likely to say it will make their situation better in the long run (22%). The percentage who say their healthcare situation will be made worse in the long run is lower than it was last fall—amid the botched opening of the healthcare exchanges.

Long-Term Effect of Healthcare Law on Americans' Healthcare Situations
In the long run, how do you think the healthcare law will affect your family's healthcare situation? Will it -- [ROTATED: make things better, not make much difference, (or will it) make things worse]?

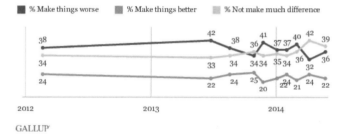

GALLUP

Bottom Line

As of yet, there is no sign that Americans think the new healthcare law is having a net positive effect on their healthcare situations. The majority say the law has not affected them, while those who do report it having an effect are more likely to say it has hurt their healthcare situation rather than helped it. Americans also remain more negative than positive when asked about their views of the potential impact of the law on their family's healthcare situation in the long run.

That so few believe the healthcare law has had a positive impact on their lives could mean most Americans would not be upset if lawmakers change the law. Democrats running for office this year appear to be adopting a "keep and improve" position that acknowledges that the law needs changes. The Republican House announced Wednesday that it plans to put forward its own healthcare plan for a vote this year that would radically change how the healthcare system works. This proposal almost certainly has little chance of becoming law this year, and it is far from clear if the proposed plan would be any more popular than Obamacare. But given the widespread perception that Obamacare has not benefited Americans so far, politicians on both sides of the aisle would appear to have little to lose by advocating changes to some elements of the law.

Survey Methods

Results for this Gallup poll are based on telephone interviews conducted May 21–25, 2014, with a random sample of 2,538 adults, aged 18 and older, living in all 50 U.S. states and the District of Columbia.

For results based on the total sample of national adults, the margin of sampling error is ±3 percentage points at the 95% confidence level.

May 30, 2014
NEW RECORD HIGHS IN MORAL ACCEPTABILITY
Premarital sex, embryonic stem cell research, euthanasia growing in acceptance

by Rebecca Riffkin

WASHINGTON, D.C.—The American public has become more tolerant on a number of moral issues, including premarital sex, embryonic stem cell research, and euthanasia. On a list of 19 major moral issues of the day, Americans express levels of moral acceptance that are as high or higher than in the past on 12 of them, a group that also encompasses social mores such as polygamy, having a child out of wedlock, and divorce.

MORAL ACCEPTABILITY:
Do you believe that, in general, the following are morally acceptable?

Highly acceptable	Birth control*	90%
Largely acceptable	Divorce*	69%
	Sex between an unmarried man and woman*	66%
	Medical research using stem cells obtained from human embryos*	65%
	Gambling	62%
	The death penalty	61%
	Buying and wearing clothing made of animal fur	58%
	Having a baby outside of marriage*	58%
	Gay or lesbian relations*	58%
	Medical testing on animals	57%
Contentious	Doctor-assisted suicide*	52%
	Abortion*	42%
Largely unacceptable	Cloning animals*	34%
	Pornography	33%
	Sex between teenagers	30%
Highly unacceptable	Suicide*	19%
	Polygamy, when a married person has more than one spouse at the same time*	14%
	Cloning humans*	13%
	Married men and women having an affair	7%

% Yes, morally acceptable
*Denotes moral acceptability at or near record high

May 8-11, 2014   GALLUP

These 19 issues fall into five groups, ranging from highly acceptable to highly unacceptable. Overall, 11 of the 19 are considered morally acceptable by more than half of Americans. Ninety percent of Americans believe birth control is morally acceptable, putting it into the "highly acceptable" category, which has little moral opposition—the only such issue among the 19. Nine of the other 10 issues with majority acceptance can be put into a "largely acceptable" category, as they have smaller majorities considering them morally acceptable and sizable minorities that consider them morally wrong. Moral agreement with doctor-assisted suicide, though at the majority level this year, is separated from disagreement by fewer than 10 percentage points, and so this issue is considered "contentious."

Solid majorities of Americans consider seven of the issues morally wrong. Four of these—extramarital affairs, cloning humans, polygamy, and suicide—are considered morally wrong by more than 70% of Americans and fall into the "highly unacceptable" group. Three other issues fall into the "largely unacceptable" category, as smaller majorities of Americans consider them morally wrong, and at least three in 10 consider them morally acceptable.

Abortion receives neither majority support nor majority disapproval, making it the most contentious issue of the 19 tested. The current split is similar to what Gallup measured last year, but is a more even division than the four prior years when at least half said it was morally wrong.

Gallup has tracked Americans' views on the moral acceptability of 12 of these issues annually since 2001 and the rest annually since 2002 or later. These data are from an overall question asked each year as part of Gallup's Values and Beliefs poll, the latest of which was conducted May 8–11, 2014.

Americans' views on the morality of many of these issues have undergone significant changes over time. For example, acceptance of gay and lesbian relations has swelled from 38% in 2002 to majority support since 2010. Fifty-three percent of Americans in 2001 and 2002 said sex between an unmarried man and woman was morally acceptable, but this year it is among the most widely accepted issues, at 66%. Similarly, fewer than half of Americans in 2002 considered having a baby outside of wedlock morally acceptable, but in the past two years, acceptance has been at or near 60%.

Additionally, a few widely condemned actions, such as polygamy, have become slightly less taboo. Five percent of Americans viewed polygamy as morally acceptable in 2006, but that is now at 14%. The rise could be attributed to polygamist families being the subject of television shows—with the HBO TV show *Big Love* one example—thus removing some of the stigma.

Republicans and Democrats Divided on Moral Acceptability of Several Issues

Republicans, independents, and Democrats have differing views of the morality of several issues. Democrats are more likely than Republicans to consider issues like divorce, gambling, medical research using embryos, and having a baby outside of wedlock morally acceptable. But Republicans are more likely than Democrats to see wearing fur, the death penalty, and medical testing on animals as morally acceptable. Independents tend to fall in the middle of the two groups.

In the 12 years Gallup has asked this overall question, Democrats have become significantly more tolerant on many issues, while independents generally show a smaller shift in the same direction and Republicans' views have changed little. The percentage of

Democrats who say an issue is morally acceptable has increased for 10 issues, including abortion, sex between an unmarried man and woman, extramarital affairs, cloning humans, divorce, cloning animals, suicide, research using stem cells from human embryos, polygamy, and gay and lesbian relations.

Moral Acceptability by Party Identification

	Republicans %	Independents %	Democrats %
Birth control	88	90	93
Divorce	60	69	78
Sex between an unmarried man and woman	54	67	77
Medical research using stem cells obtained from human embryos	50	67	74
Gambling	53	64	67
The death penalty	73	62	52
Buying and wearing clothing made of animal fur	71	59	49
Having a baby outside of marriage	40	59	72
Gay or lesbian relations	39	60	71
Medical testing on animals	69	56	50
Doctor-assisted suicide	40	54	63
Abortion	28	41	59
Cloning animals	28	38	36
Pornography	21	38	37
Sex between teenagers	23	32	33
Suicide	11	18	27
Polygamy, when a married person has more than one spouse at the same time	6	15	19
Cloning humans	8	14	14
Married men and women having an affair	1	7	13

Sorted by the percentage of Americans who say each issue is "morally acceptable"
May 8–11, 2014

GALLUP

In some cases, the change among Democrats has been substantial. For example, in 2003, 52% of Democrats said having a baby outside of wedlock was morally acceptable, and 40% of Republicans and 61% of independents agreed. This year, 72% of Democrats, a 20-percentage-point increase, say it is morally acceptable. Meanwhile, Republicans have seen no change, with 40% still saying it is morally acceptable, although a higher 50% viewed it as morally acceptable last year. Independents have also not seen a change, with 60% saying having a baby out of wedlock is morally acceptable this year.

Republicans are slightly more accepting of gay and lesbian relations, sex between an unmarried man and woman, and divorce than they were in 2001, when these questions were first asked. Independents' views on the first two issues (but not divorce) also have seen small shifts, but neither group has seen changes as drastic as those among Democrats.

Bottom Line

Americans largely agree about the morality of several issues. Most say birth control is acceptable but that extramarital affairs are wrong. However, other issues show clear, substantial divides. These differences are largely explained by party identification, but previous research has shown that age also plays a factor.

Attitudes about the morality of these behaviors have in many instances changed over the past 13 years, especially among Democrats, and Americans are now more tolerant of issues previously deemed "morally wrong." Some Americans would say this new tolerance is good, because it increases acceptance. The rise of same-sex marriages across the country may be representative of that newfound acceptance. However, others may disagree. In the same poll, 74% of Americans said they thought the state of moral values in the U.S. is getting worse. Furthermore, 6% of Americans said the moral and ethical decline was the country's most important problem in May. Deep divisions exist among Americans, and clashes over the moral acceptance of certain issues will more than likely continue in the years to come.

Survey Methods

Results for this Gallup poll are based on telephone interviews conducted May 8–11, 2014, with a random sample of 1,028 adults, aged 18 and older, living in all 50 U.S. states and the District of Columbia.

For results based on the total sample of national adults, the margin of sampling error is ±4 percentage points at the 95% confidence level.

May 30, 2014
MOST AMERICANS SAY SAME-SEX COUPLES ENTITLED TO ADOPT
Right to adopt children outpaces Americans' acceptance of same-sex marriage

by Art Swift

WASHINGTON, D.C.—A clear majority of Americans (63%) say same-sex couples should have the legal right to adopt a child, the most to say so since Gallup began tracking opinions on the matter more than 20 years ago. This is higher than Americans' support for same-sex marriage (55%).

Do you think same-sex couples should or should not have the legal right to adopt a child?

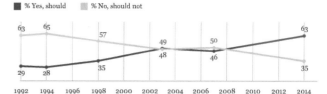

NOTE: Wording in 1992–1998 and 2007 was "legally permitted to adopt"; all questions prior to 2014 used term "homosexual couples."

GALLUP

These findings are from Gallup's May 8–11 Values and Beliefs survey. Gallup has been asking slight variations of this question since 1992. Overall, support has shifted from a clear majority in the 1990s saying same-sex or homosexual couples should not be legally permitted to adopt children to the opposite now.

Support for Same-Sex Adoption Outpaces Support for Same-Sex Marriage

Americans' support for adoption by same-sex couples is higher than their support for same-sex marriage, measured in a recent Gallup poll showing majority support for same-sex marriage at 55%. According to an expert in public policy related to lesbian, gay, bisexual, and transgender people, Gary Gates of the Williams Institute at the UCLA School of Law, this is not unusual.

"In general, adults in the U.S. continue to be more supportive of same-sex parenting than legal recognition of same-sex relationships or comfortableness with same-sex sexual behavior," said Gates. "Laws in the U.S. have reflected this pattern in public support. Many states in the U.S. that have not formally repealed sodomy laws, despite the U.S. Supreme Court declaring such statutes unconstitutional, and that do not recognize marriage for same-sex couples include jurisdictions that allow same-sex couples to adopt children."

Americans' Support for Same-Sex Adoption vs. Support for Same-Sex Marriage

■ % Yes, same-sex couples should have the legal right to adopt a child

▨ % Yes, same-sex marriages should be recognized by the law as valid

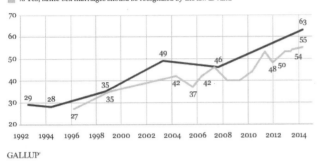

A majority of Americans across all major demographics now say same-sex couples should have the legal right to adopt a child. This includes among all key political persuasions: 80% support among Democrats, 61% support among independents, and 51% support among Republicans.

This majority support for legally permitting same-sex couples to adopt a child is also the case among different age groups. Young people between the ages of 18 and 29 are most likely to support the idea, with 77% saying same-sex couples should be allowed to adopt children.

Support for same-sex adoption declines with each successive age group, but even among those aged 65 and older, a slim majority, 52%, believe same-sex couples should be legally permitted to adopt.

Same-Sex Couples and Adoption, by Age

Do you think same-sex couples should or should not have the legal right to adopt a child?

	% Yes, should	% No, should not
18-29	77	22
30-49	65	33
50-64	59	39
65+	52	45

May 8-11, 2014

GALLUP

Bottom Line

As the question of whether same-sex parents should be allowed to adopt has been debated in the U.S. in the last decade, same-sex couples nationwide have been adopting children at a regular pace. According to the Williams Institute at UCLA, more than 16,000 same-sex couples are raising an estimated 22,000 adopted children in the U.S. While popular support for same-sex adoption is outpacing approval of gay marriage, Gates notes that even lesser forms of relationship recognition—such as civil unions and domestic partnerships—have included the right for same-sex couples to jointly adopt children. In other words, Americans have reached consensus faster about same-sex couples adopting children than about support for gay marriage in the last 20 years.

Survey Methods

Results for this Gallup poll are based on telephone interviews conducted May 8–22, 2014, with a random sample of 1,028 adults, aged 18 and older, living in all 50 U.S. states and the District of Columbia.

For results based on the total sample of national adults, the margin of sampling error is ±4 percentage points at the 95% confidence level.

June 02, 2014
U.S. CONSUMER SPENDING HITS SIX-YEAR HIGH
Daily spending average climbs $10 from April

by Justin McCarthy

WASHINGTON, D.C.—Americans' reports of daily spending spiked in May, averaging a six-year high of $98—$10 higher than the April average. This is also up from May 2013 ($90), and is the best figure for the month of May since 2008.

Daily Self-Reported U.S. Consumer Spending -- January 2008-May 2014
Monthly averages

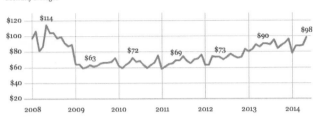

Figures shown are for May of each year

GALLUP

These figures are based on Americans' self-reports of the total amount they spent "yesterday" in stores, gas stations, restaurants, or online—not counting home and vehicle purchases, or normal monthly bills.

The May spending estimate comes as good news for the economy, in which Americans' confidence has been largely stagnant so far in 2014. Spending estimates in May have generally climbed each year since May 2009's $63 average. Before this year, the highest May average since 2008 was last year's $90.

In the previous five years, April-to-May gains in consumer spending were moderate and predictable, ranging from $3 to $6. The exception was 2012, which saw no increase. Thus, the $10 spike in average daily spending between April and May this year is the largest between those two months since 2008, when spending jumped $28.

Three-Day Spending Average Highest Since 2008

One reason average spending in May was so high is the extraordinarily high spending levels seen around Memorial Day. The three-day spending average for May 27–29 reached $134—the highest three-day average since 2008. The three-day average closest to this figure was $129, during the pre-Christmas days of Dec. 21–23, 2013.

Bottom Line

Though Americans' views of the economy on a monthly basis have been flat throughout 2014, the May increase in spending suggests the possibility of some economic improvement. The six-year-high spending average last month is an indicator that regardless of whether Americans are feeling more confident about the economy, their personal cash flows have picked up.

Where spending levels go in June is something to watch. In previous years, May to June spending has either fallen slightly or remained flat.

Survey Methods

Results for this Gallup poll are based on telephone interviews conducted May 1–31, 2014, on the Gallup Daily tracking survey, with a random sample of 15,724 adults, aged 18 and older, living in all 50 U.S. states and the District of Columbia.

For results based on the total sample of national adults, the margin of sampling error is ±1 percentage point at the 95% confidence level. The margin of error for the spending mean is ±$5.

June 02, 2014
IN U.S., 42% BELIEVE CREATIONIST VIEW OF HUMAN ORIGINS
Americans' views related to religiousness, age, education

by Frank Newport

PRINCETON, NJ—More than four in 10 Americans continue to believe that God created humans in their present form 10,000 years ago, a view that has changed little over the past three decades. Half of Americans believe humans evolved, with the majority of these saying God guided the evolutionary process. However, the percentage who say God was not involved is rising.

Which of the following statements comes closest to your views on the origin and development of human beings?

1) Human beings have developed over millions of years from less advanced forms of life, but God guided this process, 2) Human beings have developed over millions of years from less advanced forms of life, but God had no part in this process, 3) God created human beings pretty much in their present form at one time within the last 10,000 years or so

■ % Humans evolved, with God guiding   ■ % Humans evolved, but God had no part in process
■ % God created humans in present form

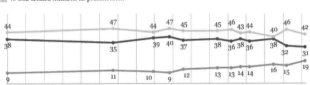

GALLUP

This latest update is from Gallup's Values and Beliefs survey conducted May 8–11. Gallup first asked the three-part question about human origins in 1982.

The percentage of the U.S. population choosing the creationist perspective as closest to their own view has fluctuated in a narrow range between 40% and 47% since the question's inception. There is little indication of a sustained downward trend in the proportion of the U.S. population who hold a creationist view of human origins. At the same time, the percentage of Americans who adhere to a strict secularist viewpoint—that humans evolved over time, with God having no part in this process—has doubled since 1999.

Religiousness, Age, Education Related to Americans' Views

Historically, Americans' views on the origin of humans have been related to their religiousness, education, and age.

- Religiousness relates most strongly to these views, which is not surprising, given that this question deals directly with God's role in human origins. The percentage of Americans who accept the creationist viewpoint ranges from 69% among those who attend religious services weekly to 23% among those who seldom or never attend.
- Educational attainment is also related to these attitudes, with belief in the creationist perspective dropping from 57% among Americans with no more than a high school education to less than half that (27%) among those with a college degree. Those with college degrees are, accordingly, much more likely to choose one of the two evolutionary explanations.
- Younger Americans—who are typically less religious than their elders—are less likely to choose the creationist perspective than are older Americans. Americans aged 65 and older—the most religious of any age group—are most likely to choose the creationist perspective.

Which of the following statements comes closest to your views on the origin and development of human beings?
By education, church attendance, and age

	Humans evolved, God guided process	Humans evolved, God had no part in process	God created humans in present form within last 10,000 years
	%	%	%
Attend church weekly	24	1	69
Attend church nearly weekly/monthly	39	9	47
Seldom/Never attend church	32	34	23
Less than high school	3	10	57
High school graduate	19	27	46
Some college	16	33	49
College graduate	27	41	27
18 to 29	35	30	28
30 to 49	27	20	46
50 to 64	38	11	44
65+	23	16	50

May 8-11, 2014

GALLUP

Americans Less Familiar With "Creationism" Now Than in 2007

Americans' self-reported familiarity with evolution as an explanation for the origin and development of life on Earth has stayed roughly the same over the past seven years. Seventy-nine percent of Americans say they are very or somewhat familiar with it, leaving 19% not too or not at all familiar.

However, significantly fewer Americans claim familiarity with "creationism" than did so seven years ago. In 2007, 86% were familiar, including 50% who were very familiar. Now, 76% are familiar, with just 38% very familiar. In short, even though the adherence to the creationist view has not changed over time, familiarity with the term "creationism" has diminished.

Familiarity With Evolution and Creationism as Explanations for Origin of Life

	Very familiar	Somewhat familiar	Not too familiar	Not at all familiar
EVOLUTION	%	%	%	%
May 8-11, 2014	42	37	13	6
Jun 1-3, 2007	41	41	12	5
CREATIONISM	%	%	%	%
May 8-11, 2014	38	38	13	7
Jun 1-3, 2007	50	36	9	4

GALLUP

Sixty-four percent of those who are very familiar with the theory of evolution choose one of the two evolutionary explanations for the origin of humans, compared with 28% among the smaller group of Americans who report being not too or not at all familiar with it. The majority of those not familiar with evolution choose the creationist viewpoint.

Which of the following statements comes closest to your views on the origin and development of human beings?
By familiarity with theory of evolution

	Humans evolved, God guided process	Humans evolved, God had no part in process	God created humans in present form within last 10,000 years
	%	%	%
Very familiar	30	34	33
Somewhat familiar	13	35	43
Not too/Not at all familiar	7	21	57

May 8-11, 2014

GALLUP

These relationships do not necessarily prove that if Americans were to learn more about evolution they would be more likely to believe in it. Those with less education are most likely to espouse the creationist view and to be least familiar with evolution, but it's not clear that gaining more education per se would shift their perspectives. Many religious Americans accept creationism mostly on the basis of their religious convictions. Whether their beliefs would change if they became more familiar with evolution is an open question.

Implications

Between 40% and 47% of Americans over the past 32 years have said the creationist explanation for the origin of human life best fits their personal views. These Americans tend to be highly religious, underscoring the degree to which many Americans view the world around them through the lens of their religious beliefs. Those who adopt the creationist view also tend to have lower education levels, but given the strong influence of religious beliefs, it is not clear to what degree having more education or different types of education might affect their views.

A number of states have been embroiled in fights in recent years over the degree to which evolution and creationism should be included in their public school curricula. Residents in the South are more likely to believe in the creationist view of the origin of humans than are those living in other regions, making it clear why the fights to have creationism addressed in the public schools might be an important political issue in that region.

Still, few scientists would agree that humans were created pretty much in their present form at one time 10,000 years ago, underscoring the ongoing discontinuity between the beliefs that many Americans hold and the general scientific consensus on this important issue.

Survey Methods

Results for this Gallup poll are based on telephone interviews conducted May 8–11, 2014, with a random sample of 1,028 adults, aged 18 and older, living in all 50 U.S. states and the District of Columbia.

For results based on the total sample of national adults, the margin of sampling error is ±4 percentage points at the 95% confidence level.

June 03, 2014

U.S. ECONOMIC CONFIDENCE TICKS UP TO –14 IN MAY

May saw the highest weekly confidence reading since January

by Justin McCarthy

WASHINGTON, D.C.—Gallup's U.S. Economic Confidence Index increased to –14 in May, its highest monthly reading in 2014 so far. May's economic confidence reading, however, remains significantly below the –7 average found in May 2013, which was the highest monthly average since Gallup began tracking the measure in 2008.

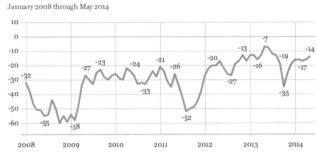

Gallup Economic Confidence Index -- Monthly Averages
January 2008 through May 2014

Gallup Daily tracking

GALLUP

The improved Economic Confidence Index score for May includes a –13 economic confidence reading for the week of May 26–June 1, which was the highest weekly reading since early January of this year.

In recent years, May has generally been an eventful month for economic confidence, sometimes seeing substantial gains from April. In May 2011, the index climbed 10 points as part of a broader increase in Americans' optimism after the death of Osama bin Laden. And May 2013 holds the record for the highest monthly economic confidence score since Gallup Daily tracking began in 2008. A seasonal boost in May isn't always the norm, however, as confidence dropped slightly in May 2010 and was flat in May 2008.

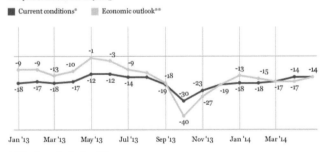

Gallup Economic Confidence Sub-Indexes -- Monthly Averages
Complete trend since January 2013

■ Current conditions*   Economic outlook**

* % (Excellent + Good) minus % Poor
** % Getting better minus % Getting worse
Gallup Daily tracking

GALLUP

Gallup's Economic Confidence Index is an average of two components: Americans' views of the current economic situation and their perceptions of whether the economy is getting better or worse. In last month's average, views of the current economic situation

remained the same as in April, with 20% rating the economy as "excellent" or "good," while 34% say it is "poor," resulting in a current conditions score of –14. Meanwhile, Americans' views about the direction of the economy improved with 40% saying the economy is "getting better," and 54% saying it is "getting worse." This results in an economic outlook score of –14, up from April's score of –17.

Bottom Line

All in all, May's two-point gain in Gallup's economic confidence reading lends credence to the idea that confidence is stable and gradually improving. However, given the propensity of economic confidence since the Great Recession to fall whenever it approaches the neutral mark, any improvement—or even stability—is positive.

The uptick in confidence comes in conjunction with a six-year high in consumer spending, and a promising Job Creation Index reading for April. Though economic confidence remains in negative territory, these other encouraging factors in the U.S. economy suggest that confidence may continue to edge higher.

Survey Methods

Results for this Gallup poll are based on telephone interviews conducted May 1–31, 2014, on the Gallup Daily tracking survey, with a random sample of 15,726 adults, aged 18 and older, living in all 50 U.S. states and the District of Columbia.

For results based on the total sample of national adults, the margin of sampling error is ±1 percentage point at the 95% confidence level.

June 04, 2014

U.S. JOB CREATION INDEX HITS NEW HIGH

Averages +27 in May

by Jeffrey M. Jones

PRINCETON, NJ—Gallup's U.S. Job Creation Index reached a new high in its more than six-year trend, registering +27 in May. The prior high had been +26 in the initial monthly measurement of January 2008, just as the recession was taking hold. The index is based on employee reports of hiring activity at their places of employment.

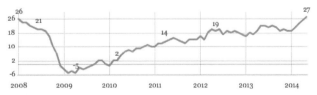

Gallup Job Creation Index Among All U.S. Workers -- January 2008-May 2014

Based on the percentage of U.S. workers who say their employer is hiring workers and expanding the size of its workforce minus the percentage who say their employer is letting workers go and reducing the size of its workforce

Based on monthly averages
Gallup Daily tracking

GALLUP

The +27 index score for May is based on 40% of employees saying their employer is hiring workers and expanding the size of its workforce and 13% saying their employer is letting workers go and reducing the size of its workforce. Another 41% report no change in staffing.

After starting out at a fairly high level in January 2008, the index quickly sank over the course of that year as the recession deepened. The index was in negative territory for much of 2009, meaning workers on average said their employers were cutting more workers than they were adding. This included record-low job creation scores of −5 in February and April 2009.

By 2010, the index began to improve, reaching +10 by October 2010 and +20 in April 2012, hovering about the +20 mark throughout 2012 and 2013. After starting this year at +19, the index has shown gains of exactly two points each month.

Hiring Lags Behind in the East, Government Sector

Job Creation Index scores were largely similar by region in May, averaging +27 in the Midwest and West and +28 in the South. Only the East showed lower job creation, at +23. Workers in the East have typically been a bit less positive about the hiring situation than workers in other parts of the country since January 2013.

Hiring activity continues to be much stronger in the private sector than in the government sector, with an index score of +29 among nongovernment employees (41% hiring and 12% letting workers go) and +14 among government employees (35% hiring and 21% letting workers go). Both indexes are improving, however, with the private sector score at a new high and the government sector score two points below the January 2008 high.

Gallup Job Creation Index, Government vs. Nongovernment Workers

Based on the percentage of U.S. workers who say their employer is hiring workers and expanding the size of its workforce minus the percentage who say their employer is letting workers go and reducing the size of its workforce

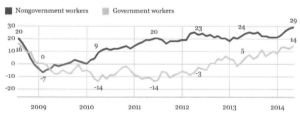

Based on monthly averages
Gallup Daily tracking

GALLUP

Nongovernment hiring has a bigger effect on the overall index score because many more workers are employed in the private sector than the government sector. According to Gallup's estimates, there are more than five private-sector workers for every one government worker.

Net hiring reports differ across the various levels of the government sector. State and local government workers continue to report a more positive hiring situation where they work than federal government workers do. In fact, federal workers are about as likely to report their employer is letting workers go (33%) as to say they are hiring workers (34%), for an index score of +1. The index score among state workers is +19 and among local government workers it is +18.

These state and local versus federal differences have been consistent since 2012.

Even though the net hiring score among federal government workers is lower on a relative basis, it is much improved from −19 in December 2011.

Implications

Job creation is undoubtedly one of the key aspects of a strong economy, and U.S. workers now report a more positive hiring situation where they work than at any point in the last six years. The trend is consistent with the government's latest four-week average of initial jobless claims, which is the lowest in more than six years.

The private sector is driving much of the improvement in hiring. Government-sector hiring has picked up, too, although this has been mostly at the state and local levels.

The more positive hiring picture, along with Americans' higher reports of spending, are important signs of a healthier U.S. economy, though Americans still rate economic conditions more negatively than positively. Americans' still-negative economic outlook is understandable because not all economic indicators are positive. These include a decline in the gross domestic product in the first quarter of 2014 and unemployment rates that, despite improvement, are still higher than pre-recession levels.

Survey Methods

Results for this Gallup poll are based on telephone interviews conducted May 1–31, 2014, on the Gallup Daily tracking survey, with a random sample of 17,993 adults, aged 18 and older, living in all 50 U.S. states and the District of Columbia, who are employed full or part time.

For results based on the total sample of workers, the margin of sampling error is ±1 percentage points at the 95% confidence level.

June 04, 2014
THREE IN FOUR IN U.S. STILL SEE THE BIBLE AS WORD OF GOD
But 21%, near the 40-year high, consider it fables and history

by Lydia Saad

PRINCETON, NJ—Twenty-eight percent of Americans believe the Bible is the actual word of God and that it should be taken literally. This is somewhat below the 38% to 40% seen in the late 1970s, and near the all-time low of 27% reached in 2001 and 2009. But about half of Americans continue to say the Bible is the *inspired* word of God, not to be taken literally—meaning a combined 75% believe the Bible is in some way connected to God. About one in five Americans view the Bible in purely secular terms—as ancient fables, legends, history, and precepts written by man—which is up from 13% in 1976.

Which of the following statements comes closest to describing your views about the Bible?
■ % The Bible is the actual word of God and is to be taken literally, word for word
■ % The Bible is the inspired word of God but not everything in it should be taken literally
■ % The Bible is an ancient book of fables, legends, history, and moral precepts recorded by man

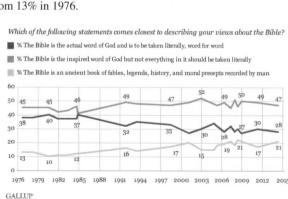

GALLUP

The latest results are from Gallup's 2014 update of its annual Values and Beliefs poll, conducted May 8–11.

Fittingly, overall acceptance of the Bible as being divinely written or inspired closely approximates the proportion of Americans identifying themselves as Christian: 76% in Gallup's 2013 religion aggregate. Meanwhile, the 21% viewing the Bible in secular terms nearly matches the combined 22% who identify with another religion or no religion.

Parsing the Debate Over Biblical Interpretation

Gallup's long-standing trend question on biblical interpretation touches on two ongoing debates in Christian theology. One is about whether the words of the Bible came directly from God—essentially using the writers as scribes—or if they are the words of men, but guided by divine inspiration. The other debate involves the meaning of the words: whether they should be taken literally, or be viewed partly—or merely—as metaphors and allegories that allow for interpretation.

To help clarify where the non-literal believers stand on God's role in the Bible, Gallup asked half of respondents in the new poll a different question that offered a fourth choice: saying the Bible is the actual word of God, but with multiple interpretations possible.

In response to this four-part question, 22% of Americans say the Bible is the actual word of God, to be taken literally—a bit lower than when using the three-part question. Twenty-eight percent believe it is the actual word of God, but with multiple interpretations possible.

Another 28% say the Bible is the *inspired* word of God but should not be taken literally. Eighteen percent say it is an ancient book of fables, legends, history, and moral precepts written by man.

Gallup Split-Sample Experiment: Two Biblical Interpretation Scales

Which of the following statements comes closest to describing your views about the Bible?

	Form A	Form B
	%	%
The Bible is the actual word of God and is to be taken literally, word for word	28	22
The Bible is the actual word of God, but multiple interpretations are possible	--	28
The Bible is the inspired word of God but not everything in it should be taken literally	47	28
The Bible is an ancient book of fables, legends, history, and moral precepts recorded by man	21	18
No opinion	4	4

May 8-11, 2014

Note: Form A was asked of a half sample of 518 U.S. adults. Form B was asked of 510 U.S. adults. Both forms are nationally representative and have a margin of sampling error of ±5 percentage points.

GALLUP'

Although the smaller sample sizes associated with the split-sample results do not allow for in-depth review by subgroup, it is important to note that at least nine in 10 Christians believe the Bible is connected in some way to God, regardless of the response options.

Also, by 58% to 34%, Christians are significantly more likely to indicate they believe the Bible is the *actual* word of God when given the additional option of saying "the Bible is the actual word of God, but multiple interpretations are possible" than when only having the option of saying "the Bible is the actual word of God and is to be taken literally, word for word." This could be an important indicator of the depth of U.S. Christians' devotion to the Bible.

Gallup Split-Sample Experiment: Two Biblical Interpretation Scales, by Religion

Which of the following statements comes closest to describing your views about the Bible?

	Form A	Form A	Form B	Form B
	Christians	Non-Christians	Christians	Non-Christians
Number of interviews:	388	130	396	114
	%	%	%	%
Actual word of God, should be taken literally	34	11	27	6
Actual word of God, multiple interpretations possible	--	--	31	21
Inspired by God, not to be taken literally	52	30	31	19
Ancient book of fables, history, precepts	10	55	7	51
No opinion	4	4	4	3

May 8-11, 2014

Note: Form A, asked of a half sample of 518 U.S. adults, allows respondents to choose from three statements about the Bible. Form B, asked of 510 U.S. adults, offers a fourth statement. "Non-Christians" includes people of other faiths as well as those with no religious affiliation.

GALLUP'

Bottom Line

The Bible is the central text in Christianity, the dominant religion in the U.S., and parts of it are also relevant to followers of Judaism and Islam, thus giving it enormous cultural significance. Despite some evidence that Americans are becoming more detached from formal religion, the vast majority of Christians, and therefore of Americans, still view the Bible as God's word. The 28% adhering to biblical literalism in the trend question is down about 10 percentage points since the late 1970s. But that decline mainly occurred in the 1980s and 1990s. Ever since, the figure has varied between 27% and 34%, with the current 28% on the low end of that range.

While the long-standing Gallup trend shows biblical literalism as ebbing, the new question indicates that the percentage of Americans taking the Bible literally is even lower, at 22%, when respondents are offered more alternatives. Still, the 78% who agree with one of the three statements linking God's word to the Bible using the four-part question nearly matches the 75% choosing one of the two statements affirming God's role in the three-part question—underscoring the validity that three in four Americans consider the Bible holy to some degree.

Ultimately, the finding that nine in 10 Christians believe the Bible emanates from God indicates that U.S. Christians are Christian in more than name only.

Survey Methods

Results for this Gallup poll are based on telephone interviews conducted May 8–11, 2014, with a random sample of 1,028 adults, aged 18 and older, living in all 50 U.S. states and the District of Columbia.

For results based on the sample of 518 national adults in Form A, the margin of sampling error is ±5 percentage points. For results based on the sample of 510 national adults in Form B, the margin of sampling error is ±5 percentage points.

June 04, 2014

SMALLER MAJORITIES IN U.S. FAVOR GOV'T POLLUTION CONTROLS
Support is down from 2007 and before

by Frank Newport

PRINCETON, NJ—More than six in 10 Americans favor setting higher emissions and pollution standards for business and industry, and imposing mandatory controls on carbon dioxide emissions and other greenhouse gases. The percentages favoring these actions, however, are lower than in 2007 and prior years.

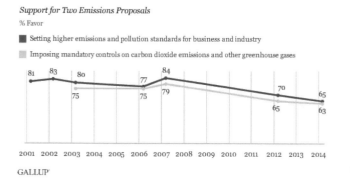

Support for Two Emissions Proposals
% Favor

■ Setting higher emissions and pollution standards for business and industry

■ Imposing mandatory controls on carbon dioxide emissions and other greenhouse gases

GALLUP'

This latest update is from Gallup's annual Environment survey, conducted March 6–9, 2014, in which Americans were asked to indicate whether they favored or opposed nine specific energy or environmental proposals, including two relating to higher emissions standards for business and controls on carbon dioxide emissions.

The poll was conducted prior to the Obama administration's announcement this week of a series of proposed carbon dioxide emissions cuts for the nation's existing power plants. The power plant and coal industries have reacted negatively to the proposed new rules, and politicians and political candidates from coal-producing states have been publicly critical of the potential economic effects.

Gallup has included these two questions about emissions in its annual environmental surveys off and on since 2001. Between 2007 and 2012, support for the two actions dropped by 14 points each. This year, support has dropped still further on both questions. Two major events occurred between 2007 and 2012 that could help explain the change—the recession and Barack Obama's election as president. Americans generally are less supportive of environmental controls when the economic environment becomes troubled, and some Americans may be less likely to favor government regulation of the environment when a Democrat, rather than a Republican, is in office.

Still, even with the downtick in support, more than six in 10 Americans continue to support both ideas, suggesting that the reaction of the general public to Obama's newly promulgated standards will most likely be more positive than negative. About three-quarters of Democrats support both proposals, and although Republicans are less positive, about half still say they favor each.

Given a Choice, Americans Tilt Toward the Environment Over Energy Production

A separate trend question Gallup has tracked each year since 2001 asks Americans to say whether the government should prioritize environmental protection "even at the risk of limiting the amount of energy supplies such as oil, gas, and coal" or favoring the development of U.S. energy supplies "even if the environment suffers to some extent."

Support for these two alternatives has fluctuated over the years. Americans were generally more supportive of the environment through 2008, but then became comparatively more supportive

of the energy production alternative through last year. This year, Americans again are more likely to prioritize the environment.

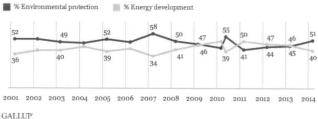

Energy Production vs. Environmental Protection

With which one of these statements about the environment and energy production do you most agree -- [ROTATED: protection of the environment should be given priority, even at the risk of limiting the amount of energy supplies -- such as oil, gas, and coal -- which the United States produces (or) development of U.S. energy supplies -- such as oil, gas, and coal -- should be given priority, even if the environment suffers to some extent]?

■ % Environmental protection   ■ % Energy development

GALLUP'

Political differences on this question are quite stark, with Democrats clearly emphasizing the environment, while Republicans emphasize energy.

Environment vs. Energy Tradeoff, by Party Identification

With which one of these statements about the environment and energy production do you most agree -- [ROTATED: protection of the environment should be given priority, even at the risk of limiting the amount of energy supplies -- such as oil, gas and coal -- which the United States produces (or) development of U.S. energy supplies -- such as oil, gas and coal -- should be given priority, even if the environment suffers to some extent]?

	Environmental protection	Energy development
	%	%
Democrats	70	21
Independents	50	41
Republicans	30	61

March 6-9, 2014

GALLUP'

Implications

Obama's recent executive actions proposing significantly stricter carbon pollution standards on energy-producing plants appear to be generally in tune with majority public opinion. Americans favor setting higher emissions and pollution standards on business and imposing mandatory controls on carbon emissions, and at this point tilt toward actions that would protect the environment even at the cost of some traditional oil, gas, and coal production.

The argument against new emissions standards is that they would ultimately require the American public to pay more for energy, that they would cost American jobs, and that they would have relatively little impact on global warming. These alternatives are not addressed directly in the trend questions reviewed here, and it is possible that when presented with specific tradeoff costs of setting higher carbon pollution standards, support would be lower.

Survey Methods

Results for this Gallup poll are based on telephone interviews conducted March 6–9, 2014, on the Gallup Daily tracking survey, with a random sample of 1,048 adults, aged 18 and older, living in all 50 U.S. states and the District of Columbia.

For results based on the total sample of national adults, the margin of sampling error is ±4 percentage points at the 95% confidence level.

June 05, 2014

U.S. UNINSURED RATE HOLDS STEADY AT 13.4%

Uninsured rate declining most among blacks and Hispanics

by Jenna Levy

WASHINGTON, D.C.—The uninsured rate for U.S. adults appears to be leveling off since the open enrollment period for buying health insurance coverage through the marketplace ended in mid-April. The uninsured rate so far in the second quarter of 2014 is 13.4%, with the rate in April and May as individual months also averaging 13.4%, respectively.

Percentage Uninsured in the U.S., by Quarter

Do you have health insurance coverage?
Among adults aged 18 and older

■ % Uninsured

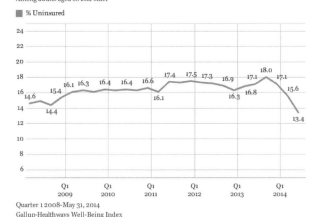

Quarter 1 2008–May 31, 2014
Gallup-Healthways Well-Being Index

GALLUP

In late March, the Obama administration extended the original April 1 deadline to buy insurance out to April 15 for those who had already begun, but not completed, the enrollment process.

The percentage of U.S. adults lacking insurance coverage in the first two months of the second quarter of 2014 is down from 17.1% in the fourth quarter of 2013 and from the 15.6% average in the first quarter of 2014. The current 13.4% average for the second quarter of 2014 is the lowest level recorded since Gallup began tracking this measure in 2008.

These data are based on more than 30,400 interviews with Americans from April 1–May 31, 2014, as part of the Gallup-Healthways Well-Being Index.

Sharpest Declines Among Blacks and Hispanics

Across nearly every major subgroup, the uninsured rate is lower now compared with the fourth quarter of 2013. The rate dropped more among blacks than it did in other major demographic groups, falling 6.2 percentage points to 14.7%.

Hispanics had the second-largest drop in the percent uninsured across demographic groups. Although the rate among Hispanics is down 5.6 points since the end of 2013 to 33.1%, this remains the highest uninsured rate across key subgroups. Hispanics are a major target of public outreach efforts, because they historically are the most likely to be uninsured among demographic groups.

Younger adults, who tend to be healthier and whose participation in the health insurance system is important to help keep costs down, are another key group targeted by outreach efforts. Those aged 26 to 34 years, however, continue to have the highest uninsured

rate among all age groups. The changes seen since the fourth quarter of 2013 for this group is similar to that of 18- to 25-year-olds and that of 35- to 64-year-olds.

Percentage Uninsured in the U.S., by Subgroup

Do you have health insurance coverage?
Among adults aged 18 and older

	Quarter 4 2013 %	Quarter 1 2014 %	April 1–May 31 2014 %	Net change Quarter 4 2013 to May 31, 2014 (pct. pts.)
National adults	17.1	15.6	13.4	-3.7
18 to 25 years	23.5	21.7	19.1	-4.4
26 to 34 years	28.2	26.4	23.9	-4.3
35 to 64 years	18.0	16.1	13.2	-4.8
65+ years	2.0	1.9	2.0	0.0
White	11.9	10.7	8.9	-3.0
Black	20.9	17.6	14.7	-6.2
Hispanic	38.7	37.0	33.1	-5.6
Less than $36,000 annual household income	30.7	27.5	24.7	-6.0
$36,000 to $89,999 annual household income	11.7	10.7	8.6	-3.1
$90,000+ annual household income	5.8	4.7	3.9	-1.9

Gallup-Healthways Well-Being Index

GALLUP

Implications

The nation's uninsured rate in both April and May was 13.4%, which is significantly lower than previous quarters. This rate, however, clearly shows a leveling off of the uninsured rate compared with the month-by-month declines seen in previous months. It remains to be seen if the uninsured rate will stay at this level, increase, or decrease between now and mid-November, when the next open enrollment begins. The rate could drop if more states elect to expand Medicaid. Gallup research shows that the uninsured rate, on average, has dropped more in states that have elected to expand Medicaid and run their own healthcare exchanges than in states that have not. Additionally, special enrollment remains an option for Americans who experience a "qualifying life event" such as a marriage, divorce, college graduation, or birth. Additionally, as employment rates pick up, the uninsured rate could further decrease.

Studies suggest that, by now, most newly insured Americans have paid their first premiums for their 2014 policies. However, without strong efforts to maintain retention, some newly insured Americans may not continue to pay for their insurance on an ongoing basis, thus potentially causing the uninsured rate to rise over time.

And although the healthcare law has brought down the number of uninsured Americans, a majority of Americans still disapprove of it, and many feel it has not helped them. More positive attitudes toward the law and its effect on Americans' healthcare situations may also help lower the uninsured rate.

Survey Methods

Results are based on telephone interviews conducted as part of the Gallup-Healthways Well-Being Index survey April 1–May 31,

2014, with a random sample of 30,430 adults, aged 18 and older, living in all 50 U.S. states and the District of Columbia.

For results based on the total sample of national adults, the margin of sampling error is ±1 percentage points at the 95% confidence level.

June 05, 2014
UTAHANS LEAST SATISFIED WITH AIR QUALITY
Fewer than three in four Nevadans and Californians satisfied

by Rebecca Riffkin

WASHINGTON, D.C.—Two in three Utah residents (65%) are satisfied with the air quality in the areas where they live, but this is the lowest percentage among residents of any of the 50 states. Residents of several of Utah's neighbors—Nevada, California, and Arizona—are also among the least satisfied. Northeastern states Delaware and New York round out the six states where less than 80% of residents are satisfied with the quality of the air.

States Where Residents Are Least Likely to Be Satisfied With Air Quality

	% Satisfied with the quality of air
Utah	65
Nevada	71
California	74
Delaware	76
Arizona	77
New York	78

Gallup 50-state poll, June-December 2013

GALLUP°

These results are based on Gallup's 50-state poll conducted June–December 2013. The poll preceded the Obama administration's proposed new emission rules released this week. The majority of residents of every state are satisfied with the air quality where they live. Median satisfaction across the 50 states is highly positive at 90%.

Some states where residents are less satisfied, such as New York and California, are known for long commutes and traffic, which could negatively affect air quality. But it may be a surprise that residents of other states, specifically Utah and Arizona, are not that satisfied with their air quality. These states are known for their natural beauty—including five national parks in Utah—and lower population densities.

Utah's 80-mile-long area known as the Wasatch Front, a mountain-surrounded valley where more than half of Utah's residents live, struggles with poor air quality, especially in the winter. A weather effect known as inversion traps air in the valley, blanketing the area with polluted air for days at time. Utah's state government has tried to combat the buildup of smog in winter months by instituting "no-burn periods" when fireplace use and driving are discouraged or banned. Despite these efforts, more than one-third of Utah residents, 35%, are dissatisfied with the air quality where they live.

Across the 50 States, Air Quality Perceptions Vary by Region

The 50 states can be categorized into five groups based on the percentage of residents who report being satisfied with the air quality in their area.

Across the U.S., residents' perceptions of air quality in their area vary by region, even though satisfaction levels are generally quite high. The states with the lowest levels of satisfaction are concentrated in the southwestern corner of the country, along with New York and Delaware.

Meanwhile, residents of the northern Midwest are the most likely to be satisfied. South Dakota, North Dakota, and Wyoming top the list, with 96% satisfied in each state. Minnesota, Iowa, Nebraska, and Wisconsin are also among this group, as are far away New Hampshire and Vermont. These regional similarities may be related to the climate or geography in these disparate parts of the country, or a matter of population density, or some combination of the three, as in Utah.

Utah Residents Least Satisfied With Air Quality

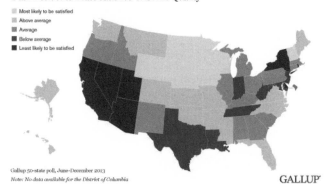

Gallup 50-state poll, June-December 2013
Note: No data available for the District of Columbia

GALLUP°

Implications

Air quality generally does not appear to be a major problem for residents of most U.S. states. Solid majorities in every state say they are satisfied with their air quality. There are differences in satisfaction, however, ranging from a low of 65% satisfied in Utah to 96% satisfied in the Dakotas and Wyoming. There may also be satisfaction differences within states—for example, between urban and rural populations. However, the sample sizes in this survey did not allow for that analysis.

Leaders in Utah have been attempting to address this issue in recent years, and leaders in other states with lower satisfaction levels have been heeding or should heed the public's dissatisfaction and work to improve air quality or at least perceptions of poor air quality, since bad air can have serious health implications. Air pollution can increase the likelihood of stroke, heart disease, lung cancer, and asthma.

Survey Methods

Results for this Gallup poll are based on telephone interviews conducted June 27–Dec. 4, 2013, with a random sample of approximately 600 adults per state, aged 18 and older, living in all 50 U.S. states.

For results based on the total sample of adults per state, the margin of sampling error is ±5 percentage points at the 95% confidence level.

June 06, 2014

IN U.S., STANDARD OF LIVING INDEX CLIMBS TO SIX-YEAR HIGH

Perceptions of current and future living standards both at record highs

by Justin McCarthy

WASHINGTON, D.C.—Gallup's U.S. Standard of Living Index climbed to 47 in May, the highest score recorded since Gallup began tracking this measure in 2008. This index score is up slightly from 44 in April.

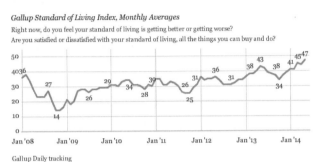

Gallup Standard of Living Index, Monthly Averages

Right now, do you feel your standard of living is getting better or getting worse?
Are you satisfied or dissatisfied with your standard of living, all the things you can buy and do?

Gallup Daily tracking
The Standard of Living Index is based on a composite of the two questions.

GALLUP'

After reaching a low of 14 in October and November 2008 during the Great Recession, the Standard of Living Index fluctuated; it generally moved in an upward direction since that time. The index dipped down to 34 during the U.S. federal government shutdown in October 2013, but has generally increased since then.

Gallup's Standard of Living Index is a composite of Americans' responses to two questions: one asking whether they are satisfied with their current standard of living, and the other asking whether their standard of living is getting better or worse. The index has a theoretical maximum of 100 (if all respondents say they are satisfied with their standard of living and say it is getting better) and a theoretical minimum of –100 (if all respondents are dissatisfied with their standard of living and say it is getting worse).

Last month, 80% of Americans said they were satisfied with their standard of living, while 20% said they were dissatisfied. This results in a net current satisfaction score of 60, a new high.

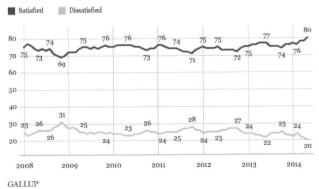

Americans' Satisfaction With Their Current Standard of Living

Are you satisfied or dissatisfied with your standard of living, all the things you can buy and do?

■ Satisfied   ▒ Dissatisfied

GALLUP'

Looking forward, 59% of Americans said they believed their standard of living was getting better—also the highest on

record—and 26% said it was getting worse. The resulting net expectations score of 33 is also the highest in Gallup's more than six-year trend. Americans' optimism about their standard of living fell to a record low in October 2008, amidst the global financial crisis, when 33% said their standard of living was getting better and 47% said it was getting worse.

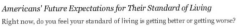

Americans' Future Expectations for Their Standard of Living

Right now, do you feel your standard of living is getting better or getting worse?

■ Getting better   ▒ Getting worse

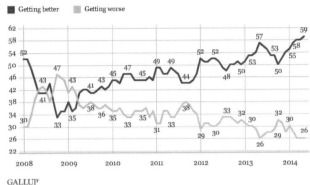

GALLUP'

Bottom Line

Americans' improved views of their standard of living mirror their increased perceptions job creation, which also reached a new high in May. Furthermore, Americans' self-reported spending increased sharply last month, and their views of the economy's current and future health improved. The lingering question is whether these improvements will continue as the year progresses.

Survey Methods

Results for this Gallup poll are based on telephone interviews conducted May 1–31, 2014, on the Gallup Daily tracking survey, with a random sample of 3,103 adults, aged 18 and older, living in all 50 U.S. states and the District of Columbia.

For results based on the total sample of national adults, the margin of sampling error is ±2 percentage points at the 95% confidence level.

June 06, 2014

FEW CONSUMERS TRUST COMPANIES TO KEEP ONLINE INFO SAFE

One in five have "a lot of trust" that companies safeguard personal data

by John H. Fleming and Elizabeth Kampf

WASHINGTON, D.C.—Recent incidents such as Target's security breach, the Heartbleed bug, and eBay's systems hack have called attention to how much consumers trust the businesses they patronize to keep their personal information safe. That trust currently appears to be hard to come by. Just 21% of Americans have "a lot of trust" in the businesses or companies they regularly interact with to keep their personal information secure.

Overall, how much trust would you say you have in the businesses or companies that you regularly do business with to keep your personal information secure? Would you say you have...?

47% some trust

22% little trust
21% a lot of trust
8% no trust at all
1% don't know/refused

How has the amount of trust you have in the businesses or companies that you regularly do business with changed in the past year? Would you say your trust has...?

52% remained the same

24% decreased a little
13% decreased a lot
7% increased a little
3% increased a lot
1% don't know/refused

GALLUP

In addition to low trust in companies' abilities to keep their data secure, Americans report decreasing trust in companies in general. Thirty-seven percent say their general level of trust in the businesses and companies they regularly do business with has declined either a little or a lot over the past year.

Banks, Credit Card Companies Top List of Institutions Consumers Trust

Consumers have more trust in the security of their information with some businesses or institutions than others. When asked how much they trust a list of nine institutions to keep their personal information secure, banks and credit card companies are the highest on the list, with 39% of consumers having a "lot of trust" in them. Following banks at a considerably lower level are health insurance companies (26%) and cellphone providers (19%). Given the rigorous data privacy provisions of HIPAA, Americans' level of trust in insurance companies is surprising. Bringing up the rear are online retailers (6%) and social networking websites or applications (2%).

How much trust do you have in each of the following to keep your personal information secure? How about _____ ? Would you say you have a lot of trust in...?

39% banks and credit card companies

26% health insurance companies
19% your cellphone carrier
16% your email provider
14% state government
14% retail stores
12% the federal government
6% online retailers
2% social networking websites or applications

GALLUP

U.S. consumers lost a great deal of confidence in banks and other financial institutions after the Great Recession. Consumer confidence hit a low point in June 2012, with 21% of Americans saying they had "a great deal" or "quite a lot" of confidence in U.S. banks. Five years earlier, however, before the financial crisis, confidence in banks stood at 41%. Today, 22% of Americans have a great deal or quite a lot of confidence in U.S. financial institutions or banks, according to a Gallup poll conducted March 7–9, 2014. While still not stellar, this improvement has been steady and substantial.

Nonetheless, consumers trust banks to protect their personal data at levels considerably higher than their overall confidence in the institutions themselves. The key differentiator here may be the protection of personal information. While, in general, the industry has suffered a negative reputation since the 2008 financial crisis, banks and credit card companies are potentially held to specific legal parameters regarding the protection of personal information. This higher standard could influence the amount of trust consumers say they have in the security of their sensitive data with financial institutions compared with other industries.

Implications

The results of this poll speak strongly to the opportunity available to the banking industry. Even in the face of an uphill battle to regain public confidence, the industry leads many other businesses that collect personal information by 13 percentage points in establishing trust with customers that their personal information will be protected. Although this represents one facet of confidence, it is potentially one that is becoming more important as consumer trust as a whole declines and threats to the security of personal information become increasingly common.

Gallup's research on customer engagement underscores the importance of confidence in building an emotional tie with consumers. But companies don't gain this emotional bond with their consumers overnight. Banks must focus on providing consistent service to meet basic customer expectations, while at the same time establishing the trust that they will always deliver on what they promise—in a market where promises are often attached to dollar amounts. Developing an emotionally engaged relationship with a customer is no doubt hard work, but it is not without reward. Trust breeds engagement, and engaged customers not only generate more revenue for banks but also have a higher number of investments and deposits with their primary bank, according to a 2013 Gallup study of the industry.

Banks can potentially capitalize on this opportunity by showing that their protection of personal information isn't just about legal ramifications. Instead, showing patrons that promises are kept because they care about their customers' financial well-being as a whole creates an opening for an emotional connection. Personal finance is *personal*, and there isn't a way around it. Banks need to assure customers that they are on their side, looking out for the security of consumers' sensitive information and keeping their best interests top of mind. In an increasingly insecure world, consumers need all the data security friends they can get.

Survey Methods

Results for this Gallup poll are based on telephone interviews conducted April 23–29, 2014, with a random sample of 1,011 adults, aged 18 and older, living in all 50 U.S. states and the District of Columbia.

For results based on the total sample of national adults, the margin of sampling error is ±4 percentage points at the 95% confidence level.

June 09, 2014

IN U.S., DEPRESSION RATES HIGHER FOR LONG-TERM UNEMPLOYED

Mental health poorest among those jobless for six months or more

by Steve Crabtree

WASHINGTON, D.C.—The longer that Americans are unemployed, the more likely they are to report signs of poor psychological well-being. About one in five Americans who have been unemployed for a year or more say they currently have or are being treated for depression—almost double the rate among those who have been unemployed for five weeks or less.

Do you currently have, or are you currently being treated for, depression?

Among unemployed, likelihood of being depressed rises steadily over time

■ Currently have/being treated for depression

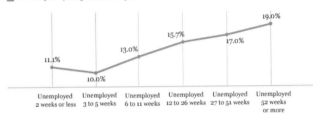

Gallup-Healthways Well-Being Index, 2013

GALLUP'

These findings are based on surveys with 356,599 Americans, including 18,322 unemployed adults, conducted in 2013 as part of the Gallup-Healthways Well-Being Index.

Gallup finds that unemployed Americans are more than twice as likely as those with full-time jobs to say they currently have or are being treated for depression—12.4% vs. 5.6%, respectively. However, the depression rate among the long-term unemployed—which the Bureau of Labor Statistics defines as those who have been seeking work for 27 weeks or more—jumps to 18.0%.

Incidence of Depression by Employment Group

Long-term unemployed more than three times as likely as full-time employed to be depressed

	Currently have/ Currently being treated for depression
All Americans	10.1%
Total unemployed	12.4%
Unemployed less than 27 weeks (short-term)	12.3%
Unemployed 27 weeks or more (long-term)	18.0%
Total employed	6.4%
Employed full time	5.6%
Employed part time, do not want full time	8.0%
Employed part time, want full time	10.3%

Gallup-Healthways Well-Being Index, 2013

GALLUP'

Psychologists have long associated unemployment with a variety of psychological ailments, including depression, anxiety, and low self-esteem. The causal direction of the relationship, though, is not clear from Gallup's data. It is possible that unemployment causes poor health conditions such as depression, or it could be that having such conditions makes it harder to land a job.

The loss of hope that can accompany long-term unemployment may be detrimental not only to job seekers' quality of life but also to their ability to find good jobs. The likelihood of unemployed Americans to agree that they will find a job within the next four weeks falls sharply the longer they are unemployed—from about seven in 10 among those unemployed for five weeks or less, to fewer than three in 10 among those who have been jobless for a year or more. This marked drop in optimism may affect job seekers' motivation, increasing the risk that they will drop out of the labor force altogether.

Do you think that in the next four weeks you will have a job?

After 27 weeks of unemployment, more job seekers are pessimistic than optimistic

■ Yes, will have a job   ■ No, will not have a job

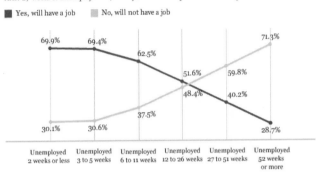

Gallup-Healthways Well-Being Index, 2013

GALLUP'

It's important to note that these results likely reflect not only attitudinal changes among job seekers but also hard realities facing those who are unemployed for an extended period. A study by economist Rand Ghayad published in 2012 found that employers preferred candidates without any relevant experience—but who had been jobless for less than six months—to those with experience who had been seeking work for longer than that.

Long-Term Unemployed Spend Less Time With Family and Friends

In general, Americans are a happy populace; 82.5% interviewed over the course of 2013 said they smiled or laughed a lot the previous day. Similarly, 81.1% of those unemployed for six months or less found things to smile or laugh about "yesterday." But among the long-term unemployed, this figure drops significantly to 70.7%.

The idea that people are less likely to experience positive emotions the longer they are unemployed may come as no surprise—but that drop may be exacerbated by a growing hesitation to seek social support. A 2011 study of the long-term unemployed published by the Heldrich Center for Workforce Development at Rutgers University found that half of participants experienced shame and embarrassment that led them to isolate themselves from friends and associates. Among the long-term unemployed, 31.1% reported spending two hours or less with family or friends the previous day, versus 21.5% among short-term unemployed adults.

Again, these results don't necessarily imply unemployment itself causes these differences. It may be that unhappy or less positive job seekers are less likely to be able to get jobs in the first place—if, for example, employers are looking for more upbeat workers. It is also possible that those who spend less time with family and friends are therefore less able to draw on their social networks for employment leads.

Approximately, how many hours did you spend, socially, with friends or family yesterday? Please include telephone or email or other online communication.

Long-term unemployed most likely to have spent no more than two hours with friends or family

	Percentage who spent two hours or less
All Americans	25.0%
Total unemployed	22.4%
Short-term unemployed	21.5%
Long-term unemployed	31.1%

Gallup-Healthways Well-Being Index, 2013

GALLUP

Bottom Line

Record-high rates of long-term unemployment remain one of the most devastating effects of the Great Recession in the U.S. The economic cost is huge—but just as tragic are signs of poor mental health among unemployed Americans. Gallup data shed light on numerous health effects likely to contribute to the long-term unemployment trap. The idea that extended unemployment causes workers' skill to atrophy is a common concern, but the effects of joblessness on candidates' health may be just as damaging to their ability to find—and, just as importantly, hang on to—a good job.

A recent study by three Princeton economists, including former White House chief economist Alan Krueger, demonstrated that many of those who find work after a long period of joblessness return to the ranks of the unemployed within a year. Previous Gallup research indicates that, in total, U.S. employees who have been diagnosed with depression miss about 68 million more days per year than those who have not, costing employers an estimated $23 billion annually. In the context of a tenuous recovery, employers may be particularly unwilling or unable to retain new employees who regularly miss work.

However, closely tracking the health effects associated with long-term unemployment may help policymakers design new interventions to reduce their severity. Programs geared toward helping American job seekers maintain psychological, physical, and social aspects of well-being over the course of their job search may help them to re-enter the workforce ready to be as productive as they were when they left.

Survey Methods

Results for this Gallup poll are based on telephone interviews conducted Jan. 1–Dec. 31, 2013, on the Gallup Daily tracking survey, with a random sample of 356,599 adults, aged 18 and older, living in all 50 U.S. states and the District of Columbia.

For results based on the total sample of national adults, the margin of sampling error is less than ±1 percentage point at the 95% confidence level.

The total number of unemployed respondents is 18,322, with 13,352 unemployed for less than 27 weeks (short-term) and 4,970 unemployed for 27 weeks or more (long-term).

June 10, 2014

IN U.S., MAJORITY "NOT OVERWEIGHT," NOT TRYING TO LOSE WEIGHT
Less than 40% of Americans report being overweight

by Joy Wilke

WASHINGTON, D.C.—A majority of Americans (55%) say they are neither overweight nor trying to lose weight, despite a recent study by the Institute for Health Metrics and Evaluation (IHME) that found two-thirds of Americans are overweight or obese.

Americans' Self-Reported Weight Status

	%
Not overweight and not trying to lose weight	55
Overweight but not trying to lose weight	18
Overweight and trying to lose weight	18
Not overweight but trying to lose weight	8

Gallup's annual Health and Healthcare survey, 2011 to 2013

GALLUP

As for Americans who report being overweight, equal percentages say they are overweight and trying to lose weight (18%) or are overweight and not trying to lose weight (18%).

These data are aggregated from Gallup's Health and Healthcare surveys from 2011 through 2013. The annual survey asks Americans about their current weight status and whether they are seriously trying to lose weight.

It is important to note that the Gallup data are based on self-descriptions of Americans' weight status from telephone interviews. Gallup-Healthways research, also conducted via telephone, takes a different approach by calculating Body Mass Index (BMI) scores based on respondents' self-reported height and weight. Another technique used to measure obesity involves in-person interviewing in which interviewers take actual height and weight measurements of study participants. These different measurement methods may result in differing estimates of the percentage of Americans who are overweight or obese.

Women, Older Americans More Likely to Say They're Trying to Lose Weight

Overall, 60% of men and 50% of women report that they are neither overweight nor trying to lose weight. Women, in general, are more likely to say they are "very" or "somewhat" overweight compared with men. Further, 21% of women say they are overweight and trying to lose weight, significantly higher than the 15% of men who say the same.

Americans' Self-Reported Weight Status, by Gender

	Men	Women
Not overweight and not trying to lose weight	60%	50%
Overweight but not trying to lose weight	18%	19%
Overweight and trying to lose weight	15%	21%
Not overweight but trying to lose weight	6%	10%

Gallup's annual Health and Healthcare survey, 2011 to 2013

GALLUP

Additionally, 10% of women say they are not overweight but are currently trying to lose weight, considerably more than the 6% of men who say the same.

Younger adults are significantly more likely than older adults to express contentment with their current weight. Among Americans aged 18 to 34, 68% state that they are neither overweight nor trying to lose weight, while 12% say they are overweight and trying to lose weight.

Just under half of Americans aged 55 and older, 47%, say they are neither overweight nor trying to lose weight, while 22% report that they are overweight and trying to lose weight.

Americans' Self-Reported Weight Status, by Age

	18 to 34	35 to 54	55+
Not overweight and not trying to lose weight	68%	51%	47%
Overweight but not trying to lose weight	11%	20%	24%
Overweight and trying to lose weight	12%	20%	22%
Not overweight but trying to lose weight	8%	9%	7%

Gallup's annual Health and Healthcare survey, 2011 to 2013

GALLUP

Implications

These data highlight the importance of perception in the battle to fight obesity in the U.S. Though several recent studies—including the global analysis released in May by IHME—have documented that two-thirds of Americans are overweight or obese, less than 40% of American adults characterize themselves as either very or somewhat overweight. Further, previous Gallup research has shown that men are more likely to be overweight or obese than women when using BMI as a metric, yet these findings indicate that women are more likely to characterize themselves as overweight.

This discrepancy may suggest that addressing the obesity crisis in America must first start by convincing overweight Americans that they are indeed overweight.

Survey Methods

Results for this Gallup poll are based on telephone interviews conducted on the annual Gallup Health and Healthcare surveys for 2011, 2012, and 2013, with a combined random sample of 3,066 adults, aged 18 and older, living in all 50 U.S. states and the District of Columbia.

For results based on the total sample of national adults, the margin of sampling error is ±2 percentage points at the 95% confidence level.

June 11, 2014
SMALLER MAJORITY OF AMERICANS VIEW HILLARY CLINTON FAVORABLY
At 54%, her favorability has slipped since February

by Justin McCarthy

WASHINGTON, D.C.—Hillary Clinton's favorability rating has dropped slightly, although a majority of Americans continue to view her in a positive light. As Clinton publicizes her new memoir, "Hard Choices," 54% of Americans view her favorably. This is down from 59% in February, and significantly less than the ratings she received as secretary of state, which were consistently above 60%.

Hillary Clinton's Favorability Ratings

Next, we'd like to get your overall opinion of some people in the news. As I read each name, please say if you have a favorable or unfavorable opinion of these people -- or if you have never heard of them. How about -- Hillary Clinton?

■ % Favorable

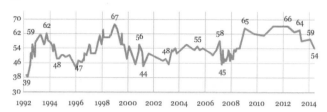

First lady (1993-2001); United States senator (2001-2009); secretary of state (2009-2013)

GALLUP

The latest findings come from a Gallup poll conducted June 5–8. Though Clinton has said she will not announce whether she'll run for president until at least later this year, her latest book has been widely framed as a preamble to another presidential bid and a move typical of White House hopefuls. Clinton already has the support of many elected officials and Democratic Party representatives if she chooses to run. Americans have named her their Most Admired Woman 18 times.

Clinton's current favorability rating is the lowest it has been since August 2008 (54%), when she was preparing to deliver a speech at the Democratic National Convention endorsing then-Sen. Barack Obama, who defeated her in a hard-fought primary battle for the party's 2008 presidential nomination.

After recovering from a contentious Democratic primary race that strapped her with campaign debt, Clinton's favorability soared while she served as secretary of state during Obama's first term. As she continued in her role, as many as two-thirds of Americans (66%) viewed her favorably, in consecutive polls in 2011 and 2012—a rating she surpassed only once before, at 67% in December 1998, shortly after her husband, President Bill Clinton, was impeached.

In her nonpolitical role as secretary of state, Clinton enjoyed extremely high ratings from her fellow Democrats, but saw her ratings increase among Republicans as well. She peaked with Republicans during this period in mid-2012, when 41% viewed her favorably. Her favorability fell with the GOP, as it did with independents, after the September 2012 attacks on the U.S. compound in Benghazi, Libya. As Democratic elected officials continue to encourage her to run for president, her name has become further politicized, thus making her less favorable to non-Democrats.

GOP operatives and media pundits have publicly questioned whether her health and age (Clinton is now 66) could hinder her ability to serve as president. Additionally, the House of Representatives has formed a select committee to investigate the attack in Benghazi. And as she wades into Obama's controversial decision to trade five Taliban prisoners held at Guantanamo Bay for U.S. soldier Bowe Bergdahl, Clinton's performance as one of Obama's top cabinet members will likely undergo greater scrutiny.

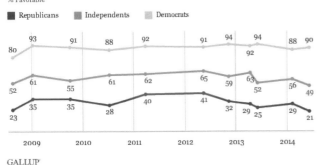

% Favorable

■ Republicans   ■ Independents   ■ Democrats

GALLUP

Bill Clinton's Effect on Hillary's Image

Bill Clinton, who in the same poll receives a 64% favorable rating, has commanded majority favorability from Americans during most of his time as president and in post-presidential life.

While some may view his high favorability ratings as an advantage for Hillary if she decides on another presidential run, Bill's favorability did take a hit when he joined her on the 2008 campaign trail. By January 2008—a year after Hillary announced her candidacy—his favorability hit a five-year low of 50%, barely ahead of Hillary's 48%.

In fact, for much of Hillary's career since Bill's presidency, their favorability ratings have been closely related.

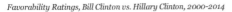

Favorability Ratings, Bill Clinton vs. Hillary Clinton, 2000-2014

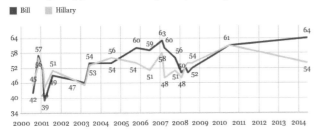

■ Bill   ■ Hillary

*Trend reflects ratings only from polls that asked about both Bill and Hillary Clinton

GALLUP

Their latest favorability ratings are separated by 10 percentage points and, with the exception of a 12-point difference in March 2007, are as far apart as they've been since Hillary independently entered the political fray as a candidate for the U.S. Senate from New York.

During Hillary's first term as New York's junior senator, her favorability was closely linked to that of her husband. But for the first three years of her second term, 2005–2007, their ratings differed by five to 12 percentage points. Then, in early 2008, when Bill became a proxy campaigner for Hillary in her bid for the presidency, his favorability fell and their ratings converged.

Bottom Line

Hillary Clinton's era of higher favorability appears to be ending even before she announces whether she will run for president. Americans typically rate non-political figures higher than political ones on this measure, and her favorable ratings before, during, and after being secretary of state are consistent with that phenomenon.

Though her husband's influence is far from Hillary's greatest selling point, he may be better positioned to help her on the campaign trail than he was last time, with his favorability up five points from what it was in mid-2006. But if Hillary does run, the boost she receives from him may be limited if it is similar to 2008, with his past favorability so closely married to her own in the backdrop of a presidential campaign.

Survey Methods

Results for this Gallup poll are based on telephone interviews conducted June 5–8, 2014, with a random sample of 1,027 adults, aged 18 and older, living in all 50 U.S. states and the District of Columbia.

For results based on the total sample of national adults, the margin of sampling error is ±4 percentage points at the 95% confidence level.

June 11, 2014
AMERICANS DIVIDED ON WISDOM OF U.S. PRISONER NEGOTIATIONS
Little change in views since 1985

by Jeffrey M. Jones

PRINCETON, NJ—Americans are evenly divided on the advisability of negotiating with terrorist groups to secure the release of American prisoners. Forty-three percent say it is more important for the U.S. to secure the safe release of prisoners, even if that means compromising with terrorist demands, while 44% say it is more important to discourage future prisoner-taking by refusing to negotiate with terrorist groups, even if that means risking the lives of the U.S. prisoners.

More Important When U.S. Prisoners Held by Terror Groups

Which is more important for the U.S. to consider when Americans are held captive by terrorist groups – [ROTATED: assuring the safe release of the American prisoners, even if it means working out some compromise on terrorist demands, (or) discouraging future prisoner-taking by refusing to deal with terrorist demands, even if that risks the lives of the American prisoners]?

	1985	2014
	%	%
Securing safe release of U.S. prisoners, even if compromising on terrorist demands	47	43
Discouraging future prisoner-taking by refusing to negotiate with terrorists, even at risk of U.S. prisoner safety	42	44
No opinion	10	13

Note: 1985 wording used "hostages" instead of "prisoners."

GALLUP

The results are based on a June 5–8 poll conducted in the first few days after the Taliban released U.S. Army Sgt. Bowe Bergdahl, whom they had held captive in Afghanistan for five years. Although the Taliban is not a terrorist group per se, it has long harbored terrorists in Afghanistan, including 9/11 mastermind Osama bin Laden. In exchange for Bergdahl, the U.S. released five Taliban detainees it was holding at the Guantanamo Bay prison in Cuba.

Gallup asked a similar question in 1985 after terrorists in Lebanon took more than 30 Americans hostage during the hijacking of a

TWA airliner. At the time, Americans were also largely divided over the trade-offs inherent in negotiating with terror groups for hostage release.

Democrats and Republicans currently have clear views of which considerations are more important when Americans are held captive. Republicans by a better than two-to-one margin believe the U.S. should not negotiate with terrorist groups, whereas by nearly the same margin Democrats believe securing the safe release of U.S. prisoners is more important.

Paramount Goal When U.S. Prisoners Are Held by Terror Groups, by Political Party Identification

	Democrats	Independents	Republicans
	%	%	%
Securing safe release of U.S. prisoners, even if compromising on terrorist demands	61	40	26
Discouraging future prisoner-taking by refusing to deal with terrorist demands, even at risk of U.S. prisoner lives	26	45	64
No opinion	12	14	10

June 5-8, 2014

GALLUP'

In 1985, Republicans and Democrats did not show as much consensus in their views as they do now. Back then, Democrats saw the safe release of hostages as the higher priority, by 53% to 37%. Republicans said discouraging future hostage taking was more important, by 48% to 40%.

Americans' Attention to Bergdahl Case Above Historical Norms for News Stories

Thirty-one percent of Americans say they are following the news about the Bergdahl release "very closely," and an additional 34% say they are following it "somewhat closely." The combined 65% following the story closely is slightly higher than the 60% average Gallup has measured for more than 200 news events since 1991.

Americans who are most engaged in the Bergdahl story—those following it "very closely"—come firmly down on the side of refusing to negotiate with terrorists. This relationship is partly because more Republicans (39%) than Democrats (27%) are following the story very closely.

Those who are not following the story closely see the safe release of prisoners as the more important objective.

Paramount Goal When U.S. Prisoners Are Held by Terror Groups, by How Closely Following News of Bowe Bergdahl Release

	Very closely	Somewhat closely	Not closely
	%	%	%
Securing safe release of U.S. prisoners, even if compromising on terrorist demands	30	46	50
Discouraging future prisoner-taking by refusing to deal with terrorist demands, even at risk of U.S. prisoner lives	56	43	35
No opinion	14	10	14

June 5-8, 2014

GALLUP'

Americans Critical of Bergdahl, as Well as Obama's Handling of the Situation

The Bergdahl release has been controversial not just because of the terms of his release but also for the circumstances surrounding his capture, including allegations that he was captured after deserting his post. A majority of Americans, 51%, do not have an opinion of Bergdahl, however those who do are decidedly more negative than positive toward him. Thirty-seven percent of Americans say they have an unfavorable opinion of Bergdahl, while 13% have a favorable one.

Those following the news about Bergdahl's release "very closely" are much more likely to have an opinion of him, and it is overwhelmingly negative, with a 65% unfavorable and 15% favorable rating among this group.

Americans' opinions about how President Barack Obama has handled the situation are also negative, with 38% approving and 50% disapproving. Among those following the story very closely, 28% approve and 69% disapprove.

Implications

The Bergdahl situation has proved to be highly controversial and Obama continues to be questioned about his decision to exchange prisoners with the Taliban. The president has emphasized the United States' desire to bring home all of its captive soldiers as a rationale for his decision.

Americans' divided opinion on the proper course of action in these matters underscores the complexity of the situation. Obama's ultimate choice in the matter was more in line with the view of his political base, given Democrats' belief that securing the safe release of Americans is more important than the potential risks involved in meeting terrorist demands. The fact that Republicans take an opposing view on how to handle such a situation is one reason Bergdahl's release has not been universally hailed. Republican congressional leaders have already called for hearings to look into the matter, and Defense Secretary Chuck Hagel testified before a House Committee on Wednesday.

Importantly for the president, despite the criticism he has received over Bergdahl and Americans' disapproval of his handling of the situation, his overall job approval rating has held steady as the controversy has evolved.

Survey Methods

Results for this Gallup poll are based on telephone interviews conducted June 5–8, 2014, with a random sample of 1,027 adults, aged 18 and older, living in all 50 U.S. states and the District of Columbia.

For results based on the total sample of national adults, the margin of sampling error is ±4 percentage points at the 95% confidence level.

June 12, 2014
SOLID MAJORITY OF AMERICANS CLOSELY FOLLOWING VA SCANDAL
Providing timelier care, firing all VA employees top list of fixes

by Art Swift

WASHINGTON, D.C.—Americans are closely following the scandal engulfing the U.S. Department of Veterans Affairs, amid allegations that thousands of veterans were denied healthcare because of false record-keeping and long waiting lists at VA facilities nationwide. Sixty-nine percent of Americans say they are following the situation "very" or "somewhat closely" in the wake of the resignation of VA Secretary Eric Shinseki and the department's widening scope of troubles.

The Situation at the VA in the United States

How closely are you following the news about the quality of medical care provided by Veterans Administration hospitals around the country, also known as the VA -- very closely, somewhat closely, not too closely or not at all?

	Very closely %	Somewhat closely %	Not too closely %	Not at all %
Jun 5-8, 2014	33	36	20	10

GALLUP

The VA situation became known this spring after reports asserted that some veterans died waiting for care, shining a spotlight on fundamental staffing problems across many Veterans Health Administration facilities. Media and political attention grew as the scandal widened, with more revelations emerging about the widespread nature of the problems. Americans are quite aware of the story, yet the 69% who have been following it isn't as high as have followed other news events this century, such as 9/11 (97%), Hurricane Katrina (96%), or the 2012 school shootings in Newtown, Connecticut (87%). But the level of attention to the VA scandal does exceed the average 60% who report closely following more than 200 major news stories since 1991.

Providing Better Care, Firing All VA Employees Top List of Fixes

As President Barack Obama considers candidates to replace Shinseki and tackle the problems at the VA, Gallup asked Americans, using an open-ended question, how they would fix the VA. No single answer is dominant, but the most common response, mentioned by 16% of Americans, is "provide better care in a more timely manner." Firing all VA employees, cleaning house, and better accountability came next, along with improving administration and supervision of the department.

Ways to Fix Problems With the Department of Veterans Affairs

There has been a great deal of attention to problems with the way in which the VA provides healthcare services to veterans. Just from what you know and have read, what would you say is the best way to fix the problems with the VA? (OPEN ENDED, by percent)

	Jun 5-8, 2014 %
Provide better care in a more timely manner	16
Fire all employees of VA/Clean house/Better accountability	11
Improve administration/Better supervision/More authority to make changes	10
Allow veterans choice in care/Not tied to VA/Provide vouchers	9
Additional/adequate funding/Better pay, resources	9
Need to overhaul veterans' health system	9
More/Better staff, doctors, nurses, caregivers	7
Better management/leadership of VA	6
Privatize veterans health system/Keep government out of it	3
Improve communication/Make more information available to veterans	2
Eliminate bonus system/Encourages falsifying of records	1
Already on the right track/moving forward	1
Change U.S. healthcare system (non-specific)	1
Get rid of unions working at VA centers	1
Other	3
Nothing	6
No opinion	20

GALLUP

Although 9% mentioned more funding for the VA, it was not Americans' top solution, suggesting that the public believes there are other remedies to be tried before more money is spent to fix the problem. Congress is currently considering proposals to allow veterans to seek care outside the VA system, something 9% of Americans mentioned as a solution. Three percent of Americans suggest privatizing the entire VA health system.

Americans Do Not Approve of Obama's Handling of Situation

As the situation continues to unfold at the VA, 29% of all Americans say they approve of the way Obama is handling the situation involving veterans at VA hospitals, with 63% disapproving. When asked to rate the president on a variety of issues, more Americans approve of his handling of other issues, including the environment (47%), terrorism (42%), and the release of U.S. Army Sgt. Bowe Bergdahl (38%). While approval is not high on any of these matters, the rather low rating of Obama's handling of the VA scandal is significant, especially paired with how closely Americans are following the issue. To date, though, it has not seemed to have had a noticeable effect on his overall job approval rating, which has been fairly steady at 44% even as the controversy has unfolded.

Bottom Line

The VA scandal could remain on the minds of Americans for quite some time. With several news reports noting that the alleged inadequate healthcare preceded the Obama administration, it may take years for any potential fix to work, even as Congress is urgently working on legislation to address the issue.

At the moment, a strong majority of Americans are following this matter closely, and Americans give the president low marks for his handling of it. This may have implications for policies and politics in 2014 and beyond.

It is clear that Americans have thoughtful responses as to how to fix the situation. From allowing veterans choice in their healthcare to improving the timeliness of treatment, there are several potential fixes to this imbroglio, some of which members of Congress will likely ponder in the months ahead.

Survey Methods

Results for this Gallup poll are based on telephone interviews conducted June 5–8, 2014, on the Gallup Daily tracking survey, with a random sample of 1,027 adults, aged 18 and older, living in all 50 U.S. states and the District of Columbia.

For results based on the total sample of national adults, the margin of sampling error is ±4 percentage points at the 95% confidence level.

June 12, 2014
AMERICANS' RATINGS OF PRESIDENT OBAMA'S IMAGE AT NEW LOWS
More view him unfavorably than favorably

by Jeffrey M. Jones

PRINCETON, NJ—Americans' views of President Barack Obama as a person have turned slightly negative, with 47% saying they have a favorable opinion of him and 52% an unfavorable one. That net favorable rating of –5 is the least positive personal assessment of Obama to date.

Barack Obama Favorable Ratings

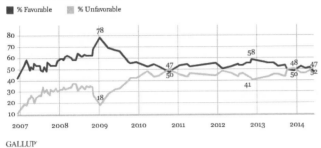

Americans have generally maintained a positive opinion of Obama personally throughout his presidency even as his job approval ratings have averaged no higher than 48% in each of his last four years in office. In addition to the current June 5–8 favorable ratings, there have been only three other times when his favorable rating did not exceed his unfavorable rating: once in October 2010, just prior to that year's midterm elections, and twice in late 2013 during the troubled rollout of major provisions of the Affordable Care Act.

In recent weeks, the president has been dogged by a scandal involving medical care for U.S. military veterans at Veterans Affairs hospitals as well as the controversy surrounding the release of Army Sgt. Bowe Bergdahl. These events to date do not appear to have dragged down his job approval rating in Gallup Daily tracking. However, they may be having a slight negative impact on his personal image.

In addition to his lower favorable rating, Americans now rate Obama less positively on each of six personal characteristics Gallup asked about than they did last year. The declines are not large, ranging from two percentage points on being "a strong and decisive leader" since last November to six points on "understanding the problems Americans face in their daily lives." But on all six dimensions, the public's ratings of Obama are now below the majority level and are the worst Gallup has measured for him to date.

Barack Obama Character Ratings

Figures are percentage who say each characteristic applies to Barack Obama

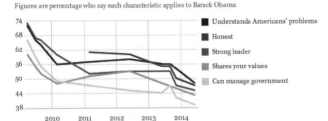

Note: Trend for "Has clear plan for solving problems" not shown.

GALLUP

Americans are most likely to say Obama understands the problems Americans face in their daily lives (48%), that he is honest and trustworthy (47%), and that he is a strong and decisive leader (45%). They are less likely to say he shares their values (43%), can manage government effectively (39%), and has a clear plan for solving the country's problems (34%).

By comparison, his ratings on four of these characteristics measured in April 2009, roughly 100 days into his presidency, ranged from 60% for shares your values to 73% for being a strong and decisive leader.

Implications

Recent controversies may be taking a modest toll on President Obama, but more so on his personal ratings than in evaluations of the job he is doing as president. While his favorable rating and assessments on six different personal dimensions are the lowest to date, his job approval rating is still a few points above his personal lows.

To some degree, an improving economy may be holding up his job approval rating and offsetting any potential negative effect from the VA and Bergdahl situations. Still, his average 44% job approval rating since April is not particularly good. Given the strong influence that presidential approval has on midterm election outcomes, Democratic candidates face a strong headwind as they campaign in this year's elections.

Survey Methods

Results for this Gallup poll are based on telephone interviews conducted June 5–8, 2014, with a random sample of 1,027 adults, aged 18 and older, living in all 50 U.S. states and the District of Columbia.

For results based on the total sample of national adults, the margin of sampling error is ±4 percentage points at the 95% confidence level.

June 13, 2014

MOST IN U.S. WANT TO PRIORITIZE IMPROVING VETERANS' HEALTH
Investigating Bergdahl matter ranks last out of nine issues

by Lydia Saad

PRINCETON, NJ—Improving healthcare for U.S. veterans is Americans' top legislative priority for Washington to focus on, out of nine issues now or recently in the national spotlight. Nearly nine out of 10 Americans say it is "extremely" (41%) or "very important" (46%) that the president and Congress deal with veterans' healthcare in the next year.

Americans' Issue Priorities

How important is it to you that the president and Congress deal with each of the following issues in the next year -- is it extremely important, very important, somewhat important, or not important?

	Extremely/ Very important
	%
Improving the way in which healthcare services are provided to U.S. military veterans	87
Passing new legislation to require equal pay for women	72
Passing new legislation providing access to high-quality preschool to every child in America	65
Conducting further investigations into the attacks on U.S. diplomatic outposts in Benghazi, Libya, in 2012 in which four Americans were killed	59
Passing new immigration reform legislation	58
Passing a bill to raise the minimum wage	57
Enforcing new limits on carbon emissions from the nation's power plants	54
Passing new legislation that would scale back parts of the 2010 healthcare law	53
Conducting investigations into the capture and recent release of Army sergeant Bowe Bergdahl, who was held captive in Afghanistan by the Taliban for five years	52

June 9-10, 2014

GALLUP

After veterans' healthcare, 72% of Americans see a strong need for equal pay legislation for women, and 65% view expanding high-quality preschool as a top government priority.

Each of the six lower-ranked issues are rated extremely or very important by just over half of U.S. adults, ranging from 59% who want to conduct further investigations into the 2012 attacks on the U.S. diplomatic outpost in Benghazi, Libya, down to 52% wanting investigations into the circumstances surrounding the capture and release of Army Sgt. Bowe Bergdahl by the Taliban in Afghanistan.

These results are from a Gallup poll conducted June 9–10. The list focuses on specific policy issues currently being proposed or debated in Congress, rather than on the more basic policy areas that face the country. Gallup measured the perceived importance of 19 such broad policy areas in January, with the economy and education coming out on top.

Democrats and Republicans Agree on Importance of VA Repairs

Republicans and Democrats agree more about the importance of some issues than others, but they are completely unified in assigning high importance to improving veterans' healthcare. Nine in 10 Americans from each party consider the veterans issue highly important for the president and Congress to address, including more than four in 10 calling it extremely important.

Although majorities of all party groups say passing legislation to require equal pay for women is highly important, this ranges from a simple majority of Republicans (58%) to the vast majority of Democrats (88%). Additionally, about six in 10 Democrats and Republicans, alike, consider passing new immigration reform legislation highly important, although it is not clear from this question whether the two groups agree on what that reform should involve.

All other issues measured in the poll are more polarizing. Large majorities of Democrats, but fewer than half of Republicans, rate providing access to high-quality preschool, raising the minimum wage, and enforcing new limits on carbon emissions as top priorities. On the other hand, conducting further investigations into the Benghazi attacks, investigating the circumstances surrounding Bergdahl's capture and release, and scaling back the 2010 healthcare law are all issues that most Republicans, but not most Democrats, see as important.

Not surprisingly, there is a slight gender gap on the equal pay issue: 80% of women consider it extremely or very important that Washington enact legislation requiring equal pay for women, compared with 64% of men.

Bottom Line

Just weeks after new information about mismanagement and corruption at a number of Veterans Health Administration hospitals around the country came to light, the Senate and House of Representatives are poised to send legislation to start remedying the situation to President Barack Obama for his signature. The strong show of bipartisanship in this quick action is mirrored in Americans' nearly universal agreement that federal lawmakers need to focus on improving how the country provides healthcare to veterans. Whether Americans are ultimately satisfied that the Veterans Affairs bill goes far enough remains to be seen, as only some of the policy prescriptions Americans had for the VA in a recent Gallup poll are included in the legislation.

Meanwhile, proposals that would strengthen the ability of women working in the private sector to receive equal pay, such as the Paycheck Fairness Act, could potentially gain some momentum in Congress this year, considering the broad bipartisan support Gallup finds among the public. However, given their lopsided political constituencies, a number of other proposals—particularly raising the minimum wage, passing new pollution regulations, and scaling back the 2010 healthcare law—are almost certain to languish as the midterm elections near.

Survey Methods

Results for this Gallup poll are based on telephone interviews conducted June 9–10, 2014, on the Gallup Daily tracking survey, with a random sample of 1,012 adults, aged 18 and older, living in all 50 U.S. states and the District of Columbia.

For results based on the total sample of national adults, the margin of sampling error is ±4 percentage points at the 95% confidence level.

Americans' Issue Priorities -- by Party ID

% Extremely/Very important that the president and Congress deal with each

	Democrats	Independents	Republicans
	%	%	%
BIPARTISAN PRIORITIES			
Improving veterans' healthcare	90	84	91
Requiring equal pay for women	88	69	58
Passing immigration reform	57	57	60
DEMOCRATIC PRIORITIES			
Ensuring access to high-quality preschool	83	63	46
Raising the minimum wage	80	52	33
Enforcing new limits on carbon emissions by power plants	71	52	36
REPUBLICAN PRIORITIES			
Investigating Benghazi attacks	48	61	75
Investigating Bowe Bergdahl capture/release	44	51	65
Scaling back the 2010 healthcare law	37	54	75

June 9-10, 2014

GALLUP'

June 13, 2014
AMERICANS CONTINUE TO OPPOSE CLOSING GUANTANAMO BAY
Opinions on closing the prison have changed little since 2009

by Justin McCarthy

WASHINGTON, D.C.—Twenty-nine percent of Americans support closing the terrorist detention camp at Guantanamo Bay, Cuba, and moving its prisoners to U.S. prisons, while two in three (66%) oppose the idea. Despite the recent controversy surrounding the release of five Taliban prisoners held at Guantanamo Bay in exchange for U.S. Army Sgt. Bowe Berghdal's release from Afghanistan, Americans' views have barely budged since 2009.

These results are from a June 5–8 Gallup poll conducted days after the release of Sgt. Bergdahl. Gallup found that Americans are divided on the wisdom of negotiating with terrorist groups to secure the release of Americans prisoners.

As you may know, since 2001, the United States has held people from other countries who are suspected of being terrorists in a prison at Guantanamo Bay in Cuba. Do you think the United States should -- or should not -- close this prison and move some of the prisoners to U.S. prisons?

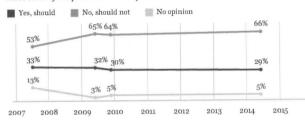

July 2007 wording: Do you think the United States should -- or should not -- close the prison at the Guantanamo Bay military base in Cuba?

GALLUP

President Barack Obama made the closing of Guantanamo Bay a part of his 2008 campaign platform, but he has yet to do so. However, he recently reiterated his desire to close the prison at the West Point graduation ceremony. Despite the president's continued commitment to its closure, Americans' views have not changed much in the four times Gallup has asked them about this issue.

Republicans remain more likely than Democrats to oppose closing the detention facility, although the majority of Democrats remain opposed.

Do you think the United States should -- or should not -- close this prison and move some of the prisoners to U.S. prisons?

By party ID

	Yes, should	No, should not
Republicans	13%	84%
Independents	30%	64%
Democrats	41%	54%

June 5-8, 2014

GALLUP

A consistent minority of Republicans have supported closing the prison since 2007, when 16% felt the prison should be closed. Republicans were even less likely to support the prison's closure by 2009, as Obama continued his pledge to close the facility, reaching its lowest at 8% in November of that year.

Like Republicans, independents' support for closing the prison has fallen since 2007, from 37% in 2007 to 28% by November 2009.

Support for Closing Guantanamo Bay and Moving Prisoners to U.S. Prisons

Do you think the United States should -- or should not -- close this prison and move some of the prisoners to U.S. prisons? % Yes, should

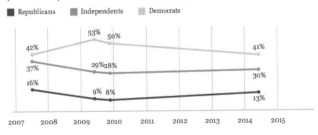

GALLUP

As of this year, Democrats have shown their lowest support for closing the prison at Guantanamo Bay. Currently, 41% support the idea, while 54% oppose it. Previously, Democrats were split in their views, sometimes differing by as little as two percentage points.

Bottom Line

Though President Obama has long backed plans to close the prison at Guantanamo Bay, he did not have the support of Americans on the issue when taking office in 2009. Today, he still does not have their support, even among those in his own party.

According to a spokeswoman for the National Security Council, 17 inmates from the detention facility have been moved out in the past 13 months, including the five Taliban officials who were recently swapped for Bergdahl. This leaves 149 remaining detainees at the facility, and the White House is currently exploring plans to transfer more of them on a case-by-case basis.

Though public opinion on what to do with the facility has been consistent, it could change as prisoner numbers dwindle. Further, as more information regarding the Bergdahl case emerges—including whether the recently freed Taliban detainees re-emerge as terror threats to the U.S.—ideas about what to do with Guantanamo Bay could shift.

Survey Methods

Results for this Gallup poll are based on telephone interviews conducted June 5–8, 2014, with a random sample of 1,027 adults, aged 18 and older, living in all 50 U.S. states and the District of Columbia.

For results based on the total sample of national adults, the margin of sampling error is ±4 percentage points at the 95% confidence level.

June 16, 2014
KEY MIDTERM ELECTION INDICATORS AT OR NEAR HISTORICAL LOWS
Approval of Congress at 16%; national satisfaction at 23%

by Jeffrey M. Jones

PRINCETON, NJ—The election environment for congressional incumbents in 2014 will be challenging, with several key public opinion indicators as negative or nearly as negative as they have been in any recent midterm election year. This includes congressional job approval, which, at 16%, is on pace to be the lowest in a midterm election year since Gallup first measured it in 1974.

Congressional Job Approval,
Midterm Election Years, 1974-2014

Year	% Approve
1974	35
1978	29
1982	29
1986	42
1990	26
1994	22
1998	44
2002	50
2006	26
2010	21
2014	16

Figures are for June 2014 and final poll before election for prior years

GALLUP

In years when congressional job approval is low, there tends to be greater turnover in House membership. The prior low job approval rating in a midterm election year was 21% in 2010, a year in which 15% of House incumbents seeking re-election were defeated. In 1994, when 22% approved of Congress, 10% of incumbents lost. By comparison, just 4% of incumbents lost in 2002, when Congress enjoyed a 50% approval rating.

The potential vulnerability of congressional incumbents was clear last week, when House Majority Leader Eric Cantor suffered a stunning defeat in his primary election in Virginia, losing to an underfunded GOP "outsider."

Fewer Than One in Four Satisfied With State of Nation

Americans are not just down on Congress but also quite unhappy with the direction of the country more generally. Currently, 23% of Americans are satisfied with the way things are going in the U.S., on par with the 22% satisfaction at the time of the 2010 elections and the 24% before the 1982 elections. Both of those elections saw significant turnover in congressional membership.

Satisfaction With Way Things Are Going in the
United States, Midterm Election Years, 1982-2014

Year	% Satisfied
1982	24
1986	58
1990	32
1994	30
1998	60
2002	48
2006	35
2010	22
2014	23

Figures are for June 2014 and final poll before election for prior years

GALLUP

Obama Approval Rating at 2010 Level

Although the president is not a candidate in midterm election years, his standing with voters is usually a significant predictor of election outcomes. When presidents are unpopular, their party typically loses a substantial number of seats in the House of Representatives. Conversely, in the 1998 and 2002 elections, when Presidents Bill Clinton and George W. Bush had approval ratings above 60%, their parties gained House seats, providing rare exceptions to the historical trend of midterm seat losses for the president's party.

Presidential Job Approval Ratings,
Midterm Election Years, 1982-2014

Year (President)	% Approve
1982 (Reagan)	42
1986 (Reagan)	63
1990 (G.H.W. Bush)	58
1994 (Clinton)	46
1998 (Clinton)	66
2002 (G.W. Bush)	63
2006 (G.W. Bush)	38
2010 (Obama)	44
2014 (Obama)	44

Figures are for June 2014 and final poll before election for prior years

GALLUP

President Barack Obama's job approval rating from Gallup Daily tracking has averaged 44% thus far in June. That is the same as his approval rating at the time of the 2010 elections, when Democrats lost more than 60 seats in the House. Only two presidents have had lower job approval ratings in recent midterm elections—George W. Bush in 2006 and Ronald Reagan in 1982. In those years, the president's party lost more than 20 seats, suggesting seat loss is not always proportional to presidential job approval, but underscoring the peril the president's party faces when his approval rating is below 50%.

Economic Concern Above Average

Poor economic conditions are often a major reason why Americans are dissatisfied with the state of the nation and disapprove of government leaders. Earlier this year, Gallup found the economy ranking ahead of other issues when voters were asked which will be most important to their vote.

Although Americans' confidence in the economy is improving slightly, the public still shows greater concern over it than in prior midterm election years. Specifically, 44% mention an economic issue when asked to name the most important problem facing the country. That is significantly higher than in the 1998, 2002, and 2006 elections, but is down sharply from 2010, reflecting improvements in the economy since then.

Percentage of Americans Mentioning an Economic
Issue as the Most Important Problem Facing the
U.S., Midterm Election Years, 1998-2014

Year	% Mentioning economic issue
1998	27
2002	29
2006	19
2010	69
2014	44

Figures are for June 2014 and final poll before election for prior years

GALLUP

The major aspects of the economy most troubling to Americans are the state of the economy in general and unemployment, mentioned by 20% and 16%, respectively, as the most important problem.

Implications

The political environment in which the 2014 elections are being contested promises to be difficult for congressional incumbents, as public attitudes on key indicators that predict election outcomes are comparatively worse than in prior midterm election years. The likelihood of significant improvement in any of these indicators between now and the fall is fairly low; the dominant trend for congressional approval, presidential approval, and satisfaction is that the measures become more negative by the eve of the midterm elections than they were in January of the same year.

Recently, Gallup found 50% of voters saying their own member of Congress deserves re-election, and 22% saying most members deserve re-election, both among the lowest Gallup has measured. Some members have chosen to retire from Congress rather than seek another term, and others are leaving to run for other offices, which means there will already be a significant change in membership in the next Congress regardless of what voters do in the fall. But voters may be poised to send even more incumbents home. Although every House election is based on idiosyncratic local personalities and factors, Cantor's defeat last Tuesday can serve as a pointed reminder for incumbents seeking re-election of just how vulnerable they may be this year.

Survey Methods

Results for this Gallup poll are based on telephone interviews conducted June 5–8, 2014, with a random sample of 1,027 adults, aged 18 and older, living in all 50 U.S. states and the District of Columbia.

For results based on the total sample of national adults, the margin of sampling error is ±4 percentage points at the 95% confidence level.

June 17, 2014
AMERICANS NOT CLOSELY FOLLOWING NEWS ON BENGHAZI HEARINGS
More approve than disapprove of hearings investigating the attack

by Lydia Saad

PRINCETON, NJ—As the Republican-led House of Representatives launches the eighth congressional investigation into the 2012 terrorist attack against American diplomats in Benghazi, Libya, fewer than one in five Americans say they are following the story "very closely." Another 24% say they are following it "somewhat closely," while the slight majority, 57%, are paying little or no attention.

Americans' Attention to News About Congressional Benghazi Hearings

How closely are you following the news about upcoming congressional hearings into the 2012 attack on U.S. diplomatic outposts in Benghazi, Libya -- very closely, somewhat closely, not too closely, or not at all?

	Very closely	Somewhat closely	Not too closely	Not at all	No opinion
	%	%	%	%	%
U.S. adults	19	24	26	31	-
Republicans	31	27	27	15	-
Independents	18	23	23	36	-
Democrats	8	25	29	37	1

June 5-8, 2014

GALLUP

The combined 43% of Americans who report paying very or somewhat close attention to news about the upcoming Benghazi hearings in Gallup's June 5–8 poll falls well short of the average 60% attention-to-news rating in Gallup's data bank of major news stories measured since 1991. In fact, it ranks 189th out of the 224 news events Gallup has measured.

And although attention may rise once the hearings get under way, it is not much lower than in May 2013 during a previous set of Benghazi hearings. At that time, barely half of Americans (53%)

were following the ongoing congressional hearings very or somewhat closely.

Currently, Republicans are significantly more likely than Democrats and independents to say they are following this news story very closely. However, even Republicans' combined "close attention" score of 58% falls short of Gallup's historical average for all major news stories.

Party-Based Support Ranges From Broad, to Mixed, to Tepid

The upcoming hearings are part of a Republican-led U.S. House Select Committee investigation that was launched last month to further review the terror incident at the Benghazi consulate. Though the Democratic-led Senate has also held hearings on the matter, many Democrats see the newest House investigations as an attempt to weaken either Democratic President Barack Obama or Hillary Clinton, the possible future Democratic presidential nominee and the secretary of state at the time of the attack.

Given the relatively light attention that Americans say they are paying to the Benghazi investigations, it is understandable that they issue no decisive judgment about the hearings themselves. Slightly more Americans say they approve than disapprove of the hearings—45% vs. 38%, respectively—but neither position garners majority support, in part because 18% have no opinion on the matter.

Americans' Approval of Congressional Benghazi Hearings

Based on what you know or have read about the hearings into the Benghazi attack, do you approve or disapprove of these hearings?

	Approve	Disapprove	No opinion
	%	%	%
U.S. adults	45	38	18
Republicans	75	20	5
Independents	40	38	22
Democrats	30	52	18

June 5-8, 2014

GALLUP

Independents' views are especially ambiguous, with about four in 10 approving as well as disapproving. Democrats are also fairly mixed: Just over half, 52%, say they disapprove of the hearings, while 30% approve and 18% have no opinion. Republicans are the most opinionated on the matter, and the most supportive of the hearings, with three-quarters approving.

Bottom Line

Despite much partisan debate in May about whether a new round of congressional investigations into the deadly 2012 terrorist attack against American diplomats in Benghazi should proceed, relatively few Americans say they are paying very close attention to the matter. As the hearings get under way, that could change, but the initial results suggest these hearings have a long way to go to reach the level of attention paid to a different investigation 16 years ago—congressional impeachment hearings against then-President Bill Clinton. In December 1998, Gallup found 77% of Americans following those hearings very or somewhat closely.

The comparison is important because Republicans' decision to impeach Clinton is often credited—or blamed, depending on the political vantage point—for temporarily harming the Republican Party's image, and in the process boosting Clinton's standing with the American people. Many observers now wonder whether Republicans risk making the same mistake with Benghazi, by looking like they are engaged in a partisan-based effort to discredit former Secretary of State Hillary Clinton.

For now, given Americans' relatively low attention to and moderate public approval of the hearings, the risk-to-reward ratio may be favorable for the GOP. Should the hearings produce no new findings, they may be quickly forgotten, whereas if Republicans uncover new evidence that supports their claims of incompetence or cover-up by the administration, the public seems open to learning about it. Indeed, in May 2013, Gallup found 69% of Americans agreeing that the issues being raised in the Benghazi hearings at the time were serious matters that needed to be investigated.

Tuesday's news that U.S. special operations forces captured one of the key suspects in the attack could, however, change the dynamic.

Survey Methods

Results for this Gallup poll are based on telephone interviews conducted June 5–8, 2014, on the Gallup Daily tracking survey, with a random sample of 1,027 adults, aged 18 and older, living in all 50 U.S. states and the District of Columbia.

For results based on the total sample of national adults, the margin of sampling error is ±4 percentage points at the 95% confidence level.

June 18, 2014
OBESITY LINKED TO LONG-TERM UNEMPLOYMENT IN U.S.
High blood pressure, cholesterol also more common among long-term unemployed

by Steve Crabtree

WASHINGTON, D.C.—Americans who have been out of work for a year or more are much more likely to be obese than those unemployed for a shorter time. The obesity rate rises from 22.8% among those unemployed for two weeks or less to 32.7% among those unemployed for 52 weeks or more.

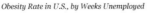

Obesity Rate in U.S., by Weeks Unemployed

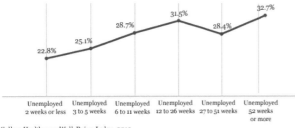

22.8%   25.1%   28.7%   31.5%   28.4%   32.7%

| Unemployed 2 weeks or less | Unemployed 3 to 5 weeks | Unemployed 6 to 11 weeks | Unemployed 12 to 26 weeks | Unemployed 27 to 51 weeks | Unemployed 52 weeks or more |

Gallup-Healthways Well-Being Index, 2013

GALLUP

Gallup tracks U.S. obesity levels daily using Americans' self-reported height and weight to calculate body mass index (BMI) scores as part of the Gallup-Healthways Well-Being Index. Individuals with BMI scores of 30 or higher are considered obese. The Gallup-Healthways Well-Being Index also tracks the percentages of Americans who report that they have ever been diagnosed with various health conditions related to obesity, including high blood pressure, high cholesterol, and diabetes.

These results are based on nearly 5,000 interviews throughout 2013 with the long-term unemployed (defined by the Bureau of Labor Statistics as being unemployed for 27 weeks or more) and more than 13,000 interviews with the short-term unemployed (those out of work for less than 27 weeks).

For Long-Term Unemployed, Obesity-Related Health Problems Also More Common

Gallup and Healthways also track the percentages of Americans who say they currently have or are being treated for health conditions such as high blood pressure and high cholesterol. In both cases, the differences between the short-term unemployed and the long-term unemployed are striking: Those who have been jobless for 27 weeks or more are nearly twice as likely to say they currently have high blood pressure, and to say they have high cholesterol.

Notably, Americans who have been unemployed for less than 27 weeks are somewhat *less* likely than those with jobs to have each of these conditions—but this is because they tend to be younger than those who have jobs (33.6 years vs. 42.6, on average).

Risk Factors for Cardiovascular Disease, by Employment Group

	Currently have/ being treated for high blood pressure	Currently have/ being treated for high cholesterol	Obese
Total unemployed	15.0%	9.7%	27.8%
Unemployed less than 27 weeks (short-term)	13.2%	7.9%	27.0%
Unemployed 27 weeks or more (long-term)	23.6%	15.0%	31.5%
Total employed	16.7%	11.8%	25.6%
Employed full time	16.0%	11.2%	25.1%
Employed part time, do not want full-time	23.7%	18.3%	19.7%
Employed part time, want full-time	14.3%	9.3%	23.6%

Gallup-Healthways Well-Being Index, 2013

GALLUP

While these results offer evidence of a strong relationship between unemployment and obesity-related health concerns, the causal direction is not clear. Unemployment may cause some people to engage in behaviors that lead to health problems, while preexisting health conditions may make it harder for others to find and keep work. For many individuals, both dynamics may be at work, perpetuating a negative cycle of declining job prospects and worsening health.

Health Problems May Have Critical Consequences for Long-Term Unemployed

Jobless Americans may be more likely to fall into such a cycle if a higher incidence of health problems hinders their efforts to find a good job. Those out of work for 27 weeks or more report experiencing an average of 4.7 days out of the past 30 when poor health kept them from doing their usual activities. That compares with an average of 2.8 lower-productivity days for those unemployed for a shorter period, and just 1.4 days for full-time workers.

During the past 30 days, for about how many days did poor health keep you from doing your usual activities?

	Average response
Full-time employed	1.4 days
Total unemployed	3.2 days
Short-term unemployed	2.8 days
Long-term unemployed	4.7 days

Gallup-Healthways Well-Being Index, 2013

GALLUP'

Over the longer term, one of the most worrisome implications of these relationships is that many of those who have been unemployed for a prolonged period may suffer chronic health problems even if they successfully re-enter the workforce. A 2009 study of Pennsylvania workers laid off in the 1970s and 1980s found that even 20 years later, these workers were 10% to 15% more likely to die in a given year than those who had not suffered a job loss.

Bottom Line

With record-setting rates of long-term unemployment in most U.S. states, the health consequences of extended periods of joblessness have become a rising concern for policymakers. The Gallup-Healthways Well-Being Index makes it possible to examine health and well-being conditions associated with long-term unemployment more closely than is possible using smaller-scale studies. Importantly, the tracking data can be aggregated to produce the large sample sizes necessary for studying well-being among specific employment groups.

One key concern raised by the current analysis is that employers in industries that require manual labor, such as manufacturing and construction, may be less likely to hire candidates who are clearly out of shape. If so, workers in these industries—who already earn lower wages, on average, than those in knowledge-based sectors—may be even more likely to be caught in a negative cycle of joblessness and poor health.

More broadly, private employers' high healthcare costs might lead them to avoid taking chances on those who pose greater health risks, particularly in a tenuous economic climate. As a result, candidates who are obese and who have been unemployed for 27 weeks or more may have two strikes against them even before they sit down for an interview.

Survey Methods

Results for this Gallup poll are based on telephone interviews conducted Jan. 1–Dec. 31, 2013, on the Gallup Daily tracking survey, with a random sample of 356,599 adults, aged 18 and older, living in all 50 U.S. states and the District of Columbia.

For results based on the total sample of national adults, the margin of sampling error is less than ±1 percentage point at the 95% confidence level. The total number of unemployed respondents is 18,322, with 13,352 unemployed for less than 27 weeks (short-term) and 4,970 unemployed for 27 weeks or more (long-term).

June 18, 2014
SEVEN IN 10 AMERICANS BACK EUTHANASIA
Support strong for past two decades

by Justin McCarthy

WASHINGTON, D.C.—Most Americans continue to support euthanasia when asked whether they believe physicians should be able to legally "end [a] patient's life by some painless means." Strong majorities have supported this for more than 20 years.

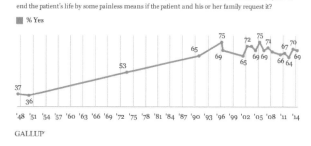

Support for Physician-Assisted Euthanasia
When a person has a disease that cannot be cured, do you think doctors should be allowed by law to end the patient's life by some painless means if the patient and his or her family request it?

GALLUP'

Although these are largely private family matters, controversy about euthanasia and other end-of-life situations has often become public—most recently, regarding the death of iconic radio host Casey Kasem. His children and his wife fought in court over what to do in the final stages of Kasem's battle with Lewy body disease, a form of dementia. Ultimately, a judge granted his daughter the authority to have doctors remove his infusions of water, food, and medicine.

These data are from Gallup's May 8–11 Values and Beliefs poll, conducted before Kasem's death. Gallup began asking this question about euthanasia in 1947. At that time, Americans were about half as likely (37%) to support euthanasia as they are today. Support had grown by 1990, and since then, a large majority of Americans have backed euthanasia.

Support for euthanasia is related to Americans' underlying religiosity. The more frequently an American attends religious services, the less likely he or she is to support euthanasia. Less than half (48%) of those who frequent their places of worship weekly are likely to support the idea of a doctor "ending a patient's life by some painless means," compared with three in four Americans who attend services nearly weekly (74%) and 82% of those who go less often.

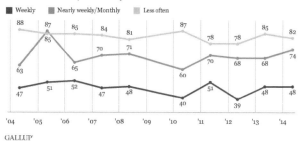

Support for a Doctor to End a Patient's Life Through "Painless Means," by Church Attendance
% Yes, should be allowed by law to end the patient's life

Weekly   Nearly weekly/Monthly   Less often

GALLUP'

Diminished Majority Favors "Doctor-Assisted Suicide"

Americans are less likely to support euthanasia when the question emphasizes that the doctor would "assist the patient to commit suicide" than when the question does not mention the word suicide.

Four states—Oregon, Washington, Montana, and Vermont—have legalized physician-assisted suicide, with the most recent being Vermont, in 2013.

In the most recent poll, 58% of Americans favor doctor-assisted suicide when the question is asked in this way. Support has varied between 51% and 68% since Gallup first asked about it in 1996.

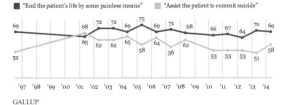

Support for Physician-Assisted Suicide -- Two Question Wordings

(Form A) When a person has a disease that cannot be cured, do you think doctors should be allowed by law to end the patient's life by some painless means if the patient and his or her family request it?

(Form B) When a person has a disease that cannot be cured and is living in severe pain, do you think doctors should or should not be allowed by law to assist the patient to commit suicide if the patient requests it?

■ "End the patient's life by some painless means" ▨ "Assist the patient to commit suicide"

GALLUP

Bottom Line

Americans have consistently maintained their support for euthanasia in recent decades. Prior to that, as far back as 1947, Americans were not in favor.

Although religious convictions often play a large role in one's support or opposition, the way the act of euthanasia is worded affects Americans' views on it, underscoring the issue's sensitivity. Life-ending scenarios are real for many Americans and their loved ones. And while the majority of Americans clearly support euthanasia—a fairly rare moral issue for which there is widespread support—that support is not unanimous. This is a reminder that these divisions play out in family decision-making every day.

Survey Methods

Results for this Gallup poll are based on telephone interviews conducted May 8–11, 2014, with a random sample of 1,028 adults, aged 18 and older, living in all 50 U.S. states and the District of Columbia. For results based on the total sample of national adults, the margin of sampling error is ±4 percentage points at the 95% confidence level.

For results based on the sample of 518 national adults in Form A, the margin of sampling error is ±5 percentage points.

For results based on the sample of 510 national adults in Form B, the margins of sampling error is ±5 percentage points.

June 19, 2014
PUBLIC FAITH IN CONGRESS FALLS AGAIN, HITS HISTORIC LOW
Of major U.S. institutions, Americans most confident in the military

by Rebecca Riffkin

WASHINGTON, D.C.—Americans' confidence in Congress has sunk to a new low. Seven percent of Americans say they have "a great deal" or "quite a lot" of confidence in Congress as an American institution, down from the previous low of 10% in 2013. This confidence is starkly different from the 42% in 1973, the first year Gallup began asking the question.

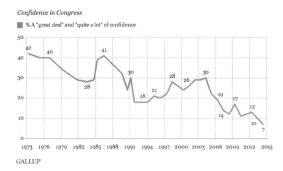

Confidence in Congress

■ % A "great deal" and "quite a lot" of confidence

GALLUP

These results come from a June 5–8 Gallup poll that updated Americans' confidence in 17 U.S. institutions that Americans either read about or interact with in government, business, and society.

Americans' current confidence in Congress is not only the lowest on record but also the lowest Gallup has recorded for any institution in the 41-year trend. This is also the first time Gallup has ever measured confidence in a major U.S. institution in the single digits. Currently, 4% of Americans say they have a great deal of confidence in Congress, and 3% have quite a lot of confidence. About one-third of Americans report having "some" confidence, while half have "very little," and another 7% volunteer that they have "none."

Confidence in Congress has varied over the years, with the highest levels in the low 40% range recorded in the 1970s and again in the mid-1980s. Confidence rose in the late 1990s and early 2000s, but has declined since 2004, culminating in this year's historic low.

Three in Four Americans Have High Confidence in the Military

The military continues to rank at the top of this year's list, with 74% of Americans having either a great deal or quite a lot of confidence in the institution. Another 20% of Americans have "some" confidence in the military. Seven percent have very little or no confidence. The military has ranked at the top of the list all but one year since 1989. Prior to that, the church or organized religion, now with 45% confidence, typically finished first.

Now I am going to read you a list of institutions in American society. Please tell me how much confidence you have in each one -- a great deal, quite a lot, some, or very little?

Sorted by most to least confidence in 2014

	% A "great deal" and "quite a lot" of confidence
The military	74
Small business	62
The police	53
The church or organized religion	45
The medical system ^	34
The U.S. Supreme Court	30
The presidency	29
The public schools	26
Banks	26
The healthcare system †	23
The criminal justice system	23
Newspapers	22
Organized labor	22
Big business	21
News on the Internet	19
Television news	18
Congress	7

June 5-8, 2014

^ Based on 510 respondents
† Based on 517 respondents

GALLUP

As is the case with confidence in Congress, Americans' confidence in many of these institutions has changed over time. The current 74% of Americans who have high levels of confidence in the military is actually lower than it has been in the past. Confidence in the military spiked in March 1991 to 85%, just after the first Persian Gulf War, but fell back through the 1990s. It also spiked in 2002 and 2003, after 9/11, and again in 2009, just before U.S. troops began withdrawing from Iraq.

Still, the current 74% confidence level is significantly higher than the average 67% rating given the military since it was first measured in 1975. The lowest was in 1981, when half of Americans had high levels of confidence in the military.

Confidence in the Military

■ % A "great deal" and "quite a lot" of confidence

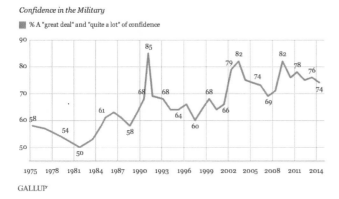

GALLUP'

While confidence in the military has been higher than confidence in Congress since Gallup began tracking both institutions, they used to be much closer. Until the late 1980s, between 50% and 63% of Americans had high levels of confidence in the military. At the same time, between 28% and 42% of Americans had high levels of confidence in Congress. Since then, the percentage of Americans who have confidence in the military has generally increased, while confidence in Congress has decreased.

Bottom Line

The current 7% of Americans who place confidence in Congress is the lowest of the 17 institutions Gallup measured this year, and is the lowest Gallup has ever found for any of these institutions. The dearth of public confidence in their elected leaders on Capitol Hill is yet another sign of the challenges that could face incumbents in 2014's midterm elections—as well as more broadly a challenge to the broad underpinnings of the nation's representative democratic system.

Survey Methods

Results for this Gallup poll are based on telephone interviews conducted June 5–8, 2014, a random sample of 1,027 adults, aged 18 and older, living in all 50 U.S. states and the District of Columbia.

For results based on the total sample of national adults, the margin of sampling error is ±4 percentage points at the 95% confidence level.

June 19, 2014
AMERICANS' CONFIDENCE IN NEWS MEDIA REMAINS LOW
Across newspapers, TV, and Internet, confidence no higher than 22%

by Andrew Dugan

WASHINGTON, D.C.—Americans' faith in each of three major news media platforms—television news, newspapers, and news on the Internet—is at or tied with record lows in Gallup's long-standing confidence in institutions trend. This continues a decades-long decline in the share of Americans saying they have "a great deal" or "quite a lot" of confidence in newspapers or TV news, while trust in Internet news remains low since the one prior measure in 1999.

Americans' Confidence in News Media, 1994-2014
% Who have a "great deal" or "quite a lot" of confidence

■ Newspapers ■ Television news News on the Internet

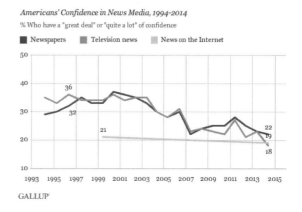

GALLUP'

These results are from a Gallup poll conducted June 5–8. The three major sources of news ranked in the bottom third of 17 different U.S. institutions measured in the poll.

Confidence in newspapers has declined by more than half since its 1979 peak of 51%, while TV news has seen confidence ebb from its high of 46% in 1993, the first year that Gallup asked this question. Gallup's only previous measure of Internet news was in 1999, when confidence was 21%, little different from today.

Conservatives' Confidence in Newspapers Tied at 10-Year Low

Slightly less than one-fifth of self-identified conservatives (15%) say they have a great deal or quite a lot of confidence in newspapers, tied with the 10-year low. In the past decade, the percentage of conservatives expressing a strong degree of confidence in newspapers has fallen by nearly half. Liberals are far more likely than conservatives—or than the adult population in general—to be confident in newspapers (34%). Nearly a quarter of moderates (24%), meanwhile, have confidence in newspapers.

Americans' Confidence in Newspapers, by Ideology, 2004-2014 Trend
% Who have a "great deal" or "quite a lot" of confidence

■ Conservatives ■ Moderates Liberals

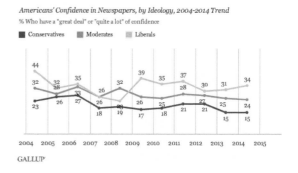

GALLUP'

While liberals are more likely to have confidence in newspapers than conservatives, conservatives are slightly more likely to express confidence in TV news (19%) than liberals (15%). For liberals, this 2014 reading represents an 11-percentage-point decline from 2013.

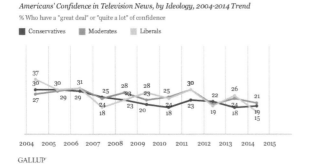

Americans' Confidence in Television News, by Ideology, 2004-2014 Trend
% Who have a "great deal" or "quite a lot" of confidence

■ Conservatives ■ Moderates ▨ Liberals

GALLUP

Over the past year, the Internet has seen the acceleration of website-only news sources that focus on empirical, data-driven analysis, including Ezra Klein's Vox website or the relaunching of Nate Silver's FiveThirtyEight site. But this quantitative approach to telling the news has not, in of itself, persuaded the major ideologies to express strong confidence in news from the Internet. More than a fifth of liberals (22%) and moderates (22%) say they have a great deal or quite a lot of confidence in news from the Internet, while slightly fewer conservatives (17%) say this.

Bottom Line

The field of news media has changed dramatically since Gallup first began measuring the confidence the public held in newspapers or TV news decades ago. The circulation of newspapers continues to shrink to the point that University of Southern California's Annenberg Center for the Digital Future estimates that most print newspapers will not exist in five years. Television news continues to see a proliferation of new cable news networks, including the launch of Al-Jazeera America in August 2013. Meanwhile, news from the Internet now figures prominently in the average American's news diet, whereas not so long ago this mode did not even exist.

Amid this rapid change, Americans hold all news media platforms in low confidence. How these platforms can restore confidence with the American public is not clear, especially as editorial standards change and most outlets lack the broad reach once available to major newspapers and broadcasters.

Survey Methods

Results for this Gallup poll are based on telephone interviews conducted June 5–8, 2014, with a random sample of 1,027 adults, aged 18 and older, living in all 50 U.S. states and the District of Columbia.

For results based on the total sample of national adults, the margin of sampling error is ±4 percentage points at the 95% confidence level.

June 20, 2014
APPROVAL OF OBAMA'S HANDLING OF IMMIGRATION FALLS TO 31%
Americans' approval falls eight percentage points since August

by Justin McCarthy

WASHINGTON, D.C.—Americans' approval of President Barack Obama's handling of immigration has dropped to 31%, one of the lowest readings since 2010, when Gallup began polling on his handling of the issue. Meanwhile, two in three Americans (65%) disapprove of his handling of immigration.

Americans' Views of President Obama's Handling of Immigration
Do you approve or disapprove of the way Barack Obama is handling immigration?

■ % Approve ▨ % Disapprove

GALLUP

These data are from a June 5–8 Gallup poll. Disapproval of the president's handling of immigration has climbed 10 points since August 2013, when more than half of Americans (55%) disapproved.

Recent developments contributing to the ongoing debate about immigration include Obama's delay of a review of deportation policies by the Department of Homeland Security in the hope of striking a legislative deal on immigration reform with Congress. Also, House Majority Leader Eric Cantor's recent primary loss was widely viewed as a defeat rooted in Cantor's perceived stance on immigration. The primary loss and subsequent shakeup in House leadership could spell greater challenges for Obama as he tries to work with Republicans. Additionally, the media has recently enlarged its spotlight on the increasing numbers of unaccompanied Central American children who have crossed the U.S. border, seeking their already immigrated family members and a generally better life.

Obama's approval on immigration has dropped since last August across all political affiliations, even among those in his own party. Democrats' approval has fallen eight points to the current 60%. Approval among independents has also fallen eight points, to 25%. A mere 8% of Republicans approve of the president's handling of the issue, and though this is not their lowest rating on the measure, their disapproval of the president's handling of immigration has reached its highest, at 90%.

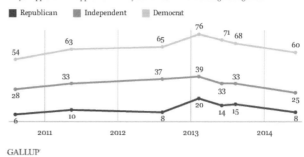

Approval of President Obama's Handling of Immigration, by Party
Do you approve or disapprove of the way Barack Obama is handling immigration?

■ Republican ■ Independent ▨ Democrat

GALLUP

Bottom Line

Though Americans largely do not see immigration as a high-priority issue for the president and Congress, Obama has said passing an immigration bill is one of his legislative priorities.

In order to accomplish this feat, he will need the support of congressional Republicans, who could hold both chambers of Congress come January, and who are understandably shaky on the issue after seeing one of their most powerful leaders fall, partly because of his stance on immigration.

For Republicans' part, the composition of their new House leadership and the potential of taking the reins of both houses of Congress could empower them to take ownership of the issue, and make immigration reform a truly bipartisan effort. They will still need the president's signature on any legislation. If they don't make a serious effort to create reform legislation, they could find themselves punished by Latino voters, who tilt Democratic, in 2016.

Survey Methods

Results for this Gallup poll are based on telephone interviews conducted June 5–8, 2014, on the Gallup Daily tracking survey, with a random sample of 1,027 adults, aged 18 and older, living in all 50 U.S. states and the District of Columbia.

For results based on the total sample of national adults, the margin of sampling error is ±4 percentage points at the 95% confidence level.

June 20, 2014
CLINTON, ELDER BUSH MOST POSITIVELY RATED LIVING PRESIDENTS
*Americans view all former presidents
more positively than negatively*

by Jeffrey M. Jones

PRINCETON, NJ—Americans view each of the four former living presidents more positively than negatively, while giving Bill Clinton and George H.W. Bush higher favorable ratings than George W. Bush and Jimmy Carter. Current President Barack Obama has a net-negative favorable rating.

Americans' Favorable Ratings of Living U.S. Presidents

	Favorable	Unfavorable	No opinion
	%	%	%
Bill Clinton	64	34	2
George H.W. Bush	63	31	6
George W. Bush	53	44	2
Jimmy Carter	52	32	16
Barack Obama	47	52	1

June 5-8, 2014

GALLUP

The younger Bush's current favorable rating is likely lower than other former presidents' ratings because his term, marked by job approval ratings well below 40% during his final two years in office, is the freshest in Americans' minds.

Though Carter left office with similarly poor job approval ratings, his lower favorable ratings today are mostly attributable to one in six Americans not having an opinion of him. That includes 36% of those younger than 30, all of whom were born after Carter left

office in 1981. The only other time Gallup measured opinions of Carter with this question format, in 2007, 69% rated him favorably, 27% unfavorably, and 4% had no opinion.

The data are based on a June 5–8, 2014, Gallup poll and represent Americans' current opinions of the four former living presidents and the current president. The elder Bush recently turned 90, and Carter will do so later this year, making them among the longest living former presidents.

In addition to these personal favorable ratings, Gallup has previously measured Americans' views of how each president's term will be judged by history and retrospective job approval ratings of former presidents. Clinton and the elder Bush also fared better than Carter and the younger Bush on those metrics.

Partisanship Drags Down Rating of Current President

Americans typically rate presidents more positively after they leave office, so Obama's relatively worse standing than his predecessors is not surprising. However, the current poll represents Obama's worst favorable rating to date.

The public likely views the incumbent president in more strongly partisan terms than former presidents, given the chief executive's role in negotiating the prevailing political and policy disputes of the day. Past presidents largely stay away from those contentious matters but still serve a public but largely ceremonial role, often using their high profile for charitable work.

As evidence of the more partisan evaluations of the current commander in chief, Republicans give Obama a much lower favorable rating (7%) than the two former Democratic presidents, Clinton and Carter (both 28%).

Still, partisanship is a major factor in how Americans view expresidents, with former presidents rated much more highly by supporters of their own party than by supporters of the other party.

Americans' Favorable Ratings of Living U.S. Presidents, by Political Party
Figures are the percentage holding a favorable view of the president

	Republican	Independent	Democrat
	%	%	%
Barack Obama	7	42	90
George W. Bush	88	52	26
Bill Clinton	28	64	95
George H.W. Bush	89	62	44
Jimmy Carter	28	50	77

June 5-8, 2014

GALLUP

George W. Bush Back Above 50%

George W. Bush appears to be reaping the public opinion benefits of being a former president. His current 53% favorable rating marks the first time it has been above the majority level since 2005, early in his second term as president.

Bush began his first term in office in 2001 as a relatively popular figure with a 64% favorable rating. After the Sept. 11 terrorist attacks that year, his favorability surged to 87%. His ratings stayed high, above 60%, until 2004, the year he sought re-election.

A difficult second term—dominated by the ongoing war in Iraq and including domestic difficulties such as the response to Hurricane Katrina, rising gas prices, and an economic recession—contributed to a steep drop in Bush's personal popularity. By April 2008, 32% of Americans had a favorable opinion of Bush and 66% had an unfavorable one. After leaving office with a slightly higher 40% favorability score, his rating improved to the mid-40s in 2010 and the high 40s in 2013 before the most recent increase.

Americans' Favorable Ratings of George W. Bush

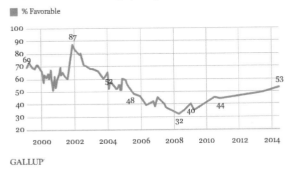

Bush's favorable rating has improved by nearly the same amount among all party groups since he left office, up 11 percentage points among Republicans (77% to 88%), 15 points among independents (37% to 52%), and 15 points among Democrats (11% to 26%).

Implications

Americans are largely forgiving of former presidents, as each of the four living ex-presidents had times in office when they had job approval ratings below 40%, if not 30%. Clinton and the elder Bush recovered and left office with majority job approval, while Carter and the younger Bush stayed unpopular through the end of their terms.

Despite the different circumstances of those presidents, a majority of Americans now have mostly positive opinions of all four, although they do rate the elder Bush and Clinton more favorably than they do the younger Bush and Carter.

Obama's current favorable ratings are the worst of his presidency, and they are worse than former presidents' ratings. No matter how popular or unpopular he is when he leaves office in a little more than two years, Americans' views of Obama personally should improve once he becomes a former president.

Survey Methods

Results for this Gallup poll are based on telephone interviews conducted June 5–8, 2014, with a random sample of 1,027 adults, aged 18 and older, living in all 50 U.S. states and the District of Columbia.

For results based on the total sample of national adults, the margin of sampling error is ±4 percentage points at the 95% confidence level.

June 22, 2014
AMERICANS SAY SOCIAL MEDIA HAVE LITTLE SWAY ON PURCHASES
Vast majority use social media to connect with friends, family

by Art Swift

WASHINGTON, D.C.—A clear majority of Americans say social media have no effect at all on their purchasing decisions. Although

many companies run aggressive marketing campaigns on social media, 62% in the U.S. say Facebook and Twitter, among other sites, do not have any influence on their decisions to purchase products.

Influence of Social Media on Americans' Purchasing Decisions
How much do social media typically influence your purchasing decisions?

	Total
A great deal of influence	5%
Some influence	30%
No influence at all	62%
Don't know	3%

Gallup Mobile Retail Panel Study, December 2012-January 2013

GALLUP'

Despite tremendous numbers of Americans using social media institutions such as Facebook, Google+, LinkedIn, and Twitter, only 5% say social media have "a great deal of influence" on their purchasing decisions, while another 30% say these channels have "some influence." These data, from Gallup's new *State of the American Consumer* report, are based on Americans' self-reported estimates of how much social media campaigns affect their purchasing decisions. While social media may have more influence than some Americans realize or will admit, these data show that relatively few consumers consciously take into account what they learn from social media when making purchases.

Millennials, a Key Social Media Audience, Not Influenced Much Either

Even millennials—a generation that many companies regard as a key social media audience—tend to say that social media marketing is not much of a factor in their decision-making. Among the four major generation groups that Gallup surveyed, millennials (those born after 1980) were the most likely to say that social media have at least some influence on their buying decisions (50%). But millennials were nearly as likely to say social media have no influence at all.

Influence of Social Media on Purchasing Decisions, by Generation
How much do social media typically influence your purchasing decisions?

	% No influence at all	% Some influence	% Great deal of influence
Millennials	48	43	7
Generation X	57	34	7
Baby Boomers	68	26	4
Traditionalists	75	16	3

Gallup Mobile Retail Panel Study, December 2012-January 2013

GALLUP'

Social media's influence on Americans' purchasing decisions decreases with age. Among traditionalists (those born prior to 1946), a solid 75% say that social media do not have any impact on whether they purchase a product or service. The generational differences may reflect varying degrees of social media use across age groups.

Overwhelmingly, Americans Use Social Media to Connect With Friends, Family

Not surprisingly, an overwhelming 94% of social media users say they use these channels to connect with friends and family, illustrating the primary need that social media fulfill. Far less, 29%, say they use social media to follow trends and find product reviews and information, while 20% say they visit social networking sites to comment on what's new or write product reviews.

Americans' Reasons for Social Media Use

Please indicate whether or not you use social networking websites such as Facebook, Twitter, and LinkedIn for any of the following purposes.

	Total
To connect with friends and family	94%
To share with others what you know	53%
To find out information about a company or organization	40%
To find others who have similar interests or careers	32%
To follow trends/To find user reviews or product information	29%
To play games	23%
To network or search for a job	22%
To comment on what's hot or new/To write reviews of products	20%
To build your own reputation or brand	17%
Other	8%

Note: Asked of those who have used social media in the past year

Gallup Mobile Retail Panel Study, December 2012-January 2013

GALLUP·

Even among American consumers who "like" or follow a company on Facebook or Twitter, 34% say that social media have no influence at all on their buying decisions, while 53% say they have some influence. Gallup research shows that when it comes to making purchasing decisions, consumers are much more likely to turn to friends, in-store displays, television commercials, and even mail catalogs and magazines than to consult a company-sponsored Facebook page or Twitter feed.

Bottom Line

U.S. companies spent a combined $5.1 billion on social media advertising in 2013, and they obviously believe that this presents them with a return on investment. However, a solid majority of American adults say that social media have no influence at all on their purchasing decisions—suggesting that the advertising may be reaching smaller segments of the market, or that the influence on consumers is indirect or goes unnoticed.

In the *State of the American Consumer* report, Gallup reveals that consumers who engage with brands often do so when they are already attached to a product or service. Companies that engage their customers—by providing exceptional service and a pleasurable in-store experience—will, in turn, drive those customers to interact with them on social media. Simply promoting products and services on Facebook or Twitter is unlikely to lead to sales.

However, companies can use social media to engage and boost their customer base. Consumers appreciate the highly personal and conversational nature of social media sites, and they prefer interacting in an open dialogue as opposed to receiving a hard sell. And companies' use of social media to provide timely responses to questions and complaints accelerates brand loyalty and, eventually, sales. When it comes to social media efforts, businesses stand to benefit when they utilize a more service-focused approach rather than one dedicated to simply pushing their products.

Survey Methods

These results are based on a Gallup Panel Web and mail study of 18,525 U.S. adults, aged 18 and older, conducted Dec. 12, 2012, to Jan. 22, 2013. All surveys were completed in English.

The Gallup Panel is a probability-based longitudinal panel of U.S. adults who are selected using random-digit-dial (RDD) telephone interviews that cover landline and cellphone telephone numbers. Address-based sampling methods are also used to recruit panel members. The Gallup Panel is not an opt-in panel, and members are not given incentives for participating. The sample for this study was weighted to be demographically representative of the U.S. adult population, using 2012 Current Population Survey figures.

For results based on this sample, the margin of sampling error is ±1 percentage point at the 95% confidence level. Margins of error are higher for subsamples.

June 23, 2014

AFTER EXCHANGES CLOSE, 5% OF AMERICANS ARE NEWLY INSURED
More than half of newly insured in '14 got insurance through exchanges

by Steve Ander and Frank Newport

PRINCETON, NJ—Five percent of Americans report being newly insured in 2014. More than half of that group, or 2.8% of the total U.S. population, say they got their new insurance through the health exchanges that were open through mid-April.

Health Insurance Status in the U.S.

Based on self-reports

	%
Newly insured in 2014	5
--Newly insured in 2014 through exchanges	2.8
--Newly insured in 2014 but not through exchanges	2.2

Gallup Daily tracking, April 15-June 17, 2014

GALLUP·

These data are based on Gallup Daily tracking interviews with more than 31,000 adults conducted between April 15 and June 17. Those who say they have health insurance were asked if their policy was new for 2014, and if so, whether they obtained their policy through a state or federal health exchange or in some other way. The exchanges officially closed on March 31, although people who indicated they had begun the process prior to that date were allowed to continue to enroll through April 15.

The preliminary April 16 Gallup update on the newly insured was based on data collected from March 4–April 14, and showed that 4% of all adults on average during that period reported being newly insured, with 2.1% reporting that they gained their insurance through an exchange.

The March-April report was based on interviews conducted evenly across that six-week period, and thus, many in that sample who ultimately got insurance may not yet have had it at the time they were interviewed—particularly earlier in March. All of the April–June interviews were conducted after the exchanges closed, and therefore these reports provide a representative portrait of the post-enrollment health coverage of the population. The increase in self-reported newly insured status from the preliminary report also dovetails with recent stories reporting surges in enrollments as the exchange enrollment period came to a close.

Many of those who enrolled in the first half of April would not see policy coverage begin until May 1 or, in some cases, one month after enrollment. Thus, the earlier report may have included individuals who did not report having insurance this year because their policies had not yet taken effect. That same situation may apply to a lesser degree to those interviewed in the current group, meaning the estimate that 5% are newly insured may itself underrepresent the percentage of Americans who ultimately will have new insurance this year.

Newly Insured Through Exchanges Are Younger

The age distribution of those who report newly obtaining health insurance this year through the exchanges is generally similar to what Gallup found in the preliminary report. The newly insured using exchanges are mostly under age 65, as would be expected, given that most Americans 65 and older are covered by Medicare. Thus, the representation of newly insured Americans is higher across all three age groups younger than 65 than is true for the general population. More specifically, newly insured Americans using the exchanges in the 18 to 29 age category are eight percentage points more prevalent than their percentage in the overall adult population, while representation of those 30 to 49 and 50 to 64 are five and four points higher, respectively.

Profile of Newly Insured Through Exchanges, by Age

	Newly insured in 2014 + used exchange	Age distribution of national adult population
	%	%
18 to 29	29	21
30 to 49	39	34
50 to 64	30	26
65+	3	19

Gallup Daily tracking, April 15-June 17, 2014

GALLUP

Newly Insured Report Being Less Healthy Than Average Adults

One catalyst for the individual healthcare mandate was to bring healthy people who otherwise chose not to have health insurance into the healthcare system using the exchanges. However, as was the case in the previous sample, the newly insured using exchanges in the April–June reporting period are less likely than those in the general population to report being in "very good" or "excellent" health.

Thirty-eight percent of those using an exchange for their new policies reported being in very good or excellent health, compared with 50% of the general population.

Profile of Newly Insured Through Exchanges, by Self-Reported Health Status

	Newly insured in 2014 + used exchange	Health of national adult population
	%	%
Excellent	16	21
Very good	22	29
Good	33	29
Fair	16	13
Poor	8	5

Gallup Daily tracking, April 15-June 17, 2014

GALLUP

Implications

The 5% of the adult population who report getting health insurance this year and who did not have it last year is roughly commensurate with the overall drop in the uninsured percentage of the overall population between the third quarter of 2013 and April–May of this year. Still, even after meeting and exceeding established goals of 7 million enrollees through healthcare.gov and with probable spillover effects into non-exchange-based new enrollments, millions of Americans still are without health insurance: the total percentage of the adult population who are uninsured remains above 13%.

If the federal government wishes to continue to expand the pool of enrollees in the next open enrollment period, which begins on Nov. 15, it may have to intensify its current outreach strategies to motivate resistant citizens to enroll. Investing resources into attracting more enrollees would align with the plan to increase fines in the coming enrollment period for those without minimum essential coverage.

Survey Methods

Results for this Gallup poll are based on telephone interviews conducted April 15–June 17, 2014, on the Gallup Daily tracking survey, with a random sample of 31,438 adults, aged 18 and older, living in all 50 U.S. states and the District of Columbia.

For results based on the total sample of national adults, the margin of sampling error is ±1 percentage point at the 95% confidence level.

June 24, 2014
WEEKLY OBAMA JOB APPROVAL DIPS TO 41%, NEAR PERSONAL LOW
Approval drop coincident with Iraq crisis intensifying

by Jeffrey M. Jones

PRINCETON, NJ—The situation in Iraq seems to be taking a toll on President Barack Obama's public standing. His weekly job approval rating is down a total of three percentage points over the last two weeks, to 41%. While this drop is not large in absolute terms, it is notable because it follows nearly three months in which his job approval averaged 44% with little week-to-week variation.

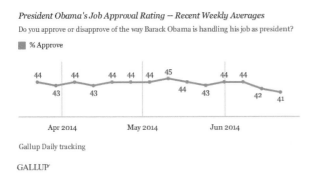

President Obama's Job Approval Rating -- Recent Weekly Averages

Do you approve or disapprove of the way Barack Obama is handling his job as president?

■ % Approve

Gallup Daily tracking

GALLUP

The long stretch of stability from mid-March to early June occurred during a period that was hardly uneventful for the president, including controversies over medical care for U.S. military veterans at Veterans Affairs hospitals and a prisoner exchange of five Taliban detainees for U.S. Army Sgt. Bowe Bergdahl. But Iraq may be the issue weighing most heavily on Obama's public support given the timing of the drop in approval.

Obama's approval rating in Gallup Daily tracking first showed signs of decline (from the mid- to the low 40s) in the immediate days after Islamic militants took control of Mosul, the second-largest city in Iraq, on June 10. The Gallup Daily tracking three-day average for June 11–13, based on fully post-Mosul interviewing, was 41%, and Obama's approval rating has been either 40% or 41% in each subsequent measurement up through June 22 interviewing.

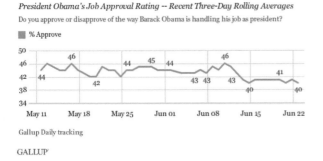

President Obama's Job Approval Rating -- Recent Three-Day Rolling Averages

Do you approve or disapprove of the way Barack Obama is handling his job as president?

■ % Approve

Gallup Daily tracking

GALLUP

Obama Job Approval Close to Personal Low

Obama's latest weekly job approval average of 41% is just one point higher than his low. His average 55% disapproval last week is the worst so far in his administration.

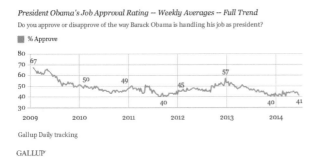

President Obama's Job Approval Rating -- Weekly Averages -- Full Trend

Do you approve or disapprove of the way Barack Obama is handling his job as president?

■ % Approve

Gallup Daily tracking

GALLUP

Obama's 40% weekly approval averages have occurred several times during his presidency, including last fall after the troubled rollout of major provisions of the healthcare law, and in late summer and early fall of 2011 after the contentious agreement to raise the debt ceiling.

Obama's lowest approval rating among Gallup's three-day rolling averages to date is 38%, slightly lower than his worst weekly average. The 38% reading has been recorded several times, all in August and October 2011 after the debt-limit agreement led to the downgrading of the U.S. credit rating and a period of volatility in the stock market. His Gallup Daily tracking approval rating has yet to drop below 40% in recent days.

Democrats', Independents' Support for President Dipping

An average of 76% of Democrats now approve of the job President Obama is doing, down from 80% before the recent slide. Independents show a drop of three points, from 38% to 35%. Republican approval—extremely low to begin with, at 10%—averaged 9% last week.

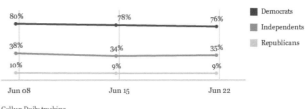

President Obama's Job Approval Rating -- Recent Weekly Averages, by Political Party

Do you approve or disapprove of the way Barack Obama is handling his job as president?

■ Democrats
■ Independents
■ Republicans

Gallup Daily tracking

GALLUP

Democratic approval of Obama has been solid throughout his presidency, only dropping to as low as 72% in late October 2011.

Implications

President Obama has already decided to send military advisers to Iraq, and he and his foreign policy team are weighing other options short of sending combat troops to stabilize the situation there. The difficult situation, more so than other recent controversies, seems to be taking a toll on his public support.

The drop in public support is unwelcome news for his party this election year, given that presidential approval ratings are an important predictor of midterm election outcomes. If Obama's 41% weekly job approval rating persists through November, it would be higher than only George W. Bush's 38% approval at the time of the 2006 election, for recent midterm election years. That year, Republicans lost control of both houses of Congress. Should Obama's approval rating not improve between now and the fall, that would certainly weaken Democrats' ability to retain control of the U.S. senate in this fall's elections.

Survey Methods

Results for this Gallup poll are based on telephone interviews conducted June 16–22, 2014, on the Gallup Daily tracking survey, with a random sample of 3,553 adults, aged 18 and older, living in all 50 U.S. states and the District of Columbia.

For results based on the total sample of national adults, the margin of sampling error is ±4 percentage points at the 95% confidence level.

June 25, 2014
FEWER IN U.S. SUPPORT IRAQ
WITHDRAWAL DECISION NOW VS. 2011
A majority, 57%, say 2003 war was a mistake

by Andrew Dugan

WASHINGTON, D.C.—More than three if five Americans (61%) still support President Barack Obama's 2011 decision to remove nearly all U.S. troops from Iraq—a move that congressional critics and former Bush administration officials have heavily scrutinized as Iraq falls into crisis. However, public support for the U.S. withdrawal from Iraq has fallen 14 percentage points from October 2011, a few months before nearly all troops left the country.

Americans' Opinions on Withdrawal of Nearly All U.S. Troops From Iraq

Turning to Iraq, do you approve or disapprove of President Obama's 2011 decision to withdraw nearly all U.S. troops from Iraq?

	% Approve	% Disapprove	% No opinion
Jun 20-21, 2014	61	34	4
Oct 29-30, 2011^	75	21	5

^Question wording: Turning to Iraq, do you approve or disapprove of President Obama's decision to withdraw nearly all U.S. troops from Iraq by the end of the year?

GALLUP'

The government of Iraq has faced an existential crisis as Sunni militant groups capture major portions of the country and press onward to Baghdad, the capital. The Islamic State of Iraq and the Levant (ISIL), a terrorist organization with previous ties to al-Qaida, is a leading force behind this violent insurgency. In response to these threats, Obama has sent 275 military troops to help secure the U.S. embassy in Iraq and 300 military advisors to assist the Iraqi government, the latter decision announced as this June 20–21 Gallup poll was conducted.

Looking back, do you think the United States made a mistake sending troops to fight in Iraq?

National adults

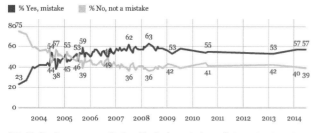

Note: Wording from 2003-2010: "In view of the developments since we first we sent our troops to Iraq, do you think the United States made a mistake in sending troops to Iraq, or not?"

GALLUP'

One factor that undoubtedly contributes to the broad support for the withdrawal of troops from Iraq is the enduring unpopularity of the decision to send troops there in the first place. A majority

(57%) see the U.S. decision to send troops to Iraq in 2003 as mistake. This reading is identical to what Gallup found in February of this year before the latest round of devastating attacks against the Iraqi government.

Republicans Least Likely to Approve of Withdrawal Decision

One-third of self-identified Republicans approve of Obama's 2011 decision to withdraw troops from Iraq, by far the lowest level of support for the decision across partisan groups. Support is highest among Democrats, at 87%, followed by independents, at 59%.

Percentage in U.S. Who Approve of Withdrawal From Iraq, by Party ID

Turning to Iraq, do you approve or disapprove of President Obama's 2011 decision to withdraw nearly all U.S. troops from Iraq?

	Oct 29-30, 2011^	Jun 20-21, 2014	Net change
	%	%	pct. pts.
Republicans	43	33	-10
Independents	77	59	-18
Democrats	96	87	-9

^Question wording: Turning to Iraq, do you approve or disapprove of President Obama's decision to withdraw nearly all U.S. troops from Iraq by the end of the year?

GALLUP'

All three partisan groups are less likely to back the withdrawal now than they did in 2011, with independents showing the greatest change in opinion—approval fell by 18 points. Approval among Democrats and Republicans also saw decreases by significant amounts, nine and 10 points, respectively.

Bottom Line

Undertaken with overwhelming public support and a major campaign promise, Obama's 2011 withdrawal of nearly all U.S. troops from Iraq is now slightly more controversial as the country edges toward civil war. Although a majority of Americans still back the decision, support for it has dropped 14 points since 2011, even as public opinion remains unchanged on the underlying invasion that brought U.S. troops to Iraq.

Survey Methods

Results for this Gallup poll are based on telephone interviews conducted June 20–21, 2014, on the Gallup Daily tracking survey, with a random sample of 1,012 adults, aged 18 and older, living in all 50 U.S. states and the District of Columbia.

For results based on the total sample of national adults, the margin of sampling error is ±4 percentage points at the 95% confidence level.

June 25, 2014
SUPPORT FOR IRAQ MILITARY ACTION
LOW IN HISTORICAL CONTEXT
Americans oppose Iraq military action by 54% to 39%

by Jeffrey M. Jones

PRINCETON, NJ—Americans mostly oppose direct U.S. military action to help the Iraqi government fight Islamic militants threatening to take control of that country. A June 20–21 Gallup poll finds 54% of Americans opposed to and 39% in favor of taking such action, lower than the level of support for other potential U.S. military actions in recent decades.

Opinion of Potential U.S. Military Actions

Country/Region	Polling dates	Favor	Oppose	No opinion
		%	%	%
Iraq	Jun 20-21, 2014	39	54	7
Syria	Sep 3-4, 2013	36	51	13
Iraq	Mar 14-15, 2003	64	33	3
Afghanistan	Oct 5-6, 2001	82	14	4
Kosovo/The Balkans	Feb 19-21, 1999	43	45	12
Iraq/Persian Gulf	Jan 11-13, 1991	55	38	4

GALLUP'

Americans were much more likely to favor taking military action against Iraq before the previous wars in 1991 and 2003, although both of those efforts were undertaken to oppose Saddam Hussein's regime.

After Iraq invaded Kuwait in August 1990, the percentage in favor of sending U.S. troops there started out low at 23%. By the fall, after President George H.W. Bush built an international coalition in favor of military action, a majority of Americans were in favor, including 55% in January 1991 just before the Persian Gulf War began.

A consistent majority of Americans supported sending U.S. ground troops to Iraq "in an attempt to remove Saddam Hussein from power" from the time the question was first asked in 1992 until the U.S. actually did so in March 2003. A March 14–15, 2003, poll conducted on the eve of the war found 64% of Americans in favor of taking such action.

President Barack Obama has ruled out the use of combat troops to address the current situation in Iraq, consistent with U.S. public opinion on the matter. However, the administration is still considering other actions, including airstrikes, and has already sent more than 100 U.S. military advisers to Iraq.

The current low level of support for military action now in Iraq is similar to what Gallup measured last fall for Syria. In September, the president was prepared to take military action in response to the Syrian government's use of chemical weapons on opposition forces there. At the time, Obama said he would not send U.S. ground troops to Syria, planning to limit the operations to airstrikes. Before the U.S. proceeded with military action, though, Russia brokered an agreement between the U.S. and Syria to resolve the dispute.

The highest level of support Gallup has measured for a potential military action was 82% prior to the war in Afghanistan, reflecting Americans' desire to retaliate against terrorists for the Sept. 11 attacks and the rally in support for U.S. government leaders after those attacks.

Gallup has measured American opinion on other military actions the U.S. has taken in recent decades, although most of those questions were asked in an approve/disapprove format after the action had begun. There is often an uptick in support for military action after the U.S. government has taken it, compared with the period when it is contemplating such action. As an example, support for the 2003 Iraq war increased from 64% prior to its start to more than 70% afterward. Thus, questions asked about support for military action before and after a war starts are generally not comparable.

Republicans Most Likely to Back Military Action

A slim majority of Republicans, 52%, are in favor of U.S. military action in Iraq, while the majority of independents and Democrats are opposed.

Support for Military Action in Iraq, by Political Party

Do you favor or oppose the United States taking direct military action in Iraq to assist the Iraqi government in fighting militants there?

	Favor	Oppose
	%	%
Republicans	52	45
Independents	39	54
Democrats	34	60

June 20-21, 2014

GALLUP'

One reason Republicans may favor military action in the current situation, whereas Democrats and independents do not, is that Republicans are much more likely to say they are worried about the situation in Iraq. Thirty-four percent of Republicans say they are "very worried" about Iraq, compared with 22% of independents and 18% of Democrats.

Twenty-three percent of all Americans are very worried about the situation in Iraq, with another 44% saying they are somewhat worried.

Republicans also were most likely to favor military action against Iraq prior to the 1991 and 2003 wars, and in Afghanistan in 2001. Republicans were not more likely than other party groups to favor military action in Kosovo or Syria.

Implications

Obama has ruled out sending U.S. combat troops to fight in Iraq, but is leaving open other possible U.S. actions to prevent Islamic militants from expanding their influence on Iraq beyond the parts of the country they now control.

But Americans are reluctant to support U.S. military action in Iraq, perhaps because of a desire not to get involved further in Iraq after the U.S. recently removed its troops from there. A majority still approve of the 2011 decision to withdraw U.S. troops from Iraq, and most continue to regard the 2003 invasion as "a mistake."

After the long U.S. engagements in Iraq and Afghanistan, Americans may also be war weary at this time and thus less supportive of any proposed new military action. Their level of support for the two most recent potential military actions, Syria in 2013 and Iraq now, and their approval of the most recent U.S. military involvement—in Libya in 2011—all rank among the lowest Gallup has measured.

Survey Methods

Results for this Gallup poll are based on telephone interviews conducted June 20–21, 2014, on the Gallup Daily tracking survey, with a random sample of 1,010 adults, aged 18 and older, living in all 50 U.S. states and the District of Columbia.

For results based on the total sample of national adults, the margin of sampling error is ±4 percentage points at the 95% confidence level.

June 26, 2014
IN U.S., CONFIDENCE IN BANKS REMAINS LOW
Twenty-six percent have a "great deal"
or "quite a lot" of confidence

by Rebecca Riffkin

WASHINGTON, D.C.—Twenty-six percent of Americans have "a great deal" or "quite a lot" of confidence in banks—unchanged from last year, but up from the record low of 21% found in 2012. Americans' confidence in banks is still far below the pre-recession level of 41% measured in June 2007.

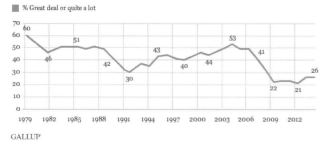

Americans' Confidence in Banks, 1979-2014 Trend

Now I am going to read you a list of institutions in American society. Please tell me how much confidence you, yourself, have in each one -- a great deal, quite a lot, some, or very little?

GALLUP

While slightly more than a quarter of Americans have a great deal or quite a lot of confidence in banks, an additional 43% express "some" confidence. On the other hand, 28% have "very little" confidence, and 2% volunteer that they have no confidence, all consistent with the percentages seen last year.

Furthermore, while 26% is a low percentage in absolute terms, banks actually rank in the middle of a list of 17 U.S. institutions Gallup asked Americans to rate on the confidence scale. In fact, in the June 5–8 survey, more Americans have confidence in banks than in the news media.

When Gallup first measured confidence in banks in 1979, 60% of Americans had a great deal or quite a lot of confidence—a level that has not been matched since. That year, banks ranked second out of nine institutions, landing only behind organized religion. By October 1991, confidence in banks fell to 30%, likely a result of the Savings and Loan Crisis of the late 1980s, but climbed to 53% by 2004 after almost a decade in the 40% range.

Confidence in banks stayed relatively high at 49% in 2005 and 2006, but dropped eight percentage points to 41% in 2007, a year in which confidence in nearly all institutions fell. Confidence in banks fell a combined nineteen points in 2008 and 2009, likely in response to the Great Recession, the collapse of Lehman Brothers bank, and the subsequent government intervention to save several other lending institutions. After bottoming out at 21% in 2012, confidence recovered slightly last year, and remained at that same low level this year.

Many More Americans Confident in Small Business Than Big Business

Consistent with recent years, small business was among the institutions earning the highest public confidence this year, at 62%. Big business, remains near the bottom of the list, at 21%. Few Americans have expressed confidence in big businesses since Gallup began asking about it in 1973, with the percentage who have a great deal or quite a lot of confidence never exceeding 35%. Meanwhile, confidence in small business has consistently been over 55%.

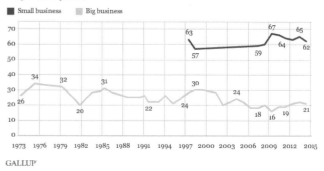

Americans' Confidence in Small Business vs. Confidence in Big Business

Now I am going to read you a list of institutions in American society. Please tell me how much confidence you, yourself, have in each one -- a great deal, quite a lot, some, or very little?

GALLUP

In 2009, 16% of Americans had a great deal or quite a lot of confidence in big business—the lowest ever measured—while 67%, a record high, expressed confidence in small business. Since then, confidence in small business has come down slightly, while confidence in big business generally increased until this year.

Bottom Line

Confidence in big business has dropped and then recovered multiple times in the 41 years Gallup has tracked it, but the current rut, with consistently 20% or less of Americans confident in big business, is new. Notably, however, the start of this rut predates the 2008 financial crisis, indicating that the image challenges facing big business will not necessarily go away as the economy continues to recover from that crisis.

By contrast, banking's image clearly stumbled during this period, with its confidence rating falling roughly 10 points each year from 2006 to 2009—a period spanning the emergence of the sub-prime mortgage crisis in 2007 and 2008, the fall of Lehman Brothers in 2008, and the broader financial crisis that ensued. But there are no easy fixes for the banking industry either. Banks were at the epicenter of the financial crisis that has had a devastating effect on the U.S. economy, and therefore, on consumers. And even though the economy appears to be recovering slowly from the depths of the recession, the percentage of Americans expressing high confidence in U.S. banks has not.

Survey Methods

Results for this Gallup poll are based on telephone interviews conducted June 5–8, 2014, with a random sample of 1,027 adults, aged 18 and older, living in all 50 U.S. states and the District of Columbia.

For results based on the total sample of national adults, the margin of sampling error is ±4 percentage points at the 95% confidence level.

June 27, 2014

**MORE IN U.S. WOULD DECREASE
IMMIGRATION THAN INCREASE**

*Support for increasing immigration is
up, yet more would still curb it*

by Lydia Saad

PRINCETON, NJ—While illegal immigration typically dominates debates over immigration policy, the issue of legal immigration came to the forefront in the recent Virginia Republican primary when House Majority Leader Eric Cantor was soundly defeated by Tea Party favorite Dave Brat. Brat highlighted Cantor's support for expanding visas for skilled immigrants in his blistering charge that Cantor is soft on immigration. Brat's case may have been a fairly easy one to make, as new Gallup polling finds fewer than one in four Americans favor increased immigration.

In your view, should immigration be kept at its present level, increased, or decreased?

	Increased	Present level	Decreased	No opinion
	%	%	%	%
National adults	22	33	41	4
Republicans	14	34	50	3
Independents	23	30	43	3
Democrats	27	37	32	4

June 5-8, 2014

GALLUP

The small amount of Americans who favor increased immigration include just 14% of Republicans. In fact, more Americans think immigration should be decreased than increased, and by a nearly two-to-one margin, 41% vs. 22%. A third in the U.S. are satisfied with the level as it is.

Americans' views on immigration have varied a bit in the past 15 years, with the dominant view shifting between decreasing immigration and maintaining it at the current level. Some of these changes may reflect the ebb and flow of Americans' reactions to the 9/11 attacks in 2001 as well as rocketing unemployment in 2009, with both events triggering a temporary surge in anti-immigration sentiment.

However, the Gallup trend also chronicles a separate narrative: a steady increase in public support for increasing immigration, rising from 10% in 1999 to 21% in 2012 and 22% today.

In your view, should immigration be kept at its present level, increased, or decreased?
Trend since 1999

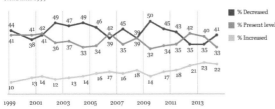

■ % Decreased
■ % Present level
■ % Increased

1999 2001 2003 2005 2007 2009 2011 2013

This is a selected trend based on Gallup's annual June/July measurement

GALLUP

The long-term rise in support for expanding immigration could reflect growing public sympathy for the argument made by some prominent business leaders that the current cap on the number of work visas granted to highly skilled foreign nationals each year—the

so called H-1B visa program—needs to be raised. In 2013, Gallup found about three-quarters of Americans were in favor of expanding the number of short-term work visas for highly skilled workers as part of a comprehensive immigration reform package.

Support for increasing immigration has grown significantly more among Americans with college degrees—those more likely to be tuned in to the discussion about the need for importing highly skilled workers—than it has among those with less formal education.

Since 2000, support for increased immigration rose 13 percentage points—from 17% to 30%—among adults with a postgraduate education, and it rose 19 points among those who stopped at an undergraduate degree. It grew comparatively less among those with only some college education (eight points) as well as those with no more than a high school education (four points).

2014 vs. 2000 Views on Immigration, by Highest Level of Education
In your view, should immigration be kept at its present level, increased, or decreased?

	Increased	Present level	Decreased
	%	%	%
June 5-8, 2014			
Postgraduate	30	36	28
College graduate	30	35	34
Some college	19	34	44
High school degree or less	19	31	47
Sept. 11-13, 2000			
Postgraduate	17	51	24
College graduate	11	49	32
Some college	11	43	36
High school degree or less	15	33	46

GALLUP

Despite Americans' resistance to increasing immigration, the great majority continue to view immigration in positive terms for the country, with 63% calling it a good thing. That is down from 2013's high of 72%, but still exceeding the sub-60% readings found during the recent recession and, before that, in the wake of 9/11.

Impact of Immigration on the U.S.
On the whole, do you think immigration is a good thing or a bad thing for this country today?

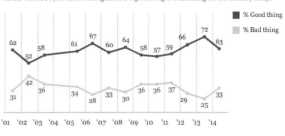

■ % Good thing
■ % Bad thing

'01 '02 '03 '04 '05 '06 '07 '08 '09 '10 '11 '12 '13 '14

GALLUP

This upbeat view of immigration is held by 72% of Democrats, 63% of independents, and 55% of Republicans.

Bottom Line

Immigration is central to who Americans are as a people, and what the United States represents, and by and large Americans view immigration as positive for the country. But deciding how many new immigrants to welcome each year can be controversial, particularly when unemployment is high, and seeming competition for good jobs already fierce.

Facebook's Mark Zuckerberg has taken a lead role in championing the cause of expanding H-1B visas on the grounds that hiring a highly skilled foreign national isn't a zero sum proposition—simply erasing a job opportunity for an American citizen. Rather, he argues, it is needed to help the country's high-tech sector make critical advances that will strengthen the economy to everyone's benefit.

Zuckerberg's critics have their own counter-arguments about his financial motives with regard to the pay scale for U.S. vs. foreign workers. Nevertheless, it's not clear how much Americans are tuning in to this debate, and thus how much it is influencing their overall views about the general volume of immigrants that should be allowed into the U.S. each year. To the extent the H-1B visa debate has influenced public opinion, it has been at the margins, with support for increasing immigration rising from 10% to 22% over the past 15 years. But reducing immigration remains the far more popular choice—potentially aiding political attacks on supporters of expanding the H-1B visa program, as former Majority Leader Eric Cantor might attest.

Survey Methods

Results for this Gallup poll are based on telephone interviews conducted June 5–8, 2014, on the Gallup Daily tracking survey, with a random sample of 1,027 adults, aged 18 and older, living in all 50 U.S. states and the District of Columbia.

For results based on the total sample of national adults, the margin of sampling error is ±4 percentage points at the 95% confidence level.

June 27, 2014
MAJORITY STILL SAYS RELIGION CAN ANSWER TODAY'S PROBLEMS
Increasing numbers of Americans say religion is out of date

by Frank Newport

PRINCETON, NJ—Fifty-seven percent of Americans say that religion can answer all or most of today's problems, while 30% say that religion is largely old fashioned and out of date. Americans have in recent decades become gradually less likely to say that religion can answer today's problems and more likely to believe religion is out of date.

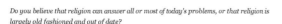

Do you believe that religion can answer all or most of today's problems, or that religion is largely old fashioned and out of date?

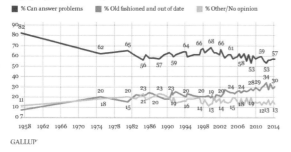

GALLUP

The latest update on this long-term Gallup trend comes from Gallup's May 8–11 Values and Beliefs survey. Gallup asked this question once in the 1950s, once in the 1970s, and multiple times in the 1980s and each subsequent decade.

The 82% choosing the "can answer today's problems" options in 1957 is in line with a number of other measures from that decade showing a high level of religiosity, including religious service attendance, importance of religion, and the percentage of Americans with a formal religious identity.

But Americans' belief that religion can answer most problems dropped—to 62%—when Gallup next asked the question in the 1970s, and it remained at about this level in the 1980s and 1990s. Americans' belief that religion offers answers fell to 60% in the 2000s, while those stating the secular belief rose to 25%.

So far this decade, an average of 57% of Americans have held this view, representing a small but notable decline.

Americans' Belief in Ability of Religion to Answer Today's Problems, by Decade

	% Can answer problems	% Old fashioned and out of date	% Other/ No opinion
1950s*	82	7	11
1970s**	62	20	18
1980s	60	21	20
1990s	63	21	16
2000s	60	25	16
2010s	57	30	14

*March 1957
**December 1974

GALLUP

Americans also appear to have a somewhat higher degree of certainty about their views on religion now than in the past, with the percentage not choosing "can answer today's problems" or "old fashioned" dropping in recent years compared with previous decades. Additionally, because the 2014 data match the overall average for the current decade, it is possible that the trend toward the belief that religion is out of date may be abating.

Highly Religious Groups Most Likely to Say Religion Relevant to Today's Problems

Americans' views on the overall relevance of religion in terms of answering today's problems are naturally related to their own personal religiosity, including measures of religious service attendance, self-reported importance of religion, and having a formal religious identity.

Americans' Belief in Ability of Religion to Answer Today's Problems, by Religiosity

	% Can answer problems	% Old fashioned and out of date	% Other/No opinion
National adults	57	30	13
Attend church weekly	84	11	4
Attend church nearly weekly/Monthly	68	20	11
Attend church less often	36	45	19
Religion very important	82	8	10
Religion fairly important	40	41	19
Religion not very important	11	76	13
Have a religious identity	64	23	13
No religious identification	21	67	12

May 8-11, 2014

GALLUP

The relationships between views on the relevance of religion and other demographic groupings of the population largely reflect how the underlying religiosity of each of those categories. Older Americans, women, those living in the South, and political conservatives are among the most religious groups in the U.S. based on measures of church attendance and importance of religion. These groups, in turn, are also the most likely to say that religion can answer most or all of today's problems. Still, across almost all of the demographic and political categories in the table below, the percentage saying that religion can answer most or all of today's problems is higher than the percentage saying that it is out of date. The exception is liberals, comprising about 25% of this sample, who are more likely to say religion is out of date than to say it can answer today's problems.

Americans' Belief in Ability of Religion to Answer Today's Problems, by Demographic

	% Can answer problems	% Old fashioned and out of date	% Other/No opinion
National adults	57	30	13
Men	52	34	14
Women	62	26	13
18-29	48	39	13
30-49	58	35	8
50-64	60	24	16
65+	62	19	18
East	47	33	20
Midwest	56	34	10
South	68	21	11
West	51	37	12
Conservative	72	16	12
Moderate	58	31	11
Liberal	36	49	15

May 8-11, 2014

GALLUP

Implications

Over the past 40 years, there has been a gradual shift in Americans' views of the relevance of religion in answering today's problems, with an increasing, but still minority, segment saying that religion is old fashioned and out of date.

The question itself is a broad take on Americans' views of the relevance of religion in today's society, and clearly, the 30% who say it is not relevant today differs markedly from the 7% who felt that way in 1957 or the 15% who felt that way in 1981. Still, the majority of Americans continue to believe that religion can answer today's problems, another indicator that the nation, by far, remains a religious country. And, with the trend leveling off in recent years, it appears this aspect of the secularization of U.S. society may have slowed, if not halted, for the foreseeable future.

Survey Methods

Results for this Gallup poll are based on telephone interviews conducted May 8–11, 2014, on the Gallup Daily tracking survey, with a random sample of 1,028 adults, aged 18 and older, living in all 50 U.S. states and the District of Columbia.

For results based on the total sample of national adults, the margin of sampling error is ±4 percentage points at the 95% confidence level.

June 30, 2014

AMERICANS LOSING CONFIDENCE IN ALL BRANCHES OF U.S. GOV'T

Confidence hits six-year low for presidency; record lows for Supreme Court, Congress

by Justin McCarthy

WASHINGTON, D.C.—Americans' confidence in all three branches of the U.S. government has fallen, reaching record lows for the Supreme Court (30%) and Congress (7%), and a six-year low for the presidency (29%). The presidency had the largest drop of the three branches this year, down seven percentage points from its previous rating of 36%.

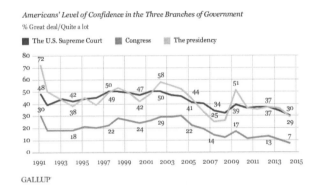

Americans' Level of Confidence in the Three Branches of Government
% Great deal/Quite a lot

GALLUP

These data come from a June 5–8 Gallup poll asking Americans about their confidence in 16 U.S. institutions—within government, business, and society—that they either read about or interact with.

While Gallup recently reported a historically low rating of Congress, Americans have always had less confidence in Congress than in the other two branches of government. The Supreme Court and the presidency have alternated being the most trusted branch of government since 1991, the first year Gallup began asking regularly about all three branches.

But on a relative basis, Americans' confidence in all three is eroding. Since June 2013, confidence has fallen seven points for the presidency, four points for the Supreme Court, and three points for Congress. Confidence in each of the three branches of government had already fallen from 2012 to 2013.

Americans' Level of Confidence in the Three Branches of Government, 2012-2014

I am going to read you a list of institutions in American society. Please tell me how much confidence you, yourself, have in each one -- a great deal, quite a lot, some, or very little?
% Great deal/Quite a lot

	2012	2013	2014	Change, 2012 to 2014
	%	%	%	Pct. pts.
The U.S. Supreme Court	37	34	30	-7
The presidency	37	36	29	-8
Congress	13	10	7	-6

GALLUP

Confidence in the presidency is now the lowest it has been under President Barack Obama, as is confidence in Congress and the Supreme Court, given their historical lows. When Obama first took office in 2009, each of the three branches saw a jump in confidence from their dismally low ratings in George W. Bush's final two years in the White House.

Confidence in the Presidency, From George H.W. Bush to Obama

The president in office is not mentioned by name when the presidential confidence question is asked, but how positively Americans evaluate the current president has a direct impact on how much confidence Americans place in the presidency as an institution.

Gallup began asking regularly about the presidency in March 1991, when George H.W. Bush was in office. At that time, 72% of Americans had confidence in the presidency—the highest confidence rating the institution has received. This was immediately following his leadership in the successful first Persian Gulf War, and at a time when his job approval rating hit the then all-time high of 89%. But the elder Bush also saw the largest drop in confidence for the institution that same year, when it fell to a still relatively high 50% in October 1991.

The three presidents who would succeed him would go on to be elected to two terms, with varying degrees of confidence in the executive branch of the U.S. government during those terms. Obama garnered the greatest first-year confidence rating, at 51% in 2009, but has held lower ratings than both Bill Clinton and George W. Bush in each subsequent year of his presidency so far.

Americans' Level of Confidence in the U.S. Presidency, by Term Year
% Great deal/Quite a lot

	Bill Clinton	George W. Bush	Barack Obama
Year 1	43	48	51
Year 2	38	58	36
Year 3	45	55	35
Year 4	39	52	37
Year 5	49	44	36
Year 6	53	33	29
Year 7	49	25	--
Year 8	42	26	--

GALLUP'

George W. Bush's presidency commanded the highest first-term confidence ratings due to the post-9/11 surge in support for government leaders and institutions, marked by a record job approval rating of 90% for Bush in September 2001 and continued high ratings for him in the months thereafter. His second-term approval ratings plummeted, however, and so did confidence in the presidency, reaching an all-time low of 25% in 2007.

Clinton had higher approval ratings during his second term thanks to a strong economy, and confidence ratings for the presidency improved as well. Compared with the sixth-year low that the presidency has reached under Obama this year, confidence in the institution registered at 53% for Clinton in June 1998. Even in the thick of the Monica Lewinsky scandal that year, Americans' confidence in the presidency remained higher than for either of his successors in their sixth years in office.

New Low for Confidence in the U.S. Supreme Court

Gallup has tracked confidence in the Supreme Court since 1973. The institution's record high of 56% was reached twice, in 1985 and 1988—both times under former President Ronald Reagan. By 1988, Reagan had made all four of his contributions to the Supreme Court's roster of confirmed justices.

From 1973 to 2006, the Supreme Court maintained confidence ratings in the 40s and 50s in all but one poll. That changed in 2007, a year after George W. Bush's second confirmed nominee to the court—the Supreme Court's confidence rating dropped sharply to 34%, along with similar declines in confidence in the other two branches of government. It has not reached 40% since.

In recent years, the presidency and the Supreme Court have often been closely rated in confidence by Americans, and in most polls since 1991, the two branches of government have been within six or seven points of each other in confidence ratings.

Bottom Line

While Americans clearly have the lowest amount of confidence in the legislative branch, ratings for all three are down and are at or near their lowest points to date. At this point, Americans place much greater faith in the military and the police than in any of the three branches of government.

Members of Congress are likely resigned to the fact that they are the most distrusted institution of government, but there should be concern that now fewer than one in 10 Americans have confidence in their legislative body. And Obama, like the younger Bush before him, is surely aware that the presidency's low confidence rating is not auspicious for his ability to govern and rally the public behind his favored policies.

While the Supreme Court, with unelected justices serving indefinite terms, is immune to the same public pressures that elected members of Congress and the president must contend with, it is not immune to the drop in confidence in U.S. government institutions that threatens and complicates the U.S. system of government.

Survey Methods

Results for this Gallup poll are based on telephone interviews conducted June 5–8, 2014, with a random sample of 1,027 adults, aged 18 and older, living in all 50 U.S. states and the District of Columbia.

For results based on the total sample of national adults, the margin of sampling error is ±4 percentage points at the 95% confidence level.

July 01, 2014
IN U.S., VETERANS REPORT LESS STRESS, WORRY THAN CIVILIANS

Retired veterans have even lower levels than discharged veterans

by Justin McCarthy

This article is part of a weeklong series analyzing the veteran experience in the United States, especially how returning veterans transition from the military to civilian life.

WASHINGTON, D.C.—Americans may understandably believe that the nation's veterans are suffering emotionally given news reports of high levels of post-traumatic stress disorder and other mood or anxiety disorders among those who have served in the military. However, Gallup finds that among employed Americans, active-duty and veteran populations are more emotionally resilient than their civilian counterparts.

Percentages Experiencing Daily Stress, by Military Service and Age

Did you experience the following feelings during a lot of the day yesterday? How about stress?

	18 to 44	45 to 64
	% Yes	% Yes
Civilians	46	40
Discharged veterans	46	36
Retired veterans	42	32
Active-duty service members	39	25

Gallup-Healthways Well-Being Index
Jan. 2, 2013-June 22, 2014

GALLUP

Gallup analyzed the responses of active-duty service members and working Americans who have served in the military—including discharged veterans and retired veterans—as well as civilians on a number of questions designed to assess emotional well-being, such as levels of stress and worry. The results are reported separately among 18- to 44-year-olds and 45- to 64-year-olds, given the strong relationship of age to emotional well-being, and the fact that a far greater number of older than younger Americans have served in the military.

In terms of daily stress, active-duty service members aged 18 to 44 are least likely to report experiencing stress (39%) among working Americans in their age group, followed by retired veterans (42%), discharged veterans (46%), and civilians (46%). Stress is lower among older workers in each service group, with active-duty members aged 45 to 64 reporting the least stress of all subgroups, at 25%.

The large majority of active-duty service members are 18 to 44 years old, but those who stay in the military longer and reach the 45-to-64 age group fare best in emotional well-being. This suggests that those who serve the longest could be poised to have the least stress.

Although younger civilians and younger discharged veterans report similar levels of stress, both civilian age groups generally report higher levels of stress than their veteran and active-duty counterparts. To many who have served in the military, this comes as no surprise, as military life braces its members for difficult adversities for which civilian life has no equivalent.

"What do I have to worry about back in the civilian world? A missed report, a client I failed to sign? The penalties for failure to perform in combat are far more severe," says Gallup Senior Consultant David Goldich, a discharged veteran who served two tours in Iraq. "The military experience is defined by resilience. Your fellow troops are counting on you to perform under pressure at all times. Quitting is not an option."

Retired veterans, those who receive full pension benefits after serving 20 or more years, tend to experience slightly less worry and stress than discharged veterans—those who have not met the military's requirements for receiving pensions.

Percentages Experiencing Daily Worry, by Military Service and Age

Did you experience the following feelings during a lot of the day yesterday? How about worry?

	18 to 44	45 to 64
	% Yes	% Yes
Civilians	31	30
Discharged veterans	26	26
Retired veterans	20	20
Active-duty service members	20	13

Gallup-Healthways Well-Being Index
Jan. 2, 2013-June 22, 2014

GALLUP

Among those aged 45 to 64, 26% of discharged veterans experience worry daily, compared with 20% of retired veterans in the same age group. Retired veterans in this age group also report less stress (32%) than their discharged counterparts (36%).

Discharged veterans do not complete the requirements for pension benefits for a variety of reasons, many of which are self-elected. For retired veterans, the benefits are wide in scope, including significantly less expensive healthcare, and this can make retired life much more comfortable.

Bottom Line

Although many veterans face very serious and unique mental health challenges, that does not seem to be the experience of most of the veteran community, which in fact fares better than working civilians in many aspects of emotional well-being.

According to the Department of Veterans Affairs, about 7% of civilians have PTSD in their lifetime, while the percentage ranges from 11% to 20% for veterans who served in the early years of the current conflicts in Afghanistan and Iraq. The VA also reports that as of 2010, more than half of veterans who sought mental healthcare (53%) had problems related to PTSD, and that more than a third (38%) suffered from depression.

On the whole, however, veterans appear more emotionally resilient than the general civilian population. As the nation works to find employment for returning veterans after two wars, it's important not to view veterans as emotionally scarred or damaged. They are, in fact, a lot more emotionally sound than those who have never served. Reasons for this may include the military attracting people more emotionally sound to begin with, or there may be an emotional benefit directly related to military service.

Survey Methods

Results are based on telephone interviews conducted as part of the Gallup-Healthways Well-Being Index survey Jan. 2, 2013–June 22,

2014, with a random sample of 128,285 adults, aged 18 and older, living in all 50 U.S. states and the District of Columbia.

Sample Sizes for Reported Groups

	18 to 44	Margin of error	45 to 64	Margin of error
Employed discharged veterans	2,828	±2.0	5,767	±1.3
Employed retired veterans	333	±5.5	1,882	±2.3
Active-duty service members	1,407	±3.0	183	±8.5
Employed civilians	58,666	±0.4	57,219	±0.4

GALLUP

For results based on the total sample of national adults, the margin of sampling error is ±0.25 percentage points at the 95% confidence level.

July 01, 2014

MAJORITY OF U.S. VETERANS SAY ACCESS TO VA CARE DIFFICULT

Fifty-five percent say it is difficult to access care; 30% say it is easy

by Jeffrey M. Jones

This article is part of a weeklong series analyzing the veteran experience in the United States, especially how returning veterans transition from the military to civilian life.

PRINCETON, NJ—Amid reports of long delays and inadequate medical care for U.S. military veterans at Veterans Affairs (VA) health centers, a new Gallup poll of U.S. veterans finds the majority, 55%, saying it is either "very" or "somewhat difficult" to access medical care through the VA. Thirty percent say it is "very" or "somewhat easy" to do so.

Military Veterans' Views of Ease of Accessing Medical Care From VA Medical Centers

Regardless of whether or not you have accessed medical care through the VA, in your opinion, how easy or difficult is it to access medical care through the VA? Would you say it is very easy, somewhat easy, somewhat difficult, or very difficult?

	%
Very easy	10
Somewhat easy	20
Somewhat difficult	28
Very difficult	27
No opinion	14

June 16-20, 2014

GALLUP

The results are based on a June 16–20 poll of 1,268 U.S. military veterans who had participated in a prior Gallup Daily tracking survey.

The VA came under heavy criticism this spring for its treatment of veterans, most notably for long delays to get medical care. Some veterans died before they could get the treatment they were seeking. The probe of the VA revealed that some VA officials falsified records, with media speculation that it was perhaps due to financial

incentives tied to providing timely medical care. The Obama administration, which released a report of its own investigation into the matter on Friday, is set to appoint former Procter & Gamble executive Robert McDonald as the new head of the VA.

Fifty-one percent of U.S. veterans say they are following news about the quality of medical care provided at VA hospitals very closely, with an additional 39% saying they are following it somewhat closely. That is a much higher level of attention than the general population reports paying to the story, based on an earlier June 5–8 Gallup poll.

The common perception of most veterans about the difficulty of accessing VA care, many of whom have personally used the VA system, confirms that the department is failing to meet the medical needs of many of those it is designed to serve. At the same time, that is not the belief or experience of all veterans, with three in 10 saying it is easy to get access to medical care through the VA.

Veterans' perceptions of VA medical access seems to be colored by their political leanings. Military veterans who identify politically as Democrats are significantly more likely to say it is easy to get medical care from the VA (40%) than Republican veterans (23%), with independents falling in between (33%). Democrats may perceive conditions as better given that a Democrat is president.

There are not significant regional differences in the perceived ease or difficulty of accessing VA care, suggesting the perceived difficulties are more a system-wide issue than one confined mostly to VA centers in particular parts of the U.S.

Veterans' Confidence in VA Shaken

The poll finds the VA controversy has negatively affected how veterans view the VA. Sixty percent say they are now less confident in the ability of the VA to care for veterans, while 34% say it has not affected their views. Four percent say they are more confident.

Effect of Recent News of VA Hospitals on Confidence in VA to Care for Veterans, Among Veterans

How has the recent news about the VA hospitals affected your view of the ability of the VA to care for veterans? Would you say it has made you -- [ROTATED: more confident, less confident, or has not made a difference]?

	More confident	Less confident	No difference
	%	%	%
2014 Jun 16-20	4	60	34

GALLUP

Despite the obvious effect on their confidence in the VA, veterans favor an expansive role for the VA in meeting veterans' care over a more limited one. Fifty-six percent say the VA should care for all veterans' medical needs for the duration of their lives, while 38% believe the VA should only care for those medical issues related to the veterans' military service.

View of Proper Role for the VA, Among Veterans

In your opinion, which of the following should be the responsibility of the VA? Is the responsibility of the VA to -- [ROTATED: only take care of health problems directly related to a military service member or veteran's service (or) should it be to take care of all of military service members' and veterans' healthcare needs for the rest of their lives]?

	Take care of medical needs related to military service	Take care of all healthcare needs for rest of veterans' lives
	%	%
2014 Jun 16-20	38	56

GALLUP

Veterans' views on the proper role for the VA are similar among those paying more and those paying less attention to the controversy.

Implications

Veterans are probably best positioned to assess how the VA is doing its job in terms of caring for them, and most report that is difficult for those who served in the military to get medical care through the VA. While that is the majority view, a substantial minority of veterans say it is easy to get medical care. It is unclear whether veterans have always believed access to medical care at the VA is difficult to get, or if they are more likely to believe this now in light of the controversy.

The controversy has shaken veterans' confidence in the VA, although not to the point that they favor a more limited role for the VA in meeting veterans' medical needs.

The Obama administration has chosen a new VA chief, and many more top officials in the administration have resigned or are expected to lose their jobs. The controversy certainly means medical care for veterans at VA hospitals will get increased scrutiny from Congress, the media, and the Obama administration, which should lead to improvements in the treatment of veterans. Both the House and Senate have passed bills designed to address delays in care, and the president is expected to sign a reconciled bill into law this year.

Survey Methods

Results are based on telephone interviews conducted June 16–20, 2014, with a random sample of 1,268 veterans, aged 18 and older, living in all 50 U.S. states and the District of Columbia.

For results based on the total sample of veterans, the margin of sampling error is ±3.3 percentage points at the 95% confidence level.

Interviews were conducted using Gallup Daily Tracking Survey Recontact Sample. Gallup Daily Tracking Survey Recontact Sample includes respondents that previously participated in the Gallup Daily Tracking Survey, and agreed to future contact. The sample universe for this study included Gallup Daily Tracking Recontact respondents that previously reported they were veterans.

July 03, 2014
MOST VETERANS ARE SATISFIED WITH GI BILL EDUCATION BENEFITS
Half of younger veterans have used modern GI Bill and are highly satisfied with it

by Lydia Saad

PRINCETON, NJ—As the original GI Bill turns 70, Gallup finds nearly eight in 10 American veterans saying they are "very satisfied" (32%) or "satisfied" (46%) with the education benefits the bills provide. Relatively few—16%—are dissatisfied to any degree.

While older veterans may be answering in terms of the GI programs available decades ago, younger veterans—those aged 18 to 49—are more likely to be answering with the current programs in mind. The broad satisfaction younger veterans express toward the program comes at a time when the federal government and some states, particularly California, are peering closely into how GI education money is being spent, and not liking what they see.

U.S. Veterans' Satisfaction With GI Bill Education Benefits

How satisfied or dissatisfied are you with the education benefits provided by the GI bills? Are you very satisfied, satisfied, dissatisfied, or very dissatisfied?

	All veterans	18 to 49	50 to 64	65 to 75	76 and older
	%	%	%	%	%
Very satisfied	32	38	28	35	29
Satisfied	46	35	48	45	55
Dissatisfied	10	12	12	8	5
Very dissatisfied	6	10	6	3	3
No opinion	7	6	5	9	8
Total satisfied	78	73	76	80	84
Total dissatisfied	16	22	18	11	8

June 16-20, 2014

GALLUP

Studies show that many veterans are failing to graduate from college before their money runs out. Others are financially unable to meet the GI Bill's requirement to attend college full time, pushing them into lower quality part-time programs. Still others turn to for-profit education programs that offer quick, but sometimes subpar degrees that fail to provide the academic leg-up in the workforce that veterans need.

These critiques could explain why overall satisfaction with GI education benefits is slightly lower among younger veterans than among those who served in the Korean War or during World War II: 73% of those younger than 50 are satisfied compared with 84% of those aged 76 and older. However, the percentage "very satisfied" is highest among the younger age group, indicating more intensity of opinion toward the program on their part.

Gallup's new survey of U.S. military veterans was conducted June 16–20. The 1,268 veterans included in the study were originally interviewed as part of Gallup Daily tracking between January 2011 and May 2014, and agreed to be recontacted. All of the veteran respondents identified themselves as either discharged or retired from the military.

Three in 10 Veterans Have Used the Newer GI Benefits

President Franklin D. Roosevelt signed the first GI Bill into law on June 22, 1944. Congress has since passed updated versions to help returning soldiers keep up with the rising cost of living and college tuition, including the Montgomery GI Bill in 1984 and the Post-9/11 GI Bill in 2009.

Thirty percent of all U.S. veterans today say they have personally used GI education benefits provided through either the Montgomery or Post-9/11 GI Bills. That includes nearly half of veterans between the ages of 18 and 49. And an additional 6% in this group say that a spouse or other dependent used the benefit.

U.S. Veterans' Use of GI Bill Education Benefits

Have you, your spouse, or a dependent used education benefits provided through the Montgomery GI Bill or the Post-9/11 GI Bill?

	All veterans	18 to 49	50 to 64	65 to 75	76 and older
	%	%	%	%	%
Yes, veteran used the benefits	30	48	32	23	18
Yes, a spouse or dependent used the benefits	5	6	5	4	3
No, not used the benefits	63	46	62	71	75
No opinion	2	0	1	2	5

June 16-20, 2014

GALLUP

Satisfaction with the government's GI education benefit is especially high among veterans who report using benefits through the Montgomery or Post-9/11 GI Bills. The slight majority of this group—51%—reports being very satisfied with the benefit, with another 35% satisfied. In contrast, 22% of veterans who have not used the benefit are very satisfied with it, and another 52% are satisfied.

U.S. Veterans' Satisfaction With GI Bill Education Benefits, by Personal Use of the Benefits

	Veteran personally used education benefits	Veteran did not personally use education benefits
	%	%
Very satisfied	51	22
Satisfied	35	52
Dissatisfied	7	12
Very dissatisfied	5	5
No opinion	3	9

June 16-20, 2014

GALLUP'

Bottom Line

The story of America's World War II GIs enrolling in college en masse after returning home from battle is often told in halcyon terms, as an example of a government policy success. President Barack Obama recently credited the GI Bill with helping to "lay the foundation for the largest middle class in history." Its passage reflected the strong commitment of many key individuals in and outside of Congress to prevent World War II veterans from suffering the same neglect that World War I veterans experienced a generation earlier.

That impulse likely continues to drive Obama and lawmakers to craft policy that provides veterans with sufficient means to not only survive but also thrive after serving their country, ultimately contributing to the nation's economic strength. At the same time, the government's promise of a college education is the lure that draws many men and women into the modern military. Thus, fulfilling that promise to today's veterans has strong moral implications.

While there is substantial evidence to suggest that the modern GI education benefit is far from perfect, the broad satisfaction that younger veterans express toward the benefit, and the particularly high satisfaction among veterans who have experience using the recent GI Bills, is a positive sign that the program may be achieving its goals.

Survey Methods

Results are based on telephone interviews conducted June 16–20, 2014, with a random sample of 1,268 veterans, aged 18 and older, living in all 50 U.S. states and the District of Columbia.

For results based on the total sample of veterans, the margin of sampling error is ±3.3 percentage points at the 95% confidence level.

July 07, 2014
AMERICANS' FINANCIAL WELL-BEING IS LOWEST, SOCIAL HIGHEST
Older Americans and women have high well-being across more elements

by Alyssa Brown and Lindsey Sharpe

WASHINGTON, D.C.—Americans are most likely to be considered thriving in their social well-being and suffering in their financial well-being across five elements of well-being measured by the newly updated Gallup-Healthways Well-Being Index. In general, more Americans are suffering or struggling than are thriving across all five elements.

State of Well-Being in the U.S.

SUFFERING: Well-being that is low and inconsistent. STRUGGLING: Well-being that is moderate or inconsistent. THRIVING: Well-being that is strong and consistent.

PURPOSE: Liking what you do each day and being motivated to achieve your goals
16% | 48% | 37%

SOCIAL: Having supportive relationships and love in your life
16% | 43% | 41%

FINANCIAL: Managing your economic life to reduce stress and increase security
23% | 38% | 39%

COMMUNITY: Liking where you live, feeling safe, and having pride in your community
15% | 47% | 38%

PHYSICAL: Having good health and enough energy to get things done daily
12% | 56% | 33%

Gallup-Healthways Well-Being Index
Jan. 1–June 23, 2014

GALLUP'

Gallup and Healthways, which have partnered to track Americans' well-being since 2008, added 27 new, actionable questions to the Gallup-Healthways Well-Being Index in January 2014. The updated index is organized into five elements of well-being:

- *Purpose well-being* is composed of questions about having an inspiring leader, daily activity, goals, and strengths.
- *Social well-being* includes questions about relationships with friends and family, personal time, and received encouragement and support.
- *Financial well-being* is made up of questions about standard of living, ability to afford basic necessities, and financial worry.
- *Community well-being* includes questions about community pride, involvement, and safety and security.
- *Physical well-being* includes questions related to alcohol, drug, and tobacco use; current disease burden and past diagnoses; exercise; and eating habits.

Extensive research by Gallup and Healthways shows that, taken together, these five elements are the core components of the best possible life.

The calculations pertaining to these elements are based on over 80,000 interviews conducted from Jan. 2–June 23, 2014. Gallup classifies respondents, at the element level, as "thriving" (well-being that is strong and consistent), "struggling" (well-being that is moderate or inconsistent), or "suffering" (well-being that is low and inconsistent).

Older Americans, Women, Southerners Are Thriving Across More Elements

Demographic, regional, and other subgroup variations in well-being on these five elements provide a valuable basis for better understanding the nature of well-being in the U.S. and can be instructive in conceiving strategies for improving it.

Well-being differed by age, gender, and geographic region in the first half of 2014, similar to patterns Gallup and Healthways have seen previously. Americans aged 65 or older are more likely than younger adults to be thriving in each of the five elements of well-being. The percentage of women who are thriving eclipsed the percentage of men who are thriving in all elements except financial well-being, where they are about the same.

Southerners have an edge over those living in all other regions in terms of the percent who are thriving in three of the five elements: purpose, social, and community well-being. Westerners are the most likely to thrive in physical well-being. Midwesterners and westerners essentially tie as highest on financial well-being.

Percentage of Americans Thriving in Each Element of Well-Being

AGE	Purpose	Social	Financial	Community	Physical
18-29 years	38	38	34	30	36
30-44 years	35	36	30	34	31
45-64 years	33	38	35	37	28
65+	44	53	62	53	40

GENDER	Purpose	Social	Financial	Community	Physical
Men	33	39	39	36	30
Women	40	42	39	40	35

REGION	Purpose	Social	Financial	Community	Physical
East	34	40	38	35	33
Midwest	35	38	40	36	31
South	39	42	38	40	32
West	37	41	40	39	35

Gallup-Healthways Well-Being Index
Jan. 1–June 23, 2014

GALLUP'

Implications

Americans are more likely to be struggling or suffering than thriving across all five elements of well-being, underscoring the significant challenges Americans face in bettering their quality of life. Gallup and Healthways research also shows that half of Americans are thriving in only one well-being element or none at all. And fewer than one in five U.S. adults are thriving in four or five elements, which indicates that many individuals are not maximizing their well-being.

While Americans likely can do more to improve their sense of purpose, social relationships, financial security, connection to community, and physical health, government leaders and employers can do a lot to encourage and support their efforts. Each of the five elements of well-being are interrelated, and working to improve one element can contribute to growth in other areas. For example, an individual or company with strong social well-being might integrate social networks and support into an exercise program aimed at bolstering physical well-being. Companies can integrate personal finance education into their broader wellness programs for employees. And individuals with strong purpose can apply their unique strengths to local volunteer activities, thereby increasing their sense of community.

These efforts to boost individual well-being are critically important to the health of communities, workplaces, and the U.S. economy overall. Previous Gallup research has shown that well-being predicts key health outcomes such as healthcare utilization, life expectancy, new onset disease burden, and change in obesity status. Additionally, the Well-Being Index predicts important business outcomes including absenteeism, turnover, and workplace safety.

Survey Methods

Results are based on telephone interviews conducted as part of the Gallup-Healthways Well-Being Index survey Jan. 1–June 23, 2014, with a random sample of 85,145 adults, aged 18 and older, living in all 50 U.S. states and the District of Columbia.

For results based on the total sample of national adults, the margin of sampling error is ±1 percentage points at the 95% confidence level.

July 09, 2014
OBESITY LINKED TO LOWER SOCIAL WELL-BEING
Americans with high social well-being exercise more frequently

by Rebecca Riffkin

WASHINGTON, D.C.—Obese and underweight adults in the U.S. are somewhat less likely to be "thriving" socially and are more likely to be "suffering" than those who are normal weight or are overweight, but not obese.

State of Americans' Social Well-Being, by BMI Category

	% Thriving	% Struggling	% Suffering
Obese	36.5	45.2	18.4
Overweight	41.6	42.9	15.6
Normal weight	43.0	42.3	14.8
Underweight	39.3	41.2	19.5

Gallup-Healthways Well-Being Index
Jan. 1–June 23, 2014

GALLUP'

In fact, those who are obese are the least likely across all weight groups to be thriving socially and underweight individuals are the most likely to be suffering, underscoring the risk of being at either extreme of the weight spectrum when it comes to social well-being.

These data, collected Jan. 1–June 23, 2014, as part of the Gallup-Healthways Well-Being Index, are based on more than 80,000 interviews, with U.S. adults, aged 18 and older. The social well-being scores are based on respondents' answers to items about the strength of their relationship with their spouse, partner, or closest friend; positive energy gained from family and friends; making time for trips or vacations with family and friends; and having someone who encourages them to be healthy. Gallup then categorizes respondents as "thriving" (well-being that is strong and consistent), "struggling" (well-being that is moderate or inconsistent), or "suffering" (well-being that is low and inconsistent) in their social well-being.

Overall, 41% of Americans are thriving, with 43% struggling and 16% suffering in their social well-being. Gallup previously found that more Americans are thriving in social well-being than in the other four elements measured as part of the Gallup-Healthways Well-Being Index.

Body Mass Index (BMI) scores are based on respondents' self-reported height and weight. A BMI of 30 or greater is considered obese, 25.0 to 29.9 is overweight, 18.5 to 24.9 is normal weight, and less than 18.5 is underweight. The majority of Americans are either overweight (35.3%) or obese (27.7%), and just over a third of Americans (34.9%) are a normal weight. The current obesity rate is significantly higher than the 25.5% found in 2008, when Gallup and Healthways began tracking it. A small percentage of the population today, 2.1% vs 1.8% in 2008, is underweight.

Although these data reveal a clear link between extreme weight and lower social well-being, the direction of the relationship is unclear. It is possible that those who are obese or underweight are less likely to have strong social relationships. These Americans may lack self-confidence or be negatively stereotyped based on their weight, making it harder to form or maintain relationships. It is also possible, however, that Americans who are struggling in their relationships with their friends or family are more likely to either eat too much or too little, making it difficult to maintain a healthy weight. Those who lack social support may also have a harder time correcting their eating habits if they veer off course.

High Social Well-Being Linked to Frequent Exercise and Produce Consumption

One possible explanation for the link between weight and lower social well-being is that Americans who have higher social well-being are more likely to eat produce regularly and exercise frequently. Americans who are thriving in their social well-being are more likely to eat at least five servings of fruits and vegetables four or more days per week than are those who are suffering in social well-being, 66.4% vs. 44.3%, respectively.

The results are similar for Americans who exercise regularly. While 57.9% of Americans who are thriving in social well-being exercise at least 30 minutes on three or more days per week, 40.2% of those who are suffering socially say the same.

Again, the direction of these relationships are not clear. Americans who eat well and exercise more frequently may have an easier time developing close social relationships. Or those with high

social well-being may receive emotional and practical support that makes exercising and eating produce easier.

State of Americans' Social Well-Being and Healthy Habits

	Thriving	Struggling	Suffering
% Ate fruits and vegetables 0-3 days	32.5	44.2	54.5
% Ate fruits and vegetables 4-7 days	66.4	54.6	44.3
% Exercised 30+ minutes 0-2 days	41.5	50.4	59.1
% Exercised 30+ minutes 3-7 days	57.9	48.9	40.2

Gallup-Healthways Well-Being Index
Jan. 1-June 23, 2014

GALLUP'

Bottom Line

It is well known that obesity puts individuals at higher risk for chronic diseases such as high blood pressure, diabetes, and some cancers, but obesity also appears to be related to lower social well-being. It is not clear whether obesity leads to lower social well-being, or if low social well-being triggers lifestyle choices that lead to excessive weight gain. And the same issues and questions apply to underweight Americans.

Overweight Americans do not seem to suffer from lower social well-being, so whatever dynamic is at play—either weight hampering social relations, or subpar social relations triggering weight gain—is clearly specific to weight extremes.

Studies show that when someone gains weight, their close friends, regardless of whether they live close by, tend to gain weight also. Social networks and weight are clearly related, but how to harness this relationship and use it to help combat the rising obesity rate requires further research.

Survey Methods

Results are based on telephone interviews conducted as part of the Gallup-Healthways Well-Being Index survey Jan. 1–June 23, 2014, with a random sample of 84,890 adults, aged 18 and older, living in all 50 U.S. states and the District of Columbia.

For results based on the total sample of national adults, the margin of sampling error is ±1 percentage points at the 95% confidence level.

July 10, 2014
OLDER AMERICANS FEEL BEST ABOUT THEIR PHYSICAL APPEARANCE
Whites' satisfaction with their appearance erodes during middle age

by Justin McCarthy

WASHINGTON, D.C.—Though many may pine for the physical appearance they had in their younger years, America's seniors are the most confident in their looks. Two-thirds (66%) of Americans aged 65 and older "agreed" or "strongly agreed" that they always feel good about their physical appearance, compared with 61% of

18- to 34-year-olds. Middle-aged Americans (54%) are the least likely to report feeling good about their appearance.

Americans Who Always Feel Good About Their Physical Appearance, by Age

On a 5-point scale, where 5 means strongly agree and 1 means strongly disagree, please rate your level of agreement with the following item: You always feel good about your physical appearance.

	% Who rated 4 and 5
All ages	58
18-34 years	61
35-64 years	54
65+ years	66

Gallup-Healthways Well-Being Index
Jan. 1–June 23, 2014

GALLUP'

For both men and women, confidence in their physical appearance is lower in middle age than in young adulthood, yet gets higher during their senior years.

Americans' Perceptions of Their Physical Appearance, by Gender and Age

On a 5-point scale, where 5 means strongly agree and 1 means strongly disagree, please rate your level of agreement with the following item: You always feel good about your physical appearance.

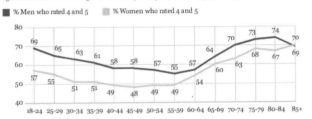

■ % Men who rated 4 and 5   ▨ % Women who rated 4 and 5

Gallup-Healthways Well-Being Index
Jan. 1–June 23, 2014

GALLUP'

At nearly every age level, men are more likely than women to feel good about their appearance, though this margin narrows among older age groups. More than two in three men aged 18–24 (69%) say they feel good about their physical appearance, compared with the 57% of women in the same age group—a 12-percentage-point gap. But by retirement age, the gap shrinks to a four-point difference: 64% of men feel good about their looks compared with 60% of women.

This analysis is based on more than 80,000 interviews with U.S. adults from Jan. 1–June 23, 2014, as part of the Gallup-Healthways Well-Being Index. Specifically, Americans are asked to rate their level of agreement with the statement, "I always feel good about my physical appearance," on a five-point scale where five means strongly agree and one means strongly disagree. Overall, more than half of Americans, 58%, agreed that they always feel good about their looks, answering with a four or five. Far fewer disagreed that they always feel good about their appearance, with 15% answering with a one or two. About one in four Americans (27%) neither agreed nor disagreed, responding with a three.

Blacks and Hispanics More Confident Than Whites in Physical Appearance

Blacks and Hispanics are much more likely than whites and, to a lesser extent, Asians to say they always feel good about their

appearance. More than two-thirds of blacks (68%) and Hispanics (67%) report that they are confident in their physical appearance compared with 55% of whites and 62% of Asians.

These patterns by race and ethnicity hold true across most age categories, except that middle-aged blacks and Hispanics are just as happy with their appearance as are middle-aged Asians.

Americans Who Always Feel Good About Their Physical Appearance, by Race and Age

On a 5-point scale, where 5 means strongly agree and 1 means strongly disagree, please rate your level of agreement with the following item: You always feel good about your physical appearance.

	% Whites who rated 4 and 5	% Blacks who rated 4 and 5	% Asians who rated 4 and 5	% Hispanics who rated 4 and 5
	%	%	%	%
All ages	55	68	62	67
18-34 years	56	68	60	67
35-64 years	49	65	65	67
65+ years	65	75	70	75

Gallup-Healthways Well-Being Index
Jan. 1–June 23, 2014

GALLUP'

Additionally, only whites' confidence in their appearance drops sharply in middle age. Blacks, Asians, and Hispanics all maintain their positive perspective on their physical appearance through middle age, and then become even more confident in their golden years.

Bottom Line

Americans' concern about their physical appearance fuels a huge component of the U.S. economy, extending across clothing, makeup, hair care, weight control, and cosmetic surgery industries. This concern about physical appearance is not totally ill founded, given that research studies show that attractive people fare better than those perceived as less attractive in many business and social situations.

One's concern about their appearance is clearly rooted in a combination of subjective and objective factors, and thus it differs according to a variety of demographic and cultural variances, including gender, age, and racial and ethnic background.

Additionally, as people age, perhaps a different set of societal expectations and appearance standards lead to a renewed sense of confidence. In an image-conscious society where beautiful men and women flood the screens and pages of Americans' various mediums, it isn't surprising that many are left feeling inadequate. For whites, who are the least likely to feel confident in their physical appearance across all age groups, societal pressure to conform to conventional standards of physical attractiveness takes an even bigger toll.

This study did not include a measure of the actual physical attractiveness of the respondents, so there is no way to judge the relationship between Americans' confidence in their physical appearance and how others regard them. However, older Americans' looks are generally out of sync with the youthful standard of beauty that prevails in American culture, and yet they are most happy with what they see in the mirror. Perhaps it will come as a relief to many who toil over minute details of their appearance that they could become happier with their looks in years to come.

Survey Methods

Results are based on telephone interviews conducted as part of the Gallup-Healthways Well-Being Index survey Jan. 1–June 23, 2014, with a random sample of 85,145 adults, aged 18 and older, living in all 50 U.S. states and the District of Columbia.

For results based on the total sample of national adults, the margin of sampling error is ±.39 percentage points at the 95% confidence level. Sample sizes for reported sub-groups, however, get smaller and the margin of error can get much higher. The smallest sub-group (Asians 65+) is comprised of 130 respondents, and carries a margin of error of ±10.5%.

July 10, 2014

IN U.S., UNINSURED RATE SINKS TO 13.4% IN SECOND QUARTER

Significant decline in uninsured rate across age groups since the end of 2013

by Jenna Levy

WASHINGTON, D.C.—The uninsured rate in the U.S. fell 2.2 percentage points to 13.4% in the second quarter of 2014. This is the lowest quarterly average recorded since Gallup and Healthways began tracking the percentage of uninsured Americans in 2008. The previous low point was 14.4% in the third quarter of 2008.

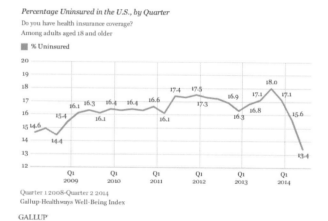

Percentage Uninsured in the U.S., by Quarter
Do you have health insurance coverage?
Among adults aged 18 and older

Quarter 1 2008-Quarter 2 2014
Gallup-Healthways Well-Being Index

GALLUP

The uninsured rate has decreased sharply since the Affordable Care Act's requirement for most Americans to have health insurance went into effect at the beginning of 2014. In fact, the uninsured rate has dropped by 3.7 points since the fourth quarter of 2013, when it averaged 17.1%.

The decline in the uninsured rate last quarter took place at the start of the quarter. The drop reflected a surge of health plan enrollees in early April, prior to the April 15 extended enrollment deadline for people who had previously experienced technical difficulties with the federal healthcare exchange website. In April and May, the uninsured rate hovered at 13.4%, and it remained at that level in June—clearly indicating that the decline seen since late 2013 has leveled off.

The second-quarter results are based on more than 45,000 interviews with U.S. adults from April 1 to June 30, 2014, as part of the Gallup-Healthways Well-Being Index.

Uninsured Rate Continues to Drop Across Age Groups

Gallup's quarterly trends show that the uninsured rate dropped by about three points from the fourth quarter of 2013 among each

major age group under 65. The uninsured rate in the second quarter averaged 18.7% among 18- to 25-year-olds, 23.9% among 26- to 34-year-olds, and 13.4% among 35- to 64-year-olds.

Given the availability of Medicare and Medicaid benefits, very few seniors report being without health insurance, although the uninsured rate among those 65 and older is now 2.0%, down from 2.8% in the third quarter of 2013.

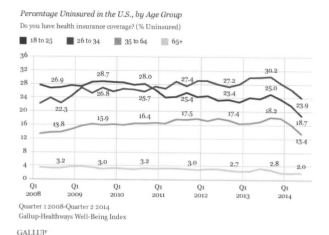

Percentage Uninsured in the U.S., by Age Group
Do you have health insurance coverage? (% Uninsured)

■ 18 to 25   ■ 26 to 34   ■ 35 to 64   ■ 65+

Quarter 1 2008-Quarter 2 2014
Gallup-Healthways Well-Being Index

GALLUP

More 18- to 64-Year-Olds Have Self-Funded Insurance Now Than in 2013

While 18- to 64-year-olds are most likely to have health insurance through a current or former employer (43.5%), more reported having self-funded insurance coverage in the second quarter than did before the healthcare exchanges opened in October 2013. For Americans younger than 65, 20.7% say they have a health insurance plan they or a family member pays for, compared with 16.7% in August–September 2013.

There has also been a slight increase in the percentage who have Medicaid insurance, perhaps because a provision of the 2010 healthcare law expanded the qualifying income levels for Medicaid. Thus, the reduction in the percentage of uninsured Americans has been accompanied by increases in the percentages who now have Medicaid or self-funded insurance, through a government exchange or on their own.

Type of Health Insurance Coverage in the U.S.
Is your insurance coverage through a current or former employer, a union, Medicare, Medicaid, military or veteran's coverage, or a plan fully paid for by you or a family member?
Among 18- to 64-year-olds

	Aug-Sept 2013 %	Quarter 4 2013 %	Quarter 1 2014 %	Quarter 2 2014 %
Current or former employer	44.4	44.2	42.5	43.5
Plan paid by self or family member	16.7	17.6	19.3	20.7
Medicaid	6.8	6.9	7.9	8.4
Medicare	6.4	6.1	6.3	6.9
Military or veteran's coverage	4.3	4.6	4.8	4.7
Union	2.8	2.5	2.6	2.5
(Something else)	3.8	3.5	3.7	3.8
(No insurance)	21.2	20.8	19.0	16.2

Gallup-Healthways Well-Being Index

GALLUP

Gallup and Healthways began asking about insurance types using the current question wording in August 2013. Respondents are asked, "Is your primary health insurance coverage through a current or former employer, a union, Medicare, Medicaid, military or veteran's coverage, or a plan fully paid for by you or a family member?" Respondents who say they have a secondary form of health insurance are also asked, "Thinking about this secondary health insurance coverage, is it through a current or former employer, a union, Medicare, Medicaid, military or veteran's coverage, or a plan fully paid for by you or a family member?" The results reported here are a combined estimate of primary and secondary insurance types.

Implications

The uninsured rate fell 2.2 points in the second quarter, evidently due to a surge in the percentage of Americans who completed their enrollment in healthcare plans just before the mid-April deadline. The uninsured rate has since been flat at about 13.4%, suggesting that there won't be further reductions in the rate until after the open enrollment period for 2015 begins on Nov. 15. And although Medicaid has added to the increase in health insurance coverage as more states have adopted expansion provisions over the past few months, it remains unclear how many Americans were previously insured and moved to Medicaid to reduce costs.

Throughout the enrollment period for 2014, the Obama administration increased outreach efforts to young Americans, including 26- to 34-year-olds, and Hispanics. It is likely these groups will be targeted again in the months leading up to the enrollment period for 2015 as they are the subgroups with the highest uninsured rates.

Survey Methods

Results are based on telephone interviews conducted as part of the Gallup-Healthways Well-Being Index survey April 1–June 30, 2014, with a random sample of 45,125 adults, aged 18 and older, living in all 50 U.S. states and the District of Columbia.

For results based on the total sample of national adults, the margin of sampling error is ±1 percentage point at the 95% confidence level.

July 10, 2014
PARTY IDENTIFICATION VARIES WIDELY ACROSS THE AGE SPECTRUM
Young Americans lean Democratic, independent as well

by Frank Newport

PRINCETON, NJ—Young Americans in their 20s and 30s today share two important political characteristics—they are the most likely of any age group to eschew identification with either party, and, among those who do have a political identity, they are the most likely, along with older baby boomers, to tilt toward the Democratic Party.

Americans aged 18 to 40 are least likely to identify with a party or even lean toward one, with almost one out of five falling into that category. At the same time, among those who do identify with or lean toward one of the two major parties, there is a double-digit Democratic advantage among those at each age point from 18 to 35. These are in fact the only ages—across the entire age spectrum—at which Democrats hold a 10-point or higher advantage.

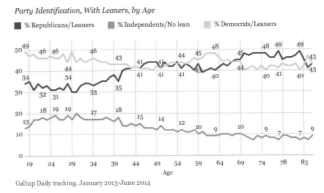

Party Identification, With Leaners, by Age

■ % Republicans/Leaners   ▓ % Independents/No lean   ░ % Democrats/Leaners

Gallup Daily tracking, January 2013-June 2014

GALLUP

These results represent both good news and bad news for Democrats. While Democrats enjoy a decided advantage in partisan identification among today's young adults, the higher percentages who don't identify with or even lean toward a party are symptomatic of young Americans' distance from the political system. This, in turn, reflects the political reality that this group is less likely than older age groups to vote. Additionally, while Democrats have a decided identification advantage among those younger than 40, it is hardly monolithic, given that more than 30% of the group identifies with or leans toward the Republican Party.

These findings are based on more than 267,000 interviews conducted as part of Gallup's Daily tracking from January 2013 through June 2014, using Gallup's standard party identification question: "In politics, as of today, do you consider yourself a Republican, a Democrat [order rotated], or an independent?" Those who initially identify as independents are subsequently asked if they lean toward either party, and the combined party preferences, including "leaners," are presented in the first graph.

A Gallup analysis from earlier this year demonstrated how different age groups have, over time, shifted in their political party preferences. The 2013–2014 data analyzed here allow for a more fine-grained analysis of current party affiliation at each individual age. A Gallup report on 2009 data by age showed broadly similar patterns, although the overall population at that point was significantly more Democratic in orientation.

There is no sign of a pending reduction in Democratic strength among even the very youngest adult Americans. Those 18 and 19 years of age, many of whom may still be living at home, are slightly more likely to identify with or lean toward one of the two major parties than those between 20 and 30 years of age. But among those 20 to 30, the Democratic tilt is fairly consistent.

As noted in previous Gallup research, Democrats also perform relatively well among baby boomers aged 60 to 63. Democrats have a seven- to eight-percentage-point average advantage among this group of Americans who were born between about 1950 and 1953, and who came of age during the late 1960s and early 1970s. The Democratic Party does slightly less well among younger baby boomers, those aged 57 to 59, while the oldest baby boomers, aged 64 to 67, are much less Democratic than other boomers in their party identification.

Republicans Do Best Among Middle-Aged and Older Americans

Republicans do best among two age segments, the first of which is Americans aged 43 to 56—among whom the GOP has a slight edge, breaks even, or is at only a slight disadvantage compared with Democrats. These Americans were born between 1957 and 1970, and straddle the Gen X and the baby boomer generations. The second area of relative GOP strength is among Americans 69 and older, with the exception of a Democratic tilt among 84-year-old Americans. Although not represented on the accompanying graphs because of low sample sizes, Democrats do better as a rule among the smaller segments of Americans aged 86 and up into their 90s.

The GOP edge among seniors is not as pronounced as is the Democratic edge among young Americans, and at no point across the entire age spectrum do Republicans enjoy a double-digit party identification advantage. However, seniors are the most likely to turn out and vote in elections, meaning the modest Republican advantage among older Americans translates into disproportionate power at the ballot box.

The Partisan Gap Reflects Varied Political Sensibilities

A broad portrait of the political shape of today's electorate is provided in the accompanying graph, which summarizes the party identification gap at each age point from 18 to 85. Democrats' decided youth advantage begins to erode as Americans enter their late 30s and 40s, picks up again (though to a lesser extent) among Americans in their 50s and early 60s, and then erodes further among those in their mid-60s and older.

Partisan Gap by Age

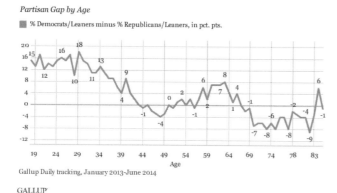

Gallup Daily tracking, January 2013-June 2014

GALLUP

Almost Half of Young Americans Initially Identify as Independents

The party identification results reviewed above are based on the combined percentages who identify with a party and those who initially claim to be independent but lean toward either party when probed. The results of the initial party identification question—before independents are probed as to their leanings—are presented in the next graph. The results provide an insight into those who can be classified as "core" Republicans (those who initially identify themselves as Republicans), "core" Democrats (those who initially identify themselves as Democrats) and those who identify themselves as independents in the initial question, even if many of these later indicate they lean to a particular party.

These results highlight, again, the political detachment of the younger generation, with almost half of the very youngest initially identifying themselves as independents. The percentage of Americans who are independent drops at a remarkably steady rate across the entire age spectrum.

Party Identification by Age

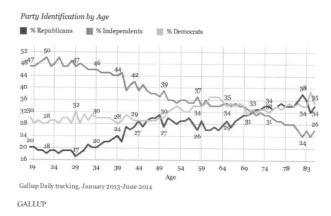

Gallup Daily tracking, January 2013-June 2014

GALLUP

The percentage of the population who are core Democrats and core Republicans generally reflects the patterns seen previously when leaners are taken into account. Republican identification is low among young Americans, rises somewhat among middle-aged Americans, and rises again among Americans who are 70 and older. The representation of those who identify as a core Democrat is more stable across age, reaching a slightly higher point among older baby boomers and among a smaller segment of Americans in their mid-80s.

Implications

Democrats have a general advantage in American politics today, with 44% of American adults interviewed in 2013 and the first half of 2014 identifying with or leaning toward the Democratic Party, contrasted with 39% who identify with or lean toward the Republican Party. These overall numbers, however, mask highly important differences across the age spectrum. Young Americans are more detached from the political system in general, but still tilt strongly toward the Democratic Party, particularly when those who initially identify as independents are asked to which party they lean. Middle-aged Americans from about 40 to their mid-50s are more Republican in their political leanings, while older baby boomers tilt back toward a Democratic political orientation. Finally, seniors in today's world for the most part constitute Republicans' strongest age group.

Survey Methods

Results for this Gallup poll are based on telephone interviews conducted Jan. 2, 2013–June 30, 2014, on the Gallup Daily tracking survey, with a random sample of 267,321 adults, aged 18 and older, living in all 50 U.S. states and the District of Columbia.

For results based on the total sample of national adults, the margin of sampling error is ±1 percentage point at the 95% confidence level.

The margin of sampling error for the samples of those at each age varies depending on the sample size, which varies from a high of 6,583 of those aged 65, to a low of 1,749 of those aged 85, but in all instances is no more than ±3 percentage points at the 95% confidence level.

July 11, 2014
U.S. MUSLIMS MOST APPROVING OF OBAMA, MORMONS LEAST
Relative rank order of religious groups stable throughout his presidency

by Jeffrey M. Jones

PRINCETON, NJ—Seventy-two percent of U.S. Muslims approved of the job President Barack Obama was doing as president during the first six months of 2014, higher than any other U.S. religious group Gallup tracks. Mormons were least approving, at 18%. In general, majorities of those in non-Christian religions—including those who do not affiliate with any religion—approved of Obama, while less than a majority of those in the three major Christian religious groups did.

Obama Job Approval, by Religion

January-June 2014 Gallup Daily tracking

	Approve	Disapprove
	%	%
Muslim	72	20
Other non-Christian	59	34
Jewish	55	41
No religion/Atheist	54	38
Catholic	44	51
Protestant/Other Christian	37	58
Mormon/Latter-day Saints	18	78

GALLUP

The results are based on aggregated data from more than 88,000 Gallup Daily tracking interviews conducted in the first six months of 2014—a time when the president averaged 43% job approval among all Americans. Gallup interviewed 552 Muslims and at least 1,700 respondents in every other religious group during this time.

The United States remains a predominantly Christian nation, with roughly half of Americans identifying with a Protestant religion and another quarter identifying as Catholics. Thus, the opinions of these Christian groups are by far the most influential in determining Obama's overall ratings.

The relative rank order of the religious groups on job approval has been consistent throughout Obama's presidency. In fact, the current rank order, with Muslims most approving and Mormons least, exactly matches the order seen over the more than five years he has been in office since January 2009.

Comparison of President Obama's January-June 2014 Job Approval to His Presidency's Average, by Religion

	% Approve, January 2009-June 2014	% Approve, January-June 2014	Difference (pct. pts.)
All Americans	48	43	-5
Muslim	77	72	-5
Other non-Christian	64	59	-5
Jewish	62	55	-7
No religion/Atheist	60	54	-6
Catholic	50	44	-6
Protestant/Other Christian	43	37	-6
Mormon/Latter-day Saints	25	18	-7

Gallup Daily tracking

GALLUP

Moreover, current job approval among each religious subgroup is between five and seven percentage points lower than the full 2009–2014 average for each. Obama's current 43% overall job approval average is five points lower than his 48% average so far in his presidency.

In general, when Obama's approval rating has dropped among all Americans, his approval rating in each religious subgroup has dropped by a similar amount. The accompanying graph shows how Obama's average approval rating among Protestants, Catholics, and Mormons has compared with the average among all Americans over time. Because the movement in each religious group has shadowed the national movement, Mormons have been least approving of Obama in each time period. Protestants have been consistently below the national average, and Catholics slightly above it.

Trend in President Obama Approval Among Protestants, Catholics, and Mormons

% Approve

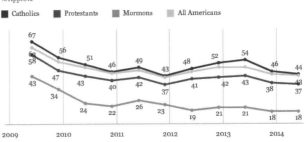

Gallup Daily tracking; figures are half-year averages

GALLUP

Similarly, Muslims have been the most approving among the religious groups in each time period. Jewish Americans and Americans with no religious preference have also exceeded the national average job approval in each time period, tracking each other closely.

Trend in President Obama Approval Among Muslims, Jews, and Those With No Religious Affiliation

% Approve

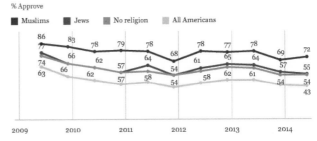

Gallup Daily tracking; figures are half-year averages

GALLUP

Implications

The patterns in Obama's job approval by religion have prevailed throughout his presidency, with Muslim, Jewish, and nonreligious Americans giving him higher ratings, and Mormons and Protestants giving him the lowest ratings. Catholics have typically been closest to the national average, but slightly above it.

As Obama's overall job approval rating has had its ups and downs over the five-plus years he has been president, his ratings among religious groups have moved in tandem. That is, Americans of various faiths seem to react similarly to the factors that cause the president's popularity to wax and wane, rather than reacting in idiosyncratic ways tied to their religious beliefs.

Clearly, members of various religions view the president quite differently, but this may be attributable more to whether Obama's Democratic affiliation matches the political leanings of each religious group, and less to the specific policies and actions he has taken throughout his presidency.

Survey Methods

Results for this Gallup poll are based on telephone interviews conducted January–June 2014, on the Gallup Daily tracking survey, with a random sample of 88,801 adults, aged 18 and older, living in all 50 U.S. states and the District of Columbia.

For results based on the total sample of national adults, the margin of sampling error is ±1 percentage point at the 95% confidence level.

Results for religious subgroups are based on the following sample sizes and margins of error:

Sample Sizes and Margins of Error for Religious Groups

	N	Margin of error
Protestant/Other Christian	46,202	±1 pct. pt.
Catholic	20,326	±1 pct. pt.
Mormon	1,724	±3 pct. pts.
Jewish	2,059	±3 pct. pts.
Muslim	552	±6 pct. pts.
Other non-Christian	2,205	±3 pct. pts.
None/Atheist/Agnostic/No response	15,733	±1 pct. pt.

January–June 2014 Gallup Daily tracking

GALLUP'

Recession and still reeling from a stagnant economy. This is the first time Gallup has measured household spending in this way, so it is unclear whether the current patterns are typical, or if the results on discretionary spending are better now than during the recession. Gallup's daily measure of consumer spending has been significantly higher the last two years than in 2009 through 2011—although this could be partly the result of higher spending on essentials.

The Items Americans Spend Money on, Summer 2014

	% Spending more	% Spending about the same	% Spending less	Net spending more (% more minus % less)
Groceries	59	31	10	49
Gasoline or fuel	58	27	12	46
Utilities	45	44	10	35
Healthcare	42	45	8	34
Household goods such as toilet paper or cleaning supplies	32	63	5	27
Rent or mortgage	32	55	9	23
Telephone services	32	55	11	21
Personal care such as toothpaste or cosmetics	26	67	7	19
Cable or satellite	33	44	15	18
Home maintenance	32	48	16	16
Internet	21	57	8	13
Automotive expenses not including gas	27	51	15	12
Retirement investments	18	49	17	1
Leisure activities	28	37	31	-3
Clothing	25	44	30	-5
Consumer electronics	20	41	31	-11
Travel	26	27	38	-12
Dining out	26	31	38	-12

Gallup poll, June 9-15, 2014

GALLUP'

Americans Traveling More This Summer, Especially Since Recession

Americans' summer travel plans clearly demonstrate the tension between increased spending on essentials and reduced spending on discretionary items. While substantially more Americans say they are traveling this summer (69%) than said so in 2009 during the Great Recession (52%), over one-third of travelers plan to travel less (36%) than last year. This is roughly comparable to Gallup's findings in the summers of 2010 and 2011 (33% and 35%, respectively).

Americans' Summer Travel Plans

Are you planning to travel this summer?

	% Planning to travel
2014	69
2009	52
2008	59
2006	62

GALLUP'

Also, many travelers plan to stay close to home: More than two-thirds of those traveling this summer intend to take a trip longer than an overnight trip. Among those, most will travel by car (81%), whereas slightly less than half will take at least one trip by air

July 11, 2014
CONSUMERS SPENDING MORE, JUST NOT ON THINGS THEY WANT
Groceries, gasoline top list; leisure, travel, dining out at bottom

by John Fleming

PRINCETON, NJ—Slightly less than half of all Americans (45%) report spending more than they did a year ago, while 18% report spending less. A closer look at these numbers reveals Americans' increased spending is on household essentials, such as groceries, gasoline, utilities, and healthcare, rather than on discretionary purchases.

At the other end of the spectrum, roughly one-third of Americans report spending less on discretionary items such as travel (38%), dining out (38%), leisure activities (31%), consumer electronics (31%), and clothing (30%). More than half of Americans say they are spending about the same for rent or mortgage, household goods, telephone, automobile expenses other than fuel, personal care products, and the Internet.

All of this suggests that the increasing cost of essential items is further constraining family budgets already hit hard by the Great

(47%). Less than 10% intend to travel by bus or train this summer. Slightly more than half expect both transportation and non-transport expenses for their summer trips to cost more this year than last.

In U.S., Methods of Summer Trips or Vacations, Summer 2014

How are you traveling on vacation this summer?

	% Yes	% No
Your own vehicle	81	19
Airplane	47	52
Rental car vehicle	29	71
Boat or ship	12	88
Train	9	90
Bus or motor coach	9	91

Gallup poll, June 9-15, 2014

GALLUP

Implications

These results paint a picture of consumers straining against rising prices on daily essentials to afford summer travel, dining out, and discretionary household purchases—the kinds of purchases that ordinarily keep an economy humming. And while the two-thirds of Americans who plan to travel this summer is the highest level Gallup has measured since 2006, nearly one-third plan to spend just one night or less away from home, meaning it is not much of a vacation.

Those who do intend to travel this summer expect to spend more in all travel categories—transportation, food, lodging, and entertainment—than last year, further pressuring their already strained budgets. Most will take their own cars despite relatively high gas prices. If there was any doubt that the U.S. economy is still struggling to get back on its feet, the results of this poll reinforce that reality. Because consumer spending is the lifeblood of a healthy economy, these findings suggest that discretionary spending still has a ways to go before it will fuel the kind of economic growth Americans have been hoping for.

Survey Methods

Results for this Gallup poll are based on telephone interviews conducted June 9–15, 2014, on the Gallup Daily tracking survey, with a random sample of 1,029 adults, aged 18 and older, living in all 50 U.S. states and the District of Columbia.

For results based on the total sample of national adults, the margin of sampling error is ±4 percentage points at the 95% confidence level.

July 14, 2014
AMERICANS' APPROVAL OF THE SUPREME COURT REMAINS DIVIDED
Approval among Republicans up 21 percentage points from 2013

by Rebecca Riffkin

WASHINGTON, D.C.—Americans remain divided in their assessments of the U.S. Supreme Court, with 47% approving of the job it is doing, and 46% disapproving. These ratings are consistent with approval last September, when 46% approved and 45% disapproved, and rank among the lowest approval ratings for the court in Gallup's 14-year trend.

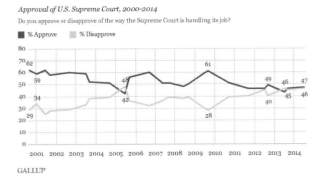

Approval of U.S. Supreme Court, 2000-2014

Do you approve or disapprove of the way the Supreme Court is handling its job?

GALLUP

Since Gallup began asking the question in 2000, Americans have typically been more likely to approve than to disapprove of the job the Supreme Court is doing. However, the margin between the two has been narrowing since its recent high point in 2009, and Americans were divided over the court in 2012 and again in 2013. Separate polling found that confidence in the Supreme Court also fell to record lows this year, as Americans' confidence in all three branches of government is down.

The current approval ratings were measured July 7–10, after a controversial 2013–2014 term. Several recent court decisions allowed prayers in city council meetings; determined that the buffer zones around abortion and contraception medical centers in Massachusetts were too large and hampered free speech; said a public union could not force home-care workers to join the union and pay dues; and, perhaps the most well known, permitted family-owned businesses (in a suit brought by Hobby Lobby) to opt out of providing certain types of contraceptive coverage for employees if doing so was in conflict with the owners' religious beliefs.

Republican Approval for the Supreme Court Increases

Republican approval of the Supreme Court is up 21 percentage points since last September, from 30% in 2013 to 51%. Independents' approval shows little change, going from 47% to 46%. Support among Democrats, on the other hand, is down. In September, Democrats were the most approving group, at 58%, while in the current survey their approval is as low as independents', at 44%. Democrats are now slightly more likely to disapprove (50%) than approve (44%).

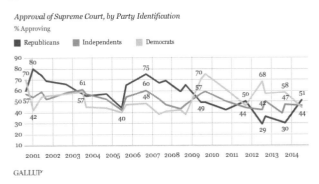

Approval of Supreme Court, by Party Identification

% Approving

GALLUP

Support among Republicans may have increased this year in response to the court's 5–4 decision in Hobby Lobby's favor. At the same time, that decision likely cost the court some support from Democrats. Democratic leaders in Congress have expressed public disagreement with this ruling and are trying to pass a bill to override it.

Prominent Supreme Court decisions have led to changes in approval by party in the past. For example, in early 2001, just weeks after the *Bush v. Gore* decision effectively made George W. Bush the winner of the 2000 presidential election, Republican approval of the high court reached 80%. In 2012, after a landmark decision about the Affordable Care Act, support among Democrats increased to 68%, close to a record high among that group.

Bottom Line

Americans remain split on the job the Supreme Court is doing, and the current approval rating is on the low end of what Gallup has measured since it began asking the question in 2000. The biggest change in Americans' views of the court this year has been the flip in partisan approval.

Controversial decisions since 2012 have resulted in dramatic changes in views of the court among Americans of different party affiliations. However, this term, nearly two-thirds of the court's decisions were unanimous, in contrast to the 5-4 split in the two high-profile cases at the end. Americans' current views more closely reflect the court's own ideological divisions in these two recent decisions, rather than its bipartisan unanimity.

Survey Methods

Results for this Gallup poll are based on telephone interviews conducted July 7–10, 2014, on the Gallup Daily tracking survey, with a random sample of 1,013 adults, aged 18 and older, living in all 50 U.S. states and the District of Columbia.

For results based on the total sample of national adults, the margin of sampling error is ±4 percentage points at the 95% confidence level.

July 15, 2014
CONGRESSIONAL APPROVAL RATING LANGUISHES AT LOW LEVEL
More than one in five say replacing all members is best way to fix it

by Andrew Dugan

WASHINGTON, D.C.—Fifteen percent of Americans approve of the way Congress is handling its job. Congressional ratings show little sign of substantial recovery from last year's record low as November's midterm elections draw closer.

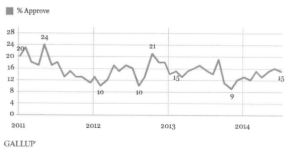

Do you approve or disapprove of the way Congress is handling its job?
Recent trend
■ % Approve

These findings come from a July 7–10 Gallup poll, with this most recent reading virtually unchanged from June's 16% approval. The stability in this metric—it has not fluctuated much over the course of this year—suggests that the 435 House members and one-third of the Senate who face re-election could do so amid the lowest congressional approval ratings for a midterm election in modern political history. Gallup historically has found that low congressional approval ratings are associated with higher congressional turnover.

The current divided control of Congress complicates the picture, however. In one sense, divided control has contributed to Congress's sickly approval ratings, as it denies the Hill the usual reservoir of partisan support that traditionally comes with one-party control. Republicans and Democrats approve of Congress at similarly (low) levels—17% and 16%, respectively. Congress is, as Gallup Senior Editor Jeff Jones put it, a "political orphan" that neither Republicans nor Democrats will adopt as their own.

The divided control of Congress combined with Americans' bipartisan disapproval portend an electoral outcome that may not be as straightforward as was true in previous midterms when the party in control of both houses was electorally routed, as in 1994, 2006, and 2010. The historical record offers few data points to consult on this matter. In post–World War II politics, there have been three midterm elections featuring a divided Congress: 1982, 1986, and 2002. In two of these instances, the party controlling the House won the keys to the Senate, but in 1986 this was a blow to the sitting president, and in 2002 it was a boon. In 1982, there was no change in party control of Congress after the elections. The 1986 example is probably the most germane to today's situation: It saw a sixth-year president (Ronald Reagan) trying to keep his party in power in the Senate, to no avail.

Public Ready to Start Over to Fix Congress

Congress's low approval ratings for the past several years underscore the idea that Americans think their representative bodies need dramatic changes. Gallup in the current poll asked respondents in an open-ended format what their most important recommendation to fix Congress would be. More than one in five Americans (22%) are ready to start over entirely, saying all members should be fired or replaced. Clearly, there won't be a wholesale turnover in congressional representation in any election, but the general idea of replacing the old with the new does speak to the public's immense frustration with the legislative branch.

One in seven (14%) say bipartisan cooperation is the ticket to fixing Congress. About one in 10 (9%) want to "make members accountable to people, not their own agendas," an umbrella category that includes specific reforms such as limiting the number of recesses Congress takes, ending gerrymandering, or requiring balanced budgets. Another 11% favor enacting term limits or shorter terms, an action Congress could take if it were willing. A bill has been introduced this legislative session that would amend the Constitution to impose on legislators a 12-year limit for serving in the House and an additional 12 years for the Senate. Gallup found several other items receiving smaller levels of support, including "regulate campaign finance laws" (3%), "elect more Democrats" (2%), and "get rid of President Obama" (1%).

Still, for some Americans, the remedy is elusive—16% have no opinion on how to fix Congress, and another 3% say "nothing."

Americans on How to Fix Congress

What is the most important thing you would recommend be done to fix Congress? [OPEN-ENDED]

	%
Fire/Replace all members/Get all new people	22
More bipartisan cooperation/Work together/Get along better	14
Term limits/Shorten terms	11
Make members accountable to people, not their own agendas	9
Regulate campaign finances/Limit special interest contributions	3
Follow the Constitution/Live by the rules	3
Reduce influence of parties/Get a third party/More independents	3
Change the benefit/pay structure	2
Elect more Democrats	2
Elect more Republicans	1
Get rid of President Obama	1
Other	10
Nothing	3
No opinion	16

Based on a half sample
July 7-10, 2014

GALLUP

Americans who say they affiliate with one of the two major political parties have somewhat differing perspectives on the best recourse to rehabilitating Congress. A plurality of Republicans (21%) want to fire all members, and another 18% would impose term limits and/or shorten terms. Fewer than one in 10 Republicans (8%) suggest bipartisan cooperation.

How to Fix Congress, Top Recommendations by Party Identification

% of Republicans and Democrats recommending each item

	% Mentioning, Republicans		% Mentioning, Democrats
Fire them all/ Get rid of all of them	21	More bipartisan cooperation/Work together/Get along better	25
Term limits/Shorten terms	18	Fire them all/ Get rid of all of them	17
Don't know	17	Make them accountable to constituents/Not have their own agendas	15
More bipartisan cooperation/Work together/Get along better	8	Don't know	12
Make them accountable to constituents/Not have their own agendas	7	Other	7

July 7-10, 2014

GALLUP

The highest percentage of Democrats, on the other hand, advocates bipartisan cooperation (25%) as the remedy for Congress's ills. Seventeen percent want to fire or replace all members; 15% believe it is important to make members more accountable to people, instead of having their own agendas.

Bottom Line

With less than four months remaining before the 2014 midterms, the parties in control of each chamber are pushing through legislative priorities their base supports. These include the House Republican leadership's announcement that it will pursue a bill that would initiate a lawsuit against President Barack Obama. Meanwhile, Senate Majority Leader Harry Reid has said he would like to see his chamber pass legislation that reverses the Supreme Court's recent decision allowing "closely held" corporations to refuse to provide some types of contraceptive coverage to their employees, an action that could boost Democratic enthusiasm for the coming elections.

But while these moves may fire up partisans, only 15% of Americans overall approve of the job Congress is doing, including

about equal shares of Democrats and Republicans. That so many advocate voting into office a completely new Congress is perhaps a sign of anti-incumbency fervor. Others want to see bipartisan cooperation take over the Hill, an unlikely event as election-year agendas become front and center. This mixture of disapproval and disappointment that so many Americans feel toward Congress could produce unpredictable results this fall.

Survey Methods

Results for this Gallup poll are based on telephone interviews conducted July 7–10, 2014, on the Gallup Daily tracking survey, with a random sample of 1,013 adults, aged 18 and older, living in all 50 U.S. states and the District of Columbia.

For results based on the total sample of national adults, the margin of sampling error is ±4 percentage points at the 95% confidence level.

For results based on the sample of 494 national adults in Form A, the margin of sampling error is ±6 percentage points.

July 16, 2014
ONE IN SIX SAY IMMIGRATION MOST IMPORTANT U.S. PROBLEM
Immigration concerns surged in July, while economic mentions ebbed

by Lydia Saad

PRINCETON, NJ—With thousands of undocumented immigrant minors crossing the nation's southern border in recent months, the percentage of Americans citing immigration as the top problem has surged to 17% this month, up from 5% in June, and the highest seen since 2006. As a result, immigration now virtually ties "dissatisfaction with government," at 16%, as the primary issue Americans think of when asked to name the country's top problem.

Percentage Naming Immigration as the United States' Most Important Problem

Based on U.S. adults

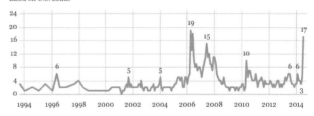

GALLUP

This is not the first time that immigration has spiked in the public's consciousness. Most recently, Gallup found the issue increasing to 10% in 2010, at a time when a new immigration law in Arizona was making news. And prior to that, it increased twice in 2006 to 15% or higher, amid congressional debate over immigration reform.

Signaling that public mentions of immigration today could be stemming more from concern about illegal immigration than from support for immigration reform, mentions of the issue are significantly higher among Republicans (23%) than Democrats (11%). Gallup polling earlier this year showed Republicans with a preference for focusing on sealing the border, while Democrats prioritized addressing the status of illegal immigrants already here.

Additionally, older Americans are more likely than those younger than 50 to name immigration as the top issue. Regionally, concern is highest in the West.

The Economy Still Ranks High

The economy and unemployment rank just below immigration and dissatisfaction with government in perceived importance, at 15% and 14%, respectively. However, no other issue reaches double-digit concern this month. This includes healthcare, which declined by half as a perceived top problem since the open-enrollment period to buy health insurance through health exchanges (and the associated press coverage of the enrollment process) ended in April. Gallup's monthly trend shows mentions of healthcare dropping from 16% in January and 15% in April to 11% in May, 10% in June, and 8% today.

U.S. Most Important Problem -- Recent Selected Trend

What do you think is the most important problem facing this country today? ^

	July 2014	June 2014	January 2014
	%	%	%
Immigration/Illegal aliens	17	5	3
Dissatisfaction with government/Congress/politicians; Poor leadership/Corruption/Abuse of power	16	19	21
Economy in general	15	20	18
Unemployment/Jobs	14	16	16
Poor healthcare/hospitals; High cost of healthcare	8	10	16
Federal budget deficit/Federal debt	6	5	8
Education/Poor education/Access to education	5	4	4
Ethics/moral/religious/family decline; Dishonesty	4	7	5
Poverty/ Hunger/Homelessness	3	2	4
Foreign aid/Focus overseas	3	3	3
Judicial system/Courts/Laws	3	2	1
Lack of money	2	2	4
Taxes	2	1	1
Wage issues	2	1	1
Crime/Violence	2	3	1
Race relations/Racism	2	1	1
Lack of respect for each other	2	2	2

Problems mentioned by at least 2% of Americans; for full results see survey methodology.

GALLUP

Overall mentions of the economy also have been eased in 2014, driven by modest drops in those citing unemployment/jobs and "the economy," generally. As a result, the percentage of Americans naming at least one economic problem—what Gallup terms "net economic mentions"—is now 41%, down from 53% in February, and well below the recent high of 76% seen in late 2011. This is also the lowest net economic mentions has been since January 2008.

Net Mentions of the Economy as U.S. Most Important Problem

Percentage of Americans naming at least one economic problem

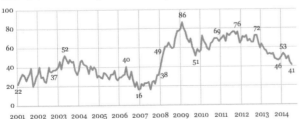

GALLUP

These results are from a Gallup survey conducted July 7–10.

Americans Divided Over Which Party Better for Top Issue

After naming the nation's top problem, respondents were asked to say which party can better handle that issue. And, based on history, the results are relatively positive for the Republicans, who are now at parity with Democrats, each chosen by 35% of Americans. This is similar to the Republicans' positioning on this question in 2010, shortly before voters gave their party a sweeping victory in the midterm House elections. Republicans were also practically tied with Democrats in 1994 and 2002—both years when the GOP fared well in the midterms. By contrast, in 2006, the Democrats held a record 15-percentage-point advantage on this measure and went on to retake control of both houses of Congress.

The only recent midterm election year in which Republican parity with the Democrats on this measure did not foretell Republican gains in the midterms was in 1990, but that year an unusually high proportion chose neither party as the best for handling the top issue.

Party Perceived as Better Able to Handle Most Important Problem

Which political party do you think can do a better job of handling the problem you think is most important -- the Republican Party or the Democratic Party?

	Republican Party	Democratic Party	Same/Other/ No opinion
	%	%	%
2014 Jul 7-10	35	35	29
2010 Sep 13-16	40	38	22
2006 Sep 7-10	34	49	16
2002 Jul 26-28	38	36	26
1998 Apr 17-19	40	42	18
1994 Oct 22-25	41	37	22
1990 October	30	29	41

Figures are for June 2014 and final pre-election poll for prior years

GALLUP

Bottom Line

Americans' perception of the main problem ailing the country continued its gradual shift away from the economy in July, while healthcare is also fading as a top-of-mind concern. At the same time, immigration has clearly captured public attention given the political and humanitarian crisis building at the border with the influx of thousands of children from Central and South America seeking refugee status.

Each previous spike in mentions of immigration as the nation's top problem was fairly short-lived. But with no solution to the current crisis in sight, and less than four months to go before the midterm elections, it is easy to believe the issue could still be a factor come November.

If so, the recent shifts in what Americans perceive to be the nation's top problem could be important. While the 17% of Americans naming immigration as the top problem is not large in absolute terms, the fact that the issue is of particular concern to Republicans and older Americans—both groups that Republicans need to turn out in force in the midterms—could be critical to the outcome.

Survey Methods

Results for this Gallup poll are based on telephone interviews conducted July 7–10, 2014, with a random sample of 1,013 adults, aged 18 and older, living in all 50 U.S. states and the District of Columbia.

For results based on the total sample of national adults, the margin of sampling error is ±4 percentage points at the 95% confidence level.

July 16, 2014
IN U.S., QUALITY JOBS OUTLOOK BEST IN MORE THAN SIX YEARS
Thirty-five percent say now is a good time to find a quality job

by Rebecca Riffkin

WASHINGTON, D.C.—More than one in three Americans (35%) say now is a good time to find a quality job. While not high on an absolute basis, this percentage is the highest since December 2007, the starting point of the Great Recession. The jobs measure has been improving in the past few months, and increased seven percentage points between June and July alone.

Percentage in U.S. Saying Now Is a Good Time to Find a Quality Job
Thinking about the job situation in America today, would you say that it is now a good time or a bad time to find a quality job?

■ % Good time to find a quality job

GALLUP'

Gallup first asked this question in August 2001, when 39% of Americans said it was a good time to find a quality job. Gallup has updated it monthly since October of that year; the most recent data come from Gallup's July 7–10 survey.

The average percentage saying it is a good time to find a quality job is 26% since polling began in 2001, depressed by the lower percentages from 2008 to 2011. Prior to the recession, the August 2001–November 2007 average was 34%, similar to July's 35% reading. Optimism about finding a quality job has been as high as 48% in early 2007, before the Great Recession began. Gallup did not measure this trend in earlier periods such as the dot-com boom of the late 1990s, when it could have been even higher. Sentiment sank as low as 8% in late 2009 and again in late 2011.

While Americans are as positive about the job market as they have been in more than six years, the majority of Americans, 61%, continue to say it is a bad time to find a quality job. That has improved, however, from the 70% seen in May 2014 and the 90% in November 2011.

The percentage saying now is a good time to find a quality job has increased at least marginally since June among all major

demographic groups Gallup looks at. Currently, 27% of Republicans say now is a good time, compared with 43% of Democrats and 34% of independents.

Is Now a Good Time or a Bad Time to Find a Quality Job?

	Good time	Bad time	Good time, June 2014
	%	%	%
Republicans	27	72	26
Independents	34	61	22
Democrats	43	52	38
18 to 29	49	50	36
30 to 49	37	58	32
50 to 64	28	68	25
65+	24	71	16
Postgraduate	45	48	33
College graduate	40	58	33
Some college	31	65	28
High school or less	32	64	23
$75,000 or more	43	53	39
$30,000-$74,999	28	68	23
Less than $30,000	38	60	20

July 7-10, 2014

GALLUP'

In July, young Americans, wealthier Americans, Democrats, and those with advanced degrees are the most optimistic groups about finding a quality job. In March, Gallup reported that Democrats have been more positive than Republicans about jobs since President Barack Obama came into office, while Republicans were more positive than Democrats when George W. Bush was in office. While this trend is still true, with a 16-point gap between Democrats and Republicans this month, Americans of all political persuasions have become more optimistic about jobs over the past several months.

The quality jobs measure is just one more indication of an improving job market, along with Gallup's recent updates on employee reports of hiring at their companies. Gallup's latest monthly Payroll to Population rate is 45.0%, near the high of 45.7% found in October 2012.

Bottom Line

The percentage of Americans saying now is a good time to find a quality job is increasing, and has reached levels not seen since the very beginning of the recession. While the percentage is still much lower than what was typically seen in the years right before the recession, the higher percentage is a promising sign for the U.S. economy. There are a host of others as well: the percentage of U.S. adults who are employed, as measured in Gallup's Payroll to Population rate, has been rising. Gallup's Job Creation Index, which measures employee reports of hiring or firing in the companies where they work, has also been increasing and in June held steady at a six-year high. Furthermore, Gallup's 30-day rolling averages of unemployment (6.3%) and underemployment (15.1%) are the lowest Gallup has measured since it began tracking these in 2010.

These positive employment signs are good news for the economy in general; however, if they continue, it may take a while for them to ripple through to consumers and the rest of the U.S. population. Consumer spending dipped slightly in June but may be showing signs of improving in July. Gallup's Economic Confidence Index has been largely steady throughout 2014, but also may be recovering this week after a slight dip last week. But Americans' ability to find good jobs and be hired is important for coming out of the recession and growing the economy again.

Survey Methods

Results for this Gallup poll are based on telephone interviews conducted July 7–10, 2014, with a random sample of 1,013 adults, aged 18 and older, living in all 50 U.S. states and the District of Columbia.

For results based on the total sample of national adults, the margin of sampling error is ±4 percentage points at the 95% confidence level.

July 17, 2014
CLINTON IS BEST KNOWN, BEST LIKED POTENTIAL 2016 CANDIDATE
Huckabee's image is slightly better than other GOP contenders

by Jeffrey M. Jones

PRINCETON, NJ—Hillary Clinton is currently the best known and best liked of 16 potential 2016 presidential candidates tested in a July 7–10 Gallup poll, due to her 91% familiarity score and +19 net favorable rating. The net favorable is based on her 55% favorable and 36% unfavorable ratings.

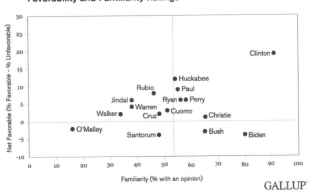

POTENTIAL 2016 PRESIDENTIAL CANDIDATES
Favorability and Familiarity Ratings

In the graph seen above, those potential candidates in the upper-right quadrant are viewed more positively than negatively by Americans and have above average familiarity. The further candidates in that quadrant are away from the intersecting lines, the higher their scores are on both dimensions. The graph clearly shows Clinton's strong image positioning relative to other candidates at the moment for the general election. Gallup will report on candidate images among rank-and-file Republicans and Democrats in the coming days to see how the 2016 hopefuls stack up for their respective party's nomination.

Those potential candidates in the other three quadrants have weaknesses in familiarity, favorability, or both. Those in the lower-right quadrant are better known but less well liked, and must work to change people's opinions about them. Those in the upper-left quadrant are better liked but less well known, and their challenge lies more in becoming nationally known figures.

Huckabee May Have Slight Edge in GOP Field for General Election

Former Arkansas governor and current talk show host Mike Huckabee is arguably in a slightly better position image-wise among the national adult population than other potential Republican presidential candidates. His +12 net favorable rating edges out Kentucky Sen. Rand Paul's +9 for the highest among Republican candidates. Huckabee's 54% familiarity score trails those for New Jersey Gov. Chris Christie (65%) and former Florida Gov. Jeb Bush (65%), but is above the 52% average for the 11 Republicans measured in the poll. Christie's and Bush's net favorable ratings are among the lowest.

Familiarity and Favorable Ratings of Potential 2016 Republican Presidential Candidates, Based on National Adults

Ranked by net favorable

	% Familiar (have an opinion)	% With favorable opinion	% With unfavorable opinion	Net favorable (pct. pts.)
Mike Huckabee	54	33	21	+12
Rand Paul	55	32	23	+9
Marco Rubio	46	27	19	+8
Rick Perry	58	32	26	+6
Paul Ryan	56	31	25	+6
Bobby Jindal	38	22	16	+6
Ted Cruz	48	25	23	+2
Scott Walker	34	18	16	+2
Chris Christie	65	33	32	+1
Jeb Bush	65	31	34	-3
Rick Santorum	48	22	26	-4

July 7-10, 2014

GALLUP

Florida Sen. Marco Rubio has an above average +8 net favorable among national adults, but lags other Republican candidates with 46% familiarity. Texas Gov. Rick Perry and Wisconsin Rep. Paul Ryan are slightly above average in terms of both of favorability and familiarity.

Louisiana Gov. Bobby Jindal has the same +6 net favorability as Perry and Ryan, but is among the least well-known Republicans included in the poll with 38% familiarity. Texas Sen. Ted Cruz, Wisconsin Gov. Scott Walker, and former Pennsylvania Sen. Rick Santorum are below average in both favorability and familiarity, with Santorum viewed more negatively than positively.

Biden Is Well-Known, Not Well-Liked

Two of the five Democrats included in the poll have net negative favorable ratings—Vice President Joe Biden and Maryland Gov. Martin O'Malley. O'Malley is the least known potential candidate in the survey, with 83% of Americans not having an opinion of him. Biden's net negative favorable rating could be more troubling in terms of his 2016 prospects, as 80% of Americans have an opinion of him, second only to Clinton among the 16 candidates in the poll.

Americans are slightly more likely to have a positive than negative view of Massachusetts Sen. Elizabeth Warren (21% favorable, 17% unfavorable) and New York Gov. Andrew Cuomo (27%

favorable, 24% unfavorable). Cuomo is the better known of those two, but still has below average familiarity.

Familiarity and Favorable Ratings of Potential 2016 Democratic Presidential Candidates, Based on National Adults

Ranked by net favorable

	% Familiar (have an opinion)	% With favorable opinion	% With unfavorable opinion	Net favorable (pct. pts.)
Hillary Clinton	91	55	36	+19
Elizabeth Warren	38	21	17	+4
Andrew Cuomo	51	27	24	+3
Martin O'Malley	16	7	9	-2
Joe Biden	80	38	42	-4

July 7-10, 2014

GALLUP'

Perry, Christie, Cruz Images Recovering

The candidates with net negative favorable ratings can take some solace in knowing that Americans are quick to forgive—or perhaps to forget—when politicians do things that reflect negatively on them. Three of the potential candidates in the current survey—Perry, Christie, and Cruz—were rated much more negatively than positively the last time Gallup asked about them, and all are back to at least a slightly more positive than negative favorable rating.

- Perry's recovery may be the most impressive. When Gallup last measured him in December 2011, with his 2012 presidential campaign sputtering due to poor debate performances, he had a net favorable rating of −28 (27% favorable, 55% unfavorable). His familiarity scores are down since then, from 82% to 58%, but those able to rate him are now more positive than negative.
- Christie became a prominent and well-regarded national figure known for taking on the Democratic legislature in New Jersey and for his response to Superstorm Sandy. In June 2013 he had a +32 net favorable rating. The "Bridgegate" scandal last fall sent Christie's image plummeting, to a net −9 favorable rating earlier this year, before improving to +1 in the current poll.
- Cruz, a central figure in the government shutdown last fall, had a net favorable rating of −10 in an October 2013 Gallup poll. Eight months later, his net favorable rating is back to +2.

Biden is the only potential candidate whose image is notably worse than the last time Gallup measured him, with his net favorable rating slipping to −4 from +4 in February.

Implications

The viability of a candidate's chances depends both on voters knowing who the candidate is, but also on voters having a positive impression of the candidate. Candidates usually become better known over the course of a campaign, but those who are better known at the outset have an advantage in that they don't have to work as hard to attract attention to, or raise money for, their campaigns. On the other hand, those who are well-known may have more difficulty improving their image during a campaign.

Although Clinton is the best-liked potential candidate in the poll—18 months before the first primaries or caucuses—her favorable ratings are lower now than when she was secretary of state. They are, however, better than in July 2006, a year-and-a-half before the 2008 primaries, when she had a +6 net favorable rating (50%

favorable, 44% unfavorable), before running a competitive but ultimately unsuccessful bid for the Democratic presidential nomination.

So while Clinton's image has lost some of its luster as she has moved from a less overtly political role as secretary of state to her current role as a book author and potential presidential candidate, she is in an arguably stronger position with the public now than she was before her 2008 presidential campaign.

Survey Methods

Results for this Gallup poll are based on telephone interviews conducted July 7–10, 2014, with a random sample of 1,013 adults, aged 18 and older, living in all 50 U.S. states and the District of Columbia.

For results based on the total sample of national adults, the margin of sampling error is ±4 percentage points at the 95% confidence level.

July 18, 2014
AMERICANS WHO EXERCISE MOST FEEL BEST ABOUT APPEARANCE
Link between exercising regularly and feeling good about appearance

by Justin McCarthy

WASHINGTON, D.C.—Americans who report exercising for 30 minutes every day in the past week feel best about their physical appearance, while those who exercise no more than one day in a given week feel the worst. Seventy percent of Americans who exercised for at least 30 minutes every day the prior week express agreement that they "always feel good" about their appearance, compared with half of those who say they exercised for at least 30 minutes one day (50%) or no days (49%). For the most part, each additional day per week that Americans exercise for 30 minutes or more is associated with at least a small increase in feeling good about their appearance.

Americans' Perceptions of Their Physical Appearance, by Weekly Exercise Frequency

On a 5-point scale, where 5 means strongly agree and 1 means strongly disagree, please rate your level of agreement with the following item: You always feel good about your physical appearance.

■ % who gave 4 or 5 rating

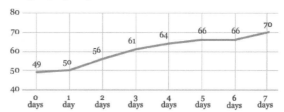

Gallup-Healthways Well-Being Index
Jan. 1–June 23, 2014

GALLUP'

These data are based on more than 80,000 interviews with U.S. adults from Jan. 1–June 23, 2014, as part of the Gallup-Healthways Well-Being Index. Gallup asks Americans to rate their level of agreement with the statement, "I always feel good about my physical appearance" on a five-point scale, where "5" means strongly agree and "1" means strongly disagree. Overall, more than half of

Americans, 58%, agree that they always feel good about their looks, answering with a 4 or a 5.

Fifty-six percent of Americans who exercise two days per week feel good about their looks. This jumps to the 60% range among those who exercise three to six times per week.

According to the U.S. Department of Health and Human Services, adults should engage in at least 2 hours and 30 minutes of "moderate intensity" physical activity "spread throughout the week." While fitness professionals often frown on working out too frequently, and HHS does not offer guidance on how many days a week Americans should exercise, those who exercise daily seem to feel the best about their appearance.

Daily exercisers make up only about one in seven Americans (14%), however, while 29% report not exercising for 30 minutes on any day in the past week. A third of Americans (34%) report exercising for 30 minutes or more up to three days weekly, while 23% report exercising about four to six days per week, which is closer to the HHS recommendation.

Frequency of Americans' Exercise

In the last seven days, on how many days did you exercise for 30 or more minutes?

	%
None	29
One to three days	34
Four to six days	23
Every day	14

Gallup-Healthways Well-Being Index
Jan. 1–June 23, 2014

GALLUP

The link between Americans' frequency of exercise and feeling good about their appearance could reflect a variety of concurrent patterns. Exercise produces a number of benefits, including in particular lower weight, better health, higher muscle mass, and improved mood. Any or all of these perks could result in exercisers' feeling better about the way they look. Plus, more self-confident people could feel good about their looks and therefore be more likely to want to maintain those looks.

Americans at Normal Weight Feel Best About Appearance

Weight status is clearly associated with how Americans feel about their physical appearance. Those who are obese are the least likely to feel good about their appearance (44%), while those who maintain a normal weight are most likely to feel this way (67%). Those who are overweight but not obese (60%) are much more likely to feel good about their appearance than those who are obese. Meanwhile, 62% of those who are underweight feel good about their appearance.

Americans' Perceptions of Their Physical Appearance, by Weight Category

On a 5-point scale, where 5 means strongly agree and 1 means strongly disagree, please rate your level of agreement with the following item: You always feel good about your physical appearance.

	% who gave 4 or 5 rating
Underweight	62
Normal weight	67
Overweight	60
Obese	44

Gallup-Healthways Well-Being Index
Jan. 1–June 23, 2014

GALLUP

Bottom Line

These results underscore yet another reason why regular exercise is good for Americans—those who exercise more than once a week are significantly more likely to feel good about their physical appearance than those who don't.

At the same time, the mechanisms at work in this relationship are not totally clear. Certainly, while regular exercise can help Americans maintain a normal weight and thus make them feel good about their appearance, those who are most concerned about their physical appearance may also be more motivated to exercise to maintain their appearance.

Physical activity releases endorphins into the brain that act as natural pain killers, and reduces stress, anxiety, and depression. In addition to helping individuals control their weight, exercise could also have a positive effect on how confident they are in their looks.

But 63% of Americans exercise for at least 30 minutes on three or fewer days per week—likely falling short of HHS's recommended amount of exercise. In addition to weight control and other health benefits, exercising more frequently would likely improve Americans' perceptions of their appearance.

Survey Methods

Results are based on telephone interviews conducted as part of the Gallup-Healthways Well-Being Index survey Jan. 1–June 23, 2014, with a random sample of 85,143 adults, aged 18 and older, living in all 50 U.S. states and the District of Columbia.

For results based on the total sample of national adults, the margin of sampling error is ±0.4 percentage points at the 95% confidence level. There error range is larger, however, for the subgroups reported here. For reporting relevant to days exercised per week, the maximum expected error ranges from about 1 to 2 percentage points. For reporting of the four BMI weight classes, the maximum expected error range is ±2.8 points for underweight and less than one point for all other weight classes.

July 18, 2014
HUCKABEE, PAUL, RYAN, PERRY BEST KNOWN AND LIKED IN GOP
Chris Christie has lowest net favorable rating among Republicans

by Frank Newport

PRINCETON, NJ—Four potential GOP candidates for president in 2016 stand above seven others as the best known and best liked among Republicans at this early juncture in the nominating process. Former Arkansas Gov. Mike Huckabee, Kentucky Sen. Rand Paul, Wisconsin Rep. Paul Ryan, and Texas Gov. Rick Perry are all familiar to more than 60% of Republicans and Republican-leaning independents and have net favorable ratings of +40 or better. Huckabee has slightly higher familiarity and net favorability than the other 10 potential Republican candidates tested.

These findings are based on Gallup interviewing conducted July 7–10. The graph above displays Republicans' familiarity with each candidate on the horizontal axis and the net favorable rating on the vertical axis, which is based on the percentage of Republicans who have a favorable opinion minus those who have an unfavorable opinion. Those candidates in the upper-right quadrant have familiarity and net favorable ratings that are both above average. By contrast, those in the lower left quadrant have familiarity and net favorable ratings that are both below average.

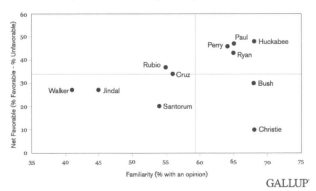

POTENTIAL 2016 REPUBLICAN PRESIDENTIAL CANDIDATES
Favorability and Familiarity Ratings Among Republicans/leaners

Three of the four leading Republicans have previously competed in Republican presidential contests, and all four are highly visible on the national stage.

- **Mike Huckabee** ran for the GOP nomination in 2008, and he has been an active radio and television personality in the years since. At this point, he reigns as the single candidate with the best combination of familiarity and net favorability among Americans who identify with or lean toward the Republican Party nationwide.
- **Paul Ryan** was Mitt Romney's vice presidential nominee in 2012, and as chairman of the House Budget Committee, he is regarded as the GOP's resident expert on budget issues.
- **Rand Paul** has been active in nationwide politics since winning the U.S. Senate seat in Kentucky in 2010, taking strong libertarian-oriented positions on several issues, similar to his father Ron Paul, the former Texas representative, who had multiple presidential bids.
- **Rick Perry** unsuccessfully sought the 2012 GOP nomination. He has recently been in the news regarding the border crisis in his state of Texas, where many young immigrants from Mexico and Central America have crossed the border.

Two other possible GOP candidates are as familiar to Republicans as these four, but they both have below-average net favorable scores: Florida Gov. Jeb Bush and New Jersey Gov. Chris Christie. Despite **Jeb Bush's** staus as the son of a former president and the brother of another, Republicans' familiarity with him is no higher than any of the other possible candidates tested. Perhaps because some Republicans continue to have less than positive memories of his brother, Bush's unfavorable rating of 19% is the second highest of any of those tested. **Chris Christie** has the lowest net favorable (+10) of any candidate tested, with 39% holding a positive opinion and 29% a negative opinion.

Three other candidates have below-average familiarity, Texas Sen. **Ted Cruz**, Florida Sen. **Marco Rubio**, and former Pennsylvania Sen. **Rick Santorum**. Of these, Santorum, a very active candidate for the GOP nomination in 2012, has the lowest net favorable rating.

The final two candidates measured—Louisiana Gov. **Bobby Jindal** and Wisconsin Gov. **Scott Walker**—are familiar to less than half of Republicans and have net favorable scores that are slightly below average.

Democrats Like Jeb Bush Least and Christie and Jindal Most

All of the candidates measured have net negative favorable scores among Democrats and Democratic-leaning independents, as would be expected. Democrats are least positive about Jeb Bush, giving him a −34 net favorable rating, no doubt reflecting Democrats' associating him with the two Republicans who have served as president. Several of the other potential GOP candidates have net favorable scores among Democrats that are almost as low.

Favorable Ratings of Potential 2016 Republican Presidential Candidates
Ranked by net favorable among Republicans/leaners

	Net favorable Republicans/leaners (pct. pts.)	Net favorable Democrats/leaners (pct. pts.)
Mike Huckabee	+48	-17
Rand Paul	+47	-26
Rick Perry	+46	-31
Paul Ryan	+43	-31
Marco Rubio	+37	-16
Ted Cruz	+34	-29
Jeb Bush	+30	-34
Bobby Jindal	+27	-12
Scott Walker	+27	-21
Rick Santorum	+20	-27
Chris Christie	+10	-12

July 7-10, 2014

GALLUP

At the other end of the spectrum are Jindal and Christie, both of whom have the least negative net favorable scores among Democrats, at −12. Jindal is not as well-known as Christie among Democrats, with only a 38% familiarity score. Christie, on the other hand, has accomplished the remarkable feat of being as well-known among Democrats as he is among Republicans, with a 68% familiarity score among both. While Christie is the least well-liked among Republicans, he is least disliked among Democrats of any of the GOP candidates tested. Christie's favorability profile presents a challenge for him in securing the Republican nomination, given his lower relative popularity among the party base, but would potentially put him in a more advantageous position in a general election setting, given Democrats' lesser dislike for him than other GOP candidates.

Bottom Line

Less than 70% of Republicans and Republican leaners nationwide are familiar with any of the 11 potential GOP candidates tested, even though several actively campaigned for the Republican nomination in 2012, one was the 2012 vice presidential nominee, and others have been visible in the news in recent months. None of them has the same level of name recognition as Hillary Clinton or Joe Biden among all adults. This suggests that many Republicans have not yet turned their attention to the next presidential race.

The four candidates who have somewhat better images than others at this early stage—Huckabee, Paul, Ryan, and Perry—all have managed to keep themselves in the news over the past year and maintained a positive position in Republicans' eyes. Bush and Christie are as well-known nationally as these four, but they are not nearly as well-liked. Christie in particular has the distinction of being the least liked of the candidates measured among Republicans. Two candidates often mentioned as possible 2016 candidates—Jindal and Walker—have the most ground to gain because Republicans are less familiar with them than the other candidates measured.

Although the 2016 presidential election is more than two years away, active campaigning and preliminary debates will begin as early as the fall of 2015, meaning that next year is the real starting point for GOP candidates to intensify their quest to capture their party's nomination. While Hillary Clinton is regarded as a strong front-runner for the Democratic nomination should she choose to run, there is no clear leader at this point on the Republican side—indicating that the race for the GOP nomination is essentially wide open.

Survey Methods

Results for this Gallup poll are based on telephone interviews conducted July 7–10, 2014, with a random sample of 1,013 adults, aged 18 and older, living in all 50 U.S. states and the District of Columbia.

For results based on the total sample of national adults, the margin of sampling error is ±4 percentage points at the 95% confidence level.

July 18, 2014
CUOMO, WARREN, O'MALLEY STILL UNKNOWN TO MANY DEMOCRATS
Hillary Clinton solidly leads Democrats in favorability

by Art Swift

WASHINGTON, D.C.—Out of a field of five potential 2016 presidential candidates, only Hillary Clinton and Joe Biden are viewed favorably by a majority of Democrats and Democratic-leaning independents. The other possible contenders are less well-known to Democrats. In fact, nearly seven in 10 Democrats say they have never heard of Maryland Gov. Martin O'Malley.

Favorable Ratings of Potential 2016 Democratic Presidental Candidates, Based on Democrats/Leaners

Ranked by percentage favorable

	Favorable	Unfavorable	Never heard of	Heard of, but no opinion
Hillary Clinton	84	9	2	5
Joe Biden	65	16	8	10
Andrew Cuomo	39	14	29	19
Elizabeth Warren	38	6	39	18
Martin O'Malley	9	7	69	15

July 7-10, 2014

GALLUP

The results are based on a July 7–10 Gallup poll. Gallup previously reported on the current public images of 16 different potential 2016 presidential candidates from both parties, and on how Republicans rate the field of the major GOP contenders.

While speculation about the 2016 campaign may be premature, especially in advance of the November midterm elections, Democrats' have clear-cut opinions of two candidates: Clinton and Biden. Ninety-three percent of Democrats have an opinion of Clinton, who has been on the national stage for 22 years as secretary of state, as a U.S. senator from New York, and first lady. As for the vice president, 81% of Democrats have an opinion of Biden, who previously served as a U.S. senator from Delaware for 36 years and ran unsuccessfully for president in 1988 and 2008.

Massachusetts Sen. Elizabeth Warren, New York Gov. Andrew Cuomo, and O'Malley do not have the long political careers that Biden and Clinton have, and at this point they are struggling to attain a high profile on the national stage.

- **Andrew Cuomo**, son of three-term New York Gov. Mario Cuomo, is running for his second term as governor this year after previously being the state's attorney general and Secretary of Housing and Urban Development under President Bill Clinton. Despite that long career and being in a prominent family that includes his brother Chris Cuomo, a CNN news personality, nearly half of Democrats (48%) have never heard of or don't have an opinion of the governor.
- **Elizabeth Warren**, a first-term senator, was a former Harvard Law professor and served in the Obama administration as a special adviser to the Consumer Financial Protection Bureau. She has been campaigning nationally for Democratic candidates, some of whom are running in traditionally strong Republican states, such as West Virginia and Kentucky. Warren has said that she is touting her populist message to ensure the Democratic agenda succeeds in the next Congress. However, Warren is still far from a household name among Democrats: 57% of Democrats nationally have never heard of or don't have an opinion of the senator.
- **Martin O'Malley** is finishing his second term as governor of Maryland, having been elected in 2006 after eight years as the mayor of Baltimore. While he counts as a success signing same-sex marriage into state law in 2012, O'Malley has not gained much traction with the American public. The vast majority of Democrats (84%) have neither heard of O'Malley or don't have an opinion of him.

POTENTIAL 2016 DEMOCRATIC PRESIDENTIAL CANDIDATES
Favorability and Familiarity Ratings Among Democrats/leaners

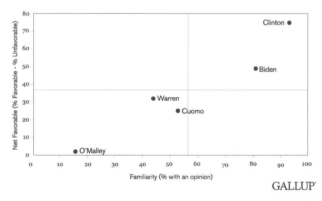

Clinton and Biden enjoy high familiarity and high favorability ratings with Democrats and Democratic-leaning independents. By subtracting her unfavorable rating from her favorable rating, Clinton has a net favorable rating of +75, far higher than any other potential presidential candidate, including Republican candidates. As would be expected, Democrats rate all of these Democratic politicians more positively than negatively, with Biden at +49 net favorable, Warren at +32, Cuomo at +25, and the little-known O'Malley at +2.

Clinton, Despite Potential Missteps, Maintains Favorability Nationwide

Clinton, who has been on a tour promoting her memoir of her term as secretary of state, *Hard Choices*, has maintained her high favorability rating on a national scale as well, with 55% of all Americans having a positive view of her and 36% an unfavorable view. This is despite potential missteps on the book tour where she referred to herself and her husband as "dead broke" when they left the White House in 2001. As a result, Clinton has been under increased scrutiny over her speaking fees, including the revelation that the State University of New York at Buffalo paid her $275,000 to speak there.

Clinton's favorable rating among Americans has been as high as 67% in 1998, at the time of her husband's impeachment. Her favorable ratings were in that same territory during her years as secretary of state, but have declined since she left that post and speculation began about her 2016 presidential intentions. Several times throughout the last 20+ years, Clinton's favorable ratings have dipped below 50%. This includes in 1994 when her attempt to institute national healthcare failed, throughout much of the 1996 election year prior to the Democratic convention, in 2001 after the Clintons' messy White House departure, and at various times in 2007 and 2008 during her quest for the party's presidential nomination.

Hillary Clinton's Favorability Ratings Among National Adults

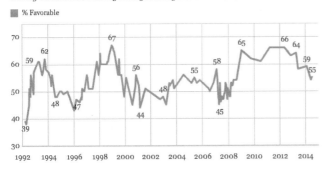

First lady (1993–2001); United States senator (2001–2009); secretary of state (2009–2013)

GALLUP

Bottom Line

Hillary Clinton dominates the Democratic field for the 2016 presidential nomination. Even though she has not announced a second run for the presidency and may decide not to run again, she is clearly better known and better perceived among Democrats than any other potential challenger for the party's nomination. That may not be good news for Biden, who in most years would have the inside track to the nomination as a sitting vice president. The last vice president who wanted to run for his party's nomination but failed was Alben Barkley, President Harry Truman's vice president in 1952. Barkley was dismissed as "too old" to run at age 74, which would be the same age Biden would be if he were inaugurated as president.

Warren, Cuomo, and O'Malley have work to do to raise their familiarity and favorability ratings among Americans—let alone among their own party's base. Overshadowed by Clinton at this point, it could be difficult for these Democrats to boost their profiles enough to mount a serious challenge to Clinton should the former secretary decide to run. O'Malley would have a particularly uphill climb in raising awareness as he prepares to exit his platform as governor; at this point, fewer than two in 10 Democrats know enough about him to have an opinion.

Survey Methods

Results for this Gallup poll are based on telephone interviews conducted July 7–10, 2014, with a random sample of 1,013 adults, aged 18 and older, living in all 50 U.S. states and the District of Columbia.

For results based on the total sample of national adults, the margin of sampling error is ±4 percentage points at the 95% confidence level.

July 18, 2014
MANY U.S. SMOKERS SAY HIGHER CIGARETTE TAXES ARE UNJUST
But many smokers think smoking restrictions in public places are justified

by Andrew Dugan

WASHINGTON, D.C.—Governments have increased taxes on cigarettes in recent years at least partly to discourage smoking, but more than half of U.S. smokers (58%) see these tax hikes as an act of unjust discrimination. About two in five smokers (39%) think the tax increases are justified. Smokers are now slightly less likely to feel discriminated against on this basis than they were in 2002.

As a result of increased taxes on cigarettes, do you feel unjustly discriminated against as a smoker, or do you think these tax increases are justified?
Based on smokers

	Yes, unjustly discriminated against	No, tax increases are justified	No opinion
	%	%	%
Jul 7-10, 2014	58	39	3
Jul 9-11, 2002	68	29	3

GALLUP

The latest result comes from Gallup's 2014 Consumption Habits survey, conducted July 7–10. The median state cigarette tax is $1.36 per pack, and the federal government tacks on another $1.01. In places such as New York City, the combined city and state tax is as high as $5.85—often higher than the price of a pack of cigarettes itself.

One reason various levels of government have increased these levies on cigarettes in recent years is that many public health advocates believe cigarette taxes can reduce smoking. But the large majority of smokers, 71%, do not believe they personally smoke less because of the tax increases. However, 26% admit that the higher taxes discourage them from lighting up, a finding that policy advocates might see as a success because cigarettes are notoriously addictive.

Independent research on the effectiveness of tax increases for reducing smoking rates is mixed. A study published by the National Bureau of Economic Research says, "It will take sizable tax increases, on the order of 100%, to decrease adult smoking by as much as 5%." Still, other researchers conclude that higher cigarette prices do reduce smoking rates among certain subgroups, such as the young.

Many Smokers Think Smoking Restrictions in Public Places Are Justified

While a majority of smokers think higher taxes on cigarettes are unjustly discriminatory, a solid majority of smokers say increased restrictions on smoking in public places are justified (58%). Meanwhile, 37% say these restrictions unjustly discriminate against smokers. These attitudes are similar to those in previous years.

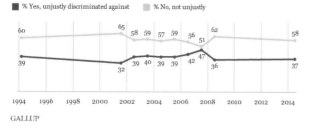

As a result of increased restrictions on smoking in public places, do you feel unjustly discriminated against as a smoker, or do you think the restrictions are justified?
Based on smokers

■ % Yes, unjustly discriminated against   ■ % No, not unjustly

GALLUP

And while these restrictions certainly make it more challenging for smokers to light up in public places, they generally do not seem to lead to smokers cutting back. Three-quarters of smokers say they are not smoking less because of these restrictions. But as was the case with cigarette taxes, some smokers have responded to these policies. A quarter say restrictions on smoking in public places have reduced their smoking.

Smokers Lighting Up Less Frequently Each Day

Alongside this raft of anti-smoking measures, the percentage of "heavy smokers," defined as those who smoke more than a pack a day, has retreated. Fewer than one in 10 smokers (7%) say they smoke more than a pack a day—down from a little less than 20% of smokers in the 1990s. And over two-thirds of smokers (68%) say they consume less than a pack per day, on par with historical highs seen in recent years.

A consistent majority of smokers since 1999 have said they smoke less than a pack per day. A fifth smoke one pack per day, also a figure that has declined considerably over time.

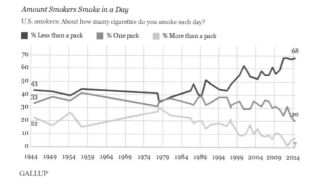

Amount Smokers Smoke in a Day
U.S. smokers: About how many cigarettes do you smoke each day?

■ % Less than a pack   ■ % One pack   ■ % More than a pack

GALLUP

Nationally, a fifth of Americans (21%) report having a cigarette in the past week, close to the historical low on this Gallup measure dating back to 1944, but on par with recent readings.

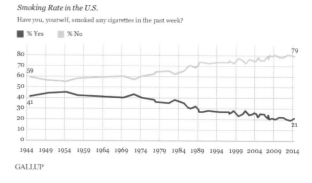

Smoking Rate in the U.S.
Have you, yourself, smoked any cigarettes in the past week?

■ % Yes   ■ % No

GALLUP

Fifteen percent of smokers say they worry about their smoking all of the time and another 41% confess to worrying about it some of the time. About a quarter indicate they seldom worry about their smoking, and 21% of smokers say they never worry about it.

How often do you worry about your smoking? Would you say you worry all of the time, some of the time, not too often or never?
Based on smokers

	All of the time	Some of the time	Not too often	Never
	%	%	%	%
Jul 7-10, 2014	15	41	23	21

GALLUP

Bottom Line

Many smokers take exception to at least one anti-smoking policy—higher taxes. A majority of smokers believe paying higher excise taxes on packs of cigarettes unjustly discriminates against them as smokers, and an overwhelming majority do not believe tax increases have discouraged them from lighting up. However, more smokers think restrictions on smoking in public places are justified than do not think so, a sign that smokers do not uniformly oppose all anti-smoking measures.

Survey Methods

Results for this Gallup poll are based on telephone interviews conducted July 7–10, 2014, on the, with a random sample of 1,013 adults, aged 18 and older, living in all 50 U.S. states and the District of Columbia.

For results based on the total sample of national adults, the margin of sampling error is ±4 percentage points at the 95% confidence level.

For results based on the sample of 176 smokers, the margin of sampling error is ±9 percentage points at the 95% confidence level.

July 21, 2014
OBAMA AVERAGES 43.2% JOB APPROVAL IN 22ND QUARTER
Slight improvement from 42.4% average in 21st quarter

by Jeffrey M. Jones

PRINCETON, NJ—President Barack Obama averaged 43.2% job approval during his 22nd quarter in office, from April 20 through

July 19. That is a minimal increase from the prior quarter's 42.4% average, but still ranks among the lowest for Obama to date. His worst quarterly average thus far is 41.0% in quarter 11.

Barack Obama's Quarterly Job Approval Averages

■ % Approve

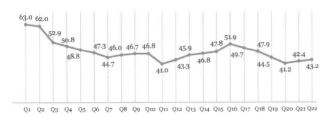

Gallup Daily tracking

Obama's 22nd quarter was largely characterized by remarkable stability in his job ratings, which ranged narrowly between 43% and 45% each week throughout April and May into early June. His job approval showed a notable dip to 41% in mid-June, about the time Islamic militants took control of major portions of Iraq. His approval has recovered slightly since then, averaging 43% last week, but has yet to get back to 44%. His late-quarter slump prevented slightly greater improvement in his overall 22nd-quarter average.

Obama is the sixth twice-elected president since World War II to serve 22 quarters in office. His 22nd-quarter averages are lower than those of three other presidents—Dwight Eisenhower, Ronald Reagan, and Bill Clinton—and higher than those of two others, Richard Nixon and George W. Bush. Nixon's 22nd quarter was his last full quarter before he resigned in August 1974 because of his involvement in the Watergate scandal and the mounting threat of an impeachment vote in the House of Representatives.

Quarterly Job Approval Averages for Presidents During Their 22nd Quarter in Office, Presidents Elected to Two Terms

President	Dates of 22nd quarter	22nd-quarter job approval average	Number of polls
Eisenhower	Apr 20–Jul 19, 1958	53.0%	3
Nixon	Apr 20–Jul 19, 1974	26.0%	7
Reagan	Apr 20–Jul 19, 1986	64.0%	4
Clinton	Apr 20–Jul 19, 1998	61.6%	5
G.W. Bush	Apr 20–Jul 19, 2006	35.8%	8
Obama	Apr 20–Jul 19, 2014	43.2%	88

Harry Truman was not elected to his first term in office but was elected to a second term and served a 22nd quarter in office. Truman averaged 39.0% approval from July 20-Oct 19, 1950.

A seventh post–World War II president, Harry Truman, served a 22nd quarter in office, though he was not elected to his first term. During that quarter, from July to October 1950, when the U.S. was fighting the Korean War abroad and dealing with a struggling economy and McCarthyism domestically, Truman's average job approval was 39%.

All of these presidents' 22nd quarters in office occurred with the second midterm elections of their presidencies looming. Historically, the president's party typically suffers heavy losses in the House in the second midterm. But Clinton's and Reagan's relatively high popularity likely helped mitigate midterm seat losses for their parties in the elections.

In 1998, the Democrats bucked the historical trend and gained seats in the House of Representatives, at a time when Republicans

were undertaking efforts to impeach Clinton in the aftermath of his affair with a former White House intern. In 1986, Republicans lost only a small number of House seats. However, Republicans did lose enough seats in the Senate that year to yield partisan control to the Democrats.

Obama's approval rating is unlikely to improve much before the 2014 midterm elections, based on history. Eisenhower, Clinton, and Bush saw modest improvements in their 23rd-quarter ratings of between two and three percentage points, while Reagan saw a modest decrease. Reagan's 22nd-quarter average proved to be the high-water mark of his presidency.

Although Obama's lower job approval rating does make Democratic candidates vulnerable this fall, it is not clear from a structural perspective how many more seats Republicans could gain in the House after they gained more than 60 in the 2010 midterms. Obama's unpopularity is likely to be a greater factor in the Senate elections, as Democratic Senate incumbents elected in a strong Democratic year of 2008 must face re-election this year in a much less favorable election environment for them.

Implications

The relative stability in Obama's job approval ratings can be looked at both from a glass-half-empty and a glass-half-full perspective. On the negative side, his ratings are not increasing much despite an improving economy. On the positive side, they have held steady despite a series of challenging events during the last quarter, including the controversy about medical care for military veterans at Veterans Affairs hospitals, the prisoner exchange with the Taliban, the Iraq situation, and the crisis of illegal immigrant children from Central America crossing the U.S. border.

At a similar point in his presidency, George W. Bush's support had eroded to mostly below 40% in the face of a series of second-term challenges including the war in Iraq, Hurricane Katrina, and the failed nomination of Harriet Miers to the Supreme Court.

Obama may be able to keep his ratings above the 40% mark as long as he maintains strong levels of support among Democrats. Although Democrats' approval ratings of Obama are down from earlier in his presidency, they still consistently approach 80%.

Survey Methods

Results for this Gallup poll are based on telephone interviews conducted April 20–July 19, 2014, on the Gallup Daily tracking survey, with a random sample of 44,622 adults, aged 18 and older, living in all 50 U.S. states and the District of Columbia.

For results based on the total sample of national adults, the margin of sampling error is ±1 percentage point at the 95% confidence level.

July 22, 2014
HIRING DISCRIMINATION FOR SMOKERS, OBESE REJECTED IN U.S.
Americans say higher health insurance rates for smokers are justified

by Rebecca Riffkin

WASHINGTON, D.C.—Fewer than one in eight Americans, 12%, say companies should be allowed to refuse to hire people because they are significantly overweight. Similarly, 14% of Americans say companies should be allowed to refuse to hire smokers.

Hiring Smokers and Those Who Are Significantly Overweight

Do you think companies should be allowed to refuse to hire people just because they smoke, or not?
Do you think companies should be allowed to refuse to hire people just because they are significantly overweight, or not?

■ % Yes, should be allowed to refuse to hire smokers

▨ % Yes, should be allowed to refuse to hire those who are significantly overweight

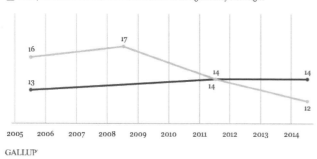

GALLUP'

While Americans are just as likely now to say that companies should be able to refuse to hire smokers as when Gallup first asked the question in 2005, they are slightly less likely to say that companies should be able to refuse to hire those who are significantly overweight. The 12% of Americans who say companies should be able to refuse to hire those who are significantly overweight is down slightly from 16% in 2005 and 17% in 2008.

These results come from Gallup's July 7–10 Consumption Habits survey, in which 21% of Americans reported having at least one cigarette in the week prior to being interviewed, near the historical low. Furthermore, in the same poll, 40% of Americans said they consider themselves to be "very" or "somewhat" overweight.

Majority Agree With Higher Health Insurance Rates for Smokers

While Americans overwhelmingly reject the idea of hiring discrimination against smokers and those who are significantly overweight, they are more amenable to the idea of charging these individuals more for health insurance. In fact, a majority of Americans, 58%, say that it would be justified to set higher health insurance rates for smokers. Fewer Americans—but still a substantial minority, at 39%—say higher rates would be justified for those who are significantly overweight.

Higher Health Insurance for Smokers, Those Who Are Significantly Overweight

Do you think it would be justified or unjustified to set higher health insurance rates for people who smoke?
Do you think it would be justified or unjustified to set higher health insurance rates for people who are significantly overweight?

■ % Justified for smokers   ▨ % Justified for those who are significantly overweight

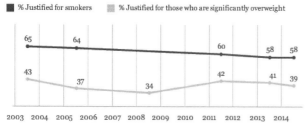

Note: In 2005 and 2008, asked of a half sample

GALLUP'

These figures are both slightly lower than in 2003, when Gallup first asked these questions. At that time, 65% of Americans said that smokers should pay higher health insurance rates, and 43% said the same about those who are significantly overweight.

Smokers, Overweight Adults More Opposed Than Other Americans

Smokers are much more likely than nonsmokers to oppose hiring discrimination and higher insurance rates for those who smoke. While a quarter of smokers say that higher insurance rates are justified, only 3% say companies should be allowed to refuse to hire smokers. Former smokers' views are similar to those of nonsmokers in general, indicating that current smoking status is a larger determinant of views on these issues than is past history of smoking.

Smokers, Nonsmokers Differ Largely in Their Views

	Smokers	Nonsmokers	Former smokers
Higher health insurance rates justified for smokers	26%	66%	59%
Higher health insurance rates not justified for smokers	73%	31%	37%
Companies should be allowed to refuse to hire smokers	3%	16%	17%
Companies shouldn't be allowed to refuse to hire smokers	97%	82%	81%

Note: "Nonsmokers" includes former smokers and Americans who have never smoked.

GALLUP'

While similar differences exist between Americans who say they are overweight and those who say they are "about right," they are not as pronounced. Thirty-two percent of overweight Americans say higher health insurance rates for those who are overweight are justified, compared with 44% of Americans who say their weight is about right. Overweight Americans are just as likely as those who say their weight is about right to say that companies should be allowed to refuse to hire overweight Americans.

Americans' Views on Hiring/Health Insurance Rates, by Self-Reported Weight Status

	Significantly overweight	Weight "about right"
Higher health insurance rates justified for overweight	32%	44%
Higher health insurance rates not justified for overweight	66%	55%
Companies should be allowed to refuse to hire overweight	11%	12%
Companies shouldn't be allowed to refuse to hire overweight	87%	85%

GALLUP'

Implications

Most Americans oppose hiring policies that would allow companies to refuse to hire smokers or those who are significantly overweight. It is unclear if those views are because Americans do not think smoking and obesity negatively affect workplace performance or they simply reject discrimination of any kind in hiring. Some workplaces, many of which are hospitals, justify policies of not hiring smokers by saying they increase productivity and cut down on healthcare costs. A Texas hospital began extending this policy to those who are obese for similar reasons, but later reversed the decision.

While higher health insurance rates are acceptable to more Americans, particularly for smokers, it is still a controversial idea, even though smokers have long had to pay higher life insurance rates. However, smoking and being overweight are associated with higher healthcare costs. The Affordable Care Act allows for higher insurance premiums for smokers, and while the majority of Americans say this type of policy is acceptable, nearly four in 10 say it is not.

Advocates for both of these ideas—allowing companies to refuse to hire smokers and those who are overweight, and charging these individuals higher health insurance rates—say the tactics would help encourage people to live healthier lives. So far, however, Americans are only on board with charging smokers higher insurance premiums.

Survey Methods

Results for this Gallup poll are based on telephone interviews conducted July 7–10, 2014, with a random sample of 1,013 adults, aged 18 and older, living in all 50 U.S. states and the District of Columbia.

For results based on the total sample of national adults, the margin of sampling error is ±4 percentage points at the 95% confidence level.

For results based on the sample of 176 smokers, the margin of sampling error is ±9 percentage points.

For results based on the sample of 837 nonsmokers, the margin of sampling error is ±4 percentage points.

For results based on the sample of 249 former smokers, the margin of sampling error is ±8 percentage points.

July 23, 2014
AMERICAN CONSUMERS CAREFUL WITH SPENDING IN SUMMER 2014
Consumers using multiple methods to reduce expenses and save money

by John Fleming

WASHINGTON, D.C.—In the face of increasing demands on their pocketbooks for spending on household essentials this summer, Americans have various ways of dealing with the continuing budget crunch.

Saving and Spending Money in the U.S., Summer 2014

In the past four weeks, have you ... ?

	% Yes	% No
Purchased generic or store brand goods	83	16
Shopped at more than one store for similar items to get the best deal	61	39
Gone online to compare prices and find the best deal	59	41
Used coupons when shopping	58	42
Purchased more at the store than you originally intended	58	42
Followed a strict budget	55	45
Purchased used goods	40	60
Made an impulse purchase	38	61
Gone shopping for fun	31	69
Made a major purchases that cost at least one week's pay	27	73

June 9-15, 2014

GALLUP

More than half of American consumers Gallup polled say in the past four weeks they purchased generic or store brand goods (83%), shopped at more than one store for similar items to get the best deal (61%), gone online to compare prices and find the best deal (59%),

used coupons when shopping (58%), and followed a strict budget (55%). But, perhaps surprisingly, a majority also say they purchased more at the store than they originally intended to (58%).

American consumers have not embraced all cost-saving measures, however. Four out of 10 respondents say they have purchased used goods to save money (40%). Equally interesting is what consumers are not doing: About a third of consumers report making an impulse purchase (38%), going shopping for fun (31%), or making a major purchase that cost at least one week's pay (27%). These results are consistent with the sentiments expressed in the Gallup Daily tracking poll.

Consumers' spending decisions this summer underscore the tension between doing what is right for the larger economy (more spending) and doing what is right for their own personal or household economy (spending responsibly and reducing expenses). Overall, Americans' spending habits are bad news for the larger U.S. economy. This is the first time Gallup has measured household saving in this way, so it is unclear whether the current patterns are typical, or if the results about saving strategies are better now than during the recession.

Americans' Attitudes Show Inclination Toward Saving Money

Americans' seem to be leaning toward saving their money instead of spending it. More than half of Americans (53%) "strongly agree" (giving a rating of 5) that they are careful about how they spend their money, with another 22% agreeing less strongly (giving a rating of 4). Forty-five percent strongly agree they always save some of their money when they get some and about one-third say they only shop for exactly what they need. In contrast, 28% rank convenience over saving money (strongly agree + a rating of 4), and 16% say they spend the money they get right away (strongly agree + a rating of 4).

Americans' Attitudes About Saving Money

Still thinking about your spending, on a scale of 1 to 5 where 5 is strongly agree and 1 is strongly disagree, please indicate your level of agreement with each of the following.

	% Strongly disagree	2	3	4	% Strongly agree	Net agree (4+5)
I am careful about how I spend my money.	6	4	15	22	53	75
When I get some money, I always save some of it.	10	8	19	17	45	62
I only shop for exactly what I need.	10	13	26	18	34	52
Convenience is more important to me than saving money.	29	18	24	13	15	28
When I get some money, I spend it right away.	52	20	12	6	10	16

June 9-15, 2014

GALLUP

Bottom Line

Americans' careful spending habits characterize an economy still struggling to get on its feet and households continuing to find ways to pinch pennies to make ends meet. The poll results underscore the tension between doing what is right for the larger economy—spending more—and doing what is right for one's personal economy—spending responsibly and reducing expenses. Using coupons, price shopping, buying store brands or generics, and sticking to a budget are some of the ways Americans are trying to do more with less. A majority of consumers are using coupons when they shop, suggesting that coupon use, as well as other ways of obtaining price discounts, is firmly entrenched in the American consumer's mindset.

Discounting has become so ubiquitous that it is possible that consumers will avoid retailers who do not discount. While Americans are spending more on household essentials, they have less available to spend on discretionary items, such as leisure activities, travel, dining out, and consumer electronics. Even more to the point, American consumers are foregoing major purchases and rarely shopping for fun. It is likely that a more robust economy will see the return of the joy of shopping, but, paradoxically, the joy of shopping for fun, making major purchases, and spending on discretionary items is what fuels economic growth.

Survey Methods

Results for this Gallup poll are based on telephone interviews conducted June 9–15, 2014, with a random sample of 1,029 adults, aged 18 and older, living in all 50 U.S. states and the District of Columbia.

For results based on the total sample of national adults, the margin of sampling error is ±4 percentage points at the 95% confidence level.

July 23, 2014

BEER IS AMERICANS' ADULT BEVERAGE OF CHOICE THIS YEAR

More than six in 10 adults say they drink, similar to recent averages

by Lydia Saad

PRINCETON, NJ—As they have for most of the past two decades, Americans who drink alcohol choose beer over wine and liquor as the type of alcohol they imbibe most often. This year, 41% of U.S. drinkers report they typically drink beer; 31% name wine and 23% name liquor.

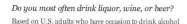

Do you most often drink liquor, wine, or beer?
Based on U.S. adults who have occasion to drink alcohol

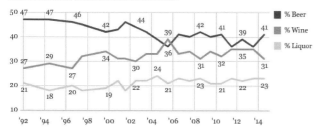

GALLUP

At 41%, Americans' current preference for beer is among the highest Gallup has recorded since beer tumbled to 36% on this measure in 2005—although still not as highly favored as it was in the 1990s, when nearly half preferred it.

The 2005 dip for beer occurred at the peak of an apparent increase in American drinkers' preference for wine between 2002 and 2005. Since then, drinkers' tastes have reverted somewhat, with beer back on top. Slightly more drinkers still choose wine today than did so in the early to mid-1990s; however, wine shows no upward momentum.

Consistent with recent years, wine continues to be the top choice for women, at 46%. Among men, wine (17%) trails both beer (57%) and liquor (20%). Wine edges out beer among older adults: 38% of those 55 and older drink wine most often, compared with 32% who most often drink beer. By contrast, the plurality of 18- to 34-year-olds (48%) and those aged 35 to 54 (43%) prefer beer.

The latest results are from Gallup's July 7–10 Consumption Habits survey, and are based on telephone interviews with U.S. national adults, aged 18 and older.

Nearly Two-Thirds of U.S. Adults Drink Alcohol

Sixty-four percent of U.S. adults say they "have occasion to use alcoholic beverages," whereas 36% identify as total abstainers. The percentage of drinkers is about the same—65%—among adults 21 and older, those for whom drinking is legal.

The current percentage of drinkers among the general population is similar to the 63% average across Gallup's long-term trend, which started in 1939. However, in the three-quarters of a century Gallup has tracked this, self-reported drinking has been as low as 55% in 1958, and as high as 71% in the mid- to late 1970s. By contrast, since 1997, the percentage of drinkers has narrowly ranged between 60% and 67%.

Percentage of U.S. Adults Who Drink Alcohol
Do you have occasion to use alcoholic beverages such as liquor, wine or beer, or are you a total abstainer?

GALLUP

Most Americans who drink alcohol appear to do so fairly regularly, as 67% report having had at least one drink in the past week. Another quarter most recently drank within the last three months, while 10% say it was further back in time. Some of these less-frequent drinkers include people who say they drink only on special occasions.

When did you last take a drink of any kind of alcoholic beverage?
Based on adults who drink alcoholic beverages

	Jul 7-10, 2014
	%
Within the last 24 hours	27
Within the last 2 to 4 days	25
Within the last 5 to 7 days	15
Between a week and a month ago	17
One to three months ago	6
Four to 12 months ago	5
More than a year ago	3
Only drink on holidays/special occasions	2

GALLUP

Reported Drinking Rises on Weekends

More Americans are drinking on the weekends than on weekdays. This is evident in an analysis of Gallup's alcohol consumption data from 2001 through 2014, encompassing nearly 10,000 interviews with adult drinkers. Over this period, the percentage of drinkers who report having had alcohol in the past 24 hours varies according to the day of week on which respondents were interviewed.

Adults interviewed on Sundays were the most likely to say they had had an alcoholic drink in the prior 24 hours, at 44%, followed by those interviewed on Saturdays, at 40%. Those interviewed on Tuesdays were the least likely to have had a drink in the past day, at 27%. This was followed by Thursdays (30%) and Wednesdays (31%). Reported drinking was slightly higher on Mondays, at 32%, likely because of more frequent drinking on Sundays.

Reports of most recently having had a drink "two days ago" reinforce the finding that drinking is higher on weekends, while, regardless of the day of interview, roughly two-thirds indicate they had a drink within the previous seven days.

Self-Reported Time U.S. Drinkers Last Had an Alcoholic Drink

Based on day of interview

	Last 24 hours	Two days ago	Total within last 2 days	Total within last week
Day interviewed:	%	%	%	%
Monday	32	14	46	69
Tuesday	27	9	36	66
Wednesday	31	5	37	68
Thursday	30	7	37	66
Friday	34	6	40	68
Saturday	40	5	44	67
Sunday	44	9	53	66

Data from 2001-2014 annual Consumption Habits surveys

GALLUP

Average Drinks Consumed Weekly Holds Steady at 4.1

Gallup measures the amount Americans drink by asking those who ever drink to report how many drinks they had in the past seven days. This year, the average consumed by drinkers in the past week is 4.1, similar to the average in recent years. This includes 35% who had no drinks in the past week, and 50% who had between one and seven drinks. The average is pushed higher by the 9% who had between eight and 19 drinks, and the 5% who had 20 or more.

Reported alcohol consumption is a bit lower today than it was from 2002 to 2010, when the average approached five drinks, but it is higher than in the late 1990s, when drinkers consumed closer to 3.5 drinks per week, on average.

Average Number of Drinks Consumed in Past Week by U.S. Drinkers

Approximately how many drinks of any kind of alcoholic beverages did you drink in the past seven days?

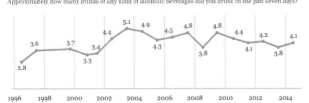

Mean includes zero drinks for those who did not drink in past seven days

GALLUP

Bottom Line

Drinking is the norm for about four in 10 Americans. That includes 32% who say they had between one and seven drinks in the past

week and another 9% who consumed eight or more drinks. Another 22% appear to drink less routinely, while slightly more than one-third don't drink at all.

On average, U.S. drinkers consume about four drinks per week. And to the extent they drink, it is more likely to be on the weekend than any day during the week.

No single type of alcohol dominates American culture, but beer edges out wine as the preferred drink, although by a smaller margin than it did a decade or so ago.

Survey Methods

Results for this Gallup poll are based on telephone interviews conducted July 7–10, 2014, with a random sample of 1,013 adults, aged 18 and older, living in all 50 U.S. states and the District of Columbia.

For results based on the total sample of national adults, the margin of sampling error is ±4 percentage points at the 95% confidence level.

For results based on the total sample of 645 adults who drink alcoholic beverages, the margin of sampling error is ±4 percentage points at the 95% confidence level.

July 24, 2014
AMERICANS STILL OPPOSE LOWERING THE DRINKING AGE
Reject lowering age to 18 by 74% to 25%

by Jeffrey M. Jones

PRINCETON, NJ—Thirty years after federal legislation established 21 as a uniform minimum age to drink alcohol in all states, Americans are widely opposed to lowering the legal drinking age to 18. Seventy-four percent say they would oppose such legislation, while 25% would favor it. The level of opposition is similar to what Gallup has measured in the past.

Would you favor or oppose a federal law that would lower the drinking age in all states to 18?

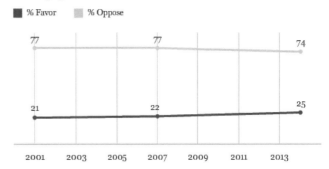

In 1984, President Ronald Reagan signed into law a bill that withheld a portion of federal highway funds from states that did not have a minimum drinking age of 21. A Gallup Poll conducted weeks before Reagan signed the law found Americans widely favored raising the drinking age to 21, by 79% to 18%.

One of the major aims of the 1984 law was to reduce the amount of driving fatalities involving young adults. That was especially a concern when neighboring states had different minimum drinking ages. Those those old enough to drive, but not old enough to drink in their own state, would drive to a neighboring state with a lower drinking age to purchase or consume alcohol. Research shows the 1984 law did help reduce vehicle fatalities involving alcohol, particularly among young adults.

Despite the progress made in reducing traffic deaths involving alcohol, drunk driving remains a factor in many automobile fatalities. Also, one of the major concerns with alcohol today is binge drinking among young adults, and it is not clear that having a higher drinking age helps in that regard. Rather, some experts suggest lowering the drinking age, and teaching teens and young adults to drink responsibly at a younger age, would help to reduce the allure of alcohol to those forbidden by law to possess it.

But Americans are either not aware of or not persuaded by such arguments, given that public support for a minimum drinking age of 21 seems pretty solid and consistent over the past three decades.

Liberals, Drinkers Least Likely to Oppose Lower Drinking Age

All major subgroups are opposed to lowering the drinking age. Political ideology is one of the major dividing lines on the issue, with liberals (34%) among the most supportive of lowering the drinking age and conservatives (18%) among the least supportive subgroups. There are only minor differences by political party.

Favor/Oppose Federal Law to Lower Drinking Age in All States to 18, by Subgroup

	% Favor	% Oppose
Postgraduate	37	63
Drink alcohol weekly	35	64
Political liberal	34	66
Drink alcohol (ever)	29	71
Male	28	72
30-49 years old	28	72
Seldom/Never attend church	28	71
Political independent	28	72
College graduate only	27	72
West	27	72
18-29 years old	26	74
White	25	73
Midwest	25	75
Political moderate	25	74
Have children under 18	25	75
Do not have children under 18	25	74
50-64 years old	24	74
East	24	75
Some college education	24	75
Attend church nearly weekly/monthly	24	75
Nonwhite	23	77
South	23	75
Democrat	23	75
Female	22	77
High school education or less	21	78
Republican	21	79
65+ years old	19	79
Attend church weekly	19	80
Conservative	18	81
Do not drink alcohol	18	81

July 7-10, 2014

Another major predictor of support for lowering the drinking age is whether one personally drinks alcohol. Twenty-nine percent of those who drink alcohol at least on occasion favor lowering the drinking age compared with 18% who never drink. Support is even higher among those who drink regularly—on a weekly basis—at 35%.

Also, support for lowering the drinking age tends to be higher among those who have higher levels of education, with 37% of those with a postgraduate degree supporting such a change in the law.

Although younger adults in the current poll are no more likely to favor lowering the drinking age than their older counterparts, Gallup has found this relationship in past surveys in 2001 and 2007.

Implications

It is widely known that underage drinking remains common in the U.S., despite the uniform minimum drinking age of 21 in all states. One proposed solution to the problem is to lower the drinking age to 18. Although such a move could be seen as giving in to lawbreaking, it may also encourage those under 21 who drink to do so in public settings where their alcohol intake can be better monitored.

The United States' minimum age of 21 is higher than in nearly every other country. Further, there are questions about why those under 21 cannot legally drink alcohol when they are permitted to drive, vote, and serve in the military. In fact, that was the rationale that led many states to lower the drinking age to below 21 in the 1970s. Of course, those changes in the law created their own set of problems with drunk driving, although that may have been partly a result of the lack of uniformity in state drinking laws as well as irresponsible drinking by those between the ages of 18 and 20.

In any case, the public is widely opposed to lowering the drinking age, and has been for some time. Thus, any proposed legislation to legalize drinking at the age of 18 is unlikely to succeed unless Americans' attitudes on the proper minimum drinking change. Even change in public attitudes alone may not be enough to change the law, as tying federal highway funds to a minimum drinking age of 21 is an incentive for states to leave their laws unchanged.

Survey Methods

Results for this Gallup poll are based on telephone interviews conducted July 7–10, 2014, with a random sample of 1,013 adults, aged 18 and older, living in all 50 U.S. states and the District of Columbia.

For results based on the total sample of national adults, the margin of sampling error is ±4 percentage points at the 95% confidence level.

July 24, 2014
NO VACATION FOR ONE IN FIVE MICROBUSINESS OWNERS LAST YEAR
Lack of vacation leaves U.S. microbusiness owners less satisfied but still energized

by Ben Ryan

WASHINGTON, D.C.—One in five U.S. microbusiness owners (20%) report not taking any vacation days in the past 12 months, with another 21% saying they took a week or less. These owners are also the most likely to say they will not be vacationing anytime soon—with almost half (9% of microbusiness owners overall) saying they don't expect to take a vacation in the next year either.

Microbusiness Owners and Their Amount of Vacation

How many vacation days did you take in the past 12 months?

	Percent
No vacation days	20%
One week or less	21%
One to two weeks	20%
Two to three weeks	10%
One month	10%
Two months	9%
More than two months	9%

June 2014 (n=1,004)

GALLUP'

The Sam's Club/Gallup Microbusiness Tracker follows micro-business owners'—those with five or fewer workers, including the owner—basic preparedness and state of mind, highlighting their unique concerns and needs as well as their readiness to meet the day-to-day challenges of being a microbusiness owner. Although virtually all businesses begin as microbusinesses, only some grow into the small, medium, or large enterprises that employ most American workers. Understanding microbusinesses' unique challenges and concerns can provide important insights into the factors shaping the future of the American economy.

The median annual vacation for microbusiness owners is 12 days, comparable with average vacations across the general workforce. By contrast, the average number of annual vacation days for microbusiness owners in the U.S. is 29 days. That average is pulled higher by the 18% who report taking two months or more of vacation time in the past 12 months.

Microbusiness Owners' Vacation Days, by Demographic Group

	Average vacation days per year	Median vacation days per year
Revenue of less than $10,000	32	10
Revenue of $10,000 to less than $50,000	30	10
Revenue of $50,000 to less than $100,000	32	14
Revenue of $100,000 to less than $500,000	24	12
Revenue of $500,000 or more	21	10
Has no employees	32	14
Has employees	24	10
In business one year or less	19	7
In business two to five years	26	10
In business six to 10 years	28	14
In business 11 to 20 years	27	12
In business more than 20 years	33	14
18 to 34 years old	16	7
35 to 49 years old	19	10
50 to 64 years old	25	10
65+ years old	45	15

December 2013-June 2014 (n=2,683)

GALLUP'

Microbusiness owners reporting higher revenue and those who employ other workers take fewer vacation days, on average, than owners with lower revenue and those who have no employees. Also, those who started their businesses within the past year report taking much less vacation in that time than those running more established businesses. Business owners operating a company for 20 years or more take the most vacation time.

While microbusiness owners bringing in lower annual revenue report taking more vacation, on average, the median amount of vacation increases with higher business revenue. This indicates that a number of microbusiness owners earning lower revenue are vacation "outliers" who take much more vacation per year than their peers. However, among those with the highest revenue (over $500,000 per year) the median number of vacation days drops back down to only 10, while the average number also falls to the lowest number among any revenue bracket. Among these highest-earning microbusiness owners, far fewer take large amounts of vacation.

Microbusiness owners who report taking less vacation in the past 12 months also work more hours per week. Those who say they took no vacation in the past year report working an average of 42 hours per week for the past month, three hours more per week than the average microbusiness owner (39 hours). Owners past retirement age (65+) are the most likely to say they work fewer than 10 hours per week (20%, vs. 15% overall) and to say they take more than two months of vacation (15%, vs. 8% overall).

Microbusiness Owners' Hours Per Week, by Demographic Group

	Average hours per week	Median hours per week
Revenue of less than $10,000	27	20
Revenue of $10,000 to less than $50,000	34	30
Revenue of $50,000 to less than $100,000	41	40
Revenue of $100,000 to less than $500,000	47	50
Revenue of $500,000 or more	51	50
Has no employees	36	30
Has employees	43	45
In business one year or less	40	40
In business two to five years	38	35
In business six to 10 years	37	40
In business 11 to 20 years	39	40
In business more than 20 years	41	40
18 to 34 years old	40	40
35 to 49 years old	44	45
50 to 64 years old	40	40
65+ years old	34	30

December 2013-June 2014 (n=2,683)

GALLUP'

Lack of Vacation Leaves U.S. Microbusiness Owners Less Satisfied But Still Energized

Microbusiness owners who do not take any vacation days are less satisfied with their standard of living and struggle more to balance their work and personal life.

Microbusiness Owners and Their Level of Satisfaction

Thinking about your life in general, please rate your level of agreement with each of the following using a five-point scale, where 5 means "strongly agree" and 1 means "strongly disagree." (Percentage of those in different vacation groupings rating each statement 1 through 5)

		1	2	3	4	5
I struggle to balance my work and personal life.	All microbusiness owners	23%	16%	27%	16%	18%
	No vacation last year	21%	13%	24%	13%	29%
	No vacation next year	20%	14%	22%	18%	26%
	No vacation either year	19%	14%	23%	10%	32%
I am satisfied with my standard of living.	All microbusiness owners	6%	11%	23%	28%	32%
	No vacation last year	14%	14%	24%	22%	26%
	No vacation next year	17%	11%	27%	22%	23%
	No vacation either year	21%	10%	28%	19%	22%

All microbusiness owners/No vacation last year n=2,683; No vacation next year n=160; No vacation either year n=88

GALLUP'

However, compared with all microbusiness owners, just as many of those who neither took nor expect to take a vacation "strongly agree" that they are in excellent health (36%, vs. 37% overall), even while more of them "strongly disagree" (11%, vs. 4% overall). Similarly, just as many of these owners strongly agree that they have the ideal job (42%, vs. 40% overall) even while more strongly disagree (10%, vs. 4% overall). They are also more likely to strongly agree that they feel energized by their work.

Microbusiness Owners and Their Level of Engagement

Thinking about your life in general, please rate your level of agreement with each of the following using a five-point scale, where 5 means "strongly agree" and 1 means "strongly disagree." (Percentage of those in different vacation groupings rating each statement 1 through 5)

		1	2	3	4	5
I have the ideal job.	All microbusiness owners	4%	7%	19%	29%	40%
	No vacation last year	7%	10%	17%	27%	39%
	No vacation next year	8%	10%	18%	23%	41%
	No vacation either year	10%	8%	19%	21%	42%
I am in excellent health.	All microbusiness owners	4%	7%	21%	32%	37%
	No vacation last year	5%	6%	27%	26%	36%
	No vacation next year	7%	9%	21%	30%	33%
	No vacation either year	11%	8%	22%	22%	36%
I feel energized by my work.	All microbusiness owners	3%	7%	20%	34%	37%
	No vacation last year	4%	8%	18%	34%	35%
	No vacation next year	5%	8%	17%	31%	38%
	No vacation either year	4%	10%	11%	33%	42%

All microbusiness owners/No vacation last year n=2,683; No vacation next year n=160; No vacation either year n= 88

GALLUP

Bottom Line

While microbusiness owners who don't take vacation time are more likely than their peers who do vacation to report struggling with their work/life balance and being dissatisfied with their standard of living, some appear to be energized by the workload. This polarization may point to two groups of microbusiness owners who take little to no vacation—those who are energized by their ideal job and might choose not to take time away from it, and those who are struggling and might not be able to afford to take time away.

Indeed, microbusiness owners who have just started out and those younger than 35 report taking the fewest median vacation days per year, while median vacation increases with business revenue up to the $100,000- to $500,000-per-year range. These findings suggest that as microbusinesses become more established and bring in more revenue, owners can afford to increase the amount of vacation time they take away from their businesses. Among this group, those who cannot afford (whether in terms of financial ability or available time) to take vacations do not—and those who can, do.

However, among those with the highest revenue (over $500,000 per year) the median number of vacation days drops back down to only 10, while the average number also falls to the lowest number among any revenue bracket. Owners making the most revenue also report working the most hours per week. Despite higher revenues that should enable them to take as much or more vacation than their smaller-budget peers, these microbusiness owners continue to invest more time and energy into their businesses.

Read more Sam's Club/Gallup Microbusiness Tracker findings at samsclub.com/newsroom.

Survey Methods

Results for the Sam's Club/Gallup Microbusiness Tracker are based on telephone interviews conducted on a quarterly basis with a random sample of microbusiness owners aged 18 and older, living in all 50 U.S. states and the District of Columbia. Business owners selected were those who reported owning a "microbusiness" with five or fewer workers, including the owner. Results from the Quarter 2, 2014, study are based on 1,004 interviews conducted May 8–23, 2014. Results from the Quarter 1, 2014, study are based on 868 interviews conducted Feb. 18–March 2, 2014, and results from the Quarter 4, 2013, study are based on 864 interviews conducted Dec. 2–11, 2013.

July 24, 2014
AMERICANS' REACTION TO MIDDLE EAST SITUATION SIMILAR TO PAST
Divided on whether Israel's actions against Hamas justified

by Jeffrey M. Jones

PRINCETON, NJ—Americans are divided in their views of whether Israel's actions against the Palestinian group Hamas is "mostly justified" or "mostly unjustified," but they widely view Hamas' actions as mostly unjustified. Those results are similar to what Gallup measured 12 years ago during another period of heightened Israeli-Palestinian violence, and they are consistent with Americans' generally more positive views of the Israelis than of the Palestinians.

Americans' Views of Actions in Current Middle East Conflict

	Justified	Unjustified	No opinion
	%	%	%
July 22-23, 2014			
Israel's actions against Hamas	42	39	20
Hamas' actions against Israel	11	70	20
April 3, 2002			
Israel's actions against Palestinians	44	34	22
Palestinians' actions against Israel	17	62	21

NOTE: 2014 wording "Palestinian group Hamas"; 2002 wording "Palestinians"

GALLUP

The latest escalation of violence in the Middle East occurred after the militant Palestinian group Hamas captured and killed three Israeli students and a Palestinian teen was subsequently murdered in an alleged revenge killing. The tensions erupted into bombings, missile attacks, and armed conflict. The two sides have not agreed to a cease-fire so far despite the international community's efforts to end the fighting.

Americans do not view the current round of violence as substantially worse than the 2002 fighting, when Israel invaded areas under Palestinian control while Palestinian suicide bombers targeted Israel. A separate question in the new July 22–23 Gallup poll underscores the finding that Americans' see the current round of fighting as no worse than usual: 45% of Americans say the current Israeli-Palestinian conflict is "more serious than past conflicts between them," 43% about as serious as past conflicts, and 3% as "less serious."

Republicans See Israel's Actions as Justified; Democrats Disagree

There are not substantial differences across major demographic and attitudinal subgroups as to whether Hamas' actions are justified;

significant majorities of all major subgroups say what Hamas is doing is unjustified. However, there are significant differences in opinions of Israel's actions by subgroup.

Consistent with Republicans' more pro-Israel outlook, the majority of Republican identifiers back what Israel is doing. Meanwhile, Democrats take the opposing view, with nearly half saying Israel's actions are unjustified.

Americans' Views of Israel's Actions in Current Middle East Conflict, by Political Party

	Justified	Unjustified	No opinion
	%	%	%
Republicans	65	21	14
Independents	36	46	18
Democrats	31	47	22

July 22-23, 2014

GALLUP

Other subgroup differences may stem from the basic party divisions. Men, older Americans, and whites are more likely than women, younger Americans, and nonwhites to say Israel's actions are justified. Although Americans with postgraduate education tend to be politically Democratic, they are the most likely education group to endorse Israel's actions.

Americans' Views of Israel's Actions in Current Middle East Conflict, by Subgroup

	Justified	Unjustified	No opinion
	%	%	%
Men	51	32	17
Women	33	44	22
White	50	34	16
Nonwhite	25	49	27
18-29 years old	25	51	24
30-49 years old	36	43	22
50-64 years old	53	29	18
65+ years old	55	31	14
High school or less	34	45	21
Some college	43	38	19
College graduate only	49	33	18
Postgraduate	53	27	20

July 22-23, 2014

GALLUP

A majority of Americans interviewed July 22–23 say they are following news of the conflict very (22%) or somewhat (37%) closely. The more closely Americans are following the news about the Middle East situation, the more likely they are to think Israel's actions are justified.

There are not large partisan differences in terms of whether the current round of violence is more serious than in the past. However, 65% of those following the story very closely, and 54% following it somewhat closely, say the current conflict is more serious than past Israeli-Palestinian fighting.

Americans' Views of Israel's Actions in Current Middle East Conflict, by How Closely Following News About the Situation

	Justified	Unjustified	No opinion
	%	%	%
Very closely	71	24	5
Somewhat closely	51	42	7
Not closely	18	43	39

July 22-23, 2014

GALLUP

Implications

Americans are generally pessimistic about the Israelis and Palestinians being able to settle their differences and live in peace, and while the escalated tensions between the two sides have been a major news story the last two weeks, the American public does not view it as any more serious than past conflicts.

Americans continue to exhibit more positivity toward Israel than the Palestinians, but also stop short of saying Israel's actions in the current situation are justified.

At this point, more than two weeks into the conflict, it is not clear how long the increased violence will continue, as efforts to broker a cease-fire have been unsuccessful.

Survey Methods

Results for this Gallup poll are based on telephone interviews conducted July 22–23, 2014, on the Gallup Daily tracking survey, with a random sample of 1,016 adults, aged 18 and older, living in all 50 U.S. states and the District of Columbia.

For results based on the total sample of national adults, the margin of sampling error is ±4 percentage points at the 95% confidence level.

July 25, 2014
NEARLY HALF IN U.S. REMAIN WORRIED ABOUT THEIR WEIGHT
Two-thirds of overweight Americans express concern about their current weight

by Joy Wilke

WASHINGTON, D.C.—Almost half of Americans (45%) worry about their weight "all" or "some of the time," significantly higher than the 34% who reported this level of worry in 1990. Naturally, Americans who consider themselves to be overweight are much more likely to worry about their weight than are those who say their weight is "about right," 67% vs. 32%, respectively.

About the same percentage of Americans report worrying about their weight now as did in 2012, when Gallup last asked the question, and nearly half of American adults remain preoccupied with their weight. These data are from the Gallup Consumption Habits survey, conducted July 7–10.

Different segments of the population are more preoccupied with their weight than others. Women (21%) are significantly more likely than men (9%) to say they worry about their weight all of the time.

Almost one-third of men (32%) say they never worry about their weight, compared with just 16% of women.

Percentage of Americans Who Worry About Their Weight All or Some of the Time
How often do you worry about your weight?
How would you describe your own personal weight situation right now?

■ National adults ■ Self-described as overweight ■ Self-described as weight is about right

GALLUP

Young adults are also more likely to worry about their weight all of the time, compared with other age groups. Americans aged 65 and up are the most likely to report "never" worrying about their weight.

How often do you worry about your weight?

	% All of the time	% Some of the time	% Not too often	% Never
GENDER				
Men	9	26	33	32
Women	21	34	29	16
AGE				
18-29 years	21	18	33	28
30-49 years	14	34	29	24
50-64 years	14	39	32	14
65+ years	12	25	32	30

July 7-10, 2014

GALLUP

Losing Weight Remains a Priority for Some Americans

Although 45% of Americans say they worry about their weight, a smaller percentage, 29%, say they are seriously trying to lose weight. The percentage of Americans actively trying to lose weight was much lower, 18%, in 1990. Since 2003, at least one-quarter of Americans have reported they are seriously trying to lose weight.

At this time are you seriously trying to lose weight?
% Yes

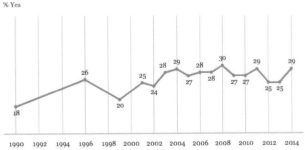

GALLUP

A majority of Americans who see themselves as overweight, 54%, report they are trying to lose weight at this time. Over one-third

of women (35%) and nonwhite Americans (41%) say they are seriously trying to lose weight, compared with 22% of men and 24% of whites.

Trying to Lose Weight, Among Select Groups
At this time are you seriously trying to lose weight?

	% Yes, trying to lose weight	% No, not trying
CURRENT WEIGHT		
Overweight	54	45
About right	12	88
Underweight	5	95
GENDER		
Men	22	78
Women	35	65
RACE		
White	24	76
Nonwhite	41	59

July 7-10, 2014

GALLUP

Gallup asked the 29% of Americans who say they are trying to lose weight to share one or two of the primary reasons why they are doing so. About half of those trying to lose weight say it is to be healthier in general, and another 29% say they are trying to lose weight for specific medical or health reasons. About one-quarter report they want to lose weight to improve their physical appearance. About one in 10 say they are doing so simply to feel better.

Reasons Americans Are Trying to Lose Weight
What are one or two of the most important reasons why you are trying to lose weight? (Asked of those trying to lose weight)

	%
To be healthier	49
For medical/health reasons (diabetes, high blood pressure, etc.)	29
To look better/improve physical appearance	23
To feel better	11
For family/loved ones	6
To be more fit/improve athleticism	5
To improve energy level	4
To prolong [my] life	4
Other	2

July 7-10, 2014

GALLUP

Implications

Almost half of Americans say that they worry about their weight all or some of the time, including two-thirds of those who see themselves as overweight. This finding suggests that weight plays a major role in the American public's psyche, particularly for those who are overweight. Those who are actively trying to lose weight generally say they are doing so for health reasons, suggesting Americans are aware that carrying extra pounds can negatively affect their health.

Still, only 29% of the American public say they are seriously trying to lose weight, which is significantly below the 45% who see themselves as overweight. Furthermore, the 45% who admit to being overweight is lower than the 63% of Americans who are overweight or obese according to the Gallup-Healthways Well-Being Index, which uses self-reported height and weight to calculate body mass index (BMI). These findings underscore previous Gallup research showing that even viewing yourself as overweight is not enough to prompt some Americans to try to lose weight.

Survey Methods

Results for this Gallup poll are based on telephone interviews conducted July 7–10, 2014, with a random sample of 1,013 adults, aged 18 and older, living in all 50 U.S. states and the District of Columbia.

For results based on the total sample of national adults, the margin of sampling error is ±4 percentage points at the 95% confidence level.

For results based on the total sample of 292 adults who are trying to lose weight, the margin of sampling error is ±7 percentage points at the 95% confidence level.

July 28, 2014
RELIGION REMAINS A STRONG MARKER OF POLITICAL IDENTITY IN U.S.
Little change in basic relationship over last six and a half years

by Frank Newport

PRINCETON, NJ—Even as overall party identification trends in the U.S. have shifted over the past six and half years, the relationship between religion and party identification has remained consistent. Very religious Americans are more likely to identify with or lean toward the Republican Party and less frequently identify with or lean toward the Democratic Party, compared with those who are moderately or nonreligious.

Political Party Affiliation, by Religiousness, Monthly Trend, February 2008-June 2014
% Identifying as Democrats or leaning Democratic minus % identifying as Republicans or leaning Republican

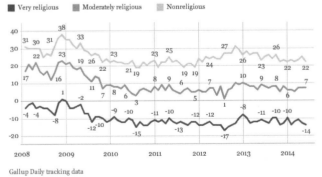

Gallup Daily tracking data

GALLUP

Gallup classifies Americans as "very religious" if they say religion is an important part of their daily lives and that they attend religious services every week or almost every week. That group constituted 41% of all U.S. adults in the first half of 2014.

"Nonreligious" Americans (30% of Americans in 2014) are those who say religion is not an important part of their daily lives and that they seldom or never attend religious services. The remaining group, 29%, are classified as "moderately religious." These people say religion is important in their lives but that they do not attend services regularly, or that religion is not important but that they still attend services.

From 2008 to June 2014, nonreligious Americans have been the most Democratic of the three religious groups, with a net Democratic value ranging between +38 and +19 over that period. Those who are moderately religious have also tilted Democratic, with net values ranging from +23 to +1. Those who are very religious are least Democratic, with net values in the negative range, meaning that on average, this group identifies with or leans toward the Republican Party more than the Democratic Party.

All three groups were more Democratic and less Republican in 2008 and early 2009, reflecting the generally more Democratic tilt of the country at that time, but the differences among those who are very, moderately, or nonreligious were as significant then as they are now. In short, the religious gap in party identification has persisted over nearly seven years.

These data are based on Gallup Daily tracking samples of approximately 30,000 interviews per month from 2008 to 2012, and 15,000 per month in 2013 to 2014.

About Half of Very Religious Americans Are Republicans

Data from the first six months of 2014 provide more detailed insights into the underlying relationship between religiousness and partisanship. Republican identification (including leaners) drops from 49% to 29% among those who are very religious versus those who are unreligious, respectively, while Democratic identification rises from 36% to 52% between these two groups.

Political Party Affiliation, by Religiousness: June 2014

	Republicans/Leaners	Independents/No leaners	Democrats/Leaners	Difference: Democrats minus Republicans
	%	%	%	
Very religious Americans	49	11	36	-13
Moderately religious Americans	38	14	44	+6
Nonreligious Americans	29	15	52	+23

Gallup Daily tracking data

GALLUP

Black Democratic Partisanship Unaffected by Religiousness

The relationship between religiosity and party identification in the U.S. has been both constant across time and most demographic groups within the population, including age, gender, region, and socio-economic status. Within each category of these groups, Americans who are the most religious are the most likely to be Republican, while those who are the least religious are the most likely to be Democratic.

The one exception to the basic religiousness and party identification relationship occurs among black Americans, who tend to be the most Democratic of any major race and ethnic group measured. Blacks are very religious on average, but the political orientation of blacks who are nonreligious does not vary significantly from those who are very religious. Democratic affiliation among black

Americans hovers near 75% within all three religious groups of black Americans.

Political Party Affiliation, by Religiousness, Among Black Americans

	Republicans/ Leaners	Democrats/ Leaners	Difference: Democrats minus Republicans
	%	%	
Very religious	9	77	+68
Moderately religious	10	76	+66
Nonreligious	9	73	+64

Gallup Daily tracking data

GALLUP

On the other hand, non-Hispanic whites, Hispanics, and Asians follow the basic pattern observed in the general population, with more religious members of each group skewing more Republican. The relationship is most pronounced among non-Hispanic whites, among whom the swing in the net Democratic advantage goes from +18 points among those who are unreligious to −39 points among those who are very religious.

Very religious Hispanics and very religious Asians are also significantly less likely to identify with or lean toward the Democratic Party than those in each group who are less religious. Americans in both of these groups show a Democratic preference overall, but that preference is significantly less pronounced among very religious Hispanics and Asians than among the others.

Political Party Affiliation, by Religiousness, Race and Ethnicity

	Republicans/ Leaners	Democrats/ Leaners	Difference: Democrats minus Republicans
	%	%	
WHITE AMERICANS			
Very religious	64	25	-39
Moderately religious	51	35	-16
Nonreligious	33	51	18
HISPANIC AMERICANS			
Very religious	26	46	20
Moderately religious	20	51	31
Nonreligious	20	55	35
ASIAN AMERICANS			
Very religious	32	50	18
Moderately religious	19	59	40
Nonreligious	22	61	39

Gallup Daily tracking, January-June 2014

GALLUP

Bottom Line

The relationship between Americans' religiousness and their party preference is a persistent and well-documented social pattern that has remained extraordinarily stable over the last six and a half years. The basic nature of the relationship—in which those who are the most religious are the most likely to identify as Republicans—has changed little. With few exceptions, Americans' religiousness remains a major predictor of their political orientation.

The underlying explanations for the relationship are complex, and have to do with the historical development of partisan politics in the decades since Jimmy Carter and Ronald Reagan were president, differing positions of the parties on moral and values issues such as abortion and same-sex marriage, and geographic patterns

of residency that are simultaneously related to religiousness and partisanship.

From a practical politics standpoint, Republicans face the challenge of expanding their party's appeal beyond the minority of Americans who are very religious, and appealing to Hispanics and Asians given that even the most religious of these growing groups tilt Democratic, albeit not as much as others in these groups who are less religious. Democrats face the challenge of attempting to broaden their party's appeal beyond the base of those who are moderately or nonreligious, a tactic that most likely will require effort to frame the party's positions on social justice and equality issues in a way that is compatible with a high degree of religiousness.

Survey Methods

Results for this Gallup poll are based on telephone interviews conducted from January 2008 through June 2014 on the Gallup Daily tracking survey, with monthly random samples of between 15,000 and 30,000 national adults, aged 18 and older, living in all 50 U.S. states and the District of Columbia.

For results based on the total sample of 87,023 national adults interviewed January–June 2014, the margin of sampling error is ±1 percentage point at the 95% confidence level.

July 28, 2014
AMERICANS MORE LIKELY TO AVOID DRINKING SODA THAN BEFORE
More than nine in 10 try to include fruits or vegetables in diet

by Justin McCarthy

WASHINGTON, D.C.—Nearly two-thirds of Americans say they avoid soda in their diet, while more than half say they avoid sugar. Meanwhile, more than nine in 10 Americans claim they try to include fruits (92%) or vegetables (93%) in their diet—slightly more than said this previously.

Americans' Dietary Habits of Drinking Soda

Thinking about the food you eat, for each of the following please say if it is something you actively try to include in your diet, something you actively try to avoid, or something you don't think about either way. How about soda or pop?

	Include	Avoid	Don't think about
	%	%	%
Jul 7-10, 2014	23	63	13
Jul 8-11, 2004	25	51	24
Jul 9-11, 2002	36	41	23

GALLUP

These data are from a July 7–10 Gallup poll that asked Americans about their consumption habits. Americans have become increasingly wary of drinking soda since Gallup began asking them about their dietary choices in 2002. At that time, only 41% said they actively tried to avoid soda, a percentage that has now jumped to 63%.

Studies continue to reveal the adverse health effects of consuming soda, and high-profile attempts to ban the purchase of large individual servings of soda or to tax it have apparently raised Americans' consciousness about drinking it, even if closer to half still consume the beverage. At this point, 13% of Americans say they don't think about soda intake, down from 24% a decade ago.

Americans More Likely to Include Vegetables and Fruits Than Organic Foods

The data generally show that Americans are highly aware of what they should and should not be including in their diet, including their almost universal claim that they include fruits and vegetables in their daily eating plans. Because it is not clear that such a high proportion of Americans really do eat this healthily, the challenge appears to be one of changing their actual behavior rather than their underlying knowledge of what is good and bad for their health.

Less than half of Americans, 45%, try to include organic foods—which have become increasingly available in stores in recent years—in their diet. Nearly as many, 38%, do not give much consideration to including or avoiding organic foods, a higher percentage than for any other type of food on the list.

Americans' Dietary Choices

Thinking about the food you eat, for each of the following please say if it is something you actively try to include in your diet, something you actively try to avoid, or something you don't think about either way.

	% Include	% Avoid	% Don't think about
Vegetables	93	1	5
Fruits	92	1	6
Chicken and other poultry	84	5	10
Fish and other seafood	75	9	15
Grains such as bread, cereal, pasta, and rice	70	15	14
Dairy products	69	13	17
Beef and other red meat	62	22	16
Organic foods	45	15	38
Carbohydrates	41	29	28
Salt	28	46	25
Sugar	27	52	19
Soda or pop	23	63	13
Fat	22	56	21

July 7-10, 2014

GALLUP

Americans Also Avoiding Sugar, But Change Not as Evident as It Is for Soda

Avoidance of sugar has also increased since 2002, most likely for similar reasons. Sugar has a wide variety of negative effects on the body, and many experts say Americans consume too much of it. While the percentage of Americans who actively include sugar in their diet hasn't changed significantly since 2002, the number avoiding it has reached a new high. Meanwhile, the number of Americans who don't think about their sugar intake has reached a new low (19%).

Americans' Dietary Habits of Consuming Sugar

	Include	Avoid	Don't think about
	%	%	%
Jul 7-10, 2014	27	52	19
Dec 8-10, 2006	22	51	27
Jul 8-11, 2004	21	51	28
Jul 9-11, 2002	29	43	27

GALLUP

But while Americans are attempting to adjust their consumption of soda and sugar, minding their salt intake hasn't changed much over the years, with the current level of avoidance about the same as in 2002. Today, 28% of Americans say they try to include salt in their diet, 46% avoid it, and 25% do not think about it either way.

Americans' Dietary Habits of Consuming Salt

	Include	Avoid	Don't think about
	%	%	%
Jul 7-10, 2014	28	46	25
Dec 8-10, 2006	24	49	27
Jul 8-11, 2004	23	47	30
Jul 9-11, 2002	27	45	28

GALLUP

Dietary Choices Among Food Groups Virtually Unchanged Since 2002

Among protein-rich foods, chicken and other poultry remain what the largest proportion of Americans try to include (84%), followed by fish and other seafood (75%), and beef and other red meat (62%)—all largely unchanged since 2002. Still, some Americans avoid these foods, with 5% avoiding chicken, 9% avoiding seafood, and more than one in five (22%) avoiding red meat. Between 10% and 16% don't think about whether any of these high-protein foods are on their personal menus.

Seven in 10 Americans try to include grains (70%) and dairy products (69%) in their diet. While dietary trends for dairy have not fluctuated greatly since 2002, avoidance of grains more than doubled between 2002 (6%) and 2004 (14%). Since then, the percentage who avoid grains has remained virtually unchanged (it's now 15%) despite the introduction of the Paleo diet, which discourages carbohydrates. Currently, 41% include carbs in their diet, while 29% avoid them.

Bottom Line

Since 2002, soda and sugar have moved into the category of food a majority of Americans appear to consider bad for them. This year, more Americans than ever say they try to avoid drinking soda, while there has been little change in sentiment about avoiding sugar intake. At the same time, avoidance of salt—something close to half the public tries to do—has not increased. And despite a series of diet fads that frown on carbohydrates, the percentage of Americans avoiding grains has increased only at the margins since 2004; the vast majority of Americans still view these as important to include in their diet.

A promising note is that almost all Americans say they try to include fruits and vegetables. But this doesn't necessarily reflect their success in doing so.

In a nation that struggles with obesity, Americans' words about what they eat likely need to be followed up with actions.

Survey Methods

Results for this Gallup poll are based on telephone interviews conducted July 7–10, 2014, on the Gallup Daily tracking survey, with a random sample of 1,013 adults, aged 18 and older, living in all 50 U.S. states and the District of Columbia.

For results based on the total sample of national adults, the margin of sampling error is ±4 percentage points at the 95% confidence level.

July 29, 2014

AMERICANS STILL AVOID FAT MORE THAN CARBS

Share saying they avoid fat has fallen as new research suggests fat can be healthy

by Andrew Dugan

WASHINGTON, D.C.—Nearly twice as many Americans say they are actively trying to avoid fat in their diet (56%) as say they are actively avoiding carbohydrates (29%). However, fewer Americans are avoiding fat now than a decade ago.

Americans' Dietary Habits Regarding Fat and Carbohydrates

Thinking about the food you eat, for each of the following please say if it is something you actively try to include in your diet, something you actively try to avoid, or something you don't think about either way.

How about carbohydrates/fat?

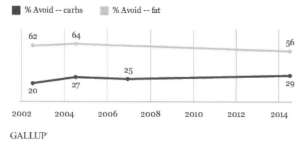

These results are from the Gallup Consumption Habits survey, conducted July 7–10. With nearly half of Americans worrying about their weight "some" or "all" of the time, finding the right diet is an important challenge for many U.S. adults.

Two common types of diets on the market are low-fat and low-carb diets, and the two are often seen as competing with each other. Low-fat diets instruct users to avoid fatty foods, such as red meat, while low- or no-carb diets, popularized by the Atkins diet, allow high-fat foods in place of carbohydrates.

Americans' Dietary Habits of Eating Fat

Thinking about the food you eat, for each of the following please say if it is something you actively try to include in your diet, something you actively try to avoid, or something you don't think about either way.

How about fat?

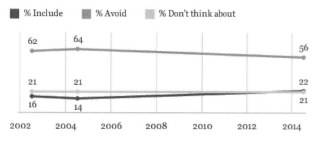

Both types of diets have been on the nutritional scene for decades, though low-fat diets enjoy more support in the form of U.S. government dietary guidelines. An opposing view asserts that processed carbohydrates—not saturated fats—are a key driver of weight gain, and this has gotten some scientific traction lately. *Time*

magazine recently featured an article saying new research showed why "it's time to end the war [against fat]."

But despite the high-profile dietary debate, the public's attitudes about fats and carbohydrates have changed only marginally over the last decade, though perhaps they are now closer to the low-carb mentality. Twenty-two percent of Americans say they actively try to include fat in their diet, a percentage lower than for any of the 12 other foods Gallup measured in the poll. However, this percentage is slightly higher than in 2004 (14%), while the percentage who say they try to avoid fat is down since then.

More than four in 10 Americans (41%) say they try to include carbohydrates, and this is down slightly from the half who said so in 2002, but up from 33% in 2004, when the Atkins diet was fashionable.

Americans' Dietary Habits of Eating Carbohydrates

Thinking about the food you eat, for each of the following please say if it is something you actively try to include in your diet, something you actively try to avoid, or something you don't think about either way.

How about carbohydrates?

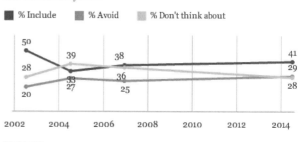

Twenty-eight percent of Americans say they don't think about actively including or avoiding carbohydrates as part of their diet, down from what Gallup found in the mid-2000s. A smaller 21% say they don't think about whether they include or avoid fat in their diet.

Americans Trying to Lose Weight Strongly Avoid Fats

Twenty-nine percent of Americans say they are trying to lose weight. Of these, nearly three-fourths (73%) say they are actively trying to avoid fats. Slightly more than one in 10 (12%) say they are actively trying to *include* fats. However, individuals seeking to lose weight are more likely than the typical American to say they are avoiding carbohydrates (44%), suggesting many dieting Americans do not see an either/or proposition when it comes to determining how much fat and carbohydrates they should consume.

Americans' Dietary Habits Regarding Carbohydrates and Fat by Whether They Are Trying to Lose Weight

July 7-10, 2014

	Yes, seriously trying to lose weight	No, not seriously trying to lose weight
FAT	%	%
Actively try to include	12	26
Actively try to avoid	73	49
Do not think about either way	13	24
CARBOHYDRATES		
Actively try to include	32	44
Actively try to avoid	44	23
Do not think about either way	21	30

GALLUP

Bottom Line

Americans are still more likely to say they are avoiding fat rather than carbohydrates, but they are avoiding carbs more than they once were. Notably, the largest increase in the percentage who actively avoid carbohydrates occurred in 2004, coinciding with the general time the Atkins diet was most popular.

However, avoidance of fat is lower than it was a decade ago, perhaps reflecting new scientific research that is calling into question the supposed insalubrious effects of fat.

Individuals who say they are seriously trying to lose weight are more likely than other Americans to say they avoid both fats and carbohydrates, though fats are clearly the more pressing priority to exclude for dieters. Nonetheless, many dieters appear to take advice from both schools of thought, a reminder that dieters must customize and improvise to find the right balance for themselves.

Survey Methods

Results for this Gallup poll are based on telephone interviews conducted July 7–10, 2014, on the Gallup Daily tracking survey, with a random sample of 1,013 adults, aged 18 and older, living in all 50 U.S. states and the District of Columbia.

For results based on the total sample of national adults, the margin of sampling error is ±4 percentage points at the 95% confidence level.

July 29, 2014
REPORTS OF ALCOHOL-RELATED FAMILY TROUBLE REMAIN UP IN U.S.
Thirty-six percent say alcohol has been a cause of trouble in their family

by Jeffrey M. Jones

PRINCETON, NJ—More than one in three Americans (36%) say drinking alcohol has been a cause of problems in their family at some point, one of the highest figures Gallup has measured since the 1940s. Reports of alcohol-related family troubles have been much more common in recent decades than they were prior to 1990.

Has drinking ever been a cause of trouble in your family?

Gallup updated its longstanding trend on this question in its July 7–10 Consumption Habits poll. When first asked in 1947, 15% of Americans said alcohol had been a cause of family problems. The percentage remained low in the 1960s and 1970s, before it ticked up—to an average of 21%—during the 1980s.

Reports of family problems due to drinking increased further in the 1990s (27%) and 2000s (32%). The average has leveled off at 32% since 2010, although this year's 36% exceeds the current decade's average.

The increase in reported alcohol-related family problems is not due to an increase in drinking among Americans. Since the 1980s, an average of between 62% and 64% of U.S. adults have reported that they drink alcohol on occasion.

Moreover, the frequency with which U.S. drinkers consume alcohol has declined slightly. During the 1980s, an average of 66% of U.S. drinkers reported having one or more drinks in the past seven days, compared with 64% since 2010. Also, the percentage of drinkers reporting having eight or more alcoholic drinks in the past week has declined from an average of 17% during the 1980s to 13% in the current decade.

Thus, it may just be that those who drink are now more likely to do so in a manner that creates problems in their family than in the past. However, other societal factors may have helped cause the increase as well.

First, Americans have a greater understanding and awareness of alcoholism than in the past, and thus there is less of a social stigma attached to it. As such, families who have dealt with alcoholism may be more open about their experiences, and more likely to disclose that information in a survey. Also, in recent decades there has been greater attention paid to alcohol-related crimes, and stricter enforcement of drunken driving–related laws—thus, alcohol-related legal troubles may be more common, pushing up the percentage reporting family troubles. Finally, media attention to "binge drinking" and alcohol-related deaths among young adults may have increased public awareness of newer types of problems stemming from overdrinking.

In recent Gallup surveys, there have been few consistent differences by key demographic groups in the percentage reporting alcohol-related trouble in their family, including by gender, age, education, income, political affiliation, or church attendance.

Drinking Rates Lower Among Those Experiencing Family Troubles

One consistent difference Gallup has found in recent years is that the percentage of Americans who say they drink alcohol varies by whether they report alcohol being a cause of family problems. In Gallup's 2013 and 2014 Consumption Habits surveys, an average of 49% of Americans who say drinking has been a source of family problems say they drink alcohol on occasion. Among those who report no such trouble, a higher average of 66% say they drink.

Alcohol Use, by Reports of Drinking Being a Cause of Family Problems

	Alcohol has been a cause of family trouble	Alcohol has NOT been a cause of family trouble
	%	%
Drink alcohol on occasion	49	66
Abstain from alcohol	50	33

Note: Based on aggregated data from 3,000 interviews in Gallup's 2013 and 2014 Consumption Habits surveys

Gallup also found higher rates of abstinence from alcohol among those who say drinking has been a source of family problems in surveys prior to 2013. That relationship persists even when controlling for factors that predict drinking such as age, gender, education, and church attendance.

These results merely indicate a relationship between past family troubles and current drinking behavior. They cannot, however, establish that those who have experienced alcohol-related problems firsthand intentionally avoid drinking as a consequence, although that would be one potential explanation for the relationship. It is also possible that those who abstain from alcohol may be more likely to characterize incidents arising from alcohol consumption as "trouble" than those who drink.

Implications

In more than seven decades of tracking Americans' drinking behavior, one of the major changes Gallup has seen is an increasing percentage of Americans saying alcohol has caused problems in their family. Though it still remains a minority of the population, the percentage reporting such trouble has more than doubled since the 1970s.

The increase in alcohol-related family troubles may be one factor in Americans' reluctance to lower the drinking age to 18. And while greater awareness of alcohol-related troubles, in addition to an actual increase in the behavior, may be driving up the percentage who report family troubles due to alcohol, the trend does not suggest that the U.S. is making progress curbing some of the problems associated with alcohol use.

Survey Methods

Results for this Gallup poll are based on telephone interviews conducted July 7–10, 2014, with a random sample of 1,013 adults, aged 18 and older, living in all 50 U.S. states and the District of Columbia.

For results based on the total sample of national adults, the margin of sampling error is ±4 percentage points at the 95% confidence level.

July 30, 2014

AMERICANS FAVOR BAN ON SMOKING IN PUBLIC, BUT NOT TOTAL BAN
Nineteen percent favor making smoking totally illegal in U.S.

by Rebecca Riffkin

WASHINGTON, D.C.—A majority of Americans, 56%, are in favor of making smoking in public places illegal. This is in line with what Gallup has measured since 2011. By contrast, until 2008, Gallup found most Americans were opposed to a ban on smoking in public places, with as few as 31% in favor of such a ban in 2003.

The latest results come from Gallup's July 7–10 Consumption Habits survey, in which 21% of Americans report smoking cigarettes, near the historical low. Gallup first began asking about banning public smoking in 2001. At that time, 39% of Americans were in favor of making smoking in public places illegal, while 60% were against it.

Sometime between 2008 and 2011, when Gallup did not ask this question, attitudes shifted from a majority of Americans being *against* making smoking in public places illegal to a majority being in *favor* of making it illegal.

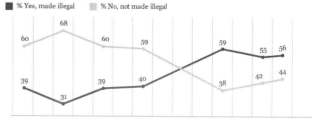

Should smoking in all public places be made totally illegal, or not?

All data based on a half sample

GALLUP

While the majority of Americans are currently in favor of making smoking in public places illegal, only 19% are in favor of making smoking in the U.S. completely illegal. The percentage who are in favor of making smoking totally illegal in the country has been largely steady since Gallup began asking this question in 1990, but it has ticked up slightly in recent years. From 1990 to 2001, an average 13% of Americans supported banning smoking completely. However, in the last two years, the average rose to 21%.

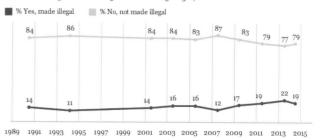

Should smoking in this country be made totally illegal, or not?

2001, 2003, 2005, 2007, 2011, 2013. 2014 data based on a half sample

GALLUP

Young Less Likely Than Old to Support Banning Smoking in Public

Slightly more than a quarter of Americans aged 18 to 29 favor making all smoking illegal in the country, higher than the percentage of older Americans who say the same.

By contrast, a majority of Americans aged 30 and older support banning smoking in public places. Gallup's combined smoking attitudes data from 2011, 2013, and 2014 show that 46% of Americans aged 18 to 29 support banning smoking in public, more than 10 percentage points lower than what is found among older age groups.

Views on the Legality of Smoking, by Age

Should smoking in all public places be made totally illegal, or not?
Should smoking in this country be made totally illegal, or not?

	18-29	30-49	50-64	65+
% Yes, made illegal to smoke in public places	46	57	57	67
% No, not made illegal to smoke in public places	52	41	42	30
% Yes, smoking should be totally illegal	26	20	15	22
% No, smoking should not be totally illegal	73	79	83	74

Combined responses from 2011, 2013, and 2014

GALLUP

These age differences may reflect Americans' different experiences with smoking, especially in public. While smoking in public was far more common a few decades ago, many states have recently enacted smoking bans, especially in public places like bars and restaurants, to protect residents from the harm of secondhand smoke. As a result, younger Americans may have grown up in places where smoking in public was already uncommon, if not illegal, and thus not feel as much of a need to ban it in public now or in the future.

Even though it is part of their lives, this year, one in 10 smokers say that smoking should be totally illegal in this country. Furthermore, about three in 10 smokers say that smoking in public places should be illegal. Other Gallup research has shown that most smokers want to quit and have tried. So smokers may want to make smoking illegal to either help them quit or to discourage others from picking up the habit.

Implications

Few Americans say that smoking should be totally illegal in this country, but a majority support making smoking in public places illegal. Smoking is already illegal in many public places, such as at airports, public parks, schools, bars, and restaurants, but these restrictions vary by state.

According to the U.S. Centers for Disease Control and Prevention, 25 states and the District of Columbia prohibit smoking indoors at worksites, restaurants, and bars. Seven states, Indiana, Kentucky, Mississippi, South Carolina, Texas, West Virginia, and Wyoming, have no statewide smoking restrictions. Gallup found that two of those states, Kentucky and West Virginia, have the highest smoking rates in the nation, with slightly less than a third of the adult population saying they smoke.

Furthermore, a 2013 Associated Press article reported that outdoor smoking bans in places such as parks and playgrounds have doubled in the last five years, which is in line with the increase in public support for banning smoking in public places that Gallup has measured.

Gallup has also found a link between bans on smoking and lower smoking rates. A majority of Americans are OK with banning smoking in public places, which would likely lower smoking rates. But nearly one in five Americans are willing to go even further and say that smoking should be completely banned in this country. Overall, however, most Americans, although they are aware of the health risks, say that smoking should not be made totally illegal.

Survey Methods

Results for this Gallup poll are based on telephone interviews conducted July 7–10, 2014, with a random sample of 1,013 adults, aged 18 and older, living in all 50 U.S. states and the District of Columbia.

For results based on the total sample of national adults, the margin of sampling error is ±4 percentage points at the 95% confidence level.

For results based on the sample of 494 national adults in Form A, the margin of sampling error is ±6 percentage points.

For results based on the sample of 519 national adults in Form B, the margins of sampling error is ±5 percentage points.

For results based on the sample of 176 smokers, the maximum margin of sampling error is ±9 percentage points.

July 30, 2014
LGBT AMERICANS CONTINUE TO SKEW DEMOCRATIC AND LIBERAL
More than six in 10 approve of Obama, while 33% disapprove

by Frank Newport

PRINCETON, NJ—Americans who identify as lesbian, gay, bisexual, or transgender remain significantly more likely than non-LGBT Americans to identify as Democrats. More than six in 10 LGBT Americans identify as Democrats or are Democratic-leaning independents, while 21% identify with or lean toward the Republican Party. Non-LGBT Americans are more evenly divided in their politics, tilting just slightly more Democratic than Republican.

Party Identification
By LGBT status

	Republicans/ Leaners	Independents/ No lean	Democrats/ Leaners
	%	%	%
LGBT	21	15	63
Non-LGBT	42	13	44

January-June 2014

GALLUP

The political orientation of LGBT individuals is virtually unchanged since Gallup's June–September 2012 report, when 21% identified as Republicans, and 65% as Democrats.

These results are based on 88,802 Gallup Daily tracking interviews conducted between Jan. 2 and June 30, 2014. In this period, 3.6% of adults who were asked the political questions identified themselves as "lesbian, gay, bisexual, or transgender." Self-reported LGBT status has been generally stable in Gallup polling since October 2012, when 3.4% of all adults identified as LGBT.

The federal government recently released its own report on the percentage of Americans in 2013 who identified as lesbian, gay, or bisexual in its National Health Interview Survey (NHIS), and estimated that total as 2.3%. Various methodological differences between the two surveys may account for the differences in the estimates, including that the NHIS survey was conducted in person, asked about lesbian/gay status and bisexual status separately, and did not ask for identification as transgender. The NHIS study also did not measure political variables.

LGBT Individuals' Approval of Obama 19 Percentage Points Higher Than Non-LGBT

As would be expected from their Democratic skew in party identification, LGBT individuals are significantly more likely than are non-LGBT adults to approve of the overall job President Barack Obama is doing. Obama's job approval is 61% among the LGBT population, compared with 42% among all others.

Obama Job Approval
By LGBT status

	Approve	Disapprove
	%	%
LGBT	61	33
Non-LGBT	42	53

January-June 2014

GALLUP

Obama's overall job approval rating has dropped among both groups since Gallup reported on these measures using June–September 2012 data, but is down slightly more among LGBT individuals. In the 2012 data, 68% of LGBT individuals approved of Obama, seven points higher than now. Among non-LGBT individuals, approval was 45%, three points higher than it is now. The approval gap between LGBT and non-LGBT individuals has shrunk from 23 to 19 points during this period.

Obama has actively promoted LGBT causes, as outlined on the White House website: "The president and his administration are dedicated to eliminating barriers to equality, fighting discrimination based on sexual orientation and gender identity, and engaging LGBT communities across the country." Underscoring this commitment, Obama recently signed an executive order that gave workplace protection to LGBT employees working for the federal government and federal contractors. Still, support for Obama is not monolithic in the LGBT community, with 33% disapproving of his job performance. By contrast, disapproval among black Americans, one of the groups that most strongly support Obama, was 9% during the same period.

LGBT Population Skews Liberal, But More Than Half Are Conservative or Moderate

LGBT individuals are twice as likely as other Americans to identify themselves as politically liberal, and about half as likely to identify as conservatives. This is a notable departure from the rest of the population because Americans as a whole have been historically much more likely to identify as conservative than as liberal, though the gap has shrunk in recent years.

Ideology

By LGBT status

	Conservative	Moderate	Liberal
	%	%	%
LGBT	20	33	46
Non-LGBT	38	37	23

January–June 2014

GALLUP'

Still, a not insignificant 20% of LGBT Americans are conservatives and another third are moderates, underscoring the finding that the LGBT population in the U.S., while definitely skewing to the left end of the political spectrum, is by no means without ideological diversity.

LGBT-Political Relationship Holds Across Age Groups

Americans who identify as LGBT are much younger than the overall population. In the January–June 2014 sample, 48% of the LGBT population is between the ages of 18 and 34, compared with 28% of non-LGBT individuals.

Because younger Americans are significantly more likely to identify as Democrats than those who are older, some of the Democratic orientation of the LGBT population could theoretically reflect its relative youth. That does not appear to be the case, however, as the large majority of LGBT adults in every age category are Democratic or lean Democratic, with relatively little variation. In fact, middle-aged LGBT adults are just as Democratic as those aged

18 to 34. This contrasts with the pattern among non-LGBT individuals, whose Democratic leanings decrease at each age level, to the point that the older category leans Republican.

Party Identification

By age and LGBT status

	Republicans/ Leaners	Independents/ No lean	Democrats/ Leaners
	%	%	%
AGE 18 to 34			
---LGBT	18	17	63
---Non-LGBT	36	17	46
AGE 35 to 54			
---LGBT	18	14	67
---Non-LGBT	42	14	42
AGE 55+			
---LGBT	29	10	59
---Non-LGBT	46	9	44

January–June 2014

GALLUP'

Implications

LGBT individuals in the U.S. today constitute a small percentage of the U.S. population and as such will not be a major voting bloc in most state and national elections, although they could be a factor in close races. Taken as a whole, LGBT individuals are not unusually active on the political front. Research conducted before the 2012 presidential election showed that as a group, LGBT individuals were slightly less likely to be registered to vote and slightly less likely to say they were going to vote than non-LGBT individuals. Still, it is clear that any political effect that LGBT voters do have will benefit the Democratic Party and Democratic candidates more than the Republicans.

LGBT activists in recent years have been a significant part of engendering a major shift in American attitudes on one issue of great interest to the LGBT community—same-sex marriage. The public's attitudes have shifted significantly toward acceptance of legalized same-sex marriage, which is legal in a growing number of states. This suggests that the LGBT population and its supporters can help affect political policy.

Survey Methods

Results for this Gallup poll are based on telephone interviews conducted Jan. 2–June 30, 2014, on the Gallup Daily tracking survey, with a random sample of 88,802 adults, aged 18 and older, living in all 50 U.S. states and the District of Columbia.

For results based on the total sample of national adults, the margin of sampling error is ±1 percentage point at the 95% confidence level.

For results based on the total sample of 2,767 national adults who identify as LGBT, the margin of sampling error is ±2 percentage points at the 95% confidence level.

July 31, 2014
PARTISANSHIP POINTS TO TOUGH MIDTERM ENVIRONMENT FOR DEMS
Democrats have narrow, two-percentage-point edge in partisanship

by Jeffrey M. Jones

PRINCETON, NJ—An average of 42% of Americans currently identify as Democrats or say they are independent but lean to the Democratic Party. Slightly fewer, 40%, are Republicans or Republican leaners. That narrow two-percentage-point Democratic edge is closer to what Gallup measured in the third quarter of strong Republican midterm years such as 1994, 2002, and 2010 than in the strong Democratic years of 1998 and 2006.

Party Identification and Leaning, Third Quarter, Recent Midterm Election Years

Year	% Democrat/ Lean Democratic	% Republican/ Lean Republican	Democratic advantage (pct. pts.)
2014*	42%	40%	2
2010	44%	45%	-1
2006	50%	40%	10
2002	46%	44%	2
1998	48%	41%	7
1994	46%	45%	1

*Based on July 2014 data

GALLUP

Gallup began to regularly measure Americans' party identification, including a follow-up question asking political independents whether they lean Democratic or Republican, in 1993. The combined measure of initial party identification plus the political leanings of independents is useful because it more closely resembles the Republican or Democratic choice voters have in elections. Since 1993, Gallup has found considerable variation in Americans' party preferences during midterm election years. These differences, particularly in the third quarter, have provided a good indication of which party would fare better in that fall's midterm elections.

Over the last two decades, Democrats have typically enjoyed an advantage in partisanship among the U.S. adult population. However, Republicans usually vote at higher rates than Democrats. That Republican Party turnout advantage leaves the Democratic Party politically vulnerable in midterm election years when they do not have a significant cushion in partisanship.

In years when the Democrats had a narrow advantage in partisanship among all adults, the usual Republican turnout advantages have resulted in a voting electorate composed of more Republicans than Democrats. Such years include 1994, 2002, and 2010, when Republicans gained seats in the House of Representatives.

In years when Democrats enjoyed a wide lead in partisanship, even as Democrats turned out at lower rates than Republicans, the electorate still included more Democrats than Republicans. The two years that fit that description—1998 and 2006—are the years in which Democrats gained seats in the House. The Democrats also picked up Senate seats in 2006, but 1998 saw no net change in Republican vs. Democratic seats in the Senate.

While the third-quarter partisanship figures provide a broad indication of which party is likely to gain seats in a midterm election, they are less likely to shed light on how many seats a party will win. For example, Republicans gained far more seats in 1994 and 2010 than in 2002, although the partisanship gap was similar in all three years. And Democrats gained many more seats in 2006 than in 1998, with fairly similar Democratic edges in partisanship each year.

The number of seats gained may be determined more by structural factors such as the political makeup of the government and how the parties performed in the prior election. For example, Republicans may have gained more seats in the 1994 and 2010 elections because each followed two years in which a Democratic president and Democratic House and Senate governed the country, after strong Democratic election years in 1992 and 2008. Additionally, Presidents Bill Clinton and Barack Obama were relatively unpopular in 1994 and 2010, respectively, with approval ratings in the mid-40s.

The 2006 elections followed four years of unified Republican government after strong Republican showings in the 2002 and 2004 elections.

Although President Obama is currently unpopular, Republicans have the majority in the House of Representatives after making big gains in the 2010 elections, which were largely maintained in 2012. Thus, it is not clear how much larger the Republican majority could get after this year's elections. Republicans may be poised for more significant gains in the Senate, especially because many of the Democratic incumbents defending their seats were elected in 2008, a very favorable political year for Democrats.

Implications

Democrats currently have a narrow advantage in terms of Americans' identification with the two major parties, but based on historical turnout and other structural patterns, this small advantage suggests that the Democrats face a tough election environment this year. As Gallup demonstrated earlier this summer, President Obama's below-average job approval rating and Americans' low level of satisfaction with the way things are going in the country are also ominous signs for the Democrats. Historically, these indicators are unlikely to change in a short period of time such as the three months between now and Election Day.

With Democrats' advantage in partisanship currently consistent with where it has been in previous strong GOP midterm election years, it is imperative that Democrats match or exceed Republican turnout this fall if they hope to keep control of the Senate and minimize the size of the Republican majority in the House.

Survey Methods

Results for this Gallup poll are based on telephone interviews conducted July 1–30, 2014, on the Gallup Daily tracking survey, with a random sample of 14,713 adults, aged 18 and older, living in all 50 U.S. states and the District of Columbia.

For results based on the total sample of national adults, the margin of sampling error is ±1 percentage point at the 95% confidence level.

August 01, 2014

RELIGION PLAYS LARGE ROLE IN AMERICANS' SUPPORT FOR ISRAELIS

Religious Americans, Jews, and Mormons most likely to support Israelis

by Frank Newport

PRINCETON, NJ—Religious Americans are significantly more likely than less religious Americans to be sympathetic to the Israelis in the Middle East situation. Over the past 14 years, on average, 66% of Americans who attend church weekly or almost every week are sympathetic to the Israelis, compared with 13% who are sympathetic to the Palestinians. Sympathy for Israel drops to 46% among those who never attend church, still twice as many as the 23% who are sympathetic to the Palestinians.

Americans' Sympathies in Mideast Situation, by Church Attendance

	Israelis	Palestinians	Both/Neither/No Opinion
	%	%	%
Weekly/Almost weekly	66	13	21
Monthly/Seldom	58	16	26
Never	46	23	31

Aggregated sample, 2001-2014

GALLUP

These results are from an aggregated sample of more than 14,000 adults interviewed each February from 2001 to 2014 as part of Gallup's Foreign Affairs survey, and asked in the survey, "In the Middle East situation, are your sympathies more with the Israelis or more with the Palestinians?" Although Americans' sympathies have fluctuated over the years, more have been sympathetic toward the Israelis than the Palestinians every time they have been asked. Overall, an average of 59% of Americans have been sympathetic to the Israelis and 16% sympathetic to the Palestinians, with the rest saying "both" or not having an opinion.

Religious Americans' higher levels of sympathy for the Israelis have been consistent over the past 14 years, although percentages have fluctuated some from year to year. The difference between weekly church attenders and those who never attend has widened slightly in recent years, although it narrowed again in 2014.

Trend in Americans' Sympathy for Israelis, by Church Attendance

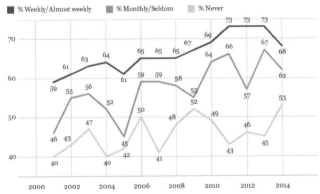

■ % Weekly/Almost weekly ■ % Monthly/Seldom ■ % Never

GALLUP

Religious Groups Vary in Sympathy Toward Israelis

Sympathy for Israelis is—not surprisingly—higher among U.S. Jews than among Americans in any other major religious group. More than nine in 10 Jews across the time span surveyed expressed sympathy for Israelis, while only 2% were more sympathetic to the Palestinians.

Seventy-nine percent of Mormons are more sympathetic to Israelis, followed by Protestants (66%) and Catholics (59%). The lowest level of sympathy is among the "nones"—those without a formal religious identity—among whom 45% express more sympathy for Israelis and 25% for the Palestinians.

Americans' Sympathies in Mideast Situation, by Religious Identification

	Israelis	Palestinians	Both/Neither/No Opinion
	%	%	%
Jewish	93	2	5
Mormon	79	11	10
Protestant/Other Christian	66	14	20
Catholics	59	17	24
Other	54	18	28
No religious identity	45	25	30

Aggregated sample, 2001-2014

GALLUP

Religiousness Has Effect Within Both Major Political Parties

Americans' political party identification is strongly related to their sympathies for the two sides in the conflict, with Republicans much more sympathetic to Israelis than Democrats are. This relationship is also evident when Gallup recently asked Americans about the justification of the Israeli and Hamas military actions in the current conflict in Gaza.

Because Republicans on average attend religious services more frequently than Democrats, it is reasonable to assume that religiousness could be part of the explanation for why Republicans are more sympathetic to Israelis. But both party identification and religion independently affect Americans' sympathies. Church attendance is related to sympathies for Israelis among Republicans *and* Democrats, although the relationship is somewhat stronger among Republicans.

Americans' Sympathies in Middle East Situation, by Political Party and Church Attendance

	Israelis	Palestinians	Both Neither/No Opinion
	%	%	%
REPUBLICANS/LEANERS			
Weekly/Almost weekly	80	7	13
Monthly/Seldom	70	12	18
Never	65	13	22
DEMOCRATS/LEANERS			
Weekly/Almost weekly	55	20	25
Monthly/Seldom	52	20	28
Never	42	30	28

Aggregated sample, 2001-2014

GALLUP

As many as 80% of weekly church-attending Republicans are more sympathetic toward Israelis, with this number dropping to 65% among Republicans who never attend church. Among Democrats, there is little difference in sympathy for Israelis between those who attend weekly and monthly or seldom, but sympathy drops significantly to 42% among Democrats who never attend church.

Underscoring the possibility that partisanship is likely more influential than religion on these attitudes, nonreligious Republicans are more likely to sympathize with Israelis than highly religious Democrats.

Bottom Line

How religious Americans are, as measured by their religious service attendance, is a reliable indicator of their relative sympathy for Israelis over the Palestinians in the Middle East conflict. This relationship is evident among both Republicans and Democrats. Support for Israelis is also higher among U.S. Jews, Mormons, and Protestants than among other religious groups.

There are several possible reasons for the relationship between religiousness and support for Israelis. Many explanations focus on roles that Israel and Israelis play in the Bible, the centrality of the saga of the Israelites in the Old Testament, and the promises God made in the Old Testament to the ancient prophets that he would create a promised land for them. Some evangelical Christians also connect Israel to their views of the second coming of Christ at Armageddon.

Although highly religious Christians in the U.S. strongly tilt toward the Republican Party, and U.S. Jews tilt strongly toward the Democratic Party, support for Israelis over the Palestinians in the Middle East conflict is one issue that unites these otherwise politically disparate groups.

Survey Methods

Results for this Gallup poll are based on telephone interviews conducted as part of 14 separate Gallup polls conducted each February from 2001 to 2014, each based on a random sample of approximately 1,000 adults, aged 18 and older, living in all 50 U.S. states and the District of Columbia.

For results based on the total sample of national adults, the margin of sampling error is ±1 percentage points at the 95% confidence level.

The margin of sampling error for results based on the total sample of each year's survey, and for subgroups based on church attendance, religious identification, and political identification, will vary depending on the sample size involved.

August 05, 2014
MIDDLE EAST UPDATE: U.S. SUPPORT FOR ISRAEL, HAMAS IS STABLE
Four in 10 say Israel's attacks are justified, 14% say Hamas' attacks are justified

by Frank Newport

PRINCETON, NJ—Americans' views of the military actions of Israel and Hamas in the current conflict in Gaza have changed little over the past 10 days. The public remains closely divided over whether Israel's actions have been justified, but is mostly critical of Hamas' actions.

Americans' Views of Actions in Current Middle East Conflict

	Justified	Unjustified	No opinion
	%	%	%
Aug 2-3, 2014			
Israel's actions against Hamas	42	38	21
Hamas' actions against Israel	14	66	19
Jul 22-23, 2014			
Israel's actions against Hamas	42	39	20
Hamas' actions against Israel	11	70	20
Apr 3, 2002			
Israel's actions against Palestinians	44	34	22
Palestinians' actions against Israel	17	62	21

NOTE: 2014 wording is "Palestinian group Hamas"; 2002 wording is "Palestinians"

GALLUP

These results from Gallup Daily tracking interviews conducted Aug. 2–3 are also similar to what Gallup measured for another period of heightened Israeli-Palestinian violence in 2002. This stability suggests that Americans' underlying attitudes about the region may be anchoring their reaction to the Gaza conflict, even as raw images of the fighting and civilian casualties pour in.

Although the latest explosion of violence has been going on for nearly a month prior to the temporary cease-fire agreed to on Monday, Americans appear to be paying no more or less attention to the conflict now than they were in late July. Six in 10 say they are following the conflict "very" or "somewhat closely."

The advent of social media has changed the dynamics of the way news unfolds worldwide. Some observers have argued that this more real-time news, often including more graphic coverage of the fighting, destruction, injuries, and deaths in Gaza, could affect public opinion about the conflict.

The evidence to support that hypothesis is not strong. Not only is opinion little different now than it was during a similar 2002 conflict, but just 19% of Americans report using Facebook, Twitter, or other social media to follow news of the conflict "a lot" or "some," significantly lower than those who are using newspapers, the Internet, and in particular television (including cable) news.

How much have you read, heard, or seen about the current conflict between the Israelis and Hamas from each of the following sources -- a lot, some, a little, or nothing at all?

	A lot/Some	A little/Nothing at all	Not following
	%	%	%
Television or cable news	55	26	19
News on the Internet	39	40	19
Newspapers	27	52	19
Facebook, Twitter, or other social media	19	61	19

Aug 2-3, 2014

GALLUP

The attitudes of those following the conflict on social media are only marginally different from the attitudes of those following the conflict using other sources of news and information, although many Americans may be exposed to multiple sources of news content.

Those who are paying closest attention to the conflict in general are more likely to say that Israel's actions are justified. It follows that the four groups who use each of the four sources of information are also more likely than the average respondent to say Israel's actions are justified. There is a slight tendency for those using social media to be less likely than those using other media to say Israel's actions are justified, but even among this group, the percentage is higher than the average of national adults. Those using the Internet and social media are slightly more likely to say that Hamas' actions are mostly justified, but these differences are again slight.

Views of Israeli and Hamas Actions by Use of Specific Media to Follow News of the Middle East Conflict

	Israeli actions mostly justified	Hamas actions mostly justified
	%	%
National adults	42	14
Read or seen a lot or some news about conflict on television and cable news	55	15
Read or seen a lot or some news about conflict on Internet	53	18
Read or seen a lot or some news about conflict in newspapers	54	14
Read or seen a lot or some news about conflict on Facebook, Twitter, or other social media	49	18

Aug 2-3, 2014

GALLUP

Implications

Despite the vividness of news and social media images emanating from the conflict in the Middle East, Americans' attention to the conflict and their attitudes about the actions on both sides have remained remarkably unchanged compared with almost two weeks ago, and also compared with results from the period of Israeli-Palestinian violence 12 years ago. This suggests that Americans may have responded to both crises in ways that reflect their basic attitudes toward Israel and the Palestinians rather than the specifics of either conflict. In general, Americans rate Israel much more favorably as a country than the Palestinian Territories, and are much more likely to say they sympathize with the Israelis than the Palestinians when asked to choose between the two sides.

Americans remain roughly divided on the issue of whether the actions of the Israelis against the Hamas are justified. While this is unchanged from previous updates, it is important to note that the pro-Israel sentiment on this measure is significantly below the percentage who routinely say that their sympathies are more broadly with the Israelis rather than the Palestinians in the Middle East.

Survey Methods

Results for this Gallup poll are based on telephone interviews conducted Aug. 2–3, 2014, on the Gallup Daily tracking survey, with a random sample of 1,019 adults, aged 18 and older, living in all 50 U.S. states and the District of Columbia.

For results based on the total sample of national adults, the margin of sampling error is ±4 percentage points at the 95% confidence level.

August 05, 2014

IN U.S., ECONOMIC CONFIDENCE DIPS TWO POINTS IN JULY
Americans' economic outlook worsens

by Rebecca Riffkin

WASHINGTON, D.C.—Gallup's Economic Confidence Index fell two points in July to −17, which is the lowest index reading since March.

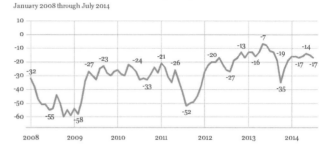

Gallup Economic Confidence Index — Monthly Averages
January 2008 through July 2014

Gallup Daily tracking

GALLUP

Despite small monthly ups and downs, U.S. economic confidence has generally been quite stable so far in 2014, with monthly index averages ranging between −14 and −17. By contrast, at the end of 2013, confidence plunged 16 points in October during the federal government shutdown, followed by a 10-point increase in November after the shutdown ended.

Economic confidence was −15 for the week of July 28 through Aug. 3, slightly better than the July average. It also marked a sharp improvement from the −21 score the week prior—the lowest economic confidence reading in any week this year. The rapid recovery last week suggests a short-term downtick, rather than lasting change. Americans' confidence in the economy improved last week despite sharp drops in the major stock market indexes.

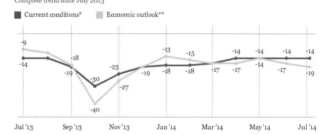

Gallup Economic Confidence Sub-Indexes -- Monthly Averages
Complete trend since July 2013

■ Current conditions* ▨ Economic outlook**

* % (Excellent + Good) minus % Poor
** % Getting better minus % Getting worse
Gallup Daily tracking

GALLUP

Gallup's Economic Confidence Index is the average of two components, Americans' ratings of current economic conditions in the nation, and their perceptions of whether the economy is getting better or getting worse. In July, 20% of Americans said current economic conditions were "excellent" or "good" while 34% said they were "poor," resulting in a −14 net current conditions score. Americans' views of current economic conditions have been unchanged since April.

Meanwhile, 38% of Americans last month said the economy is getting better while 57% said it is getting worse. This results in a net economic outlook score of −19, the lowest score since last December. Thus, the drop in overall U.S. economic confidence in July was the result of souring views of the economy's direction rather than changing assessments of current conditions.

Implications

The July dip in economic confidence reflects a dimming of Americans' confidence in the economy's direction, even as their views of current conditions remained steady.

The drop in the index last month was partly a function of the sharply lower confidence for the week of July 21–27—a time when the stock market stumbled and a number of international events may have rattled Americans' outlook. Confidence bounced back in the last few days of July and first few days of August, despite drops in the stock market. This increase in economic confidence is perhaps because of generally positive reports on the nation's gross domestic product and job growth.

Survey Methods

Results for this Gallup poll are based on telephone interviews conducted July 1–31, 2014, on the Gallup Daily tracking survey, with a random sample of 15,193 adults, aged 18 and older, living in all 50 U.S. states and the District of Columbia.

For results based on the total sample of national adults, the margin of sampling error is ±1 percentage point at the 95% confidence level.

August 05, 2014
ARKANSAS, KENTUCKY REPORT SHARPEST DROPS IN UNINSURED RATE
Medicaid expansion, state exchanges linked to faster reduction in uninsured rate

by Dan Witters

WASHINGTON, D.C.—Arkansas and Kentucky lead all other states in the sharpest reductions in their uninsured rate among adult residents since the healthcare law's requirement to have insurance took effect at the beginning of the year. Delaware, Washington, and Colorado round out the top five. All 10 states that report the largest declines in uninsured rates expanded Medicaid and established a state-based marketplace exchange or state-federal partnership.

As Gallup previously reported, the states that chose to expand Medicaid and set up their own health exchanges had a lower uninsured rate to begin with: 16.1% compared with 18.7% for the remaining states—a difference of 2.6 percentage points. The already notable gap between the two groups of states widened through the first quarter to 4.3 points, as states that have implemented these core mechanisms of the Affordable Care Act reduced their uninsured rates three times more than states that did not implement these core mechanisms.

These data, collected as part of the Gallup-Healthways Well-Being Index, are based on respondents' self-reports of health insurance status based on the question, "Do you have health insurance coverage?"

10 States With Largest Reductions in Percentage Uninsured, 2013 vs. Midyear 2014
"Do you have health insurance?" (% no)

State	% Uninsured, 2013	% Uninsured, midyear 2014	Change in uninsured (pct. pts.)	Medicaid expansion AND state/partnership exchange in 2014
Arkansas	22.5	12.4	-10.1	Yes
Kentucky	20.4	11.9	-8.5	Yes
Delaware	10.5	3.3	-7.2	Yes
Washington	16.8	10.7	-6.1	Yes
Colorado	17.0	11.0	-6.0	Yes
West Virginia	17.6	11.9	-5.7	Yes
Oregon	19.4	14.0	-5.4	Yes*
California	21.6	16.3	-5.3	Yes
New Mexico	20.2	15.2	-5.0	Yes
Connecticut	12.3	7.4	-4.9	Yes

Gallup-Healthways Well-Being Index

GALLUP

Uninsured Rates Continue to Drop More in States Embracing Multiple Parts of Health Law

The uninsured rate in the states that have chosen to expand Medicaid *and* set up their own state exchange in the health insurance marketplace has declined significantly more in the first half of 2014 than in the remaining states that have not done so. The uninsured rate declined 4.0 points in the 21 states that have implemented both of these measures, compared with a 2.2-point drop across the 29 states that have implemented only one or neither of these actions.

Change in Uninsured Rate Between 2013 and Midyear 2014
Among states with Medicaid expansion AND state exchange/parternship compared with all others

State type	% Uninsured, 2013	% Uninsured, midyear 2014	Change in uninsured (pct. pcts.)
States with Medicaid expansion AND state exchange/partnerships	16.1	12.1	-4.0
States with only one or neither	18.7	16.5	-2.2

Gallup-Healthways Well-Being Index

GALLUP

Some states have chosen to implement state-federal "partnership" exchanges, where states run certain functions and make key decisions based on local market and demographic conditions. For the purposes of this analysis, these partnerships are included with the state exchanges. New Hampshire, which manages a state-based exchange but has only recently voted to expand Medicaid, is not included, as its eligible residents were not privy to expanded Medicaid through the first six months of 2014. Four states—North Dakota, New Jersey, Ohio, and Arizona—have decided to expand Medicaid without also administering a state-based exchange or partnership, while several others continue to debate its expansion. The District of Columbia, which has expanded Medicaid and has implemented a locally managed exchange, is not included in this analysis.

Implications

While a majority of Americans continue to disapprove of the Affordable Care Act, the uninsured rate is declining, as the law intended. Nationally, 17.3% of U.S. adults reported being without health insurance in 2013, a rate that had slowly increased from 14.8% in 2008. The uninsured rate peaked at 18.0% in the third quarter of

2013—the three months immediately preceding the opening of the healthcare exchanges—and has since declined to 13.4% in the second quarter of 2014, the lowest quarterly rate in more than six years of Gallup-Healthways Well-Being Index trending.

At the state level, those that have implemented two of the law's core mechanisms—Medicaid expansion and state health exchanges—are seeing a substantially larger drop in the uninsured rate than states that did not take both of these actions. Consequently, the gap in uninsured that existed between the two groups in 2013 has now nearly doubled through the first half of 2014.

Many states continue to debate implementing these actions. New Hampshire recently became the 26th state (plus the District of Columbia) to expand Medicaid, which takes effect this summer. Utah, a conservative state with a Republican governor, Gary Herbert, continues negotiation with the Centers for Medicare and Medicaid Services to have revised, more flexible terms than what is detailed in the Affordable Care Act. Utah expanding Medicaid could serve as a blueprint for other red states to follow, as could similar scenarios playing out in Indiana and Pennsylvania.

Other states, in turn, are debating dropping their state-based exchanges and moving to the federal exchange because of technological issues or unexpected cost-related challenges. Oregon will be designated as a supported state-based marketplace in 2015 that leverages federal technology, while Maryland is modifying its troubled website to model Connecticut's. Officials from the states of Massachusetts and Hawaii—both of which had comparatively low uninsured rates to begin with but show little or no change since 2013—are also considering switching to the federal exchange, indicating that locally managed exchanges are not necessarily optimal for insurance sign-ups in some states.

Survey Methods

Results are based on telephone interviews conducted as part of the Gallup-Healthways Well-Being Index survey Jan. 2–Dec. 29, 2013, with a random sample of 178,068 adults, aged 18 and older, living in all 50 U.S. states and the District of Columbia. A total of 88,678 respondents were interviewed Jan. 2–June 30, 2014.

The 2013 margin of sampling error for most states is ±1 to ±2 percentage points, but it is as high as ±3.5 points for states with smaller population sizes, such as Wyoming, North Dakota, South Dakota, Delaware, and Hawaii. For midyear 2014 results, the error range increases to as high as ±5.0 points for these smallest states.

August 06, 2014
U.S. JOB CREATION INDEX ADVANCES TO SIX-YEAR HIGH IN JULY
For the first time since 2008, plurality of workers say employer is hiring

by Lydia Saad

PRINCETON, NJ—Gallup's U.S. Job Creation Index rose in July to its highest level in more than six years, hitting +28. This is up from +27 in June, and from +21 a year ago. The index has been inching up most of the year.

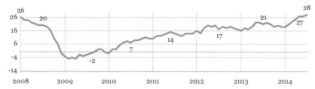

Gallup Job Creation Index Among All U.S. Workers -- January 2008-July 2014

Based on the percentage of U.S. workers who say their employer is hiring workers and expanding the size of its workforce minus the percentage who say their employer is letting workers go and reducing the size of its workforce

Based on monthly averages
Gallup Daily tracking

GALLUP

The Job Creation Index is a measure of net hiring in the U.S. as indicated by a nationally representative sample of full- and part-time workers, including those employed at all levels of government. In July, 41% of workers reported that their employer is hiring and expanding the size of its workforce, while 13% said their employer is letting workers go and reducing the size of its workforce, resulting in the +28 net hiring score.

Gallup has been tracking net hiring since January 2008. After tumbling that year amid the deepening recession and Wall Street financial crisis, the index started to recover in 2009 and has continued to improve every subsequent year. However, the pace of improvement thus far in 2014 has been significantly better than at the same point in any year since 2010. The index has gained nine points since January, well exceeding the one- to five-point gains between January and July of each of the preceding three years. In 2010, Gallup saw an eight-point index jump from January to July, but that was starting from a bleak jobs assessment in January 2010 rather than the much more positive situation in January 2014.

Gallup Job Creation Index

Midyear improvement for each year

	January of each year	July of each year	Change
2014	19	28	+9
2013	16	21	+5
2012	16	17	+1
2011	10	14	+4
2010	-1	7	+8
2009	-3	-2	+1
2008	26	20	-6

Gallup Daily tracking

GALLUP

Bottom Line

The progress seen this year in job creation was punctuated in July as the Gallup Job Creation Index averaged a new high in the more than six years of tracking this metric. The +28 index score still barely exceeds the +26 Gallup found at the start of 2008, which itself was not a highly favorable time for the economy. As such, there is still significant room for this critical measure of the nation's economic health to improve.

Regardless, it's promising that the percentage of workers who are witnessing hiring in their workplaces has reached a new high. That could help buoy workers' economic confidence, which could in turn have a positive ripple effect on the economy. One note of caution is that Gallup has previously seen the Job Creation Index peak at midyear, only to level off or falter in the second half. That was the case in each of the past three years, but not in 2010. The index's direction in August could thus be telling as to whether the momentum to date is taking on a life of its own, or still sensitive to any negative economic signals that may arise. An initial indication is encouraging: Gallup's latest weekly average, for the week ending Aug. 3, finds the index hitting +30, a weekly record since 2008.

Survey Methods

Results for this Gallup poll are based on telephone interviews conducted July 1–31, 2014, on the Gallup Daily tracking survey, with a random sample of 17,088 employees, aged 18 and older, living in all 50 U.S. states and the District of Columbia.

For results based on the total sample of employees, the margin of sampling error is ±1 percentage point at the 95% confidence level.

August 06, 2014
U.S. HISPANICS POSITIVE ABOUT THEIR STANDARD OF LIVING
Ratings have improved more than those of blacks and whites since 2011

by Jeffrey M. Jones

PRINCETON, NJ—Blacks, whites, and Hispanics in the U.S. have grown steadily more positive about their standard of living since 2011, as measured by Gallup's Standard of Living Index. Hispanics have seen the greatest increase of the three groups, and are now significantly more upbeat about their standard of living than whites or blacks.

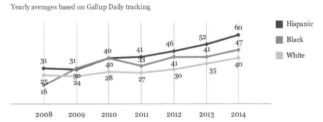

Standard of Living Index, by Racial and Ethnic Group
Yearly averages based on Gallup Daily tracking

2014 averages are based on January-July data

The Standard of Living Index is based on the average difference between the percentage who are satisfied minus the percentage who are dissatisfied with their standard of living, and the percentage who say their standard of living is getting better minus the percentage who say it is getting worse. The index has a theoretical range of -100 to +100.

GALLUP

These results are based on yearly averages of Gallup Daily tracking interviews from January 2008 through July 2014. The 2014 data include interviews with more than 1,800 interviews each with blacks and Hispanics.

Gallup asks Americans if they are satisfied or dissatisfied with their standard of living, and if their standard of living is getting better or worse. The Standard of Living Index has a theoretical maximum of +100, which would indicate all respondents are satisfied rather than dissatisfied with their standard of living, and think it is getting better rather than worse. The theoretical minimum is −100.

All major U.S. racial and ethnic groups are generally positive about their standard of living. The index score among all Americans in 2014 to date is +44, which includes record monthly highs of +47 in May and July.

By comparison, the index score among all Americans was +24 in the recessionary year of 2008, including +31 among Hispanics, +25 among whites, and +16 among blacks. Blacks' perceptions of their standard of living greatly improved in 2009, coincident with Barack Obama's taking office as president, while whites' and Hispanics' ratings were generally stable.

Standard-of-living ratings rose among all three groups in 2010, before stalling in 2011, but the scores began to rise again in 2012 as the economy improved.

Hispanics Lead Whites, Blacks on Both Standard-of-Living Items

Hispanics have the highest score on Gallup's Standard of Living Index because they score higher than the other groups on both components of the index—being satisfied rather than dissatisfied with their standard of living, and saying their standard of living is getting better rather than worse.

Currently, 82% of Hispanics say they are satisfied with their standard of living, compared with 79% of whites and 70% of blacks.

Meanwhile, 74% of Hispanics say their standard of living is getting better, slightly higher than the 72% of blacks who say this and significantly better than the 52% among whites.

All three groups' 2014 ratings on both standard-of-living items represent highs in Gallup's trend of more than six years.

Hispanics' Relative Youth a Key Factor in Standard-of-Living Ratings

Hispanics are more positive about their standard of living than whites or blacks, although that appears to be more of a perceptual difference rather than one grounded in reality. Whites report much higher annual household incomes on average than Hispanics or blacks. And Hispanics' unemployment rate is nearly twice that of whites.

One major reason Hispanics nevertheless rate their standard of living positively is that U.S. Hispanic adults as a whole tend to be much younger than whites or blacks, and younger Americans tend to be quite upbeat about their standard of living improving. Specifically, 85% of Americans between the ages of 18 and 29 say their standard of living is getting better, compared with 66% of those aged 30 to 49, 44% of those aged 50 to 64, and 33% of those aged 65 and older. These differences by age in standard-of-living ratings are apparent among blacks, Hispanics, and whites, but roughly three-quarters of U.S. Hispanic adults are younger than age 50, whereas a little more than half of U.S. non-Hispanic white adults are.

Also, although Hispanics tend to come from lower-income households, given the higher standard of living in the U.S. compared with most other countries, even a low income by U.S. standards may be significantly higher than what workers can earn in most other countries. Because a high percentage of U.S. Hispanics are recent immigrants, often from poorer countries in Latin America, their reference point may be one of a generally low standard of living. In contrast, non-immigrants in the U.S. would be more likely to evaluate their own standard of living against historical U.S. living standards.

Indeed, Hispanics whose annual household incomes are $36,000 or less are much more likely to be positive about their standard of living than whites or blacks at the same income level.

Implications

Although Hispanics are currently more upbeat about their standard of living than whites or blacks, this may be related more to the demographics of each group as well as their immigrant status. Thus, the differences in standard-of-living ratings by race and ethnic group may be something specific to the current generation of Hispanics living in the U.S. Those differences may not hold as U.S. Hispanics as a group get older, or as future generations of U.S. Hispanics become further removed from the original U.S. immigrants in their family tree.

Survey Methods

Results for this Gallup poll are based on telephone interviews conducted January–July 2014, on the Gallup Daily tracking survey, with a random sample of 20,616 adults, aged 18 and older, living in all 50 U.S. states and the District of Columbia.

For results based on the total sample of national adults, the margin of sampling error is ±1 percentage point at the 95% confidence level.

For results based on the total sample of 15,491 non-Hispanic whites, the margin of sampling error is ±1 percentage point at the 95% confidence level.

For results based on the total sample of 1,836 non-Hispanic blacks, the margin of sampling error is ±3 percentage points at the 95% confidence level.

For results based on the total sample of 1,835 Hispanics, the margin of sampling error is ±3 percentage points at the 95% confidence level.

August 07, 2014
STUDENT DEBT LINKED TO WORSE HEALTH AND LESS WEALTH
Those with over $50,000 in debt have lower well-being than debt-free peers

by Andrew Dugan and Stephanie Kafka

WASHINGTON, D.C.—College graduates who carry a high amount of student debt appear to face long-term challenges that stretch beyond just their finances. A new analysis of Americans who graduated college between 1990 and 2014 shows that graduates who took on the highest amounts of student debt, $50,000 or more, are less likely than their fellow graduates who did not borrow for college to be thriving in four of five elements of well-being: purpose, financial, community, and physical.

Percentage of U.S. College Graduates Thriving in Five Elements of Well-Being, by Amount of Student Loan Debt

Among adults who graduated between 1990 and 2014

	No student debt	$25,000 and below	$25,001 to $50,000	Over $50,000
Purpose	49	46	40	40
Social	47	45	42	45
Financial	40	31	26	25
Community	43	42	35	38
Physical	34	30	26	24

Feb. 4-March 7, 2014; debt applies only to undergraduate degree

GALLUP

Although graduates with no student loan debt are slightly more likely than their indebted peers to be thriving socially, the differences are not statistically significant.

Gallup finds the starkest differences among these groups in the areas of financial and physical well-being. Higher debt signifies lower likelihood of thriving in these two areas of well-being. Graduates who went the deepest into debt to obtain their college degree, for instance, are far less likely to be thriving than graduates who took out no debt, by 15 percentage points in financial well-being and 10 points in physical well-being. The pattern is similar for graduates' sense of purpose, although those who borrowed over $50,000 are just as likely to be thriving in this element as those who borrowed $25,001 to $50,000. The relationship is less straightforward for graduates' community well-being, though again, graduates who took on the most debt for their degree are less likely to be thriving in this element than those who did not take out any loans for their undergraduate education.

These results are based on the inaugural Gallup-Purdue Index, a joint-research effort with Purdue University and Lumina Foundation to study the relationship between the college experience and college graduates' lives. The Gallup-Purdue Index is a comprehensive, nationally representative study of U.S. college graduates with Internet access. According to a 2013 Census Bureau report, 90% of college graduates in the U.S. have access to the Internet. This analysis is based on a Web study conducted Feb. 4–March 7, 2014, with more than 11,000 adults who graduated college between 1990 and 2014.

Using the Gallup-Healthways Well-Being Index, the Gallup-Purdue Index measures key outcomes to determine whether college graduates have good lives. The Well-Being Index is organized into five elements of well-being:

- *Purpose*: liking what you do each day and being motivated to achieve your goals
- *Social*: having supportive relationships and love in your life
- *Financial*: managing your economic life to reduce stress and increase security
- *Community*: liking where you live, feeling safe, and having pride in your community
- *Physical*: having good health and enough energy to get things done daily

Gallup classifies those who respond, at the element level, as "thriving" (well-being that is strong and consistent), "struggling" (well-being that is moderate or inconsistent), or "suffering" (well-being that is low and inconsistent).

The student loan debt figures this analysis uses are reported by the respondents and are adjusted for inflation to today's dollars.

Figures only apply to undergraduate student loan debt. Gallup did not ask respondents about the status of their student debt or inquire into how much of their loan they have repaid.

As college costs rise and enrollment increases, the amount of outstanding undergraduate student debt in the U.S. continues to climb. The amount of student debt now stands at over $1 trillion for both undergraduate and graduate loans and exceeds Americans' overall credit card debt, according to the Federal Reserve. In particular, estimates put the average amount of undergraduate student loan debt for the class of 2014 at just over $33,000, a substantial increase from $18,600 in 2004.

Most degree earners in Gallup's survey graduated with debt: 59% of those graduating between 1990 and 2014 had borrowed at least some amount for educational expenses, including 21% who borrowed between $25,001 and $50,000 and 11% who borrowed over $50,000. The remaining 27% borrowed less than $25,000.

Student Loan Debt Among U.S. College Graduates Who Graduated Between 1990 and 2014

Approximately how much money did you borrow in student loans to obtain your undergraduate degree at (name of university)?

	%
No student debt	41
$1-$25,000	27
$25,001-$50,000	21
Over $50,000	11

Feb. 4-March 7, 2014

GALLUP

As the amount of money students are borrowing continues to grow, the importance of student debt as a U.S. political issue has increased. Politicians and higher education leaders express concern that highly indebted graduates are unable to forge an economic identity after graduation, putting off major purchases and suffering from low savings. Congress, for instance, has debated proposals that could bring down the cost of monthly student debt payments for borrowers. The U.S. Treasury, for its part, is also exploring ways to help make debt repayments more affordable for some student borrowers.

The findings from the Gallup-Purdue Index raise another important concern about student debt: its link to lower well-being. However, the findings do not necessarily demonstrate that higher amounts of student loan debt causes lower well-being among graduates. Other factors that often determine whether students take out loans for college and how much they borrow—the family's household income, socio-economic status, the type of school attended, the chosen field of study, and the student's ability to get scholarships and financial aid—may be the same factors that influence graduates' future well-being.

While many—including Secretary of Education Arne Duncan—refer to a college degree as "the great equalizer" that puts workers on a level playing field, some studies show that the salutary economic effects of a college degree can be mitigated by other factors, such as a person's background. But it is worth noting that even after controlling for the highest level of education obtained by the respondent's mother, a common proxy for socio-economic status, the relationship between higher undergraduate student loan debt and lower well-being holds true.

Link Between Student Debt and Lower Well-Being Holds Across Graduation Classes

This study's large sample includes U.S. adults who graduated college over a 25-year time span, allowing Gallup to see how the interaction of well-being and student debt holds over time. Given standard repayment plans, graduates earning their degrees in the 1990s might consider their student loans a distant memory, as opposed to more recent graduates who are still chipping away at their educational debt. Nonetheless, Gallup's analysis shows that important well-being differences still exist between the heaviest borrowers and those with no loan debt, and this applies to 1990s graduates as well as the more recent 2000–2014 cohort.

Relatively recent college graduates—those who earned their degree from 2000 to 2014—who have more than $50,000 in student debt are significantly less likely to be thriving financially and physically than their counterparts without loans. They are also less likely to have a strong sense of purpose and to be thriving in their community well-being. Notably, for 2000–2014 graduates, the most indebted degree holders are less likely to be thriving in social well-being, something that is not true of the larger sample.

Well-Being Among College Graduates, by Amount of Undergraduate Student Loan Debt

"Thriving gap" equals percentage thriving for individuals with over $50,000 in debt minus percentage thriving for those with no student loans

	No student loans	Over $50,000	Thriving gap
2000-2014 Graduates			
	%	%	pct. pts.
Purpose	47	38	-9
Social	49	45	-4
Financial	38	22	-16
Community	41	35	-6
Physical	33	22	-11
1990-1999 Graduates			
	%	%	pct. pts.
Purpose	51	45	-6
Social	44	45	+1*
Financial	44	31	-13
Community	45	44	-1*
Physical	35	27	-8

*Not statistically significant
Feb. 4-March 7, 2014

GALLUP

But older graduates who took out large student loans also differ from their fellow graduates in their current well-being. Though their student debt is likely paid off, those who graduated in the 1990s and borrowed more than $50,000 have lower financial, physical, and purpose well-being compared with those who never took out loans.

In financial well-being, older graduates that had large student loans trail behind their debt-free peers by 13 points in terms of thriving rates, nearly as large as the gap among the two of graduate types for the 2000–2014 cohort.

Large "thriving gaps"—the difference between the percentage of graduates with $50,000 or more in student loans thriving in one element from the percentage of debt-free graduates thriving in that element—exist for physical well-being (-8 points) and purpose well-being (-6 points). In both instances, these differences are comparable to discrepancies observed in the younger group of graduates. On the other hand, unlike the younger group of college graduates, graduates of the 1990–1999 era have little differences in thriving in the elements of community and social well-being, regardless of how much they borrowed to get their degree.

There are many possible reasons why those who took out student loans more than 20 years ago still have lower financial, physical, and purpose well-being today. The possession and repayment of debt is known to have negative ripple effects that might not disappear once the financial obligation does. It may be, for example, that the years spent paying down debt rather than securing savings leads to financial insecurity, or that the physical health problems that are often associated with debt persist.

Implications

President Barack Obama recently commented on the challenge of paying for college, saying, "At a time when higher education has never been more important, it's also never been more expensive. Over the last three decades, the average tuition at a public university has more than tripled." But, as Obama conceded in the same speech, college is a "smart investment." The wisdom of this investment is often framed in terms of the economic benefits a degree can bring, rather than on a broader set of criteria, such as if a college degree—and its associated costs—leads to a rewarding, healthy life in the long run.

Recent research suggests that most college graduates will eventually pay down their debt, partly because of the increased earning power commanded by those degrees. And, indicating that the loan process may be working, the vast majority of student loan accounts are not in delinquency—though the rate is rising. But findings from the Gallup-Purdue Index show that there may be costs associated with considerable levels of undergraduate debt that go beyond repayment. Student debt is linked to lower financial, purpose, physical, and community well-being. Notably, well-being is worse for students taking out more than $50,000 worth of student debt, suggesting student debt is most problematic when it is substantial. This pattern is consistent across two decades of graduates, meaning it includes many individuals who have paid off their debt entirely.

Although the analysis clearly shows a link between student debt and well-being that continues later in life, the mechanisms driving that relationship are unclear and cannot be established by this study. Specifically, it is unclear if the debt itself and its effect on future life events drags down a person's well-being, or if the conditions that lead one to borrow for college, such as family income, are related to well-being and have effects that persist later in life.

Studies show that high student debt can result in the deferral of major life events, such as marriage and homeownership. High student debt can also result in a graduate pursuing a career path he or she would not have taken otherwise. These new insights from the Gallup-Purdue Index suggest the legacy of high student debt may be lower well-being that lasts for many years after graduates receive their diploma.

More broadly, there are many factors to consider when measuring the outcomes of a college education—not just salaries or employment rates. The Gallup-Purdue Index provides the most comprehensive examination of the relationship between the college experience and whether college graduates have great jobs *and* great lives.

Survey Methods

Results for the Gallup-Purdue Index are based on Web surveys conducted Feb. 4–March 7, 2014, with a random sample of 29,560 respondents with a bachelor's degree or higher, aged 18 and older, with Internet access, living in all 50 U.S. states and the District of Columbia.

For results based on the total sample of 1990–2014 college graduates, the margin of sampling error is ±1.4 percentage points at the 95% confidence level.

The Gallup-Purdue Index sample was compiled from two sources: the Gallup Panel and the Gallup Daily tracking survey.

The Gallup Panel is a proprietary, probability-based longitudinal panel of U.S. adults who are selected using random-digit-dial (RDD) and address-based sampling methods. The Gallup Panel is not an opt-in panel. The Gallup Panel includes 60,000 individuals who Gallup surveys via phone, mail, or Web. Gallup Panel members with a college degree and access to the Internet were invited to take the Gallup-Purdue Index survey online.

August 07, 2014

FORTY-FIVE PERCENT OF AMERICANS SEEK OUT ORGANIC FOODS

More people in cities or in the West actively include organic foods

by Rebecca Riffkin

WASHINGTON, D.C.—A little less than half of Americans, 45%, actively try to include organic foods in their diets, while 15% actively avoid them. More than a third, 38%, say they "don't think either way" about organic foods.

Eating Organic Foods

Thinking about the food you eat, for each of the following please say if it is something you actively try to include in your diet, something you actively try to avoid, or something you don't think about either way. How about organic foods?

	% Actively try to include	% Actively try to avoid	% Don't think about either way
Americans	45	15	38

July 7-10, 2014

GALLUP

Organic agriculture is monitored and certified by the U.S. Department of Agriculture and must adhere to strict regulations to be certified as "organic." Organic food is free of man-made additions like antibiotics, and organic farming is supposed to be better for the environment than traditional farming. Organic foods often cost more than non-organic foods, which could keep some Americans from including them in their diets.

This is the first year Gallup has asked about eating organic foods in the annual Consumption Habits survey. Forty-five percent actively try to include organic foods, putting such foods in the middle of the list of 12 others measured—trailing fruits and vegetables by a wide margin, but well ahead of fat, soda, and sugar. The 38% who say they "don't think either way" about organic foods is higher than the percentage for any of the other food products.

In the West, Over Half Include Organic Foods in Their Diets

In the U.S., inclusion of organic foods is highest in the West (54%) and lowest in the East (39%). Americans who report living in a big or small city are more likely to eat organic foods than those who describe their location as a town or rural area, 50% versus 37%, respectively, while those who live in suburban areas fall between these two groups.

Location and Eating Organic Foods

Thinking about the food you eat, for each of the following please say if it is something you actively try to include in your diet, something you actively try to avoid, or something you don't think about either way. How about organic foods?

	% Actively try to include	% Actively try to avoid	% Don't think about either way
East	39	18	41
Midwest	47	17	34
South	43	13	41
West	54	12	34
Big/Small city	50	16	32
Suburb	46	8	44
Town/Rural	37	19	41

July 7-10, 2014

GALLUP

Younger Americans More Likely Than Older to Eat Organic Foods

More than half of 18- to 29-year-old Americans actively try to include organic foods in their diets, compared with one-third of Americans who are 65 and older. Older Americans are slightly more likely than other age groups to "think either way" about organic foods.

Eating Organic Foods Among Various Demographic Groups

Thinking about the food you eat, for each of the following please say if it is something you actively try to include in your diet, something you actively try to avoid, or something you don't think about either way. How about organic foods?

	% Actively try to include	% Actively try to avoid	% Don't think about either way
18 to 29 years	53	13	32
30 to 49 years	48	13	38
50 to 64 years	45	16	38
65+ years	33	19	44
Republican	40	20	40
Independent	45	14	38
Democrat	48	12	36
Household annual income $75,000+	49	11	39
Household annual income $30,000 to $74,999	45	13	40
Household annual income under $30,000	42	24	31

July 7-10, 2014

GALLUP

Household income is a factor in food choices, with almost half of upper-income Americans actively including organic foods, compared with 42% of lower-income Americans. Almost a quarter of lower-income Americans, however, actively avoid organic foods, while among upper-income Americans it is closer to one in 10. This could be a reaction to cost, as organic foods typically cost 20% to 100% more than non-organic foods. So lower-income Americans could be actively avoiding organic foods because they are trying to save money on food purchases, rather than avoiding them because of health reasons or dietary preferences.

Implications

Organic foods are subject to strict government regulations in order to earn that title. They can't be treated with chemical pesticides, and growers of organic foods must use natural fertilizers. Often this results in more expensive food, a major downside to organic foods. However, advocates praise organic foods as better for the environment and free of potentially harmful aspects like pesticides and additives. Studies are still inconclusive about whether organic foods are actually healthier.

Given that almost half of Americans actively try to include organic foods in their diets, they may view the benefits of organic foods as greater than their downsides, such as the higher cost or limited access. Income and location appear to be factors in preference for organic foods, although that may be changing. Wal-Mart, the largest retailer and grocer in the U.S., and known for its low-price business strategy, has announced plans to begin selling organic food. Organic food could soon become more easily accessible and more affordable, and this in turn could encourage more Americans to include it in their diets.

Survey Methods

Results for this Gallup poll are based on telephone interviews conducted July 7–10, 2014, with a random sample of 1,013 adults, aged 18 and older, living in all 50 U.S. states and the District of Columbia.

For results based on the total sample of national adults, the margin of sampling error is ±4 percentage points at the 95% confidence level.

August 11, 2014
LGBT POPULATION IN U.S. SIGNIFICANTLY LESS RELIGIOUS
Almost half are classified as nonreligious

by Frank Newport

PRINCETON, NJ—Americans who identify as lesbian, gay, bisexual, or transgender are significantly less likely than non-LGBT Americans to be highly religious, and significantly more likely to be classified as not religious. The same percentage of each group is moderately religious.

These results are based on more than 104,000 Gallup Daily tracking interviews conducted between Jan. 2 and July 31, 2014, including 3,242 adults who identified themselves as lesbian, gay, bisexual, or transgender.

Gallup classifies Americans as "very religious" if they say religion is an important part of their daily lives and that they attend religious services every week or almost every week. That group constituted 41% of all U.S. adults between January and July 2014. "Nonreligious" Americans (30% of U.S. adults) are those who say religion is not an important part of their daily lives and that they seldom or never attend religious services. The remaining group, 29% of Americans, are classified as "moderately religious." These people say religion is important in their lives but that they do not attend services regularly, or that religion is not important but that they still attend services.

Religiosity Among National Adults

By LGBT status and gender

	Highly religious	Moderately religious	Not religious
	%	%	%
NATIONAL ADULTS			
LGBT	24	29	47
Non-LGBT	41	29	30
MALE			
LGBT	25	26	49
Non-LGBT	36	28	35
FEMALE			
LGBT	24	31	46
Non-LGBT	45	30	25

January-July 2014

LGBT and non-LGBT individuals differ on both dimensions that make up the religiosity classification. About a quarter of LGBT individuals attend religious services regularly, contrasted with 42% of non-LGBT individuals.

Religious Service Attendance

By LGBT status

	At least once a week/ Almost every week	About once a month	Seldom/Never
	%	%	%
LGBT	26	11	62
Non-LGBT	42	12	44

January-July 2014

In similar fashion, although about half of LGBT individuals say religion is important in their daily lives, this is significantly less than the 66% of non-LGBT individuals who say religion is important.

Is Religion Important in Your Daily Life?

By LGBT status

	Yes	No
	%	%
LGBT	49	51
Non-LGBT	66	34

January-July 2014

There are a number of possible explanations for the lower level of religiosity among the U.S. LGBT population. LGBT individuals may feel less welcome in many congregations whose church doctrine, church policy, or ministers or parishioners condemn same-sex relations, and for the same reasons may be less likely to adopt religion into their own daily lives and beliefs.

Other possible explanations have to do less with church doctrine and more with the demographics of the LGBT population. LGBT individuals may be more likely to live in areas and cities where religion and religious service attendance are less common, and may adopt the practices of those with whom they share geography.

The LGBT population skews substantially younger than the non-LGBT population, and because younger people are the least religious of any age group in the U.S. today, age could be an explanation. However, a look at the relationship between LGBT status and religiousness across age groups shows that while older individuals in both groups are more religious than those who are younger, differences in religiousness are evident within all three age groups. In short, even if the LGBT population had the same age divisions as the non-LGBT population, the former's lower levels of religiousness would most likely still be evident.

Religiosity, by Age

By LGBT status

	Highly religious	Moderately religious	Not religious
	%	%	%
18 TO 34			
LGBT	17	27	56
Non-LGBT	33	28	39
35 TO 54			
LGBT	27	29	44
Non-LGBT	41	30	29
55+			
LGBT	37	30	33
Non-LGBT	46	29	25

January-July 2014

LGBT Americans More Likely to Be "Nones," Less Likely to Be Protestants or Catholics

Overall, 67% of LGBT Americans identify with a specific or general religion, lower than the 83% of non-LGBT adults who identify with one—with fewer LGBT individuals identifying as Protestants, and, to a lesser degree, as Catholics. While slightly more than half of the non-LGBT population is Protestant, that percentage shrinks to 35% among the LGBT population. The LGBT Catholic percentage is five points lower than the non-LGBT group. LGBT individuals are as likely as others to identify as Jews or Muslims, while they are more likely to identify with all other non-Christian religions combined—8% vs. 2%.

Religious Identification

By LGBT status

	Pro-testant	Catholic	Mormon	Jewish	Muslim	Other non-Christian religion	No religious identity
	%	%	%	%	%	%	%
LGBT	35	20	1	2	1	8	33
Non-LGBT	51	25	2	2	1	2	17

January-July 2014

Bottom Line

The under-representation of LGBT Americans in the ranks of the religious in the U.S. today has a number of possible causes. Some of these center on the effect of church policies and doctrine, which have historically been disapproving of non-heterosexual love and relations, while others may reflect demographic and geographic differences in the LGBT population compared with the rest of the population.

Societal attitudes toward same-sex relations have become more accepting, and recent stances taken by several churches and religions reflect this. Just this summer, the Presbyterian Church (USA) voted to allow that denomination's ministers to perform same-sex marriages in states where it is legal. If these types of shifts continue, LGBT adults may be more likely to feel welcome in attending churches and other religious institutions, as well as in identifying as religious, personally.

Survey Methods

Results for this Gallup poll are based on telephone interviews conducted January to July 2014, on the Gallup Daily tracking survey, with a random sample of 104,024 adults, aged 18 and older, living in all 50 U.S. states and the District of Columbia. For results based on the total sample of national adults, the margin of sampling error is ±1 percentage point at the 95% confidence level.

For results based on the total sample of 3,242 LGBT adults, the margin of sampling error is ±2 percentage points at the 95% confidence level.

For results based on the total sample of 93,324 non-LGBT adults, the margin of sampling error is ±1 percentage point at the 95% confidence level.

August 12, 2014

AMERICANS SERVING THEIR COMMUNITIES GAIN WELL-BEING EDGE

Community volunteers are less likely to report feeling daily stress and worry

by Lindsey Sharpe

WASHINGTON, D.C.—Americans who actively work to better their communities have higher overall well-being than those who do not. U.S. adults who agree that they have received recognition for helping to improve their communities in the last year have an average Well-Being Index score of 70.0, while those who disagree have an average of 58.5. Importantly, this relationship between well-being and receiving recognition for community involvement persists even after controlling for the effects of age and income—two factors that are related to higher community well-being.

While wealthier Americans typically have higher well-being than their lower-income counterparts, lower-income Americans who have received recognition for community work have a higher average index score than even the highest-income earners who have not received community recognition, at 67.2 vs. 62.6, respectively. Similarly, older Americans typically have higher well-being than those who are younger. But younger adults who have received recognition for community involvement have higher well-being than older Americans who have not received recognition.

Americans' Well-Being Index Average Scores, by Community Involvement

	Have received community service recognition	Have not received community service recognition
Well-Being Index score	70.0	58.5
Score by age group:		
18 to 29	70.3	58.4
30 to 45	68.8	57.2
46 to 64	68.6	56.8
65+	73.0	62.9
Score by annual household income:		
Less than $36,000	67.2	52.4
$36,000 to less than $90,000	69.9	58.7
$90,000 or more	71.3	62.6

Gallup-Healthways Well-Being Index
Jan. 2-July 30, 2014

GALLUP

Although the data indicate a link exists between community involvement and high well-being, the direction of the relationship is not clear. It is possible that those who already have higher well-being might be more likely to volunteer in their communities.

These data are based on more than 100,000 interviews with U.S. adults from Jan. 2 to July 30, 2014, as part of the Gallup-Healthways Well-Being Index. Gallup asks Americans to rate their level of agreement with the following statement using a five-point scale, where "5" means strongly agree and "1" means strongly disagree: "In the last 12 months, you have received recognition for helping to improve the city or area where you live."

Overall, 19% of U.S. adults report receiving recognition for their community involvement, answering with a 4 or a 5, while two-thirds of U.S. adults disagree that they have received recognition by answering with a 1 or a 2.

Active Community Participation Inoculates Against Stress and Worry

U.S. adults who say they have received recognition for work in their communities in the past year are also less likely to say they experienced stress or worry the day before being interviewed.

Overall, 40% of American adults report feeling stressed "yesterday." However, the rate drops to 34% among those who say they have received recognition for community involvement, and rises to 42% among those who say they have not received such recognition. Similarly, a quarter of adults who say they have received recognition report feeling worry on any given day, compared with 32% of those who indicate they have not received recognition.

Americans' Daily Emotional Health, by Community Involvement

Did you experience the following feelings during a lot of the day yesterday? How about [worry/stress]?

	Have received community service recognition	Have not received community service recognition	Difference (pct. pts.)
Experienced worry	25%	32%	-7
Experienced stress	34%	42%	-8

Gallup-Healthways Well-Being Index
Jan. 2-July 30, 2014

GALLUP

The same patterns hold true across age and income groups. At each age or income level, those who agree that they have received recognition for community work consistently report less daily stress and worry than those who do not agree.

Implications

These findings, in addition to previous Gallup research, suggest that community involvement may help improve well-being and may protect individuals from daily stress and worry. However, the causal relationship remains unknown. It is possible that those who already have higher well-being and less stress—possibly indicating they have more free time to be involved in community activities—are simply more likely to volunteer in their communities.

Still, working to better the community may help bolster key areas of well-being. Volunteering to improve a community can foster a sense of purpose and meaning, help volunteers build social relationships and connections, increase physical activity, and provide a fresh perspective on life. Looking beyond the day-to-day struggles of one's own life and focusing externally may help decrease stress, worry, and other negative emotions.

Given that two-thirds of U.S. adults say they have not been recognized for improving their communities in the past 12 months, there are a considerable number of Americans who could still benefit from volunteering. Local governments should consider promoting existing community service opportunities and causes within their communities. Doing so clearly benefits the community directly through the services provided, and also may boost volunteers' well-being. Similarly, business leaders could help their employees' well-being by organizing workforce community service efforts and encouraging and recognizing participation.

Survey Methods

Results are based on telephone interviews conducted as part of the Gallup-Healthways Well-Being Index survey Jan. 2–July 30, 2014, with a random sample of 103,301 adults, aged 18 and older, living in all 50 U.S. states and the District of Columbia.

For results based on the total sample of national adults, the margin of sampling error is ±1 percentage point at the 95% confidence level.

August 12, 2014
CONGRESSIONAL JOB APPROVAL STAYS NEAR HISTORICAL LOW
Thirteen percent of Americans approve, 83% disapprove

by Jeffrey M. Jones

PRINCETON, NJ—Americans' dismal evaluations of Congress continue, with 13% approving and 83% disapproving of the job it is doing. That approval rating is just four percentage points above the all-time low of 9% measured last November.

This month, Gallup followed up its standard congressional job approval question by asking Americans whether they hold that opinion strongly or only moderately. A majority, 55%, say they strongly disapprove of Congress, while 2% strongly approve.

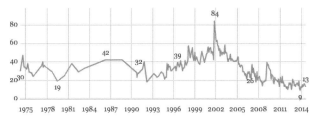

Congressional Job Approval -- Full Trend

GALLUP

Gallup previously asked about strength of Congress approval twice in 1994 and once in 1998. In October 1994, just before Republicans took control of Congress after 40 years as the minority party in the House of Representatives, 42% strongly disapproved of Congress.

Strength of Congressional Approval and Disapproval -- Full Gallup Trend

Do you approve or disapprove of the way Congress is handling its job?
Do you [approve/disapprove] strongly or only moderately?

	Strongly approve	Moderately approve	Moderately disapprove	Strongly disapprove
	%	%	%	%
Aug 7-10, 2014	2	11	28	55
Oct 29-Nov 1, 1998	8	36	26	21
Oct 22-24, 1994	2	21	28	42
Oct 7-9, 1994	2	19	33	40

GALLUP

Congress Approval on Pace to Be Lowest in Midterm Year

Since hitting the low point in Gallup's 40-year trend on congressional approval last fall—just after the partial federal government shutdown ended—Congress' ratings have barely improved. This year, Congress' approval has ranged between 12% and 16%, averaging 14%.

Although Congress has not had stellar approval ratings historically—the average since 1974 is 33%—it has never been as low in a midterm election year as it is now. The prior low at any point in a midterm election was 16% in March 2010. The lowest in the last few days before a midterm election, as voters were finalizing their vote choices, was 21%, also in 2010.

Gallup has found a strong relationship between congressional approval and seat change in Congress, with much more membership turnover when Congress' approval rating is below 40% at the time of the midterm elections. Voters typically take out their wrath more on the president's party than on the majority party in Congress (if the two differ) when Congress is unpopular, as was the case in the 1974 and 1982 elections. As a result, Democrats are probably more vulnerable than Republicans to losing seats this year. On average, the president's party has lost 34 seats in the House of Representatives when Congress' approval rating is below 40%, with a range of eight to 63 seats.

While a loss of 30 or more House seats is not out of the question this year, there are certain structural factors that may work against it. One is divided control of Congress, with Democrats currently having the majority in the Senate and Republicans in the House. That has almost certainly depressed Congress' approval ratings compared with what they would be if one party controlled both chambers. When one party controls the House and Senate, supporters of that party typically give Congress higher ratings than supporters of the other party do. In the current era of divided party control of Congress, the party gaps have disappeared. The Aug. 7–10 Gallup poll, for example, shows 14% of Republicans, 12% of independents, and 13% of Democrats approving of Congress.

Congressional Approval Ratings and President's Party Seat Changes, Recent Midterm Elections

Year	President's party	Majority party in House	% Approve of Congress ^	Seat gain/loss in U.S. House for president's party
2010	Democrat	Democrat	21	-63
2006	Republican	Republican	26	-30
2002	Republican	Republican	50	+6
1998	Democrat	Republican	44	+5
1994	Democrat	Democrat	23	-53
1990	Republican	Democrat	26	-8
1986	Republican	Democrat	42	-5
1982	Republican	Democrat	29	-28
1978	Democrat	Democrat	29	-11
1974	Republican*	Democrat	35	-43

^ In last pre-election poll

* The president (Ford) took office less than three months before the midterm elections

GALLUP

A second factor working against a large seat change in the House this year is that partisan redistricting in many states has led to a situation in which fewer districts are competitive. So even if strong national forces shave five or 10 percentage points off an incumbent's usual voting percentage, that still may not be enough to tip the election to the challenger's party. And it is not clear how many more seats Republicans might be able to pick up after winning so many in 2010, and keeping most of those in the 2012 elections.

Also, perhaps because redistricting effectively limits the number of seats each party can reasonably expect to hold, since the 1960s no two-term president has had two midterm "wave elections" occur during his presidency. And Democrats' 63-seat loss in 2010 certainly qualifies as a Republican wave during the Barack Obama presidency.

Implications

Americans' dismal views of Congress are well-documented. Along with their near-historically low job approval ratings of Congress, with a majority strongly disapproving, Americans' confidence and trust in the institution, and ratings of its members as honest and ethical, are also among the lowest Gallup has measured.

That certainly makes incumbents vulnerable to defeat if they run for re-election. To date, many members of Congress have retired or decided to run for higher office, and a few others have been defeated in primary elections. This has already guaranteed that there will be some new faces in Congress. And although the vast majority of incumbents seeking re-election will win in the fall general elections, they arguably will have a more challenging run than in past years. Incumbents from more competitive districts, and those facing a strong challenger from the other party, are especially vulnerable to losing their seats this fall.

Survey Methods

Results for this Gallup poll are based on telephone interviews conducted Aug. 7–10, 2014, with a random sample of 1,032 adults, aged 18 and older, living in all 50 U.S. states and the District of Columbia.

For results based on the total sample of national adults, the margin of sampling error is ±4 percentage points at the 95% confidence level.

August 13, 2014
FEAR FOR CHILD'S SAFETY NEARLY BACK TO PRE–SANDY HOOK LEVELS
Twenty-seven percent of parents worry for their children's safety at school

by Justin McCarthy

WASHINGTON, D.C.—The percentage of U.S. parents who say they fear for their oldest child's safety at school has fallen to 27% after being elevated for more than a year following the massacre at Sandy Hook Elementary School in Newtown, Connecticut. Parents' concern jumped eight percentage points from 25% in August 2012 to 33% after the December massacre, and remained there in a poll conducted nearly a year after the shootings.

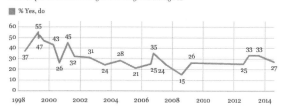

Thinking about your oldest child, when he or she is at school, do you fear for his or her physical safety?

Based on parents of children in grades kindergarten through 12

■ % Yes, do

Note: 1977 result of 24% not shown

GALLUP

These data are based on Gallup's annual Work and Education poll, conducted Aug. 7–10.

The percentage of American parents who feared for their oldest child's physical safety in school peaked at 55% in 1999 after the Columbine High School shootings in Colorado. In the first decade of the 2000s, parents' fears waned overall, though they spiked accordingly with reports of school shootings. In 2008, parents' fear fell to an all-time low of 15%. This low level of worry was short-lived, however, because by 2009, it had climbed back to 26%, and remained at this level until late 2012.

Fears for children's safety have spiked after tragic events in schools, but the short-term increases in parents' concerns also appear to get smaller each time. After reaching 55% after the Columbine High School shootings in 1999, there was a spike to 45% after the 2001 Santana High School shootings in California. By 2006, safety fears increased to 35% after a shooting at an Amish schoolhouse in Pennsylvania. And after an Alabama killing spree in homes and businesses that left 10 dead in 2009, 26% of parents feared for their children's safety.

Relatively Few Parents Say Their Children Have Expressed Fear to Them

While 26% of parents worry about the safety of their sons and daughters at school, a much smaller 8% report that their children have expressed worry to them about feeling unsafe at school. This gap between parents' and children's views has been evident each time Gallup has asked the questions. This figure, however, accounts only for children who have told their parents about their fears, and may not represent all children's feelings.

The percentage of parents who say their children have expressed fear to them about school safety has been quite stable over time, ranging narrowly between 8% and 12% since 2003.

At times, children have been more likely to express fear to their parents about feeling unsafe at school. In August 1999, roughly four months after Columbine, 18% of parents said they had heard such worries from their children, and in March 2001, after the Santana High School shootings, 22% said this.

Have any of your school-aged children expressed any worry or concern about feeling unsafe at their school when they go back to school this fall?

Based on parents of children in grades kindergarten through 12

■ % Yes, have

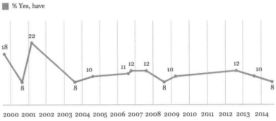

GALLUP'

Bottom Line

Although the trauma of Sandy Hook clearly stuck with Americans in the following year, Americans have, overall, shown increasing resilience in their reactions to school shootings since Columbine, becoming less likely to have greater fear about their own child's safety. According to a CNN analysis, there had been 15 "Newtown-like" school shootings since Sandy Hook as of June 2014, although none has attracted as much attention as Newtown.

It is unclear whether the delayed decline in fear after Newtown is attributable to stepped-up security measures at schools, which could help allay parents' fears, or if it is mainly attributable to Newtown's being further in the past and thus less top-of-mind for parents.

Survey Methods

Results for this Gallup poll are based on telephone interviews conducted Aug. 7–10, 2014, with a random sample of 221 parents with children in kindergarten through grade 12, living in all 50 U.S. states and the District of Columbia.

For results based on the total sample of parents, the margin of sampling error is ±9 percentage points at the 95% confidence level.

August 14, 2014
SLIM MAJORITY IN U.S. CALL SECONDHAND SMOKE VERY HARMFUL
Views differ between parents who smoke vs. don't smoke

by Lydia Saad

PRINCETON, NJ—Less than half of U.S. smokers with children younger than 18, 44%, believe exposure to secondhand smoke is "very harmful" to adults. That contrasts with two-thirds of parents

who don't smoke, and 61% of adult nonsmokers without children younger than 18. Meanwhile, relatively few smokers who don't have minor-aged children, 29%, consider secondhand smoke very harmful.

Perceived Seriousness of Health Risk Posed by Secondhand Smoke

In general, how harmful do you feel secondhand smoke is to adults -- very harmful, somewhat harmful, not too harmful, or not at all harmful?

	Smokers, have children under 18	Nonsmokers, have children under 18	Smokers, no children under 18	Nonsmokers, no children under 18
	%	%	%	%
Very harmful	44	66	29	61
Somewhat harmful	41	24	41	29
Not too harmful	8	7	18	6
Not harmful at all	5	2	10	2
Not sure	2	1	1	1

Based on aggregated 2010-2014 Gallup data

GALLUP'

Essentially, solid majorities of nonsmokers believe secondhand smoke is very harmful, and whether a nonsmoker has children makes little difference. By contrast, less than half of smokers consider secondhand smoke a significant health hazard, although smokers with children are more likely to rate it very harmful than are smokers without children. Roughly one in five parents of children in the U.S. smoke—22%—similar to the 20% found among adults with no minor-aged children.

These findings are based on combined data from Gallup's annual updates on smoking and tobacco from 2010 through 2014. The question about secondhand smoke refers to its health effects on adults, specifically. While concern could be higher if the question asked about the effects on children, it's likely that gaps between smokers and nonsmokers would persist.

Additionally, it's not clear that the risks of secondhand smoke are any greater to children than to adults. According to the U.S. surgeon general's 2006 report on secondhand smoke, "Children exposed to secondhand smoke are at an increased risk for sudden infant death syndrome, acute respiratory infections, ear problems, and more severe asthma." And the report offers this summary of the health consequences for adults: "Exposure of adults to secondhand smoke has immediate adverse effects on the cardiovascular system and causes coronary heart disease and lung cancer."

Public Concern About Secondhand Smoke Remains Steady

Americans' awareness of the risks of secondhand smoke is significantly higher today than it was 20 years ago when barely a third (36%) called it very harmful. However, despite the surgeon general's strong warnings in 2006, recognition has consistently hovered near 55% since the late 1990s, apart from one slightly lower reading in 1999.

Seriousness of Health Risk From Secondhand Smoke

In general, how harmful do you feel secondhand smoke is to adults -- very harmful, somewhat harmful, not too harmful, or not at all harmful?

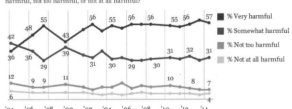

GALLUP'

Despite the broad stability of views over the past 15 years, smokers who have children younger than 18 have become slightly more likely to see secondhand smoke as at least somewhat harmful—at 85% in the 2010–2014 period, up from an average 79% in 2003–2008. However, the percentage calling it very harmful is barely higher, at 44% in the last five years versus 42% in the prior decade.

Overall, Americans' awareness of the dangers of secondhand smoke continues to lag far behind their acknowledgment that smoking is dangerous to smokers themselves. Since Gallup initiated this trend in 2002, a steady eight in 10 Americans have described smoking as very harmful to adults who smoke.

Seriousness of Health Risk of Smoking to Smokers Themselves

In general, how harmful do you feel smoking is to adults who smoke -- very harmful, somewhat harmful, not too harmful, or not at all harmful?

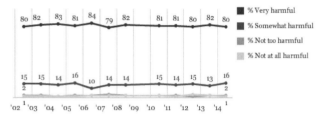

- ■ % Very harmful
- ■ % Somewhat harmful
- ▨ % Not too harmful
- ▨ % Not at all harmful

GALLUP

Bottom Line

Gallup has long documented a chasm in smokers' and nonsmokers' stated belief that smoking is very harmful to smokers. This could be a matter of smokers downplaying the risks because they don't want to believe smoking is dangerous. Or it could be tied to smokers' lower levels of education, on average, compared with nonsmokers. In any case, the awareness gap is a detriment to smokers themselves.

The dynamic is completely different with respect to secondhand smoke. The failure of many smokers to fully appreciate the health risks of so-called involuntary smoking may make them less careful about avoiding nonsmokers when they light up. And when they smoke around children, those who suffer are both faultless and helpless.

With fewer than six in 10 adults perceiving secondhand smoke as very harmful, significant room exists for public awareness to grow. Whatever information has been available over the past decade has evidently not been persuasive enough to increase public understanding about the extent of the risks, so a different approach may be necessary. Also, developing messages that elevate smokers' concern about the dangers their habit poses to others would seem to be particularly important.

Survey Methods

Results for the most recent Gallup findings are based on telephone interviews conducted July 7–10, 2014, with a random sample of 1,013 adults, aged 18 and older, living in all 50 U.S. states and the District of Columbia.

For results based on the total sample of national adults, the margin of sampling error is ±4 percentage points at the 95% confidence level.

August 15, 2014
U.S. INVESTORS OPT FOR HUMAN OVER ONLINE FINANCIAL ADVICE
Just one in three are very comfortable using online technology for investing

by Lydia Saad

PRINCETON, NJ—Even as access to the Internet has become ubiquitous in the U.S. and data analytics is highly touted for use in finance, U.S. investors are more likely to have a dedicated financial adviser than to use a financial website for obtaining advice on investing or planning for their retirement, 44% vs. 20%.

Resources U.S. Investors Use for Seeking Financial Advice

Now thinking about financial advice on investing or planning for retirement, do you use any of the following, or not?

	Yes, use	No, don't use
	%	%
A dedicated personal financial adviser	44	56
A financial advisory firm, where you can call into a call center and speak to a financial adviser	35	64
A friend or family member who advises you	29	71
An online financial planning or investing website	20	80

Wells Fargo/Gallup Investor and Retirement Optimism Index
June 27-July 9, 2014

GALLUP

More investors also report using either a financial advisory firm that gives them access to live advice through a call center (35%) or a friend or family member (29%) to advise them than using a financial website.

These findings are based on a Wells Fargo/Gallup Investor and Retirement Optimism Index survey conducted in late June and early July. The survey is based on a nationally representative sample of U.S. investors with $10,000 or more in stocks, bonds, mutual funds, or in a self-directed IRA or 401(k).

Retirees, High-Value Investors Gravitate Toward Dedicated Financial Advisers

Among U.S. investors, retirees and investors with $100,000 or more in invested assets are significantly more likely than their counterparts to use a dedicated financial adviser. Nonretirees are more likely than retirees to use financial websites or to rely on friends and family.

Resources U.S. Investors Use for Obtaining Financial Advice

	Dedicated financial adviser	Financial advisory firm	Friend or family member	Financial website
Men	41%	34%	26%	25%
Women	46%	36%	32%	14%
Retired	53%	39%	16%	11%
Not retired	40%	33%	34%	24%
$100,000 or more in investments	53%	33%	28%	23%
Less than $100,000 in investments	32%	36%	32%	18%

Wells Fargo/Gallup Investor and Retirement Optimism Index
June 27-July 9, 2014

GALLUP

Men and women are about equally likely to report using three of the four advice resources. The exception is financial websites, which men are about twice as likely as women to say they use, 25%

vs. 14%. There is little difference across types of investors in the use of financial advisory firms, with about a third of each demographic group saying they use one.

Eight in 10 Investors Receive Advice Somewhere

Overall, 79% of investors report using at least one of the four financial advice resources tested, while 21% don't use any of the four. The largest percentage of investors—40%—rely on just one source, but almost a third (30%) rely on two, 7% on three, and 2% on all four.

The following chart details how investors fall into all 16 possible combinations of the four resources. Of particular note is that many more investors rely on a financial adviser to the exclusion of a financial website than the reverse: 37% vs. 14%. Only 7% rely on both, either alone or in combination with other resources.

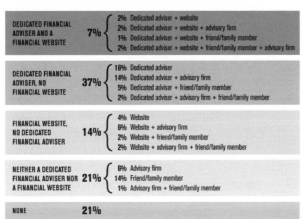

Which of four resources do U.S. investors rely on for financial advice on investing or planning for retirement?

DEDICATED FINANCIAL ADVISER AND A FINANCIAL WEBSITE	7%	2% Dedicated adviser + website 2% Dedicated adviser + website + advisory firm 1% Dedicated adviser + website + friend/family member 2% Dedicated adviser + website + friend/family member + advisory firm
DEDICATED FINANCIAL ADVISER, NO FINANCIAL WEBSITE	37%	16% Dedicated adviser 14% Dedicated adviser + advisory firm 5% Dedicated adviser + friend/family member 2% Dedicated adviser + advisory firm + friend/family member
FINANCIAL WEBSITE, NO DEDICATED FINANCIAL ADVISER	14%	4% Website 6% Website + advisory firm 2% Website + friend/family member 2% Website + advisory firm + friend/family member
NEITHER A DEDICATED FINANCIAL ADVISER NOR A FINANCIAL WEBSITE	21%	6% Advisory firm 14% Friend/family member 1% Advisory firm + friend/family member
NONE	21%	

Based on 509 U.S. adults with $10,000 or more in invested assets
Wells Fargo/Gallup Investor and Retirement Optimism Index survey, June 27-July 9, 2014

GALLUP'

Part of what may be suppressing investors' use of online financial resources is that less than a third of investors—30%—say they are "very comfortable" using online or mobile technology for their investing or financial advice needs. While another 27% are somewhat comfortable, 43% say they are not comfortable with this.

There is a strong generational skew in these attitudes, with 66% of nonretirees indicating at least some level of comfort with online financial advice tools, compared with 35% of retirees. Additionally, men have a higher comfort level than women.

And while people may not always be the best judge of their own likelihood of adopting technology in the future, just one in four investors—24%—say they expect to use online or mobile technology more in the next two to three years than they do currently.

Implications

The most recent Wells Fargo/Gallup survey shows that the great majority of investors feel they need expert advice to help them invest in the stock market, and the desire for professional input would likely be greater when advice needed for other types of financial matters (such as planning for retirement, college expenses, and healthcare) is factored in. Accordingly, eight in 10 investors report that they do receive advice in some form, spanning the four sources of advice tested in the poll. And despite lots of buzz about online financial tools that allow users to submit their portfolios to computer algorithms, most investors still feel more comfortable involving a human, whether in the form of a dedicated personal adviser or a financial advisory firm that gives them access to live counselors in a call center.

This shouldn't be an either-or situation. Investors who want the best of both worlds can probably get it by seeking a partnership with financial advisers who are tapping into the same powerful analysis tools being offered to consumers online. In fact, such a marriage of humans and computers could be a strong selling point for the financial services industry—bridging consumers' reluctance to go it alone online with their desire for a human connection and the best possible performance for their investments.

Survey Methods

These findings are part of the Wells Fargo-Gallup Investor and Retirement Optimism Index, which was conducted June 27–July 9, 2014, by telephone. The sample for the Index included 1,036 investors, aged 18 and older, living in all 50 states and the District of Columbia. For this study, the American investor is defined as any person or spouse in a household with total savings and investments of $10,000 or more. About two in five American households have at least $10,000 in savings and investments in stocks, bonds, mutual funds, or in a self-directed IRA or 401(k). The sample consists of 72% nonretired investors and 28% retired investors.

Questions about how investors get financial advice were asked of a random half-sample of 509 U.S. investors. The margin of sampling error for these results is ±5 percentage points at the 95% confidence level.

August 18, 2014
CONGRESSIONAL RE-ELECT MEASURE REMAINS NEAR ALL-TIME LOW
American voters not as negative about their own member of Congress

by Frank Newport

PRINCETON, NJ—Nineteen percent of U.S. registered voters say most members of Congress deserve re-election, roughly the same as in two measures earlier this year. This is on pace to be the lowest such "re-elect" sentiment in a midterm election year over Gallup's history of asking this question since 1992.

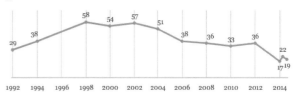

Please tell me whether you think each of the following political officeholders deserves to be re-elected, or not. How about – most members of Congress?

Among registered voters

■ % Yes, deserve re-election

1992	1994	1996	1998	2000	2002	2004	2006	2008	2010	2012	2014
29	38		58	54	57	51	38	36	33	36	22 17 19

1992-2012 figures are final reading before election. 2014 figures are based on polls conducted in January, April, and August. The question was not asked in 1996.

GALLUP'

The latest update on this measure comes from Gallup's Aug. 7–10 survey in which congressional job approval was 13%, just a few percentage points higher than the all-time low on that measure.

This congressional re-elect measure is related to overall congressional seat change in a midterm election and to the percentage of House members seeking re-election who are returned to Congress. Assuming that these attitudes remain similarly sour over the next 2 1/2 months, history would suggest above-average turnover in Congress in the November elections. Two other years in which this measure was relatively low—1994 and 2010—saw major shakeups, although the same party (Democrats) controlled the House and the Senate in both of those years, which may have made it easier for voters to take out their frustrations. Still, the 19% of American voters who on average this year say most members do not deserve re-election is significantly lower than in 1994 or 2010, providing a negative general context for the coming elections.

Americans Not as Negative About Their Own Representative

A separate question asks voters if "the U.S. representative in your congressional district" deserves to be re-elected. Currently, 50% of voters say yes, he or she does. This percentage essentially ties with the response to this question in 2010, and is just slightly higher than the 48% in 1992. So while this measure is historically low, it has not dropped to the record-low depths of the "most members" question.

Please tell me whether you think each of the following political officeholders deserves to be re-elected, or not. How about -- the U.S. representative in your congressional district?

Among registered voters

■ % Deserves re-election

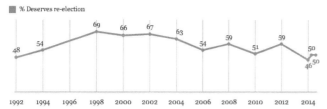

1992-2012 figures are final reading before election. 2014 figures are based on polls conducted in January, April, and August. The question was not asked in 1996.

GALLUP

Americans' views of most members of Congress have always been more negative than their views of their own member. But as noted, voters' views this year about most members of Congress have descended to the lowest levels ever seen, while their views of the advisability of re-electing *their* member, although historically low, are no lower than they have been in previous midterm election years. This has resulted in a 31-percentage-point gap between the re-elect measure for "your member" versus "most members" of Congress—the widest such gap in a midterm year in Gallup's history. In 2010, for example, the gap in the final poll before that year's elections was 18 points, and in 1994, it was 16 points.

Previous research shows that the "most members" and the "your member" measures are related to the percentage of incumbents seeking re-election who are in fact re-elected. How voters will manifest their historically distinct views of Congress at the national versus the local level this year will be one important key to the outcome of the elections.

Thoughts About Voting for Local Representative Specific to Job

The August survey included two questions asking Americans to explain in their own words why they do or do not think their member deserves re-election this year. Their responses center mainly on assessments of the specific performance of their House member—including many statements about the member doing a good job or not doing a good job. Those who say their member deserves to be re-elected also mentioned that he or she works for the district, shares the respondent's views, and listens to the people and relates to them. Those who say the member does not deserve re-election also say the member had been in Congress too long and that a change is needed, that the member does not work for the people or the district, that he or she has not followed through on promises, and that he or she only votes the party line.

What are some of the reasons why you think the U.S. representative in your congressional district deserves re-election?

Based on 500 adults who say their representative deserves re-election

	% Deserves re-election
Doing a good job	29
Works for/Stands up for/Supports district, state	18
Shares my views, values	6
Listens to people/communicates/relates	6
Has not been in Congress long/Needs more time	4
Is conservative	4
Been there a long time/Experienced/Good record	3
Honest/Good person	2
Haven't heard anything bad about/No mistakes	2
Focus on economy, employment	2
Focus on immigration, border security	1
Is a Democrat	1
No one better/All the same/Need someone in Congress	1
Protects environment, resources	1
Is a Republican	1
Stood against Obama/his agenda	1
Takes positions whether popular or not	1
Focus on military, veterans	1
Focus on education	1
Other	6
No opinion	16

Aug. 7-10, 2014

GALLUP

What are some of the reasons why you think the U.S. representative in your congressional district does not deserve re-election?

Based on 392 adults who say their representative does not deserve re-election

	% Does not deserve re-election
Not doing his/her job/Bad record	26
Been there too long/Need a change	15
Does not work for/represent people/district/state	12
Not followed through on promises	11
Only votes with his/her party	7
Does not share my views, values	6
Does not listen/communicate/relate/Out of touch	5
Supports Obama, Obamacare	3
Not dealing with economy	3
Not fiscally responsible	2
Questionable actions/Dishonest	2
A politician/Just running for office	2
Is a conservative	1
Is a liberal/Too far left	1
Is a Democrat	1
Immigration issue	1
Is a Republican	*
Other	7
No opinion	8

* Less than 0.5%
Aug. 7-10, 2014

GALLUP

Americans' responses seem to be quite specific to the performance of their individual representative rather than suggesting they are taking out their broad dissatisfaction with Congress in making a decision on their local vote. In short, it appears Americans are evaluating representatives on how they are doing their job and representing the district, while evaluating the institution as a whole on its collective inability to get much done.

Bottom Line

The percentage of American voters who believe most members of Congress deserve re-election is at an all-time low. Their views of whether their own representative deserves re-election are also low, but not nearly as sour as their views of Congress more generally. These negative evaluations of Congress have historically been related to lower rates of incumbent re-election in midterm elections and a higher turnover of congressional seats.

Survey Methods

Results for this Gallup poll are based on telephone interviews conducted Aug. 7–10, 2014, with a random sample of 897 registered voters, aged 18 and older, living in all 50 U.S. states and the District of Columbia.

For results based on the total sample of registered voters, the margin of sampling error is ±4 percentage points at the 95% confidence level.

For results based on the total sample of 1,032 national adults, the margin of sampling error is ±4 percentage points at the 95% confidence level.

August 18, 2014
FEWER WORKERS IN THE U.S. ARE WORRIED ABOUT JOB SETBACKS
Job worries still higher than before 2008 financial collapse

by Andrew Dugan

WASHINGTON, D.C.—Fewer than one in five U.S. full- and part-time workers currently worry that they will be laid off in the near future, down sharply from 29% last year. This marks a return of worker confidence to the upper end of the range Gallup saw in the years prior to the financial collapse in late 2008. Workers' concerns about maintaining their current level of benefits and compensation have also eased, though they remain higher than pre-2008 levels.

Workers Worried About Job Events, 2004-2014

Next, please indicate whether you are worried or not worried about each of the following happening to you, personally, in the near future. How about that ____?

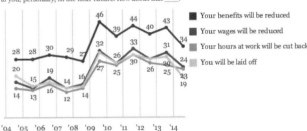

Based on U.S. workers, aged 18 and older, employed full or part time

GALLUP

The results are based on Gallup's annual Work and Education poll, conducted Aug. 7–10. These data come at a crucial time, as the Federal Reserve openly debates when to begin raising interest rates, which have been at record lows for six years in an effort to spur economic growth. The health of the labor market is a key variable in the Fed's analysis of when to raise interest rates.

While conventional metrics such as the unemployment rate and speed of economic activity—both of which have painted a brighter economic picture lately—are helpful in assessing the labor market's vitality, measures of American workers' feelings of security are also telling. Since 2009, Gallup has seen a heightened, persistent fear among U.S. workers about their job status, pay, and benefits, even as the economy slowly recovered—pointing to a difficult job market. This year may tell a different story—one of a more confident workforce—as seen by the large drop in the proportion of U.S. workers saying they are worried about having their benefits and wages reduced and being laid off. The data still show, however, that worries about several key job-related issues remain higher than before the financial collapse.

The worry that is probably most workers' biggest fear—being laid off—has dropped precipitously. Today's 19% worried is 10 percentage points lower than last year, and is nearly on par with layoff worries between 1997 and 2008, when an average of 17% worried about losing their job.

Reductions in benefits (34%) remain the most common job-related worry, as they have been since Gallup first asked this question in 1997. Even so, this year's reading is down nine points from last year and the lowest level since this figure nearly doubled after the financial crisis. In a similar vein, about a quarter of workers say they worry that their wages will be reduced (24%), down from 31% last August. However, both measures remain slightly elevated relative to where they were prior to the financial crisis.

Change in Worry About Job Events
% Worried

	Aug 7-10, 2014	2009-2013 average	1997-2008 average
That your benefits will be reduced	34	42	30
That your wages will be reduced	24	30	16
That your hours at work will be cut back	23	27	14
That you will be laid off	19	29	17

Based on U.S. workers employed full or part time

GALLUP

At 23%, the percentage of employed Americans saying they are worried that their hours at work will be cut is the only item that did not see a noteworthy decline from last year. It is, however, down significantly from its 2011 high of 30%, although still higher than its 1997–2008 average (14%).

Although "outsourcing" often receives significant political attention, most American workers do not fear that their jobs will be shipped overseas. Fewer than one in 10 U.S. workers (8%) say they worry their company "will move jobs to countries overseas," down slightly from 11% in the previous two years.

U.S. Workers Worried About Outsourcing Where They Work

Next, please indicate whether you are worried or not worried about each of the following happening to you, personally, in the near future. How about -- that your company will move jobs to countries overseas?

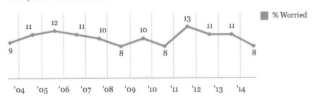

Based on U.S. workers, 18 and older, employed full or part time

GALLUP

Young Workers More Anxious About Being Laid Off

Young adult workers aged 18 to 34 are more likely to express signs of job insecurity than older workers. Nearly three in 10 young

American workers (29%) say they worry about being laid off, almost double the 15% of 35- to 54-year-olds and the 13% of workers aged 55 and older (13%). Moreover, young workers' fear of being laid off has not decreased from last year, whereas this year, fewer older workers say they are worried about being laid off. Younger workers also are more likely than older workers to worry that their hours will be cut back.

Worry About Job Events, by Age
% Worried

	18 to 34	35 to 54	55 and older
That your benefits will be reduced	33	40	26
That your wages will be reduced	31	23	17
That your hours at work will be cut back	33	20	11
That you will be laid off	29	15	13

Aug. 7-10, 2014; based on U.S. workers employed full or part time

GALLUP

Bottom Line

Determining to what extent the labor market still has "slack"—room for improvement—will be an important part in guiding the Fed's decision on whether to raise interest rates. The state of the job market will be a key topic at this week's meeting of top monetary officials and economists in Jackson Hole, Wyoming. A vigorous debate is expected. On one hand, the number of jobs added to the U.S. economy has picked up steam this year and the unemployment rate, at 6.2%, has fallen from its recessionary heights. On the other hand, the labor force participation rate remains as low as it has been since 1978, and wages remain stagnant.

The confidence of American workers themselves is also important to consider in this discussion. After the financial crisis and the grueling recession, the share of workers fearing layoffs or reductions in wages or benefits spiked, and these numbers failed to retreat over the past five years even as the economy came out of recession and the unemployment rate slowly improved. For many workers, even if the economy was improving, it wasn't making them feel any less anxious about their employment or compensation situation, a telling sign of the recovery's weakness.

Now, for the first time since the financial collapse, the percentage of U.S. workers worried about being laid off has fallen by double digits, and drops in those worried about having wages or benefits reduced are nearly as large. While workers still are more likely to say they worry on several questions now than before the financial crisis, these figures are down considerably. For the first time in a long time, fewer U.S. workers are worried in some way about their job, meaning the job market could finally be turning in favor of the employee.

Survey Methods

Results for this Gallup poll are based on telephone interviews conducted Aug. 7–10, 2014, with a random sample of 474 adults who are employed full or part time, aged 18 and older, living in all 50 U.S. states and the District of Columbia.

For results based on the total sample of national adults, the margin of sampling error is ±6 percentage points at the 95% confidence level.

August 19, 2014
AMERICANS WARY OF FEDERAL INFLUENCE ON PUBLIC SCHOOLS
Prefer local school boards over federal government, 56% to 15%

by Valerie J. Calderon

WASHINGTON, D.C.—Americans' trust in U.S. leaders has slipped amid partisan gridlock that has led to federal government inaction on pressing issues at home and abroad. Americans' weak confidence in the federal government extends to issues surrounding public education.

When asked to reflect on who should have the greatest influence on what is taught in the public schools, Americans prefer local school boards over the federal government by a wide margin, 56% to 15%. Twenty-eight percent believe state government should have the greatest say on curriculum.

In your opinion, who should have the greatest influence in deciding what is taught in the public schools here -- the federal government, the state government, or the local school board?

	All Americans	Democrats	Independents	Republicans
	%	%	%	%
Federal government	15	28	16	3
State government	28	26	28	28
Local school board	56	44	55	68
Don't know/Refused	1	1	1	*

* Less than 0.5%
May 29-June 20, 2014
46th Annual PDK/Gallup Poll of the Public's Attitudes Toward the Public Schools

GALLUP

While about nine times as many Democrats as Republicans say the federal government should have the greatest influence, the local school board is still the most popular choice among Democrats.

These findings are from the 46th Annual PDK/Gallup Poll of the Public's Attitudes Toward the Public Schools. Results are based on a Gallup Panel telephone study of 1,001 adults, aged 18 and older, conducted from May 29–June 20, 2014.

Majority of Americans Oppose Common Core to Guide Teaching

Common Core is one of the dominant topics in American public education this decade. About eight in 10 Americans say they have heard at least a little about the Common Core State Standards. Of those, the majority oppose using the standards in their community to guide teaching. Those who report they know "a great deal" about the Common Core are somewhat less likely to favor them (24%) than those who only know a little (39%).

How much, if anything, have you heard about the new national standards for teaching reading, writing, and math in grades K through 12, known as the Common Core State Standards -- a great deal, a fair amount, only a little, or nothing at all?

	%
Great deal	17
Fair amount	30
Only a little	34
Nothing at all	19

May 29-June 20, 2014
46th Annual PDK/Gallup Poll of the Public's Attitudes Toward the Public Schools

GALLUP

Majority opposition to the use of the Common Core State Standards to guide instruction persists across age, income, and education levels, but opinion diverges by political affiliation. Republicans who have heard of Common Core are twice as likely as Democrats to oppose use of the standards to guide teaching.

Do you favor or oppose having the teachers in your community use the Common Core State Standards to guide what they teach?

	All Americans	Democrats	Independents	Republicans
	%	%	%	%
Favor	33	53	34	17
Oppose	59	38	60	76
Don't know/Refused	7	9	6	7

Among those who have heard a great deal, a fair amount, or only a little about the Common Core State Standards
May 29-June 20, 2014
46th Annual PDK/Gallup Poll of the Public's Attitudes Toward the Public Schools

GALLUP'

Results from the Gallup Daily tracking survey earlier this year show that 52% of public school parents who had heard at least a little about the Common Core Standards were somewhat or very positive about them. The PDK/Gallup poll item is somewhat more specific, but results show that only about one in three (32%) public school parents favor having teachers in their community use the Common Core Standards to guide what they teach.

Common Core Limits Teachers, Opponents Say

Respondents who oppose having the teachers in their community use the Common Core were given four reasons they might oppose them. About two-thirds (65%) say a very important reason is that it will limit the flexibility teachers have to teach what they think is best.

Would you say that each of the following is a very important, somewhat important, not very important, or a not at all important reason that you oppose the use of the Common Core State Standards to guide what teachers in your community teach? How about [ITEMS ROTATED]?

Among those who have heard a great deal, a fair amount, or only a little about the Common Core State Standards and who oppose having teachers use Common Core to guide what they teach

	Very important	Somewhat important	Not very important	Not at all important	Don't know/ Refused
	%	%	%	%	%
The Common Core State Standards will limit the flexibility that teachers have to teach what they think is best.	65	22	6	5	3
The teachers in our community do not support the Common Core State Standards.	51	26	13	8	2
The federal government initiated the Common Core State Standards.	40	22	18	20	1
The Common Core State Standards will result in a national curriculum and national tests.	38	30	18	14	1

May 29-June 20, 2014
46th Annual PDK/Gallup Poll of the Public's Attitudes Toward the Public Schools

GALLUP'

Though the Common Core State Standards were developed by the National Governors Association, it is possible that Americans associate the initiative with the federal government because of support from the Department of Education and President Barack

Obama. Despite declining trust in federal agencies and government generally, federal involvement with the Common Core State Standards does not emerge as a chief reason for opposition among the few that were proposed in this study. Just four in 10 opponents say the fact that the federal government originated the Common Core State Standards Initiative is a very important reason that they oppose them.

Common Core Is Important for Education Equity, Supporters Say

Those who favor use of the Common Core to guide teachers are most enthusiastic about the opportunity for education equity that the standards may afford. Three in four say a very important reason they favor the standards is that they will help students learn regardless of where they go to school.

Would you say that each of the following is a very important, somewhat important, not very important, or a not at all important reason that you favor the use of the Common Core State Standards to guide what teachers in your community teach? How about [ITEMS ROTATED]?

Among those who have heard a great deal, a fair amount, or only a little about the Common Core State Standards and who favor having teachers use Common Core to guide what they teach

	Very important	Somewhat important	Not very important	Not at all important	Don't know/ Refused
	%	%	%	%	%
The Common Core State Standards will help more students learn what they need to know regardless of where they go to school.	73	23	2	1	*
Common Core State Standards will yield student tests that give parents a better understanding of what students have learned.	53	28	14	5	*
The Common Core State Standards are more challenging than other academic standards used in the past.	42	42	12	2	2
Teachers in our community support the Common Core State Standards.	40	47	11	2	*

* Less than 0.5%
May 29-June 20, 2014
46th Annual PDK/Gallup Poll of the Public's Attitudes Toward the Public Schools

GALLUP'

Implications

Americans are generally distrusting of the federal government these days, and this suspicion colors opinions concerning its involvement in public education as well. This is consistent with studies that show Americans' generally higher trust in local over national government, and the results align with the last time this question was asked on the PDK/Gallup poll.

The majority of those who have heard about the Common Core State Standards oppose their use to guide teaching, though opinions on this question are clearly divided along political party lines. While the Common Core Standards are not a federal initiative per se, Americans may see the program as overreaching. Those who oppose the standards for guiding teaching value teacher flexibility and perceive the standards as a threat to teachers' autonomy in the classroom; and those who favor the Common Core see a framework for teaching that could address the well-documented achievement gap, increase rigor in lagging schools, and set students on equal footing with those in higher-achieving schools.

The jury is out about whether the initiative is making a positive impact on student learning. Meanwhile, education agencies need to better articulate how the Common Core standards align with the purpose and plan to help all students learn what they need to know to be successful in college, career, and life.

Survey Methods

Results are based on a Gallup Panel telephone study completed by 1,001 national adults, aged 18 and older, conducted May 29–June 20, 2014. All interviews were conducted in English. The Gallup Panel is a probability-based longitudinal panel of more than 60,000 U.S. adults that are selected using random-digit-dial (RDD) phone interviews that cover landline and cellphones. Address-based sampling methods are also used to recruit panel members. The Gallup Panel is not an opt-in panel and members are not given incentives for participating. The sample for this study was weighted to be demographically representative of the U.S. adult population, using 2013 Current Population Survey figures. For results based on this sample, one can say that the maximum margin of sampling error is ±4.6 percentage points at the 95% confidence level. The margin of error accounts for the design effect from weighting. Margins of error are higher for subsamples.

August 20, 2014
GALLUP REVIEW: BLACK AND WHITE ATTITUDES TOWARD POLICE
Criminal justice system viewed skeptically by blacks

by Frank Newport

PRINCETON, NJ—The death of 18-year-old African-American Michael Brown at the hands of a white police officer in Ferguson, Missouri, has reopened the subject of black Americans' relationship with the police, and more generally the differences in the way blacks and whites look at the criminal justice and civil rights situations in the U.S.

A review of Gallup data provides a social and cultural context for these issues.

1. Confidence in Police

Blacks in the U.S. have a significantly lower level of confidence in the police as an institution than do whites.

Combined 2011–2014 data measuring Americans' confidence in the police shows that 59% of whites have a great deal or quite a lot of confidence in the police, compared with 37% of blacks.

Confidence in Police

	A great deal/ Quite a lot	Some	Very little/None
	%	%	%
National adults	56	30	14
Whites	59	29	12
Blacks	37	37	25

Gallup poll aggregate from surveys conducted in June 2011, June 2012, June 2013, and June 2014

GALLUP

The police are among the three highest-rated institutions out of 17 tested in terms of whites' confidence, behind only the military and small business. Among blacks, police drop to seventh on the list, behind not only the military and small business but also the presidency, the church or organized religion, the medical system, and television news.

This racial gap in confidence in the police has been evident in the data throughout the past decade and a half that Gallup has been measuring these trends on an annual basis.

Notably, this substantial racial gap is much more muted in terms of confidence in the criminal justice system. Those confidence ratings are low in general, but there is no difference between the views of blacks and whites in terms of positive confidence in the criminal justice system. Blacks are, however, somewhat more likely to say they have very little or no confidence in the justice system than are whites.

Confidence in Criminal Justice System

	A great deal/ Quite a lot	Some	Very little/None
	%	%	%
National adults	27	40	31
Whites	27	42	30
Blacks	27	32	40

Gallup poll aggregate from surveys conducted in June 2011, June 2012, June 2013, and June 2014

GALLUP

2. Honesty and Ethics of Police Officers

Blacks give police officers lower honesty and ethics ratings than do whites.

Gallup data on a different question—asking Americans to rate the honesty and ethics of various professions—show a significant black-white divide in views of police officers, although the gap is not as large as the overall confidence gap in police as an institution reviewed above. In Gallup data from 2010–2013, 59% of whites say the honesty and ethics of police officers is very high or high, compared with 45% of blacks.

Perceived Honesty and Ethics of Police Officers

	Very high/High	Average	Low/Very low
	%	%	%
National adults	56	33	11
Whites	59	31	10
Blacks	45	38	17

Gallup poll aggregate from surveys conducted in December 2010, December 2011, December 2012, and December 2013

GALLUP

3. Perceptions of Treatment by Police

Younger black males are more likely than older black men or black women to report having been treated unfairly by police within the past 30 days. Among young black men, this is the highest level of perceived unfair treatment out of five situations measured.

About one in four young black men interviewed in Gallup's June 2013 Minority Rights poll said they had been treated unfairly in dealings with police in the past 30 days. This was one of five situations asked about in the survey, and incidence of unfair treatment by the police was more common than any of the other four among 18- to 34-year-old black men. The other situations measured included unfair treatment while shopping, while dining out or in attendance at theaters or other entertainment venues, at work, and while getting healthcare.

Can you think of any occasion in the last thirty days when you felt you were treated unfairly in the following places because you were black? How about in dealings with the police, such as traffic incidents?

		Yes, treated less fairly	No, not treated less fairly
18 to 34	Male	24%	76%
	Female	18%	82%
35 to 54	Male	22%	74%
	Female	12%	83%
55 and older	Male	11%	86%
	Female	10%	84%

June 13-July 5, 2013

GALLUP°

Perceptions of having received unfair treatment from the police were almost as high among 35- to 54-year-old black men as among those 18 to 34, but much lower among older black men. Black women were less likely than black men to perceive unfair treatment at each age.

At the same time, the reports among all blacks of having received unfair treatment by police was lower last year than in most of the previous years. Seventeen percent of all blacks said they had been treated unfairly in 2013, down from a high of 25% in 2004.

Blacks: Treated Unfairly by Police Within Last 30 Days?

■ % Yes

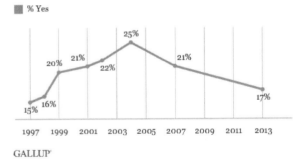

GALLUP°

4. Black-White Differences in Views of the Need for New Civil Rights Laws

Blacks in the U.S. have consistently been more likely than whites to say new civil rights laws are needed to reduce discrimination against blacks.

Black Americans are much more likely than whites to say that new civil rights laws are needed to reduce discrimination against blacks. In Gallup's Minority Rights poll in 2013, 53% of blacks said such new laws are necessary, compared with 17% of whites.

Are New Civil Rights Laws Needed to Reduce Discrimination Against Blacks?

	% Yes
National adults	27
Whites	17
Blacks	53

June 13-July 5, 2013

GALLUP°

5. Views of Discrimination Against Blacks in the Criminal Justice System

Blacks are more than 2 1/2 times as likely as whites to say the higher rates of incarceration among black men than among white men is attributable to discrimination against blacks.

Americans were asked in Gallup's Minority Rights poll last summer about their perceptions of why black males constitute a disproportionately high percentage of those incarcerated in the nation's prisons. Overall, 80% of whites said the cause was not discrimination but something else, while blacks were divided roughly 50–50 in their responses.

On the average, black males are more likely to go to prison than white males. Do you think this is mostly due to discrimination against blacks, or is it mostly due to something else?

	Mostly discrimination	Mostly something else
	%	%
National adults	25	74
Whites	19	80
Blacks	50	48

June 13-July 5, 2013

GALLUP°

The disproportionality of black men's contact with the criminal justice system has become a focal point of the debate that has arisen out of the Ferguson police shooting incident. In 2011, U.S. Department of Justice statistics indicate that more than 3% of all black males were in prison, compared with 0.5% of white males and 1.2% of Hispanic males. Other estimates find that one in three black males can expect to be in prison at some point in their lifetime, compared with one in 17 white men.

Bottom Line

Polling conducted after the shooting death of Trayvon Martin, a young black male killed in 2012 at the hands of a neighborhood watch coordinator for a residential development, showed major black-white differences in perceptions of the case and the way the criminal justice system was handling it. Going back further in time, blacks and whites had similarly starkly different views of the criminal justice system and the murder case involving O.J. Simpson in the 1990s. Preliminary surveys conducted by several research organizations after the recent Ferguson, Missouri, shooting death of Brown have shown similar racial divisions in opinions on the matter.

All of these reactions are symptomatic of the underlying gap in the ways whites and blacks view the police in the U.S. today. Blacks have significantly lower levels of confidence in the police as an institution, and lower assessments of the honesty and ethics of police officers specifically.

This underlying structural negativity toward the police among blacks has been starkly evident in the black community's reactions to the Missouri shooting death, as has been the case in each previous such incident that has received national attention.

August 20, 2014
AMERICANS' SATISFACTION WITH JOB SECURITY AT NEW HIGH
Satisfaction with many job aspects returns to high pre-recession levels

by Rebecca Riffkin

WASHINGTON, D.C.—In the U.S., 58% of full- or part-time workers are completely satisfied with their job security. This represents an increase from the levels recorded during the aftermath of the Great Recession—from 2009 to 2013—when roughly 50% of Americans said they were completely satisfied.

U.S. Workers' Satisfaction With Job Security

Are you completely satisfied, somewhat satisfied, somewhat dissatisfied, or completely dissatisfied with your job security?

■ % Completely satisfied

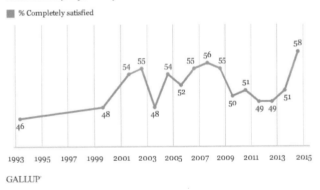

GALLUP

While workers' satisfaction with their job security has varied at least slightly from year to year, it has been consistently lower in the past five years than in the period immediately prior to the 2007–2009 recession. The weak economy and soft job market during that period appear to have caused workers to feel less secure in their employment, even after the U.S. unemployment rate fell from its peak in 2010. Now, with unemployment down to nearly 6%, Americans are finally showing more confidence in their job security—in fact, more confidence than at any point in Gallup's trend. This trend complements the decline in worker concern about being laid off, which dropped this year to levels not seen since the recession.

Workers' overall satisfaction with several specific aspects of their jobs increased between 2013 and 2014. Last year, 54% of workers were completely satisfied with the amount of vacation time they receive. This increased by five percentage points to 59% in

2014. In 2013, 56% were satisfied with their boss or immediate supervisor. In 2014, 60% are satisfied—a four-point increase.

U.S. Workers' Satisfaction With All Job Aspects

Now I'll read a list of job characteristics. For each, please tell me how satisfied or dissatisfied you are with your current job in this regard. First, are you completely satisfied, somewhat satisfied, somewhat dissatisfied, or completely dissatisfied with ...

	% Completely satisfied 2013	% Completely satisfied 2014	Difference (pct. pts.)
The physical safety conditions of your workplace	70	74	4
Your relations with coworkers	70	71	1
The flexibility of your hours	64	63	-1
Your boss or immediate supervisor	56	60	4
The amount of vacation time you receive	54	59	5
Your job security	51	58	7
The amount of work that is required of you	51	56	5
The recognition you receive at work for your work accomplishments	48	53	5
Your chances for promotion	38	38	0
The health insurance benefits your employer offers	35	39	4
The retirement plan your employer offers	33	36	3
The amount of money you earn	29	31	2
The amount of on-the-job stress in your job	28	27	-1

Sorted by % Completely satisfied in 2014

GALLUP

Compared with 2013, three job aspects did not see an increase in the percentage of workers who are completely satisfied: on-the-job stress, chances for promotion, and flexibility of hours. However, satisfaction with these measures stayed almost the same as in 2013; none saw more than a one-point drop. Many aspects had seen drops in satisfaction levels toward the beginning of the recession. For example, satisfaction with the amount of vacation time one receives showed a four-point drop, from 55% completely satisfied in 2007 to 51% in 2008.

Worker satisfaction with different job aspects varies widely. One in four workers, 27%, are completely satisfied with their amount of on-the-job stress, while three in four (74%) are satisfied with physical safety conditions in the workplace. Satisfaction with safety has always been high—its lowest point was 63% completely satisfied in 1999. Satisfaction with amounts of job stress, on the other hand, has historically been low. In 2007, 32% were satisfied with their job stress, the highest point for this measure.

Implications

Americans are more satisfied with most job aspects than they were last year. It is not clear, however, if employers have worked to improve working conditions and benefits, or if general improvements in the economy and job market have made workers more satisfied. The latter seems to be the case when thinking about job security, but the reasons behind the increases in satisfaction with other job aspects are less evident.

Separately, Gallup has conducted extensive research on employee engagement and on how to make employees happier and more productive in their jobs. Gallup's *State of the American Workplace* report analyzes employee engagement and productivity in workplaces across the U.S. This research shows that less than a third of U.S. employees (30%) are engaged at work. Thus, while Americans may be satisfied with their job security, and with other aspects of their jobs such as vacation time and retirement benefits, it does not necessarily mean they are engaged at work.

Results for this Gallup poll are based on telephone interviews conducted Aug. 7–10, 2014, with a random sample of 1,032 adults, aged 18 and older, living in all 50 U.S. states and the District of Columbia.

For results based on the total sample of 474 adults who are employed full or part time, the margin of sampling error is ±6 percentage points at the 95% confidence level.

August 21, 2014
OBAMA JOB APPROVAL TOPS ECONOMY, FOREIGN AFFAIRS RATINGS
Pattern has existed throughout his second term in office

by Jeffrey M. Jones

PRINCETON, NJ—Throughout his second term, President Barack Obama's overall job approval rating has exceeded his approval ratings on both the economy and foreign affairs, arguably the two most important areas of focus for presidents. Obama's 36% approval rating for handling foreign affairs and 35% approval on the economy in Gallup's Aug. 7–10 poll, compares with a higher 44% overall job approval rating in the same poll.

Barack Obama's Overall, Economic, and Foreign Affairs Approval Ratings During His Second Term

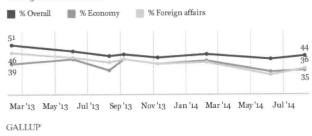

GALLUP

Obama's job approval rating has been a bit lower—averaging 42% in Gallup Daily tracking—since that Aug. 7–10 poll, which was conducted as the U.S. commenced airstrikes against Islamic militants in Iraq.

That Obama's overall approval rating is higher than his ratings on foreign affairs or the economy is evidence he is getting a more positive review from the public than would be expected given his ratings on the two major issues. This is a change from his first term, when his average overall approval rating (50%) matched his average foreign affairs approval rating, but still exceeded his economic approval rating (41%).

All these ratings are lower for Obama in his second term than in his first term, but his average foreign affairs rating has dropped more than his economic approval rating or his overall job approval rating.

Gallup regularly began measuring presidential approval for handling the economy and foreign affairs during Ronald Reagan's presidency. Since then, there have been different patterns in how these measures compare for the various presidents. For some, like Obama, George W. Bush, and Bill Clinton, the patterns varied across the presidents' two terms.

Presidents' Overall Job Approval Average vs. Averages for Handling Economy and Foreign Affairs, by Term

President and term in office	Overall job approval average*	Average approval rating for handling the economy	Average approval rating for handling foreign affairs
	%	%	%
Reagan I	50	43	42
Reagan II	55	47	47
G.H.W. Bush	59	35	63
Clinton I	49	45	46
Clinton II	60	69	55
G.W. Bush I	63	52	57
G.W. Bush II	40	41	38
Obama I	50	41	50
Obama II	45	38	39

*Based on polls in which both economy and foreign affairs approval were also asked. May differ slightly from overall job approval average based on all polls in which it was asked during president's term.

GALLUP

Looking at the last nine presidential terms, three basic patterns emerge in how Americans rate the president on the economy and foreign affairs in comparison to how he is handling his job overall.

1. Presidents are generally rated higher overall than on both the economy and foreign affairs.

This has been the most common pattern, describing five of the nine presidential terms since 1981, including Obama's second term to date, in which his average foreign affairs and economic approval ratings are six and seven percentage points lower, respectively, than his overall approval rating.

This pattern was apparent in both of Reagan's terms. Reagan's average overall approval rating was roughly eight points higher than either his average economic or foreign affairs approval ratings in both his terms in office.

Notably, even though Reagan is remembered for presiding over a strong economy near the end of his first term and throughout his second term, his economic approval ratings were never that high. Even when his overall job approval rating exceeded 60% for much of 1985 and 1986, his economic approval rating peaked at only 52%.

During Clinton's first term, his overall approval rating slightly exceeded his foreign affairs and economic approval ratings.

George W. Bush's overall approval rating of 63% during his first term also surpassed his ratings on the two main issues by healthy margins. After 9/11, Bush's job approval rating was likely more closely tied to his approval for handling terrorism, which usually exceeded 60%, than his handling of the economy or foreign affairs.

2. A president's overall job approval rating falls between his economic and foreign affairs ratings.

If Americans were mostly judging presidents based on their handling of the economy and foreign affairs, one would expect their overall approval rating to fall in between those two ratings. That has been the case for some recent presidents, but is not the norm. This pattern seems to occur most often when economic conditions or U.S. foreign policy are doing very well, or very poorly.

Obama's first term best fits in this category. He received lower ratings on handling the economy, as would be expected given the state of the economy when he took office, but his foreign affairs rating was higher and matched his overall job approval rating.

George H.W. Bush entered office with extensive foreign policy experience, and Americans credited him for his handling of foreign affairs as he navigated the U.S. through the end of the Cold War and a decisive victory in the 1991 Persian Gulf War with Iraq. His 63% average foreign affairs approval rating is the highest for any recent president, and exceeded his overall approval rating.

On the other hand, Bush was never judged well for handling the economy, only exceeding majority approval one time early in his presidency. His average 35% approval for handling the economy is the worst of any recent president.

Clinton defeated Bush in 1992 largely due to the poor economy, and Clinton's average economic approval ratings in his first term were also not strong. It wasn't until late in his first term that Americans consistently gave Clinton positive economic approval ratings. Clinton's economic approval ratings got even better as the economy continued to grow in his second term, averaging 69% with a high of 81% in January 1999.

The strong economy also helped lift Clinton's overall job approval rating during his second term, to a 60% average, but his foreign affairs approval rating was lower, at 55%.

3. A president's overall job approval rating is similar to his economic and foreign affairs ratings.

The only clear example of a president receiving an overall job approval rating similar to his ratings on both the economy and foreign affairs occurred during George W. Bush's second term. The war in Iraq dominated Bush's second term, but he also dealt with major economic troubles such as record-high gas prices, the recession, and the financial crisis near the end of his presidency. Not surprisingly, his approval ratings across the board were low.

Clinton's first term could arguably be included in this category as well.

To date, no president's overall approval rating has averaged lower than his ratings on the economy and foreign affairs.

Implications

Even though Obama's overall job approval rating is not stellar, it is higher than his rating on handling the economy and foreign affairs. The deficit cannot be explained on the basis of Americans evaluating Obama more favorably on other issues that may be more important to them. Education is the only one of seven issues measured in the Aug. 7–10 poll on which Obama's approval for handling the issue (48%) exceeded his overall approval rating.

There are two possible explanations for the discrepant approval ratings. The first is Americans may be evaluating Obama on factors other than his handling of these issues. For example, in June, Gallup found that Obama's ratings on personal characteristics, such as being a strong and decisive leader, understanding problems Americans face in their daily lives, and being honest and trustworthy—though lower than in the past—still exceeded his overall job approval rating. Also, the public typically gives presidents higher personal favorable ratings than job approval ratings.

The second possibility is that Americans may just rate presidents more positively in a general sense than they do when focusing

on specifics. Although that has not been the case for every recent president, there are exceptions when there are strong and obvious differences in how a president handles foreign affairs versus the economy, as with the elder Bush, or if conditions in one or the other area are exceptionally good or exceptionally bad.

Survey Methods

Results for this Gallup poll are based on telephone interviews conducted Aug. 7–10, 2014, with a random sample of 1,032 adults, aged 18 and older, living in all 50 U.S. states and the District of Columbia.

For results based on the total sample of national adults, the margin of sampling error is ±4 percentage points at the 95% confidence level.

August 22, 2014
REPUBLICANS MORE FOCUSED ON IMMIGRATION AS TOP PROBLEM
Republicans, Democrats agree on government, economy as top problems

by Frank Newport

PRINCETON, NJ—Although both Republicans and Democrats name dysfunctional government, the economy, and unemployment as top problems facing the country today, they attach different importance to other issues. Republicans and Republican-leaning independents are significantly more likely than Democrats and Democratic-leaning independents to say that immigration and moral decline are top problems in the U.S., while Democrats are more likely to mention poverty and education.

Most Important Problem, Republicans	Republicans/ Republican leaners
Immigration	22%
Dysfunctional government	20%
Economy	17%
Unemployment	12%
Healthcare/Hospitals	9%
Ethical/Moral decline	8%
Foreign aid/ Focus overseas	7%
Federal budget deficit/Debt	7%

July-August 2014

GALLUP

Most Important Problem, Democrats	Democrats/ Democratic leaners
Dysfunctional government	16%
Economy	13%
Unemployment	13%
Immigration	11%
Healthcare/Hospitals	8%
Poverty/Hunger/ Homelessness	7%
Education	7%
Gap between rich and poor	5%

July-August 2014

GALLUP

The differences between partisan groups are most evident in terms of immigration, with an 11-percentage-point spread between Republicans (22%) and Democrats (11%) mentioning the issue. Two issues show a six-point gap in mentions between party groups, with Democrats more likely to mention poverty/hunger/homelessness and Republicans more likely to mention ethical decline.

These data are from an aggregated sample of 2,001 national adults interviewed in Gallup's July and August Gallup Poll Social Series surveys. In those two months, immigration ranked near the top of the list after the wave of Central Americans illegally entering the country became a major national news story. Prior to July, immigration ranked much lower on the most important problem list.

Most Important Problem Facing the U.S.

	National adults	Republicans/ Republican leaners	Democrats/ Democratic leaners
	%	%	%
Dysfunctional government	17	20	16
Immigration	16	22	11
Economy	15	17	13
Unemployment	13	12	13
Healthcare/Hospitals	8	9	8
Federal budget deficit/Debt	5	7	3
Foreign aid/Focus overseas	5	7	4
Ethical/Moral decline	5	8	2
Education	5	2	7
Poverty/Hunger/Homelessness	4	1	7

July–August 2014

GALLUP'

Dissatisfaction With Government Based on Different Viewpoints

Dissatisfaction with government was Americans' top-mentioned problem in July and August, exceeding all other issues in public perceptions of the most important problem facing the country, although just slightly above mentions of immigration. Dissatisfaction with government appears to be germane to both Republicans and Democrats, ranking as the top issue for Democrats and second for Republicans, behind immigration.

But a closer look at the data shows that Republicans and Democrats view this problem from different perspectives. Republicans are more likely to talk about problems with overall leadership of the country, which translates in many instances into criticisms of President Barack Obama, while Democrats are more likely to talk about problems with Congress and the lack of bipartisan cooperation, which often translates into criticism of the Republican-controlled House.

Americans who mention criticisms of dysfunctional government focusing on presidential leadership give such comments as:

"a president who doesn't know how to sit down with Congress and negotiate"
"no one is leading this country"
"country is in a downward spiral due to our president"
"the way the president is running our country"
"Obama thinking he can circumvent everybody"

Americans who mention criticisms of dysfunctional government but with a focus on Congress offer such comments as:

"obstructionism of Congress, especially in the House of Representatives"
"Congress, they're not getting anything done"
"dysfunctional Republican House of Representatives"
"the fact that the Republicans will not do the job they are elected for"
"most important thing facing the country today is the do-nothing Congress"
"House Republicans"

Thus, the American public's views regarding dysfunctional government tend to illustrate the issue, with the two political groups likely to present opposing views on which aspect of government is at the root of this problem.

Bottom Line

Republicans and Democrats, despite being politically opposed to each other, share some common concerns when asked to name the most important problem facing the country. Both groups' top five categories of responses include the economy and unemployment, as well as concerns about healthcare and dysfunctional government.

But differences are apparent as well, both among categories such as immigration, moral and ethical decline, and poverty, and within the category dealing with dysfunctional government. Democrats tend to place the blame for dysfunctional government on Congress, specifically on the Republican majority in the House of Representatives, while Republicans tend to place the blame on the president and lack of leadership. These differences in priorities among rank-and-file partisans could be a factor in determining their reactions to candidates in the midterm elections this November, and also may be a significant factor in determining the priorities adopted by Republican and Democratic members of Congress.

Survey Methods

Results for this Gallup poll are based on telephone interviews conducted July 7–10 and Aug. 7–10, 2014, with a combined random sample of 2,001 adults, aged 18 and older, living in all 50 U.S. states and the District of Columbia.

For results based on the total sample of national adults, the margin of sampling error is ±2 percentage points at the 95% confidence level.

For results based on the total sample of 945 Republicans and Republican-leaning independents, the margin of sampling error is ±4 percentage points at the 95% confidence level. For results based on the total sample of 854 Democrats and Democratic-leaning independents, the margin of sampling error is ±4 percentage points at the 95% confidence level.

August 22, 2014
IN U.S., 55% OF WORKERS GET SENSE OF IDENTITY FROM THEIR JOB
Seven in 10 college graduates get a sense of identity from their job

by Rebecca Riffkin

WASHINGTON, D.C.—U.S. workers continue to be more likely to say they get a sense of identity from their job, 55%, as opposed to having their job just be something they do for a living, 42%. These results have been consistent throughout multiple Gallup polls since 1989.

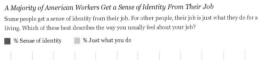

A Majority of American Workers Get a Sense of Identity From Their Job

Some people get a sense of identity from their job. For other people, their job is just what they do for a living. Which of these best describes the way you usually feel about your job?

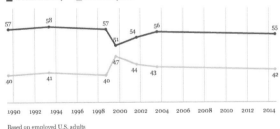

Based on employed U.S. adults

GALLUP'

As part of Gallup's annual Work and Education poll, employed Americans were asked if they get a sense of identity from their job. Gallup asked this question on an occasional basis from 1990 through 2003, and then again this year. Although there was a downtick in the percentage who said they get a sense of identity from their work in 1999, the results over time have been generally stable, and the 2003 results are almost identical to those this year.

Education is one of the most significant predictors of how workers approach their job, with 70% of college graduates saying they get a sense of identity from their job, compared with the 45% of Americans who don't hold a college degree who say the same.

Job Identity, by Socio-Economic Group

Some people get a sense of identity from their job. For other people, their job is just what they do for a living. Which of these best describes the way you usually feel about your job?

	% Sense of identity	% Just what you do
College graduate	70	29
Didn't graduate college	45	51
Annual household income of $50,000 or more	63	36
Annual household income of less than $50,000	43	52

Aug. 7-10, 2014

GALLUP

American workers in households with higher annual incomes are also more likely to receive a sense of identity from their job. Sixty-three percent of those whose annual household income is $50,000 a year or more get a sense of identity from their job, compared with 43% of Americans who live in households with lower annual incomes. However, as this question measures household rather than individual income, the results do not necessarily mean that Americans with higher paychecks get a sense of identity from their job, particularly because those in upper-income households predominantly have two working adults in the household and those in lower-income households have only one.

Older working Americans, those aged 45 and older, are slightly more likely than younger workers to get a sense of identity from their job. This difference may be generational, reflecting older workers coming of age during a time when occupation mattered more to employees than it does today. Or it may be that older Americans have been in the workforce longer and may be more established in their careers, thus gaining more of their identity from their job.

Job Identity, by Demographics

Some people get a sense of identity from their job. For other people, their job is just what they do for a living. Which of these best describes the way you usually feel about your job?

	% Sense of identity	% Just what you do
18 to 44 years old	52	45
45+ years old	58	39
Men	50	48
Women	61	35
Republicans	56	41
Independents	54	44
Democrats	55	41

Aug. 7-10, 2014

GALLUP

Women are slightly more likely to get a sense of identity from their job than men. However, in past polling, these differences were less pronounced.

Implications

More American workers get a sense of identity from their job as opposed to saying it is just what they do for a living. Americans who graduated college are the most likely group to get a sense of identity from their job, perhaps because advanced education opens up more job opportunities for them than someone without a college degree, meaning they could find a better fit between their interests and the type of work they do.

Survey Methods

Results for this Gallup poll are based on telephone interviews conducted Aug. 7–14, 2014, with a random sample of 1,032 adults, aged 18 and older, living in all 50 U.S. states and the District of Columbia.

For results based on the total sample of 474 adults who are employed full or part time, the margin of sampling error is ±6 percentage points at the 95% confidence level.

August 25, 2014
LGBT AMERICANS REPORT LOWER WELL-BEING
Significant differences seen in financial and physical well-being elements

by Gary J. Gates

WASHINGTON, D.C.—Americans who identify as lesbian, gay, bisexual, or transgender (LGBT) report lower well-being than non-LGBT Americans. LGBT Americans have an average Well-Being Index score of 58, lower than non-LGBT adults' score of 62. Importantly, these differences hold true even after taking into account the effects of gender, age, race and ethnicity, educational attainment, state of residence, and population density.

Gallup-Healthways Well-Being Index Scores, by LGBT Status

	LGBT	Non-LGBT	Difference
National adults	58	62	-4
Men	59	61	-2
Women	57	63	-6

Jan. 1-June 23, 2014
Gallup-Healthways Well-Being Index

GALLUP

The disadvantage in overall well-being is more acute for LGBT women than for LGBT men. LGBT women have a Well-Being Index score of 57, well below the score of 63 for non-LGBT women. LGBT men also lag behind their non-LGBT counterparts in overall well-being, but not by as much—59 vs. 61, respectively.

These findings are based on 2,964 interviews with LGBT adults and 81,134 interviews with non-LGBT adults conducted Jan. 1– June 23, 2014, as part of the Gallup-Healthways Well-Being Index survey. The Well-Being Index is constructed on a scale of 0 to 100, with higher scores indicating better overall well-being. The index includes questions that fall into five broad areas: purpose, social, financial, community, and physical. Each of these well-being elements consists of multiple questions on related topics that Gallup uses to categorize respondents into three groups: thriving, struggling, and suffering.

Across all five elements of well-being, LGBT Americans—particularly LGBT women—trail their non-LGBT counterparts, even after taking into account possible differences in the demographic and geographic characteristics of LGBT and non-LGBT adults.

Financial Well-Being: LGBT Americans' Biggest Hurdle

The financial element is where the LGBT community falls furthest behind the non-LGBT population. LGBT Americans are 10 percentage points less likely to be thriving financially than their non-LGBT counterparts. For women, the difference is slightly above average, while for men it is slightly below.

Financial well-being is made up of questions about standard of living, ability to afford basic necessities, and financial worry.

Financial Well-Being Scores, by LGBT Status
% Thriving

	LGBT	Non-LGBT	Difference
	%	%	(pct. pts.)
National adults	29	39	-10
Men	32	40	-8
Women	27	39	-12

Jan. 1-June 23, 2014
Gallup-Healthways Well-Being Index

GALLUP

These findings are consistent with research from UCLA's Williams Institute, which shows that the LGBT population is at a disproportionate risk for poverty and food insecurity.

Physical Well-Being: A Sore Spot for LGBT Women

Physical well-being is another area in which there are stark differences between LGBT and non-LGBT Americans, particularly among women. One in three non-LGBT Americans are thriving physically, compared with about one in four LGBT Americans. This difference is entirely driven by LGBT women, as differences by LGBT status among men are not statistically significant.

Physical Well-Being Scores, by LGBT Status
% Thriving

	LGBT	Non-LGBT	Difference
	%	%	(pct. pts.)
National adults	26	33	-7
Men	28	30	-2
Women	24	36	-12

Jan. 1-June 23, 2014
Gallup-Healthways Well-Being Index

GALLUP

Physical well-being includes questions related to alcohol, drug, and tobacco use; current disease burden and past diagnoses; exercise; and eating habits.

A variety of factors could contribute to LGBT women's disproportionately lower physical well-being. A recent analysis of the 2013 National Health Interview Survey reported higher levels of smoking and alcohol consumption among LGB women than among non-LGB women, as well as elevated weight and psychological distress among bisexual women.

Social Well-Being: LGBT Americans Less Likely to Thrive

LGBT Americans are less likely than their non-LGBT counterparts to be thriving in their social lives. Thirty-five percent of LGBT adults are thriving socially, compared with 41% of non-LGBT adults. The gaps for men and women are the same.

Social well-being includes questions about relationships with friends and family, personal time, and received encouragement and support.

Social Well-Being Scores, by LGBT Status
% Thriving

	LGBT	Non-LGBT	Difference
	%	%	(pct. pts.)
National adults	35	41	-6
Men	33	39	-6
Women	36	42	-6

Jan. 1-June 23, 2014
Gallup-Healthways Well-Being Index

GALLUP

Community Well-Being: LGBT Women Less Connected to Where They Live

LGBT Americans are less likely than their non-LGBT counterparts to be thriving in community well-being—32% vs. 38%, respectively. This difference by LGBT status is largely driven by women. LGBT status is not a significant factor in men's assessments of their communities.

Community well-being includes questions about community pride, involvement, and safety and security.

Community Well-Being Scores, by LGBT Status
% Thriving

	LGBT	Non-LGBT	Difference
	%	%	(pct. pts.)
National adults	32	38	-6
Men	33	36	-3
Women	31	40	-9

Jan. 1-June 23, 2014
Gallup-Healthways Well-Being Index

GALLUP

Purpose Well-Being: LGBT Women Lagging Behind

Overall, LGBT Americans trail non-LGBT Americans in reporting a strong sense of purpose in life (33% vs. 37%, respectively). This gap reflects the substantial difference that exists between LGBT women and non-LGBT women. The comparable figures for men do not vary by LGBT status.

Purpose well-being is composed of questions about having an inspiring leader, daily activity, goals, and strengths.

% Thriving

	LGBT	Non-LGBT	Difference
	%	%	(pct. pts.)
National adults	33	37	-4
Men	33	33	0
Women	32	40	-8

Jan. 1-June 23, 2014
Gallup-Healthways Well-Being Index

GALLUP

Bottom Line

Despite evidence of decreasing social stigma directed toward the LGBT community in the U.S., LGBT Americans—particularly LGBT women—show a wide range of well-being disparities compared with their non-LGBT counterparts. In measures of physical health, financial security, sense of purpose, social life, and community attachment, data from the Gallup-Healthways Well-Being Index reveal that LGBT adults experience a wide range of well-being challenges.

These disparities associated with sexual orientation and gender identity highlight the ongoing need for the inclusion of sexual orientation and gender identity measures in data collection focused on health and socio-economic outcomes. Availability of better data that identify the LGBT population will help researchers, healthcare policymakers, and healthcare providers craft better strategies to understand and prevent well-being disparities associated with sexual orientation and gender identity.

Gary J. Gates is a Williams Distinguished Scholar at the Williams Institute, UCLA School of Law. A national expert in LGBT demographics, he has a Ph.D. in public policy from Heinz College, Carnegie Mellon University.

Survey Methods

Results are based on telephone interviews conducted as part of the Gallup-Healthways Well-Being Index survey Jan. 1–June 23, 2014, with a random sample of 2,964 LGBT adults and 81,134 non-LGBT adults, aged 18 and older, living in all 50 U.S. states and the District of Columbia.

For results based on the total sample of LGBT adults, the margin of sampling error is ±2 percentage points at the 95% confidence level.

For results based on the total sample of non-LGBT adults, the margin of sampling error is ±0.4 percentage points at the 95% confidence level.

August 25, 2014
NORTH DAKOTA: LEGENDARY AMONG STATES
Residents highly satisfied with economy, education, air quality

by Art Swift

WASHINGTON, D.C.—"Oil boom" is probably the first phrase that comes to mind when one thinks about North Dakota. Yet North Dakotans see their state as much more than oil. They are highly satisfied with their schools, their air quality, their ability to find a quality job, and their overall standard of living. In Gallup's comprehensive survey of all 50 states, North Dakota ranks No. 1 on a variety of indicators spanning economics, public affairs, education, the environment, and well-being. In 2014, North Dakota is a complex, thriving state that is adapting rapidly to the economic and social factors that are transforming this population of roughly 725,000 people.

These findings are based on a special 50-state Gallup poll conducted June–December 2013, including interviews with approximately 600 residents in every state.

"Oil is a very thick frosting on a very nicely baked cake."

North Dakotans are more likely than residents of any other state to say that their state's economic conditions are excellent or good, that the state's economy is getting better, and that they have not lacked money for adequate housing in the last 12 months. In addition, more residents than anywhere else say it is a good time to find a quality job and that their state is a good place for people starting a new business.

To an outsider, the answer seems clear: the North Dakota oil boom has expanded wealth and opportunity to the point that there is a chicken in every pot. To leading officials in North Dakota, the story has its roots in prudent long-term planning statewide that Democrats and Republicans began in the early 1990s. North Dakota Gov. Jack Dalrymple says well before oil was discovered in the Parshall Oil Field in 2006, the state was on its way to economic prosperity. Dalrymple, who served as former Gov. John Hoeven's lieutenant governor, credits his boss with taking these efforts to the next level.

"We needed to get our state economy going," Dalrymple says. "We basically set about creating a state for more opportunities . . . energy, agriculture, technology, advanced manufacturing, tourism."

In 2000, North Dakota was 38th in personal per capita income, at $25,872. By 2008, that figure had risen to $40,880, or 19th in the nation. According to Andy Peterson, president and CEO of the North Dakota Chamber of Commerce, the growth in advance manufacturing, value-added food processing, and tourism, in addition to traditional bases such as agriculture, accounted for North Dakota's vaulting ahead of other states. It was only in 2009 that oil became a factor in the state's finances, but the groundwork for a boom had already been laid.

"Oil is a very thick frosting on a very nicely baked cake," Peterson says.

Oil had been found in North Dakota before, but Dalrymple, Peterson, and Al Anderson, North Dakota state commerce commissioner, agree that the volume and velocity of the boom was unexpected. Dalrymple says there were 200,000 barrels a day in 2009, compared with 1 million barrels a day now.

"The rapid evolution of the oil industry was not foreseen," says Anderson.

"We had seen oil booms come and go but now the technology has changed," Peterson says. "We didn't realize how much oil was in the ground. We found ways to extract oil that we could never expect."

In addition to oil, success in agriculture, manufacturing, and tourism are contributing factors to North Dakota's having the lowest unemployment in the U.S. for the past four years. Per capita income in North Dakota rose to $57,084 last year, second in the nation to Connecticut at $60,847. The state has added 116,000 jobs since 2000, a job-growth increase of 35.6%. Net migration in the state is up 12.7% since 2000. This onrush of new jobs and workers has strained the housing market. North Dakota residents are fully aware of this, as 61% say they are satisfied with the availability of affordable housing in their state, one of the lowest in the nation.

Anderson says North Dakota has been building 2,000 to 3,000 new housing units per year and that hotel occupancy has dropped from 95% to 65%, as more houses are being built. Dalrymple says his state is building apartment buildings with controlled rents to meet demand.

"I consider that one of the solvable challenges," Dalrymple says. "We're mostly spending money for infrastructure needs."

North Dakotans Give Their Schools an "A"

North Dakotans are not just satisfied with their economy, however. Across the 50 states, North Dakotans are the most likely to rate their K–12 education as excellent or good, to agree that their schools prepare students to get a good job, and to be satisfied with the education system or schools overall.

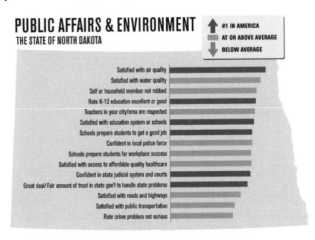

According to the North Dakota officials, there are various reasons for this high satisfaction with education in the state.

"Sheer volume of school districts helps because there are many local school districts," says Peterson. "Schools are more accessible to students and teachers."

Anderson added that "education has always been extremely important to North Dakota," though he would like to see a continued focus on education for STEM jobs, to keep pace with the growth in the state.

In contrast to their mostly positive—in many cases, nation-leading—views about the economy and education, North Dakotans exhibit mixed views on the social climate in their state. While residents were first in the nation in saying they were "treated with respect all day yesterday," and "experienced enjoyment a lot of the day yesterday," they reported low levels of their state being a "good place for racial and ethnic minorities" and a "good place for gay or lesbian people." Gallup reported last year that North Dakota has the lowest percentage of residents in the nation who identify as gay, lesbian, bisexual or transgender.

In offering his view on why his state residents might make these assertions, Dalrymple spoke in general terms about how North Dakota is in a process of evolution.

"There's a tendency for people not being immediately comfortable with new people until they have had a chance to meet them and evaluate them," Dalrymple says. "We're evolving every year and becoming more accustomed to different people and lifestyles."

"We've had a pretty homogenous society in the past," Anderson says. "Ninety percent is probably the white Caucasian split, but minorities are increasing." Anderson added, "I truly believe our rankings will go up. We will adjust and improve. I think it is embraced by the vast majority of people in North Dakota."

Peterson says where North Dakota is located plays a major factor in evaluating newcomers and different lifestyles.

"The rest of the country, especially the coasts, change the pace of life quicker than we do," he says. "Doesn't surprise me that we are slower to change. But I think the state is changing. We reflect the Midwest and I think we're going to change last. But there isn't hostility to these groups. Once you interact with these groups, you realize that people are people."

The North Dakota Experience

North Dakotans are, by and large, satisfied with their state and the direction in which it is going. Certainly the oil boom, after years of strategic economic planning, may be one of the chief contributors to this statewide contentment. North Dakota may now be on the map as an economic power, but it is still a rural state with a large land mass and relatively few residents, with room to grow. Anderson estimated that oil output could rise to 1.7 million barrels per day in the near future. He says North Dakota is now second behind Texas in oil production and that "a few years ago, we saw a 20-year run with oil (but) this can be a 60-year-play."

When asked to sum up the North Dakota experience, each official offered this reflection of the state:

- Peterson: "The North Dakota experience is one of quiet fortitude and self-reliance, pull yourself up by your bootstraps, equal opportunity for all—at least in our minds, even if it isn't the case. It is about individual responsibility and self-reliance."
- Dalrymple: "North Dakota has been discovered. When I travel around the country, people are no longer clueless about what's going on here—people coming here and investing here—it's prospering and there are opportunities here."
- Anderson: "[People] can truly make a difference in North Dakota and they can't necessarily do it everywhere. I've lived in eight states and outside the country. You see a lot of people giving back [in North Dakota]. Our legislators are truly part-time legislators. Everybody matters here and I don't think people get that in a larger community all the time."

North Dakota is evolving—and its residents are now more positive about their state than any other state in the nation is on economics, well-being, and public affairs.

Survey Methods

Results for this Gallup poll are based on telephone interviews conducted June–December 2013, with a random sample of approximately 600 adults per state, aged 18 and older, living in all 50 U.S. states.

For results based on the total sample of adults per state, the margin of sampling error is ±5 percentage points at the 95% confidence level.

August 25, 2014
DISAPPROVAL OF CONGRESS LINKED TO HIGHER VOTER TURNOUT
Turnout generally higher when congressional job approval is low

by Jeffrey M. Jones

PRINCETON, NJ—Americans' disenchantment with Congress may lead to higher voter turnout on Election Day this year. In the last five midterm elections, voter turnout has exceeded 40% when Congress' approval rating was low, but turnout was below 40% when Americans were more approving.

Congressional Job Approval and Voter Turnout, Recent Midterm Elections

	Congressional job approval	Voter turnout
	%	%
2010	21	40.9
1994	23	41.1
2006	26	40.4
1998	44	38.1
2002	50	39.5

Congressional job approval is based on the final Gallup estimate before each midterm election. Turnout is the percentage of the voting eligible population who voted, based on estimates from The United States Elections Project website.

GALLUP

Congressional job approval, currently 13%, is on pace to be the lowest it has been in a midterm election year. Moreover, a near-record-low 19% of registered voters say most members of Congress deserve re-election. This latter measure shows a similarly strong relationship to voter turnout as does job approval.

Voter turnout in midterm elections has ranged narrowly between 38.1% and 41.1% since 1994, considerably lower than the 51.7% to 61.6% range for the last five presidential elections. But there has been a clear pattern of turnout being on the higher end of the midterm year range when Americans were less approving of Congress. The correlation between turnout and congressional approval since 1994 is −.83, indicating a strong relationship.

The disapproval-turnout link is a fairly recent phenomenon. From 1974—the first year Gallup measured congressional job approval—until 1990, there was only a weak relationship between turnout and approval, with turnout higher when approval was higher, the opposite of the current pattern. But that weak relationship was driven mostly by the 1974 midterm elections, when turnout was among the higher ones for midterms and Congress was relatively popular after the Watergate hearings that led to President Richard Nixon's resignation that summer.

The pre-1994 congressional landscape was characterized by Democratic Party dominance of Congress, as it enjoyed a 40-year reign as the majority party in the House of Representatives until the 1994 elections.

Voters Feeling More Empowered to Make Change in Recent Elections?

Since 1994, majority control of the House has changed hands three times in five midterm elections: after the 1994, 2006, and 2010 elections. Not coincidentally, congressional approval was low and turnout was high in those three elections, which suggests voters were motivated to change the direction of national policy, perhaps something that didn't seem likely to occur in midterm elections prior to 1994.

The 1994, 2006, and 2010 elections took place with a relatively unpopular president paired with a Congress controlled by the same party. While President Barack Obama is unpopular at the moment, averaging 42% approval in August to date, he is governing at a time when Republicans hold a majority in the House, while his fellow Democrats are the majority party in the Senate. In 2010, his job approval rating just before the elections was similar, at 45%.

As a result, it is unclear how the current frustration with Congress will manifest itself in terms of party control of the two houses of Congress. Because the president's party usually loses seats in the House in midterm elections, few give the Democrats much chance of reclaiming the majority there. The Senate appears to be the more important battleground, as Democrats, expected to lose seats, are trying to avoid losing the six seats that would give the Republicans the majority.

Implications

Since 1994, voters may have a greater belief that they can change the federal government and its policies by their choices of members of Congress in midterm elections. That belief in turn may help drive up turnout when voters feel a change is needed.

Voters likely feel a change in government is needed this year, given their historically low congressional approval ratings. Past patterns suggest this should lead to above-average turnout in the midterm elections this November. But there may be less consensus this year on what that change should be, given the divided control of Congress. In some recent elections, one party was clearly vulnerable to voters' wrath when they were upset with Congress because that party had control of the presidency and both houses.

If many voters see little possibility of changing the partisan makeup of government after this fall's elections—given that a divided government is already in place and almost certainly will be after the elections—there could be no increase in turnout this year despite Americans' frustration with Congress. However, if voters have designs on changing the government and see a good chance that they can do so—perhaps by voting against incumbents of both parties—then turnout may rise, as in similar past elections.

Survey Methods

Results for this Gallup poll are based on telephone interviews conducted Aug. 7–10, 2014, with a random sample of 1,032 adults, aged 18 and older, living in all 50 U.S. states and the District of Columbia.

For results based on the total sample of national adults, the margin of sampling error is ±4 percentage points at the 95% confidence level.

August 26, 2014
IN U.S., LGBT MORE LIKELY THAN NON-LGBT TO BE UNINSURED
LGBT adults more likely to lack a personal doctor and enough money for healthcare

by Gary J. Gates

WASHINGTON, D.C.—Americans who identify as lesbian, gay, bisexual, or transgender (LGBT) are more likely than non-LGBT Americans to report that they lack health insurance. While the percentage of LGBT adults without health insurance has decreased significantly since the Affordable Care Act's provisions requiring Americans to have health insurance took effect at the beginning of 2014, they are still more likely to be uninsured than their non-LGBT counterparts.

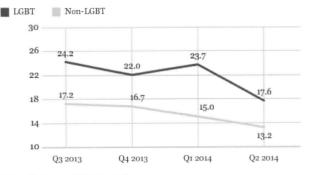

Percentage Uninsured in the U.S., by LGBT Status
Do you have health insurance coverage? (% Uninsured)

Gallup-Healthways Well-Being Index

GALLUP

The LGBT community is one of the many constituencies targeted by the Obama administration for participation in open enrollment for health insurance under the provisions of the Affordable Care Act, commonly known as "Obamacare." Gallup-Healthways Well-Being Index data suggest that both LGBT and non-LGBT populations saw similar drops in their uninsured rates. The most useful time periods for comparison are the fourth quarter of 2013—the three months before provisions requiring insurance took effect—and the second quarter of 2014, after open enrollment ended. Between those two periods, the percentage of uninsured LGBT adults fell by 4.4 percentage points, similar to the 3.5-point drop among non-LGBT Americans.

For LGBT Adults, Struggling to Afford Healthcare More Common

One possible symptom of the health insurance gap by LGBT status is that LGBT adults are significantly more likely to say they did not have enough money for healthcare needs at least once in the past year. One-quarter of LGBT adults report they did not have enough money for healthcare needs at least once in the last year, compared with 17% of non-LGBT individuals. This disparity is evident for both men and women.

Percentage in U.S. Struggling to Afford Healthcare or Medicine, by LGBT Status and Gender

Have there been times in the past 12 months when you did not have enough money to pay for the healthcare and/or medicines that you or your family needed? (% Yes)

	LGBT %	Non-LGBT %	Difference (pct. pts.)
All adults	25	17	8
Men	21	15	6
Women	29	19	10

Gallup-Healthways Well-Being Index
Jan. 1-June 23, 2014

GALLUP

LGBT Women More Likely Than Non-LGBT Women to Lack a Personal Doctor

LGBT adults are more likely than non-LGBT adults to report that they do not have a personal doctor (29% vs. 21%, respectively).

But this difference is driven primarily by LGBT women, who are nearly twice as likely as non-LGBT women to lack a personal doctor, 29% vs. 16%. The difference between LGBT men and their non-LGBT counterparts is not significant.

Percentage in U.S. Without a Personal Doctor, by LGBT Status and Gender

Do you have a personal doctor? (% No)

	LGBT %	Non-LGBT %	Difference (pct. pts.)
All adults	29	21	8
Men	29	27	2
Women	29	16	13

Gallup-Healthways Well-Being Index
Jan. 1–June 23, 2014

GALLUP

Implications

Gallup-Healthways Well-Being Index data suggest that LGBT adults experience hurdles in accessing health insurance and resources. These findings are consistent with a 2013 NHIS report showing that LGB individuals experience some disadvantages in their access to healthcare. Compared with their straight counterparts, bisexual adults, both men and women, and lesbians were less likely to report a usual place to go for medical care and more likely to report not seeking needed medical care because they could not afford it. However, unlike the results from the Gallup-Healthways Well-Being Index, there were no differences in health insurance coverage by sexual orientation in that study.

Population-based data sources that provide insights into the health and well-being of Americans and include the measurement of sexual orientation and gender identity remain rare. More routine inclusion of these data on demographic, economic, and health-related surveys would improve the ability of researchers to document not only whether LGBT Americans experience negative health and well-being disparities but also why that might be the case. Understanding the "why" is crucial information to assist policymakers and health advocates in the development of policies and programs designed to reduce health and well-being disparities associated with LGBT status.

Gary J. Gates is a Williams Distinguished Scholar at the Williams Institute, UCLA School of Law. A national expert in LGBT demographics, he has a Ph.D. in public policy from Heinz College, Carnegie Mellon University.

Survey Methods

Results for Quarter 3 and Quarter 4, 2013, insurance rates are based on telephone interviews conducted as part of the Gallup-Healthways Well-Being Index survey July 1–Dec. 29, 2013, with a random sample in Quarter 3, 2013, of 1,831 LGBT adults, and 43,906 non-LGBT adults, and a random sample in Quarter 4, 2013, of 1,569 LGBT adults, and 41,222 non-LGBT adults. All samples are based on those aged 18 and older, living in all 50 U.S. states and the District of Columbia.

For results based on the total sample of LGBT adults in the 3rd and 4th quarters in 2013, the margin of sampling error is ±3 percentage points at the 95% confidence level.

For results based on the total sample of non-LGBT adults in the 3rd and 4th quarters in 2013, the margin of sampling error is ±1 percentage point at the 95% confidence level.

Results for the questions asking about healthcare or medicine affordability and having a personal doctor are based on telephone interviews conducted as part of the Gallup-Healthways Well-Being Index survey Jan. 1–June 23, 2014, with a random sample of 2,964 LGBT adults and 81,134 non-LGBT adults, aged 18 and older, living in all 50 U.S. states and the District of Columbia.

For results based on the total sample of LGBT adults interviewed Jan. 1–June 23, 2014, the margin of sampling error is ±2 percentage points at the 95% confidence level.

For results based on the total sample of non-LGBT adults Jan. 1–June 23, 2014 , the margin of sampling error is ±0.4 percentage points at the 95% confidence level.

August 27, 2014
NORTH CAROLINA'S POLITICAL AND ECONOMIC ENVIRONMENT IN 2014
Major parties are nearly tied in self-reported political identification

by Andrew Dugan

WASHINGTON, D.C.—With a critical midterm U.S. Senate election approaching—one that could help decide which party controls the upper chamber—about as many North Carolinians lean or identify Democratic (42%) as they do Republican (41%). This effective draw between the two major parties demonstrates the extent to which political attitudes have shifted in North Carolina since 2008, when Democrats had a 10-percentage-point advantage over Republicans in party leanings (49% vs. 39%, respectively). That same year, Democratic Sen. Kay Hagan, who is currently competing for re-election, was initially elected by roughly nine points amid a strong Democratic year, nationally.

North Carolina -- Self-Reported Party Identification
Lean/Identify as Democratic or Republican

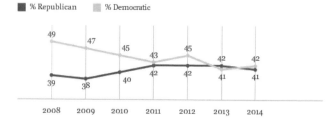

Data for 2014 collected Jan. 1–June 30

GALLUP

Party identification and a number of other political and economic measures for North Carolina are included in Gallup's new State Scorecard assessments, which present data for 14 key measures for each of the 50 states. Within each assessment, the state's performance on the measure is compared with the national average for the same time period.

Democrats were extremely successful in North Carolina in 2008. Barack Obama was the first Democratic presidential candidate since Jimmy Carter to carry the state, and Hagan defeated incumbent Republican Sen. Elizabeth Dole. But Democrats' luck in North Carolina has since wavered, with Republicans scoring a number of state electoral victories, including takeover of the state legislature in 2010 and winning the governor's race in 2012, which broke the GOP's 20-year losing streak for that office. President Obama also narrowly failed to carry North Carolina in his 2012 re-election bid.

Despite these setbacks, current polling shows Hagan running neck and neck against her Republican opponent, Thom Tillis, and many analysts consider the race a toss-up. Nonetheless, Democrats have lost their huge advantage in party identification that was extant in 2008—though official state data still show them leading in voter registration—and political attitudes, as measured by self-reported political party identification, today are closer to where the state was in 2010 and 2012, both good years for North Carolina Republicans.

These results come from aggregated Gallup Daily tracking data for the first six months of 2014, from Jan. 1 to June 30. Party identification has followed a similar pattern nationally, with Democrats' lead over Republicans shrinking from 13 points in 2008 (50% vs. 37%, respectively) to four points thus far in 2014 (43% vs. 39%).

Obama's Job Approval in North Carolina Near National Average

A key indicator included in each State Scorecard is presidential job approval, always an important predictor of midterm election outcomes. At 41% in North Carolina, Obama's job approval rating for the first six months of this year is middling at best, but close to the national average for the same period (43%) and much higher than in other Southern states that Senate Democrats hope to win, such as Arkansas (33%). Among the states that Mitt Romney won in the 2012 presidential election, North Carolina gives Obama one of his highest approval ratings, along with Georgia at 42%. Certainly, Obama is not a particularly popular figure in North Carolina—a state he is visiting on Tuesday—but his support is not cratering either. This could mean that attempts to sink Hagan by linking her to Obama only carry so much traction.

Confidence in State Government Lower Than National Average

According to Gallup's State Scorecard, North Carolina lags behind the 50-state average of 58% confidence in state government: 51% of North Carolinians have a "great deal" or "fair amount" of trust in their state government, while 47% express low or no confidence.

North Carolina -- Confidence in State Government, by Party Identification
How much trust and confidence do you have in the government of the state where you live when it comes to handling state problems -- a great deal, a fair amount, not very much, or none at all?

	Democrats	Republicans	Independents
	%	%	%
A great deal	7	16	5
A fair amount	34	46	48
Not very much	38	24	28
None at all	20	12	20

June-December 2013

GALLUP

Consistent with their party's complete control of the state government, over six in 10 North Carolina Republicans say they have a great deal or fair amount of trust in the state government (62%). Less than half of Democrats (41%) express similar confidence. Though

the Senate election represents a run for federal office, confidence in state government could prove especially relevant, as Hagan's opponent, Tillis, is the state House speaker.

Confidence in North Carolina's Economy Trails 50-State Average

On several metrics, North Carolina's economy is rated worse than average by its residents. While confidence in the state's economy is in positive territory (+8), it ranks far lower than the average economic confidence index score for all states (+23). Additionally, less than a third of North Carolinians (30%) believe it is a good time to find a job in their local area—10 points below the 50-state average.

Meanwhile, at −20, North Carolinians' confidence in the national economy ranks 30th among the states and is slightly worse than the national figure of −16.

Bottom Line

North Carolina's midterm Senate race looks to be one of the most competitive in the country. Gallup data show that North Carolina has lost the Democratic tilt it possessed in 2008, and that the two major parties are now nearly tied in self-reported party identification. As with all elections, especially midterm, turnout will be a deciding factor—revealing which party or constituency is most motivated to vote.

The dynamics of internal North Carolina politics could make this race especially interesting. As Republican Thom Tillis runs a campaign linking his opponent to President Obama—a fairly unpopular figure in North Carolina—and other national Democrats, Democrat Kay Hagan is trying to run against the Republican-led state government and its perceived excesses. Both campaigns see themselves as a way to fight back against political extremism: either the alleged liberalism of Obama and his allies, or the supposed radicalism of the GOP state government.

Given this framing, North Carolinians would appear to be making a monumental decision when they go to the ballot box in 10 weeks, and one that could help determine which party controls the U.S. Senate. But given their sour ratings of the state's economy, many voters may be thinking about economic issues rather than the larger political message of their vote. The determining factor for this race may be whether more North Carolinians fault Obama and Senate Democrats such as Kay Hagan for the state's underwhelming economic performance, or the Republican officials in charge of the state government in Raleigh.

Use Gallup Analytics to explore state political, economic, and well-being data collected since 2008.

Survey Methods

Results for this Gallup poll are based on telephone interviews conducted Jan. 1–June 30, 2014, on the Gallup Daily tracking survey, with a random sample of 88,802 adults, aged 18 and older, living in all 50 U.S. states and the District of Columbia, and Gallup's recent 50-state poll conducted June–December 2013, with a random sample of approximately 600 adults per state, aged 18 and older, living in all 50 U.S. states.

For results based on the 2014 sample of 2,886 North Carolina residents, the margin of sampling error is ±2 percentage points at the 95% confidence level.

For results based on the 2013 sample of adults per state, the margin of sampling error is ±5 percentage points at the 95% confidence level.

August 27, 2014
REPUBLICANS' "THOUGHT" TO 2014 ELECTION EXCEEDS DEMOCRATS'
GOP advantage more similar to those in 2002 and 2010 than in 2006

by Jeffrey M. Jones

PRINCETON, NJ—One in three Americans (33%) say they have given "quite a lot" or "some" thought to the 2014 midterm election, up from 26% in April. Importantly, Republicans (42%) are much more engaged than Democrats (27%) in the election at this point.

Thought Given to Upcoming Election for Congress, by Political Party
Figures represent percentages giving "quite a lot" or "some" thought to election

	April 2014	August 2014
	%	%
National adults	26	33
Republicans	37	42
Independents	23	32
Democrats	24	27
Republican-Democratic gap	13	15

GALLUP'

Just as Americans' thought given to the election has increased from April, it should continue to increase between now and Election Day, as has been the case in prior midterm election years. Although Gallup does not have much historical data on this question prior to the fall months, there is some evidence suggesting Americans' attention to this year's election is lower than in 2006 and 2010. In June 2006 (41%) and June 2010 (37%), more Americans said they had given at least some thought to the election than say so now.

The question about the thought Americans are giving to the election is one that Gallup uses to identify those Americans most inclined to vote in a coming election. Consistent with their usually higher voter turnout, typically more Republicans than Democrats say they have given thought to the election.

The gaps in election thought by party can change throughout the course of an election. There was no consistent pattern in how Republican versus Democratic thought changed leading up to Election Day in the past three midterm election years.

- The 10-percentage-point GOP advantage just prior to the 2010 election was actually a bit smaller than Gallup had measured earlier in the fall, peaking at 19 points in early October and averaging 14 points during the fall months.
- There were relatively small differences in Republican versus Democratic thought in 2006, apart from a higher GOP advantage in mid-September that vanished quickly. The GOP held a slight four-point advantage by the end of the campaign in what was a Democratic "wave" election.
- In 2002, the parties were basically even through much of the fall campaign, before Republicans surged at the end—perhaps due

to the intense campaigning of then-popular President George W. Bush on behalf of Republican candidates.

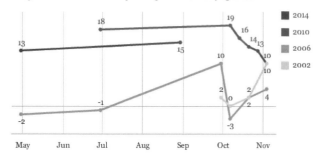

GOP Advantage in Thought Given to Election -- Recent Midterm Election Years
Figures represent the percentage of Republicans saying they give "quite a lot" or "some" thought to the election minus the percentage of Democrats saying the same

GALLUP'

Overall, the changes in the election thought gap by party in the final months before previous elections suggest that the gap in late summer or early fall is by no means what will be in place on Election Day. If there is no significant narrowing of the Republican-Democratic thought gap between now and Election Day, the Republican advantage in turnout could surpass that on Election Day 2010.

One difference, though, is that registered voters were more likely to say they were going to vote for Republican candidates in 2010 than they are now. In Gallup's final 2010 pre-election poll, Republicans led Democrats by 48% to 44% among all registered voters in their vote intention for the House of Representatives. In the recent Aug. 7–10 poll, Democrats held a slight edge among registered voters in congressional voting preference, 47% to 45%. So even if Republican turnout is as strong or stronger this year than in 2010, that may not mean Republican candidates will do as well as they did four years ago.

Implications

Democrats need strong turnout to minimize the potential seat losses in Congress that occur in nearly every midterm election for the president's party. But with Republicans much more engaged in the election at this point than Democrats—and by one of the larger margins in recent midterm election years—the odds of strong Democratic turnout seem low, suggesting 2014 could be a good year for Republicans. Even if the Republican advantage narrows considerably by Election Day, as seen in 2010, Republicans seem poised to have the upper hand in turnout.

To some degree, the Democratic deficit in election thought may reflect not just their turnout intentions but also their beliefs about the likelihood their party will perform well in the election. From that standpoint, the measure may overstate the Republican advantage in potential turnout this year. Even if that is the case, it is clear Democrats are operating at a deficit in voter motivation that looks more like recent strong Republican midterm years in 2002 and 2010 than the strong Democratic one in 2006.

Survey Methods

Results for this Gallup poll are based on telephone interviews conducted Aug. 7–10, 2014, with a random sample of 1,032 adults, aged 18 and older, living in all 50 U.S. states and the District of Columbia.

For results based on the total sample of national adults, the margin of sampling error is ±4 percentage points at the 95% confidence level.

For results based on the total sample of 897 registered voters, the margin of sampling error is ±4 percentage points at the 95% confidence level.

August 28, 2014
AMERICANS' SATISFACTION WITH EDUCATION SYSTEM INCREASES
In 2014, 48% of Americans are satisfied with the quality of K–12 education

by Rebecca Riffkin

WASHINGTON, D.C.—As students return to school in the U.S., 48% of Americans are "completely" or "somewhat satisfied" with the quality of kindergarten through high school education in the country, the highest Gallup has measured since 2004. For the first time since 2007, Americans are now about as likely to say they are satisfied as dissatisfied.

Americans' Satisfaction With K-12 Education in U.S.

Overall, how satisfied are you with the quality of education students receive in kindergarten through grade 12 in the U.S. today -- would you say you are completely satisfied, somewhat satisfied, somewhat dissatisfied or completely dissatisfied?

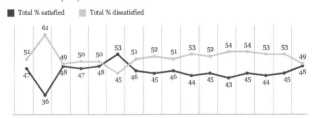

Satisfied percentage is those completely and somewhat satisfied; dissatisfied percentage is those somewhat and completely dissatisfied

GALLUP

Gallup has asked U.S. adults about their satisfaction with education since 1999, including each August since 2001, as part of its annual Work and Education poll. The high of 53% satisfaction was reached in 2004, the only year more Americans were satisfied with education than dissatisfied. Americans were most negative about the state of education in 2000, when education was a major presidential campaign issue and more than six in 10 said they were dissatisfied.

Satisfaction has largely been stable in recent years, ranging from 43% to 46% in 2005–2013. However, satisfaction ticked up this year, and is now similar to what was seen in the early 2000s.

Americans who have children in grades K–12 are generally more satisfied than U.S. adults as a whole. A majority of these parents (57%) are satisfied with education in the country. Parents may be basing their evaluations at least partly on their own child's education, not just on what they hear in the news.

Three in Four Parents Are Satisfied With Their Child's Education

Parents' tendency to be more positive than the general public about education is vividly evident when Gallup asks parents with a child

in grades K–12 about their satisfaction with their own child's education. Three in four parents say they are satisfied with the quality of education their oldest child is receiving in 2014, significantly higher than the 48% of Americans who are satisfied with U.S. K–12 education in general.

U.S. Parents' Satisfaction With Their Child's Education

How satisfied are you with the quality of education your oldest child is receiving? Would you say you are completely satisfied, somewhat satisfied, somewhat dissatisfied or completely dissatisfied?

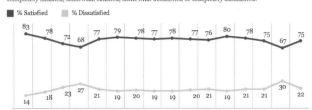

Asked of parents with children in grades kindergarten through 12

GALLUP

The 75% of parents who are satisfied with their own child's education is consistent with what Gallup has measured in prior years, although satisfaction was a bit lower last year, at 67%.

Implications

For as long as Gallup has measured it, U.S. parents of school-aged children are more likely to be satisfied with the quality of their child's education than Americans are with the quality of education in the country. Most parents are satisfied with their child's education, while historically the majority of Americans have been dissatisfied with the quality of U.S. education. This long-evident "optimism gap" may result from Americans focusing on press reports of inadequate schooling in problem school districts when they are asked about education nationally, but focusing on what they perceive as a much more positive local situation when asked about the education of their own children.

Survey Methods

Results for this Gallup poll are based on telephone interviews conducted Aug. 7–10, 2014, a random sample of 1,032 adults, aged 18 and older, living in all 50 U.S. states and the District of Columbia.

For results based on the total sample of national adults, the margin of sampling error is ±4 percentage points at the 95% confidence level.

For results based on the sample of 221 parents with children in kindergarten through grade 12, the margin of sampling error is ±9 percentage points at the 95% confidence level.

August 28, 2014
OBAMA'S "STRONG DISAPPROVAL" DOUBLE HIS "STRONG APPROVAL"
Republicans are more likely to strongly disapprove now than in 2010

by Justin McCarthy

WASHINGTON, D.C.—Americans are more than twice as likely to say they "strongly disapprove" (39%) of President Barack Obama's job performance as they are to say they "strongly approve" (17%). The percentage of Americans who strongly disapprove of Obama has increased over time, while the percentage who strongly approve has dropped by almost half.

In the first year of Obama's presidency, the percentages of Americans who had strong views about the job he was doing were essentially tied, but the strongly negative responses now significantly outweigh the strongly positive ones. The largest segment of Americans today, 39%, strongly disapprove of Obama's job performance, while 14% moderately disapprove. Another 27% moderately approve, while 17% strongly approve.

Strong disapproval of the president's job performance has been within 30% to 39% the four times Gallup has asked the question—in 2009, 2010, 2011, and now this year—but has risen by five percentage points since 2011, and by nine points since the first month Obama was in office. At the same time, strong approval has fallen by nine points in the last three years, and by 15 points since January 2009.

The overall changes reflect larger shifts in opinion within the president's own Democratic base, as well as among Republicans, whose already widespread strong disapproval of Obama has expanded.

Three in Four Republicans Strongly Disapprove of Obama's Job Performance

Since 2009, a majority of Republicans have strongly disapproved of Obama's performance, ranging between 58% and 75%. Gallup has not asked this intensity question frequently, but in its recent Aug. 7-10 poll, this percentage jumped 13 points from the January 2011 measure, suggesting that extreme dissatisfaction among the president's opposing party is higher than it has ever been.

Notably, Republicans are even more likely to say they strongly disapprove of Obama now than in 2010, a year when a tide of anti-Obama sentiments led to major Democratic losses in the House and Senate in that year's midterm election. Part of that increase may be attributable to the passage of time, in that Republicans are simply more solid in their views of Obama six years into his presidency

than two years in. But those strong negative views of Obama could boost Republican turnout this fall when the Democratic majority in the Senate is in peril.

Though Republicans who moderately or strongly approve of Obama have always been in the minority, a sizable one in five (21%) approved of the president in 2009. Today, however, this percentage is less than half of what it was then, with only 9% of Republicans saying they approve—moderately or strongly—of Obama's performance.

Enthusiastic Support for Obama Among Democrats Wanes

Democrats are also less likely to approve of Obama now than during his honeymoon period in 2009 (78% vs. 88%, respectively). Additionally, whereas Democrats were nearly three times as likely to strongly approve as moderately approve of Obama in 2009, the ratio is now about 1-to-1.

Margin Widens Between Independents' Strong Approval, Disapproval

Compared with Democrats and Republicans, independents have been more consistent in the intensity of their views of Obama, particularly among independents who disapprove of the president. Currently, 39% of independents say they strongly disapprove of Obama's performance—a slight increase from the 2009 through 2011 polls, when one in three (33% to 34%) said the same.

In previous years, one in five or more independents (19% to 23%) strongly approved of the president's performance. In 2014, however, the percentage of independents who strongly approve has shrunken to 11%.

Bottom Line

It remains to be seen whether strong disapproval of Obama's performance will continue to grow during his final two years in office, or if it will ease once the heightened partisanship that midterms can bring ends, and the 2016 election season begins.

Clearly, the trajectory in his overall ratings will determine much of that. But if Americans' overall opinion of him grows more positive, his strong disapproval numbers may fall. More generally, the intensity of opinions about the president could affect both the forthcoming midterm election and the presidential election of 2016.

Survey Methods

Results for this Gallup poll are based on telephone interviews conducted Aug. 7–10, 2014, on the Gallup Daily tracking survey, with a random sample of 1,032 adults, aged 18 and older, living in all 50 U.S. states and the District of Columbia.

For results based on the total sample of national adults, the margin of sampling error is ±4 percentage points at the 95% confidence level.

August 28, 2014
AMERICANS APPROVE OF UNIONS BUT SUPPORT "RIGHT TO WORK"
Union approval at 53% while 71% favor right-to-work laws

by Jeffrey M. Jones

PRINCETON, NJ—A slim majority of Americans, 53%, approve of labor unions, although approval remains on the low end of Gallup's nearly 80-year trend on this question. Approval has been as high as 75% in the 1950s. Currently, 38% disapprove of unions.

Do you approve or disapprove of labor unions?

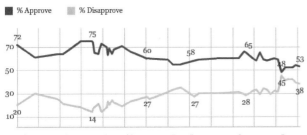

■ % Approve   ■ % Disapprove

GALLUP

At the same time Americans express greater approval than disapproval of unions, they widely support right-to-work laws. Those laws allow workers to hold jobs in unionized workplaces without joining a union. Currently, 10% of Americans identify as union members according to Gallup's Aug. 7–10 poll.

Opinion of Right-to-Work Laws

Some states have passed right-to-work or open shop laws that say each worker has the right to hold his job in a company, no matter whether he joins a labor union, or not. If you were asked to vote on such a law, would you vote for it, or against it?

	Vote for	Vote against	No opinion
	%	%	%
Aug 7-10, 2014	71	22	7
Jul 18-23, 1957	62	27	11

GALLUP

In an update of a question asked in 1957, 71% of Americans said they would "vote for" a right-to-work law if they had the opportunity to do so, while 22% said they would vote against such a law.

That is a slightly higher level of support than Gallup measured nearly 60 years ago.

The popularity of right-to-work laws may be a result of Americans' greater agreement with a major argument put forth by right-to-work proponents than by one of the main arguments put forth by opponents of such laws. The poll finds 82% of Americans agreeing that "no American should be required to join any private organization, like a labor union, against his will," a position advanced by right-to-work proponents. Pro-union forces partly oppose right-to-work laws because of the "free-rider" problem, with non-union workers benefiting as much as union workers when unions negotiate pay and benefit increases with employers. But by 64% to 32%, Americans disagree that workers should "have to join and pay dues to give the union financial support" because "all workers share the gains won by the labor union."

Currently, 24 U.S. states have right-to-work laws in place, including Indiana and Michigan who passed theirs in 2012. The Indiana law's fate is uncertain given recent legal challenges to it. The states with right-to-work laws tend to be Republican-leaning states, mostly in the South, Mountain West, and Plains areas of the country. That is consistent with the preferences of rank-and-file Republicans nationally, who disapprove of unions by 57% to 32%, and support right-to-work laws by 74% to 18%. Democrats, meanwhile, overwhelmingly approve of labor unions. Interestingly, though, most Democrats favor right-to-work laws, and their support nearly matches that of Republicans.

Opinions of Labor Unions, by Political Party

	Democrats	Independents	Republicans
	%	%	%
UNION APPROVAL			
Approve	77	47	32
Disapprove	19	40	57
RIGHT-TO-WORK LAWS			
Would vote for	65	77	74
Would vote against	30	17	18

Aug. 7-10, 2014

GALLUP

Democrats' widespread approval of unions, and their support for right-to-work laws, appear at odds. It is possible they may be sympathetic to the concept of unions and what they stand for in theory, but may disagree with some of the specific policies unions favor that could interfere with the opportunities for non-union members to secure employment.

Gallup has a limited sample of union members in its poll, and the data suggest that they are divided in their views of right-to-work laws rather than being outright opposed to them.

Implications

Although Americans widely favor right-to-work laws, only about half of the states have passed such laws. The right-to-work debate is ongoing in states like Ohio and Wisconsin, and New Mexico and Kentucky may adopt those laws if Republicans win control of the legislatures in those states in the next election.

The evidence for whether right-to-work laws are a net positive or net negative to states is mixed. On the one hand, consistent with the arguments of proponents, right-to-work states do appear to attract more business than states without such laws. On the other hand, consistent with the arguments of proponents, workers in right-to-work states appear to be worse off in terms of pay and benefits than workers in other states.

It is clear that whether a state has a right-to-work law in place is a reflection of the politics surrounding labor unions, with Democrats showing much greater support for labor unions than Republicans. Political leaders in states that tend to be politically Democratic and where Democrats are currently in power are unlikely to pursue laws strongly opposed by unions. Most Republican-leaning states already have such laws in place, consistent with Republicans' more anti-union stance. States that are more competitive politically may enact right-to-work laws if Republicans can win party control of the state government, as occurred in Michigan and may happen in Kentucky and New Mexico.

Americans, though, are clearly less supportive of labor unions, and somewhat more supportive of right-to-work laws, than in the past. Union membership is also on the decline, which in turn makes unions less of a political force than they used to be. If these trends continue, more states could adopt right-to-work laws in the future.

Survey Methods

Results for this Gallup poll are based on telephone interviews conducted Aug. 7–10, 2014, with a random sample of 1,032 adults, aged 18 and older, living in all 50 U.S. states and the District of Columbia.

For results based on the total sample of national adults, the margin of sampling error is ±4 percentage points at the 95% confidence level.

August 29, 2014
THE "40-HOUR" WORKWEEK IS ACTUALLY LONGER—BY SEVEN HOURS
Full-time U.S. workers, on average, report working 47 hours weekly

by Lydia Saad

PRINCETON, NJ—Adults employed full time in the U.S. report working an average of 47 hours per week, almost a full workday longer than what a standard five-day, 9-to-5 schedule entails. In fact, half of all full-time workers indicate they typically work more than 40 hours, and nearly four in 10 say they work at least 50 hours.

Average Hours Worked by Full-Time U.S. Workers, Aged 18+

In a typical week, how many hours do you work?

	Employed full-time
	%
60+ hours	18
50 to 59 hours	21
41 to 49 hours	11
40 hours	42
Less than 40 hours	8

Based on Gallup data from the 2013 and 2014 Work and Education polls, conducted in August of each year

GALLUP

The 40-hour workweek is widely regarded as the standard for full-time employment, and many federal employment laws—including the Affordable Care Act, or "Obamacare"—use this threshold to define what a full-time employee is. However, barely four in 10 full-time workers in the U.S. indicate they work precisely this much. The hefty proportion who tell Gallup they typically log more than 40 hours each week push the average number of hours worked up to 47. Only 8% of full-time employees claim to work less than 40 hours.

These findings are based on data from Gallup's annual Work and Education Survey. The combined sample for 2013 and 2014 includes 1,271 adults, aged 18 and older, who are employed full time.

While for some workers the number of hours worked may be an indicator of personal gumption, for others it may be a function of their pay structure. Hourly workers can be restricted in the amount they work by employers who don't need or can't afford to pay overtime. By contrast, salaried workers generally don't face this issue. And, perhaps as a result, salaried employees work five hours more per week, on average, than full-time hourly workers (49 vs. 44, respectively), according to the 2014 Work and Education survey.

Average Hours Worked by Full-Time U.S. Workers, Aged 18+

Self-reported hours typically worked each week, based on pay structure

	Paid a salary	Paid hourly
	%	%
60+ hours	25	9
50 to 59 hours	25	17
41 to 49 hours	9	12
40 hours	37	56
Less than 40 hours	3	8
Weekly average	49 hours	44 hours

Based on Gallup's 2014 Work and Education poll, conducted Aug. 7-10, 2014

GALLUP

Another factor in lengthening Americans' workweek is individuals taking on more than one job. According to past Gallup data, 86% of full-time workers have just one job, 12% have two, and 1% have three or more. However, even by restricting the analysis to full-time workers who have only one job, the average number of hours worked is 46—still well over 40.

Average Number of Hours Logged by Full-Time Workers Remains Steady

The amount of hours that all U.S. full-time employees say they typically work each week has held fairly steady over the past 14 years, except for a slight dip to just under 45 hours in Gallup's 2004–2005 two-year average. Part-time workers have averaged about 20 hours per week less than full-timers, although the precise figure shifts more for part-timers. This is partly due to the lower sample size of this group, resulting in greater volatility in the measure.

Forty-three percent of U.S. adults in the August 2014 survey tell Gallup they are employed full time, down from about 50% in the Work and Education polls conducted each August before the 2007–2009 recession. Meanwhile, the percentage who work part time has consistently hovered near 9%.

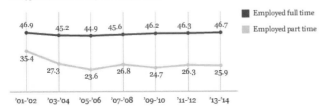

Average Number of Hours Worked by U.S. Workers, Aged 18+

In a typical week, how many hours do you work?

■ Employed full time

▨ Employed part time

46.9   45.2   44.9   45.6   46.2   46.3   46.7

35.4
    27.3   23.6   26.8   24.7   26.3   25.9

'01-'02 '03-'04 '05-'06 '07-'08 '09-'10 '11-'12 '13-'14

Based on Gallup Work and Education polls conducted each August; data combined in two-year increments

GALLUP'

Shifts in labor force participation can reflect a number of underlying factors in addition to the strength of the economy, including changes in the demographic composition of the population.

Bottom Line

The percentage of full-time workers in the U.S. has dwindled since the recession began in 2007, but the number of hours they say they work each week has held steady, at about 47. While four in 10 workers put in a standard 40-hour workweek, many others toil longer than that, including nearly one in five (18%) who work a grueling 60 hours or more. That translates into 12-hour days from Monday to Friday—or into shorter weekdays with lots of time spent working on the weekends.

Salaried workers, on average, work even more, with a full 25% saying they put in at least 60 hours per week. Thus, while workers earning a salary may enjoy greater income than their counterparts who are paid hourly, they do pay a price in lost personal time.

But this doesn't necessarily mean that workers logging long hours are suffering. According to Gallup workplace management scientists Jim Harter and Sangeeta Agrawal, certain workplace polices—including the number of hours worked—can affect employee well-being. However, having an engaging job and workplace still trumps these factors in fostering higher overall well-being in workers. Highly engaged workers who log well over 40 hours will still have better overall well-being than actively disengaged workers who clock out at 40 hours. In other words, hours worked matters, but it's not all that matters.

Survey Methods

Results for the latest Gallup Work and Education poll are based on telephone interviews conducted Aug. 7–10, 2014, with a random sample of 1,032 adults, aged 18 and older, living in all 50 U.S. states and the District of Columbia.

For results based on the total sample of national adults, the margin of sampling error is ±4 percentage points at the 95% confidence level.

For results based on the sample of 400 adults who work full time, the margin of sampling error is ±6 percentage points at the 95% confidence level.

For results based on the 2013–2014 combined sample of 1,271 adults who work full time, the margin of sampling error is ±3 percentage points at the 95% confidence level.

September 03, 2014

BUSINESS AND INDUSTRY SECTOR IMAGES CONTINUE TO IMPROVE

Images of 24 business sectors are most positive since 2003

by Frank Newport

PRINCETON, NJ—Americans' views of 24 business and industry sectors continue to grow more positive after falling precipitously in 2008 during the Great Recession. The average net-positive rating of the 24 sectors is now +18, up from −1 in 2008, and the highest since 2003.

Average Net Positive Ratings of 24 Business and Industry Sectors: 2001-2014

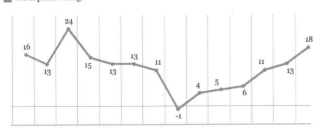

GALLUP'

These results are based on Gallup's annual Work and Education poll, conducted Aug. 7–10. Each year since 2001, Gallup has asked Americans to rate 24 different business sectors and industries on a scale ranging from "very positive" to "very negative." The net-positive ratings are the difference between the positive and negative ratings for each industry. Ratings of "the federal government," included in the list since 2003, are not included in the yearly averages.

Americans' views of individual business and industry sectors included in the average have varied over the years, and future articles on Gallup.com will explore these differences. But, overall, the trend in the combined average clearly shows that these business sectors have steadily recovered from the blow they took in 2008. Business and industry—at least as represented by these industries—have returned to the relative good graces of the American public. This increase since 2008 is similar to the general recovery in other Gallup measures, including economic confidence, job creation, and Payroll to Population and unemployment.

Restaurant Industry Has Top Image; Oil and Gas, Federal Gov't, the Worst

Americans have widely differing views of the specific sectors included in Gallup's annual list. The relative rank order of the sectors stays fairly consistent from year to year, particularly for the sectors rated best and worst.

The two "well above average" sectors—the restaurant and computer industries—are the only sectors with net-positive scores higher than 50. At the other end of the scale, three sectors are rated "negative" or "very negative": the healthcare industry, the legal field, and—at the bottom of the list—the oil and gas industry. The federal government, not a business sector or industry per se, but included on this list in recent years for comparison purposes, is dead last with a net-positive image of −36.

Net Positive Ratings of Business and Industry Sectors: 2014

	Net positive
	Pct. pts.
WELL ABOVE AVERAGE	
Restaurant industry	60
Computer industry	56
ABOVE AVERAGE	
Farming and agriculture	48
Retail industry	40
Travel industry	37
Grocery industry	34
Accounting	31
Internet industry	27
AVERAGE	
Sports industry	21
Automobile industry	20
Publishing industry	18
Education	15
Telephone industry	15
Real estate industry	12
BELOW AVERAGE	
Movie industry	8
Television and radio industry	8
Banking	8
Airline industry	6
Pharmaceutical industry	4
Advertising and public relations industry	4
Electric and gas utilities	3
NEGATIVE	
Healthcare industry	-9
The legal field	-9
VERY NEGATIVE	
Oil and gas industry	-27
The federal government	-36

Aug 7-10, 2014

GALLUP'

This rating system taps into Americans' initial top-of-mind reactions to these industries, much as favorable/unfavorable ratings measure general feelings about individual politicians. Americans' ratings of these business and industry sectors thus may reflect a wide variety of factors. In addition to the economy's overall health, these can include people's personal involvement with the industries, news stories about real-world incidents involving the industries, the types of services each industry provides, the costs of these services, legal issues involving the industries, and general perceptions about how well each is doing its job.

The perennially negative image of the oil and gas industry, for example, may reflect concerns about the effect this industry has on the environment, as well as about the sometimes seemingly unexplainable increases in gasoline prices at times when the industry is making high levels of profits. The positive image of the restaurant industry could reflect the wide variety of restaurants available for the public to choose from, particularly in regard to cost, and that dining out is often associated with pleasure and friends or family.

The negative image of the healthcare industry could reflect the reaction some of the public has had to the controversial Affordable Care Act, along with general concerns about steadily increasing healthcare premiums and costs. Gallup's honesty and ethics of professions ratings show that healthcare professionals per se rate well, suggesting the relative contempt is focused more on the healthcare system than on the people involved. That the legal profession scores low is no surprise given the generally low rating of the honesty and ethics of lawyers in the same survey.

The "computer" industry does significantly better than the Internet industry, suggesting that Americans differentiate between the makers of computer products and the Internet, particularly given the recent revelations of invasions of privacy and breaches of data and email accounts.

Implications

Americans' images of various business and industry sectors matter for several reasons, including the effect such images have on consumers' decisions about spending money in these sectors. A positive or negative industry image can also affect investment decisions, and indirectly affect decisions on the passage of regulatory legislation, taxation, and government rules that in turn can affect the operating environment of a business.

The oil and gas industry's relatively negative image is apparently no secret to that industry, as shown by the television and print and online advertising campaigns designed to improve British Petroleum's image after the Gulf oil spill in 2010. If the Internet industry's image continues to deteriorate in coming years because of concerns about privacy and hacking, the industry may attempt to burnish its reputation, although Americans are still on balance quite positive toward it, which is not the case for oil and gas.

Overall, however, the continuing six-year recovery of the images of major businesses is good news for the business sector in the U.S., and suggests that improving economic conditions are making Americans feel more positive about the businesses that are the engine of the nation's economy.

Survey Methods

Results for the latest Gallup Work and Education poll are based on telephone interviews conducted Aug. 7–10, 2014, with a random sample of 1,032 adults, aged 18 and older, living in all 50 U.S. states and the District of Columbia.

For results based on the total sample of national adults, the margin of sampling error is ±4 percentage points at the 95% confidence level.

September 05, 2014

U.S. BANKS HAVE POSITIVE IMAGE FOR FIRST TIME SINCE 2007

Real estate industry also has positive views for first time since 2006

by Rebecca Riffkin

WASHINGTON, D.C.—Americans' views of the banking industry are positive for the first time since 2007, at a net positive rating of 8. The public also has an improved view of the real estate industry (12), marking the first time Americans' image of this industry has been positive since 2006. Net positive views of banking increased 18 points from 2013, while opinions of real estate rose 11 points.

Americans' Views of Banking and Real Estate Industries

For each of the following business sectors in the United States, please say whether your overall view of it is very positive, somewhat positive, neutral, somewhat negative, or very negative.

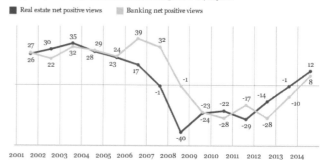

Net positive views are the total percentage of positive views minus the total percentage of negative views.

GALLUP

Each year since 2001, Gallup has asked Americans to rate 24 different business sectors and industries on a five-point scale ranging from "very positive" to "very negative." The net ratings are the difference between the positive and negative ratings for each industry, reflecting Americans' overall attitudes toward each industry. The most recent data were collected from Aug. 7–10 as part of Gallup's annual Work and Education poll.

The average net positive rating across all 24 industries this year is 18, up significantly from previous years. The images of both the banking and real estate industries remain below the overall average, continuing a pattern seen since 2007.

Americans' views of the banking and real estate industries worsened from 2003 to 2005. While views of banks then improved and reached a high of 39 in 2006, net positive views of real estate continued to deteriorate and fell into negative territory in 2007. Its image plummeted in 2008 to −40, the lowest Gallup has found for the real estate industry. In late 2006, real estate prices in the U.S. began falling rapidly, and continued to drop. Many homeowners saw their home values plummet, likely contributing to real estate's image taking a hard hit.

Views of the banking industry did not worsen until 2008 and did not plunge deeply into negative territory until 2009. Many banks suffered financially as a result of falling home prices as some were heavily involved in offering risky mortgage loans, and thus closed or faced significant hardship in 2008 and 2009. This may have been a key reason why Americans' image of the banking industry overall went downhill.

The large drops in the positive images of banking and real estate in 2008 and 2009 reflect both industries' close ties to the recession, which was precipitated in large part because of the mortgage-related housing bubble. U.S. government programs like TARP (Troubled Asset Relief Program) provided government money to banks, credit markets, and the automobile industry to stabilize these markets during the recession. At the time, many Americans were against this program, claiming it would waste taxpayer dollars, which may have negatively affected views of the industries—like the banking and real estate industries—that benefited from the program. However, recent reports indicate that TARP did help stabilize the economy, with the government recovering much of its investment.

Americans viewed banks and the real estate industry negatively from 2008 through 2013. The real estate industry started to recuperate in 2012, and views of the banking industry grew more positive in 2013.

Views of Automobile Industry Also Deteriorated From 2008 Through 2009

Americans have a more positive view of the automobile industry than they do for either banking or real estate. The automobile industry this year has a net positive view of 20, down slightly from 26 last year, but still well above where it was during the recession. Prior to the recession, Americans viewed the automobile industry positively.

Automobile Industry Positive Views, 2001-2014

For each of the following business sectors in the United States, please say whether your overall view of it is very positive, somewhat positive, neutral, somewhat negative, or very negative.

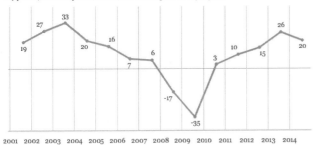

Net positive views are the total percentage of positive views minus the total percentage of negative views.

GALLUP

The recession hit the automobile industry hard, with three of America's largest companies requesting government bailouts to avoid bankruptcy. While Americans' views for most industries grew negative in 2008, the −17 and −35 net positive views for the automobile industry in 2008 and 2009, respectively, were significantly below the industry's ratings before the bailouts. The improvement in Americans' image of the automobile industry in 2010 is one of the largest and most rapid Gallup has found. Increasing car sales may have spurred part of this improvement. Many reports say auto sales returned to pre-recession levels in 2013, and the bailouts have ended. This financial improvement in the automobile industry seems to coincide with the improvement in Americans' views of the industry.

Bottom Line

The positive images of most industries have returned to pre-recession levels, including three business sectors that the recession most directly affected: banking, real estate, and the automobile industry. The real estate and banking industries both have positive images for the first time since before the recession. Americans' views of the automobile industry reached positive territory in 2010 and have

bounced back to pre-recession levels. Although the images of banking and real estate remain below the average of 24 industries Gallup has tracked, their sharp recovery from their previous extreme low points suggests they are heading in the right direction.

Survey Methods

Results for this Gallup poll are based on telephone interviews conducted Aug. 7–10, 2014, with a random sample of 1,032 adults, aged 18 and older, living in all 50 U.S. states and the District of Columbia.

Each industry was rated by a randomly selected half sample of respondents. The sample sizes for each industry are approximately 500 national adults. For results based on the total sample of national adults, the margin of sampling error is ±5 percentage points at the 95% confidence level for each industry.

September 05, 2014
IOWA: AS MIDTERM ELECTION LOOMS, OBAMA'S SUPPORT DROPS
Republican identification in Iowa rises six points since 2008

by Andrew Dugan

WASHINGTON, D.C.—As a key U.S. Senate race unfolds in Iowa, President Barack Obama's declining job approval rating may be one factor making it such a close battle. Obama's approval rating among Iowans for the first half of the year stood at 38%, five percentage points below the national average and the lowest rating Gallup has measured in Iowa during his presidency. The Senate race pits current Democratic Rep. Bruce Braley against Republican state Sen. Joni Ernst. Several polls show a close race—perhaps closer than many analysts would expect, given Ernst's relatively unknown background as a new state senator versus Braley's background as a four-term U.S. Representative.

Iowa: Presidential Job Approval

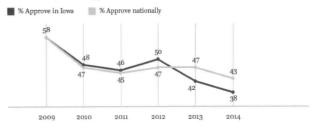

■ % Approve in Iowa   ■ % Approve nationally

Gallup Daily tracking

GALLUP

Perhaps more than any state other than Obama's home state of Illinois, Iowa has been important to the president's political career. His win in the 2008 Iowa caucus transformed him from a decided underdog to a contender for the Democratic nomination. He would go on to win this key swing state's Electoral College votes twice, in the 2008 and 2012 general elections.

But despite the integral role the Hawkeye State has played in Obama's political career, Iowans could cause Obama a severe second-term setback if they elect a Republican to succeed retiring Democratic Sen. Tom Harkin. A GOP victory would help increase the chances for Republicans to take control of the Senate, hindering Obama's agenda for his remaining two years in office.

Further complicating matters for Braley is the surge in Republican identification in Iowa since 2008, as measured by self-reported party affiliation and independents who report "leaning" toward the GOP. While the percentage of national adults identifying as or leaning Republican was two percentage points higher in the first half of 2014 than in 2008 (39% vs. 37%, respectively), it was six points higher among Iowans (40% vs. 34%).

Iowa: Lean or Identify as Republican

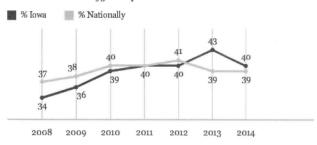

■ % Iowa   % Nationally

Gallup Daily tracking

GALLUP

Meanwhile, in the first half of 2014, 41% of Iowans said they identify as or lean Democratic—slightly below the national average of 43%. Put simply, Iowa was more Democratic than the rest of the nation in 2008; it is now less Democratic than the rest of the nation.

Presidential job approval, partisanship, and a number of other political and economic measures for Iowa are included in Gallup's new State Scorecard assessments, which present data for 14 key measures for each of the 50 states. Within the scorecard, the state's performance on each measure is compared with the national average.

As GOP Gov. Runs for Re-Election, Confidence in State Gov't Is High

Iowa is one of a handful of states to feature both a Senate and gubernatorial election in 2014. Republican Gov. Terry Branstad is running for re-election and is considered by many analysts a solid favorite to win his sixth term as Iowa's governor, previously having served from 1983 to 1999 and then again from 2011 to the present. Gallup's State Scorecard data show a few major reasons why Branstad has been so popular, as confidence in the state government is very high. However, these data were collected before a scandal surfaced alleging the governor fired state employees for political reasons—leaving open the possibility that confidence in state government has fallen in the wake of these alleged abuses.

Iowa: State Government Performance

How Iowa's state government compares with the nation

	Iowa	50-state average
Great deal/Fair amount of trust in state government	67%	58%
State taxes not too high	53%	47%
Best/One of the best states to live in	56%	46%

Gallup Daily tracking
June-December 2013

GALLUP

Despite dealing with a series of scandals, polling continues to show Branstad ahead in his race for re-election, and this may be another cause for concern in the Braley campaign. Just as an unpopular Democratic president may be a drag on Braley's U.S. Senate campaign, a popular Republican governor on the ballot may be a boost for Ernst's. Further, Ernst's position as a state senator connects her to a popular and well-regarded state government, which may be a plus in comparison with Braley's link to a very unpopular U.S. Congress.

Economic Confidence High in Iowa

Gallup's Economic Confidence Index, which measures attitudes toward the national economy, stood at −9 in Iowa for the first six months of the year, better than the national average of −16 for the same period.

Iowans' confidence in their state's economy is at a robust +50—significantly higher than the 50-state average of +23—and places Iowa near the top of the list on this measure.

Gallup's Payroll to Population rate, which measures the percentage of the adult population who are employed full time for an employer, is 48% in Iowa, higher than the national average of 43%.

In most respects, Iowa's economic perceptions are more positive than other states'—which would usually play to the advantage of the party currently occupying the White House. But with Obama's crestfallen approval and Democrats' sagging support in party identification, that does not necessarily appear to be the case.

Bottom Line

Iowans launched Obama's presidential primary campaign from a quixotic, unlikely bid to instant frontrunner—and, eventually, to the Democratic nominee. The state also voted for Obama in the general elections, helping to cement his Electoral College victory twice.

But now, in a strange twist of fate, Iowa is on the verge of making an electoral decision that could deal a political blow to President Obama in his final two years in office. The race for Iowa's first open Senate seat in decades is competitive, and a GOP victory is a very real prospect. If Republicans prevail in Iowa, this will go a long way in bolstering their chances of gaining control of the upper chamber.

A Democratic defeat in Iowa could be at least partially attributed to Obama's diminishing popularity in the state—a true reversal of fortunes for a state that did so much to help make Obama a national figure. At the same time, the GOP Senate candidate may receive a boost in support because of her connection to the well-regarded state government being run by a Republican.

Survey Methods

Results for this Gallup poll are based on telephone interviews conducted on the Gallup Daily tracking survey with a random sample of 88,802 adults, aged 18 and older, living in all 50 U.S. states and the District of Columbia. Results are also based on Gallup's recent 50-state poll conducted June–December 2013 with a random sample of approximately 600 adults per state, aged 18 and older, living in all 50 U.S. states.

For results based on the 2014 sample of 2,066 Iowa residents, the margin of sampling error is ±2 percentage points at the 95% confidence level.

For results based on the 2013 sample of adults per state, the margin of sampling error is ±5 percentage points at the 95% confidence level.

September 05, 2014
AMERICANS RATE COMPUTER INDUSTRY BETTER THAN INTERNET
In a 14-year trend, computer business consistently tops online industry

by Art Swift

WASHINGTON, D.C.—Americans have solidly positive views of the computer industry, which have stayed consistently high since 2001. Yet fewer Americans feel the same way about the Internet industry, with a drop off in net positive ratings in this area since last year.

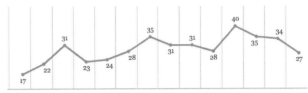

Americans' Net Positive Views of the Internet Industry, 2001-2014

For each of the following business sectors in the United States, please say whether your overall view of it is very positive, somewhat positive, neutral, somewhat negative, or very negative.

Net positive views are the total percentage of positive views minus the total percentage of negative views.

GALLUP

Americans' Views of the Computer and Internet Industries

For each of the following business sectors in the United States, please say whether your overall view of it is very positive, somewhat positive, neutral, somewhat negative, or very negative.

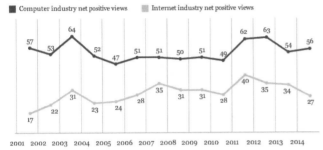

Net positive views are the total percentage of positive views minus the total percentage of negative views.

GALLUP

This question was part of the Aug. 7–10 annual Work and Education poll, in which Gallup asks Americans about their attitudes toward 24 distinct businesses and industries. Although the question did not define the "computer industry" for those responding, Americans could have been thinking about companies that make computer hardware and software when answering this question. The net ratings are the difference between the positive and negative ratings for each industry, reflecting Americans' overall attitudes toward each business.

Since 2001, Americans' overall views of the computer industry have generally been quite positive. There is a one-point difference in attitudes now compared with 2001, and although views were slightly less positive between 2004 and 2010, they returned to generally higher levels over the past four years. In general, the net-positive trend has remained in the 50s and 60s for 14 years. The computer industry is now the second most positively evaluated industry of 24 tested, second only to the restaurant industry.

The reasons for Americans' positive views may be related to advancements in the computer industry throughout the past 15 years. The computer industry is an ever-evolving business that continually produces more powerful and faster computers, enhancing Americans' productivity and ability to use technology almost anywhere and keeping American consumers highly interested for years.

Internet Industry Not as Well Regarded

Views of the "Internet industry" may be more complicated, possibly because of the mixed reactions many Americans have toward the Internet itself. The Internet makes it easy for Americans to search for information or buy merchandise, but using it comes with risks—from the threat of hacking to identity theft to general privacy concerns.

Americans have consistently rated the Internet industry less positively than the computer industry in Gallup's 14-year trend. Since 2001, the highest sentiment for the industry was a net positive of 40 in 2011.

Currently, the net-positive view of the Internet industry is 27, which is toward the lower end of the trend. Still, this is not as low as its nadir of 17 after the dot-com bust in 2001. But in 2014, the net-positive view of the industry is down seven points from last year. The downward drift in Americans' positive image of the Internet industry compared with the uptick in the positive images of most other industries is perhaps related to revelations about the National Security Agency's domestic surveillance on the Internet in the past year, along with various hacking scandals. Other reasons for the decrease could be one-time Internet giants such as AOL reducing to a fraction of their former size and companies such as Yahoo! garnering headlines in recent years for their financial struggles.

Bottom Line

At first blush, one might assume the "computer industry" and the "Internet industry" are interchangeable, and as such would elicit the same views from the American public. Since 2001, that has not been the case, as Americans have always rated the computer industry higher than the Internet industry. In fact, the worst year for the computer industry (net positive 47 in 2005) was higher than the best year for the Internet industry (40 in 2011) since Gallup began asking this question.

Americans' views could change in years to come. If hacking and privacy concerns about the Internet continue to weigh on Americans' minds, it may be some time before they feel secure enough to boost their positive opinions of the Internet industry. As for the computer industry, it is likely that positive views will stay high as long as computer makers continue to innovate and produce new tablets, laptops, and desktops that the American public buys and enjoys.

Survey Methods

Results for this Gallup poll are based on telephone interviews conducted Aug. 7–10, 2014, with a random sample of 1,032 adults, aged 18 and older, living in all 50 U.S. states and the District of Columbia.

For results based on the total sample of national adults, the margin of sampling error is ±4 percentage points at the 95% confidence level.

September 08, 2014

CONGRESS APPROVAL SITS AT 14% TWO MONTHS BEFORE ELECTIONS

Lowest approval in fall before an election since 1974

by Frank Newport

PRINCETON, NJ—With less than two months to go before the midterm congressional elections, 14% of Americans approve of how Congress is handling its job. This rating is one of the lowest Gallup has measured in the fall before a midterm election since 1974.

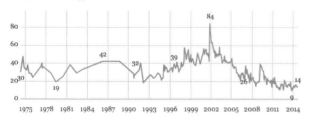

Congressional Job Approval -- Full Trend

GALLUP

Americans' rating of Congress, from Gallup's latest Social Series survey, conducted Sept. 4–7, is barely changed from the August reading, and matches the 14% average so far in 2014. The all-time low congressional approval rating is 9%, measured in November 2013.

In September 2010, just before that year's midterm elections in which the Republicans took control of the House with a sweeping 63-seat change, congressional approval was 18%, slightly higher than it is today. Four years before that, Congress' approval was 29% in September 2006—an election in which the Democrats did well and took control of both houses.

Previous Gallup analysis shows that low Congress approval is associated with higher seat turnover. That review also suggested that when the president's party and the majority party in Congress are different, as they are now, voters' frustration with Congress is more likely to be taken out on the party of the president, although this conclusion is based on a limited number of recent elections.

Most observers believe the Republicans are in little jeopardy of losing control of the House this year, so more of the focus has been on the states with Senate races. Given the idiosyncratic nature of the particular senators and states that have Senate seats up for election this year, the impact of the negative attitudes about Congress in general on specific Senate races is difficult to predict.

Still, when asked directly, two-thirds of those who disapprove of Congress say this makes them more likely to vote in the congressional elections; only 11% say it makes them less likely to vote in the elections. Taken at face value, these responses suggest that the historic disapproval ratings in a midterm year may bring more voters to the polls. There is little difference in these responses by partisan identification.

Does your disapproval of Congress make you more likely or less likely to vote in the congressional elections, or does it make no difference?

Asked of those who disapprove of the way Congress is handling its job

	More likely to vote in congressional elections	Makes no difference	Less likely to vote in congressional elections
Sep 4-7, 2014	66%	22%	11%

GALLUP

Approval Is Lower Among Those Paying the Most Attention to National Politics

Members of Congress can take little comfort in the finding that those who are paying closest attention to national politics are the most negative about the institution's performance. Only 8% of the one-third of all Americans who are following national politics "very closely" approve of the way Congress is handling its job. On the other hand, Americans who say they are not following national politics closely are the most positive, with 23% saying they approve.

Congressional Job Approval, by How Closely Respondents Are Following National Politics

	Approve	Disapprove	Don't know/ Refused
	%	%	%
Following national politics very closely	8	89	3
Following national politics somewhat closely	13	84	3
Not following national politics closely	23	70	7

Sept. 4-7, 2014

GALLUP

Implications

The current 14% congressional job approval rating is one of the lowest Gallup has recorded in the fall of a midterm election year since Gallup first measured approval of Congress in the current format in 1974. Americans indicate that these negative attitudes will increase their probability of voting this fall, and history suggests it is more likely that more Democrats than Republicans will suffer as a result, given Democratic control of the White House.

Survey Methods

Results for this Gallup poll are based on telephone interviews conducted Sept. 4–7, 2014, on the Gallup Daily tracking survey, with a random sample of 1,017 adults, aged 18 and older, living in all 50 U.S. states and the District of Columbia.

For results based on the total sample of national adults, the margin of sampling error is ±4 percentage points at the 95% confidence level.

September 10, 2014

TRUST IN FEDERAL GOV'T ON INTERNATIONAL ISSUES AT NEW LOW

Americans' trust in government handling of domestic problems also at record low

by Jeffrey M. Jones

PRINCETON, NJ—Americans' trust in the federal government to handle international problems has fallen to a record-low 43% as President Barack Obama prepares to address the nation on Wednesday to outline his plan to deal with ISIS. Separately, 40% of Americans say they have a "great deal" or "fair amount" of trust in the federal government to handle domestic problems, also the lowest Gallup has measured to date.

The results are based on Gallup's annual Governance poll, conducted Sept. 4–7. This year's poll was conducted at a time when the government is faced with instability in many parts of the world, including Iraq and Syria, the Middle East, and Ukraine. President Obama, who recently said he had "no strategy" for dealing with ISIS—the Islamic extremists who have taken control of parts of Iraq and Syria and recently captured and beheaded two American journalists—is set to present his plan for dealing with the group Wednesday.

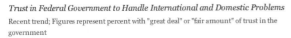

Trust in Federal Government to Handle International and Domestic Problems

Recent trend; Figures represent percent with "great deal" or "fair amount" of trust in the government

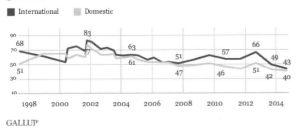

Americans' confidence in the government to handle international problems slid 17 percentage points last year, when the Obama administration was planning military action against Syria. Russia later brokered an agreement to avert that action. Last year's poll marked the first time that fewer than half of Americans trusted the federal government's ability to deal with international threats. With the world stage seemingly more unstable now, the public's trust has dipped an additional six percentage points this year.

Likewise, trust in the government's ability to handle domestic problems dropped slightly this year after a larger decline in 2013. Although the economy has improved, it may be overshadowed by partisan gridlock in Washington, which has led to little formal government action to deal with important domestic challenges facing the United States. Indeed, Americans have consistently mentioned dissatisfaction with government as one of the most important problems facing the country in 2014.

The level of trust in the government to handle both domestic and international matters is nearly half what it was at the high point Gallup measured, shortly after the 9/11 terror attacks. In October 2001, 83% trusted the government's ability to deal with international problems and 77% trusted its ability to handle domestic ones.

Gallup asked the trust items three times in the 1970s, and at least once every year since 1997 with the exception of 1999. Prior to 2013, the low point in domestic trust was 43% in 2011, shortly after contentious negotiations to raise the federal debt limit, and the low point in international trust was 51% in 2007, as the Iraq war dragged on.

Democrats Maintain High Level of Trust in Government

Democrats' trust in the federal government has been far less shaken than that of Republicans and independents in the last two years. That likely stems from a Democratic president being in office—supporters of the president's party typically show much more trust in government than other Americans do. That pattern is illustrated by the dramatic shifts in trust by party between 2008 and 2009, when Democrat Obama replaced Republican George W. Bush as president.

Currently, 70% of Democrats trust the government's ability to handle international problems, compared with 39% of independents and 27% of Republicans. Since 2012, Democrats' trust is down 11 points, compared with a 24-point drop for independents and a 26-point drop for Republicans.

Trust in Federal Government to Handle International Problems, by Political Party

Figures represent percent with "great deal" or "fair amount" of trust in the government

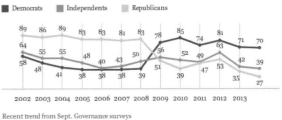

Recent trend from Sept. Governance surveys

Meanwhile, 63% of Democrats trust the federal government to handle domestic problems it faces, compared with 34% of independents and 28% of Republicans. In contrast to the declines in trust on international matters, the drops in trust on domestic matters since 2012 are similar by party group, with each down between six and 10 percentage points. This is, in part, because international trust was higher than domestic trust in 2012, and thus had more room to fall.

Trust in Federal Government to Handle Domestic Problems, by Political Party

Figures represent percent with "great deal" or "fair amount" of trust in the government

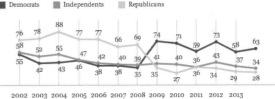

Recent trend from Sept. Governance surveys

Implications

Gallup has never measured lower levels of trust in the federal government to handle pressing issues than now. That includes the Watergate era in 1974, when 51% of Americans trusted the government's ability to handle domestic problems and 73% trusted its ability to deal with international problems, and also at the tail end of the Bush administration when his job approval ratings were consistently below 40% and frequently below 30%.

The key question going forward is whether Americans' trust in the federal government can be restored. Although there have been short-lived increases in recent years, including in Obama's first year in office and in his re-election year, these were not maintained. The general trend since the post-9/11 surge has been toward declining trust. Simply voting new people into office may not be sufficient to restore trust in government. Rather, given the public's frustration with the way the government is working, it may be necessary to elect federal officials who are more willing to work together with the other party to find solutions to the nation's top problems.

Survey Methods

Results for this Gallup poll are based on telephone interviews conducted Sept. 4–7, 2014, with a random sample of 1,017 adults, aged 18 and older, living in all 50 U.S. states and the District of Columbia.

For results based on the total sample of national adults, the margin of sampling error is ±4 percentage points at the 95% confidence level.

September 10, 2014
SINCE 9/11, FEWER AMERICANS SAY TERRORISM TOP PROBLEM
Government and the economy most commonly cited problems now

by Rebecca Riffkin

WASHINGTON, D.C.—Four percent of Americans currently mention terrorism as the most important problem facing the U.S. Although low on an absolute basis, it is the highest percentage naming this issue since May 2010. Mentions of terrorism have been near 1% for the past four years.

Views of Terrorism as the Most Important U.S. Problem

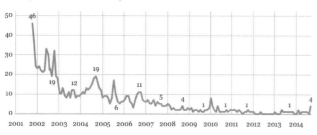

Data shown for October 2001, and September 2002-2014

Relatively few Americans—usually less than 0.5%—mentioned terrorism as the most important problem facing the U.S. prior to 9/11. But that changed quickly after the 9/11 attacks. Mentions jumped to 46% the month after the attacks, the highest percentage Gallup has found for terrorism since it began asking Americans monthly to name the most important problem facing the nation in March 2001.

Mentions of terrorism have spiked several times since 2001, generally in reaction to new threats or potential attacks. The most recent surge, to 8% in early 2010, came after the "Christmas Day bomber" failed to blow up a commercial U.S. flight. Each spike since 2001 has been smaller than the one before, and mentions have been lower in the months afterward.

The current increase in mentions of terrorism follows a great deal of media attention about Iraq, Syria, and the terrorist group the Islamic State in Iraq and Syria (ISIS), most notably the group's beheading of two U.S. journalists. President Barack Obama will speak to the nation about these threats on Wednesday, and many analysts predict he will outline a new counterterror strategy.

Gallup's open-ended "most important problem" question measures concern about terrorism as a top-of-mind issue in relation to many other issues. That a relatively low 4% mention terrorism doesn't mean Americans are not concerned about it, but rather that these concerns have not risen to the point where Americans are more likely to see it as the top problem over economic problems and other issues.

Government Dissatisfaction, Economy Continue to Be Most Important Problems

In September, the issues Americans most commonly mention as the nation's top problems are dissatisfaction with government and the economy, followed closely by unemployment and immigration. Although down slightly after an initial spike in July, mentions of immigration remain elevated.

Most Important Problem Facing the U.S.

What do you think is the most important problem facing this country today?

	Jul 7-10, 2014	Aug 7-10, 2014	Sep 4-7, 2014
	%	%	%
Dissatisfaction with government	16	18	18
Economy in general	15	14	17
Immigration/Illegal aliens	17	15	12
Unemployment/Jobs	14	12	12
Foreign policy/Foreign aid/Focus overseas	3	7	6
Federal budget deficit/Federal debt	6	3	6
Healthcare	8	9	5
Ethics/Moral/Religious decline	4	6	5
Terrorism	1	*	4
Poverty/Hunger/Homelessness	3	5	3
Education	5	4	3
Gap between rich and poor	1	3	3
Wars/War (nonspecific)/Fear of war	1	3	3
Situation in Iraq	*	1	3
Judicial system/Courts/Laws	3	1	3
Race relations/Racism	2	1	3

Responses listed by at least 3% of Americans are shown.

* Less than 0.5%

Mentions of foreign policy and foreign aid increased in August, and remain higher in September. The ISIS situation is likely behind the increase in mentions of terrorism and foreign policy, and is also most likely related to a slight increase in mentions of Iraq, up to 3% this month. Meanwhile, mentions of healthcare have been dropping over the past six months, from 15% of mentions in April to 5% in September.

Bottom Line

Thirteen years after the 9/11 terrorist attacks in New York City and Washington, D.C., terrorism is far less top-of-mind for Americans than it was immediately after those attacks. Mentions of terrorism did increase slightly this month as terrorist groups such as ISIS took actions that directly affect the U.S., prompting calls for U.S. action from many politicians and some journalists.

While terrorism may be less top-of-mind to Americans—and less likely to register as the most important problem facing the nation—many still see it as important when asked about it specifically. In January polling, 72% of Americans said they felt terrorism was an important issue for Congress and the president to deal with this year. In February, 77% said international terrorism was a critical threat to the U.S. The economy or dissatisfaction with government may trump terrorism as the most important problem at the moment, but many Americans still see terrorism as a threat that must be dealt with, even 13 years after 9/11.

Survey Methods

Results for this Gallup poll are based on telephone interviews conducted Sept. 4–7, 2014, with a random sample of 1,017 adults, aged 18 and older, living in all 50 U.S. states and the District of Columbia.

For results based on the total sample of national adults, the margin of sampling error is ±4 percentage points at the 95% confidence level.

September 11, 2014

REPUBLICANS EXPAND EDGE AS BETTER PARTY AGAINST TERRORISM

GOP also holds advantage as party better able to keep country prosperous

by Frank Newport

PRINCETON, NJ—The Republican Party has expanded its historical edge over the Democratic Party in Americans' minds as being better able to protect the U.S. from international terrorism and military threats. At this point, 55% of Americans choose the GOP on this dimension, while 32% choose the Democratic Party. This is the widest Republican advantage in Gallup's history of asking this question since 2002.

Party Better Able to Protect U.S. From Terrorism, September 2002-September 2014

Looking ahead for the next few years, which political party do you think will do a better job of protecting the country from international terrorism and military threats -- [the Republican Party or the Democratic Party]?

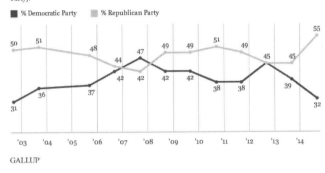

GALLUP

The latest update on this 12-year trend comes from Gallup's Sept. 4–7 Governance poll, finished just days before President Barack Obama's speech to the nation Wednesday night, in which he outlined his plans for addressing the challenges presented by the Islamic State in Iraq and Syria (ISIS) and other international threats.

Republicans have held a perceptual edge on this question in all but two of the 12 years that it has been asked—2007 and 2012. The GOP's edge has been significant in many of the other years, although the 19-percentage-point gap measured in 2002, which was previously the largest, is eclipsed by this year's 23-point Republican edge.

The strong Republican advantage this year is most likely related to the increasing news coverage of ISIS and its beheadings of two American journalists. Although the Obama administration has initiated air attacks against terrorist positions in Iraq, the president's widely quoted comments that he had "no strategy" for dealing with the issue may help explain why Americans have become less likely to say the Democrats could better protect the U.S. from terrorism and military threats.

Republicans Have Edge as Party Better Able to Keep Country Prosperous

In addition to the GOP advantage on matters of security, Americans also give the Republican Party an edge as the party better able to keep the country prosperous, with 49% choosing the Republicans and 40% the Democrats.

This is one of Gallup's oldest measures of relative party strength, and, as might be expected, it has produced widely differing results over the years, mirroring changes in the relative strength of the two parties more broadly.

Looking ahead for the next few years, which political party do you think will do a better job of keeping the country prosperous -- [ROTATED: the Republican Party or the Democratic Party]?

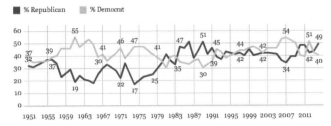

Chart represents yearly averages for years in which the question was asked multiple times.

GALLUP

- Democrats held sway as the party better able to keep the country prosperous through most of the 1950s, 1960s, and 1970s—a time when Democrats were the strong majority party in Congress.
- Republicans gained the upper hand on the measure during the Reagan years, but the two parties moved closer together, with ups and downs, during the George H.W. Bush and Clinton administrations.
- Democrats moved ahead during the George W. Bush years, in particular during his second term.
- The pattern has been sharply mixed during the Obama years, with the Democrats holding an edge in 2009 and 2012, but the Republicans having at least a slight edge in the other years.

The current nine-point GOP edge on this measure is up from 2013, but similar to where it was in 2010 and 2011.

Implications for Midterm Elections

While these measures are by no means perfect predictors of how well a party will do in a midterm election year, the Republican Party's strength this year does not bode well for Democratic chances to outperform already low expectations.

Gallup has a long trend on the "prosperous" question, and the chart shows the two parties' standings on this dimension in September before each of last five midterm elections, along with the outcome of the House vote in the corresponding year.

Relationship Between Party Seen as Better Able to Keep Country Prosperous and Midterm Congressional Outcome

	% Democratic	% Republican	President's party	Edge of president's party	House seats won/lost by president's party
2014	40	49	Democrat	-9	?
2010	40	48	Democrat	-8	-63
2006	53	36	Republican	-17	-30
2002	42	42	Republican	0	+6
1998	46	37	Democrat	9	+5
1994	38	48	Democrat	-10	-53

GALLUP

There is a clear relationship between these perceptions and the outcome of midterm elections, with the president's party losing substantial seats when it has a deficit as the better party for economic prosperity, even though each election has its own unique dimensions. These results are thus best seen as providing an estimate of the direction of an election, rather than any precise outcome.

The president's actions internationally and domestically in the coming weeks, and the actions or lack thereof on the part of Congress during the short time it will be in session before the elections, could both affect the election's dynamics. But the historical pattern suggests that the GOP's current edge as the party better able to keep the country prosperous and safe from terrorism would translate into gains in the midterm elections—if Americans' perceptions of the two parties stay pretty much as they are now over the next two months.

Survey Methods

Results for this Gallup poll are based on telephone interviews conducted Sept. 4–7, 2014, with a random sample of 1,017 adults, aged 18 and older, living in all 50 U.S. states and the District of Columbia.

For results based on the total sample of national adults, the margin of sampling error is ±4 percentage points at the 95% confidence level.

September 11, 2014
AMID CRUCIAL SENATE RACE, ALASKANS' INDEPENDENCE GROWS
Nearly six in 10 Alaskans identify as independents, up from 47% in '13

by Justin McCarthy

WASHINGTON, D.C.—Amid a tight race for a U.S. Senate seat from Alaska, a growing proportion of Alaskans, now 59%, identify as political independents. At the same time, there are recent lows in the percentage of Alaskans identifying as Republicans (25%) and the percentage identifying as Democrats (13%). These shifts create a more challenging political landscape for the campaigns of both incumbent Democratic Sen. Mark Begich and his Republican challenger, former Alaska Attorney General Dan Sullivan.

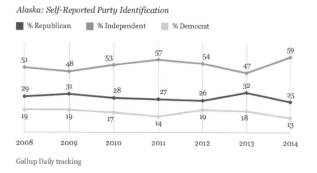

Alaska: Self-Reported Party Identification

Gallup Daily tracking

GALLUP

The race between Begich and Sullivan has been highly watched as national Republicans and Democrats hone in on competitive elections. The campaign is similar to those in North Carolina and Iowa that could decide the majority in the U.S. Senate. Alaska has traditionally been among the states with the highest percentages of residents who identify as independents, and the current Alaskan independent percentage far exceeds the national average of 40%.

Historically, however, the state has leaned right. Despite Alaskans' initial inclination to identify as politically independent, when

examined closer, more Alaska independents say they "lean" to the Republican Party than to the Democratic Party. That leaves a situation in which 42% of Alaskan adults identify as Republican or lean Republican, compared with 34% who identify as Democrats or lean Democratic. At the same time, the current Republican advantage is less than Gallup has measured in recent years. Still, the comparable national percentages are 43% who identify with or lean Democrat, and 39% who identify with or lean Republican. This underscores Alaska's generally more Republican orientation.

Party identification and several other political and economic measures for Alaska are included in Gallup's new State Scorecard assessments, which present data for 14 key measures for each of the 50 states. Within each assessment, the state's performance on the measure is compared with the national average for the same time period.

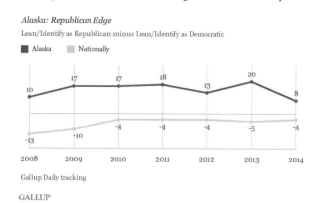

Alaska: Republican Edge

Lean/Identify as Republican minus Lean/Identify as Democratic

Gallup Daily tracking

GALLUP

Historically, the state has leaned to the right, with Republicans exerting firm control over both of the state's U.S. Senate seats. Prior to Begich's historic victory in 2008, former Republican Sen. Ted Stevens held his seat for four decades before losing to Begich amidst an extensive federal corruption investigation. Former Sen. Frank Murkowski and his daughter, incumbent Sen. Lisa Murkowski—both Republicans—have occupied the other seat since the early 1980s. The state's at-large congressman, Republican Don Young, has owned Alaska's single House seat since 1973.

One of the Lowest Obama Approval Scores in the Nation

Despite being the state's first Democrat in Congress in nearly three decades, Begich has done much to distance himself from President Barack Obama, a fellow Democrat also elected in 2008. Given Alaska's political climate, this is a smart move if not a political necessity for the vulnerable incumbent. One in three Alaskans (34%) approve of Obama's job performance—well below the national average of 43%.

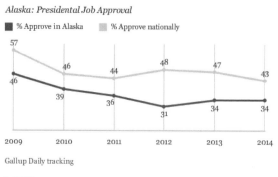

Alaska: Presidental Job Approval

Gallup Daily tracking

GALLUP

Alaskans Have Low Confidence in U.S. Economy, But High Confidence at Home

In the gubernatorial election, too, the surge in independents could muddy the path to re-election for Republican Gov. Sean Parnell. Parnell is being challenged by a joint ticket led by former Republican Valdez Mayor Bill Walker, an independent candidate for governor, and a Democratic running mate for lieutenant governor. Parnell successfully won election in 2010 after taking over for former Gov. Sarah Palin, who resigned. However, a unique challenge from a bipartisan ticket could threaten his standing with a swath of independent voters.

Parnell, however, has some advantages on his side. Alaskans' confidence in their state's economy, as measured in Gallup's 2013 50-state poll, was well above that in the other states. Alaskans' confidence in the national economy based on January through June 2014 polling is similar to the national average.

Alaska: Economic Measures

	Alaska	Nationally
Confidence in the U.S. economy (Economic Confidence Index)	-15	-16
Confidence in your state's economy (Economic Confidence Index)^	47	23
% Good time to get a job in city or area^	54%	40%
% State taxes not too high^	69%	47%
% Payroll to Population rate*	48%	43%

^ Overall average of the 50 individual state averages. The 50-state average measures are from a 50-state Gallup poll conducted June–December 2013 with at least 600 residents in each state.
*% of population employed full time by an employer

GALLUP'

Most residents of Alaska also view their state as among the best places to live. While 46% of Americans say their state is the best or one of the best places, more than three in four Alaskans (77%) feel this way about where they live, putting Alaska along with Montana at the top of the list of states on this dimension.

Additionally—and crucially for Parnell—Alaskans were among the most trusting of their state government, according to the 2013 50-state poll. Part of this may come from the fact that more than one in four residents work for the government in some capacity—the highest figure in the nation—including the government of the state of Alaska.

This culmination of factors gives Parnell—who has been in office for five years now—a favorable climate with which to run for re-election—one that many other governors likely wish they could enjoy in their own states.

Bottom Line

The shifts in party identification among Alaskans make a complicated landscape for all candidates running for statewide office in the Last Frontier this November. For incumbent Sen. Mark Begich, the shifts could serve to his benefit as a result of the decline in those who identify as Republicans. Those who identify as Democrats are also on the decline.

However, the large percentage of independents also leaves many question marks in this unpredictable election season, particularly for the re-election race of Gov. Parnell. Largely, voters in Alaska treat incumbents well. But the unprecedented independent-Democratic ticket attempting to unseat Parnell could provide the upset to a statewide incumbent that Alaska has not seen since Ted Stevens' loss in 2008.

Survey Methods

Results for this Gallup poll are based on telephone interviews conducted on the Gallup Daily tracking survey with a random sample of 88,802 adults, aged 18 and older, living in all 50 U.S. states and the District of Columbia. Results are also based on Gallup's recent 50-state poll conducted June–December 2013, with a random sample of approximately 600 adults per state, aged 18 and older, living in all 50 U.S. states.

For results based on the 2014 sample of 278 Alaska residents, the margin of sampling error is ±7 percentage points at the 95% confidence level.

For results based on the 2013 sample of adults per state, the margin of sampling error is ±5 percentage points at the 95% confidence level.

September 12, 2014
U.S. INVESTORS SEEK ADVICE FOR SOME THINGS MORE THAN OTHERS
Nearly half of investors have created a financial plan with professional advice

by Lydia Saad

PRINCETON, NJ—U.S. investors have made a number of important financial decisions in their lives, but their propensity to seek advice, and particularly professional advice, varies widely depending on the activity. Purchasing a car is the most common financial decision of five tested, but it is the one investors are the least likely to say they have done with any sort of advice. Investors are most likely to have sought advice when creating a personal financial plan, with 63% doing so, and three-quarters of these saying it was professional, as opposed to informal, advice.

U.S. Investors' Use of Advice for Various Financial Decisions

For each of the following, please tell me if it is something you have done with advice from others; something you have done, but without advice from others; or not something you have done. When you got advice, did you seek any professional advice, or only informal advice from people you know?

	Total, have done	Have done with advice^	Used professional advice^^	Used informal advice^^
	%	%	%	%
Bought a car	82	28	19	81
Planned a major vacation	80	31	23	76
Bought a house	77	39	50	48
Created a personal financial plan	76	63	74	24
Created a college savings plan	38	42	48	49

^ Based on U.S. investors (adults with $10,000 or more in investments) who have done each
^^ Based on investors who got advice for each

Wells Fargo/Gallup Investor and Retirement Optimism Index
June 27–July 9, 2014

GALLUP'

These findings are based on the Wells Fargo/Gallup Investor and Retirement Optimism Index survey conducted June 27–July 9, 2014. The survey is based on a nationally representative sample of U.S. investors with $10,000 or more in stocks, bonds, mutual funds, or self-directed IRAs or 401(k) accounts.

Roughly four in five investors have experience with most of the activities asked about in the poll. This includes 82% buying a car, 80% planning a major vacation, 77% purchasing a house, and 76%

creating a personal financial plan. The only activity that is significantly less common is creating a college savings plan—something 38% of investors say they have done.

Of those who have experience with each financial decision or activity, the percentage who have sought some sort of advice in the process ranges from 63% for creating a personal financial plan to 28% for buying a car. Close to half of investors have sought advice for creating a college savings plan, about three in 10 have sought advice for planning a major vacation, and 39% have done so for buying a house. While few investors—38%—say they have ever created a college savings plan, a relatively large proportion of those who have—42%—say they sought advice when doing so.

Separately, the poll finds a wide range of reliance on professional advice among those who have sought any type of advice for each activity. As noted, three-quarters of those who have sought advice for a personal financial plan used professional advice, as opposed to informal advice from people they know. About half of advice-seekers for buying a house and creating a college savings plan used professional advice. But the percentage goes way down for those planning a major vacation—less than a quarter (23%) of those who have sought advice sought it from a professional—as well as for buying a car (19%).

Women More Likely Than Men to Ask for Help

While men and women report similar levels of experience with most of the activities, women are more likely to say they have sought advice for three of them. The gap is especially large for purchasing a car: 22% of men versus 35% of women have sought advice when buying one. Women are also more likely than men to have sought advice when buying a house and creating a college savings plan. However, among advice-seekers, there is no difference in men's and women's likelihood of getting professional advice versus informal advice from people they know.

U.S. Investors' Financial Decisions and Use of Advice, by Gender

For each of the following, please tell me if it is something you have done with advice from others; something you have done, but without advice from others; or not something you have done.

	Men	Women
HAVE EVER DONE	%	%
Bought a car	82	84
Planned a major vacation	79	81
Bought a house	75	79
Created a personal financial plan	76	75
Created a college savings plan	42	34
HAVE DONE WITH ADVICE^	%	%
Bought a car	22	35
Planned a major vacation	32	30
Bought a house	36	43
Created a personal financial plan	61	66
Created a college savings plan	39	47

^ Based on U.S. investors (adults with $10,000 or more in investments) who have done each

Wells Fargo/Gallup Investor and Retirement Optimism Index
June 27-July 9, 2014

GALLUP'

The poll also finds that investors with $100,000 or more in investable assets are slightly more likely than those with less than $100,000 to have experience with each type of financial decision. However, the two groups are relatively similar in reporting that they sought advice for each. The only exception is that investors with less than $100,000 in investments are more likely than those with greater investments to say they have sought advice when buying a house: 45% vs. 35%.

U.S. Investors' Financial Decisions and Use of Advice, by Amount Invested

For each of the following, please tell me if it is something you have done with advice from others; something you have done, but without advice from others; or not something you have done.

	Less than $100,000	$100,000 or more
HAVE EVER DONE	%	%
Bought a car	79	84
Planned a major vacation	77	82
Bought a house	71	81
Created a personal financial plan	71	80
Created a college savings plan	35	40
HAVE DONE WITH ADVICE^	%	%
Bought a car	28	29
Planned a major vacation	28	33
Bought a house	45	35
Created a personal financial plan	61	65
Created a college savings plan	44	42

^ Based on U.S. investors (adults with $10,000 or more in investments) who have done each

Wells Fargo/Gallup Investor and Retirement Optimism Index
June 27-July 9, 2014

GALLUP'

Bottom Line

Even if it costs something, seeking professional advice for major financial decisions can be a great strategy if the advice saves or makes one money in the long run. But more often than not, U.S. investors seek advice informally from friends and family, or get no advice.

The one major exception to this is when creating a personal financial plan. Three-quarters of investors (76%) report having created a personal financial plan at some point. Of those who did, 63% say they sought advice from others—and among those who sought advice, roughly three-quarters (74%) say they sought professional advice. This is much higher than the percentage of advice-seekers who sought professional advice when buying a car (19%), planning a major vacation (23%), buying a house (50%), or even creating a college savings plan (48%).

Higher proportions of investors have made some of these other major financial decisions than have created a financial plan, but none of these decisions is nearly as likely to compel investors to seek professional advice. Whether this is because of the perceived complexity of planning out one's finances, because of the importance of it, or because of the amount of money involved isn't clear.

Survey Methods

These findings are part of the Wells Fargo/Gallup Investor and Retirement Optimism Index survey, conducted June 27–July 9,

2014, by telephone. The sample included 1,036 investors, aged 18 and older, living in all 50 states and the District of Columbia. For this study, the American investor is defined as any person or spouse in a household with total savings and investments of $10,000 or more. About two in five American households have at least $10,000 in savings and investments in stocks, bonds, mutual funds, or self-directed IRAs or 401(k) accounts. The sample consists of 72% non-retired investors and 28% retired investors.

Questions about investors' use of professional advice were asked of a random half-sample of 509 U.S. investors. The margin of sampling error for these results is ±5 percentage points at the 95% confidence level.

September 15, 2014
AMERICANS' TRUST IN EXECUTIVE, LEGISLATIVE BRANCHES DOWN
Trust in all branches of federal government at or near record lows

by Jeffrey M. Jones

PRINCETON, NJ—Americans' trust in each of the three branches of the federal government is at or near the lows in Gallup's trends, dating back to the early 1970s. Americans' trust in the legislative branch fell six percentage points this year to a new low of 28%. Trust in the executive branch dropped eight points, to 43%, and trust in the judicial branch, at 61%, is also the lowest measured to date.

Americans' Trust in the Three Branches of the Federal Government

Figures represent the percentage with a "great deal" or "fair amount" of trust in the branch

GALLUP

The data are part of Gallup's annual update on trust in government, conducted in the Sept. 4–7 Governance poll. Gallup previously documented that Americans' trust in the federal government to handle both domestic and international problems slid to new lows this year.

Americans have generally had the least trust in the legislative branch, consisting of the House of Representatives and the Senate, but never lower than the 28% who do so now. The prior low was the 31% measured in 2011, shortly after Congress and the president engaged in contentious debt-ceiling negotiations.

Trust in the legislative branch had recovered slightly during the previous two years, to 34%, but is down significantly this year. As recently as 2007, 50% of Americans trusted Congress, but that trust has eroded amid a struggling economy and an era of intense partisan gridlock. This has been particularly acute since Congress was divided between a Republican House and a Democratic Senate after the 2010 elections.

After a sharp drop from last year, trust in the executive branch is the lowest it has been during President Barack Obama's tenure, at 43%. The historical low of 40% was measured in April 1974, months before Richard Nixon resigned amid the Watergate scandal. Trust in the executive branch was also in the low 40s during the last two years of George W. Bush's presidency.

Americans' trust in the executive branch has surpassed 70% on two occasions in Gallup's trend—in 1972, the year Nixon was re-elected in a landslide, and in 2002 under Bush, shortly after the 9/11 terrorist attacks. The high during Obama's presidency so far is 61%, measured during his first year in office.

Trust in the judicial branch has usually been higher on a relative basis than trust in the other branches of the federal government, and remains so. Although essentially the same as last year's 62%, the 61% who trust the judicial branch this year is the lowest to date. Trust in the judicial branch generally exceeded 70% in the late 1990s and early 2000s, and was in the high 60% range for much of the period from 2003 to 2012.

Republicans and Democrats Differ in Trust in Executive Branch, Similar on Legislative

Republicans (35%) and Democrats (31%) exhibit similarly low trust in the legislative branch, with independents even less trusting at 23%. There has been a relatively narrow Republican-Democratic gap in trust in Congress, averaging six points, since party control of the Senate and the House became divided in 2011.

Prior to that, Democrats showed greater trust in the legislature when the Democratic Party held the majority of both houses from 2007 to 2010, with an average 24-point higher trust rating than Republicans. Republicans, likewise, exhibited far greater trust in Congress than Democrats when the GOP had control of Congress prior to 2007, with an average 11-point gap from 2004 to 2006.

Recent Trend in Trust in the Legislative Branch of the Federal Government, by Political Party

Figures represent the percentage with a "great deal" or "fair amount" of trust in the branch

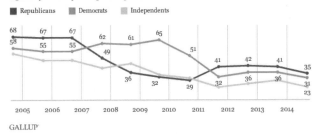

GALLUP

After the Republican Party gained control of the House in 2011, Republicans' trust in the legislative branch increased in comparison to what it was under Democratic control of both houses from 2007 to 2010. But both Republicans' and Democrats' trust in the legislative branch is far lower under the divided Congress than it was when their respective parties held full control of Congress.

Americans' trust in the executive branch seems to be influenced mostly by the party of the president, at least for those with a party preference. Currently, 83% of Democrats and 13% of Republicans say they have a great deal or fair amount of trust in the executive branch at a time when a Democrat resides in the White House. Independents' trust (37%) is currently closer to the level of Republicans than of Democrats. When Republican Bush was president, a similar partisan division was seen, with the trust levels of the parties reversed.

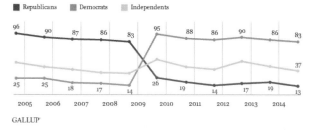

Recent Trend in Trust in the Executive Branch of the Federal Government, by Political Party
Figures represent the percentage with a "great deal" or "fair amount" of trust in the branch

■ Republicans ■ Democrats ■ Independents

GALLUP

Trust in the judicial branch currently shows modest partisan variation, with 67% of Democrats and 59% of Republicans saying they trust it. Independents' trust is also 59%. When there have been party differences in trust in the federal judiciary in the past, those who identify with the president's party have typically expressed greater trust.

Implications

Americans' trust in the three branches of the federal government is collectively lower than at any point in the last two decades. Although trust in the executive branch was lower during the Watergate era, the erosion of trust at that time was limited to that branch. Today, less than a majority trust the executive and legislative branches, and judicial trust, though still high on a relative basis, is the lowest Gallup has measured.

The frustration with government is also evident in near-historical-low job approval ratings for Congress, below-average job approval ratings for Obama, and Americans' consistently ranking the government itself as one of the most important problems facing the country.

U.S. voters will have a chance to alter the balance of power in Congress in the midterm elections, which could in theory affect their level of trust in the government more generally. However, it is not clear how much the government will change once the elections are over. Republicans are expected to keep majority control of the House, meaning there will be some form of divided government for Obama's last two years, regardless of which party wins control of the Senate.

Survey Methods

Results for this Gallup poll are based on telephone interviews conducted Sept. 4–7, 2014, with a random sample of 1,017 adults, aged 18 and older, living in all 50 U.S. states and the District of Columbia.

For results based on the total sample of national adults, the margin of sampling error is ±4 percentage points at the 95% confidence level.

September 15, 2014
FEW AMERICANS WANT MORE GOV'T REGULATION OF BUSINESS
About half say there is too much regulation; 22% say there is too little

by Frank Newport

PRINCETON, NJ—Less than one quarter of Americans (22%) say there is too little government regulation of business and industry, while about half (49%) say there is too much regulation.

An additional 27% say the level of regulation is about right. These attitudes have been consistent over the past five years. Prior to that, the percentage who said there was too much regulation rose between 2008 and 2010.

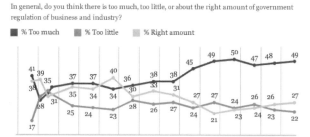

Americans' Overall Perceptions on Government Regulation of Business
In general, do you think there is too much, too little, or about the right amount of government regulation of business and industry?

■ % Too much ■ % Too little ■ % Right amount

GALLUP

The latest data are from Gallup's annual Governance survey, conducted Sept. 4–7. The Governance poll this year shows general declines in Americans' trust in all three branches of government, and a dip in Americans' trust in the federal government to handle domestic and international problems.

Gallup has been tracking attitudes toward government regulation of business annually since 2001. The low point in the perception that there was too much regulation came in 2002, the year after the 9/11 terrorist attacks. This reflected a "rally effect," in which Americans became more positive about all aspects of government, including record-high job approval ratings of the president and Congress. In fact, the only times that a higher percentage of Americans said there was too little rather than too much government regulation of business were in February and June 2002, the first two times Gallup asked this question after 9/11.

From 2003 through the remainder of the George W. Bush administration, however, these attitudes settled into a pattern in which Americans were more likely to say there was too much rather than too little government regulation of business. After Barack Obama took office in 2009, the percentage saying "too much" regulation rose into the high 40s, including a reading of 50% in 2011, and has remained at these relatively high levels since.

Less than a quarter of Americans have perceived in the last two years that there is too little government regulation of business and industry, while slightly more have said regulation is about right.

Partisan Gap in Views of Regulation Wider Than Before Obama Took Office

As is the case with most attitudes about government and government use of power, Republicans and Democrats have sharply differing views on government regulation of business. About three-quarters of Republicans (76%) say there is too much regulation, compared with less than one quarter (22%) of Democrats.

The rise in the overall percentage of Americans who say there is too much regulation of business is driven in large part by Republicans' views in the years since Obama took office. The percentage of Republicans saying "too much" rose from the 40% to 50% range under Bush to as high as 84% in 2011, then dropping to the current 76%. Democrats' views have been much more stable across the Bush and Obama administrations to date, but are, on average, slightly lower under Obama than under Bush, 23% vs. 28%, respectively.

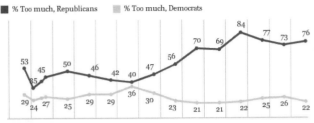

Americans' Views on Government Regulation of Business, by Party

In general, do you think there is too much, too little, or about the right amount of government regulation of business and industry?

■ % Too much, Republicans   ▨ % Too much, Democrats

84 77 73 76
70 69
56
53 50 47
45 46 42 40
36
35   30
29   27 25 29 29   23 21 21 22 25 26 22
24

2001 2002 2003 2004 2005 2006 2007 2008 2009 2010 2011 2012 2013 2014

GALLUP

Given that these trends stretch back to 2001 and there are data for only one Republican and one Democratic presidential administration, it is not clear whether Republicans' shift toward "too much" regulation is unique to their views of regulations under the Obama administration, or would be apparent for Republicans under any Democratic president.

The majority of Democrats who don't think there is too much regulation are split between the "about right" (35%) and "too little" responses (39%).

Implications

A number of Americans view the federal government negatively, and it's likely that for many in this group, their negative perceptions of government regulation of business at least partially reflect their doubts that government's getting more involved in such endeavors would produce positive outcomes.

Americans' interest in having more government regulation of business and industry did not increase after the recession began in 2008, even though that economic meltdown was caused in large part by mortgage companies and banks engaging in what turned out to be disastrous mortgage lending and mortgage buying and selling practices. Government did step in during the recession under both Presidents Bush and Obama, taking a number of extraordinary actions that many have credited as helping stave off even worse consequences for the banking industry, the housing industry, the automotive industry, and the economy more broadly.

The Dodd-Frank bill was passed by Congress and signed into law by the president in July 2010, largely in response to the recession, and was one of the most far-reaching financial regulatory pieces of legislation in U.S. history. Yet even as these actions were taken and this legislation passed, Americans didn't become more likely to say the amount of government regulation was about right, but instead increasingly said there was too much regulation. This may have reflected Republicans' views that Dodd-Frank and other actions went too far, or it could have been a more general reaction to having a Democrat in the White House. Whatever the reason, it is clear that the financial upheaval caused by the recession did not result and has not resulted in a significant jump in the number of Americans who say there is too little government regulation of business.

Gallup recently found a record-high percentage of Americans saying "big government" is a greater threat to the U.S. than big business or big labor. Thus, even though Americans don't have a great deal of confidence in "big business" as an institution, they have even less in big government, and express little desire for the latter to become more involved in regulating the former.

Survey Methods

Results for this Gallup poll are based on telephone interviews conducted Sept. 4–7, 2014, with a random sample of 1,017 adults, aged 18 and older, living in all 50 U.S. states and the District of Columbia.

For results based on the total sample of national adults, the margin of sampling error is ±4 percentage points at the 95% confidence level.

September 16, 2014
THOUGH INSURED, MANY U.S. ASIANS LACK A PERSONAL DOCTOR
Hispanics are the least likely to have a personal doctor

by Diana Liu and Lindsey Sharpe

WASHINGTON, D.C.—In the U.S., Hispanic and Asian adults are significantly less likely than white and black adults to report having a personal doctor. While Hispanics' lower rates of having health insurance can partially explain their lower rates of having a personal doctor, Asians are among the groups most likely to have health insurance.

Personal Doctor and Health Insurance Coverage, by Race

Do you have _____?

	Personal doctor (%)	Health insurance (%)	Difference (pct. pts.)
White	84	90	6
Black	76	84	8
Asian	64	89	25
Hispanic	57	65	8

Gallup-Healthways Well-Being Index
Jan. 2-Aug. 10, 2014

GALLUP

Further illustrating the varying degree to which having health insurance is related to having a personal doctor for Asians and Hispanics, Gallup finds that more than three-quarters of Asians (78%) who lack a personal doctor are insured vs. 35% of Hispanics who lack a personal doctor. This pattern has been consistent since Gallup and Healthways began tracking these measures in 2008.

These data, collected as part of the Gallup-Healthways Well-Being Index, are based on respondents' self-reports of personal doctor and health insurance status based on the questions, "Do you have a personal doctor?" and "Do you have health insurance coverage?"

One possible reason why Asians, despite being among the groups most likely to be insured, are less likely to have a personal doctor is because they are, on average, healthier. Previous Gallup research has found that Asians are the least likely racial and ethnic group to say they have been diagnosed with chronic health conditions such as high blood pressure, high cholesterol, depression, asthma, diabetes, cancer, and heart attack. However, it is also possible that Asians are less likely to say they have been diagnosed with these conditions because they lack a personal doctor who would make such a diagnosis in the first place. Independent of conditions that may be diagnosed by a doctor, Asians are also less likely than other racial and ethnic groups to be obese and to smoke.

The gap between the percentage of Asians who have health insurance and the percentage who have a personal doctor has been much higher than among other racial and ethnic groups in every year since 2008. Asians' self-reports of having a personal doctor has gradually decreased over the past seven years, even as their rate of having health insurance has remained steady or increased. The gap between Asians who have health insurance and Asians who have a personal doctor has increased significantly in 2014 to date, to 25 percentage points.

Personal Doctor and Health Insurance Coverage Over Time, Asians

Do you have _____?

	Personal doctor (%)	Health insurance (%)	Difference (pct. pts.)
2008	71	89	18
2009	71	86	15
2010	70	89	19
2011	66	84	18
2012	66	83	17
2013	65	86	21
2014	64	89	25

Gallup-Healthways Well-Being Index
Jan. 2, 2008-Aug. 10, 2014

GALLUP

On the other hand, Hispanics' self-reports of having a personal doctor and having health insurance have generally increased since 2012. Over the same time period, the gap between Hispanics with health insurance and Hispanics with a personal doctor increased, indicating that they are purchasing health insurance at faster rate than they are finding a personal doctor.

Personal Doctor and Health Insurance Coverage Over Time, Hispanics

Do you have _____?

	Personal doctor (%)	Health insurance (%)	Difference (pct. pts.)
2008	55	62	7
2009	55	60	5
2010	56	61	5
2011	55	58	3
2012	53	59	6
2013	55	60	5
2014	57	65	8

Gallup-Healthways Well-Being Index
Jan. 2, 2008-Aug. 10, 2014

GALLUP

Both Asian and Hispanic Americans may have cultural and logistical barriers that decrease their likelihood of having a personal doctor. Both cultures have a long history of preferring non-Western medicine, which may lead to reluctance in accepting American healthcare and selecting a personal doctor. Asians, particularly those from China, believe in traditional Chinese medicine, which relies more heavily on acupuncture and herbal remedies. Similarly, Hispanics often utilize herb-based treatments to treat common ailments.

Logistical barriers may also exist, such as language. Particularly for the older generations, learning English medical terms and communicating with a doctor or health insurance company can prove challenging. Culture shock and unfamiliar reservation systems might also reduce their likelihood of seeking out personal doctors.

Finally, it is possible that Asians may actually see doctors often, but instead of having a "personal doctor" as asked in the question, they use storefront clinics, emergency rooms, or other ways of accessing healthcare on an ad hoc basis.

Older, High-Income, Married Are Most Likely to Have Personal Doctor

Older Asians and Hispanics are more likely to have a personal doctor than are those who are younger. Among those who are 65 years and older, 86% of Hispanics and 91% of Asians have a personal doctor. Further, the percentage who have a personal doctor increases steadily with age for both groups.

As income levels increase, both Asian and Hispanic adults become more likely to have a personal doctor. Within the highest income group, about 80% of both Asians and Hispanics say that they have a personal doctor. The likelihood of having a personal doctor also increases among those who are married in both groups—61% of married Hispanics report having a personal doctor, and 79% of Asians who are married do the same.

Hispanics with children in their household are less likely to have a personal doctor (50%) than those who do not have kids at home (62%). Conversely, Asians with children in the home are more likely to have a personal doctor than those who do not, 73% vs. 64%, respectively.

Personal Doctor Among Hispanics and Asians by Demographics, 2008-2014

Do you have a personal doctor?

	Hispanic (% yes)	Asian (% yes)
AGE		
18-29	44	53
30-44	51	73
45-64	67	84
65+	86	91
ANNUAL HOUSEHOLD INCOME		
Less than $36,000	44	51
$36,000-$90,000	61	66
$90,000 and above	81	80
MARITAL STATUS		
Married	61	79
Unmarried	50	58
KIDS IN HOUSEHOLD		
No kids	62	64
Have kids	50	73

Gallup-Healthways Well-Being Index
Jan. 2, 2008-Aug. 10, 2014

GALLUP

Income Boosts the Likelihood of Having Personal Doctors for Hispanics With Kids at Home

For Hispanics with children in the household, income may be the determining factor behind the lower percentage who have a personal doctor compared with those who do not have children in the home. Within the lowest income group, those who do not have kids are

15 percentage points more likely to have a personal doctor. Most likely those with children in the home are spending their income on items necessary for child rearing. Among the highest income group, however, there is no difference in the percentage who report having a personal doctor between those who do and do not have children at home.

Personal Doctor Among Hispanics by Income, 2008-2014

Do you have a personal doctor?

ANNUAL HOUSEHOLD INCOME	No kids (% yes)	Kids in household (yes)	Difference (pct. pts.)
Less than $36,000	53	38	15
$36,000-$90,000	65	57	8
$90,000 and above	81	81	0

Gallup-Healthways Well-Being Index
Jan. 2, 2008-Aug. 10, 2014

GALLUP'

Implications

One of the main objectives of the Affordable Care Act is to increase the percentage of the population with health insurance, which in turn could be expected to increase access to healthcare. The increasing gap between the percentage who are insured and those who have a personal doctor for both Asians and Hispanics suggests that factors other than health insurance—including income, having children, and cultural and logistical barriers—may play a role in increasing access to care.

Understanding the factors that decrease the likelihood of having a personal doctor, beyond insurance and income, for Asians and Hispanics is important. Gallup research shows that the majority of Americans with personal doctors have conversations with them about preventative care and healthy behaviors, including exercise, eating healthy, and not smoking. This is particularly important among those with lower incomes, as those in poverty are more likely to suffer from chronic disease.

Removing known barriers to having a personal doctor may help increase access to care. One potential approach is to provide current U.S. personal doctors with more resources and connections to various Asian and Hispanic treatments, like Chinese acupuncture clinics, for example, and for insurance companies to cover such services.

To decrease logistical barriers to finding a personal doctor, medical communities, insurers, and local governments might partner to create online healthcare communities that offer advice to Asians and Hispanics. This type of community might also increase familiarity with the healthcare system and support doctor-patient relationships. To overcome language barriers, communities and medical associations could consider recruiting Chinese or Spanish translators as volunteers to help non-English speakers communicate with their personal doctors. Further, areas with larger Hispanic or Asian populations could seek to hire doctors who are bilingual.

Finally, governments and communities could also partner with medical care facilities to create solutions specifically aimed at ensuring that low-income families, particularly Hispanics with children, are able to find personal doctors. Information about programs could be posted in both Spanish and English within communities.

Survey Methods

Results are based on telephone interviews conducted as part of the Gallup-Healthways Well-Being Index survey Jan. 2, 2014–Aug. 10, 2014, with a random sample of 108,440 adults, including 9,669 and 2,299 self-identified Hispanics and Asians respectively, aged 18 and older, living in all 50 U.S. states and the District of Columbia.

For results based on the total sample of national adults, the margin of sampling error is ±0.09 percentage points at the 95% confidence level.

September 16, 2014
U.S. ECONOMIC CONFIDENCE INDEX REMAINS ON PLATEAU
Index has hovered around –16 since early August

by Rebecca Riffkin

WASHINGTON, D.C.—Gallup's U.S. Economic Confidence Index measured –16 for the week ending Sept. 14, 2014. The index has stayed within one point of –16 for the past seven weeks.

Gallup's Economic Confidence Index -- Weekly Averages for the Past 12 Months
Latest results for week ending Sept. 14, 2014

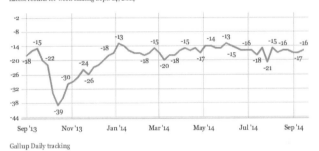

Gallup Daily tracking

GALLUP'

The index has been –20 or lower only twice so far in 2014: in early March and again for a week in late July. It quickly recovered both times, reaching the –16 and –15 scores seen throughout 2014 within a few weeks of each dip. The average weekly index for 2014 is –16, the same as the most recent weekly index.

Economic Confidence Index Components -- Weekly Averages for the Past 12 Months
Latest results for week ending Sept. 14, 2014

■ Current conditions   ▨ Economic outlook

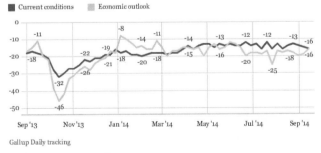

Gallup Daily tracking

GALLUP'

Gallup's Economic Confidence Index is the average of two components: Americans' views of current economic conditions and their opinions on whether the economy is getting better or worse. For the week ending Sept. 14, 19% of Americans said the economy was "excellent" or "good," while 35% said the economy was "poor." This resulted in a current conditions index score of −16, compared with −15 the week before.

Gallup's economic outlook score improved slightly. While 39% of Americans said the economy was "getting better," 55% said it was "getting worse." This resulted in an economic outlook score of −16, up from −19 the week prior.

Bottom Line

While economic confidence remains stable in the U.S., the current level is a noticeable improvement over the scores in the −40s and −50s seen through much of 2009 until 2011. The index has stayed within an eight-point range so far in 2014. This lack of variation between weekly index scores is unusual compared with prior years. Last year, weekly scores were within a 31-point range from January through September—from a high of −3 in May to a low of −34 in the last week of September. And in 2009, in the depths of the recession, scores were within a 39-point range between January and the end of September, dropping to a low of −59 for two weeks in February but reaching a high of −20 in the second-to-last week of September.

The more stable economic confidence scores in 2014 are an improvement from the drastic drops seen in previous years, but also indicate that confidence is not growing. Americans remain more negative than positive about the current economy, and most think the economy will get worse in the future, indicating that Americans' pessimistic views of the economy persist.

Survey Methods

Results for this Gallup poll are based on telephone interviews conducted Sept. 8–14, 2014, on the Gallup Daily tracking survey, with a random sample of 3,532 adults, aged 18 and older, living in all 50 U.S. states and the District of Columbia.

For results based on the total sample of national adults, the margin of sampling error is ±2 percentage points at the 95% confidence level.

September 17, 2014
TRUST IN MASS MEDIA RETURNS TO ALL-TIME LOW
Six-percentage-point drops in trust among
Democrats and Republicans

by Justin McCarthy

WASHINGTON, D.C.—After registering slightly higher trust last year, Americans' confidence in the media's ability to report "the news fully, accurately, and fairly" has returned to its previous all-time low of 40%. Americans' trust in mass media has generally been edging downward from higher levels in the late 1990s and the early 2000s.

Prior to 2004, Americans placed more trust in mass media than they do now, with slim majorities saying they had a "great deal" or "fair amount" of trust. But over the course of former President George W. Bush's re-election season, the level of trust fell significantly, from 54% in 2003 to 44% in 2004. Although trust levels

rebounded to 50% in 2005, they have failed to reach a full majority since.

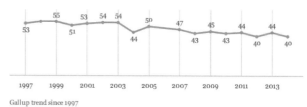

Americans' Trust in the Mass Media

In general, how much trust and confidence do you have in the mass media -- such as newspapers, TV, and radio -- when it comes to reporting the news fully, accurately, and fairly -- a great deal, a fair amount, not very much, or none at all?

■ % Great deal/Fair amount

Gallup trend since 1997

GALLUP

Americans' trust in the media in recent years has dropped slightly in election years, including 2008, 2010, 2012, and again this year—only to edge its way back up again in the following odd-numbered years. Although the differences between the drops and the recoveries are not large, they suggest that something about national elections triggers skepticism about the accuracy of the news media's reporting.

Among Democrats, Trust in Media at a 14-Year Low

Trust among Democrats, who have traditionally expressed much higher levels of confidence in the media than Republicans have, dropped to a 14-year low of 54% in 2014. Republicans' trust in the media is at 27%, one percentage point above their all-time low, while independents held steady at 38%—up one point from 37% in 2013.

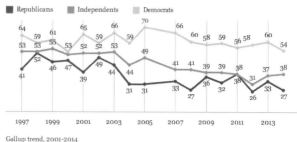

Trust in Mass Media, by Party

% Great deal/Fair amount of trust

■ Republicans ■ Independents ▨ Democrats

Gallup trend. 2001-2014

GALLUP

Sharp Uptick in Americans Who Think News Media Are "Too Conservative"

As has been the case historically, Americans are most likely to feel the news media are "too liberal" (44%) rather than "too conservative," though this perceived liberal bias is now on the lower side of the trend. One in three (34%) say the media are "just about right" in terms of their coverage—down slightly from 37% last year.

Nearly one in five Americans (19%) say the media are too conservative, which is still relatively low, but the highest such percentage since 2006. This is up six points from 2013—the sharpest increase in the percentage of Americans who feel the news skews too far right since Gallup began asking the question in 2001.

Americans' Perceptions of Media Bias

In general, do you think the news media are -- [ROTATED: too liberal, just about right, or too conservative]?

■ % Too liberal   ■ % Just about right   ▨ % Too conservative

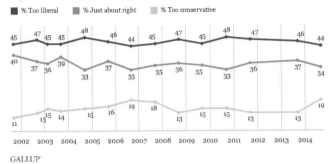

GALLUP'

Conservatives (70%) are far more likely than liberals (15%) to perceive the media as too liberal. Moderates' views are closer to liberals, with 35% calling the media too liberal. Likewise, relatively few moderates—similar to conservatives—think the media are too conservative.

Democrats—with a small majority of 52%—are most likely to think the media are just about right, while a mere 18% of Republicans feel this way about the news. More than seven in 10 Republicans say the media are too liberal.

Perceptions of Media Bias, by Party and Ideology

	% Too liberal	% Just about right	% Too conservative
Democrats	20	52	24
Independents	42	33	21
Republicans	71	18	9
Liberals	15	49	33
Moderates	35	44	18
Conservatives	70	16	12

Sept. 4-7, 2014

GALLUP'

Bottom Line

Though a sizable percentage of Americans continue to have a great deal or fair amount of trust in the media, Americans' overall trust in the Fourth Estate continues to be significantly lower now than it was 10 to 15 years ago.

As the media expand into new domains of news reporting via social media networks and new mobile technology, Americans may be growing disenchanted with what they consider "mainstream" news as they seek out their own personal veins of getting information. At the same time, confidence is down across many institutions, and a general lack in trust overall could be at play.

Americans' opinions about the media appear affected in election years, however. Americans' trust in the media will likely recover slightly in 2015 with the absence of political campaigns. But the overarching pattern of the past decade has shown few signs of slowing the decline of faith in mass media as a whole.

Survey Methods

Results for this Gallup poll are based on telephone interviews conducted Sept. 4–7, 2014, with a random sample of 1,017 adults, aged 18 and older, living in all 50 U.S. states and the District of Columbia.

For results based on the total sample of national adults, the margin of sampling error is ±4 percentage points at the 95% confidence level.

September 17, 2014

AMERICANS SAY FEDERAL GOV'T WASTES 51 CENTS ON THE DOLLAR
Consider state and local governments a bit less wasteful

by Rebecca Riffkin

WASHINGTON, D.C.—Americans estimate that the federal government wastes 51 cents of each tax dollar. This matches their prior estimate in 2011, which was the highest Gallup had measured since 1979. Americans are less harsh about their state and local governments, viewing them as wasting 42 cents and 37 cents, respectively.

Americans Say the Federal Government Wastes More of Each Tax Dollar Than They Say State and Local Governments Waste

How many cents of each tax dollar would you say are wasted?

■ Cents wasted by the federal government (mean)   ■ Cents wasted by state government (mean)
■ Cents wasted by local government (mean)

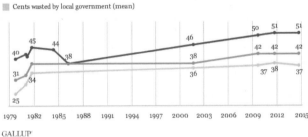

GALLUP'

When Gallup first asked the question in 1979, Americans estimated that the federal government wasted 40 cents of every dollar, their state government wasted 31 cents, and their local government wasted 25 cents. Those are the lowest figures for state and local levels of government in any year since, while the lowest waste estimate for federal spending was a slightly lower 38 cents in a 1986 survey.

Gallup didn't ask these questions during the next decade, but when it next asked them in 2001, the "wasted cents" estimates were roughly in line with those in the 1980s. Since 2001, however, the proportion of the tax dollar Americans say the federal and state governments waste has increased, while the estimate for local governments has remained roughly the same.

Americans historically have always seen local governments as wasting the lowest proportion of each dollar, while seeing the federal government as wasting the most. This is consistent with Gallup research showing that Americans' trust in state and local governments is significantly higher than their trust in the executive and legislative branches of the federal government.

Republicans More Likely Than Democrats to See More Waste in Federal Government

Republicans' average government waste estimates are higher than Democrats' and independents' for all three levels of government, although the gap is particularly wide with respect to federal tax dollars. These gaps are much narrower at the local and state levels.

Views of Tax Dollars Wasted, by Americans' Party Identification

	Republicans	Independents	Democrats
Mean federal taxes wasted (cents per dollar)	59	51	42
Mean state taxes wasted (cents per dollar)	44	42	39
Mean local taxes wasted (cents per dollar)	39	37	35

Mean includes responses that zero cents are wasted
Sept. 4-7, 2014

GALLUP

Bottom Line

Most Americans are currently not satisfied with the way things are going in the country, and approval of government bodies, such as Congress, continues to be close to all-time lows. Americans' views that half of federal tax dollars are wasted underscore this lack of confidence in and satisfaction with the federal government. State and local governments fare better, but their perceived waste is still more than one-third of each dollar. Even Democrats, who have higher trust in government than independents and Republicans, see all levels of government as wasting at least 35 cents per dollar.

Congress is in the process of passing a new budget bill, which it failed to do this time last year, causing the partial government shutdown, which lasted several weeks. Although Americans see a lot of waste in government, it is unclear if they feel this is from wasteful programs, or if they feel the government spends too much on things that don't deserve funding to begin with.

Past polling, however, has found that a majority of Americans oppose funding cuts to almost all programs Gallup has asked about. So while Americans say the federal government wastes large amounts of tax dollars, they are also unwilling to cut funding to many programs. Americans do seem to feel the government generally needs to rein in its spending and do a better job of spending tax dollars wisely.

Survey Methods

Results for this Gallup poll are based on telephone interviews conducted Sept. 4–7, 2014, on the Gallup Daily tracking survey, with a random sample of 1,017 adults, aged 18 and older, living in all 50 U.S. states and the District of Columbia.

For results based on the total sample of national adults, the margin of sampling error is ±4 percentage points at the 95% confidence level.

September 17, 2014
BLACK COLLEGE GRADS MORE LIKELY TO GRADUATE WITH DEBT
Black graduates have lower levels of well-being than other college graduates

by Andrew Dugan & Scott Vanderbilt

WASHINGTON, D.C.—Half of 2000–2014 black college graduates in the U.S. report graduating with more than $25,000 in undergraduate student loan debt. By comparison, 34% of recent white graduates report similar levels of debt, revealing a large borrowing gap between the races.

Undergraduate Student Loan Debt, by Race: 2000-2014 Graduates

Approximately how much money did you borrow in student loans to obtain your undergraduate degree?

	2000-2014
	%
BLACKS	
No loans	22
$1-$25,000	28
More than $25,000	50
WHITES	
No loans	39
$1-$25,000	28
More than $25,000	34
TOTAL	
No loans	37
$1-$25,000	28
More than $25,000	35

Feb. 4- March 7, 2014
Figures adjusted for inflation in 2014 dollars

GALLUP

In total, just over a fifth of recent black college graduates (22%) report leaving school with no debt, about half the rate among white college graduates (39%). About three in 10 recent black college graduates (28%) and the same percentage of whites say they borrowed up to $25,000. Overall, 35% of 2000–2014 U.S. college graduates report graduating with more than $25,000 in student debt, in inflation-adjusted dollars.

These results are based on the inaugural Gallup-Purdue Index, a joint research effort with Purdue University and Lumina Foundation to study the relationship between the college experience and college graduates' lives. The Gallup-Purdue Index is a comprehensive, nationally representative study of U.S. college graduates with Internet access, conducted Feb. 4–March 7, 2014. According to a 2013 Census Bureau report, 90% of college graduates in the U.S. have access to the Internet.

The student loan debt figures on which this analysis is based are reported by those responding to the survey and are adjusted for inflation to today's dollars. Figures only apply to undergraduate student loan debt. Gallup did not ask respondents about the current status of their student debt or how much of their loan they had repaid at the time of the interview.

Racial Borrowing Gap for Recent Grads
Nearly as Wide as in Past

Mirroring the overall population of college graduates, black college graduates have increasingly relied on at least some student loans to finance their education. Less than half (48%) of blacks who graduated from college in the 1970s say they took on student loan debt to obtain their undergraduate degree, but this grew to 63% for graduates in the 1980s, 67% in the 1990s, and 78% for the 2000–2014 cohort.

While there has also been a concurrent rise in the amount of undergraduate debt for whites as well as blacks, the gap between white and black college graduates has remained roughly the same over the timespan, at nearly 20 percentage points. Recent black college graduates are 17 points more likely to have graduated with student loan debt than white college graduates, close to the differences that existed between white and black college graduates in the 1970s (20 points), 1980s (20 points), and 1990s (17 points).

Borrowing Gap Between the Races

Percentage of college graduates with student loan debt of any amount

	Whites	Blacks	Gap
	%	%	(pct. pts.)
2000-2014	61	78	-17
1990-1999	50	67	-17
1980-1989	43	63	-20
1970-1979	28	48	-20

Feb. 4-March 7, 2014

GALLUP

Many black college graduates are "first-generation" college graduates—meaning neither parent graduated from college with an undergraduate degree. Nearly three in five black college graduates (58%) report being first-generation graduates, whereas 44% of white graduates say the same.

First-Generation College Graduate, by Race and Time

% First generation (neither parent graduated from college)

	1970-1979	1980-1989	1990-1999	2000-2014	Total
	%	%	%	%	%
Whites	58	47	43	37	44
Blacks	77	68	59	48	58
Total	60	49	45	40	46

Feb. 4-March 7, 2014

GALLUP

But college is fast becoming an expectation in many black families, with larger percentages of black college graduates saying they were *not* the first in their family to graduate college. Less than half of black college graduates say they are first-generation graduates (48%), down from 77% in the 1970s. Given the known relationship between a college education and increased earning power, it might seem puzzling that even as more blacks graduate college and come from college-educated families, the need for college tuition borrowing has not declined. In fact, borrowing has increased—78% of recent black college graduates report that they borrowed for their undergraduate education, compared with 49% of their 1970s counterparts.

On one hand, this dynamic is not exclusive to black college graduates. Recent white college graduates report borrowing at higher rates and levels than their 1970s antecedents, even though just over a third are first-generation graduates (37%). The cost of tuition has, on average, risen over time, and this has forced many households to take on college-related debt.

Then there is the larger issue of the income and wealth gap between the races that has failed to close, according to several studies. Indeed, a 2011 study by the Center on Education and the Workforce at Georgetown University showed that even when educational attainment is the same between whites and blacks, blacks consistently earn less. This could help create a vicious cycle for many black graduates whereby they are compelled by economic necessity

to take on student debt when they attend college and then subsequently spend a substantial period of their professional life paying down this debt, minimizing the ability to save for a child's college education.

Less Than a Fifth of Recent Black College Graduates Thrive Financially

Previous Gallup-Purdue Index research looking at 1990–2014 college graduates reveals that the more student debt a graduate has, the lower his or her likelihood of thriving in four of the five elements of well-being—purpose, financial, community, and physical.

Consistent with those findings, recent black college graduates, with their significant probability of carrying more than $25,000 in debt, also show lower rates of well-being compared with all other recent college graduates, particularly in the area of financial well-being. Fewer than one in five 2000–2014 black college graduates (17%) are classified as thriving in the area of financial well-being, compared with 31% of 2000–2014 white college graduates and 29% of all college graduates during this time period.

Recent black college graduates also trail in purpose well-being—defined as liking what you do each day and being motivated to achieve your goals. About a third of recent black college graduates (34%) are thriving in this area, compared with 43% of recent white graduates. In community well-being—liking where you live, feeling safe, and having pride in your community—recent black college graduates are again less likely to be thriving compared with whites, by a gap of 12 percentage points.

Well-Being Among College Graduates, by Race and Time

% Thriving

	Purpose	Social	Financial	Community	Physical
	%	%	%	%	%
2000-2014					
Whites	43	45	31	39	28
Blacks	34	44	17	27	25
All graduates	42	45	29	38	28
1990-1999					
Whites	50	44	41	45	34
Blacks	42	40	33	41	28
All graduates	50	44	40	45	33
1980-1989					
Whites	53	46	44	48	38
Blacks	45	56	40	36	30
All graduates	53	48	44	47	38
1970-1979					
Whites	62	53	53	52	41
Blacks	64	52	42	48	37
All graduates	62	53	53	53	41
Total (all years)					
Whites	50	46	40	45	34
Blacks	41	46	28	35	28
All graduates	49	47	38	44	33

Feb. 4-March 7, 2014

GALLUP

These well-being disparities are apparent to some degree among graduates of earlier eras, particularly in the element of financial well-being. Black college graduates of every decade are less likely to be thriving financially than white graduates in the same decade. For 1980s and 1990s graduates, as well as more recent graduates, there is also a sharp gulf between the races in purpose well-being, with whites more likely to be thriving. Discrepancies in physical well-being are witnessed for every cohort studied.

This is not to suggest that these lower levels of well-being can be explained solely by the fact that black college graduates borrow at higher rates than other graduates do. Many variables may contribute to these observed differences in well-being between these two similarly educated groups—including, but not limited to, the income gap between the races as well as discrimination against black Americans. But these findings are significant in that they reveal well-being differences between the races even among college graduates, a segment of the population that has achieved the same propitious milestone in life—namely, a college degree.

Bottom Line

Even as an increasing percentage of black Americans graduate from college—often, the first in their family to do so—they remain more likely to need to borrow to finance their undergraduate education, and the borrowing gap between the races has stayed, in percentage-point terms, about as wide for 2000–2014 graduates as in earlier decades. Over half of recent black college graduates acquired more than $25,000 of student debt—a concerning statistic, given previous Gallup findings showing a link between large undergraduate student loan debt and lower well-being.

Survey Methods

Results for the Gallup-Purdue Index are based on Web surveys conducted Feb. 4–March 7, 2014, with a random sample of 29,560 respondents with a bachelor's degree or higher, aged 18 and older, with Internet access, living in all 50 U.S. states and the District of Columbia.

The Gallup-Purdue Index sample was compiled from two sources: the Gallup Panel and the Gallup Daily tracking survey.

The Gallup Panel is a proprietary, probability-based longitudinal panel of U.S. adults who are selected using random-digit-dial (RDD) and address-based sampling methods. The Gallup Panel is not an opt-in panel. The Gallup Panel includes 60,000 individuals. Panel members can be surveyed by phone, mail, or Web. Gallup Panel members with a college degree and with access to the Internet were invited to take the Gallup-Purdue Index survey online.

The Gallup Daily tracking survey sample includes national adults with a minimum quota of 50% cellphone respondents and 50% landline respondents, with additional minimum quotas by time zone within region. Landline and cellular telephone numbers are selected using RDD methods. Landline respondents are chosen at random within each household on the basis of which member had the most recent birthday. Gallup Daily tracking respondents with a college degree, who agreed to future recontact, were invited to take the Gallup-Purdue Index survey online.

Gallup-Purdue Index interviews are conducted via the Web, in English only. Samples are weighted to correct for unequal selection probability and nonresponse. The data are weighted to match national demographics of gender, age, race, Hispanic ethnicity, education, and region. Demographic weighting targets are based on the most recent Current Population Survey figures for the aged 18 and older U.S. population with a bachelor's degree or higher.

All reported margins of sampling error include the computed design effects for weighting.

For results based on the total sample of 1990–2014 college graduates, the margin of sampling error is ±1 percentage point at the 95% confidence level.

For results based on the total sample of 23,942 1970–2014 college graduates, the margin of sampling error is ±1 percentage point at the 95% confidence level.

September 18, 2014
DEMOCRATIC, REPUBLICAN PARTY FAVORABLE RATINGS NOW SIMILAR
Ratings of GOP improve, but are still negative

by Jeffrey M. Jones

PRINCETON, NJ—Americans' views of the Democratic and Republican parties are now similar, mainly because of their more positive ratings of the GOP. Since bottoming out at 28% last fall during the government shutdown, Americans' opinions of the Republican Party have grown more positive and are nearly back to pre-shutdown levels. Over the same time period, ratings of the Democratic Party have generally held steady.

Favorable Ratings of the Major U.S. Political Parties: Recent Trend

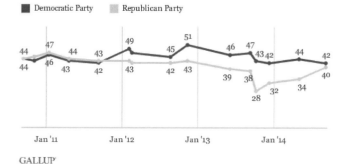

Americans view both parties negatively overall, with a 40% favorable and 57% unfavorable rating for the Republican Party, and a 42% favorable and 54% unfavorable rating for the Democratic Party. This net-negativity toward both major political parties has generally been the case since 2010, apart from President Barack Obama's re-election year in 2012, when on several occasions Americans had slightly more positive than negative views of the Democrats.

There are encouraging and discouraging signs for both parties in the latest poll, conducted Sept. 4–7, just two months before the important midterm elections.

Americans have typically rated the Democratic Party more positively than the Republican Party since the question was first asked in 1992, so the current parity between the two is a positive sign for the GOP and a negative one for the Democratic Party. Indeed, current opinions of the Democratic Party are among the worst Gallup has measured in the past 20 years. The only time Gallup measured a lower favorable rating for the Democrats was 41% in late March 2010, just after Obama signed the Affordable Care Act into law.

At the same time, Democrats can take some solace in the fact that Americans are not rating the GOP any more positively than they rate the Democratic Party, even at a time when Americans believe the Republican Party is better than the Democratic Party both at keeping the U.S. prosperous and at keeping the U.S. secure from international threats.

The situation is similar to what occurred in 2010. Even as Republicans were making large gains in federal and state offices nationwide, Americans did not view the GOP any more positively than the Democratic Party. As such, the Republicans may have merely benefited from public frustration with Obama and the Democrats in 2010, rather than having been truly embraced by Americans. Thus, if Republicans do well on Election Day this year, it does not necessarily equate to a voter mandate for the party and its policies.

All Partisan Groups More Positive Toward GOP

The gains, or perhaps recovery, in the GOP's image over the past year are evident among Democrats, independents, and Republicans. Notably, Republicans' favorable views of their own party are still not back to pre-shutdown levels.

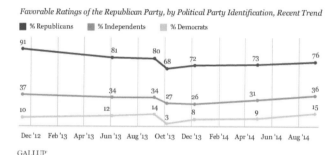

Favorable Ratings of the Republican Party, by Political Party Identification, Recent Trend

■ % Republicans ▨ % Independents ▨ % Democrats

GALLUP

As would be expected given the stability in overall views of the Democratic Party, the ratings of it by respondents' political identity are also generally steady over the past 12 months. However, Democrats and independents are less positive toward the Democratic Party than they were in late 2012, after Obama's re-election.

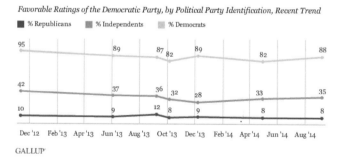

Favorable Ratings of the Democratic Party, by Political Party Identification, Recent Trend

■ % Republicans ▨ % Independents ▨ % Democrats

GALLUP

Favorable ratings of the Democratic Party are more politically polarized than ratings of the Republican Party. There is an 80-percentage-point party gap in ratings of the Democratic Party, based on an 88% favorable rating from Democrats compared with an 8% favorable rating from Republicans. The comparable gap in ratings of the Republican Party is 61 points, due to 76% favorable rating of the GOP among Republicans and 15% among Democrats.

Implications

Americans now view the Republican Party as favorably as they view the Democratic Party. While the Democratic Party's rating has been steady, the GOP's rating has improved, restoring their image to what it was prior to the federal government shutdown in the fall of 2013. But neither party is viewed positively overall, and thus voters may be choosing between two unappealing options this fall rather than between two appealing ones, and thus claims of a voter mandate by the party that does better in the Nov. 4 elections may be more wishful thinking than reality.

Survey Methods

Results for this Gallup poll are based on telephone interviews conducted Sept. 4–7, 2014, with a random sample of 1,017 adults, aged 18 and older, living in all 50 U.S. states and the District of Columbia.

For results based on the total sample of national adults, the margin of sampling error is ±4 percentage points at the 95% confidence level.

September 19, 2014

FEWER CONSERVATIVE DEMS IN ARKANSAS ADDS TO TIGHT MIDTERM
Arkansas residents confident in state government

by Andrew Dugan

WASHINGTON, D.C.—As Democratic U.S. Sen. Mark Pryor battles to keep the seat to which he was re-elected in 2008, the Democratic Party's declining ability to attract conservatives in Arkansas may complicate his re-election prospects. In a state that is consistently more conservative than the nation, conservative Democrats may have been the critical ingredient to the party's 2008 success in statewide elections. Fifteen percent of Arkansans were conservative Democrats in 2008—four percentage points higher than the national rate, and a substantial share of the Democratic base. Since then, their numbers have dwindled, and, perhaps not coincidentally, the overall share of Arkansans identifying as or leaning Democratic has dropped by eight percentage points.

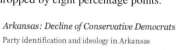

Arkansas: Decline of Conservative Democrats

Party identification and ideology in Arkansas

■ % Conservative Democrat ▨ % Moderate Democrat ▨ % Liberal Democrat

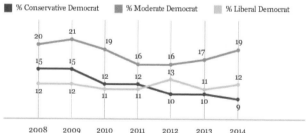

Aggregated Gallup Daily tracking; 2014 data from Jan. 1-June 30, 2014

GALLUP

As the percentage of conservative Democrats has dropped, the percentage of conservative Republicans has risen. In the first six months of 2014, 28% of Arkansans said they identify as conservative Republicans, compared with less than a quarter (24%) in 2008. As is the case nationally, conservatives are the dominant ideology among Republicans.

Arkansas has been a reliably red state in each of the last four presidential elections. But this predictability in presidential elections belies the seismic political shift in the Razorback State over the past four years. Federal and state offices once dominated by Democrats are now filled with Republicans. Before the 2010 election, Democrats held five out of six federal offices—in both the Senate and three of the four House seats—and also controlled both chambers of the state legislature.

But beginning with the 2010 midterm election, Republicans seized the state legislature, defeated a Democratic U.S. senator, and took all four U.S. House seats. One of these House seats is held by Rep. Tom Cotton, the Republican candidate challenging Pryor for his Senate seat. Pryor, the sole remaining Democrat in the Arkansas congressional delegation, is a main target for Senate Republicans as they look to claim a majority in the nation's upper chamber.

Despite the shifting political winds, Arkansas' underlying ideology remains unchanged; it has consistently been more conservative than the rest of the nation. In the first six months of 2014, 41% of Arkansans said they identify as conservative, five points higher than the national average. In 2008, when Pryor was re-elected with no serious opposition, Arkansans were more conservative than the U.S. by a six-point margin.

Arkansas: Ideology

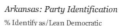

	% Conservative	% Moderate	% Liberal
Arkansas	41	35	17
Nation	36	36	23

Jan. 1-June 30, 2014

GALLUP

So while the state's ideology has not changed in the last six years, what appears to have changed is the state Democratic Party's ability to appeal to conservative-minded individuals. In 2008, conservative Democrats were the second largest bloc of Democrats in Arkansas, but they have since retreated into third place. This may have driven down Democratic support, with the percentage identifying as or leaning Democratic falling to 41% in the first half of 2014, from 49% in 2008.

Arkansas: Party Identification

% Identify as/Lean Democratic

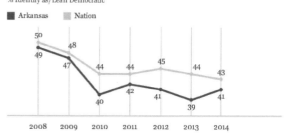

Aggregated Gallup Daily tracking; 2014 data from Jan. 1- June 30, 2014

GALLUP

Party identification and a number of other political and economic measures for Arkansas are included in Gallup's new State Scorecard assessments, which present data for 14 key measures for each of the 50 states. Within each assessment, the state's performance on the measure is compared with the national average for the same time period.

Obama Very Unpopular in Arkansas

One-third of Arkansans (33%) approved of President Barack Obama's job performance in the first six months of 2014, lower than his approval rating in the previous election years of 2012 (37%) and 2010 (39%), both of which resulted in widespread Democratic defeats across the state. Residents of Arkansas give Obama one of the lowest approval ratings in the nation—his approval rating is currently 10 points below the national average, and that gap has held steady even as Obama's approval nationally has ebbed and flowed since he took office in 2009.

Arkansas: Presidential Job Approval

% Approve

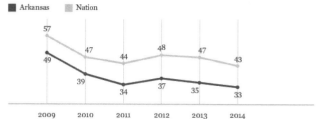

Aggregated Gallup daily tracking; 2014 data from Jan. 1-June 30, 2014

GALLUP

Arkansans Confident in State Gov't Despite Economy, Taxes

One Democrat who survived the Republican tide of 2010, retiring two-term Democratic Gov. Mike Beebe, appears to be ending his tenure in good standing: 65% of Arkansas residents say they have a great deal or fair amount of trust in their state government. The race to replace Beebe is between two former congressmen, Republican Asa Hutchinson and Democrat Mike Ross. Polls taken in the state indicate a close race, but Hutchinson typically has a slight advantage. Ross, nonetheless, has attempted to capitalize on Beebe's well-rated performance by featuring the governor in his television ads.

Arkansas: Important State Measures

	Arkansas	50-state average^
Great deal/Fair amount of trust and confidence in state government	65%	58%
State taxes NOT too high	47%	47%
Good time to get a job in city or area where you live	32%	40%
Confidence in your state's economy (Economic Confidence Index)	+8	+23
Best state in nation to live in	37%	46%

^ Overall average of the 50 individual state averages. The 50-state average measures are from a 50-state Gallup poll conducted June-December 2013 with at least 600 residents in each state.

GALLUP

Despite their high regard for the state government, Arkansans are comparatively down on several aspects of their state that could reflect poorly on the Beebe administration, or at least provide the Hutchinson campaign with some possible critiques to make against the outgoing government:

- Less than half of Arkansans say state taxes are *not* too high (47%)—lower than in most Southern states.
- One-third of the state's residents (32%) believe it is a good time to find a job in their city or area, below the 50-state average of 40%.
- Arkansans also have low confidence in their state's economy compared with other states' residents.
- Fewer than four in 10 Arkansans (37%) say their state is the best state to live in, nine points below the 50-state average.

Bottom Line

In the upcoming midterm election that could help determine control of the U.S. Senate, the Razorback State may vote out the last remaining Democrat in the state's congressional delegation—a delegation that Democrats recently dominated. In many respects, the deck seems stacked against Pryor: Obama's approval rating is slumping in Arkansas, Democratic affiliation has declined, and residents tilt conservative.

Nonetheless, polling within the state shows a tight race—a testament to the state's relatively strong Democratic Party that has historically been able to field conservative to moderate candidates, such as Pryor, who appeal to Arkansans of various political stripes, including conservatives. Whether Pryor is able to hold on to his Senate seat or Democrat Mike Ross comes from behind to win the governor's race will be a significant indicator as to whether Arkansas Democrats can still succeed using the same playbook, or if the political ground beneath them has completely shifted.

Survey Methods

Results for this Gallup poll are based on telephone interviews conducted Jan. 1–June 30, 2014, on the Gallup Daily tracking survey, with a random sample of 88,802 adults, aged 18 and older, living in all 50 U.S. states and the District of Columbia. Results are also based on Gallup's recent 50-state poll conducted June–December 2013, with a random sample of approximately 600 adults per state, aged 18 and older, living in all 50 U.S. states.

For results based on the 2014 sample of 1,030 Arkansas residents, the margin of sampling error is ±2 percentage points at the 95% confidence level.

For results based on the 2013 sample of adults per state, the margin of sampling error is ±5 percentage points at the 95% confidence level.

September 19, 2014
IN U.S., MORE HISPANICS NAME IMMIGRATION AS TOP PROBLEM
Ranks second to economy in general among Hispanics

by Andrew Dugan

WASHINGTON, D.C.—Over the summer, the percentage of U.S. Hispanics naming immigration as the most important issue facing the U.S. nearly doubled from the first half of the year, as the issue received heavy media attention related to the surge of unaccompanied migrant children from Central America. Concern among the general public about the issue intensified as well, rising over threefold, but Hispanics remained more likely to name this issue as one of the country's top problems.

Most Important Problem: All Americans Compared With Hispanic Americans

	January-June 2014		July-September 2014	
	National adults	Hispanics	National adults	Hispanics
Economy	49%	47%	40%	40%
Immigration	4%	13%	15%	25%
Dissatisfaction with government	19%	13%	18%	13%
Poverty	4%	5%	4%	5%
Healthcare	13%	11%	7%	6%
Terrorism	3%	5%	6%	4%
Moral/Ethical/Family decline	5%	2%	5%	5%

GALLUP

These latest results come from a combined sample of Gallup polls conducted in July, August, and September, consisting of 3,062 adults.

U.S. Hispanics' mentions of immigration as the top problem rose from 13% to 25% between the first half of the year and the past three months, while immigration rose from 4% to 15% among all adults. Apart from the importance they place on immigration, there is little difference in how U.S. Hispanics and all Americans describe the nation's challenges.

Immigration Gains Momentum as a Top Issue for Republicans

Hispanic turnout and support will be instrumental in several key U.S. Senate races in November's midterm elections, but despite the importance of the immigration issue to the Hispanic community, some Democrats have been less than willing to make the subject a major plank of their campaign. But this is, as always, a complicated topic that has put Democrats in a tough spot.

Despite Hispanics' Democratic bent—54% of Hispanics in the total January–September sample leaned or identified with the Democratic Party, compared with 29% who identified with or leaned Republican—immigration is actually now more likely to be a top concern among all Republicans. In the past three months, 20% of national adults who self-identify as Republican named immigration as a top issue, compared with 8% of Democrats. In the first half of the year, a nearly identical 4% of Republicans and 3% of Democrats named immigration as the country's most important problem.

Immigration as Most Important Problem, by Party Affiliation
% of national adults naming immigration as most important problem

	Republican	Democrat	Republican-Democratic gap
January-June 2014	4%	3%	+1
July-September 2014	20%	8%	+12

GALLUP

The Obama administration was reportedly considering issuing a series of executive actions that would ease the number of deportations. However, likely a result of pressure from vulnerable Senate Democrats in states such as North Carolina, the administration backed off announcing such measures.

Bottom Line

Hispanics are more likely than the general public to see immigration as a major problem facing the country, suggesting that this issue could be a significant factor for many Hispanic voters in the fall election. However, other issues matter to Hispanics as well, especially the economy. The Obama administration may have been trying to specifically appeal to Hispanic voters when it floated the possibility of executive action to repair perceived problems with the current immigration system. After many objections from fellow Democrats, however, the administration has backed away from doing anything before the midterm election. Meanwhile, Republicans now seem more focused on the topic of immigration than Democrats do, though the GOP faces the challenge of attempting to take actions that U.S. Hispanics would support.

This lack of action on policymakers' behalf could result in a Hispanic surge at the ballot box in November, or, alternatively, it could be a reason why many Hispanics choose not to vote. Regardless, these findings make it clear that immigration remains a potent issue for Hispanics across the country.

Survey Methods

Results for this Gallup poll are based on telephone interviews conducted July–September 2014, with a random sample of 3,062 adults, aged 18 and older, living in all 50 U.S. states and the District of Columbia.

For results based on the total sample of national adults, the margin of sampling error is ±2 percentage points at the 95% confidence level.

For results based on the total sample of 212 U.S. Hispanics, the margin of sampling error is ±8 percentage points at the 95% confidence level.

September 22, 2014
IN U.S., FOUR IN 10 SAY PARTY CONTROL OF CONGRESS MATTERS
Similar proportion knowledgeable about who controls House and Senate

by Lydia Saad

PRINCETON, NJ—Two months ahead of the midterm elections that may very well change the balance of power in Congress, four in 10 Americans say the specific party that controls Congress matters a great deal to them, while 29% say it matters a moderate amount and another 30% say it generally doesn't matter to them.

Percentage Who Care "a Great Deal" About Who Controls Congress

How much does it matter to you which political party controls Congress -- a great deal, a moderate amount, not much, or not at all?

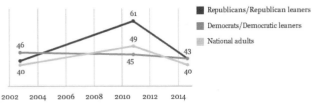

■ Republicans/Republican leaners
■ Democrats/Democratic leaners
■ National adults

Note: Averages for national adults include the views of independents who don't lean toward either party, which are not shown in this graph

GALLUP'

The 40% of national adults now highly concerned about control of Capitol Hill equals what Gallup found a month before the 2002 midterms, but is lower than the 49% seen in late October 2010.

While the views of Democrats (including independents who lean Democratic) on this question have been steady across the three midterms—roughly 45% each year have said the party in control mattered a great deal to them—Republicans' concern has varied. Currently, 43% of Republicans (including Republican leaners) say party control matters a great deal. It was a whopping 61% in 2010, but that was up from 42% in 2002.

The 2002 and 2010 elections were favorable to Republicans, as the GOP retained majority control of the U.S. House of Representatives and regained control of the Senate in 2002, and recaptured control of the House in 2010 with an enormous seat gain. Thus, while rank-and-file Republicans' concern about party control is not nearly as high today as it was in 2010, when Democrats controlled both houses, it is comparable to 2002—which could suggest that conditions are still favorable for the GOP. Missing from this midterm trend, however, is 2006, which was a strong Democratic year. Therefore, it is not entirely clear how levels of concern on this question relate to each party's performance.

These results are from the 2014 update of Gallup's annual Governance survey, conducted Sept. 4–7.

Close to Four in 10 Also Knowledgeable About Control of Congress

The same poll asked respondents to identify the party currently holding a majority of seats in the U.S. Senate as well as in the U.S. House of Representatives. About half of Americans can correctly identify the majority party for each: 49% say the Democrats control the Senate, and 51% say the Republicans control the House. Somewhat fewer—36%—can correctly identify the majority in both chambers, although this knowledge is somewhat higher, at 41%, among registered voters.

Another 14% of Americans are aware that party control of Congress is divided, but match each party to the wrong chamber, believing Republicans control the Senate and Democrats control the House.

A relatively large subset of Americans, 28%, can correctly identify the majority party for only one chamber (while being wrong or unsure about the other), while 22% are either unsure about both, or name the wrong party for one chamber and are unsure about the other.

Summary of Americans' Knowledge of Which Party Controls U.S. Senate and U.S. House of Representatives

	House – GOP, Senate -- Democratic (correct response)	House -- Democratic, Senate – GOP (incorrect response)	Correct on one house	Unsure^
	%	%	%	%
U.S. adults	36	14	28	22
Republicans/ Lean Republican	38	15	30	17
Democrats/ Lean Democratic	38	14	27	21
Registered to vote	41	15	25	19
Not registered	15	11	39	35

^ Unsure includes respondents unsure of both, or wrong on one and unsure on the other

Sept. 4-7, 2014

GALLUP'

Americans who are knowledgeable about who controls each house of Congress are significantly more likely than others to say party control of Congress matters greatly to them: 55% of the well-informed group say this, versus about a third or less of those who can't properly identify party control. This highlights the divide in midterm politics between the politically concerned and informed subset of Americans—a proportion similar to the typical midterm turnout rate, near 40%—and the rest of the population that is less engaged politically.

Survey Methods

Results for this Gallup poll are based on telephone interviews conducted Sept. 4–7, 2014, with a random sample of 1,017 adults, aged 18 and older, living in all 50 U.S. states and the District of Columbia.

For results based on the total sample of national adults, the margin of sampling error is ±4 percentage points at the 95% confidence level.

September 22, 2014
AMERICANS STILL TRUST LOCAL GOVERNMENT MORE THAN STATE
Republicans maintain highest levels of confidence

by Justin McCarthy

WASHINGTON, D.C.—As they have for more than a decade, Americans continue to trust their local governments (72%) more than their state governments (62%). Both levels of confidence in 2014 are unchanged from last year, and are only a few percentage points off from their historical averages.

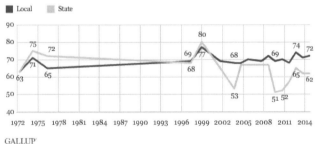

Americans' Trust in State and Local Government

Figures are percentages with a great deal/fair amount of trust in the level of government

The stability in state and local government trust, as measured in the Sept. 4–7 Governance poll, contrasts with this year's declines in trust in the federal government to handle international and domestic problems, and in two of the three branches of the federal government.

Since 2001, local government has consistently garnered more trust from Americans than state government. When Gallup first asked Americans the question in 1972, a record low of 63% said they had a "great deal" or "fair amount" of confidence in their local government. Confidence reached a high of 77% in 1998, amid a national economic boom.

Trust in state government, on the other hand, has been more varied and vulnerable to economic downturns, reaching lows in 2009

(51%) and 2010 (52%) as states struggled to pass budgets during the recent recession. Just like on the local level, the robust economy in 1998 spurred confidence in state government, which peaked at 80% that year and marginally surpassed trust in local government for the last time before the new millennium.

Republicans Significantly More Likely Than Dems, Independents to Trust State Government

Nearly three in four Republicans (73%) currently have a great deal or fair amount of trust in their state government—much higher than the 59% among Democrats and independents. Since 1997, Republicans have typically expressed more confidence in state government than their Democratic and independent counterparts have, with a few exceptions between 2005 and 2010, when they tied with Democrats. But the partisan disparity in trust has grown wider in recent years, with Republicans now leading the other groups by 14 points.

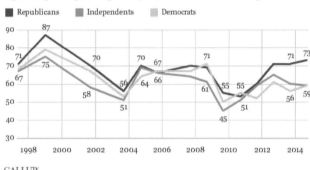

Trust in State Government, by Party

Figures are percentages with a great deal/fair amount of trust in the level of government

Independents have generally been less likely than Republicans and Democrats to express confidence in state government. They also are the only group whose trust in state government has ever fallen below the 50% mark, in 2009. But independents' and Democrats' scores have often been similar. They tied this year and their historical average—61%—is on par with Democrats' average of 62%.

More Than Four in Five Republicans Have Confidence in Local Government

Republicans have also expressed generally higher levels of confidence in local government than independents and Democrats have. This year, 81% of Republicans have a great deal or fair amount of trust in their local governments, similar to the previous high in 1998.

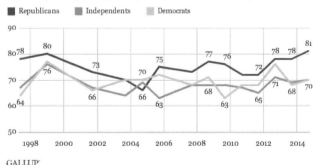

Trust in Local Government, by Party

Figures are percentages with a great deal/fair amount of trust in the level of government

Independents have shown the least confidence in local government in all but a few polls—though they maintained a majority level of trust each time. Independents' and Democrats' record-low confidence is 63%, and each group's trust peaked in 1998, along with that of Republicans.

In 2004, when Republican President George W. Bush was in office, Democrats' confidence in local government (70%) was similar to that of independents (69%) but they had a slight edge over Republicans (66%).

Bottom Line

Though Americans' current confidence ratings in state and local governments are nothing out of the ordinary, Republicans' trust in each is increasing. Republicans have typically expressed the most trust in these levels of government in the past, but the widening gap between Democrats and Republicans could have several significant explanations and implications.

For one, the GOP's mantra of smaller government could translate literally to higher levels of trust in governments that are both smaller and closer to the citizens they are designed to serve. Republicans are most likely to see the federal government as wasteful, and are least confident in its ability to handle international and domestic issues. But their level of confidence grows with each descending level of government, with local government receiving the highest rates of trust.

But the GOP's increasing trust in state and local levels of government could also reflect a shift in the GOP's power players, who are resigned to showcasing the party's ideas on the state level as Democratic control of the White House as well as the U.S. Senate keeps Republican influence on the federal level at bay. Prior to 2012, the previous highs in confidence among Republicans took place in the late '90s, when another Democrat was president.

While the GOP has had limited power at the federal level in recent years, some of the party's stars—and prospective 2016 presidential candidates—have been governors who have taken the national spotlight for their firm, and often controversial, Republican stances on issues in their home states. On issues including taxes, union contracts, immigration, same-sex marriage, voter ID bills, and restrictions to abortion, Republican governors have been the party's most powerful representatives of national GOP ideals during the Democratic Obama administration.

Survey Methods

Results for this Gallup poll are based on telephone interviews conducted Sept. 4–7, 2014, with a random sample of 1,017 adults, aged 18 and older, living in all 50 U.S. states and the District of Columbia.

For results based on the total sample of national adults, the margin of sampling error is ±4 percentage points at the 95% confidence level.

September 23, 2014
SLIGHTLY FEWER BACK ISIS MILITARY ACTION VS. PAST ACTIONS
More than six in 10 Republicans and Democrats approve

by Jeffrey M. Jones and Frank Newport

PRINCETON, NJ—Americans' 60% approval for U.S. military action against Islamic militants in Iraq and Syria, commonly known

as ISIS, is slightly below their average 68% approval for 10 other U.S. military operations Gallup has asked about using this question format. Americans have been a bit less supportive of recent military actions after prolonged engagements in Afghanistan and Iraq.

Approval/Disapproval for U.S. Military Actions After They Began

Country/Region	Polling dates	% Approve	% Disapprove
Iraq and Syria	2014 Sept 20-21	60	31
Libya	2011 Mar 21	47	37
Iraq	2003 Mar 20	76	20
Afghanistan	2001 Oct 7	90	5
Kosovo/The Balkans	1999 Apr 30-May 2	51	45
Afghanistan and Sudan	1998 Aug 20	66	19
Somalia	1993 Jun 18-21	65	23
Iraq	1993 Jan 13	83	9
Persian Gulf	1991 Jan 16	79	15
Libya	1986 Apr 17-18	71	21
Grenada	1983 Oct 26-27	53	34

Wording of 2014 question: "Next, we have a question about the military action the United States is taking in Iraq and Syria against Islamic militants, commonly known as ISIS. Do you approve or disapprove of this U.S. military action?"

Note: Gallup did not ask an approve/disapprove question after the 1989 invasion of Panama.

GALLUP'

The most recent results are based on a Sept. 20–21 Gallup poll, conducted after the U.S. had launched airstrikes in Iraq but before military action began in Syria on Sept. 22. President Barack Obama announced his intention in a nationally televised address on Sept. 10 to use U.S. military force to "degrade and destroy" ISIS, also known as ISIL, in those two countries.

Notably, there is little partisan difference in opinions of the U.S. military action, with 64% of Democrats and 65% of Republicans approving. Independents are somewhat less likely to approve, but a majority (55%) still do.

Next, we have a question about the military action the United States is taking in Iraq and Syria against Islamic militants, commonly known as ISIS. Do you approve or disapprove of this U.S. military action?

	Favor	Oppose
	%	%
Democrats	64	28
Independents	55	38
Republicans	65	27

Sept. 20-21, 2014

GALLUP'

Now that military action is already under way, Americans' support for it is significantly higher than in June when Gallup asked about proposed U.S. military actions to "aid the Iraqi government in fighting militants there." At that time, after ISIS gained control of parts of Iraq, 39% of Americans were in favor of direct U.S. military action in Iraq and 54% opposed.

This increase is not atypical, as support commonly increases from the time military action is first discussed as an option until it is taken. For example, 23% of Americans favored U.S. military action to drive the Iraqis out of Kuwait in August 1990. By January 1991, just before the U.S. began the Persian Gulf War, 55% were in favor. Immediately after the U.S. began the war, 79% approved of it.

The increase in support is likely also tied to ISIS being perceived as a more direct threat to the U.S., which may not have been as clear in June. In recent weeks, ISIS has captured and beheaded two U.S. journalists. In fact, the current poll finds 50% of Americans describing ISIS as a "critical threat" to U.S. vital interests, with an additional 31% saying the group is an "important threat."

About one in three Americans (34%) say they are following the news about the Islamic militants' actions in Iraq and Syria "very closely," while 41% say they are following it "somewhat closely." Approval of the U.S. military action is significantly higher among those following it very or somewhat closely.

Americans Not Backing U.S. Ground Troops to Fight ISIS

Despite their overall approval of U.S. military action in Iraq and Syria, more Americans oppose (54%) than favor (40%) sending U.S. ground troops there. The relatively low level of support for ground troops could be related to Americans' reluctance to engage in another extended fight in Iraq. A majority of Americans continue to describe the 2003 Iraq war as a mistake for the U.S. And, as of June, a majority still backed President Obama's decision to withdraw all U.S. troops from Iraq.

Would you favor or oppose the United States sending ground troops to Iraq and Syria in order to assist groups in those countries that are fighting the Islamic militants?

	Favor	Oppose	No opinion
	%	%	%
National adults	40	54	6
Democrats	30	63	7
Independents	35	59	6
Republicans	61	36	3

Sept. 20-21, 2014

GALLUP

Although Republicans and Democrats both approve of the current U.S. military action, Republicans are twice as likely as Democrats to favor the use of ground troops, 61% to 30%. Independents' views are in line with those of Democrats, at 35% approval. Democrats may be taking their cue from President Obama, who is ruling out the use of U.S. ground troops. Republicans, on the other hand, may be more sympathetic to the idea of ground troops in Iraq because the 2003 Iraq war was initiated by a Republican president.

Bottom Line

Americans' level of support for the current military action against Islamic militants in Iraq and Syria is below the historical average for support for other U.S. military interventions over the past 31 years, but still represents a majority of Americans. This marks a rare instance in which Republicans and Democrats share basically the same attitudes. However, partisanship comes back into play on the issue of potentially using ground troops in Iraq and Syria, which Republicans support and Democrats do not.

Survey Methods

Results for this Gallup poll are based on telephone interviews conducted Sept. 20–21, 2014, on the Gallup Daily tracking survey, with a random sample of 1,013 adults, aged 18 and older, living in all 50 U.S. states and the District of Columbia.

For results based on the total sample of national adults, the margin of sampling error is ±4 percentage points at the 95% confidence level.

September 24, 2014
AMERICANS CONTINUE TO SAY A THIRD POLITICAL PARTY IS NEEDED
Views little changed from last year

by Jeffrey M. Jones

PRINCETON, NJ—A majority of U.S. adults, 58%, say a third U.S. political party is needed because the Republican and Democratic parties "do such a poor job" representing the American people. These views are little changed from last year's high. Since 2007, a majority has typically called for a third party.

Americans' Opinions of a Need for a Third U.S. Political Party

In your view, do the Republican and Democratic parties do an adequate job of representing the American people, or do they do such a poor job that a third major party is needed?

GALLUP

The results are based on Gallup's Sept. 4–7 Governance poll. The first time the question was asked in 2003, a majority of Americans believed the two major parties were adequately representing the U.S. public, which is the only time this has been the case. Since 2007, a majority has said a third party is needed, with two exceptions occurring in the fall of the 2008 and 2012 presidential election years.

The historical 60% high favoring a third party came in a poll conducted during the partial federal government shutdown last October. At that time, 26% of Americans said the parties were doing an adequate job. That figure is up to 35% now, but with little change in the percentage calling for a third party.

Americans' current desire for a third party is consistent with their generally negative views of both the Republican and Democratic parties, with only about four in 10 viewing each positively. Americans' views toward the two major parties have been tepid for much of the last decade. However, even when the party's images were more positive in the past, including majority favorability for the Democrats throughout 2007 and favorability for the GOP approaching 50% in 2011, Americans' still saw the need for a third party.

Independents Maintain Solid Preference for Third Party

Political independents, as might be expected given a lack of allegiance to either major party, have shown a far greater preference for a third political party than those who identify as Republicans or Democrats. Currently, 71% of independents say a third party is needed, on the upper end of the trend line. That compares with 47% of Democrats and 46% of Republicans who say the same.

Support for a Third Major U.S. Political Party, by Political Party Affiliation
Numbers in percentages

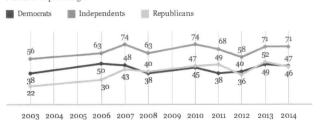

Note: 2007 and 2011 data represent average of two polls

GALLUP

For most of the past 11 years, Republicans and Democrats were about equally as likely to favor a third party. From 2003 to 2006—when Republicans had control of the presidency and both houses of Congress—Democrats were more likely than Republicans to see the need for a third party. And in 2011, after the rise of the Tea Party movement, Republicans were a bit more inclined than Democrats to see a third party as necessary.

Implications

Although Americans express a desire for a viable alternative to the Democratic and Republican parties, third political parties have had little success in American politics. The U.S. political system makes it difficult for third parties to hold elected office given the Electoral College system of electing presidents and election of members of Congress from individual states and districts based on the candidate getting the most votes. Such a system generally favors two parties—a center-right and a center-left party—that have the ability to assemble a winning plurality or majority in districts and states across the country. Also, some states have restrictive laws on ballot access that make it difficult for third-party candidates to appear on the ballot.

Third parties have had success in other countries when they had strong support in a particular region, or if members of the legislature were allocated proportionately to the nationwide vote each party received. This allowed third parties to hold seats with national vote shares usually well less than 30%.

Given the U.S. political system, those whose ideology puts them to the left of the Democratic Party or the right of the Republican Party are better served trying to work within a major political party than establishing their own party. Supporters of the Tea Party movement generally took this approach, with some success, by trying to get their preferred candidates nominated as Republicans in the last few election cycles. But as with most U.S. third parties historically, the Tea Party's influence appears to be waning as the movement did not play a pivotal role in the 2012 Republican presidential nomination and was less successful in defeating more moderate Republican candidates in the 2014 congressional primaries than in 2010.

Though the desire for a third party exists, it is unclear how many Americans would actually support a third party if it came to be. Americans' preference for a third party may reflect their frustration with the way the Republican and Democratic parties are performing, as well as the idea that the system ought to be open to new parties, regardless of whether this is viable in practice.

Survey Methods

Results for this Gallup poll are based on telephone interviews conducted Sept. 4–7, 2014, with a random sample of 1,017 adults, aged 18 and older, living in all 50 U.S. states and the District of Columbia.

For results based on the total sample of national adults, the margin of sampling error is ±4 percentage points at the 95% confidence level.

September 24, 2014
SATISFACTION WITH U.S. GOVERNANCE LOWER THAN PRE-SHUTDOWN
Republicans are less likely to be satisfied than Democrats

by Rebecca Riffkin

WASHINGTON, D.C.—More than one in four Americans are satisfied with the way the nation is being governed, while nearly three in four are dissatisfied. Americans' satisfaction has varied widely in recent years. Although the 27% who are currently satisfied is higher than the record-low satisfaction seen last October during the partial government shutdown, it is still below where it was in September 2013, before the shutdown began.

Americans' Satisfaction With the Way the Nation Is Being Governed
On the whole, would you say you are satisfied or dissatisfied with the way the nation is being governed?

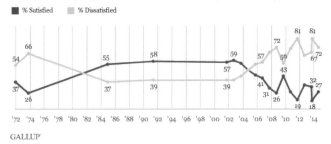

GALLUP

Gallup first asked Americans about their satisfaction with the way the country is governed in 1971 and has done so at least annually since 2001. Prior to 2008, the record low was 26% in 1973, during the Watergate scandal. In two measurements in the 1980s and 1990s, and from 2001 until 2003, more Americans were satisfied with the government than were dissatisfied.

However, in 2004, Americans were evenly divided, and more have been dissatisfied than satisfied since then. Satisfaction has been a highly fluid measure, reaching as high as 43% in 2009 before plummeting below 20% in 2011 and in late 2013, both years in which Congress faced heated budget discussions.

Satisfaction Hasn't Returned to Pre-Shutdown Levels Among Democrats

The month before the partial shutdown, more than half of Democrats (54%) were satisfied with the way the U.S. was governed. This dropped to 28% in October 2013, and now has partially recovered to 46%. Republicans and independents are as likely to be satisfied today as they were in September 2013, although satisfaction among both groups is much lower than among Democrats.

Satisfaction With the Way the Country Is Being Governed, by Party
% Satisfied

	Republicans	Independents	Democrats
September 2013	11%	26%	54%
October 2013	8%	15%	28%
September 2014	11%	25%	46%

GALLUP

During the last year, about one in 10 Republicans have been satisfied with the way the country is governed. Republicans' satisfaction had the smallest drop during the partial government shutdown, mainly because it was already so low.

Historically, Americans who affiliate with the president's political party are more likely than others to be satisfied with the way the nation is being governed. In 2007, when George W. Bush was president, six in 10 Republicans were satisfied, compared with 18% of Democrats and independents. In 2009, after President Barack Obama took office, 72% of Democrats were satisfied with the way the nation was governed, but Republican satisfaction had fallen to 16% and independents were in the middle at 34%.

Bottom Line

The partial government shutdown affected Americans' views of many things, including a sharp drop in economic confidence and a rise in the percentage saying dysfunctional government was the most important problem in the country. While views on a number of these issues have improved since the shutdown ended, many Americans continue to have low opinions of the country's government. Currently, Americans are not satisfied with the way things are going in the country and are less trusting of the executive and legislative branches than they were in 2013. With voters set to go to the polls in a little more than a month, incumbents seeking re-election may face a more challenging fight than in the past.

Survey Methods

Results for this Gallup poll are based on telephone interviews conducted Sept. 4–7, 2014, with a random sample of 1,017 adults, aged 18 and older, living in all 50 U.S. states and the District of Columbia.

For results based on the total sample of national adults, the margin of sampling error is ±4 percentage points at the 95% confidence level.

September 25, 2014
COLORADO'S POLITICS ARE AS DIVIDED AS THEY GET
Obama no more popular in the Centennial State than elsewhere

by Lydia Saad

PRINCETON, NJ—Of the handful of extremely close U.S. Senate races this year, the battle over the Colorado seat being defended by Democratic Sen. Mark Udall is one of the closest, mirroring the sharply divided politics of the state. Forty-two percent of Coloradans in the first half of 2014 identified as or leaned Republican and 42% identified as or leaned Democratic.

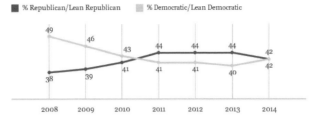

Colorado: Self-Reported Party Identification

■ % Republican/Lean Republican ▨ % Democratic/Lean Democratic

Data for 2014 collected Jan.1–June 30

GALLUP

Colorado's political environment may be a bit better for the Democrats now than in the three previous years when Republicans outnumbered Democrats in the state by a slight margin. But, as is the case nationally, the environment is significantly worse for Democrats now than it was in 2008—the year Udall first captured his seat with 53% of the vote after a decade serving Colorado in the U.S. House. That same year, Americans overall were significantly more likely to identify as Democrats, and Barack Obama won Colorado in the presidential election, with 53.5% of the vote.

Udall faces Republican Rep. Cory Gardner, a former member of the Colorado Statehouse who won the election for Colorado's 4th congressional district seat in 2010, beating an incumbent Democrat.

Coloradans' Approval Ratings of Obama Near National Average

While Obama may have aided Udall's 2008 bid, he is widely seen as a drag on Democrats' chances across the country given his much lower approval ratings in 2014 compared with 2008. In this respect, Colorado is no exception. Obama's job approval rating in the state averaged 41% between January and June of this year—just slightly below the 43% average seen nationally over the same time period, and 11 percentage points lower than Obama's approval in Colorado in 2009.

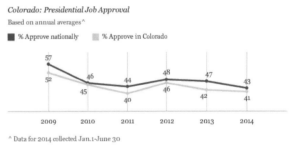

Colorado: Presidential Job Approval
Based on annual averages^

■ % Approve nationally ▨ % Approve in Colorado

^ Data for 2014 collected Jan.1–June 30

GALLUP

A majority of Coloradans, 55%, disapproved of Obama's job performance in the first half of 2014. And given the stability in Obama's approval rating nationally since then, his disapproval rating in Colorado likely remains about the same.

As is usually the case in midterm elections, turnout will be a major factor in deciding the outcome of the Senate race in Colorado, and as a result, the campaigns are battling hard to raise issues that could help spur their bases to the polls. Gardner is doing his best to tie Udall to Obama generally, as well as to the Affordable Care Act, or Obamacare, specifically.

One potentially positive angle on the situation for Udall, however, is that Obama's job approval rating in Colorado is not significantly lower than the total percentage of Democrats in the state, suggesting that Colorado Democrats are fairly loyal to the party. This contrasts with Arkansas, Louisiana, and, to a lesser extent, Iowa, where Obama's approval ratings in each state have been running several points lower than the total percentage of Democrats and Democratic-leaners in each state. Thus, it would appear that Democrats running in these states—Sen. Mark Pryor, Sen. Mary Landrieu, and Rep. Bruce Braley, respectively—run a greater risk of forfeiting a certain amount of support from their own party members, particularly if they appear too closely linked with Obama.

Democratic Party Identification vs. Obama Job Approval in Close 2014 Senate Races
States listed by difference between Obama approval rating and Democratic identification

	Democratic/ Lean Democratic	Approve of Obama	Difference (pct. pts.)
	%	%	
Georgia	40	42	+2
Michigan	45	45	0
Alaska	34	34	0
Colorado	42	41	-1
North Carolina	42	41	-1
Iowa	41	38	-3
Louisiana	45	40	-5
Arkansas	41	33	-8

Based on Gallup Daily tracking Jan. 1-June 30, 2014

GALLUP

So, while Gardner's strategy of linking Udall with Obama may be an effective way to get his Republican base to the polls, it could backfire a bit with Colorado Democrats, who like the president and who would view Udall's connection to him as plus. Also, while Obama may be as unpopular in Colorado as he is nationally, the state as a whole is a bit less conservative than the rest of the country. One in three adults in Colorado (33%) describe their political views as conservative, compared with 36% of adults nationally. A quarter of Coloradans vs. 23% of adults nationally identify themselves as liberal.

These political assessments are available in Gallup's new State Scorecard assessments, which present data on 14 political, economic, and social measures for each of the 50 states. Each state's ratings are presented alongside the national average for the same time period, to provide an easy way to gauge whether the state is performing at, above, or below par on each.

Democratic Tilt Among Women in Colorado Could Aid Udall

Meanwhile, Udall has placed his bets on reproductive rights as the issue that will activate women on his behalf. Udall has heavily focused his offense on Gardner's opposition to abortion, as well as Gardner's positions on birth control and "personhood" for fetuses.

The reasoning behind targeting women is clear, given women's relatively strong Democratic orientation in Colorado, which is similar to women's political leanings nationally. Women in the state tilt Democratic by 46% to 37%, nearly as strongly as Colorado men tilt Republican: 47% vs. 37%.

While national issues will undoubtedly be paramount in who voters back for the U.S. Senate in Colorado, conditions within the state could affect the race, mainly because of the gubernatorial election happening at the same time. Colorado residents appear a bit more positive about their state's economy than are residents of the 50 states on average. For instance, Gallup polling in the last half of 2013 showed 44% of Coloradans saying it is a good time to get

a job where they live, compared with the 50-state average of 40%. And 59% said their state taxes are not too high, versus 47% on average across the states. And more broadly, residents in Colorado are highly positive about their state, with 65% describing their state as the best or one of the best states to live in, much higher than the 46% 50-state average.

Party Identification by Gender in Colorado and Nationally

	All adults	Men	Women
COLORADO ADULTS	%	%	%
Republican/Lean Republican	42	47	37
Independent (no lean)	13	13	13
Democratic/Lean Democratic	42	37	46
U.S. ADULTS			
Republican/Lean Republican	39	43	36
Independent (no lean)	14	14	13
Democratic/Lean Democratic	43	38	47

Based on Gallup Daily tracking Jan. 1-June 30, 2014

GALLUP

The Democratic incumbent, Gov. John Hickenlooper, ought to be benefiting most from these sentiments, in which case the entire Democratic ticket, including Udall, could do better. However, recent local polling in the state has shown Hickenlooper at best tied with his opponent, and at worst 10 points behind. Thus, if the relatively positive views residents have toward their state aren't helping the sitting governor, it's not clear how they would help Udall as the incumbent senator.

Bottom Line

Udall was elected to the Senate in a strong Democratic year, and Gardner was elected to the House in a strong Republican year. Now they are fighting for the same Senate seat at a time when the population of Colorado is sharply divided, but with the political profile of the state closer to what was seen in 2010 than in 2008.

Accordingly, most of the recent horserace polls conducted in Colorado, roughly two months out from the election, have found the Senate race too close to call. But, of course, given that turnout in midterm elections is typically near 40%, the political profile of voters in midterms can differ markedly from the general public. Any edge either candidate can get in turning out his base, such as by activating conservatives or women, could be decisive.

Survey Methods

Results for this Gallup poll are based on telephone interviews conducted Jan. 1–June 30, 2014, on the Gallup Daily tracking survey, with a random sample of 88,802 adults, aged 18 and older, living in all 50 U.S. states and the District of Columbia. Results are also based on Gallup's recent 50-state poll conducted June–December 2013, with a random sample of approximately 600 adults per state, aged 18 and older, living in all 50 U.S. states.

For results based on the 2014 sample of 1,706 Colorado residents, the margin of sampling error is ±2 percentage points at the 95% confidence level.

For results based on the 2013 sample of adults per state, the margin of sampling error is ±5 percentage points at the 95% confidence level.

IN U.S., SUPPORT FOR DAILY PRAYER IN SCHOOLS DIPS SLIGHTLY
Many Americans still support proposals concerning religion in schools

by Rebecca Riffkin

WASHINGTON, D.C.—Sixty-one percent of Americans support allowing daily prayer to be spoken in the classroom. Though still solidly above the majority level, this is down slightly from 66% in 2001 and 70% in 1999.

Percentage of Americans Who Favor Daily Prayer in the Classroom Down Slightly

Next I'm going to read a variety of proposals concerning religion and public schools. For each one, please tell me whether you would generally favor or oppose it. Allowing daily prayer to be spoken in the classroom.

	% Favor	% Oppose
2014 Aug 7-10	61	37
2001 Feb 9-11	66	34
2000 Sep 11-13	68	30
1999 Jun 25-27	70	28

GALLUP

These data are from Gallup's Aug. 7–10 Work and Education survey.

In the same survey, Gallup asked questions about two other aspects of religion and schools, and the results indicate that more Americans favor allowing prayers at graduation ceremonies and making public school facilities available after hours for student religious groups to use than daily prayer in the classroom.

Three-quarters of Americans (75%) support allowing students to say prayers at school graduation ceremonies, down slightly from 83% in 1999. The 77% of Americans who support making public school facilities available after hours for student religious groups to use is essentially unchanged from 78% in 1999.

Americans in Favor of Graduation Prayers and Religious Groups Using School Facilities

Next I'm going to read a variety of proposals concerning religion and public schools. For each one, please tell me whether you would generally favor or oppose it.
% Favor shown

	2014 Aug 7-10	2001 Feb 9-11	2000 Sep 11-13	1999 Jun 25-27
Making public school facilities available after school hours for use by student religious groups	77	72	N/A	78
Allowing students to say prayers at graduation ceremonies as part of the official program	75	80	77	83
Allowing daily prayer to be spoken in the classroom	61	66	68	70

Religious groups using school facilities was not asked about in 2000

GALLUP

As would be expected, Americans' attitudes toward religion in schools are highly related to their underlying religiosity. Those who seldom or never attend church are split on daily prayer in the classroom, while those who attend church monthly or weekly are generally in favor. Similar patterns exist in terms of attitudes toward prayers at graduation and use of school facilities by student religious groups.

Opinions on these issues vary by religious preference. Americans who identify with no religion are the least likely to support daily prayer in classrooms, prayer at graduation ceremonies, and use of school facilities for prayer groups. Protestants and those who identify with other non-Catholic Christian religions are more strongly in favor of these ideas than are Catholics.

Frequent Church Attendees More Likely to Favor Religion in Schools

Next I'm going to read a variety of proposals concerning religion and public schools. For each one, please tell me whether you would generally favor or oppose it.
% Favor shown

	Daily prayer in the classroom	Students say prayers at graduation ceremonies	Public school facilities available after hours for student religious groups
Attend church weekly	82	93	87
Attend church monthly	67	80	79
Seldom attend church	49	62	69
Protestant or other Christian	77	89	85
Catholic	57	78	66
No religious preference	35	44	69

Aug. 7-10, 2014

GALLUP

Republicans in the U.S. are significantly more religious than other Americans, so it follows that Republicans are considerably more likely to favor each proposal on religion in schools than are independents or, in particular, Democrats. A large majority of Republicans favor these proposals, with at least 80% supporting all three. Independents also support the various proposals on religion in schools, but to a lesser extent than Republicans do. A majority of Democrats do not support daily school prayers (45%), but a majority do support graduation prayers (65%) and using school facilities for student religious groups (76%).

Republicans Much More Likely Than Democrats to Favor Daily Prayer in Classrooms

Next I'm going to read a variety of proposals concerning religion and public schools. For each one, please tell me whether you would generally favor or oppose it.
% Favor shown

	Republican	Independent	Democrat
Allowing daily prayer to be spoken in the classroom	80	64	45
Allowing students to say prayers at graduation ceremonies as part of the official program	92	75	65
Making public school facilities available after school hours for use by student religious groups	83	76	76

Aug. 7-10, 2014

GALLUP

The decline in Americans' overall support for daily prayer in school over time is driven, in part, by a dip in support among Democrats. In 2000, 67% of Democrats supported this idea. This dropped to 59% in 2001 and fell to 45% by 2014. Meanwhile, support among Republicans has stayed consistent, and independents' support increased slightly.

Bottom Line

Religion continues to be important to many Americans. The vast majority of Americans identify with a religion, a majority of Americans say religion can solve today's problems, and three in four Americans see the Bible as the actual or inspired word of God.

Thus, it is not surprising that a majority of Americans are in favor of religion having a larger presence in schools. In fact, previous

Gallup research showed that in 2005, three in four Americans supported a constitutional amendment to allow voluntary prayer in public schools. While support for saying a daily prayer in school has dropped slightly since 2001, a majority still favors this idea. There is also widespread support for having prayers as part of graduation ceremonies and for the use of school facilities by student religious groups.

Survey Methods

Results for this Gallup poll are based on telephone interviews conducted Aug. 7–10, 2014, with a random sample of 1,032 adults, aged 18 and older, living in all 50 U.S. states and the District of Columbia.

For results based on the total sample of national adults, the margin of sampling error is ±4 percentage points at the 95% confidence level.

September 26, 2014
HISPANICS' APPROVAL OF OBAMA DOWN SINCE '12
In U.S., 52% of Hispanics approve,
compared with 42% of all adults

by Frank Newport

PRINCETON, NJ—Hispanics' approval of the job being done by President Barack Obama has settled in at about 10 percentage points above the national average, well below the Hispanic advantage of over 20 points that the president enjoyed in late 2012 and 2013. Obama's approval rating among Hispanics has averaged 13 points above the national average since he first took office in 2009.

Obama Job Approval -- Monthly Averages
% Approve

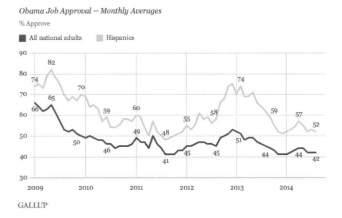

Hispanics' generally higher approval of Obama reflects their overall Democratic orientation. From January through August of this year, for example, 49% of Hispanics identified with or leaned toward the Democratic Party, compared with 43% of Americans overall. Twenty-two percent of Hispanics identified with or leaned toward the Republican Party, compared with 39% of the nation as a whole. In the 2012 presidential election, Hispanics voted for Obama over Mitt Romney by a 71% to 27% margin, according to exit polls.

The size of Obama's approval advantage among Hispanics has varied significantly over the course of his administration, from as low as six points in some months in 2011 to more than 20 points

in late 2012 and early 2013. In December 2012, just after the election, 75% of Hispanics approved, compared with 53% among all Americans. By August of this year, Obama's Hispanic approval gap dwindled to 10 points—52% among Hispanics versus 42% among the overall population.

Still, even with the recent drop, Obama's support remains higher among Hispanics than among the national population, and is proportionately higher now than it has been at other points such as in 2010, 2011, and early 2012.

Obama Job Approval -- Hispanic Gap Over National Average

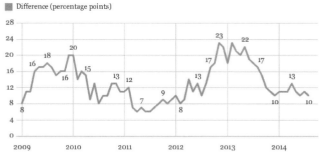

Hispanics were clearly most positive about Obama on a relative basis in the months leading up to his successful bid for reelection in late 2012 and into the first months of 2013. In some of these months, Hispanic approval ratings were in the mid-70s, compared with ratings in the low 50s among the national population. This surge in Hispanic approval in and around the 2012 election likely reflects the Obama reelection campaign's attention to Hispanics and its focus on increasing Hispanic turnout in key battleground states. During his campaign, for example, Obama said he was confident that he would get immigration reform done over the next year. Immigration reform has not yet come to pass, suggesting that the disproportionate drop in Obama approval among Hispanics since the election reflects at least in part the failure of the president—and Congress—to enact these promised legislative changes.

This hypothesis is reinforced by data showing that Hispanics are much more likely than U.S. adults overall to say immigration is the most important problem facing the country. Moreover, previous Gallup research also shows that variation in Hispanics' approval of Obama is tied to significant events in the immigration debate.

Bottom Line

President Obama has lost significantly more support among Hispanics than among the national population since the months following his reelection in November 2012, although Hispanics' ratings of Obama remain 10 points above the national average. The significant uptick in Hispanics' approval at the time of the 2012 election, and the subsequent significant drop, may reflect unfulfilled promises that Obama made during the campaign about immigration reform.

Survey Methods

Results for this Gallup poll are based on telephone interviews conducted from January 2009 through August 2014 on the Gallup Daily tracking survey, with random monthly samples of approximately 15,000 adults and 1,300 Hispanics, aged 18 and older, living in all 50 U.S. states and the District of Columbia.

For results based on the total monthly sample of national adults, the margin of sampling error is ±1 percentage point at the 95% confidence level. For results based on the total monthly sample of Hispanics, the margin of sampling error is ±3 percentage points at the 95% confidence level.

September 29, 2014
AMERICANS REMAIN DIVIDED ON PREFERENCE FOR GOV'T ACTIVITY
Thirty-five percent prefer a less active role, 32% a more active one

by Jeffrey M. Jones

PRINCETON, NJ—Americans continue to divide almost evenly when asked to rate their preference for government activity on a 1-to-5 scale. Currently, 35% rate themselves a "1" or "2," indicating that they favor a limited government that "provides only the most basic government functions." Meanwhile, 32% rate themselves a "4" or "5," tending to prefer a government that "takes active steps in every area it can to try and improve the lives of its citizens." The remaining one-third of Americans fall in the middle.

Preferences Regarding Federal Government's Role

Next, I'd like you to think more broadly about the purposes of government. Where would you rate yourself on a scale of 1 to 5, where 1 means you think the government should do only those things necessary to provide the most basic government functions, and 5 means you think the government should take active steps in every area it can to try and improve the lives of its citizens? You may use any number from 1 to 5.

	2010	2011	2013	2014
	%	%	%	%
5/Gov't should take active steps in every area it can	19	21	19	17
4	15	14	15	15
3	33	27	33	32
2	15	18	16	19
1/Gov't should provide only the most basic functions	18	19	16	16

GALLUP

Gallup has asked this question four times since 2010, and each time, Americans have divided themselves roughly into thirds favoring a more active government, a less active government, or something in between. This division is especially noteworthy because the government's role in solving the nation's problems has been arguably more salient in recent years during the housing crisis, financial crisis, economic recession, and passage of the Affordable Care Act.

Party Differences in Preference Regarding Government Activity

	Democrats	Independents	Republicans
	%	%	%
Prefer a more active government (4,5)	53	29	16
Neutral (3)	38	31	26
Prefer a less active government (1,2)	9	39	58

Sept. 4-7, 2014

GALLUP

Consistent with their respective parties' platforms, a majority of Democrats favor a more active government, while a majority of Republicans favor a more limited government. But party supporters are not entirely consistent with the approach to governing that the elected leaders from their party usually take. Substantial percentages of each party's supporters—38% of Democrats and 26% of

Republicans—place themselves in the middle on the 5-point scale. And one in six Republicans say they favor a more active government, while one in 10 Democrats favor a less active one.

Americans Say Government Doing Too Much Currently

When asked in a separate question about the government's current activity level, 54% of Americans say the government is "trying to do too many things that should be left to individuals and businesses." Meanwhile, 41% say the government should "do more to solve our country's problems."

Gallup has asked this question since 1992, including during four different presidential administrations—two Republican and two Democratic. Americans' opinions appear to be influenced by which party is in the White House, and whether the president prefers a more active or a less active government. During the two Republican administrations, an average of 49% of Americans said the government was doing too much, compared with 55% during the two Democratic administrations.

Americans' preferences for government activity are highly related to their opinions of whether the government is currently doing too much. Those who prefer a limited government role on the 5-point scale overwhelmingly say the government is doing too much now (86%). At the same time, most of those who prefer an active government, 74%, say the government should be doing *more* right now. Those without a clear preference on this matter tilt in the direction of saying the government is currently doing too much.

Views of Whether Government Is Doing Too Much or Should Be Doing More, by Preference for Government Activity

	Prefer a more active government (4,5)	Neutral (3)	Prefer a less active government (1,2)
	%	%	%
Gov't doing too much	21	51	86
Gov't should be doing more	74	41	10

Sept. 4-7, 2014

GALLUP

Implications

Americans as a whole do not have a clear preference for whether the government should take an active role or a limited one. The public generally divides into equal thirds in favoring an active government, a limited government, or something in between. This division has been consistent during the five years Gallup has asked Americans to indicate their preferences.

The divided preferences on government activity do not give elected leaders clear direction in deciding whether to rely on government or nongovernment solutions to the nation's biggest problems. To some degree this may help explain why the president and Congress have had difficulty in addressing some of the major issues facing the country in recent years.

Survey Methods

Results for this Gallup poll are based on telephone interviews conducted Sept. 4–7, 2014, with a random sample of 1,017 adults, aged 18 and older, living in all 50 U.S. states and the District of Columbia.

For results based on the total sample of national adults, the margin of sampling error is ±4 percentage points at the 95% confidence level.

September 30, 2014

LOUISIANA TILTING DEMOCRATIC IN 2014

Landrieu's re-election bid could suffer from smaller party edge, low Obama approval

by Justin McCarthy

WASHINGTON, D.C.—In 2014, more Louisianans identify themselves as or lean Democratic (45%) than Republican (41%), a shift from the slight edge Republicans have held for past three years. The shift in party preferences is likely a welcome indicator for Democratic Sen. Mary Landrieu as she attempts to win her fourth term in one of this year's most highly watched U.S. Senate races.

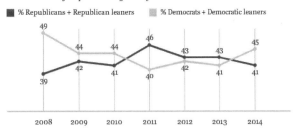

Louisiana -- Self-Reported Party Identification

■ % Republicans + Republican leaners   ■ % Democrats + Democratic leaners

Data for 2014 collected Jan. 1–June 30

GALLUP

Still, the Democratic Party's current edge in Louisiana is smaller than its 10-point advantage in 2008, when Landrieu last won re-election.

Without allocating the leanings of independents, 35% of Louisianans in the first half of 2014 identified themselves as Democrats, 33% as independents, and 28% as Republicans, giving the Democrats a seven-percentage-point edge. That compares with a 10-point edge in unleaned party ID in 2008, when 39% identified as Democrats and 29% as Republicans. Nationally, for the first six months of this year, the split was 30% Democrats, 40% independents, and 25% Republicans.

Either way, Louisiana Democrats have a smaller advantage this year than in 2008, similar to the party identification trends nationally. That is not good news for Landrieu, who has clung to her seat with relatively narrow victories since her initial 1996 bid for the Senate. If Landrieu fails to get 50% of the vote in the November election, by state law, it would force a December runoff election between the two top vote-getters—likely against the Republican front-runner, Rep. Bill Cassidy. This scenario could leave her vulnerable if the anti-Landrieu votes are consolidated in the runoff.

Though Landrieu narrowly avoided a runoff in 2008, two Republicans—Cassidy and Air Force Col. Rob Maness—are challenging her in the November general election, making a subsequent runoff election likely because of the split votes. For Landrieu, the risk of a runoff is only magnified by the smaller Democratic advantage this year than in 2008. For national Democrats and Republicans, it could mean that the majority party in the U.S. Senate would not be decided until December.

However, given that 2014 may be a slightly more favorable Democratic environment in Louisiana than in 2010 or 2012, the news is not all bad for Landrieu. Of course, the Democratic advantage in party preferences helps her only if the turnout of Democrats (and Landrieu supporters) comes close to matching that of non-Democrats (and Landrieu opponents).

Despite Democratic Edge, Louisianans Most Likely to Identify as Conservatives

Although Democrats currently outnumber Republicans in the state, Louisianans are most likely to describe their political views as conservative (45%), rather than moderate (34%) or liberal (17%).

Louisiana is among the six most conservative states in the country, and has the distinction of being one of four states whose residents are more likely to identify as conservatives than they are as Republicans (including leaners). The other three states all have 2014 Senate races: In Mississippi and West Virginia, Republicans are expected to win, while the outcome of the Arkansas contest is uncertain.

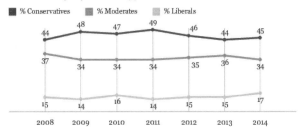

Louisiana -- Self-Reported Ideology

■ % Conservatives   ■ % Moderates   ■ % Liberals

Data for 2014 collected Jan. 1–June 30

GALLUP

This conservative bent may seem contradictory, given the lower percentage identifying as Republicans in Louisiana. But with the GOP's grip on five of the state's six congressional districts, as well as the governor's office and the other U.S. Senate seat (held by David Vitter since 2005), the high number of conservatives suggests that right-leaning Louisianans may be voting along ideological rather than partisan lines.

Obama's Effect on the Louisiana Senate Race

President Barack Obama's job approval rating in Louisiana has consistently been below the national average. In the first half of this year, 40% of Louisianans approved of the president's performance, compared with 43% nationally. In some years, his rating in Louisiana has been as many as seven points below the national average.

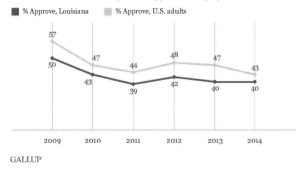

Louisiana vs. National Average -- Job Approval Ratings of President Obama

■ % Approve, Louisiana   ■ % Approve, U.S. adults

GALLUP

Low Obama approval in Louisiana is a new challenge for Landrieu, who has not run for re-election during Obama's tenure until this year. Though she has attempted to distance herself from the president, her opponents have tried to tie Landrieu to his policies, including her vote that helped pass the Affordable Care Act.

But the president isn't the only external political figure who could play into the Senate race—former Democratic Gov. Edwin

Edwards is running for a seat in Cassidy's former congressional district. Edwards, who served eight years in federal prison for corruption, could negatively affect the Democratic line for some voters who react against the scandals that have plagued many of the state's political figures. According to Gallup's 2013 50-state poll, 48% of Louisianans express trust in their state government, 10 points lower than the 50-state average.

Additionally, Louisianans have a gloomier view of the nation at large. Gallup's Economic Confidence Index for the first half of 2014 puts the 50-state average at −16, but for Louisiana, it's an even lower −27. At the state level, the 50-state average for Americans' confidence in their state's economy in 2013 was 23; for Louisiana it was 10. This lower confidence in the economy, especially the national economy, could affect whom voters choose to send to Congress.

Bottom Line

The road to winning the Louisiana U.S. Senate seat is marked with many potholes that could sink Landrieu's path to re-election. From the less favorable political climate to Obama's unpopularity, and from the conservative tilt of the state to the complicated three-way contest in the so-called "jungle primary," there are many obstacles for the incumbent to navigate. Though she has squeezed through some highly contested races in the past, Landrieu's chances of doing so again in 2014 appear to be slimmer, given the variety of factors going against her.

Obama's name will not appear on the 2014 ballot, but he is clearly a presence in the race—and his low approval rating suggests that he is more of a detriment than an asset to Landrieu's re-election bid. These factors culminate in a stormy political climate that gives Cassidy an opportunity to take the seat Landrieu has held for three terms.

Survey Methods

Results for this Gallup poll are based on telephone interviews conducted on the Gallup Daily tracking survey with a random sample of 88,802 adults, aged 18 and older, living in all 50 U.S. states and the District of Columbia. Results are also based on Gallup's recent 50-state poll conducted June–December 2013 with a random sample of approximately 600 adults per state, aged 18 and older, living in all 50 U.S. states.

For results based on the 2014 sample of 1,396 Louisiana residents, the margin of sampling error is ±3 percentage points at the 95% confidence level.

For results based on the 2013 sample of adults per state, the margin of sampling error is ±5 percentage points at the 95% confidence level.

September 30, 2014
SMALL-BUSINESS OWNERS SATISFIED, BUT FEWER FEEL SUCCESSFUL
U.S. small-business owners cite the freedom of being their own boss as top job perk

by Coleen McMurray and Frank Newport

PRINCETON, NJ—U.S. small-business owners are more likely now to say they are satisfied with being a small-business owner than they were at the tail end of the recession, but are less likely to see themselves as successful. According to a Wells Fargo/Gallup survey of small-business owners conducted earlier this year, 56% of small-business owners, up from 45% in 2010, are either extremely or very satisfied with being a small-business owner. But fewer owners, 37%, say they feel extremely or very successful as a small-business owner—the lowest figure in a decade.

U.S. Small-Business Owners: Satisfaction vs. Success
Wells Fargo/Gallup survey of small-business owners

■ % Feel extremely/very satisfied with being a small-business owner
□ % Feel extremely/very successful as a small-business owner

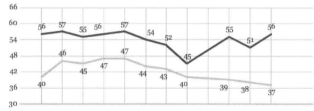

GALLUP'

While small-business owners' satisfaction dropped in 2009 and fell even further in 2010, it rebounded in 2012 to where it was prior to the recession. After dipping again in 2013, it returned this year to the level seen in 2012. On the other hand, owners' perceptions of being extremely or very successful have trended downward since 2007 and have yet to recover. This is the case even as Gallup has observed improvements in many of its economic measures on employment, hiring, economic confidence, and consumer spending in recent years.

One explanation for this paradox may lie in the fact that small-business owners tend to like the basic lifestyle and self-sufficiency that come with being an entrepreneur, and therefore may tend to be satisfied even when they don't perceive themselves as particularly successful. Over four in 10 say that the most rewarding thing about starting and running their business is being their own boss and being independent—by far the most frequently mentioned response to this open-ended question.

What would you say has been the most rewarding thing about starting and running your own business?
Wells Fargo/Gallup survey of U.S. small-business owners

	Total
	%
Being my own boss/Independence/Being the decision-maker	42
Job satisfaction/Sense of accomplishment/Pride	17
Work my own schedule/Flexible/Having more family time	12
Interaction with customers	11
Financial rewards/Money	7
Creating jobs/employment	2
Community involvement/Giving back to community	1
Working with family	0
Other	3
None/Nothing	4
Don't know	1

March 31-April 4, 2014

GALLUP'

Separately, when given a list of reasons that might motivate people to start their own business, the most popular answers are the desire to secure their financial future (69%), to be their own boss (66%), and to set their own hours (51%). Owners are less likely to rate many other reasons as being important in their decision to open a small business, including the desire to take advantage of new business opportunities, continuing a family business, providing jobs for children and/or family members, or pursuing a hobby.

Thinking about your motivations for opening a small business, please tell me how important each of the following were as a reason to start your own business.

Wells Fargo/Gallup survey of U.S. small-business owners

	Very important	Somewhat important	Not very important	Not at all important
	%	%	%	%
To secure your financial future	69	21	5	4
To be your own boss	66	22	6	5
To set your own hours	51	24	10	14
To have a job/source of income until the job market improves	30	18	19	31
To take advantage of new business opportunities available in the marketplace	29	28	22	20
To continue the family business	26	10	14	46
To provide jobs for children and/or family members	21	19	20	39
To pursue a hobby	15	17	23	44

March 31-April 4, 2014

GALLUP'

Owners Recognize the Difficulties of Being an Entrepreneur

Even while the majority of small-business owners are satisfied with their occupation choice, they clearly recognize the difficulties of being an entrepreneur and a self-employed business owner. Many owners say they would advise young people to work for someone else (47%) rather than start their own business (42%), underscoring the challenges that today's entrepreneurs face.

Would you recommend to a young person that they start their own business, or go to work for someone else?

Wells Fargo/Gallup survey of U.S. small-business owners

	Total
	%
Start their own business	42
Go to work for someone else	47
Don't know	11

March 31-April 4, 2014

GALLUP'

Implications

Small-business owners convey their strong desire to be their own boss and to set their own hours, and report feeling mostly satisfied with being a small-business owner. But fewer today say they feel successful as a small-business owner, even as the economy has improved in the last few years. And although other Wells Fargo/Gallup research shows that most would do it all over again if given the chance, owners are divided on whether they would recommend to young people that they start their own business, perhaps recognizing the significant challenges that come with the territory of being an entrepreneur in today's economy.

For more information, please see:

- https://wellsfargoworks.com/run/optimism-continues-to-slowly-improve
- https://wellsfargoworks.com/File/Index/DFC0D5uow02DtLPw5ZtGxw

About the Wells Fargo/Gallup Small Business Index

Since August 2003, the Wells Fargo/Gallup Small Business Index has surveyed small-business owners on current and future perceptions of their business' financial situation.

Wells Fargo serves more than 2.5 million small-business owners across the United States and loans more money to America's small businesses than any other bank (2002–2012 CRA government data). To help more small businesses achieve financial success, in 2014 Wells Fargo introduced Wells Fargo Works for Small Business—a broad initiative to deliver resources, guidance, and services to business owners—and a goal to extend $100 billion in new lending to small businesses by 2018. For more information about Wells Fargo Works for Small Business, visit wellsfargoworks.com.

Survey Methods

Results for the total data set are based on telephone interviews conducted March 31–April 4, 2014, with a random sample of 601 small-business owners, living in all 50 U.S. states and the District of Columbia.

For results based on the total sample of small-business owners, the margin of sampling error is ±4 percentage points at the 95% confidence level.

Gallup uses a Dun & Bradstreet sample of small businesses nationwide having $20 million or less in sales or revenues. The data are weighted to be representative of U.S. small businesses within this size range nationwide.

In addition to sampling error, question wording and practical difficulties in conducting surveys can introduce error or bias into the findings of public opinion polls.

October 01, 2014
TEA PARTY SUPPORT HOLDS AT 24%
Ideology is the major factor in Tea Party support within the GOP

by Frank Newport

PRINCETON, NJ—One in four Americans now say they are supporters of the Tea Party. This is down from 2010, but support has been fairly stable since late 2011. The percentage of Americans classifying themselves as Tea Party opponents is slightly higher now than it was in 2010. The lower support for the Tea Party reflects the group's more limited impact in primary election contests this midterm election year, compared with its major role in 2010.

Americans' Affiliation With the Tea Party

Do you consider yourself to be -- [ROTATED: a supporter of the Tea Party movement, an opponent of the Tea Party movement], or neither?

■ % Supporter   % Opponent

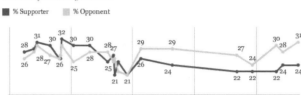

Percentage "neither" not shown

GALLUP'

The latest update is from Gallup's Sept. 4–7 Governance survey. The Tea Party came into national prominence in 2010, when its supporters were widely credited with helping elect candidates they supported to Congress. Support among Americans was 30% or higher in a number of polls in 2010 and the first part of 2011, but began to drop later that year. It reached a low of 21% in two late 2011 surveys, followed by a slight recovery in 2012. After declining slightly in three surveys in 2013 and early 2014, support then edged up to 24% in surveys conducted in May and September of this year. Thirty-one percent of Americans now classify themselves as Tea Party opponents—by one percentage point, the highest opposition level Gallup has measured—leaving about 44% of Americans who are neither supporters nor opponents, or who do not answer the question.

Strength of Support for and Opposition to Tea Party

Are you a strong [supporter/opponent] of the Tea Party movement, or not?

	%
SUPPORTER	
Strong supporter	11
Not strong supporter	13
OPPONENT	
Strong opponent	19
Not strong opponent	12
NEITHER	42
NO OPINION	2

Sept. 4-7, 2014

GALLUP'

Tea Party opponents feel more strongly about their position than do supporters. More than half say they are "strong opponents," while less than half of supporters say they are "strong supporters." This pattern has been evident to one degree or the other since 2011.

Tea Party Republicans Much More Conservative Than Other Republicans

The Tea Party movement's major influence has been within the Republican Party, particularly in terms of Republican primaries. Eight in 10 Tea Party supporters in the September survey are Republicans or lean toward the Republican Party, with the rest divided between independents and Democrats.

Gallup has asked about Tea Party support in five surveys conducted over the past year, consisting of more than 6,000 interviews, with 18% of adults in that large sample saying they are Tea Party Republicans, 25% who are Republicans who do not support the Tea Party, and 58% who are not Republicans.

Overall, 77% of Tea Party Republicans are conservative, including 28% who say they are *very* conservative. That presents a sharp contrast with the 52% of non–Tea Party Republicans who are conservative, including only 10% who classify themselves as very conservative.

Tea Party Support, by Ideology

	Tea Party Republicans	All other Republicans	All others
	%	%	%
Very conservative	28	10	4
Conservative	49	42	16
Moderate	19	38	42
Liberal	3	7	25
Very liberal	1	3	9

Aggregrated polls conducted from September 2013 to September 2014

GALLUP'

Demographically, 31% of Tea Party Republicans are men aged 50 and older, compared with 21% of other Republicans. Tea Party Republicans are also more likely to be married. There are only minor differences between the two groups of Republicans in terms of region and education. Republicans overall are much more likely than other Americans to be non-Hispanic whites, as are Tea Party Republicans, 86% of whom are white.

Bottom Line

Tea Party support is down from where it was at the time of the last midterm elections in 2010, although it has remained relatively stable over the last year or two—while opposition is up from 2010. These trends may help explain the diminished impact of the Tea Party in 2014 Republican primary elections this year, and could mean the Tea Party will have less of an impact in the forthcoming November general elections.

Most Tea Party supporters are Republicans, and within the Republican Party, Tea Party supporters are clearly defined by their conservative ideology, meaning they are generally indistinguishable from conservative Republicans. Tea Party supporters within the Republican Party also tend to be older, are more likely to be male, and are more likely to be married than other Republicans.

Results for this Gallup poll are based on telephone interviews conducted in surveys from Sept. 5–8, 2013, Dec. 5–8, 2013, April 24–30, 2014, June 5–8, 2014, and Sept. 4–7, 2014, with a total random sample of 6,098 adults, aged 18 and older, living in all 50 U.S. states and the District of Columbia.

For results based on the total sample of national adults, the margin of sampling error is ±1 percentage point at the 95% confidence level.

For results based on the Sept. 4–7, 2014, sample of 1,017 national adults, the margin of sampling error is ±4 percentage points at the 95% confidence level.

October 03, 2014
KANSAS: GOP HAS NUMBERS ADVANTAGE, BUT SUPPORT DROPS
Among states with the most Republicans, Kansas has the fewest conservatives

by Andrew Dugan

WASHINGTON, D.C.—Kansas has emerged as an unlikely battleground state in the 2014 midterm election, with two longtime Republican fixtures, U.S. Sen. Pat Roberts and Gov. Sam Brownback, facing competitive races. These races threaten to sweep the GOP out of two of the state's most prominent positions. Adding to the element of surprise is the fact that residents of the Sunflower State still strongly favor the GOP in terms of party identification, although the Republican edge dropped in the first half of this year to its lowest point since 2009.

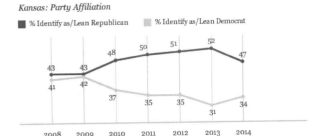

Kansas: Party Affiliation

Data for 2014 collected Jan. 1–June 30

GALLUP

In the first six months of 2014, nearly half of Kansans (47%) said they leaned toward or identified with the GOP—down five percentage points from 2013, but still giving Republicans a wide margin over Democrats in party affiliation.

The GOP is unquestionably the dominant political party within the state of Kansas, holding both Senate and all four House seats and controlling supermajorities in the state legislature. Any Republican nominee for president can consider Kansas a sure bet—the state last voted for a Democrat, Lyndon Johnson, in 1964.

Kansas' Republican leanings have generally intensified throughout Barack Obama's presidency, as Gallup's Daily tracking data evince, though the first half of 2014 saw a slight retreat in Republican support. Republicans have held a near or actual majority in party affiliation since the first year of Obama's presidency.

Undoubtedly, Kansas' low ratings of Obama's job performance have helped drive this trend. In the first half of 2014, just 32% of Kansans approved of Obama's performance—11 points below the national average. Kansas' approval of Obama is among the lowest in the nation.

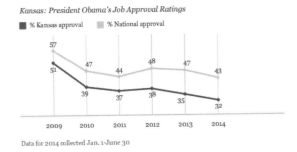

Kansas: President Obama's Job Approval Ratings

Data for 2014 collected Jan. 1-June 30

GALLUP

These data generally suggest Republicans should be in a strong position for the midterm election, despite this year's drop in GOP identification. But statewide polling shows that both Roberts and Brownback have a real race on their hands. Roberts, who is battling for his fourth term in the Senate, finds himself in an unenviable position—after once clearly leading a three-way race, he now trails independent candidate Greg Orman after Democrat Chad Taylor dropped out.

Kansas Least Conservative of Top 10 Republican States

Nearly as many Kansans describe their ideology as moderate (36%) as they do conservative (38%), which may be one reason the self-described moderate Orman is performing so well in the polls. The percentage of Kansas moderates is on par with the national figure, but higher than in other conservative-leaning states with key Senate elections this year, including North Carolina and Arkansas. And despite the conservative flavor of many Kansas politicians—its delegation to the U.S. House was named by *National Journal* in 2012 as the most conservative of all delegations—the state is not as conservative as other ruby-red states. Of the 10 states with the highest proportion of the population identifying with or leaning toward the GOP, Kansas has the lowest share of the population describing their political views as conservative. In other words, there is reason to believe a candidate stressing a moderate platform could be successful.

Republican Affiliation and Conservative Ideology, by State

	% Identify as/ Lean Republican	% Identify as conservative
Utah	61	46
Wyoming	59	42
Idaho	54	46
South Dakota	51	41
Montana	49	42
Alabama	49	46
Nebraska	48	40
Mississippi	47	49
Kansas	47	38
Tennessee	47	42

Jan. 1- June 30, 2014

GALLUP

Additionally, one-fifth of Kansans (20%) describe themselves as liberal, meaning a solid majority (56%) describe themselves as either moderate or liberal.

Ideology, party identification, and several other political and economic measures for Kansas are included in Gallup's new State Scorecard assessments, which present data for 14 key measures for each of the 50 states. Within each assessment, the state's performance on the measure is compared with the national average for the same time period.

Despite Brownback's Tax-Cutting Agenda, Few Say Taxes Not Too High

Sam Brownback, a former U.S. representative and senator, was elected governor of Kansas in 2010 after pledging to reduce taxes—and over the course of his term, he has delivered on that pledge. The governor, along with the GOP-led state legislature, cut personal income tax rates and made various other changes to the tax code to reduce liabilities. Despite the fact that many of these changes went into effect at the start of 2013, only 42% of Kansans said in a 2013 poll that state taxes are *not* too high, below the 50-state average of 47%.

Kansans' Views of State Taxes

Do you consider the amount of state taxes you have to pay as too high, or not too high?

	Kansas	50-state average
Not too high	42%	47%
Too high	57%	50%

June-December 2013

GALLUP

Brownback promoted the tax-cutting legislation as actions that would create jobs and grow the state economy. However, Kansans had a relatively small amount of confidence in their state economy by the end of 2013. The state's Economic Confidence Index averaged +15, below the 50-state average of +23. And Kansans' views of the local job market were no more positive than those in most other states. For both questions, Kansas performed worse than three of the four states that border it—Nebraska, Colorado, and Oklahoma. Only Missouri performed worse.

About Three in 10 Say Kansas Is Best State to Live in

One issue dogging Sen. Roberts stems from reports earlier this year that he does not have his own house in Kansas, leaving him open to one of the most deadly attacks in the political playbook—that he is out of touch with his state. Yet it seems a sizable percentage of Kansans wouldn't mind having a home located elsewhere in the country either: Almost four in 10 Kansans (37%) say that if they had the opportunity, they would move to another state. About six in 10 (63%) say they would like to remain in Kansas. And just 34% of Kansans say their state is the best state to live in, well below the 50-state average of 46%.

Bottom Line

Kansas is not a state that usually comes up in discussions of battleground states—the state last voted for a Democrat for president

in 1964, and the last Democratic senator won his term in 1932. And given the national environment that appears to favor Republicans this fall, Kansas would seem an unlikely candidate for tight midterm races that could throw out two well-known Republican officials. For all the suspense, though, the GOP's strengths in this state could very well carry its candidates come November—Republicans have a huge lead in self-reported political identification, and Obama registers one of his lowest job approval ratings in the country.

Yet a GOP victory is not a foregone conclusion, and this must be quite a shock to the typically triumphant Kansas Republican Party. The political drama in Kansas is, if nothing else, a reminder that ideology and job performance matter, even in states with well-rooted political identities.

Survey Methods

Results for this Gallup poll are based on telephone interviews conducted Jan. 1–June 30, 2014, on the Gallup Daily tracking survey, with a random sample of 88,802 adults, aged 18 and older, living in all 50 U.S. states and the District of Columbia. Results are also based on Gallup's recent 50-state poll conducted June–December 2013, with a random sample of approximately 600 adults per state, aged 18 and older, living in all 50 U.S. states.

For results based on the 2014 sample of 866 Kansas residents, the margin of sampling error is ±4 percentage points at the 95% confidence level.

For results based on the 2013 sample of adults per state, the margin of sampling error is ±5 percentage points at the 95% confidence level.

October 03, 2014

OBAMA FACTOR IN 2014 VOTE SIMILAR TO 2010

As in 2010, more say they will vote to oppose rather than support him

by Jeffrey M. Jones

PRINCETON, NJ—Registered voters are more likely to view their choice of candidate in this year's midterm elections as a message of opposition (32%) rather than support (20%) for President Barack Obama. That 12-percentage-point margin is similar to what Gallup measured for Obama in 2010 and George W. Bush in 2006, years in which their parties performed poorly in the midterm elections.

Registered Voters' Use of Midterm Election Vote to Send Message to President

Will your vote for a candidate be made in order to send a message that you SUPPORT [Barack Obama], be made in order to send a message that you OPPOSE [Barack Obama], or will you NOT be sending a message about [Barack Obama] with your vote?

	% Message to Support	% Message to Oppose	% Not Sending a Message
Obama 2014	20	32	46
Obama 2010	22	30	44
Bush 2006	18	31	46
Bush 2002	28	15	53
Clinton 1998	24	19	54

Based on registered voters.

GALLUP

Gallup first asked this question in 1998, the year Republicans were moving toward impeaching President Bill Clinton for lying about his affair with a White House intern. That year, when Clinton's approval rating was 63%, more voters said their choice of candidate in the fall election would be made to show support rather than opposition to Clinton. Democrats had a strong showing in that fall's elections, gaining seats in the House of Representatives, bucking the historical pattern by which the president's party loses seats in Congress in midterm elections.

In the next midterm election, voters by an even larger margin said their vote would be made to support rather than oppose President George W. Bush, who had a 66% approval rating at the time of the elections. These attitudes were consistent with the eventual outcome, as Republicans increased their majority in the House and gained majority control of the Senate.

The presidents in the next two midterm elections were not popular, including Bush's second midterm election in 2006 (38%) when Democrats won control of the House and Senate and Obama's first midterm in 2010 (44%) when Republicans won back control of the House. Reinforcing that the 2014 midterms look more like 2006 and 2010 than 1998 or 2002, Obama's approval ratings have been in the low 40% range, including 42% in the most recent Gallup Daily tracking three-day rolling average.

Republican Opposition to Obama Overshadows Democrats' Support

A majority of Republican registered voters, 58%, say they will be sending a message of opposition to Obama with their vote this fall. In contrast, 38% of Democratic voters say they will support the president. Rather than supporting Obama, most Democrats, 53%, say they will not be sending a message with their vote.

Democrats are a bit less likely now (38%) than in 2010 (45%) to say they will be sending a message of support to Obama, while Republican opposition to the president is the same.

Registered Voters' Use of Midterm Election Vote to Send Message to President, by Political Party

	% Support	% Oppose	% No message
OBAMA 2014			
Democrats/Democratic leaners	38	8	53
Republicans/Republican leaners	4	58	37
OBAMA 2010			
Democrats/Democratic leaners	45	4	48
Republicans/Republican leaners	2	58	38
BUSH 2006			
Democrats/Democratic leaners	2	57	37
Republicans/Republican leaners	39	4	54
BUSH 2002			
Democrats/Democratic leaners	8	31	57
Republicans/Republican leaners	51	1	46
CLINTON 1998			
Democrats/Democratic leaners	40	4	52
Republicans/Republican leaners	6	39	52

Based on registered voters.

GALLUP

Obama's current numbers by party mirror Bush's numbers in his second midterm in 2006. A majority of Democrats at that time said they were voting to oppose Bush, and Republicans were more likely to say they were not sending a message with their vote than to say they were casting it to show support for Bush. The 2006 Bush numbers represented a shift from 2002 when most Republicans said they were voting to support Bush.

Implications

The president is always a major factor in midterm elections, with his party typically losing seats in Congress. And it is clear, based on his lower approval ratings and that more voters say they will be voting as a means of showing opposition rather than support for the president, that Obama is more of a liability than an asset to Democratic candidates this year. Republican operatives are aware of this, trying to link Democratic candidates to the president, particularly in key senate races that will determine whether the Democrats or Republicans hold the majority in the Senate next year. Contrary to Bush's active campaigning on behalf of Republicans in fall 2002, Obama himself may choose to be less active in campaigning for Democrats to avoid hurting Democratic candidates' chances.

Survey Methods

Results for this Gallup poll are based on telephone interviews conducted Sept. 25–30, 2014, with a random sample of 1,095 registered voters, aged 18 and older, living in all 50 U.S. states and the District of Columbia.

For results based on the total sample of registered voters, the margin of sampling error is ±4 percentage points at the 95% confidence level.

October 06, 2014

LOW FAVORABLE RATINGS STILL PLAGUE TOP DOGS ON CAPITOL HILL
Net favorability toward Sen. Harry Reid is his lowest yet

by Lydia Saad

PRINCETON, NJ—Relatively few Americans have a favorable impression of U.S. Senate Majority Leader Harry Reid or Speaker of the U.S. House of Representatives John Boehner—the two top-ranking members of Congress. But as weak as both men's ratings have been in recent years, Reid's has recently gotten worse, with his favorable score dropping from 27% in April to 21% today.

Americans' Overall Opinion of Senate Democratic Leader Harry Reid
Based on U.S. adults

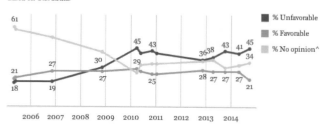

^ No opinion includes those who say they have never heard of Reid

GALLUP

Reid's image has consistently tilted negative since he emerged as a nationally known figure in 2008. Before that, the majority of Americans had either not heard of him, or had no opinion of him. But now his net favorable score (the percentage viewing him favorably minus the percentage viewing him unfavorably) is the worst of his career, at −24.

While Reid's image took a hard hit since April, Boehner's rating is down only slightly. Twenty-eight percent of Americans view him favorably, down from 31%, and 50% view him unfavorably. This is roughly equivalent to his ratings since late 2013, but far worse than his image prior to that.

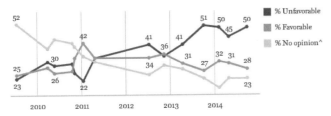

Americans' Overall Opinion of Speaker of the House John Boehner
Based on U.S. adults

Prior to 2011, the question read "House Republican Leader, John Boehner"
^ No opinion includes those who say they have never heard of Boehner

GALLUP

The latest results are based on a Gallup telephone survey conducted Sept. 25–30 with 1,252 national adults.

Reid's favorable image has dimmed among all party groups since April, although most notably among Democrats, dropping eight percentage points to 46%. Smaller declines occurred among Republicans and independents, reflecting the fact that his scores were already so low among these groups that they didn't have much further to fall.

From a longer-term perspective—at least since 2012—Reid's favorable rating has hovered near 50% among Democrats, while it has declined among independents and Republicans.

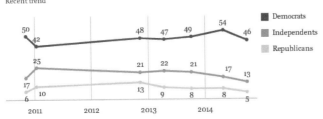

Percentage Viewing Senate Democratic Leader Harry Reid Favorably, by Party ID
Recent trend

GALLUP

Boehner's Image Nearly Underwater With Republicans

While Reid's favorable ratings are far from stellar, he can at least boast a relatively positive net favorable score among rank-and-file Democrats, as only 16% of Democrats have an unfavorable view of the Democratic leader. Boehner, by contrast, is in a far worse position with his political base with a full 40% of Republicans viewing him unfavorably, versus 46% viewing him favorably.

Boehner's image among Republicans started to sour in 2012, along with the broader slide in the Republican Party's image.

However, after recovering somewhat earlier this year, his favorability recently got significantly worse, with his unfavorable score among Republicans rising 11 points since April.

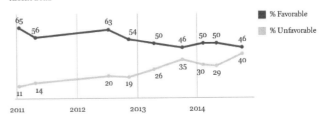

Opinion of House Majority Leader John Boehner -- Among Republicans
Recent trend

GALLUP

Boehner's image likely suffered in 2013 from Americans' disaffection with Congress over the budget shutdown, and Republicans' disappointment with the lack of spending cuts in the final budget deal that Boehner supported. His troubles within the GOP this year could stem from the mounting criticism he has faced from conservatives—including three Tea Party Republicans who challenged Boehner in the primary election in his district this spring—partly over his support for pursuing comprehensive immigration reform.

Like Reid, Boehner has also seen a clear decline in support from independents, with his favorable rating falling to 22% among this group, from 32% in late 2012—while his rating among Democrats is largely unchanged, at 21%.

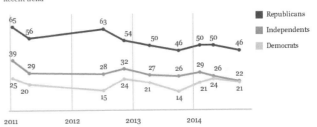

Percentage Viewing House Majority Leader John Boehner Favorably, by Party ID
Recent trend

GALLUP

Bottom Line

As voters prepare to go to the polls in November, neither party's leader in Congress offers his members a positive face with the American public. Boehner's 28% favorable rating is slightly higher than Reid's 21%, but Boehner's unfavorable rating is also slightly higher (50% vs. 45%). Essentially, the situation is a draw—not significantly disadvantaging either party.

Beneath the surface, however, both men appear to have significant problems. While Reid is managing to maintain close to 50% favorability among Democrats, he is becoming far less palatable to independents, a trend that could compel his colleagues who want to repair their party's image with voters after the election to consider their alternatives. Boehner's status with his own party is even worse than Reid's, with nearly as many Republicans viewing him unfavorably as favorably. That could inspire opponents within the GOP caucus to challenge Boehner for the speakership, although overcoming the House rules to mount such a challenge would be daunting.

Survey Methods

Results for this Gallup poll are based on telephone interviews conducted Sept. 25–30, 2014, with a random sample of 1,252 adults, aged 18 and older, living in all 50 U.S. states and the District of Columbia.

For results based on the total sample of national adults, the margin of sampling error is ±3 percentage points at the 95% confidence level.

October 07, 2014

ONE-FIFTH OF AMERICANS WORRY ABOUT GETTING EBOLA

Level of concern on par with that seen in 2009 H1N1/swine flu outbreak

by Andrew Dugan

WASHINGTON, D.C.—Twenty-two percent of Americans say they worry about getting the Ebola virus, matching or exceeding the number of U.S. adults who worried about contracting the H1N1 virus throughout its 2009 outbreak, despite the higher prevalence of H1N1 in the U.S.

Public Concern About Contracting Ebola Compared With H1N1/Swine Flu

Now, thinking about the Ebola virus that has been in the news, did you, personally, worry yesterday about getting the Ebola virus, or not?

Now, thinking about the H1N1 virus, also known as the swine flu virus, that has been in the news, did you, personally, worry yesterday about getting swine flu, or not?

	% Yes, worried	% No, did not worry	Number of Americans believed to have virus
EBOLA VIRUS			
2014 Oct 4-5	22	77	6
H1N1/SWINE FLU VIRUS			
2009 Apr 28	22	78	~14 million to ~34 million
2009 Apr 30	25	75	~14 million to ~34 million
2009 May 3	19	81	~14 million to ~34 million
2009 May 5	17	83	~14 million to ~34 million
2009 May 19	13	87	~14 million to ~34 million
2009 Jun 13-15	8	92	~14 million to ~34 million
2009 Aug 26	17	82	~14 million to ~34 million

Note: H1N1 data for "Number of Americans believed to have virus" provided by CDC

GALLUP

In total, six Americans are known to have contracted Ebola since the outbreak began this spring. All of these infections occurred in West Africa, the epicenter of the outbreak. By contrast, many more Americans contracted the H1N1 virus during the 2009 outbreak, though it is not as virulent as the deadly Ebola virus.

These results come from an Oct. 4–5 Gallup poll, conducted shortly after the first diagnosed case of Ebola in the U.S.—a Liberian man staying in Texas—was discovered. This poll was conducted prior to news reports of a Spanish woman becoming the first known case of a person to contract Ebola outside of Africa in the current outbreak, which could agitate public concerns further.

By and large, most Americans do not think it is likely that they or someone in their family will get the Ebola virus—34% deem it "not too likely," and 49% say "not likely at all." Four percent of Americans think it is very likely they will contract the Ebola virus, and another 10% consider it somewhat likely.

Perceived Likelihood of Getting Ebola Compared With H1N1

How likely do you think it is that you or someone in your family will get the Ebola virus -- very likely, somewhat likely, not too likely, or not likely at all?

How likely do you think it is that you or someone in your family will get swine flu -- very likely, somewhat likely, not too likely, or not likely at all?

	% Very likely	% Somewhat likely	% Not too likely	% Not likely at all
EBOLA VIRUS				
2014 Oct 4-5	4	10	34	49
H1N1/SWINE FLU				
2009 May 5	4	16	37	42
2009 Aug 26	8	28	36	26

GALLUP

By comparison, Americans were similarly confident that they would escape the reach of the H1N1 flu when news of that virus started to mount in May 2009. One-fifth of U.S. adults at that time (20%) thought it was very or somewhat likely they would catch H1N1, the seasonal flu virus that received the sobriquet "swine flu" because it resembled viruses found in pigs. Nearly eight in 10 were not particularly concerned (79%). However, that figure fell to 62% by August.

Majority Have Confidence in Federal Government to Handle Outbreak

Americans have slightly less confidence in the federal government's ability to handle an outbreak of the Ebola virus in the U.S. (61%) than they did about its ability to contain the swine flu in May 2009 (74%). More specifically, 26% today are very confident the government can handle Ebola, and 35% are somewhat confident. However, confidence in the federal government's ability to handle the swine flu in 2009 did diminish as the outbreak progressed.

Confidence in Federal Government to Handle Public Health Risk

How confident are you that the federal government will be able to handle an outbreak of [the Ebola virus/swine flu/bird flu^] in this country -- very confident, somewhat confident, not too confident, or not confident at all?

	% Very confident	% Somewhat confident	% Not too confident	% Not confident at all
EBOLA VIRUS				
2014 Oct 4-5	26	35	20	17
H1N1/SWINE FLU				
2009 May 5	29	45	14	11
2009 Aug 26	10	49	25	14
BIRD FLU				
2005 Oct 21-23	14	38	25	22

^ Question wording: As you may know, a virus known as "bird flu" or "avian flu" has killed some people in Asia. How confident are you that the federal government could handle an outbreak of bird flu in this country -- very confident, somewhat confident, not too confident, or not confident at all?

GALLUP

These ratings come amid allegations that a Dallas-area hospital released the Liberian man who had gone there with severe flu-like symptoms—despite the hospital's awareness that he had recently traveled from Liberia. Although the hospital is private, the situation has raised questions about the government's oversight capabilities. As a result, pressure has amplified, including from Texas Gov. Rick Perry, for the federal government to enhance the screening process at all U.S. points of entry.

In stark contrast to the American public's reaction to Ebola and the swine flu is the 2005 scare involving the "avian" or "bird" flu, which never actually hit U.S. shores. In October 2005, 47% of Americans said they were "not too confident" or "not confident at all" in the government's ability to combat the bird flu. This widespread lack of confidence in the federal government may have been related to the perception that the federal government poorly handled the response to Hurricane Katrina, which hit the Gulf Coast in August of that year.

As has been seen in other public health scares, confidence in the federal government's abilities does vary with party affiliation. Today, with a Democrat serving as president, Democrats are more likely to have confidence in the federal government's ability to handle the Ebola virus (74% somewhat or very confident) than are Republicans (49%). In 2005, by contrast, with a Republican in the White House, self-identified GOP supporters were more likely to express confidence in the federal government's response capabilities than were Democrats.

Just 12% Say Ebola Will Not Strike U.S.

While there is no evidence that any person has contracted the Ebola virus while in the United States, Americans are not optimistic that the country will avoid a rendezvous with the disease in some form, although most do not expect a major outbreak. Just 12% say Ebola will not strike the U.S. Meanwhile, 65% say there will be a minor outbreak, and nearly a fifth say we will have either a major outbreak (9%) or a crisis (9%). These numbers are largely in line with public forecasts regarding the bird flu at the time, a disease that never materialized in the U.S.

Public Views on Whether Ebola Will Strike the U.S.

Which comes closest to your view about [the Ebola virus/the bird flu virus] -- it will not strike the United States at all; there will be a minor outbreak in the United States; there will be a major outbreak in the United States, but it will not create a crisis; or it will strike the United States and create a crisis?

	% Will not strike U.S.	% Minor outbreak	% Major outbreak	% Crisis
EBOLA VIRUS				
2014 Oct 4-5	12	65	9	9
BIRD FLU				
2005 Dec 9-11	14	63	13	8

GALLUP

Bottom Line

About as many Americans worry about contracting the Ebola virus today as worried about getting the H1N1 flu during the 2009 flu season. Of course, H1N1 was a more prevalent force in the U.S., both in terms of the number of Americans who contracted it and the fact that most were exposed in the U.S. But what Ebola lacks in sheer number of cases, it makes up for in its deadliness.

Survey Methods

Results for this Gallup poll are based on telephone interviews conducted Oct. 4–5, 2014, on the Gallup Daily tracking survey, with

a random sample of 1,016 adults, aged 18 and older, living in all 50 U.S. states and the District of Columbia.

For results based on the total sample of national adults, the margin of sampling error is ±4 percentage points at the 95% confidence level.

October 08, 2014
VOTER ENGAGEMENT LOWER THAN IN 2010 AND 2006 MIDTERMS
Turnout indicators more similar to 1998, 2002 than to 2006, 2010

by Jeffrey M. Jones

PRINCETON, NJ—Turnout in the midterm elections this fall could be lower than in the past two midterm elections, based on current voter engagement. On each of three indicators of voter engagement in midterm elections—how much thought Americans have given to them, their expressed motivation to vote, and their enthusiasm about voting compared with past elections—2014 looks more like lower-turnout years 1998 and 2002 than higher-turnout years 2006 and 2010.

Midterm Voting Indicators and Voter Turnout in Recent Election Years

	Given "quite a lot of"/"some" thought to election	"Extremely motivated" to vote	"More enthusiastic about voting than usual"	Voter turnout
	%	%	%	%
2014	33	32	37	n/a
2010	46	50	46	40.9
2006	42	45	43	40.4
2002	33	30	38	39.5
1998	36	31	35	38.1

Indicators are from Sept. 25-30, 2014, poll and mostly from late September/early October polls in prior years.
Turnout is the percentage of the voting eligible population that voted, based on figures from the United States Elections Project website.

GALLUP

The latest results are based on Gallup's Sept. 25–30 poll, which includes updates on several key election indicators. Although voter turnout has not varied greatly in recent midterm elections—ranging from a low of 38.1% of eligible voters in 1998 to a high of 40.9% in 2010—there is a positive correlation between greater voter engagement on these measures and higher voter turnout.

One likely reason voter turnout was higher in 2006 and 2010 was that Americans were deeply dissatisfied with the state of the nation, as well as the jobs the president and Congress were doing. In those elections, the same party controlled the presidency and both houses of Congress, so voters looking to change the government had a clear and obvious way to do so—voting against members of Congress from the majority party. And that is precisely what happened, with Democrats winning control of both houses of Congress in 2006, and Republicans winning control of the House of Representatives in 2010.

In 1998 and 2002, in contrast, Americans were generally pleased with the way things were going in the country and with the job performance of the president and Congress—even with divided party control—and were thus less motivated to use their vote to try to change the government. Accordingly, there was little change in the party composition of Congress after those elections.

This year presents a different set of circumstances. Americans are dissatisfied with the state of the nation and generally unhappy with the job the president is doing and even more so with the job Congress is doing. Earlier Gallup research suggested that low approval of Congress is associated with higher voter turnout in midterms. However, with a Democratic president and divided party control of Congress, there is no clear remedy to inspire voters to change things this year, and that may be keeping Americans' motivation to vote and enthusiasm about voting in check.

Republicans Poised for Stronger Turnout

Usually, Republicans vote at higher rates than Democrats, and this is evident in higher scores for Republicans than for Democrats on the voter engagement questions, including this year. In fact, the Republican advantages on each of the three turnout measures at this point approach what Gallup measured in the strong GOP year of 2010 rather than in other midterm election years. As a result, even if overall turnout is depressed compared with prior years, Republicans appear poised to turn out in greater numbers than Democrats.

Midterm Voting Indicators by Political Party in Recent Election Years

	Republican/ Republican leaner	Democrat/ Democratic leaner	Republican advantage
	%	%	Pct. pts.
THOUGHT GIVEN TO ELECTION (% Quite a lot/Some)			
Sep 25-30, 2014	40	28	+12
Sep 26-Oct 3, 2010	58	40	+18
Oct 6-8, 2006	42	44	-2
Oct 3-6, 2002	33	34	-1
Sep 23-24, 1998	42	33	+9
MOTIVATED TO VOTE (% Extremely)			
Sep 25-30, 2014	44	25	+19
Aug 27-30, 2010	62	42	+20
Oct 22-23, 2006	44	49	-5
Oct 3-6, 2002	34	29	+5
Sep 23-24, 1998	36	30	+6
ENTHUSIASM ABOUT VOTING (% More enthusiastic)			
Sep 25-30, 2014	48	30	+18
Oct 21-24, 2010	63	37	+26
Oct 6-8, 2006	39	48	-9
Oct 31-Nov 2, 2002	42	38	+4
Oct 9-12, 1998	45	41	+4

GALLUP'

It is possible that each of these turnout items is not a pure measure of intention to vote, but also picks up partisans' sense of how their preferred party will perform in the elections. In other words, Democrats may be less likely to report thinking about the elections, being motivated to vote, or being enthusiastic about voting if they expect their party to perform poorly in the elections, even if they fully intend to vote. Most political indicators point to 2014 being a stronger Republican year, and political experts expect the Republicans to increase their majority in the House and pick up seats in the Senate, possibly enough to win control of the upper chamber. The prospect of Republican control of both houses

of Congress may make rank-and-file Republicans feel more motivated to vote, particularly in states that have important Senate elections in which their vote should matter more in determining the balance of power.

As a result, these turnout indicators may exaggerate the likely Republican turnout advantage on Election Day. However, even if that is the case, these data certainly do not suggest that Democratic turnout will be able to match or exceed Republican turnout.

Implications

Although the current political environment in many respects is more similar to the anger and frustration that led to higher voter turnout in 2006 and 2010 than to the generally content electorates that voted at lower rates in 1998 and 2002, Gallup's key indicators point to voter turnout that more closely approaches the latter elections than the former. The key to explaining that may lie in the current divided party control of Congress, with voters having no clear way to act on their frustrations with the state of the nation and the government. With little hope of 2014 being a "change" election—even if Republicans win the Senate, the GOP-controlled Congress will have to contend with a Democratic president—more Americans appear to be willing to sit out this fall's elections than was the case in the previous two midterm election years.

Survey Methods

Results for this Gallup poll are based on telephone interviews conducted Sept. 25–30, 2014, with a random sample of 1,252 adults, aged 18 and older, living in all 50 U.S. states and the District of Columbia.

For results based on the total sample of national adults, the margin of sampling error is ±4 percentage points at the 95% confidence level.

October 09, 2014
ECONOMY, GOVERNMENT TOP ELECTION ISSUES FOR BOTH PARTIES
Differ most widely on climate change, deficit

by Frank Newport

PRINCETON, NJ—Republican and Democratic voters see the economy, jobs, and fixing the federal government as important to their congressional vote this year, but prioritize other issues quite differently. Republicans and Republican leaners rate the situation with Islamic militants and the deficit in their top five issues. For Democrats and Democratic leaners, the top five issues include equal pay for women and the way income and wealth are distributed in the U.S.

This update is based on Gallup's Sept. 25–30 survey, which asked U.S. voters to rate the importance of each item in a series of 13 issues to their vote for Congress this year.

Much election campaigning focuses on targeting partisan groups, based largely on the need to get known Democratic or Republican voters to the polls in the typically lower-turnout midterm elections. Analyzing which issues are important to each of these two groups thus becomes particularly vital.

Top Priority Issues, by Party Identification -- Registered Voters

% Extremely/Very important

Democrats/ Democratic leaders	%	Republicans/ Republican leaders	%
The availability of good jobs	89	The economy	91
Equal pay for women	87	The situation with Islamic militants in Iraq and Syria	85
The economy	86	The availability of good jobs	83
The way the federal government is working	81	The federal budget deficit	82
The way income and wealth are distributed in the U.S.	75	The way the federal government is working	82
The situation with Islamic militants in Iraq and Syria	72	Taxes	77
The Affordable Care Act, also known as "Obama-care"	64	Immigration	75
Foreign affairs	64	Foreign affairs	73
Taxes	63	The Affordable Care Act, also known as "Obama-care"	64
The federal budget deficit	63	Equal pay for women	58
Climate change	61	The way income and wealth are distributed in the U.S.	54
Abortion and access to contraception	60	Abortion and access to contraception	43
Immigration	57	Climate change	19

Sept. 25-30, 2014

GALLUP

Clearly, the two issues that top the overall list—the economy and the availability of good jobs—are relevant for Republicans and Democrats, who assign similar importance to each. This economic focus on the part of voters mirrors the responses to Gallup's open-ended "most important problem" question asked each month, which shows that economic concerns usually rank near the top of the list.

How important will each of the following issues be to your vote for Congress this year -- will it be -- Registered Voters

% Extremely/Very important

	Democrats/ Democratic leaders	Republicans/ Republican leaders	Difference (pct.pts.)
	%	%	
Climate change	61	19	42
Equal pay for women	87	58	29
The way income and wealth are distributed in the U.S.	75	54	21
Abortion and access to contraception	60	43	17
The availability of good jobs	89	83	6
The Affordable Care Act, also known as "Obama-care"	64	64	0
The way the federal government is working	81	82	-1
The economy	86	91	-5
Foreign affairs	64	73	-9
The situation with Islamic militants in Iraq and Syria	72	85	-13
Taxes	63	77	-14
Immigration	57	75	-18
The federal budget deficit	63	82	-19

Sept. 25-30, 2014

GALLUP

Once beyond the economy and the way the federal government is working, the two partisan groups rate other issues quite differently. Two of the top five issues for Republicans—the federal budget deficit and the Islamic militant situation—are given much lower importance by Democrats, with gaps of 19 and 13 percentage points between the two groups, respectively. Two of Democrats' top five issues—equal pay for women and the way income and wealth are distributed in the U.S.—are much less important for Republicans, with gaps of 29 points on equal pay and 21 points on income distribution.

More broadly, in addition to equal pay for women and income and wealth inequality, the issues of climate change and abortion and access to contraception are relatively much more important to Democrats than to Republicans. And, in addition to the deficit, taxes, and the situation with the Islamic militants, immigration is significantly more important to Republicans.

Economy, Fixing Government, Islamic Militants Most Important Overall

When all voters' attitudes are combined, the highest levels of importance are assigned to the economy and jobs, the way in which the federal government is working, the Islamic militant situation, and equal pay for women. The least important issues to voters are climate change and abortion and access to contraception, which appear near the bottom of the list for both political groups—although on absolute terms each are rated as much more important by Democrats than by Republicans.

Implications

No candidate for office in this year's midterm elections will go wrong in emphasizing what he or she would do to fix the economy and create more jobs in the U.S. These are the top issues for all voters, and also are rated highest in importance among both Republicans and Democrats. Gallup's previous assessments of issue priority have also shown that the economy is nearly always toward the top of the list, and economic concerns in general are generally always the top concern of voters when they are asked to name the most important problems facing the nation.

Focusing on the way the federal government is working, or not working, also would appear to be a solid and fruitful focus for candidates, given that it ranks high among all voters, including among Republicans and Democrats.

Beyond these issues, however, candidates hoping to activate interest and turnout among Democrats would do well to focus on inequality-related issues, including unequal pay for women. Candidates looking to increase turnout among Republicans would do better to focus on the Islamic militant situation in Iraq and Syria, the deficit, and on taxes and immigration.

Survey Methods

Results for this Gallup poll are based on telephone interviews conducted Sept. 25–30, 2014, with a random sample of 1,252 adults, aged 18 and older, living in all 50 U.S. states and the District of Columbia.

For results based on the total sample of registered voters, the margin of sampling error is ±4 percentage points at the 95% confidence level.

October 09, 2014
INVESTORS SAY POLITICAL DISCORD HURTS INVESTMENT CLIMATE
Income inequality also mentioned as negative factor

by Art Swift

WASHINGTON, D.C.—The biggest factor rattling investors' confidence today is the hyper-partisan atmosphere in the nation's capital. Two-thirds of U.S. investors say political discord in Washington is hurting the U.S. investment climate a lot, eclipsing investors' level of worry about eight other issues.

Political Factors and the Investment Climate
Is the following situation hurting the investment climate in the United States a lot, hurting it a little, having no effect on it, helping it a little, or helping the investment climate a lot?

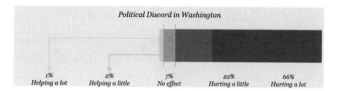

Political Discord in Washington

| 1% Helping a lot | 2% Helping a little | 7% No effect | 22% Hurting a little | 66% Hurting a lot |

GALLUP

These results are from the most recent Wells Fargo/Gallup Investor and Retirement Optimism Index, conducted Aug. 15–24 with 1,011 investors, including 374 retirees and 631 nonretirees. The index is a measure of broad economic and financial optimism among U.S. investors with $10,000 or more in any combination of stocks, bonds, mutual funds, self-directed IRAs, and 401(k) retirement accounts. This index was up in the third quarter, but is still far below pre-recession levels.

Political discord, income inequality, and tensions in the Middle East top a list of nine issues that Gallup asked about as part of the Wells Fargo/Gallup Investor and Retirement Optimism Index. Investors considered most of the factors asked about as harmful to the investment climate, except the current level of interest rates. Investors were evenly split in their views on whether the current level of interest rates is helping or hurting the situation for investors. The Federal Reserve has been consistently keeping interest rates low since the advent of the Great Recession.

Political Factors and the Investment Climate -- Complete List
Now I am going to read you some possible situations that could affect the investment climate in the United States. For each one, please tell me whether you think that situation is hurting the investment climate in the United States a lot, hurting it a little, having no effect on it, helping it a little, or helping the investment climate a lot. How about ____?
Sorted by % hurting

	% Hurting	% No effect	% Helping
Political discord in Washington	88	7	3
Events in the Middle East	82	10	5
Unemployment above 6%	80	11	6
The widening gap between wealthy and middle-class Americans	78	16	4
The conflict involving Russia and the Ukraine	74	20	3
U.S. immigration policy	70	21	6
Financial conditions in Europe	65	19	9
Federal policy and decisions on interest rates	51	13	31
The current level of interest rates	40	16	40

Aug. 15-24, 2014

GALLUP

Income Inequality Cited as Hurting Investment Climate in U.S.

Roughly half of investors mentioned the widening wealth gap in the U.S. or events in the Middle East as hurting the investment climate a lot. This survey was conducted as tensions between Israel and Hamas flared, which may have elevated investors' anxiety about the stability of the global market. Political and economic developments such as these potentially explain why U.S. investors continue to express concern about the stock market, even as it continues to hover at historic highs.

President Barack Obama has made income inequality a hallmark of his second-term agenda amid reports from the U.S. Census Bureau that the income gap between the richest and the poorest grew to its widest in 2011. Investors may be taking note of an increased governmental focus on this issue, as 78% said the widening gap between wealthy and middle-class Americans is hurting the investment climate at least a little, including 50% who say it is hurting American investing a lot. There is a small divide between investors with particular amounts invested in the market: 46% with more than $100,000 in investments say the income divide is hurting American investing a lot, while 55% of those with less than $100,000 in investments say the same thing.

Political Factors and the Investment Climate
Is the following situation hurting the investment climate in the United States a lot, hurting it a little, having no effect on it, helping it a little, or helping the investment climate a lot?

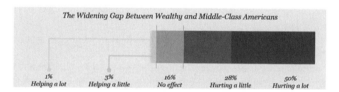

The Widening Gap Between Wealthy and Middle-Class Americans

| 1% Helping a lot | 3% Helping a little | 16% No effect | 28% Hurting a little | 50% Hurting a lot |

GALLUP

Middle East Tensions Having Significant Impact on Investors' Views

Increased tensions in the Middle East—especially the conflict between the Israelis and Hamas—have been a prominent issue in 2014. This boiling cauldron of pressures has likely affected investors' views of the investment climate in the U.S. Forty-seven percent say events in the Middle East are hurting the climate a lot, while 35% say these events are hurting a little. Ten percent say they are having no effect.

Political Factors and the Investment Climate
Is the following situation hurting the investment climate in the United States a lot, hurting it a little, having no effect on it, helping it a little, or helping the investment climate a lot?

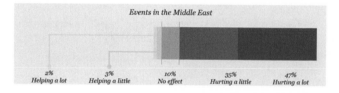

Events in the Middle East

| 2% Helping a lot | 3% Helping a little | 10% No effect | 35% Hurting a little | 47% Hurting a lot |

GALLUP

Aside from broad-based concerns with warring factions in the Middle East, investors may be concerned about oil production fluctuation and the economic vitality of the region.

Political discord is a top factor harming American investors' views of the current investment climate. It is clear that investors are paying attention to events in the U.S and abroad and these developments are having an impact on their views about investing.

While the discord in Washington is not a new phenomenon, it gained special prominence during the 2012 election when both Republican candidate Mitt Romney and President Obama highlighted how the contentious environment in government might be problematic for small businesses.

Perhaps surprisingly, 75% of those with $100,000 or more invested in the market say that income inequality is hurting the investment climate to some degree. With a Congressional Budget Office report stating that between 1979 and 2007 household income of the top 1% of earners grew by 275%, compared with 65% for the next 20%, less than 40% for the next 60%, and 18% for the 20% of the population with the lowest income, the new Gallup survey results suggest that wealthier investors might be bothered by the growing gap between wealthy and middle-class Americans.

Overall, these concerns may help explain investors' continued reluctance to view the stock market as a good place to invest. This is despite the market mostly holding steady in the upper 16,000 or low 17,000s all year.

Survey Methods

Results for this Wells Fargo/Gallup Investor and Retirement Index survey are based on questions asked Aug. 15–24, 2014, on the Gallup Daily tracking survey, with a random sample of 1,011 adults, having investable assets of $10,000 or more.

For results based on the entire sample of investors, the margin of sampling error is ±3 percentage points at the 95% confidence level.

October 10, 2014

INDEPENDENTS, PARTY SPLIT COULD MEAN RUNOFFS IN GEORGIA

Georgians slightly more likely to lean or identify as Republican

by Justin McCarthy

WASHINGTON, D.C.—With two hotly contested seats on the ballot in Georgia this midterm election, four in 10 Georgians (40%) identify as independent, while the rest are closely split between Republicans (27%) and Democrats (28%). Moreover, nearly as many Georgia independents say they lean toward the Democratic Party (12%) as say they lean Republican (15%), resulting in a tight party division in the state.

Since neither major party has a clear advantage and the state requires a candidate to get more than 50% of the votes, it is likely that the races for both U.S. Senate and governor will be decided in December and January runoff elections.

The Georgia GOP is on the defensive this year. With incumbent Gov. Nathan Deal up for re-election and Sen. Saxby Chambliss retiring, this leaves an opening for Democrats to take seats that have been in Republican hands for over a decade.

Georgia: Party Affiliation, Including Leaners

	%
Identify as Republican	27
Independent, lean Republican	15
Independent, no lean	13
Independent, lean Democratic	12
Identify as Democratic	28

Data for 2014 collected Jan. 1–June 30

GALLUP

Democrats saw their grip on Georgia disintegrate in 2002, when Sonny Perdue became the state's first Republican governor since Reconstruction. In the years that followed, both chambers of the Georgia state legislature came under Republican control, and each of the state's U.S. Senate seats became red as well. The Peach State has been dominated by the GOP ever since.

Democrats are hoping to reverse this trend, and given the nearly even split between Democrats and Republicans in Georgia's partisanship, it is a realistic endeavor. In the gubernatorial election, Democratic state Sen. Jason Carter, grandson of former President Jimmy Carter, is challenging Deal. In the Senate race, family ties are even more amplified. Democrat Michelle Nunn—daughter of former U.S. Sen. Sam Nunn, who once held the seat she's competing for—is running against Republican David Perdue, cousin of the former governor.

Georgia's election laws will complicate both parties' efforts this fall. Just like in Louisiana, a candidate must garner more than 50% of the votes; if no candidate reaches this mark, a runoff election is held between the top two competitors. In addition to the state's closely divided political landscape, with neither major party claiming close to 50% and with third-party candidates in each of the statewide races, runoffs are a distinct possibility.

Georgia has shown a close party division between Republicans and Democrats in recent years, with neither party—including leaners—having more than a five-percentage-point edge in any given year since 2008. The two-point gap in the first half of 2014 ties the margin Gallup measured in 2010, when Deal defeated his opponent in the general election (53% to 43%), thus avoiding a runoff.

Georgia: Trends in Party Affiliation

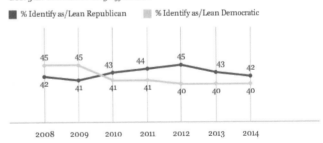

■ % Identify as/Lean Republican   % Identify as/Lean Democratic

Data for 2014 collected Jan. 1–June 30

GALLUP

Georgia's proportion of Republican identifiers and leaners is slightly higher than the nation's overall (42% vs. 39%, respectively), while its proportion of Democratic identifiers and leaners is slightly lower (40% vs. 43%).

Meanwhile, Georgians—who have been increasingly more likely to describe themselves as conservative in recent years—are exhibiting a slight dip in this ideological preference. Nearly four in 10 residents (39%) describe their views as conservative; this is the lowest percentage recorded since Gallup began asking the question in 2008. One in five (20%) describe their views as liberal—the highest figure to date.

Georgia: Trends in Self-Reported Ideology

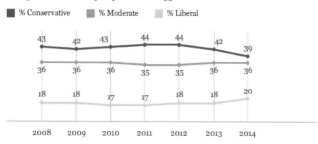

Data for 2014 collected Jan. 1-June 30

GALLUP

Conservatives have held at least a 24-point edge over liberals in years past, but the lead has diminished to 19 points this year. Though this is still a significant ideological advantage, it reinforces that Georgia's political competitiveness has tightened this year amid these crucial elections.

This mirrors the national trend toward a narrower conservative-liberal gap in recent years.

Georgia a Bellwether for Nationwide Presidential Approval

Since 2009, President Barack Obama's approval rating in Georgia has been within two points of the national average. In the first half of 2014, both nationally (43%) and in Georgia (42%), Obama received his lowest average approval ratings since entering office.

Georgia: Trends in Presidential Job Approval

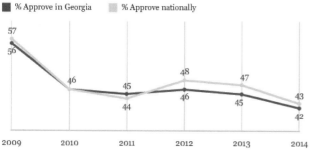

Data for 2014 collected Jan. 1-June 30

GALLUP

While this could hurt Nunn, whose views Perdue has tried to tie to the president's, Georgia's average approval rating is higher than in other states with close races, including Louisiana (40%), Arkansas (33%), and Kansas (32%). And it is certainly higher than in very strong Republican states such as Wyoming, whose residents are less than half as likely as Georgians to approve of the president's performance.

Bottom Line

Georgia has been under the firm grip of Republican control for well over a decade, and recent polls show that Republican candidate Perdue has a slight advantage, although the race is still considered to be a toss-up. Georgia could end up being one of the tightest Senate races this year, and could also leave the nation waiting on a January runoff election that may determine which party controls Congress' upper chamber.

While Republicans typically use low approval ratings against the president, and against those who share his Democratic affiliation, their attacks on the president's performance might not be as fruitful in the Peach State as it is in other states with close Senate races. Though Obama is unpopular with Georgians, his approval is on par with that of the 50-state average, and therefore might not be the most convincing case to make against a Democratic candidate. For her part, Nunn has reminded voters that Obama will only be in office for the first two years of the elected senator's term, and that his name will not appear on the 2014 ballot.

Survey Methods

Results for this Gallup poll are based on telephone interviews conducted Jan. 1–June 30, 2014, on the Gallup Daily tracking survey, with a random sample of 88,802 adults, aged 18 and older, living in all 50 U.S. states and the District of Columbia. Results are also based on Gallup's recent 50-state poll conducted June–December 2013 with a random sample of approximately 600 adults per state, aged 18 and older, living in all 50 U.S. states.

For results based on the 2014 sample of 2,647 Georgia residents, the margin of sampling error is ±2 percentage points at the 95% confidence level.

For results based on the 2013 sample of adults per state, the margin of sampling error is ±5 percentage points at the 95% confidence level.

October 10, 2014

SLIM MAJORITY IN U.S. EXPECT REPUBLICANS TO WIN THE SENATE

Parties even among registered voters on generic congressional ballot

by Lydia Saad

PRINCETON, NJ—Fifty-two percent of Americans say they expect the Republican Party to win in the U.S. Senate, while an even larger majority, 63%, say Republicans will retain their majority in the House of Representatives.

Partisans on both sides show signs of wishful thinking when assessing which party will win control of the U.S. House and Senate this fall. Nearly two-thirds of Democrats interviewed in the Sept. 25–30 survey say their own party will win the Senate—not an unreasonable conjecture given that Democrats currently control the upper chamber and would need to lose a net of six seats to lose the majority. But the slight majority of Democrats, 51%, also believe their party will win in the House—an outcome out of step with the Republican gains most pundits are expecting.

Americans' Predictions for Who Will Win Control of U.S. House and Senate

Regardless of how you, yourself, plan to vote, which party do you think will win control of the U.S. House of Representatives in the congressional elections this fall -- [the Republicans (or) the Democrats]?

And which party do you think will win control of the U.S. Senate in the congressional elections this fall -- [the Republicans (or) the Democrats]?

	U.S. adults	Republicans	Independents	Democrats
	%	%	%	%
CONTROL OF U.S. SENATE				
Republicans will win	52	76	55	30
Democrats will win	42	19	39	65
No opinion	6	5	6	5
CONTROL OF U.S. HOUSE				
Republicans will win	63	87	61	46
Democrats will win	33	11	34	51
No opinion	4	2	5	3

Sept. 25-30, 2014

GALLUP'

Likewise, despite the closeness of several races that Republicans must win if they are to gain control of the Senate, the vast majority of Republicans, 76%, are optimistic the Republicans will take the U.S. Senate. Meanwhile, 87% of Republicans believe the Republican Party will control of the House, possibly reflecting their awareness that their party already has a firm hold on it.

The more objective predictions may be those made by political independents, which mirror the national averages. More than half of independents predict Republicans will win the Senate, and a solid majority—61%—say Republicans will win the House.

All Five Previous House Predictions Have Been Right

This is the first time Gallup has asked Americans about the likely party outcome in the U.S. Senate, and thus it has uncertain value as a forecasting tool. However, as Gallup has noted in the past, Americans' predictions for the U.S. House, albeit limited in number, have been remarkably accurate, aligning with the winning party in all five midterms in which the question was asked. This includes the 2010 and 2006 midterms—particularly notable since party control changed after both elections—as well as in three earlier midterms: 1962, 1958, and 1946.

Historical Predictions About Party Control of U.S. House of Representatives
Based on national adults

	Republicans will win	Democrats will win	No opinion	National vote winner
	%	%	%	
Sep 25-30, 2014	63	33	4	?
Sep 23-26, 2010	52	32	15	Republicans
Oct 20-22, 2006	38	54	8	Democrats
Sep 20-25, 1962	16	60	24	Democrats
Sep 10-15, 1958	12	67	22	Democrats
Sep 27-Oct 2, 1946	63	37	0	Republicans

Selected trend, based on final poll in each election from 1946-2010

GALLUP'

Relatedly, Gallup has also found that Americans as whole have a good track record of predicting which presidential candidate will win the popular vote, forecasting the correct winner in each of the four elections since 1996.

The midterm prediction trend spans relatively few elections, and only two recent ones. However, the results reinforce research

that suggests prediction markets (including polls asking the public to predict election outcomes) can be more accurate than other forecasting tools, such as expert predictions, heavily engineered models, and voter-preference polls.

Although Americans are fairly strong in their view that the Republicans will retain control of the House, the new poll finds registered voters are more closely divided in their actual intentions to vote for the Republican versus the Democratic candidate in their congressional district. Forty-seven percent of registered voters say they would vote for the Republican in their district if the election were held today, while 46% would vote for the Democrat. This is similar to what Gallup found in August, but more favorable to the Republicans than in April when the Democrats were ahead by five percentage points, 49% to 44%, respectively.

Political parity on the generic ballot among registered voters is typically a positive sign for Republicans in midterm years. That is because Republican voters tend to turn out in greater numbers than Democratic voters do in these lower-turnout elections.

Republicans' actual turnout advantage in 2014 will be highly dependent on the degree to which Democrats can inspire their base closer to the election. Right now, rank-and-file Republicans are showing about average engagement in the election relative to the past four midterms, while Democrats' attention is somewhat below average.

Bottom Line

Gallup's new question asking Americans who they think will win control of the Senate offers some hope for Republicans, as they lead on this by 10 points, 52% to 42%. But with no trends available for comparison, and control of the Senate likely coming down to a handful of races that are too close to call—such as in Arkansas, Alaska, Colorado, Louisiana, North Carolina, Kansas, Georgia, and Iowa—it is not clear how useful this national perceptual measure really is.

An even larger majority of Americans expect the Republicans to retain control of the House, a projected outcome supported by the political parity in registered voters' vote intentions. Still, the Republicans' 33-seat advantage is small by historical standards, and Gallup analysis suggests that Americans' low satisfaction with the direction of the country could fuel high seat turnover. But the conformity of the new poll findings with other important signals—including President Barack Obama's subpar approval rating, Obama's net-negative effect on voters' choice of candidates, and Republicans' current advantage on several indicators of potential turnout—adds weight to their significance.

Survey Methods

Results for this Gallup poll are based on telephone interviews conducted Sept. 25–30, 2014, with a random sample of 1,252 adults, aged 18 and older, living in all 50 U.S. states and the District of Columbia.

For results based on the total sample of national adults, the margin of sampling error is ±4 percentage points at the 95% confidence level.

For results based on the sample of 1,095 registered voters, the margin of sampling error is ±4 percentage points at the 95% confidence level.

October 13, 2014
U.S. VOTERS GIVE GOP EDGE VS. DEMS ON HANDLING TOP ISSUES
Prefer GOP on seven of 13 election issues; Democrats, on just four

by Andrew Dugan

WASHINGTON, D.C.—The Republicans in Congress hold significant leads over the Democrats on four of the six issues that U.S. registered voters say are most important in determining how they will vote in November: the economy, the way the federal government is working, the situation with Islamic militants in Iraq and Syria, and the federal budget deficit. Democrats, by contrast, top their Republican rivals on just one of the six: "equal pay for women."

2014 Midterm Issues: Importance and Party Advantage

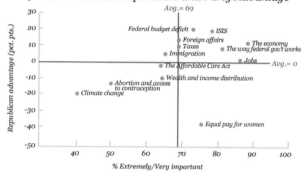

These results are from a Sept. 25–30 poll in which Gallup asked registered voters to rate the importance of 13 issues to their vote for Congress, and then to indicate which party would do a better job on each issue. The accompanying graph simultaneously displays the rankings of these issues on both dimensions. The higher an issue is, the greater the Republican Party's advantage. And the farther to the right an issue is, the more important it is to the electorate.

The 13 issues measured in the new poll include eight that appeared in a Gallup Poll conducted in April, before the midterm campaign season came into full bloom, plus five new ones. In total, six issues were rated above the average of 69%, in terms of the percentage of voters saying they are extremely or very important to their vote:

1. the economy (88%)
2. the availability of good jobs (86%)
3. the way the federal government is working (81%)
4. the situation with Islamic militants in Iraq and Syria (78%)
5. equal pay for women (75%) and
6. the federal budget deficit (73%)

On the No. 1 issue, the economy, Republicans have more than doubled their April lead over Democrats, to 11 percentage points.

Notably, as the GOP tries to gain control of the Senate, the current GOP advantage on the economy nearly matches the 12-point advantage the party held in August 2010, shortly before the midterm elections that gave the Republicans control of the House of Representatives.

The GOP's lead on the federal budget deficit has also widened, to 20 points from 14 points in April, and is now higher than at any other time during Barack Obama's presidency.

Party Advantage on the Economy Ahead of Midterms

Do you think the Republicans in Congress or the Democrats in Congress would do a better job of dealing with each of the following issues and problems?

How about the economy?

	Republicans	Democrats	Republican advantage
	%	%	(Pct. pts.)
Sep 25-30, 2014	50	39	+11
Apr 24-30, 2014	48	43	+5

GALLUP

Republicans are also in a better position than Democrats on several new items included in the poll, including the way the federal government works and the situation in Iraq and Syria. Republicans hold a solid eight-point advantage on how the federal government functions, despite gripes from Senate Majority Leader Harry Reid (D-Nev.) that "Republican obstruction" is the source of federal dysfunction.

Voters also prefer the GOP by a commanding 19-point margin regarding Islamic militants in Iraq and Syria. The GOP has historically held an edge over Democrats on terrorism and national security, and they continue to lead in this arena, even as the Obama administration conducts airstrikes against Islamic militant targets in Iraq and Syria.

In terms of "the availability of good jobs," the two parties are essentially tied, with a one-point Republican lead.

Voters clearly favor Democrats only on securing equal pay for women among issues of above-average importance. Democrats have an outsized 38-point advantage—the largest lead either party holds on any issue.

On the two issues that are of average importance to voters, "foreign affairs," and "taxes," voters give Republicans the nod.

Democrats Strong on Issues Voters Think Are Less Important

For the five issues rated below average in importance, voters largely view Democrats as the better party—perhaps scant comfort to Democrats. At the same time, these issues are more important to self-identified Democrats than to other voters, meaning they are potentially good issues to help bring Democrats to the polls.

Bottom Five Issues and Party Advantage

How important will each of the following issues be to your vote for Congress this year -- will it be -- extremely important, very important, moderately important, or not that important? How about -- [RANDOM ORDER]?

Do you think the Republicans in Congress or the Democrats in Congress would do a better job of dealing with each of the following issues and problems? How about -- [RANDOM ORDER]?

	% Extremely/ Very important	Democratic advantage
Immigration	65	-5
The Affordable Care Act, also known as "Obamacare"	64	+2
The way income and wealth are distributed in the U.S.	64	+10
Abortion and access to contraception	50	+13
Climate change	40	+20
AVERAGE	57	+8

Note: Democratic advantage = % saying Democrats would do a better job of handling the issue minus % saying Republicans would
Sept. 25-30, 2014

GALLUP

Democrats are the clear favorites to handle wealth and income distribution, abortion and access to contraception, and climate change; the party holds double-digit advantages on these issues. But only one of the three has more than half of voters assessing it as extremely or very important, and all three rank well below the top issues.

Bottom Line

Republicans lead Democrats on a number of issues of high importance to the electorate, including the economy, the situation in Iraq and Syria, and the federal budget deficit. Democrats are not without electoral strengths—equal pay for women is an issue that voters judge as important, and that a wide swath think Democrats are most adept to handle. But as the two parties enter the final campaign stretch, the electoral environment increasingly appears to favor the GOP.

Survey Methods

Results for this Gallup poll are based on telephone interviews conducted Sept. 25–30, 2014, with a random sample of 1,095 registered voters, aged 18 and older, living in all 50 U.S. states and the District of Columbia.

For results based on the total sample of voters, the margin of sampling error is ±4 percentage points at the 95% confidence level.

October 13, 2014
AMERICANS SAY EQUAL PAY TOP ISSUE FOR WORKING WOMEN
Equal opportunity for advancement is second

by Jeffrey M. Jones

This article is featured in "Women and the Workplace," a week-long series exploring a variety of issues affecting modern working women.

PRINCETON, NJ—Nearly four in 10 Americans say equal pay is the top issue facing working women in the United States today, a sentiment shared by roughly the same proportions of men, women, and working women. About twice as many Americans mention equal pay as cite the second-ranked issue—equal opportunity for advancement. No other issue is cited by more than 10% of Americans.

The results are based on an open-ended question asked in a Sept. 25–30 Gallup poll. There are almost as many working women as working men in the U.S. And many women today seek not only to have jobs but also to establish their careers and advance in them. But working women continue to face challenges that differ from those of working men. As an example, last week, Microsoft's CEO sparked controversy when asked about one of the major challenges for working women—pay equity—when he suggested that women should not ask for raises but rely on the system to deliver fair pay to them.

Americans clearly see norms of fairness and equality—in terms of pay and the opportunity to get ahead—as the greatest challenges for working women. These surpass issues such as how women are treated in the workplace and balancing parenthood with work, but these more practical concerns certainly are not absent from the list of issues facing women. For example, 8% of Americans mention that respectful treatment of female employees, including sexual harassment, is an issue in the workplace. Another 7% mention access to childcare, and 6% mention balancing work and home life.

What do you think are the most important issues facing working women in this country today? [OPEN-ENDED]

	All Americans	Women	Men	Working women
	%	%	%	%
Equal pay/Fair pay	39	41	37	42
Equal opportunity for promotion, advancement/No gender discrimination	20	20	21	24
Jobs/Unemployment/Availability of jobs	8	8	8	8
Sexual harassment/Better treatment, more respect in workplace	8	7	9	9
Access to childcare/Better childcare	7	10	3	12
Balancing work and home life	6	9	3	10
Healthcare	5	7	3	9
Maternity leave/Family leave/Time off for family matters	3	3	3	2
Abortion/Access to contraception	2	2	2	2
The economy (nonspecific)	2	2	2	3
Education/Access to education	1	1	1	1
Equal benefits	1	*	1	*
Other	5	5	6	4
No opinion	16	12	20	8

* Less than 0.5%
Sept. 25-30, 2014
Responses total more than 100% because of multiple mentions.

GALLUP'

For the most part, men, women, and working women have similar ideas about the challenges facing working women. The greatest perceptual differences appear between men and working women with respect to the top-of-mind importance of childcare, work-home balance, and healthcare. Few men, no more than 3%, mention these as the most important challenges for working women. But 9% of working women mention healthcare, 10% mention balancing work and home life, and 12% mention childcare.

Men in general are also less likely than women and working women to cite any issue, as 20% of men do not have an opinion, compared with 12% of all women and 8% of working women.

While there are not wide differences by gender in perceptions of the key issues for working women, the views of political liberals and conservatives diverge. Liberals are nearly twice as likely as conservatives, 51% to 28%, to mention equal pay as the biggest challenge working women face. Despite this difference, it is still the most commonly mentioned issue for conservatives.

View of Most Important Issues Facing Working Women in United States Today, by Political Ideology

	Liberals	Moderates	Conservatives
	%	%	%
Equal pay/Fair pay	51	44	28
Equal opportunity for promotion, advancement/No gender discrimination	26	24	15
Jobs/Unemployment/Availability of jobs	4	6	12
Sexual harassment/Better treatment, more respect in workplace	10	6	8
Access to childcare/Better childcare	6	9	6
Balancing work and home life	6	4	7
Healthcare	5	7	3
Maternity leave/Family leave/Time off for family matters	6	2	1
Abortion/Access to contraception	4	1	3
The economy (nonspecific)	1	2	3
Education/Access to education	1	1	*
Equal benefits	1	*	1
Other	5	5	5
No opinion	8	9	26

* Less than 0.5%
Sept. 25-30, 2014
Responses total more than 100% because of multiple mentions.

Liberals are also much more likely than conservatives to mention equal opportunity. In contrast, conservatives are more likely than liberals to mention the availability of jobs as the top issue for working women.

Conservatives are also much more likely than liberals not to offer a response—26% of conservatives do not have an opinion, compared with 8% of liberals.

Implications

Americans regard basic norms of fairness and equality—specifically in terms of pay and opportunities to advance—as the greatest issues facing working women today. Although there are almost as many working women as working men in the U.S. today, and women are increasingly rising to positions of prominence in business, they still as a group lag behind men in pay and in the percentage of upper management positions they hold.

In fact, equal pay for women has become a major issue this year. In addition to the controversy regarding the Microsoft CEO's comments, pay equity has also become a significant issue in this year's political campaigns. And it resonates with voters—ranking among the most important issues in this year's elections. The prominence of the issue in this year's campaign may also explain why it is top-of-mind for Americans as the most important issue facing working women.

Survey Methods

Results for this Gallup poll are based on telephone interviews conducted Sept. 25–30, 2014, with a random sample of 1,252 adults, aged 18 and older, living in all 50 U.S. states and the District of Columbia.

For results based on the total sample of national adults, the margin of sampling error is ±4 percentage points at the 95% confidence level.

For results based on the total sample of 233 working women, the margin of sampling error is ±8 percentage points at the 95% confidence level.

October 14, 2014
AMERICANS STILL PREFER A MALE BOSS TO A FEMALE BOSS
Women are more likely than men to prefer a female boss

by Rebecca Riffkin

WASHINGTON, D.C.—Americans are still more likely to say they would prefer a male boss (33%) to a female boss (20%) in a new job, although 46% say it doesn't make a difference to them. While women are more likely than men to say they would prefer a female boss, they are still more likely to say they would prefer a male boss overall.

These results are based on Gallup's annual work and education poll, conducted Aug. 7–10. In 1953, Gallup first asked Americans, "If you were taking a new job and had your choice of a boss, would you prefer to work for a man or a woman?" At that time, 66% of Americans said they preferred a male boss. Five percent said they preferred a female boss, and 25% volunteered that it made no difference.

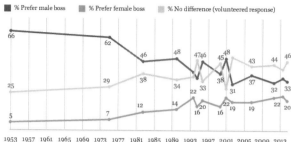

Americans Slightly More Likely to Prefer a Male Boss

If you were taking a new job and had your choice of a boss, would you prefer to work for a man or a woman?

■ % Prefer male boss   ■ % Prefer female boss   ▨ % No difference (volunteered response)

GALLUP

Women More Likely Than Men to Prefer a Female Boss

In an age when women are told to "lean in" to get positions of power at work, even women are more likely to prefer a male boss to a female boss. However, women have historically been more likely than men to prefer a female boss, although support for preferring a female boss has grown among both groups over time. In 2014, 25% of women say they would prefer a female boss, compared with 14% of men.

Men and Women Differ in Their Preference for Boss' Gender

If you were taking a new job and had your choice of a boss, would you prefer to work for a man or a woman?

	Men	Women	Difference
	%	%	(pct. pts.)
Prefer male boss	26	39	-13
Prefer female boss	14	25	-11
No difference	58	34	24

Aug. 7-10, 2014

GALLUP

The percentage of women who would prefer a female boss has never surpassed 30%. Currently, both genders would prefer a male boss, with 26% of men and 39% of women saying they would prefer a male boss if they were to take a new job. Men are more likely than women to say they have no preference—58% mention this response, compared with 34% of women.

The survey indicates that 51% of working Americans currently have a male boss and 33% have a female boss. Those who have a female boss are more likely than those with a male boss to say they would prefer a female boss if they got a new job (27% vs. 15%, respectively).

Boss Preference, by Gender of Current Boss

Asked only of Americans who are employed part time or full time

	Currently have male boss	Currently have female boss
	%	%
Prefer male boss	41	33
Prefer female boss	15	27
No preference	43	38

Aug. 7-10, 2014

GALLUP

As Gallup has previously noted, younger Americans are slightly more likely than older Americans to prefer a female boss; however, preference for a male boss is consistent between the two groups. Republicans are more likely to prefer a male boss (42%) to a female boss (16%), while Democrats break even between the two—29% prefer male, while 25% prefer female.

Bottom Line

In June, *Fortune* reported that the number of female CEOs of Fortune 500 companies had reached a historic high, yet only 4.8% of this elite group are women. And while bestselling books like *Lean In* by Sheryl Sandberg push women to achieve their goals and focus on their careers, Americans' views about wanting female bosses haven't changed since Gallup began asking about them regularly in the 1980s. More Americans continue to prefer a male boss to a female boss—although, since 2002, the greatest percentage continue to say it does not make a difference to them. While the percentage who prefer a female boss has grown over the last 60 years, it has never passed 25%.

Women, however, are more likely than men to prefer a female boss, even if more women overall still prefer a male boss. Furthermore, workers who currently have a female boss are more likely than those who have a male boss to prefer a female boss in the future. This could mean that as more women enter management, preference for female bosses could continue to rise.

Survey Methods

Results for this Gallup poll are based on telephone interviews conducted Aug. 7–10, 2014, with a random sample of 1,032 adults, aged 18 and older, living in all 50 U.S. states and the District of Columbia.

For results based on the total sample of national adults, the margin of sampling error is ±4 percentage points at the 95% confidence level.

October 15, 2014
AMERICANS: MY MEMBER OK, MOST IN CONGRESS ARE NOT
Dueling views helps explain why most incumbents are re-elected

by Frank Newport

PRINCETON, NJ—In the U.S., the majority believes that most members of Congress are out of touch with average Americans, more focused on special interests than the needs of their constituents, and are corrupt. Americans are slightly more likely to say each of these things than they were in the past. At the same time, they are much less likely to say these descriptions fit their local member of Congress than to say they fit most members.

Gallup first asked these questions in 1994, re-asked them twice in 2006, and then asked again this year in a survey conducted Sept. 25–30.

A substantial majority of Americans have said that most members of Congress are out of touch and beholden to special interests each time Gallup has asked the questions. This year marks the second time that half or more of Americans agree that most members of Congress are corrupt.

Americans' Views of Congress: Most Members and Your Member

	Most members of Congress	Your member of Congress
OUT OF TOUCH		
	%	%
2014	81	47
2006	77	38
2006	69	38
1994	75	41
FOCUSED ON NEEDS OF SPECIAL INTERESTS		
	%	%
2014	69	46
2006	65	40
2006	54	40
1994	58	42
CORRUPT		
	%	%
2014	54	27
2006	47	22
2006	38	22
1994	50	27

GALLUP

Taken together, these responses add to the list of findings underscoring Americans' lack of confidence in Congress as a body, including low overall approval ratings, low trust in the legislative branch of government, and a confidence rating for Congress at the bottom of the list of American institutions.

Americans' cynicism about their own member of Congress is slightly higher than in the past. For the first time, more Americans say their member is focused on the need of special interests than on the needs of his or her constituents.

Additionally, Americans are now equally divided on whether their own member is out of touch with average Americans, and the 27% who say their member is corrupt ties the percentage from 1994.

Americans Typically More Positive About Their Own Member of Congress

The fact that Americans are more negative about most members of Congress than they are about their local member reflects an established pattern in which Americans' assessments of many entities and situations becomes more positive the closer they are to home. These include healthcare, schools, and crime. This pattern helps explain a central paradox in American politics: Although the public is extremely negative about Congress as an institution and has little confidence in its ability to get things done, Americans still send the vast majority of members of Congress who seek re-election back to Washington.

This disjuncture between Americans' views of most members and their own member of Congress is underscored by the finding in the Sept. 25–30 survey that 54% of Americans say they approve of the job their local member is doing. Gallup's September job approval rating for Congress as a whole was 14%.

Despite Americans' relatively high approval rating for their own member of Congress, 63% of Americans say it is bad for the country that nearly all members of Congress seeking re-election are likely to win in November. In addition, 78% of Americans say it would change Congress for the better if the present members of Congress are replaced with new members after the November elections.

Americans' Attitudes Toward Congressional Elections

	Sep 25-30, 2014
As you may know, nearly all members of Congress who are seeking re-election are likely to win this November. Do you think this is good for the country or bad for the country?	
	%
Good for country	29
Bad for country	63
No opinion	8
Suppose that after the November elections most of the present members of Congress are replaced with new members. Do you think it would change Congress for the better or change Congress for the worse?	
	%
Better	78
Worse	11
No opinion	10

GALLUP

In other words, while the majority of Americans approve of the job their member is doing, and thus would presumably vote for this person's re-election, an even greater percentage say it is a bad thing that most members of Congress will be re-elected.

Implications

Americans remain negative about most members of Congress, with majorities perceiving that members are out of touch with their local constituents and that they pay too much attention to special interests. A majority says that most members are corrupt.

Given that Congress consists of members elected from districts across the U.S., the only real action Americans can take to change the makeup of Congress is to vote against their incumbent. But Americans are much less likely to have harsh views of their own local member of Congress than they do of Congress as a whole. Even if Americans in some abstract way believe that their member is contributing to the partisan gridlock that frustrates Americans so much, they might approve of their member for the things he or she does to help the district, his or her party affiliation, or for being their official voice in Washington.

Furthermore, the majority of Americans might believe that their member is above average or the exception. Or, it could be that the average American perceives that systems and procedures in Washington need to be changed in fundamental ways that transcend the particular group of people who are elected to serve in Congress at any given time.

All in all, Americans' relatively positive attitudes about their local representatives, spread out across 435 congressional elections, help explain why so many members of Congress return to Washington year after year—even while these same Americans so negatively assail the institution to which these members belong.

Survey Methods

Results for this Gallup poll are based on telephone interviews conducted Sept. 25–30, 2014, with a random sample of 1,252 adults, aged 18 and older, living in all 50 U.S. states and the District of Columbia.

For results based on the total sample of national adults, the margin of sampling error is ±4 percentage points at the 95% confidence level.

October 15, 2014

WOMEN'S WELL-BEING SUFFERS MORE WHEN MARRIAGE ENDS
Stress, substance use jump more for women who are divorced, separated

by Dan Witters and Lindsey Sharpe

PRINCETON, NJ—Married Americans tend to have higher well-being than nonmarried Americans, particularly those who are divorced or separated, according to the Gallup-Healthways Well-Being Index. Women typically have higher well-being than men across all marital statuses, including a notable 2.2-point gap in the overall Well-Being 5 score among those who are married. The significant exception is that there is essentially no gender difference in well-being among those who are separated, the group with the lowest well-being.

U.S. Well-Being 5 Score and Marital Status, by Gender

	TOTAL	Married	Domestic partnership	Single	Divorced	Separated
ALL ADULTS	61.7	63.9	60.2	59.6	56.5	54.8
Women	62.4	65.0	60.8	59.9	57.1	54.5
Men	60.9	62.8	59.5	59.4	55.7	55.1
Difference between women and men (pct. pts.)	1.5	2.2	1.3	0.5	1.4	-0.6

Gallup-Healthways Well-Being Index, Jan. 2-Sept. 25, 2014

GALLUP

These findings are based on 131,159 interviews with American adults, aged 18 and over, from Jan. 2–Sept. 25, 2014, conducted as part of the Gallup-Healthways Well-Being Index, which organizes well-being into five elements: purpose, social, financial, community, and physical.

Daily Stress Jumps Among Those Who Are Separated

Gallup and Healthways measure daily reports of stress, which affects all five elements, as a component of overall well-being. Married Americans are far less likely than those who are not married to report that they felt stress "a lot of the day yesterday." Whereas 36.8% of married Americans say they felt stress the prior day, the percentage increases significantly for other marital statuses, and jumps to 51.0% among those who are separated.

U.S. Daily Stress and Marital Status, by Gender
"Did you experience stress a lot of the day yesterday?" (% Yes)

	TOTAL	Married	Domestic partnership	Single	Divorced	Separated
ALL ADULTS	39.9	36.8	46.7	45.3	44.1	51.0
Women	42.0	39.7	48.5	47.6	47.0	56.0
Men	37.6	34.0	44.9	43.3	40.3	44.5
Difference between women and men (pct. pts.)	4.4	5.7	3.6	4.3	6.7	11.5

Gallup-Healthways Well-Being Index, Jan. 2-Sept. 25, 2014

GALLUP

Women are more likely than men to carry stress on any given day across all marital status groups, but there is a visibly pronounced stress gap by gender when one compares women who are separated to men who are separated. In this case, while both groups are significantly higher in daily stress than their married counterparts, the increase in stress among separated women compared with married women is about 55% greater than what is found among the same groups of men—up 16.3 percentage points among women, compared with 10.5 points among men.

Elevated Drug/Medication Use Linked to Divorce, Separation

Another factor in overall well-being is the self-reported use of drugs to relax. Roughly 17% of adults who are married, in domestic partnerships, or single say they use drugs or other medications (including prescription drugs) "almost every day" to aid in relaxation. That compares with a much higher three in 10 separated or divorced Americans who do the same.

Women are somewhat more likely than men across all marital groups to report using drugs or medicine to relax. However, the gender gaps are notably greater among divorced and separated Americans than among those who are married, single, or in a domestic partnership.

U.S. Drug/Medication Use and Marital Status, by Gender
"How often do you use drugs or medications, including prescription drugs, which affect your mood and help you relax?" (% Almost every day)

	TOTAL	Married	Domestic partnership	Single	Divorced	Separated
ALL ADULTS	19.0	17.0	17.1	16.4	28.1	29.3
Women	21.1	18.6	18.1	17.9	30.4	31.7
Men	16.8	15.5	16.0	15.1	25.0	26.2
Difference between women and men (pct. pts.)	4.3	3.1	2.1	2.8	5.4	5.5

Gallup-Healthways Well-Being Index, Jan. 2-Sept. 25, 2014

GALLUP

Implications

Marriage is associated with higher well-being for both men and women, particularly when compared with divorce or separation. Entering into a marriage can foster a sense of purpose through a shared perspective on life and a need to support another person. Similarly, marriage can expand a person's social connections and relationships, increase household wealth, and lead to a more permanent housing selection and a related connection to the community. In addition, multiple studies have confirmed that married adults have better health outcomes, likely attributable to reduced stress and having a partner to encourage healthy behaviors and to hold one accountable for choices affecting one's health.

The data suggest, however, that women's well-being may suffer more if the marriage ends. For example, typically, married men in the U.S. earn more than married women, and while this could be attributable to men's postponing marriage until they earn higher salaries, it results in women's seeing a significant household income bump after marriage. This particularly results from the disparity between men and women's average wages. Married women, therefore, may see more significant financial benefits from marriage than married men do, resulting in a boost to their financial well-being that may outpace what is found among men.

Married adults—but particularly married women—have far lower daily rates of stress and substance use than their divorced or separated counterparts. Though married men have somewhat lower rates overall, married women's stress levels compare quite favorably with those of women in other marital statuses. Reduced stress,

coupled with a non-elevated use of drugs to relax found in divorced or separated settings, likely plays a significant role in married women's higher overall well-being.

Survey Methods

Results are based on telephone interviews conducted as part of the Gallup-Healthways Well-Being Index survey Jan. 2–Sept. 25, 2014, yielding a random sample of 131,159 adults, aged 18 and older, living in all 50 U.S. states and the District of Columbia, selected using random-digit-dial sampling. Of this sample, 37,381, 5,983, and 1,146 interviews were with men who were married, divorced, and separated, respectively, while 31,101, 8,205, and 1,350 interviews were with women who were married, divorced, and separated, respectively.

For results based on the sample sizes noted below, married respondents for each gender will have a maximum expected error range of about ±0.6 percentage points at the 95% confidence level, while divorced respondents for each gender will have a margin of error of about ±1.3 percentage points and separated respondents for each gender will have a margin of error of about ±3.4 percentage points at the 95% confidence level.

October 16, 2014
IN U.S., NO PREFERENCE FOR DIVIDED VS. ONE-PARTY GOVERNMENT
Thirty percent prefer one-party government, 28% divided government

by Jeffrey M. Jones

PRINCETON, NJ—Americans lack consensus on whether it is better to have one party holding the presidency and the majority in Congress, or better to have control of each branch of government split between the two major political parties. Currently, 30% say it is better to have a one-party government, 28% say a divided government is better, and the highest percentage, 37%, say it makes no difference.

Do you think it is better for the country to have a president who comes from the same political party that controls Congress, does it make no difference either way, or do you think it is better to have a president from one political party and Congress controlled by another?

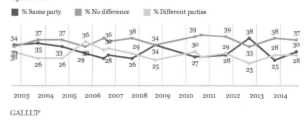

GALLUP

The results are based on Gallup's annual Governance poll, conducted Sept. 4–7. Since Gallup first asked the question in 2002, Americans have not shown a clear preference on the most desirable form of government. Most often, the highest percentage have said it "makes no difference." The highest percentage in favor of one-party government was 38% in 2012 and the highest in favor of divided government was 36% in 2005.

Divided government has been the norm in U.S. politics for most of the last 45 years, with one party controlling both houses of Congress and the presidency for only 12 of those years—1977–1980, 1993–1994, 2003–2006 and 2009–2010, as well as part of 2001.

As such, Americans may simply be used to divided government and do not see it as better or worse than the alternative. But Americans have also seemingly rejected one-party government in the midterm elections that took place in 1994, 2006, and 2010, when a single party controlled Congress and the presidency and the public was dissatisfied with the way things were going in the country. In those midterms, the president's party lost control of one or both houses of Congress in highly successful elections for the opposition party.

Partisans' Preferences Influenced by Party of President

To a large degree, Americans' opinions on the desirability of divided versus unified party government may not be based on a theoretical or normative preference, but on which form of government would give their favored party the most power. Since a Democrat is currently president, Americans may now equate one-party government with a *Democratic* one-party government. Consistent with this, Republicans currently say they favor divided government over unified government by 33% to 24%, and Democrats favor one-party government by an even larger 29-percentage-point margin, 47% to 18%.

Preference for Party Control of Congress and the Presidency, by Political Party

	Republicans	Independents	Democrats
	%	%	%
Same party	24	23	47
Different parties	33	32	18
Makes no difference	38	39	33
Same party - different parties (pct. pts.)	-9	-9	+29

Sept. 4-7, 2014

GALLUP

Underscoring that these preferences for divided versus unified government are influenced by which party is in the White House, Republicans have, on average, favored divided government during the Obama administration, but preferred one-party government when George W. Bush was president. Democrats, who favored divided government under Bush, now prefer one-party government with Barack Obama in office.

Preference for Party Control of Congress and the Presidency, by Political Party and Presidential Administration

	Republicans	Independents	Democrats
	%	%	%
OBAMA PRESIDENCY (2009-2014)			
Same party	26	22	42
Different parties	34	33	15
Makes no difference	34	39	38
Same party - different parties (pct. pts.)	-8	-11	+27
BUSH PRESIDENCY (2001-2008)			
Same party	45	21	28
Different parties	18	35	34
Makes no difference	35	39	34
Same party - different parties (pct. pts.)	+27	-14	-6

GALLUP

Independents' preferences have been consistent—in favor of divided rather than unified government—regardless of the party of the president.

Implications

Party control of the political branches of the U.S. government has typically been divided over the last 45 years. This has included times when a Republican president had to work with a Democratic Congress and when a Democratic president had to work with a Republican Congress. There have also been times, including currently, when party control of the two houses of Congress was divided.

There are certainly arguments to be made in favor of either divided or one-party government. If one party controls the presidency and Congress, it will have a much easier time passing legislation on policy that addresses the major issues facing the country. That arrangement also gives voters clear lines of accountability if people are happy or unhappy with the direction of the government, as was evident in voters' decisions to change party control of Congress in the 1994, 2006, and 2010 midterm elections.

Of course, if one party controls the federal government it may pursue policies that certain segments of the public do not like, and it could be up to two years before voters have the opportunity to change the partisan make-up of the government.

Divided government may also be seen as a way to ensure moderation in government policy, rather than it moving too far in a liberal direction if Democrats are in full control or too far in a conservative direction if Republicans are control. And having divided party control of government may be seen as another way to have checks and balances on the power of the various government institutions, in addition to those the founding fathers laid out in the Constitution.

Regardless of Americans' preferences, the U.S. is virtually certain to have divided government after this year's midterm elections, with President Obama in office for two more years and Republicans widely expected to retain their majority in the House of Representatives and with a reasonable chance of winning the majority in the Senate.

Survey Methods

Results for this Gallup poll are based on telephone interviews conducted Sept. 4–7, 2014, with a random sample of 1,017 adults, aged 18 and older, living in all 50 U.S. states and the District of Columbia.

For results based on the total sample of national adults, the margin of sampling error is ±4 percentage points at the 95% confidence level.

October 16, 2014
MORE WOMEN THAN MEN IN U.S. WORKFORCE ARE IRKED BY PAY

by Lydia Saad

PRINCETON, NJ—When asked to rate 13 different aspects of their job and work environment, women employed full time in the U.S. differed most from their male counterparts in reaction to their pay. Twenty-eight percent of full-time working women are completely satisfied with their pay, compared with 34% of men.

Satisfaction With 13 Workplace Factors Among Full-Time U.S. Workers -- by Gender

Ranked by percentage of women completely satisfied with each factor

	Women (work full time)	Men (work full time)	Women's net satisfaction
	%	%	(pct. pts.)
Physical safety conditions	74	73	+1
Relations with coworkers	70	70	0
Flexibility of work hours	65	61	+4
Amount of vacation time	60	56	+4
Boss or immediate supervisor	57	55	+2
Job security	54	52	+2
Amount of work required	52	52	0
Recognition received at work	50	46	+4
Health insurance benefits	40	40	0
Chances for promotion	39	40	-1
Retirement plan employer offers	36	36	0
Amount of money earned	28	34	-6
Amount of on-the-job stress	26	27	-1

Based on combined 2010-2014 data

GALLUP'

Men and women have nearly identical reactions to the other 12 aspects of work measured—or at least the differences (up to four percentage points) are not statistically significant. This includes differences in satisfaction with their chances for promotion, the amount of on-the-job stress they have, and the flexibility of their work hours. Accordingly, the rank order of issues according to satisfaction is similar between the genders, with physical safety at the top for both, and stress and the amount of money earned at the bottom.

These finding are based on 2,076 full-time workers interviewed as part of Gallup's annual Work and Education poll between 2010 and 2014, including 1,281 men and 795 women.

According to the full range of responses, 71% of women versus 76% of men are completely or somewhat satisfied with their earnings, while 29% of women and 23% of men are completely or somewhat dissatisfied. Thus, whether the standard is "complete satisfaction" or the lower bar of "satisfaction," women still lag men.

Satisfaction With Amount of Money Earned

Based on adults employed full time

	Women	Men	Net result among women
	%	%	(pct. pts.)
Completely satisfied	28	34	-6
Somewhat satisfied	43	42	+1
Somewhat dissatisfied	18	14	+4
Completely dissatisfied	11	9	+2
Total satisfied	71	76	-5
Total dissatisfied	29	23	+6

Based on combined 2010-2014 data

GALLUP'

These results closely mirror last year's finding from Gallup's 2013 Work and Education poll that among all workers—including those employed full and part time—women are about as satisfied as men with all of the job aspects evaluated in the survey, except for pay.

Further analysis of the five-year aggregate reveals no major gender differences in men's and women's satisfaction with earnings according to age (those 18–29 vs. 50 and older), or whether they work in the private sector or for government.

Bottom Line

Earlier this week Gallup reported that four in 10 Americans consider equal or fair pay to be the top issue facing working women today. That seems borne out in the lower satisfaction that working women have relative to men with their earnings. While the majority of both groups are at least somewhat satisfied with their earnings, neither gender is highly satisfied with what they earn, but women are even less so than men.

Survey Methods

Results for this analysis are based on telephone interviews with a random sample of U.S. workers, aged 18 and older, employed full time and living in the 50 U.S. states and District of Columbia. The data is based on combined interviews from Gallup's 2010 through 2014 annual Work and Education polls, conducted each August. This includes interviews with 1,281 men employed full time and 795 women employed full time.

For results based on the total sample of men employed full time, the margin of sampling error is ±3 percentage points at the 95% confidence level.

For results based on the total sample of women employed full time, the margin of sampling error is ±4 percentage points at the 95% confidence level.

October 17, 2014
WEEKS BEFORE ELECTIONS, CONGRESSIONAL APPROVAL STILL LOW
Approval remains at 14%

by Rebecca Riffkin

WASHINGTON, D.C.—Less than one month before the 2014 midterm elections, 14% of Americans approve of the way Congress is handling its job. This is unchanged from September and is only five percentage points above the historical low of 9% found in November 2013.

Congressional Job Approval -- Full Trend

Do you approve or disapprove of the way Congress is handling its job? (% Approve shown)

GALLUP'

Congressional job approval in October matches the 14% average found so far in 2014.

The current approval figure is the lowest found in October of a midterm election year since Gallup began tracking this measure in 1974. Gallup has found that low congressional approval ratings before midterm elections are linked to higher seat turnover, especially for members of the president's party. For example, congressional job approval in October was 21% in 2010, and 23% in 1994, two years when the president's party lost a large number of seats. However, in other years when approval of Congress was in the 20% range, seat loss was not as extreme. This suggests that although low congressional approval is related to seat loss for the president's party, it is not a perfect predictor of what will happen in the upcoming elections. There likely are other factors at play, such as low presidential job approval and whether the president's party is the majority party in Congress.

Congressional Approval Ratings and President's Party Seat Changes, Recent Midterm Elections

Year	President's party	Majority party in House	% Approve of Congress ^	Seat gain/loss in U.S. House for president's party
2014	Democrat	Republican	14	NA
2010	Democrat	Democrat	21	-63
2006	Republican	Republican	26	-30
2002	Republican	Republican	50	6
1998	Democrat	Republican	44	5
1994	Democrat	Democrat	23	-53
1990	Republican	Democrat	26	-8
1986	Republican	Democrat	42	-5
1982	Republican	Democrat	29	-28
1978	Democrat	Democrat	29	-11
1974	Republican*	Democrat	35	-43

^ 2014 is based on Oct. 12-15, 2014, poll; prior years based on final estimate before elections
* The president (Ford) took office less than three months before the midterm elections

GALLUP

Democrats are slightly more likely to approve of Congress, at 19% in October, than are Republicans and independents, both at 11%. This gap is the largest it has been since February; from March to September, there was little difference in congressional approval by party identification. An increase in approval among Democrats is mostly responsible for this month's gap.

Congressional Approval Ratings by Political Affiliation Over the Last Year

Do you approve or disapprove of the way Congress is handling its job? (% Approve shown)

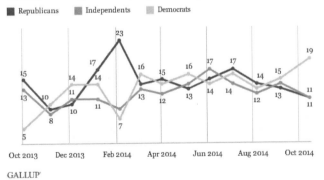

GALLUP

Bottom Line

In the fast-approaching midterm elections, all 435 House seats and 36 Senate seats are up for election. While Americans get to vote

only for the member of Congress in their own district and, if applicable this year, a senator or senators from their own state, the Congress' dismal approval rating could signal high congressional seat turnover, based on history. That will likely fall disproportionately on Democrats because voters often turn their frustrations on members of the president's political party.

One variable working against a big shakeup is the current divided party control of Congress. In contrast to most past elections, those unhappy with Congress cannot as clearly direct their frustrations at one party because currently, there is divided party control of Congress. This blurred line of responsibility—and the presently small likelihood that the Democrats will gain control of the House and maintain control of the Senate, along with the presidency, after the elections—may be why voters are not as motivated to show up at the polls this year as in past elections, when frustration with Congress was high.

Survey Methods

Results for this Gallup poll are based on telephone interviews conducted Oct. 12–15, 2014, with a random sample of 1,017 adults, aged 18 and older, living in all 50 U.S. states and the District of Columbia.

For results based on the total sample of national adults, the margin of sampling error is ±4 percentage points at the 95% confidence level.

October 17, 2014
KENTUCKIANS NOW MORE LIKELY TO ALIGN WITH GOP
Democratic presence, Obama approval at six-year lows in Kentucky

by Justin McCarthy

WASHINGTON, D.C.—A series of disheartening figures could make Democratic Kentucky Secretary of State Alison Lundergan Grimes' attempt to unseat Senate Minority Leader Mitch McConnell all the more difficult. Kentuckians are now more likely to identify as or lean toward Republicans (45%) than Democrats (39%). In the prior six years, Gallup found Democrats held at least a slight advantage.

Kentucky: Party Affiliation, Including Leaners

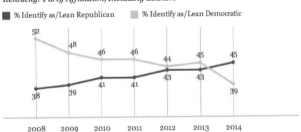

Data for 2014 collected Jan. 1-June 30

GALLUP

The six-percentage-point edge favoring Republicans, based on interviewing conducted in Kentucky from January through June of this year, underscores the uphill battle Grimes faces in trying to unseat McConnell. And given typical Republican advantages in voter turnout, the Democratic deficit on partisanship among those Kentucky residents who actually turn out to vote may be even greater than six points.

Although the Senate race has been considered a potential Democratic takeover, that possibility now seems a bit more remote after the Democratic Senatorial Campaign Committee announced it will stop running television ads in support of Grimes' bid to defeat the long-serving Republican incumbent.

The shift toward Republican Party affiliation certainly aids McConnell's chances. McConnell narrowly won in 2008, 53% to 47%, in a year when Democrats had a decided advantage in party affiliation both nationally and in Kentucky. That close outcome may have emboldened Democrats to initially invest party resources in an effort to unseat the highest-ranking Republican in the Senate. With 2014 shaping up as a better year for Republicans, a McConnell upset may not be in the cards—and Democrats' decision to withdraw ads from the state may be an admission of that.

If Democrats are not successful overall in this year's midterm election, McConnell is poised to become Senate majority leader.

Obama's Impact on the Kentucky Race for U.S. Senate

It has been common for Republican candidates throughout the 2014 election season to exploit the unpopularity of Democratic President Barack Obama by linking the president to their Democratic opponents. But as of recently, the Bluegrass State has become the political epicenter of the president's burden on competing Democrats.

Kentucky's 29% job approval rating for Obama in the first six months of this year is one of the lowest in the nation, and is among just a handful of states where approval has dipped below 30%. That compares to a 43% approval rating nationally during the same period. Though the state has typically fallen well below the average in approval of Obama's performance, the difference is larger in 2014 than in any previous year since he took office.

Kentucky: Presidential Job Approval

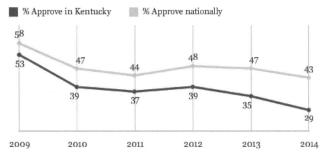

Data for 2014 collected Jan. 1-June 30

GALLUP'

Obama's dire unpopularity in Kentucky has been a vulnerable point for Grimes throughout the race, but has become even more of an issue since she declined in two media appearances to say whether she voted for him in the presidential election. Perhaps these figures shed some light on why Grimes would be reluctant to divulge her vote—but regardless, the apprehension she expressed has put a spotlight on the president in a race Grimes would likely prefer he not be a part of.

The reality, however, is that Obama and his policies are very much at the center of the race. Kentucky has been one of the shining stars of Obama's Affordable Care Act, and the sharp drop in the state's uninsured rate has been touted as one of the program's greatest successes. This is especially noted given that Kentucky has the highest smoking rate in the country and one of the highest levels of obesity.

In theory, the success of the healthcare law in Kentucky should give Grimes a leg up in the race since McConnell and the GOP have vehemently opposed the act. However, the state's branding of its exchange, Kynect, has allowed Kentuckians to disassociate the program from the president, even if it was his leadership that spearheaded it in the first place.

In Kentucky, Very Low Confidence in the National Economy

Underscoring Kentuckians' decision in November are the dismal views they have of the economy. Kentucky is among the bottom five states when it comes to residents' views of the national economy's current condition and future prospects, based on Gallup's Economic Confidence Index. Kentucky's index score of −31 is 15 points lower than the national average.

Kentuckians were significantly more positive in their views of their state's economy (+6) in a Gallup poll conducted last year, but still lagged behind the 50-state index reading (+23).

Kentucky: Economic Confidence Index

Gallup's Economic Confidence Index is the average of two components: Americans' views of current economic conditions and whether they think the economy will get better or will get worse.

	In Kentucky	Nationally
Confidence in the U.S. economy	-31	-16
Confidence in your state's economy^	+6	+23

June-December 2013

^ The national figure for "Confidence in your state's economy" is the overall average of the 50 individual state averages.

GALLUP'

Bottom Line

As a candidate taking on a powerful, long-serving incumbent senator, Grimes undoubtedly has a lot going against her.

Though she has taken many opportunities to remind voters that Obama isn't on the ballot with her, Grimes' recent refusal to say whether she voted for the president has put a spotlight on an area she probably would like to avoid, given the president's very low approval rating in her state—one of the lowest in the nation. At the same time, Kentucky is among the states showing the most positive impact from Obama's healthcare law; however, if residents do connect this directly with the president, it is not apparent in his approval rating.

While Democratic presence in the state has gradually shrunk over the past several years, 2014 saw a sharp drop in the percentage of Kentuckians who identify with or lean toward the party. In some respects, this decline might not mean much, as Republicans have still managed to control five of the state's six congressional seats despite the state having a Democratic edge. And this is likely due to greater average turnout among Republicans to overcome

Democrats' numerical advantage in partisanship among all Kentucky adults.

A continued drop in Democratic Party affiliation could mean more damage to the party next year, however, as the state's leading Democrat, Gov. Steve Beshear, is not eligible for re-election due to state term limits. This gives Republicans yet another opening to tighten their grip on Kentucky if they succeed in getting McConnell re-elected.

Survey Methods

Results for this Gallup poll are based on telephone interviews conducted Jan. 1–June 30, 2014, on the Gallup Daily tracking survey, with a random sample of 88,802 adults, aged 18 and older, living in all 50 U.S. states and the District of Columbia. Results are also based on Gallup's recent 50-state poll conducted June–December 2013, with a random sample of approximately 600 adults per state, aged 18 and older, living in all 50 U.S. states.

For results based on the 2014 sample of 1,419 Kentucky residents, the margin of sampling error is ±2 percentage points at the 95% confidence level.

For results based on the 2013 50-state poll, the margin of sampling error is ±5 percentage points at the 95% confidence level.

October 20, 2014
U.S. ADULTS WITH CHILDREN AT HOME HAVE GREATER JOY, STRESS

by Dan Witters

WASHINGTON, D.C.—American adults who have children younger than 18 at home are more likely than adults who don't live with children to say they smile or laugh a lot on any given day, 84.1% vs. 79.6%. At the same time, by an even greater margin—45.1% vs. 36.8%—adults with children at home also experience greater stress, according to the Gallup-Healthways Well-Being Index.

U.S. Adults Daily Smiling/Laughter and Daily Stress, by Whether Children Are in Household
"Did you experience [smiling and laughter/stress] a lot of the day yesterday?" (% Yes)

Daily emotion	All adults %	Adults with children under 18 in household %	Adults with no children under 18 in household %	Difference between the two groups (pct. pts.)
Smiled or laughed a lot "yesterday"	81.2	84.1	79.6	4.5
With stress a lot of day "yesterday"	39.9	45.1	36.8	8.3

Gallup-Healthways Well-Being Index, Jan. 2-Sept. 25, 2014

GALLUP

These findings are based on 131,159 interviews with American adults, aged 18 and older, including 36,043 adults who reported having a child under age 18 living in the household. Interviews were conducted from Jan. 2–Sept. 25, 2014, as part of the Gallup-Healthways Well-Being Index, which organizes well-being into five elements: purpose, social, financial, community, and physical.

Daily emotions such as smiling/laughter and stress are affected by all five elements of well-being. The 8.3-percentage-point gap in reports of daily stress between those with and those without children under 18 at home is nearly double the 4.5-point gap in reports of

smiling and laughter. On a relative basis, then, it appears children do more to boost negative than positive emotions. These patterns also hold true after controlling for age.

Differences in Emotions Similar in Both Women and Men

The relationship between children in the household and daily emotions is similar among men and women. Although women as a whole report more stress than men on any given day, the difference in stress rates between those with and those without children is almost identical for each gender—around eight points. Likewise, daily smiling and laughter, which men and women report similarly, is enhanced by comparable levels for each gender.

U.S. Daily Smiling/Laughter and Daily Stress, by Whether Children Are in Household and by Gender
"Did you experience [smiling and laughter/stress] a lot of the day yesterday?" (% Yes)

Daily emotion	All respondents %	Children in household %	No children in household %	Difference between those with children and those with no children (pct. pts.)
WOMEN				
Smiled or laughed a lot "yesterday"	81.9	84.5	80.3	4.2
With stress a lot "yesterday"	42	47.1	39	8.1
MEN				
Smiled or laughed a lot "yesterday"	80.5	83.6	78.8	4.8
With stress a lot "yesterday"	37.6	42.9	34.7	8.2

Gallup-Healthways Well-Being Index, Jan. 2-Sept. 25, 2014

GALLUP

Bottom Line

As many parents will attest, raising children is a task filled with great joys as well as great challenges. This extends to emotional outcomes, which are a part of well-being. The parenting experience of having children living at home is filled with many moments of joy, typically driven by love and buttressed by the satisfaction that comes with children's growth and successes as students, artists, athletes, friends, and citizens—inside and outside the home.

Parenting, in turn, also comes with many challenges that can catalyze stress on a daily basis. These range from managing normal behavioral struggles about mealtime, household routines, and homework, along with loss of sleep, to more serious issues faced by many parents—including teen rebellion, addressing special needs, eating disorders, peer issues, substance abuse, and self-injury. The stress associated with grappling with these issues may be further magnified for the parent upon separation or divorce, especially for women.

Ultimately, the simultaneous increase in positive and negative emotions when one lives with children is something many parents will invariably encounter. That these elevated emotions are common to women as well as men underscores the shared parenting that occurs in many families, and can play a part in helping spouses recognize a shared set of experiences in this role.

Survey Methods

Results are based on telephone interviews conducted as part of the Gallup-Healthways Well-Being Index survey from Jan. 2–Sept. 25, 2014, yielding a sample of 131,159 adults, aged 18 and older, living in all 50 U.S. states and the District of Columbia, selected using random-digit-dial sampling. Of this sample, 64,468, 46,525, and 18,738 were with all men, men without children younger than 18 in the household, and men with children younger than 18 in the household, respectively, while 65,673, 48,220, and 17,305 were with all women, women without children in the household, and women with children in the household, respectively.

For results based on the sample sizes noted above, respondents for each gender will have a maximum expected error range of about ±0.5 percentage points, while respondents for each gender without children at home will have a margin of error of about ±0.5 percentage points and respondents for each gender with children at home will have a margin of error of about ±0.9 percentage points. Each sample of national adults includes a minimum quota of 50% cellphone respondents and 50% landline respondents, with additional minimum quotas by time zone within region. Landline and cellular telephone numbers are selected using random-digit-dial methods.

October 20, 2014
OBAMA AVERAGES 41.5% JOB APPROVAL IN HIS 23RD QUARTER
Among the lowest quarterly averages of his presidency

by Jeffrey M. Jones

WASHINGTON, D.C.—President Barack Obama's job approval rating averaged 41.5% during his 23rd quarter in office, which began on July 20 and ended on Oct. 19. That ranks as one of his lowest quarterly approval ratings to date. The only two that were lower were the 41.2% in his 20th quarter—after the troubled launch of the health insurance exchanges last fall—and the 41.0% in his 11th quarter during the negotiations to raise the federal debt limit and its fallout on the U.S. economy.

Barack Obama's Quarterly Job Approval Averages
■ % Approve

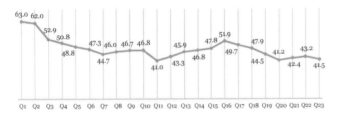

Gallup Daily tracking

GALLUP

Obama's first quarter in office, when his approval rating averaged 63.0%, still ranks as his best. Since his first year, his average quarterly approval ratings have all been below 50%, with one important exception—in the fall and early winter of 2012, the quarter in which he won re-election. Obama's job approval rating has averaged 48% throughout his nearly six full years in office.

During his 23rd quarter, Obama's Gallup Daily tracking job approval ratings fell to as low as 38% in early September, tying his personal low. That came after the Islamic militant group ISIS beheaded two American journalists. His approval rating did rise to

45% in Sept. 19–21 polling, shortly after he announced an expanded U.S. program of military airstrikes against ISIS in Iraq and Syria.

Obama 23rd Quarterly Average Among Lowest

Five post–World War II presidents have been elected to office twice and served a full 23rd quarter in office. Among these, George W. Bush has the lowest 23rd quarter average approval rating at 39.1%, just slightly lower than Obama's. In contrast, Dwight Eisenhower, Ronald Reagan and Bill Clinton were much more popular at this stage in their presidencies, with average 23rd quarter approval ratings of 56% or better.

Quarterly Job Approval Averages for Presidents During Their 23rd Quarter in Office, Presidents Elected to Two Terms

President	Dates of 23rd quarter	23rd quarter job approval average	Number of polls
Eisenhower	Jul 20–Oct 19, 1958	56.4%	5
Reagan	Jul 20–Oct 19, 1986	61.7%	3
Clinton	Jul 20–Oct 19, 1998	63.9%	8
G.W. Bush	Jul 20–Oct 19, 2006	39.1%	8
Obama	Jul 20–Oct 19, 2014	41.5%	90

Richard Nixon resigned during his 23rd quarter in office. He had a 24% job approval rating in the only poll conducted during that quarter prior to his resignation.
Harry Truman was not elected to his first term in office but was elected to a second term and served a 23rd quarter in office. Truman averaged 37.3% approval from Oct. 20, 1950–Jan. 19, 1951.

GALLUP

The importance of a president's 23rd quarter average cannot be understated, as it signifies his political standing heading into the second midterm election of his presidency. Typically the president's party's fortunes in the midterms are heavily tied to his popularity.

For example, the Republicans suffered heavy losses in the 2006 midterm elections under Bush, losing majority control of both the House of Representatives and the Senate. Republicans also performed poorly in the 1974 midterms, just after what would have been Richard Nixon's 23rd quarter in office. He resigned in August just after his 23rd quarter began, with his only job approval rating measured during that quarter at 24%.

In contrast, presidents who were relatively popular in their 23rd quarters—including Reagan and Clinton—saw their parties perform better in the midterms. In fact, in 1998, Democrats gained seats in the House in 1998 under Clinton, a rare occurrence for the president's party in midterm elections.

Implications

Obama's job approval rating continues to languish near his personal lows, creating a strong headwind for Democratic candidates in next month's midterm elections.

Based on the historical record, it would not be surprising if Obama's approval ratings decline further over the next three months. Although there are only four twice-elected presidents who have served 24 quarters in office since Gallup began polling on presidential approval, in three out of four cases their 24th quarter average was lower than their 23rd quarter average. Clinton was the exception, as his approval rating went up, which may have been the result of a strong economy and a rally in support in reaction to Republicans' attempts to impeach him and remove him from office—which Americans opposed. By contrast, Reagan's 24th quarter approval rating took a nosedive of 10 percentage points as the Iran-Contra scandal exploded. Bush and Eisenhower saw more modest declines.

This limited historical pattern suggest the odds are against Obama's approval ratings improving in the next quarter. And if Democrats have a poor showing on Election Day, Nov. 4—including possibly losing their Senate majority—Obama will likely be politically weakened. If his job approval rating declines as a result, he may end the next quarter with his lowest quarterly average.

Survey Methods

Results for this Gallup poll are based on telephone interviews conducted July 20–Oct. 19, 2014, on the Gallup U.S. Daily survey, with a random sample of 45,640 adults, aged 18 and older, living in all 50 U.S. states and the District of Columbia. For results based on the total sample of national adults, the margin of sampling error is ±1 percentage point at the 95% confidence level.

Each sample of national adults includes a minimum quota of 50% cellphone respondents and 50% landline respondents, with additional minimum quotas by time zone within region. Landline and cellular telephone numbers are selected using random-digit-dial methods.

October 21, 2014
AMERICANS' CONFIDENCE IN GOVERNMENT TO HANDLE EBOLA DROPS

by Frank Newport

PRINCETON, NJ—Americans are no more worried about getting Ebola now than they were two weeks ago, but they have become somewhat less confident in the federal government's ability to deal with an outbreak of the virus. Fifty-two percent of Americans are now very or somewhat confident in the government's ability to handle Ebola, down from 61% in early October.

Attitudes About Ebola

■ % Worried yesterday about getting Ebola

■ % Very/Somewhat likely that you or someone in your family will get Ebola

□ % Very/Somewhat confident in federal government's ability to handle Ebola

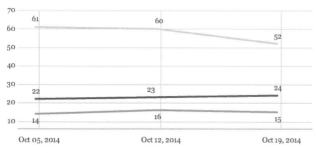

GALLUP'

Twenty-four percent of Americans say they worried yesterday about getting Ebola, little changed from 22% two weeks ago. Similarly, the percentage believing it is at least somewhat likely that they or someone in your family will get Ebola has also remained stable, now at 15%.

The drop in Americans' confidence in the federal government to handle the Ebola situation has occurred in part because the issue has become politicized. Republicans were already less confident than Democrats in the government's ability to handle Ebola two weeks ago, but the gap between the two has grown larger. Now, 37% of Republicans are confident in the government compared with 71% of Democrats; two weeks ago, 48% of Republicans and 74% of Democrats were confident in the government's ability to handle an Ebola outbreak.

How confident are you that the federal government will be able to handle an outbreak of the Ebola virus in this country?
% Very/Somewhat confident

	Republicans/Leaners	Democrats/Leaners
	%	%
Oct 18-19, 2014	37	71
Oct 11-12, 2014	45	78
Oct 4-5, 2014	48	74

GALLUP'

In recent days, several Republican Senate and House candidates running for election have adopted criticisms of the administration's response to the Ebola situation as talking points in their campaign, and rank-and-file Republicans appear to have picked up on this theme. Perhaps in reaction to these criticisms, and to give Democratic candidates something concrete to point to, President Barack Obama on Friday appointed Ron Klain as "Ebola czar" to head up the government's efforts to address Ebola. However, Republicans have responded with criticisms of that appointment as well, including Arizona Sen. John McCain's questions about the fact that Klain lacks a medical background and has mainly served as a high-ranking assistant to Democratic officeholders during his professional career.

Few Americans Think Ebola Will Be a Crisis or Major Outbreak

Most Americans continue to say that the Ebola virus ultimately will not strike the U.S. at all—even though cases have already been reported in the U.S.—or predict only a minor outbreak. Two in 10 now say it will be a major outbreak or a crisis. These attitudes are similar to those measured two weeks ago.

Which comes closest to your view about the Ebola virus?

	Will not strike U.S.	Minor outbreak	Major outbreak	Crisis	No opinion
	%	%	%	%	%
Oct 18-19, 2014	9	65	10	10	6
Oct 4-5, 2014	12	65	9	9	6

GALLUP'

Implications

The Ebola situation has been a constant presence in news coverage over the past two weeks. The first person diagnosed with Ebola in the U.S. died in a Dallas hospital, and two American healthcare workers were identified as having contracted the virus. Politicians and pundits have debated possible travel bans and immigration restrictions.

Throughout all of this, Americans' concerns about getting the virus have remained stable, and have been similar to their worries about contracting swine flu five years ago. Further, few Americans appear worried that Ebola will spread to the point of producing a major outbreak or a crisis in the U.S.

Over the last two weeks, however, the American public has lost some confidence in the federal government's ability to handle Ebola, although the confidence level still remains at a majority level. It is mainly Republicans who have lost confidence in the government to handle Ebola, suggesting that this health and medical situation—as is the case with so much else in American society today, particularly during election season—has become a politicized issue.

Survey Methods

Results for this Gallup poll are based on telephone interviews conducted Oct. 18–19, 2014, on the Gallup U.S. Daily survey, with a random sample of 1,017 adults, aged 18 and older, living in all 50 U.S. states and the District of Columbia. For results based on the total sample of national adults, the margin of sampling error is ±4 percentage points at the 95% confidence level.

Each sample of national adults includes a minimum quota of 50% cellphone respondents and 50% landline respondents, with additional minimum quotas by time zone within region. Landline and cellular telephone numbers are selected using random-digit-dial methods.

Over the last two decades, Democrats' support for the death penalty has dropped significantly, from 75% to 49%. Now, Democrats are divided on whether it should be administered to convicted murderers. Republicans' and independents' support is also lower now—down nine and 18 percentage points, respectively—though both groups still solidly favor the death penalty.

Views of Death Penalty for Convicted Murderers, 1994 vs. 2014, by Political Party

	1994	2014	Change
	%	%	pct. pts.
DEMOCRATS			
In favor	75	49	-26
Not in favor	22	46	+24
INDEPENDENTS			
In favor	80	62	-18
Not in favor	14	32	+18
REPUBLICANS			
In favor	85	76	-9
Not in favor	12	22	+10

GALLUP

October 23, 2014
AMERICANS' SUPPORT FOR DEATH PENALTY STABLE

by Jeffrey M. Jones

WASHINGTON, D.C.—Six in 10 Americans favor the death penalty for convicted murderers, generally consistent with attitudes since 2008. Since 1937, support has been as low as 42% in 1966 and as high as 80% in 1994.

Are you in favor of the death penalty for a person convicted of murder?

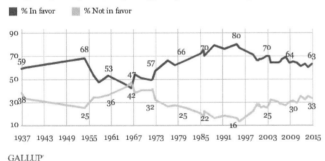

GALLUP

Americans' support for the death penalty has varied over time, but apart from a single reading in 1966, the public has consistently favored it. Support ebbed from the 1960s to the mid-1970s, when the application of the death penalty was questioned and ultimately led to the Supreme Court's invalidating state death penalty laws. Subsequent to that, newly written laws passed constitutional muster and states began to use the death penalty again in the late 1970s, with support among Americans increasing to 70% or more in the mid-1980s to the late 1990s.

The broader trend over the last two decades has been diminished support for the death penalty, including a 60% reading last year, the lowest since 1972.

Americans Tilt in Favor of Death Penalty Over Life Imprisonment

Gallup's long-standing question asks about basic support for the death penalty, but does not explicitly mention an alternative punishment for murderers. Gallup separately asks Americans to choose between the death penalty and "life imprisonment with absolutely no possibility of parole" as the better punishment for murder. Support for the death penalty has been significantly lower using this approach, but Americans still tilt in favor of it by 50% to 45%. These attitudes are similar to recent years, but show reduced support for the death penalty from the 1980s and 1990s.

If you could choose between the following two approaches, which do you think is the better penalty for murder -- [ROTATED: the death penalty (or) life imprisonment, with absolutely no possibility of parole]?

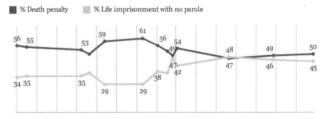

GALLUP

Democrats' opinions have also shifted markedly on the death penalty vs. life imprisonment question. Two decades ago, Democrats preferred the death penalty by a wide margin, but they now prefer life imprisonment by nearly the same margin. Independents' and Republicans' views have changed less, although both show increases in support for life imprisonment.

Better Punishment for Murderer, 1993 vs. 2014, by Political Party

	1993	2014	Change
	%	%	pct. pts.
DEMOCRATS			
Death penalty	55	37	-18
Life imprisonment	33	60	+27
INDEPENDENTS			
Death penalty	56	50	-6
Life imprisonment	29	44	+15
REPUBLICANS			
Death penalty	68	68	0
Life imprisonment	23	29	+6

GALLUP'

Implications

The death penalty has always been controversial, and this year, the issue made headlines again amid a botched execution attempt in Oklahoma.

Americans' support for the death penalty has stabilized at a lower level than was the case prior to 2008, and is well below the highs from the mid-1980s to mid-1990s. And in recent years the public has shown only a slight preference for the death penalty over life imprisonment as the better penalty for murder. These trends toward diminished support seem to be reflected in state death penalty laws, as six U.S. states have abolished the death penalty since 2007, and no new states have adopted it.

Democrats are mostly responsible for this shift in attitudes, and thus it is not surprising that most of the states that have abolished the death penalty in recent years are Democratic leaning. The death penalty is another example of how Democrats' and Republicans' opinions on political matters have become increasingly divergent compared with recent decades, including their views of the job the president is doing and on issues such as global warming and labor unions.

Survey Methods

Results for this Gallup poll are based on 1,017 telephone interviews conducted Oct. 12–15, 2014 (for the favor/not in favor question), and 1,252 telephone interviews conducted Sept. 25–30, 2014 (for the death penalty vs. life imprisonment question). Each is based on a random sample of adults, aged 18 and older, living in all 50 U.S. states and the District of Columbia.

For results based on the total sample of national adults, the margin of sampling error is ±4 percentage points at the 95% confidence level.

October 23, 2014
AMERICANS: "EYE FOR AN EYE" TOP REASON FOR DEATH PENALTY

by Art Swift

WASHINGTON, D.C.—Americans who favor the death penalty most often cite "an eye for an eye" as the reason they hold their position, with 35% mentioning it. "Save taxpayers money" and "they deserve it" tie as the second-most-popular reasons Americans volunteer in this open-ended measure, at 14% each.

Reasons to Support the Death Penalty (Open-Ended)
Why do you favor the death penalty for persons convicted of murder?

	1991 %	2001 %	2003 %	2014 %
An eye for an eye/They took a life/Fits the crime	50	48	37	35
Save taxpayers money/Cost associated with prison	13	20	11	14
They deserve it	--	6	13	14
They will repeat crime/Keep them from repeating it	19	6	7	7
Deterrent for potential crimes/Set an example	13	10	11	6
Depends on the type of crime they commit	--	6	4	5
Fair punishment	--	1	3	4
Serve justice	3	1	4	4
If there's no doubt the person committed the crime	--	2	3	3
Support/believe in death penalty	--	6	2	3
Don't believe they can be rehabilitated	--	2	2	3
Biblical reasons	--	3	5	3
Life sentences don't always mean life in prison	--	2	1	2
Relieves prison overcrowding	--	2	1	2
Would help/benefit families of victims	--	1	2	1
Other	11	3	4	1
No opinion	2	1	2	4

Based on sample of those who favor the death penalty in murder convictions

GALLUP'

A solid majority of Americans (63%) still favor using the death penalty in murder convictions, generally consistent with the level of support found over the last decade.

This is the fourth time Gallup has probed Americans to state, in their own words, why they hold the position they do on the death penalty.

Americans who say they support the death penalty have given a variety of responses over the years, but the biblical phrase "an eye for an eye," or retaliation, consistently has been named as the No. 1 reason why the death penalty should be applied. However, this reason's pre-eminence has waned since Gallup first asked this question in 1991, when half of Americans who favor the death penalty mentioned it.

"An Eye for an Eye," 1991-2014
% Mentioning this as reason they support death penalty

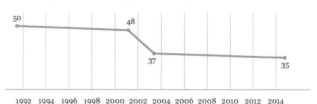

GALLUP'

The No. 2 response to this question has fluctuated over the years. Originally in 1991, the idea of the death penalty as a way to stop someone from repeating a crime was second at 19%. That concept has seemingly lost favor over the years, and this year, only 7% say deterrence is their top reason for supporting the death penalty. Instead, "save taxpayers money" and simply, "they deserve it," have emerged as the second-most-popular responses to why the death penalty should be used in murder convictions.

Several practical reasons including the belief that the prisoners "cannot be rehabilitated," that "life sentences don't always mean life in prison," and that the death penalty "relieves prison overcrowding" are mentioned less frequently, by between 2% and 3% of death penalty proponents.

Those Opposed to Death Penalty Cite "Wrong to Take a Life" as Top Reason

While a majority of Americans tilt in favor of the death penalty, the one in three Americans who oppose it also have a diversity of views as to why the ultimate penalty should not be used. "Wrong to take a life" has been the top reason for opposing it since 1991, by comfortable margins.

Reasons to Oppose the Death Penalty (Open-Ended)

Why do you oppose the death penalty for persons convicted of murder?

	2001 %	2003 %	2014 %
Wrong to take a life	41	46	40
Persons may be wrongly convicted	11	25	17
Punishment should be left to God/religious belief	17	13	17
Need to pay/suffer longer/think about their crime	--	5	9
Depends on the circumstances	--	4	9
Unfair application of death penalty	6	4	5
Does not deter people from committing murder	7	4	4
Costs more to keep prisoners on death row	--	--	2
Possibility of rehabilitation	6	5	2
Other	16	3	1
No opinion	6	4	3

Based on sample of those who oppose the death penalty in murder convictions

GALLUP

In two of the three times Gallup has asked this question, "persons may be wrongly convicted" has been the No. 2 justification Americans give for opposing the death penalty, along with reasons grounded in religious beliefs, including that "punishment should be left to God." Yet "wrong to take a life" is still the most popular open-ended response by a more than 2-to-1 margin.

As with the reasons for favoring the death penalty, subjective attitudes often outrank practical concerns in terms of why people oppose the death penalty. Some of the practical reasons offered for death penalty opposition include the "possibility of rehabilitation," the cost of keeping a prisoner on death row, and unfair application of the death penalty.

Bottom Line

Americans' top reasons for supporting the death penalty, including most prominently that it is necessary to take "an eye for an eye" when a murder is committed, demonstrate that Americans are less concerned with using the tool as a deterrent for future crimes and more so with using it as a means of punishment.

For those who oppose the death penalty, moral and religious reasons such as it is "wrong to take a life" are most popular. Considering the numerous accounts of death-row inmates being found innocent through the use of DNA evidence, it may be surprising that wrongful conviction is only tied for second as a reason cited by death penalty opponents. Practical reasons like the cost of keeping a prisoner on death row—for decades, potentially—do not factor

as much into why Americans oppose the death penalty. Additionally, few opponents cite cruelty as a reason for their beliefs, despite recent news stories of botched executions in which lethal injections did not work as planned.

Throughout the 23 years Gallup has asked Americans why they hold their views on the death penalty, the responses have been generally consistent, with a few changes at the margins. For those studying the death penalty, these beliefs suggest many Americans have not only made up their minds about it but also coalesced around defined reasons for holding those beliefs.

Survey Methods

Results for this Gallup poll are based on telephone interviews conducted Oct. 12–15, 2014, with a random sample of 1,017 adults, aged 18 and older, living in all 50 U.S. states and the District of Columbia. For results based on the total sample of national adults, the margin of sampling error is ±4 percentage points at the 95% confidence level. For results based on the total sample of 634 who favor the death penalty, the margin of sampling error is ±5 percentage points at the 95% confidence level. For results based on the total sample of 335 who oppose the death penalty, the margin of sampling error is ±7 percentage points at the 95% confidence level.

October 24, 2014
THE STATE OF NEW HAMPSHIRE: POLITICALLY IN FLUX

by Andrew Dugan

WASHINGTON, D.C.—A hallmark of the current era of politics is that many of the 50 states, indeed a majority of them, have reliable political identities. Their presidential vote is a foregone conclusion, and they typically elect federal officeholders of their preferred brand—but not so in New Hampshire, one of the most politically schizophrenic states in the nation. In seven years, it has vacillated between a large Democratic lead on party preferences to a clear Republican advantage, and now to a tie.

New Hampshire: Party Identification

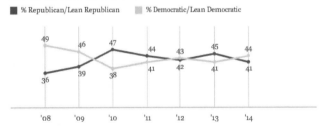

Aggregated Gallup U.S. Daily tracking; 2014 data collected Jan. 1-June 30

GALLUP

This year, with a competitive Senate race raising the state's political profile, 44% of New Hampshire residents lean or identify as Democratic, while 41% opt for the GOP.

Granite State politics are far from predictable. The only northeastern state to vote for George W. Bush in 2000, it instead backed Bush's opponent in his 2004 re-election campaign. But things have really heated up recently. In 2008, the state lurched further toward the Democratic column, voting for Barack Obama by about nine percentage points and electing a Democrat to the Senate for the first time in decades, Jeanne Shaheen. That year, Gallup found that almost half of New Hampshire residents leaned or identified Democratic (49%) and, more broadly, Democrats enjoyed a 13-point lead over the GOP.

But New Hampshire residents quickly switched gears, as Republicans took an ample lead in party identification in 2010, mirroring the same general pattern across the country. In that year's midterm election, a Republican was easily elected to the Senate, Republicans won both of the state's seats in the U.S. House and both chambers of the state legislature transferred to GOP control after four years of Democratic management. Then in 2012, Democrats enjoyed a large enough rebound in party support to bring the two parties to parity—43% Democratic, 42% Republican. New Hampshire again gave Obama its electoral votes, Democrats regained their seats in Congress and the state House flipped back to the Democrats.

This year, Republicans and Democrats are once more running neck and neck. Shaheen's re-election bid against erstwhile Massachusetts Sen. Scott Brown remains a tight race, with just over a week until Election Day.

As close as the race is, Gallup data suggest that the New Hampshire political environment is somewhat more hospitable to Democrats compared with other states with close Senate races. Democrats at least hold a nominal, if not statistically significant, lead in the state. And President Obama is less of a liability here than in states where his approval rating is below the national average. In New Hampshire, it matches the national average—still subpar in absolute terms, but not in relative terms.

New Hampshire: Presidential Approval

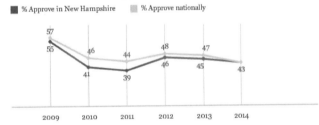

■ % Approve in New Hampshire   ▨ % Approve nationally

Aggregated Gallup U.S. Daily tracking; 2014 data collected Jan. 1–June 30

GALLUP'

Majority of New Hampshire Residents Say State Is Best to Live In

Scott Brown, formerly a senator from neighboring Massachusetts, is sensitive to a crippling political charge: the out-of-touch out-of-stater looking for a political launch pad. With 67% of Granite State residents saying New Hampshire is the best state in the country to live in, these attacks—which Shaheen drove home in the Oct. 20 debate—could prove especially persuasive to New Hampshire–loving residents. Additionally, three-quarters of New Hampshire residents say they would like to remain in the state and not move, 10 points higher than the 50-state average. In other words, New Hampshire residents are especially happy and content to be in the Granite State, and Brown's status as a recent arrival may hinder his ability to connect with these proud people. In Brown's defense, far fewer individuals from Massachusetts say it is the best state to live in (46%) or that they would like to remain there (58%). Thus, Brown could

retort he was acting on a common desire of many Massachusetts residents: moving out of the Bay State.

New Hampshire: Important State Measures

	New Hampshire	50-state average^
Great deal/Fair amount of trust and confidence in state government	66%	58%
State taxes NOT too high	52%	47%
Good time to get a job in city or area where you live	36%	40%
Confidence in your state's economy (Economic Confidence Index)	+36	+23
Best state in nation to live in	67%	46%
Would like to remain in state and not move	75%	65%

^ The 50-state averages are from a 50-state Gallup poll conducted June–December 2013 with at least 600 residents in each state.

GALLUP'

New Hampshire residents give the state strong marks on many other important metrics. According to Gallup's 2013 50-state poll, New Hampshire residents believe their state economy is in good shape and exhibit above-average levels of trust in state government. Accordingly, even as the Senate race remains close, incumbent Gov. Maggie Hassan, a Democrat, looks like a good bet for re-election.

Bottom Line

Political winds shift very quickly in New Hampshire—probably quicker than in any other state in the country. Democrats swept the major offices in 2008, while Republicans won big in 2010. In the last presidential election, Democrats rebounded, though New Hampshire was considered a battleground state throughout the contest. With just over a week until voters decide on a crucial Senate election, Granite State residents' party leanings continue to be closely divided, meaning this contest could be decided by a razor-thin margin.

Survey Methods

Results for this Gallup poll are based on telephone interviews conducted June–December 2013, with a random sample of approximately 600 adults, aged 18 and older, living in all 50 U.S. states and the District of Columbia. Results are also based on telephone interviews conducted as part of the Gallup U.S. Daily survey Jan. 1–June 30, 2014, with a random sample of 349 New Hampshire adults, aged 18 and older.

For results based on the 50-state poll and the total sample of adults per state, the margin of sampling error is ±5 percentage points at the 95% confidence level.

For results based on the total sample of New Hampshire residents, the margin of sampling error is ±8.3 percentage points at the 95% confidence level.

October 24, 2014
TEA PARTY REPUBLICANS HIGHLY MOTIVATED TO VOTE IN MIDTERMS

by Frank Newport

PRINCETON, NJ—Although the Tea Party has not been as visible in this year's midterm elections as it was in 2010, Tea Party

Republicans have given more thought to this year's elections and are much more motivated to vote than are non–Tea Party Republicans or other Americans. About one in four Americans continue to say they support the Tea Party.

Midterm Elections: Thought Given to and Motivation to Vote

	Tea Party Republicans	Other Republicans	Non-Republicans
	%	%	%
Given quite a lot/Some thought to elections	54	31	27
Extremely/Very motivated to vote	73	57	42

Sept. 25-30, 2014

GALLUP'

These results, from a Sept. 25–30 Gallup poll, demonstrate that despite what appears to be a lower profile this year, the Tea Party wing of the Republican Party—about 18% of all national adults—remains a powerful force, given their higher interest in the election and higher motivation to vote. This is not a new phenomenon; Republican Tea Party supporters gave the 2010 midterm elections more thought and were more motivated to vote than other Republicans, although all voters in general were paying more attention that year.

Previous Gallup research has shown that Tea Party Republicans are considerably more likely than other Republicans, as well as the rest of the population, to identify as conservatives. As befits this ideological orientation, Tea Party Republicans interviewed in a Sept. 4–7 survey were significantly more likely than other Republicans and the rest of the population to believe the government is doing too much, that there is too much government regulation of business and too much federal government power, and that government should be limited to providing only the most basic functions.

Views of Government's Role in U.S.

	Tea Party Republicans	Other Republicans	Non-Republicans
	%	%	%
Government doing too much that should be left to individuals and businesses	88	69	33
Federal gov't has too much power	87	73	43
Too much government regulation of business	84	66	27
Government should provide only most basic functions	71	45	18

Sept. 4-7, 2014

GALLUP'

Tea Party Republicans also differ from other Republicans in the importance they place on a number of specific issues in terms of their midterm election vote. In particular, Tea Party Republicans are much more likely than other Republicans to say the federal budget deficit and the Affordable Care Act are "extremely important" to their vote, and they view a number of other issues as at least somewhat more important than do non-Tea-Party-supporting Republicans. At the other end of the spectrum, Tea Party Republicans place somewhat less importance than other Republicans on equal pay for women and the availability of good jobs as issues.

Even with these differences, the top issues for Tea Party Republicans are generally the same as the top issues for other Republicans, except that Tea Party Republicans—reflecting their overall higher levels of interest in the elections—generally give the top issues at least a slightly higher importance rating.

Importance of Issues to Your Vote in Midterm Elections

How important will each of the following issues be to your vote for Congress this year -- will it be -- extremely important, very important, moderately important, or not that important?

% Extremely important

	Tea Party Republicans	Other Republicans	Non-Republicans
	%	%	%
Situation with Islamic militants in Iraq and Syria	57	51	34
Federal budget deficit	55	40	31
The way the federal government is working	48	39	42
The economy	47	40	43
Taxes	42	35	25
Immigration	42	35	26
Affordable Care Act	41	30	30
Foreign affairs	40	34	25
Availability of good jobs	39	43	47
The way income and wealth are distributed	24	25	35
Abortion and access to contraception	24	22	26
Equal pay for women	15	22	43
Climate change	7	9	26

Sept. 25-30, 2014

GALLUP'

More broadly, compared with all non-Republicans, Tea Party Republicans differ most in the importance they place on the deficit and the situation with the Islamic militants, and the lack of importance they place on equal pay for women.

Implications

During the 2010 midterm election campaign, the Tea Party had its greatest influence in the Republican primaries, pushing for and succeeding in nominating candidates who reflected its underlying ideology. This aspect of the Tea Party's influence has lessened in this election cycle, and the actual representation of Tea Party supporters in the general population has dropped slightly from 2010 levels. Still, although the Tea Party has been less visible in the election campaigning that has taken place this year in both the primaries and the lead-up to the general election, Tea Party supporters' stronger motivation to vote underscores the group's importance to the election outcome. Because most Tea Party supporters are Republicans or Republican leaners, and because it is unlikely that they will be voting for anyone other than a Republican candidate, the main effect of Tea Party supporters in the general election will be to provide a motivated base for the GOP to build on as it focuses on getting out the vote.

It is clear that Tea Party Republicans are defined by a strong belief in the need to curb the federal government's power and influence—a belief that they are more likely than other Republicans to hold. This makes it logical that the two issues of importance to Tea Party Republicans on which they differ most compared with other Republicans are the federal budget deficit and the Affordable Care Act—both of which are directly related to government spending and government power. It follows that the Tea Party's emphasis in future election years will likely continue to be nominating and electing candidates who embrace this "less government is better" mentality.

Survey Methods

Results for this Gallup poll are based on telephone interviews conducted Sept. 4–7, 2014, with a random sample of 1,017 adults, and telephone interviews conducted Sept. 25–30, 2014, with a random sample of 1,252 adults. Both samples were based on respondents

18 and older, living in all 50 U.S. states and the District of Columbia. For results based on the both samples of national adults, the margin of sampling error is ±4 percentage points at the 95% confidence level.

Each sample of national adults includes a minimum quota of 50% cellphone respondents and 50% landline respondents, with additional minimum quotas by time zone within region. Landline and cellular telephone numbers are selected using random-digit-dial methods.

October 27, 2014
HACKING TOPS LIST OF CRIMES AMERICANS WORRY ABOUT MOST

by Rebecca Riffkin

WASHINGTON, D.C.—As the list of major U.S. retailers hit by credit card hackers continues to grow this year, Americans are more likely to worry about having credit card information they used in stores stolen by computer hackers than any other crime they are asked about. Sixty-nine percent of Americans report they frequently or occasionally worry about this happening to them. Having a computer or smartphone hacked (62%) is the only other crime that worries the majority of Americans.

Crime Worries in U.S.

How often do you, yourself, worry about the following things -- frequently, occasionally, rarely or never? How about ...

	% Frequently or occasionally worry
Having the credit card information you have used at stores stolen by computer hackers	69
Having your computer or smartphone hacked and the information stolen by unauthorized persons	62
Your home being burglarized when you are not there	45
Having your car stolen or broken into	42
Having a school-aged child physically harmed attending school	31
Getting mugged	31
Your home being burglarized when you are there	30
Being the victim of terrorism	28
Being attacked while driving your car	20
Being a victim of a hate crime	18
Being sexually assaulted	18
Getting murdered	18
Being assaulted/killed by a coworker/employee where you work	7

Oct. 12-15, 2014

GALLUP

Less than half of Americans worry at least occasionally about other crimes, ranging from 45% who worry about their home being burglarized when they are not there to 7% who worry about being assaulted by a coworker on the job.

Gallup updated its measure of Americans' worry about a number of crime scenarios in its annual Crime poll, conducted Oct. 12–15. Trends on Americans' worries about most of these crimes extend back to 2000, although this was the first year Gallup asked Americans about having credit card information stolen or a smartphone or computer hacked.

Upper-income Americans, those whose household incomes are $75,000 or more a year, are more likely than lower-income Americans to worry frequently or occasionally about hacking of their credit card information, 85% to 50%. Americans between the ages of 30 and 64 worry about this more than younger and older Americans do.

Upper-Income More Likely Than Lower-Income Americans to Worry About Hacking
% Frequently or occasionally worry

	Credit card info hacking at stores	Computer/ Smartphone hacking
	%	%
Annual household income less than $30,000	50	46
Annual household income $30,000 to $74,999	71	64
Annual household income $75,000+	85	76
18 to 29 years old	62	55
30 to 49 years old	72	69
50 to 64 years old	77	63
65+ years old	62	53

Oct. 12-15, 2014

GALLUP

Higher levels of worry about credit card and computer-related crimes among upper-income Americans may result from their higher daily spending. Additionally, lower-income Americans are less likely to own credit cards or smartphones. In April, 58% of Americans whose annual household incomes are less than $30,000 said they owned no credit cards, compared with 11% of upper-income Americans. In December 2013, Gallup found that upper-income Americans are also more likely than lower-income Americans to own a smartphone, 84% vs. 46%.

More Than One in Four Americans Say They Have Been Hacked

Americans may be more worried about hacking because a relatively high percentage of them say they have had their information hacked. A quarter of Americans, 27%, say they or another household member had information from a credit card used at a store stolen by computer hackers during the last year—making this the most frequently experienced crime on a list of nine crimes. Eleven percent say they or a household member have had their computer or smartphone hacked in the last year, also in the top half of crimes on the list.

Although a relatively high percentage of Americans say they have been hacking victims, relatively low percentages say they reported it to the police. Slightly less than half of Americans (45%) who say they had credit card information stolen say they reported it to the police. And about a quarter of victims say they notified police about their computer or smartphone being hacked. Of Americans who say they were victims of other crimes in the last year, including stolen cars, muggings, or burglaries, an average of two-thirds say they reported them to police, higher than what Gallup finds for hacking crimes.

One reason reporting of credit card information theft may be lower is that some Americans who are victims of these crimes may not have seen monetary losses. The Department of Homeland Security estimates that more than 1,000 U.S. businesses have been hit by cyberattacks similar to the one that hit U.S. retailer Target; the Target breach alone is estimated to have affected 40 million credit and debit card accounts. Although this is a large proportion of Americans whose information could have been affected, it is unknown how many actually saw these cards used for fraudulent purchases.

Bottom Line

Americans today are more worried about their credit card information being hacked from stores than about any other crimes they are asked about, and a relatively high percentage say they have been victims of this hacking. Many high-profile and popular stores and restaurants have had major hacking problems in 2013 and 2014, something that no doubt has helped kindle such fears.

With credit card hacking clearly a concern to many Americans, it may affect their shopping habits as they take measures to protect their identities and finances. Consumers may avoid stores that have been hacked, and begin paying more frequently with cash or prepaid cards to protect their identities. To protect their customers and themselves, some credit card companies are switching to security chips, which are more secure than the magnetic strips currently common in the U.S., and are cautioning customers to check their accounts for suspicious activity.

Survey Methods

Results for this Gallup poll are based on telephone interviews conducted Oct. 12–15, 2014, with a random sample of 1,017 adults, aged 18 and older, living in all 50 U.S. states and the District of Columbia.

For results based on the total sample of national adults, the margin of sampling error is ±4 percentage points at the 95% confidence level.

October 28, 2014
PUBLIC SCHOOL PARENTS NOW DIVIDED ON COMMON CORE

by Justin McCarthy

WASHINGTON, D.C.—Parents of U.S. public school students in grades K–12 are about evenly divided over the Common Core State Standards. Thirty-five percent view them negatively and 33% view them positively, while another third aren't familiar with them or don't have an opinion. This reflects a slight shift since April, when parents were slightly more positive (35%) than negative (28%).

U.S. Public School Parents' Overall Impressions of Common Core Standards

For those who have heard a great deal/fair amount/a little about Common Core: And from what you know about them, do you have a positive or negative impression of the Common Core standards? Is that very [positive/negative], or somewhat [positive/negative]?

	April 2014	September 2014
	%	%
Very positive	9	6
Somewhat positive	26	27
Somewhat negative	15	17
Very negative	13	18
No opinion	4	5
Not heard of	33	27
Total positive	35	33
Total negative	28	35
No opinion/Not heard of	37	32

Results based on parents of students in public school, grades K-12

April 3-9, 2014, and Sept. 16-21, 2014

GALLUP

The overall proportion of public school parents who report having heard at least a little about the new standards has not changed appreciably since April, now at 73%. However, nearly half (49%) of public school parents now say they have heard a great deal or fair amount about the new standards, up from 38% in April.

The data suggest that this increase in awareness has led to an increase in negativity, given the seven-percentage-point increase in those viewing the standards negatively and the two-point decrease in those viewing them positively.

The April and September Gallup polls gauged public school parents' general reactions to the Common Core standards. A Phi Delta Kappa/Gallup poll on Common Core conducted in May and June elicited views about the standards that were more negative, although the questions were worded differently. That survey found 29% of public school parents in favor of "having teachers in your community use the Common Core State Standards to guide what they teach" and 57% opposed to that, with 6% unsure and 8% completely unfamiliar with Common Core. The majority opposition found with that measure could reflect parents' concern about the standards limiting teachers' flexibility in the classroom.

Support for Standards, Testing Has Waned

Though most public school parents still support the three key components of Common Core—the curriculum standards, the student testing, and using student test scores to evaluate teachers—support for the curriculum standards and student testing has declined since April, consistent with the more negative views of the standards overall.

Today, 65% of public school parents view having one set of national educational standards for reading, writing and math positively, but this is down from 73% in April. About six in 10 currently view standardized computer-based testing of students positively, as well as linking teacher evaluations to their students' Common Core test scores. Closer to two-thirds of parents favored both of these elements in April.

Parents' Views on Specific Aspects of Common Core

Now I'd like to mention several aspects of the Common Core. For each, please tell me if you think it will have a very positive, somewhat positive, somewhat negative or very negative impact on education in the United States?

	Total positive, April	Total positive, September
	%	%
Having one set of educational standards across the country for reading, writing and math	73	65
Using standardized computer-based tests to measure all students' performance and progress	65	59
Linking teacher evaluations to their students' Common Core test scores	67	62

Based on parents of students in public school, grades K-12

April 3-9, 2014, and Sept. 16-21, 2014

GALLUP

Opposition to Common Core Solidifies Among Parents Who Lean Republican

Today, as in April, public school parents who identify with or lean toward the Democratic Party are more supportive than Republicans of Common Core. However, as both groups have grown slightly more aware of the program, the balance of Republicans' views has become much more negative, while Democrats' views have stayed about the same.

The majority of Republican parents—58%—now hold a negative view of Common Core, up from 42% in April, and leaving just 19% viewing it positively. Additionally, significantly more Republicans now have a very negative view of Common Core than a somewhat negative view, 35% vs. 23%.

Republican and Republican-Leaning Public School Parents' Impressions of Common Core

	April 2014	September 2014
	%	%
Very positive	4	2
Somewhat positive	22	17
Somewhat negative	20	23
Very negative	22	35
Not heard of/No opinion	31	24
Total positive	26	19
Total negative	42	58

April 3-9, 2014 and Sept. 16-21, 2014

GALLUP

Meanwhile, Democratic parents remain in favor of Common Core by about 2-to-1, with 48% viewing it positively and 23% negatively, similar to their views in April. However, unlike Republican opposition, which is relatively strong, Democrats' support is tepid, with most supporters saying they have a somewhat rather than a very positive view of it, 37% vs. 11%.

Democratic and Democratic-Leaning Public School Parents' Impressions of Common Core

	April 2014	September 2014
	%	%
Very positive	13	11
Somewhat positive	32	37
Somewhat negative	15	17
Very negative	8	6
Not heard of/No opinion	33	30
Total positive	45	48
Total negative	23	23

April 3-9, 2014, and Sept. 16-21, 2014

GALLUP

Bottom Line

At least a year into its implementation in most states, the Common Core State Standards initiative has received a great deal of discussion, review and pushback—with Indiana and Oklahoma becoming the first states to drop the math and reading standards through legislation, bringing the number of states that are not participating to seven.

This might not be the end of major opposition among the states. Common Core has been an issue in many of the gubernatorial elections taking place this November, the outcomes of which could affect how the standards are implemented—if at all. In New York and Connecticut, the rollout of Common Core has become an issue for the Democratic governors who supported it, and has given some ammunition to their Republican challengers who oppose the initiative.

In Florida, meanwhile, Republican Gov. Rick Scott has said he is opposed to Common Core but has received flak for not waging political war on the initiative. His stance is further complicated by former Republican Gov. Jeb Bush's support for the standards—a rogue stance for a prospective 2016 GOP presidential candidate. In some states, an attempt to repeal Common Core is under way—such as Pennsylvania, where vulnerable Republican Gov. Tom Corbett has reversed his support for the initiative.

While parents' attitudes about Common Core have soured a bit since April, most of that shift comes from solidifying opposition among Republicans. This likely means that leaders in Republican states will continue to feel grassroots pressure to resist the standards, even if implementation proceeds apace elsewhere. However, without a larger proportion of Democratic parents backing the initiative, it's conceivable that serious repeal efforts could take hold anywhere.

Survey Methods

Results for this poll are based on telephone interviews conducted Sept. 16–17, 2014, on Gallup Daily tracking, with a random sample of 532 public school K–12 parents, aged 18 and older, living in all 50 U.S. states and the District of Columbia.

For results based on the total sample of public school parents, the margin of sampling error is ±6 percentage points at the 95% confidence level.

October 28, 2014
U.S. TEACHERS OFFER SPLIT DECISION ON COMMON CORE

by Lydia Saad

PRINCETON, NJ—In a new Gallup survey of teachers, U.S. public school teachers are closely split in their overall reaction to the Common Core State Standards: 41% view the program positively and 44% negatively. Even in terms of strong reactions, teachers' attitudes are divided, with 15% saying their perceptions of the initiative are "very positive" and 16% saying "very negative."

U.S. Public School Teachers' Impressions of the Common Core State Standards

	%
Very positive	15
Somewhat positive	26
Somewhat negative	28
Very negative	16
No opinion	16
Total positive	41
Total negative	44
No opinion	16

Aug. 11-Sept. 7, 2014

GALLUP

Underscoring this parity in views, more than half of teachers say their peers' perceptions vary. When asked how most teachers they know personally feel about the Common Core, 56% say the reaction is "mixed." Another 7% say it is positive, while 32% say it is negative.

These findings are based on an online Gallup Panel survey with 854 public school teachers in grades K–12 across the country. Teachers in the Gallup Panel were selected at random from Gallup Daily tracking. Those teachers available to take surveys by Web (95% of teacher panelists) were invited to take the Common Core survey online between Aug. 11 and Sept. 7.

Teachers Most Familiar With Common Core Like It Best

Teachers' attitudes toward the Common Core are not much different in the 43 states (plus the District of Columbia) where the standards have been adopted than they are nationally. Forty-four percent of those working in these states view the program positively, and 40% view it negatively—still roughly evenly divided.

However, within these Common Core states, the majority of teachers who say they work in schools where the Common Core standards were fully implemented in the 2013–2014 school year feel good about it: 61% view it positively versus 35% negatively. Among teachers in Common Core states whose schools had not yet fully implemented the standards last year, views are 37% positive versus 43% negative.

U.S. Public School Teachers' Impressions of the Common Core State Standards
Based on status of Common Core in their schools as of 2013-2014 school year

	Fully implemented	Partially/Not yet implemented	Not in a Common Core state
	%	%	%
Positive	61	37	26
Negative	35	43	59
No opinion	5	20	16

Aug. 11-Sept. 7, 2014

GALLUP'

While these differences in teachers' attitudes may partially reflect the underlying political climate in each state or school district that led to the adoption or rejection of the Common Core there to begin with, it is also possible that teachers feel more positively about the Common Core once they fully use it.

Gallup's polling of public school parents reveals strong partisan differences in parental attitudes toward the Common Core, with Democrats significantly more supportive of it than Republicans. Teachers display the same pattern. A little over half of those who identify as or lean Democratic have a positive impression of the Common Core, while six in 10 Republican teachers have a negative impression.

U.S. Public School Teachers' Impressions of the Common Core State Standards – by Party ID

	Republican/ Lean Republican	Democratic/ Lean Democratic
	%	%
Very positive	8	22
Somewhat positive	17	31
Somewhat negative	33	24
Very negative	25	9
No opinion	17	14
Total positive	25	53
Total negative	58	33
No opinion	17	14

Aug. 11-Sept. 7, 2014

GALLUP'

This pattern helps explain some of the differences between teachers in Common Core states versus those in non–Common Core states, as teachers in the latter lean more toward the GOP.

Elementary School Teachers Most Positive About Common Core

The poll also shows some variation in teachers' reactions to the Common Core according to the school level at which they teach. Elementary school teachers are, on average, the most positive about the Common Core, with a net +2 viewing it positively (43% positively minus 41% negatively). Among middle school teachers, attitudes tilt negative with a net –4, and among high school teachers they tilt even more negative with a net –11.

U.S. Public School Teachers' Impressions of the Common Core State Standards
Based on level of school taught in 2013-2014 school year

	Elementary	Middle school	High school
	%	%	%
Very positive	23	15	9
Somewhat positive	20	23	29
Somewhat negative	30	22	25
Very negative	10	20	24
No opinion	16	20	13
Positive	43	38	38
Negative	41	42	49
Net positive	+2	-4	-11

Aug. 11-Sept. 7, 2014

GALLUP'

Teachers' Views on the Pros and Cons of the Common Core

Teachers were given an opportunity on the poll to state what they consider to be the most positive aspect of the Common Core, as well as the most negative aspect.

These open-ended responses paint an unambiguous picture of what teachers consider to be the most positive aspect, as 56% of all public school teachers say that sharing the same standards across states is the main advantage. This is followed by 12% saying the Common Core fosters critical thinking, and 10% saying it sets higher standards or is more rigorous.

What do you think is the most positive thing about the Common Core?
Based on U.S. public school teachers in grades K-12

	Most positive thing
	%
Unified standards throughout the U.S.	56
Good critical thinking techniques	12
Higher standards/More rigorous	10
Improves reading and writing	3
In-depth learning	3
Attempting to make positive change/Fostering good conversations about education	3
Covers the basics	2
Holds teachers/schools/districts accountable	2
Has a good curriculum	2
Improves students' ability to communicate their thoughts	2
Allows for creativity/for teachers to teach as they see fit	1
Improves learning	2
Improves teaching/Instructs teachers how to teach	2
Focuses on students/their individual needs	1
Teaches real-life concepts/Prepares students for life	1
Integrates subjects	1
Other	6
Nothing positive	5
Don't know	1

Aug. 11-Sept. 7, 2014

GALLUP'

Teachers' views about the most negative aspects of the Common Core are more varied. The largest percentage of responses, 15%, is focused on the view that the Common Core is not practical, while 14% say it is being implemented poorly. The latter category includes many teachers who believe the Common Core should have been phased in with the younger grades to allow students to grow into the curriculum, rather than put into effect for everyone in kindergarten through high school at the same time.

Twelve percent cite the standardized testing that goes along with the Common Core as the worst aspect, and another 12% take issue with the curriculum standards themselves, saying they are inadequate, inaccurate, or biased.

Rounding out the top five complaints, 11% say the system is unfair to students in its "one size fits all" approach.

What do you think is the most negative thing about the Common Core?

Based on U.S. public school teachers in grades K-12

	Most negative thing
	%
Not practical/Unrealistic/Lacks common sense/Too much pressure	15
Poor planning and implementation/Shouldn't apply to older students	14
Don't believe in standardized testing/assessments	12
The curriculum testing standards are subpar/Dumbs down education/Inaccurate/Changes history	12
Unfair to students/One size fits all/Not student driven	11
Too bureaucratic/Stifles creativity/Doesn't empower teachers	8
Has unwarranted negative image/Poor public image	6
Should allow states to set their own standards/Too much government regulation	6
Has become too political	6
Need more training	6
Should cover more subjects/Leaves out important information	4
Need to provide materials/resources	4
Should be based on teachers' needs/created by teachers	5
Need more information on the program/Don't know enough about it/Too vague	3
Unfair to teachers/Shouldn't be tied to assessments or pay	4
Doesn't work for children with special needs/atypical learners	2
Takes too much time away from actual learning	3
Too difficult to understand/Too complicated/Creates more work	3
Not enough funding/Not a wise use of money	2
Out to make stakeholders wealthy	2
Poor technology/Don't have access to technology or computers	2
Doesn't work for lower socio-economic schools	1
Doesn't take student's lifestyle/home-life attitude into account	1
Too much change/Need more consistency with programs	1
Not effective for ESL students or students from other countries	1
Doesn't address real problems	1
Other	6
Nothing negative	2
Don't know	2

Aug. 11-Sept. 7, 2014

GALLUP

Bottom Line

Teachers in the 43 states that have adopted the Common Core State Standards are going through major shifts in how they teach reading, writing, grammar and math—as well as other subjects in which these skills come into play. Although some states have already worked these changes into their curricula, others started phasing them in last year, and others are just starting now. As the process unfolds, policymakers should pay close attention to how teachers themselves view the program, and whether it is working for both students and educators.

This initial survey on the Common Core reveals teachers' attitudes are sharply split, giving no clear advantage to the standards' proponents or opponents. However, regardless of the politics of the issue, the findings suggest some teachers may be experiencing a stressful work environment as they start the 2014–2015 school year—especially if staff members within their own schools are at odds over the Common Core.

On a positive note, the teachers who have the most experience teaching with the new standards are much more positive about it than others. Also, a solid majority of teachers applaud the fundamental goal of unifying standards across states. However, many express concerns that the program is unwieldy, not being implemented well, or simply bad policy. Further, although the initiative began as a bipartisan effort among the states, it has clearly become politicized among teachers, as it has with the general public. And that could mean attitudes will grow rigid rather than be receptive to change as new information about the Common Core—whether positive or negative—emerges over time.

Survey Methods

Results are based on Web interviews conducted Aug. 11–Sept. 7, 2014, via the Gallup Panel, with a random sample of 854 public K–12 school teachers, aged 18 and older, with Internet access, living in all 50 U.S. states and the District of Columbia. The data are weighted to match national teacher demographics of gender, age, race, Hispanic ethnicity, education and region.

Demographic weighting targets are based on the weighted demographic distribution of Gallup's nationally representative nightly poll respondents identified as teachers over a period of four years.

For results based on the sample of 854 public school teachers, the margin of sampling error is ±5 percentage points.

October 29, 2014
TEACHERS FAVOR COMMON CORE STANDARDS, NOT THE TESTING

by Linda Lyons

WASHINGTON, D.C.—The large majority of U.S. public school teachers, 76%, react positively to the primary goal of the Common Core—to have all states use the same set of academic standards for reading, writing and math in grades K–12. However, this positivity fades when the topic turns to using computerized tests to measure student performance (27%) and linking those test scores to teacher evaluations (9%).

A Michigan high school teacher who took part in Gallup's August and September 2014 survey of 854 K–12 public school teachers summarized these broadly held attitudes: "The standards were positive until standardized testing was involved."

These findings from the survey, as well as others, reveal a large disconnect between the solid support for the goals of the Common Core initiative among the teachers interviewed—68% of whom have been teachers for 10 or more years—and their serious concerns about how it will affect students and teachers.

Public School Teachers' Reactions to Main Elements of Common Core State Standards

For each of the following aspects of the Common Core, please indicate whether you think its impact on education in the United States will be very positive, somewhat positive, somewhat negative or very negative?

	Total positive	Total negative	No opinion
	%	%	%
Having one set of educational standards across the country for reading, writing, and math	76	24	1
Using standardized computer-based tests to measure all students' performance and progress	27	72	1
Linking teacher evaluations to their students' Common Core test scores	9	89	2

Aug. 11-Sept. 7, 2014

GALLUP

This gap in attitudes is also evident in what teachers feel is the appropriate time frame for introducing different aspects of the Common Core. The majority of teachers interviewed would prefer to start using the curriculum standards either this school year (28%) or later (32%), while 26% say they would never do so.

This contrasts with their preferences for implementing the student testing. About half would implement the testing component either this school year (8%) or eventually (41%), while a substantial 40% say they would never implement it. Far fewer (17%) would ever implement the teacher evaluation component; 79% would never implement it.

Public School Teachers' Preference for Implementing Each Aspect of the Common Core

Next, we want to know when you think different aspects of the Common Core should be implemented, focusing separately on the curriculum standards, testing and linking testing to teacher evaluations.

	Implement in fall 2014	Delay until fall 2015 or later	Never implement	No opinion
	%	%	%	%
Curriculum standards	28	32	26	14
Student testing	8	41	40	12
Linking teacher evaluation to test scores	2	15	79	5

Aug. 11-Sept. 7, 2014

GALLUP

Teachers Rate New Math Standards Better Than New English Standards

Praise for the Common Core curriculum standards is widespread among teachers whose schools used the standards in 2013–2014—that's one in four teachers—and who are familiar enough with the standards to offer an opinion about the academic rigor of its two main components. Sixty percent of these teachers believe the Common Core math standards are more rigorous than the math standards their schools used previously, and half (51%) believe the English language arts (ELA) standards are more rigorous. Relatively few believe either set of standards is less rigorous than what was in place previously, while the rest say they are about the same.

*Public School Teachers' Views of Common Core English and Math Standards^*

How do you feel the Common Core standards [for English Language Arts -- that is, reading, writing and grammar/for mathematics] compare with the previous standards used most recently at your school?

	English language arts	Mathematics
	%	%
More rigorous than the previous standards	51	60
About the same	40	29
Less rigorous than the previous standards	9	11

^ Based on teachers in schools that used Common Core standards in the 2013-2014 school-year, and who are familiar enough with them to have an opinion.

Aug. 11-Sept. 7, 2014

GALLUP

Elementary and middle school teachers see more rigor in the new standards than high school teachers do. This is particularly true for math. Sixty percent or more of elementary and middle school teachers say these standards are more rigorous than what their school used previously, but about half as many high school teachers (34%) agree. And, while few elementary school teachers, 4%, say the Common Core math standards are less rigorous than what their school had before, this more than triples to 14% among high school teachers.

*Public School Teachers' Views of Common Core English and Math Standards -- by School Level Taught^*

	Elementary school	Middle school	High school
	%	%	%
MATH STANDARDS			
More rigorous	64	60	34
Same	33	31	51
Less rigorous	4	9	14
ENGLISH (ELA) STANDARDS			
More rigorous	65	65	49
Same	24	25	38
Less rigorous	11	11	14

^ Based on 194 elementary school, 113 middle school, and 232 high school teachers in schools that used Common Core standards in the 2013-2014 school year, and who are familiar enough with them to have an opinion.

Aug. 11-Sept. 7, 2014

GALLUP

Teachers See Some Advantages, More Disadvantages to Common Core

The majority of teachers agree with four main arguments in favor of the Common Core that were tested in the survey, as well as four main arguments against it. However, teachers more broadly agree with the four statements describing possible disadvantages of Common Core than with the four statements highlighting its possible advantages.

In terms of advantages, teachers are most likely to agree (76%) that having unified standards helps teachers to better educate students who move from different states. "Regardless of what state an American child lives in, he or she will be held to the same standards and be offered the same opportunities to learn," says a middle school teacher in Texas. An elementary school teacher in Washington state who took part in the survey offered an example of why this is needed: "I had students move into my class recently from Florida and Wisconsin. Both were bright, but far behind Washington in math."

Six in 10 teachers agree that Common Core standards will facilitate better teacher training, and half say it will improve student assessment or ensure equality of educational opportunity throughout the U.S. One Pennsylvania high school teacher summed up her view of Common Core's benefits: "The idea that we should be raising expectations for all students is most positive."

Public School Teachers' Reactions to Four Arguments in Favor of Common Core

Please indicate how much you agree or disagree with each of the following possible advantages of the Common Core.

	Strongly agree	Somewhat agree	Somewhat disagree	Strongly disagree
	%	%	%	%
Enable teachers to better educate students who move from different states	29	47	10	13
Help colleges/professional development programs better prepare teachers for the classroom	15	45	18	17
Provide more accurate measurement of student achievement than by the current standardized testing	10	42	20	16
Help ensure that all students get the same high-quality level of education regardless of school district or location	14	38	20	27

Aug. 11-Sept. 7, 2014

GALLUP'

On the flip side, nearly nine in 10 teachers (89%) agree that linking teacher evaluations to student testing is unfair, and three-quarters (78%) agree that the tests take too much time away from teaching. Nearly two-thirds agree that Common Core gives students too little time for creative learning (63%) and takes too much control away from teachers (64%).

Public School Teachers' Reactions to Four Arguments Against Common Core

Please indicate how much you agree or disagree with each of the following possible disadvantages of the Common Core.

	Strongly agree	Somewhat agree	Somewhat disagree	Strongly disagree
	%	%	%	%
Takes too much control away from teachers over how they teach in their own classrooms	37	27	19	13
Results in students getting too little time for recess, art and music	35	28	13	9
Testing done to monitor student progress takes too much classroom time away from teaching	45	33	10	4
Linking teacher evaluations to student test scores is unfair to teachers	67	22	6	4

Aug. 11-Sept. 7, 2014

GALLUP'

Teachers Say Linking Teacher Evaluation to Student Test Scores Is Unfair

Given that nearly nine in 10 public school teachers (89%) agree with the statement, "Linking teacher evaluations to student test scores on the Common Core is unfair to teachers," Gallup recontacted some respondents to provide more qualitative detail on what is behind this widely held sentiment.

"Linking teacher evaluations without taking a student's mindset into the mix when taking a test is unfair to the teacher," said a Nevada high school teacher. "What about a student who is hungry, homeless, being abused, has MIA (missing-in-action) parents, etc.?"

An elementary school teacher from South Carolina said, "Student populations are not spread evenly among teachers. Some students will have learning disabilities and some will have familial and environmental factors that do not allow them to progress at the same rate as others. If I have to be so concerned about a test score, I cannot address the needs of individual students." And a Texas high school teacher concludes, "We must have different yardsticks for

different student circumstances so teachers can focus on individual student growth."

Yet despite these types of serious concerns that emerged in teacher follow-up comments, teachers as a whole are evenly divided about the merits of Common Core, with 41% saying their overall impression of it is positive and 44% negative—hardly an outright rejection of the program.

Bottom Line

Maeve Ward, Senior Program Officer, U.S. Policy and Advocacy Team at the Bill and Melinda Gates Foundation, is not surprised by teachers' resistance to any single-measure evaluation, including the Common Core test. As an education expert who has conducted extensive studies with teachers about how they view the evaluation process, Ward says, "Teachers want two criteria in the components of their evaluations—multiple measures and actionable feedback. Few teachers have real experience with Common Core–aligned assessments because states are just starting to replace their old bubble tests with these new tests that measure real-world skills like problem solving and critical thinking. Teachers need time to familiarize themselves with the standards and the assessments and see how they can provide that actionable feedback."

Survey Methods

Results are based on Web interviews conducted Aug. 11–Sept. 7, 2014, via the Gallup Panel, with a random sample of 854 public K–12 school teachers, aged 18 and older, with Internet access, living in all 50 U.S. states and the District of Columbia. The data are weighted to match national teacher demographics of gender, age, race, Hispanic ethnicity, education and region. Demographic weighting targets are based on the weighted demographic distribution of Gallup's nationally representative nightly poll respondents identified as teachers over a period of four years.

For results based on the sample of 854 public school teachers, the margin of sampling error is ±5 percentage points.

October 30, 2014

NARROW EDGE IN PARTISANSHIP IS BAD ELECTION SIGN FOR DEMOCRATS

by Jeffrey M. Jones

WASHINGTON, D.C.—Americans' party preferences during the third quarter of a midterm election year give a good indication of which party will perform better in that year's election. Democrats' narrow two-percentage-point advantage in party affiliation this year—45% to 43%—shares a greater similarity with strong Republican midterm years, such as 1994, 2002 and 2010, than with the advantage held in better Democratic years like 1998 and 2006.

Democrats typically hold an advantage in party affiliation among the national adult population—Republicans have held a slight numerical advantage in only three years since 1993. But since Republicans and Republican leaners typically vote at higher rates than Democrats and Democratic-leaning independents, the voting electorate will usually be much less Democratic than the larger adult population. Thus, if Democrats start out with only a slim advantage among all adults, the voting electorate may very well end up being more Republican than Democratic.

Party Identification and Leaning, Third Quarter, Recent Midterm Election Years

Year	% Democrat/ Lean Democratic	% Republican/ Lean Republican	Democratic advantage (pct. pts.)
2014	45	43	+2
2010	44	45	-1
2006	50	40	+10
2002	46	44	+2
1998	48	41	+7
1994	46	45	+1

GALLUP

Although party affiliation and vote choice are not the same thing, they are strongly related. Typically upward of nine in 10 voters who identify or lean with a party will vote for that party's candidate for Congress, emphasizing the importance of voter turnout among the major party groups.

The accompanying table shows how the national vote for Congress compares with the initial party leanings of the adult population. This gives a sense of the impact of turnout and how Republicans can easily overcome a slight deficit in partisanship with superior voter turnout.

Party Identification and Leaning, Third Quarter, and Vote for U.S. House, Recent Midterm Election Years

Year	Party affiliation, all national adults — Democrat-Republican	Democratic advantage (pct. pts.)	Midterm vote for House of Representatives — Democrat-Republican	Democratic advantage (pct. pts.)	Net shift toward Republicans, party affiliation to midterm House vote (pct. pts.)
2014	45%-43%	2	n/a	n/a	n/a
2010	44%-45%	-1	45%-52%	-7	6
2006	50%-40%	10	53%-45%	8	2
2002	46%-44%	2	46%-51%	-5	7
1998	48%-41%	7	48%-48%	0	7
1994	46%-45%	1	46%-52%	-6	7

Party affiliation figures are based on Gallup third quarter average for party identification (including independent leaners) in midterm election years.
Midterm vote figures based on national vote for U.S. House in the midterm election.

GALLUP

In each of the past five midterm elections, Republicans appeared to have stronger turnout, based on how voters nationwide cast their votes for the House of Representatives versus the party affiliation among the larger national adult population. The differences in national party affiliation versus the national vote by party show a shift in the Republican direction that ranges between two and seven percentage points in these elections. The smallest difference occurred in 2006, when Democrats had a 10-point advantage in partisanship among all adults and a slightly smaller eight-point advantage in the voting electorate's candidate choices.

In the other four elections, the Republican turnout advantage was large enough to wipe out the Democratic advantage in partisanship, including in 1998 when Democrats gained seats in the House of Representatives but the Republicans maintained their majority.

With Republicans currently trailing by two points in national party affiliation, if turnout patterns by party in this year's election are similar to the past, that would suggest Republican House candidates would get more votes nationwide than Democrats. Unless turnout is unusually heavy for Democrats—something Gallup's turnout indicators suggest is not likely to be the case—Republicans will hold on to their majority in the House of Representatives.

Implications

Democrats have big challenges in convincing voters to support their party in this year's midterm congressional elections with President Barack Obama's generally low job approval ratings and Americans' feelings of dissatisfaction with the way things are going in the country. In addition to that, the Democrats face some structural disadvantages, including their typically lower voter turnout than Republicans, but also a congressional seat map that appears tilted in Republicans' favor.

In 2012—the first year in which congressional candidates competed in newly drawn districts after the 2010 census—Democrats received a majority of the two-party votes for the House of Representatives, but not a majority of seats. In fact, Democrats netted 46% of House seats despite winning 51% of the popular vote for the House. As a result, not only must Democrats outpoll Republicans this fall, they must do so by a healthy margin to regain the majority in the House.

With little seeming to be in their favor, the real drama in the 2014 midterms is likely not to be if Nov. 4 will be a difficult day for Democrats, but just how difficult it will be.

Survey Methods

Results for this Gallup poll are based on combined telephone interviews conducted July–September 2014, with a random sample of 4,314 adults, aged 18 and older, living in all 50 U.S. states and the District of Columbia.

For results based on the total sample of national adults, the margin of sampling error is ±1 percentage points at the 95% confidence level.

October 31, 2014
TEACHERS CONCERNED ABOUT COMMON CORE'S COMPUTER TESTING

by Lydia Saad

PRINCETON, NJ—After overseeing the introduction of the Common Core curriculum standards in their schools for at least a year, most states must now start assessing student learning in English and math with new standardized online tests. Yet the majority of U.S. public school teachers whom Gallup surveyed believe their own students are not well prepared for these computer-based assessments, given their typing and computer skills.

Considering their students' typing and computer skills, 54% of teachers working in states where the Common Core State Standards are being used say their students are not well prepared to take the Common Core assessment tests by computer.

The issue is particularly concerning for elementary school teachers, as well as teachers who say they work in schools where most of the students are from low-income families. Roughly seven in 10 teachers in both of these categories say their students are not well prepared for the tests from the standpoint of their keyboarding or computer skills. This contrasts with about four in 10 teachers of higher grade levels, or of students mainly from middle- or high-income backgrounds.

Public School Teachers' Perceptions of Their Students' Computer Testing Readiness
Now, thinking about the typing and computer skills of your students, how well prepared are most of your students to take the Common Core assessment tests by computer?

	Very well prepared	Somewhat well prepared	Not well prepared
	%	%	%
All public school K-12 teachers	10	34	53
Teachers in Common Core states	9	35	54
Teach elementary school	4	23	71
Teach middle school/high school	14	42	42
Teach in low-income school	2	22	73
Teach in middle-/high-income school	15	41	41
Teachers in SBAC states*	9	41	46
Teachers in PARCC states**	8	26	66

Aug. 11-Sept. 7, 2014

* Teachers in the 22 states currently affiliated with the Smarter Balanced Assessment Consortium (SBAC) assessment
** Teachers in the 12 states plus District of Columbia currently affiliated with the Partnership for Assessment of Readiness for College and Careers (PARCC) assessment

GALLUP

In responding to an open-ended survey question, an elementary school teacher working in a rural district in Washington state commented, "Computer-based testing will punish lower-income students without regular access to computers—now we have to teach the content AND the computer?"

These findings are based on a Gallup Panel survey conducted via the Web with 854 public school teachers in grades K–12 across the country. Teachers in the Gallup Panel are selected at random from Gallup Daily tracking to become panelists. Teachers available to take surveys by Web (95% of teacher panelists) were invited to take the Common Core survey online between Aug. 11 and Sept. 7.

Nearly Half Indicate School Technology Isn't Adequate

Teachers in Common Core states are only slightly less concerned about their school's technical preparedness to administer the Common Core tests than they are about their students' readiness. Close to half, 47%, say their school is not well prepared to administer the online assessment tests, given its computer hardware or networking abilities. A third say their school is somewhat well prepared to do this, while 17% say it is very well prepared.

These views are similar among teachers at the elementary vs. middle and high school levels; however, teachers in schools where the students are mostly low income are a bit more likely to report lack of preparedness than those in schools with more well-to-do populations, 54% vs. 42%.

The two major state confederations assembled to create Common Core–aligned tests are working to provide districts with clear guidelines for the technology requirements needed to administer the exams in a reasonable time. However, from the data, it appears that the Partnership for Assessment of Readiness for College and Careers (PARCC) states may have a more difficult task than those aligned with the Smarter Balanced Assessment Consortium (SBAC), as teachers in the states affiliated with PARCC are much less likely than those in the SBAC states to believe their schools are technologically prepared.

Public School Teachers' Perceptions of Their School's Readiness for Computer-Based Tests
Thinking about the number and quality of computers at your school, as well as its Wi-Fi or network capabilities, how well prepared is your school to administer the Common Core computer-based assessment tests?

	Very well prepared	Somewhat well prepared	Not well prepared
	%	%	%
All public school K-12 teachers	17	34	46
Teachers in Common Core states	17	34	47
Teach elementary school	21	31	47
Teach middle school/high school	14	35	48
Teach in low-income school	11	34	54
Teach in middle-/high-income school	21	34	42
Teachers in SBAC states*	20	37	38
Teachers in PARCC states**	15	32	52

Aug. 11-Sept. 7, 2014

* Teachers in the 22 states currently affiliated with the Smarter Balanced Assessmsent Consortium (SBAC) assessment
** Teachers in the 12 states plus District of Columbia currently affiliated with the Partnership for Assessment of Readiness for College and Careers (PARCC) assessment

GALLUP

Six in 10 Teachers Report That Field Testing Went Smoothly

Forty-eight percent of teachers nationally, including 49% of those in Common Core states, report that their school participated in the field tests held last spring for both exams. And when asked how this practice testing went, the majority nationwide say it went very smoothly (10%) or mostly smoothly (51%), while 21% say it did not go smoothly and 11% say it went badly.

Teacher Review of Common Core Field Tests, Based on Those Whose Schools Participated
Did your school participate in the practice tests, also called field tests, for the Common Core exams that were conducted around the country this spring? And, as far as you know, how did the testing process go in your school?

	Went very/mostly smoothly	Went not very smoothly	Went badly
	%	%	%
All public school K-12 teachers	61	21	11
Teachers in Common Core states	61	19	11

Aug. 11-Sept. 7, 2014

GALLUP

These findings are important, because the testing consortia themselves have not reported any nationally representative data on how the field testing went in all of the states they work with. The Gallup data on perceptions from teachers at least provide a rough confirmation that the experience has been positive overall, but with a sizable minority reporting problems.

Bottom Line

From their vantage point on education's front lines, U.S. public school teachers see the potential for problems with the computer testing of students that has become integral to the Common Core program. The majority of teachers in Common Core states indicate that the students they work with lack the level of typing and computer skills needed to perform well on the tests. And nearly half say their school is ill prepared when it comes to the computer hardware or network capabilities needed to administer them.

The testing consortia are clearly aware of these problems. According to the report on its spring 2014 field test, SBAC documented a variety of computer-related problems that schools encountered, including lost Internet access during testing, test sessions timing out during extended pauses in student input, problems with logging in or resetting passwords, and complaints about the keyboarding challenges some students experienced during extended writing-based tasks. PARCC's review of its testing describes some student confusion over how to submit answers and difficulties in using the interactive tools, as well as breakoffs that required some students to start over.

Despite these sorts of issues, the solid majority of teachers in Gallup's survey who experienced firsthand the field testing last spring report that it went at least fairly smoothly. Nevertheless, a third had more negative experiences with the test, possibly intensifying their broader concerns about the testing component of Common Core—which the majority of teachers don't like—and these may be contributing to teachers' so-so review of Common Core overall.

Survey Methods

Results are based on Web interviews conducted Aug. 11–Sept. 7, 2014, via the Gallup Panel, with a random sample of 854 public K–12 school teachers, aged 18 and older, with Internet access, living in all 50 U.S. states and the District of Columbia. The data are weighted to match national teacher demographics of gender, age, race, Hispanic ethnicity, education and region. Demographic weighting targets are based on the weighted demographic distribution of Gallup's nationally representative nightly poll respondents identified as teachers over a period of four years.

For results based on the sample of 854 public school teachers, the margin of sampling error is ±5 percentage points.

October 31, 2014
LESS THAN HALF OF AMERICANS SUPPORT STRICTER GUN LAWS

by Art Swift

WASHINGTON, D.C.—Less than half of Americans, 47%, say they favor stricter laws covering the sale of firearms, similar to views found last year. But this percentage is significantly below the 58% recorded in 2012 after the school shooting in Newtown, Connecticut, spurred a nationwide debate about the possibility of more stringent gun control laws. Thirty-eight percent of Americans say these laws should be kept as they are now, and 14% say they should be made less strict.

The percentage favoring stricter gun sale laws in the two years since Newtown occurred has declined despite steady and tragic high-profile shootings in the U.S at schools, malls and businesses. This past week, shootings occurred at a Seattle-area school and of police officers in Sacramento and Placer County, California. Amidst events like these in 2014, and the resulting calls for stricter gun sale laws, the 47% who favor stricter laws is just above the historical low of 43% measured in 2011.

Ten years ago, three in five Americans (60%) said they favored stricter laws regulating the sale of firearms, but support fell to 44% in 2009 and remained at that level in polls conducted in the next two years. Days after the Newtown shooting, support for stricter gun sale laws swelled. Since 2012, however, Americans have retreated from those stronger attitudes about the need for more gun control,

and the percentage of Americans who say the laws should be less strict—although still low—has edged up.

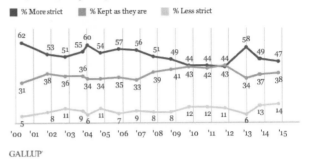

Laws Covering the Sale of Firearms -- Americans' Preferences Since 2000

In general, do you feel that the laws covering the sale of firearms should be made more strict, less strict, or kept as they are now?

These findings come from a new Gallup Poll Social Series survey, conducted Oct. 12–15.

Americans Say Possessing Handguns Should Not Be Banned

As support for stricter laws regulating the sale of guns has dwindled, the percentage of Americans who say handguns should be banned has remained low. About one in four Americans say handgun possession should be banned for everyone except the police and "other authorized persons" such as security or the military. A near-record high of 73% of Americans now say that handguns should not be banned.

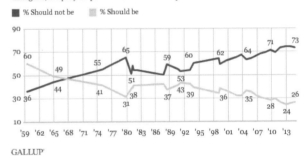

Support for Ban on Possession of Handguns, 1959-2014

Do you think there should or should not be a law that would ban the possession of handguns, except by the police and other authorized persons?

While Americans overwhelmingly say that there should not be a ban on handguns, this has not always been the case. When Gallup first asked this question in 1959, 60% favored a ban on handguns, except for those carried by police officers and similar authorities. By 1975, that number had slipped to 41%, with 55% saying they opposed such a ban. The percentage opposing has stayed above 50% ever since.

Support for Stricter Gun Sale Laws Drops Across Most Groups

Americans vary by demographic group as to whether they favor more stringent laws covering the sale of firearms. Among these groups, support is generally down across the board compared with the poll taken after the Newtown tragedy.

Democrats still express the most support for stricter gun sale laws, at 71%, down from 79% two years ago. Republicans, liberals, nonwhites, women and whites all show substantially less support on this measure compared with 2012.

Views on Gun Sale Laws, by Demographic Group

Ranked by percentage favoring stricter laws covering the sale of firearms

	2012	2014
	%	%
Democrats	79	71
Liberals	75	67
Nonwhites	65	60
Women	69	55
Moderates	61	53
U.S. ADULTS	58	47
Whites	56	42
Men	47	40
Independents	35	36
Conservatives	44	32
Republicans	39	29

Oct. 12-15, 2014

GALLUP'

Bottom Line

Public demand for stricter gun sale laws is returning to levels seen throughout the past decade. After seeing a spike in support for stricter laws following the Newtown school shooting in 2012, the call for more stringent laws has settled to near-record lows. The percentage of Americans who say that handguns should not be banned is at a near-record high as well. This suggests that while shootings may still occur with disturbing regularity in the U.S., there is a disconnect between those events and support for making gun laws stricter.

Survey Methods

Results for this Gallup poll are based on telephone interviews conducted Oct. 12–15, 2014, with a random sample of 1,017 adults, aged 18 and older, living in all 50 U.S. states and the District of Columbia. For results based on the total sample of national adults, the margin of sampling error is ±4 percentage points at the 95% confidence level.

November 03, 2014
U.S. VOTERS DIVIDED ON PARTY BETTER TO CONTROL CONGRESS

by Jeffrey M. Jones

PRINCETON, NJ—U.S. registered voters do not have a clear preference on whether the country would be better off if Republicans (29%) or Democrats (27%) controlled Congress, with 40% saying it would be the same regardless of which party is in power. In the 2006 Democratic and 2010 Republican "wave" elections, voters had a clear preference for the party that won. Today's views are most similar to the 2002 elections, which saw more modest change in the party composition of Congress.

Do you think the country would be better off if the Republicans controlled Congress, if the Democrats controlled Congress, or would the country be the same regardless of which party controlled Congress?

Based on registered voters

	Better if Republicans controlled	Better if Democrats controlled	Same regardless	Republican–Democratic gap
	%	%	%	pct. pts.
2014	29	27	40	+2
2010	35	23	38	+12
2006	27	35	33	−8
2002	27	28	40	−1

Note: Each poll was conducted in late October/early November, in the final days before the midterm elections.

GALLUP'

The 2006 and 2010 elections were contested at a time when one party had control of the presidency and both houses of Congress, and voters were more likely to think the country would benefit from shifting control of Congress away from the majority party than keeping it with that party. In 2002, as now, party control was divided, with the president's party having control of one house of Congress but not the other. The blurred lines of accountability could explain why voters did not more clearly show a preference for which party controlled Congress in 2002 or this year.

But other aspects of Americans' current mood look more like they did in 2006 and 2010—and in other years, such as 1982 and 1994, in which there were major shakeups in congressional membership—than in 2002. These include their subpar ratings of the job performance of the president and of Congress, and their low satisfaction with the direction of the country as a whole.

Key Election Indicators in Recent Midterm Election Years

Based on national adults

	Approve of job president is doing	Approve of job Congress is doing	Satisfied with way things are going in the U.S.	Net seat loss for president's party in U.S. House
	%	%	%	
2014	44	20	27	n/a
2010	44	21	22	−63
2006	38	26	35	−30
2002	63	50	48	+6
1998	66	44	60	+5
1994	46	22	30	−53
1990	58	26	32	−8
1986	63	42	58	−5
1982	42	29	24	−28

Note: 2014 estimates are based on an Oct. 29-Nov. 2 Gallup poll. Obama job approval in Gallup Daily tracking was 42% for Oct. 27-Nov. 2. Prior years' estimates are based on final Gallup estimates before the midterm elections, usually in October or early November.

GALLUP'

The president's party typically loses seats in midterm elections, but those losses tend to be greater when Americans' approval ratings of the president, and of Congress, are relatively poor, and when Americans are not satisfied with the way things are going in the United States. In years like 1986, 1998 and 2002, when Americans were generally upbeat about the state of the nation, there tended to be less change in the membership of Congress in the midterm elections.

Importantly, though these key indicators are still low on an absolute basis, most of the current updates are a bit more positive than what Gallup measured earlier this year. For example, congressional job approval has averaged 14% so far in 2014 and has not been as high as the current 20% since just before the 2012 elections.

Also, the current 27% satisfied with the way things are going in the United States exceeds the 2014 average to date of 23%; satisfaction was last at this level in July 2013.

President Barack Obama's job approval rating, 44% in the Oct. 29–Nov. 2 poll, is nominally more positive, but not significantly different from, the 42% he has averaged in Gallup Daily tracking over the past week.

Americans' improving economic confidence may be one reason the current national mood indicators are a bit more positive than they have been. And while the level of improvement is not enough to fundamentally erase the Republicans' advantage going into Tuesday's elections, it does suggest the negative climate that has been providing the wind at the GOP's back may not be quite as strong as it was a few months, or even weeks, ago.

Implications

The national political climate, as measured by several key indicators of Americans' satisfaction with current conditions in the country and how the nation is being governed, usually gives a strong sense of which way a midterm election will go. And this year, with a Democratic president in office and Americans in a generally negative mood, the fundamentals point to 2014 being a better year for the Republican Party than the Democratic Party. Indeed, the general consensus among political experts is that the Republicans will increase their majority in the House of Representatives and could win control of the Senate.

And though the key indicators are about as negative this year as they have been in past wave elections, 2014 may not see the same level of shakeup in Congress as was the case in 2006, 2010 and other years. The key variable working against a 2014 wave may be that divided party control in Washington already exists when it did not in 1994, 2006 and 2010, and thus, frustrated voters this year have no clear way to act on their frustration by changing the party composition of the federal government. With Obama in office for two more years and little chance of Republicans losing their House majority, divided government should still be in place regardless of which party has the Senate majority, and the way the nation is governed over the next two years may not materially change.

Survey Methods

Results for this Gallup poll are based on telephone interviews conducted Oct. 29–Nov. 2, 2014, with a random sample of 1,832 adults, aged 18 and older, living in all 50 U.S. states and the District of Columbia.

For results based on the total sample of national adults, the margin of sampling error is ±3 percentage points at the 95% confidence level.

For results based on the total sample of 1,590 registered voters, the margin of sampling error is ±3 percentage points at the 95% confidence level.

November 03, 2014

OBAMA EFFECT LIKELY NEGATIVE IN KEY SENATE RACES

by Andrew Dugan

WASHINGTON, D.C.—In an election in which President Barack Obama's mediocre approval ratings have cast a shadow on Democrats' efforts to maintain their slim Senate majority, his image has remained generally weak in six states featuring competitive races. This includes sub-40% approval ratings over the last several months in Iowa (38%), Kansas (33%) and Arkansas (29%). In two other states, North Carolina (42%) and Georgia (41%), Obama's approval ratings have been about equal to his national average. Among these six states, only in Colorado has Obama's approval rating (46%) been higher than his national rating.

Presidential Approval: Six Major Senate Races

% Approve

	Iowa	Kansas	North Carolina	Georgia	Arkansas	Colorado
Jan. 1- June 30, 2014	38	32	41	42	33	41
July 1-Oct. 15, 2014	38	33	42	41	29	46

Gallup U.S. Daily tracking

GALLUP

These results come from aggregated Gallup U.S. Daily tracking data collected July 1 through Oct. 15, 2014, among adults living in six states featuring high-profile Senate races this year. Sample sizes range from 513 in Kansas to 1,744 in North Carolina. Each state sample is weighted to be demographically representative of the state.

Obama's enervated approval rating has undoubtedly benefited Republican candidates across the country, particularly in terms of motivating turnout, but in a few key states, Democrats' association with the unpopular president has the potential to be particularly troublesome. In Iowa and Arkansas, where fewer than two in five residents approve of the president, Republicans have strong possibilities of taking Senate seats from Democrats. In Kansas, another state with a sub-40% Obama approval rating, one reason the Republican incumbent is having a hard time profiting from the anti-Obama environment is because there is *no* Democrat in the race, rather an independent challenger whose ultimate partisan allegiance is unclear.

But even in states where Obama's approval rating is higher— like in North Carolina and Georgia, where it matches the national average, or in Colorado, where Obama scores slightly better than the national average—Democratic candidates are still fighting an uphill battle.

The Senate races in these six states are among the closest in the country. Democrats currently hold four of the seats up for election in these states, while Republicans cling to two. Every race is distinct, but all will take place with a relatively unpopular second-term president as a backdrop.

Democratic Party Losing Supporters in Arkansas; Others Stable

Party identification among adults in these six states has been generally stable in recent months, with one important exception: Arkansas residents now decidedly tilt Republican after being balanced between the two parties in the first half of the year. Over the last four months, 47% of Arkansas residents have identified as Republican or have said they are independents with Republican leanings, compared with 31% identifying as or leaning Democratic. This shift in political attitudes seems to augur good things for the GOP Tuesday in the Natural State.

Party Identification: Six Major Senate Races

% Lean/Identify as

	Jan. 1- June 30, 2014	July 1-Oct. 15, 2014	CHANGE
IOWA			
Republican	40	43	+3
Democratic	41	40	-1
KANSAS			
Republican	47	47	0
Democratic	34	37	+3
NORTH CAROLINA			
Republican	41	40	-1
Democratic	42	43	+1
GEORGIA			
Republican	42	43	+1
Democratic	40	37	-3
ARKANSAS			
Republican	39	47	+8
Democratic	41	31	-10
COLORADO			
Republican	42	40	-2
Democratic	42	44	+2

Gallup U.S. Daily tracking

GALLUP

In Iowa, Republicans have held a nominal lead in party affiliation (43%) compared with 40% leaning or identifying Democratic. Republican Senate candidate Joni Ernst now enjoys a small but durable lead in state polls.

In Kansas, Republicans have continued to show an advantage in party affiliation. However, simple party allegiances may not be as informative given the unique dynamics of the race, which features an independent who has not specified which party he would caucus with if elected to the Senate facing a long-serving Republican senator. The key in that race may be whether party leanings or frustration with incumbents is the bigger factor in voters' decisions.

In North Carolina, party identification has been essentially tied, while Democrats have maintained a small lead in Colorado and Georgia. North Carolina has the dubious distinction of being the country's most expensive Senate race, with total spending projected to surpass $100 million. This bullion appears to have been spent in vain—party preferences for July through October mirror those observed in the first six months of the year.

Bottom Line

Obama is not doing the Democratic candidates in these six states any favors with his sub-par approval ratings. Only in one state is the president's approval rating above his national figure, or anywhere close to approaching the majority level. Party preferences, meanwhile, are generally stable compared with the first half of the year, despite the onslaught of political advertising occurring in these states. The one exception is Arkansas, which has seen a breathtaking rise in Republican identification compared with earlier this year when political identification was more evenly divided.

Though each of these Senate races has its own character, they do not occur in a vacuum. Obama's lackluster approval rating will probably be a deterrent in motivating less-attached Democratic adults to vote, while in turn providing a turnout motivator for Republicans who are eager to deliver a blow to the president by making him deal with a unified Republican Congress in his last two years.

Also worth noting is that of these six states, only North Carolina is not also conducting a gubernatorial race this year, a race that can have an additional effect on turnout. In two states, Arkansas and Iowa, Republican gubernatorial candidates appear to have the upper hand as voters head to the ballot box, which could have positive ripple effects on other Republican candidates elsewhere on the ticket. In the other three states, the gubernatorial contests, just as with the Senate matches, are currently neck and neck, a sign that truculent political division is hardly confined to the Senate elections.

Survey Methods

Results for this Gallup poll are based on telephone interviews conducted July 1–Oct. 15, 2014, on the Gallup U.S. Daily survey, with a random sample of adults, aged 18 and older, living in Arkansas, Colorado, Georgia, Iowa, Kansas and North Carolina. Sample sizes and margins of error for each state sample are listed below.

State	Sample size	Margin of sampling error (95% confidence level)
Arkansas	594	±5 percentage points
Colorado	1,135	±4 percentage points
Georgia	1,629	±3 percentage points
Iowa	613	±5 percentage points
Kansas	513	±5 percentage points
North Carolina	1,744	±3 percentage points

November 04, 2014
U.S. ECONOMIC CONFIDENCE INDEX HIGHEST IN OVER A YEAR

by Justin McCarthy

WASHINGTON, D.C.—Gallup's U.S. Economic Confidence Index jumped to a monthly reading of −12 in October. This is the most positive score since the −12 of July 2013, though it is still lower than the record high of −7 in May 2013. The three-point increase from September is the largest monthly improvement seen this year so far.

The October reading is the third-highest monthly figure Gallup has found since it began tracking the Economic Confidence Index on a daily basis in 2008. Confidence in October was buoyed by two

weekly readings of −10—the highest such readings since August of last year. Last week's index score of −11, based on Oct. 27–Nov. 2 interviewing, suggests that confidence has stabilized at a more positive level compared with most of 2014.

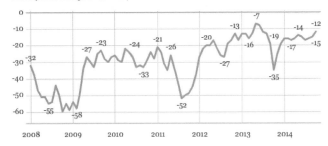

Gallup Economic Confidence Index -- Monthly Averages
January 2008 through October 2014

Gallup Daily tracking

GALLUP'

Though the monthly index remains negative, this is the closest it has come to a positive reading in some time. The record monthly high for the Economic Confidence Index is −7, recorded in May 2013, and June of that year saw a −8, before confidence plummeted in the fall.

Gallup's Economic Confidence Index is the average of two components: how Americans view current economic conditions, and their perceptions of whether the economy is getting better or worse. In October, 22% said the economy is "excellent" or "good," while 32% said it is poor. This resulted in a current conditions dimension score of −10, the highest current conditions score since February 2008.

Meanwhile, 41% of Americans said the economy is getting better, while 54% said it is getting worse. This resulted in an economic outlook score of −13—the best outlook score since January.

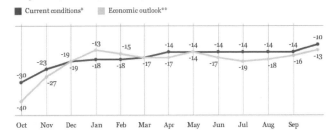

Gallup Economic Confidence Sub-Indexes -- Monthly Averages
Complete trend, October 2013-October 2014

■ Current conditions*   ■ Economic outlook**

* % (Excellent + Good) minus % Poor
** % Getting better minus % Getting worse
Gallup Daily tracking

GALLUP'

Upper-Income Americans' Confidence Reaches Positive Territory

The confidence of both upper-income Americans (+2) and middle- and lower-income Americans (−14) reached levels in October that have not been seen since July 2013.

Upper-income Americans had a particularly large climb in confidence, gaining eight index points from the previous month and reaching positive territory.

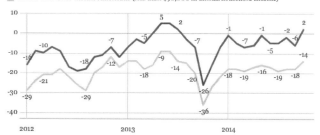

Economic Confidence Index Scores by Income

Monthly averages from January 2012 through October 2014

■ Upper-income Americans ($90,000+ in annual household income)

▓ Middle- and lower-income Americans (less than $90,000 in annual household income)

Gallup Daily tracking

GALLUP®

Confidence Up Among Dems, Independents; Flat for Republicans

In the waning days of the 2014 campaign season, confidence improved by six points for both Democrats (+20) and independents (−15), while Republicans' confidence in the economy remained flat—and much lower—at −37. These stark partisan differences reflect a typical pattern by which those who identify with the party of the president are generally much more positive than others.

Economic Confidence Index Scores by Political Party

■ Democrats   ■ Independents   ▓ Republicans

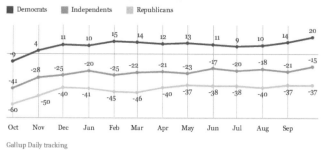

Gallup Daily tracking

GALLUP®

Bottom Line

October's improvement in economic confidence comes in the final stretch of a year with index readings that, although negative, approached seven-year highs and were remarkably stable. After months of stagnant confidence, Americans may be becoming more positive in their views of the economy's current state and future prospects.

With the stock market having ended last month on a positive note and gas prices continuing to drop, it is reasonable to expect the gains made in October to be sustained in November.

Survey Methods

Results for this Gallup poll are based on telephone interviews conducted Oct. 1–31, 2014, on the Gallup U.S. Daily survey, with a random sample of 15,168 adults, aged 18 and older, living in all 50 U.S. states and the District of Columbia.

For results based on the total sample of national adults, the margin of sampling error is ±1 percentage point at the 95% confidence level.

November 04, 2014

VOTERS, ESPECIALLY INDEPENDENTS, LACK INTEREST IN ELECTION

by Lydia Saad

PRINCETON, NJ—Two of Gallup's long-term indicators of voter turnout show that Americans are much less interested in the midterm election today than they were on the eve of the election in 2010. Moreover, the 41% of U.S. adults saying they have given "quite a lot" or "some" thought to this year's election is the lowest Gallup has recorded on the eve of any of the last six midterms. The 58% saying they are absolutely certain they will vote ties with 1998 for the lowest.

Indicators of U.S. Adults' Propensity to Vote in Midterm Election

Recent final pre-election trends

■ % Absolutely certain will vote   ▓ % Given quite a lot/some thought to the election

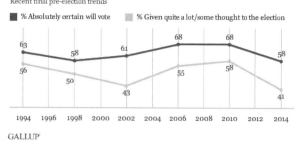

GALLUP®

Additionally, after two midterm elections with above-average voter enthusiasm, the percentage of Americans saying they feel *less* enthusiastic than usual about voting this year (48%) now exceeds the percentage who say they are *more* enthusiastic (40%). This is similar to the pattern seen in each midterm from 1994 through 2002.

Enthusiasm About Voting -- Final Pre-Election Results

Compared to previous elections, are you more enthusiastic about voting than usual, or less enthusiastic?

■ % More enthusiastic   ■ % Less enthusiastic   ▓ % Same

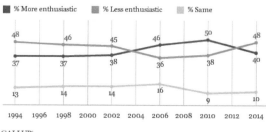

GALLUP®

The clearest indication that turnout will be lower than four years ago is that more than a quarter of U.S. adults—27%—say they do not plan to vote in this year's election, up from 20% in 2010. This does not mean that all others will in fact vote, but it is a useful metric to gauge relative turnout across elections.

Americans' 2014 Midterm Voting Intentions

Which of the following applies to you -- you have already voted in this year's election, either by absentee ballot or early voting opportunities in your state; you plan to vote before Election Day, either by absentee ballot or early voting opportunities in your state; or you plan to vote on Election Day itself?

	Already voted	Plan to vote early	Will vote on Election Day	Do not plan to vote/ Not registered
	%	%	%	%
Oct 29-Nov 2, 2014	13	8	51	27
Oct 28-31, 2010	16	6	57	20

GALLUP®

Independents' Voter Engagement Declines Sharply

One of the most striking findings in the poll is that intent to vote has plummeted among political independents. The 41% saying they are "absolutely certain" they will vote is down 19 percentage points from 2010, easily the lowest level of independents' intended turn-out in any midterm since 1994. Meanwhile, intent to vote among core Republicans and Democrats has subsided to normal levels after matching or hitting new highs in 2010.

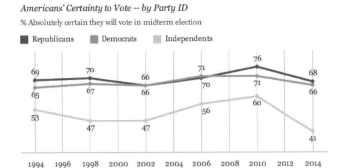

Americans' Certainty to Vote -- by Party ID
% Absolutely certain they will vote in midterm election

GALLUP

To elaborate on this point, intent to vote has declined substantially since 2010 among independents who lean toward each of the major political parties: it is down 25 points among independents who lean Republican and down 20 points among independents who lean Democratic. Meanwhile, intent to vote among pure independents—those who do not lean toward either party, and who generally are the least likely to say they plan to vote—has declined by just eight points. Thus, the hard-core partisans on both sides have generally maintained high interest in voting this year, albeit somewhat reduced, while those less attached to either party have significantly downgraded their interest.

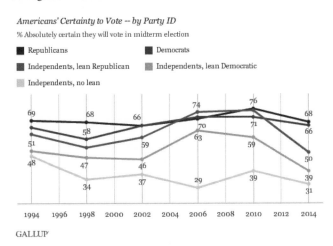

Americans' Certainty to Vote -- by Party ID
% Absolutely certain they will vote in midterm election

GALLUP

Bottom Line

The 2014 election has provided politicos with great political theater, including a number of close Senate races that will determine whether Republicans capture the majority in the upper chamber and numerous hard-charging Republican candidates aiming to expand the GOP majority in the House. But somehow this has failed to ignite the interest of independents, and even core partisans' attention has

waned a bit. One explanation could be the near certainty that the outcome will not transform the balance of power in Washington. Even if the Republicans win the Senate and hold the House, there will still be a division of power in Washington with a Democratic president. Without the opportunity to effect more major change, Republican- and Democratic-leaning independents may see less of a reason to pay attention or vote.

Another explanation could be the lack of a galvanizing issue for either party—such as the Iraq war provided the Democrats in 2006 and "Obamacare" provided the Republicans in 2010. A third reason could be the lack of a popular figurehead for either party driving their base to the polls. President Barack Obama is surely trying to do what he can, but with his approval rating hovering near 40% nationally, and now below 60% among conservative Democrats, his pull is limited. Plus, neither party's leader in Congress is highly popular nationally, or among his own party base. Finally, the hyper-partisan nature of politics over the past few years could be a turnoff to some voters, particularly independents.

As discouraging as low turnout may be for those who care deeply about citizen engagement, and who would like to see more Americans exercising their right to vote, the trends make it clear that voter participation has the capacity to spring back. The 2014 midterm represents a year when many of the variables that can affect turnout conspired to suppress it; however, a change in even one of these factors next time—a popular party leader, a strong issue-based platform or a clear opportunity for either party to consolidate power in Washington—could make all the difference.

Meanwhile, the drop in interest in the 2014 election among independents leaves the outcome more directly dependent than ever on partisans of both sides, and in that regard underscores the obvious efforts of late to increase turnout among voters whose political predilections are already known, rather than attempting to change voters' minds about whom to vote for.

Survey Methods

Results for this Gallup poll are based on telephone interviews conducted Oct. 29–Nov. 2, 2014, with a random sample of 1,832 adults, aged 18 and older, living in all 50 U.S. states and the District of Columbia.

For results based on the total sample of national adults, the margin of sampling error is ±3 percentage points at the 95% confidence level.

November 05, 2014
AMERICANS WANT NEW CONGRESS TO FIX ITSELF, FOCUS ON ECONOMY

by Frank Newport

PRINCETON, NJ—After returns from Tuesday's midterm elections confirmed that the Republicans will maintain control of the House and take control of the Senate, attention now turns to what actions the new Congress should take. Nearly a third of Americans, 31%, say their newly elected representatives should not focus on a specific issue, but rather on fixing the way Congress operates, including paying more attention to constituents, compromising and getting things done.

Americans' Priorities for the New Congress

Regardless of which candidate wins in your district, what is the most important thing you want your representative in Congress to do when Congress begins its new session in January?

	National adults %
HOW REPRESENTATIVES/CONGRESS WORK	
Listen to the people/Represent the people	10
Compromise/Cooperate/Get along/Work together/End gridlock	9
Follow through on promises	4
Do your job/Pass some legislation	4
Be honest	2
Abide by/Follow the Constitution	2
ECONOMIC-RELATED ISSUES	
Create jobs/Employment/Bring jobs home	7
Balance the budget/Reduce the deficit/Cap spending	5
Lower taxes/Cut taxes	4
Improve the economy	2
Improve wages/Raise the minimum wage	2
OTHER SPECIFIC ISSUES	
Improve healthcare	7
Pass immigration reform/Secure the borders	6
Improve education/school systems	5
Stop the wars/Bring troops home	3
Stop terrorism/Improve national security	2
Improve foreign policy	2
Pass Social Security reform	1
Pass gun control	1
Address police brutality/Curb police power	1
Address climate change/environmental issues/water shortages	1

Sept. 25-30, 2014

GALLUP

These data are from a late September survey in which Gallup asked Americans to look beyond whoever might win in their congressional district, and name what they want their representative to do on their behalf in Washington once the new Congress is gaveled into session.

Beyond the general issues relating to how members of Congress do their jobs, 20% of Americans want their elected congressional representative to focus on some aspect of the economy—including creating jobs and increasing employment, raising wages, balancing the budget and lowering taxes.

Another 29% of Americans listed specific priorities other than those directly related to the economy—including healthcare, immigration, education, wars, terrorism and foreign policy in general. No more than 7% of Americans mention any of these issues, suggesting there is no single non-economic issue that dominates the public's thinking at this time.

Across major demographic groups, Americans' desires for what they want their member of Congress to do are generally similar. Nonwhites are somewhat more likely to mention jobs and employment, along with schools and education, as their top priority; young people—particularly younger women—are more likely to mention education; seniors are more likely than young people to mention compromise and stopping wars; and those with postgraduate educations are more likely than those with high school educations or less to mention compromise. Otherwise, Americans mention the same types of priorities regardless of their demographic status.

Also surprising—given the often acrimonious debates and arguments on issues and priorities between Republican and Democratic candidates for office—there is little difference on most issues between Americans affiliated with the two major parties in their priorities for Congress.

Implications

Republicans maintained control of the House and gained the majority in the Senate as a result of Tuesday's midterm elections. Now the newly constituted Republican majority leaders will need to focus on what they are going to do with their new mandate from the voters. The campaigns themselves did not necessarily provide major direction for these leaders. Other than Republican candidates' tactic of tying their Democratic opponents to President Barack Obama, there was no single dominant issue in terms of what candidates emphasized on the campaign trail or in debates and advertisements.

Prior to the elections, Americans also did not overwhelmingly name any issue they wanted their newly elected representatives to focus on when the new Congress is sworn in at the beginning of the new year. Instead, many indicated that Congress' highest priority should be operating better as a body, paying more attention to constituents and cooperating more and getting things done. They mentioned economic concerns—ranging from creating more jobs to lowering the deficit—more frequently than others. Small segments named healthcare, immigration, education and foreign policy as their desired No. 1 focus for their representative, and some of these would be more important in some districts and states than in others. But none of these rises to the level that would suggest Americans consider it a major priority for the new Congress.

Survey Methods

Results for this Gallup poll are based on telephone interviews conducted Sept. 25–30, 2014, with a random sample of 1,252 adults, aged 18 and older, living in all 50 U.S. states and the District of Columbia. For results based on the total sample of national adults, the margin of sampling error is ±4 percentage points at the 95% confidence level.

November 05, 2014
FEWER AMERICANS STRUGGLING TO AFFORD FOOD

by Rebecca Riffkin

WASHINGTON, D.C.—Fewer Americans say they are struggling to afford food now than did so during the depths of the recession. On average, 17.2% of U.S. adults so far in 2014 report that in the last 12 months they have struggled to afford food for themselves or their families. This percentage is on track to be the lowest measured since the Gallup-Healthways Well-Being Index started in 2008.

This year's decrease in the percentage of Americans reporting a struggle to afford food is a positive sign that the economic recovery now could be reaching those who previously struggled to afford the basics. Furthermore, while food prices increased more in the first six months of 2014 than they did for all of 2013, this does not appear to be resulting in more Americans struggling to afford food.

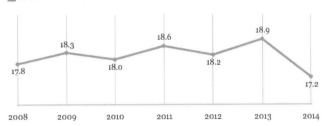

Percentage of Americans Who Struggled to Afford Food in Past Year

Have there been times in the past 12 months when you did not have enough money to buy food that you or your family needed?

▨ % Yes

17.8 (2008) 18.3 (2009) 18.0 (2010) 18.6 (2011) 18.2 (2012) 18.9 (2013) 17.2 (2014)

Year-to-date 2014 data are from Jan. 1-Oct. 31, 2014
Gallup-Healthways Well-Being Index

GALLUP

Earning at Least $24K Reduces Likelihood of Struggling to Afford Food

While the percentage who lack enough money to buy food at all times over a 12-month period is directly related to household income, earning an annual household income of at least $24,000 significantly reduces the likelihood that individuals will struggle to pay for the food that they or their families need. Those whose households earn $24,000 to $47,999 a year are half as likely to report struggling to afford food as those who earn less than $24,000, 19.9% vs. 40.3%, respectively. The rate is cut in half again at the next income level, with 10.5% of those earning $48,000 to $59,999 saying they lacked enough money for food. The rate continues to diminish at higher income levels, although not as steeply.

Percentage of U.S. Adults Struggling to Afford Food, by Household Income Level

Have there been times in the past 12 months when you did not have enough money to buy food that you or your family needed?

	2014	2013	Difference
	%	%	pct. pts.
Less than $24,000	40.3	42	-1.7
$24,000 to $47,999	19.9	22.4	-2.5
$48,000 to $59,999	10.5	12.5	-2
$60,000 to $89,999	6.6	7.9	-1.3
$90,000 or more	4.4	5.2	-0.8

Year-to-date 2014 data are from Jan. 1-Oct. 31, 2014
Gallup-Healthways Well-Being Index

GALLUP

Since 2013, the percentage of Americans struggling to afford food has declined in each income group. The drop was highest among Americans whose household annual income is between $24,000 and $47,999. The improvement across all income groups indicates that the economic recovery is not only reaching upper-income Americans but also seems to be benefiting those with lower incomes, at least when it comes to affording food.

Blacks More Than Twice as Likely as Whites to Struggle to Afford Food

Across racial and ethnic groups, blacks are the most likely to report struggling to afford food, followed by Hispanics. These groups are about twice as likely as whites to report lacking the money they need

to buy food for themselves or their families. Asians are the least likely to report struggling to afford food.

Black and Hispanic Americans More Likely to Report Struggling to Afford Food

Have there been times in the past 12 months when you did not have enough money to buy food that you or your family needed?

	% Yes
Black	29.0
Hispanic	25.5
White	13.3
Asian	7.4

Year-to-date 2014 data are from Jan. 1-Oct. 31, 2014
Gallup-Healthways Well-Being Index

GALLUP

This pattern may be partially related to income. Black households make 67% of the national average. According to the U.S. Census Bureau, in 2013, the median household income among whites was $58,270, while it was $40,963 among Hispanics and $34,598 among blacks. It was highest among Asians, at $67,065.

Bottom Line

Americans are less likely to say they are struggling to afford food so far in 2014 than they have said so in the past five years. The percentage of Americans who say they lacked enough money to afford food over the previous 12 months has returned to pre-recession levels, an encouraging sign that those who previously struggled to meet their basic needs may be feeling the positive effects of the recovery.

Fewer Americans are unemployed or underemployed in 2014, which may be related to the improvement in Americans' struggles to afford food. On average, Americans spend about 10% of their disposable annual income on food, according to the U.S. Department of Agriculture. The improvement in 2014 could mean that Americans have more disposable income to spend on food, reducing affordability struggles. Or it is possible that if other expenses are down, such as lower gas prices, Americans can simply put more of their disposable income toward food.

Survey Methods

Results are based on telephone interviews conducted Jan. 1–Oct. 31, 2014, as part of the Gallup-Healthways Well-Being Index survey, with a random sample of 148,854 adults, aged 18 and older, living in all 50 U.S. states and the District of Columbia. For results based on the total sample of national adults, the margin of sampling error is ±0.3 percentage points at the 95% confidence level.

November 05, 2014
ABOUT ONE IN FOUR U.S. HOUSEHOLDS VICTIMIZED BY CRIME

by Jeffrey M. Jones

PRINCETON, NJ—Twenty-six percent of Americans say they or another member of their household were the victim of some type of property or physical crime in the last 12 months, ranging from theft to sexual assault, according to Gallup's index of crime victimization. Since 2000, the percentage of households that have been victimized by crime has ranged narrowly between 22% and 27%. The percentage of Americans who have been personally victimized has ranged from 14% to 19%.

Gallup Crime Victimization Rates, 2000-2014

■ Household Victimization Index (% of U.S. Households)

▨ Personal Victimization Index (% of Americans)

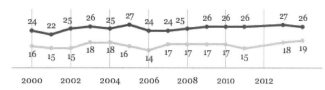

Based on Gallup annual Crime poll and percentage reporting being victimized by one or more of seven different crimes.
Poll was not conducted in 2012.

GALLUP'

Since 2000, with the exception of 2012, Gallup has asked Americans in its annual Crime poll to say whether they or anyone in their households have been the victim of seven different crimes—burglary, property theft or larceny, car theft, vandalism, robbery, physical assault and sexual assault. Gallup's household crime victimization index represents the percentage of Americans who say that they or a member of their household was a victim of one or more of these crimes in the last 12 months. The personal crime victimization index is based on the same summary, only reduced to those who say each crime happened to them personally.

Of these seven crimes, property theft (15%) and vandalism (14%) are the most common for U.S. households, followed by burglary (6%). The other crimes are rare, with only as many as 3% saying each occurred to a household member in the last 12 months.

Household/Self Victim of Crime in Last 12 Months

	U.S. Households Victimized	U.S. Adults Victimized
	%	%
Money or property stolen from you or another member of your household	15	11
A home, car, or property owned by you or another household member vandalized	14	8
Your house or apartment broken into	6	6
A car owned by you or another household member stolen	3	2
You or another household member mugged or physically assaulted	3	2
Money or property taken by force, with gun, knife, weapon or physical attack	1	1
You or another household member sexually assaulted	*	*

Oct. 12-15, 2014.
* = Less than 0.5%

GALLUP'

The incidence of each of these crimes has been fairly consistent throughout Gallup's 14-year trend, with property theft and vandalism most common at about 15% each year.

"Cyber-Crime" Not Uncommon

In addition to the seven core crimes asked each year since 2000, this year's Crime poll asked about two so-called cyber-crimes that have been in the news recently—theft of credit card information from store database and hacking of computers or smartphones.

Twenty-seven percent of households and 19% of U.S. adults say they have been affected by stolen credit card information, such as those that affected Target and Home Depot customers in the past 12 months—far more than said they had been victimized by any of the traditional crimes.

Meanwhile, 11% of U.S. households and 7% of Americans say they had a computer or smartphone hacked and information stolen by unauthorized users.

The newer cyber-crimes are not included in Gallup's victimization index in order to preserve the long-term trendability of the index. If they were included, the household victimization rate would surge to 46% (from 26%) and the individual victimization rate would jump to 34% (from 19%).

Two in Three Traditional Crimes Reported, Less than Half of Cyber-Crimes

Although Americans are somewhat more likely to report being victimized by these cyber-crimes than by traditional crimes, cyber-crime victims are much less likely to alert the police to their occurrence. Whereas 67% of respondents victimized by the traditional crimes said they reported these incidents to the police, only 45% who had credit card information stolen and 26% who had a computer or smartphone hacked said they reported those crimes to the police. It is possible that those victimized by hacking or stolen credit card information may report those to their bank or service provider rather than to the legal authorities, if they feel a need to alert an institution about the crime.

The roughly two-thirds of traditional property or physical crimes reported to the police is in line with Gallup's historical estimates.

Crime Reporting to Police, 2000-2014, Gallup Polls

■ % Reported   ▨ % Not reported

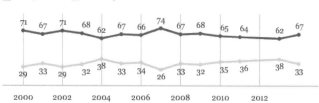

Figures are based on the percentages of those who said they were a victim of burglaries, property thefts, car thefts, vandalism, robberies, physical assaults or sexual assaults.
Survey not conducted in 2012.

GALLUP'

The rate of unreported crimes is important as it indicates that crime statistics based on compilation of police records may significantly underestimate the amount of crime that occurs in the United States. It is also possible that many of the crimes not reported to authorities may be less severe—for example, many acts of vandalism or theft of a small amount of money. If that is the case, the official reports may mainly be measuring the incidence of more significant crimes.

Implications

Traditional crimes against property or physical assaults are not uncommon in the U.S. but typically affect one in four U.S. households and just under one in five Americans each year. The reported crime rates are generally stable, suggesting a fairly constant level of crime that varies only at the margins.

These traditional forms of crime, though, appear to be less likely to happen to Americans than cyber-crime involving electronic theft of personal information. Americans are as likely or more likely to report being affected by these types of crimes in the past 12 months than traditional crimes. And the public does worry more about these high-tech crimes than other forms of crime.

However, the relative infrequency with which these crimes are reported to police could indicate that the impact of cyber-crimes on Americans may not be as severe as traditional crimes. In other words, if the incident was serious enough to cause significant harm against a person, they very well might report it to the traditional legal authorities.

Survey Methods

Results for this Gallup poll are based on telephone interviews conducted Oct. 12–15, 2014, with a random sample of 1,017 adults, aged 18 and older, living in all 50 U.S. states and the District of Columbia.

For results based on the total sample of national adults, the margin of sampling error is ±4 percentage points at the 95% confidence level.

November 06, 2014

MAJORITY CONTINUES TO SUPPORT POT LEGALIZATION IN U.S.

by Lydia Saad

PRINCETON, NJ—A slim majority of Americans, 51%, favor legalizing the use of marijuana—similar to the 50% who supported it in 2011 and 2012, but down from a reading of 58% last year.

Americans' Support for Legalizing the Use of Marijuana -- Recent Trend
Do you think the use of marijuana should be made legal, or not?

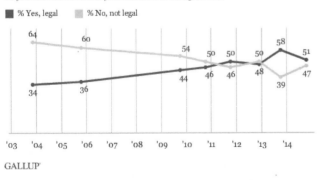

GALLUP

The new result is based on an Oct. 12–15 Gallup poll, conducted in the run-up to the midterm elections in which various pro-marijuana policy initiatives went before voters in Oregon, Washington,

D.C. and Florida, as well as in several cities in Maine, Michigan and elsewhere. Most of those initiatives succeeded, although a proposed Constitutional amendment in Florida to legalize medical marijuana failed with 57% of the vote, just shy of the 60% needed.

Gallup's long-term trend on Americans' support for legalizing marijuana (the full trend is available here) shows that in 1969, just 12% of U.S. adults were in favor. But that swelled to 28% by the late 1970s, and 34% by 2003. Since then, support steadily increased to the point that 50% supported it in 2011. Last year was the first time Gallup found a solid majority in favor, at 58%. That poll was conducted amid heavy news coverage of the imminent implementation of Colorado's marijuana legalization law, which may have contributed to what appears to have been a temporary jump in support. This year, support at 51% is still a majority, but closer to where it was in 2011 and 2012.

Conservatives Still Resist Legalization

Gallup's trend data also makes it clear that legalizing marijuana remains a much easier task in certain places than others. Chiefly, in contrast to high levels of support among liberals and solid support among moderates, less than a third of conservative Americans think marijuana should be legal. As a result, such measures are likely to be more viable in relatively liberal locales, including in Oregon and Washington, D.C., where they have already succeeded, than in conservative bastions like Wyoming, Utah or Arkansas.

Support for Legalizing the Use of Marijuana -- Recent Trend by Political Ideology
% Yes, should be legal

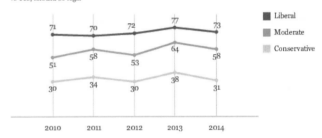

GALLUP

This pattern is echoed in the results by party ID, with the same implications about the outlook for marijuana legalization being tied to a state's partisan makeup. Currently, 64% of Americans who identify as or lean Democratic side with legalization, compared with 39% of Republicans.

Support for Legalizing the Use of Marijuana -- Recent Trend by Region
% Yes, should be legal

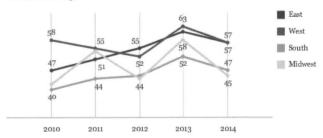

GALLUP

And in accordance with the regional distribution of red and blue states, with most of the blue—heavily Democratic—states clustered on the coasts, and most of the red—Republican-oriented—states concentrated in the middle and southern regions of the country, Gallup finds a solid majority supporting legalization of marijuana in the East and West, while in 2014, fewer than half support it in the South and Midwest.

Bottom Line

Public support for legalizing the use of marijuana has clearly increased over the past decade. The question now is whether the momentum will continue to build or level off at a bare majority supporting it.

Last year's finding of 58% in favor was recorded as Colorado was preparing to become the first state to implement a law decriminalizing the use of small amounts of marijuana for recreational use. Although the law passed in November 2012, it did not go into effect until January 2014. Americans may have warmed some to proponents' arguments in 2013 in the ongoing discussion around the Colorado law. More recently, Colorado has been in the news over the sale of marijuana-infused edibles—everything from brownies to gummy bears—and the risk they pose to children, possibly sparking public concern. Also, a year ago, proponents in California were poised to launch a ballot initiative for 2014 to legalize marijuana in the Golden State, adding to the sense of momentum for legalization, but later decided to wait until 2016 for fear of losing at the polls, as they did in 2010. The relative lack of attention to new legalization initiatives throughout 2014 may have caused public support to subside.

As long as support hovers around the 50% mark, it will be difficult for proponents to promote legalization beyond the more Democratic and liberal-oriented states. The South and Midwest are likely to remain less hospitable, at least for the time being. But with a super-majority of younger Americans supportive—64% of those aged 18 to 34, contrasted with 41% of those 55 and older—it seems inevitable that this will eventually change.

Survey Methods

Results for this Gallup poll are based on telephone interviews conducted Oct. 12–15, 2014, with a random sample of 1,017 adults, aged 18 and older, living in all 50 U.S. states and the District of Columbia. For results based on the total sample of national adults, the margin of sampling error is ±4 percentage points at the 95% confidence level.

November 07, 2014
MORE THAN SIX IN 10 AMERICANS SAY GUNS MAKE HOMES SAFER

by Justin McCarthy

WASHINGTON, D.C.—The percentage of Americans who believe having a gun in the house makes it a safer place to be (63%) has nearly doubled since 2000, when about one in three agreed with this. Three in 10 Americans say having a gun in the house makes it a more dangerous place.

Having a Gun in the House -- Safer or More Dangerous?

Do you think having a gun in the house makes it a safer place to be or a more dangerous place to be?

	% Safer	% More dangerous	% Depends
Oct 12-15, 2014	63	30	6
Oct 9-12, 2006	47	43	7
Oct 11-14, 2004	42	46	10
Aug 29-Sep 5, 2000	35	51	11

GALLUP'

Gallup originally asked Americans about their views on the implications of having a gun in the home in 1993, and then updated the measure in 2000. Between 2000 and 2006, less than half of Americans believed having a gun at home makes it safer—but since then, this percentage has significantly increased to a majority.

Republicans (81%) are about twice as likely as Democrats (41%) to believe having a gun improves home safety. About half of Democrats say having a gun makes a home a more dangerous place to be.

Although there is a gender gap in the results for this question, majorities of both men (67%) and women (58%) believe having a gun improves home safety. While one in three women say it makes for a more dangerous place to be, only one in four men say the same about guns in the home.

About two-thirds of whites and Southerners endorse having a gun to improve home safety, as do majorities of nonwhites (56%) and residents of the other three regions.

Having a Gun in the House -- Safer or More Dangerous?

Do you think having a gun in the house makes it a safer place to be or a more dangerous place to be?

	% Safer	% More dangerous
Men	67	26
Women	58	34
Whites	65	28
Nonwhites	56	37
East	59	34
Midwest	62	30
South	68	26
West	59	33
Republicans	81	15
Independents	64	26
Democrats	41	53

Oct. 12-15, 2014

GALLUP'

Since 2000, Americans of all political stripes have become more inclined to believe a gun makes a home more secure. But the rate of increase has been greatest among Republicans, with 81% now holding this position, up from 44% in 2000.

While those who identify with the GOP have seen a 37-percentage-point growth in this sense of safety, independents show a 29-point climb and Democrats show a 13-point increase.

Do you think having a gun in the house makes it a safer place to be or a more dangerous place to be?

% Safer

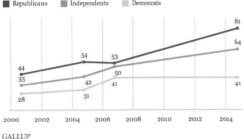

■ Republicans ■ Independents ■ Democrats

GALLUP

More Than Four in 10 Americans Keep a Gun in Their Home

Forty-two percent of Americans report having a gun in their home, similar to the average reported to Gallup over the past decade. This self-reported measure has fluctuated from survey to survey, but is consistent with trends since 2004. Longer term, Gallup has found that household gun ownership has ranged from a low of 34% in 1999 to a high of 51% in 1993.

Percentage of Americans Who Have a Gun in Their Home

Do you have a gun in your home?

■ % Yes

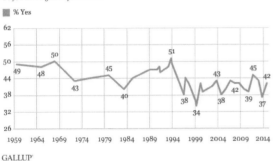

GALLUP

Republicans are twice as likely as Democrats to have a gun in their house. A majority of Southerners say there is a gun in their home, much higher than the rate among those in the West and East.

Men are about equally as likely to have or not have a gun at home. About six in 10 women say they do not have a gun in the home.

Percentage of Americans Who Have a Gun in Their Home, by Demographic Group

Do you have a gun in your home?

	% Yes	% No
Men	47	48
Women	38	59
Whites	49	46
Nonwhites	28	70
East	31	66
Midwest	44	49
South	51	45
West	39	57
Republicans	55	38
Independents	43	53
Democrats	27	72

Oct. 12–15, 2014

GALLUP

Most survey respondents report that the gun in their household belongs to them personally (30%), as opposed to another household member (14%). This means that about one in three people who have a gun in their home are not personally owners, but are aware the gun is there. The personal ownership trend has been generally stable over the past 13 years.

Gun Ownership in Household

Do you personally own a gun, or do the gun or guns in your household belong to another household member?

■ % Personally own ■ % Other household member owns ■ % No gun owned

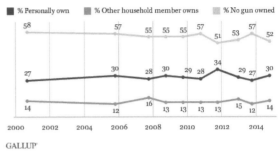

GALLUP

Americans who have a gun in their household are significantly more likely than others to say that having a gun makes a home safer (86%), though one in 10 believe it makes a household more dangerous.

Bottom Line

While Gallup figures on U.S. gun ownership have not shifted much since 2006, the percentage of Americans who say that having a gun in the home makes that household safer has drastically climbed over the past eight years.

Americans own guns for a wide array of reasons, but the increase in the perceived safety value of owning them suggests that guns are taking on more of a protective role than they have in the past. Florida passed the nation's first "Stand Your Ground" law in 2005, followed by dozens of states that passed different versions of the law. In the decade since, Americans have become more likely to view guns as a means of self-protection.

Regardless of Americans' perceptions of crime and their need to protect themselves, violent crime rates fell significantly from 1993 to 2012. While it may be a contentious assertion, some attribute falling crime rates to increased gun sales.

Survey Methods

Results for this Gallup poll are based on telephone interviews conducted Oct. 12–15, 2014, on the Gallup U.S. Daily survey, with a random sample of 1,017 adults, aged 18 and older, living in all 50 U.S. states and the District of Columbia. For results based on the total sample of national adults, the margin of sampling error is ±4 percentage points at the 95% confidence level.

November 10, 2014
THE NEW ERA OF COMMUNICATION AMONG AMERICANS

by Frank Newport

PRINCETON, NJ—Texting, using a cellphone and sending and reading email messages are the most frequently used forms of nonpersonal communication for adult Americans. Between 37% and 39% of all Americans said they used each of these "a lot" on the day prior to being interviewed. That compares with less than 10% of the population who said they used a home landline phone or Twitter "a lot."

Use of Communication Devices Among Americans

Thinking just yesterday, how much did you do each of the following yesterday?

	A lot	A little	Not at all
	%	%	%
Send or read a text message	39	34	27
Make or receive a phone call using a cellphone	38	44	18
Send or read an email message	37	33	29
Post or read messages on Facebook, Instagram, or some other social media site	20	35	45
Make or receive a phone call using a business landline phone	15	21	64
Make or receive a phone call using a home landline phone	9	37	53
Use Twitter, including posting or reading "tweets"	4	9	86

Sept. 9-10, 2014

GALLUP

The ways Americans communicate vary significantly by age. Sending and receiving text messages is the most prevalent form of communication for Americans younger than 50. More than two-thirds of 18- to 29-year-olds say they sent and received text messages "a lot" the previous day, as did nearly half of Americans between 30 and 49. Younger Americans are also well above average in their use of cellphones, email and social media on a daily basis.

Among Americans aged 65 and older, the most-used methods of communication are cellphones, landline phones and email, although this older group is generally much less likely than those who are younger to use any form of communication.

Use of Communication Devices Among Americans, by Age

% Who did this "a lot" the previous day

Sorted by % among 18- to 29-year-olds

	18 to 29	30 to 49	50 to 64	65+
	%	%	%	%
Send or read a text message	68	47	26	8
Make or receive a phone call using a cellphone	50	41	40	18
Send or read an email message	47	44	38	16
Post or read messages on Facebook, Instagram or some other social media site	38	20	17	6
Use Twitter, including posting or reading tweets	14	3	2	0
Make or receive a phone call using a business landline phone	13	19	15	8
Make or receive a phone call using a home landline phone	7	6	10	17

Sept 9-10, 2014

GALLUP

These results are based on a survey Gallup conducted Sept. 9–10, in which Americans were asked to say how frequently they used each of seven modes of communication "yesterday." The survey's interviewing days were Tuesday and Wednesday, meaning respondents answered the questions in terms of weekday, not weekend, communication patterns. The survey did not ask Americans how often they communicated in person or by traditional letters.

These data clearly show that staying in touch with others using most of these forms of communication is an inverse function of age. There are no historical trends on these measures, so it is not possible to measure how much more likely young people were to communicate using whatever means were available in decades past. But in the present era, the percentage of 18- to 29-year-olds who used the

seven methods "a lot" the previous day averages 34%, and that percentage drops to 26% among those aged 30 to 49, 21% among those aged 50 to 64, and down to 10% among those aged 65 and older.

- Texting is the most frequently used form of communication among Americans younger than 50. Texting drops off significantly after age 50, and is used infrequently among those aged 65 and older.
- Use of cellphones and email to communicate is highest among the youngest age group, with little dropoff among those 30 to 64, and is lowest among those aged 65 and older. Still, despite seniors' relatively infrequent use of cellphones and email, both are essentially tied with landline phone use as the most frequently used method of communication even in this oldest age group.
- The use of social media to communicate is in the top four among those aged 18 to 29, but its use drops off significantly among those 30 or older.
- Few Americans of any age report using Twitter frequently, although its use is higher among the younger group. Three percent or less of those aged 30 and older report using Twitter a lot, including virtually no Americans aged 65 and older.
- The use of home landline phones shows a different pattern by age than the other communication methods: it is low across all age groups, albeit slightly higher among those 65 and older. Business landline use is slightly lower among seniors.

Bottom Line

One of the most striking cultural and social changes in the U.S. in recent decades has been the revolution in the ways Americans communicate. Until recently, humans were confined to communicating face to face and through letters and the traditional landline phone. Now, computer and smartphone use has dramatically accelerated, and texting, cellphones and email are the most commonly used modes of communication out of seven tested in this research. The use of social media is fourth.

The younger the American, the more likely he or she is to communicate using these newer technologies, meaning millennials today are a generation that is highly "in touch" with their friends and relatives. It is possible that older Americans make up for their lack of use of these modes of communication by talking to others in person, or perhaps by traditional mail, but seniors' low relative use of even the landline phone suggests they are basically less likely than those who are younger to be in touch with others on a daily basis.

Part of the higher level of communication among young Americans could reflect lifestyle considerations, particularly their higher probability of being unmarried. It is also possible that younger Americans have simply been the quickest to embrace the communication capabilities that new technology represents, and that use of such technology will increase in older age cohorts as the millennials age in the years ahead. The youthful skew in these results may also to some degree reflect that the data were collected during the week, although it is not clear whether all but the business landline form of communication would be lower on Saturdays and Sundays.

Although the use of email and these other forms of communication could be considered a positive way for more physically isolated older Americans to stay in touch with others, these results suggest that use of these devices is not yet extremely common among seniors. That could reflect their lack of access to tools such as computers, tablets or smartphones to send and receive email or text messages, because they simply are less accustomed to using these forms of communication.

Survey Methods

Results for this Gallup poll are based on telephone interviews conducted Sept. 9–10, 2014, with a random sample of 1,015 adults, aged 18 and older, living in all 50 U.S. states and the District of Columbia. For results based on the total sample of national adults, the margin of sampling error is ±4 percentage points at the 95% confidence level.

Each sample of national adults includes a minimum quota of 50% cellphone respondents and 50% landline respondents, with additional minimum quotas by time zone within region. Landline and cellular telephone numbers are selected using random-digit-dial methods.

November 10, 2014
AMERICANS SATISFIED WITH HOW HEALTH SYSTEM WORKS FOR THEM

by Rebecca Riffkin

WASHINGTON, D.C.—Over the last seven and a half months, two-thirds of Americans, on average, have been satisfied with how the healthcare system is working for them. Less than a week before the health insurance exchanges reopen, these results show that Americans who have health insurance (70%) are almost twice as likely as those who don't (37%) to be satisfied with the healthcare system.

Are you satisfied or dissatisfied with how the healthcare system is working for you?

	Satisfied	Dissatisfied	No opinion
	%	%	%
National adults	66	33	2
Have health insurance	70	28	1
Do not have health insurance	37	59	4

March 21-Oct. 31, 2014

GALLUP

In the third quarter of 2014, the uninsured rate in the U.S. was 13.4%, the lowest quarterly average Gallup has found in daily measurement of this metric going back to 2008. The health insurance exchanges open again on Nov. 15 to enable those who are uninsured to shop for insurance coverage for 2015. If more Americans gain health insurance, general satisfaction with the way the system is working may rise, given that insured Americans are much more likely to be satisfied than the uninsured are.

Monthly averages of Americans' satisfaction with how the healthcare system works for them have been largely consistent since daily tracking began toward the end of March. In April, average monthly satisfaction was highest at 67%, while several months, including May, September and October, tied for lowest, at 65% satisfied.

Gallup has previously found that Americans' level of satisfaction with the healthcare system partly depends on their party identification. Currently, about three in four Democrats and Democratic-leaning independents are satisfied with their healthcare situation, compared with 60% of Republicans and Republican leaners.

Democrats More Satisfied With Healthcare System Than Republicans
Are you satisfied or dissatisfied with how the healthcare system is working for you?

	% Satisfied	% Dissatisfied
Republicans/Leaners	60	39
Democrats/Leaners	74	25

March 21-Oct. 31, 2014

GALLUP

Americans younger than age 30 are more likely to be satisfied with how the healthcare system works for them than Americans aged 30 to 64, but Americans 65 and older are the age group most likely to be satisfied, at 79%. Americans at higher income levels are also more likely to be satisfied. Among Americans with annual household incomes of $90,000 or more, 70% are satisfied. This drops to 62% among Americans with annual household incomes under $36,000.

Satisfaction Varies Among Demographic Groups
Are you satisfied or dissatisfied with how the healthcare system is working for you?

	% Satisfied	% Dissatisfied
AGE		
18 to 29	66	33
30 to 49	61	38
50 to 64	63	35
65 and older	79	20
RACE		
Non-Hispanic whites	64	34
Blacks	73	26
Hispanics	68	30
Asians	70	28
ANNUAL HOUSEHOLD INCOME		
Less than $36,000	62	37
$36,000 to $89,999	67	32
$90,000 or more	70	29

March 21-Oct. 31, 2014

GALLUP

Younger and older Americans' greater likelihood to be satisfied may be a result of the unique coverage experiences among those groups. Older Americans can qualify for Medicare health insurance and have high rates of being insured, which helps explain their overall higher levels of satisfaction. And the Affordable Care Act expanded coverage to many young Americans by allowing them to be covered under their parents' health insurance until age 26. However, Americans aged 26 to 34 are the least likely to be insured, which could be affecting this group's satisfaction rates.

The differences in satisfaction across age and racial/ethnic groups most likely reflect their political orientation. Non-Hispanic white Americans—the racial group least likely to be satisfied, at

64%—are more likely than other races to be or lean Republican. Among blacks, who are largely Democratic, 73% are satisfied. Past Gallup research has found that while most Asians have health insurance, they often lack a personal doctor. Seven in 10 Asians are satisfied with how the healthcare system works for them, and they are more likely to be Democrats than Republicans.

One of the major goals of the Affordable Care Act was to expand health insurance coverage among Hispanics. Gallup has found that only 65% of Hispanics have health insurance, compared with 90% of non-Hispanic whites. Satisfaction among Hispanics is slightly lower than what is seen among blacks and Asians, at 68% satisfied. Hispanics are also more likely to lean Democratic than Republican.

Bottom Line

Last year, the health insurance exchanges first opened to a wave of technical problems but ultimately were credited with helping millions of previously uninsured Americans gain health insurance. However, the Affordable Care Act remains unpopular among the American people. In October, Gallup found that more Americans say the law has hurt them, rather than helped them. On Nov. 15 the exchanges will open again, allowing Americans to purchase healthcare coverage for 2015.

At this time, two-thirds of Americans are satisfied with how the U.S. healthcare system works for them. With the insured generally much more likely to be satisfied than the uninsured, it is possible that—if the uninsured rate continues to decline—overall satisfaction with the way the healthcare system is treating Americans will increase in the months ahead.

Survey Methods

Results for this Gallup poll are based on telephone interviews conducted March 21–Oct. 31, 2014, on the Gallup U.S. Daily survey, with a random sample of 110,835 adults, aged 18 and older, living in all 50 U.S. states and the District of Columbia. For results based on the total sample of national adults, the margin of sampling error is ±1 percentage point at the 95% confidence level.

November 11, 2014
MAJORITY IN U.S. WANT GOP IN CONGRESS TO SET NATION'S COURSE

by Lydia Saad

PRINCETON, NJ—Following the midterm election that some have termed a Republican wave, the majority of Americans want the Republicans in Congress—rather than President Barack Obama—to have more influence over the direction the country takes in the coming year. This is a switch from early 2012 when a slim plurality, 46%, wanted Obama to prevail in steering the nation.

Republicans' 17-percentage-point edge over Obama on this measure exceeds what they earned after the 2010 midterm, when Americans favored Republicans by an eight-point margin (49% to 41%). It also eclipses the nine-point advantage Republicans had over Bill Clinton following the 1994 midterm in which Republicans captured the majority of both houses.

Americans' Preference for Who Should Lead U.S. Direction

Who do you want to have more influence over the direction the nation takes in the next year -- Barack Obama or the Republicans in Congress?

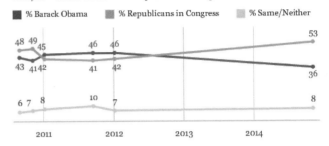

Note: "Same/Neither" is a volunteered response.

GALLUP'

Republicans' current edge, however, is still bested by Democrats' 30-point lead over George W. Bush (61% to 31%) following the 2006 midterm election. Democrats regained majority control of both houses that year.

The similarity across all three of these elections is that they resulted in the president's opposing party acquiring majority control of one, if not two, chambers of Congress. By contrast, a month after the 1998 midterm election in which the Republican majority survived—but only barely, given a decline in their House seat margin—Americans favored Clinton over the Republicans in Congress for leading the nation by a hefty 29-point margin.

Another factor likely influencing Americans' post-election preferences for whose leadership should prevail is the president's job approval rating. Obama in 2014 and 2010, Bush in 2006 and Clinton in 1994 all had approval ratings under 50%—or even below 40%—whereas Clinton's in December 1998 was a soaring 73%.

Americans' Preference for Who Should Lead U.S. Direction

	Prefer sitting president	Prefer opposing party in Congress	President's lead/deficit	President's approval rating
	Barack Obama	Republicans in Congress		
November 2014	36%	53%	-17	37%
November 2010	41%	49%	-8	44%
	George W. Bush	Democrats in Congress		
November 2006	31%	61%	-30	33%
	Bill Clinton	Republicans in Congress		
December 1998	60%	31%	+29	73%
January 1995	40%	49%	-9	47%

Results shown are the first conducted after each midterm election, as available.

GALLUP'

More Say the Country Will Now Be Better Off Than Worse Off

Although Americans are presumably happy with the outcome of the election—as it gave full control of Congress to the party they want in charge of the nation's direction—most are not expecting a major upturn in national conditions as a result of the Republicans' success at the polls. While more say the country will be better off now that the Republicans have won control than say it will be worse off (34% vs. 19%), close to half say it won't make a difference.

Americans' Perception of Nation's Future, by Party ID

Now that the Republicans have won control of Congress in this November's elections, do you think the country will be better off, worse off or will it not make any difference?

	Better off	Worse off	No difference	No opinion
	%	%	%	%
National adults	34	19	44	2
Republicans	67	2	31	1
Independents	28	16	55	2
Democrats	12	44	43	2

Nov. 6-9, 2014

GALLUP'

Americans' expectations about the outcome are a bit subdued compared with 2006, when 48% thought the country would be better off as a result of Democrats' victories in that midterm election. Another 16% thought it would be worse off, leaving just 33% saying the election would not make a difference.

The main factor accounting for the difference between 2006 and today could be that the 2006 midterm shifted the balance of power in Washington from unified Republican control to divided control, whereas this year the outcome only strengthened the Republicans' hand within an already divided government. As a result, Democrats in 2006 were more likely than Republicans are today—79% vs. 67%—to believe the country would be better off as a result of their party's victory. And there has been an even bigger change among independents, with 43% in 2006 versus 28% today expecting things to improve.

Bottom Line

The midterm election provided a clear signal as to which party voters want to control Congress. That message is echoed in the results of the latest Gallup poll showing Americans expressly asking for the Republicans—rather than Obama—to guide the direction the country takes in the next year. But after four years of partisan gridlock, most Americans are not optimistic that the election's outcome will improve things.

Survey Methods

Results for this Gallup poll are based on telephone interviews conducted Nov. 6–9, 2014, with a random sample of 828 adults, aged 18 and older, living in all 50 U.S. states and the District of Columbia. For results based on the total sample of national adults, the margin of sampling error is ±4 percentage points at the 95% confidence level.

November 12, 2014
DEMOCRATIC PARTY FAVORABLE RATING FALLS TO RECORD LOW

by Andrew Dugan

WASHINGTON, D.C.—After the midterm elections that saw the Democratic Party suffer significant losses in Congress, a record-low 36% of Americans say they have a favorable opinion of the party, down six percentage points from before the elections.

The Republican Party's favorable rating, at 42%, is essentially unchanged from 40%. This marks the first time since September 2011 that the Republican Party has had a higher favorability rating than the Democratic Party.

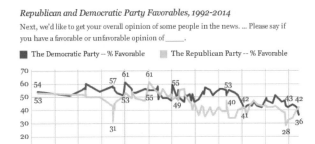

Republican and Democratic Party Favorables, 1992-2014

Next, we'd like to get your overall opinion of some people in the news. ... Please say if you have a favorable or unfavorable opinion of _____.

GALLUP'

These results come from a Nov. 6–9 Gallup poll, conducted after Republicans enjoyed a breathtaking sweep of important contests throughout the country in this year's midterms. The party gained control of the Senate and will likely capture its largest House majority in nearly a century. Additionally, the GOP now controls 31 governorships and two-thirds of state legislative chambers.

The descent in Democrats' ratings caps a wild political ride for both parties over the past two years. After President Barack Obama's re-election in 2012, the Democratic Party's favorable rating spiked to 51%, the first time either party had enjoyed majority support since 2009. However, after the post-election glow wore off, the party's image settled back down near the 45% average for the Obama presidency. Meanwhile, Americans' favorable ratings of the Republican Party collapsed to 28% during the fall 2013 federal government shutdown, the lowest such rating for either party since Gallup first asked the question in 1992.

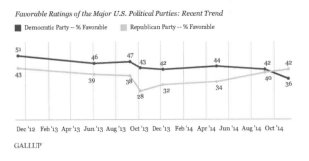

Favorable Ratings of the Major U.S. Political Parties: Recent Trend

GALLUP'

Because of congressional Republicans' apparent political miscalculation in allowing the shutdown, some raised the possibility of a Democratic takeover of the House of Representatives in the 2014 midterms. But the speculation was short lived. While Republicans agreed to a compromise that ended the shutdown, the Obama administration made a number of political blunders, including the botched rollout of the federal government's healthcare website; a series of international crises in Ukraine, Iraq and Syria; the Veterans Affairs hospitals scandal; and a criticized response to the first appearance of the Ebola virus on U.S. soil. Whatever momentum the Democrats gained during the government shutdown was lost. The Democratic Party's image stagnated as Republicans' slowly improved, putting the parties at rough parity heading into the midterms.

The GOP currently has an image advantage over the Democratic Party; still, neither party is held in particularly high regard. This is yet another sign of Americans' dissatisfaction with their political system.

Democrats Now Less Likely to Have Positive Image of Own Party

Across party groups, the Republican Party's image held steady from Gallup's last update in September. But support for the Democratic Party dropped among independents and among Democrats themselves. Currently, 81% of self-identified Democrats have a favorable view of their party, down from 88% in September and 95% shortly after the 2012 election. Independents' ratings of the Democratic Party, at 25%, are down 10 points from September.

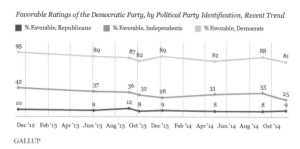

Favorable Ratings of the Democratic Party, by Political Party Identification, Recent Trend

GALLUP

Bottom Line

After the 2012 election, many political analysts focused on the GOP's "image problem." Now, it is the Democrats who appear to have the more battered image. Their favorability rating has never been lower, and they are reeling from defeats that cost them control of the U.S. Senate and strengthened the Republican House majority to levels likely not seen in 90 years.

On the other hand, the American public does not admire Republicans more, their numerous election victories notwithstanding. Neither party can say it is making significant progress in improving its image among the U.S. population, but undoubtedly the 2014 elections augmented the GOP's ability to shape the agenda in Washington and in state capitals across the country. This newfound power could pose its own problems for the GOP. The party could be on the verge of winning over a greater segment of the country or, not unlike the Democrats this year, could see its brand go into a free fall. This will depend on what Republican leaders do in the coming two years.

Survey Methods

Results for this Gallup poll are based on telephone interviews conducted Nov. 6–9, 2014, with a random sample of 828 adults, aged 18 and older, living in all 50 U.S. states and the District of Columbia. For results based on the total sample of national adults, the margin of sampling error is ±4 percentage points at the 95% confidence level.

November 12, 2014
AMERICANS SAY GOVERNMENT, ECONOMY MOST IMPORTANT PROBLEMS

by Rebecca Riffkin

WASHINGTON, D.C.—The economy in general and government are the issues Americans are most likely to name as the most important problems facing the country in November. These are followed closely by mentions of immigration and unemployment.

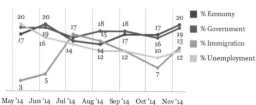

Recent Trends in Top Four "Most Important" U.S. Problems
What do you think is the most important problem facing this country today? [OPEN-ENDED]

■ % Economy ■ % Government % Immigration % Unemployment

GALLUP

Government, unemployment and the economy in general have ranked among the most frequently named problems since the beginning of the year. Mentions of immigration increased sharply in July, in response to a large wave of young immigrants crossing the U.S.-Mexico border. Mentions dipped from 12% in September to 7% in October, perhaps because the issue was overshadowed by the Ebola crisis. However, immigration is now back up to 13%.

Mentions of disease, and Ebola specifically, rose to 5% in October, debuting on the list of issues that at least 3% of Americans mention. However, in November, 2% mention Ebola, perhaps because they perceive the threat as less severe than it was a month ago.

Recent Trend for Most Important U.S. Problem
What do you think is the most important problem facing this country today? [OPEN-ENDED]

	September 2014	October 2014	November 2014
	%	%	%
Economy in general	17	17	20
Dissatisfaction with government	18	16	19
Immigration/Illegal aliens	12	7	13
Unemployment/Jobs	12	10	12
Healthcare	5	8	7
Federal budget deficit/Federal debt	6	5	5
Education	3	5	4
Poverty/Hunger/Homelessness	3	3	4
Terrorism	4	3	4
Ethical/Moral/Family decline	5	5	3
Situation in Iraq/ISIS	3	5	3
Foreign aid/Focus overseas	6	3	3
National security	2	2	3

Note: Issues mentioned by 2% or fewer not shown

GALLUP

As is typically the case, Americans of differing party affiliations often have dissimilar ideas of the most important problem. For example, Republicans and Republican-leaning independents (27%) are more likely than Democrats and Democratic leaners (14%) to list the economy in general. And Republicans are slightly more likely than Democrats to mention immigration.

Party differences are smaller on government dissatisfaction, healthcare and unemployment.

Top Five U.S. Problems, by Party
What do you think is the most important problem facing this country today? [OPEN-ENDED]

	Republican/Lean Republican	Democrat/Lean Democratic
	%	%
Economy in general	27	14
Dissatisfaction with government	21	19
Immigration/Illegal aliens	16	10
Unemployment/Jobs	10	13
Healthcare	9	6

Nov. 6-9, 2014

GALLUP

Mentions of immigration increased similarly between October and November for Republicans (from 9% to 16%) and Democrats (from 4% to 10%). Although it is a pressing issue in many Americans' minds, the prospects for government action are unclear. President Barack Obama is discussing executive action on immigration reform and says he is tired of waiting for Congress to act. Some Republicans are pushing for compromise, and party leaders may be waiting for January, when the GOP takes full control of Congress, but have not issued a plan for action on immigration.

Bottom Line

Government and the economy in general continue to be the most commonly cited problems facing the U.S. Mentions of immigration increased in November after a dip in October. During the current "lame duck" session, congressional leaders may be hesitant to act on these issues—though this would be the last chance to act for members of Congress who were not re-elected. For their part, Republicans may be waiting until January, when their new Senate majority is sworn in.

Americans are more likely to say they want the new Republican Congress rather than Obama to set the nation's course in January. But more than anything, Americans want Congress to fix itself and begin compromising, a view reinforced by Americans' continuing to name the government itself as the most important problem facing the nation.

Survey Methods

Results for this Gallup poll are based on telephone interviews conducted Nov. 6–9, 2014, with a random sample of 828 adults, aged 18 and older, living in all 50 U.S. states and the District of Columbia. For results based on the total sample of national adults, the margin of sampling error is ±4 percentage points at the 95% confidence level.

November 13, 2014
IN U.S., 55% OF UNINSURED PLAN TO GET HEALTH COVERAGE

by Jeffrey M. Jones

PRINCETON, NJ—More than half of uninsured Americans say they plan to sign up for health coverage, a promising sign as the open enrollment period for obtaining health insurance through state and federal exchanges opens. Specifically, 55% of Americans who currently lack insurance say they plan to sign up for coverage while 35% of the uninsured say they will not get insurance and instead pay the fine as required by the Affordable Care Act, also known as "Obamacare."

The results are based on Oct. 22 through Nov. 12 Gallup Daily tracking interviews with 976 uninsured Americans.

Most uninsured Americans, 70%, say they are aware of the requirement to have health insurance or pay a fine, the "individual mandate" provision of the 2010 healthcare law that the Supreme Court upheld in a 2012 ruling. However, that leaves nearly 30% who were not aware they must have insurance or pay a fine at the

time that Gallup interviewers asked them about it. This suggests that more than a year after the healthcare exchanges opened and more than four years after the healthcare law was passed, challenges remain in regard to educating uninsured Americans about the new requirements.

As I mentioned, Americans without health insurance either have to get health insurance or pay a fine. Given what you know, as of right now, would you say you are -- [ROTATED: more likely to get health insurance (or) more likely to pay the fine]?

Based on U.S. adults without health insurance

	%
More likely to get insurance	55
More likely to pay the fine	35
No opinion	10

Gallup Daily tracking, Oct. 22-Nov. 12, 2014

GALLUP®

A key part of the law was the establishment of insurance exchanges to make it easier for Americans not eligible for employer-provided insurance or government programs to obtain insurance. And the exchanges are the preferred method for obtaining insurance among the uninsured who plan to do so, but not overwhelmingly so, at 50%. Another 29% who plan to get insurance say they will get coverage outside of an exchange, leaving 21% who are unsure of where they might get insurance.

Uninsured Americans' familiarity with the exchanges is low, with 46% saying they are "not familiar at all" with the exchanges, and another 19% claiming they are "not too familiar" with the exchanges. Eight percent say they are "very familiar" and 22% are "somewhat familiar."

Gallup asked the same set of questions of the uninsured late in 2013 and early in 2014 during the last open enrollment period. The current reported intentions to get insurance, awareness of the requirement to obtain insurance or pay a fine, familiarity with the exchanges and plans to obtain insurance through an exchange are similar to what Gallup measured before.

For example, from January through March 2014, an average of 55% of uninsured said they planned to sign up, matching the current percentage intending to do so. But from October through December 2013, an average of 61% of uninsured planned to sign up.

The decline from late last year may have as much to do with changes in the uninsured population as it had to do with changes in the uninsured's desire to get insurance. After the first wave of insurance sign-ups late last year and early this year, the uninsured population has declined to 13% of U.S. adults, down from 18% in the third quarter of 2013. Those who signed up late last year—and who are no longer counted among the uninsured—may have been the most eager to obtain insurance. And so, as the uninsured population gets smaller, those still in it are probably less motivated to become insured.

The fact that intentions to get insurance are similar to what they were earlier this year (at the end of the last enrollment period) is notable, given that the fine for not having insurance in 2015 will increase. So either the amount of the fine is still not high enough to compel the uninsured to get coverage—or the uninsured may be unaware of the stiffer penalty in 2015 for being uninsured.

Politics Remains a Factor in Health Insurance Intentions

One consistent finding from Gallup's 2013–2014 tracking of health insurance intentions was that uninsured Republicans were less likely than uninsured Democrats to say they planned to get insurance. And that is still the case today, as 62% of uninsured Democrats (including Democratic-leaning independents) and 47% of uninsured Republicans (including Republican-leaning independents) say they plan to get insurance.

Intentions to Get Health Insurance, by Party Affiliation

Based on U.S. adults without health insurance

	Uninsured Democrats/Democratic leaners	Uninsured Republicans/Republican leaners
	%	%
More likely to get insurance	62	47
More likely to pay the fine	31	44
No opinion	7	9

Gallup Daily tracking, Oct. 22-Nov. 12, 2014

GALLUP

Uninsured Republicans' stated reluctance to sign up for insurance may reflect Republicans' overwhelmingly negative opinions of the Affordable Care Act.

Overall, 43% of uninsured Americans are Democrats or Democratic leaners, 28% are Republicans or Republican leaners and the remainder have no party preference or leaning.

Implications

A majority of Americans who lack insurance say they plan to sign up for coverage rather than pay a fine, which is an encouraging sign that more progress will be made toward the Affordable Care Act's major goal of reducing the uninsured rate. And, in fact, data from the Gallup-Healthways Well-Being Index clearly show a reduction in the percentage of Americans who lack health insurance, compared with a year ago.

Importantly, though, the measures of people's current intentions may not reflect their ultimate behavior, whether that is because they have not come to a final decision, or circumstances prevent them from following through or if they just never take the necessary steps to sign up for insurance even though they say they plan to. If in fact a little more than half of uninsured Americans had signed up for coverage in the past year—similar to their stated intentions—then the reduction in the uninsured rate would have been closer to eight or nine percentage points than the five points Gallup estimated.

Given a current uninsured rate of roughly 13%, and with 55% of uninsured Americans saying they plan to get insurance, if all followed through on their intentions the uninsured rate would fall another seven percentage points. And while that large of a reduction may not be realized, it seems that with a sufficiently large percentage of uninsured planning to get insurance that the uninsured rate should fall at least a bit in the coming year.

Survey Methods

Results for this Gallup poll are based on telephone interviews conducted Oct. 22–Nov. 12, 2014, on the Gallup U.S. Daily survey, with a random sample of 976 adults, aged 18 and older, living in all 50 U.S. states and the District of Columbia, who do not currently have health insurance.

For results based on the total sample of uninsured adults, the margin of sampling error is ±4 percentage points at the 95% confidence level.

November 14, 2014
NEWLY INSURED THROUGH EXCHANGES GIVE COVERAGE GOOD MARKS

by Frank Newport

PRINCETON, NJ—Over seven in 10 Americans who bought new health insurance policies through the government exchanges earlier this year rate the quality of their healthcare and their healthcare coverage as "excellent" or "good." These positive evaluations are generally similar to the reviews that all insured Americans give to their health insurance.

Ratings of Quality of Healthcare and Healthcare Coverage

Among those newly insured through a government exchange this year, and among all who have health insurance

	Newly insured this year*	All with health insurance**
	%	%
QUALITY OF HEALTHCARE		
Excellent	32	38
Good	42	43
Only fair	20	15
Poor	5	4
HEALTHCARE COVERAGE		
Excellent	25	29
Good	46	43
Only fair	19	22
Poor	9	5

* Oct. 22-Nov. 11, 2014
** Nov. 6-9, 2014

GALLUP

Among those who bought new health insurance policies through the exchanges, the majority are about as satisfied with their coverage and healthcare as are other Americans—suggesting that the end result of the exchange enrollment process is a generally positive one for those who take advantage of it. Americans who still lack health insurance will have the opportunity to buy coverage when the national insurance marketplace exchanges open again on Nov. 15.

These data reflecting newly insured Americans' attitudes toward their healthcare coverage are based on interviews conducted Oct. 22 through Nov. 12 on Gallup Daily tracking. Gallup asked all Americans with health insurance if their coverage was new for 2014, and if so, whether they had obtained their coverage through federal or state exchanges. About 4% of the adult population classify themselves as being newly insured this year through the exchanges. The comparison group of all Americans with insurance is from Gallup's annual healthcare survey, conducted this year Nov. 6–9.

In addition to newly insured Americans rating their coverage and the quality of their healthcare positively, they are more satisfied than the average insured American with the cost of their health coverage. Three in four of the newly insured say they are satisfied with this aspect of their healthcare experience, compared with 61% among the general population of those with insurance. To some degree, this could reflect the fact that many who get insurance through the exchanges receive government subsidies to help reduce the overall cost of their health insurance.

Satisfaction With Cost of Healthcare

Among those newly insured through a government exchange this year, and among all who have health insurance

	Newly insured this year*	All with health insurance**
	%	%
Satisfied with cost of healthcare	75	61
Dissatisfied with cost of healthcare	25	37

* Oct. 22-Nov. 11, 2014
** Nov. 6-9, 2014

GALLUP'

Newly insured Americans' positive attitudes toward their health coverage are manifested in their coverage intentions going forward. Among those who bought a new policy through a government exchange this year, 68% say they will renew their current policy, while 7% say they plan to get a different policy through a state or federal exchange. Meanwhile, 15% say they will get a different policy from another source, and 2% say they will drop their health insurance altogether.

Newly Insured Americans' Plans for Health Insurance in 2015

Among those newly insured through a government exchange this year

	%
Renew current policy	68
Get different policy from healthcare exchange	7
Get different policy from somewhere else	15
Not have health insurance at all	2
Don't know	8

Oct. 22-Nov. 11, 2014

GALLUP'

Bottom Line

Americans who obtained new health insurance policies in 2014 using the government exchanges are roughly as positive about their healthcare coverage and the quality of healthcare they receive as the average insured American, and are more satisfied with the cost of their coverage. More than two-thirds of the newly insured who purchased coverage through federal or state exchanges intend to renew their exchange policies, while another 7% plan to look for a different policy through the exchanges.

As the healthcare exchanges reopen on Nov. 15, these data suggest that the currently uninsured will mostly be pleased with the outcome if they opt to use the exchanges to obtain insurance on this second go-around.

Survey Methods

Results for this Gallup poll are based on telephone interviews conducted Oct. 22–Nov. 12, 2014, on the Gallup U.S. Daily survey, with a random sample of 407 adults, aged 18 and older, living in all 50 U.S. states and the District of Columbia, who are newly insured in 2014 through a government health insurance exchange.

For results based on this sample, the margin of sampling error is ±6 percentage points at the 95% confidence level.

November 17, 2014
EBOLA RANKS AMONG AMERICANS' TOP THREE HEALTHCARE CONCERNS

by Lydia Saad

PRINCETON, NJ—Healthcare costs (19%) and access (18%) continue to rank among the leading issues Americans cite when asked what they consider to be the country's "most urgent health problem." But Ebola, mentioned by 17%, now joins these perennial concerns as one of Americans' top health worries.

What would you say is the most urgent health problem facing this country at the present time?

	Nov 7-10, 2013	Nov 6-9, 2014
	%	%
Affordable healthcare/health insurance; Costs	23	19
Access to healthcare/universal health coverage	16	18
Ebola virus	--	17
Obesity	13	10
Cancer	10	10
Finding cures for diseases	1	3
Diabetes	2	2
Heart disease	2	2
Government interference	9	2
Drug/Alcohol abuse	1	1
Flu	--	1
Mental illness	2	1
AIDS	1	1
Other	6	3
No opinion	13	10

GALLUP'

Obesity and cancer are the only other issues garnering double-digit percentages of mentions this year, each cited by 10%. Other specific diseases or health problems—including diabetes, heart disease, drug and alcohol abuse, flu, mental illness and AIDS—receive minimal mentions of 1% or 2%.

Gallup has measured public perceptions of the leading U.S. health problem annually since 1999, and, prior to that, periodically starting in 1987. This year's results are based on Gallup's annual Health and Healthcare survey, conducted Nov. 6–9.

At the time of the new survey, only one of the four people who had been diagnosed with Ebola in the U.S. was still being treated, and the other two surviving patients had already been declared virus-free. Several U.S. healthcare workers who were infected abroad and flown to the U.S. for treatment had also recovered by the time of the survey, while the outbreak in West Africa seemed to be slowing. Thus, it is a testament to the gravity of the Ebola virus that it still sparks relatively high public concern several weeks after the peak of the U.S. scare.

Similar percentages of men and women, as well as younger versus older Americans, consider Ebola the nation's top health concern right now. But this view does differ by level of education. Twenty-two percent of adults who never attended college, as well as 19% of those with some college experience, name Ebola as the top problem, compared with 11% of those with least a four-year college degree.

Ebola Joins Flu, Bioterrorism and AIDS as National Health Scares

Gallup's long-term trend documents a handful of episodic health concerns over the years, where the issue spiked as a public concern one year, only to disappear the next. The flu has twice captured public attention when specific flu strains attracted widespread publicity, including with the bird flu scare in 2005 and the H1N1 virus in 2009. Bioterrorism was the top-ranking concern in 2001, mentioned by 22% of Americans as the nation was riveted by an ongoing anthrax attack, but it fell to 1% the next year.

AIDS stands apart, as a concern that dominated the health landscape for a number of years, until it subsided, partly due to progress in the control and treatment of the illness. AIDS registered 68% concern in Gallup's inaugural asking and continued to dominate the list through the 1990s. However, it dwindled as a public concern after 2000, and is now hardly mentioned.

These issues contrast with cancer, which has rarely been a top-ranking issue, but has consistently appeared in the top three or four health problems in Americans' minds, almost always registering at least 10%, and reaching a high of 23% in 1999. Obesity has emerged as a steady concern in recent years, including 16% mentioning it in 2012 after it gradually rose from 1% in 1999.

Bottom Line

Ebola may not be the dominant news story it was a month ago, but it is still on the minds of Americans, 17% of whom cite it when asked to name the top health problem facing the U.S. Still, Gallup's history of asking this question strongly suggests that without continued incidents of Americans catching the virus on U.S. soil, this flare of concern will be temporary.

Meanwhile, a year after the Affordable Care Act began to offer all Americans healthcare through government healthcare exchanges, with discounts given to some based on financial need, nearly one in five Americans continue to name healthcare costs as the most urgent health problem facing the country, and a similar proportion name healthcare access. These issues have been prominent on the list for over a decade, and are likely to remain so.

Survey Methods

Results for this Gallup poll are based on telephone interviews conducted Nov. 6–9, 2014, with a random sample of 828 adults, aged 18 and older, living in all 50 U.S. states and the District of Columbia. For results based on the total sample of national adults, the margin of sampling error is ±4 percentage points at the 95% confidence level.

November 17, 2014
AS NEW ENROLLMENT PERIOD STARTS, ACA APPROVAL AT 37%

by Justin McCarthy

WASHINGTON, D.C.—As the Affordable Care Act's second open enrollment period begins, 37% of Americans say they approve of the law, one percentage point below the previous low in January. Fifty-six percent disapprove, the high in disapproval by one point.

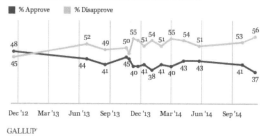

Americans' Views of the Affordable Care Act

Do you generally approve or disapprove of the 2010 Affordable Care Act, signed into law by President Obama that restructured the U.S. healthcare system?

Americans were slightly more positive than negative about the law around the time of the 2012 election, but they have consistently been more likely to disapprove than approve of the law in all surveys that have been conducted since then. Approval has been in the low 40% or high 30% range after a noticeable dip that occurred in early November 2013. This was shortly after millions of Americans received notices that their current policies were being canceled, which was at odds with President Barack Obama's pledge that those who liked their plans could keep them. The president later said, by way of clarification, that Americans could keep their plans if those plans didn't change after the ACA was passed.

The current 37% reading comes on the heels of last week's midterm elections, in which Republicans won full control of both houses of Congress. Already, party leaders are discussing efforts to repeal the unpopular law.

Repeal is highly unlikely, given Obama's veto power, but the law's new low in approval—and new high in disapproval (56%)—could potentially have an impact on its future. The president himself has acknowledged he will consider modifications to the law, which could include repealing the tax on medical devices.

Approval Among Independents at 33%

Approval of the law continues to diverge sharply by party, with 74% of Democrats and 8% of Republicans approving of it. Independents have never been particularly positive toward the law, with approval ranging between 31% and 41%. Currently, 33% of independents approve.

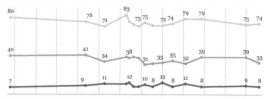

Approval of the Affordable Care Act, by Party ID

Do you generally approve or disapprove of the 2010 Affordable Care Act, signed into law by President Obama that restructured the U.S. healthcare system?

Nonwhites, who disproportionately identify as Democrats, have maintained majority approval since the ACA's inception, now at 56%. Though this is still about double the level of approval among whites (29%), it is the first time nonwhites have fallen below the 60% mark.

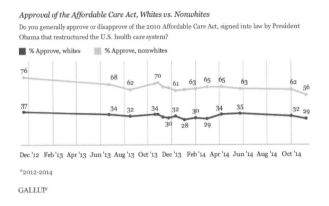

Approval of the Affordable Care Act, Whites vs. Nonwhites

Do you generally approve or disapprove of the 2010 Affordable Care Act, signed into law by President Obama that restructured the U.S. health care system?

■ % Approve, whites   ▨ % Approve, nonwhites

Dec '12 Feb '13 Apr '13 Jun '13 Aug '13 Oct '13 Dec '13 Feb '14 Apr '14 Jun '14 Aug '14 Oct '14

*2012-2014

GALLUP

Bottom Line

Americans have never been overly positive toward the ACA, at best showing a roughly equal division between approval and disapproval early on in the law's implementation. The percentage of Americans who approve of the law represents a new numerical low, which could indicate a loss of faith in the law amid the aftermath of the 2014 midterms. Although the ACA, also called Obamacare, was not as dominant an issue in this year's congressional elections as it was in 2010, the issue was part of Republicans' campaign efforts to oppose the president's agenda overall. In doing that, many of the party's candidates were successful.

Though the law's implementation suffered setbacks last fall, government officials have greater optimism for the health insurance website's usability this time around. Importantly, though, approval of the law has remained low throughout the year even as it has had obvious success in reducing the uninsured rate. And with approval holding in a fairly narrow range since last fall, it may be that Americans have fairly well made up their minds about the law, and even a highly successful second open enrollment period may not do much to boost their approval.

Survey Methods

Results for this Gallup poll are based on telephone interviews conducted Nov. 6–9, 2014, on the Gallup U.S. Daily survey, with a random sample of 828 adults, aged 18 and older, living in all 50 U.S. states and the District of Columbia. For results based on the total sample of national adults, the margin of sampling error is ±4 percentage points at the 95% confidence level.

November 17, 2014
NONWHITES LESS LIKELY TO FEEL POLICE PROTECT AND SERVE THEM

by Justin McCarthy

WASHINGTON, D.C.—As a grand jury decides whether to indict a white police officer for shooting an unarmed black teen in Ferguson,

Missouri, Americans' confidence in their local police to protect them from violent crime continues to differ by race, as it has since Gallup started measuring it. White Americans (60%) surveyed last month expressed more trust in police than nonwhites did (49%), although the 11-percentage-point gap is slightly smaller than the average 14-point gap seen since 1985.

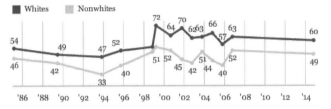

Confidence in Police to Protect Them From Violent Crime,
U.S. Whites vs. Nonwhites

How much confidence do you have in the ability of the police to protect you from violent crime -- a great deal, quite a lot, not very much, or none at all?

% A great deal/Quite a lot of confidence

■ Whites   ▨ Nonwhites

'86 '88 '90 '92 '94 '96 '98 '00 '02 '04 '06 '08 '10 '12 '14

*Recent trend: 1985-2014

GALLUP

Since 1985, Gallup has generally found double-digit differences between the percentages of U.S. whites and nonwhites who say they have "a great deal" or "quite a lot" of confidence in the ability of their local police to protect them. Just three times—in 1985, 1989 and 1998—has the gap been below 10 percentage points.

Confidence in police protection plummeted to its lowest on record for both whites (47%) and nonwhites (33%) in 1993—months after two police officers were given 30-month prison sentences for violating the civil rights of Rodney King and arresting him with excessive force. However, even as confidence has since increased among both groups, a significant gap has persisted.

Although there have been high-profile shootings of unarmed black teenagers in recent years, the current 11-point gap between white and nonwhite opinions is narrower than in most years. The difference between whites' and nonwhites' views has ranged from four to 25 points, with the largest gap in 2001.

Current confidence in police protection among nonwhites—which encompasses Hispanics and other communities of color—is just a few points off from the average since 1985, suggesting that it has not seen any significant improvements over the past three decades.

Overall, Americans Trust Police to Protect Them From Violent Crime

Aside from the differences by race, the majority of Americans have generally had confidence in their local police to protect them from violent crime since Gallup began polling on the question in 1981. Americans' current level of confidence in police protection—57%—is slightly higher than the average for all previous polls.

Since 1995, solid majorities of Americans have expressed confidence in police to protect them from violent crime, with the largest majority found in 1999, when 70% of Americans said they had confidence. Prior to 1995, trust in police among Americans ranged from 45% to 52%.

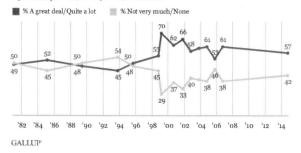

Americans' Confidence in Police to Protect Them From Violent Crime

How much confidence do you have in the ability of the police to protect you from violent crime -- a great deal, quite a lot, not very much, or none at all?

■ % A great deal/Quite a lot ■ % Not very much/None

GALLUP

Americans More Likely to Respect Police Than Express Confidence in Them

Six in 10 Americans (61%) say they have "a great deal" of respect for the police in their area, while 29% have "some" respect and 9% have "hardly any."

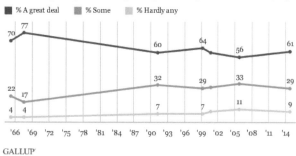

Americans' Respect for Police in Their Areas

How much respect do you have for the police in your area -- a great deal, some, or hardly any?

■ % A great deal ■ % Some ■ % Hardly any

GALLUP

Respect for police was significantly higher in the 1960s. Roughly three in four Americans (77%) had "a great deal" of respect for police in 1967. In subsequent polls, Americans' respect for police has ebbed, though it has always remained a majority sentiment. The current reading is up slightly from 56% in the prior measurement in 2005.

Bottom Line

The case stemming from the August shooting of black teen Michael Brown is yet another example of the strained relations between police and the black community in the U.S. With its mostly white police force in a largely black municipality and some citizens' allegations of prolonged police harassment, Ferguson has been at the center of conversations about the challenges many blacks face in their relationship with their local police.

While about half of nonwhites hold some higher degree of confidence in the local law enforcement to protect them, a sizable number don't have any faith in police at all.

Nonwhites' confidence level is at about the historical average—but this lack of improvement could trouble those who seek to strengthen the police's relationship with particular communities.

Survey Methods

Results for this Gallup poll are based on telephone interviews conducted Oct. 12–15, 2014, on the Gallup U.S. Daily survey, with a random sample of 1,017 adults, aged 18 and older, living in all 50 U.S. states and the District of Columbia. For results based on the total sample of national adults, the margin of sampling error is ±4 percentage points at the 95% confidence level. For results based on the total sample of 776 whites, the margin of sampling error is ±4 percentage points at the 95% confidence level. For results based on the total sample of 218 nonwhites, the margin of sampling error is ±8 percentage points at the 95% confidence level.

November 19, 2014
AMERICANS' VIEWS OF JOB MARKET HOLD STEADY

by Jeffrey M. Jones

PRINCETON, NJ—Americans' perceptions of the job market are holding steady, with 30% saying now is "a good time to find a quality job," matching the average since August. Although not positive on an absolute basis, that assessment is much brighter than was the case during periods of elevated unemployment from 2009 to 2012, including lows of 8% in November 2009 and November 2011. The high for finding a quality job was 48% in January 2007.

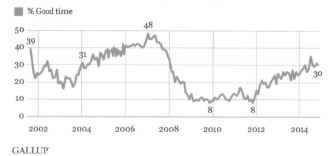

Thinking about the job situation in America today, would you say that it is now a good time or a bad time to find a quality job?

■ % Good time

GALLUP

Gallup has asked Americans to evaluate the job market monthly since October 2001, including the current data based on a Nov. 6–9 poll. This attitudinal measure differs from Gallup's tracking of the unemployment and underemployment rates based on respondent self-reports of their employment status and Gallup's Job Creation Index based on worker reports of hiring activity at their places of work. Although those three measures take different approaches to measuring the health of the U.S. job market, they all show a better situation than was the case in the recession and immediate post-recession years.

While Gallup has found a strong partisan influence on Americans' opinions of whether it is a good time to find a quality job, those perceptions are also a reflection of what is going on in the U.S. job market. The quality job measure has shown a strong relationship with changes in the Bureau of Labor Statistics' official unemployment measure, with Americans' perceptions of the job market tending to improve when unemployment is down and to decline when unemployment is up.

Specifically, when the unemployment rate averaged 4.6% in 2006 and 2007, more than four in 10 Americans thought it was a good time to find a quality job. When unemployment hovered around 9% in 2009 through 2011, barely more than one in 10

Americans thought it was a good time to find a quality job. In the last three years, as the unemployment rate has dropped more than two full percentage points, the percentage of Americans believing the job market is good has risen an average of six points per year, to 29% for 2014 to date.

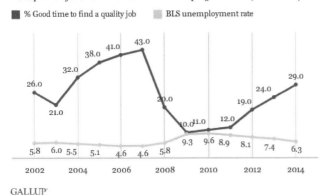

Perceptions of the Job Market and the Unemployment Rate, 2002-2014

■ % Good time to find a quality job ■ BLS unemployment rate

GALLUP

Although the unemployment rate and quality job measure are not perfectly correlated, the data suggest perceptions of the job market may improve further once the unemployment rate dips into the mid-5% range, and may surpass 40% believing it is a good time to find a quality job when the unemployment rate drops below 5%.

Implications

While Americans are not overly positive about the U.S. job market, they are much more upbeat about it than they were a few years ago when the unemployment rate was around 9%. It may take another one- to two-point reduction in the unemployment rate for Americans' perceptions to approach the highs near 40% that Gallup measured in 2006 and 2007.

The ceiling on the quality jobs measure could reach even higher, as surveys of working Americans conducted by the University of Connecticut and Rutgers University during the dot-com boom in the late 1990s and early 2000 found readings between 69% and 78%.

Survey Methods

Results for this Gallup poll are based on telephone interviews conducted Nov. 6–9, 2014, with a random sample of 828 adults, aged 18 and older, living in all 50 U.S. states and the District of Columbia. For results based on the total sample of national adults, the margin of sampling error is ±4 percentage points at the 95% confidence level.

November 19, 2014
IN U.S., RATINGS OF HEALTHCARE COVERAGE GENERALLY STEADY

by Rebecca Riffkin

WASHINGTON, D.C.—Americans' ratings of healthcare coverage in the U.S. have generally held steady, despite the opening of the healthcare exchanges in 2013 and the decline in the uninsured

rate this year. Thirty-eight percent of Americans now rate healthcare coverage in the U.S. as "excellent" or "good," within the range of the combined positive ratings seen since 2009, but more positive than what Gallup found from 2001 to 2008.

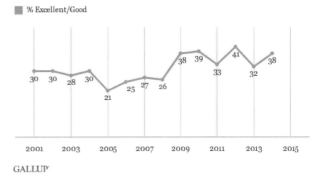

Ratings of Healthcare Coverage in U.S. Generally Stable Since 2009

Overall, how would you rate healthcare coverage in this country?

■ % Excellent/Good

GALLUP

Since 2001, Gallup has asked Americans each November to rate healthcare coverage in the country as a whole. Americans' positive ratings of coverage jumped from 26% in November 2008 to 38% November 2009, after President Barack Obama took office and vowed to make healthcare a priority. Ratings generally remained more upbeat after the Affordable Care Act was passed in 2010, though they did dip slightly in 2011 and 2013.

When positive ratings of healthcare coverage increased in 2009, they improved about equally among Republicans (including independents who lean Republican) and Democrats (including Democratic leaners). Since then, however, Republicans' ratings have waned, while Democrats' have increased. Democrats' positive ratings have risen particularly sharply in the past year, possibly because of the implementation of the healthcare exchanges, which have broadened Americans' access to health insurance. As a result, for the first time, Democrats and Republicans are about equally likely to rate healthcare coverage in the U.S. positively, 41% vs. 35%, respectively.

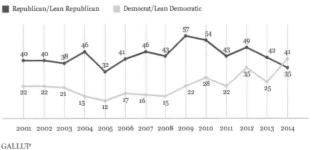

Americans' Positive Ratings of Healthcare Coverage in the U.S., by Party

% Excellent/Good

■ Republican/Lean Republican ■ Democrat/Lean Democratic

GALLUP

Similar Party Switch in Ratings on Quality of Healthcare

Broadly speaking, 54% of Americans overall rate the quality of healthcare in the U.S. as "excellent" or "good" in 2014, unchanged from last year and generally stable since Gallup began asking Americans to rate the quality of healthcare in 2001.

Just as Republicans' and Democrats' relative ratings of U.S. healthcare *coverage* have shifted during the past year, so have their ratings of U.S. healthcare *quality*. Fifty-eight percent of Democrats rate healthcare quality as excellent or good, compared with 52% of Republicans—a much smaller difference than in previous years. Prior to this year, Republicans and Republican leaners consistently rated the quality of healthcare more positively than Democrats and Democratic leaders, sometimes by margins of 20 percentage points or more, such as in 2012 and 2010.

Americans' Positive Ratings of Healthcare Quality in the U.S., by Party

Overall, how would you rate the quality of healthcare in this country?

% Excellent/Good

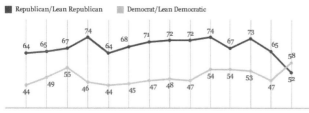

Democrats' ratings of healthcare quality generally moved above 50% beginning in 2010. In contrast, since 2012, Republicans' ratings have plummeted. This is likely a result of the passage of the healthcare law, which Democrats are far more likely than Republicans to support. Republicans may have been less likely to see the law as necessary or helpful, because they already were more likely than Democrats to rate U.S. healthcare positively.

Bottom Line

While more Americans rate healthcare coverage in the U.S. positively than did so prior to Obama's taking office in 2009, less than half say healthcare coverage is "excellent" or "good." This is despite a large drop in the U.S. uninsured rate in 2014, a sign that the Affordable Care Act is successfully meeting its goal of expanding coverage.

Political leanings are a strong predictor of how Americans feel about the healthcare law. Accordingly, the relative stability in ratings of national coverage since 2009 is driven almost entirely by Democrats' greater positivity, which has compensated for a sharp drop in positive reviews among Republicans over the same period.

Survey Methods

Results for this Gallup poll are based on telephone interviews conducted Nov. 6–9, 2014, with a random sample of 828 adults, aged 18 and older, living in all 50 U.S. states and the District of Columbia. For results based on the total sample of national adults, the margin of sampling error is ±4 percentage points at the 95% confidence level.

Each sample of national adults includes a minimum quota of 50% cellphone respondents and 50% landline respondents, with additional minimum quotas by time zone within region. Landline and cellular telephone numbers are selected using random-digit-dial methods.

November 20, 2014
MAJORITY SAY NOT GOV'T DUTY TO PROVIDE HEALTHCARE FOR ALL

by Frank Newport

PRINCETON, NJ—For the third consecutive year, a majority of Americans (52%) agree with the position that it is not the federal government's responsibility to ensure that all Americans have healthcare coverage. Prior to the start of Barack Obama's presidency in 2009, a majority of Americans consistently took the opposite view.

The Role of the Federal Government in Ensuring Americans Have Healthcare Coverage

Do you think it is the responsibility of the federal government to make sure all Americans have healthcare coverage, or is that not the responsibility of the federal government?

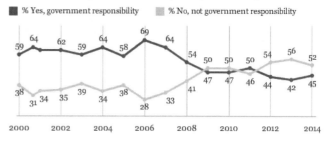

The most recent data were collected in Gallup's annual Health and Healthcare poll, conducted Nov. 6–9. Gallup first asked this question in 2000, when 59% of Americans said it was the federal government's responsibility to make sure all Americans have healthcare. This sentiment peaked at 69% in 2006. Americans' attitudes began to shift in the 2008 poll, conducted just after Obama was elected, and became evenly divided after Obama took office in 2009. During this time, Republicans and independents became more likely to say universal healthcare was not the government's responsibility, most probably in reaction to Obama's campaign promise that he was going to attempt to do just that. This non-government-involvement view became more pronounced in 2012 and has been the majority opinion in the U.S. over the past three years.

Do you think it is the responsibility of the federal government to make sure all Americans have healthcare coverage, or is that not the responsibility of the federal government?

	Yes	No
	%	%
National adults	45	52
Republicans/Leaners	24	75
Democrats/Leaners	70	28
Approve of Affordable Care Act	79	19
Disapprove of Affordable Care Act	22	76

Nov. 6-9, 2014

GALLUP

The political divide on this fundamental issue is evident—although not universal. While seven in 10 Democrats and Democratic leaners agree that providing healthcare coverage to all is the federal government's job, three-quarters of Republicans and Republican leaners disagree.

The federal government's role in ensuring healthcare for all of its citizens is at the heart of the political controversy over the Affordable Care Act—given the mandate it places on individuals to participate in the system. Views of the ACA are themselves highly partisan, making it no surprise that 79% of those who approve of the ACA also say it is the government's responsibility to ensure universal healthcare, while 76% of those who disapprove of the ACA say the opposite.

Differences in views of government's role in health coverage by race and age mirror the political orientations of these populations. Two-thirds of nonwhites and 60% of 18- to 34-year-olds, both significantly Democratic constituencies, believe it is the government's responsibility. This sentiment drops well below the majority level among whites and those aged 35 and older, who tend to be more Republican. Even among the group of Americans aged 55 and older, many of whom have government-provided Medicare but who lean Republican politically, 58% say it is not the government's responsibility to provide healthcare.

Do you think it is the responsibility of the federal government to make sure all Americans have healthcare coverage, or is that not the responsibility of the federal government?

	Yes	No
	%	%
National adults	45	52
Whites	36	62
Nonwhites	66	31
18 to 34	60	39
35 to 54	40	57
55+	39	58

Nov. 6-9, 2014

GALLUP

Bottom Line

Americans' attitudes about the federal government's role in ensuring that all Americans have healthcare coverage shifted significantly after Obama was elected in 2008 and first took office in 2009. Given that Obama campaigned on a pledge to expand the government's role in ensuring healthcare coverage for Americans, and then pushed for and obtained passage of the landmark ACA in 2010, these tangible manifestations of a larger government role in healthcare most likely created a significant backlash, particularly among Republicans and independents.

Americans' attitudes about the government's role in ensuring healthcare coverage help explain their reactions to the ACA. The act's proponents have pointed out that Americans favor a number of the act's provisions when tested in isolation, and that the act has already lowered the nation's uninsured rate. Yet a majority of Americans continue to say they disapprove of it, even as the ACA is making progress toward its stated goal of expanding health insurance coverage. That more than half of Americans think it is not the government's role to make sure Americans have healthcare

coverage suggests that opposition to the ACA may be centered more on its philosophical underpinnings, rather than on the specifics of its actual provisions and outcomes.

Survey Methods

Results for this Gallup poll are based on telephone interviews conducted Nov. 6–9, 2014, with a random sample of 828 adults, aged 18 and older, living in all 50 U.S. states and the District of Columbia. For results based on the total sample of national adults, the margin of sampling error is ±4 percentage points at the 95% confidence level.

November 20, 2014
AMERICANS' RATINGS OF CDC DOWN AFTER EBOLA CRISIS

by Jeffrey M. Jones

PRINCETON, NJ—Americans' ratings of the job being done by the Centers for Disease Control (CDC) are down significantly from last year, from 60% saying it is doing an "excellent" or "good" job to 50%. None of the other eight government agencies measured in both years showed a decline.

Changes in Government Agency Job Ratings
Figures are the percentage rating each agency as doing an "excellent" or "good" job

	May 2013	November 2014	Change
	%	%	pct. pts.
The Centers for Disease Control and Prevention, or the CDC	60	50	-10
The Food and Drug Administration, or FDA	45	45	0
The Department of Homeland Security	46	48	2
The Federal Bureau of Investigation, or the FBI	55	58	3
The Environmental Protection Agency, or EPA	41	44	3
The Federal Reserve Board	33	38	5
NASA, the U.S. space agency	42	50	8
The Central Intelligence Agency, or the CIA	40	49	9
The Internal Revenue Service, or the IRS	27	41	14

GALLUP

Americans' lower job evaluations of the CDC come as the agency continues to deal with the threat posed by the deadly Ebola virus. Although Ebola has largely been confined to Africa, there have been four confirmed cases in the United States, including two nurses assigned to treat the first U.S. Ebola patient in Dallas. The nurses have now recovered, but their contracting the virus generated criticism of the government's response to the threat.

Republicans' views of the CDC have worsened since last year—more so than Democrats' views have—perhaps because the recent criticism of the agency has come under a Democratic presidential administration. In May 2013, 71% of Democrats and 65% of Republicans said the CDC was doing an excellent or good job. Since then, Democrats' ratings have fallen eight percentage points to 63% while Republicans have dropped 25 points to 40%.

Now that the possibility of a widespread Ebola outbreak in the U.S. seems less likely than it did a month ago, the CDC's image may actually be recovering from lower levels when it was the dominant news story. A CBS News poll from October asking the same question found 37% of Americans saying the CDC was doing an excellent or good job, 13 points lower than in the current Gallup poll.

Just as the CDC's image appears to be recovering, so has the IRS' from the scandal in 2013 that sent its ratings tumbling. After the IRS was accused of targeting Republican-aligned groups for greater scrutiny when applying for tax exempt status, its job ratings fell from 40% excellent or good in 2009 to 27% in May 2013. Now, their ratings have recovered to their prior level, at 41%.

U.S. Postal Service Gets High Marks, VA Rated Poorly

In addition to updating the nine agencies measured last year, the Nov. 11–12 poll included first-time ratings of four other agencies—the U.S. Postal Service, the Secret Service, the FEMA, and the Veterans' Administration, or VA. The U.S. Postal Service received the most positive job ratings of any of the 13 agencies rated, and the VA the worst, while the Secret Service and IRS came in near the bottom of the list.

Ratings of Job Government Agencies are Doing

How would you rate the job being done by – []? Would you say it is doing an excellent, good, only fair, or poor job?

	Excellent/ Good	Only fair	Poor
	%	%	%
The U.S. Postal Service	72	20	8
The Federal Bureau of Investigation, or the FBI	58	27	8
The Centers for Disease Control and Prevention, or the CDC	50	30	16
NASA, the U.S. space agency	50	25	8
The Central Intelligence Agency, or the CIA	49	28	11
The Department of Homeland Security	48	32	16
The Federal Emergency Management Agency, or FEMA	47	31	14
The Food and Drug Administration, or FDA	45	34	19
The Environmental Protection Agency, or EPA	44	32	20
The Secret Service	43	30	16
The Internal Revenue Service, or the IRS	41	29	27
The Federal Reserve Board	38	35	14
The Veterans Administration, or VA	29	29	35

Nov. 11-12, 2014

GALLUP

Even with the decline in the CDC's ratings, it still rates among the most highly regarded agencies, joining the postal service, FBI and NASA with 50% or more of Americans saying it is doing an excellent or good job. The CIA, Department of Homeland Security and FEMA fall just below 50% positive ratings.

The VA is the only one of the 13 government agencies to have "poor" ratings that exceed its "excellent"/"good" ratings. The VA faced widespread criticism this year for prolonged delays in medical care for veterans and allegations that managers falsified records to cover up those delays and gain incentives for speedy care.

There are not large party differences in ratings of the agencies, averaging an 11-point gap in Democrats' versus Republicans' ratings of the 13 agencies, usually with Democrats' ratings exceeding those of Republicans. The largest differences come in evaluations of the IRS, with a 26-point difference in excellent or good ratings (56% among Democrats and 30% among Republicans), and the CDC, with a 23-point difference.

Implications

Americans appear to be responsive to news that reflects on government agencies, as evidenced by the drop in the image of the CDC this year, and the drop in the image of the IRS last year. The CDC's image already appears to be recovering, and, like the image of the IRS, may return to prior pre-crisis levels once the controversy subsides.

Although Americans have highly negative opinions of the federal government overall, they are more likely to give positive than highly negative ratings for many of the agencies that make up the federal government. Of the 13 agencies tested in the latest poll, Americans gave only the VA a net negative rating, and that may very well be a much more negative image than was the case in the past due to the controversy over medical care for veterans.

Survey Methods

Results for this Gallup poll are based on telephone interviews conducted Nov. 11–12, 2014, on the Gallup U.S. Daily survey, with a random sample of 1,020 adults, aged 18 and older, living in all 50 U.S. states and the District of Columbia. For results based on the total sample of national adults, the margin of sampling error is ±4 percentage points at the 95% confidence level.

November 21, 2014
AMERICANS RATE POSTAL SERVICE HIGHEST OF 13 MAJOR AGENCIES

by Steve Ander and Art Swift

WASHINGTON, D.C.—While the U.S. Postal Service has recently withstood a barrage of negative attention, from getting hacked to announcing continued multibillion-dollar deficits, it enjoys the most positive image of 13 high-profile government agencies Gallup recently tested. Younger Americans are more likely than older Americans to review the Postal Service favorably.

Approval of U.S. Postal Service, by Age

How would you rate the job being done by the U.S. Postal Service -- excellent, good, only fair or poor?

	% Excellent/Good
18 to 29	81
30 to 49	75
50 to 64	65
65+	65

Nov. 11-12, 2014

GALLUP

The Postal Service is the nation's second-largest employer, and an agency virtually all Americans interact with to some extent in their daily lives. Younger Americans, who may have accumulated less experience with the service, have a very positive image of the job it is doing. All age groups give solid approval ratings to the Postal Service—however, their ratings decline from 81% among the youngest age group to 65% among the oldest.

Seniors' ratings of the Postal Service, however, still exceed the ratings they give to all other federal government agencies tested in the Nov. 11–12 survey.

No Gender Gap Overall, or by Age

Overall, 73% of women and 70% of men in the U.S. rate the job the Postal Service is doing as "excellent" or "good." Additionally, although Gallup documents clear generational differences in the Postal Service's image, men and women within each age group give the agency similar ratings. Among those under 50 years of age, 80% of women and 75% of men give it positive reviews. And there is virtually no difference in men's and women's views of the Postal Service among those 50 and older, with just under two-thirds of each group rating it favorably.

Approval of U.S. Postal Service, by Age and Gender

How would you rate the job being done by the U.S. Postal Service -- excellent, good, only fair or poor?

	% Excellent/Good
Women overall	73
Men overall	70
Women under 50	80
Men under 50	75
Women 50+	65
Men 50+	64

Nov. 11-12, 2014

GALLUP'

Implications

Discovering that Americans rate the U.S. Postal Service ahead of 12 other major government agencies could be good news for an organization that has been battered by bad publicity for quite some time. Americans are probably more likely, to some degree, to come into direct contact with the Postal Service and the IRS than with any of the other agencies tested—and clearly that experience has resulted in a very positive image for the service, compared with Americans' negative image of the IRS.

While the post office has been forced to address concerns over competitiveness and budget woes by consolidating installations, limiting Saturday delivery and increasing revenue through raising stamp prices, the overall image of the agency has remained remarkably positive. This reservoir of goodwill may serve the Postal Service well as it strives to adapt to the changing world in which electronic communication and commerce are rapidly replacing the traditional mailed letter. While more than six in 10 Americans overall back cost-cutting measures, less than a majority of the youngest age group say they support eliminating Saturday delivery. Perhaps not surprisingly, this youngest segment has the highest approval rating of the Postal Service. One might expect older Americans to be the age group viewing the service most favorably, at least out of nostalgia. The fact that the opposite is true could mean that the agency has the opportunity to establish itself as a trusted brand with this new generation, putting the baggage of any tarnished image with older Americans behind them.

A possible explanation for reconciling these opinions may be the difference in how these age groups interact with the post office.

A recent Gallup report shows that 18- to 49-year-olds are nearly universal in their reporting of Internet usage on a day-to-day basis, while over a third of older Americans report not using the Internet. Thus, it is also possible that while younger Americans may be mailing and receiving fewer traditional letters, they could be more connected to the Postal Service as a result of e-commerce and receiving goods purchased online. Older Americans are more likely to consume Postal Service goods and services in person and to receive more hard copy mail such as bills and cards. Receiving packages purchased online may be a more positive customer experience than performing interactions in person at postal locations—thus providing a reason why younger Americans have a more positive view of the Postal Service. In fact, from the standpoint of the recipient, the Postal Service may be making even more package deliveries than customers expect, as it will frequently deliver millions of packages for UPS and FedEx in their "last mile," thereby increasing these touchpoints and reinforcing these ratings over time.

With the country becoming more reliant on the Internet and rapidly embracing e-commerce, the increased amount of shipping and packaging could prove even more beneficial for the Postal Service both in its image ratings and financial performance. If the way in which Americans consume the agency's services affects its image, future ratings could trend upward as the market shifts. And the Postal Service has actually seen significant growth and profitability in its shipping and packaging business year over year. The agency's current leadership team has recognized this trend and opportunity and has even partnered with Amazon to deliver packages on Sundays. In the meantime, the Postal Service could benefit from learning more about how to further convert these positive feelings into increased share of wallet and customer retention among the younger segment of the population, and from determining how to optimize the interactions that may impact older Americans' perceptions.

Survey Methods

Results for this Gallup poll are based on telephone interviews conducted Nov. 11–12, 2014, on the Gallup U.S. Daily survey, with a random sample of 1,020 adults, aged 18 and older, living in all 50 U.S. states and the District of Columbia. For results based on the total sample of national adults, the margin of sampling error is ±4 percentage points at the 95% confidence level.

November 21, 2014
MOST AMERICANS STILL SEE CRIME UP OVER LAST YEAR

by Justin McCarthy

WASHINGTON, D.C.—A majority of Americans say there is more crime in the U.S. than there was a year ago, as is typical for this long-term Gallup trend. The current 63% of Americans who believe this is well below the recent high of 74% in 2009 and is one of the lowest percentages since 2004. However, it is still much higher than the historic low points between 1999 and 2001.

As the percentage of Americans who say crime is up hits one of its lowest points in the past 10 years, more than one in five Americans (21%) say crime is down. This is the highest since 2005. Meanwhile, 9% of Americans say the level of crime has remained the same.

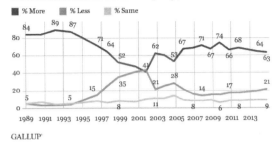

Perceptions of Crime in the U.S., 1989-2014

Is there more crime in the U.S. than there was a year ago, or less?

■ % More   ■ % Less   ■ % Same

GALLUP

Americans are historically less likely to believe crime is up in their area than believe this to be the case nationally, and that remains true today, with 44% saying local crime is up. Nearly one in three Americans (32%) say crime is down in their area, while about one in five (19%) say it has remained the same. These figures have not changed much over the past decade, with each of this year's figures just a percentage point off from its respective 10-year average.

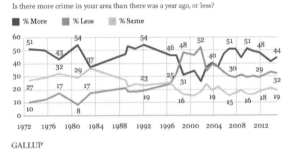

Perceptions of Crime in Local Area, 1972-2014

Is there more crime in your area than there was a year ago, or less?

■ % More   ■ % Less   ■ % Same

GALLUP

Perceptions of Crime Still Detached From Reality

With a handful of exceptions, government statistics show serious crime has decreased nearly every year from 1994 through 2010. According to the U.S. Department of Justice, Bureau of Justice Statistics, the overall violent crime rate for rape, sexual assault, robbery, aggravated assault and simple assault fell from 80 victimizations per 1,000 persons in 1994 to 19 per 1,000 in 2010. In the first decade of that trend, public opinion followed, with the percentage perceiving crime was up falling from 87% in 1993 to 41% in 2001. But this shot up to 62% in 2002—around the time of the Washington, D.C.-area sniper shootings—and has remained fairly high ever since.

Though serious crime did increase in 2011 and 2012, Americans' perceptions of crime did not grow in subsequent polls, underscoring that federal crime statistics have not been highly relevant to the public's crime perceptions in recent years.

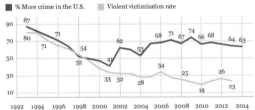

U.S. Violent Crime Rate^ vs. Americans' Perception of Crime Rate vs. Year Ago

■ % More crime in the U.S.   ■ Violent victimization rate

^ Violent crime rate is number of victimizations per 1,000 persons that occurred during the year. Source: Bureau of Justice Statistics, National Crime Victimization Survey, 1996-2013

GALLUP

Bottom Line

For more than a decade, Gallup has found the majority of Americans believing crime is up, although actual crime statistics have largely shown the crime rate continuing to come down from the highs in the 1990s and earlier.

Compared with previous decades, perceptions of crime in the U.S. have calmed somewhat. Still, majorities of Americans maintain that there has been an increase in crime from the previous year. Because Americans are more pessimistic about crime in the U.S. as a whole as opposed to their own localities, this could suggest that many base their views on what they hear about crimes that take place outside of their own hometowns. Some argue that consumption of news media plays a role in this by exposing Americans to crimes that they may perceive as more widespread than actually is the case.

But even in their own localities, sizable portions of the population view crime in their area as having increased over the past year, and at several points over the past few decades, majorities have held these views.

Survey Methods

Results for this Gallup poll are based on telephone interviews conducted Oct. 12–15, 2014, on the Gallup U.S. Daily survey, with a random sample of 1,017 adults, aged 18 and older, living in all 50 U.S. states and the District of Columbia. For results based on the total sample of national adults, the margin of sampling error is ±4 percentage points at the 95% confidence level.

November 24, 2014
AMERICANS' PROJECTED HOLIDAY SPENDING UP SLIGHTLY FROM 2013

by Lydia Saad

PRINCETON, NJ—Gallup's latest measure of Americans' Christmas spending plans finds U.S. adults projecting they will spend an average of $720 on gifts this year, up slightly from their $704 estimate in November 2013, pointing to an OK holiday season for retailers.

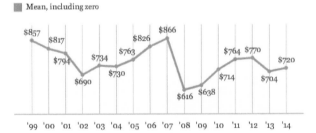

Americans' Christmas Spending Estimate in November of Each Year

■ Mean, including zero

Question: Roughly how much money do you think you personally will spend on Christmas gifts this year?

GALLUP

Overall, a quarter of Americans plan to spend $1,000 or more on gifts, and another 21% will spend at least $500. At the other end of the spectrum, 24% expect to spend less than $250, and 15% will spend between $250 and $499. Nine percent of Americans tell Gallup this year that they won't spend anything or don't celebrate Christmas.

Americans' Christmas Spending Estimate

Roughly how much money do you think you personally will spend on Christmas gifts this year?

	Nov 19-20, 2014
	%
$1,000 or more	25
$500 to $999	21
$250 to $499	15
$100 to $249	19
Less than $100	5
None/Don't celebrate	9
Not sure	6
Average (including zero)	$720
Average (excluding zero)	$790

GALLUP'

Shoppers May Be Getting Cold Feet

Though up from 2013, the current spending estimate is well below the November reading in several earlier years, particularly in 2006 and 2007, when the figure exceeded $800. It is also below what Gallup found in October, when Americans predicted they would spend $781 this holiday season.

The $61 decline in Americans' forecasted spending over the past month is similar to the $82 decline that occurred last year, and might be seen as something of a "cold feet" syndrome. Although Americans' spending estimate increased between October and November in 2011 and held steady in 2010, Gallup saw similar declines in 2006 and 2007. The steeper declines in 2008 and 2009 may have related more directly to mounting economic problems in the country at those times.

Americans' Average Christmas Spending Estimates for October and November of Each Year

	October	November	Change
2014	$781	$720	-$61
2013	$786	$704	-$82
2012	--	$770	
2011	$712	$764	+$52
2010	$715	$714	-$1
2009	$740	$638	-$102
2008	$801	$616	-$185
2007	$909	$866	-$43
2006	$907	$826	-$81
2005	--	$763	
2004	--	$730	
2003	--	$734	
2002	$695	$690	-$5
2001	--	$794	
2000	--	$817	
1999	--	$857	

Averages include zero, for those who plan to spend nothing

GALLUP'

Spending on Track to Increase by Roughly 3%

According to Gallup's modeling of how prior years' spending forecasts compare with the final November–December retail sales figures for each year, Americans' latest Christmas spending estimate points to an increase of between 2.2% and 3.5% in U.S. holiday retail sales, with the most likely outcome around 3%. Even at the low end, this would be an improvement over 2013, but this isn't saying much, because last year's sales were up only 1.5%, according to the Census Bureau's GAFO (General merchandise, Apparel and accessories, Furniture and Other sales) retail sales estimates.

Gallup Christmas Spending Estimate vs. U.S. Holiday Sales — Annual Percentage Changes

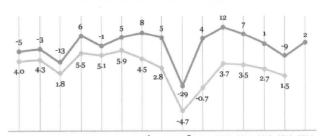

Gallup data represent the annual percentage change in Americans' average spending estimate.

U.S. retail data are based on the Census Bureau's GAFO retail sales data, which reflect sales at general merchandise, apparel, furniture and other retail stores.

*Gallup data for 2014 are based on final November measure.

GALLUP'

Since posting a solid 3.7% gain in 2010 after the highly anemic recession-era sales of 2008 and 2009, holiday retail sales have grown by smaller amounts each year. Thus, given last year's disappointing sales gains, an increase of 2% or larger may be a welcome sign for retailers, who may be wondering if the ho-ho-ho has gone out of Christmas shopping altogether.

Bottom Line

Barring a major economic crisis or winter weather event that curbs Americans' willingness to shop, consumers seem on track to outlay a bit more on Christmas gifts this year than they did in 2013. But even if consumers' spending reaches the high end of the range indicated by their current spending forecast, U.S. retail sales growth for November and December would still barely hit the 14-year average of 3.1%, suggesting Christmas sales still aren't what they used to be.

Survey Methods

Results for this Gallup poll are based on telephone interviews conducted Nov. 19–20, 2014, on the Gallup U.S. Daily survey, with a random sample of 1,019 adults, aged 18 and older, living in all 50 U.S. states and the District of Columbia. For results based on the total sample of national adults, the margin of sampling error is ±4 percentage points at the 95% confidence level.

IN U.S., 37% DO NOT FEEL SAFE WALKING AT NIGHT NEAR HOME

by Andrew Dugan

WASHINGTON, D.C.—Fewer than four in 10 adults in the U.S. (37%) say there is an area within a mile of where they live where they would be afraid to walk alone at night, similar to Americans' attitudes over the last decade and a half. Most Americans continue to feel safe in their immediate communities, with 63% saying they would not be afraid to walk alone there at night.

Americans' Feelings of Safety in Walking Alone at Night in Their Communities

Is there any area near where you live -- that is, within a mile -- where you would be afraid to walk alone at night?

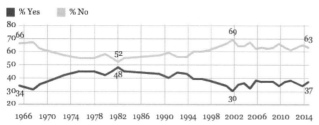

GALLUP

These results come from Gallup's annual Crime survey, conducted Oct. 12–15. The 37% of U.S. adults who say they would not feel safe walking alone near their home is in line with the historical average for the question (39%), which dates back to 1965. But responses to this question have not always been so stable. In the 1970s and 1980s, there was a steep rise in the percentage of U.S. adults feeling unsafe in their communities, culminating in the 1982 survey, when nearly *half* (48%) of Americans said they were afraid to walk alone at night in their neighborhood.

In tandem with plunging crime rates in the 1990s, Americans increasingly reported feeling safe in walking alone in their area at night. By 2001, a record low of 30% said they would not feel safe walking alone at night, and the percentage has risen only marginally since then.

Gallup's World Poll asks a similar question: "Do you feel safe walking alone at night in the city or area where you live?" In 2013, 75% of Americans answered affirmatively, which is higher than the global average of 64% for all 133 countries surveyed. The U.S. score is also slightly higher than average for wealthy countries in the Organization for Economic Co-operation and Development (69%).

"Gender Gap" in Security Still Exists

Nearly half of all women, 45%, say they do not feel safe walking alone at night, compared with 27% of men. Though substantial, this 18-percentage-point "safety gap" between the genders is in line with historical trends, and larger gulfs have been measured in the recent past. For instance, in 2010, 50% of women said they did not feel safe walking at home at night, compared with 22% of men, for a difference of 28 points.

This is not to say the gender safety gap hasn't narrowed somewhat in this era of lower crime rates. In 1982, more than six in 10 women (64%) said they did not feel safe walking alone at night, compared with 31% of men—a 33-point gap.

Americans' Feelings of Safety in Walking Alone at Night in Their Communities, by Gender

% No, do not feel safe

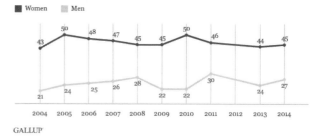

GALLUP

The previously mentioned Gallup World Poll question about perceptions of safety also finds that the gaps in the U.S. are not atypical for high-income countries; still, those results show that the U.S. has one of the largest gaps between men and women saying they don't feel safe walking alone at night.

Young, Lower-Income Feel Less Safe Walking Alone

Other groups also feel less secure when walking alone at night, including young adults aged 18 to 29 and individuals earning less than $30,000 annually (compared with those making at least $75,000). Reasons for their relative sense of insecurity when walking alone may be that these groups are more likely to live in urban areas, or to live in lower-income housing where crime may be more prevalent than in more secluded high-income housing.

Not Feeling Safe Walking Alone at Night

Is there any area near where you live -- that is, within a mile -- where you would be afraid to walk alone at night?

	% Yes, afraid
18 to 29	48
30 to 49	35
50 to 64	34
65 or older	31
Household income less than $30,000	40
$30,000 to less than $75,000	37
$75,000 or more	31

Oct. 12-15, 2014

GALLUP

Bottom Line

While the percentage of Americans saying they do not feel safe walking alone within a mile of their home at night has remained steady over the past decade, there has been a considerable shift in Americans' views on this question over the past 30 years. While falling crime rates have not necessarily affected Americans' perceptions of crime on a national level, they have been felt in neighborhoods and communities across the country.

Nonetheless, women are among the groups that feel the least safe, suggesting the benefits of falling crime rates have not been evenly felt by all. Other groups, such as the young and lower-income individuals, are also more likely to worry about their own safety.

Survey Methods

Results for this Gallup poll are based on telephone interviews conducted Oct. 12–15, 2014, with a random sample of 1,017 adults, aged 18 and older, living in all 50 U.S. states and the District of Columbia. For results based on the total sample of national adults, the margin of sampling error is ±4 percentage points at the 95% confidence level.

November 25, 2014
OBAMA APPROVAL DROPS AMONG WORKING-CLASS WHITES

by Frank Newport

PRINCETON, NJ—President Barack Obama's job approval rating among white non-college graduates is at 27% so far in 2014, 14 percentage points lower than among white college graduates. This is the largest yearly gap between these two groups since Obama took office. These data underscore the magnitude of the Democratic Party's problem with working-class whites, among whom Obama lost in the 2012 presidential election, and among whom Democratic House candidates lost in the 2014 U.S. House voting by 30 points.

Obama Job Approval Ratings, by Education

% Approve, among non-Hispanic whites only

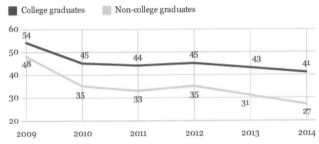

Data for 2014 collected January through October

GALLUP'

Obama's overall job approval rating has dropped throughout the first six years of his administration, and this downward trajectory is seen both among white Americans who are college graduates and those who are not. But the gap between his approval ratings among college-educated and non-college-educated whites has grown. It was six points in 2009, when Obama had the overall highest ratings of his administration, then expanded to 10 points in 2010 and to 12 points in 2013. The gap between these two groups is at its highest yet, at 14 points so far this year.

Whites in general constitute a political challenge for Democrats and the president given their Republican orientation, as evidenced by Obama's job approval ratings so far this year of 84% among blacks, 64% among Asians, 53% among Hispanics and 32% among whites. About two-thirds of adult whites have not graduated from college, making working-class whites a particularly important group politically because of its sheer size.

Gender and Age

Democrats and the president do better among white women than among white men, and this gender gap is evident among those who are college graduates and those who are not. Obama's approval

rating ranges from a high of 45% among white female college graduates to a low of 25% among white male non-college graduates. The eight-point gender gap among white college graduates is twice that among white non-college graduates.

Obama Job Approval Ratings, by Education and Gender

% Approve, among non-Hispanic whites only

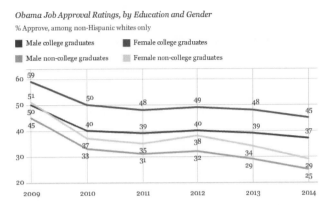

Data for 2014 collected January through October

GALLUP'

The larger decline in approval among non-college graduates than among college graduates is evident among both men and women.

Among whites, Obama does better with younger Americans than with those who are older, but the education gap is evident across all age groups. Approval among 18- to 29-year-old white college graduates is 17 points higher than among 18- to 29-year-old white non-college graduates. Gaps by education are somewhat smaller among those aged 50 and older.

Obama Job Approval Ratings, by Education and Age

% Approve, among non-Hispanic whites only

	College graduates	Non-college graduates
	%	%
18 to 29	47	30
30 to 49	40	24
50 to 64	41	28
65+	40	28

January-October 2014

GALLUP'

Implications

Given its sheer size, the working-class white population in the U.S. is of keen importance to politicians and strategists on both sides of the aisle, and many discussions and strategy sessions have focused on the complex set of attitudes and life positions which, as evidenced by these data, have pushed this group further from the Democratic president over the past six years. Discussions have also focused on the value of a populist approach to appeal to these voters' economic situations, and the impact of the cultural positions taken by a Democratic Party that has as one of its core segments a coalition of minority race and ethnic group members, along with liberals and a smaller segment of highly educated whites. These discussions will continue as the 2016 election campaigns ramp up in the coming two years. At the moment, working-class whites exhibit weak support for the

Democrats and their president, and it's not clear how likely that is to change as time goes on.

Survey Methods

Results for this Gallup poll are based on telephone interviews conducted on the Gallup U.S. Daily survey from 2009 through October 2014, with random samples of approximately 355,000 adults, aged 18 and older, living in all 50 U.S. states and the District of Columbia for each of the 2009–2012 yearly samples; approximately 175,000 adults for 2013; and 149,150 adults for January–October 2014. For results based on the total sample of national adults in each yearly average, the margin of sampling error is ±1 percentage point at the 95% confidence level.

November 26, 2014
AMERICANS' EFFORT TO LOSE WEIGHT STILL TRAILS DESIRE

by Justin McCarthy

WASHINGTON, D.C.—As has generally been the case for the past decade, Americans continue to be about twice as likely to want to lose weight (51%) as to say they are seriously trying to do so (26%).

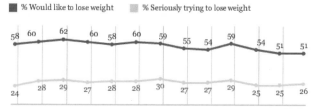

Americans' Weight-Loss Desires and Behaviors, 2002-2014

Would you like to lose weight, stay at your present weight or put on weight?
At this time, are you seriously trying to lose weight?

■ % Would like to lose weight   ■ % Seriously trying to lose weight

GALLUP'

However, despite the increasing focus on the negative consequences of obesity, the percentage of Americans who would like to lose weight has gone down, not up, since the early 2000s, while the percentage saying they are making a serious effort to lose it has been consistent. The margin between those who want to lose weight and those who are trying has shrunk an additional point from last year, reaching its smallest yet of 25 percentage points.

These results are from Gallup's Health and Healthcare survey, conducted Nov. 6–9. Gallup has asked American adults about their weight and their attitudes toward it since 1990, and on a yearly basis since 2002.

Desire to lose weight was relatively consistent between 2002 and 2008, at about the 60% level—peaking at 62% in 2004. But this desire has flagged in recent years, down to its lowest level of 51% in the past two years. The percentage of Americans who would like to stay at their present weight has varied even less, ranging from 32% to 41% since 1990. The current reading of 40% is one of the highest percentages of Americans who are happy with their weight since 1996.

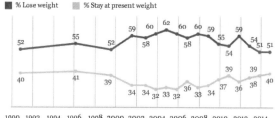

Americans' Attitudes Toward Their Weight

Would you like to lose weight, stay at your present weight or put on weight?

■ % Lose weight   ■ % Stay at present weight

GALLUP'

Americans' Ideas of Personal Weight Don't Match Obesity Statistics

Americans' descriptions of their current weight situation are also at odds with reality. Although slightly more than half of Americans would like to lose weight, only 36% describe themselves as either "somewhat" or "very overweight." More than half of Americans say their current weight is "about right" (56%). This doesn't mesh with actual figures. In reality, 35% of Americans are overweight, and 28% are obese.

Mirroring the decline in the percentage who say they want to lose weight, Americans have become more likely to say they their weight is "about right" in recent years, peaking at 60% in 2012. At the same time, Americans have become less likely to say they are very or somewhat overweight. In 1990, 48% admitted to being overweight to some degree, but this fell to 39% by 1999. This figure has hovered in the 30s since 2009.

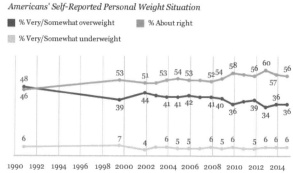

Americans' Self-Reported Personal Weight Situation

■ % Very/Somewhat overweight   ■ % About right
■ % Very/Somewhat underweight

GALLUP'

Ideal vs. Actual Weight

Although most Americans don't describe themselves as overweight, six in 10 say they are heavier than they would like to be, based on self-reports of their actual weight and ideal weight. A majority of men (56%) and a greater majority of women (65%) are at least a pound heavier than what they describe as their ideal weight.

Americans' Current Weight Compared With Ideal Weight

Actual/Ideal weight is self-reported and in pounds

	Under ideal weight	At ideal weight	Over ideal weight
National adults	15%	20%	60%
Men	19%	21%	56%
Women	10%	19%	65%

Nov. 6-9, 2014

GALLUP'

On average, American women are further (20 pounds) from their ideal weight than men (12 pounds). While the average ideal weight for a man is 182 pounds, the average actual self-reported weight is 193 pounds. Women's average ideal weight is 137 pounds, while 157 pounds is their self-reported average actual weight. It is not known how accurately Americans report their weight; if their reports tend to be lower than reality, the discrepancy between actual and ideal could be higher than these reports indicate.

Americans' Average Actual vs. Ideal Weight

Actual/Ideal weight is self-reported and in pounds

	Average actual weight	Average ideal weight	Difference between actual and ideal
National adults	175	159	16
Men	193	182	11
Women	157	137	20

Nov. 6-9, 2014

GALLUP

Bottom Line

These data show several interesting and important discrepancies in the ways that Americans look at their weight situations. For whatever their personal reasons, about half of Americans want to lose weight, while only half of that percentage are actively trying to. Additionally, only a little more than a third of Americans describe themselves as overweight, even though the majority say that their ideal weight is less than their actual weight.

These results suggest that many Americans don't want to present or view themselves as overweight even while being more forthcoming about the fact that they weigh more than their ideal weight and would like to lose weight.

Perhaps most importantly, the longer-term trends in these results show that fewer Americans now than in the past say they are overweight, and fewer say they want to lose weight—even though the negative medical effects of being overweight have increasingly become evident.

Survey Methods

Results for this Gallup poll are based on telephone interviews conducted Nov. 6–9, 2014, on the Gallup U.S. Daily survey, with a random sample of 828 adults, aged 18 and older, living in all 50 U.S. states and the District of Columbia. For results based on the total sample of national adults, the margin of sampling error is ±4 percentage points at the 95% confidence level. For results based on the total sample of 430 men, the margin of sampling error is ±6 percentage points at the 95% confidence level. For results based on the total sample of 398 women, the margin of sampling error is ±6 percentage points at the 95% confidence level.

November 28, 2014
COST STILL A BARRIER BETWEEN AMERICANS AND MEDICAL CARE

by Rebecca Riffkin

WASHINGTON, D.C.—One in three Americans say they have put off getting medical treatment that they or their family members need because of cost. Although this percentage is in line with the roughly 30% figures seen in recent years, it is among the highest readings in the 14-year history of Gallup asking the question.

Percentage of Americans Putting Off Medical Treatment Because of Cost

Within the last 12 months, have you or a member of your family put off any sort of medical treatment because of the cost you would have to pay?

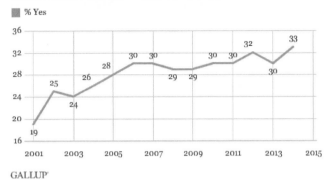

GALLUP

Since 2001, Gallup has asked Americans each November if they have put off any sort of medical treatment for themselves or their families in the past 12 months. Last year, many hoped that the opening of the government healthcare exchanges and the resulting increase in the number of Americans with health insurance would enable more people to seek medical treatment. Despite a drop in the uninsured rate, a slightly higher percentage of Americans than in previous years report having put off medical treatment, suggesting that the Affordable Care Act has not immediately affected this measure.

Among Americans with varying types of medical coverage (including no coverage), uninsured Americans are still the most likely to report having put off medical treatment because of cost. More than half of the uninsured (57%) have put off treatment, compared with 34% with private insurance and 22% with Medicare or Medicaid. However, the percentage of Americans with private health insurance who report putting off medical treatment because of cost has increased from 25% in 2013 to 34% in 2014.

Income and Healthcare Coverage Factors in Putting Off Treatment

Within the last 12 months, have you or a member of your family put off any sort of medical treatment because of the cost you would have to pay?

	2013 % Yes	2014 % Yes
ANNUAL HOUSEHOLD INCOME		
Under $30,000	43	35
$30,000 to $74,999	33	38
$75,000 or more	17	28
HEALTHCARE COVERAGE		
Private	25	34
Medicare/Medicaid	22	22
Uninsured	59	57

GALLUP

Thirty-five percent of lower-income Americans—those with annual household incomes under $30,000—report putting off medical treatment in the past 12 months, down from 43% in 2013. More upper-income Americans, on the other hand, report delaying treatment, with percentages rising from 17% in 2013 to 28% this year. The percentage of middle-income Americans who have put off medical treatment remains roughly the same as last year, at 38%.

Americans More Likely to Put Off Treatment for Serious Conditions

Those who indicate that they have put off medical treatment in the past 12 months are asked to rate the seriousness of the underlying condition or illness. This year, 22% of Americans say they have put off medical treatment for a "very" or "somewhat serious" condition. This is double the 11% who say they have put off treatment for a non-serious condition. Furthermore, the percentage who have put off treatment for a serious condition has increased slightly since 2013.

Putting Off Treatment for a Serious vs. Non-Serious Condition

When you put off this medical treatment, was it for a condition or illness that was very serious, somewhat serious, not very serious or not at all serious?

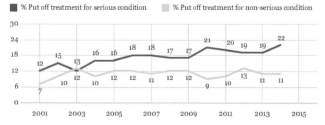

Note: Combined question results among all Americans; percentage who have not put off treatment is not shown.

GALLUP'

More Americans have put off treatments for serious conditions than for non-serious conditions every year except 2003, when similar percentages of Americans put off treatments for both types of conditions. The current 11-percentage-point gap between the two is one of the widest Gallup has found, second only to the 12-point gap found in 2010. On average, the gap has been less than 10 points.

Bottom Line

One of the goals of opening the government exchanges was to enable more Americans to get health insurance to help cover the costs of needed medical treatments. While many Americans have gained insurance, there has been no downturn in the percentage who say they have had to put off needed medical treatment because of cost. This may reflect high deductibles or copays that are part of the newly insured's plans, although separate research has shown that most of the newly insured in 2014 are satisfied with their health coverage.

Variation in the pricing for medical treatments, not to mention differences in how much insurance plans cover, could be confusing Americans or making them fear a needed treatment is too expensive. And while the costs of medical procedures aren't rising as rapidly as they once were, it is still too early to tell if that is an effect of the Affordable Care Act and how prices may change in the future.

Survey Methods

Results for this Gallup poll are based on telephone interviews conducted Nov. 6–9, 2014, with a random sample of 828 adults, aged 18 and older, living in all 50 U.S. states and the District of Columbia. For results based on the total sample of national adults, the margin of sampling error is ±4 percentage points at the 95% confidence level.

December 02, 2014

U.S. ECONOMIC CONFIDENCE INDEX AT 17-MONTH HIGH

by Justin McCarthy

WASHINGTON, D.C.—Gallup's U.S. Economic Confidence Index climbed to −8 in November, the highest monthly reading in nearly a year and a half. The index in November essentially matches the post-recession high of −7 in May 2013.

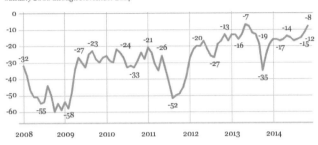

Gallup Economic Confidence Index -- Monthly Averages

January 2008 through November 2014

Gallup Daily tracking

GALLUP

This is the monthly index's fourth consecutive improvement after a long year of fairly stagnant readings. Until October, the index had remained in a narrow range of −14 to −17.

Though the index remains in negative territory, November is the closest it has come to breaking into positive territory in quite some time. The current reading is the second-highest monthly reading since Gallup began tracking the index daily in January 2008. November saw higher weekly scores than at any point in the past year and a half, with a weekly high of −6 for the week ending Nov. 16. The month ended with a score of −8 for the week ending Nov. 30.

Gallup's Economic Confidence Index is the average of two components: how Americans view current economic conditions, and their perceptions of whether the economy is getting better or worse. In November, 24% said the economy is "excellent" or "good," while 30% said it is "poor," resulting in a current conditions score of −6, the highest current conditions score since January 2008.

Meanwhile, 43% of Americans said the economy is "getting better," while 52% said it is "getting worse." This resulted in an economic outlook score of −9—the best outlook score since July 2013.

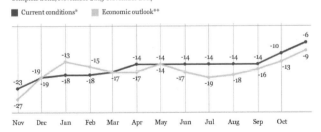

Gallup Economic Confidence Sub-Indexes -- Monthly Averages

Complete trend, November 2013-November 2014

■ Current conditions* ■ Economic outlook**

* % (Excellent + Good) minus % Poor
** % Getting better minus % Getting worse
Gallup Daily tracking

GALLUP

Upper-Income Americans Show Highest Economic Confidence to Date

Confidence among lower- and middle-income Americans climbed three points from October, to a current score of −11, and among higher-income Americans, it rose four points to +6. Upper-income Americans, those who make $90,000 a year or more, also had positive index scores of +5 in May and June of 2013.

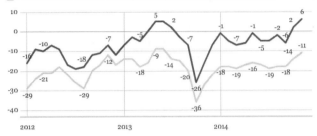

Economic Confidence Index Scores by Income

Monthly averages from January 2012 through November 2014

■ Upper-income Americans ($90,000+ in annual household income)

■ Middle- and lower-income Americans (less than $90,000 in annual household income)

Gallup Daily tracking

GALLUP

Democrats Continue to Be More Confident Than Republicans

Democrats' index scores continue to be in positive territory, averaging +16 in November, down slightly from +20 in October. This reflects a common pattern in which Americans who identify with the political party controlling the White House tend to score much higher than others on economic confidence.

Republicans continue to be much more negative about the economy than Democrats, with an index score of −33 for November, but this does show a slight improvement from −37 in October. Independents' economic confidence, which, at −9, registers about halfway between that of Republicans and Democrats, is significantly better than at any other point in the past year.

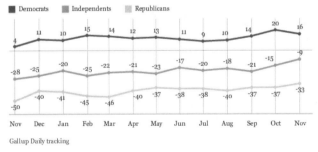

Economic Confidence Index Scores by Political Party

■ Democrats ■ Independents ■ Republicans

Gallup Daily tracking

GALLUP

Bottom Line

November's economic confidence reading brings more promising news for those watching the index's movement. The consecutive monthly increases in economic confidence come as gas prices continue to drop and are slated to fall below $2 a gallon in some parts of the country. Additionally, the Dow rose 2.5% in November.

There's no question that Americans' economic confidence has improved since the recession, but they still evaluate the economy negatively overall, as has been the case consistently over the past seven years.

Survey Methods

Results for this Gallup poll are based on telephone interviews conducted Nov. 1–30, 2014, on the Gallup U.S. Daily survey, with a random sample of 14,683 adults, aged 18 and older, living in all 50 U.S. states and the District of Columbia. For results based on the total sample of national adults, the margin of sampling error is ±1 percentage points at the 95% confidence level.

Each sample of national adults includes a minimum quota of 50% cellphone respondents and 50% landline respondents, with additional minimum quotas by time zone within region. Landline and cellular telephone numbers are selected using random-digit-dial methods.

December 02, 2014

U.S. PARTISANSHIP SHIFTS TO GOP AFTER MIDTERMS

by Jeffrey M. Jones

PRINCETON, NJ—Since the Republican Party's strong showing on Election Day last month, Americans' political allegiances have shifted toward the GOP. Prior to the elections, 43% of Americans identified as Democrats or leaned toward the Democratic Party, while 39% identified as or leaned Republican. Since then, Republicans have opened up a slight advantage, 42% to 41%, representing a net shift of five percentage points in the partisanship gap.

U.S. Partisanship Before and After the 2014 Midterm Elections

	Pre-election	Post-election	Change
Identify as/Lean Democratic	43%	41%	-2
Identify as/Lean Republican	39%	42%	+3
Democratic advantage	+4	-1	-5

Pre-election results are based on Gallup U.S. Daily tracking interviews conducted Oct. 1-Nov. 4. Post-election results are based on interviews conducted Nov. 5-30.

GALLUP

The pre-election results are based on Gallup Daily tracking interviews with 17,259 U.S. adults, conducted between Oct. 1 and Nov. 4. The post-election interviews are based on 12,671 interviews conducted Nov. 5–30.

There have been similar "bandwagon" effects for the winning party in the past, including after the 1994 and 2002 midterm elections, when Republicans benefited, and after the 2006 election, when Democrats made gains.

The most dramatic shift occurred after the 1994 midterms, in which Republicans picked up more than 50 seats in the House of Representatives to gain a majority in that chamber for the first time in 40 years. Before the 1994 elections, Democrats enjoyed a four-point advantage in party affiliation, but after the GOP wave, Republicans emerged with a 12-point margin, for a total shift of 16 points in the gap.

U.S. Partisanship Before and After Recent Midterm Elections

Partisanship figures include independents who lean toward the party.

	Pre-election (Party with advantage, margin)	Post-election (Party with advantage, margin)	Change in Democratic advantage
1994	Democratic, 48-44	Republican, 53-41	-16
1998	Democratic, 49-40	Democratic, 51-40	+2
2002	Democratic, 48-43	Republican, 47-43	-9
2006	Democratic, 52-38	Democratic, 56-34	+8
2010	Democratic, 43-41	Democratic, 43-41	0
2014	Democratic, 43-39	Republican, 42-41	-5

Pre-election data for 1994-2006 based on average of Gallup polls conducted from October through Election Day; pre-election data for 2010-2014 based on Gallup U.S. Daily tracking for October through Election Day.

Post-election data for 1994-2006 based on average of Gallup polls conducted after Election Day through end of November; post-election data for 2010-2014 based on Gallup U.S. Daily tracking from day after election through end of November.

GALLUP

In 2002, Republicans capitalized on the popularity of George W. Bush to accomplish the rare feat of having the president's party gain seats in Congress in a midterm election. After that strong showing, partisanship moved from a five-point Democratic edge to a four-point Republican margin.

Four years later, with Bush's job approval rating stuck below 40%, Democrats gained control of both houses of Congress. An already strong Democratic partisanship advantage of 14 points swelled to 22 points after the election.

Not every "wave" election has produced a distinct shift in a party's advantage. The 1998 and 2010 midterms were also notable for their outcomes, but did not produce any apparent change in Americans' basic party loyalties. In 1998, Democrats gained seats in the House even with a Democratic president in office. In 2010, Republicans gained a net of 63 seats in the House to win back control of that chamber. That year, the shifts in party allegiances seemed to be in place before the election, with the smallest Democratic edge seen in any recent midterm year. Consequently, in 2010 it appeared that shifts in party allegiances drove the election results, whereas in other years the election results seemed to produce shifts in party affiliation after the election.

The bandwagon effect can largely be explained by the amount of positive publicity given to the victorious party after its success. However, it is unclear why there would be a bandwagon effect following most midterm elections but not all of them.

No Clear Historical Pattern on How Long Post-Midterm Party Gains Last

One key question is how long the effects persist when they do occur. A review of the three elections with obvious bandwagon effects reveals no consistent pattern.

- The 1994 Republican surge in partisanship was the largest and the longest lasting. Republicans maintained a healthy eight-point advantage in partisanship through December 1994, and an average four-point advantage from January through March 1995. By April, Democrats had regained a slight edge, and for the most part held it throughout the remainder of the year.
- The 2002 Republican gains were fairly short-lived, evident in November and December and largely gone by January 2003. However, when the Iraq war commenced in March, Republicans saw another surge in partisanship.

- The 2006 Democratic gains were the most brief, disappearing by December—though that still left the party with a healthy 12-point edge in partisanship.

Implications

The 2014 midterms were an unqualified success for the Republican Party. The GOP took control of the Senate and expanded its majority in the House, giving Republicans control of both houses of Congress for the first time since 2006. And that success has caused Americans to view the Republican Party more favorably than the Democratic Party, as well as to say congressional Republicans should have more influence than President Barack Obama over the direction the nation takes in the next year. Americans are also now more likely to align themselves politically with the Republican Party than the Democratic Party.

It is not clear how long these good feelings toward the GOP will last. That could be influenced by what Republicans do with their enhanced power. While they are unlikely to achieve many of their major policy objectives with a Democratic president in office, how they and the president navigate the key issues facing the nation over the next two years will go a long way toward determining where each party stands heading into the 2016 presidential election.

Survey Methods

Results for this Gallup poll are based on telephone interviews conducted Nov. 5–30, 2014, on the Gallup U.S. Daily survey, with a random sample of 12,671 adults, aged 18 and older, living in all 50 U.S. states and the District of Columbia. For results based on the total sample of national adults, the margin of sampling error is ±1 percentage point at the 95% confidence level.

Each sample of national adults includes a minimum quota of 50% cellphone respondents and 50% landline respondents, with additional minimum quotas by time zone within region. Landline and cellular telephone numbers are selected using random-digit-dial methods.

December 04, 2014
U.S. SMALL BUSINESS OPTIMISM HIGHEST SINCE EARLY 2008

by Coleen McMurray and Frank Newport

PRINCETON, NJ—Small-business owners in the U.S. are more optimistic now than at any time since early 2008, according to the latest Wells Fargo/Gallup Small Business Index. The overall Index score rose to 58 in November, up from 49 in July. The Index was last this high in the first quarter of 2008 when it was at 83. Despite these significant gains, the overall Index is still well below pre-recession levels.

These latest results are from the fourth quarter Wells Fargo/Gallup Small Business Index survey of small-business owners nationwide, conducted Nov. 10–14. The all-time high for the index over its 13-year history is 114, reached in late 2006, while the Index was at its all-time low of −28 in the third quarter of 2010. This increase shows that small-business owners are reacting positively to the same rising economic tides that have lifted overall economic confidence in the U.S. and optimism about jobs.

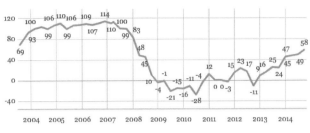

Wells Fargo/Gallup Small Business Index

Small-business owners continue to be somewhat more positive about the future than the present, although both components of the index have risen steadily over the past two years. Owners' future expectations are now at 37, while the present situation rating is at 21. Both of these are, like the basic index, higher than at any point since the first quarter of 2008.

Wells Fargo/Gallup Small Business Index

Prospects for Increased Jobs at Small Businesses Improve

Small businesses are responsible for employing the vast majority of all workers in the country, with the Small Business and Entrepreneurship Council estimating that 90% of workers are employed at firms with 20 or fewer employees. Thus, it is an encouraging sign for the job market and U.S. economy overall that small-business owners' expectations about hiring over the next year are at their highest point since 2007.

Overall Number of Jobs Next 12 Months
Wells Fargo/Gallup Small Business Index

The current survey finds that 26% of small-business owners say the number of jobs at their companies will increase in the next 12 months, while 8% say the number of jobs will go down.

The resulting +18 in net staff increase this quarter compares with +10 last quarter when 20% anticipated an increased workforce, and 10% said their staff would decrease. The low point in hiring plans occurred in 2008 when net hiring intentions were underwater, with 18% saying their workforce would decrease and only 14% anticipating an increase.

The current 26% who say their workforce will increase is within four points of the high on this measure recorded in 2006.

Financial Expectations and Anticipated Capital Spending Up

Small-business owners' expectations for their financial situations have been improving steadily and have returned to a level not seen since the first quarter of 2008. Currently, 71% of business owners expect their companies' financial situation in the next 12 months to be "very good" or "somewhat good," up from 50% just two years ago, and the highest since 2007. At the same time, 11% now expect their financial situation to be "very poor" or "somewhat poor," the lowest since 2007.

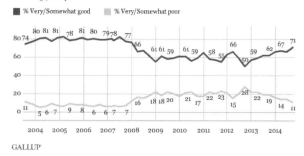

Financial Situation 12 Months From Now
Wells Fargo/Gallup Small Business Index

GALLUP

Another positive indicator for the overall U.S. economy comes from small-business owners' increased expectations about making capital investments in 2015. Half of all small-business owners say they plan on making investments next year, up from 43% in 2013 and 41% in 2012.

Does your business plan any capital investments over the NEXT 12 months, such as purchasing new equipment or new facilities, but also including any technology upgrades such as new mobile devices, new computers, new software, or a new website?
Wells Fargo/Gallup Small Business Index

	Yes	No	Don't know/ Refused
	%	%	%
4th Quarter, 2014	50	49	1
3rd Quarter, 2013	43	56	1
3rd Quarter, 2012	41	57	2

GALLUP

Bottom Line

The gains in small-business owners' optimism found in this quarter's Wells Fargo/Gallup Small Business Index mirror improvements in Americans' ratings of their overall economic confidence, workers' reports of job creation and the lower rate of U.S. unemployment. All of these indicators show an economy that is continuing to recover from the negative depths to which it descended in the years following the recession. Still, the over-time trend of the Small Business

Index shows that small-business owners' optimism has a ways to go before it recovers to where it was in the pre-recession years of the last decade.

Survey Methods

Since August 2003, the Wells Fargo/Gallup Small Business Index has surveyed small-business owners on current and future perceptions of their business financial situation. The Index consists of two dimensions: 1) owners' ratings of the current situation of their businesses, and 2) owners' ratings of how they expect their businesses to perform over the next 12 months. Results are based on telephone interviews with 601 small-business owners in all 50 United States conducted Nov. 10–14, 2014.

The overall Small Business Index is computed using a formula that scores and sums the answers to 12 questions—six about the present situation and six about the future. An Index score of zero indicates that small-business owners, as a group, are neutral—neither optimistic nor pessimistic—about their companies' situations. The overall Index can range from –400 (the most negative score possible) to +400 (the most positive score possible), but in practice spans a much more limited range. The margin of sampling error is ±4 percentage points.

December 04, 2014
NONTRADITIONAL GRADS IN U.S. NOT AS ATTACHED TO ALMA MATER

by Andrew Dugan

WASHINGTON, D.C.—A growing presence in the university ranks, nontraditional graduates, or individuals who complete college at age 25 or older, are less likely to be emotionally attached to their alma mater (14%) than are traditional graduates (20%).

Alumni Attachment: Traditional vs. Nontraditional College Graduates

"Emotionally attached" means the individual strongly agrees with the statements "I can't imagine a world without [University]" and "[University] was the perfect school for people like me."
"Emotionally unattached" means the individual strongly disagrees with both statements.

	Traditional graduates	Nontraditional graduates
	%	%
Emotionally attached	20	14
Emotionally unattached	11	9
Neither attached nor unattached	70	77

Gallup-Purdue Index, Feb. 4-March 7, 2014
Among graduates who completed college between 1990 and 2014

GALLUP

Graduates are determined to be emotionally attached to their alma mater if they simultaneously strongly agree that they "can't imagine a world without" their degree-awarding university and that their university "was the perfect school." These results come from the Gallup-Purdue Index study, a joint research effort with Purdue University and Lumina Foundation to study the relationship between the college experience and college graduates' lives. The results are based on surveys with nearly 4,000 nontraditional graduates and approximately 7,500 traditional college graduates as part of the Gallup-Purdue Index.

Alumni attachment is important—both for the graduate and the graduate's college or university. The Gallup-Purdue Index finds that graduates who are emotionally attached to their school are two times more likely to be thriving in all five elements of the Gallup-Healthways Well-Being Index. That is, emotionally attached graduates are twice as likely to be thriving in purpose, social, financial, community and physical well-being. Research from the Gallup-Purdue Index also finds that emotionally attached graduates are twice as likely to be engaged in their jobs.

And in the competitive world of university fundraising, having an emotionally attached alumni network could prove invaluable. Given the rising number of nontraditional college students, it is clearly important for schools to find ways to engender emotional attachment among this crucial bloc. However, this could prove challenging, since nontraditional students are less likely to live on campus or participate in extracurricular activities—suggesting typical methods of connecting with undergraduates will not be as useful in reaching out to older enrollees.

Nontraditional Graduates Less Likely to Have Experiential Learning

In addition to being less emotionally attached to their alma mater, nontraditional graduates report having fewer opportunities for "experiential learning" while in college than traditional graduates—in other words, they are less likely to strongly agree that they had a semester-long project, had an internship or a job that allowed them to apply what they were learning, or were extremely active in extracurricular activities.

Experiential Learning: Traditional vs. Nontraditional College Graduates

Based on responses to the following three items:
"While attending [University] I worked on a project that took a semester or more to complete."
"While attending [University] I had an internship or job that allowed me to apply what I was learning in the classroom."
"I was extremely active in extracurricular activities and organizations while attending [University]."

	Traditional graduates	Nontraditional graduates
	%	%
Experiential learning (strongly agree with all three statements)	10	3
Mixed (strongly agree with one or two statements)	82	80
No experiential learning (do not strongly agree with any of the three statements)	8	17

Gallup-Purdue Index, Feb. 4-March 7, 2014
Among graduates who completed college between 1990 and 2014

GALLUP

Just 3% of nontraditional graduates strongly agree that they had all three types of experiential learning opportunities, compared with 10% of traditional graduates. And the rate of nontraditional graduates who strongly agree that they had none of the three experiential learning opportunities is double that of traditional graduates (17% vs. 8%, respectively). The vast majority of graduates fall somewhere in between, neither strongly agreeing with all three statements nor strongly disagreeing with all three.

Experiential learning has been linked to higher work engagement. Finding ways to ensure nontraditional graduates enjoy experiential learning, however, will be no easy task for colleges. Older

students may have less time for an internship, as they may be working full time to support themselves. They may feel less compelled to be active in extracurricular activities or organizations, or simply just not have the availability to participate.

Bottom Line

With the U.S. Department of Education estimating that 40% of today's college-attending population is older than age 25, universities must find ways to connect with this different type of student. Currently, nontraditional graduates are less emotionally attached to their university and report having had fewer experiential learning opportunities than traditional graduates. Finding ways to engage this increasingly common type of student should be an important priority for universities.

Survey Methods

Results for this Gallup-Purdue Index study are based on Web interviews conducted Feb. 4–March 7, 2014, with a random sample of 29,560 respondents with a bachelor's degree or higher, aged 18 and older, with Internet access, living in all 50 U.S. states and the District of Columbia. For results based on the total sample of bachelor's degree or higher respondents who graduated between 1990 and 2014, and are traditional college students, the margin of sampling error is ±1.8 percentage points at the 95% confidence level. For results based on the total sample of bachelor's degree or higher respondents who graduated between 1990 and 2014, and are nontraditional college students, the margin of sampling error is ±2.5 percentage points at the 95% confidence level.

The Gallup-Purdue Index sample was compiled from two sources: the Gallup Panel and the Gallup U.S. Daily survey.

December 05, 2014
AS ACA TAKES EFFECT, MAJORITY OK WITH PERSONAL HEALTH COSTS

by Andrew Dugan

WASHINGTON, D.C.—Nearly six in 10 Americans (57%) say they are satisfied with the total cost they pay for healthcare, on par with other readings over the last five years. So far, there is little indication that the Affordable Care Act (ACA), also known as "Obamacare," has affected the way Americans view their healthcare costs, either positively or negatively.

Americans' Satisfaction With Their Personal Healthcare Costs

Are you generally satisfied or dissatisfied with the total cost you pay for your healthcare?

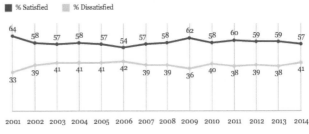

GALLUP

Healthcare has been the focus of political and economic debates since at least the start of President Barack Obama's first term, when Obama and congressional Democrats passed the controversial healthcare law in an attempt to increase the number of Americans with health insurance. This law also aimed to stop or at least lessen the ever-rising costs of healthcare in the country, though costs continue to climb.

Despite this backdrop, the majority of Americans have been serene about the cost of *their* healthcare for over a decade, and there is little evidence of change in those perceptions from recent years. Conversely, few are satisfied with the total cost of healthcare across the U.S., indicating that while most Americans believe the cost of healthcare is too expensive nationally, they don't consider it a problem for themselves.

Oldest Americans Most Satisfied With Cost of Their Healthcare

Americans aged 65 and older are by far the most satisfied with the cost of their healthcare, at 77%, compared with any other major demographic group. The poorest Americans, those reporting a yearly household income of less than $20,000, are slightly above average in terms of their satisfaction with healthcare costs, at 61%. Interestingly, a significant share of both groups are eligible for the country's two government-run social healthcare programs, Medicare and Medicaid. Notably, about three-quarters of U.S. adults who have insurance via these two programs are satisfied with the cost of healthcare—16 percentage points higher than adults using private insurance (58%).

Are you generally satisfied or dissatisfied with the total cost you pay for your healthcare?

By demographics and characteristics

	% Satisfied
AGE	
18-29	56
30-49	52
50-64	55
65+	77
TYPE OF HEALTH INSURANCE HELD	
Private insurance	58
Medicaid or Medicare, no private insurance	74
No insurance	28

Aggregated data from 2012-2014

GALLUP

Meanwhile, some types of Americans appear to be feeling the pinch of healthcare costs more than others. The uninsured are the least satisfied (28%), for reasons that are not so mysterious. Americans younger than 65 are much less likely to be satisfied with the total cost of their healthcare, revealing a huge disparity between U.S. adults of working age and those in their retirement years on this item.

Strong Majorities Positive on Quality of Healthcare and Coverage

Nearly eight in 10 U.S. adults rate the quality of healthcare they receive as "excellent" or "good" (79%), a continued sign that Americans are largely content with the services they receive, whatever the

cost considerations might be. Again, there has been no significant change in these perceptions since the 2010 passage of the ACA.

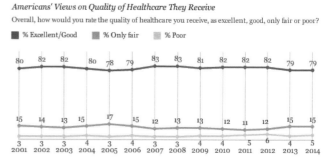

Americans' Views on Quality of Healthcare They Receive

Overall, how would you rate the quality of healthcare you receive, as excellent, good, only fair or poor?

GALLUP

While U.S. adults rate the healthcare services they receive positively, some Americans struggle with what services or doctors their health insurance plans allow, or their healthcare "coverage." But the vast majority rate their overall healthcare coverage as excellent or good (67%). This hovers around where it has been for as long as Gallup has measured this question—both before the healthcare law took effect and after. The percentage who say their coverage is "only fair" is up slightly, but from a big picture perspective, the main takeaway from this trend is one of little change in recent years.

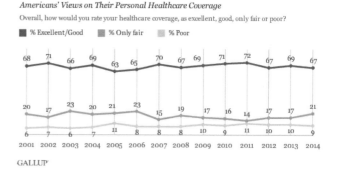

Americans' Views on Their Personal Healthcare Coverage

Overall, how would you rate your healthcare coverage, as excellent, good, only fair or poor?

GALLUP

U.S. adults holding health insurance via a private insurance plan are about as likely to rate their coverage positively (77%) as Americans holding either Medicare or Medicaid (75%), suggesting both groups are about equally happy with their plans. But, as noted earlier, Medicare and Medicaid holders are far more satisfied with the cost of their plan.

As Gallup has found in the past, Americans are far less effusive with their praise for healthcare coverage in the U.S. as a whole. This year is not an exception: Fewer than four in 10 Americans now rate healthcare coverage in the U.S. as excellent or good.

Bottom Line

Before passing the ACA, the large majority of Americans who had health insurance were broadly satisfied with their medical care and coverage *and* their healthcare costs. Thus, a major test of the ACA will be whether it succeeds in expanding affordable healthcare to the previously uninsured while doing "no harm" to the large majority of Americans who are already highly satisfied with their healthcare coverage. So far, the verdict is positive. Gallup finds no decrease in insured Americans' satisfaction with their healthcare services and their costs. At the same time, the uninsured are as negative as ever, but their numbers have dwindled. Gallup's annual November updates of these trends will monitor whether this positive outcome persists as implementation of the ACA progresses.

Survey Methods

Results for this Gallup poll are based on telephone interviews conducted Nov. 6–9, 2014, with a random sample of 828 adults, aged 18 and older, living in all 50 U.S. states and the District of Columbia. For results based on the total sample of national adults, the margin of sampling error is ±4 percentage points at the 95% confidence level.

Each sample of national adults includes a minimum quota of 50% cellphone respondents and 50% landline respondents, with additional minimum quotas by time zone within region. Landline and cellular telephone numbers are selected using random-digit-dial methods.

December 08, 2014
URBAN BLACKS IN U.S. HAVE LITTLE CONFIDENCE IN POLICE

by Jeffrey M. Jones

PRINCETON, NJ—As controversy continues to swirl about police officers' treatment of blacks, an analysis of Gallup data underscores how much less likely U.S. blacks are than whites or Hispanics to express confidence in the police. The analysis also reveals that blacks living in urban areas are significantly less likely than blacks in non-urban areas to say they are confident in the police.

Confidence in Police, by Race and Place of Residence

Figures are percentages saying they have a great deal or quite a lot of confidence in the police

	All Americans	Non-Hispanic whites	Non-Hispanic blacks	Hispanics
	%	%	%	%
Total	57	61	34	57
Live in urban area	54	62	26	54
Live in non-urban area	58	60	38	59

2006-2014 aggregated data

GALLUP'

The results are based on aggregated data from Gallup's 2006 through 2014 annual updates on confidence in major U.S. institutions. Over this time, an average of 57% of Americans have said they have "a great deal" or "quite a lot" of confidence in the police, typically placing it near the top of the list of institutions. This includes confidence ratings of 61% among whites and 57% among Hispanics, but just 34% among blacks.

Racial differences in views of the police are long-standing, but have been brought to the forefront again after white police officers' actions resulted in the deaths of black men in Ferguson, Missouri, and Staten Island, New York. Grand juries did not indict either officer.

Blacks living in highly urban areas are even less likely to have confidence in the police, 26%, than those living in non-urban areas (38%). For this analysis, urban residents are those living in the

47 U.S. counties that include the nation's largest cities, using the definition of "Big Cities" from the American Communities Project and the American University School of Public Affairs. These counties are highly urban and include a high proportion of racial and ethnic minorities. About one in three blacks nationwide live in these highly urban counties.

Because many of the high-profile racial incidents involving police have occurred in urban settings, blacks living in and around big cities may be more sensitive to these tensions with police than blacks living in non-urban areas. It is possible that these high-profile events were not isolated incidents but more extreme examples of ongoing and widespread tensions between police and blacks, which many urban blacks may experience firsthand.

Although blacks' views of police vary depending on where they live, there is little meaningful difference in the views of whites or Hispanics living in urban versus non-urban areas.

Democrats Less Confident in Police

While race clearly influences how Americans view the police, the public's political leanings also have an effect. Republicans have significantly more confidence in the police than do Democrats or independents, and these political differences are apparent among white and nonwhite Americans. Race and politics interact such that nonwhite Democrats and independents have far less confidence in police than Republicans of any race, or than Democrats and independents who are white.

Confidence in Police, by Race and Party Identification

Figures are percentage saying they have a great deal or quite a lot of confidence in the police

	All Americans	Non-Hispanic whites	Nonwhites
	%	%	%
Total	57	61	46
Democrats	52	59	41
Independents	52	55	44
Republicans	69	70	67

2006-2014 aggregated data

GALLUP'

Democrats' tendency to view matters of race and racism as a greater priority for government may help explain these political differences.

Implications

Tensions between blacks and police officers have been an unfortunate but not uncommon issue in the U.S. for decades. These tensions have resulted from a wide-ranging set of historical and contemporary factors that have been the subject of much debate.

Blacks, particularly those living in urban areas, view the police much less positively than whites do. In addition to the basic confidence-in-institutions data reported here, Gallup has also shown racial differences in other attitudes about police, including a report last month showing large and consistent racial differences over time in a separate question that asked about Americans' confidence in the police to protect them from violent crime, specifically. Most blacks also believe the U.S. justice system more broadly is biased against blacks.

Whites and blacks have divergent attitudes in many other areas, particularly matters that touch on race, including racial equality and opportunity. Thus, one reason for blacks' more negative views of police may be that they evaluate the police against the backdrop of real or perceived unequal treatment of their race, while racial sensitivities do not come into play when other Americans evaluate the police.

Survey Methods

Results for this Gallup poll are based on aggregated telephone interviews conducted from 2006 to 2014, with a random sample of 9,442 adults, aged 18 and older, living in all 50 U.S. states and the District of Columbia. For results based on the total sample of national adults, the margin of sampling error is ±1 percentage point at the 95% confidence level.

For results based on the total sample of 7,671 whites, the margin of sampling error is ±1 percentage point at the 95% confidence level.

For results based on the total sample of 730 blacks, the margin of sampling error is ±4 percentage points at the 95% confidence level.

For results based on the total sample of 568 Hispanics, the margin of sampling error is ±5 percentage points at the 95% confidence level.

Each sample of national adults includes a minimum quota of 50% cellphone respondents and 50% landline respondents, with additional minimum quotas by time zone within region. Landline and cellular telephone numbers are selected using random-digit-dial methods.

December 08, 2014
OBAMA LOSES SUPPORT AMONG WHITE MILLENNIALS

by Frank Newport

PRINCETON, NJ—President Barack Obama's job approval rating in 2014 among white 18- to 29-year-olds is 34%, three points higher than among whites aged 30 and older. This is the narrowest approval gap between the president's previously strong support base of white millennials and older white Americans since Obama took office.

Obama Job Approval, Younger vs. Older Whites, and All Americans

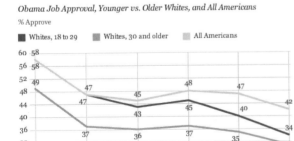

Note: 2009-2010 percentages for the 18 to 29 group are the same as those for all Americans

Gallup Daily tracking

GALLUP

By contrast, the president's approval rating was nine percentage points higher among younger whites in 2009, and 10 points higher in 2010. Additionally, while the president's approval among younger whites matched his overall national rating in his first two years in office, it is now eight points below the national average. These data underscore the gradual erosion of the disproportionately strong support Obama received from young white voters as he took office in 2009 and ran for re-election in 2012.

The data are based on yearly averages from Gallup's Daily tracking, including 2014 data through November.

Obama's support among white millennials has factored into his two presidential election successes. Exit polls conducted after the 2012 election, for example, showed that Obama received 44% of the vote of white 18- to 29-year-olds, about six points higher than he received among whites aged 30 and older. Obama's 45% job approval rating among 18- to 29-year-old whites in 2012 mirrored these voting results closely. But the president's 11-point drop among white 18- to 29-year-olds since 2012 is almost double the six-point drop among the national population and among older whites.

Younger Whites' Approval Now Closer to All Other Age Groups

From a broader perspective, there is relatively little difference today in Obama's job approval ratings among whites in any of the four major age groups. Whites aged 30 to 49, as well as those 65 and older, have given Obama a 31% approval rating so far in 2014, with 50- to 64-year-olds coming in at 32% and 18- to 29-year-olds at 34%. The spread among age categories was slightly larger in the earliest years of the Obama administration.

Obama Job Approval Among Whites, by Age

% Approve

■ Whites 18 to 29   ■ Whites 30 to 49   ■ Whites 50 to 64   ▨ Whites 65+

Note: 2011-2014 percentages for the 30 to 49 group are the same as those for the 65+ group

Gallup Daily tracking

GALLUP

Support Down, But Still Higher Among Nonwhite Than Among White Young People

Although Obama's approval rating has dropped among black, Hispanic and Asian 18- to 29-year-olds from 2009 to 2014, just as it has among white millennials, the president maintains a much higher level of support among these groups than among whites. Specifically, Obama's approval is 80% among young blacks, 68% among young Asians, and 55% among Hispanic 18- to 29-year-olds—contrasted with his 34% approval among white young adults.

Age affects Obama's approval ratings differently among each of these racial and ethnic groups. Obama does slightly less well among black young people than among older blacks, and significantly better among Asians younger than 50 than among those who are older. There is little significant difference in his approval rating by age within the Hispanic population.

Obama Job Approval, by Age and Race/Ethnicity

	18 to 29	30 to 49	50 to 64	65+
	%	%	%	%
Non-Hispanic whites	34	31	32	31
Non-Hispanic blacks	80	84	87	88
Hispanics	55	52	51	53
Asians	68	64	53	53

Gallup Daily tracking, January-November 2014

GALLUP'

Implications

While Obama is significantly more popular among nonwhites than among whites, he was able to count on proportionately stronger support from young whites than older whites in his 2008 and 2012 presidential election campaigns. Now, his support among white millennials appears to be waning, and these young Americans give Obama an approval rating that is only marginally higher than that among older whites.

These findings demonstrate the general importance of race and ethnicity when one talks about Obama's job approval ratings by age. Obama continues to enjoy higher approval ratings among all 18- to 29-year-olds—regardless of race or ethnicity—than he does among the general population, but this is largely attributable to younger age groups in the U.S. being disproportionately composed of nonwhites. In other words, a big part of the age gap in Obama's approval ratings today is attributable not so much to differences in approval *within* racial or ethnic groups, but to the fact that the white population in the U.S. skews older, while the nonwhite population skews younger.

The white vote has become an increasing challenge for Democratic presidential candidates in recent years, as well as Senate candidates in many Southern and swing states. Just this past weekend, a lack of strong support among white voters was instrumental in incumbent Democratic Sen. Mary Landrieu's loss in Louisiana's senatorial runoff election. That loss gives the Republicans control of every southern Senate seat from Texas to the Carolinas. While Democrats are likely to be helped in coming years by a growing Hispanic population, Democratic presidential candidates—and senatorial candidates in many states—will continue to need the votes of a substantial minority of white voters in order to put together a winning coalition. Thus, Obama's continuing loss of support among younger white voters highlights one of the potential challenges ahead for Democratic candidates in 2016.

Survey Methods

Results for this Gallup poll are based on telephone interviews conducted on the Gallup U.S. Daily survey from 2009 through November 2014, with random samples of approximately 355,000 adults, aged 18 and older, living in all 50 U.S. states and the District of Columbia for each of the 2009–2012 yearly samples; approximately 175,000 adults for 2013; and 163,847 adults for Jan. 2–Nov. 30, 2014. For results based on the total sample of national adults in each yearly average, the margin of sampling error is ±1 percentage point at the 95% confidence level. The margin of sampling error for each year's age subgroups varies by sample size.

Each sample of national adults includes a minimum quota of 50% cellphone respondents and 50% landline respondents, with additional minimum quotas by time zone within region. Landline and cellular telephone numbers are selected using random-digit-dial methods.

December 10, 2014
U.S. HISPANICS BACK OBAMA IMMIGRATION ACTIONS

by Jeffrey M. Jones

PRINCETON, NJ—Americans overall say they disapprove (51%) rather than approve of (41%) the executive actions President Barack Obama plans to take to deal with undocumented immigrants living in the U.S. However, Hispanics, U.S. immigrants and blacks approve of the actions by wide margins, whereas whites are oppose them.

Views of President Obama's Executive Actions on Immigration

	Approve	Disapprove
	%	%
All Americans	41	51
Non-Hispanic whites	30	62
Non-Hispanic blacks	68	24
Hispanics	64	28
U.S. immigrants	69	23

Gallup Daily tracking, Nov. 24-Dec. 7

GALLUP'

These results are based on Gallup Daily tracking interviews conducted between Nov. 24 and Dec. 8, including interviews with more than 6,000 U.S. adults and more than 500 Hispanics, blacks and U.S. immigrants—those who report they were born outside the U.S.

Obama outlined his planned steps in a nationally televised address Nov. 20. He intends to grant legal resident status to undocumented immigrants who have been in the U.S. five years or longer, have children born here and who do not have a criminal record. Republican leaders in Congress widely oppose the move, in particular his use of executive actions rather than the legislative process to change the policy.

The Gallup Daily tracking question did not address the specifics of the actions, but rather asked Americans for their views on the "executive actions President Obama plans to take dealing with certain categories of undocumented immigrants living in the U.S." Recent polls other organizations have conducted since Obama's speech, as well as past polls by Gallup, show Americans favor plans to allow illegal immigrants to remain in the U.S. if they meet certain requirements, rather than deporting them. Thus, opposition to Obama's policy may have as much to do with his use of executive actions rather than the legislative process, or simply political opposition to Obama and his agenda more generally, as to the specifics of what he is proposing.

Roughly two-thirds of Americans say they are following news about Obama's immigration actions closely, with relatively little variation in attention paid by whites, blacks, Hispanics and immigrants.

Three in Four Hispanic Immigrants Back Obama's Actions

Obama's actions on immigration will likely help him politically with the growing Hispanic population in the U.S. because Hispanics favor the proposal by a better than 2-to-1 margin. Notably, support is higher among Hispanics who migrated to the U.S. (75%) than among Hispanics who were born in this country (51%), but both groups show greater approval than disapproval.

More generally, those of all racial and ethnic backgrounds who were born outside the U.S. are far more supportive of Obama's proposed actions than those born in this country.

Views of President Obama's Executive Actions on Immigration, by Country of Birth

	Approve	Disapprove
	%	%
ALL AMERICANS		
Born in U.S.	37	56
Born in another country	69	23
HISPANICS		
Born in U.S.	51	42
Born in another country	75	17
NON-HISPANICS		
Born in U.S.	36	57
Born in another country	60	32

Gallup Daily tracking, Nov. 24-Dec. 7

GALLUP'

The biggest divide in opinions on the president's immigration actions is political. Whereas 70% of Democrats approve of the actions, 85% of Republicans disapprove. Independents also show greater disapproval than approval.

Views of President Obama's Executive Actions on Immigration, by Political Party Identification

	Approve	Disapprove
	%	%
Democrats	70	22
Independents	38	53
Republicans	11	85

Gallup Daily tracking, Nov. 24-Dec. 7

GALLUP'

Implications

Obama made clear in his address to the nation that he believes he has the legal authority to use executive actions to address the status of illegal immigrants living in the U.S. However, many disagree, and his actions are already facing challenges. The Republican-led House of Representatives last week passed a bill to block Obama's actions. And 17 states are joining a legal challenge to Obama's proposed actions.

The Gallup data clearly underscore the divisiveness of Obama's actions, both politically and along racial and ethnic lines. However, the groups most opposed to what Obama is doing are also the groups least likely to support him. As a result, even with the overall negative reaction to his immigration plans, his job approval rating has held fairly steady since he announced them.

Survey Methods

Results for this Gallup poll are based on telephone interviews conducted Nov. 24–Dec. 7, 2014, on the Gallup U.S. Daily survey, with a random sample of 6,084 adults, aged 18 and older, living in all 50 U.S. states and the District of Columbia. For results based on the total sample of national adults, the margin of sampling error is ±2 percentage points at the 95% confidence level.

For results based on the total sample of 4,539 non-Hispanic whites, the margin of sampling error is ±2 percentage points at the 95% confidence level.

For results based on the total sample of 584 Hispanics, the margin of sampling error is ±5 percentage points at the 95% confidence level.

For results based on the total sample of 553 non-Hispanic blacks, the margin of sampling error is ±5 percentage points at the 95% confidence level.

For results based on the total sample of 574 U.S. immigrants, the margin of sampling error is ±5 percentage points at the 95% confidence level.

Each sample of national adults includes a minimum quota of 50% cellphone respondents and 50% landline respondents, with additional minimum quotas by time zone within region. Landline and cellular telephone numbers are selected using random-digit-dial methods.

December 10, 2014
HISPANICS' SUPPORT FOR OBAMA CLIMBS AFTER EXECUTIVE ACTIONS

by Justin McCarthy

WASHINGTON, D.C.—Hispanic Americans' approval of President Barack Obama's job performance is up 12 points, to 64%, since he issued executive actions protecting some immigrants who are living in the U.S. illegally from deportation. Whites' and blacks' ratings of the president did not change meaningfully during this time.

Obama Job Approval Ratings, by Race and Ethnicity
% Approve

	Nov 1-20, 2014	Nov 21-Dec 8, 2014	Change (pct. pts.)
Total	41	43	+2
Hispanic	52	64	+12
White	31	31	0
Black	83	80	-3

Gallup Daily tracking

GALLUP'

Obama's executive actions, issued Nov. 20, will create a program that allows immigrants who are in the U.S. illegally to apply to work legally—as long as they have no criminal record, have lived in the U.S. for at least five years and have children. The 4 to 5 million immigrants that qualify could also become eligible for Medicare and Social Security. Obama has said that his efforts to overhaul the immigration system could be supplanted by congressional action.

Since that announcement, his job approval ratings among all Americans have climbed two points. Given no change in approval rating among whites, and a small but not statistically meaningful decline among blacks, the increase in his overall job approval rating appears to be largely driven by Hispanics' opinions.

Although Americans overall are more likely to disapprove than approve of the executive action, a majority of Hispanics (64%) approve of it.

Hispanics' Presidential Approval Has Fluctuated More Than Whites', Blacks'

Hispanic Americans' opinions of the president's performance have varied more since he took office than has been the case among blacks and whites. Monthly approval ratings among Hispanics reached a high of 82% early in Obama's term in May 2009, and a low of 47% in September 2014. This 35-percentage-point range is wider than the 27-point range among whites and the 14-point range among blacks.

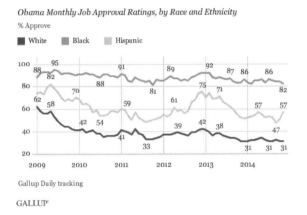

Obama Monthly Job Approval Ratings, by Race and Ethnicity

% Approve

■ White   ■ Black   ■ Hispanic

Gallup Daily tracking

GALLUP

Whites' approval of the president peaked at 62% upon his first month in office, and has reached a low of 31% seven times since November 2013. Blacks, however, have been significantly more approving of Obama's performance, reaching a high of 95% in June 2009, and with a low of 81% in October 2011.

Bottom Line

The president's executive action on immigration may have clear supporters and detractors among racial, ethnic and political subgroups. Even though Americans are more likely to disapprove than approve of the actions Obama plans to take on immigration, his overall job approval rating has not suffered largely because Hispanics have responded so positively.

It's uncertain whether those actions will continue to engender Hispanics' goodwill toward Obama. As a group, Hispanics' opinions of Obama have tended to vary more than those of other subgroups. His approval rating among Hispanics for the week of Dec. 1–7 was 60%, compared with 68% the prior week, although the smaller sample sizes on those weekly estimates make it premature to conclude that the surge in approval seen among Hispanics is staring to fade.

Survey Methods

Results for this Gallup poll are based on telephone interviews conducted Nov. 21–Dec. 8, 2014, on the Gallup U.S. Daily survey, with a random sample of 8,116 adults, aged 18 and older, living in all 50 U.S. states and the District of Columbia. For results based on the total sample of national adults, the margin of sampling error is ±1 percentage points at the 95% confidence level.

For results based on the total sample of 795 Hispanics, the margin of sampling error is ±4 percentage points at the 95% confidence level.

All reported margins of sampling error include computed design effects for weighting.

Each sample of national adults includes a minimum quota of 50% cellphone respondents and 50% landline respondents, with additional minimum quotas by time zone within region. Landline and cellular telephone numbers are selected using random-digit-dial methods.

December 11, 2014
HISPANICS' DAILY SPENDING WELL ABOVE U.S. AVERAGE

by Rebecca Riffkin and Frank Newport

WASHINGTON, D.C.—Hispanic adults in the U.S. in 2014 have reported spending more money on a daily basis, on average, than is typical for the U.S. adult population: $96 vs. $90, respectively.

Average Daily Consumer Spending -- by Race and Ethnicity

Next, we'd like you to think about your spending yesterday, not counting the purchase of a home, motor vehicle, or your normal household bills. How much money did you spend or charge yesterday on all other types of purchases you may have made, such as at a store, restaurant, gas station, online, or elsewhere?

	Average daily spending
Hispanics	$96
Asians	$95
Non-Hispanic whites	$88
Non-Hispanic blacks	$87
All U.S. adults	$90

Gallup Daily tracking, January-November 2014

GALLUP

These results are based on interviewing conducted as part of 2014 Gallup Daily tracking, which asks Americans how much they spent "yesterday," excluding normal household bills and major purchases. It provides an indication of discretionary consumer spending. So far in 2014, daily spending averages for most months have been slightly higher than in the corresponding month in 2013, and overall average daily spending to date in 2014 is slightly higher than what was found in 2013.

President Barack Obama's recent executive action would defer the deportation of millions of immigrants who are in the U.S. illegally, many of them Hispanic. This raises the question of the potential effect this move will have on the U.S. economy. Hispanics are joined by Asians as the largest spenders this year among major racial and ethnic groups, reporting significantly higher spending than non-Hispanic whites or blacks. This suggests a potential benefit to the consumer spending component of the economy if these Hispanic immigrants remain in the U.S. rather than being returned to their native countries.

Children Large Part of Reason for Higher Hispanic Spending

One likely reason Hispanics report higher average spending than whites and blacks is that they are more likely to have children younger than 18 living in their households. Half of Hispanics report having children younger than 18, compared with 29% of whites, 39% of blacks and 36% of Asians. Previously, Gallup has found that having children is associated with higher daily spending, and analysis of 2014 data shows that within each major racial and ethnic group, those who have children spend substantially more than those who do not.

Average Daily Consumer Spending Affected by Having Children Under 18

Next, we'd like you to think about your spending yesterday, not counting the purchase of a home, motor vehicle, or your normal household bills. How much money did you spend or charge yesterday on all other types of purchases you may have made, such as at a store, restaurant, gas station, online, or elsewhere?

	% Have children under 18	Average daily spending, those without children under 18	Average daily spending, those with children under 18
Hispanics	50	$76	$116
Asians	36	$82	$119
Non-Hispanic whites	29	$79	$108
Non-Hispanic blacks	39	$72	$111
All U.S. adults	33	$79	$111

Gallup Daily tracking, January-November 2014

GALLUP

The significant proportion of Hispanics with children gives this group—with its higher spending average—a major representation in Hispanics' overall spending average. On the other hand, the lower level of spending associated with not having children under 18 has much higher weight among the overall total of all Americans. Thus, Hispanics' youthful average age and their resulting higher likelihood of having children in the home translate into higher overall spending.

Implications

One major element of Obama's executive action on immigration would allow immigrants whose children meet certain qualifications to avoid active deportation efforts and thus to remain in the U.S. Many of those who would avoid deportation would be Hispanics with children. If these immigrants are similar to Hispanics in general, they are likely to spend more than the average American, helping to contribute to the U.S. retail economy, particularly in cities and regions where Hispanics constitute a higher percentage of the population than in others. There are certainly other, countervailing economic implications of allowing these individuals to remain in the U.S., but in terms of the consumer economy, the net effect would likely be a positive one.

Survey Methods

Results for this Gallup poll are based on telephone interviews conducted Jan. 1–Nov. 30, 2014, on the Gallup U.S. Daily survey, with a random sample of 159,068 adults, aged 18 and older, living in all 50 U.S. states and the District of Columbia. For results based on the total sample of national adults, the margin of sampling error is ±1 percentage point at the 95% confidence level. For results based

on the total sample of 14,538 Hispanics, the margin of sampling error is ±1 percentage point at the 95% confidence level. For results based on the total sample of 6,358 Hispanics with children, the margin of sampling error is ±2 percentage points at the 95% confidence level. All reported margins of sampling error include computed design effects for weighting.

Each sample of national adults includes a minimum quota of 50% cellphone respondents and 50% landline respondents, with additional minimum quotas by time zone within region. Landline and cellular telephone numbers are selected using random-digit-dial methods.

December 12, 2014
IN U.S., STANDARD OF LIVING RATINGS IMPROVING IN 2014

by Andrew Dugan

WASHINGTON, D.C.—In line with a recent raft of good economic news—including robust gross domestic product growth in the third quarter and November's strong jobs report—nearly six in 10 Americans said in November that their standard of living was getting better (58%). This is close to the highest monthly value in the question's seven-year history (60%), and nearly double the estimates seen at the depths of the recession.

Standard of Living in U.S. -- Monthly Averages

Right now, do you feel your standard of living is getting better or getting worse?

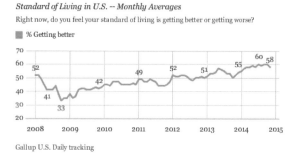

Gallup U.S. Daily tracking

GALLUP

These findings come on the heels of other broad economic indicators pointing to renewed vitality. Gallup's Economic Confidence Index, for example, nearly matched its highest monthly post-recession score of −8 in November, a huge improvement from the drop to −60 measured in October 2008.

Gallup Economic Confidence Index -- Monthly Averages

How Americans rate economic conditions in this country today, and whether they think economic conditions in the country as a whole are getting better or getting worse

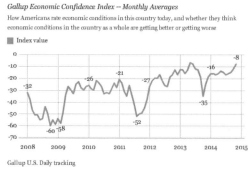

Gallup U.S. Daily tracking

GALLUP

Despite Good Economic News, Small
Changes in Personal Finance

Even as Gallup's indicators of the public's views of the national economy approach new heights, Americans' views about their own finances and self-reported financial habits have shown, at best, only moderate improvement compared with their two-year averages. Importantly—as has consistently been the case—large majorities of Americans continue to say they are watching their spending very closely (88%) and are cutting back on spending (61%). These attitudes appear to be fundamental to the way Americans approach their spending, and thus are not subject to much change. Meanwhile, many still feel uneasy about their personal financial situation—half of U.S. adults say they would be able to make an emergency purchase, while less than half (47%) say they are feeling pretty good about the amount of money they have to spend. Less than half of Americans also report that they are feeling better about their financial situation (47%)—even as the prices of critical necessities decline.

Americans' Views on Saving and Spending -- November 2014

Percentage saying "Agree" or "Yes"

	November 2014	2013-2014 average	Difference
	%	%	(pct. pts.)
Do you agree or disagree with the following statement? You are watching your spending very closely.	88	88	0
Would you be able right now to make a major purchase, such as a car, appliance or furniture, or pay for a significant home repair if you needed to?	50	48	2
At this time, are you cutting back on how much money you spend each week, or not?	61	64	-3
Are you feeling pretty good these days about the amount of money you have to spend, or not?	47	45	2
Did you worry yesterday that you spent too much money, or not?	31	32	-1
Do you agree or disagree with the following statement? You have more than enough money to do what you want to do.	32	29	3
Do you have enough money to buy the things you need, or not?	70	68	2
Are you feeling better about your financial situation these days, or not?	47	44	3

Gallup U.S. Daily tracking

GALLUP'

While the general thrust of Americans' responses to these questions reveals a financially cautious public focused more on saving than spending—potentially trouble for an economy that relies heavily on consumer spending to generate economic growth—there is evidence that Americans felt marginally more secure in November relative to the recent past, perhaps a sign that improved national economic indicators are being felt more locally. For instance, the 47% saying they are feeling better about their financial situation is up by three percentage points over the 2013–2014 average. Likewise, the percentage of Americans saying they are cutting back on the amount of money they spend is down by three points over the same two-year average.

The history of asking these personal financial questions indicates much more stability in Americans' minds than when they are asked about the national economy. In other words, they are much more willing to shift their views of what is happening at the national level than they are to do so regarding their own financial situation. These data do show a slight change in favor of Americans feeling more economically secure and thus comfortable in their spending, but by no stretch can it be said that Gallup has measured a sea change in Americans' perceptions of their personal financial status.

Bottom Line

Last week's jobs report from the Bureau of Labor Statistics seemed a signal to many economic commentators that the recovery may now become easier for average Americans to appreciate. Nationally, Gallup's economic and standard of living data support this notion, as more Americans now say their standard of living is getting better than say it is getting worse. Meanwhile, Gallup's Economic Confidence Index is perking up, even if it is still in negative territory.

But when measuring the personal spending and saving habits—the life and blood of the U.S. economy—of individual U.S. residents, the intensifying recovery narrative becomes less compelling. Of course, there may be a lag in how quickly propitious macroeconomic data trickle out into the larger economy. But stagnant feelings about personal finances may provide one explanation as to why President Barack Obama has not seen a marked bump in his job approval rating even as good economic news continues to materialize.

Survey Methods

Results for this Gallup poll are based on telephone interviews conducted Nov. 1–30, 2014, on the Gallup U.S. Daily survey, with a random sample of 14,607 adults, aged 18 and older, living in all 50 U.S. states and the District of Columbia. For results based on the total sample of national adults, the margin of sampling error is ±1 percentage point at the 95% confidence level.

Each sample of national adults includes a minimum quota of 50% cellphone respondents and 50% landline respondents, with additional minimum quotas by time zone within region. Landline and cellular telephone numbers are selected using random-digit-dial methods.

December 12, 2014
GALLUP REVIEW: BLACK AND WHITE DIFFERENCES IN VIEWS ON RACE

by the Gallup Editors

PRINCETON, NJ—The outcry after grand juries in Ferguson, Missouri, and Staten Island, New York, decided not to indict police officers in the deaths of unarmed black men has refocused Americans' attention on the continuing, contentious issue of race relations in the U.S. Gallup has measured black and white Americans' attitudes about race for more than 50 years, and both groups continue to look at race relations in significantly different ways, even today.

Gallup data help show how black Americans' and white Americans' views continue to differ in four crucial areas: views of race relations in general, views of discrimination against blacks, views on the need for new civil rights laws and more government intervention, and, finally, views of the police and justice system.

1. Attitudes About Race Relations in General

Since the late 1990s, blacks' optimism that there will be a solution to the country's racial problems has consistently trailed whites' by about 12 percentage points. Most recently, in June 2013, Gallup found 58% of whites versus 48% of blacks believing a solution to black-white relations would eventually be worked out. By contrast, in December 1963—at the end of what some describe as "the defining year of the civil rights movement"—a U.S. poll conducted by NORC found 70% of blacks in the U.S. believing a solution would eventually be worked out, while barely half of whites—53%—agreed. When Gallup repeated this question in the early 1990s, blacks' outlook had dimmed to match whites', with 44% of both groups feeling optimistic. Now, the gap has expanded, primarily because whites have become more positive.

Do you think that relations between blacks and whites will always be a problem for the United States, or that a solution will eventually be worked out?

% Eventually worked out

■ Blacks ▨ Whites

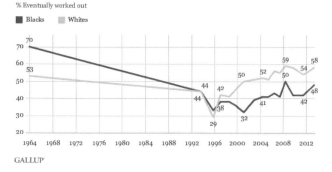

GALLUP'

Perhaps one reason for this racial gap in optimism is the even greater gulf between how blacks and whites perceive society's treatment of blacks. In the same 2013 poll, 67% of whites versus 47% of blacks said they were either very or somewhat satisfied with how blacks are treated in society. And blacks' satisfaction dipped further, to 41%, in a special Gallup poll of blacks two months later—after the acquittal of a neighborhood security watchman in Florida, George Zimmerman, in the shooting death of a 17-year-old black teenager, Trayvon Martin.

Despite blacks' general pessimism about the outlook for racial harmony, and their dissatisfaction with how blacks are treated, the majority are broadly positive about white-black relations. Two-thirds of blacks in June 2013 described white-black relations as very good (8%) or somewhat good (58%), while one-third called them very bad (24%) or somewhat bad (9%). These views were largely unchanged after the Zimmerman verdict, with 62% rating relations as good.

Meanwhile, whites were slightly more positive than blacks in June 2013 about race relations, with 72% calling them good, and 27% calling them bad. This is consistent with whites' slightly more positive perceptions of race relations over the past decade.

2013 Attitudes About U.S. Black-White Relations
June 13-July 5, 2013

	Blacks (non-Hispanic)	Whites (non-Hispanic)	Racial gap
	%	%	Pct. pts.
Rating of relations between whites and blacks			
Very/Somewhat good	66	72	-6
Very/Somewhat bad	33	27	
Outlook for relations between blacks and whites in the U.S.			
Solution will eventually be worked out	48	58	-10
Relations will always be a problem	49	39	
Satisfaction with how blacks are treated in society			
Very/Somewhat satisfied	47	67	-20
Very/Somewhat dissatisfied	52	33	

GALLUP'

2. Views of Discrimination Against Blacks in U.S. Society

Blacks and whites in the U.S. reject the idea that discrimination is the major reason blacks tend to have worse housing, employment and income situations on average than do whites. But even while this view is in the minority, blacks (37%) are more inclined than whites (15%) to see discrimination as the main factor. Whites and blacks are slightly less likely now than in 1993 to see racial discrimination as the major reason for blacks' objectively worse outcomes in these areas.

Most whites believe that blacks living in the U.S. have the same opportunities as whites for jobs (74%), education (80%) and housing (85%). Blacks, on the other hand, are far more divided, with only slim majorities saying blacks have equal opportunities in housing (56%) and education (55%). Many fewer blacks, 40%, say people of their race have equal job opportunities. The racial gap is largest—34 percentage points—on this question.

2013 Measures of Perceived Discrimination
June 13-July 5, 2013

	Blacks (non-Hispanic)	Whites (non-Hispanic)	Racial gap
	%	%	Pct. pts.
Do blacks have as good a chance as whites in your community to get any kind of job for which they are qualified?			
Yes	40	74	-34
No	59	25	
Do black children have as good a chance as white children in your community to get a good education?			
Yes	55	80	-25
No	44	19	
Do blacks have as good a chance as whites in your community to get any housing they can afford?			
Yes	56	85	-29
No	43	15	
What is to blame for blacks' inferior jobs, income and housing situation?			
Mostly discrimination	37	15	
Mostly something else	60	83	-23

GALLUP'

The major long-term change in these attitudes is that blacks and whites now view job opportunities as better for blacks than they did in the 1960s. Whites' positive views have risen more than blacks' views, however, and the gap in these perceptions is actually about as large now as it has been at almost any point. And, although these attitudes among both racial groups are more positive compared with the early 1960s—before the passage of major civil rights legislation—they have not changed appreciably since the 1970s.

In general, do you think that blacks have as good a chance as whites in your community to get any kind of job for which they are qualified, or don't you think they have as good a chance?

% Have as good a chance

■ Blacks ▨ Whites

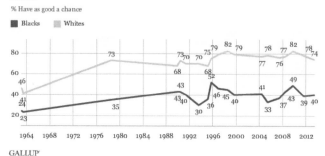

GALLUP'

3. Civil Rights and the Need for Government Intervention and New Civil Rights Laws

While white and black Americans agree that civil rights for blacks have improved in the U.S. over their lifetimes, whites are much more likely to say that they have "greatly improved." Barely a third of whites in October 1995—two weeks after that year's O.J. Simpson verdict—thought civil rights had greatly improved, but that swelled to 48% by 2003 and reached the majority level in 2011, where it remains.

Blacks, on the other hand, are much more likely to say civil rights for blacks have improved "somewhat," with 52% holding that view in the most recent Gallup update. The percentage of blacks perceiving that civil rights have "greatly improved" is 29%, essentially unchanged from earlier Gallup estimates as far back as 1995, including two measurements since President Barack Obama became the country's first black president.

Blacks' Views of Civil Rights for Blacks

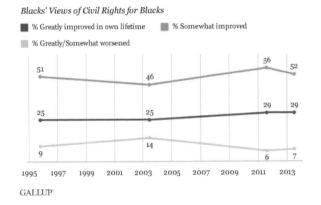

■ % Greatly improved in own lifetime   ■ % Somewhat improved

■ % Greatly/Somewhat worsened

GALLUP

Reflecting their differences on the current civil rights situation for blacks, the two racial groups differ sharply on the issue of whether new civil rights laws are needed to reduce discrimination against blacks. Blacks are essentially split, with a little more than half saying new laws are needed. Whites, on the other hand, overwhelmingly say they are not.

2013 Attitudes About Civil Rights Laws
June 13-July 5, 2013

	Blacks (non-Hispanic)	Whites (non-Hispanic)	Racial gap
	%	%	Pct. pts.
How have civil rights for blacks changed in this country over your lifetime?			
Greatly improved	29	54	-25
Somewhat improved	52	35	
Stayed the same	11	7	
Greatly/Somewhat worsened	7	3	
Are new civil rights laws are needed to reduce discrimination against blacks?			
No	45	81	-36
Yes	53	17	
Preferred government role in trying to improve the social and economic position of blacks and other minority groups			
Major role	54	22	+32
Minor role	36	49	
No role	10	29	

GALLUP

In similar fashion, whites and blacks differ significantly on the need for government intervention to deal with the situation of blacks in America. White Americans generally favor a minor government role in attempting to "improve the social and economic position of

blacks and other minorities in this country," while most blacks prefer more significant government involvement. Fifty-four percent of blacks say government's role should be a major one, while only 22% of whites agree. About three in 10 whites say that the government should play no role at all in this.

Substantial racial differences have always been apparent in this question. But whites are now less likely to favor a major government role in assisting minorities than they were during the previous decade. Blacks, though still supportive of a major government role, are also a bit less likely now than they were in 2004–2005 to think that.

4. Blacks and Whites Diverge Widely on Opinions About Police and Justice System

The high-profile incidents in Ferguson and New York City have thrust the issue of race relations and the police into the national spotlight in a powerful way in 2014. Many Americans have noted how differently the races view the police, especially when considering the question of whether black Americans receive fair treatment from law enforcement.

The disparity is greatest when Americans are asked, as Gallup did last year, if the American justice system is biased against black people. Sixty-eight percent of black Americans said the system is biased and 26% said it was not. Whites' attitudes were almost exactly the opposite—25% said the system is biased and 69% not biased.

Yet black Americans were more positive toward law enforcement when evaluating the honesty and ethical standards of police officers. Less than half of black Americans, 45%, said officers' standards are high or very high, while 59% of white Americans said the same. Only 17% of blacks said police officers' standards were low or very low, suggesting that at least last year, before Ferguson, blacks held the police in reasonably high regard.

Along the same lines, as of this June, 74% of black Americans said they had at least "some" confidence in the police, while 88% of white Americans said the same. Black Americans' confidence in the police is softer, however, when examining those who said they have a "great deal" or "quite a lot" of confidence—the percentage drops to 37% of blacks (compared with 59% of whites). Recent analysis also shows that blacks living in urban areas have less confidence in the police than those living elsewhere, underscoring the negative context in which encounters between blacks and police are carried out in the nation's metropolitan areas.

Recent Attitudes About the Police

	Blacks (non-Hispanic)	Whites (non-Hispanic)	Racial gap
	%	%	Pct. pts.
Is American justice system biased against black people?*			
No	26	69	-43
Yes	68	25	
How would you rate the honesty and ethical standards of police officers?*			
Very high/High	45	59	-14
Average	38	31	
Very low/Low	17	10	
How much confidence do you have in the police?*			
A great deal/Quite a lot	37	59	-22
Some	37	29	
Very little/None	25	12	

* July 16-21, 2013; ** Combined data from 2010-2013; *** Combined data from 2011-2014

GALLUP

Yet despite the high-profile nature of incidents involving blacks and the police in recent decades, when Gallup asked blacks directly if they had felt they were treated unfairly by the police in the last 30 days because they were black, 81% said no. The 17% who said they had been treated unfairly was down from responses gathered between 1999 and 2007—including 2004, when 25% of blacks said they had been treated unfairly within the previous month. There are differences in these views by age and gender, and an analysis in 2013 showed that young black men were more likely than other blacks to report having been treated unfairly by police within the previous 30 days. It remains to be seen, given the current intense media attention toward police treatment of blacks, whether these percentages will rise.

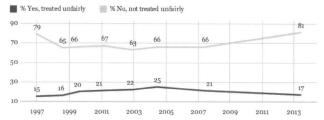

Can you think of any occasion in the last thirty days when you felt you were treated unfairly in the following places because you were black?
In dealings with the police, such as traffic incidents

■ % Yes, treated unfairly   % No, not treated unfairly

Based on non-Hispanic blacks

GALLUP

December 15, 2014
2014 U.S. APPROVAL OF CONGRESS REMAINS NEAR ALL-TIME LOW

by Rebecca Riffkin

WASHINGTON, D.C.—Americans' job approval rating for Congress averaged 15% in 2014, close to the record-low yearly average of 14% found last year. The highest yearly average was measured in 2001, at 56%. Yearly averages haven't exceeded 20% in the past five years, as well as in six of the past seven years.

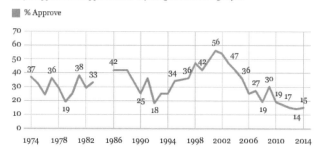

Congress' Job Approval Ratings, Yearly Averages
Do you approve or disapprove of the way Congress is handling its job?

■ % Approve

Note: Gallup did not measure congressional job approval in 1984-1985.

Congress' approval rating has averaged less than 20% each year since 2010. In 2009, President Barack Obama's first year in office in which he governed with a large Democratic majority in Congress, an average of 30% approved. Prior to 2008, Congress' job approval over the 40-year history of Gallup's measure had been below 20% only twice before, in 1979 and 1992.

After peaking in 2001 at 56%, a high figure that reflected the rally in support for government institutions after the 9/11 terror attacks, Americans' approval of Congress has generally been dropping each year, with the exception of the spike in 2009.

Similar Approval Rates Among Americans of All Political Affiliations

This past year, Congress' approval ratings averaged 15% among both Republicans and Democrats, while averaging 14% among independents. These lower approval ratings among those identifying with both major parties are partly attributable to the divided control of Congress in 2014. Control has been divided since 2011, and neither party's supporters have averaged above 20% approval of Congress.

In the past, including in 2009 and 2010 under unified Democratic control of Congress, and for most of 1995 through 2006 under unified Republican control, the majority party's supporters had a much more favorable opinion of the job Congress was doing.

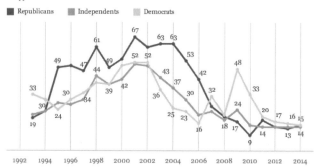

Congress' Job Approval Ratings, Yearly Averages by Party
% Approve

■ Republicans   ■ Independents   Democrats

Note: Gallup did not compile approval by party prior to 1993.

Congress Approval Averaged 16% in December

Gallup's most current *monthly* rating of Congress, from a Dec. 8–11 poll, shows 16% of Americans approving of Congress. That is little changed from November, but remains down from a slightly higher 20% reading just before this year's midterm elections. That is the only time Congress' monthly approval rating has reached the 20% mark over the last two years. Approval fell to an all-time monthly low of 9% in November 2013 after the partial government shutdown.

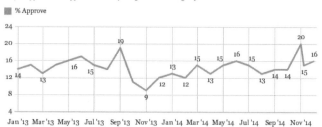

Congress' Monthly Job Approval Ratings in 2013 and 2014
Do you approve or disapprove of the way Congress is handling its job?

■ % Approve

GALLUP

Bottom Line

Over the past four years, Congress' approval ratings have been among the lowest Gallup has measured. Part of this may be attributed to the divided control of Congress, with neither party controlling both the House and Senate—thus leaving both Republicans and Democrats with divided sentiments when asked to rate Congress as a whole. However, in January, when newly elected Republican senators are sworn in and Republicans begin controlling both houses of Congress, approval may increase as Americans who identify as Republicans become more positive. This has happened in the past, with Republican approval of Congress surging in 1995 and Democratic approval increasing in 2007.

Survey Methods

Results for this Gallup poll are based on telephone interviews conducted Dec. 8–11, 2014, on the Gallup U.S. Daily survey, with a random sample of 805 adults, aged 18 and older, living in all 50 U.S. states and the District of Columbia. For results based on the total sample of national adults, the margin of sampling error is ±4 percentage points at the 95% confidence level.

Each sample of national adults includes a minimum quota of 50% cellphone respondents and 50% landline respondents, with additional minimum quotas by time zone within region. Landline and cellular telephone numbers are selected using random-digit-dial methods.

December 15, 2014
BLACKS' APPROVAL OF PRESIDENT OBAMA REMAINS HIGH

by Frank Newport

PRINCETON, NJ—President Barack Obama's job approval rating among U.S. blacks has stayed consistently about 40 percentage points higher than his approval among all Americans since 2010. So far in 2014, blacks' approval of Obama has averaged 84%, which is down from previous years but in line with the drop among the overall American population.

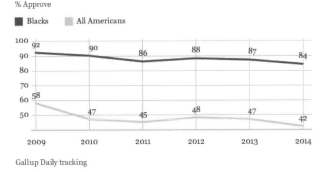

Obama Job Approval, Among Blacks and All Americans

% Approve

■ Blacks   ■ All Americans

Gallup Daily tracking

GALLUP

These data are based on Gallup Daily tracking, consisting of about 15,000 interviews with blacks from January through November 2014, and larger samples of blacks in previous years.

Blacks in the U.S. are strongly Democratic in political orientation. Gallup's pre-election surveys and the national exit polls suggest that well over 90% of blacks voted for Obama in the 2008 and 2012 presidential elections, and Obama enjoys higher levels of support among blacks than among any other racial or ethnic group. Thus, analysis of Obama's job approval among blacks is not based on expectations that it is going to change dramatically, but rather on relative variations in that high level of support over time and changes among blacks relative to other racial groups.

Black Drop in Approval Parallels Overall Drop

Americans overall were significantly more positive about Obama in his first year in office, 2009, than they have been in the years since—reflecting the honeymoon period that most presidents enjoy when they first take office. Black approval in 2009 was 92%, also the highest among this group of any of the Obama years so far. Obama's overall job approval rating dropped in 2010 and 2011, and it rose again in 2012 when Obama was re-elected. It stayed at about that level in 2013, before falling this year to what will be the lowest annual average of his administration. Black approval has generally followed the same pattern, dropping slightly in 2011, rising slightly in 2012 and staying about the same in 2013, and falling this year to its lowest average so far.

On a near-term basis, black job approval trended somewhat lower in November of this year, which included the weeks after the president's executive actions on immigration. But for the first two weeks of December, black approval is back at 84%, exactly at his yearly average.

Obama Losing Support Among Younger Blacks

As is the case for younger Americans in general, Obama's support has been dropping disproportionately among younger blacks in recent years. In the first two years of his administration, Obama's approval rating among 18- to 29-year-old blacks was just a few points lower than his approval among older blacks. That approval gap by age has widened. In 2014, Obama's job approval rating among 18- to 29-year-old blacks (80%) is seven points lower than among blacks aged 50 to 64 (87%), and eight points lower than among blacks 65 and older (88%). Similarly, the gap between Obama's job rating among 30- to 49-year-old blacks and those who are aged 50 and older has widened slightly in the past two years.

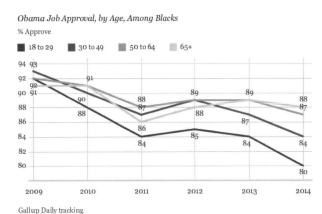

Obama Job Approval, by Age, Among Blacks

% Approve

■ 18 to 29   ■ 30 to 49   ■ 50 to 64   ■ 65+

Gallup Daily tracking

GALLUP

Politically, black Americans are reliably Democratic, and have consistently given Obama the highest job approval ratings of any racial or ethnic group in the U.S. That high level of support for Obama has drifted somewhat lower in recent years, but is generally in line with the drop in Obama's support overall. Black approval so far in 2014 remains more than 40 points higher than his overall average. Obama has lost more support among younger blacks than among those aged 50 and older, but this too follows the pattern observed among all Americans.

The relative stability in Obama's support among blacks contrasts with the more fluid support he receives among Hispanics. As a case in point, Obama's approval rating had fallen among Hispanics earlier this fall, but rose significantly in the weeks after his executive actions on immigration. Black support during this time underwent much less change, and, for the first two weeks in December, is exactly where it has been all year.

Survey Methods

Results for this Gallup poll are based on telephone interviews conducted Jan. 2–Nov. 30, 2014, on the Gallup U.S. Daily survey, with a random sample of 163,847 adults, aged 18 and older, living in all 50 U.S. states and the District of Columbia. For results based on the total sample of national adults, the margin of sampling error is ±1 percentage point at the 95% confidence level. For results based on the total sample of 15,084 non-Hispanic blacks, the margin of sampling error is ±1 percentage point at the 95% confidence level. All reported margins of sampling error include computed design effects for weighting.

Each sample of national adults includes a minimum quota of 50% cellphone respondents and 50% landline respondents, with additional minimum quotas by time zone within region. Landline and cellular telephone numbers are selected using random-digit-dial methods.

December 16, 2014
U.S. FEDERAL EMPLOYEES LESS ENGAGED THAN THE REST

by Steve Ander and Art Swift

WASHINGTON, D.C.—U.S. federal government workers are less engaged than the rest of the U.S. workforce. On average, 27% of federal government employees are engaged in their jobs in 2014, compared with 31% of all other workers in the U.S. With more than 2 million federal employees, this lack of engagement is costing the federal government an estimated $18 billion in lost productivity annually, or approximately $9,000 per employee.

Engagement Differences, by Type of Worker

	% Federal Workers	% All Other Workers
Engaged	27	31
Not Engaged	53	51
Actively Disengaged	19	17

GALLUP

According to Gallup, engaged employees feel a profound connection to their organization and move the organization forward. Not engaged employees may meet expectations of their jobs but do not expend discretionary energy or feel passion for their work. Actively disengaged employees typically are unhappy at work, but more than that, they will actually undermine the progress that their engaged co-workers make.

Those federal government employees who are actively disengaged, combined with those employees who are not engaged, translates into 11% lost productivity across the government, according to a Gallup analysis. This suggests that nearly $9,000 of the average $78,467 federal employee salary is not producing benefits for the agency or the general public.

Gallup determines this estimate of lost productivity by comparing it to a theoretical workplace where all employees are engaged. For obvious reasons, a fully engaged workplace is unlikely to exist, but this estimate also does not take into account other costs of disengaged employees to their employers, such as increased workers' compensations claims, greater turnover, and increased costs for hiring and onboarding new employees.

These lower federal engagement results follow the U.S. Office of Personnel Management's (OPM) recent release of their annual Federal Employee Viewpoint Survey (FEVS) Report that documents federal employee satisfaction. OPM reports that their satisfaction numbers continue to drop and are currently at their lowest levels since 2003. Employee satisfaction means that an employee may have his or her overall needs met but may not have an incentive to excel. Yet employee engagement means that employees have an emotional investment in the organization, looking upon their work as fulfilling a mission. In general, it is more difficult for an organization to achieve true employee engagement as opposed to satisfaction.

These findings are based on more than 68,000 interviews conducted, with U.S. adults aged 18 and older who were employed full time from Jan. 2–Nov. 2, as part of the Gallup-Healthways Well-Being Index.

Federal Workers Less Engaged Across Age Groups

The difference in engagement between the federal and non-federal sectors becomes even starker when comparing by age group. Each age group within the federal government is less engaged than its counterpart outside the federal government, with the gap widest among the oldest workers. Engagement increases with age in both sectors until the ages of 51 to 60, when it dips slightly. It climbs back up somewhat for those aged 61 and older in the federal government, but increases significantly for those outside the government—two versus eight points, respectively.

Levels of Worker Engagement, by Age

	% Federal Workers	% All Other Workers
Younger than 30	25	28
31–40	27	32
41–50	30	33
51–60	27	31
61+	29	39

GALLUP

These trends in federal workers' engagement align with previous Gallup research showing that older federal employees use their strengths less than younger federal workers. Given that employees who use their strengths every day are six times more likely to be engaged in their jobs, older federal workers' low engagement is not surprising.

Implications

With the federal government's educated workforce carrying out many different roles and mission-rich responsibilities, it has the potential to be the best place to work in America, or even the world. However, these data suggest the government has not converted these roles and responsibilities into higher engagement.

Low engagement is causing the federal government to lose value from its employees in terms of productivity, arguably more than those in all other work sectors per employee. Gallup research shows that measuring and improving engagement is linked to positive organizational outcomes such as improved retention, higher customer satisfaction and loyalty metrics, increased productivity, fewer safety claims, and minimized absenteeism. For example, Gallup estimates that absenteeism due to low engagement costs U.S. companies approximately $1 billion per year.

The current OPM budget allocates less than $30 million to administer FEVS and direct efforts to improve engagement in the federal government, and individual agencies are probably spending much less than that.

While the size of the government's employee base may be large and diverse, this budget item at these levels is not likely to promote much positive change. If OPM and the rest of the federal government is looking for a simple way to increase federal workers' engagement and reap the benefits of doing so, they could start by managing to employees' strengths, which directly contributes to engagement.

Survey Methods

Results are based on telephone interviews conducted Jan. 2–Nov. 2, 2014, as part of the Gallup-Healthways Well-Being Index survey, with a random sample of 68,684 adults, aged 18 and older, living in all 50 U.S. states and the District of Columbia. For results based on the total sample of national adults, the margin of sampling error is ±2 percentage points at the 95% confidence level.

Each sample of national adults includes a minimum quota of 50% cellphone respondents and 50% landline respondents, with additional minimum quotas by time zone within region. Landline and cellular telephone numbers are selected using random-digit-dial methods.

December 17, 2014
U.S. INVESTOR OPTIMISM REMAINED POSITIVE IN NOVEMBER

by Lydia Saad

PRINCETON, NJ—Prior to the recent slide in the stock market, American investors' mood remained fairly upbeat this quarter, with the Wells Fargo/Gallup Investor and Retirement Optimism Index coming in at +48 in mid-November, similar to the +46 reading in August. While still far from the +178 high point recorded in early 2000, the index is notably improved from +25 a year ago and at a seven-year high.

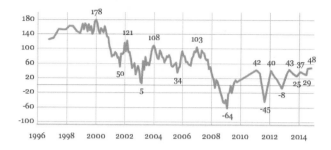

Wells Fargo/Gallup Investor and Retirement Optimism Index
October 1996-November 2014

GALLUP'

The fourth quarter Wells Fargo/Gallup Investor and Retirement Optimism Index is based on a nationally representative telephone survey of 1,009 U.S. adults with $10,000 or more in investable assets, conducted Nov. 14–23, 2014. About two in five American households have at least $10,000 in savings and investments.

The index has two components: economic and personal. The economic dimension improved slightly this quarter, rising to +5 from −1. At the same time, the personal dimension was steady but positive at +43 versus +47 in August.

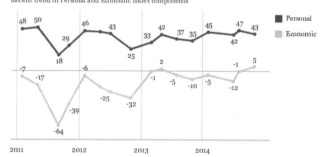

Wells Fargo/Gallup Investor and Retirement Optimism Index
Recent trend in Personal and Economic Index components

GALLUP'

The economic dimension is based on investors' expectations about the performance of four aspects of the economy over the next year. Of these, investors are most upbeat about the stock market, with a net optimism score of +31 (out of a possible +200), similar to +29 last quarter. Gallup also finds positive net optimism about economic growth, at +4 up from −1. Investors' ratings of unemployment (−3) and inflation (−14) are lower but slightly improved from August.

Compared with a year ago, investor optimism has shown some improvement on all dimensions except for the stock market, which is about as positive today as it was then.

U.S. Investor Optimism About the Economy -- Selected Trend
Net optimism (optimism minus pessimism)

	2014, Quarter 4	2014, Quarter 3	One year ago
The stock market	+31	+29	+29
Economic growth	+4	-1	-17
Unemployment rate	-3	-8	-24
Inflation	-14	-20	-23

Wells Fargo/Gallup Investor and Retirement Optimism Index

GALLUP'

Personal Financial Outlook Flat But Positive

On the personal dimension, the fourth quarter survey finds investors quite optimistic about their ability to maintain or increase their income in the next 12 months (+54). That is similar to last quarter, but up 14 points from a year ago. At the same time, the +43 net optimism score for achieving five-year investment goals and +30 for achieving 12-month investment targets have shown less change in the past year.

U.S. Investor Optimism About Personal Finances -- Selected Trend

Net optimism (optimism minus pessimism)

	2014, Quarter 4	2014, Quarter 3	One year ago
Maintaining or increasing your income	+54	+54	+40
Achieving five-year investment goals	+43	+50	+42
Achieving 12-month investment targets	+30	+36	+25

Wells Fargo/Gallup Investor and Retirement Optimism Index

GALLUP'

Outlook Improves Among Retired Investors

After trailing nonretirees' optimism last quarter, the level among retired investors rose 19 points in November to +54, edging past nonretired investors' optimism, which fell slightly this quarter to +46. This marks only the third time in three years that retirees' optimism has exceeded nonretirees'.

Wells Fargo/Gallup Investor and Retirement Optimism Index

Recent trend, by retirement status

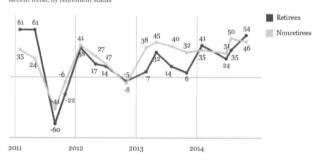

GALLUP'

Retirees' increased optimism reflects major gains in their confidence on all four aspects of the economic dimension, with no improvement in their personal dimension ratings. While the reason for this is unclear, it could reflect retirees' greater exposure to the stock market given their higher average asset level and reliance on investments for current income. The performance of the stock market in the fourth quarter, bouncing back in November after plunging in October, may have encouraged retirees to feel better about the economy overall at the time of the survey.

Bottom Line

Investors have had some scares in 2014, with significant market declines in January, July, October and now December interrupting an otherwise encouraging market ride. Also, retirees who are reliant on interest income have had to endure another year of low rates, possibly hampering their overall outlook. At the same time, recent strength in the economy and labor market may be helping to offset concerns about low interest rates with some investors.

Whatever forces are at play, investors, overall, managed to remain fairly optimistic in the past quarter, at a level slightly better than a year ago and the highest the Wells Fargo/Gallup Investor and Retirement Optimism Index has reached since 2007. Whether that continues into early 2015 will greatly depend on whether the latest market turbulence is as short-lived as the prior episodes this year, or if it proves to be the beginning of the end of the bull market.

Survey Methods

Results for the Wells Fargo/Gallup Investor and Retirement Optimism Index survey are based on questions asked Nov. 14–23, 2014, on the Gallup Daily tracking survey, of a random sample of 1,009 U.S. adults having investable assets of $10,000 or more.

For results based on the entire sample of investors, the margin of sampling error is ±3 percentage points at the 95% confidence level.

In addition to sampling error, question wording and practical difficulties in conducting surveys can introduce error or bias into the findings of public opinion polls.

December 18, 2014
DROP AMONG NONWHITES DRIVES U.S. POLICE HONESTY RATINGS DOWN

by Jeffrey M. Jones

PRINCETON, NJ—A new Gallup poll finds that Americans are less likely now than in 2013 to view police officers as having high honesty and ethical standards after grand juries did not indict white police officers whose actions resulted in the deaths of black men. The overall drop of six percentage points in honesty and ethics ratings is the result of a sharp, 22-point drop in nonwhites' ratings of police officers; whites' views haven't changed.

Honesty/Ethics Ratings of Police Officers, by Race

Figures are the percentage rating the honesty and ethical standards of police officers as "very high" or "high"

	2013	2014	Change
	%	%	(pct. pts.)
All Americans	54	48	-6
Non-Hispanic whites	58	59	+1
Nonwhites	45	23	-22

GALLUP'

Earlier this year, a white officer in Ferguson, Missouri, shot and killed an unarmed black teen, and a white officer in Staten Island, New York, held a black man in a chokehold that resulted in his death. Those incidents, and, importantly, grand juries' decisions not to indict either officer, have ignited controversy over racial bias and the police's use of force to apprehend suspects.

Although those incidents involved blacks, a single standard poll of U.S. national adults does not usually include a large enough sample of blacks to provide reliable estimates of that specific group's attitudes. However, the Dec. 8–11 poll does include a sufficiently large sample of nonwhites—consisting mainly of blacks and Hispanics—to look at differences among this broader racial group.

Even before this year, whites have consistently held more positive views of the police than nonwhites. So the much greater likelihood of whites than nonwhites to view police officers as honest and ethical is not new.

But the data from the Dec. 8–11 poll show that whites and nonwhites are reacting very differently to the recent events—with nonwhites' already less positive views of police eroding further, while there is little apparent impact on the way whites view the police. Consequently, the gap in white versus nonwhite ratings of the honesty and ethics of police has expanded from 13 points last year (58% to 45%) to 36 points this year (59% to 23%).

Ratings of Police Lowest in Two Decades

The six-point drop in all Americans' ratings of the honesty and ethics of police gives the profession its worst rating since 1995, a time when crime was among Americans' greatest concerns. Still, the current 48% rating of police officers is substantially higher than the all-time low of 37% measured in 1977, the first year Gallup asked the question.

Honesty/Ethics Ratings of Police Officers

Figures denote the percentage rating the honesty and ethical standards of police officers as "very high" or "high"

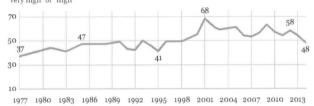

GALLUP

The long-term trend shows two clear phases in Americans' ratings of police officers. From 1977 through 1998, their honesty and ethics scores were consistently 50% or below. From 1999 to 2013, perhaps as a result of sharply declining crime rates, the ratings were consistently above 50%. That includes a record-high 68% in 2001, likely aided by the rally in support for public institutions after the Sept. 11 terrorist attacks.

The recent controversy over the police's use of force has thus eroded much of the increased positivity the police had built up in recent decades.

Implications

Blacks and whites, perhaps because of historical racial discrimination in the U.S. as well as their own life experiences, have largely differing views on matters that touch on race in U.S. society. Ongoing tensions between police and black citizens, commonly in urban areas, also factor into blacks' (and other nonwhites') more negative views of police.

These factors help explain why nonwhites' views of police nosedived after the Ferguson and Staten Island incidents, whereas whites' views have largely held steady. It is certainly possible that as these incidents fade from memory, nonwhites' views of the police—as well as those of Americans more broadly—will return to their

prior levels. However, improved relations between blacks and police would also go a long way toward improving the way Americans of all racial and ethnic backgrounds view the police.

Survey Methods

Results for this Gallup poll are based on telephone interviews conducted Dec. 8–11, 2014, with a random sample of 805 adults, aged 18 and older, living in all 50 U.S. states and the District of Columbia. For results based on the total sample of national adults, the margin of sampling error is ±4 percentage points at the 95% confidence level.

For results based on the total sample of 606 non-Hispanic whites, the margin of sampling error is ±5 percentage points at the 95% confidence level.

For results based on the total sample of 174 nonwhites, the margin of sampling error is ±9 percentage points at the 95% confidence level.

All reported margins of sampling error include computed design effects for weighting.

Each sample of national adults includes a minimum quota of 50% cellphone respondents and 50% landline respondents, with additional minimum quotas by time zone within region. Landline and cellular telephone numbers are selected using random-digit-dial methods.

December 18, 2014
AMERICANS RATE NURSES HIGHEST ON HONESTY, ETHICAL STANDARDS

by Rebecca Riffkin

WASHINGTON, D.C.—In 2014, Americans say nurses have the highest honesty and ethical standards. Members of Congress and car salespeople were given the worst ratings among the 11 professions included in this year's poll. Eighty percent of Americans say nurses have "very high" or "high" standards of honesty and ethics, compared with a 7% rating for members of Congress and 8% for car salespeople.

U.S. Views on Honesty and Ethical Standards in Professions

Please tell me how you would rate the honesty and ethical standards of people in these different fields -- very high, high, average, low, or very low?

	% Very high or high	% Average	% Very low or low
Nurses	80	17	2
Medical doctors	65	29	7
Pharmacists	65	28	7
Police officers	48	31	20
Clergy	46	35	13
Bankers	23	49	26
Lawyers	21	45	34
Business executives	17	50	32
Advertising practitioners	10	44	42
Car salespeople	8	46	45
Members of Congress	7	30	61

Dec. 8-11, 2014
Rated in order of % Very high or high

GALLUP

Americans have been asked to rate the honesty and ethics of various professions annually since 1990, and periodically since 1976. Nurses have topped the list each year since they were first included in 1999, with the exception of 2001 when firefighters were included in response to their work during and after the 9/11 attacks. Since 2005, at least 80% of Americans have said nurses have high ethics and honesty. Two other medical professions—medical doctors and pharmacists—tie this year for second place at 65%, with police officers and clergy approaching 50%.

Historically, honesty and ethics ratings for members of Congress have generally not been positive, with the highest rating reaching 25% in 2001. Since 2009, Congress has ranked at or near the bottom of the list, usually tied with other poorly viewed professions like car salespeople and—when they have been included—lobbyists, telemarketers, HMO managers, stockbrokers and advertising practitioners.

Although members of Congress and car salespeople have similar percentages rating their honesty and ethics as "very high" or "high," members of Congress are much more likely to receive "low" or "very low" ratings (61%), compared with 45% for car salespeople. Last year, 66% of Americans rated Congress' honesty and ethics "low" or "very low," the worst Gallup has measured for any profession historically.

Other relatively poorly rated professions, including advertising practitioners, lawyers, business executives and bankers, are more likely to receive "average" than "low" honesty and ethical ratings. So while several of these professions rank about as low as members of Congress in terms of having high ethics, they are less likely than members of Congress to be viewed as having low ethics.

No Professions Improved in Ratings of High Honesty, Ethics Since 2013

Since 2013, all professions either dropped or stayed the same in the percentage of Americans who said they have high honesty and ethics. The only profession to show a small increase was lawyers, and this rise was small (one percentage point) and within the margin of error. The largest drops were among police officers, pharmacists and business executives. But medical doctors, bankers and advertising practitioners also saw drops.

U.S. Views on Honesty and Ethical Standards in Professions Compared With 2013

Please tell me how you would rate the honesty and ethical standards of people in these different fields -- very high, high, average, low, or very low?

	% 2014 very high or high	% 2013 very high or high	Difference (pct. pts.)
Nurses	80	82	-2
Medical doctors	65	69	-4
Pharmacists	65	70	-5
Police officers	48	54	-6
Clergy	46	47	-1
Bankers	23	27	-4
Lawyers	21	20	1
Business executives	17	22	-5
Advertising practitioners	10	14	-4
Car salespeople	8	9	-1
Members of Congress	7	8	-1

Dec. 8-11, 2014

GALLUP

Honesty and ethics ratings of police dropped six percentage points since last year, driven down by many fewer nonwhite Americans saying the police have high honesty and ethical standards.

The clergy's 47% rating last year marked the first year that less than 50% of Americans said the clergy had high ethical and honesty standards—and the current 46% rating is, by one percentage point, the lowest Gallup has measured for that profession to date.

Bottom Line

Americans continue to rate those in medical professions as having higher honesty and ethical standards than those in most other professions. Nurses have consistently been the top-rated profession—although doctors and pharmacists also receive high ratings, despite the drops since 2013 in the percentage of Americans who say they have high ethics. The high ratings of medical professions this year is significant after the Ebola outbreak which infected a number of medical professionals both in the U.S. and in West Africa.

At the other end of the spectrum, in recent years, members of Congress have sunk to the same depths as car salespeople and advertising practitioners. However, in one respect, Congress is even worse, given the historically high percentages rating its members' honesty and ethics as being "low" or "very low." And although November's midterm elections did produce a significant change in membership for the new Congress that begins in January, there were also major shakeups in the 2006 and 2010 midterm elections with little improvement in the way Americans viewed the members who serve in that institution.

Previously in 2014, Gallup found that Americans continue to have low confidence in banks, and while Americans continue to have confidence in small businesses, big businesses do not earn a lot of confidence. This may be the result of Americans' views that bankers and business executives do not have high honesty and ethical standards, and the fact that their ratings dropped since last year.

Survey Methods

Results for this Gallup poll are based on telephone interviews conducted Dec. 8–11, 2014, with a random sample of 805 adults, aged 18 and older, living in all 50 U.S. states and the District of Columbia. For results based on the total sample of national adults, the margin of sampling error is ±4 percentage points at the 95% confidence level.

Each sample of national adults includes a minimum quota of 50% cellphone respondents and 50% landline respondents, with additional minimum quotas by time zone within region. Landline and cellular telephone numbers are selected using random-digit-dial methods.

December 19, 2014
AS A MAJOR U.S. PROBLEM, RACE RELATIONS SHARPLY RISES

by Justin McCarthy

WASHINGTON, D.C.—The percentage of Americans naming "race relations" or "racism" as the most important problem in the U.S. has climbed dramatically to 13%, the highest figure Gallup has recorded since a finding of 15% in 1992, in the midst of the Rodney King verdict. In November, race relations/racism was cited by 1% of the public as the most important problem.

Trend for "Race Relations/Racism" as Most Important Problem in U.S.

What do you think is the most important problem facing this country today?

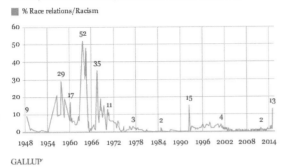

■ % Race relations/Racism

GALLUP

Since 1992, the percentage of Americans saying race relations/racism is America's biggest problem has ranged from 0% to 5%. The jump to 13% this month comes on the heels of national protests of police treatment of blacks in the wake of incidents in Ferguson, Missouri, and Staten Island, New York, among others.

Concurrently, Gallup has found recent drops in nonwhites' confidence in police to protect them as well as nonwhites' ratings of the honesty and ethical standards of police officers.

Nonwhites (22%) are more than twice as likely as whites (9%) to view racial issues as the nation's largest problem.

"Race Relations/Racism" as Most Important Problem, by Race

What do you think is the most important problem facing this country today?

	Among whites	Among nonwhites
Race relations/Racism	9%	22%

Dec. 8-11, 2014

GALLUP

Prior to this month and the spring of 1992, the last time race relations was a significant top-of-mind issue for Americans was in the 1950s and 1960s, when race was front and center of national policy discussions on civil rights. In 1963, more than half of Americans (52%) said race relations was the country's biggest problem.

By the 1970s and 1980s, the percentage of Americans naming racial issues as the nation's biggest problem tapered off, before erupting in a single poll in the early 1990s.

After barely registering with Americans as the top problem for two decades, race relations now matches the economy in Americans' mentions of the country's top problem, and is just slightly behind government (15%). Eight percent of Americans now identify unemployment as the nation's greatest problem, down slightly from November.

Recent Trends in Top Four "Most Important" U.S. Problems

What do you think is the most important problem facing this country today?

■ % Government   ■ % Racism   ■ % Economy   ■ % Unemployment

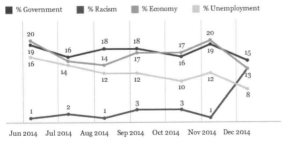

GALLUP

Bottom Line

With the news in recent weeks filled with protestors angry about high-profile grand jury decisions involving race, Americans have turned their attention to the issue of racial discord in this country. Race relations is now tied with the economy in general—and nearly matches issues with the government—as the nation's top perceived problem.

At 13%, the percentage now mentioning racism is nowhere near as high as Gallup found in the 1950s and 1960s, but is similar to the level found in the midst of the Rodney King case. It remains to be seen whether this public concern persists, as it did during the civil rights era, or recedes as quickly as it did in 1992.

Survey Methods

Results for this Gallup poll are based on telephone interviews conducted Dec. 8–11, 2014, on the Gallup U.S. Daily survey, with a random sample of 805 adults, aged 18 and older, living in all 50 U.S. states and the District of Columbia. For results based on the total sample of national adults, the margin of sampling error is ±4 percentage points at the 95% confidence level.

Each sample of national adults includes a minimum quota of 50% cellphone respondents and 50% landline respondents, with additional minimum quotas by time zone within region. Landline and cellular telephone numbers are selected using random-digit-dial methods.

December 19, 2014
SATISFACTION WITH DIRECTION OF U.S. CONTINUES TO LANGUISH

by Jeffrey M. Jones

PRINCETON, NJ—In 2014, an average of 23% of Americans said they were satisfied with the way things were going in the U.S., similar to their views in recent years but on the lower end of what Gallup has measured since 1979.

Americans' Satisfaction With the Way Things Are Going in the U.S., Annual Gallup Averages

■ % Satisfied

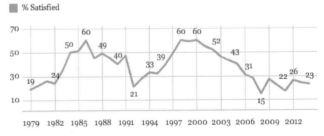

GALLUP

These results are based on aggregated data from 13 different Gallup polls conducted in 2014—one per month with an additional conducted in late October and early November. This includes the reading from December, which is also 23%.

Although Americans are relatively dissatisfied with the way things are going, the 2014 average is substantially better than the all-time low of 15% in 2008, a year marked by a recessionary economy and the financial crisis.

Still, the 2014 average is well below Gallup's historical average satisfaction rating of 38%. The all-time highs were 60% readings in 1986, 1998, and 2000, which all came at times of sustained economic growth.

Democrats Much More Satisfied Than Republicans

Thirty-eight percent of Democrats, compared with 10% of Republicans and 21% of independents, said they were satisfied with the way things were going in the U.S. throughout 2014. Those party averages are similar to what they have been since 2009, when President Barack Obama took office. They are also consistent with the historical pattern by which supporters of the president's party are more likely to be pleased with the direction of the country than non-supporters.

Satisfaction With the Way Things Are Going in the U.S., Annual Gallup Averages 1993-2014, by Political Party

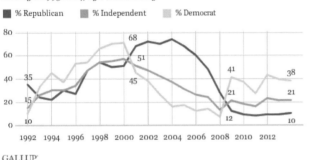

GALLUP

In 1992, the last year of George H.W. Bush's presidency and a year of generally low satisfaction overall, Republicans were significantly more satisfied than Democrats. That changed in 1993, when Bill Clinton took office and Democrats began reporting higher levels of satisfaction than Republicans. During Clinton's time in office, satisfaction increased among both Republicans and Democrats, but with Democrats consistently expressing satisfaction. When George W. Bush succeeded Clinton, Republicans once again became more satisfied, and they continued to be so even as satisfaction fell precipitously during his second term. During Obama's term, the party gap has held close to 30 percentage points, apart from 2011, when Democratic satisfaction dipped before recovering the next year.

Satisfaction Low But Improving as Economic Confidence Improves

As Gallup's 35-year trend on satisfaction makes clear, Americans are relatively more pleased with the state of the nation during good economic times—like the mid-1980s, late 1990s and early 2000s. And they are much more dissatisfied with national conditions when the economy is poor—as in the late 1970s and early 1980s, early 1990s and late 2000s.

As the economy has modestly improved in recent years, so has satisfaction, from 15% in 2008 to 23% this year—a 53% increase. Over the same time period, Gallup's Economic Confidence Index has improved from −48 in 2008 to −14 so far in 2014, representing an 71% increase. Both satisfaction and economic confidence, however, remain below where they were in 2006 and 2007 before the recession.

Importantly, even as economic confidence has improved, it, too, remains low in absolute terms, as evidenced by the negative score on the index: −14. Gallup calculates the index such that negative scores indicate Americans are more negative than positive about the state of the economy, and positive scores indicate Americans are more upbeat than pessimistic. Therefore, satisfaction might not grow appreciably until Americans are more optimistic about the economy *and* evaluate it positively overall.

Even though Americans are more positive about the economy than they have been in recent years, it still ranks at or near the top of their list of the most important problems facing the country. In addition to the economy, dissatisfaction with the government has also consistently ranked among the most important problems facing the country in the last two years. As a result, Americans' frustration with Washington's ability to address the country's major issues could be holding satisfaction down, as it likely did in 2006 and 2007 when the economy was relatively good. With Republicans taking control of the Senate and the House in January, the prospects for greater cooperation in Washington are not bright.

Survey Methods

Results for this Gallup poll are based on aggregated data from telephone interviews conducted in 2014, with a random sample of 13,714 adults, aged 18 and older, living in all 50 U.S. states and the District of Columbia. For results based on the total sample of national adults, the margin of sampling error is ±1 percentage points at the 95% confidence level.

Each sample of national adults includes a minimum quota of 50% cellphone respondents and 50% landline respondents, with additional minimum quotas by time zone within region. Landline and cellular telephone numbers are selected using random-digit-dial methods.

December 22, 2014
U.S. QUALITY JOB OUTLOOK BACK AT PRE-RECESSION LEVELS

by Rebecca Riffkin

WASHINGTON, D.C.—The percentage of Americans saying now is a good time to find a quality job jumped to 36% in December, up six percentage points from November. This is by one point the highest percentage found since November 2007, prior to the start of the Great Recession.

Percentage in U.S. Saying Now Is a Good Time to Find a Quality Job

Thinking about the job situation in America today, would you say that it is now a good time or a bad time to find a quality job?

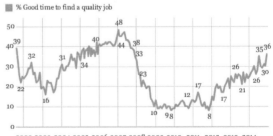

GALLUP

When Gallup first asked this question in August 2001, 39% of Americans said it was a good time to find a quality job. Gallup began updating this question monthly in October of that year. The highest "good time" percentage Gallup has found since was the 48% in January 2007, while the lowest was 8%—found several times, most recently in November 2011.

While Americans are as positive about the job market as they were in December 2007, the majority, 61%, continue to say it is a bad time to find a quality job. That has improved, however, from the 66% seen last month and the 73% in December 2013.

Among groups of Americans, younger adults continue to be more optimistic than older Americans about the quality job situation (43% "good time" vs. 29%, respectively). Possibly because there is a Democratic president, Democrats and those who lean Democratic (47%) are more positive than Republicans and those who lean Republican (29%). Gallup has previously found that views of the availability of quality jobs are linked to political views.

Good Time to Find a Quality Job, by Subgroup

Thinking about the job situation in America today, would you say that it is now a good time or a bad time to find a quality job?

	% Good time
Republican/Lean Republican	29
Democrat/Lean Democratic	47
18 to 49	43
50+	29
College graduate	37
No college degree	36
Employed	45
Not employed	27

Dec. 8-11, 2014

GALLUP

Americans with a college degree and those without one have similar views of quality job prospects. Employed Americans, however, are more positive about this than are those who are not employed. It is important to note that Americans who are not employed are not necessarily unemployed; they could also be retired or choosing not to work.

Implications

Americans' perceptions that now is a good time to find a quality job have returned to pre-recession levels, a sign that Americans are seeing improving job conditions. This follows a November increase in Gallup's Job Creation Index. That month, the Bureau of Labor Statistics' U.S. unemployment rate stayed just under 6%, at 5.8%. While these indicators are still not as good as what was seen prior to the start of the recession, they are much improved from 2009 to 2011, when the economy was still slowly recovering.

Survey Methods

Results for this Gallup poll are based on telephone interviews conducted Dec. 8–11, 2014, on the Gallup U.S. Daily survey, with a random sample of 805 adults, aged 18 and older, living in all 50 U.S. states and the District of Columbia. For results based on

the total sample of national adults, the margin of sampling error is ±4 percentage points at the 95% confidence level. All reported margins of sampling error include computed design effects for weighting.

Each sample of national adults includes a minimum quota of 50% cellphone respondents and 50% landline respondents, with additional minimum quotas by time zone within region. Landline and cellular telephone numbers are selected using random-digit-dial methods.

December 22, 2014
ONE IN FIVE INVESTORS HAVE TAPPED INTO 401(K) PREMATURELY

by Art Swift

WASHINGTON, D.C.—The majority of nonretired investors in the U.S. say their employer offers a 401(k) plan, and of these, 89% say they participate in it. Yet 21% of those who participate in such a plan say they have either taken out a 401(k) loan or even taken an early withdrawal from the plan in the last five years.

401(k) Plans, Loans and Early Withdrawals

In the last five years, have you taken out a loan from your 401(k)-type plan for any reason? In the last five years, have you had to take an early withdrawal from your 401(k)-type plan for any reason?

	Yes	No
Loan	16%	84%
Early withdrawal	9%	91%
Total % who have taken a loan/early withdrawal/both	21%	80%

Nov. 14-23, 2014
Wells Fargo/Gallup Investor and Retirement Optimism Index

GALLUP

The latest findings from the Wells Fargo/Gallup Investment and Retirement Optimism Index show nonretired investors are generally enthusiastic about 401(k) plans, but there are some troubling signs and uncertainty regarding the investment vehicle. As long-term savings, 401(k) plans are not intended to be accounts from which contributors can make early withdrawals. However, not only have a fifth of investors tapped into 401(k) funds prematurely, but barely more than half of those with a plan, 55%, say they understand the tax consequences of early 401(k) withdrawals "extremely well." Most of the rest, 40%, say they understand the consequences "somewhat well," and 5% say "not very well" or "not at all."

The fourth-quarter Wells Fargo/Gallup Investor and Retirement Optimism Index is based on a nationally representative telephone survey of 1,009 U.S. adults with $10,000 or more in investable assets, conducted Nov. 14–23, 2014. About two in five U.S. households have at least $10,000 in investments.

Most 401(k) Investors Actively Involved in Their Plan

With nearly 90% of nonretired investors saying they are participating in a 401(k) plan if their employer offers it, it is clear that 401(k) plans remain a popular investment option in American workplaces. Almost all investors with a plan (96%) say they are actively contributing to their plan, and 93% say they have reviewed their plan's performance in the last year. Another sign of the strength of the program is that, in a separate question, only 5% say they have lowered or stopped contributing to their 401(k) overall.

Bottom Line

Americans with $10,000 or more in investments are theoretically in a far better position than those with less or with nothing invested to get along without taking on debt. Yet 16% of this group reports having borrowed against their retirement plan in the past five years, and 9% have resorted to the more drastic option of making an early withdrawal. Five percent have done both.

Some of this may be attributable to Americans' putting less in liquid savings at a time of low interest rates, opting instead for maximizing what they can put in stock-based funds, such as those that make up the backbone of most 401(k) accounts. At a time when the U.S. savings rate is on the lower side of the historical range, investors with the capacity to save may need more guidance about how to save to avoid costly emergency measures, or having to take out loans or engage in early withdrawals.

Survey Methods

Results for the Wells Fargo/Gallup Investor and Retirement Optimism Index survey are based on questions asked Nov. 14–23, 2014, on the Gallup Daily tracking survey, of a random sample of 1,009 U.S. adults having investable assets of $10,000 or more.

For results based on the entire sample of investors, the margin of sampling error is ±3 percentage points at the 95% confidence level. All reported margins of sampling error include computed design effects for weighting.

In addition to sampling error, question wording and practical difficulties in conducting surveys can introduce error or bias into the findings of public opinion polls.

December 23, 2014
ONE IN FOUR INVESTORS STARTED YOUNG SAVING FOR RETIREMENT

by Lydia Saad

PRINCETON, NJ—Twenty-six percent of investors in the U.S. report that they started saving for their retirement before they turned 25, including 7% who had the foresight—or, more likely, the adult guidance—to start before they turned 20.

Another 23% began between the ages of 25 and 29, meaning about half of today's investors started the process of saving for retirement before turning 30. Investors who start saving for retirement by their 20s are positioned to enjoy tremendous gains because of the effect of compound interest in long-term investing, often termed "snowball savings."

While the remainder of investors might have missed these prime years for maximizing the snowball effect, a large segment—28% of all investors—say they first started saving at some point in their 30s. Relatively few, 14%, waited until their 40s or until they were 50 or older (8%).

Age at Which U.S. Investors Estimate They Started Saving for Retirement

	Nov. 14-23, 2014
	%
Younger than 20	7
20 to 24	19
25 to 29	23
30 to 39	28
40 to 49	14
50 and older	8

Based on 946 investors, including 576 nonretirees who have started saving for retirement and 370 retirees

Wells Fargo/Gallup Investor and Retirement Optimism Index

GALLUP

This question was asked of all retired investors and the 91% of nonretired investors who say they are saving for their retirement. The average age at which all of these investors started saving is 30, while it is slightly higher among retirees (age 35) than nonretirees (age 29).

The findings are from the latest Wells Fargo/Gallup Investor and Retirement Optimism Index survey of U.S. adults who have at least $10,000 invested in stocks, bonds or mutual funds. The survey was conducted Nov. 14–23.

Most Investors Could Save More

About a quarter of nonretired investors who are currently saving for their retirement say they could not possibly save any more each month than they already do. Most of the rest (69%), however, believe they could—with the median additional estimated savings among this group being $250 more each month.

U.S. Investors' Estimate of Possible Additional Retirement Savings

Thinking carefully about all of your spending and expenses, how much more money, if any, could you possibly save each month for your retirement if you made a serious effort to do so?

	Nov. 2014
	%
$1,000+	15
$400-$999	16
$200-$399	18
Less than $200	20
Nothing	26
Not sure	5

Based on 636 nonretired investors
Wells Fargo/Gallup Investor and Retirement Optimism Index

GALLUP

Another indication that investors could devote more resources to their retirement if they had to comes from a question asking, hypothetically, how knowing that they would not receive any money from Social Security in retirement might influence their savings behavior. Three in 10 say this scenario would motivate them to save a lot more money for their retirement, and another 24% say it would motivate them to save a little more. Less than half, 44%, say it would not make a difference.

Effect on Investor Savings of Hypothetically Losing Social Security

Hypothetically, if you knew you would not receive any money from Social Security when you retire, would that motivate you to save a lot more money for your retirement than you do now, a little more money or would it not make a difference in how much you save?

	Nov. 2014
	%
Would make you save a lot more	30
Would make you save a little more	24
Would not make a difference	44
No opinion	2

Based on 636 nonretired investors
Wells Fargo/Gallup Investor and Retirement Optimism Index

GALLUP'

Investors' responses to this question indicate that many are counting on Social Security as a safety net for at least some of their retirement security. More importantly, their answers reveal that despite past Wells Fargo/Gallup research showing that 38% of non-retired investors fear they are not saving enough for retirement, the truth is many probably could be saving more with careful budgeting. While there is little risk that the government will deny any of today's investors all of their Social Security benefits, additional savings are probably warranted for many, as the agency itself projects it will only be able to pay 76% of benefits come 2037 without additional revenue.

Bottom Line

In an ideal world, every employed American could start saving for retirement in his or her early 20s, using tax-advantaged accounts to shelter at least 10% of his or her income and earning interest that well outpaces inflation. Unfortunately, the reality usually falls short of these goals, and as a result, just two in five adult Americans even have the $10,000 in investments needed for inclusion in the Wells Fargo/Gallup Investor and Retirement Optimism Index. Of these investors, half tell Gallup they started saving for their retirement in their 20s.

By this point in the holiday season, spare cash can be hard to come by, but for those who have a little extra and do not yet have a retirement account, learning about compound interest could provide them the motivation to start saving. And for those investors who believe they can squeeze out more savings each month, now is the time to increase their 401(k) contributions for next year or make a catch-up contribution for 2014 if eligible.

Survey Methods

Results for the Wells Fargo/Gallup Investor and Retirement Optimism Index survey are based on questions asked Nov. 14–23, 2014, on the Gallup Daily tracking survey, of a random sample of 1,009 U.S. adults having investable assets of $10,000 or more.

For results based on the entire sample of investors, the margin of sampling error is ±3 percentage points at the 95% confidence level.

In addition to sampling error, question wording and practical difficulties in conducting surveys can introduce error or bias into the findings of public opinion polls.

December 24, 2014
THREE-QUARTERS OF AMERICANS IDENTIFY AS CHRISTIAN

by Frank Newport

PRINCETON, NJ—About three in four Americans interviewed in 2014 name a Christian faith when asked for their religious preference, including 50% who are Protestants or another non-Catholic Christian religion, 24% who are Catholic and 2% who are Mormon.

Religious Preference in the United States

	2013	2014
	%	%
Protestant/Other Christian	51	50
Catholic	24	24
Mormon	2	2
Jewish	2	2
Muslim	1	1
Other non-Christian religion	3	3
None/Atheist/Agnostic	15	16
No response given	3	3

Gallup Daily tracking

GALLUP'

These data are based on 173,490 interviews conducted from Jan. 2 through Dec. 21 as part of Gallup Daily tracking.

The proportion of Americans identifying as Protestant dropped by one percentage point from 2013 to 2014, while the Catholic and Mormon percentages stayed essentially the same.

About 6% of Americans identify with a non-Christian religion, including 2% who are Jewish, less than 1% who are Muslim and 3% who identify with other non-Christian religions. This leaves 16% who say they don't have a religious preference, along with another 3% who don't answer the question. This combined 19% without a formal religious identity is up one point from 2013.

The slight erosion of Americans' identification as Protestant and concomitantly slight increase in the percentage with no religious preference exemplifies general trends in religious identity over the past decades. In the 1950s, Gallup surveys showed that up to 71% of Americans identified as Protestant, and small percentages had no religious identity. Then, as now, however, well more than 90% of Americans who express a religious preference identify themselves as Christians.

Majority Attend Religious Services Monthly or More Frequently

More than half (53%) of Americans in 2014 report attending religious services at least monthly, including 41% who attend weekly or almost every week. Only one in five say they never attend religious services. These numbers reflect a slight shift to less frequent attendance compared with 2013.

How often do you attend church, synagogue or mosque?

	2013	2014
	%	%
At least once a week	34	33
Almost every week	9	8
About once a month	13	12
Seldom	23	24
Never	20	21
Don't know/Refused	1	2

Gallup Daily tracking

GALLUP'

Religious service attendance varies widely across segments of the U.S. population, including significant differences among specific religious groups. Mormons report the highest attendance of any of the major religious groups, with 75% attending weekly or almost every week. Protestants are next on the attendance list, followed by Muslims and Catholics. Attendance among Jews and those who identify with other non-Christian religions is significantly lower than that for Christians and Muslims. As would be expected, few of those who have no religious preference report attending services frequently.

Religious Service Attendance, by Religious Preference

	At least once a week/ Almost every week
	%
Mormon	75
Protestant/Other Christian	53
Muslim	50
Catholic	45
Jewish	19
Other non-Christian religion	19
None/Atheist/Agnostic	4

Jan. 2-Dec. 21, 2014
Gallup Daily tracking

GALLUP

Protestants make up the largest single segment of the religious landscape in the U.S., and church attendance varies among segments of this large group. The split in attendance among Protestants by race and ethnicity is particularly interesting. U.S. Hispanics are predominantly Catholic, but a substantial 27% in 2014 identified themselves as Protestants. More than seven in 10 blacks are Protestants. Both black and Hispanic Protestants report much higher attendance than do white Protestants.

There is little difference in attendance between Hispanic and non-Hispanic white Catholics. About a third of all Catholics in the U.S. are Hispanic.

U.S. Religious Service Attendance, by Religious Preference and Race/Ethnicity

	At least once a week/ Almost every week
	%
Hispanic Protestants	62
Non-Hispanic black Protestants	61
Non-Hispanic white Protestants	50
Non-Hispanic white Catholics	44
Hispanic Catholics	44

Jan. 2-Dec. 21, 2014
Gallup Daily tracking

GALLUP

Implications

The U.S. remains a largely Christian nation, with over three-quarters of Americans identifying as Protestant, Catholic or Mormon. The U.S. also remains a generally observant nation as measured by Americans' self-reported attendance at religious services. Eight in 10 Americans attend religious services at least occasionally, while more than half attend monthly or more frequently. Mormons attend religious services most frequently, while those who identify as Jewish or with some other non-Christian religions attend the least.

Survey Methods

Results for this Gallup poll are based on telephone interviews conducted Jan. 2–Dec. 21, 2014, on the Gallup U.S. Daily survey, with a random sample of 173,490 adults, aged 18 and older, living in all 50 U.S. states and the District of Columbia. For results based on the total sample of national adults, the margin of sampling error is ±1 percentage point at the 95% confidence level. Results based on smaller subgroups of the population defined by religious preference and race and ethnicity will have larger margins of sampling error, depending on sample size. All reported margins of sampling error include computed design effects for weighting.

Each sample of national adults includes a minimum quota of 50% cellphone respondents and 50% landline respondents, with additional minimum quotas by time zone within region. Landline and cellular telephone numbers are selected using random-digit-dial methods.

December 26, 2014
U.S. BLACKS SUFFER DISPROPORTIONATELY FROM CHRONIC CONDITIONS

by Dan Witters and Jade Wood

WASHINGTON, D.C.—Older Americans generally are more likely than their younger counterparts to be obese, with the rate peaking in middle age and then declining around retirement age. But for blacks in particular, obesity rates show even greater differences by age group. Between the ages of 18 to 29 and 45 to 64, blacks' obesity rate ticks up 21 percentage points, compared with 16 points for Hispanics, 15 points for whites and five points for Asians.

Percentage Obese in U.S. by Race/Ethnicity and Age

Body Mass Index values of 30 or above are classified as "obese," according to respondents self-reported weight and height

	Total	White	Black	Asian	Hispanic
18-29	17%	16%	22%	7%	19%
30-44	29%	27%	39%	10%	33%
45-64	33%	31%	43%	12%	35%
65+	27%	26%	36%	10%	28%
Difference (pct. pts.) between 65+ and 18-29 groups	16	15	21	5	16
All ages	27%	26%	35%	9%	28%

Gallup-Healthways Well-Being Index
Jan. 2, 2013-Aug. 8, 2014

GALLUP

Overall, in Gallup-Healthways Well-Being Index data captured from Jan. 2, 2013 through Aug. 8, 2014, 27% of Americans are obese. Across the four major racial and ethnic groups, blacks have the highest obesity rate (35%) and Asians have the lowest (9%)—a pattern that has been consistent over time.

These results are based on interviews with more than 272,000 Americans conducted as part of the Gallup-Healthways Well-Being Index. The resulting sample sizes for each racial and ethnic group allow for a granular look at how obesity and other chronic diseases progress with age.

The Well-Being Index uses respondents' self-reports of their height and weight to calculate standard Body Mass Index (BMI)

scores. Individual BMI values of 30 or above are classified as "obese."

High Blood Pressure Jumps Among Seniors, Especially Blacks

Unlike obesity rates, which hit their peak in middle age and then decrease among those older than 65, hypertension continues to be significantly more common among seniors. Young Americans start out on a relatively even playing field in terms of hypertension, with similar, very low, rates across all 18- to 29-year-olds. But by middle age, nearly half of blacks report having hypertension—roughly double the rates of Asians and Hispanics in the same age group. An even higher 70% of retirement-age blacks have or are being treated for high blood pressure, significantly greater than the rates seen for all other groups.

Do you currently have or are you currently being treated for high blood pressure?
% Yes, by race/ethnicity and age

	Total	White	Black	Asian	Hispanic
18-29	2%	2%	3%	1%	2%
30-44	10%	9%	17%	6%	7%
45-64	32%	30%	49%	22%	26%
65+	54%	53%	70%	59%	53%
Difference (pct. pts.) between 65+ and 18-29 groups	52	51	67	58	51
All ages	24%	26%	30%	9%	13%

Gallup-Healthways Well-Being Index
Jan. 2, 2013-Aug. 8, 2014

GALLUP'

High Cholesterol Elevated Among Older Age Groups, Regardless of Race or Ethnicity

Unlike hypertension, the percentage of adults reporting that they currently have or are currently being treated for high cholesterol is similar by age across all major racial and ethnic groups. Among those aged 45 to 64, whites and blacks (24%) are somewhat more likely to report high cholesterol than are their Asian or Hispanic counterparts. There is no gap by racial or ethnic group among those aged 65 and older, however, with all four groups at or within two points of the national level of 39%.

Do you currently have, or are you currently being treated for high cholesterol?
% Yes, by race/ethnicity and age

	Total	White	Black	Asian	Hispanic
18-29	1%	1%	1%	1%	1%
30-44	6%	6%	7%	5%	6%
45-64	23%	24%	24%	20%	19%
65+	39%	39%	40%	40%	37%
Difference (pct. pts.) between 65+ and 18-29 groups	38	38	39	39	36
All ages	17%	20%	15%	7%	9%

Gallup-Healthways Well-Being Index
Jan. 2, 2013-Aug. 8, 2014

GALLUP'

Implications

Blacks in older age groups are significantly more likely than other Americans to be obese and report having high blood pressure. This begs the question of what factors beyond genetics contribute to this pattern. Given that blacks, on average, earn a lower household income than whites, income seems to play a role. Having a lower income and the presence of more food deserts have additively been linked to obesity, a factor that would also be relevant to Hispanics.

In addition, blacks are second only to Hispanics in being uninsured, making accessing and paying for available healthcare a challenge. And the U.S. healthcare system largely focuses on treating illnesses instead of preventing them in the first place, an approach that may perpetuate incidences of chronic disease as many people do not have the tools and support to avoid these conditions. Further, early education programs tailored toward improving health and well-being are lacking in the U.S., particularly within impoverished communities.

However, a movement in healthcare known as "lifestyle medicine," which teaches individuals and populations how to reverse and prevent chronic disease through lifestyle modification, is gaining ground. Dr. Dean Ornish, founder of the Preventive Medicine Research Institute and thought leader in advocating preventive lifestyle measures as treatment, says, "The most common chronic diseases—including high blood pressure, elevated cholesterol levels and heart disease—have a common root cause: the lifestyle choices that we make each day. Most doctors prescribe a lifetime of medications to treat these conditions, but comprehensive lifestyle changes can prevent and even reverse them."

The lifestyle modifications typically consist of strategies addressing diet, exercise, stress reduction and increased social support. Given the comparatively high prevalence of these chronic conditions among blacks and the socio-economic factors driving these high rates, a lifestyle approach that allows individuals to take their health into their own hands could be extremely beneficial.

While not all American adults will fall into one of the high-risk categories for obesity, high blood pressure or high cholesterol, these conditions affect everyone, as soaring healthcare costs account for about 17% of the United States' GDP. Ultimately, long-term improvement in the rates of these illnesses partially rests on addressing the underlying factors contributing to the racial disparities in chronic condition rates. Tackling the root causes of these illnesses and empowering people to manage their own health will benefit individuals and the overall U.S. economy.

Survey Methods

Results are based on telephone interviews conducted Jan. 2, 2013–Aug. 8, 2014, as part of the Gallup-Healthways Well-Being Index survey, with a random sample of 272,347 adults, aged 18 and older, living in all 50 U.S. states and the District of Columbia. For results based on the total sample of each reported subgroup, the margin of sampling error ranges between ±0.5 and ±5.8 percentage points at the 95% confidence level. (See the table for full sample sizes.) In most cases, the margin of error is no more than ±1.5 points. All reported margins of sampling error include computed design effects for weighting.

Sample Sizes for Reported Groups

	Total	White	Black	Asian	Hispanic
All ages	272,347	213,782	24,131	5,752	24,658
18-29	38,380	22,757	5,056	2,118	7,636
30-44	49,677	34,044	5,526	1,911	7,335
45-64	102,137	83,101	9,161	1,293	7,029
65+	82,153	73,880	4,388	430	2,658

Gallup-Healthways Well-Being Index
Jan. 2, 2013-Aug. 8, 2014

GALLUP'

Each sample of national adults includes a minimum quota of 50% cellphone respondents and 50% landline respondents, with additional minimum quotas by time zone within region. Landline and cellular telephone numbers are selected using random-digit-dial methods.

December 29, 2014
BARACK OBAMA, HILLARY CLINTON EXTEND RUN AS MOST ADMIRED

by Jeffrey M. Jones

PRINCETON, NJ—Americans continue to name Hillary Clinton as the woman living anywhere in the world whom they admire most, and name Barack Obama as the man they admire most. Clinton has held the top women's spot in each of the last 13 years and 17 of the last 18, with that streak interrupted only by first lady Laura Bush in 2001 after the 9/11 terror attacks. Obama has been most admired man in each of the last seven years, beginning with 2008, the year he was elected president.

Most Admired Man and Woman, 2014

What [woman/man] that you have heard or read about, living today in any part of the world, do you admire most? And who is your second choice?

	% Mentioning
MOST ADMIRED WOMAN	
Hillary Clinton	12
Oprah Winfrey	8
Malala Yousafzai	5
Condoleezza Rice	4
Michelle Obama	3
Angelina Jolie	2
Sarah Palin	2
Princess Kate	2
Elizabeth Warren	1
Laura Bush	1
MOST ADMIRED MAN	
Barack Obama	19
Pope Francis	6
Bill Clinton	3
Rev. Billy Graham	2
George W. Bush	2
Ben Carson	1
Stephen Hawking	1
Bill Gates	1
Bill O'Reilly	1
Benjamin Netanyahu	1
Vladimir Putin	1

Dec. 8-11, 2014

Combined first and second mentions; rankings based on total mentions

GALLUP

For nearly seven decades, Gallup has asked Americans, using an open-ended question, to name the man and woman living anywhere in the world whom they admire most. The current results are based on a Dec. 8–11 poll.

In total, Clinton has been most admired woman 19 times, easily the most of any woman in Gallup's history of asking the most admired question, six more times than Eleanor Roosevelt. Clinton won the distinction from 1993 to 1994 and 1997 to 2000, when she was first lady; from 2002 to 2008, when she was a U.S. senator; and from 2009 to 2012, when she was secretary of state. Although she has had no formal public role during the last two years, she retains a high enough profile to top the list. Clinton is the presumed front-runner for the 2016 Democratic presidential nomination, should she decide to run.

Clinton's margin over second-place Oprah Winfrey is four percentage points, 12% to 8%—the smallest lead for Clinton since a two-point lead over Winfrey in 2007. During her years as most admired woman, Clinton's lead over the second-place finisher has generally been smaller when she held a partisan political role as U.S. senator or a presidential candidate than when she held a less partisan role as first lady or secretary of state. The more politicized views of Clinton have also been evident in the decline in her favorable ratings among all Americans since she resigned as secretary of state.

Clinton and Winfrey are joined in the top 10 by Nobel Prize–winning Pakistani teen Malala Yousafzai, former Secretary of State Condoleezza Rice, first lady Michelle Obama, actress and humanitarian Angelina Jolie, former Alaska Gov. Sarah Palin, Princess Kate of England, Massachusetts Sen. Elizabeth Warren, and Laura Bush.

Winfrey now has 27 top 10 appearances, the fourth most of any woman. Queen Elizabeth II of England did not finish in the top 10 this year, but still holds the record of 46 appearances for all women historically. Clinton's 23 top 10s is fifth all time, while Rice (14 times) and Laura Bush (11 times) have also frequently ranked in the top 10.

Most Top 10 Finishes on Most Admired Woman List, 1948-2014

	Number of appearances
Queen Elizabeth II*	46
Margaret Thatcher	34
Jacqueline Kennedy Onassis	28
Oprah Winfrey*	27
Hillary Rodham Clinton*	23
Mamie Eisenhower	21
Barbara Bush*	20
Margaret Chase Smith	20
Nancy Reagan*	19
Mother Teresa	18
Clare Boothe Luce	18
Betty Ford	17
Mme Chiang Kai-Shek	17
Helen Keller	17
Patricia Nixon	15

*Denotes still living

GALLUP

Obama a Solid No. 1 as Most Admired Man

Obama has appeared on the top 10 list each year since 2006, including ranking No. 1 in each of the last seven years, all by healthy margins over the second-place finisher. The incumbent president is nearly always the winner of the most admired distinction, having placed first in all but 12 of the 68 years the question has been asked.

Most of those 12 exceptions have come when the president was unpopular, including in 2008 when President-elect Obama finished ahead of George W. Bush; in 1980 when Pope John Paul II edged out Jimmy Carter; during the Watergate era of 1973–1975; in the late 1960s during the height of the Vietnam War; and for much of Harry Truman's presidency when he was overshadowed by Gens. Dwight Eisenhower and Douglas MacArthur.

The remainder of the top 10 men this year is mainly a mix of religious figures, such as Pope Francis and the Rev. Billy Graham, and political figures—including former Presidents Bill Clinton and George W. Bush, Israeli Prime Minister Benjamin Netanyahu, Russian President Vladimir Putin and potential 2016 presidential candidate Dr. Ben Carson. Businessman and philanthropist Bill Gates, astrophysicist Stephen Hawking and political commentator Bill O'Reilly also finished in the top 10.

Graham's top 10 finish this year brings his unprecedented total appearances on the list to 58. He has finished in the top 10 every year since 1963 (except 1976, when the question was not asked), as well as from 1955 to 1961. He has never ranked first, but did finish second every year from 1969 through 1974.

Clinton made the top 10 for the 23rd time, the fifth most behind Graham, Ronald Reagan, Carter and Pope John Paul II. Gates had his 15th top 10 finish this year, and Bush his 14th.

Most Top 10 Finishes on Most Admired Man List, 1946-2014

	Number of appearances
Billy Graham*	58
Ronald Reagan	31
Jimmy Carter*	28
Pope John Paul II	27
Bill Clinton*	23
Dwight Eisenhower	21
Richard Nixon	21
George H.W. Bush*	20
Harry Truman	20
Nelson Mandela	20
Edward Kennedy	18
Winston Churchill	17
Colin Powell*	16
Bill Gates*	15
Douglas MacArthur	15
George W. Bush*	14

Note: 1946-1947 version asked about "Most Admired Person"
*Denotes still living

GALLUP

Partisanship Influences Most Admired Choice

Democrats and Democratic leaners widely choose Hillary Clinton (20%) and Barack Obama (33%) as the most admired woman and man, respectively. Not unexpectedly, Republicans and Republican leaners are much less likely to name either as their most admired. In fact, former Secretary of State Rice edges out Winfrey and Clinton as the most admired woman among Republicans. Obama and Pope Francis tie as the most admired man among Republicans, at 8%.

Republicans' and Democrats' top five most admired women include both Clinton and Winfrey, and their top five most admired men include both the president and the pope. Beyond these, their choices differ.

Most Admired Man and Woman, by Political Party, 2014

	% Mentioning
MOST ADMIRED WOMAN	
Democrats/Democratic leaners	
Hillary Clinton	20
Oprah Winfrey	10
Malala Yousafzai	7
Michelle Obama	6
Elizabeth Warren	3
Republicans/Republican leaners	
Condoleezza Rice	9
Oprah Winfrey	6
Hillary Clinton	5
Sarah Palin	4
Angelina Jolie	3
MOST ADMIRED MAN	
Democrats/Democratic leaners	
Barack Obama	33
Pope Francis	5
Bill Clinton	4
Stephen Hawking	2
Bill Gates	2
Republicans/Republican leaners	
Barack Obama	8
Pope Francis	8
Billy Graham	4
George W. Bush	3
Ben Carson	3

Dec. 8-11, 2014

GALLUP

Implications

Although both Hillary Clinton and Obama saw their popularity fade this year, they remain prominent and popular enough to be the most top-of-mind people living today when Americans are asked to name the woman and man they admire most. At this time next year, Clinton may be actively campaigning to become Obama's successor as president. It is unclear whether doing so would make it more likely or less likely that she would continue her reign as most admired woman. On one hand, being a presidential candidate and the clear front-runner would ensure she stays a prominent figure in the news. On the other hand, as a presidential candidate she likely would be evaluated from a more partisan perspective, which may cause some—particularly Republicans—to view her in a less favorable light.

Survey Methods

Results for this Gallup poll are based on telephone interviews conducted Dec. 8–11, 2014, with a random sample of 805 adults, aged 18 and older, living in all 50 U.S. states and the District of Columbia. For results based on the total sample of national adults, the margin of sampling error is ±4 percentage points at the 95% confidence level. All reported margins of sampling error include computed design effects for weighting.

Each sample of national adults includes a minimum quota of 50% cellphone respondents and 50% landline respondents, with additional minimum quotas by time zone within region. Landline and cellular telephone numbers are selected using random-digit-dial methods.

December 30, 2014
GALLUP'S TOP 10 U.S. WELL-BEING DISCOVERIES OF 2014

by Alyssa Brown

WASHINGTON, D.C.—Throughout the past year, Gallup has published nearly 90 articles about Americans' health and well-being. The Gallup-Healthways Well-Being Index uncovers new insights with its daily surveys, providing the most up-to-date data available on Americans' sense of purpose, social relationships, financial security, connection to community and physical health.

The following list represents Gallup editors' picks for the top 10 most important findings in 2014:

1. Uninsured rate drops nearly four percentage points since late 2013: Gallup was among the first to report the decline in the U.S. uninsured rate, which coincided with the new requirement that Americans carry health insurance. The percentage of U.S. adults without health insurance was 13.4% in both the second and third quarters of 2014, down from 17.1% in the fourth quarter of 2013. This is the lowest quarterly uninsured rate measured since Gallup and Healthways began tracking it in 2008.

2. Uninsured rate drops more in states embracing ACA: The uninsured rate among adults in the states that have chosen to expand Medicaid *and* set up their own exchanges in the health insurance marketplace has declined significantly more this year than among those in the remaining states that have taken one or neither of these actions. This finding suggests that adopting these components is critical to lowering the uninsured rate within states.

3. Using mobile technology for work linked to more stress: Nearly half of workers who "frequently" use email for work outside of normal working hours (48%) report experiencing stress "a lot of the day yesterday," compared with 36% among those who "never" check work email outside of working hours. However, workers who email outside of normal working hours also rate their lives better than their counterparts who do not. The same patterns hold true for working remotely outside of working hours.

4. Depression rates higher for long-term unemployed: About one in five Americans who have been unemployed for a year or more say they currently have or are being treated for depression—almost double the rate among those who have been unemployed for five weeks or less. The long-term unemployed also spend less time with family and friends than other Americans. Gallup also found that Americans who have been out of work for a year or more are much more likely to be obese than those unemployed for a shorter time.

5. U.S. veterans report less stress, worry than civilians: Although many veterans face very serious and unique mental health challenges, Gallup finds that among employed Americans, active-duty and veteran populations are more emotionally resilient than their civilian counterparts.

6. In U.S., 14% of those aged 24 to 34 report living with parents: Young adults who live at home are significantly less likely to be married, to be employed full time and to have a college education than those who are the same age but don't live at home. Those aged 24 to 34 who live at home are also less likely to be "thriving" and have lower overall well-being than their peers who don't live with their parents.

7. Obesity linked to lower social well-being: In terms of social well-being, obese Americans are the least likely of all weight groups to be thriving, while underweight individuals are the most likely to be suffering. This pattern underscores the risk of being at either extreme of the weight spectrum when it comes to social relationships.

8. Older Americans feel best about their physical appearance: Two-thirds (66%) of Americans aged 65 and older agree that they always feel good about their physical appearance, compared with 61% of 18- to 34-year-olds. Middle-aged Americans (54%) are the least likely to report feeling good about their appearance. Blacks and Hispanics are much more likely than whites and, to a lesser extent, Asians to say they always feel good about their appearance.

9. LGBT Americans report lower well-being: Americans who identify as lesbian, gay, bisexual or transgender (LGBT) trail their non-LGBT counterparts in all five elements of well-being: purpose, social, financial, community and physical. The disadvantage in overall well-being is starker for LGBT women than for LGBT men.

10. Baby boomers are not maximizing their strengths at work: Although U.S. baby boomers have been in the workforce for many years, they are no more likely than younger generations to say that they are able to use their strengths to do what they do best throughout the day. About one in two baby boomers plan to delay their retirement, meaning they will remain an influential part of the workforce. Therefore, employers have an opportunity to help baby boomers identify and use their strengths to achieve higher performance outcomes.

December 30, 2014
TAKING REGULAR VACATIONS MAY HELP BOOST AMERICANS' WELL-BEING

by Justin McCarthy

WASHINGTON, D.C.—Making time for regular trips or vacations with family and friends is linked to higher overall well-being. Americans who say they take regular trips have significantly higher well-being than those who say they do not, as measured by Gallup-Healthways Well-Being Index scores, and this difference persists across all income groups. In fact, those who earn less than $24,000 annually and say they take regular trips actually have higher well-being (scoring 66.3) than those who earn $120,000 or more but say they *don't* regularly make time for vacations (55.1).

Well-Being Index Scores of Regular vs. Irregular Vacation-Takers, by Income
You always make time for regular trips or vacations with friends and family.

	Index score of those who agree/ strongly agree	Index score of those who disagree/ strongly disagree
All Americans	68.4	51.4
Income less than $24,000	66.3	49.1
Income of $24,000 to $47, 999	67.1	50.9
Income of $48,000 to $89,999	68.0	52.5
$90,000-119,999	68.4	53.6
$120,000 +	69.5	55.1

Gallup-Healthways Well-Being Index
January-November 2014

GALLUP

The link between making regular time for vacations and higher Well-Being Index scores is significant because these scores take into account Americans' self-reported sense of purpose, social relationships, financial security, connection to community, and physical health. Previous Gallup research shows that an individual's Well-Being Index score strongly relates to important health outcomes such as healthcare utilization, life expectancy, new onset disease burden, and change in obesity status.

These data are based on interviews with more than 148,000 Americans from January through November, as part of the Gallup-Healthways Well-Being Index. Gallup asked Americans to indicate whether they make time for regular trips or vacations with family or friends using a one to five agree/disagree scale where a "5" means "strongly agree" and a "1" means "strongly disagree."

About half of Americans agree they regularly take vacations with family and friends, responding "4" or "5" to the statement on the five-point scale, while 31% disagree (responding "1" or "2").

Despite the well-being benefits associated with taking regular vacations, those who make less than $24,000 a year are about half as likely (33%) to make time for such leisure as those who make $120,000 or more annually (64%). This difference is likely due to lower-income Americans' lack of funds, and possibly time, a necessary resource to go on trips or vacations.

Regularly taking vacation time is incrementally more common with each step up the income ladder.

Americans Who Regularly Make Time for Vacation, by Income Bracket
You always make time for regular trips or vacations with friends and family.

	% Agree/ strongly agree	% Disagree/ strongly disagree
All Americans	49	31
Income $120,000 and over	64	18
Income of $90,000 to $119,999	62	19
Income of $48,000 to $89,999	56	23
Income of $24,000 to $47, 999	44	35
Income less than $24,000	33	49

Gallup-Healthways Well-being Index
January-November 2014

GALLUP

While income is the top factor determining whether Americans agree that they regularly make time for vacations and trips with others, there are other differences across demographic groups.

- Asians (55%) and whites (52%) are most likely to agree that they regularly take vacations, while the figures are lower for blacks (44%) and Hispanics (42%).

- A majority (57%) of Americans over age 65, compared with less than half of those aged 18–29 (47%), 30–44 (46%), and 45–64 (49%), make time for regular trips or vacations.

- Slightly less than half (47%) of Americans with children under age 18 in their households regularly make time for vacations or trips, a bit lower than the 51% found among those who don't have children in their homes.

- Married Americans (56%) are most likely to take vacations with friends and family, followed by widowers (47%), single folks (43%), and those with a domestic partner (43%). People who are divorced (37%) or separated (30%) are least likely to regularly take such trips.

Bottom Line

Regardless of income, Americans who make time for vacations or trips with family and friends have higher overall well-being than those who don't. Some studies suggest that vacation time has positive effects on the brain and heart, and could ultimately lower healthcare costs—which would be good news for employers.

The exact causal path underneath this relationship is not clear. While it is likely that taking regular vacations may cause Americans to have higher well-being for the rest of the year, it is also possible that Americans with higher well-being to begin with are more inclined and motivated to travel than are those with lower well-being.

It would seem that those who can afford a week-long cruise or airfare to a foreign country might experience a greater boost in their overall well-being than those who can't. But for Americans on a budget, this same—or an even greater—uptick in well-being might come just as easily from a weekend camping trip or driving to visit relatives. The well-being benefits may come more from anticipating the trip, developing or deepening relationships with family and friends, and recalling fond memories of the trip than the degree of luxury involved.

This research showing a link between taking vacations and well-being suggests that employers may benefit from encouraging their workers to make time for regular trips. Higher well-being predicts key business outcomes such as lower absenteeism and turnover, as well as fewer workplace safety incidents. Employers may want to arrange for workers to take paid time off, plan regular company outings that are open to family and friends, and foster a culture that makes it acceptable to take time off for vacation.

Survey Methods

Results are based on telephone interviews conducted Jan. 1–Nov. 30, 2014, as part of the Gallup-Healthways Well-Being Index survey, with a random sample of 148,854 adults, aged 18 and older, living in all 50 U.S. states and the District of Columbia. For results based on the total sample of national adults, the margin of sampling error is ±1 percentage points at the 95% confidence level.

Sample Sizes and Margins of Error for Reported Groups:

Income Group	Sample Size	MOE	Well-Being Index MOE
Under $24,000	26,168	+/- .7%	+/- .22
$24,000-47, 999	30,906	+/- .7%	+/- .20
$48,000-89,999	35,850	+/- .6%	+/- .19
$90,000-119,999	9,999	+/- 1.2%	+/- .36
$120,000 +	19,555	+/- .9%	+/- .26

Each sample of national adults includes a minimum quota of 50% cellphone respondents and 50% landline respondents, with additional minimum quotas by time zone within region. Landline and cellular telephone numbers are selected using random-digit-dial methods.

December 31, 2014
WHAT'S AHEAD FOR AMERICANS IN 2015?

by Frank Newport

PRINCETON, NJ—As 2014 ends, the attention of a nation turns to 2015 and how Americans' attitudes and opinions may change in the months ahead.

Politics

The political focus in 2015 will inevitably turn away from lame-duck President Barack Obama, and toward the maneuverings of the multitude of politicians who are in one way or the other thinking about running for president in 2016. Still, Obama has two years to go in his second term. And despite facing a House and Senate controlled by the opposition party, he will likely continue to attempt to influence policy by using executive actions that allow him to work around Congress.

Obama's job approval rating rose slightly at the end of this year, fueled by an increase in his standing among Hispanics, who were reacting to his executive action on immigration announced in November. It also likely rose because of the increasingly positive views of the economy. Thus, Obama's approval rating in the coming year will continue to depend on his standing among Hispanics, a group that research shows is quick to change its mind about Obama. An increase in his approval rating among whites will likely depend on the economy, among other factors.

Congress' job approval rating should go up in January and in the following months because rank-and-file Republicans' views of Congress will likely rise as their party takes control of both houses. The lower rating of the divided Congress in recent years was partly because neither Republicans nor Democrats rated the institution very positively. But when one party has control of both houses, supporters of that party are typically much more positive toward Congress.

Whether Congress' approval rating remains improved may also depend on what the two chambers actually do in the new year. A number of prominent Senate members and, to a lesser degree, House members are potentially running for president and thus looking at how their every action might affect their path to the party's nomination the following year. It is possible that Congress will continue to find itself beset by partisan feuding as these members jockey for position among presidential primary voters.

Obama's approval rating likely will not be dramatically affected by what Congress does. His rating dropped a few percentage points in October and November 2013, after the government shutdown, but remained above 40%, much higher than the all-time lows on that measure, earned by Harry Truman and Richard Nixon. Congress' job approval dropped to 9% in November 2013, the lowest in Gallup's history of rating that institution. If Congress appears to be doing nothing in the months ahead, Obama could look better by comparison.

Few presidents in the modern polling era have made it to a seventh year in office, so there is not a lot of historical context for Obama in 2015. But of the four presidents since 1952 who have served seven years, three—Ronald Reagan, Bill Clinton and George W. Bush—saw a decline in approval. Reagan, beset by problems associated with the Iran-Contra affair, saw his approval rating drop from 60% in his sixth year to 48% in his seventh—a larger drop than Clinton or Bush experienced. The exception was Dwight Eisenhower, whose average in his seventh year was 64%, up from 54% the year before.

The Economy

Americans' views of Obama and Congress will partly depend on their views of what is happening to the economy. On that front, 2014 saw significant change. Americans' economic confidence shot up in the fourth quarter of the year, reflecting a stock market at record highs, lower gas prices, increasingly positive views of the job market, government data showing that unemployment is down and other positive indicators of economic growth in the U.S.

Despite this uptick in economic confidence, history suggests there is still a lot of room for improvement. Gallup began tracking economic confidence on a daily basis in January 2008 but asked the underlying questions that constitute the Economic Confidence Index for years prior to that. A review of these measures, particularly those obtained in the final years of the dot-com boom, shows just how economically positive Americans can become in the right circumstances.

Americans are now slightly more positive than negative about the economy's direction, with 49% saying the economy is getting better and 45% saying it is getting worse for the week of Dec. 22–28. This is a relatively good rating, and aside from two weeks in May 2013 when the measure was in net positive territory, last week marks the only time since January 2008 that it has been above water.

However, by comparison, the net positive gap on this getting better/getting worse measure is still low. The gap was as high as 46 points in January 2000, when 69% of Americans said the economy was getting better and 23% said it was getting worse. In similar fashion, although the current 27% who say the economy is excellent or good is an improvement from most of the readings in recent years, that percentage was above 70% multiple times in 1999 and 2000. In short, there is a lot of room for improvement in views of the current economy, based on where these views have been in fairly recent U.S. history.

Attitudes Toward Major Social Issues

It's difficult to neatly summarize current trends in Americans' views of moral, values and cultural issues, and therefore difficult to forecast what the future trends might be. While Americans have become more liberal on at least two significant issues—same-sex marriage and marijuana legalization—they show little sign of adopting a more liberal position on gun control or global warming.

As recently as 2009, 40% of Americans favored same-sex marriage, while 57% opposed it. Now, 55% favor it, and 42% oppose it—a dramatic flip of opinion in just half a decade. Young Americans are significantly more likely than older Americans to favor same-sex marriage, giving rise to the hypothesis that attitudes will move further in a favorable direction as the years go on. This assumes that

a) these young people maintain their more liberal attitudes as they move into middle age, and b) future generations of young people will have the same liberal attitudes as those who came before them.

This same age trends could affect views on marijuana. Eleven years ago, just about a third of Americans supported marijuana legalization; in contrast, majorities interviewed in 2013 and 2014 support its legalization. Younger Americans are much more likely than those who are older to support marijuana legalization, suggesting a continuing liberalization of attitudes in the years ahead—if, as noted in the context of same-sex marriage, young people maintain their views as they age, and if rising cohorts of young people continue to have more liberal views.

At the same time that the country's views of same-sex marriage and marijuana have undergone significant short-term change, attitudes toward two other significant issues have not changed. Less than half of Americans favor stricter gun laws, and while this is slightly higher than what Gallup found from 2010 to 2012, it is below the prevailing sentiment in the years prior to that time. And in a fascinating turnabout in opinion, Americans are now much more likely to say that having a gun in the house makes it a safer, rather than a more dangerous, place to be.

Clearly, the examples of horrific gun violence in recent years that resulted in the deaths of innocent victims of all ages and in a variety of settings have not produced the change in attitudes toward guns that gun-control advocates have predicted.

Gallup's in-depth research on Americans' views on climate change in 2014 did not reveal any major shift in concern or focus on this issue. This is despite continuing efforts by climate-change researchers to point out the impact of what they consider to be one of the most significant threats to humans in history. This reflects the politicization of the issue, a process by which positions on the issue have come to reflect ideology and views of government's role in daily life, as well as questions of science. One would not expect to see significant changes in these attitudes in the year ahead, unless there are highly dramatic examples of climate change's effects, or unless climate-change activists can figure out a way to make this issue transcend politics.

Population Trends

Two trends relating to the underlying American population could affect public opinion in 2015.

The U.S. Census Bureau predicts that nonwhites will represent an increasing percentage of the overall population in the years ahead, particularly in key states—driven by high nonwhite migration rates and the youthful skew of the large Hispanic population, which leads to proportionally higher numbers of Hispanic births. Additionally, the aging of the huge baby boom generation means the 65-and-older percentage of the population will continue to increase each year.

From a different perspective, state migration patterns will continue to have a significant effect on the nation in the years ahead.

The Census Bureau shows continuing major change in state populations, with six states—Illinois, West Virginia, Connecticut, New Mexico, Alaska and Vermont—actually losing population between 2013 and 2014 even as the country as a whole continued to grow. Many factors play into a state's population trends, including the relative balance between births and deaths (which is based on the age of the population) and migration into and out of the state. These migration patterns are in turn based on perceptions of job availability in a state, plus other factors that constitute a state's overall attractiveness. Gallup research shows huge differences in residents' views of their state as a place to live, ranging from 77% of residents in Montana and Alaska who rate their state as one of the best states to live in, down to only 18% of Rhode Island residents who rate their state similarly. Americans will continue to move to states where there are the best job opportunities. Additionally, if Americans continue to be less trusting of the federal government than of state governments, they may increasingly choose to live under a state government about which they hold positive views.

Index

Abbas, Mahmoud, 80
abortion
    consider yourself pro-choice or pro-life, 198–200
        demographics of, 199
        trends in, 198
    legal issues in, opinions on, 199
    as morally acceptable, 207–8
    as most important issue for working women, 387
    as priority, 17–18
    satisfaction with, 16–17
    as voting issue, 199, 381
        Tea Party and, 403
accounting, image of, 335–36
adoption, LGBT individuals and, 208–9
advertising and public relations
    image of, 335–36
    practitioners of, honesty and ethical standards of, 469–70
Affordable Care Act
    approval ratings, 44–45, 87, 138–39, 204, 434–35
        party identification and, 125
        race and, 204–5
    effects of, 86–87, 138
        in long run, 45, 87, 138, 204, 206
            race and, 205
        so far, 45, 138, 205–6
    exchanges
        familiarity with, 431
        newly insured and, 239
        ratings of healthcare and coverage, 432–33
        uninsured and, 1, 37–38, 49–50, 145–46, 431
    familiarity with, 47
    government role and, 439
    individual mandate, awareness of, 431
    newly insured and, 147–48
        plans for insurance, 433
        ratings of healthcare and coverage, 432–33
    satisfaction with, 41
    scaling back, as priority, 227–28
    states and
        Kentucky and, 395
        uninsured and, 296–97, 480
    as voting issue, 193–94, 381
        Tea Party and, 403
    websites
        Obama, Barack, and, 3
        uninsured and, 1

Afghanistan
    as greatest enemy of U.S., 69
    U.S. military action in
        as mistake, 64–65
        support for, 243
African Americans. See blacks
age
    abortion and, 199
    appearance and, 255, 480
    budget deficit and, 14
    checking work email and, 167
    chronic conditions and, 476–77
    college and, 132
    communication and, 426
    congressional priorities and, 420
    creationism and, 212
    dentist visits and, 160
    diversity and, 122
    divided government and, 198
    drinking age should/not be lowered, 278
    economy and, 107
    energy and, 126
    entrepreneurial aspirations and, 11–12
    environment and, 107
    feel safe walking alone at night, 444
    financial problems and, 152–54, 157
    gay marriage and, 195
    GI Bill and, 251
    global warming and, 95–96, 129, 156
    good/bad time to find a quality job, 105, 265, 473
    government healthcare coverage and, 439
    greatest enemy of U.S. and, 69
    healthcare and, 14, 99, 427
    healthcare costs and, 454
    health insurance and, 26, 53, 131
    ideology and, 290
    Israel and, 81
    job identity and, 320
    job worries and, 311–12
    LGBT identification and, 290, 303
    living with parents and, 58–59
    Middle East and, 63, 281
    mobile technology and, 163–64, 170
    most important issue and, 14
    newly insured and, 148, 240
    Obama, Barack, and, 445–46, 456–57, 464

obesity and, 78, 197
organic foods and, 302
parental spending and, 85
party identification and, 116–17, 257–58
    race and, 116–17
perceptions of treatment by police and, 314–15
personal doctor and, 350
Postal Service and, 440–41
religion and, 247
retail shopping and, 170
retirement expectations and, 20–21, 162, 181
retirement savings and, 474
Russia and, 120
same-sex-couple adoption and, 209
Saudi Arabia and, age and, 63
smoking bans and, 288–89
social media and purchasing decisions and, 238
spending and, 152
standard of living and, 298
Tea Party and, 373
technological devices and, 5
Ukraine and, 90
uninsured and, 173, 217, 256
vacation days of microbusiness owners and, 279
vacations and, 481
volunteering and, 304
weight and, 223, 282
well-being and, 253
workplace engagement and, 21
    federal workers and, 466
See also baby boomers; Millennials
agriculture. *See* farms/farming
AIDS, as most urgent health problem, 433–34
air, pollution of, worry about, 128
Air Force, as most important for defense, 200
airline industry, image of, 335–36
air quality, satisfaction with, states and, 218
Alabama
    Catholics and, 46
    economic confidence in, 50
    health and, 88
    ideology in, 39
    job creation in, 54
    party identification in, 35
    Protestants and, 46
    religion and, 43
    standard of living and, 56
    struggle to afford food in, 110
    struggle to afford healthcare/medicine in, 120–21
    well-being in, 66
Alaska
    dentist visits and, 169
    economic confidence in, 50–51, 345
    health and, 88
    livability, 159, 345
    minorities and, 186
    Mormons and, 46
    Obama, Barack, and, 30
    party identification in, 35, 344–45
    smoking in, 94

    standard of living and, 56–57
    state taxes and, 134
    struggle to afford food in, 109–10
    struggle to afford healthcare/medicine in, 121
    trust in state government and, 129
    underemployment and, 60
    well-being in, 67
Albright, Madeleine, favorability ratings, 86
alcohol/alcoholic beverages, 276–77
    cause of trouble in family, 287–88
    drinks consumed in past week, 277
    last took a drink, 276
    lowering drinking age, 277–78
    as most urgent health problem, 433
    trends in, 276
aliens. *See* immigrants/immigration
American people, mood of, 32–33
Anderson, Al, 323–24
animals
    cloning of, as morally acceptable, 207–8
    extinction of, worry about, 128
    fur of, buying and wearing clothing made of, as morally
        acceptable, 207–8
    medical testing on, as morally acceptable, 207–8
appearance
    exercise and, 267–68
    satisfaction with, 254–56, 480
    weight and, 268
approval ratings
    of Affordable Care Act, 44–45, 87, 138–39, 434–35
    of Bernanke, Ben, 36–37
    of Bush, George H. W., 3, 317
    of Bush, George W., 3, 22, 27, 154, 273, 317, 397
    of Clinton, Bill, 22, 27, 154, 273, 317, 397
    of Congress, 51–52, 262–63, 305–6, 340, 393–94, 464–65
        midterm elections and, 229, 305–6, 394
        trends in, 51, 305, 393, 464
        voter turnout and, 324–25
    of Eisenhower, Dwight D., 22, 27, 154, 273, 397
    of government agencies, 439–40
    of Greenspan, Alan, 36–37
    of Nixon, Richard, 22, 27, 154, 273
    of Obama, Barack, 1–3, 154, 240–41
        age and, 456–57
        Alaska and, 344
        Arkansas and, 358
        blacks and, 464–65
        Colorado and, 365
        demographics of, 445–46
        fifth year, 21–22, 26–27
        Hispanics and, 368, 458–59
        intensity of, 329–31
        Iowa and, 337–38
        issues and, 317–18
        Kansas and, 374
        Kentucky and, 395
        LGBT individuals and, 289–90
        Louisiana and, 370–71
        midterm elections and, 230, 416–17
        New Hampshire and, 402

North Carolina and, 327
partisan gap in, 26–27
quarterly averages, 22, 272–73, 397–98
race and, 456–57
religion and, 259–60
states and, 30–31
trends in, 241
presidential, Georgia and, 384
of Reagan, Ronald, 3, 22, 27, 154, 273, 317, 397
of Supreme Court, 261–62
Arizona
air quality and, 218
charitable activity and, 178
dentist visits and, 169
health and, 88
healthcare exchanges and, 49
job creation in, 54
Mormons and, 46
planning to move, 165–66
schools and, 135
prepare students for success in workplace, 136
smoking in, 94
struggle to afford food in, 110
struggle to afford healthcare/medicine in, 121
underemployment and, 60
uninsured in, 49
well-being in, 67
Arkansas, 357–59
Catholics and, 46
charitable activity and, 178
dentist visits and, 169
economic confidence in, 50, 358–59
health and, 88
healthcare exchanges and, 49
ideology in, 39
job creation in, 54
livability, 358–59
minorities and, 187
Obama, Barack, and, 30
obesity in, 84
party identification in, 416
Protestants and, 46
religion and, 43
struggle to afford food in, 110
struggle to afford healthcare/medicine in, 121
uninsured in, 49, 296
well-being in, 66
Army, as most important for defense, 200
Asian Americans
appearance and, 255, 480
chronic conditions and, 476–77
dentist visits and, 160
healthcare and, 427
health insurance and, 349–51
Obama, Barack, and, 457
party identification of, 283–84
personal doctor and, 349–51
religion and, 283–84
spending and, 459–60
struggle to afford food and, 421

vacations and, 481
atheists. *See* nonreligious persons
attentiveness
to Benghazi hearings, 231–32
to Bergdahl, Bowe, 225
to Middle East, 281, 294
to Ukraine, 90–91
to Veterans Affairs situation, 225–26
automobile(s)
alternate fuel sources for, 126
spending on, 260
automobile industry
emissions standards for, 126, 215–16
image of, 335–36
trends in, 337
sales personnel in, honesty and ethical standards of, 469–70

baby boomers
banking industry and, 22–23
checking work email and, 167
historical influences and, 28–29
party identification of, 27–29
percentage in workplace, 21
retirement and, 20–21
social media and purchasing decisions, 238
strengths usage and, 25, 480
Balkans, U.S. military action in, support for, 243
banker(s), honesty and ethical standards of, 469–70
banks and banking
baby boomers and, 22–23
confidence in, 234
trends in, 244
image of, 335–36
trends in, 336–37
trust to keep personal information secure, 220
Basic Access Index
living with parents and, 61
metro areas and, 114
states and, 67
Beebe, Mike, 358
beer, 276
Begich, Mark, 344
Benedict XVI, favorability ratings, 118
Benghazi incident
Clinton, Hillary, and, 108–9
investigation of
approval of, 231
following closely, 231–32
as priority, 227–28
Bergdahl, Bowe, 224
following closely, 225
investigation of, as priority, 227–28
opinion of, 225
Bernanke, Ben, 36–37
Beshear, Steve, 396
beverages, soda drinking habits, 284–85
Bible, literal view of, 214–15
Biden, Joe, 71
favorability ratings, 266–67, 270–71
trends in, 70

big business
confidence in, 234
trends in, 244
See also business and industry; corporations
bill paying, as most important financial problem, 153, 156–57
bin Laden, Osama, killing of, following closely, 90
bioterrorism, as most urgent health problem, 434
bipartisanship, Congress and, 262–63
bird flu, versus Ebola, 378–79
birth control. *See* contraception
blacks
Affordable Care Act and, 204–5
appearance and, 255, 480
chronic conditions and, 476–77
church attendance and, 476
civil rights perceptions and, 463
dentist visits and, 160
discrimination and, 462
first-generation college graduates, 355
healthcare and, 427
health insurance and, 131, 349
immigration and, 457
Obama, Barack, and, 457–59, 464–65
obesity and, 78, 197
party identification of, 283–84
personal doctor and, 349
police and, 314–16, 455, 463, 468–69
race and, 298–99
race relations and, 461–64, 471
religion and, 283–84
spending and, 459–60
struggle to afford food and, 421
student debt and, 354
trends in, 354–55
treated unfairly by police within last 30 days, 315, 464
uninsured and, 173, 217
vacations and, 481
voter registration and, 48
well-being and, college and, 355–56
blood pressure, high. *See* high blood pressure
blue states, 35–36
BMI (body mass index), 78, 253–54
See also obesity
Boehner, John
favorability ratings, 75–76, 187–89, 376–77
Tea Party and, 188
bonds, as best investment, 149
border security. *See* immigrants/immigration
BP oil spill, following closely, 90
Braley, Bruce, 337–38
Branstad, Terry, 338
Brown, Michael, 314
Brown, Scott, 402
Brownback, Sam, 374–75
budget, federal
sequester and, 2
stress and, 33
waste in, as concern, 353–54
budget deficit, federal
as most important issue, 13, 93, 192–93, 264, 318–19, 342, 430
trends in, 14

as priority, 420
as voting issue, 193–94, 381, 386
Tea Party and, 403
worry about, 91
Buettner, Dan, 89, 115
Bush, Barbara
admiration of, 478
favorability ratings, 83
Bush, George H. W.
admiration of, 479
approval ratings, 3, 317
favorability ratings, 237
Bush, George W.
admiration of, 479
approval ratings, 3, 22, 27, 154, 273, 317, 397
confidence in presidency and, 248
divided government preference and, 392
economy and, 113
energy and, 113
environment and, 113
favorability ratings, 237–38
voting to support/oppose, 180
Bush, Jeb
Common Core standards and, 406
favorability ratings, 266, 269, 270
Bush, Laura
admiration of, 478
favorability ratings, 83
business and industry
executives, honesty and ethical standards of, 469–70
image of, 335
leaders
confidence in, 150–51
education and, 76–77
hiring factors and, 73
online education and, 133–34
regulation of, 348–49
trust to keep personal information secure, 219–20
See also corporations

cable television, access to, 4–5
California
air quality and, 218
Catholics and, 46
economic confidence in, 50
healthcare exchanges and, 49
ideology in, 39
Obama, Barack, and, 30
obesity in, 84
party identification in, 35
Protestants and, 46
schools and, 135
prepare students for success in workplace, 136
smoking in, 94
standard of living and, 56–57
state taxes and, 134
trust in state government and, 129
underemployment and, 60
uninsured in, 49, 296
well-being in, 67
campaign finance, reform, Congress and, 262–63

cancer
    as most urgent health problem, 433–34
    obesity and, 84
capital punishment. *See* death penalty
cars. *See* automobile(s); automobile industry
Carson, Ben, admiration of, 479
Carter, Jason, 383
Carter, Jimmy
    admiration of, 479
    favorability ratings, 237
Cassidy, Bill, 370
Catholics
    church attendance and, 476
    Francis I and, 118
    identification with, 475–76
    LGBT identification and, 303
    Middle East and, 293
    states and, 45–47
CDC (Centers for Disease Control and Prevention), approval
            ratings, 439–40
cell phones, communication and, 425–27
Chambliss, Saxby, 383
charitable activity, states and, 177–78
Chiang Kai-Shek, Madame, admiration of, 478
childcare, as most important issue for working women, 387
children
    extramarital, as morally acceptable, 207–8
    joy and stress and, 396
    obesity in, 84
    school safety and, 306–7
    spending and, 85, 460
    vacations and, 481
China
    as economic leader, 68
    economic power of, as threat, 82
    as greatest enemy of U.S., 68–69
    military power of, as threat, 82
    opinion of, 67–68
        trends in, 68
    as threat, 68, 82
cholesterol, high
    demographics of, 477
    obesity and, 84
    unemployment and, 232
Christians/Christianity
    Bible and, 215
    church attendance and, 476
    identification with, 475–76
    Middle East and, 293
    Obama, Barack, and, 259
Christie, Chris, favorability ratings, 266, 267, 269
Christmas
    mood and, 32
    spending on, 442–43
        forecast versus actual, 443
Christopher, Warren, favorability ratings, 86
church/church attendance, 475–76
    confidence in, 234
    creationism and, 212
    doctor-assisted suicide and, 233
    drinking age should/not be lowered, 278

LGBT identification and, 303
    Middle East and, 293–94
    religion and, 246
    school prayer and, 367
Churchill, Winston, admiration of, 479
CIA (Central Intelligence Agency), approval ratings, 439–40
cigarettes. *See* smoking
civil rights
    government and, 463
    as improved/worsened, blacks and, 463
civil unions. *See* gay marriage
clergy, honesty and ethical standards of, 469–70
climate change
    outlook for, 483
    as priority, 420
    as voting issue, 381
        Tea Party and, 403
    weather and, 97–98
    worry about, 91, 128–29
    See also global warming
Clinton, Bill
    admiration of, 479
    approval ratings, 22, 27, 154, 273, 317, 397
    Clinton, Hillary, and, 224
    confidence in presidency and, 248
    favorability ratings, 237
    presidency of Hillary Clinton and, 108
    voting to support/oppose, 180
Clinton, Hillary Rodham
    admiration of, 478, 479
    Benghazi incident and, 231–32
    best/worst thing about presidency, 107–9
    Clinton, Bill, and, 224
    favorability ratings, 69–70, 83, 86, 223–24, 266–67, 270–71
        party identification and, 224
        trends in, 70, 223, 271
clothing, spending on, 260
coal, U.S. should emphasize, 126
Coast Guard, as most important for defense, 200
Cobb, Nathan, 95
cold, climate change and, 97–98
Cold War, return of, 119–20
college
    attachment to, 452–53
    change in
        need for, 132–33
        signs of, 132
    community, trust in, 133
    costs, as most important financial problem, 153, 156–57
    first-generation graduates, race and, 355
    importance of, 132–33
    nontraditional graduates, 452–53
    online, trust in, 133
    traditional, trust in, 133
    well-being and, 175–76
        race and, 355–56
    workplace engagement and, 175–76
    See also education; student debt
Colorado, 365–66
    health and, 88
    livability, 159

Mormons and, 46
obesity in, 84
party identification in, 365, 416
smoking in, 94
state taxes and, 134
underemployment and, 60
uninsured in, 296
well-being in, 66
would leave if could, 165
communication, technology and, 162–63, 425–27
community satisfaction, 136–38
community well-being, 252–53
    LGBT identification and, 321
    student debt and, 299
computer industry, image of, 335–36
    versus Internet industry, 338
computers
    crime and, 422
    hacking, worry about, 404–5
    online banking, 23
    possession of, 4–5
    testing, Common Core Standards and, 411–13
    use of, 167
Congress
    approval ratings, 51–52, 262–63, 305–6, 340, 393–94, 464–65
        midterm elections and, 229, 305–6, 394
        trends in, 51, 305, 393, 464
        voter turnout and, 324–25
    confidence in, 234–35, 247–48
        trends in, 247
    control of
        importance of, 360–61
        party preference for, 415
    dissatisfaction with, as most important issue, 264
    how to fix, 262–63
    members of
        deserve re-election, 29–30, 185, 309–11
            results and, 186
        honesty and ethical standards of, 469–70
        own
            deserves re-election, 29–30, 185, 310
            image of, 389–90
        should all be replaced, 262–63
        views of, 389
    as most important issue, 13, 192–93
    priorities for, 17–18, 227–28, 419–20
    trust in, 347–48
    See also Democrats in Congress; Republicans in Congress
congressional elections
    incumbents in, 185–86
        attitudes toward, 390
    indicators, 229–31, 415
    party identification and, 410–11, 416
    predictions for, 384–85
        accuracy of, 385
    thought given to, 328, 418
Connecticut
    Catholics and, 46
    dentist visits and, 169
    economic confidence in, 50

healthcare exchanges and, 49
Jews and, 46
job creation in, 54
livability, 159
Obama, Barack, and, 30
obesity in, 84
party identification in, 35
planning to move, 165–66
Protestants and, 46
religion and, 43
standard of living and, 56
state taxes and, 134
struggle to afford healthcare/medicine in, 121
uninsured in, 49, 296
would leave if could, 165
conservatives
    Affordable Care Act and, 125
    drinking age should/not be lowered, 278
    gay marriage and, 196
    global warming and, 156
    gun control and, 414
    identification with, 202–3
        trends in, 10–11
    Internet news and, 236
    LGBT identification and, 290
    marijuana legalization and, 423
    media and, 352–53
    most important issues facing working women and, 387
    newspapers and, 235
    North Korea and, 66
    party identification and, 202
    religion and, 247
    states and
        Arkansas and, 358
        Georgia and, 384
        Kansas and, 374
        Louisiana and, 370
    Tea Party and, 179, 373
    television news and, 236
Constitution, as priority, 420
consumers, spending and, 211, 260–61, 275
    trends in, 8–9
contraception
    Hobby Lobby decision, 261–62
    as morally acceptable, 207–8
    as most important issue for working women, 387
    as voting issue, Tea Party and, 403
Corbett, Tom, 406
corporations
    ratings on functions, 201–2
    tax system, perceptions of, 143
    See also business and industry
corruption
    Congress and, 389
    Illinois and, 130
    as most important issue, 13, 192–93, 264
cost of living
    as most important financial problem, 153, 156–57
    See also inflation; standard of living

Cotton, Tom, 358
courts. *See* Supreme Court
creationism, 211–12
credit cards
   having information stolen
      incidence of, 404–5, 422
      worry about, 404
   as most important financial problem, 153, 156–57
   trust businesses to keep personal information secure, 220
crime
   computer/Internet, 422
   confidence in police protection, race and, 435–36
   as most important issue, 264
   North Dakota and, 323
   perceptions of, 441–42
      versus reality, 442
   as priority, 17–18, 34
   reporting, 422
   residents feel safe
      demographics of, 444
      metro areas and, 144–45
   satisfaction with, 16–17
   victimization rates, 421–22
   worry about, 91, 404–5
   in your area, 442
criminal justice system
   confidence in, 234
      race and, 314
   views of, race and, 463
Cruz, Ted, favorability ratings, 266, 267, 269
Cuomo, Andrew, favorability ratings, 266–67, 270–71

Dalrymple, Jack, 322–24
Deal, Nathan, 383
death penalty
   versus life imprisonment, 399–400
   methods, as humane, 189–90
   as morally acceptable, 189–90, 207–8
   support for, 399–95
      reasons for, 400–401
      trends in, 399
debt
   as most important financial problem, 153, 156–57
   See also budget deficit, federal
defense
   as priority, 17–18, 34
   spending on, 79
   See also national security
deficit. *See* budget deficit, federal
Delaware
   air quality and, 218
   dentist visits and, 169
   health and, 88
   healthcare exchanges and, 49
   ideology in, 39
   job creation in, 54
   minorities and, 186
   Obama, Barack, and, 30
   obesity in, 84

party identification in, 35
state taxes and, 134
uninsured in, 49, 296
Democratic Party
   abortion and, 199
   Affordable Care Act and, 47, 87, 125, 139, 204–6, 432, 434
   Afghanistan and, 64–65
   age and, 116–17, 121–22, 257–58
      trends in, 258
   Benghazi incident and, 231
   Bernanke, Ben, and, 36–37
   Boehner, John, and, 377
   budget deficit and, 14
   Bush, George H. W., and, 237
   Bush, George W., and, 237
   business regulation and, 348–49
   candidates, favorability ratings, 266–67, 270–71
   Carter, Jimmy, and, 237
   Clinton, Bill, and, 237
   Clinton, Hillary, and, 109, 224
   Common Core standards and, 140, 405–7
   Congress and, 51–52, 263, 360, 394, 464
   death penalty and, 399–400
   defense spending and, 79
   direction of country and, 429
   divided government and, 198, 392
   drinking age should/not be lowered, 278
   Ebola virus and, 398
   economic confidence and, 418, 449
   economy and, 106–7, 343
   election of 2014 and, 291, 384–85
   energy and, 216
   enthusiasm for election and, 183
   environment and, 103–4, 106–7, 216
   executive branch and, 348
   favorability ratings, 190–91, 356–57, 429–30
      election results and, 191
      trends in, 429
   federal government and, 341
   foreign trade and, 71
   gay marriage and, 196
   gender and, 366
   generational groups and, 28–29
   global respect for Obama and, 72
   global warming and, 96, 100–103, 129, 156
   good/bad time to find a quality job, 105, 265, 473
   government and, 24, 365
   government healthcare coverage and, 438–39
   government role and, 369
   greatest enemy of U.S. and, 69
   Greenspan, Alan, and, 36
   Guantanamo Bay prison and, 229
   gun control and, 414
   gun ownership and, 424–25
   healthcare and, 14, 99–100, 427
   healthcare coverage and, 437
   healthcare quality and, 438
   Hispanics and, 47–49
   identification with, 450–51
      trends in, 6–7

ideology and, 10, 202–3
image of, 430
immigration and, 62, 236, 245, 359, 458
investments and, 149
Iraq and, 242–43
ISIS and, 362–63
Israel and, 81
job identity and, 320
labor and, 331
legislative branch and, 347
LGBT identification and, 289–90
likely to get health insurance, 122–23, 147
local government and, 361–62
media and, 352–53
Middle East and, 280–81, 293–94
midterm elections and, 380, 410–11
mobile technology and, 164
morality and, 207–8
most admired man/woman and, 479
most important issue and, 14, 193, 264, 318–19, 430
newly insured and, 148
North Korea and, 66
Obama, Barack, and, 26–27, 83, 108, 113, 236–37, 241, 329–30, 458
Obama, Michelle, and, 83
opportunity and, 20
organic foods and, 302
police and, 455
priorities and, 33–34, 228
prisoners of terrorists and, 225
race and, 48, 111
Reid, Harry, and, 377
religion and, 283–84
Republican Party and, 357
Russia and, 120
satisfaction of, 16–17, 20
satisfaction with healthcare and, 427
satisfaction with U.S. and, 13, 31, 92, 192, 472
school prayer and, 367
spending and, 152
state government and, 361
North Carolina and, 327
states and, 35–36
Alaska and, 344
Arkansas and, 357–58
Colorado and, 365
Georgia and, 383
Iowa and, 338
Kansas and, 374
Kentucky and, 394
Louisiana and, 370
North Carolina and, 326–27
Supreme Court and, 261–62
taxes and, 141–43
Tea Party and, 178–79
terrorism and, 343–44
third party and, 363–64
thought given to election, 328
U.S. as No. 1 military power and, 80
United Nations and, 75
voting certainty and, 419

voting issues and, 193–94, 381, 386–87
waste in spending and, 353–54
worrying issues and, 91–92
Democrats in Congress, economy and, 150–51
dentists, visits to, demographics of, 160–61
depression
obesity and, 84
unemployment and, 221–22, 480
diabetes
as most urgent health problem, 433
obesity and, 84
dining out, spending on, 260
discrimination
blacks and, 315, 462
criminal justice system and, 315
as most important issue for working women, 387
need new civil rights laws, 315
obesity and, 273–74
smoking and, 273–74
dishonesty, as most important issue, 13, 93, 192–93, 264
District of Columbia
economic confidence in, 50, 112
ideology in, 39
Jews and, 46
job creation in, 54
Obama, Barack, and, 30
party identification in, 35
religion and, 43
standard of living and, 56
divorce
as morally acceptable, 207–8
well-being and, 390–91
doctor(s)
honesty and ethical standards of, 469–70
personal
demographics of, 350
LGBT individuals and, 325–26
race and, 349–51
doctor-assisted suicide
as morally acceptable, 207–8
support for, 233–34
domestic issues, government and, confidence in, 340–41
drinking age, lowering, 277–78
drones
prestige of military and, 201
satisfaction with, 42
drought
climate change and, 97–98
region and, 98
drug use
divorce/separation and, 391
as most urgent health problem, 433
worry about, 91
Duncan, Arne, 300

Earth Day, 106
Easter, mood and, 32
Ebola virus
CDC approval ratings and, 439–40
government and, 378, 398
as most urgent health problem, 433–34

perceived likelihood of getting, 378, 398
will/not strike U.S., 379, 398
worry about, 378, 398
economic conditions
    Bush, George W., and, 113
    confidence in, 44, 213, 295–96, 351–52, 417–18, 449–50,
        460, 472
        metro areas and, 112
        standard of living and, 56
        states and, 50–51
            Alaska and, 345
            Arkansas and, 358–59
            Iowa and, 338
            Kentucky and, 395
            New Hampshire and, 402
            North Carolina and, 327
        trends in, 8–9, 44, 351–52, 417, 449, 460
    confidence in leaders on, 150–51
    environment and, 106–7
    ideology and, 202–3
    job creation, 176–77, 213–14, 297
        trends in, 8–9
    as most important financial problem, 153, 156–57
    as most important issue, 13, 93, 192–93, 318–19, 342, 430–31
        midterm elections and, 230
        trends in, 14, 264, 430, 471
    as most important issue for working women, 387
    North Dakota and, 322–23
    Obama, Barack, and, 112–13, 150, 317–18
    outlook for, 213, 482
        saving/spending and, 152
    party preferred to deal with, 343
        midterm elections and, 343–44
    Payroll to Population rate, 7–8
    as priority, 17–18, 34, 420
    satisfaction with, 16–17
    as voting issue, 193–94, 380–81, 386
        Tea Party and, 403
    worry about, 91–92
    See also financial situation, personal; stocks/stock market
education
    business leaders and, 76–77
    checking work email and, 167
    college
        importance of, 132–33
    Common Core standards, 139–41, 312–14, 405–6
        computer testing and, 411–13
        familiarity with, 139–40, 312, 407
        field tests, 412
        math versus English, 409
        teachers and, 406–10
    congressional priorities and, 420
    creationism and, 212
    drinking age should/not be lowered, 278
    entrepreneurial aspirations and, 11–12
    experiential learning, 453
    foreign trade and, 71
    GI Bill, satisfaction with, 251–52
    global warming and, 102, 129, 156
    good/bad time to find a quality job, 265, 473

hiring decisions and, 73
image of, 335–36
immigration and, 245
institution versus major
    importance of, 73
job identity and, 320
living with parents and, 59
Middle East and, 281
as most important issue, 13, 93, 192–93, 264, 318–19, 342, 430
as most important issue for working women, 387
North Dakota and, 323
Obama, Barack, and, 445–46
online, trust in, 133–34
preschool, as priority, 227–28
as priority, 17–18, 34, 420
satisfaction with, 16–17, 329
    trends in, 329
spending and, 152
See also college; school(s)
Edwards, Edwin, 370–71
Egypt
    following closely, 90
    opinion of, 62–63
        age and, 63
Eisenhower, Dwight D.
    admiration of, 479
    approval ratings, 22, 27, 154, 273, 397
Eisenhower, Mamie, admiration of, 478
elderly, electronic devices owned, 5
election of 1994
    congressional approval and, 306, 324, 394
    enthusiasm for, 183–84
    incumbents in, 186
    party identification and, 450
    party seen as better able to keep country prosperous and, 343
    voter turnout, 324
election of 1996, party favorable averages and, 191
election of 1998
    congressional approval and, 306, 324, 394
    enthusiasm for, 183–84
    incumbents in, 186
    indicators, 379–80, 415
    party identification and, 450
    party seen as better able to keep country prosperous and, 343
    voter turnout, 324
election of 2000
    incumbents in, 186
    party favorable averages and, 191
election of 2002
    congressional approval and, 306, 324, 394
    enthusiasm for, 183–84
    incumbents in, 186
    indicators, 379–80, 415
    party favorable averages and, 191
    party identification and, 450
    party seen as better able to keep country prosperous and, 343
    voter turnout, 324
election of 2004
    incumbents in, 186
    party favorable averages and, 191

election of 2006
congressional approval and, 306, 324, 394
enthusiasm for, 183–84
incumbents in, 186
indicators, 379–80, 415
party favorable averages and, 191
party identification and, 450–51
party seen as better able to keep country prosperous and, 343
voter turnout, 324
election of 2008
incumbents in, 186
party favorable averages and, 191
election of 2010
congressional approval and, 306, 324, 394
enthusiasm for, 183–84
incumbents in, 186
indicators, 379–80, 415
party favorable averages and, 191
party identification and, 450
party seen as better able to keep country prosperous and, 343
voter turnout, 324
election of 2012
incumbents in, 186
party favorable averages and, 191
election of 2014
abortion and, 200
congressional approval and, 305–6, 394
country will be better/worse off, 428–29
enthusiasm for, 179, 183–84, 418
indicators, 229–31, 379–80, 415
issues in, 193–94, 380–81, 386–87
Tea Party and, 403
likely voters and, 418–19
party favorable averages and, 191
party identification and, 291, 410–11, 450–51
party seen as better able to keep country prosperous and, 343
predictions for, 384–85
sending message to president, using vote for, 375–76
thought given to, 328, 418
voting to support/oppose Obama, 180
as wave election, 29
election of 2016
candidate favorability ratings
Democratic field, 266–67, 270–71
Republican field, 266, 267, 268–70
electric and gas utilities, image of, 335–36
electric chair, as humane, 189–90
electronics, devices owned, 4–5
Elizabeth II, queen of Great Britain, admiration of, 478
email
checking, demographics of, 167
communication and, 426
stress and, 171, 480
See also mobile technology
emotional health
living with parents and, 61
metro areas and, 114
states and, 67
See also mental health

employer-based health insurance
prevalence of, 53–54, 182, 256
satisfaction with, 316
employers, mobile technology and, 171
employment
depression and, 221
discrimination and
obesity and, 273–74
race and, 462
smoking and, 273–74
health and, 233
health insurance and, 26
living with parents and, 58–59
obesity and, 232–33
outlook, 221
Payroll to Population rate, 7–8
working remotely after hours is positive/negative, 166–67
See also jobs; unemployment; workplace engagement
energy
alternative, 126
Bush, George W., and, 113
conservation versus production, 125–26
costs
as most important financial problem, 153, 156–57
worry about, 91
environment and, 216
Obama, Barack, and, 112–13
as priority, 17–18
satisfaction with, 40
worry about, 91
See also gasoline; oil
enjoyment
children in household and, 396
North Dakota and, 323
See also happiness
entertainment, spending on, 260
entrepreneurs
aspirations to, 11–12
opportunities of, 12
environment
BP oil spill, following closely, 90
Bush, George W., and, 113
economy and, 106–7
energy and, 216
as most important issue, 192–93
North Dakota and, 323
Obama, Barack, and, 112–13
outlook for, 103–4
as priority, 17–18, 34
quality of, 103–4
regulation and, 126
satisfaction with, 16–17, 40
worry about, 91
See also climate change; global warming
EPA (Environmental Protection Agency), approval ratings, 439–40
equal opportunity, as most important issue for working women, 387
equal pay
as most important issue for working women, 387–88

as priority, 227–28
as voting issue, 381, 386
Tea Party and, 403
Ernst, Joni, 337–38
ethics, as most important issue, 13, 93, 192–93, 264, 318–19, 342, 430
ethnic groups. *See* race
European financial conditions, investors and, 382
European Union, as economic leader, 68
euthanasia. *See* doctor-assisted suicide
evolution, 211–12
executive branch. *See* president/presidency
exercise, participation in, last week, 268
appearance and, 267–68
obesity and, 84
social well-being and, 254
states and, 88
extinction, worry about, 128

family(ies)
drinking and, 287–88
leave, as most important issue for working women, 387
as most important issue, 13, 93, 192–93, 264, 430
North Dakota and, 323
social media and, 239
time with, unemployment and, 221–22
vacations with, well-being and, 480–81
farms/farming
Farm Bill, 110
image of, 335–36
Father's Day, mood and, 32
FBI (Federal Bureau of Investigation), approval ratings, 439–40
FDA (Food and Drug Administration), approval ratings, 439–40
federal government
Ebola virus and, 378, 398
image of, 335–36
jobs with, engagement and, 466–67
power of, worry about, 91
satisfaction with, 24
schools and, 312–14
shutdown
Obama, Barack, and, 2–3
satisfaction and, 364–65
trust to handle international/domestic problems, 340–41
trust to keep personal information secure, 220
as voting issue, 381, 386
waste in spending, perceptions of, 353–54
See also budget, federal; government
Federal Reserve Board, approval ratings, 439–40
financial situation, personal
better off next year than now, 15
better off now than year ago, 15
can buy what you need, 89
getting better/worse, 89
outlook for, age and, investors and, 468
problems, 152–54, 156–57
well-being and, 252–53
See also income; money; spending
financial well-being
LGBT identification and, 321

student debt and, 299
firing squad, as humane, 189–90
Florida
healthcare exchanges and, 49
Jews and, 46
Payroll to Population rate and, 59
state taxes and, 134
struggle to afford healthcare/medicine in, 121
underemployment and, 60
uninsured in, 49
flu
versus Ebola, 378
as most urgent health problem, 433–34
food
ate fruits and veggies last week
obesity and, 84
social well-being and, 254
states and, 88
ate healthy yesterday, obesity and, 84
carbohydrates, 286–87
choices, 285
fats, 286–87
groups, dietary choices, 285
organic, 301–2
demographics of, 302
prices, 110
struggle to afford, 420–21
states and, 109–10
Ford, Betty, admiration of, 478
foreign affairs/policy
government and, confidence in, 340–41
as most important issue, 93, 192–93, 264, 318–19, 342, 430
Obama, Barack, and, 317–18
as priority, 17–18, 34, 420
satisfaction with, 16–17
as voting issue, 193–94, 381
Tea Party and, 403
foreign aid, as most important issue, 13, 93, 192–93, 264, 318–19, 342, 430
foreign trade
approval ratings, 70–71
trends in, 71
satisfaction with, 41
fracking, U.S. should emphasize, 126
France
approval of U.S. leadership, 52
opinion of, 52–53
Francis I, pope
admiration of, 479
favorability ratings, 117–18
friends
North Dakota and, 323
social media and, 239
time with, unemployment and, 221–22
vacations with, well-being and, 480–81
fuel, prices, spending on, 260

Gadhafi, Moammar, 63
gambling, as morally acceptable, 207–8
Gardner, Cory, 365–66

gas chamber, as humane, 189–90
gasoline
    industry, image of, 335–36
    as most important financial problem, 153, 156–57
    spending on, 260
    U.S. should emphasize, 126
Gates, Bill, admiration of, 479
gay marriage
    outlook for, 482–83
    support for, 195–96
        adoption and, 209
    as voting issue, 193–94
gender
    abortion and, 199
    appearance and, 255
    boss gender preference, 388–89
    budget deficit and, 14
    checking work email and, 167
    dentist visits and, 160
    drinking age should/not be lowered, 278
    emotional impact of children in household and, 396
    feel safe walking alone at night, 444
    financial advice sources and, 308
    financial advice use and, 346
    global warming and, 156
    gun control and, 414
    gun ownership and, 424–25
    healthcare and, 14
    health insurance and, 26
    job identity and, 320
    marital status and well-being and, 390–91
    Middle East and, 281
    most important issue and, 14
    most important issues facing working women and, 387–88
    Obama, Barack, and, 83, 445–46
    Obama, Michelle, and, 83
    obesity and, 78, 197
    party identification and, 366
    Postal Service and, 441
    religion and, 247
    weight and, 222, 282, 447
    well-being and, 253
    work environment satisfaction and, 392–93
generational groups
    banking industry and, 22–23
    checking work email and, 167
    Obama, Barack, and, 456–57
    party identification and, 116
    party identification of, 27–29
    retirement and, 20–21
    social media and purchasing decisions, 238
    strengths usage and, 25
Generation X
    banking industry and, 23
    checking work email and, 167
    party identification of, 28
    percentage in workplace, 21
    social media and purchasing decisions, 238
    strengths usage and, 25
    workplace engagement and, 21

Generation Y. *See* Millennials
geographic region
    abortion and, 199
    air quality and, 218
    dentist visits and, 161, 169
    drinking age should/not be lowered, 278
    gay marriage and, 196
    gun ownership and, 424–25
    marijuana legalization and, 423
    minorities and, 187
    obesity and, 78, 197
    organic foods and, 301–2
    religion and, 247
    right-to-work laws and, 331
    spending and, 151–52
    state taxes and, 134–35
    struggle to afford food in, 110
    struggle to afford healthcare/medicine in, 121
    uninsured in, 50
    well-being and, 114, 253
    winter temperatures and, 98
Georgia, 383–84
    Catholics and, 46
    healthcare exchanges and, 49
    party identification in, 416
    Protestants and, 46
    religion and, 43
    struggle to afford food in, 110
    underemployment and, 60
    uninsured in, 49
GI Bill, satisfaction with, 251–52
global warming
    causes of, 101–3, 155–56
    opinion groups on, 155–56
        demographics of, 156
    scientists and, 101
    seriousness of, 100–101, 155–56
        trends in, 100
    as threat, 95–96, 155–56
        trends in, 95
    understanding of, 102
    as voting issue, 193–94
    when effects will happen, 95–96
    worry about, 128–29, 155–56
        demographics of, 129
        trends in, 128
    See also climate change
gold, as best long-term investment, 149
Goldich, David, 249
government
    civil rights and, 463
    dissatisfaction with
        as most important issue, 13–14, 192–93, 264, 318–19, 342, 430–31
            trends in, 430, 471
        political affiliation and, 319
    divided, 197–98, 391–92, 428
        satisfaction with Congress and, 262
        trends in, 391
    Ebola virus and, 378, 398

healthcare and, 438–39
investors and, 382–83
jobs with, 177
    hiring/letting go, 214
as most important issue, 93, 192–93
as most urgent health problem, 433
one-party control of, 391–92
power of, satisfaction with, 24
priorities for, 17–18
    party identification and, 33–34
role of, 369
    Republican Party and, 403
    Tea Party and, 403
satisfaction with, 364–65
    trends in, 23–24
size of
    satisfaction with, 24
    worry about, 91
spending by
    and alternative energy, 126
    waste in, perceptions of, 353–54
    worry about, 91
surveillance programs
    as priority, 17–18
    satisfaction with, 41
Graham, Billy, admiration of, 479
greenhouse effect. *See* global warming
greenhouse gases, regulation of, 126, 215–16
    as priority, 227–28
Greenspan, Alan, 36–37
Grimes, Alison Lundergan, 394–95
groceries
    industry, image of, 335–36
    spending on, 260
Guantanamo Bay prison, closure of, support for, 228–29
gun(s)
    ownership of, 425
        demographics of, 425
        makes house safer/more dangerous, 424–25
        trends in, 425
    violence, 42
gun control
    handgun ban, 413
    Obama, Barack, and, 2
    outlook for, 483
    support for, 413–14
        demographics of, 413–14
gun policy
    as priority, 17–18, 34, 420
    satisfaction with, 16–17
        trends in, 38–39

hacking
    incidence of, 404–5, 422
    worry about, 404–5
Hagan, Kay, 326–27
Hamas, 280–81, 294–95
hanging, as humane, 189–90
happiness, 221
    trends in, 33
    See also enjoyment

Harkin, Tom, 337
Hassan, Maggie, 402
Hawaii
    charitable activity and, 177
    health and, 88
    healthcare exchanges and, 49
    ideology in, 39
    job creation in, 54
    livability, 159
    minorities and, 186
    Mormons and, 46
    Obama, Barack, and, 30
    obesity in, 84
    party identification in, 35
    Payroll to Population rate and, 59
    Protestants and, 46
    religion and, 43
    schools and, 135
        prepare students for success in workplace, 136
    standard of living and, 56
    struggle to afford healthcare/medicine in, 121
    underemployment and, 60
    uninsured in, 49
    well-being in, 66
    would leave if could, 165
Hawking, Stephen, admiration of, 479
health/well-being
    Ebola virus, 378–79, 398
    have put off treatment for non/serious condition, 448
    living with parents and, 61
    metro areas and, 114
    newly insured and, 148, 240
    states and, 67
    well-being and, 252–53
    See also Well-Being Index
healthcare
    access to
        as most urgent health problem, 433
        satisfaction with, 16–17
        worry about, 91
    Clinton, Hillary, and, 108–9
    confidence in, 234
    costs
        as most important financial problem, 153, 156–57
            trends in, 153, 157
        as most important issue, 13, 93, 192–93, 264
        as most urgent health problem, 433
        put off care due to, 447
        satisfaction with, 16–17, 453–55
        worry about, 91
    coverage
        put off medical treatment due to cost, 447
        rated, 437–38, 454
    government and, 438–39
    industry, image of, 335–36
    as most important issue, 93, 318–19, 342, 430
        trends in, 14
    as most important issue for working women, 387
    most important issue in, 433–34
    newly insured and, 432–33
    as priority, 17–18, 34, 420

quality of, 454
    as most important issue, 13, 192–93, 264
    party identification and, 438
    satisfaction with, 16–17
satisfaction with, 99–100, 427–28
    demographics of, 427
spending on, 260
struggle to afford, 120–21
    LGBT individuals and, 325
healthcare reform. *See* Affordable Care Act
health insurance
    costs
        as most urgent health problem, 433
        newly insured and, 433
    coverage, 1, 26, 217–18, 256–57
        Affordable Care Act and, 206
        age and, 53
        dentist visits and, 169
        LGBT individuals and, 325–26
        newly insured and, 432–33
        political affiliation and, 122–23
        race and, 349–51
        satisfaction and, 99, 427
        states and, 296–97
        struggle to afford healthcare/medicine and, 121
        by type, 182, 256–57
    newly insured, 147–48, 239–40
        plans for insurance, 433
        ratings of healthcare and coverage, 432–33
    obesity and, 274
    satisfaction with, 393
    self-funded, prevalence of, 182
    smoking and, 274
    See also uninsured
health insurance companies, trust to keep personal
        information secure, 220
Healthy Behaviors Index
    living with parents and, 61
    metro areas and, 114
    states and, 67, 88–89
heart attack, obesity and, 84
heart disease, as most urgent health problem, 433
Herbert, Gary, 297
high blood pressure
    demographics of, 477
    obesity and, 84
    unemployment and, 232
hiring activity. *See* jobs
Hispanics
    Affordable Care Act and, 205
    appearance and, 255, 480
    chronic conditions and, 476–77
    church attendance and, 476
    daily spending and, 459–60
    dentist visits and, 160
    healthcare and, 427
    health insurance and, 131, 349–51
    immigration and, 359–60, 457–58
    Obama, Barack, and, 368, 457–59

obesity and, 78, 197
outlook for, 483
party identification of, 47–49, 283–84
personal doctor and, 349–51
police and, 455
religion and, 283–84
standard of living and, 298–99
struggle to afford food and, 421
uninsured and, 173, 217
vacations and, 481
holidays, mood and, 32–33
Hollande, Francois, 52–53
Homeland Security, approval ratings, 439–40
homelessness
    as most important issue, 13, 93, 192–93, 264, 318–19, 342, 430
    as priority, 17–18, 34
    satisfaction with, 16–17
    worry about, 91
home ownership, costs, as most important financial problem, 153, 156–57
homosexuals and homosexuality. *See* gay marriage; LGBT individuals and issues
honesty
    Obama, Barack, and, 227
    as priority, 420
hospitals
    as most important issue, 192–93, 318–19
    quality of, as most important issue, 13, 264
    See also healthcare
House of Representatives. *See* Congress
housing
    costs, as most important financial problem, 153, 156–57
    good/bad time to buy, 158
    with parents
        age and, 58–59
        well-being and, 60–61
    prices, predictions for, 158–59
    spending on, 260
    struggle to afford, safety and, 144–45
    worth more than when purchased, 158
Huckabee, Mike, favorability ratings, 266, 268–70
humans, cloning, as morally acceptable, 207–8
hunger
    as most important issue, 13, 93, 192–93, 264, 318–19, 342, 430
    worry about, 91
Hutchinson, Asa, 358
hypertension. *See* high blood pressure

Idaho
    charitable activity and, 177
    economic confidence in, 50
    health and, 88
    ideology in, 39
    minorities and, 187
    Mormons and, 46
    Obama, Barack, and, 30
    party identification in, 35
    Payroll to Population rate and, 59
    planning to move, 165–66

Protestants and, 46
schools and, prepare students for success in workplace, 136
state taxes and, 134
ideology
Affordable Care Act and, 125
drinking age should/not be lowered, 278
gay marriage and, 196
global warming and, 156
gun control and, 414
identification with, 202–3
trends in, 10–11
Internet news and, 236
LGBT identification and, 290
marijuana legalization and, 423
media and, 352–53
most important issues facing working women and, 387
newspapers and, 235
North Korea and, 66
party identification and, 202
religion and, 247
states and, 39–40
Arkansas and, 357–58
Georgia and, 384
Kansas and, 374
Louisiana and, 370
Tea Party and, 179, 373
television news and, 236
illegal immigration. *See* immigrants/immigration
Illinois
Catholics and, 46
charitable activity and, 177
livability, 159
Obama, Barack, and, 30
party identification in, 35
planning to move, 165–66
schools and, 135
prepare students for success in workplace, 136
smoking in, 94
state taxes and, 134
struggle to afford food in, 110
trust in state government and, 129
would leave if could, 165
immigrants/immigration
border control, 61–62
business leaders and, 77
education and, 77
as good/bad thing for country, 245
H-1B visas, 246
investors and, 382
levels of, 245–46
trends in, 245
as most important issue, 13, 93, 192–93, 263–64, 318–19, 342, 430–31
Hispanics and, 359–60
trends in, 430
North Dakota and, 323
Obama, Barack, and, 236, 457–58
as priority, 17–18, 34
reform, as priority, 227–28, 420
satisfaction with, 16–17, 40
worry about, 91

as voting issue, 193–94, 381
Tea Party and, 403
income
Affordable Care Act and, 206
Bernanke, Ben, and, 37
best investment and, 149
can buy what you need, 89
checking work email and, 167
dentist visits and, 160
distribution of
as priority, 17–18
satisfaction with, 19–20
economic confidence and, 44, 417–18, 449
feel safe walking alone at night, 444
financial problems and, 153–54
good/bad time to find a quality job, 265
hacking worries and, 404
healthcare and, 427
health insurance and, 26, 131
mobile technology and, 170
money worries and, 89
newly insured and, 148
North Dakota and, 322–23
obesity and, 78, 197
organic foods and, 302
parental spending and, 85
personal doctor and, 350
personal financial situation and, 89
put off medical treatment due to cost, 447–48
retail shopping and, 170
spending and, 151–52
standard of living and, 298–99
struggle to afford food and, 421
taxes and, 142
uninsured and, 173, 217
vacation and, 481
vacation days of microbusiness owners and, 279
volunteering and, 304
See also financial situation, personal; money; wages
income inequality. *See* inequality
income tax
fairness of, 141–42
middle-income people pay their fair share, 142–43
See also taxes
independents
abortion and, 199
Affordable Care Act and, 47, 87, 125, 139, 206, 434
age and, 257–58
trends in, 258
Benghazi incident and, 231
Bernanke, Ben, and, 36–37
Boehner, John, and, 377
budget deficit and, 14
Bush, George H. W., and, 237
Bush, George W., and, 237
Carter, Jimmy, and, 237
Clinton, Bill, and, 237
Clinton, Hillary, and, 109, 224
Congress and, 51–52, 394, 464
death penalty and, 399–400
defense spending and, 79

Democratic Party and, 357, 430
direction of country and, 429
divided government and, 198, 392
drinking age should/not be lowered, 278
economic confidence and, 418, 449
energy and, 216
environment and, 103–4, 216
executive branch and, 348
federal government and, 341
foreign trade and, 71
gay marriage and, 196
gender and, 366
global respect for Obama and, 72
global warming and, 96, 100–103, 129
good/bad time to find a quality job, 105, 265
government and, 24, 365
government role and, 369
greatest enemy of U.S. and, 69
Greenspan, Alan, and, 36
Guantanamo Bay prison and, 229
gun control and, 414
gun ownership and, 424–25
healthcare and, 14, 99–100
identification with, 6–7
ideology and, 11
immigration and, 236, 245, 458
investments and, 149
Iraq and, 242–43
ISIS and, 362–63
Israel and, 81
job identity and, 320
labor and, 331
legislative branch and, 347
LGBT identification and, 289–90
local government and, 361–62
media and, 352–53
Middle East and, 281
mobile technology and, 164
morality and, 207–8
most important issue and, 14, 193
North Korea and, 66
Obama, Barack, and, 83, 108, 113, 236–37, 241, 330, 458
Obama, Michelle, and, 83
opportunity and, 20
organic foods and, 302
police and, 455
priorities and, 228
prisoners of terrorists and, 225
race and, 48
Reid, Harry, and, 377
Republican Party and, 357
Russia and, 120
satisfaction of, 20
satisfaction with U.S. and, 13, 31, 92, 192, 472
school prayer and, 367
spending and, 152
state government and, 361
    North Carolina and, 327
states and
    Alaska and, 344
    Georgia and, 383

Supreme Court and, 261–62
taxes and, 141–43
third party and, 363–64
U.S. as No. 1 military power and, 80
United Nations and, 75
voting certainty and, 419
waste in spending and, 353–54
India
    conflict with Pakistan, as threat, 82
    as economic leader, 68
Indiana
    health and, 88
    planning to move, 165
    smoking in, 94
industry. See business and industry
inequality
    investors and, 382
    as most important issue, 13, 93, 192–93, 318–19, 342
    student debt and, 355
    as voting issue, 193–94, 381
        Tea Party and, 403
inflation
    investor optimism and, 467
    as most important financial problem, 153, 156–57
influenza
    versus Ebola, 378
    as most urgent health problem, 433–34
infrastructure, satisfaction with, 40–41
interest rates
    investors and, 382
    as most important financial problem, 153, 156–57
Internal Revenue Service, approval ratings, 439–40
international issues. See foreign affairs/policy
Internet
    crime and, 422
    industry, image of, 335–36
        versus computer industry, 338
    news
        confidence in, 234–35
        Middle East and, 294–95
    online banking, 23
    online education, 133–34
    online financial advice, 308–9
    online testing, Common Core standards and, 411–13
    spending on, 260
    trust businesses to keep personal information secure, 219–20
investments
    401(k) accounts, loans and early withdrawals, 473–74
    financial advice sources and, 308
    financial advice use and, 346
    as most important financial problem, 153, 156–57
    political factors and, 382–83
    which type is best, 18–19, 148–50
investors
    financial advice sources, 308–9
        demographics of, 308
        use of, 309
    financial advice use, 345–46
    optimism of, 96–97, 467–68
    political factors and, 382–83
    saving/spending and, 152

Iowa
  economic confidence in, 50, 338
  health and, 88
  healthcare exchanges and, 49
  job creation in, 54
  Obama, Barack, and, 337–38
  party identification in, 338, 416
  planning to move, 165
  schools and, 135
    prepare students for success in workplace, 136
  standard of living and, 56–57
  struggle to afford food in, 110
  struggle to afford healthcare/medicine in, 121
  underemployment and, 60
  uninsured in, 49
  well-being in, 66–67
Iran
  as greatest enemy of U.S., 68–69
  opinion of, 62–63
    age and, 63
  as threat, 82
Iraq
  as greatest enemy of U.S., 69
  as most important issue, 342, 430
  opinion of, 62–63
    age and, 63
Iraq war
  as mistake, 64, 242
  support for, 242–43
  withdrawal from, 242
Islam. *See* Muslims
Islamic fundamentalism, as threat, 82
Islamic State in Iraq and Syria (ISIS), 341–42
  military action against
    approval of, 362–63
    ground troops in, 363
  as most important issue, 430
  as voting issue, 381, 386
    Tea Party and, 403
Israel
  opinion of, 62–63
    age and, 63
  sympathy with, 81
  See also Middle East
issues, most important, 13–15, 93, 192–93, 342, 430–31
  Democratic Party and, 318–19
  immigration as, Hispanics and, 359–60
  party preferred to deal with, 264
  race relations as, 470–71
  Republican Party and, 318–19
  terrorism as, 342
  trends in, 14

Japan, as economic leader, 68
Jews
  church attendance and, 476
  identification with, 475–76
  LGBT identification and, 303
  Middle East and, 293–94
  Obama, Barack, and, 259
  states and, 45–47

Jindal, Bobby, favorability ratings, 266, 269
Job Creation Index, 176–77, 213–14, 297
  metro areas and, 105–6
  midyear, 297
  standard of living and, 54, 56
  states and, 54–55
  trends in, 8–9
jobs
  benefits
    as most important issue for working women, 387
    worry about, 311–12
  companies are hiring/letting go, 177
    metro areas and, 106
  creation of, 176–77, 213–14, 297
  good/bad time to find a quality job, 104–5, 265–66, 436–37, 472–73
    Arkansas and, 358–59
    demographics of, 265, 473
    New Hampshire and, 402
    trends in, 104, 265
  hours, 332–33
    satisfaction with, 316, 393
    worry about, 311–12
  identity and, 319–20
    demographics of, 320
  as most important issue, 93, 192–93, 264, 342, 430
    trends in, 430
  as most important issue for working women, 387
  North Dakota and, 323
  outlook, 221
  as priority, 420
  security, satisfaction with, 316–17
  as voting issue, 380–81, 386
    Tea Party and, 403
  worried about being laid off, 311–12
  See also employment; unemployment
John Paul II, pope
  admiration of, 479
  favorability ratings, 118
Jolie, Angelina, admiration of, 478
Jones, Jeff, 262
journalists. *See* media; news
Judaism. *See* Jews
judicial branch. *See* Supreme Court
judicial system
  confidence in, North Dakota and, 323
  as most important issue, 264, 342
  See also criminal justice system

Kansas, 374–75
  charitable activity and, 177
  health and, 88
  healthcare exchanges and, 49
  livability, 375
  Obama, Barack, and, 30
  party identification in, 35, 416
  schools and, 135
    prepare students for success in workplace, 136
  uninsured in, 49
Kasem, Casey, 233
Keller, Helen, admiration of, 478

Kennedy, Edward, admiration of, 479
Kennedy, Jacqueline, admiration of, 478
Kennedy, John F., 68, 75
Kentucky, 394–96
    charitable activity and, 178
    dentist visits and, 169
    economic confidence in, 50
    healthcare exchanges and, 49
    job creation in, 54
    minorities and, 187
    Obama, Barack, and, 30
    obesity in, 84
    party identification in, 394
    planning to move, 165
    Protestants and, 46
    religion and, 43
    smoking in, 94
    standard of living and, 56
    struggle to afford food in, 110
    struggle to afford healthcare/medicine in, 121
    uninsured in, 49, 296
    well-being in, 66
Kerry, John, 80
    favorability ratings, 85–86
        trends in, 86
Keystone XL pipeline, following closely, 90
Kim Jong-un, 66
Korean War, as mistake, 64
Kosovo, U.S. military action in, support for, 243

labor (organized; unions)
    approval ratings, 331
    confidence in, 234
    health insurance coverage, prevalence of, 53–54, 182, 256
    right-to-work laws, 331
Lacatell, Janna, 128, 197
lakes, pollution of, worry about, 128
Landrieu, Mary, 370, 457
large metro areas
    obesity in, 127
    well-being in, 115
Latinos/as. See Hispanics
Latter-Day Saints. See Mormons
law enforcement. See police
lawyer(s)
    honesty and ethical standards of, 469–70
    image of, 335–36
leadership
    as most important issue, 13, 192–93, 264
    Obama, Barack, and, 227
legislative branch. See Congress
lethal injection, as humane, 189–90
Lew, Jack, 150
LGBT individuals and issues
    adoption rights and, 208–9
    health insurance coverage, 325–26
    ideology of, 290
    nature/nurture, 203–4
    Obama, Barack, and, 289–90
    party identification of, 289–90

    as priority, 17–18
    relations, as morally acceptably, 207–8
    religion and, 302–4
    satisfaction with, 16–17
    well-being and, 320–22, 480
liberals
    drinking age should/not be lowered, 278
    gay marriage and, 196
    global warming and, 156
    gun control and, 414
    identification with, 10–11
    Internet news and, 236
    LGBT identification and, 290
    marijuana legalization and, 423
    media and, 352–53
    most important issues facing working women and, 387
    newspapers and, 235
    North Korea and, 66
    party identification and, 202
    religion and, 247
    states and, 39–40
        Arkansas and, 358
        Georgia and, 384
        Louisiana and, 370
    Tea Party and, 179, 373
    television news and, 236
Libya
    following closely, 90
    opinion of, 62–63
        age and, 63
Life Evaluation Index
    living with parents and, 61
    metro areas and, 114
    mobile technology and, 171
    states and, 67
liquor, 276
local government
    schools and, 312
    trust in, 361–62
    waste in spending, perceptions of, 353–54
Louisiana, 370–71
    charitable activity and, 178
    dentist visits and, 169
    economic confidence in, 50
    health and, 88
    healthcare exchanges and, 49
    ideology in, 370
    livability, 159
    minorities and, 187
    Obama, Barack, and, 370–71
    obesity in, 84
    party identification in, 370
    planning to move, 165–66
    religion and, 43
    schools and, 135
        prepare students for success in workplace, 136
    smoking in, 94
    struggle to afford food in, 110
    trust in state government and, 129
    uninsured in, 49

well-being in, 66
would leave if could, 165
Luce, Clare Boothe, admiration of, 478

MacArthur, Douglas, admiration of, 479
Maine
    health and, 88
    ideology in, 39
    job creation in, 54
    planning to move, 165
    religion and, 43
    standard of living and, 56
    trust in state government and, 129
    well-being in, 67
    would leave if could, 165
Mandela, Nelson, 3
    admiration of, 479
Maness, Rob, 370
Manning, Chelsea (Bradley), 33
marijuana, legalization of, 423–24
    outlook for, 483
    trends in, 423
Marines, as most important for defense, 200
marital status
    dentist visits and, 161
    living with parents and, 58
    personal doctor and, 350
    vacations and, 481
    well-being and, 390–91
marriage. See divorce; gay marriage
Martin, Trayvon, 2, 462
Maryland
    economic confidence in, 50
    Jews and, 46
    livability, 159
    Obama, Barack, and, 30
    party identification in, 35
    planning to move, 165–66
    smoking in, 94
    state taxes and, 134
    struggle to afford healthcare/medicine in, 121
    trust in state government and, 129
    would leave if could, 165
Massachusetts
    Catholics and, 46
    dentist visits and, 169
    economic confidence in, 50
    healthcare exchanges and, 49
    ideology in, 39
    Jews and, 46
    livability, 402
    Obama, Barack, and, 30
    obesity in, 84
    party identification in, 35
    Protestants and, 46
    religion and, 43
    schools and, 135
        prepare students for success in workplace, 136
    smoking in, 94
    standard of living and, 56–57

state taxes and, 134
struggle to afford food in, 110
struggle to afford healthcare/medicine in, 121
uninsured in, 49
well-being in, 67
would leave if could, 165
maternity leave, as most important issue for working women, 387
McConnell, Mitch, 394–95
    favorability ratings, 187–89
    Tea Party and, 188–89
McDonald, Robert, 250
media
    confidence in, 235–36
    ideology and, 352–53
    Middle East and, 294–95
    trust in, 352–53
    See also news; specific medium
Medicaid, prevalence of, 53–54, 182, 256
medical system
    confidence in, 234
    finding cures for diseases, as most important issue, 433
    See also healthcare
Medicare
    prevalence of, 53–54, 182, 256
    as priority, 17–18, 34
    satisfaction with, 16–17
medicine
    struggle to afford, 120–21
        LGBT individuals and, 325
    use of, divorce/separation and, 391
Memorial Day
    mood and, 32
    spending and, 211
men
    abortion and, 199
    admiration of, 478–79
    appearance and, 255
    boss gender preference and, 388–89
    budget deficit and, 14
    checking work email and, 167
    dentist visits and, 160
    drinking age should/not be lowered, 278
    emotional impact of children in household and, 396
    financial advice sources and, 308
    financial advice use and, 346
    global warming and, 156
    gun control and, 414
    gun ownership and, 424–25
    healthcare and, 14
    health insurance and, 26
    job identity and, 320
    marital status and well-being and, 390–91
    Middle East and, 281
    most important issue and, 14
    most important issues facing working women and, 387
    Obama, Barack, and, 83, 445–46
    Obama, Michelle, and, 83
    obesity and, 78, 197
    party identification and, 366
    Postal Service and, 441

religion and, 247

weight and, 222, 282, 447

well-being and, 253

work environment satisfaction and, 392–93

mental health

as most urgent health problem, 433

See also depression; emotional health

metro areas

community satisfaction in, 136–38

economic confidence in, 112

job creation in, 105–6

obesity in, 127–28

optimism and, 137

organic foods and, 302

police and, 455

residents feel safe in, 144–45

well-being in, 113–15

Michigan

healthcare exchanges and, 49

job creation in, 54

livability, 159

minorities and, 187

Payroll to Population rate and, 59

smoking in, 94

standard of living and, 56

underemployment and, 60

uninsured in, 49

microbusiness, owners

hours per week, 279

vacation days, 278–80

See also small business

Middle East

following closely, 281, 294

investors and, 382

opinion of, 80–81, 280–81, 294–95

demographics of, 281

religion and, 293–94

sympathies in, 81

as threat, 82

Middleton, Kate, admiration of, 478

military

branch most important to defense, 200

confidence in, 234–35

health insurance coverage, prevalence of, 53–54, 182, 256

as priority, 17–18, 34

satisfaction with, 16–17

stress/worry and, 249

Millennials

banking industry and, 23

checking work email and, 167

living with parents, 58–59, 480

Obama, Barack, and, 456–57

party identification of, 28

percentage in workplace, 21

social media and purchasing decisions and, 238

strengths usage and, 25

workplace engagement and, 21

minimum wage

as priority, 227–28

satisfaction with, 40

Minnesota

charitable activity and, 177

dentist visits and, 169

economic confidence in, 50

healthcare exchanges and, 49

job creation in, 54

livability, 159

obesity in, 84

planning to move, 165

schools and, 135

prepare students for success in workplace, 136

smoking in, 94

standard of living and, 56

struggle to afford food in, 109–10

struggle to afford healthcare/medicine in, 121

underemployment and, 60

uninsured in, 49

well-being in, 66

would leave if could, 165

minorities, racial

North Dakota and, 323

states and, 186–87

See also Asian Americans; blacks; Hispanics; nonwhites; race

Mississippi

Catholics and, 46

charitable activity and, 178

dentist visits and, 169

healthcare exchanges and, 49

ideology in, 39

livability, 159

minorities and, 187

obesity in, 84

Payroll to Population rate and, 59

planning to move, 165–66

Protestants and, 46

religion and, 43

schools and, 135

smoking in, 94

standard of living and, 56

struggle to afford food in, 109–10

struggle to afford healthcare/medicine in, 121

underemployment and, 60

uninsured in, 49

well-being in, 66–67

would leave if could, 165

Missouri

dentist visits and, 169

health and, 88

minorities and, 187

smoking in, 94

standard of living and, 56

well-being in, 66

mobile technology

communication and, 162–63, 425–27

financial advice sources and, 309

politics and, 162–64

shopping and, 170

use of, 167

working after hours and, 166–67

stress and, 171, 480

moderates
    Affordable Care Act and, 125
    drinking age should/not be lowered, 278
    gay marriage and, 196
    global warming and, 156
    gun control and, 414
    identification with, 10–11
    Internet news and, 236
    LGBT identification and, 290
    marijuana legalization and, 423
    media and, 352–53
    most important issues facing working women and, 387
    newspapers and, 235
    North Korea and, 66
    party identification and, 202
    religion and, 247
    states and, 39–40
        Arkansas and, 358
        Georgia and, 384
        Louisiana and, 370
    Tea Party and, 179, 373
    television news and, 236
money
    lack of
        as most important financial problem, 153, 156–57
        as most important issue, 13, 93, 264
    worry about, 89
    See also financial situation, personal; income; wages
Montana
    charitable activity and, 177
    economic confidence in, 50
    health and, 88
    healthcare exchanges and, 49
    ideology in, 39
    livability, 159
    Mormons and, 46
    Obama, Barack, and, 30
    obesity in, 84
    party identification in, 35
    Payroll to Population rate and, 59
    schools and, 135
        prepare students for success in workplace, 136
    state taxes and, 134
    underemployment and, 60
    uninsured in, 49
    well-being in, 66–67
    would leave if could, 165
morality
    acceptability of various issues, 207–8
    as most important issue, 13, 93, 192–93, 264, 318–19, 342, 430
Mormons
    church attendance and, 476
    identification with, 475–76
    LGBT identification and, 303
    Middle East and, 293
    Obama, Barack, and, 259
    smoking and, 94
    states and, 45–47
Morsi, Mohamed, 63
mosques. *See* church/church attendance

Mother's Day, mood and, 32
movies, industry, image of, 335–36
Mubarak, Hosni, 63
Murkowski, Frank, 344
Murkowski, Lisa, 344
Muslims
    church attendance and, 476
    identification with, 475–76
    LGBT identification and, 303
    Obama, Barack, and, 259
mutual funds. *See* stocks/stock market
MyRA, 42, 157

NASA (National Aeronautics and Space Administration),
        approval ratings, 439–40
national security, as most important issue, 430
National Security Agency, Obama, Barack, and, 2
natural gas, U.S. should emphasize, 126
Navy, as most important for defense, 200
Nebraska
    Catholics and, 46
    economic confidence in, 50
    health and, 88
    job creation in, 54
    party identification in, 35
    schools and, 135
        prepare students for success in workplace, 136
    standard of living and, 56
    state taxes and, 134
    struggle to afford food in, 110
    trust in state government and, 129
    underemployment and, 60
    well-being in, 66–67
Nelson, Gaylord, 106
Netanyahu, Benjamin, 80
    admiration of, 478
Nevada
    air quality and, 218
    charitable activity and, 178
    Jews and, 46
    minorities and, 186
    Mormons and, 46
    obesity in, 84
    planning to move, 165–66
    Protestants and, 46
    religion and, 43
    schools and, 135
        prepare students for success in workplace, 136
    smoking in, 94
    state taxes and, 134
    underemployment and, 60
    well-being in, 67
    would leave if could, 165
New Hampshire, 401–2
    Catholics and, 46
    charitable activity and, 177
    job creation in, 54
    livability, 159, 402
    minorities and, 187
    party identification in, 401

Protestants and, 46
religion and, 43
struggle to afford food in, 109–10
underemployment and, 60
would leave if could, 165
New Jersey
Catholics and, 46
health and, 88
ideology in, 39
Jews and, 46
livability, 159
minorities and, 186
Obama, Barack, and, 30
party identification in, 35
Protestants and, 46
smoking in, 94
state taxes and, 134
would leave if could, 165
New Mexico
Catholics and, 46
health and, 88
job creation in, 54
livability, 159
minorities and, 186
obesity in, 84
party identification in, 35
Payroll to Population rate and, 59
schools and, 135
prepare students for success in workplace, 136
underemployment and, 60
uninsured in, 296
news
highest followed stories, 90
Internet
confidence in, 234–35
Middle East and, 294–95
social media, Middle East and, 294–95
television
confidence in, 234–36
Middle East and, 294–95
newspapers
confidence in, 234–35
Middle East and, 294–95
Newtown shootings, fears about school safety and, 306–7
New York
air quality and, 218
Catholics and, 46
charitable activity and, 178
health and, 88
ideology in, 39
Jews and, 46
job creation in, 54
Obama, Barack, and, 30
obesity in, 84
party identification in, 35
planning to move, 165–66
Protestants and, 46
schools and, prepare students for success in workplace, 136
standard of living and, 56
state taxes and, 134

underemployment and, 60
would leave if could, 165
Nixon, Pat, admiration of, 478
Nixon, Richard
admiration of, 479
approval ratings, 22, 27, 154, 273
non-Christian religions
Bible and, 215
church attendance and, 476
identification with, 475–76
LGBT identification and, 303
Obama, Barack, and, 259
nonreligious persons
church attendance and, 476
Francis I and, 118
identification with, 475–76
LGBT identification and, 302–4
Middle East and, 293
Obama, Barack, and, 259
party identification and, 283–84
nonwhites
Affordable Care Act and, 435
congressional priorities and, 420
entrepreneurial aspirations and, 11–12
government healthcare coverage and, 439
gun control and, 414
gun ownership and, 424–25
health insurance and, 26
Middle East and, 281
outlook for, 483
party identification and, 111
age and, 116–17
police and, 435–36
satisfaction with U.S. and, 31
spending and, 152
weight and, 282
See also Asian Americans; blacks; Hispanics
North Carolina, 326–27
Catholics and, 46
charitable activity and, 178
healthcare exchanges and, 49
job creation in, 54
party identification in, 416
Payroll to Population rate and, 59
planning to move, 165–66
Protestants and, 46
religion and, 43
standard of living and, 56
struggle to afford food in, 110
struggle to afford healthcare/medicine in, 121
underemployment and, 60
uninsured in, 49
North Dakota
Catholics and, 46
dentist visits and, 169
economic confidence in, 50
health and, 88
job creation in, 54
livability, 159
Obama, Barack, and, 30

party identification in, 35
planning to move, 165
satisfaction with, 322–24
schools and, 135
    prepare students for success in workplace, 136
smoking in, 94
standard of living and, 56
state taxes and, 134
struggle to afford food in, 110
struggle to afford healthcare/medicine in, 121
trust in state government and, 129
underemployment and, 60
well-being in, 66–67
North Korea
    conflict with South Korea, as threat, 66, 82
    as greatest enemy of U.S., 69
    opinion of, 65
nuclear power, U.S. should emphasize, 126
Nunn, Michelle, 383
Nunn, Sam, 383
nurses, honesty and ethical standards of, 469–70

Obama, Barack
    admiration of, 478–79
    Affordable Care Act and, 3, 131
    approval ratings, 1–3, 154, 240–41
        age and, 456–57
        Alaska and, 344
        Arkansas and, 358
        Colorado and, 365
        demographics of, 445–46
        fifth year, 21–22, 26–27
        Hispanics and, 368, 458–59
        intensity of, 329–31
        Iowa and, 337–38
        issues and, 317–18
        Kansas and, 374
        Kentucky and, 395
        LGBT individuals and, 289–90
        Louisiana and, 370–71
        midterm elections and, 230, 416–17
        New Hampshire and, 402
        North Carolina and, 327
        partisan gap in, 26–27
        quarterly averages, 22, 272–73, 397–98
        race and, 456–57
        religion and, 259–60
        states and, 30–31
        trends in, 241
    Bergdahl, Bowe, and, 225
    blacks and, 464–65
    budget sequester and, 2
    can manage government effectively, 227
    confidence in, 150
    confidence in presidency and, 248
    divided government preference and, 392
    economy and, 112–13, 150, 317–18
    election of 2014 and, 180, 375–76
    energy and, 112–13
    environment and, 107, 112–13

favorability ratings, 75, 83, 227, 237
foreign affairs and, 317–18, 341
France and, 52–53
global respect for, 72
government shutdown and, 2
gun policy and, 2
healthy eating and, 79
Hispanics and, 368
honesty and, 227
image of, 226–27
immigration and, 236, 457–58
influence of, 428
Israel and, 80
leadership and, 227
NSA and, 2
party identification and, 111, 117
Putin, Vladimir, and, 55
Russia and, 119
shares your values, 227
State of the Union address, 40–42
student debt and, 301
understands problems Americans face in daily lives, 227
Veterans Affairs situation and, 226
Obama, Michelle
    admiration of, 478
    favorability ratings, 83
    healthy eating and, 79
    Let's Move campaign, 197
    opinions of, 83
Obamacare. *See* Affordable Care Act
obesity, 77–79
    appearance and, 268
    demographics of, 78, 197
    disease rates and, 84
    employment discrimination should/not be allowed, 273–74
    health insurance rates and, 274
    healthy eating habits and, 84
    metro areas and, 127–28
    as most urgent health problem, 433–34
    social well-being and, 253–54, 480
    states and, 83–84
    trends in, 196–97
    unemployment and, 232–33, 480
    See also weight
Ohio
    health and, 88
    obesity in, 84
    smoking in, 94
    standard of living and, 56
    well-being in, 66
oil
    favor drilling in off-limits areas, 126
    industry, image of, 335–36
    North Dakota and, 322, 324
    U.S. should emphasize, 126
    See also energy; gasoline
Oklahoma
    Catholics and, 46
    dentist visits and, 169
    economic confidence in, 50

health and, 88
healthcare exchanges and, 49
ideology in, 39
minorities and, 187
Obama, Barack, and, 30
obesity in, 84
party identification in, 35
Protestants and, 46
religion and, 43
smoking in, 94
struggle to afford food in, 110
struggle to afford healthcare/medicine in, 121
uninsured in, 49
well-being in, 66
O'Malley, Martin, favorability ratings, 266–67, 270–71
opportunities, satisfaction with, 19–20
optimism
    investors and, 96–97, 467–68
    metro areas and, 137
    retirement and, 96–97, 467–68
    small business owners and, 184–85, 451–52
Oregon
    health and, 88
    ideology in, 39
    livability, 159
    Mormons and, 46
    Payroll to Population rate and, 59
    religion and, 43
    schools and, 135
        prepare students for success in workplace, 136
    uninsured in, 296
    would leave if could, 165
O'Reilly, Bill, admiration of, 478
organic foods, 301–2
    demographics of, 302
Orman, Greg, 374
Ornish, Dean, 477
outsourcing, worry about, 311–12

Pakistan, as threat, 82
Palestine
    support for independent state, 80–81
    sympathy with, 81
    See also Middle East
Palestinian Authority, opinion of, 62–63
    age and, 63
Palin, Sarah, 345
    admiration of, 478
parents
    Common Core standards and, 139–41, 405–6
    drinking age should/not be lowered, 278
    joy and stress and, 396
    living with
        age and, 58–59, 480
        well-being and, 60–61
    personal doctor and, 350
    satisfaction with education, 329
    school safety and, 306–7
    secondhand smoke and, 307
    spending and, 85

vacations and, 481
Parnell, Sean, 345
partisan gap
    age and, 257–58
    economy and, 106–7
    environment and, 106–7
    foreign trade and, 71
    global warming and, 102–3
    Israel and, 81
    mobile technology and, 164
    worrying issues and, 91
party identification, 450–51
    age and, 27–29, 116–17, 121–22, 257–58
        trends in, 258
    generation and, 27–29
    LGBT identification and, 289–90
    midterm elections and, 291, 410–11
    race and, 110–11
        age and, 116–17
    states and, 35–36, 416
        Alaska and, 344–45
        Arkansas and, 357–58
        Colorado and, 365
        Georgia and, 383
        Kansas and, 374
        Kentucky and, 394
        Louisiana and, 370
        New Hampshire, 401
        North Carolina and, 326–27
    trends in, 6–7
    See also political affiliation
Paul, Rand, favorability ratings, 266, 268–70
Payroll to Population rate, 7–8
    states and, 59–60
Pelosi, Nancy, favorability ratings, 187–89
Pennsylvania
    Catholics and, 46
    healthcare exchanges and, 49
    minorities and, 187
    planning to move, 165
    standard of living and, 56
    trust in state government and, 129
    uninsured in, 49
Perdue, David, 383
Perdue, Sonny, 383
Perry, Rick, 379
    favorability ratings, 266, 267, 268–70
Persian Gulf, U.S. military action in, support for, 243
Peters, Jeremy W., 200
Peterson, Andy, 322–24
pharmaceutical industry, image of, 335–36
pharmacists, honesty and ethical standards of, 469–70
physical health. See health/well-being
physical well-being
    LGBT identification and, 321
    student debt and, 299
physicians. See doctor(s)
plant species, extinction of, worry about, 128
police
    confidence in, 234

North Dakota and, 323
place of residence and, 455
race and, 314, 435–36, 455, 463
honesty and ethical standards of, 469–70
race and, 314, 463, 468–69
trends in, 469
perceptions of treatment by, race and, 314–15, 463
as priority, 420
race and, 314–16, 463
respect the police in your area, 436
political affiliation
abortion and, 199
Affordable Care Act and, 47, 87, 125, 139, 204–6, 432, 434
Afghanistan and, 64–65
Benghazi incident and, 231
Bernanke, Ben, and, 36–37
Boehner, John, and, 377
budget deficit and, 14
Bush, George H. W., and, 237
Bush, George W., and, 237
business regulation and, 348–49
Carter, Jimmy, and, 237
Clinton, Bill, and, 237
Clinton, Hillary, and, 109, 224
Common Core standards and, 140, 405–7
Congress and, 51–52, 263, 360, 394, 464
death penalty and, 399–400
defense spending and, 79
Democratic Party and, 357, 430
direction of country and, 429
divided government and, 198, 392
drinking age should/not be lowered, 278
economic confidence and, 418, 449
economy and, 106–7
energy and, 216
enthusiasm for election and, 183
environment and, 103–4, 106–7, 216
executive branch and, 348
federal government and, 341
foreign trade and, 71
gay marriage and, 196
gender and, 366
global respect for Obama and, 72
global warming and, 96, 100–103, 128–29, 156
good/bad time to find a quality job, 105, 265, 473
government and, 24, 365
government healthcare coverage and, 438–39
government role and, 369
greatest enemy of U.S. and, 69
Guantanamo Bay prison and, 229
gun control and, 414
gun ownership and, 424–25
healthcare and, 14, 99–100, 427
healthcare coverage and, 437
healthcare quality and, 438
Hispanics and, 47–49
ideology and, 202–3
immigration and, 62, 236, 245, 359, 458
investments and, 149

Iowa and, 338
Iraq and, 242–43
ISIS and, 362–63
Israel and, 81
job identity and, 320
legislative branch and, 347–48
likely to get health insurance and, 122–23, 147
local government and, 361–62
media and, 352–53
Middle East and, 280–81, 293–94
midterm elections and, 380
mobile technology and, 164
morality and, 207–8
most admired man/woman and, 479
most important issue and, 14, 193, 318–19, 430
newly insured and, 148
North Korea and, 66
Obama, Barack, and, 26–27, 83, 108, 236–37, 241, 458
Obama, Michelle, and, 83
organic foods and, 302
police and, 455
priorities and, 33–34, 228
prisoners of terrorists and, 225
Reid, Harry, and, 377
Republican Party and, 357
Russia and, 120
satisfaction by, 20
satisfaction with issues and, 16–17
satisfaction with U.S. and, 13, 92, 192, 472
school prayer and, 367
spending and, 152
state government and, 361
Supreme Court and, 261–62
taxes and, 141–43
Tea Party and, 178–79
third party and, 363–64
U.S. as No. 1 military power and, 80
United Nations and, 75
voting certainty and, 419
voting issues and, 381
waste in spending and, 353–54
worrying issues and, 91–92
See also party identification; *specific party*
politicians, as most important issue, 13, 93, 192–93, 264
trends in, 14
politics
closely follow news about, 340
mobile technology and, 162–64
actual versus expected, 163–64
outlook for, 482
pollution
standards, support for, 126, 215–16
worry about, 128
See also environment
polygamy, as morally acceptable, 207–8
poor people. *See* inequality; poverty
Pope, James E., 84
pornography, as morally acceptable, 207–8
Postal Service, approval ratings, 440–41

post-traumatic stress disorder, incidence of, 249
poverty
    as most important issue, 13, 93, 192–93, 264, 318–19, 342, 430
    as priority, 17–18, 34
    satisfaction with, 16–17
Powell, Colin
    admiration of, 479
    favorability ratings, 86
power, abuse of, as most important issue, 13, 192–93, 264
prayer, in schools, 367–68
preschool, as priority, 227–28
president/presidency
    approval ratings, Georgia and, 384
    confidence in, 234, 247–48
    priorities for, 227–28
    trust in, 347–48
presidential candidates, favorability ratings, 266–67, 268–71
prison
    discrimination and, blacks' perceptions of, 315
    life imprisonment, versus death penalty, 399–400
prisoners
    from Guantanamo Bay, move to U.S., 229
    negotiating for release of, 224–25
problem, most important. *See* issues, most important
prosperity. *See* economic conditions
Protestants/Protestantism
    church attendance and, 476
    Francis I and, 118
    identification with, 475–76
    LGBT identification and, 303
    Middle East and, 293
    Obama, Barack, and, 259
    states and, 45–47
Pryor, Mark, 357–59
public schools. *See* school(s)
publishing industry, image of, 335–36
purpose well-being, 252–53
    LGBT identification and, 321–22
    student debt and, 299
Putin, Vladimir, 91
    admiration of, 478
    opinion of, 119
        trends in, 55–56

quality of life. *See* Life Evaluation Index

race
    Affordable Care Act and, 125, 204–5, 435
    appearance and, 255, 480
    chronic conditions and, 476–77
    church attendance and, 476
    congressional priorities and, 420
    dentist visits and, 160
    diversity of, age and, 122
    entrepreneurial aspirations and, 11–12
    first-generation college graduates and, 355
    government healthcare coverage and, 439
    gun control and, 414
    gun ownership and, 424–25
    healthcare and, 427

    health insurance and, 26, 131
    Middle East and, 281
    Obama, Barack, and, 456–59
    obesity and, 78
    party identification and, 48–49, 110–11
        age and, 116–17
    police and, 314–16, 435–36
    religion and, 283–84
    satisfaction with U.S. and, 31
    spending and, 152
    standard of living and, 298–99
    struggle to afford food and, 421
    student debt and, 354–56
        trends in, 354–55
    Tea Party and, 373
    uninsured and, 173, 217
    vacations and, 481
    weight and, 282
race relations, 461–64
    as most important issue, 192–93, 264, 342, 470–71
        trends in, 471
    as priority, 17–18
    satisfaction with, 16–17
    will always a problem/will be worked out, 462
    worry about, 91
racism. *See* discrimination
radio, industry, image of, 335–36
rain forests, loss of, worry about, 128
Reagan, Nancy, admiration of, 478
Reagan, Ronald, 277
    admiration of, 479
    approval ratings, 3, 22, 27, 154, 273, 317, 397
real estate
    as best investment, 149
    industry, image of, 335–36
        trends in, 336–37
red states, 35–36
region. *See* geographic region
Reid, Harry, favorability ratings, 187–89, 376–77
religion
    Bible, literal view of, 214–15
    can answer today's problems, 246–47
        demographics of, 247
        trends in, 246
    confidence in, 234
    identification with, 475–76
    importance of, 246
        LGBT identification and, 303
    LGBT identification and, 302–4
    Middle East and, 293–94
    as most important issue, 13, 93, 192–93, 264, 342
    Obama, Barack, and, 259–60
    party identification and, 283–84
    prayer in schools, 367–68
    smoking and, 94
    states and, 43
    See also church/church attendance
Republican Party
    abortion and, 199
    Affordable Care Act and, 47, 87, 125, 139, 204–6, 432, 434

Afghanistan and, 64–65
age and, 116–17, 121–22, 257–58
    trends in, 258
Benghazi incident and, 231
Bernanke, Ben, and, 36–37
Boehner, John, and, 377
budget deficit and, 14
Bush, George H. W., and, 237
Bush, George W., and, 237
business regulation and, 348–49
candidates, favorability ratings, 266, 267, 268–69
Carter, Jimmy, and, 237
Clinton, Bill, and, 237
Clinton, Hillary, and, 109, 224, 232
Common Core standards and, 140, 405–7
Congress and, 51–52, 263, 360, 394, 464
death penalty and, 399–400
defense spending and, 79
Democratic Party and, 357, 430
direction of country and, 429
divided government and, 198, 392
drinking age should/not be lowered, 278
Ebola virus and, 398
economic confidence and, 418, 449
economy and, 106–7, 343
election of 2014 and, 291, 384–85
energy and, 216
enthusiasm for election and, 179, 183
environment and, 103–4, 106–7, 216
executive branch and, 348
favorability ratings, 190–91, 356–57, 429–30
    election results and, 191
    trends in, 429
federal government and, 341
foreign trade and, 71
gay marriage and, 196
gender and, 366
global respect for Obama and, 72
global warming and, 96, 100–103, 129, 156
good/bad time to find a quality job, 105, 265, 473
government and, 24, 365, 403
government healthcare coverage and, 438–39
government role and, 369
greatest enemy of U.S. and, 69
Greenspan, Alan, and, 36
Guantanamo Bay prison and, 229
gun control and, 414
gun ownership and, 424–25
healthcare and, 14, 99–100, 427
healthcare coverage and, 437
healthcare quality and, 438
identification with, 450–51
    trends in, 6–7
ideology and, 11, 202–3
immigration and, 62, 236, 245, 359, 458
investments and, 149
Iraq and, 242–43
ISIS and, 362–63
Israel and, 81
job identity and, 320

labor and, 331
legislative branch and, 347
LGBT identification and, 289–90
likely to get health insurance, 122–23, 147
local government and, 361–62
media and, 352–53
Middle East and, 280–81, 293–94
midterm elections and, 380, 410–11
    sending message to president, 376
mobile technology and, 164
morality and, 207–8
most admired man/woman and, 479
most important issue and, 14, 193, 264, 318–19, 430
motivation to vote, 402–3
newly insured and, 148
North Korea and, 66
Obama, Barack, and, 26–27, 83, 108, 113, 236–37, 241, 329–31, 458
Obama, Michelle, and, 83
opportunity and, 20
organic foods and, 302
police and, 455
priorities and, 33–34, 228
prisoners of terrorists and, 225
race and, 48–49, 111
Reid, Harry, and, 377
religion and, 283–84
Russia and, 120
satisfaction of, 16–17, 20
satisfaction with U.S. and, 13, 31, 92, 192, 472
school prayer and, 367
spending and, 152
state government and, 361
    North Carolina and, 327
states and, 35–36
    Alaska and, 344
    Colorado and, 365
    Georgia and, 383
    Iowa and, 338
    Kansas and, 374
    Kentucky and, 394
    Louisiana and, 370
    North Carolina and, 326–27
Supreme Court and, 261–62
taxes and, 141–43
Tea Party and, 178–79, 373
terrorism and, 343–44
third party and, 363–64
thought given to election, 328, 402–3
U.S. as No. 1 military power and, 80
United Nations and, 75
voting certainty and, 419
voting issues and, 193–94, 381, 386–87
waste in spending and, 353–54
worrying issues and, 91–92
Republicans in Congress
    economy and, 150–51
    influence of, 428
reservoirs, pollution of, worry about, 128
respect, as most important issue, 13, 264

restaurants, image of, 335–36
retail industry
    image of, 335–36
    mobile technology and, 170
retirement
    401(k) accounts
        importance of, 172–73
        loans and early withdrawals, 473–74
    age of, 20–21, 161–62
    expectations of, 181
    financial advice sources and, 308
    income, 172–73
    optimism and, 96–97, 467–68
    plan, satisfaction with, 316
    savings
        could save more, 474–75
        as most important financial problem, 153, 156–57
            trends in, 157
        MyRA and, 42, 157
        spending on, 260
        starting age, 474
Rhode Island
    Catholics and, 46
    charitable activity and, 178
    dentist visits and, 169
    health and, 88
    job creation in, 54
    livability, 159
    Obama, Barack, and, 30
    party identification in, 35
    Protestants and, 46
    smoking in, 94
    standard of living and, 56
    state taxes and, 134
    trust in state government and, 129
    would leave if could, 165
Rice, Condoleezza
    admiration of, 478, 479
    favorability ratings, 86
rivers, pollution of, worry about, 128
Roberts, Pat, 374
Rodman, Dennis, 66
Roe v. Wade. See abortion
Roman Catholic Church. See Catholics
Roosevelt, Franklin, 251
Ross, Mike, 358
Rubio, Marco, favorability ratings, 266, 269
rural areas, organic foods and, 302
Russia
    as economic leader, 68
    as friend or foe, 118–19
    as greatest enemy of U.S., 69
    investors and, 382
    opinion of, 55–56
    return of Cold War, 119–20
    as threat, 82
    Ukraine and, 86, 90–91
Ryan, Paul, favorability ratings, 266, 268–70

salt, consumption of, 285
same-sex marriage. See gay marriage
Santorum, Rick, favorability ratings, 266, 269
satisfaction
    with abortion policies, 16–17
    with air quality, states and, 218
    with appearance, 254–56
    with crime policies, 16–17
    with economic conditions, 16–17
    with education, 16–17, 329
    with employer-based health insurance, 316
    with energy policies, 16–17
    with environment, 16–17
    with foreign affairs, 16–17
    with global position of U.S., 72–73
    with government, 364–65
        trends in, 23–24
    with gun laws, 16–17
        trends in, 38–39
    with healthcare, 16–17, 99–100, 427–28
        demographics of, 427
    with healthcare costs, 453–55
    with homelessness, 16–17
    with immigration, 16–17
    with job security, 316–17
    with LGBT acceptance, 16–17
    with Medicare, 16–17
    microbusiness owners and, 279–80
    with military, 16–17
    with opportunities, 19–20
    with poverty, 16–17
    priorities and, 18
    with race relations, 16–17
    small business owners and, 371
    with Social Security, 16–17
    with standard of living, 219
    with taxes, 16–17
    with United States, 92, 191–92, 471–72
        midterm elections and, 230
        party identification and, 31
        race and, 31
        trends in, 13, 92, 191
    with wealth distribution, 19–20
    with work environment, gender and, 392–93
    See also approval ratings
Saudi Arabia, opinion of, 62–63
savings, 461
    attitudes toward, 275
    enjoyment of, 151–52
        demographics of, 152
    lack of, as most important financial problem, 153, 156–57
    retirement
        could save more, 474–75
        as most important financial problem, 153, 156–57
        spending on, 260
        starting age, 474
savings accounts, as best investment, 149

school(s)
confidence in, 234
federal government and, 312–14
graduation prayers, 367
North Dakota and, 323
prayer in, 367–68
prepare students for success in workplace, states and, 136
preschool, as priority, 227–28
religious groups using facilities, 367
safety at, 306–7
states and, 135–36
technology and, 412
See also education
Scott, Rick, 406
Senate. *See* Congress
September 11, 2001, following closely, 90
sex/sexual activity
extramarital affairs, as morally acceptable, 207–8
LGBT, as morally acceptable, 207–8
between teenagers, as morally acceptable, 207–8
between unmarried man/woman as morally
acceptable, 207–8
sexual harassment, as most important issue for
working women, 387
Shaheen, Jeanne, 402
shopping, cost-saving measures, 275
Silent Generation
party identification of, 28
See also traditionalists
small business
confidence in, 234
trends in, 244
contributions of, 201
credit availability, 184
hiring, 451–52
outlook for, 57–58, 452
owners
biggest challenge, 195
most rewarding thing, 194, 371
motivations of, 372
optimism and, 184–85, 451–52
satisfaction and, 371
success and, 371
would do it again, 194–95
would recommend to young person, 372
present situation of, 57, 184, 452
smartphones
possession of, 4–5
use of, 167
Smith, Margaret Chase, admiration of, 478
smoking
bans on
public versus total, 288–89
smokers and, 272
states and, 94
cigarettes per day, 272
cigarette tax, 271–72
employment discrimination should/not be allowed, 273–74
as harmful, 308
health insurance rates and, 274
prevalence of, 272

secondhand smoke, as harmful, 307–8
states and, 94–95
worry about, 272
Snowden, Edward, 2, 119
social climate, North Dakota and, 323
social issues
ideology and, 202–3
See also abortion; gay marriage
social media
communication and, 426
influence on purchasing decisions, 238–39
news, Middle East and, 294–95
politics and, 163–64
trust to keep personal information secure, 220
uses of, 239
Social Security
loss of, retirement savings and, 475
as most important financial problem, 153, 156–57
as priority, 17–18, 34, 420
reliance on, 172–73
satisfaction with, 16–17
worry about, 91
social well-being, 252–53
LGBT identification and, 321
obesity and, 253–54, 480
student debt and, 299
soda, drinking habits, 284–85
soil, contamination of, worry about, 128
solar power, U.S. should emphasize, 126
South Carolina
Catholics and, 46
health and, 88
ideology in, 39
obesity in, 84
party identification in, 35
Payroll to Population rate and, 59
planning to move, 165–66
Protestants and, 46
religion and, 43
struggle to afford healthcare/medicine in, 121
South Dakota
charitable activity and, 177
dentist visits and, 169
job creation in, 54
Obama, Barack, and, 30
party identification in, 35
schools and, 135
prepare students for success in workplace, 136
standard of living and, 56
struggle to afford food in, 110
struggle to afford healthcare/medicine in, 121
trust in state government and, 129
underemployment and, 60
well-being in, 66
would leave if could, 165
South Korea
conflict with North Korea, as threat, 66, 82
opinion of, 65
spending, 174, 461
Christmas and, 442–43
forecast versus actual, 443

consumers and, 211, 260–61
  trends in, 8–9
  daily average
    parental status and, 85
    race and, 459–60
  enjoyment of, 151–52
    demographics of, 152
  as most important financial problem, 153, 156–57
  as new normal, 174
  parental status and, 85
    race and, 460
  summer and, 275
  See also financial situation, personal
sports, industry, image of, 335–36
standard of living, 219, 460–61
  getting better/worse, 219
  job creation and, 54, 56
  as most important financial problem, 157
  race and, 298–99
  satisfaction with, 219
  states and, 56–57
  trends in, 460
state government
  confidence in
    Arkansas and, 358
    Iowa and, 338
    New Hampshire and, 402
    North Carolina and, 327
  schools and, 312
  trust in, 361–62
    states and, 129–30
  trust to keep personal information secure, 220
  waste in spending, perceptions of, 353–54
state governors, confidence in, 150–51
states
  air quality and, 218
  charitable activity and, 177–78
  dentist visits and, 169
  economic confidence in, 50–51
  healthcare exchanges and, 49–50
  healthy behavior and, 88–89
  ideology and, 39–40
  job creation in, 54–55
  livability, 159
  migration patterns, outlook for, 483
  minorities and, 186–87
  Obama, Barack, and, 30–31
  obesity and, 83–84
  Payroll to Population rate and, 59–60
  planning to move, 165–66
  political affiliation, 35–36
  religion and, 43, 45–47
  schools and, 135–36
    prepare students for success in workplace, 136
  smoking in, 94–95
  standard of living and, 56–57
  state government and, 129–30
  state taxes and, 134–35
  struggle to afford food in, 109–10
  struggle to afford healthcare/medicine in, 120–21

underemployment and, 60
uninsured and, 296–97, 480
well-being and, 66–67
would leave if could, 165–66
stem cell research, as morally acceptable, 207–8
Stevens, Ted, 344
stocks/stock market
  as best investment, 149
    trends in, 18–19
  investment in, 19
  investor optimism and, 467
  as most important financial problem, 153, 156–57
strengths, use of, generation and, 25, 480
stress, 33
  children in household and, 396
  marital status and, 390–91
  satisfaction with, 393
  veterans and, 249–50, 480
  volunteering and, 304
  work and, satisfaction with, 316
  working remotely after hours and, 171, 480
student debt
  amount of, 300
  race and, 354–56
    trends in, 354–55
  well-being and, 299–301
    trends in, 300
suburban areas, organic foods and, 302
success, small business owners and, 371
sugar, consumption of, 285
suicide
  doctor-assisted
    as morally acceptable, 207–8
    support for, 233–34
  as morally acceptable, 207–8
Sullivan, Dan, 344
summer
  spending and, 275
  travel plans, 260–61
Supreme Court
  confidence in, 234, 247–48
    trends in, 247
  trust in, 347–48
synagogue. *See* church/church attendance
Syria
  as greatest enemy of U.S., 69
  military action in
    stress and, 33
    support for, 243
  opinion of, 62–63
    age and, 63

tablets, use of, 167
taxes
  Arkansas and, 358
  as most important financial problem, 153, 156–57
  as priority, 17–18, 34, 420
  satisfaction with, 16–17, 141–42
  state
    Kansas and, 375

New Hampshire and, 402
  states and, 134–35
  as voting issue, 193–94, 381
  Tea Party and, 403
teachers, Common Core standards and, 140, 313, 406–10
  computer testing and, 411–13
  field tests, 412
  negatives of, 408–10
  positives of, 407, 409–10
  teaching level and, 08, 407
Tea Party
  Boehner, John, and, 188
  demographics of, 373
  enthusiasm for election and, 179
  government and, 403
  McConnell, Mitch, and, 188–89
  motivation to vote, 402–3
  Republican Party and, 178–79
  support for, 178–79, 373
    strength of, 373
  thought given to midterm elections, 402–3
  voting issues and, 403
technology
  communication and, 162–63, 425–27
  devices owned, 4–5
  online testing, Common Core standards and, 411–13
  See also mobile technology
telephones
  cell versus landline, communication and, 426
  industry, image of, 335–36
  spending on, 260
television
  industry, image of, 335–36
  news
    confidence in, 234–36
    Middle East and, 294–95
Tennessee
  Catholics and, 46
  dentist visits and, 169
  economic confidence in, 50
  health and, 88
  ideology in, 39
  obesity in, 84
  Protestants and, 46
  religion and, 43
  smoking in, 94
  well-being in, 66
Teresa, Mother, admiration of, 478
term limits, Congress and, 262–63
terrorism
  following closely, 90
  as most important issue, 430
    trends in, 342
  negotiating for prisoners, 224–25
  party preferred to deal with, 343–44
  as priority, 17–18, 34, 420
  as threat, 81–82
    trends in, 82
  worry about, 91, 404

Texas
  dentist visits and, 169
  health and, 88
  healthcare exchanges and, 49
  Hispanics in, 47–49
  job creation in, 54
  livability, 159
  minorities and, 186
  party identification in, 47–49
  planning to move, 165
  standard of living and, 56
  state taxes and, 134
  struggle to afford healthcare/medicine in, 121
  trust in state government and, 129
  uninsured in, 49
  well-being in, 67
  would leave if could, 165
text messaging, communication and, 425–27
Thanksgiving, mood and, 32
Thatcher, Margaret, admiration of, 478
third party
  Congress and, 263
  need for, 363–64
threats, most critical. *See* issues, most important
Tillis, Thom, 327
tobacco. *See* smoking
tourism. *See* travel
toxic waste, worry about, 128
traditionalists
  banking industry and, 23
  social media and purchasing decisions, 238
  strengths usage and, 25
  workplace engagement and, 21
transportation
  costs, as most important financial problem, 153, 156–57
  North Dakota and, 323
travel
  industry, image of, 335–36
  spending on, 260
  summer plans, 260–61
  well-being and, 480–81
tropical rain forests, loss of, worry about, 128
Truman, Harry, admiration of, 479
tsunami, following closely, 90
Twitter, communication and, 426

Udall, Mark, 101, 365–66
Ukraine, 85–86
  following closely, 90–91
  as friend/foe, 119
  investors and, 382
  return of Cold War and, 119–20
underemployment
  living with parents and, 58–59
  Payroll to Population rate and, 7–8
  states and, 60
unemployment
  depression and, 221–22, 480
  health insurance and, 26

investor optimism and, 467

investors and, 382

job market perceptions and, 437

living with parents and, 58–59

as most important financial problem, 153, 156–57

as most important issue, 13, 93, 192–93, 264, 318–19, 342, 430

    trends in, 14, 430, 471

as most important issue for working women, 387

obesity and, 232–33, 480

Payroll to Population rate and, 7–8

time with family and friends and, 221–22

worry about, 311–12

See also employment; jobs

uninsured, 130–32, 173–74, 217–18, 256–57, 480

    Affordable Care Act and, 206

    age and, 53

    demographics of, 131, 217

    dentist visits and, 169

    healthcare exchanges and, 1, 37–38, 49–50, 145–46

    LGBT individuals and, 325–26

    likely to get insurance, 37–38, 431–32

        fines and, 146–47

        party identification and, 122–23

    prevalence of, 182

    states and, 49–50, 145–46, 296–97, 480

    struggle to afford healthcare/medicine and, 121

    trends in, 26, 53–54, 131

United Nations

    is doing good/poor job, 74–75

    role in world affairs, 75

United States

    country will be better/worse off following election, 428–29

    as economic leader, 68

    five years ago, 32

    five years from now, 32

    global position of, satisfaction with, 72–73

    global respect for, 72

    greatest enemy of, 68–69

    most important problem facing, 263–64

    as No. 1 military power, 79–80

        trends in, 80

    satisfaction with, 92, 191–92, 471–72

        midterm elections and, 230

        party identification and, 31

        race and, 31

        trends in, 13, 92, 191

Utah

    air quality and, 218

    Catholics and, 46

    charitable activity and, 177

    dentist visits and, 169

    ideology in, 39

    livability, 159

    Mormons and, 46

    Obama, Barack, and, 30

    party identification in, 35

    Protestants and, 46

    religion and, 43

    smoking in, 94

    trust in state government and, 129

utilities

    costs, as most important financial problem, 153, 156–57

    image of, 335–36

    spending on, 260

vacation

    microbusiness owners and, 278–80

    time, satisfaction with, 316

    well-being and, 480–81

values

    Obama, Barack, and, 227

    See also morality

Vermont

    health and, 88

    healthcare exchanges and, 49

    ideology in, 39

    job creation in, 54

    livability, 159

    minorities and, 187

    Obama, Barack, and, 30

    party identification in, 35

    planning to move, 165

    Protestants and, 46

    religion and, 43

    standard of living and, 56–57

    state taxes and, 134

    uninsured in, 49

    well-being in, 66–67

veterans

    GI Bill

        satisfaction with, 251–52

        use of, 251

    healthcare for

        access to, 250

        confidence in, 250

        as priority, 227–28

    health insurance coverage, prevalence of, 53–54, 182, 256

    stress/worry and, 249–50, 480

Veterans Affairs

    access to, 250

    confidence in, 250

    role of, 250–51

    situation

        best way to fix, 226

        following closely, 225–26

Vietnam War, as mistake, 64

violence

    as most important issue, 264

    worry about, 91

    See also crime; gun(s)

volunteering

    states and, 177–78

    well-being and, 304–5

voter registration, race and, 48

voters

    engagement, 379–80

    turnout of

        congressional approval ratings and, 324–25

        indicators and, 418–19

    See also specific elections

wages
   low, as most important financial problem, 153, 156–57
   as most important issue, 264
   as priority, 420
   satisfaction with, 316, 393
   worry about, 311–12
Walker, Bill, 345
Walker, Scott, favorability ratings, 266, 269
war
   as most important issue, 342
   as priority, 420
   See also specific wars
Ward, Maeve, 410
Warren, Elizabeth
   admiration of, 478
   favorability ratings, 266–67, 270–71
Washington (state)
   economic confidence in, 50
   health and, 88
   minorities and, 186
   Mormons and, 46
   religion and, 43
   smoking in, 94
   uninsured in, 296
   well-being in, 66
Washington Navy Yard shootings, stress and, 33
water, pollution of, worry about, 128
wealth, distribution of
   as priority, 17–18
   satisfaction with, 19–20
   See also inequality
weekends
   drinking and, 276–77
   mood and, 32–33
weight, 77–79, 222–23
   appearance and, 268
   difference between actual and ideal, 446–47
   over ideal weight, 222–23
   social well-being and, 253–54
   trying to lose, 222–23, 446
      dietary choices and, 286–87
      reasons for, 282
      seriously, 282, 446
   worry about, 281–83
   would like to lose, 446
welfare, as most important issue, 13
Well-Being Index, 252–53, 480
   charitable activity and, 178
   children in household and, 396
   chronic conditions, race and, 476–77
   college and, 175–76
      race and, 355–56
   demographics and, 253
   divorce and, 390–91
   LGBT identification and, 320–22, 480
   living with parents and, 60–61
   metro areas and, 113–15
   states and, 66–67
   student debt and, 299–301
   trends in, 66

vacations and, 480–81
volunteering and, 304–5
West Virginia
   Catholics and, 46
   charitable activity and, 178
   dentist visits and, 169
   economic confidence in, 50–51
   health and, 88
   job creation in, 54
   minorities and, 187
   Obama, Barack, and, 30
   obesity in, 84
   Payroll to Population rate and, 59
   planning to move, 165
   Protestants and, 46
   schools and, 135
   smoking in, 94
   standard of living and, 56
   struggle to afford food in, 110
   struggle to afford healthcare/medicine in, 121
   uninsured in, 296
   well-being in, 66–67
whites
   Affordable Care Act and, 204–5, 435
   appearance and, 255, 480
   chronic conditions and, 476–77
   church attendance and, 476
   civil rights perceptions and, 463
   congressional priorities and, 420
   dentist visits and, 160
   discrimination and, 462
   entrepreneurial aspirations and, 11–12
   first-generation college graduates, 355
   government healthcare coverage and, 439
   gun control and, 414
   gun ownership and, 424–25
   healthcare and, 427
   health insurance and, 26, 131, 349
   immigration and, 457
   Middle East and, 281
   Obama, Barack, and, 457–59
   obesity and, 78, 197
   outlook for, 483
   party identification of, 48–49, 111, 283–84
      age and, 116–17, 122
   personal doctor and, 349
   police and, 314–16, 435–36, 455, 463, 468–69
   race and, 298–99
   race relations and, 461–64, 471
   religion and, 283–84
   satisfaction with U.S. and, 31
   spending and, 152, 459–60
   struggle to afford food and, 421
   student debt and, 354
      trends in, 354–55
   Tea Party and, 373
   uninsured and, 173, 217
   vacations and, 481
   weight and, 282
   well-being and, college and, 355–56

WikiLeaks
  following closely, 90
  stress and, 33
wind power, U.S. should emphasize, 126
wine, 276
Winfrey, Oprah, admiration of, 478, 479
winter weather
  climate change and, 97–98
  region and, 98
Wisconsin
  Catholics and, 46
  dentist visits and, 169
  economic confidence in, 50
  healthcare exchanges and, 49
  job creation in, 54
  schools and, 135
    prepare students for success in workplace, 136
  struggle to afford food in, 110
  struggle to afford healthcare/medicine in, 121
  uninsured in, 49
  well-being in, 67
women
  abortion and, 199
  admiration of, 478–79
  appearance and, 255
  boss gender preference and, 388–89
  budget deficit and, 14
  checking work email and, 167
  dentist visits and, 160
  drinking age should/not be lowered, 278
  emotional impact of children in household and, 396
  equal pay for
    as most important issue for working women, 387–88
    as priority, 227–28
    as voting issue, 381, 386
      Tea Party and, 403
  financial advice sources and, 308
  financial advice use and, 346
  global warming and, 156
  gun control and, 414
  gun ownership and, 424–25
  healthcare and, 14
  health insurance and, 26
  job identity and, 320
  marital status and well-being and, 390–91
  Middle East and, 281
  most important issue and, 14
  most important issues facing working women and, 387–88
  Obama, Barack, and, 83, 445–46
  Obama, Michelle, and, 83
  obesity and, 78, 197
  party identification and, 366
  Postal Service and, 441
  religion and, 247

weight and, 222, 282, 447
well-being and, 253
work environment satisfaction and, 392–93
working, most important issues facing, 387–88
work environment
  boss gender preference, 388–89
    trends in, 388
  living with parents and, 61
  metro areas and, 114
  as most important issue for working women, 387
  satisfaction with, 316
    gender and, 392–93
  states and, 67
work-life balance, as most important issue for
    working women, 387
workplace engagement
  age and, 21
  college and, 175–76
  federal workers and, 466–67
  microbusiness owners and, 280
  worker type and, 466
worry, 33
  North Dakota and, 323
  See also stress
Wyoming
  economic confidence in, 50
  health and, 88
  ideology in, 39
  livability, 159
  minorities and, 187
  Mormons and, 46
  Obama, Barack, and, 30
  party identification in, 35
  schools and, 135
    prepare students for success in workplace, 136
  state taxes and, 134
  trust in state government and, 129
  underemployment and, 60
  would leave if could, 165

Yatsenyuk, Arseniy, 91
Yellen, Janet, 150
Young, Don, 344
Yousafzai, Malala, admiration of, 478
youth
  Democratic Party and, 121–22
  electronic devices owned, 5
  entrepreneurial aspirations and, 11–12
  living with parents, 58–59, 480
  Postal Service and, 440–41
  See also age

Zimmerman, George, 2, 462
Zuckerberg, Mark, 246